A COMPANION TO
SAINT THÉRÈSE OF LISIEUX

A Companion to
SAINT THÉRÈSE
OF LISIEUX

Her Life and Work
&
The People and Places
In Her Story

JOSEPH P. KOCHISS

Angelico Press

First published
by Angelico Press
www.angelicopress.com
© Angelico Press 2014

All rights reserved

No part of this book may be reproduced or transmitted,
in any form or by any means, without permission.

For information, address:
Angelico Press
4709 Briar Knoll Dr.
Kettering, OH 45429
angelicopress.com

978-1-62138-068-9 (paper)
978-1-62138-070-2 (cloth)

Cover Design: Michael Schrauzer

*This book is dedicated to my dear parents
and to my twin brother John — a steadfast companion
and indispensable helper.*

Contents

Preface xiii
Abbreviations xvi
Acknowledgements xvii

CHAPTER 1   ST. THÉRÈSE OF LISIEUX 1
   A. LIFE AND POSTHUMOUS CHRONOLOGY 1
   B. WRITINGS AND ART WORK 33
      1. Autobiography 37
      2. Letters 44
      3. Poems 47
      4. Plays 59
      5. Prayers 66
      6. Diverse Writings 69
      7. Art Work 70
   C. BEATIFICATION AND CANONIZATION 75
      1. History 75
      2. Major Steps Leading to the Canonization of St. Thérèse 77
      3. The Four Required Miracles 79
      4. Witnesses 80
      5. Leading Ecclesiastics Involved 82
   D. THÉRÈSE'S TITLES, HONORS, CONGREGATIONS, AND RELICS 98

CHAPTER 2   ST. THÉRÈSE'S FAMILY 103
   A. FAMILY TREE 103
   B. PARENTS 105
      1. Louis Martin 105
      2. Zélie Martin 114
   C. CHILDREN 122
      1. Marie-Louise Martin 122
      2. Marie-Pauline Martin 132
      3. Marie-Léonie Martin 137
      4. Marie-Hélène Martin 146
      5. Marie-Joseph-Louis Martin 149
      6. Marie-Joseph-Jean-Baptiste Martin 151
      7. Marie-Céline Martin 152
      8. Marie-Mélanie-Thérèse Martin 166
      9. Marie-Françoise-Thérèse 167
   D. GRANDPARENTS 168
      1. Captain Pierre-François Martin 168
      2. Fanie Boureau Martin 171
      3. Isidore Guérin 174
      4. Louise-Jeanne Macé Guérin 175

  E. Father's Other Relatives 177
   1. Adolphe Leriche 178
  F. Mother's Other Relatives 180
   1. Marie-Louise-Pétronille Guérin 182
   2. Isidore Guérin 185
   3. Élisa-Céline Fournet Guérin 190
   4. Jeanne-Marie-Elisa Guérin 195
   5. Marie Guérin 200
   6. Dr. Francisque-Lucien-Sulpice La Néele 208
   7. Mme. Elisa-Ernestine Petit Fournet and M. Pierre-Célestin Fournet . . 213
   8. The Maudelonde Family 215

CHAPTER 3 NON-FAMILY RELATIONS 221
  A. Family Friends. 221
   1. Mlle. Félicité Baudouin 225
   2. M. and Mme. Victor Besnard 225
   3. Paul-Albert Boul 226
   4. Auguste David 226
   5. Victor Lahaye 227
   6. Louise Magdelaine 228
   7. François Nogrix 229
   8. The Pallu du Bellay Sisters 229
   9. The Pigeon Sisters 230
   10. The Primois Sisters 231
   11. The Rabinel Family 231
   12. The Romet Family 232
   13. Mme. Léonie (Gilbert) Tifenne 234
  B. Domestic Help 238
   1. Marie-Françoise-Félicité Hubert 241
   2. Marcelline-Anna Husé 241
   3. Desiré Lejuif and Marie Lejuif 244
   4. Louise Marais 246
   5. Victoire Pasquer 250
  C. Doctors, Tutors, and Others 253
   1. Mlle. Godard and Edouard Krug 253
   2. Dr. Alphonse-Henri Notta 255
   3. Mme. Valentine Papinau 256
   4. Rose Taillé 259
   5. Tom 262
  D. Thérèse's School Companions 265
   1. Hélène Doise 268
   2. Amélie-Alexandrine and Marie Domin 269
   3. Jeanne-Louise Raoul 270
   4. Marie-Blanche Dupont 271
   5. Marguerite-Léonie-Augustine Leroy 271

CHAPTER 4   NUNS 273
   A. At the Benedictine Abbey of Notre-Dame-du-Pré 273
      1. Mère Saint François de Sales, O.S.B. 282
      2. Mère Saint Léon 284
      3. Mère Saint-Placide 285
   B. At the Carmel in Lisieux 287
      sœurs de chœur (*Choir Sisters*) 287
      1. Révérende Mère Agnès de Jésus 289
      2. Sœur Aimée de Jésus et du Cœur de Marie 289
      3. Sœur Anne du Sacré-Cœur 291
      4. Sœur Febronie de la Sainte-Enfance 293
      5. Sœur Geneviève de la Sante-Face 295
      6. Révérende Mère Geneviève de Sainte-Thérèse 295
      7. Mère Hermance du Cœur de Jésus 298
      8. Sœur Marguerite-Marie du Sacré-Cœur 300
      9. Mère Marie de Gonzague 301
      10. Sœur Marie de Jésus 309
      11. Sœur de la Trinité et de la Sainte-Face 311
      12. Sœur Marie de L'Eucharistie 317
      13. Soeur Marie de Saint-Joseph 317
      14. Sœur Marie des Anges et du Sacré-Cœur 320
      15. Sœur Marie-Emmanuel 323
      16. Sœur Marie-Philomène de Jésus 324
      17. Sœur Marie du Sacré-Cœur 326
      18. Sœur Saint-Jean Baptiste du Cœur de Jésus 326
      19. Soeur Saint-Jean de la Croix 328
      20. Sœur Saint-Raphael du Cœur de Marie 330
      21. Sœur Saint-Stanislas des Sacrés-Cœurs 332
      22. Sœur Thérèse de Jésus du Cœur de Marie 334
      23. Sœur Thérèse de Saint-Augustin 336
      sœurs converses (*Converse Sisters—Lay Sisters*) 339
      1. Sœur Marie de l'Incarnation 340
      2. Sœur Marie-Madeleine du Saint-Sacrement 342
      3. Sœur Marthe de Jésus de Bienheureux Perboyre 344
      4. Sœur Saint-Joseph de Jésus 347
      5. Sœur Saint-Pierre de Sainte Thérèse 349
      6. Sœur Saint-Vincent de Paul 351
      sœurs tourières (*Extern Sisters*) 354
      1. Sœur Marie-Antoinette 355
      2. Sister Mary Elizabeth of Saint Thérèse 355
   C. In Other Orders 357
      1. Mère Marie-Adélaid Costard 357
      2. Sœur Marie-Aloysia 359

CHAPTER 5   CHURCHMEN 363
   A. In Thérèse's Childhood 363
      1. Abbé Jean-Baptiste Crêté 366
      2. Abbé Victor-Louis Domin 367
      3. Abbé Alcide-Leoida Ducellier 370
      4. Abbé Lucien-Victor Dumaine 373
      5. Abbé Frédéric-Auguste Hurel 374
      6. Abbé Jamot 374
      7. Abbé Lepelletier 375
      8. Abbé Charles-Louis-Auguste Marie 376
      9. Père Almire-Théophile-Augustin Pichon, S.J. 378
   B. On the Pilgrimage to Rome 384
      1. Msgr. Abel-Anastase Germain 385
      2. Abbé Alcide-Victor Leconte 386
      3. Msgr. Arséne-Louis-Jean-Marie Legoux 386
      4. Pope Leo XIII 387
      5. Abbé Maurice-Joseph Révérony 389
      6. Père Vauquelin 394
   C. On the Carmel Staff 396
      1. Abbé Eugene-Auguste Baillon 396
      2. Canon Jean-Baptiste Delatroëte 397
      3. Abbé Pierre-Alexandre Faucon 399
      4. Abbé Zacharie-Jules-Eugène Hodierne 400
      5. Canon Alexandre-Charles Maupas 401
      6. Abbé Louis-Auguste Youf 403
   D. Carmel Retreat Masters 407
      1. Père Laurent Blino, S. J. 407
      2. Père Déodat De Basly 408
      3. Abbé Victor-Oscar Lechesne 409
      4. Père Armand-Constant Lemonnier 409
      5. Pere Godefroid Madelaine, O. Praem. 411
      6. Père Alexis Prou 414
      7. Père Almire Pichon, S.J. 416
   E. Others 417
      1. Abbé Maurice Bellière 417
      2. Abbé Chillart 424
      3. Abbé Joseph de Cornière 425
      4. Abbé Joseph Denis de Maroy 427
      5. Abbé Louis Gombault 428
      6. Msgr. Flavien-Abel-Antoine Hugonin 430
      7. Père Adolphe Roulland 433
      8. Frère Salutaire, F.S.C. 439
      9. Frère Siméon, F.S.C. 441
     10. Abbé Paul Troude 445

CHAPTER 6	SAINTS AND "SINNERS"	447
	Introduction	448

A. SAINTS 451
    1. Angels 451
    2. The Blessed Virgin Mary 456
    3. Carmelite Martyrs of Compiègne 462
    4. Léon-Papin Dupont 465
    5. Père Frèdéric Mazel, M.E.P. 469
    6. Saint Agnes 470
    7. Saint Aloysius Gonzaga 473
    8. Saint Cecilia 475
    9. Saint Joan of Arc 478
    10. Saint John of the Cross 483
    11. Saint Mary Magdalene 488
    12. Saint Sebastian 492
    13. Saint Stanislas Kostka 495
    14. Saint Teresa of Avila 497
    15. Saint Théophane Vénard 501

B. "SINNERS" 507
    1. Henry Chéron 507
    2. Père Hyacinthe Loyson 508
    3. Henri-Jacques Pranzini 511
    4. Léo Taxil 518
    5. René Tostain 523

CHAPTER 7	PLACES ASSOCIATED WITH ST. THÉRÈSE	525

A. IN NORMANDY 525
    1. Alençon 527
    2. Vicinity of Alençon 550
    3. Lisieux 556
    4. Vicinity of Lisieux 593
    5. Elsewhere 600

B. THE TRIP TO ROME 619
    1. Paris 623
    2. Lucerne 629
    3. Milan 630
    4. Venice 632
    5. Padua 633
    6. Bologna 634
    7. Loreto 636
    8. Rome 638
    9. Naples and Pompeii 645
    10. Assisi 646
    11. Florence 648
    12. Pisa and Genoa 649
    13. Nice 650
    14. Marseille 651
    15. Lyon and Paris 653

    C. Other Places Visited by St. Thérèse's Family 655
        1. The Basilica of Our Lady of Deliverance 655
        2. Lourdes 656
        3. The Trappist Monastery of Soligny 658
CHAPTER 8   THE CARMELITES 661
    A. History 661
    B. The Lisieux Carmel 666
        1. Formation Stages 666
        2. Daily Schedule and Regimen in St. Thérèse's Time 668
        3. Thérèse's Assignments 671
        4. Lay Staff 672

Selected Bibliography 679
Picture Credits 684
The 22 Plates 685

Preface

I love the reading of the lives of the saints very much, the account of their heroic deeds sets my courage on fire and attracts me to imitate them; but I admit that, at times, I happen to envy the blessed lot of their relatives who had the joy of living in their company and of enjoying their conversations.[1]

— *Thérèse*

PEOPLE HAVE OFTEN ASKED ME WHY I LIKE ST. THÉRÈSE AND WRITE about her. In a way my answer surprises even me: "I don't know." I guess I have a special affection for her because I have known about her since childhood, have found her story appealing and her philosophy simple but profound. Why I am writing about her is an enigma too because I do not like to write prose. For me doing so is a real chore, a burden, and frustrating. Most gifted writers of prose I presume have little difficulty in transferring their thoughts into words on paper with rapid facility. Practically every page in this book somehow required a great deal of revisions, corrections, struggles over elements of style, and choice of vocabulary, let alone involving an enormous amount of factual research, not only from English sources but also French—a language in which I am a neophyte. I must confess, though, that when I wrote three published plays for children (one with my own music), I did not face these problems. The style is different and my imagination flowed easily with no annoying restraints interfering or slowing me down. Furthermore, and this I can't quite fathom, there is the strong desire and persistence I have maintained for so many years to work at and finish this book.

My introduction to St. Thérèse originated when I was in "grammar" school where those kind, dedicated, and pedagogically eminent nuns in the order of School Sisters of Notre Dame taught. I can't remember actually when any of them specifically talked about Thérèse, but I believed that they, in their habits and holy demeanor, epitomized St. Thérèse. In fact, all of us thought our sixth grade teacher, Sister Mary Teresa, resembled St. Thérèse in her aspect and in her holiness.

As an altar boy, I spent much time in our parish church, St. John Nepomucene (c. 1350–1393, patron saint of Bohemia / Czechoslovakia). Here I really encountered her in the form of a statue on a shelf next to the altar of St. Joseph. Above her another significant object struck me and also made a lasting impact: a large mural of Christ preaching from a boat just off shore by an artist who has become one of my favorite religious painters, Heinrich Hofmann (1824–1911).

---

1 LT 178. Thérèse to her Aunt Guérin on July 20–21, 1895.

This painting ignited my abiding interest in art and its history. In addition, what intrigued me a great deal was, recessed in the wall of the left transept, a life-sized diorama of the Lourdes grotto with water gently trickling over a large stone from Lourdes below the feet of a statue of Our Lady, and kneeling figure of St. Bernadette nearby. Thérèse, Hofmann, and Lourdes remain to this day deeply engraved in my psyche.

The next vital step in my life-long fascination with Thérèse was reading about her. The first book I obtained, and I can't remember how, was Father Albert Dolan's *The Living Sisters of the Little Flower* in which he recounts his interviews with Thérèse's four sisters. His other books followed. They all completely enchanted me. The perfume of her sanctity seemed to emanate from the very pages I held in my hands as I read. After I devoured these books, I acquired her life story by Laveille and the one by Piat, followed finally by her own autobiography. From then on I was firmly entrenched in her mystique. My interest in her gradually accelerated to the point at which I decided to jot down names of people and places in her story I wanted to know more about. As a result, I delved deeper and searched wider because not one source contained all the information I craved. It slowly dawned on me that I should record this data methodically. This led me to believe that other people might also want to seek this knowledge contained in just one volume; thus I began to research for material with the aim of producing a book. Incidentally, I understand that of the hundreds of books about St. Thérèse there is not one that is similar to mine or covers the material in the manner I do.

One simple incident in my early adulthood brought to my consciousness the reality and actual nearness in time in which St. Thérèse is to us—at least to me. Despite countless visits to my dear grandmother's grave, one day I was startled when I noticed for the first time the significance of the year of her birth—1873, the same as Thérèse's!

Thérèse Martin was an actual person who appeared on earth in the last quarter of the 19th century and lived only twenty-four years. Yes, she was human in every sense of the word, but far above the ordinary in her spirituality. She experienced many of the illnesses, sorrows, and joys of young people her age: intestinal ailments, headaches, rashes, pimples, emotional upsets, extreme sensitivity, and even doubts.

Thérèse was the product of a family intensely concentrated on personal sanctity. Of the nine children born of Louis and Zélie Martin (who themselves have been beatified and are on the way to canonization), Thérèse was the youngest, most malleable, and willing clay her holy parents so easily molded into the embodiment of all their hopes and dreams, the apex of which was sainthood followed by the awesome honor of being designated a Doctor of the Universal Church.

I quote a massive amount of material from Thérèse's writings and others with the conviction that the original words, even though in translation, convey more accurately the essence and immediacy of the situations, and certainly the personality of the characters involved far better than I could possibly do with my own words. I have endeavored to find and copy all the quotations from Thérèse's writings as well as those of others that refer to or are pertinent to each subject on which I write. Some of the banalities of her life and the childish language of her early writings, so natural in little ones—even saints—may seem a bit trite or unnecessary, but they do, nonetheless, merit consideration and evaluation. They are not only imbued with charm but reflect the reality of her humanity. In a way, I consider everything she has written to be a kind of fourth class relic.

Finally, the purpose of this book is to provide facts and other information about Thérèse and the people and places connected with her that have never been collected and compiled into one book. I must emphasize that what I have produced is basically a reference, a source book, a companion, or an addendum, if you will, to the story of St. Thérèse. I do not in any way specifically delve into an analysis of her spirituality or her message to the world. This has all been thoroughly accomplished by expert theologians. At any rate, Thérèse's gems of spirituality permeate all of her writings and conversations, and obviously all that I have included in my book. The illustrations therein further enhance in their own visual manner the understanding and knowledge of each entry. I have traveled to, and recorded on film, the places Thérèse and her family visited and, when possible, I have spoken to the people presently living in the very buildings where Thérèse or her family used to live.

My sincere hope is that this book will be of interest and value to anyone wishing to gain detailed information about the life of St. Thérèse of Lisieux, her works, the many people and places connected with her, and more, all contained in one volume.

Abbreviations

CG II	*Correspondance Générale*, Vol. 1 (1877–1890) and Vol. II (1890–1897). (General Correspondence)
CF	*Correspondance familiale*. (Family Correspondence of letters from Zèlie Martin from 1863 to 1877)
ChrIG	*Cahier de M. Isidore Guérin.* (Copybook of M. Isidore Guérin containing his family genealogy and chronology)
CMG III	*Carnets manuscripts de Soeur Geneviève* (CMG I–IV). (Manuscript of Sister Geneviève)
CRM	*"Carnet rouge" de Soeur Marie de la Trinité—deposition au Procés.* ("Red Notebook" of Sister Marie of the Trinity—testimony at the Process)
DCL	*Documentation du Carmel de Lisieux.* (Documentation from the Lisieux Carmel)
LC	*Lettres des correspondants de Thérèse.* (Letters from Thérèse's Correspondents)
LT	*Lettres de Thérèse.* (Letters from Thérèse)
PA	*Procès Apostolique*, 1915–1917. (Apostolic Process)
PO	*Procès de l' Ordinaire*, 1910–1911. (Called the Ordinary Process, Bishop's or the Diocesan Process)
Pri	*Prières de Sainte Thérèse de l'Enfant-Jésus.* (Prayers by Saint Thérèse of the Child Jesus)
RP	*Récréations Pieuses de Sainte Thérèse de l'Enfant-Jésus* (Plays of Saint Thérèse of the Child Jesus: Pious Recreations of Sainte Thérèse of the Child Jesus)

Acknowledgments

WITHOUT MY TWIN BROTHER JOHN'S INDISPENSABLE HELP THIS book would not have been written. I could not have done without his invaluable editing, constant encouragement, infinite optimism, faith in my topic, patience in visiting all the places in France and Italy associated with Thérèse, and skill in taking hundreds of photographs on location.

I am profoundly indebted to the nuns of the Lisieux Carmel Archives. They graciously answered the many questions I so often bombarded them with and which only they knew the answers to; they did so with no hesitation at all, not even a hint of annoyance. They also encouraged me when I was frustrated with my slowness and discouraged with the number of pages I never dreamed would be so large. I deeply appreciate their belief in the unique merit of the book.

My earliest association with Carmelites extends back many years, though not to any in the United States, but in Canada. The first Carmel is in Montreal which I visited a number of times, followed later by the one in Trois Rivières. One day while at the monastery in Montreal I gave a brief sample of my earliest manuscript to one of the extern sisters whom I had known for a few years and who was aware of the book I was writing. She and another sister at the Trois Rivières Carmel showed much interest in it and prayed for its successful conclusion. By chance, Msgr. Guy Gaucher, then auxiliary bishop of Bayeux and Lisieux, the scholar and author *par excellence* of many books about St. Thérèse, was scheduled to see the Montreal Carmel nuns the next day. The nuns presented the sample of my work to him for his perusal and evaluation. A few days later I was introduced to him. During our conversation he advised me to send a portion of my manuscript to a religious magazine, and if it was accepted, to see what reaction the readers had to it. The first magazine I submitted it to, *The Apostolate of the Little Flower* published by the Carmelite Fathers in San Antonio, Texas, accepted it. The readers apparently liked it because I was asked to write more articles for them covering a period of ten years. During this time they selected me as one of the contributing editors, a post I held for a few years. Incidentally, the first article by me that appeared in their magazine was about St. Thérèse's pet dog, Tom. I owe a great debt of gratitude to John Lee, former assistant editor of this periodical. His continued friendship, advice, and firm belief in the value of my book have sustained and influenced me tremendously.

Many other personal friends and religious have helped me in my long and tedious efforts to write and finally finish this book. My sincere and deep gratitude is extended particularly to Father Andrew Walter who was constant in his belief in the worth of my book. He tirelessly pursued all channels, spreading the knowledge of my work, and accompanied my brother and me as we visited many of the places Thérèse journeyed through on her pilgrimage to Rome. Other kind priests also offered reassurance and prayers.

I am truly indebted to the following two nuns who willingly translated difficult French passages into English: Sister Frances and Sister Marie Lucie of the Congregation of the Hospitaler Sisters of Saint Thomas of Villanova who manage a convalescent home in Norwalk, Connecticut. Other nuns who were especially genial and obliging with their prayers and support were Sister Gregoria of the Sisters of the Holy Family of Nazareth at the motherhouse in Monroe, Connecticut, and Sister Caesaria (later called Sister Julia Foray) a member of the School Sisters of Notre Dame—my second grade teacher who many years ago chose my brother and me as altar boys, a privileged position we proudly held for several years. Another nun to whom I am particularly indebted is Sister Monique Richer of Montreal who personally introduced me to Msgr. Guy Gaucher and has always encouraged me and prayed for the success of my project.

My deep felt gratitude certainly extends to my closest friends Elvira Kaminski and Estelle Carrafiello who never ceased to have faith in my project, continued to offer their unending words of encouragement, and persisted in forcing me to work and finish the job.

I cannot omit my friends in the Community of the Beatitudes, particularly Ginette Johnson formerly at Ste. Anne de Beaupré in Canada, those in Hermival le Vaux close to Lisieux, and at St. Broladre near Mont-Saint-Michel in France at whose houses I stayed, who showed much interest in my work, and helped me along with their prayers.

One person in France who has been so friendly and helpful was the sacristan (now former) at the Carmel in Lisieux, Philippe Bannier. He willingly offered to show us around the sacristy and indicated the places there connected with St. Thérèse such as the enclosure door to the cloistered area in front of which is the same tile floor Thérèse knelt on to receive her father's last blessing, the confessional (the priest's side), the turn, and the original altar from the main chapel. Thanks go also to another Frenchman, Rodolphe Durand, a young visiting student from France, who gladly translated numerous French articles for me.

I devoted years to writing at home, but also when I was traveling in my country (U.S.A.), Canada, and abroad. In France I visited where St. Thérèse lived and every place she spent time at on vacations. In Italy too, I saw, and my brother photographed, all but two of the many sites and hotels of her sojourn there. On practically every trip I brought along material to work on, especially during those winter weeks I spent in the Florida Keys at the home of the late Anthony Deaso, a family friend and teaching colleague who was always accommodating, hospitable, and encouraging.

Cindy Perez and her colleagues at our local Staples Office Supplies Store deserve much thanks for their kindness, patience, and expertise in providing countless copies and other work I needed during many of the years I was writing this book. The fine quality of the images reproduced here is due to Marita Therese Corr Baker, the owner and the staff of Baker Graphics in Westport, Connecticut.

Two families who allowed me the extraordinary privilege of entering into the world of St. Thérèse are M. Louis Gérault and his gracious wife Christiane of Alençon and M. Jacques Hervieu and his equally hospitable wife Anne Marie of Lisieux. By sheer luck at our first meeting in each place, they cordially invited us into their homes where they explained their house's relation to Thérèse and even kindly offered us refreshments then as well as at each subsequent visit. This house in Alençon was the home of M. and Mme. Tifenne where Thérèse and Céline slept in what Thérèse called the "Cardinal's Room." The Hervieu home in Lisieux became in 1892 the residence of M. Martin and his daughters Léonie and Céline following Louis's release from a hospital in Caen where he was confined for nearly four years. They lived in this house until Louis's death in 1894. Since his beatification, a sign now indicates he stayed there.

Finally, I was indeed privileged to have spent many blissful days throughout the years working on my book in the quiet solitude of the library at the Benedictine Abbaye de Saint-Benoît-du-Lac in Austin (Québec), Canada, outside at a table under the trees, in the beautiful guest library, or in my little monastic cell inside this large abbey complex so evocative of European medieval monasteries.

Plate 1

St. Thérèse of Lisieux

A. AGE 3
1876

B. AGE 8
1881

C. AGE 13
1886

D. AGE 15
1888

E. AGE 16
1889

F. AGE 22 as Joan of Arc
1895

G. AGE 22
1895

H. AGE 23
1896

I. AGE 24
1897

J. AGE 24–Thérèse in death
1897

CHAPTER 1

ST. THÉRÈSE OF LISIEUX

A. Life and Posthumous Chronology
B. Writings and Art Work
C. Beatification and Canonization
D. Thérèse's Titles, Honors, Congregations, and Relics

A. Life and Posthumous Chronology

ALENÇON (1873–1877)

1873

JANUARY 2 (*Thursday*)
Marie-Françoise-Thérèse Martin is born at 11:30 P.M. at 36 (now 42) rue Saint Blaise.

JANUARY 4 (*Saturday*)
Thérèse is baptized in Notre Dame Church located a few blocks away from her home. Her eldest sister Marie (13 years old) becomes her godmother and Paul-Albert Boul (13 years old) her godfather.

JANUARY 17 (*Friday*)
The first symptoms of enteritis (inflamation of the intestines) appear.

MARCH 1 (*Saturday*)
Thérèse is very ill.

MARCH 15 OR 16 (*Saturday or Sunday*)
Rosalie Tailée ("Little Rose") begins nursing Thérèse at her country cottage several miles away in Semallé.

MAY 22 (*Thursday*)
Thérèse weighs fourteen pounds.

DECEMBER 13 (*Saturday*)
Thérèse walks almost all by herself.

WORLD EVENTS
- German troops finally withdraw from France where they were stationed since the Franco-Prussian War (1870–1871).
- The French elect Comte de MacMahon President of France.
- Remington & Sons produce the first commercial typewriter.
- Enrico Caruso, Italian tenor, is born.

1874 — 1 Year Old

JANUARY 8 (*Thursday*)
Thérèse walks by herself and has a sweet smile.

APRIL 2 (*Thursday*)
Thérèse returns for good to her family in Alençon.

JUNE 24 (*Wednesday*)
She is almost beginning to talk.

AUGUST 9 (*Sunday*)
She is sick for a week with teeth problems.

NOVEMBER 8 (*Sunday*)
She says her prayers "like an angel" and sings little songs.

WORLD EVENTS
- First Impressionist exhibition in Paris.
- The foundation stone of the basilica of *Sacré-Coeur* is laid.
- The first performance of these musical works: Mussorgsky's *Boris Godunov*, Johann Strauss' *Die Fledermaus*, and Verdi's *Requiem*.
- First sterilized instruments and sterilized rubber gloves used during surgeries.

1875 — 2 Years Old

FEBRUARY (*Sunday*)
Thérèse escapes from home to go to Mass.

MARCH 29 (*Monday*)
Thérèse goes with her mother by train to see her aunt, Sister Marie-Dosithée, a Visitation nun and teacher in Le Mans. She cries a lot but is very sweet and exceptionally obedient.

MAY 19 (*Wednesday*)
She has a persistent cough with a fever.

OCTOBER 8–22 (*Friday to Friday*)
The same health problems appear and last for two weeks.

OCTOBER 24 (*Sunday*)
In a letter to her friend Marie Morel, Marie Martin wrote that "Our baby is a pretty rascal; this funny little child Thérèse is attractive, impish, and darling, all in one."

NOVEMBER 5 (*Friday*)
Thérèse won't sleep until she says her prayers.

DECEMBER 5 (*Sunday*)
Mme. Martin in a letter to her daughter Pauline says that "The baby is a matchless rascal; she comes to caress me, wishing me dead: 'Oh! How I wish you were dead, dear little Mother!' We scold her, and she says: 'It is so that you may go to heaven, since you say we must die to go there.'"

DECEMBER 28 (*Tuesday*)
Thérèse knows almost all the letters of the alphabet. At this very early age, Thérèse says, "I too will be a religious."

WORLD EVENTS
- The Paris Opera House opens.
- Hans Christian Anderson dies.
- Bizet's opera *Carmen* is performed for the first time.

1876   3 Years Old

Sometime during this year Thérèse states that "at the age of three I began refusing nothing that God was asking from me."

MARCH 5 (*Sunday*)
Thérèse progresses rapidly in learning under the tutelage of her oldest sister Marie.

MAY 14 (*Sunday*)
Mme. Martin says that Thérèse "has in her an almost invincible stubbornness ... however, she has a heart of gold, she is very affectionate and very honest."

JULY 16 (*Sunday*)
Thérèse has her first picture taken which shows her pouting.

NOVEMBER 8 (*Wednesday*)
Thérèse wants to join her sisters in the practice of virtues which they counted on beads.

NOVEMBER (*Middle of*)
She has symptoms of measles which last for four days.

DECEMBER 24 (*Sunday*)
Mme. Martin consults Dr. Notta about a tumor on her breast which he says is too late to operate on.

WORLD EVENTS
- Alexander Bell invents the telephone.
- Publication of Mark Twain's *Adventures of Tom Sawyer*.
- First complete performance of Wagner's *Ring of the Nibelung*.

1877   4 Years Old

FEBRUARY 24 (*Saturday*)
Thérèse's aunt, Sister Marie-Dosithée (Guérin) dies.

MARCH 4 (*Sunday*)
Thérèse continues her chaplet of penances.

APRIL 4 (*Wednesday*)
Pauline guides Thérèse's hand as she writes her first letter (to Louise Magdelaine, Pauline's friend).

MAY

Marie tells Pauline that Thérèse "makes her prayer, leaping with joy. If you only knew how full of mischief she is, and yet not silly. I am full of admiration for this little 'bouquet.'"

JUNE 18–23 (*Monday to Saturday*)

Marie, Pauline, and Léonie travel to Lourdes with their mother who is seeking a cure for her breast cancer.

JULY 31 OR AUGUST 1 (*Tuesday or Wednesday*)

Céline and Thérèse, home schooled by Marie, are awarded prizes for their good work during the year.

AUGUST 28 (*Tuesday*)

Mme. Martin dies at 12:30 A.M. at her home in Alençon.

AUGUST 29 (*Wednesday*)

Mme. Martin is buried by the graves of her four children in the public cemetery in Alençon.

SEPTEMBER 9 (*Sunday*)

Thérèse's uncle (Isidore Guérin) finds a house for the Martin family to rent in Lisieux called "Les Buissonnets."

LISIEUX
Les Buissonnets (1877–1888)

NOVEMBER 16 (*Friday*)

The five sisters move into Les Buissonnets.

NOVEMBER 30 (*Friday*)

M. Martin joins his daughters after settling his business affairs in Alençon.

WORLD EVENTS
- Thomas Edison invents the phonograph.
- Rutherford B. Hayes is elected U.S. President.

1878   *5 Years Old*

APRIL

Thérèse understands a sermon for the first time (by Abbé Ducellier on the Passion of Our Lord).

AUGUST 8 (*Thursday*)

Thérèse travels by train to Trouville on a day trip and sees the ocean for the first time.

WORLD EVENTS
- Pope Pius IX dies and is succeeded by Pope Leo XIII.
- The Universal Exposition opens in Paris
- London has electric street lighting.
- *Pinafore*, an operetta by Gilbert and Sullivan, has its premier in London.

1879   *6 Years Old*

During this year Thérèse visits the Carmel Chapel for the first time.

In the summer of this or the next year Thérèse has the prophetic vision of her father in the garden of Les Buissonnets which foreshadows the coming trial of his mental and physical health problems to come.

At the end of this year or the beginning of 1880 Thérèse makes her first confession to Abbé Ducellier in Saint Pierre Church.

WORLD EVENTS
- Installation of the first European telephone exchange in Paris.
- Pasteur discovers the principle of vaccination.
- Premier of Tchaikovsky's opera *The Maid of Orleans*.

1880   *7 Years Old*

In the beginning of the year Thérèse writes without any help.

MAY 13 (*Thursday*)
Céline receives her First Communion which is also a great happiness for Thérèse.

JUNE 4 (*Friday*)
Céline's Confirmation.

DECEMBER 1 (*Wednesday*)
Thérèse writes all by herself a letter (the first one that is preserved) to her sister Pauline.

WORLD EVENTS
- The Boer War commences.
- Gladstone succeeds Disraeli as British Prime Minister.
- James Garfield is elected U.S. President.
- Jacques Offenbach, French operatic composer, dies.
- Anti-clerical decrees include the dissolution of the Society of Jesus and the closing of 261 religious houses.
- Siemen's electric elevator is installed.
- The first appendectomies are performed.

1881   *8 Years Old*

Sometime this year a professional photograph is taken of Céline and Thérèse holding a skipping rope.

JULY 10 (*Sunday*)
M. Martin gives a magpie to Thérèse from Eugène Taillé, Thérèse's "foster brother." This ten-year-old boy, the son of Rosalie Taillé (Thérèse's wet nurse), lives in the same cottage where Thérèse had been nursed.

OCTOBER 3 (*Monday*)
Thérèse enters for the first time the Benedictine Abbey of Lisieux (Notre-Dame-du-Pré) as a day student in the fourth or "green" class.

WORLD EVENTS
- President Garfield and Tsar Alexander are assassinated.
- Feodor Dostoyevsky, Russian novelist, dies.

1882   *9 Years Old*

JANUARY 12 (*Thursday*)
Thérèse is enrolled in the Work of the Holy Childhood.

FEBRUARY 16 (*Thursday*)
Pauline decides to become a Carmelite nun at the Lisieux Monastery.

APRIL 17 (*Monday*)
Marie takes Father Pichon, a Jesuit, as her spiritual director.

MAY 31 (*Wednesday*)
Thérèse is received into the association called "Child of the Holy Angels."

SUMMER
Thérèse learns by surprise of Pauline's leaving soon for the Carmel of Lisieux. Though greatly disturbed by this, she too feels a call to become a Carmelite.

OCTOBER 2 (*Monday*)
Pauline (age 21) enters the Lisieux Carmel and receives the name Sister Agnès of Jesus. Thérèse returns for her second school year with the Benedictines. Céline takes drawing lessons which Thérèse would love to receive but keeps silent about it.

OCTOBER
Mother Marie de Gonzague proposes the name "Sister Thérèse of the Child Jesus" for Thérèse when she becomes a Carmelite.

OCTOBER 15 (*Sunday*)
Celebrations are held commemorating the 300th anniversary of the death of St. Teresa of Avila.

DECEMBER
During this month Thérèse is pale and suffers from headaches, insomnia, pimples, and plaster patches.

> **WORLD EVENTS**
> - Ferdinand de Lesseps begins construction of the Panama Canal.
> - Robert Louis Stevenson's *Treasure Island* is published.
> - Wagner's *Parsifal* is performed for the first time.
> - Darwin, Rossetti, Emerson, and Longfellow die.

1883   *10 Years Old*

JANUARY 1 (*Monday*)
Mother Geneviève of Saint Teresa is elected prioress of the Carmel.

FEBRUARY 18 (*Sunday*)
The twenty-three year-old Paul-Albert Boul, Thérèse's godfather, dies.

MARCH 25 (*Easter Sunday*)
This is the beginning of Thérèse's strange nervous illness (trembling, hallucinations, etc.) while she is at the Guérin house when her father, Marie, and Léonie are away in Paris attending Easter services there.

APRIL 6 (*Friday*)
Pauline, after finishing her period as a postulant, receives the Carmelite habit. Thérèse, who is feeling a little better, attends the ceremony and hugs and kisses her sister in the outside speakroom.

APRIL 7 (*Saturday*)
Back home in Les Buissonnets, Thérèse has a relapse of her illness.

APRIL 8 (*Sunday*)
Thérèse's grandmother Martin dies in her home in Valframbert (near Alençon).

APRIL 13 (*Friday*)
Thérèse is suddenly cured of her illness by the smile she sees the Blessed Virgin Mary's statue gives her while she is lying in her sick bed in Les Buissonnets.

MAY
Thérèse visits Sister Agnès (Pauline) and the other Carmelites. She begins to have scruples about her illness (which lasted until May 1888) and of the smile she saw the Blessed Mother gave her.

AUGUST 20–30 (*Monday to Thursday*)
Thérèse vacations in Alençon with her father and sisters. Here she prays at her mother's grave and visits chateaux in the surrounding area.

AUGUST 22 (*Wednesday*)
Thérèse meets father Pichon in Alençon for the first time.

OCTOBER 1 (*Monday*)
Thérèse enters the new school year at the Abbey and is enrolled in the third class, second division.

WORLD EVENTS
- The Orient Express makes its initial run from Paris to Istanbul.
- The Metropolitan Opera House in New York opens.
- The Brooklyn Bridge opens.
- Manet, Gustave Doré, Karl Marx, and Wagner die.

1884 *11 Years Old*

JANUARY
Henri Chéron (future lawyer and well-known politician) spends time with Isidore Guérin at his pharmacy in Lisieux.

FEBRUARY – MAY
Thérèse prepares for her First Communion with the aid of her sister Pauline (Sister Agnès) and the booklet she arranged for her.

APRIL 2 (*Wednesday*)
Thérèse is received as a Communicant in the Catechism examination.

MAY 4 (*Sunday*)
Thérèse enters the Abbey school as a boarder for four days in preparation for her First Communion.

MAY 5–8 (*Monday to Thursday*)
This is the preparatory retreat time for Thérèse. The instructions are by Abbé Domin.

MAY 7 (*Wednesday*)
Thérèse makes her general confession.

MAY 8 (*Thursday*)
She receives her First Communion at the Abbey and experiences an interior peace for a year. Pauline's Profession at the Carmel is on the same day.

MAY 22 (*Ascension Thursday*)
Thérèse receives Communion for the second time.

JUNE 14 (*Saturday*)
Thérèse is confirmed at the Abbey by Msgr. Hugonin, Bishop of Bayeux.

JUNE 26 (*Thursday*)
She is given the spaniel Tom as a pet.

JULY–AUGUST
Thérèse has whooping cough.

JULY 16 (*Wednesday*)
Sister Agnès of Jesus takes the black veil.

AUGUST (*Beginning of*)
Thérèse stays with her cousins Jeanne and Marie Guérin at their grandmother's (Mme. Fournet) farm in Saint-Ouen-le-Pin (some 6 miles from Lisieux) where she enjoys the clean air, sketching, and exploring the countryside.

AUGUST 8 (*Friday*)
Thérèse sketches a building on Mme. Fournet's farm.

SEPTEMBER 25 (*Friday*)
She is enrolled in the Holy Rosary Confraternity.

OCTOBER 4 (*Saturday*)
Marie goes with her father Louis Martin to Le Havre to see Father Pichon who is leaving for Canada.

OCTOBER 6 (*Monday*)
Thérèse starts the new school year at the Abbey as a day student.

DECEMBER 14 (*Sunday*)
She is nominated as a counselor of the Association of the Holy Angels.

WORLD EVENTS
- Grover Cleveland is elected President of the U.S.A.
- Kodak and Eastman photography is advanced.
- Mark Twain's *Huckleberry Finn* is published.
- Massenet's opera *Manon* has its world premier.
- Pope Leo XII issues *Humanus Genus*, an encyclical against Freemasonry.

1885 *12 Years Old*

APRIL 26 (*Sunday*)
Thérèse is enrolled in the "Confraternity of the Holy Face" at Tours.

APRIL 29 (*to June 5*)
The Guérins stay at the Maison Colombe (later called Chalet des Roses) in Deauville.

MAY 3–10 (*Sunday to Saturday*)
Thérèse is on vacation in Deauville with the Guérins. She sketches the Chalet des Roses. Headaches plague her and then she understands Fontaine's fable of "the donkey and the little dog."

MAY 17–21 (*Sunday to Thursday*)
Thérèse makes a retreat in preparation for her Second Solemn Communion. The instructions are by Abbé Domin. Now also begins a period where Thérèse experiences scruples which last until the autumn of 1886.

MAY 21 (*Thursday*)
Thérèse receives her second Solemn Communion.

JULY
Thérèse is given a linnet.

JULY (*End of*)
She again vacations at the farm house of her Aunt Guérin's mother, Mme. Fournet, and has a delightful time with Céline and their cousins Jeanne and Marie.

AUGUST 4 (*Tuesday*)
Céline who is sixteen years old completes her schooling at the Abbey.

AUGUST 22 (*Saturday*)
Louis Martin, accompanied by Father Charles Marie of Saint Jacques Church in Lisieux, takes a trip to Constantinople lasting seven weeks.

SEPTEMBER 3–30 (*Sunday to Wednesday*)
The Guérins rent the Villa Rose in Trouville.

SEPTEMBER 20–30
Thérèse and Céline join the Guérins in Trouville.

OCTOBER (*Beginning of*)
Thérèse starts her fifth school year (orange) at the Abbey without Céline.

OCTOBER 10–17
M. Martin returns to Lisieux from his trip to Constantinople.

WORLD EVENTS
- Golf and football first appear in the U.S.A.
- Victor Hugo dies.
- The Statue of Liberty arrives in New York from France.

1886   *13 Years Old*

FEBRUARY 2 (*Tuesday*)
Thérèse is accepted as an aspirant into The Children of Mary. She suffers from headaches and is frequently absent from school.

FEBRUARY 3 (*Wednesday*)
Mother Marie de Gonzague is elected prioress of the Carmel.
M. Martin removes Thérèse from the abbey school because of her health (headaches, etc.). She now receives private lessons from Mme. Papinau. Thérèse arranges a study for herself in the attic of Les Buissonnets.

JUNE 15 – JULY 31
The Guérins rent the Chalet des Lilas in Trouville at 29 rue de la Cavée.

JUNE 30 (*Wednesday*)
Thérèse goes to visit the Guérins in Trouville without her sisters but leaves because of homesickness.

AUGUST
She learns of her sister Marie's leaving in October to enter the Lisieux Carmel.

SEPTEMBER 21 (*Tuesday*)
Thérèse resumes lessons with Mme. Papinau.

SEPTEMBER 29 (*Wednesday*)
M. Martin and Marie travel to Calais, Dover, and Paris to meet Father Pichon who is returning from Canada.

OCTOBER 3 (*Sunday*)
M. Martin and Marie return to Les Buissonnets.

OCTOBER 5 (*Tuesday*)
M. Martin with Thérèse and Céline go to Alençon for a few days.

OCTOBER 7 (*Thursday*)
Without any warning Léonie enters the Poor Clares in Alençon.

OCTOBER 15 (*Friday*)
Marie enters the Lisieux Carmel and assumes the name Sister Marie of the Sacred Heart.

OCTOBER (*End of*)
Thérèse finally is freed from her scruples which lasted a year-and-a-half.

DECEMBER (*Wednesday*)
Léonie returns home after fifty-five days with the Poor Clares in Alençon.

DECEMBER 25 (*Saturday*)
After Midnight Mass on Christmas morning, Thérèse experiences the grace of "conversion" at Les Buissonnets when she said God made her strong and courageous enough to "run as a giant" in life's struggles.

WORLD EVENTS
- Coca-Cola is produced for the first time in Atlanta, Georgia, U.S.A.
- The first electric street lamps are installed in Paris.
- The first sound records are made.

1887   *14 Years Old*

For Céline and Thérèse life at Les Buissonnets this year is "the ideal of happiness."

JANUARY–MAY
Céline gives Thérèse drawing lessons.

MARCH 19 (*Saturday*)
Sister Marie of the Sacred Heart (Marie) receives the Carmelite habit. Father Pichon preaches the sermon.

MARCH 19–20 (*Night of Saturday–Sunday*)
Henri Pranzini murders two women and a young girl in Paris.

APRIL 12 (*Tuesday*)
Thérèse sketches the church in Ouilly-le-Vicomte near Lisieux.

MAY 1 (*Sunday*)
Louis Martin has his first paralytic stroke giving him partial paralysis on one side.

MAY 29 (*Pentecost Sunday*)
Thérèse's father gives his consent to have her enter Carmel at the age of fifteen.

MAY 31 (*Tuesday*)
Thérèse is received into the Children of Mary.

JUNE 16 (*Thursday*)
M. Martin, Abbé Lepelletier, Léonie, Céline, and Thérèse spend a day in the Pont-l'Évêque area sketching, picking flowers, and fishing. The Abbé made a sketch of the girls in a field which shows Thérèse picking flowers.

JUNE
M. Martin takes his three daughters to Honfleur and to the International Maritime Exposition in Le Havre where Thérèse buys two bluebirds for Céline.

JUNE 21 (*Tuesday*)
Sister Agnès of Jesus (Pauline) finishes her novitiate at the Carmel.

JUNE 20–JULY 31
The Guérins are on vacation at the Chalet des Lilas in Trouville.

JULY 13 (*Wednesday*)
Henri Pranzini is condemned to death. Thérèse prays and makes sacrifices for his conversion.

JULY 16 (*Saturday*)
Léonie enters the Visitation convent in Caen again.

SEPTEMBER 1 (*Thursday*)
Thérèse reads in *La Croix* the account of Pranzini's execution (by guillotine on August 31) and is convinced of his conversion when he kisses a crucifix just before he is killed.

OCTOBER 6 (*Thursday*)
Thérèse visits her sister at the Visitation convent in Caen on a one day trip from Lisieux.

OCTOBER 6–15 (*Thursday to the second Saturday*)
Father Pichon preaches a retreat at the Carmel in Lisieux.

OCTOBER 8 (*Saturday*)
Thérèse asks her uncle Isidore Guérin for his permission to enter Carmel at Christmas, but he wants to postpone her entrance.

OCTOBER 12 (*Wednesday*)
Céline takes Father Pichon as her spiritual director.

OCTOBER 22 (*Saturday*)
Uncle Guérin, influenced by Sister Agnès of Jesus (Pauline), finally consents to Thérèse's entrance into Carmel.

OCTOBER 24 (*Monday*)
Canon Delatroëtte, ecclesiastical Superior of the Lisieux Carmel, opposes Thérèse's entrance until she is twenty-one.

OCTOBER 31 (*Monday*)
Thérèse and her father visit Bishop Hugonin in Bayeux to ask for her admittance into the Lisieux Carmel, but he delays his answer.

NOVEMBER 4 (*Friday*)
At 3 o'clock in the morning M. Martin, Céline, and Thérèse leave Lisieux for Paris where they begin their pilgrimage to Rome. They join the groups from the dioceses of Coutances and Bayeux which are going to celebrate the golden jubilee of Pope Leo XIII's ordination to the priesthood.

NOVEMBER 7–13 (*Monday to Sunday*)
In Paris Thérèse visits the Marian shrine of Our Lady of Victories where she obtains a special grace of peace. On Sunday the group assembles in the crypt of *Sacré-Coeur* (the upper part is not completed), attend services, and depart by train at 7:00 A.M.

NOVEMBER 78–13 (*Monday to Sunday*)
The pilgrim group visit Lucerne, Milan, Venice, Padua, and Bologna.

NOVEMBER 13 (*Sunday*)
Céline and Thérèse are in Loretto overnight and receive Communion at the Holy House. They arrive in Rome in the evening.

NOVEMBER 14 (*Monday*)
Among other places, the Martins visit the Colosseum, the Catacombs of Saint Calixtus, and the church of Saint Agnès Outside the Walls.

NOVEMBER 20 (*Sunday*)
The pilgrims have an audience with Pope Leo XIII. Thérèse asks the Pope for permission to become a Carmelite but he says (much to her disappointment) to "do what your Superiors tell you," followed by, "you will enter if God wills it."

NOVEMBER 21–22 (*Monday–Tuesday*)
Thérèse and Céline take a trip to Naples and Pompeii without their father who stays in Rome to visit his old friend Brother Siméon.

NOVEMBER 24 – DECEMBER 2 (*Thursday to the second Friday*)
On the return trip they visit Assisi, Florence, Pisa, Genoa, Nice, Marseille, Lyon, and Paris.

DECEMBER 2 (*Friday*)
The Martins arrive at Lisieux at 4:30 in the afternoon. They promptly visit the Carmel to talk to Pauline and Marie.

DECEMBER 16 (*Friday*)
Thérèse sends letters to the Bishop and to Father Révérony asking for permission to enter Carmel at Christmas.

DECEMBER 28 (*Wednesday*)
Bishop Hugonin finally gives his answer stating that Mother Marie de Gonzague may accept Thérèse into the monastery.

WORLD EVENTS
- Queen Victoria celebrates her Golden Jubilee.
- The construction of the Eiffel Tower begins.
- A. B. Dick & Co. introduces mimeograph duplicating machines.
- Verdi's *Otello* is first performed.

1888 — *15 Years Old*

JANUARY 1 (*Sunday*)
The Bishop gives his approval for Thérèse to enter Carmel but her entrance is postponed three months because her sister Pauline does not want her to enter during the severe penitential Lenten season.

JANUARY 6 (*Friday*)
Léonie leaves the Caen Visitation and goes home.

APRIL (*Beginning of*)
Céline says that a professional photographer takes a picture of Thérèse with her hair combed to look older. Most likely it was taken on Oct. 31, 1887

APRIL 9 (*Monday*)
Thérèse enters Carmel the same day Céline receives an offer of marriage.

AT THE CARMEL
Postulancy
(April 9, 1888 to January 10, 1889)

APRIL
Thérèse is assigned to work in the linen room and sweeping a corridor. Her postulancy is "more thorns than roses." Her sister Marie is her "Angel."

MAY 22 (*Tuesday*)
Sister Marie of the Sacred Heart (Marie) is professed. During the ceremony Thérèse crowns her with roses.

MAY 23 (*Wednesday*)
Marie takes the veil. Father Pichon gives the sermon. It is also the fiftieth anniversary of the founding of the Lisieux Carmel.

MAY 24–28 (*Thursday to Monday*)
Father Pichon gives a retreat with two instructions a day.

MAY 28 (*Monday*)
Thérèse makes a general confession to Father Pichon. She takes him as her spiritual director.

JUNE 15 (*Friday*)
Céline tells her father that she too wants to be a Carmelite.

JUNE 21 (*Thursday*)
It is the feast day of the prioress, Mother Marie de Gonzague. To celebrate it, Thérèse plays the part of St. Agnès in a play by her sister Pauline (Sister Agnès).

JUNE 23–27 (*Saturday to Wednesday*)
M. Martin flees to Le Havre in a state of confusion and amnesia.

JUNE 26 (*Tuesday*)
The house next door to Les Buissonnets catches on fire. Next month M. Martin buys the land where the burnt house stood for the purpose of enlarging his own estate.

JUNE 27 (*Wednesday*)
M. Martin is found near the General Post Office in Le Havre by Mr. Guérin, his nephew by marriage, and Céline.

JULY (*Beginning of*)
M. Martin, Léonie, and Céline stay for two weeks at Auteuil (not far from Paris) where M. Martin rented a flat.

AUGUST 12 (*Sunday*)
Louis Martin has a relapse at Les Buissonnets.

AUGUST 22 (*Wednesday*)
Auguste David, a cousin of Mme. Guérin, dies and leaves an important inheritance to the Guérins including the Chateau de La Musse.

OCTOBER 8–15 (*Monday to Monday*)
The annual community retreat is preached most likely by the Jesuit, Father Blino.

OCTOBER 31–NOVEMBER 2 (*Wednesday to Friday*)
M. Martin and Céline go to Le Havre to bid farewell to Father Pichon who is leaving for Canada. At Honfleur M. Martin has another serious relapse. They return by way of Paris where they finally meet up with Father Pichon.

NOVEMBER
Because of M. Martin's condition, Thérèse's reception of the habit is postponed.

DECEMBER 8 (*Saturday*)
Isidore Guérin sells his pharmacy in Lisieux to Victor Lahaye, a close family friend.

DECEMBER
M. Martin gives 10,000 francs for a new main altar in the cathedral of Saint-Pierre in Lisieux. He gave the same amount for Thérèse's dowry when she entered Carmel.

WORLD EVENTS
- Benjamin Harrison is elected U.S. President.
- Jack the Ripper murders several women in London.
- Wilhelm II (the "Kaiser) becomes Emperor of Germany.

1889   *16 Years Old*

JANUARY 5–10 (*Saturday to Thursday*)
Thérèse goes on retreat for six days in preparation for her reception of the habit during which she writes six notes or letters (LT 74–79). Letter 77 is the last one to her father. All the rest she wrote to him were destroyed.

JANUARY 10 (*Thursday*)
Thérèse receives the habit with her father present. She adds "of the Holy Face" to her name. To her joy, it snows. This is the last celebration that Louis Martin attends.

NOVITIATE
(January 10, 1889–September 8, 1890)

JANUARY
The new tasks for Thérèse are: work in the refectory with Sister Agnès of Jesus (Pauline) and sweeping. Two photos are taken of Thérèse in the Carmel courtyard.

JANUARY 22 (*Around this date*)
M. Martin's condition becomes worse with alternating symptoms of over excitement, inertia, indolence, and sleepiness. This lasts for some ten days and then he is confined to bed.

FEBRUARY 12 (*Tuesday*)
After a crisis of hallucinations, M. Guérin and a friend take M. Martin to Bon Sauveur, a hospital in Caen, where he will remain for three years.

FEBRUARY 13 (*Wednesday*)
Mother Marie de Gonzague is re-elected prioress for three years.

FEBRUARY 19 (*Tuesday*)
Léonie and Céline stay at the Orphanage of Saint Vincent de Paul in Caen run by the Sisters of Charity in order to visit their father frequently.

MARCH 25–JUNE 7
The Guérins (who moved out of their home above the pharmacy on Place Thiers in Lisieux) move temporarily into La Maison Sauvage at 16 rue Condorcet before they will settle into Les Buissonnets.

APRIL 20 (*Saturday*)
The Guérins buy a house at 19 rue de la Chaussée (now rue Paul Banaston).

MAY
The turn quarters of the monastery are being renovated. The speakroom is used as a confessional. Céline and Léonie will not see their Carmelite sisters for a whole year.

MAY 5 (*Sunday*)
There are big celebrations in Lisieux in remembrance of the 100th anniversary of the convocation of the Etats Généraux. The Universal Exhibition is held in Paris and the inauguration of the Eiffel Tower is held.

MAY 14 (*Tuesday*)
Léonie and Céline leave Caen and return to Les Buissonnets since they are not allowed to see their father now but once a week.

JUNE 7 (*Friday*)
The Guérins move into Les Buissonnets for a few weeks.

JUNE 18 (*Tuesday*)
The Lisieux tribunal appoints an administrator over the possessions of the now incompetent Louis Martin.

JULY 6–20 (*Saturday to Saturday*)
Céline, Léonie, and the Guérins stay for two weeks at the Château de La Musse.

JULY
Thérèse receives a Marian grace while praying at the hermitage of Saint Mary Magdalene. This place, located behind the cemetery in the garden of the monastery, consists of a grotto with a statue of the repentant Magdalene.

JULY 12 (*Friday*)
Marcelline Husé, a servant of the Guérins, enters the Benedictine Order in Bayeux.

JULY 20 (*Saturday*)
On their return from La Musse, Céline and Léonie go to live for a while with the Guérins' new home on rue Paul Banaston in Lisieux. Les Buissonnets is now abandoned.

AUGUST 27 (*Tuesday*)
Carmel's sacristan, Victor Bonaventure, dies; the two novices—Sister Thérèse and Sister Martha—assume for a while the sacristan's duty of sweeping the outside chapel open to the public.

OCTOBER
There is no preached retreat because of renovations in the turn sisters area.

OCTOBER 21 (*Around this date*)
Some furniture from Les Buissonnets is given to the Carmel. Thérèse's pet spaniel Tom comes into the cloister at this time and recognizes Thérèse even though her face is veiled.

DECEMBER 25

The lease of Les Buissonnets is ended. At Carmel Thérèse enjoys playing the part of the Blessed Virgin in the play her sister Pauline (Sister Agnès) wrote entitled *The First Dream of the Child Jesus*.

WORLD EVENTS
- The Eiffel Tower's completion opens the Universal Exposition.
- The Crown Prince of Austria, the Archduke Rudolph, commits suicide in his hunting lodge in Mayerling. His mistress Baroness Maria Vetsera also dies.
- Robert Browning dies.
- Father Damien of the leper colony in Molokai, Hawaii, dies.
- The feast of the Sacred Heart is instituted.
- Adolf Hitler is born.

1890 — *17 Years Old*

During this year Thérèse reads the works of Saint John of the Cross and discovers the texts of Isaias concerning the "Suffering Servant."

JANUARY

Thérèse's Profession is postponed.

APRIL 4 (*Good Friday*)

The foundress of the Lisiuex Carmel, Mother Geneviève, receives Extreme Unction.

MAY

Thérèse has a conversation with Father Blino, a Jesuit, who tries to moderate her great desire for holiness.

JUNE 8 (*Sunday*)

Thérèse's cousin Jeanne becomes engaged to Dr. La Néele.

JULY

The new quarters of the turn are completed. The two new Turn Sisters arrive: Sister Marie Elizabeth and Sister Marie Antoinette. The speakrooms are used as before. The novitiate is arranged on the first floor.

JULY 10–31 (*Thursday to Thursday*)

Léonie and Céline stay with the Guérins at La Musse for three weeks.

JULY 18 (*Friday*)

Thérèse writes of the hidden beauties of Jesus, of the *Song of Songs*, and of St. John of the Cross. (See LT 108 to Céline)

JULY 27–29 (*Sunday to Tuesday*)

In a letter to Marie Guérin (LT 109), Thérèse writes about her (Marie's) vocation and temptations.

AUGUST (*Beginning of*)

Thérèse is admitted for Profession by the Conventual Chapter.

AUGUST 28–SEPTEMBER 8 (*Thursday to 2nd Monday*)

Thérèse makes a ten day retreat for her profession in complete aridity.

SEPTEMBER 2 (*Tuesday*)

Thérèse undergoes the canonical examination in the chapel during which she states that she has come to Carmel "to save souls and above all in order to pray for priests." On this day a papal benediction arrives from Pope Leo XIII for Thérèse and her father.

SEPTEMBER 8 (*Monday*)

Thérèse is professed. She asks for herself "love without limits" and "martyrdom of body and heart." She prays for Léonie's vocation and for her father's cure.

SEPTEMBER 24 (*Wednesday*)

Thérèse receives the black veil with sadness because of her father's absence. Marie Guérin is assured of her Carmelite vocation.

OCTOBER 1 (*Wednesday*)

Jeanne Guérin and Dr. LaNéele are married in Caen.

DECEMBER 28 (*Sunday*)

Pope Leo XIII issues a decree on frequent communion for religious.

WORLD EVENTS
- The electric chair is invented in New York City.
- Vincent van Gogh commits suicide.
- *Cavalleria Rusticana*, an opera by Mascagni, has its world premier.
- Subways are installed in London.

1891 — *18 Years Old*

APRIL–JULY

Thérèse prays for Hyacinthe Loyson (an ex-Carmelite priest and provincial of the order) who left the Church and journeys through Normandy giving anti-Catholic conferences.

JUNE 29–AUGUST 13

Céline and Léonie stay with the Guérins at La Musse for seven weeks.

JULY 5 (*Sunday*)

Thérèse's sister Marie (Sister Marie of the Sacred Heart) leaves the novitiate quarters with Sister Martha as Thérèse's only companion there.

JULY 23 (*Thursday*)

Thérèse writes a letter (LT 130) to Céline which urges her to refuse the proposal of marriage from Henry Maudelonde.

OCTOBER 7–15 (*Wednesday to the 2nd Thursday*)

The Franciscan Father Alexis Prou preaches the community retreat. Thérèse obtains a great grace from it.

OCTOBER 10 (*Saturday*)

The vicar general of the diocese, Abbé Révérony, dies in Caen at the age of fifty-five.

NOVEMBER 23–25 (*Monday to Wednesday*)
Celebrations are held for the third centenary of the death of Saint John of the Cross. The Franciscan priest Father Déodat de Basly preaches sermons about this in the monastery during the triduum. Bishop Hugonin enters the cloister and shows a very paternal attitude toward Thérèse, "his little girl."

NOVEMBER 26 (*Thursday*)
Dr. Francis LaNéele sells his pharmacy in Caen, keeping only the medical office in order to have the right legally to practice medicine.

DECEMBER 5 (*Saturday*)
Mother Geneviève, the foundress of the Lisieux Carmel, dies.

DECEMBER 23 (*Wednesday*)
Mother Geneviève is interred in the sanctuary of the Carmel Chapel. Thérèse dreams she receives the heart of the saintly Mother.

DECEMBER 28 (*Monday*)
Beginning of the influenza epidemic that hits the Carmel. Thérèse takes care of the sacristy and is allowed to receive Communion daily.

WORLD EVENTS
- Herman Melville dies.
- The Trans-Siberian railway begins operating.
- Arthur Conan Doyle's *The Adventures of Sherlock Holmes* is published.

1892 — *19 Years Old*

JANUARY
The influenza epidemic hits the Carmel severely. Sometime in the beginning of the month Father Baillon is appointed extraordinary confessor for the community.

JANUARY 4
Thérèse is present when the sub-prioress, Sister Febronie, dies of influenza.

JANUARY 7 (*Thursday*)
Sister Madeleine of the Blessed Sacrament also dies of the flu. Thérèse finds her dead in her room.

FEBRUARY
The elections are postponed a year because of the influenza catastrophe. Mother Marie de Gonzague remains, therefore, as prioress.

APRIL 20 (*Wednesday*)
Henri Maudelonde (who had proposed to Céline last year) marries. Thérèse is pleased that Céline, following her advice, refuses to dance at his wedding.

MAY 10 (*Tuesday*)
M. Guérin takes M. Martin home from the Caen hospital since his legs are now paralyzed and therefore is unable to escape from his house.

MAY 12 (*Thursday*)
Louis Martin makes his last visit to the Carmel to talk to his three daughters there.

JULY
Céline and Léonie move into a house on rue Labbey in Lisieux with their father and two servants—Désiré and Marie.

WORLD EVENTS
- The Panama scandal erupts.
- Ellis Island opens in New York harbor.
- William Gladstone becomes England's Prime Minister.
- Alfred Lord Tennyson and Walt Whitman die.
- The opera *Pagliacci* and Tchaikovsky's ballet *The Nutcracker* have their premier performances.

1893   *20 Years Old*

FEBRUARY 2 (*Thursday*)
Thérèse writes her first poem, "The Divine Dew," requested by Sister Thérèse of Saint Augustine.

FEBRUARY 20 (*Monday*)
Mother Agnès of Jesus (Pauline) is elected prioress. Mother Marie de Gonzague, the former prioress, is now mistress of novices. Thérèse's task is to help her in the formation of the novices.

JUNE
Thérèse paints a fresco of angels in the Oratory. She becomes "second" assistant to the bursar.

JUNE 24 (*Saturday*)
Léonie again enters the Visitation convent in Caen. This is her third attempt at religious life.

JUNE 27 – AUGUST 18 (*Over 7 weeks*)
Céline and her father with their pet spaniel Tom join the Guérins for a vacation at La Musse.

SEPTEMBER
Thérèse was scheduled to leave the novitiate quarters this month but asks to stay. Her tasks include painting and working as second portress.

SEPTEMBER 15 (*Friday*)
Céline takes lessons in painting with the artist Krug.

WORLD EVENTS
- Tchaikovsky and Guy de Maupassant die.
- Puccini's first successful opera *Manon Lescaut* has its world premier in Italy.
- Dvorak's "From the New World" symphony is first performed.
- The diesel engine is invented.

1894 *21 Years Old*

This is the year of Joan of Arc. Thérèse now begins to fast according to the Rule.

JANUARY

Thérèse paints "The Dream of the Child Jesus." She also writes her first play, *The Mission of Joan of Arc.*

JANUARY 2 (*Tuesday*)

Thérèse is twenty-one years old so she has to begin fasting according to the Rule.

JANUARY 27 (*Saturday*)

Pope Leo XIII declares Joan of Arc Venerable.

SPRING

This is the beginning of Thérèse's sufferings of her throat.

MAY 8 (*Tuesday*)

Great celebrations are held in Lisieux honoring the Venerable Joan of Arc. The Guérins and Martins decorate their houses with flags for the occasion. Thérèse writes Poem 4, "Canticle to Obtain the Canonization of the Venerable Joan of Arc."

MAY 27 (*Sunday*)

M. Martin has a paralytic stroke and receives Extreme Unction.

JUNE 5 (*Tuesday*)

Louis Martin has a serious heart attack.

JUNE 8 (*Friday*)

The Guérins install Louis Martin and Céline in their home on rue Paul Banaston in the street next to the house where the Guérins are living.

JUNE 20 (*Wednesday*)

Father Pichon explains in a letter his plans for "Bethany," a religious group of women for which Céline would be the foundress.

JULY 29 (*Sunday*)

M. Martin dies at La Musse.

AUGUST 2 (*Thursday*)

M. Martin is buried in the Lisieux public cemetery. A little while later Céline divulges Father Pichon's project to her sisters who all disapprove of her involvement in his plan.

AUGUST 7 OR 8 (*Tuesday or Wednesday*)

Céline asks the superior of the Lisieux Carmel, Msgr. Delatroëtte, for permission to become a nun at the Carmel.

AUGUST 20 (*Monday*)

In a letter to Céline, Father Pichon gives up his plans for Céline and says that he "gives Céline to Carmel."

SEPTEMBER 14 (*Friday*)

Céline enters Carmel, takes the name Sister Marie of the Holy Face, and is entrusted to Thérèse.

OCTOBER 11 (*Thursday*)
The coffins of Mme. Martin, her four children, her father, and mother-in-law are transferred to the Lisieux cemetery where Louis Martin was buried.

AUTUMN
Thérèse examines the notebooks of Céline and finds scriptural texts that substantiate her "little way."

DECEMBER (*end of*)
Mother Agnès (Pauline) orders Thérèse to write her childhood memories.

WORLD EVENTS
- Captain Dreyfus, a Jew, is court-martialed for being a spy for Germany and is deported to Devil's Island.
- The first Coca Cola bottles are produced.
- Robert Louis Stevenson and Oliver Wendell Holmes die.
- Kipling's *The Jungle Book* is published.

1895   *22 Years Old*

This is the year Thérèse writes her first copybook (Manuscript A) of the *Story of a Soul*.

JANUARY 21 (*Monday*)
Thérèse takes the part of Joan of Arc in her third play, *Joan of Arc Accomplishing Her Mission*. She barely misses being severely burned during the production. Céline takes five photos of her as Joan.

JANUARY (*End of*)
Céline is given a new name—Sister Geneviève of St. Teresa.

FEBRUARY 5 (*Tuesday*)
Sister Geneviève receives the habit.

JUNE 11 (*Tuesday*)
With her sister Céline (Sister Geneviève) Thérèse pronounces the words of Prayer 6—"Act of Oblation to Merciful Love" before the statue of the Virgin of the Smile.

JUNE 13 (*Thursday*)
The supposed "conversion" of the fictitious Diana Vaughan occurs.

JULY 20 (*Saturday*)
Léonie leaves the Visitation convent in Caen and goes home to Lisieux.

AUGUST 15 (*Thursday*)
Thérèse's cousin Marie Guérin (Sister Marie of the Eucharist) enters the Lisieux Carmel on her feast day, the Assumption of Mary.

OCTOBER 7–15 (*Monday to the next Tuesday*)
The community retreat is preached by Father Lemonnier. Mother Agnès asks him to examine the text of Thérèse's Act of Oblation to Merciful Love. He and his superiors sanction its use for religious with only one change, that of "infinite desires" to "immense desires."

OCTOBER 8 (*Tuesday*)
The superior of the Lisieux Carmel, Msgr. Delatroëtte, dies.

OCTOBER 17 (*Thursday*)
Mother Agnès assigns Maurice Bellière, a 21-year-old seminarian, a future missionary to Africa, to be Thérèse's first "spiritual brother."

WORLD EVENTS
- The X-ray is discovered.
- Louis Pasteur dies.
- Oscar Wilde's *The Importance of Being Earnest* has its London premier. Wilde is sent to prison.
- The Brothers Lumière develop a motion-picture camera.
- Mark Twain's book *Joan of Arc* is published.

1896   23 Years Old

JANUARY (*Date uncertain*)
Canon Maupas is made superior of the Carmel.

JANUARY 20 (*Monday*)
Thérèse gives Mother Agnès her completed copybook of childhood memories (Manuscript A).

FEBRUARY 24 (*Monday*)
Sister Geneviève is professed.

MARCH 17 (*Tuesday*)
Sister Geneviève receives the black veil.

MARCH 21 (*Saturday*)
Mother Marie de Gonzague is elected prioress after seven separate votings. Thérèse is confirmed in her role as auxiliary mistress of novices. Mother Agnès reads Thérèse's memoirs of her childhood sometime after this date.

APRIL 3 (*Good Friday*)
On the night of April 2–3 Thérèse spits up blood for the first time and waits until morning to check.

APRIL 5 (*Easter Sunday*)
Thérèse enters into "the thickest darkness," a trial of faith that will last until her death.

MAY 30 (*Saturday*)
Mother Marie de Gonzague gives Thérèse a second "spiritual brother"— Adolph Roulland from the Paris Seminary for the Foreign Missions—who is later to become a missionary to China.

JUNE 23 (*Tuesday*)
Thérèse writes the first of seven letters to Adolph Roulland.

JULY 3 (*Friday*)
Father Roulland says his first Mass at the Carmel. He talks to Thérèse in the speakroom (parlor).

AUGUST 2 (*Sunday*)
Father Roulland leaves for China.

SEPTEMBER 8 (*Tuesday*)
Thérèse starts to write Manuscript B at the request of her sister, Sister Marie of the Sacred Heart.

SEPTEMBER 16 (*Wednesday*)
Thérèse finishes Manuscript B.

OCTOBER 21 (*Wednesday*)
Thérèse writes the first of eleven letters to Maurice Bellière.

> **WORLD EVENTS**
> - Wlliam McKinley is elected U.S. President.
> - Athens hosts the first modern Olympics.
> - Marconi gives his first public radio demonstration.
> - Puccini's opera *La Bohème* has its first performance.

1897   *24 Years Old*

JANUARY 1 (*Friday*)
In Letter 216 to her sister Mother Agnès, Thérèse makes the first allusion to a member of her family regarding her coming death.

MARCH 4–12 (Thursday to the 2nd Friday)
Thérèse makes a personal novena to Saint Francis Xavier to obtain the favor of "spending her heaven in doing good on earth."

APRIL 6 (*Tuesday*)
The beginning of *Last Conversations* is undertaken by Thérèse's sisters who record the conversations they have with Thérèse because they realize this is her final sickness.

APRIL 19 (*Monday*)
Leo Taxil reveals his impostures and hoaxes during a press conference in Paris, in particular the revelation that he had invented the person "Diana Vaughan."

MAY
Thérèse is freed from all her duties and Office in choir.

MAY (*End of*)
Thérèse is exempted from the care of the novices.

JUNE 3 (*Thursday*)
At the request of Mother Agnès, Mother Marie de Gonzague orders Thérèse to continue writing her autobiography (Manuscript C).

JUNE 9 (*Wednesday*)
Thérèse writes about her "night of darkness."

JUNE 30 (*Wednesday*)
Thérèse has her last talk with her Uncle Guérin in the parlor.

JULY 8 (*Thursday*)
Thérèse is brought to the infirmary. Céline stays in the room next door in order to take care of her. Manuscript C ("Notebook written for the Rev. Mother Marie de Gonzague"), begun about thirty-six days ago, is left unfinished with 74 autograph pages.

JULY 14 (*Wednesday*)
Thérèse writes her last letter to Father Roulland (LT 254). She receives from Rome the benediction "*In articulo mortis.*"

JULY 17 (*Saturday*)
Thérèse writes her last letter to Léonie (LT 257).

JULY 24–25 (*Saturday to Sunday*)
Thérèse writes her last letter to the Guérins (LT 260).

JULY 28 (*Wednesday*)
This is the beginning of the "great sufferings."

JULY 30 (*Friday*)
Thérèse undergoes continuous coughing up of blood, suffocations, and violent pains in her side. There is fear she will not live through the night. At 7 o'clock she receives Extreme Unction and Communion by Canon Maupas.

AUGUST (*Beginning of*)
Thérèse writes her last letter to Father Pichon (LT 263).
Thérèse writes her final letter to Father Bellière (LT 263).

AUGUST 17 (*Tuesday*)
Dr. La Nèele visits Thérèse. He discovers that her right lung is wasted away and the left one is nearly gone.

AUGUST 19 (*Thursday*)
Thérèse offers her last Communion for the apostate Carmelite priest Hyacinthe Loyson.

AUGUST 23 (*Monday*)
Thérèse says it was the worst night ever and even understands the temptation of suicide.
The last picture of Thérèse is taken of her alive (Photo 45).

SEPTEMBER 8 (*Wednesday*)
Dr. La Nèele pays his fourth and last visit to Thérèse.

SEPTEMBER 29 (*Wednesday*)
Thérèse suffers extreme agony. Father Faucon hears her last confession.

SEPTEMBER 30 (*Thursday*)
Thérèse dies around 7:30 P.M. with the community assembled around her. Her last words are, "My God ... I ... love you!"

OCTOBER 1 (*Friday*)
Céline takes Photo 46 of Thérèse in death in the infirmary.

OCTOBER 3 (*Sunday*)
Four days after Thérèse's death, the final picture (Photo 47) is taken of her in a flower-covered coffin placed on view in the Carmel choir.

OCTOBER 4 (*Monday*)
Thérèse is buried in the public cemetery in Lisieux.

> **WORLD EVENTS**
> - The U.S. warship *Maine* blows up in Havana harbor.
> - The U.S. declares war on Spain.
> - Queen Victoria celebrates her Diamond Jubilee.

POSTHUMOUS CHRONOLOGY
(1898–2008)

MARCH 7
Msgr. Hugonin, bishop of Bayeux, gives permission for the printing of *Story of a Soul*.

MAY 2
Bishop Hugonin dies.

OCTOBER 21
2,000 copies of *Story of a Soul* (475 pages) are printed (one year after Thérèse died) by Imprimerie Saint-Paul at Bar-le-Duc.

1899

JANUARY 28
Léonie definitively enters the Visitation convent in Caen.

MAY 24
The first edition of *Story of a Soul* is out of print and a second edition is authorized. By October, half of the second edition of 4,000 copies is sold.

1899–1901
The first favors and cures are reported. Pilgrims come to Sister Thérèse's grave to pray.

1901

Story of a Soul is translated into English and the 4th French edition of 2,000 copies appears.

1902

The autobiography is translated into Polish and the 5th French edition of 3,000 copies is published.

APRIL 19
Mother Agnès is re-elected prioress.

1903
The 6th edition of the autobiography appears with 3,000 copies printed.

1904
DECEMBER 17
Mother Marie de Gonzague dies of cancer of the tongue.

1905
The autobiography is translated into Dutch.

APRIL 14
Sister Marie of the Eucharist (Thérèse's cousin Marie Guérin) dies of tuberculosis.

1906
The autobiography is translated into Italian and Portuguese.

JULY 9
Françoise Veuillot reveals in the newspaper *L'Univers* that the Carmel is occupied with introducing the Cause of Sister Thérèse in Rome.

1907
OCTOBER 15
The new bishop of Bayeux, Msgr. Lemonnier, asks the Carmelites to write down their memories of Sister Thérèse.

1908
MAY 26
A little blind four-year-old girl named Reine Fauquet is cured at the grave of Sister Thérèse in the Lisieux public cemetery.

1909
JANUARY
Father Rodrique, a Carmelite in Rome, and Msgr. de Teil in Paris are named respectively postulator and vice-postulator of the cause.

APRIL 11
Beatification of Joan of Arc by Pope Pius X.

MAY 2
Beatification of Théophane Vénard by Pope Pius X.

1910
MARCH 3
Beginning of the Diocesan Informative Process at a seminary near Caen.

JULY
By now the Carmel receives well over 9,000 letters from people in France and foreign countries.

AUGUST 12

The first exhumation of the remains of Sister Thérèse in the Lisieux cemetery takes place. They are transferred to a new vault a few feet away.

1911

Story of a Soul is translated into Spanish and Japanese.

DECEMBER 12

The Diocesan Process closes.

1912

DECEMBER 10

The Holy See approves the writings of the Servant of God, Thérèse.

1913

AUGUST

The first pilgrimage to Lisieux by train.

1914

JUNE 10

Pope Pius X signs the Decree for the Introduction of the Cause. He tells a missionary bishop in private that Sister Thérèse is "the greatest saint of modern times."

AUGUST

Beginning of World War I.

1915

From 1898 to 1915 the Carmel distributes some 8,046,000 pictures of Thérèse and some 1,124,000 "sachets-souvenirs" (mementos).

MARCH 17

The Apostolic Process opens in Bayeux.

1917

AUGUST 9–10

The second exhumation and official acknowledgment of the remains of Sister Thérèse are made at the Lisieux cemetery.

OCTOBER 30

The Apostolic Process closes in Bayeux.

1918

NOVEMBER 11

End of World War I.

1920

MAY 16
Joan of Arc is canonized by Pope Benedict XV.

1921

AUGUST 14
Pope Benedict XV promulgates the decree on the heroic virtues of Sister Thérèse who can now be called Venerable.

1923

The Carmel receives 500 to 1,000 letters every day.
At the wish of Pope Pius XI, Mother Agnès will remain in office for life.

MARCH 26
Thérèse's relics are transferred from the Lisieux cemetery to the Carmel.

APRIL 29
Pope Pius XI beatifies Sister Thérèse of the Child Jesus at St. Peter's in Rome. He calls her "the star of his pontificate."

1924

JULY 13
Father Daniel Brottier (1876–1936) lays the foundation stone for the first church dedicated to St. Thérèse, an institution serving poor orphans called *Œuvre des Orphelins Apprentis d'Auteuil* (Work of the Orphan-Apprentices of Auteuil [Paris]). He worked tirelessly for this association. He was beatified in 1984.

1925

Between 1898 and this year 30,328,000 pictures of St. Thérèse are distributed.

MAY 17
Pope Pius XI canonizes St. Thérèse of the Child Jesus and of the Holy Face. As many as 500,000 pilgrims crowd into St. Peter's Square.

1927

DECEMBER 14
Pope Pius XI proclaims St. Thérèse principal patroness of the missions on a par with St. Francis Xavier.

1928

Rev. Gabriel Martin (1873–1949) founds the Missionaries of the Plain under the patronage of St. Thérèse.

1929

Pope Pius XI proclaims Thérèse Patroness of the Russicum, a seminary for training priests to evangelize Russia.

SEPTEMBER 30

The cornerstone for the Basilica of St. Thérèse in Lisieux is laid.

1932

Lisieux holds a Theresian Congress. Requests begin for Thérèse to be made a Doctor of the Church.

1933

The Oblates of Saint Thérèse, founded by Rev. Gabriel Martin, is raised to the status of a Religious Congregation.

1937

JULY 11

The Papal Legate, Cardinal Pacelli (the future Pope Pius XII), opens and blesses the Basilica in Lisieux dedicated to St. Thérèse.

1939

SEPTEMBER

Beginning of World War II.

1940

JANUARY 19

St. Thérèse's sister Marie (Sister Marie of the Sacred Heart) dies at the age of 80.

1941

JUNE 16

Thérèse's sister Léonie (Sister Françoise-Thérèse) dies at the age of 78 at the Visitation convent in Caen.

JULY 24

Cardinal Suhard founds the Mission of France. The seminary opens in Lisieux in October 1942. The first superior is Father Augros.

1944

MAY 3

Pope Pius XII names St. Thérèse Secondary Patroness of France equal to St. Joan of Arc.

JUNE

The Allied bombings of World War II partially destroy Lisieux.
Thérèse's Abbey school is completely annihilated but the Carmel, Les Buissonnets, and the Basilica are not harmed.

1945

NOVEMBER 11
End of World War II.

1947

This is the fiftieth anniversary of Thérèse's death. Her relics are taken to almost every diocese of France.
Between 1898 and this year there are 865 biographies written about St. Thérèse. Father G. Martin founds the Missionary Brothers of Saint Thérèse of the Child Jesus.

1951

JULY 28
Mother Agnès of Jesus (Pauline) dies at the age of 90.

1954

JULY 11
The solemn consecration of the Basilica in Lisieux.

1956

The edition in facsimile of the *Manuscrits autobiographiques* is published including the restoration of *Story of a Soul* according to the original writings. The editor is Father François de Sainte-Marie, O.C.D.

1959

FEBRUARY 25
Sister Geneviève (Céline) dies at the age of 90.

1971

JULY
The first volume of *l'Edition du Centenaire* (Centenary Edition). appears which contains *Derniers Entretiens* (Last Conversations). This is followed by the publication of the following:

> *Correspondance générale* (the letters) in 1972 and 1974
> *Les Poésies* (the poems) in 1979
> *Les Récréations pieuses* (the plays) in 1985
> *Les Prières* (the prayers) in 1988)

1973

The centenary of St. Thérèse's birth is celebrated this year. Between 1973 and 1976, the Carmelite Fathers in Rome publish the Process of Beatification and Canonization of St. Thérèse, hitherto not available.

1980
JUNE 2
Pope John Paul II makes a pilgrimage to Lisieux.

1988
JUNE 19
Pope John Paul II canonizes Théophane Vénard.

1992
In this year is published *Nouvelle Edition du Centenaire* (New Edition of the Century) of Thérèse's complete works in a critical edition of eight volumes. Also published is *Œuvres complètes* (Complete Works) of St. Thérèse in one volume.

1994
MARCH 25
The parents of St. Thérèse—Louis and Zélie Martin—are proclaimed "Venerable" which is the first major step toward their canonization.

1997
The world-wide journey of St. Thérèse's relics begins.

OCTOBER 19
Pope John Paul II proclaims St. Thérèse of the Child Jesus a Doctor of the Church.

2008
OCTOBER 19
Thérèse's parents Louis and Zélie Martin are beatified at the Basilica in Lisieux.

B. *Writings and Art Work*

1. Autobiography
2. Letters
3. Poems
4. Plays
5. Prayers
6. Diverse Writings
7. Art Work

ST. THÉRÈSE NEVER CONSIDERED HERSELF AN ACCOMPLISHED WRITER. Most of her writing was done for specific and pragmatic reasons. In fact, a great deal of it was thrust upon her by either request or command, written out of a sense of service, or for her own personal reasons. In all their eloquent simplicity and perhaps at times naiveté, they are outpourings of her human and spiritual experience. When her sister Céline asked her once if she ever lost the feeling of God's presence, she answered, "Oh, no. I don't think I've ever been three minutes without it."[1] Clearly then, what she wrote reflected what she thought, felt, and believed. No matter what the circumstances were, her "Beloved Spouse" was always in her thoughts whether at devotions, painting, washing clothes, or writing.

Though St. Thérèse never composed with any literary pretensions, she is known today almost solely because of her autobiography, the *Story of a Soul*. Actually her letters, plays, poems, and prayers comprise a far greater portion of her writing than the story of her life, but are not nearly as well known or as widely read. Each in its way adds to and expands upon her spiritual doctrine as well as her personality. The *Story of a Soul* informs us of her life and religious journey; the letters disclose information not only about her family and mundane experiences but also her humanity; the poems express her spiritual state in a lyrical form; the plays dramatize her spirituality and concept of her relationship with God; and the prayers crystallize her deep longings and piety.

It must be restated that though she harbored no literary ambitions, she did come to the realization after some persuasive promptings from her sisters that her autobiography had important spiritual value and therefore should be published. They thought this was perhaps how her message of spending her existence in heaven by doing good on earth would be accomplished. Convinced, Thérèse herself said to her sister Pauline a few months before she died that:

> "The manuscript must be published without delay after my death. If you delay, the devil will set all sorts of traps to stop its publication, important though it is."

---

1 O'Mahony, *St. Thérèse of Lisieux by Those Who Knew Her*, p. 128.

"So you think it is by means of the manuscript that you are going to benefit people?" I [Pauline] said.

"Yes, it is one of the means which God will use to make me heard. It will benefit all kinds of people except those who travel by extraordinary ways." [2]

After Thérèse finished her manuscript she gave her sister Pauline this very significant admonition:

> Mother, you must revise all I have written. If you find it necessary to omit some things, or to add anything I have said *viva voce*, it will be the same as if I had done this myself. Remember this later on, and do not have any scruple in the matter.
>
> You know all the innermost recesses of my soul, you alone....[3]

And so her life's story was published, became an immediate success, and has since entered the rarified category of a religious literary masterpiece. The impact on many was tremendous, particularly for writers. From the first issuance of her autobiography to only around fifty years later, multitudes of books, studies, commentaries, and biographies appeared amounting to well over 800 recorded works in many languages.

Despite tremendous interest in St. Thérèse and an ever increasing desire to know more about her, all of her writings were not published for years, primarily because her three sisters were still living and would not permit it. They felt that her other writings were of private confidences and family matters, as well as containing a number of childish comments and embarrassing spelling and grammatical errors. However reluctantly, abridged selections of the letters, poems, and conversations were sporadically published throughout the years. After the last sister died (Céline in 1959) the reasons for withholding total publication were no longer present. Then progress in printing everything got underway. Translations into English and countless languages appeared (though not in the form of her complete works, as they have in the French).

A great step forward was the publication of the superb facsimile (photocopied) edition of the *Manuscrits Autobiographiques* in 1956 by the Office Central de Lisieux. It includes copies of the three separate manuscripts written by Thérèse that comprise her autobiography which in appearance look exactly like the originals. With the same spirit of scholarly accuracy, this was followed five years later by a two volume set of the known photographs of the saint, complete and unretouched. One volume contains copious notes and the other the photos, each reproduced with excellent quality. This was followed a year later in 1961 by an English translation in one volume by P.J. Kenedy and Sons, New York, and in a London edition. Both this and the *Manuscrits Autobiographiques* were under the expert direction of François de Sainte-Marie, O.C.D. who also wrote the commentaries.

Then in 1972 a critical edition with absolute fidelity to the originals of the complete works of St. Thérèse appeared in French commemorating the centenary of her birth (1873–1973). This monumental edition—*Edition du Centenaire*

---

2 Ibid., p. 64.
3 *Novissima Verba*, July 16, 1887.

(*Poésies, Récréations pieuses, écrits divers*)—was under the direction of Jacques Lonchampt. It includes the *Manuscrits Autobiographiques*, the letters, poems, plays, and prayers. It also contains the *Histoire d'une Âme (Story of a Soul)* (1898 version), and *Derniers Entretiens* (last conversations of St. Thérèse). Each of the above is now available separately in French, also from the Office Central de Lisieux. Furthermore, Thérèse's entire works have been published in one large volume, in French but with less extensive notes.

Her complete plays have been published for the English reading public. In 2008 the ICS Publications in Washington, D.C., issued *The Plays of Saint Thérèse of Lisieux: "Pious Recreations"* in an excellent translation by Susan Conroy and David J. Dwyer. However, the poems have been published in two English translations prior to this, but neither collection is complete. The first edition of 1907 is a free translation in rhyme made by S. L. Emery entitled POEMS of *Sr. Teresa, Carmelite of Lisieux, known as "The Little Flower of Jesus"* published by the Carmelites in Boston (Angel Guardian Press). The second one, POEMS of *St. Thérèse of the Child Jesus known as "The Little Flower of Jesus,"* is the product, also in rhyming verse, of the work in 1925 of the Carmelites of Santa Clara, California. In 1996 the Institute of Carmelite Studies in Washington, D.C., published a splendid critical edition of St. Thérèse's poetry entitled *The Poetry of Saint Thérèse of Lisieux*, a translation by Donald Kinney, O.C.D.

By far the largest volume of Thérèse's writing are her letters. Selections of her letters have always been available from the first edition of *Histoire d'une Âme (Story of a Soul)* in 1898 to the present. However, it was not until 1948 that the first "complete" French edition of the letters was produced under the capable direction of the Theresian scholar, Abbé Combes. Nonetheless, it is not actually a strictly authentic collection of her letters for there are a few omissions and corrections that were made in deference to Sister Geneviève (Thérèse's sister Céline). In 1962, when that edition went out of print, a re-issuing of the letters was clearly needed. For some time before this, however, the Lisieux Carmel was deeply involved in preparing the publication of a truly complete, punctilious, and scholarly edition of Thérèse's entire literary output with the addition of *Derniers Entretiens* (Last Conversations). Work on the letters had to wait until 1972.

Finally, the ultimate critical edition of all the saint's letters, copies of lost letters, and relevant letters from her correspondents appeared entitled *Correspondance Generale I* and *II* (1972 and 1974). An English translation by John Clarke, O.C.D came out in 1982 with the title *St. Thérèse of Lisieux: General Correspondence, Volume I*, followed two years later by *Volume II*.

All of St. Thérèse's written words are treasured by scholars and ordinary devotees of the Saint, but her spoken words were valued also by those who heard them. There were no tape recorders or camcorders in those days but many of her words in conversations during the last few months of her short life were copied in notebooks by her three admiring sisters (Pauline, Marie, and Céline) and a few jotted down by her cousin Marie Guérin and some other nuns in the convent with her.

Céline's notes were originally written on slips of paper but they were eventually gathered into one large notebook in 1925 entitled *Last Conversations of Thérèse to Céline*. Her sister Marie's very few written recollections were noted down also in 1925 into a small notebook called *Last Conversations of Sister Thérèse of the Child Jesus, collected by Sister Marie of the Sacred Heart*.

The largest and most comprehensive collection of notes was that made by Pauline. Throughout her life she found it necessary to make four separate series of notes dealing with the many talks she had with her dying sister: (1) *les Cahiers verts* (1909)—(the "Green Copybooks"); (2) *le Procès informative ordinaire* (1910)—(for the bishop's process); (3) *le Carnet jaune* (1922–1923)—(the "Yellow Notebook); (4) *Novissima Verba* (1927)—("Last Words"). The first set was made specifically for Msgr. de Teil, vice-postulator for Sister Thérèse's cause, who sought information about Thérèse's last days and death. She prepared for him five green-covered copybooks containing 306 quotations. A year later she provided 275 additional bits of conversation in her second series of quotations, this time for the diocesan tribunal. The "Yellow Notebook" was put together by Mother Agnès solely for her own benefit in order to have a complete record of all 714 "last conversations." It was one of three large notebooks she assembled containing memories of her saintly sister.

In 1927, two years after Thérèse's canonization, a very selective compilation of Thérèse's conversations (about half) was finally made available to the public in a printed French edition with the title *Novissima Verba. Derniers Entretiens de Ste. Thérèse de l'Enfant-Jésus–Mai–Septembre 1897* (Paris: Editions du Cerf—Desclée de Brouwer).[4]

The Office Central de Lisieux published in 1952 some unedited reminiscences and conversations with Sister Geneviève (Céline) under the title *Sainte Thérèse de l'Enfant-Jésus—Conseils et Souvenirs*. The same year the Carmelite nuns of New York published their translation of *Novissima Verba* entitled *Novissima Verba: The Last Conversations and Confidences of Saint Thérèse of the Child Jesus*. (P. J. Kenedy & Sons). And of course the absolutely complete and annotated edition of the *Last Conversations* in French was included in the 1997 centenary edition of Thérèse's works.

In addition to the last words of the dying nun, some of the advice given to the novices under her charge was recorded by them, particularly by her sister Céline. Several conversations were available in print in a few excerpts here and there throughout the years beginning with the 1898 *Histoire d'une Âme*. In the 1899 edition the section following the Autobiography contained selections of conversations called *Conseils et Souvenirs* (*Counsels and Reminiscences* in the English translations that followed).

Another valuable collection of Thérèse's writings consists of school assignments, copies of selections from her favorite writers, and Biblical quotations, all preserved in the Archives of the Lisieux Carmel. They are presented in the "complete" French edition of Thérèse's works under the title "*Écrits Divers*."

---

4 *St. Thérèse of Lisieux: Her Last Conversations*, translated by John Clarke, O.C.D.

However, another book appeared in 2008, published by Cerf entitled *Les Cahiers d'école de Thérèse de Lisieux, 1877–1888*, containing all of Thérèse's notebooks and school manuals. It includes her drawings, maps, penmanship exercises, compositions, math work, and more. The reproductions of the illustrations, the cover of her textbooks, copies of the printed pages, and Thérèse's own writing are in beautiful and discernibly accurate color. In addition, the rarely seen photographs included are a joyous discovery. Still not available, though, are some loose papers and a few drawings by Thérèse. Many notes by her sisters are preserved also at the Carmel Archives but are not accessible.

1. Autobiography

IF IT WERE NOT FOR SISTER THÉRÈSE'S AUTOBIOGRAPHY, *Story of a Soul*, she may not have been so quickly and widely known or even canonized within such a short time. This writing was originally intended to be exclusively for her obituary notice (*Circulaire nécrologique*). Such notices were always sent to all the Carmels in France as well as to family and friends of the deceased nun. Mother Agnès, Thérèse's sister Pauline, discussed this topic with Thérèse shortly before she died. Thérèse's comment is distinctly Theresian: "I do not really understand why there are some people who do not wish to have a notice. It is so pleasant to know each other; to know something about those with whom we are going to live for ever."[5]

Thérèse's book appeared on October 21, 1898, a year after she died, with the title *Sœur Thérèse de l'Enfant-Jésus et de la Sainte-Face,/Religieuse carmélite (1873–1897)/Histoire d'une Âme écrite par elle-même. Lettres. Poésies* (Sister Thérèse of the Infant Jesus and of the Holy Face/Carmelite (1873–1897)/*Story of a Soul* written by herself. Letters. Poems.) Two thousand copies at 4 francs each were sold to those who anxiously wanted to read it. By the end of the year the first edition was out of print. Subsequent editions quickly followed resulting in millions of copies in many languages. Even up to today new editions continue to be published somewhere in the world.

The creation of this masterpiece of religious literature was conceived rather casually. One cold January evening at the Lisieux Carmel the three Martin sisters—Pauline (Mother Agnès, then prioress of the Monastery), Marie (Sister Marie), and Thérèse (Sister Thérèse)—were reminiscing about their childhood. Mother Agnès told the story of how the autobiography came about:

> At the beginning of the year 1895, two and a half years before the death of Sister Thérèse, I was with my two sisters one winter evening. Sister Thérèse was telling me about several incidents in her childhood, and Sister Marie of the Sacred Heart (my older sister Marie) said: "Ah, what a pity we don't have this in writing; if you were to ask Sister Thérèse to write down her childhood memories for you, what lasting pleasure they would provide. I answered: "I couldn't ask anything better." Then turning to Sister Thérèse, who was laughing

---

[5] From the article, "The Publication of 'The Story of a Soul,'" that appeared in the January 1998 issue of *Sicut Parvuli*. It is a translation of the article by Guy Gaucher in *Thérèse de Lisieux, Spécial Calendrier*, 1998.

because she thought we were teasing, I said: "I order you to write down for me all your childhood memories."[6]

Considering this a matter of obedience, Thérèse worked at it as often as she could during her few spare moments, usually after Compline (between 8 and 9 P.M.) in her dismally lit cell. She sat on a low stool with an old desktop on her lap and wrote with pen and ink in a cheap brown school exercise book (about 7" by 9"). The only light came from a small oil lamp that her cousin Marie Guérin (Sister Marie of the Eucharist) had given her. Amazingly, her manuscript of 170 pages contains no noticeable erasures or corrections. It took her a year to complete, starting early in January 1895 and finishing it the next January. But this was only part of the final book. It includes the first eight chapters of *Story of a Soul*. Thérèse gave her composition (now designated as Manuscript A) the title "The Springtime Story of a Little White Flower" and offered it to Mother Agnès, to whom it is addressed, on her feast day, January 20, 1896.

> I [Mother Agnès] was at evening prayer. When passing by to go to her place, Sister Thérèse knelt down and handed me this treasure. I acknowledged it with a simple nod of my head and placed it at my side without opening it. I did not read it until after the elections which took place in the spring [late March] of that year. [Mother Marie de Gonzague was now prioress.] I noticed the Servant of God's virtue: after her act of obedience, she was no longer preoccupied with the matter, never asking me whether I had read it or what I thought of it. One day, I told her that I hadn't had time to read any of it; she appeared in no way troubled.[7]

Pauline comments further:

> This holy indifference touched me so much that I found the reading of her life all the more beautiful. I said to myself: And this blessed child, who wrote these heavenly pages, is still in our midst! I can speak to her, see her, touch her. Oh! how she is unknown here! And how I am going to appreciate her more now![8]

Nine months later Sister Thérèse wrote what is called Manuscript B—a "letter"—"To my dear Sister Marie of the Sacred Heart." Sister Marie stated at the process that "I asked her myself during her last retreat [September 1896] to put in writing her little doctrine as I called it."[9] She realized even then that Thérèse had a terminal disease. The note says in part:

> I am writing not because I have something to tell you but to get something from you, from you who are so close to God, from you who are His little privileged spouse, to whom He confides His secrets.... The secrets of Jesus to Thérèse are sweet, and I would like to hear them once again. Write me a short note. This is perhaps your last retreat....[10]

---

6 *Procès Apostolique*, Bayeux, Vol. 1, p. 295.
7 Ibid.
8 *Derniers Entretiens*, 1:35, as quoted in *Ste. Thérèse of Lisieux: Her Last Conversations*, p. 18.
9 O'Mahony, *op. cit.*, p. 84 which is a quote from Sister Marie of the Sacred Heart's testimony at the Diocesan Process.
10 LC 169, dated Sunday, September 13 (1896).

Sister Marie added that Reverend Mother allowed her to do so. Thérèse's "letter," written between September 13 and 16, 1896, consists of three sheets of paper folded to form twelve pages, ten of which Thérèse wrote in ink in very small handwriting, but this time with many corrections. It forms Chapter IX in *Story of a Soul* and epitomizes the very core of her spirituality:

> Then, in an excess of my delirious joy, I cried out: O Jesus, my Love ... *my vocation*, at last I have found it.... MY VOCATION IS LOVE!
>
> Yes, I have found my place in the Church, and it is You, O my God, who have given me this place; in the heart of the Church, my Mother, I shall be *Love*. Thus I shall be everything, and thus my dream will be realized.[11]

Oddly enough, a year and a half passed before Mother Agnès (Pauline) told the new prioress, Mother Marie de Gonzague, in June 1897, that she had received Thérèse's manuscript (Ms. "A") in January 1896. She delayed doing so presumably because she considered it solely as a private family memoir. But by this time Thérèse's illness worsened and her approaching death became apparent. Since Thérèse recorded very little about her life in religion in Manuscript A or in Manuscript B, Mother Agnès felt her story should be completed:

> On the night of June 2, 1897, four months before the death of Sister Thérèse, I went to see Mother Prioress. I said to her: "Mother, it is impossible for me to sleep until I confide a secret to you: When I was prioress, Sister Thérèse wrote down the memories of her childhood in order to please me and through obedience. I read this over again the other day; it's very good, but you will not be able to obtain much information to write her circular [obituary notice] after her death, for there is almost nothing in it about her religious life. If you were to tell her to do so, she could write something of a much more serious nature, and I don't doubt that you will have something better than I do." [12]

Mother Agnès's petition worked. The next day Mother Marie de Gonzague directed Thérèse to continue her autobiography which she, obedient as ever, began on June 3 and completed a month later. This, known as Manuscript C, is dedicated to Mother Marie de Gonzague. It amounts to seventy-four autograph pages which form Chapters X and XI in the *Story of a Soul*. This time Thérèse wrote it in a little black oilcloth covered notebook of a better quality than the first manuscript. Her increasing weakness forced her to finish writing in pencil instead of pen. She wrote much of the manuscript seated in her late father's wheelchair during summer afternoons under the chestnut trees in the monastery garden. In her typically exemplary fashion, she stoically displayed patience and love, which she was writing about, even during repeated interruptions by her infirmarians and novices.

During the Process of Beatification that began in 1910, the diocesan tribunal interrogators asked Mother Agnès if Thérèse had any idea that what she was writing would perhaps be published sometime, even in her obituary circular. This is her reply:

---
[11] *Story of a Soul*, chapter IX, p. 194.
[12] Ibid., pp. xiii–xiv.

She had no such suspicion when writing the first part, which was chiefly about her childhood and youth. She thought she was writing it just for me and our two sisters, Marie and Céline, who were with us in Carmel. In fact, that was what we thought ourselves at the time. The same is true of what has become the third part; her sister Marie had asked her for this, and it was written exclusively for her. But when Mother Gonzague asked her to write about her life in Carmel, I hinted to her that this might give edification to many people, and that its publication might well be the means that God would use to realize her ambition to do good on earth after her death. She accepted this quite simply. I also told her that Mother Prioress was liable to burn the manuscript. "That wouldn't matter," she said; "it would mean that God did not wish to make use of that means but there would be others."[13]

As late as two months before her death while writing Manuscript C, Thérèse began to realize that the publication of her story was within the realm of possibility. She eventually became aware of some problems that may arise and cautioned Mother Agnès about them:

> When I am dead you must not mention my manuscript to anyone until it is published; you must not mention it to anyone but our Mother [Marie de Gonzague]. If you ignore this, you will find that Satan tries many ways to spoil Our Lord's work, and very important work it is.... I can write no more now."[14]

Thérèse was also aware of the process and necessity of editing:

> Little Mother, I entrust my manuscript to you. Our Lord will make use of it to do a great deal of good, but you must be very careful how you set about getting it ready for publication, omitting many things, and altering anything I have done badly. Whatever you do, it is I who do it."[15]

Everyone understood at this point that the work was to be published solely as an obituary circular, albeit an unusually lengthy one, and circulated among Carmelites and concerned others. Mother Agnès undertook the task of editing, which included extensive omissions, alterations, corrections, additions, and rearrangements. The most evident edit was the format changed to make it appear that all three manuscripts were dedicated to one person, Mother Marie de Gonzague, the prioress. Some claim that Mother Agnès made many variations from the original, including the elimination of thirty original pages. After obtaining the *Imprimatur* from Bishop Hugonin, it was published with 2,000 copies on October 21, 1898, a year after Thérèse's death.

In an age when established standards of literary style and conventions were absolutely required for a published work, the printing of an unedited script by an unknown young writer was not only unthinkable, but also a possible source of embarrassment to the publisher and author. Despite all the editing, St. Thérèse's basic doctrine and story remained absolutely intact. Incidentally,

---
13 As quoted in O'Mahony, *op. cit.*, p. 35.
14 *Carnet jaune*, p. 136.
15 Thérèse's words as quoted in a letter from Mother Agnès to Msgr. de Teil, vice-postulator of the cause.

one person responsible to a great degree for the financial and editorial aspects of this endeavor was Thérèse's own relative, her uncle Isidore Guérin. Dom Godefroid Madelaine, prior of the Abbey of Mondaye and staunch friend of the Carmel, was instrumental in getting the *Imprimatur* and even in supplying the title *Histoire d'une Âme (Story of a Soul)*.

The publisher of the autobiography was L'Œuvre de Saint-Paul (founded in 1873, the year of Thérèse's birth) and the printer Bar-le-Duc. Following is a summary of the contents of the first edition that included 469 pages:[16]

> SISTER THÉRÈSE OF THE CHILD JESUS AND OF THE HOLY FACE,
> RELIGIOUS CARMELITE (1873-1897)
> STORY OF A SOUL WRITTEN BY HERSELF. LETTERS. POEMS.
>
> FRONTISPIECE: a photo of Thérèse
> DECLARATION by Pope Urban VIII relating to canonization rules
> TO THE READER: a poem by Father Norbert Paysant
> LETTER: by Father Godefroy Madelaine to Mother Marie de Gonzague
> PREFACE: by Mother Marie de Gonzague signed Dec. 25, 1897
> INTRODUCTION
> THE STORY OF A SOUL: includes all 12 chapters (about 254 pages)
> APPENDIX: includes 4 Prayers by Thérèse (about 4 pages)
> LETTERS: eighteen excerpts from letters to Céline (about 33 pages)

For sixteen years the format of the early editions of the autobiography prevailed not only in French but in the many foreign language translations of it that followed, the first being in English as early as 1901. The translator was Polish professor Dziewicki who on May 29, 1899 requested authorization to translate it:

> As a mark of gratitude towards Sister Thérèse of the Child Jesus for all the good that she has done me, I have resolved to do all that is possible to make this book known in another language. English, which I teach here at the University, is my mother's tongue, and I have already written several books in that language. I have written to Burns and Oates, the Catholic publishers in London, saying that in making the translation I did not wish for any payment. They requested me to ask your permission [the Carmel's] for the translation of the book, and for the reproduction of the photographs of Sister Thérèse, etc....[17]

Corrections were made in the 1914 French edition following the recommendations made at the Diocesan Process of 1910. But it was not until after World War II that a more accurate and scholarly rendition of the autobiography was found necessary. The Definitor General of the Carmelite Order, the Very Reverend Marie-Eugène, wrote to Mother Agnès, then eighty-six, urging her to permit this undertaking:

---

16 Gaucher, *L' Histoire díune Âme de Thérèse de Lisieux*, pp. 88–90.
17 Msgr. de Teil, *The Cause of Beatification of the Little Flower of Jesus*, p. 127.

CHAPTER 1: *St. Thérèse of Lisieux*

The sainthood and the doctrinal mission of St. Thérèse of the Child Jesus are universally recognized. From now on she belongs to the Church and to history. To avoid and to refute partial or mistaken interpretations of her doctrine and in order that her doctrine and her soul should be still more deeply understood, the documents which you have so generously given us are insufficient. Only the original texts can allow us to discover the movement of her thought, its living rhythm, and disclose all the light contained in her definitions, which are usually so firm and precise.[18]

Mother Agnès continued to have reservations about publishing the entire original manuscript, thus prompting the Holy See to postpone the project while she was alive. On July 28, 1951, Mother Agnès passed away at eighty-nine. Finally, in 1956 the Office Central de Lisieux published a superb facsimile edition of the three manuscripts in three volumes including extensive notes. They strictly adhered to contemporary literary standards of research and accuracy. This amazingly beautiful reproduction entitled *Sainte Thérèse de l'Enfant Jésus—Manuscrits Autobiographiques*— was produced under the tireless and devoted direction of Father François de Sainte Marie, O.C.D. (1910–1961).[19]

This edition sufficed for a while but left a number of general readers non-receptive principally because of the format: there were no divisions into chapters, very few paragraph indentations, no prologue or epilogue, as well as other now-familiar features missing. It became apparent that another edition was necessary; accordingly, one with the familiar format appeared in 1972: *Histoire d'une Âme. Manuscrits autobiographiques* (Editions du Cerf, Desclée de Brouwer, 1972). A note from this version explains the production of the edition:

> For the occasion of the centenary of St. Thérèse's birth, January 2, 1973, many people expressed the desire for a new edition of the Autobiographical Manuscripts. While retaining the scientific tone of the Manuscripts, this new edition should meet the needs of the ordinary person and appear under the form of a biography of Thérèse similar to the *Histoire d'une Âme* (*Story of a Soul*). The team that produced this book answered this twofold request: (1) fidelity to the authentic text as it came from Thérèse's pen; (2) fidelity to the first edition of *Histoire d'une Âme* (1898) which Mother Agnès had conceived as a complete biography of Thérèse for the ordinary reader.[20]

This definitive 1972 French edition of St. Thérèse's powerful and magnetic autobiography was faithfully translated into English in 1975 by the eminent Theresian scholar John Clarke, O.C.D. and given the title *Story of a Soul. The Autobiography of St. Thérèse of Lisieux*. Besides the text itself, it contains an Introduction, Prologue, a list of family and cousins of Thérèse, and an Appendix that includes a chronology, and a letter the Saint carried next to her heart, the "Act of Oblation to Merciful love." The Table of Contents follows:

---

18 *Story of a Soul*, Introduction, p. xvi.
19 His life of fifty-one years tragically came to an end by drowning in the Loire River.
20 *Story of a Soul*, Introduction, p. xvii.

MANUSCRIPT A

[Originally called by Thérèse "The Springtime Story of a Little White Flower" and dedicated to the Rev. Mother Agnès of Jesus [Pauline]. It was written between the early part of January 1895 and January 20, 1896. The original manuscript comprises 170 autograph pages.]

CHAPTER I	Alençon (1873–1877)
CHAPTER II	At Les Buissonnets (1877–1881)
CHAPTER III	The Distressing Years (1881–1883)
CHAPTER IV	First Communion—at the Boarding School (1883–1886)
CHAPTER V	After the Grace of Christmas (1886–1887)
CHAPTER VI	The Trip to Rome (1887)
CHAPTER VII	First Years in Carmel (1888–1890)
CHAPTER VIII	From the Profession to the Offering to Merciful Love (1890–1895)

MANUSCRIPT B

[This is the "Letter to Sister Marie of the Sacred Heart," Thérèse's sister Marie, written at the request of Sister Marie between September 13 and 16, 1896. The original manuscript amounts to ten autograph pages.]

CHAPTER IX	My Vocation: Love (1896)

MANUSCRIPT C

[This is the "Notebook written for the Rev. Mother Marie de Gonzague" composed between June 3 and early July 1897. The original manuscript has 74 autograph pages.]

CHAPTER X	The Trial of Faith (1896–1897)
CHAPTER XI	Those Whom You Have Given Me (1896–1897)
EPILOGUE	
APPENDICES	

Following are some important French and English editions, translations, and abridged versions of Thérèse's autobiography:

1. 1901   The first English version by Professor Dziewicki of the University of Cracow, Poland.
2. 1902   *Une Rose effueille* (An Unpetalled Rose), a popular edition at the time.
3. 1904   *L'Appel aux petites âmes* (Call to Little Souls), a resumé of Thérèse's life and doctrine.
4. 1911   *As Little Children*, an abridgement of the autobiography by Rev. Thomas N. Taylor.
5. 1912   *Sister Thérèse of Lisieux, The Little Flower of Jesus*, the first complete edition in English by Rev. Thomas. N. Taylor. Besides 158 pages of her autobiography, there are 238 pages of other material including "Counsels and Reminiscences," "Shower of Roses," some letters, etc.
6. 1913   *Vie abrégée* (Abridged Life) in French—very short version.
7. 1925   *The Little White Flower* by Rev. Thomas N. Taylor is a revision of his 1912 translation. This also includes a prologue and an epilogue by the Carmel, a few prayers, and two poems.

8. 1958 *Autobiography of St. Thérèse of Lisieux,* a complete and authorized translation of *L'Histoire d'une Âme* by Msgr. Ronald Knox.
9. 1972 *Histoire d'une Âme: manuscrits autobiographiques,* a definitive edition.
10. 1973 *The Story of a Soul: The Autobiography of Saint Thérèse of Lisieux* translated by Michael Day.
11. 1975 *Story of a Soul,* translated by John Clarke from the 1972 definitive French edition.

Though not the autobiography itself, but of significant interest, nevertheless, in the story of Thérèse, is the seven volume set of various conversions, miracles, and favors received through the intercession of Sister Thérèse, entitled *Pluie de Roses* (Shower of Roses). These books were published from 1907 to 1925, the first of which was included in the 1907 edition of the Story of a Soul as an appendix. It is amazing that these books amount to a total of some 3,000 pages and that 400,000 copies were sold.[21]

There are more than fifty translations of St. Thérèse's autobiography since 1901. Here is a list of some of them up to the year 1976:[22]

1901	English	1934	Chaldean
1902	Polish and German	1936	Ruanda
1905	Dutch	1939	Swedish
1906	Italian and Portuguese	1947	Hebrew (modern)
1911	Spanish and Japanese	1952	Madagascan
1913	Singhalese and Latin	1955	Russian, Ukranian, and Urdu (a variety of Hindustani)
1916	Hungarian		
1920	Danish		
1925	Flemish, Bulgarian, Croatian, Chinese, and Malayan	1956	Latvian
		1959	Konkani (Goa)
1926	Madras, Arabic, Greek, and Gaelic	1960	Uganda
		1962	Thai
1927	Catalan	1964	Romansch
1928	Bengali and Greek	1973	Slovenian and Slovak
1930	Armenian	1976	Malawi
1931	Lithuanian		

The above list is decidedly not complete for after 1976 many more translations into other languages and dialects have been made and still continue to be produced.

2. LETTERS

BEFORE THE TELEPHONE, CELL PHONE, COMPUTER, SOCIAL NETWORKING, and fast means of transportation, people communicated with each other by the only possible practical way—letter writing. This was certainly true of the Martin and Guérin families and much of the bourgeois in France at the time. In fact it evolved into a kind of art form in some circles. A fortuitous point in Thérèse's

---
21 De Meester, *Saint Thérèse of Lisieux, Her Life, Times, and Teaching,* p. 261.
22 Descouvemont, *Sur les pas de Thérèse,* p. 21.

case, was the preservation of these intimate documents. Stored in the archives at the Lisieux Carmel today are a total of well over 2,000 pieces of correspondence from Thérèse, her immediate family, and her relations. Thérèse's letters that were not destroyed or lost, however, amount to only 266. After decades of her sisters' continuous resistance from having them all published, they are now available in their entirety with copious explanations and notations in both French and English editions.

The inclusion of several carefully selected portions of Thérèse's letters at the end of *Histoire d'une Âme* represented the only letters in print for years and with but slight additions in the various editions that followed until 1910. They were originally added merely to amplify certain aspects presented in the autobiography. Because of the demands of the process leading toward beatification, greater access to the letters was eagerly sought but sparingly released in 1910. Reluctance on the part of Thérèse's living sisters to submit more of them continued. They had always believed that some of Thérèse's childhood letters were "childish" and trite. Spelling and punctuation errors were embarrassing, and the revelation of family matters was an invasion of their privacy. Céline (Sister Geneviève) gave the following advice to her sister Léonie about copying Thérèse's letters to her which the ecclesiastical commission insisted on receiving since their task was to examine all of Thérèse's writings:

> Now, little Léonie, I am going to say a word about the letters you have from Thérèse. Very soon, Bishop Lemonnier will publish a letter to be read from the pulpit on three consecutive Sundays; he will ask for the Servant of God's writings, and we shall be obliged to send them to the bishop's residence, either our original or a true copy. Msgr. de Teil [Vice-Postulator of the Cause for Beatification] told us not to part with the originals but to copy them and to have the courage to make disappear what we do not want to hand in, such as family secrets, intimate conversations, etc. As for ourselves, we are hurrying up to rectify the autographs before the appeal from Monsignor. I have destroyed [not really] all the letters she wrote to Papa. As for your own, if there are any expressions like "Baby" or others, erase them and put in another word instead. Have no scruples, for we have the right, and, besides, Thérèse told us prophetically before she died that she entrusted herself to us in this matter and that she would be doing all that we did when making the changes.[23]

As late as 1926 Mother Agnès (Pauline) wrote to her sister Léonie that "I have read in these unpublished letters of our Thérèse things which the public has no right to know and to exploit; we should be able to keep certain family secrets."[24]

It was not until 1948, the fiftieth anniversary of the publication of *Histoire d'une Âme* (1898), that far more of her letters were published principally through the efforts of the Theresian scholar André Combes (1899–1969).[25] Besides a

---
23 Letter of Sister Geneviève to Léonie, May 17, 1910, cited in *Saint Thérèse of Lisieux General Correspondence*, vol. I, p. 32.
24 Letter of May 16, 1926, cited in ibid, p. 38.
25 Professor of mystical theology and research at the Sorbonne and the Catholic Institute of Paris.

number of omissions, the work contained the usual interpolations and alterations, principally at the insistence of Thérèse's blood sisters. It was, nevertheless, a truly great advance over previous editions. Finally, by the death of the last sister, Céline, in 1959, the path was cleared for publication of all the letters. Yet it took another decade for the definitive edition to be realized.

The long sought after compilation of all the intact and unaltered letters, plus notes, inscriptions on holy cards, etc., was published in French in 1972 with the title *Correspondance génèrale* (Desclée de Brouwer–Editions du Cerf, 1972). Two years later Volume II appeared. They were part of the critical edition in French of the *Œuvres complètes (texts et dernières paroles) de sainte Thérèse de l'Enfant Jésus et de la sainte-Face,* "*l'Edition du Centenaire,*" (*Complete Works [Texts and Last Words] of Saint Thérèse of the Infant Jesus and of the Holy Face,* Centenary Edition).

The English editions translated by John Clarke, O.C.D. came out with the title *St. Thérèse of Lisieux: General Correspondence*, Volume I (1877–1890) in 1982 and Volume II (1890–1897) in 1988. Included in this invaluable collection are, of course, all of Thérèse's extant 266 letters which amount to about two-thirds of her actual output. Unfortunately some of her recipients lost or threw away her letters. The notable missing ones were written to Father Pichon (at least fifty) and to Mother Marie de Gonzague (around fifteen). Of the existing letters, 78% were addressed to her family, 10% to other Carmelites, and the rest to twelve correspondents: seven ecclesiastics, three religious, and two friends. In all she wrote to thirty-six different people.

Obviously Thérèse received letters, and interspersed in the two volumes are those from thirty-one individuals, both religious and lay. Also inserted into this edition are diverse letters from family correspondence mentioning Thérèse and even some that do not, but all of which help to establish chronological data, expand upon certain situations, or round out the historical and psychological milieu in which she lived.

Thérèse's letter writing, as illustrated below, typifies her blending of the mundane with her own religious feelings. A typical example is the excerpt below from a letter to Mme. Guérin, her aunt, who assumed the role of mother for the Martin girls after their own mother died:

My dear little Aunt,

[Dear] Aunt, I would like to be the first to wish you a Happy New Year for 1889!...
    When I think, dear Aunt, that it will soon be nine months since your little daughter [Thérèse herself] is in Carmel, I can't get over it. It seems to me it was only yesterday that I was still with you!... How quickly life passes; it is already sixteen years since I have been on earth. Oh! soon we shall all be reunited in heaven. I love these words of the psalms very much: "A thousand years in the eyes of the Lord are like yesterday that has passed already" [Psalm 89:4]. What rapidity! Oh! I want to work during the day while it is still light, for afterwards will come the night when I shall be able to do nothing [John 9:4]. Pray for your

little daughter, dear Aunt, so that she does not abuse the grace which God is showering on her in the fertile valley of Carmel....

Au revoir, dear Aunt. I beg you to tell Uncle how much I love him. I should have written him at the same time as I wrote you, dear Aunt, but I am too stupid to talk to two persons together.... I beg him to pardon me, and I send to both of you the best kiss from your littlest Benjamin [a nickname].

Thérèse of the Child Jesus
post. carm. ind.

I just remembered that I haven't thanked dear Aunt for the crown [of artificial lilies to hold the "bridal veil" in place] that she wants to give me for my reception of the habit. Oh! if she only knew how grateful I am and also how dear this souvenir will be to her little daughter's heart![26]

3. Poems

As with her prose, Thérèse had no pretensions of writing poetry seriously. She wrote her verses while in the Carmel mostly as assigned or requested tasks. These were composed between the years 1893 and 1897—from the time she was twenty to twenty-four. Her poetry displays no grandiose, intellectual, or sophisticated style but rather a simple, clear, devotional expression of her thoughts as they flowed naturally from her fertile mind. In them she concentrates on the person of Christ, her wish to live and suffer for Him alone, her spousal relationship with Him, Mary, the saints, her family, the virtues, her longing for martyrdom, and her theories of abandonment and spiritual childhood. Clearly they confirm, expand, and enhance the spiritual message that she demonstrated by her life and in her other writings. Each poem indeed discloses something about her. She explained to Abbé Bellière what her purpose was in writing poetry:

> These poor poems will reveal to you not what I am but what I would like and should be.... When composing them, I have looked more at the substance than at the form, so the rules of versification are not always respected; my purpose was to translate my sentiments (or rather the sentiments of the Carmelite) in order to respond to my Sisters' desires.[27]

It should be noted that in writing poetry she could not avoid reflecting the poetic style and taste of the age in which she lived. She was familiar with some of the writings of the Romantic poets Chateaubriand, Lamartine, and Musset, who wrote the lyrics for songs. Thérèse merely substituted her own words but used the same music these poets had composers write their songs to. The renowned Swiss theologian and Theresian scholar, Father von Balthasar, made these cogent observations about her poetic skill:

> Though her poetry remains, as to form, a prisoner of the taste of her time—where, after all, would she have learned the language of Péguy or of Claudel?—her mind is a bubbling spring of the most pertinent, the most original, and the

---
26 LT 71, dated December 28, 1888.
27 LT 220, Thérèse to Abbé Bellière, February 24, 1897.

most unforgettable images which, I am not afraid to say, render her the equal of the two great Reformers of Carmel in poetic power.[28]

Though she was not exposed to a great deal of secular literature, she certainly knew Scripture, the Divine Office, hymns, and the writings of the Saints. The literature of the period ranged from the insipid to the grand. The same may be said of some of Thérèse's poems which in general are really lyrics to music. In fact, the lyrics of the popular music she based the lines of her poems on were certainly not all models of perfection. Music was very important to her. Her entire life was truly a song of praise and love to the Lord, as she acknowledged in the very outset of her autobiography: "I'm going to be doing only one thing: I shall begin to sing what I must sing eternally: 'The Mercies of the Lord.'"[29] Later on we read a similar statement:

> While I am strewing my flowers [at the cross in the cloister] I shall sing, for could one cry while doing such a joyous action? I shall sing even when I must gather my flowers in the midst of thorns, and my song will be all the more melodious in proportion to the length and sharpness of the thorns.[30]

A novice under her guidance, Sister Marie of the Trinity, explained Thérèse's *modus operandi*:

> Her ignorance [of poetic rules] was voluntary. When I entered Carmel in June 1894, I had brought a treatise on versification. She glanced at it and gave it back to me right away. She said: "I prefer not to know all those rules. My poems are spurts from my heart, inspirations. I wouldn't know how to tie myself down to toil in spirit, to study. At this price, I would prefer to renounce writing poetry."[31]

The great reformer of the Carmelites, St. Teresa of Avila, knew the value of recreation and the utilization of the nuns' talents not only as a benefit to the community but also as an additional aid in glorifying God. Thus she encouraged the arts in all their forms: literature, music, painting, and even dancing. And whenever feasible, subsequent superiors throughout the centuries certainly promoted the same policy. Thérèse, therefore, was not the only nun who wrote for the Lisieux convent. Her sister Pauline (Mother Agnès) composed poems and skits for special community recreation periods which Thérèse obviously emulated. In fact she acted in some of the plays Pauline wrote. When Pauline became prioress she had no time to engage in these matters so she assigned them to Thérèse. In most cases, Thérèse's poems were meant to be sung specifically during recreation periods. She simply replaced existing lyrics with her own words. She chose the music herself from familiar childhood melodies, arias from well-known operas, church hymns, and from contemporary songs which totaled over sixty or so separate tunes used in both the poems and plays. Her

---

28 Hans Urs von Balthasar, "The Timeliness of Lisieux," from *Carmelite Studies: Spiritual Direction* (1980), pp. 112–113.
29 *Story of a Soul*, chapter I, p. 13.
30 Ibid., chapter IX, p. 196.
31 Letter to Mother Agnès, February 28, 1932, as given in *Sicut Parvuli*, Sept. 1983, footnote 13.

cousin Marie Guérin, an accomplished amateur pianist and singer, entered the Lisieux Carmel in 1895 and brought with her a large collection of sheet music from which Thérèse chose many of her melodies. Incidentally, there was no harmonium, guitar, organ, or piano in the Lisieux Carmel.

Thérèse wrote the requested works as poems or acrostics (three) for particular occasions such as feast days, birthdays, holidays, and anniversaries. Not all the poems, though, were assigned; some were spontaneous expressions of her own creative feelings and spiritual aspirations.

The story behind the composition of her first poem, requested by Sister Teresa of St. Augustine (a nun toward whom Thérèse surprisingly had a natural antipathy), discloses much about Thérèse's state of mind at the time and her own opinion concerning her abilities:

> One day I [Sister Teresa of St. Augustine] asked her to write a canticle on our favorite subject, the Holy Infancy of Jesus. "That's impossible," she replied, "I don't know anything about poetry." I answered, "What does that matter? We're not going to send it to the Académie française. This is just to make me happy and to satisfy a desire of my soul." Sister Thérèse replied, "I still hesitate a little because I don't know if this is God's will." I then said, "Oh! I'll give you some advice about that: Before you start to write, ask Our Lord: 'My God, if this is not your will, I ask you for the grace not to be able to succeed at it. But if this is for your glory, help me.' I believe that after that you will not have to worry." She followed my advice and that is how she wrote her first poem.[32]

It is interesting and a bit surprising to realize that Thérèse's sister Pauline had her own doubts about Thérèse's poetic skills: "I was not pleased that she had the idea to write poetry. It seemed to me—and I told her so—she would not be able to succeed at it. Only reluctantly did I give her the advice she asked for on this subject."[33] She did succeed remarkably well as one can tell when reading her poetry.

The following section is a list in English and French of all sixty-two poems by St. Thérèse in chronological order, with date, reason for composition, music chosen, and other relevant information. Most sources agree on the name of the tune Thérèse selected for each of the poems she wrote to be sung. For several others, however, one source may list a certain melody whereas another source will give a different one for the same poem. In these cases, the names of both songs are given here.

PN 1. "The Divine Dew or the Virginal Milk of Mary" (*La Rosée Divine ou Le Lait Virginal de Marie*), a eucharistic poem clothed in floral symbols dealing with the Infant Jesus and Mary, the Eucharist, seraphim, dew, blood, and the rose. It was requested by Sister Teresa of Saint Augustine and given to her on February 2, 1893. It was sung to the song "*Minuit, chrétiens*" (also called "*Cantique de Noël*"—"O Holy Night") by Adolphe Adam.

---

32 See p. 36 in *The Poetry of Saint Therese of Lisieux* translated by Donald Kinney.
33 Ibid., footnote 5, p. 37 which quotes p. 28, vol II in *Poésies*.

PN 2. **"To Our Mistress and Dear Mother for her Sixtieth Birthday"** (*A Notre Maitresse et Mère Chérie pour fêter ses 60 ans*), honoring Mother Marie de Gonzague on her birthday and signed by three novices—Sisters Thérèse, Martha, and Mary Magdalene—on February 20, 1894. This poem was perhaps not intended to be sung though the air "*Je suis crétien*" has been assigned to it.

PN 3. **"Saint Cecilia"** (*Cécile*) written for her sister Céline at home on her twenty-fifth birthday, April 28, 1884. It really expresses Thérèse's own ideas on abandonment, virginity, apostolic zeal, and martyrdom that is ideally exemplified by one of Thérèse's favorite saints, Cecilia. This was sung to a hymn of consecration to the Blessed Virgin entitled "*Prends mon Coeur, le voilà*." An alternative hymn chosen was "*Hymne à l'Eucharistie*" composed by Père Ligonnet.

PN 4. **"Canticle to Obtain the Canonization of the Venerable Joan of Arc"** (*Cantique pour obtenir la Canonisation de la Vénérable Jeanne d'Arc*) is a religious as well as patriotic poem dated May 8, 1894. In it she praises Joan's virtues and martyrdom rather than her warrior aspect. She dedicated it to her sister Céline, the "Gallant Knight, C. Martin" and sung to "*Pitié, mon Dieu*," with music by A. Kunc.

PN 5. **"My Song for Today"** (*Mon Chant d'Aujourd'hui*), requested by Sister Marie of the Sacred Heart (Thérèse's sister Marie), is about the brevity of life and Thérèse's longing for the "Eternal Today" of heaven. It is dated June 1, 1894. Two melodies were indicated by Thérèse: (1) "*Un religieuse à son Crucifix*," music by J. Hodierne, and/or (2) "*Hymne à l'Eucharistie*" by P. Ligonnet.

PN 6. **"The Portrait of a Soul I Love"** (*Le Portrait d'une Âme que j'Aime*), an acrostic—"MARIE DU SACRE COUR"—written solely for her blood sister, Sister Marie of the Sacred Heart, on her feast day, June 1, 1894. This is Thérèse's poetic portrait of the soul of her oldest sister and thus not to be sung.

PN 7. **"Song of Gratitude to Our Lady of Mount Carmel"** (*Chant de Reconnaissance à Notre-Dame du Mont-Carmel*) is dedicated to Thérèse's companion in the novitiate, Sister Martha of Jesus, and dated July 16, 1894. It reviews Martha's indebtedness to the Virgin Mary for her protection during a mostly parentless early life and for giving her this marvelous choice of vocation. No melody was indicated.

PN 8. **"Prayer of a Child of a Saint"** (*Prière de l'Enfant d'un Saint*), was written for herself in August 1894 and dedicated to her father who just recently died on July 29, 1894. It tenderly recalls sweet memories of events connected with her father and each of her sisters. She signed it "The Orphan of Bérésina"—one of Thérèse's nicknames. This was sung to "*Rappelle-toi*," music by Georges Rupès.

PN 9. **"Prayer of an Exiled Child"** (*Prière d'une enfant exilée*), composed at the request of Thérèse's sister, Sister Marie of the Sacred Heart, for Father Almire Pichon, her spiritual director, on his feast day, September 11, 1894. This acrostic—ALMIRE—that was not intended to be sung, urges him to return home to France from Canada to resume being their spiritual guide.

PN 10. **"Story of a Shepherdess Who Became a Queen"** (*Histoire d'une Bergère devenue Reine*) is dated November 20, 1894. The first part is dedicated to Sister Mary Magdalene of the Blessed Sacrament (one of two converse novices, formerly a shepherdess herself), and the second part to the Reverend Mothers of the monastery. The novice appropriately is the shepherdess who became a queen (nun) to the king (Christ). The air is "*Tombé du nid*," music by L. Clapisson.

PN 11. "**The Time of Tears Has Passed at Last**" [For Marie of the Trinity's reception of the habit] is the first of eight poems written for and actually sung by her on her Clothing Day, December 18, 1884. (The others are #12, 20, 29, 30, 31, 49, and 53). In it she asks the Blessed Virgin to help her as a nun. In 1896 she changed her name from Sr. Marie-Agnès of the Holy Face to Sr. Marie of the Trinity. According to her, the words of the poem were sung to "*Nina la glaneuse*," music by Théodore Labarre.

PN 12. "**It's Close to You, Virgin Mary**" (*C'est près de vous, Vierge Marie*) was also written for Sister Marie of the Trinity's reception of the habit. It is the second poem written for Sister Marie for December 18, 1894, as a response to PN 11 and sung by the community following the solo singing of Poem 11. In it she expresses her gratitude to Mary and the community for becoming a Carmelite and hopes to be His forever. No actual melody is indicated.

PN 13. "**The Queen of Heaven to Her Beloved Child Marie of the Holy Face**" (*La Reine du Ciel à son Enfant bien-aimée Marie de la Ste. Face*) was written for Thérèse's sister Céline (then called Sister Marie of the Holy Face), and given as a gift on Christmas night, 1894. It is a sweet carol-like poem beginning with, "I'm looking for a little girl who resembles / Jesus, my only lamb / So I can keep them both / Together in the same cradle." The music is from the song, "*Le petit mousse noir*" composed by P. Chéret.

PN 14. "**To Our Father St. Joseph**" (A *Notre Père St. Joseph*), written sometime in 1894 at the request of Sister Marie of the Incarnation (converse sister), equates the poverty and hidden life of St. Joseph with that of the Carmelites. The poem was sung to the melody of "*Nous voulons Dieu*" with music by the Abbé F.X. Moreau.

PN 15. "**The Atom of the Sacred Heart**" (*L'Atome du Sacré-Coeur*), written in 1894, was the first of four poems requested by Sister Saint Vincent de Paul who in this poem considers herself an "atom" in relation to Jesus in the Eucharist. No music is indicated. The three other poems are # 19, 25, and 32.

PN 16. "**Song of Gratitude of Jesus' Fiancée**" (*Chant de Reconnaissance de la Fiancée de Jésus*), written for Céline's Clothing Day, February 5, 1895. It expresses the gratitude Céline has for having suffered before entering Carmel and the joy that Jesus has chosen her to be a Carmelite. The music is by Monsigny for the hymn, "*O Saint Autel*."

PN 17. "**Living on Love!**" (*Vivre d'Amour!*), probably Thérèse's best and most profound poem, is not dedicated to anyone in particular. Composed on February 26, 1895, it consists of fifteen stanzas of eight lines each. Near July 16, 1897, Thérèse composed a sixteenth stanza (the last piece of poetry she wrote), the first line of which is, "You who know my extreme Littleness." (See PS 8). She enumerates all the glories of living on love but ends with the words "Dying of love is what I hope for." Three months later she died. Thérèse used the music by A. Gerbier from his song, *"Il est à moi."*

PN 18. **"The Canticle of Céline"** (*Le Cantique de Céline*). Thérèse wrote it for Céline's twenty-sixth birthday, April 28, 1895. This long poem consisting of fifty-five verses is considered one of Thérèse's best. In it she recalls loving memories of her family life and lists the beautiful things of nature that infatuated her as a child which she discovers again but now changed into her true love, Jesus. Two years later Thérèse made a shortened revised version with ten stanzas entitled "He Who Has Jesus Has Everything" (PN 18A) and sent it to Abbé Bellière, her spiritual brother in Africa. The music is from a popular song from the Auvergne that Louis Martin loved, *"Combien j'ai douce souvenance"* with words by F.R. de Châteaubriand.

PN 18A. **"He Who Has Jesus Has Everything"** (*Qui a Jésus a Tout*), written in March 1887, is a shortened, revised version of Poem 18 that Thérèse sent to Abbé Bellière. The first verse tells all: "Scorning earthly joys, / I've become a prisoner [in Carmel]. / I've seen that all pleasures are passing. / You are my only joy, / Lord!"

PN 19. **"The Atom of Jesus Host"** (*L'Atome de Jésus Hostie*) was written at the request of Sister Saint Vincent de Paul who provided Thérèse with the basic ideas for it. Thérèse wrote this poem possibly in the summer of 1895. Again, as in Poem 15, the "atom" is Sister Saint Vincent's conception of herself in the presence of Jesus in the host. The title of the air is *"Par les chants les plus magnifiques."* Composer unknown.

PN 20. **"My Heaven on Earth"** (*Mon Ciel ici-bas!*), later published as "Canticle to the Holy Face" (*Cantique à la Sainte Face*), was written for Sister Marie of the Trinity and of the Holy Face (Thérèse's novice) to celebrate her twenty-first birthday, August 12, 1895. She focuses on the face of Jesus as her homeland, kingdom, wealth, sweetness, etc. The music is by Frederic Boissiere for the song he wrote, *"Les regrets de Mignon."*

PN 21. **"Canticle of a Soul Having Found the Place of Its Rest"** (*Cantique d'une Âme ayant trouvé le Lieu de son Repos!*) was written for Thérèse's cousin Marie Guérin (Sister Marie of the Eucharist) for the day she entered Carmel—the place of her rest—and sung by Marie on August 15, 1895. The melody, *"Connais-tu le pays,"* is from Ambroise Thomas' most known opera *Mignon*. Thérèse wrote two other poems for her—Poems 36 and 48.

PN 22. **"To My Dear Mother, the Fair Angel of My Childhood"** (*A ma Mère chérie le Bel Ange de mon Enfance*) is a tender biographical poem composed with love and gratitude for her older sister Pauline (Mother Agnès) on her thirty-fourth birthday, September 7, 1895. For Thérèse, her sister is still an angel as she was when they were both at home: "I'm not alone on earth, / For in this life's exile / A fair Angel guides my steps." Later on she adds, "And now I can hear / Her sweet song every day [in the monastery]." No melody was indicated. Thérèse wrote three more poems for her—Poems 26, 34, 45.

PN 23. **"To the Sacred Heart of Jesus"** (Au *Sacré-Coeur de Jésus*), dated June or October 1895, was written at the request of Sister Marie of the Sacred Heart (Thérèse's blood sister Marie). It is a profound expression of Thérèse's intense love for Jesus. The music this was sung to is "*Le petit soulier de Noël,*" composed by O. Pradère (or L. Amat)

PN 24. **"Jesus My Beloved, Remember!"** (*Jésus mon Bien-Aimé, rappelle-toi!*), a long and great poem of 33 stanzas totaling 297 lines, was written at the request of Sister Geneviève (Céline) for her feast day—Saint Céline, October 21, 1896. This is a meditation on events in the life of Christ which were all sacrifices and thus gifts to us from Him. The music this was sung to is "*Rappelle-toi,*" composed by Georges Rupès.

PN 25. **"My Desires Near Jesus Hidden in His Prison of Love"** (*Mes Désirs auprès de Jésus caché dans sa Prison d'Amour*) was composed at the request of Sister Saint Vincent de Paul in the autumn of 1895. Thérèse says in this eucharistic poem that though she envies the inanimate objects at the altar (tabernacle, lamp, altar stone, corporal, paten, chalice), she is more precious to Jesus than they are for she is His spouse. The music that was used was "*Je me meurs de ne point mourir*" and/or "*Par les chants les plus magnifiques.*"

PN 26. **"The Responses of Saint Agnes"** (*Les Répons de Sainte Agnès*) is a kind of betrothal poem written for the prioress, Mother Agnès (her blood sister), for her feast day, January 21, 1896. In the first two lines Thérèse is really expressing her own belief. "Christ is my Love, He is my whole life. / He is the Fiancé who alone delights my eyes." The music sung is from the air "Le Lac" composed by L. Niedermeyer or else from "*Dieu de paix et d'amour*" composed by P. Ligonnet.

PN 27. **"Remembrance of February 24, 1896"** (*Souvenir du 24 Février 1896*) was written for Céline's profession, February 24, 1896. Consisting of only six quatrains, it was given to her privately and not to be read by anyone else, along with four other gifts. The melody sung to was "*Sur terre tout n'est pas rose,*" by de Yradier or possibly sung to the air "Ay Chiquita."

PN 28. **"The Eternal Canticle Sung Even in Exile"** (*Le Cantique éternel chanté dès l'Exil*) was written for a nun with psychological problems, Sister Marie of St. Joseph, for her feast day, March 19. In it Thérèse speaks of love and the fact that the Carmelite, exiled in a convent, is the spouse of Christ. Thérèse did not indicate the music but we understand it was sung to the air "*Mignon regrettant sa patrie,*" composed by Luigi Bordèse. Thérèse wrote Poem 42 also for her.

PN 29. **"How Sweet It Is For Us"** (*Souvenir du 30 Avril 1896*). The subtitle is the dedication—"To our dear little Sister Marie of the Trinity and of the Holy Face." Thérèse wrote it for Sister Marie's profession on April 30, 1896. The first two lines summarize the rest: "O dear Sister! how sweet it is for us / To sing on this radiant day ..." This was sung to the music of P. Lambillotte's song "*O Coeur de notre aimable Mère.*"

PN 30. **"A Gloss on the Divine"** (*Glose sur le Divin*) was based on a composition by St. John of the Cross and put into verse by Thérèse to celebrate the profession of Sister Marie of the Trinity, April 30, 1896. The concept Thérèse favored is in the lines: "Love, I have experienced it, / Knows how to use (what power!) / The good and the bad it finds in me." This was sung to "*Seigneur quand de ma froide couche*" or "*Par les chants les plus magnifiques.*"

PN 31. **"The Canticle of Sister Marie of the Trinity and of the Holy Face"** (*Le Cantique de Soeur Marie de la Trinité et de la Sainte Face*), known also as "I thirst for Love," was written for Sister Marie of the Trinity on her feast day—the Most Holy Trinity—May 31, 1896. It is a reciprocal expression of love between Christ and His spouse—Sister Marie of the Trinity (and Sister Thérèse too). There is no indication of the music but Sister Marie of the Trinity claimed it was sung to the air "*Au sein de l'heureuse patrie.*"

PN 32. **"My Heaven to Me!"** (*Mon Ciel à moi!*) are thoughts of Sister St. Vincent de Paul put into verse by Thérèse for the feast of the Holy Sacrament, June 7, 1896. The last two lines embody Thérèse's deepest aspirations: "To suffer while waiting for Him to look at me again / That is heaven for me!" Thérèse wrote three more poems for Sister St. Vincent—Poems 25, 19, and 15. The music chosen was to the hymn, "*Dieu de paix et d'amour*" (a hymn to the Eucharist) composed by Père Ligonnet.

PN 33. **"What I'll Soon See for the First Time"** (*Ce que je verrai bientôt pour la Première fois*) was written for her sister, Sister Marie of the Sacred Heart, June 12, 1896. It is an anticipation of Thérèse's imminent death: "I no longer feel the weight of exile, / Since soon toward my only Homeland / I'll fly for the first time." There is no record that Thérèse indicated a melody, but the Carmel tradition is that it was sung to "*O saint autel qu'environnent les Anges*" composed by Monsigny.

PN 34. **"Strewing Flowers"** (*Jeter des Fleurs!*) written at the request of her sister Pauline (Mother Agnès of Jesus) for her feast day, that of St. Paul, June 29, 1896. It evokes the quintessential concept of Thérèse in heaven showering roses (blessings) down to earth. This was sung to the music of P. Lambillotte for "*Oui, je crois, elle est immaculée.*"

PN 35. **"To Our Lady of Victories, Queen of Virgins, of Apostles and of Martyrs"** (*A Notre-Dame des Victoires Reine des Vierges, des Apôtres et des Martyrs*) was composed on July 16, 1896, for Père Roulland who celebrated one of his first masses at the Church of Our Lady of Victories in Paris before he visited Thérèse on his way to China. She maintains in the poem that her great desire to be a missionary and even a martyr will be fulfilled through him. No melody was indicated.

PN 36. **"Jesus Alone"** (*Jésus Seul*). Sister Marie of the Eucharist, asked her cousin Thérèse to write this poem for the first anniversary of her entrance into Carmel, August 15, 1896. It is a passionate song of love in human terms for Jesus: "Lord, I want to overwhelm you with my caresses." The melody sung was composed by Hippolyte Louel for the song "*Près d'un berceau.*"

PN 37. **"For Jeanne and Francis La Néele"** (*Pour Jeanne et Francis La Néele*), consisting of only twelve lines, was written at the request of Thérèse's cousin Jeanne (Guérin) La Néele and her husband, Dr. Francis La Néele, for Jeanne's special day, August 21, 1896, the feast day of St. Jeanne de Chantal. Thérèse sent it to the Chateau de La Musse where they were vacationing. Not intended to be sung.

PN 38. **"Confidential Message from Jesus to Thérèse"** (*Confidence de Jésus à Thérèse*), a second poem sent to Thérèse's cousins, Dr. and Mme. La Néele, for Jeanne La Néele's feast day, August 21, 1896, asking Jesus to "give Jeanne a little baby." Not intended to be sung.

PN 39. **"A Holy and Famous Doctor"** (*Un Docteur Saint et Célèbre*), an acrostic—"FRANCIS"—formed from Dr. La Néele's first name and sent with the two preceeding poems to the La Néeles at La Musse on August 21, 1896. As an example of the form, the first two lines are: "F—*Francis* took this motto: / R—(*Rien*) Nothing for man, everything for my God." Not intended to be sung.

PN 40. **"The Sacristans of Carmel"** (*Les Sacristines du Carmel*) was originally written in November 1896 at the request of Sister Marie Philomena of Jesus, the sacristan sister in charge of making altar breads. The other sacristans were Thérèse, Sister Marie of the Angels, and Sister Marie of the Eucharist. Thérèse announces that by having the privilege of making hosts these nuns share in the mission of the priesthood. She also affirms that "Our happiness and our glory / Is to work for Jesus." Thérèse did not leave a record of what she wanted sung, but Carmel tradition holds that it was sung to "*Par les chants les plus magnifiques.*"

PN 41. **"How I Want to Love"** (*Comment je veux aimer*). At the request of Sister Saint John of the Cross, Thérèse composed this religious love poem toward the end of 1896. The first verse commences with "Divine Jesus, listen to my prayer. / By my love I want to make you rejoice.... / It's your love, Jesus, that I crave." The air indicated by Thérèse is uncertain. It was sung either to "*Je crois au Dieu*" or to the "*Credo*" from the now forgotten opera *Herculanum* by F. David.

PN 42. **"Child, You Know My Name"** (*Enfant Tu Connais Mon Nom*) Thérèse wrote this in December 1896, requested by Sister Marie of St. Joseph, a nun with a fiery temperament who left the convent thirteen years later. Thérèse strove to tame her character by the use of affectionate and even childlike terms in dealing with her in person as well as in writing. Music: "*Où vas-tu quand tout est noir.*"

PN 43. **"The Aviary of the Infant Jesus"** (*La Volière de l'Enfant-Jésus*) was written for the Christmas night recreation period of 1896. The aviary represents Carmel and the birds are the nuns who "for you [Jesus] alone we want to sing." The images of childhood and ideas of abandonment presented here are typically Theresian. Charles Gounod wrote the music to "*Au rossignol*" that this poem was sung to.

PN 44. **"To My Little Brothers in Heaven"** (A *mes Petits Frères du Ciel*), a poem about Thérèse's four little brothers and sisters who died as babies, was intended for the recreation period on the feast of the Holy Innocents, December 28, 1896. She addresses her deceased siblings as "Dear little Lilies" concerning whom "no genius here below knows as many things / As you, Children! [in heaven]" She calls them Holy Innocents and wants to be their "faithful likeness" here on earth. The music sung to this poem was either from "*La Rose-Mousse*" by Malliot or from "*Le fil de la Vierge*" composed by P. Scudo.

PN 45. **"My Joy!"** (*Ma Joie!*) was requested by Mother Agnès for her feast day, January 21, 1897, concerning which Thérèse said, "My whole soul is in that [poem]." For example, "Oh! How many charms there are in suffering / When one knows how to hide it with flowers! / I truly want to suffer without saying so." The poem was sung to "*Où vas-tu, petit oiseau?*" by the composer Léopold Amat.

PN 46. **"To My Guardian Angel"** (*A mon Ange Gardien*) was composed in January 1897 and given to Sister Marie Philomena, former novice with Thérèse, thirty-four years her senior. It reads like a tribute to Thérèse's own guardian angel coupled with her expectations for the joys of heaven after the sacrifices of this life are over. Thérèse specified this poem to be sung to the music of "*Par les chants les plus magnifiques.*"

PN 47. **"To Théophane Vénard"** (*A Théophane Vénard*) was written for the thirty-sixth anniversary of his martyrdom, February 2, 1897. He was canonized in 1988. She saw a great deal in him that she saw in herself. In this poem she "sings" of the many virtues of this heroic martyr who died at the age of thirty-one in Vietnam (then called Tonkin). This poem was sung to the music by A. G. de Sainbris of "*Les adieux du Martyr.*"

PN 48. **"My Weapons"** (*Mes Armes*) was written for her cousin Marie Guérin, Sister Marie of the Eucharist, for the day of her profession, March 25, 1897, and sung to Charles Gounod's "Song at the Departure of the Missionaries" ("*Chant du depart des Missionnaires.*") It is a strong statement about Thérèse's own final spiritual conflicts. She ends with "And in your arms, O my Divine Spouse, / I shall die singing on the battlefield, My Weapons [poverty, chastity, obedience] in hand!"

PN 49. **"To Our Lady of Perpetual Help"** (*A Notre-Dame du Perpétuel Secours*) was written in March 1897 at the request of Sister Marie of the Trinity who had a special devotion to Mary under this title. No music indicated.

PN 50. **"To Joan of Arc"** (*A Jeanne d'Arc*), written in May 1897, is a short poem in which Thérèse identifies herself with Joan in her spiritual and physical trials. No melody indicated.

PN 51. **"An Unpetalled Rose"** (*Un Rose effeuillée*), symbolic of Thérèse herself, is one of her best poems. It was requested by a nun in the Paris Carmel and dated May 18, 1897. In stanza two Thérèse tells us that "This unpetalled rose is the faithful image, / Divine Child, / Of the heart that wants to sacrifice itself for you unreservedly at each moment." This was sung to P. Scudo's "*Le fil de la Vierge*" or possibly to Mailliot's "*La Rose-Mousse.*"

PN 52. **"Abandonment Is the Sweet Fruit of Love"** (*L'Abandon est le Fruit délicieux de l'Amour*) was requested by Sister Teresa of Saint Augustine, May 31, 1897. It is an allegory about abandonment even in the throes of death. "Abandonment alone brings me / Into your arms, O Jesus. / It alone makes me live / The life of the Elect." Thérèse did not mention a melody but Carmel tradition holds that it was sung to "*Si j'étais grande dame*," music by Louis Abadie.

PN 53. **"For Sister Marie of the Trinity"** (*Pour Sr. Marie de la Trinité*) was written in May 1897. A second title is "A Lily in the Midst of Thorns" (*Un Lys au Milieu des Épines*). The eighth and last poem for this sister, it sings of the mercies that the Lord has showered on her. It was sung to the music composed by W. Moreau for "*L'envers du ciel.*"

PN 54. **"Why I Love You, O Mary!"** (*Pourquoi je t'aime, ô Marie*) is a long prayerful poem (195 lines) that Thérèse's sister Marie (Sister Marie of the Sacred Heart) asked her to write. Composed in May 1897, it is considered to be the Saint's swan song. After explaining why she loves Mary, she concludes with "Soon I'll go to beautiful Heaven to see you. / ... With you I've suffered, and now I want / To sing on your lap, Mary, why I love you." This was sung to Louis Abadie's "*La plainte du mousse*."

The following eight poems, called "Supplementary Poems," are nearly all unfinished works or fragments, some perhaps partially written by St. Thérèse, the others by unnamed nuns from the Lisieux Carmel:

PS 1. **"O Hidden God"** (*O Dieu caché*) is an unfinished poem possibly written for the community's recreation period on the feast of Epiphany, January 6, 1895, or 1896. The first line is "O God hidden under the guise of childhood." Possibly it was sung to *"Joseph inconnue sur terre."*

PS 2. **"In the Orient"** (*En Orient*) is an incomplete poem of twelve lines intended for the community's evening recreation time on the feast of Epiphany, January 6, 1895 or 1896. No melody is indicated.

PS 3. **"For Fifty Years"** (*Depuis cinquante Ans*), dated January 15, 1896, is a short poem honoring Sister Saint Stanislas, the oldest nun in the convent, for her loving kindness and other virtues. Sung to P. Fonteneau's air *"Je suis chrétien."*

PS 4. **"Heaven's the Reward"** (*Le Ciel en est le Prix*) is a humorous and uncharacteristically ironic commentary of twenty-one quatrains on the sacrifices Carmelites make. Some doubt that Thérèse composed it; in any case, it survives in her handwriting and was written especially for her novices who sang it during a recreation period, probably in the summer of 1896. For example, the humorously paradoxical fourth stanza tells us that "Heaven's the reward. / Nothing, no table or chair. / To feel uncomfortable / Is happiness here." This was sung to the air *"Le ciel en est le prix."*

PS 5. **"For a Feast of Saint Martha"** (*Pour une Sainte-Marthe*), was composed for the lay sisters who were annually honored by the whole community on their special feast day, that of St. Martha, July 29, 1896. Each of the four sisters had four comical lines written for her telling about the gift she will receive: toy dog, pig, boat, or some little useful thing. No melody indicated.

PS 6. **"To Mother Marie de Gonzague"** (*A Mère Marie de Gonzague*) was written for the prioress' feast day, June 21, 1897. Despite the intense weakness Thérèse endured during her last illness, she lovingly wrote these eight lines mentioning the three gifts she was giving her: a photo album, her toque, and her heart. This was not intended to be sung.

PS 7. **"Silence is the Sweet Language..."** (*Le Silence est le doux langage*), composed in June 1896, is a tender poem of only eight lines intended perhaps for one of the nuns. This "silence" is the language of angels, the elect, and those who love each other in Jesus. This was not meant to be sung.

PS 8. **"You Who Know My Extreme Littleness"** (*Toi qui connais ma Petitesse extrême*), consisting of only eight lines, was sung by Sister Marie of the Eucharist (Marie Guérin) just before the very sick Thérèse received communion in the infirmary on July 16, 1897, the feast of Our Lady of Mount Carmel. This was sung to A. Gerbier's air *"Il est à moi."*

Besides the sixty-two poems recorded above, Thérèse composed others that are integrated within her recreational plays. These have been extracted and used throughout the years in various publications as independent poems not connected with the plays. Most of them come from the two plays about Joan of Arc.

The poems of Thérèse have been variably classified by critics as brilliant, mediocre, and poor. One may justly place among the brilliant poems "An Unpetalled Rose" (PN 51), "My Song for Today" (PN 5), "My Weapons" (PN 48), "The Divine Dew" (PN 1), "Living on Love" (PN 17), and "Why I Love You, O Mary" (PN 54). Together with their poetic, religious, and sentimental qualities, each of St. Thérèse's poems, in its own way, provides additional details to the remarkable doctrine that she unfolds for us in her own distinctive, poetical way.

Melodious harmonies resound throughout her poems with their exuberant praises of the Divine and their profound and passionate expressions of her love. But in reading about her actual state of mind when creating them, one is truly jarred by the discordant note one hears on page 214 in her autobiography *Story of a Soul*:

> [If] you are judging according to the sentiments I express in my little poems composed this year, I must appear to you as a soul filled with consolations and one for whom the veil of faith is almost torn aside; and yet it is no longer a veil for me, it is a wall which reaches right up to the heavens and covers the starry firmament. When I sing of the happiness of heaven and of the eternal possession of God, I feel no joy in this, for I sing simply what I WANT TO BELIEVE. It is true that at times a very small ray of sun comes to illumine my darkness, and then the trial ceases for *an instant*, but afterwards the memory of this ray, instead of causing me joy, makes my darkness even more dense.

Thérèse's bitter trial of faith continued from Easter 1896 until her death in September 1897, thereby placing nearly the last half of all her poems within the time frame of this tormented phase of her spiritual journey. The dark night of her soul's anguish persisted even as death stared her in the face, yet moments before death claimed her life, Thérèse triumphantly uttered her last words, a final redeeming act of faith: "Oh! I love Him! My God, I love you!"

Many of Thérèse's poems were published in the 1898 edition of her autobiography, but the absolutely complete collection of her poems in the original French were first published in their entirety in two volumes including notes in 1979.

The English translation of her poems by Donald Kinney, O.C.D., was used here almost exclusively. The names of the songs Thérèse had her lyrics sung to were obtained from *Les Musiques de Thérèse* published in 1997 by Les Éditions du Cerf and from *Thérèse de l'Enfant-Jésus et de la Sainte-Face ŒUVRES COMPLÈTES*, editions du Cerf, 2001. Of utmost importance too was the information obtained from Tome I, Introduction, pp. 7–20 of *Manuscrits Autobiographiques*, 1955 (the facsimile edition).

4. Plays

RP 1	*The Mission of Joan of Arc*
RP 2	*Angels at the Crib of Jesus*
RP 3	*Joan of Arc Accomplishing Her Mission*
RP 4	*Jesus at Bethany*
RP 5	*The Divine Little Beggar at Christmas*
RP 6	*The Flight Into Egypt*
RP 7	*The Triumph of Humility*
RP 8	*Saint Stanislas Kostka*

ONE SEGMENT OF ST. THÉRÈSE'S WRITINGS ALMOST COMPLETELY UNKNOWN to English-speaking readers are her plays. These skits or "pious recreations" (*récéations pieuses*), as they are termed, were meant to entertain as well as edify the nuns during their recreational periods on particular holidays, feast days, and anniversaries. It was a Carmelite custom actually mandated by St. Teresa of Avila to provide free time each day as a balance to the rigors of the cloistered and meditative life. St. Teresa of Avila particularly encouraged the nuns who had artistic and literary talents to use them in writing and painting. She maintained that not only did they add to the good of the community life but they were also a means of glorifying God. Two holidays of particular importance were Christmas and the Holy Innocents (December 28), the special day for the novices. The lay sisters too were honored every July 29 on the feast of St. Martha. The feast day of the prioress was always celebrated as well as the golden jubilee of a nun's profession. For these occasions, nuns with writing ability often wrote short plays which included dialogue and lyrics for singing. Only the novices, however, acted in the performances. When Thérèse was a novice she took the leading role in five of her own eight plays.[34]

Pauline, Thérèse's blood sister whose religious name was Sister Agnès, had the task of writing these playlets at the time Thérèse entered Carmel in 1888. Five years later, when Sister Agnès became prioress (and named Mother Agnès), she assigned the play writing to Thérèse who had acted in two of Sister Agnès's plays: the lead role in one about St. Agnès (June 21, 1888) called simply *St. Agnès* and the other a Christmas play, *The First Dream of the Child Jesus*, performed in the evening of Christmas Day 1889 in which she portrayed Mary with "much piety and simplicity." In both she is said to have been a beautiful and impressive actress. No doubt this experience helped her to write her own plays. In them she focuses on the Incarnation and Passion of Christ, Mary, the spousal relationship of the nuns to Christ, her favorite saints, the Carmelite life, the virtues (especially love and humility), abandonment, and her doctrine of spiritual childhood. In short, she reveals in each one her own religious preferences and her incomparable spirituality.

Thérèse never attended a professionally produced play and perhaps never read the script of one. She, however, may have seen a school performance though she certainly never participated in one; yet some of her writing displays a strong

---

34 These extra-liturgical forms of religious activity are referred to in canon law as "paraliturgies."

flair. These "pious recreations" were obviously modest productions but generally contained all the basics of play construction and production. A few severe critics consider them not quite suitable for a mature and sophisticated audience, though in their simplicity they are beguilingly appealing. Her plays, especially those about Joan of Arc, have on occasion been performed since 1894, particularly by other Carmelite communities and also by some children's groups.

Dialogue in each is interspersed with verses or poems sung by the actors to melodies which Thérèse chose herself. The number of songs selected for all the plays amount to well over sixty with a handful used more than once. In essence, or at least in concept, these works are plays with music which one might even make the stretch to say resemble medieval mystery plays or even old-time English ballad operas with spoken parts and song texts set to folk or popular tunes.

No one in Thérèse's immediate family was musically gifted except her father who had a beautiful sonorous voice and loved to sing his favorite songs at home and on trips. Her cousin Marie Guérin, on the other hand, was a rather accomplished amateur pianist and singer who entertained not only her own family and the Martins but also performed in public places. Everyone was familiar with the many hymns sung in church and in other religious venues. In that era the parlor piano was the frequent and perhaps only source of music for rural, provincial families. Here were introduced, by way of sheet music and a family musician, popular as well as classical music to these families who otherwise would have no other means of hearing them. Of course there was Paris, the brilliant center of the French theatrical and musical world with its opera houses, concert halls, cafes, music and dance halls, etc. Religious and deeply pious families like the Martins shunned such places of entertainment. Nonetheless, they and the Guérins certainly must have casually encountered sundry musical events at the beach resorts of Deauville and Trouville. Regardless of where Thérèse managed to gain familiarity with the music of her time, she later on capitalized on it for her own use in the convent. In addition, when Marie Guérin joined the Carmelites in Lisieux she brought with her some of the music from her own personal collection. Thérèse's repertoire, therefore, was rather large, not only encompassing music by composers of hymns and songs unknown today but also by world famous operatic composers.

Music was not absent in monasteries for the Carmelite's regimen included hours of singing the Divine Office (*recto tono* mode — singing on one note). Above all, it must be understood that Thérèse considered her life as "one great song," as she put it, of love and praise to God. She announced it clearly in the second sentence of her autobiography: "I'm going to be doing only one thing: I shall begin to sing what I must sing eternally: 'The Mercies of the Lord.'" And in another deeply personal identification, she painted at the end of this same manuscript her "coat of arms of Jesus and Thérèse" where next to a drawing of the Holy Face she placed a harp on which she symbolically was playing melodies of love to Him.

St. Thérèse's eight plays are given here in chronological order with date, cast, synopsis, and other pertinent data:

RP 1 *The Mission of Joan of Arc or the Shepherdess of Domrémy Listening to Voices* was staged on January 21, 1894, for Mother Agnès's feast day. It included ten different melodies.[35] In preparing for this play (and RP 3), Thérèse read and studied Henri Wallon's life of Joan of Arc published in 1860. The characters in her play are Joan of Arc (played by Thérèse), St. Michael the Archangel, St. Catherine, St. Margaret, Catherine (Joan of Arc's sister), and Germaine (a young shepherdess). Since childhood Thérèse had a great love for and identified with Joan of Arc whose popularity was greatly increased by the introduction of her cause at the very time Thérèse wrote and staged her play. Joan was proclaimed Venerable just a few days before this play was performed. Her beatification took place in 1909 and canonization in 1920.

Much research went into this play and its sequel. It deals with Joan's early visions and her mission to save France from the English. St. Michael the Archangel appears to the frightened Joan and urges her to take up arms for her country. She eventually agrees amid the joyous refrains of the Saints. The players sang some ten different melodies, one of which is the well- known "The Palms" ("*Les Rameaux*") by Faure. Actually Thérèse voiced her own sentiments and convictions about herself and the Carmelite life through the characters she created. The dialogues between Joan and her sister Catherine seem to echo those between Thérèse and her sister Céline, especially her injunction to remain always simple and humble. Joan sings another Theresian tenet: "Yes, I desire the cross; the sacrifice is light; / To suffer for Thee, Lord, ready and glad am I."[36]

The Saints then offer Joan the palm and crown of martyrdom. In the epilogue, St. Michael foretells Joan's imminent glorification by the Church.

> I [St. Michael] hear the universe declare
> The virtues of this maid in warlike armor drest;
> I hear God grant to her the rare
> And grand and glorious title, Jeanne the Blest.[37]

RP 2 *Angels at the Crib of Jesus* was staged for the recreation period on Christmas night, 1894. Thérèse wove nine different melodies into the story.[38] The characters in the play are: The Infant Jesus [a polychrome plaster figure], the Angel of the Infant Jesus (played by Thérèse), the Angel of the Holy Face, the Angel of the Resurrection, the Angel of the Eucharist, and the Angel of the Last Judgment. Jesus also appears at the end. The doctrine that Thérèse so fervently espoused, spiritual childhood, is the central concept that emerges through the dialogue between the Angel of the Infant Jesus and the four other Angels. Various manifestations of God as love, a baby, a face with tears, etc., demonstrate that Jesus even as a child was aware of His eventual suffering, death, and resurrection, as well as His future presence in the Eucharist. The

---

35 One of the melodies is by Charles Gounod.
36 Emery, *Poems*, p. 149.
37 Ibid., p. 151.
38 Two of the melodies are by Adolphe Adam and Giovanni Pergolesi.

Angel of the Last Judgment at the end intervenes to remind the Infant and the others that sinners should be punished. Jesus replies with: "'Tis I shall judge the human race"[39] and two stanzas later "The souls I choose, the souls I spare, / Shall reign in glory like the sun." In the final refrain, the Angels express envy toward humans who can become like Him, a child, while they cannot.

RP 3. ***Joan of Arc Accomplishing Her Mission*** is the commonly known short title of Thérèse's third play. The full title has this addition: "*or The Victories, the Captivity, the Martyrdom and Triumphs in Heaven of the Venerable Joan of France.*" It was staged on January 21, 1895, for the feast day of the prioress, Mother Agnès of Jesus. Again Thérèse heavily relied on Wallon's life of Joan of Arc for basic facts. This is the only play of which we have pictures. Céline took five photos of Thérèse as Joan which include one of herself as Saint Margaret with Joan in prison. (Photos 11–15)

Her play originally had two parts, but subsequently has been arranged into three parts (acts), with fifteen characters. Part I is entitled "The Victories" with six scenes; Part II is called "The Captivity, the Martyrdom" and has eleven scenes; Part III has the title "The Triumph in Heaven" and consists of two scenes. Thérèse used fourteen melodies, more than for any of her other plays. This is her longest recreation piece (forty-three pages of script), the most elaborately produced, and for which the community gave more applause than for any of her other plays. It included costumes, wigs, props, and special effects that at one point caused a fire which they fortunately extinguished in time. They used an alcohol stove at the stake on which Joan died. The fire resulting from it set the screen next to it aflame which Sister Marie of the Angels explained: "She [Thérèse] almost was actually burned alive, following an imprudence that lighted the beginning of a fire, while we did our best to put out the fire around her, she remained calm and immobile in the middle of the danger [out of obedience to Mother Agnès who told her to stay still], making the sacrifice of her life to God, as she said afterward."[40]

The plot concerns Joan's military victories, her crowning of King Charles VII, imprisonment, death, and glorification in heaven. Again, as in the first Joan of Arc play, the parallels between Joan and Thérèse are unmistakable. Joan in prison (as Thérèse in Carmel) exclaims: "My voices this foretold: I am a prisoner here, / No aid can I expect, except my God from Thee; / For love of Thee alone, I left my father dear...."[41] Shortly after she (Joan/Thérèse) repeats her great longing: "Now but one wish is mine,—to see Thee face to face, / No more to part from Thee:—behold my heart's desire! / To die for love of Thee,—what happier lot than this?"[42] Later on the Saints call Joan "the spouse of Christ" just as Thérèse considered herself and all the Carmelites with her. In the final scene of Joan's glorification in heaven, the saints urge Joan to spend her time there helping those on earth—just as Thérèse likewise wished to do after her death. France personified appears and implores Joan to help her:

---
39 Emery, *op. cit.*, p. 144.
40 Chalon, *Thérèse of Lisieux: A Life of Love*, p. 186.
41 Emery, *op. cit.*, p. 153.
42 Ibid., p. 154.

> I come to you, all loaded down with chains,
> With face veiled and with eyes bathed in tears.
> I am no longer counted among the queens
> And my children swamp me in sorrows.
> They have forgotten God!... They've left their mother!...
> O Joan! Take pity on my bitter sadness
> Come, comfort my heart,
> Liberating angel.
> I hope in you! I hope in you!
> ...
> Joan, it's you, my sweet Sovereign
> Daughter of God, who has come to rule the French! [43]

This is perhaps the best constructed of Thérèse's eight plays. The last pages of the script somewhat resemble opera librettos where music, drama, and meaningful lyrics blend, producing a rather impressive, almost operatic finale.

RP 4. *Jesus at Bethany* was presented on July 29, 1895, the feast of St. Martha, to honor the lay sisters of the community. The cast includes only three people: Jesus (played by Thérèse), Martha (played by Sr. Geneviève), and Mary Magdalen (played by Sr. Marie of the Trinity). (Thérèse mistakes this Mary for the sister of Lazarus and Martha.) This playlet consists of dialogue in verse with but two (possibly more) different melodies. The repentant Mary thanks God for forgiving her: "What have I ever done / To win from Thee such grace?" [44] Jesus replies with "Those pure, repentant tears; ... Thy guilt is washed away." [45] He also admonishes her: "But first, on earth a while / In prayer live silently." [46] Martha intervenes and tells Jesus that her sister should help her. He reminds her that work is necessary but "One must transfigure work with prayer." [47] In the end, the two sisters come to realize that the most important thing in life is the gift of their love. Jesus summarizes it:

> Yes, 'tis thy loving heart I crave;
> For this I came from heaven above.
> The glories 'tis My right to have,
> I left, to seek your love, your love! [48]

RP 5. *The Divine Little Beggar at Christmas* was presented for the recreation of Christmas 1895. Only five melodies were sung.[49] Actually this is not a play in the strict sense of the word but a solo performance by the Angel who sings verses that each nun gives her. Thérèse's cousin, Marie Guérin, who had a lovely voice, assumed the part of the Angel. The play's theme is Thérèse's own vocation philosophy—that the Divine Child is a beggar beseeching us to save

---

43 *The Plays of St. Thérèse of Lisieux*, pp. 194–195.
44 Emery, p. 108.
45 Ibid.
46 Ibid., p. 111.
47 Ibid., p. 112.
48 Ibid., p. 113.
49 One is a song by Jules Massenet, "Sérénade de Zanetto," and another is an air, "Au Rossignol," by Charles Gounod.

others by offering our lives to Him. The entire community of twenty-six nuns participated. The Angel enters carrying a figure of the Infant Jesus in her arms and places it in a crib. She then presents a basket to the nuns filled with folded pieces of pink and blue papers in envelopes. Each nun, beginning with the prioress, after showing respect to the Infant, picks one, and without looking at it, gives it to the Angel who opens it and sings the twelve or fourteen lines written on it. The title of each stanza and the lines below disclose Thérèse's own preferences written in her own metaphorical manner: "Roses," "A Crown of Lilies," "A Smile," "A Caress," "Little Birds," "A Lyre," "A Lamb," "A Bunch of Grapes" (the one Thérèse drew), etc.

RP 6. *The Flight into Egypt* was given on January 21, 1896, and written for the feast day of Mother Agnès, the prioress. Thérèse makes about seventy references to, or quotations from, Scripture in it. It is the second longest play and the only one in which Thérèse introduces some humor through two outwardly unsavory but sympathetic robbers. Her subject matter again shows confidence in God's love and mercy, the merits of poverty and the hidden life—all aspects of the Carmelite vocation. She wrote it in verse and prose with only six different melodies blended into the story.[50]

The play is divided into two "Acts." The first with five scenes represents the home of the Holy Family in Nazareth where the characters are the Holy Virgin (played by Thérèse), Joseph (Sr. Geneviève), Jesus (figure of an infant), and an Angel. The Angel urges the holy couple to flee to Egypt in order to escape the forthcoming slaughter of little boys at the hands of Herod's men. The second act with seven scenes shows the thieves' cavern where Susanna (Sr. Marie of the Eucharist), the wife of the robber chief Abramin (Sr. Marie of the Trinity), worries about her infant son, Dismas, suffering from leprosy. The two semi-comic characters Torcol (an old man) and Izarn (a young man) enter with their loot and express their opinions to the music of the sprightly waltz "Estudiantina."[51] Mary, Joseph, and Jesus arrive seeking shelter for the night. Because of their poverty, the thieves claim they must engage in stealing. Joseph says he is also poor but exclaims: "We're not fleeing poverty. Happiness does not consist in possessing wealth but in humbly submitting one's will to God who gives to each one of us all that is necessary to save one's soul."[52] After Mary washes the Infant Jesus, Susanna uses the same water to cleanse her baby who is instantly cured. She reacts exuberantly with much gratitude and joy.

The Angel appears again at the end and, with a typical Theresian thrust, declares "Then Satan shall, in frantic jealousy, / Seek to deplete these houses [convents] of our Lord."[53] This is followed shortly by "It may be that one day, Thy Spouses dear [nuns] / Must share Thy exile, O Thou Holy Child."

Actually the performance was not given in its entirety because Mother Agnès abruptly ordered Thérèse to stop before it was over complaining that

---

50 One is a section from a trio in Giuseppi Verdi's opera *Il Trovatore* ("*Giorni poveri vivea*") and another the "Soldiers' Chorus" from Gounod's *Faust*.
51 Music by P. Lacome but made popular by Waldteufel's 1886 arrangement.
52 RP, p. 225, as translated by John Russell in "Religious Plays of St. Thérèse" in the Carmelite studies book *Experiencing Saint Thérèse Today*, p. 51.
53 Emery, *op. cit.*, p. 120.

it was too long and tiring for the nuns. Thérèse and the other "actresses" felt humiliated and disheartened by such an action but Thérèse quickly dried her tears and regained her usual serenity. Furthermore, Mother Agnès objected to the use of such a profane composition as "Estudiantina." As a matter of fact, Thérèse used elsewhere three other "secular" tunes, all from operas: an aria from Verdi's *Il Trovatore*, the "Soldiers' Chorus" from Gounod's *Faust*, and a Credo from the now totally forgotten opera *Herculanum* by F. David.

RP 7. *The Triumph of Humility* was written for Mother Gonzague, the new prioress, and performed on June 21, 1896, the feast day of St. Aloysius Gonzaga, after whom the prioress was named. Thérèse selected three melodies for the play. The only setting is the recreation room of the convent with three novices, using their own religious names, as the main characters: Sister Thérèse of the Child Jesus (novice mistress), Sister Mary Magdalene (professed with a white veil), and Sister Martha of Jesus.

The three nuns begin the play by discussing, under the leadership of Thérèse, the prioress' feast, evil, and even mention the intriguing Diana Vaughan, a much discussed contemporary personality in France who converted from anti-Catholicism and Satanism to a believer and possible candidate for a religious vocation. At this point no one knew that Diana Vaughan was the fictitious creation of an anti-religious, salacious, sensationalist writer and hoaxer Leo Taxil. St. Michael appears and calms the nuns' concerns. Dreadful noises (made by the zealous novices) explode from behind a screen representing hell and the realm of the devils Lucifer, Beelzebub, and Asmodeus (a demon in Jewish demonology). Heard but not seen, these evil ones converse heatedly about virtue, the Church, Carmelites, and also Diana Vaughan. The frightened novices invoke St. Michael to help them which he does by throwing a lance into the abyss (behind the screen). St. Michael and Lucifer forthwith engage in a verbal exchange in which Lucifer, the prince of pride (as he calls himself) is vanquished by the power of Christ and the humility of the Blessed Virgin. Lucifer and his minions cry out "We are defeated!" and disappear. Angels sing the final refrain:

> You desire, fervent Carmelites
> To win hearts for Jesus, your Spouse.
> Well, for Him always remain little.
> Humility puts hell into a rage.[54]

RP 8. *Saint Stanislas Kostka*, presented on February 8, 1897, was composed for the golden jubilee of Sister St. Stanislas Kostka's profession. She was the oldest member of the community (73) who later served as Thérèse's infirmarian during her last illness. Thérèse wrote it in prose except for nine quatrains of music sung to two different melodies (one by Gounod) at the end by celestial voices: an Angel, St. Barbara, and the Blessed Virgin. All the saints who particularly impressed Thérèse died young as did St. Stanislas Kostka (1550–1568). The pious and humble son of a Polish senator, Stanislas entered the Jesuit novitiate in Rome and died there nine months later at eighteen.

---

54 Author's translation of the verse from RP, p. 927 in *Œuvres completes*.

The entire play takes place in the chamber of St. Francis Borgia (1510–1572), the general of the order. Thérèse covers the major events in Stanislas' life: namely his family opposition, travel to Germany, his entrance into the community, and the vision he experienced of angels accompanied by St. Barbara who administered Communion to him. Thérèse harbored two strong desires in her life which she reveals here: the wish to exercise priestly duties (like St. Barbara) and the hope (like Stanislas) of doing good on earth after death. In the vision Stanislas has at the very end, the Blessed Virgin assures him that his wish will be granted:

> Dear child, you will protect
> The souls struggling in this world
> The more the harvest will become fruitful
> And the more in heaven you will glitter.[55]

Plays were customarily put on in the recreation room located in the southern end of the main monastery building off the covered cloister walk. Next door was the kitchen and then the refectory. The pleasantly lit recreation room containing four big windows and three doors made it fairly well suited for dramatic presentations. Besides the infirmary, this, appropriately named the "warming room," was the only heated room in the convent. The nuns, however, performed two of Thérèse's plays—*The Divine Little Beggar at Christmas,* and *The Flight into Egypt*—elsewhere in the convent, both possibly in the chapter room on the second floor where during the Christmas season a large crèche was installed. They stored costumes, wigs, and props in the attic.

5. Prayers

ANOTHER TYPE OF CREATIVE WRITING THÉRÈSE FOUND INVALUABLE WAS composing prayers that seemed to flow quite naturally from her pen. She began writing them during her school days and continued until the time of her death. All those we know of are preserved in the archives of the Lisieux Monastery. Totaling twenty-one, some consist of only a few words while others are much longer, though a relatively small amount compared, for instance, to her poetic output. Despite their small number, they contain the very essence of her spirituality in miniature as her biography and other literary output do in great length. They unfold during the various periods of her spiritual journey from childhood, profession, mistress of novices, spiritual sister for two missionaries, and finally to her dying days.

In the course of the years after her death, these prayers were slowly released to St. Thérèse's readers. In the Appendix to the first edition of *Histoire d'une Âme* (1898) just four of them were included. The 1907 edition added four more, and the 1953 issue comprised fourteen. It was not until the publication of the *Complete Works* (*Œuvres Complètes*) in 1972 that all Thérèse's known prayers were accessible to the French speaking public. Finally in 1997, the complete and annotated English edition of the prayers entitled *The Prayers of Saint Thérèse*

---

[55] Author's translation of the verse from RP, p. 945 in *Œuvres completes*.

of Lisieux was published by the Institute of Carmelite Studies in Washington, D.C., in a splendid translation by Aletheia Kane, O.C.D.

Thérèse defines prayer in her autobiography: "For me, prayer is an aspiration of the heart, it is a simple glance directed to heaven, it is a cry of gratitude and love in the midst of trial as well as joy; finally, it is something great, supernatural, which expands my soul and unites me to Jesus."[56] Thérèse wrote her prayers in a practical and easily repeated form of devotion. In them she reveals her deep seated beliefs and spiritual longings.

Below is a list of all twenty-one prayers with the date of composition, for whom composed, and an explanation of each. All excerpts are from Kane's book:

> Pri 1. **"O My Good Blessed Virgin,"** composed in June 1884 for herself. This is the complete prayer: "O my good Blessed Virgin, grant that your little Thérèse may stop tormenting herself." It is a reference to her doubts about the cure she had on May 13, 1883, when the statue of Our Lady smiled at her.
>
> Pri 2. **[Profession Note]**, written by Thérèse for her own Profession Day, September 8, 1890. She lists in some two dozen lines all her desires as a nun and prays they will be achieved with the help of her divine spouse, Jesus.
>
> Pri 3. **"A Look of Love at Jesus,"** written in 1883 for Sr. Martha of Jesus and herself, it tells Jesus that they, following the Carmelite rule, are determined to keep their eyes always lowered in the refectory and by so doing they will be honoring and imitating Him.
>
> Pri 4. **"Homage to the Blessed Trinity,"** written in February 1894 for herself and Sr. Martha. She hopes that by their prayers and sacrifices in Carmel, all the indifference and the blasphemies committed against God by lay people and religious can be atoned for.
>
> Pri 5. **"Mystical Flowers,"** composed on Nov. 20, 1894, for Sr. Magdalene (one of Thérèse's novices), it is a collection of holy aspirations with symbolic titles of flowers, fifteen of them, representing sacrifices, hopes, and expressions of love made by the ones saying them.
>
> Pri 6. **"Act of Oblation to Merciful Love,"** composed on June 9, 1895 (Feast of the Most Holy Trinity), for herself and Céline (Sr. Geneviève). The subtitle summarizes the content of this famous prayer: "Offering of myself as a Victim of Holocaust to God's Merciful Love."
>
> Pri 7. **[Prayer to Jesus in the Tabernacle]**, composed at the request of Sister Martha for her 30th birthday, July 16, 1895, as an aid for her evening examination of conscience.
>
> Pri 8. **[Prayer for Abbé Bellière]**, composed in joyful response to having him assigned to her as her "spiritual brother" in October 1895. He was then a twenty-one-year-old seminarian who later became a missionary in Africa.
>
> Pri 9. **"Prayer of Céline and Thérèse,"** composed for and given to Céline on Christmas night, 1895, asking God that the spiritual kinship between them never be broken.

---

56 *Story of a Soul*, chapter XI, p. 242.

Pri 10. [**Morning Offering**], written sometime in 1895 for Thérèse's sister Marie's old-time school friend—Mme. De Mesmay—who had a special devotion to the Sacred Heart of Jesus.

Pri 11. "**Make Me Resemble You, Jesus!**" These five words form the complete and shortest prayer Thérèse composed. It was composed sometime in 1895–1896. She wrote it on a paper which she enclosed in a container she wore over her chest.

Pri 12. "**Consecration to the Holy Face**," written on August 6, 1896, The Transfiguration of Christ, one of the major feasts of the Confraternity of the Holy Face which Thérèse was a member of since 1885. It was intended for herself and two of her novices—Sister Geneviève (Céline) and Sr. Marie of the Trinity. By this somewhat long prayer, they consecrated themselves to the "Adorable Face of Jesus."

Pri 13. "**Eternal Father, Your Only Son**," composed for herself, possibly for her retreat in September 1896, in which she asks God in some fifty-five French words to grant to little children the salvation of their souls and the final joys of heaven.

Pri 14. [**To the Child Jesus**], comprising only six lines, it was written in September 1896 and begins with "I am the Jesus of Thérèse."

Pri 15. "**Eternal Father, Since You Have Given Me**," written for herself in September 1896 (at the same time as Prayers 13, 14, and 16) in which she implores God in fifteen lines "to forget the ingratitude" of priests and religious and to "pardon poor sinners."

Pri 16. [**To the Holy Face**], composed for herself in September 1896 wherein she focuses her prayer on the various aspects of the "Holy Face," the title that is part of her religious name.

Pri 17. "**Lord God of Hosts**," composed for herself in the winter of 1896–1897. It is a prayer inspired by an image of Joan of Arc, one of Thérèse's favorite saints.

Pri 18. "**O Holy Innocents, O Saint Sebastian**," composed for Céline (Sr. Geneviève) in the beginning of 1897 in which she invokes the help of the Holy Innocents and St. Sebastian in her struggles as a young Carmelite.

Pri 19. [**Act of Faith**], composed in June or July 1897 during the period of her "trial of faith." The complete prayer is: "My God, with the help of your grace I am ready to shed all my blood to affirm my faith."

Pri 20. "**Prayer for Acquiring Humility**," composed for Sr. Martha of Jesus for her 32nd birthday, July 16, 1897, at the end of which she urges Sr. Martha to repeat often, "O Jesus, sweet and humble of heart, make my heart resemble yours!"

Pri 21. "**If I Were Queen of Heaven**," the complete prayer is: "O Mary, if I were Queen of Heaven and you were Thérèse, I would want to be Thérèse so that you might be Queen of Heaven." Written on September 8, 1897, these were the very last words she was able to jot down before she died twenty-three days later.

As a sample of her prayers, below are three paragraphs out of eleven from Thérèse's famous and most important prayer that appeared in the first English edition of her autobiography. It was found after her death in a book of the Gospels she kept next to her heart day and night.[57]

PRAYER 6 (EXCERPTS)

Act of Oblation to Merciful Love
J.M.J.T
Offering of Myself as a Victim of Holocaust
To God's Merciful Love

O my God, O Most Blessed Trinity, I desire to *love* you and to make you Loved, to work for the glory of Holy Church by saving souls on earth and liberating those suffering in Purgatory. I desire to accomplish your will perfectly and to reach the degree of glory you have prepared for me in your kingdom. I desire, in a word, to be a Saint, but I feel my helplessness and I beg you, O my God! to be yourself my Sanctity.

[In] order to live in one single act of perfect Love, I offer myself as a victim of holocaust to your merciful love, asking you to consume me incessantly, allowing the waves of infinite tenderness shut up within you to overflow into my soul, and that thus I may become a Martyr of your Love, O my God! . . .

[I] want, O my Beloved, at each beat of my heart to renew this offering to you an infinite number of times, until the shadows having disappeared I may be able to tell you of my Love in an Eternal Face to Face!

*Marie, Françoise, Thérèse of the Child Jesus
and the Holy Face, unworthy Carmelite religious*

Ever since the publication of Thérèse's autobiography in 1898, her most significant poems have been printed on millions of holy cards, in novena prayers, and in other devotional material.

6. Diverse Writings

A valuable collection of Thérèse's writings consists of school assignments, copies of selections from her favorite writers, or Biblical quotations, all preserved in the Archives of the Lisieux Carmel. Practically all are presented in the complete French edition (1992) of Thérèse's works under the title "*Écrits Divers*." All of course are in French with a precious few in English translation. They include notebooks and school papers in which she wrote homework assignments (*devoirs*), little prayers, diary-like notes, comments, drawings, and notes and observations at retreats and at her First Communion. They total about seventeen pages in *Œuvres Complètes,* 2001 edition.

Below is an outline of Thérèse's diverse writings classified into two categories listed chronologically:

---

57 Morteveille, *The Rose Unpetaled*, p. 261.

DIVERSE WRITINGS (*ÉCRITS DIVERS*)

I. At Les Buissonnets (1880 to 1888)
   A. First Childhood Notebook (1880)
      Mostly vocabulary and other school-type writings.
   B. Beige Notebook (1884 to 1886)
      1. Diary notes mentioning her pet dog Tom, her father's trip to Constantinople, etc.
      2. List of days and dates she received Communion.
   C. Blue Notebook (1884 to 1885)
      Notes at 3 retreats, all conducted by Abbé Domin.
      1. May 5–7 1884.
      2. May 17–20, 1885.
      3. October 6–10, 1885.
   D. Red Diary (1885 to 1887)
      Includes expenses, proverbs, charades, etc.
   E. Program of school lessons, homework, extracts from Arminjon's *The End of the Present World and the Mysteries of the Future Life*.

II. At the Carmel (1888 to 1897)
   A. Religious pictures on which Thérèse wrote Biblical quotations.
   B. Texts from the writings of St. John of the Cross.
   C. Selections from other authors: Suso, Arminjon, Tissot, etc. and from the lives of the saints.
   D. Extracts from *Isaiah* and from Theophane Vénard.
   E. Some texts from Mother Agnès and Céline.
   F. Notes on Thérèse's conversations with Mother Geneviève.
   G. Notes on the retreats of Father Pichon, exhortations of Abbé Delatroëtte, letters of Théophane Vénard, and notes on Abbé Baillon's spiritual counseling, etc.
   H. Biblical selections, Easter concordance writings, etc.

In 2008 a book entitled *Les Cahiers d'école de Thérèse de Lisieux: 1877–1888* (*The School Notebooks of Thérèse of Lisieux: 1877–1888*) was published by Les Éditions du Cerf.

7. Art Work

MOST PEOPLE INTERESTED IN ST. THÉRÈSE KNOW HER AS A SPIRITUAL WRITER, a Doctor of the Church, poet, and even a playwright. Few, however, are aware of her artistic accomplishments. In the study and literature about her throughout the years after her death, her art has been almost totally ignored. She produced a number of works of art during her lifetime that are fortunately still preserved today.

If the function of an artist is to put drawings in pencil or paint on paper, cloth, or even sea shells; to record an impression; to depict a scene or object; to decorate; or to represent a concept symbolically, as she did, then Thérèse can be considered an artist in her own right. We now live in a democratic era that heartily acknowledges and indeed exalts the individual and his or her artistic accomplishments. Often artists are acclaimed regardless of their skills or background, whether it is that of a self-taught folk artist or an academically trained professional. If that is truly the case, then St. Thérèse's works should likewise be recognized for their individualistic merit. Her artistic output may be considered amateurish by some just as folk art is, for example. Nonetheless, they are pleasing to look at, and when originally done (especially in her convent years) they were the happy result of a specific request or need. Most importantly, they reflect in pictorial form some of the same unique thoughts she conveyed so effectively in writing.

Thérèse and the girls in her family, like many young ladies of that period and social standing, sketched and painted as a pastime. Not surprisingly, Thérèse showed artistic potential since both parents were professional craftsmen: her father was a jeweler and watchmaker, and her mother a lace maker noted for her exquisitely intricate designs. Her older sisters, especially Céline, exhibited considerable artistic talent and was the only Martin girl, unfortunately, who received any formal art training. Her teacher was the elderly and somewhat eccentric Mlle. Godard of Lisieux who had been a student in Paris of the painter Léon Cogniet. She gave drawing, painting, and clay modeling instructions to Céline for some time beginning in 1882. Incidentally, one of Cogniet's other pupils was Edouard Krug whose painting "The Guardian Angel" (1875) hangs in one of the side chapels in the cathedral of St. Pierre in Lisieux. He had studied under the famous religious painter Hippolyte Flandrin. One of Krug's commissions (1893) was the fresco on the interior of the dome above the chapel in the Benedictine Abbey in Lisieux where the Martin girls attended school. It was destroyed during the Second World War. Céline thought that she might take some lessons from him also. Her uncle Isidore, who knew the artist, told him about Céline. Krug gave her a few lessons and she in turn instructed Thérèse. In fact, he thought quite highly of her and even gave her, later on, one of his own large palettes as a personal memento.

Despite her limited art training, Céline received orders for religious paintings including a large picture of the Assumption that was placed above the main altar of the Hôtel-Dieu (the chief hospital) in Bayeux which she painted in 1892, two years before she entered Carmel. Since her religious vocation became the all-important goal in her life, she never pursued her art studies any further. Yet after becoming a cloistered nun, she did not abandon her hobby. Her artistic attainments, including her photography, were quite substantial. She made many drawings, paintings, decorations, miniatures, some sculpture, and most significantly, took a number of invaluable photographs of Thérèse and others.

Thérèse loved drawing and wished she could have received art lessons also, but never did. Céline explains why:

> I was thirteen when my father told me he was going to have me take drawing lessons. We were together, Thérèse and I, and I saw her eyes light up with envy, expecting to receive the same favor. In fact, my father said: "And you, my little Queen, would you like to learn how to draw?" She was about to answer when Marie spoke up, saying that the house was already cluttered with "smearings" that had to be framed, and she won the case. Thérèse didn't answer, and we

did not think about what she was experiencing. Later on, some weeks before her death, she recalled this incident, and she told me that she experienced such a strong desire to complain that she wondered still, after so many years, how she had the strength to resist.[58]

Thérèse never told anyone when she was a child of her strong desire to learn how to draw until she alluded to it years later in her autobiography:

> As I have always looked upon you, dear Mother [Agnès], as my *ideal*, I desired to be like you in everything; when I saw you do beautiful paintings and delightful poems, I said to myself: How happy I would be if I were able to paint and to know how to express my thoughts in verse and thus do good to souls. I would not have wanted to *ask* for these natural gifts and my desires remained *hidden away* at the bottom of my *heart*. To the great astonishment of the Sisters [when she was in the monastery] I was told to paint, and God permitted that I profit by the lessons my dear Mother gave me.[59]

Also in her autobiography Thérèse makes an interesting reference to her art work while she was in the monastery when she discusses the role of poverty and patience in her life:

> I have renounced the goods of this earth through the Vow of Poverty, and so I haven't the right to complain when one takes a thing that is not mine. On the contrary, I should rejoice when it happens that I feel the pinch of poverty.... I see on occasions that I am very imperfect. For example, in my work of painting there is nothing that belongs to me, I know. But if, when I am preparing some work, I find that the brushes and the paints are in disorder, if a rule or a penknife has disappeared, patience is very close to abandoning me and I must take my courage in both hands in order to reclaim the missing object without bitterness.... If anyone takes something which is for my use, I must not appear to be sorry about this but happy at being relieved of it.... I am very far from practicing what I understand, and still the desire alone I have of doing it gives me peace.[60]

As a youngster Thérèse, with her sisters and cousins, often sketched the picturesque Norman countryside on short trips and holiday visits to her Aunt Guérin's mother, Mme. Fournet. She lived on a large farm in the beautiful countryside of Saint-Ouen-le-Pin, a hamlet not far from Lisieux. Mme. Guérin recounted in a letter to her husband one such sketching excursion on August 7, 1884, when Thérèse was eleven:

> We are all very happy here. Thérèse's face is always radiant with joy. She is enjoying herself very much at sketching; she and Marie [Guérin, her daughter] have undertaken to do the house on the farm. I am [assuming the role of] Mademoiselle Godard [their private tutor] and I supervise my pupils closely. Like her, I am very severe but also very much inclined to complements, so I see two future *artists* in my pupils.

---
58 Page 77 from Céline's preparatory notes for the Bishop's Process of 1908.
59 *Story of a Soul*, chapter VIII, p. 175.
60 Ibid., chapter X, pp. 226–227.

Thérèse learned indirectly from the lessons Céline received for she tells us, "I studied, took lessons in drawing from Céline [in the first semester of 1887], and my clever teacher recognized in me an aptitude for her art."[61] She drew about a dozen sketches of heads dated between January and May of 1887, a year before she entered Carmel. Prior to that she made a number of drawings for school projects and for her own personal enjoyment at home and on trips, especially to Deauville and Trouville where she (and, incidentally, many of the Impressionists, especially Eugène Boudin [1824–1898]) sketched the seaside, boats, gardens, and buildings. Thérèse also dabbled with sculpture, having done some clay modeling with Céline.

As a nun, Thérèse continued her art work: drawings, miniatures, oil paintings on silk, canvas, and paper; work on vestments, decorations on holy cards, and painting of statues. She executed in oils a large mural depicting angels above the oratory in the infirmary. Concerning this picture and Thérèse's innate ability Céline said:

> I have always looked upon it as an entirely supernatural grace that she was able to paint, without ever having learnt how, a picture on the oratory wall composed of a group of little angels, each with his proper attribute [one of which represents Thérèse herself—sleeping!]. The work, which had to be carried out in a place so dark that an expert would scarcely have succeeded, is not a copy, but an original composition, which is utterly disarming.[62]

One of Thérèse's oil paintings that created perhaps the most comment is "The Dream of the Infant Jesus" which she did to illustrate some ideas Mother Agnès expressed in a few of her own poems. The picture was accompanied by a letter Thérèse wrote that included an allegory with the same title which fancifully describes and explains the painting:

THE DREAM OF THE CHILD JESUS

While playing in His crib with the flowers His dear spouse [Thérèse] brought Him, Jesus is thinking of what He will do to thank her.... Up above, in the celestial gardens, the angels, servants of the divine Child, are already weaving crowns His Heart has reserved for His beloved.

However, the night has come. The moon sends out its silvery rays, and the gentle Child falls asleep.... His little hand does not let go the flowers that delighted Him during the day, and His Heart continues dreaming about the happiness of His dear spouse.

Soon, He sees in the distance strange objects bearing no resemblance to the springtime flowers. A cross!... a lance!... a crown of thorns! [also a sponge, reed, and whips]. And yet the divine Child does not tremble; this is what He chooses to show His spouse how much He loves her!... But it is still not enough; His infant face is so beautiful. He sees it disfigured, covered with blood!... unrecognizable!... Jesus knows that His spouse will always recognize Him,

---

61 Ibid., chapter V, pp. 111–112.
62 Petitot, *Saint Teresa of Lisieux, A Spiritual Renascence*, p. 176.

so the divine Child smiles at his bloodstained image, He smiles at the chalice filled with the wine giving birth to virgins. He knows that, in His Eucharist, the ungrateful will desert Him; but Jesus is thinking of His spouse's love, her attention. He sees the flowers of her virtues as they scent the sanctuary, and the Child Jesus continues to sleep on peacefully.... He awaits the shadows to lengthen ... the night of life to give way to the bright day of eternity!...

Then Jesus will give back to His beloved spouse the flowers she had given Him, consoling Him on earth.... Then He will lower His divine Face to her, radiant with glory, and He will allow His spouse to taste eternally the ineffable sweetness of His divine kiss!!!...

Dear Mother,

You have just read the *dream* that your child wanted to reproduce for your feast day. But, alas! Only your artistic brush could paint such a sweet mystery!... I trust you will look only upon the good will of her who would be happy to please you....[63]

Mother Agnès in turn sent the picture to her former teacher at the Visitation school in Le Mans, Sister Marie-Aloysia, together with her own startlingly candid opinion of the picture:

> This humble sketch was painted by Thérèse of the Child Jesus and given to me *for you* on the 21st by this dear little Angel. I assure you she was very secretive about it, for I suspected nothing.... But, alas! when taking up the brush, she believed she was doing something marvelous, wanting to copy the Divine Child, whom she saw in her heart, so easy to render, she thought, *for she saw* Him so *clearly*! The brush misguided her! And the result cost her much in tears; this was not what she wanted to give her dear Aunt Maria-Aloysia ["Aunt" affectionately].... Really, this painting is a real daubing, but when we think it was made according to an inspiration, we are more indulgent, especially towards a child who has never learned sketching or painting. Well, I am sending it to you, in spite of the contrary opinion of Mother Marie de Gonzague, who does not like it.... She has painted such pretty things in flowers and landscapes, and the little Jesus could have been so attractive according to a model!...[64]

This is not the end of the picture's history. The painting we see today is not quite like it was originally done by Thérèse. When it was returned to the Lisieux Carmel in 1927, Sister Geneviève (Céline) repainted the face, changing it considerably from its original baby look to one that was more to her liking.

Regardless of the level of St. Thérèse's artistic skills, her entire creative legacy—spiritual as well as literary and artistic—should be studied fully in order to understand, define, and evaluate the totality of her being.

---

63 LT 156, Thérèse to Mother Agnès, January 21, 1894.
64 LT 160, Thérèse to Sister Marie-Aloysia, April 3, 1894.

C. Beatification and Canonization

1. History
2. Major Steps Leading to the Canonization
3. The Four Required Miracles
4. Witnesses
5. Leading Ecclesiastics Involved

1. History

BY 1910, ONLY THIRTEEN YEARS AFTER SISTER THÉRÈSE OF THE CHILD JESUS died, the fame of this young saintly Carmelite nun reached millions of people worldwide. Her prominence was attributed primarily to the dissemination of her autobiography, *Story of a Soul*, first published in 1898, one year after her death. The many miraculous cures and temporal blessings accredited to her intercession had by then amounted to untold numbers. Urgent pleas to introduce her cause for beatification besieged the Vatican. As a result, on February 10, 1910, the Sacred Congregation of Rites in Rome sent official notification to Msgr. Lemonnier, Bishop of Bayeux and Lisieux, authorizing him to begin the lengthy process toward beatification and eventual canonization of this beloved disciple of Christ which resulted in the speediest canonization since 1588.

For centuries before the new legislation of 1983, the Cause of Beatification and the Cause of Canonization were two separate procedures. The first cause was divided in the past into two distinct stages called processes: the Diocesan Process and the Apostolic Process. The Diocesan, sometimes referred to as the Ordinary Process and also as the Episcopal Process, included the Informative Process and was held in the diocese where the candidate for sainthood lived and died. Proceedings were under the authority of the diocesan bishop (the "ordinary" or "competent" bishop) but were directly carried out by a "vice-postulator" chosen by the bishop to promote the cause. The following information was carefully gathered and studied relative to the holy person (candidate) under consideration who was at this time referred to as the "Servant of God": (1) sanctity of life while alive and reputation for holiness after death; (2) writings; (3) evidence of heroic virtues; (4) miracles; (5) martyrdom—if applicable; (6) proof that no public devotion to the candidate existed; and (7) sworn testimony from witnesses—if available. As to the evidence of heroic virtues, each witness was questioned as to how he or she observed the Servant of God lived these virtues to an heroic degree:

1. The theological virtues of faith, hope, love of God, and love of neighbor.
2. The cardinal virtues of prudence, justice, fortitude, and temperance.
3. The religious vows of poverty, chastity, and obedience.
4. Humility.

When all the documents from the Diocesan Process were completed they were presented to the Sacred Congregation of Rites in Rome by the vice-postulator. The pope thereupon appointed a cardinal called a "relator" to take charge of the cause from then on.

The Apostolic Process—the second stage of the beatification process—commenced at this point and consisted of further inquiries transacted under the jurisdiction of the Holy See through the Sacred Congregation of Rites. It involved in depth investigation of the heroic virtues and miracles of the candidate. What followed during both processes were procedures similar to those of civil court cases that included defense and prosecuting attorneys with the candidate for sainthood "on trial," as it were. The Promoter of the Faith, popularly but inappropriately called the "Devil's Advocate," was then, one might say, the prosecuting attorney. He prepared his case and eventually submitted his objections to the Sacred Congregation of Rites. The Advocate, or the defense attorney, defended his client—the "Venerable Servant of God," as the candidate was called at this point. What ensued was virtually an ecclesiastical tribunal complete with legal dialectics. This juridical system was also followed during the interrogation of witnesses. Finally, two authentic miracles had to be presented and approved before beatification was proclaimed by the Supreme Pontiff. After beatification the Venerable Servant of God had the honor of being called "Blessed" and was entitled to a limited form of public devotion.

The time between beatification and canonization depended upon the emergence, selection, and verification of two new miracles, which in many instances never occurred; thus official sainthood was not attained. This interval could extend over decades or centuries. In the situation with Blessed Thérèse of the Child Jesus, a remarkably short period of two years elapsed. After the miracles were approved, the pope would issue a Bull of Canonization and declare the blessed a saint in a solemn ceremony at St. Peter's Basilica in Rome.

The centuries-old rules involved with canonization were clearly ponderous and intricate; therefore, under the climate generated by the Second Vatican Ecumenical Council (1962–1965), one of the first steps in revision occurred when in 1969 the Sacred Congregation of Rites was replaced by the Congregation for the Causes of Saints. Later more rulings regarding beatification and canonization were promulgated on January 25, 1983, by Pope John Paul II that dispensed with many of the procedures followed in the cause of St. Thérèse. What resulted is a simpler, shorter, more scholarly, more "collegial," and non-juridical methodology. Now, instead of having two separate causes, there is one—the Cause of Canonization. The name Cause of Beatification was eliminated but not the general investigative process itself which was incorporated under the one all-inclusive title. Furthermore, the local bishop or ordinary is entirely responsible for introducing a cause, not the Vatican as formerly. The office of Devil's Advocate was eliminated and one miracle for beatification and one for canonization are required today instead of two for each as in the past.

2. Major Steps Leading to the Canonization of St. Thérèse

YEAR	POPE	DATE	STEPS
1910	Pius X	FEB 10	Bishop Lemonnier of Bayeux and Lisieux is authorized by the Sacred Congregation of Rites in Rome to have the writings of Thérèse collected and examined. She is now called the "Servant of God."
		AUG 3	The Diocesan Process (*Procés Informatif Ordinaire*) for beatification opens at the little seminary of Saint-Marie near Caen under the leadership of the Postulator, Father Rodrigo (a Carmelite in Rome), and the Vice-Postulator, Msgr. Francis Roger de Teil. This process consists of three phases: (1) the INFORMATIVE which investigates the sanctity and miracles connected with Sister Thérèse, (2) the NON-CULTUS which is to prove that no public worship has been offered to her, and (3) the examination of all of Sister Thérèse's writings.
		AUG 12	The first witnesses are questioned, requiring 109 sessions, some lasting from four to five hours.
		SEP 6	Thérèse's body is exhumed (a requirement) and transferred to another grave in the Lisieux public cemetery, very close to the first plot, with Bishop Lemonnier, Msgr. de Teil, Canon Dubosq, and others present.
1911		AUG 29	The last witness appears before the tribunal for interrogation
		AUG 30–SEP 7	The process dealing with the *non-cultus* phase is held with 11 sessions.
		DEC 12	The 109th session, held in the Grand Seminary in Bayeux, marks the solemn closing of the Diocesan Process.
1912		FEB 6	All documents are delivered by Msgr. de Teil to the Sacred Congregation of Rites in Rome.
		DEC 6	The Pope nominates Cardinal Antonio Vico with the title Relator to take charge of the cause in Rome. He submits Thérèse's writings for examination by theologians.
		DEC 10	The decree approving the writings of Sister Thérèse is published.
1913		MAR 8	The Advocates Canon Dubosq and Father Marie (for the defense of Thérèse) prepare the arguments designed to obtain the introduction of the cause in Rome. This document is called the *positio* which summarizes all the diocesan inquiries.
		JAN 10	The decree authorizing the examination of the diocesan reports is published. The usual 10 years delay in doing so is abrogated.
		JUN 9	The Sacred Congregation of Rites approves of the Diocesan Process.
		JUN 10	Pope Pius X signs the decree authorizing the introduction of the Cause of Beatification for Thérèse in Rome which will now be directly under the Holy See.

CHAPTER 1: *St. Thérèse of Lisieux*

YEAR	POPE	DATE	STEPS
1915	Benedict XV	MAR 17–18	The Apostolic Process (*Procés Apostolique*) regarding the virtues and miracles attributed to the Servant of God, Sister Thérèse of the Child Jesus, is inaugurated at the Cathedral of Bayeux.
		APR 9	The interrogation of 55 witnesses begins (*procés ne pereant*).
1916		SEP 22	The Apostolic Process continues with the 59th and 60th session taking place in the chapel of the Lisieux Carmel (*procés continuative*).
1917		AUG 9–10	The second exhumation occurs for official identification of remains which are then re-buried in the same plot.
		OCT 30	The Apostolic Process closes in the Bayeux Cathedral after 90 sessions.
		NOV 4	The official papers of the Apostolic Process consisting of some 2,500 pages are delivered by Msgr. De Teil to the Sacred Congregation of Rites in Rome.
1918		DEC 10	The Sacred Congregation of Rites approves the procedures adopted in both processes: the Diocesan and the Apostolic.
1919		SEP 22	The fifty years' delay to examine the heroic virtues of Thérèse is dispensed with by Pope Benedict XV.
1920		FEB 18	The Promoter of the Faith ("Devil's Advocate"), Canon Dubosq, presents objections to the claim of heroic sanctity made for Thérèse.
1921		AUG 14	The Promulgation by Benedict XV of the heroic virtues of the Servant of God, Sister Thérèse, entitles her now to be called "Venerable."
1922	Pius XI	JAN 15– OCT 15	Many sessions are held during the year with the Promoter of the Faith and the Advocate concerning the miracles relating to the Venerable Thérèse of the Child Jesus.
1923		FEB 11	The two miracles required for beatification are approved.
		MAR 26–27	Thérèse's body is transferred (translated) from the public cemetery in Lisieux to the Carmel.
		APR 29	The BEATIFICATION by Pope Pius XI is solemnized at a Pontifical Mass in the Basilica of St. Peter in Rome. The Venerable Thérèse of the Child Jesus is now called Blessed Thérèse of the Child Jesus.
		JUL 25	The resumption of the cause of the Blessed Thérèse commences in anticipation of her canonization.
1924		AUG 12	Two new miracles proposed for canonization are examined in the diocese of Parma (Italy) and of Malines (Belgium).
1925		MAR 19	The two miracles are approved.
		MAY 17	The solemn canonization is proclaimed by Pope Pius XI followed by a Pontifical Mass in the Basilica of St. Peter in Rome.
			Blessed Thérèse is henceforth called Saint Thérèse of the Child Jesus and of the Holy Face. (At the same ceremony Blessed Peter Canisius [1521–1597], a Jesuit, was also canonized. The Venerable Vincenzo Strambi [1745–1824], a Passionist, Bishop of Macerata and Tolentino was beatified.)

3. The Four Required Miracles

TWO FOR BEATIFCATION

1. The seminarian Charles Albert Prosper Anne of Lisieux was cured of acute pulmonary tuberculosis, hemoptic in the cavitary period in 1906.

2. Sister Louise of St. Germain, a nun in the Congregation of the Daughters of the Cross, was cured of stomach ulcers of an hemorrhagic character in 1916 in Ustaritz, Basses-Pyrénées—a department in southern France.

TWO FOR CANONIZATION

3. Mlle. Maria Pellemans, a young Belgian girl, was cured instantly of tuberculosis of the lungs and intestines at Blessed Thérèse's grave in Lisieux on March 22, 1923.

4. Sister Gabriella Trimusi of the Poor Daughters of Jesus and Mary (also called Chieppine after the name of its founder, Msgr. Chieppi) in Parma, Italy, was cured of tuberculosis of both knees and in the spine (tubercular spondylitis) in 1923.

Plate 2

4. Witnesses

Who Gave Testimony at the Diocesan Process (1910–1911), The Apostolic Process (1915–1917), or Both

CATEGORY	NAME
FAMILY	1. Mother Agnès de Jésus, O.C.D., Lisieux Carmel—sister of St. Thérèse (Pauline Martin). 2. Sr. Geneviève de Sainte-Thérèse, O.C.D., Lisieux Carmel—sister of St. Thérèse (Céline Martin). 3. Sr. Marie du Sacré-Coeur, O.C.D., Lisieux Carmel—sister of St. Thérèse (Marie Martin). 4. Sr. Françoise-Thérèse, Ord. Visit., Caen—sister of St. Thérèse (Léonie Martin). 5. Jeanne-Guérin La Néele—wife of Dr. La Néele and cousin of St. Thérèse.
NUNS WHO KNEW THÉRÈSE	6. Sr. Aimée de Jésus, O.C.D., Lisieux Carmel. 7. Sr. Marie des Anges du Sacré-Coeur, O.C.D., Lisieux Carmel. 8. Sr. Marie-Elizabeth, O.C.D., (extern sister) Lisieux Carmel—was present at the burial and both exhumations of St. Thérèse. 9. Sr. Marie-Madeleine du Saint-Sacrement, O.C.D., Lisieux Carmel. 10. Sr. Marie de la Trinité, O.C.D., Lisieux Carmel. 11. Sr. Marthe de Jésus, O.C.D., Lisieux Carmel. 12. Sr. Thérèse de Saint-Augustin, O.C.D., Lisieux Carmel. 13. Sr. Saint Jean-l'Evangéliste (Marie Dupont), O.S.B., Lisieux—former school companion of St. Thérèse. 14. Sr. Marie du Saint-Rosaire (Marguérite Leroy), O.S.B., Lisieux—former school companion of St. Thérèse.
NUNS WHO KNEW THÉRÈSE	15. Mother Saint André, O.S.B., Lisieux—teacher and later prioress at the Abbey School when Thérèse attended classes there. 16. Sr. Saint François de Sales, O.S.B., Lisieux—teacher at the Abbey School where Thérèse attended classes. 17. Sr. Marie-Joseph de la Croix (Marcelline Husé), O.S.B., Lisieux—former maid of the Guérins.
PRIESTS WHO KNEW THÉRÈSE	18. Rev. Victor Domin, Lisieux—chaplain and instructor at the Abbey School. 19. Rev. Alcide Ducellier, Lisieux—Thérèse's first confessor. 20. Rev. Lucien Dumaine, vicar-general of Sées—baptized Thérèse. 21. Rev. Pierre-Alexandre Faucon, Lisieux—heard Thérèse's last confession. 22. Rev. Armand Lemonnier (Le Monnier), Douvres-la Délivrande—gave retreats at the Lisieux Carmel. 23. Rev. Godefroy Madelaine, O. Praem., Leffe, Belgium—gave retreats at the Lisieux Carmel and edited Thérèse's autobiography. 24. Canon Alexandre Maupas, Lisieux—ecclesiastical superior of the Lisieux Carmel who gave last rites to Thérèse, said her funeral mass, and was present at the exhumation of her coffin in 1910. 25. Rev. Almire Pichon, S.J.—Martin family spiritual director, friend, and retreat preacher at the Lisieux Carmel. 26. Rev. Adolph Roulland, M.E.P., Paris—Thérèse's "spiritual brother," missionary to China, and at that time bursar of the Paris Foreign Mission Society in Paris.
OTHER PRIESTS	27. Rev. Jean Auriault, S.J., Paris—professor consulted to examine Thérèse's reputation for holiness, and to appraise her doctrine and writings.

C. Beatification and Canonization

CATEGORY	NAME
OTHER PRIESTS	28. Rev. Anatole Flamérion, S.J., Angers—testified to the importance, in relation to Church teachings, of Thérèse's spirituality, doctrines, writings, sanctity, and miracles attributed to her. 29. Rev. Polydore Morel, Pont-l'Evêque—curé-doyen where Abbé Anne was vicar. 30. Rev. Thomas Nimmo Taylor, Glasgow—one of the first to urge the cause of Thérèse, fostered her devotion, and translated her auto-biography into English. 31. Rev. Jean Valadier, canon of Notre-Dame in Paris—gave significant details about the execution of Pranzini.
MIRACLE A	32. Rev. Charles Anne, vicar at the church of St. Michael in Pont-l'Evêque—miraculously cured of tuberculosis through St. Thérèse's intercession. 33. Prosper Anne, Lisieux—father of Charles Anne. 34. Joséphine Anne, Lisieux—mother of Charles Anne. 35. Sr. Marie St. Ignace, Congregation of the Immaculate Conception in Nogent-le-Rotrou, Lisieux—Charles Anne's nurse.
MIRACLE B	36. Sr. Saint Charles Borromée, superior of the Little Sisters of the Poor in Lisieux who conducted a hospital where an old man, Ferdinand Aubry, was a patient cured of cancer of the tongue through the intercession of St. Thérèse. 37. Sr. Laurentine Thérèse, Little Sisters of the Poor in Lisieux—Ferdinand Aubry's nurse. 38. Sr. Sainte Martine, Little Sisters of the Poor in Lisieux—Ferdinand Aubry's nurse. 39. Sr. Domitille de Saint Laurent, Little Sisters of the Poor in Lisieux—Ferdinand Aubry's nurse.
MIRACLE C	40. Rev. Etienne Frapereau, Community of St. Martin of Beaupréau, Angers—testified about the apparition of St. Thérèse to an old dying priest, Rev. Rossignol. 41. Rev. Jean Gaignet, Sulpician in Paris and professor of theology—attested to the apparition of St. Thérèse to Rev. Rossignol.
MIRACLE D	42. Rev. Claude Weber, Bayonne—his eyesight was restored as a result of praying to St. Thérèse.
MIRACLE E	43. Nicolas Giannattasio, bishop of Nardô, Italy—testified to Thérèse's apparition to Sr. M. Carmelo, a Carmelite prioress, and the financial help she gave to her Carmel in Gallipoli.
MIRACLE F	44. Rev. Elie de la Mère de Miséricorde, O.C.D., Milan—gave testimony concerning several miracles and graces obtained through the intercession of St. Thérèse.
MIRACLE G	45. Pierre Derrien, sacristan of the Lisieux Carmel since 1913—cured of serious aliments through the intercession of St. Thérèse.
MIRACLE H	46. Helene Knight Dorans, Glasgow—was suddenly cured of a large cancerous tumor through the intercession of St. Thérèse.
CONVERSIONS	47. Alexander Grant, Edinburg, Scotland—Scotch Presbyterian minister converted to Catholicism through the inspiration of St. Thérèse. (His wife also converted and they both went to live in Alençon, France, where they became caretakers of the house in which Thérèse was born.)
DOCTORS	48. Dr. Alexandre-Demase de Cornière, Lisieux—the Carmel doctor who cared for Thérèse and was Charles Anne's doctor. He was present at the first exhumation of Thérèse's coffin (1910), and examined her remains at the second exhumation (1917).

CATEGORY	NAME
DOCTORS	49. Dr. Francis La Néele, Lisieux, Thérèse's cousin by marriage—examined her in her last days, witnessed both exhumations, inspected Thérèse's remains at the second one, and gave testimony about the cure of Ferdinand Aubry and Charles Anne. 50. Dr. Adolphe-Jean Leprévost, Lisieux—gave testimony about Charles Anne and examined the remains of St. Thérèse. 51. Dr. Paul Loisnel, Lisieux—gave testimony about Charles Anne, was present at the first exhumation, and examined Thérèse's remains at the second exhumation. 52. Dr. Victor-Eugène-Albert Viel, Lisieux—Ferdinand Aubry's doctor.
OTHERS	53. Jeanne Bonnelle, Lisieux—caretaker of the Lisieux Cemetery since 1912. 54. Sr. Jeanne-Marie de l'Enfant-Jésus, O.C.D.—reported some extraordinary indications of Thérèse's presence, assistance, and solace that she experienced at the Carmel after she entered in 1905. 55. Sr. Marie-Thérèse Isabelle du Sacré-Cœur, Lisieux, O.C.D.—wrote much to spread information about Thérèse, added greatly to the Carmel Archives, and gave testimony regarding Thérèse's influence in the 10 years following her death.

Father Charles Anne is the only one miraculously cured who came with four people who witnessed the miracle. Witnesses are not obligatory since medical certificates produced in those cases constitute sufficient "proof" for the Vatican.

5. Leading Ecclesiastics Involved

a. **Msgr. Thomas Lemonnier:** *Bishop of Bayeux and Lisieux who introduced Thérèse's cause*
b. **Msgr. Francis-Roger de Teil:** *Vice-Postulator for the cause of Thérèse's beatification*
c. **Msgr. Pierre-Théophile Dubosq:** *Promoter of the Faith— "Devil's Advocate"*
d. **Canon Deslandes:** *Notary*
e. **Antonio Cardinal Vico:** *Headed the cause for Sister Thérèse in Rome*
f. **Pope St. Pius X:** *Authorized the introduction of Thérèse's cause*
g. **Pope Benedict XV:** *Proclaimed Thérèse "Venerable"*
h. **Pope Pius XI:** *Beatified and canonized St. Thérèse of the Child Jesus*

a. MSGR. THOMAS PAUL HENRI LEMONNIER (1853–1927)
Bishop of Bayeux and Lisieux who introduced Thérèse's cause

AS THE REPUTATION OF SISTER THÉRÈSE'S REMARKABLE AUTOBIOGRAPHY, sanctity, and the extraordinary graces and cures occurring through her intercession spread around the world, so did the resulting desire of many to submit her name as a candidate for canonization. Canon law required the Vatican to authorize the bishop of Thérèse's diocese, Msgr. Lemonnier, to introduce and control all the beatification procedures that were to be carried out in his diocese. It must be noted that in the beginning he, like his predecessor Bishop

Léon-Adolphe Amette, saw little in her life that would warrant such a pretentious undertaking. Msgr. Amette gave the limp excuse that a potential problem for them would involve finances, time, and the personnel to carry it all out. However, the instantaneous and miraculous cure on May 26, 1908, of a four-year-old blind girl, Reine Fauquet, after visiting Thérèse's grave must have had a measure of influence in changing the bishop's attitude toward Thérèse.

The first one, though, who requested the bishop to obtain permission to start Thérèse's cause was the new young prioress of the Lisieux Carmel, Mother Marie-Ange of the Child Jesus (1881–1909), who had entered the order primarily because of Thérèse's holy example. As a consequence of her strong urgings, that of many others, and of his own study of Thérèse, the bishop became convinced of her holiness and concurred. In 1908 Mother Agnès wrote of his feelings: "Monseigneur seems well disposed towards Thérèse, he is going to Rome in April almost exclusively to deal with her cause. It is touching that the first steps in Thérèse's cause should coincide with the beatification of her little friend Joan of Arc."[1] On February 10, 1910, the Sacred Congregation of Rites in Rome authorized him to begin the preliminary steps. Mother Marie-Ange wrote of his final conviction in a circular letter dated February 15, 1909:

> Msgr. Lemonnier, Bishop of Bayeux and Lisieux, prompted by his own devotion to her whom he calls "one of the most delicate flowers of his diocese," thought that he ought to delay no longer in taking the first steps.[2]

In a speech delivered in October 1917 when the Apostolic Process ended, he continued his praise of the Servant of God:

> It is not for us to call Sister Thérèse a "saint," but, nevertheless, we know that here was a soul greatly beloved by God. May she use her influence with Our Lord to obtain the advancement of true religion in this diocese of ours! I recommend to her especially the recruitment and caliber of my own clergy, as well as the preservation, in both body and soul, of those of my priests and seminarians who the misfortunes of this terrible war [World War I] have kept under arms for so long.[3]

Bishop Lemonnier attended all the major procedures of the cause including the three times Thérèse's remains were exhumed and finally transferred to the Carmel. One of the necessary steps in the canonization process consisted of the examination and preservation of the remains of the candidate for sainthood. The first exhumation of Thérèse's coffin took place at 3 o'clock in the afternoon of September 6, 1910 in the public cemetery of Lisieux. All the members of the Tribune connected with the Ordinary Informative Process accompanied Msgr. Lemonnier. The workmen had to dig over eleven feet down to bring up the coffin. When opened it revealed that only Thérèse's bones remained. During the raising, Bishop Lemonnier intoned Psalm 112. After studying the remains/

---

[1] As quoted in *Sicut Parvuli*, May 1983, which is a translation of an article in *Les Annales de Ste. Thérèse*, March 1982.
[2] Ibid.
[3] *Sicut Parvuli*, January 1984, which is a translation of an article in *Les Annales de Ste. Thérèse*, Sept. 1982.

relics, they were deposited in a coffin of lead and that within another one of oak. This new coffin was then transferred to a new grave, this time only six feet deep, just a few feet away from the original one.

The second exhumation took place seven years later on August 9–10, 1917. This time, according to the official church rulings, an anatomical study of the remains had to be accomplished by competent doctors under oath. The coffin was taken to the cemetery chapel and examined again. Though intended to be private, an estimated 3,000 people came to the cemetery. The remains were then replaced in the same grave.

The final translation of Thérèse's coffin occurred on March 26–27, 1923, a month before Thérèse's solemn beatification, when it was brought to the Carmel where it has found its permanent home. This time too, Bishop Lemonnier took a leading role.

Besides intimate involvement with the exhumation matters, Bishop Lemonnier was associated with many of the canonization procedures, particularly those regarding the celebrations and official functions carried out in his diocese before and after Thérèse's canonization.

In the 1924 edition of *Story of a Soul*, Bishop Lemonnier stated that the truthfulness to life of Thérèse's face is better depicted in the charcoal drawing of Thérèse by Céline than in the photographs where she seems too self-conscious and not naturally relaxed. He saw Céline's work as "a very conscientious and careful synthesis of the most expressive aspects of the aforementioned photographs. That is why we have not the least bit of hesitancy in calling this *a true and authentic portrait* of the Servant of God at about the age of twenty-three." [4]

In the course of time, Bishop Lemonnier saw the need for the construction of a basilica dedicated to St. Thérèse in Lisieux. Many of the local clergy objected to this proposal believing that, since devotion to Thérèse reached its peak in World War I, such a project would in a short time prove pointless. Besides, they contended that they had enough religious buildings in Lisieux. Persuaded by Pope Pius XI's strong desire to have a basilica built, the local clergy gave in. In 1925 Msgr. Lemonnier commissioned among others the internationally known and respected Parisian architect Louis-Marie Cordonnier to submit a plan. On September 21, 1927, the bishop approved Cordonnier's design. Construction began in 1929 under Bishop Suhard, Msgr. Lemonnier's successor, and in 1937 under Bishop Picaud it was opened and blessed by Cardinal Pacelli, the future Pope Pius XII.

Thomas-Paul-Henri Lemonnier was born on September 16, 1853, in Etretat, a popular fishing and resort town in northern Normandy near Le Havre, noted for its high cliffs and jutting out stone arches that has fascinated artists for many generations. In 1906 he was appointed bishop of Bayeux and died in that position twenty-one years later on December 29, 1927, two years after Thérèse's canonization. He had spent his childhood among the local fishermen and after he became bishop he participated in the annual Benediction of the Sea, a custom begun in 1908.

---

4 François de Sainte-Marie, *The Photo Album of St Thérèse of Lisieux*, p. 53.

b. MSGR. FRANCIS-ROGER DE TEIL, O.C.D. (1848–1922)
Vice-Postulator for the cause of Thérèse's beatification

THÉRÈSE MET MSGR. DE TEIL, CANON OF NOTRE DAME IN PARIS, IN SEPTEMber 1896, when he came to the Lisieux monastery to speak to the community about his work for the cause of the sixteen Carmelite nuns of Compiègne martyred in 1794. He asked if the nuns had heard of any miracles obtained through the intercession of those intrepid French nuns guillotined during the French Revolution. Thérèse, very impressed by the monsignor's talk and manner, remarked: "How touching is the zeal of this postulator! How glad one would be to have miracles to make known to him!"[5] Little did any one imagine then that just fourteen years later this same priest would be chosen postulator for the cause to canonize Thérèse herself. He was outstanding in this field of inquiry. In addition to the Campiègne nuns (popularly celebrated in the 1957 Poulenc opera *Dialogue of the Carmelites*), he was working on the causes of Louise of France (Sister Teresa of St. Augustine—Carmelite daughter of King Louis XV), and others.

The thought of martyrdom deeply impressed Thérèse practically all her life. Once she made this pertinent comment to one of her novices, Sister Marie of the Trinity: "Our Mother just told me of the persecution raging on all sides against religious communities.... What joy! God will answer the most beautiful dream of my life!... When I think that we are living in the age of martyrs!"[6]

The first stage in the process of the cause of a candidate for sainthood required the appointment of a postulator and a vice-postulator. In 1909 Bishop Lemonnier chose as postulator (or postulator-general) the superior general of the Carmelites, Father Rodrigue de Saint-François de Paule, O.C.D (1850–1931); and as vice-postulator, Msgr. Francis-Roger de Teil (Canon of Notre Dame de Paris). After these two selections, the institution of the Diocesan Process (or Ordinary Process) proceeded through the supervision of the vice-postulator who had to make inquiries about the candidate for sainthood (called the "Servant of God"), in this case, Sister Thérèse. It concerned her sanctity, miracles obtained through her intercession, that no public worship had been given her, and examination of all her writings.

His major responsibility as vice-postulator was gathering and collating all the writings of Thérèse. Subsequently, he drew up an account of her life and miracles called "Articles" which he personally delivered to the Prefect of the Sacred Congregation of Rites in Rome on February 6, 1912. The English edition distributed to the general public has the title *The Cause of Beatification of the Little Flower of Jesus*.

Msgr. de Teil worked closely with Bishop Lemonnier, the Lisieux Carmel, and the Sacred Congregation of Rites in Rome. In 1910 and 1917 they were present at the two exhumations of Thérèse's body—a procedure required for beatification. Interestingly, at one time he functioned as director-general of the Society of the Holy Childhood of which Thérèse had been a member. The

---
5 Laveille, *Life of the Little Flower*, p. 331.
6 Gaucher, *The Passion of Thérèse of Lisieux*, footnote "m" on p. 60.

correspondence between the Carmel and him was voluminous, amounting to over 1,400 letters. Marie (Sister Marie of the Sacred Heart) in Lisieux kept her sister Léonie in Caen informed about everything concerning the cause of their sister Thérèse. This extract from one of her letters details Msgr. de Teil's busy schedule and involvement with Thérèse's cause:

> Monsignor de Teil is completely devoted to the cause: the thing holding up the convening of the Diocesan Tribunal is that he himself is having to frame all the articles, or questions, which we shall have to answer on oath. Mgr. de Teil has had to undertake this task because of the death, two months ago, of the tribunal lawyer, Mgr. Martini, and he has been unable to find the time for it. He has had to ask Mgr. Amette [Archbishop of Paris] to take over his chaplaincy duties—for Mgr. de Teil is chaplain to a large almshouse in Paris. Furthermore, he not only has Thérèse's cause to consider, but also the Causes of the Martyrs of the Revolution, Pope Pius IX, Louise of France and someone else whose name I cannot now recall. Thérèse's cause interests him very much indeed because she has performed all the miracles almost exactly as prescribed (except for us). Consequently, he always refers to her as "our little healer." [7]

In another letter dated April 14, 1910, Marie reveals again how closely and in complete harmony the sisters were with Msgr. de Teil:

> I have spent all my working hours today, revising the manuscript of our little Saint, who little thought that one day it would be read by the Sacred Congregation. And, on Msgr. de Teil's advice, we have struck out certain passages dealing with her childhood, and are not going to copy these, because, as Mgr. de Teil wrote to us: "That your consciences may rest easy regarding the investigation into the writings, you may treat as *non existent* those extracts which have already been struck out, being those you consider unimportant, dealing, for example, with childhood pursuits, and similar things, and not really qualifying as "Letters" in the real sense of the term, though to your own eyes these rank as real memories and therefore you prefer to erase them rather than actually destroy them: let this be done before the ecclesiastical authority takes back the writings." [8]

On October 28, 1910, Msgr. de Teil gave Pope Pius X a letter (LT 92) written by Thérèse to her cousin Marie Guérin on May 30, 1889, in which she urged her to receive Holy Communion often. "Holy Father," he said, "this little saint has made the following 'anticipated' commentary on your Holiness' decree on 'frequent communion.'" After reading the letter the pontiff exclaimed, "Most opportune.... Oh, this is a great joy—*gaudio magno!*... This Process must be undertaken quickly." [9]

As vice-postulator, Msgr. de Teil promoted the cause of Thérèse tirelessly and lovingly for thirteen years until his death in Paris on May 18, 1922. On his deathbed he clasped in his hands a picture of his beloved Thérèse. Sadly, he did not live to witness Thérèse's beatification or canonization for which he labored so fervently.

---

[7] *Les Annales de Ste. Thérèse de Lisieux*, April and June 1982, as translated into English in *Sicut Parvuli*, September 1983.
[8] Ibid.
[9] *The Saint of Lisieux*, July 1953, p. 53.

c. Msgr. Pierre-Théophile Dubosq, S.S. (1860–1932)
Promoter of the Faith—"Devil's Advocate"

CANON PIERRE DUBOSQ, A MEMBER OF THE SOCIETY OF ST. SULPICE, SERVED as the Promoter of the Faith in the Process of Beatification for Sister Thérèse of the Child Jesus. Before joining the Sulpicians, he studied in Rome where he received a doctorate in theology and in canon law. He was a teacher for eighteen years at the Major Seminary in Bayeux and eventually held the post of superior there from 1905 until 1931. He also served as vicar-general of the diocese of Bayeux for many years. He died in Thérèse's town of Lisieux on May 10, 1932, at the age of seventy-two.

He drew up a set of instructions and questions for the witnesses interrogated during the Diocesan Process. He was also present in 1910 at the first exhumation of Thérèse's remains and in 1923 when her coffin was brought to the Carmel for its permanent home.

By virtue of his office as "Devil's Advocate," he had to carefully investigate every aspect in detail of a candidate for sainthood and thereby arrive at the accurate truth about him or her. And in such a capacity he asked some very tough questions. Sister Geneviève (Céline) wrote about her staunch remarks to Msgr. Dubosq's inquiries addressed to her:

> At the second Process (1915–1917), when the judges questioned me as to my motive in wanting my sister canonized, I answered that "it was solely in order to advance the Little Way of Spiritual Childhood that she had taught us."
>
> Then, they took fright, and every time I spoke these words "Little Way," they gave a start, and the Promoter of the Faith, M. Dubosq, said to me: "If you speak of a "Way," you will defeat the cause; you know very well that the cause of Mother Chapuis was abandoned for that reason."
>
> "Too bad!" I answered resolutely. "If it is defeated, it is defeated; but since I have sworn to tell the truth, I must give witness to what I have seen and heard, no matter what happens!"....
>
> [It] was all the more difficult to get this accepted since at the first Process—the Informative Process (1910–1911)—the members of the Ecclesiastical Tribunal had misgivings about the proposed cause.... But most often, I protested and told them things like this: "That I would not let Sister Thérèse of the Child Jesus be placed in the circle where custom aligned the other saints, that she had practiced only simple and hidden virtues, and that it would be necessary to get used to it...."
>
> I ask myself how I was able to be so firm; I who, because of my timidity, had once not wanted to go through my exams, certain that I would become flustered and no longer know anything in front of the examiners. It was necessary for God to arm me for the battle, because it certainly was one. M. Dubosq told me I wanted to bring my sister down to my level; and thereupon, he related some very witty stories that appeared to condemn me.[10]

Msgr. Dubosq certainly distressed Céline by his line of questioning and his gratuitous comments. Nonetheless, he became a staunch devotee of St. Thérèse and at one time wrote a pamphlet, *St. Thérèse of the Child Jesus as she*

---
10 Excerpts from a letter Céline wrote requested by her sister Pauline (Mother Agnès) dated January 10, 1938.

was, refuting a defamatory article about Thérèse by a Capuchin priest entitled "St. Thérèse of the Child Jesus as I knew her."[11]

Msgr. Dubosq was not only an admirer of St. Thérèse but a friend of her sister Céline and an advisor to the Lisieux Carmel. During the controversy over the pictures that Céline painted of Thérèse and the photographs she took of her and even retouched, Msgr. Dubosq took Céline's side:

> Our ideas and our tastes are in absolute agreement regarding the photographic question. There are many who say that photography, because it acts mechanically, is a witness to pure truth, while the work of the artist must be suspected of fantasy and caprice because of the artist's own activity. Well, I believe just the opposite. Very often it is the photograph which is false, while the artist, if he be sensitive and honest, can make his subject live. He can study, feel, observe sentiments and affections, indeed, the very character of his subject; then he gathers these fleeting and most indicative expressions of the face which best reflect the soul of his subject.[12]

For years, St. Thérèse has usually been portrayed in paintings and statuary as an overly sweet, beautiful young nun holding lovely cascading roses in her arms. Msgr. Dubosq gave some wise and pertinent advice on how this depiction has been disseminated and how it should be taken:

> I have seen all kinds of unbelievable things—brochures, images, everything. What shall we do about it, then? Nothing! We must endure it. As the cult and admiration of our dear little Sister spreads, we shall see more and more merchandising of those horrible portraits which are only caricatures of Thérèse. We shall see pictures brightly painted in canary yellow and Persian blue. Believe me, Sister Thérèse would laugh at them heartily. You can no more stop this business than you could stop birds from eating the cherries in a garden by putting a padlock on the gate.[13]

Eventually in 1927, Mother Agnès allowed the publication of Thérèse's last words to her from May to September 1897 that she copied in her notebook entitled *Novissima Verba*. Msgr. Dubosq's glowing words of praise follow:

> [With] what loving care did you not, as you took your station at her bedside, note down, day by day, and hour by hour, during her last months of agony, all she said and did! You did not omit the shortest syllable or overlook the least gesture which might reveal the dispositions of her heart.... Perhaps you hesitated to divulge without further consideration the pages of a diary which you instinctively felt contained sacred confidences of a very intimate nature.... But now you realize that the numerous souls whom your little sister must conquer and guide in "her way" are eager to know her better.... Yet, this little book you have given us is a treasure, in truth, the very testament of our dear saint. We find here her character more truly manifested than in any other record. Thank you for not having kept the treasure for yourself alone.[14]

---
11 O'Mahony, *op. cit.*, p. 9.
12 From a letter he wrote to Céline in January of 1911 quoted on p. 26 in *The Photo Album of St. Thérèse of Lisieux*.
13 Ibid., p. 50.
14 *Novissima Verba*, pp. v–vi.

d. Canon Eucher Deslandes (1849–1922))
Notary

An "advocate" involved with a cause for the beatification and canonization of a candidate for sainthood is in reality a defense attorney who upholds the cause. *Advocatus Dei* (Advocate of God) is the Latin term for this position whereas *Advocatus Diaboli* (The Devil's Advocate) is the term for Promoter of the Faith in the cause leading to sainthood.

Canon Deslandes from Bayeux and Abbé Charles Marie[15] from the church of St. Jacques in Lisieux were selected notaries during Thérèse's beatification. The former was a diocesan scholar, researcher, and archivist. As a writer, several of his works won him academic honors. He also had the distinction of being an *Officier de l'Instruction Publique*. The Sacred Congregation of Rites entrusted to Bishop Lemonnier the task of examining Thérèse's written material. He delegated the work to the above two clerics. On May 9, 1910, they were sent to the Carmel as part of this assignment. Mother Agnès observed amusingly their procedures with interest and commented to Msgr. de Teil:

> Since yesterday, in the afternoon, Monsieur le Chanoine Deslandes and M. l'abbé Marie have been in the speakroom, examining the writings. But how slow they are!!! I can hardly keep from laughing. I noticed that M. le Chanoine, when he arrived, believed it would take a day or two, but should he continue at this pace, I am afraid the "Last Judgment" will surprise him at his copybooks. He is making M. l'abbé Marie put in as many periods, commas, and underlining as the autographs before him already have. Meanwhile, he admires and he speaks joyfully at having to do this work; this consoles me very much, for, really, he puts great fervor into his work in spite of his scruples and his slowness. I was going to say he puts a real enthusiasm into it.[16]

In Msgr. de Teil's reply to Mother Agnès he expressed his appreciation and value of their "enthusiasm": "M. Deslandes' enthusiasm will exert a great influence on the bishop and his *entourage*, for they consider M. Deslandes as a real scholar and not a dreamer, and so they will attach all the more credibility to my own affirmations which surprised them; I have really experienced this."[17] Sister Marie of the Sacred Heart (Thérèse's sister Marie) was also amazed at the exceptionally fine work of the two notaries: "Never would I have believed that anyone would give these writings such meticulous care. It was necessary to copy not only the manuscript but all the letters, even those addressed to Uncle and Aunt."[18]

The examination of all the writings ended at the last session of the Informative phase of the Diocesan Process on June 12, 1910. The official, authoritative *Copy of the Writings* comprised four volumes with a total of 491 pages. Volume 2

---
15 For his biography see p. 376.
16 Mother Agnès to Msgr. de Teil, May 10, 1910, as quoted in *General Correspondence*, vol. I, p. 34.
17 Msgr. de Teil to Mother Agnès, May 10, 1910, as quoted in *General Correspondence*, p. 35.
18 Marie of the Sacred Heart to Sister Françoise-Thérèse (Léonie). May 19, 1910, as quoted in the above source.

contained the *Letters* which amounted to 184 pages. By order of Bishop Lemonnier, Canon Deslandes then went to Rome and with justifiable pride presented the manuscript to the Sacred Congregation of Rites.[19]

On November 13, 1922, a year before Thérèse's beatification, Canon Deslandes passed away. The death notice reported the important part he played in Thérèse's cause:

> ... as *notary* in the preparation and writing of the material required for the various canonical processes set up for the beatification of little Sister Thérèse of the Child Jesus. He collated these with such a scrupulous care, with such a clear and precise methodology, that we can attribute, in part, the rapidity with which the cause advanced at Rome to the perfection of his voluminous *dossier*.[20]

e. Antonio Cardinal Vico (1847–1928)
Headed the cause for Sister Thérèse in Rome

A MOST IMPORTANT PERSON IN THE PROCESS OF PROCLAIMING BLESSED Sister Thérèse of the Child Jesus a saint was Antonio Cardinal Vico, Prefect of the Sacred Congregation of Rites. When all the documents from the Diocesan Process were delivered to the Sacred Congregation of Rites, he assumed the leadership of the cause in Rome. Pope Pius X appointed him Ponent (also termed Cardinal Relator) of the cause in 1912. He served in this capacity until her canonization in 1925. Besides involvement in the official duties of this position, he also participated actively in the various triduums, ceremonies, and other functions honoring the Saint of Lisieux before and after her elevation to sainthood.

In 1919 on the occasion of his going to France to consecrate the Basilica of Sacré-Cœur of Montmartre in Paris, he visited the Lisieux Carmel and claimed that if they "were living in the early centuries of the Church, when the Servants of God were beatified by acclamation, Sister Thérèse would long ago have ranked among the Blessed."[21]

On August 14, 1921, Pope Benedict XV promulgated the decree on the heroicity of the virtues of the Venerable Sister Thérèse of the Child Jesus and gave a discourse on her Way of Spiritual Childhood. Cardinal Vico likewise praised her and anticipated her marvelous shower of spiritual blessings and miracles:

> May she exercise every day more and more her influence with the court of heaven on behalf of those who love her and who strive to follow in her footsteps. May she win over also by the charm of her voluntary childhood those whom subtle vanity, or ignorance of truth, turns aside from her luminous and sure way.
>
> "Now is the time of her conquests," and the past has proved beyond a doubt that she will be for many an angel of salvation.[22]

---

19 *General Corresponcence*, vol. I, p. 36.
20 *Semaine Religieuse de Bayeux*, December 3, 1922, p. 488.
21 Taylor (translator), *Saint Thérèse of Lisieux, the Little Flower of Jesus*, p. 248.
22 Vico, *The Spirit of Saint Thérèse de l'Enfant Jésus*, p. vi.

C. Beatification and Canonization

Thérèse was beatified on April 29, 1923, after which a number of grand celebrations were held in her honor. The next month, Pope Pius XI addressed a letter to Cardinal Vico, the Pontifical Legate for the solemnities of the beatification which were to be celebrated on May 28, 29, and 30, 1923, in Lisieux. Part of the letter follows:

Venerable brother, health and Apostolic Benediction....

Now that the solemnities have been celebrated at the Vatican, it remains for the Discalced Carmelites and the Diocese of Bayeux and Lisieux to celebrate the triduum of supplications in accordance with traditional usage, which we are confident will not only contribute to the greater glory of Blessed Thérèse but also to the greater spiritual profit of all faithful Christians.

You are well aware with what pleasure we have heard of the request made to you, our Venerable brother, to go to Lisieux and preside at the solemnities in that city....

Set out with joy. Exhort the citizens of Lisieux with our words; they possess within their walls as a precious pledge the body of this Blessed Carmelite, from which they will find a noble inspiration for the Christian virtues, and urge them to address unceasing prayers before *sepulcrum ejus gloriosum* (her glorious tomb) for the Common Father of all.

As a pledge of divine favors, and the mark of our fatherly benevolence, we give you from our heart the Apostolic Benediction.

Given at Rome at St. Peter's, on the 14th day of the month of May of the year 1923, and the second of our Pontificate.[23]

Pius, PP. XI

For the second time, Cardinal Vico was sent to Lisieux as a major participant in celebrating the supreme glorification of Thérèse as a saint. Public homage was shown to her throughout the elaborately decorated town during the double triduum with masses, processions, and other forms of devotion and adulation. At the Carmelite Chapel on September 30, 1925, the Cardinal officiated at the pontifical solemnities after which he proceeded to the special oratory in the church where he placed in the hand of the recumbent effigy of Thérèse a precious golden rose given and blessed by Pope Pius XI.

In the Epilogue of his book about St. Thérèse, Cardinal Vico had this to say about her:

Now, where is the soul of Thérèse?

Holy Church has spoken: she is canonized, she is triumphant.

But she is at the same time on earth; God has given proof of this. She is fulfilling her mission of making Love, the merciful love of the Lord, His paternal goodness towards us sinners. From the heart of the beatific vision she keeps watch over us, accomplishing wonders which surpass infinitely her immeasurable desires of love and of zeal to make God loved.[24]

In 1927 the Feast of St. Thérèse was extended to the whole Church. The Sacred Congregation of Rites issued a decree announcing this great honor signed by Cardinal Vico. Part of the text follows:

---
23 Verde, *The Story of the Canonization of S. Thérèse of Lisieux*, pp. 113–116.
24 Vico, *op. cit.*, p. 211.

URBIS ET ORBIS

From the time that by the supreme judgement of the Holy See heavenly honors were decreed to be given to S. Thérèse of the Child Jesus, there has been everywhere manifested an increasing devotion towards this blessed virgin. This devotion has been nourished by innumerable miracles and benefits which have descended like a rain of roses, and have made it ever more fruitful and wonderful.

For this reason many bishops, and not a few Cardinals, of the Roman Church have manifested the desire that S. Thérèse of the Child Jesus should be honored by an Office and Mass ordered by the Supreme Authority for the whole world.

The Supreme Pontiff, Pope Pius XI, received this request favorably....

His Holiness was pleased to approve the aforesaid Office and Mass and ordered that the clergy, both Secular and Regular, in the whole Church, should observe the Feast of S. Thérèse, Virgin, on October 3 beneath the rite of a minor double, all the rubrics being duly observed. All things to the contrary notwithstanding.

The 13th Day of July, 1927.

A. Cardinal Vico,
Bishop of Porto and Santa Rufina,
Prefect of the Sacred Congregation of Rites
Angelo Mariani, Secretary[25]

In December of the same year, the Sacred Congregation of Rites declared Thérèse Patroness of Missions for the whole Church. The decree, part of which follows, was signed by Cardinal Vico:

With what intense joy the canonization of S. Thérèse of the Child Jesus was received by the faithful throughout the world, is clearly manifested by the ever-increasing and universal devotion towards her....

Therefore our Most Holy Lord, Pope Pius XI, favorably received the petitions humbly presented to him from the whole world requesting that he would ratify their common desire by his apostolic Authority.

His Holiness informed the below-written Lord Cardinal, Prefect of the Sacred Congregation of rites, that he, acceding to the desire of the innumerable bishops who had besought him, has been pleased to declare S. Thérèse of the Child Jesus, Principal Patroness of all missionaries, whether men or women, and of all missions existing through the world, the equal of S. Francis Xavier with all the rights and liturgical privileges which belong to that title. All things to the contrary notwithstanding.

The 14th day of December, 1927.

A. Card. Vico
Bishop of Porto and Santa Rufina
S.C.R. Prefect
Angelo Mariani, Secretary[26]

---

25 Verde, *op. cit.*, pp. 171–172.
26 Ibid., pp. 172–173.

Antonio Vico was born in Agugliano, Italy, on January 9, 1847. He studied for the priesthood and was ordained at twenty-six on September 20, 1873, the same year of Thérèse's birth. After serving his regular priestly duties with distinction for twenty-four years, he began to rise rapidly and successfully up the hierarchical ladder beginning with his assignment as Apostolic Delegate to Columbia (1897), followed by ordination as Titular Archbishop of Philippi. In 1904 he was appointed Apostolic Nuncio to Belgium then, in the same capacity, to Spain in 1907. The great honor of becoming a cardinal took place on November 27, 1911, which he held for seventeen years. The posts he assumed thereupon included Cardinal-Priest of St. Callisto (1911), Pro-Prefect of Rites in the Roman Curia (1915), Cardinal-Bishop of Porto and Santa Rufino (1915), and Prefect of Rites of the Roman Curia (1918). At the time of his death at eighty-two (February 25, 1929), he had completed fifty-five years as an accomplished and hardworking priest, bishop, and cardinal of the Catholic Church.

f. Pope St. Pius X (1835–1914, Pontificate: 1903–1914)
Authorized the Introduction of Thérèse's cause

SAINT PIUS X HAD ALWAYS BEEN A STRONG ADVOCATE FOR THE FREQUENT and early reception of Holy Communion which was decidedly not the custom of the time. By a decree in 1905, *Sacra Tridentina Synodus*, he recommended frequent Communion and in 1910 (*Quam singulari*) he authorized the reception by first Communicants who had reached the age of reason. For this reason he is often referred to as the Pope of the Eucharist.

Throughout her life, Thérèse lamented the fact that she could not receive Holy Communion more frequently and even when she was a young child she believed she should be able to receive the Body of Christ. On her deathbed she predicted that the daily reception of this sacrament would be permitted in her monastery and surprisingly soon after her death it was allowed.

The first contact Pope Pius X had with Thérèse occurred in 1906 through a Canadian priest, Father Eugène Prevost, who had a strong interest in a painting (grisaille) Céline (Sister Geneviève) made of the Holy Face of Jesus based on the 1898 photograph of the Shroud of Turin. He printed many copies of a holy card with Céline's painting on one side and on the other Thérèse's prayer, "O Jesus, your face is the only beauty that delights my heart." Father Prevost, who founded a house in Rome for priests, distributed these pictures as a pious aid for priests in difficulty. The pope imparted an indulgence for the picture and prayer. The next year Father Prevost gave a copy of *Story of a Soul* to the pope in which he recognized the picture Céline painted.[27]

Years later when the cause for her beatification was in progress, Monsignor de Teil, the Vice-Postulator of her cause, presented to Pius X a copy of his *Articles of the Process of Beatification*. He particularly urged him to read an excerpt in it from a letter Thérèse wrote to her cousin Marie Guérin who

---
27 Descouvemont, *Therese and Lisieux*, p. 312.

was then suffering from scruples concerning the reception of the Eucharist. Thérèse said in it: "... don't listen to the devil, mock him, and go without any fear to receive Jesus in peace and love! That is the *only remedy* if you want to be healed." [28]

The Supreme Pontiff, deeply impressed by what he read in the *Articles*, requested that the book be left with him. Msgr. de Teil related many details of Thérèse's life and wonders after her death including her prophesy: "I want to spend my Heaven doing good on earth." [29] Whereupon, at another time in a private conversation with a missionary bishop, he revealed that he considered Thérèse to be "the greatest saint of modern times."

Pius X was born Giuseppi Sarto in Riese, Italy, into a very humble family on June 2, 1835. His mother worked as a seamstress and his father obtained at various times work as a cobbler, a church janitor, and a postman. Gifted and devout as a youth, Giuseppi entered the seminary in Padua and was eventually ordained at twenty-five in 1858. He performed admirably for seventeen years as a parish priest in Tombolo and Salzano and was consequently chosen spiritual director of a seminary and chancellor of a diocese. His holiness, humility, ability, and very successful career led to his rise to the status of bishop of Mantua and, eight years later, to his transfer to Venice as Cardinal Patriarch in 1893.

Not long before he died, Pope Leo XIII predicted that Cardinal Sarto would succeed him as pope. He was right, for on August 9, 1903, the College of Cardinals elected him pope. He, as Pope Pius X, immediately had to struggle with the French Republic which suppressed religious orders, assaulted religious education, confiscated Church property, and advocated the complete separation of church and state. During the same period, anti-Catholic furor existed elsewhere in Spain, Portugal, Italy, and elsewhere in Europe, as well as in South America; but Pope Pius X was adamant in his solicitude for the rights of religion and the Church.

Subversion within the Church itself from liberal clerics infatuated with the ideas of "modernism" wounded the pope deeply but through persistent and rigorous efforts he averted any possible calamities. His papal motto "to restore all things to Christ" found realization in his reformation of the breviary and Church music, as well as in his work on codifying canon law.

Pius X's life and work of seventy-nine years were so infused with faith, humility, and sanctity that the cardinals themselves requested the introduction of his cause in 1923 just nine years after his death in 1914 at the outbreak of World War I. He was beatified by Pope Pius XII on June 3, 1951, and canonized by him on May 29, 1954. He thus became the first canonized pope since St. Pius V who reigned nearly two and a half centuries before him.

---

28 LT 92, May 30, 1889.
29 *Last Conversations*, July 17, 1897.

g. Pope Benedict XV (1854–1922, Pontificate: 1914–1922)
Proclaimed Thérèse "Venerable"

THÉRÈSE'S LIFE AND WRITINGS, ESPECIALLY HER CONCEPT OF "SPIRITUAL childhood," so deeply stirred Pope Benedict XV that he exempted the beatification process from the customary fifty years' delay required at the time between the death of the Servant of God and the opening of the debate on the heroic nature of her virtues. In a solemn decree proclaimed on September 22, 1919, he exhorted the Catholic Church to yield to the wishes and petitions of the faithful. By then Thérèse's autobiography was read by millions who were likewise deeply moved. The Vatican had been besieged by countless numbers of letters petitioning for her canonization. During the First World War the pope took an unusual step by having a medal struck (June 10, 1915) in Thérèse's honor particularly for the soldiers, including German ones, who manifested a strong attachment to this young Norman nun they called their "little sister in the trenches."

On August 14, 1921, Pope Benedict XV read his allocution on the promulgation of the decree regarding the heroic virtues of the "Venerable Thérèse of the Child Jesus" from which these excerpts are taken:[30]

- In fact there is not a soul in the whole world who, if ever so slightly acquainted with the life of little Thérèse, does not hasten to unite his voice to that admirable choir which proclaims her life as one adorned with all the gifts of spiritual childhood. Here is the secret of sanctity, not only for the French but for all the faithful of the Catholic world.
- She was not nourished by any learned studies, yet she became so rich in the science of the saints that she was able to point out to others the true way of salvation.
- But where did she reap this copious harvest? Where did she gather such an abundance of ripe fruit? In the garden of spiritual childhood. Whence was derived this vast treasure of knowledge? From the secrets which God reveals to little ones.
- Let us recognize that this sanctity was the effect of heroic virtue, attained by constant and practical love of the graces of spiritual childhood.
- The more this new heroine of sanctity is known, the greater will become the number of her imitators who will give glory to God by rendering practical homage to the luster of spiritual childhood.
- We desire, therefore, that the secret of the sanctity of sister Thérèse of the Child Jesus may be revealed to all our children.

Pope Benedect XV was born Giacomo Della Chiesa on November 21, 1854, of patrician parents in Pegli (Genoa), Italy. His early education consisted of private tutoring and instruction from diocesan priests. He attended the Royal University of Genoa and received a doctorate in civil law in 1875. Following this he studied for the priesthood in Rome, was ordained in 1878, earned a doctorate in theology in 1879, and a year later received a doctorate in canon law. Because of his distinguished service as secretary to the papal nuncio in Spain, Pope Pius X chose him archbishop of Bologna (1907). Seven years later he was

---
30 Verde, *op. cit.*, pp. 46–63.

elevated to cardinal. In the same year (1914) he had the honor of being crowned Pope Benedict XV in the Sistine Chapel.

During the eight years of his pontificate he earned the title "the good Samaritan of humanity" because of his many acts of charity and mercy in relieving human suffering during the First World War. In particular he established at the Vatican an international missing persons bureau relative to prisoners of war. He offered many peace proposals to the warring nations but no one heeded them except the U.S.A. under the presidency of Woodrow Wilson. Furthermore, a new Code of Canon Law was eventually formulated in 1917 largely through the persistence of Benedict XV. He was also responsible for creating a better understanding between the Latin and Oriental Churches at the time.

A sudden but short attack of influenza led to his death from pneumonia at age sixty-seven on January 22, 1922.

h. POPE PIUS XI (1857–1939, Pontificate: 1922–1939)
Beatified and Canonized St. Thérèse of the Child Jesus

POPE PIUS XI CAN JUSTIFIABLY BE CALLED THE THERESIAN POPE FOR HE beatified and canonized her. For the rest of his life he lavished the highest honors and praises on her. To a group of American pilgrims he once exclaimed that she was "the little Saint whom you in America call the Little Flower, but whom I call my guiding star."[31] He went so far as to proclaim, "verily God has spoken good things through her who has become as His living word." At other times he remarked that "even this Eternal City is not accustomed to such wonders," that she has become "a prodigy of miracles," and was "the consoling angel in my trials."[32]

In his allocution of February 11, 1923, on the approbation of the miracles needed for canonization, he characterized Thérèse as:

- "this ethereal heroine of today"
- "this silent flower who fills earth and heaven with the fragrance of her perfume"
- "an exquisitely delicate miniature of perfect sanctity"[33]

In various discourses relative to her canonization in 1925, Pope Pius XI discerned precisely the essence of Thérèse's charisma:

- In an age of insolent sensuality and impurity of life, behold Blessed Thérèse of the Child Jesus, an enchanting vision of simplicity and purity, who uplifts that which essentially constitutes the Kingdom of Purity, that is to say humility and mortification. (March 29, 1925)[34]
- Who is there who does not realize that if this way of spiritual childhood be followed, how very easily human society would be reformed and restored, a work to which we have given ourselves from the very first days of our Pontificate. (May 17, 1925)[35]

---

31 Dolan, *Collected Little Flower Works*, p. 124.
32 Ibid., p. 126.
33 Verde, *op. cit.*, p. 74–76.
34 Ibid., p. 129.
35 Ibid., p. 136.

- Whosoever honors Thérèse honors the divine model she reproduced.
- Today from the depths of the cloister she has fascinated the entire world by the magic of her example, an example of sanctity which all the world can follow, for all the world can enter on this "little way"—a way of golden simplicity which is infantine only in name—this "way of spiritual childhood," all purity, simplicity of heart and of mind, of irresistible love of goodness, of truth, and of sanctity.
- Lisieux [industrially] is not the least amongst the cities of the fair land of France.... But what is that beside the storm, the deluge of glory that has descended upon Lisieux today. And this glory shall never pass away but will endure forever. (May 18, 1925) [36]

After her beatification, Pius XI declared Blessed Thérèse Patronesss of All Carmelite Missions (1923). Also, in 1925, he proclaimed her Patroness of the Pius Association of St. Peter the Apostle established to educate native priests. Two years after her canonization he extended the Feast of St. Thérèse to the entire Church and decreed her Patroness of all Missions and Missionaries on a par with St. Francis Xavier—a stupendous honor for one who never stepped foot on missionary soil.

Like Pius X, Ambrogio Damiano Achille Ratti was born into an ordinary Italian family on May 31, 1859, in Desio, a little town near Milan. A bright and pious youngster, Achille studied for the priesthood, was ordained at twenty-two (1879) and attended the Gregorian University in Rome where he earned several doctorates. Having gained a justly deserved reputation for his early pastoral work, seminary professorship, and scholarship in paleography at the Ambrosian Library in Milan, he was appointed head of the Vatican Library by Pius X. Before his election as pope on February 6, 1922, he functioned as papal nuncio to Poland, and archbishop and cardinal of Milan.

When Cardinal Ratti became pope, he chose the name Pius XI. He endeavored during the seventeen years of his pontificate to strengthen the postwar peace and to restrain the three great evils that emerged—Russian Communism, Italian Fascism, and German National Socialism (Nazism).

In the thirty encyclicals he issued during his pontificate, he dealt with all the major contemporary problems: Catholic education, marriage, non-Catholic Christendom, social order, and the international arms race. In 1929, through his wise leadership, he settled the nearly sixty year long "Roman question" which reconciled the papacy with the Italian states and established Vatican City as a sovereign state. He also instituted the honored feast of Christ the King.

Pius XI, perhaps the most notable and capable pope of the first part of the twentieth century, died just before the beginning of the Second World War on February 10, 1936 at the age of eighty-one.

---

36 Ibid., pp. 138–139.

D. Thérèse's Titles, Honors, Congregations, and Relics

THE FIFTEEN-YEAR-OLD THÉRÈSE MARTIN CHOSE AS HER RELIGIOUS NAME "Sister Thérèse of the Child Jesus and of the Holy Face." She never left the confines of her cloistered monastery during the nearly ten years of her life at the Lisieux Carmel. This twenty-four-year-old nun died an unknown, humble, and simple nun yet her extraordinary holiness, message, and spirituality soon became recognized, loved and imitated the world over. Her phenomenal rise to fame, miracles attributed to her intercession, conversions, and religious vocations because of her have reached astronomical heights. A few years before her beatification she received her first posthumous titles. After her canonization in 1925, Saint Thérèse of the Child Jesus acquired an unprecedented number of other titles and honors culminating with that of Doctor of the Church (1997)—the third woman so honored in the entire 2,000 years of Church history.

More than fifty congregations and institutes following the spirituality of St. Thérèse of the Child Jesus exist throughout the world. They number about 5,000 members.[1] The following lists the major congregations and missionary groups in France:

- **Les Missionnaires de la Plaine** (The Missionaries of the Plain)—founded by Father Gabriel Martin (1873–1949) in 1921 and recognized by the Church in 1928. These missionaries work for the evangelization of the Plain (plains) and the Marais (marshes) in the Department of the Vendée.
- *Sœurs Oblates de Sainte Thérèse de l'Enfant-Jésus* (Oblates of Saint Thérèse of the Child Jesus)—founded by Father Gabriel Martin in 1924 and recognized by the Church in 1933. The official title is "Congregation of the Oblate Sisters of St. Thérèse of the Child Jesus." They act as guides at Les Buissonnets, the birthplace house, and formerly at the Hermitage.
- *Œuvre des Orphelins Apprentis d'Auteuil* (Work of the Orphan-Apprentices of Auteuil, Paris)—founded in 1866 by Father Roussel[2] to serve the poor children of Paris. His successor, Father Brottier (1876–1936)[3] was the first to construct a church in honor of St. Thérèse.
- *Union Sacerdotale de Sainte Thérèse de l'Enfant-Jésus* (Priestly Union of Saint Thérèse of the Child Jesus)—founded in 1933 and known in England as "The Association of Priests of Saint Thérèse of the Child Jesus."
- *Frères Missionnaires de Ste. Thérèse de l'Enfant-Jesus* (The Society of Missionaries of Saint Thérèse of the Child Jesus)—founded in 1947 by Father Gabriel Martin.
- *Deus Caritas*—a secular institute for single women or widows founded in 1963 by Father Puaud (chaplain of pilgrimages to Lisieux) and approved by Rome in 1979.

---

1 Gaucher, *Saint Thérèse of Lisieux: From Lisieux to the Four Corners of the World*, p. 41.
2 Originally called the "Work of First Communion."
3 Daniel Brottier was beatified by Pope John Paul II on November 25, 1984, at the same time as the Carmelite nun Sister Elizabeth of the Trinity.

Most of the other associations in the world are apostolic congregations that follow Thérèse's little way of spiritual childhood. Here are eight representative examples with pertinent data included:

- **Carmelite Sisters of St. Thérèse of the Infant Jesus**, founded in 1917 in Oklahoma, United States.
- **Congregation of St. Thérèse of the Child Jesus**, located in India, was founded for Brothers in 1931.
- **Congrégation Maronite des Sœurs de Ste Thérèse de l'Enfant-Jésus**, founded in 1935, and located in Lebanon.
- **Zgromadzenie Sióstr sw. Teresy od Dzieciatka Jezus**, founded in 1936 and located in Podkowie Lenej, Poland.
- **Sisters of Saint Thérèse**, located in Papua-New Guinea, founded in 1954.
- **Petits frères de Ste Thérèse de l'Enfant-Jésus**, founded in Haiti in 1960.
- **I Sacerdoti oblati di S. Teresa del Bambino Gesù**, located in Ravenna, founded in 1965.
- **Teresian Sisters**, located in Lilongwe, Malawi[4] and founded in 1984.

Thérèse received an amazing amount of titles after her death beginning with Servant of God, Venerable, Blessed, Patroness, followed by Saint, Protectress, and Doctor of the Church. The titles she holds today appear below in chronological order of reception:

1923   Patroness of the Carmelite Novitiate
       Patroness of all Carmelite Missions
1924   Patroness of the Discalced Carmelites
1925   Canonized Saint Thérèse of the Child Jesus and of the Holy Face
       Patroness of the Native Missions
       Patroness of the Pious Association of St. Peter
       Patroness for the Training of Native Priests
1927   Patron Saint, along with Saint Francis Xavier, of all Missionaries
1928   Protectoress of the Church in Mexico
1929   Patron Saint of Christian Working Class Youth (CWCY)
       Patron Saint of the Apostolic Delegation to Mexico
       Patroness of the Lateran Treaty
       Patron Saint of Russicum, a seminary founded in Rome by Pope Pius XI for the education of future Russian priests.
1932   Protectress of Russia
       Patron Saint of the Christian Seafaring Youth and Colonial Infantry Soldiers
       Patron Saint of the Missions to the Sick and Infirm
       Patroness of all Novitiates
1941   Patron Saint of the Mission de France
1944   Secondary Patroness of France along with Joan of Arc
       Second Patron Saint of Australia
1997   Doctor of the Universal Church

---

4 Thérèse's first "spiritual brother" Maurice Bellière did his missionary work in Malawi.

More than seventy seminaries around the world have designated St. Thérèse of Lisieux as their patroness. The astounding number of more than 1,700 churches, chapels, and charities are named in her honor. This includes eight cathedrals and six minor basilicas ranging from Cairo[5] to the United States. Uncountable numbers of parochial schools on every academic level have taken Thérèse as their name. In addition, thousands of girls were named Thérèse at baptism and chosen at confirmation. The following have also come under her patronage: AIDS sufferers, aviators, florists, loss of parents, tuberculosis sufferers, and towns like Fresno (CA), Pueblo (CO), Kisumo (Kenya), Juneau and Fairbanks (Alaska) and Witbank (South Africa).

St. Thérèse was not only a nun, a saint, a Doctor of the Church, but a prophet as well. One of her desires in life was to become a missionary and spread the Word of God. This quotation from her autobiography foretells exactly what has come to pass within a hundred years since she passed into eternal life. She has traveled to all corners of the world in the form of her earthly remains:

> I have the *vocation of the Apostle*. I would like to travel over the whole earth to preach Your Name and to plant Your glorious Cross on infidel soil. But O my Beloved, one mission alone would not be sufficient for me, I would want to preach the Gospel on all the five continents simultaneously and even to the most remote isles. I would be a missionary, not for a few years only but from the beginning of creation until the consummation of the ages.[6]

Monasteries in many countries of the world welcomed the presence of Thérèse in their midst. Among them was the Benedictine Abbey of Fleury whose abbot announced:

> Saint Thérèse wanted to be a missionary throughout the whole world. One century after her death, her wish has come true and she has become a frontline participant in the new evangelization promoted by John Paul II. To those involved in laborious pastoral work she teaches that holiness and the poorest means are still the most powerful ways of diffusing the Good News.[7]

At the time of the grand festivities in March of 1923, preparatory to the beatification of St. Thérèse, the country of Brazil offered to the Lisieux Carmel a beautiful large reliquary, known as the Brazilian Reliquary, splendidly decorated in gold and other costly materials, in which are enclosed a significant portion of the skeletal remains of the Little Flower. This is permanently located in Lisieux. This casket, however, had to be duplicated in every detail, also embellished with precious metals but constructed mainly of a hard, fine-textured wood from the sub-tropical Brazilian Jacaranda tree. Called the Centenary Reliquary because Thérèse died exactly one hundred years before, it is the one used on all the

---

5 The Muslims of Cairo sponsored this edifice in honor of the "little Saint of Allah." These statistics have been obtained from Conrad de Meester's *Saint Thérèse of Lisieux: Her Life, Times, and Teaching*, p. 264.
6 *Story of a Soul*, chapter IX, pp. 192–193.
7 From an article "From the Carmel in Lisieux" by R. Zambelli, rector of the Basilica of Lisieux, obtained from the internet under the title "Lisieux's St. Thérèse."

worldwide journeys of Thérèse's relics. The relics from the Brazilian Reliquary were separated into two parts: one half put in each of the two reliquaries.

During the time after Thérèse's coffin was transferred from the Lisieux public cemetery to the Carmel, her relics were divided: one portion was brought to the Holy Father in Rome, the breast bone was placed in the reclining figure of Thérèse in the Carmel chapel, and later on Thérèse's right arm and hand bones were encased in a beautiful reliquary, donated by Pope Pius XI, that stays in the Lisieux Basilica.

The fragile remaining evidence of Thérèse's humanity formed part of her body when she was alive and in which she thought, loved, and suffered. When we are in the presence of these relics we can more easily summon to mind her humanity, spirituality, and message. And that is precisely what is occurring today in the minds and hearts of the viewers of her reliquary. Fervent unending crowds of adults and the elderly, teenagers and children, sick and distressed go to see and touch the reliquary. They open their hearts to her, revealing their problems, joys, sufferings, and wishes. Through her they come closer to God and His word, a hope she held all her life and which is now so manifestly being realized.

It was not until October 14, 1994, that Thérèse's missionary journey began with a visit to Lyon and the church of Notre-Dame-de-Fourvière, atop the Fourvière Hill. This was followed by stops in Marseille and Paris—all three cities Thérèse visited on her pilgrimage to Rome in 1887. Then in November of 1997, the centenary of her death, the reliquary commenced its travels to every continent on the earth which started by going to Switzerland, Austria, Slovenia, then far away to Brazil. It is still in the process of visiting thousands of large cities and tiny hamlets spreading the word of God through the example of one of His humblest servants.

CHAPTER 2

ST. THÉRÈSE'S FAMILY

A. Family Tree
B. Parents
C. Children
D. Grandparents
E. Father's Other Relatives
F. Mother's Other Relatives

A. Family Tree

THE GENEALOGY OF ST. THÉRÈSE'S FAMILY ON HER FATHER'S SIDE, THE Martins, can be traced through records as far back as the 16th century. The Martins came from Athis-de-l'Orne, south of Caen in the Department of the Orne. They were all noted for their firm faith in the Catholic Church, their piety, and even some for their genuine sanctity. A few of the men sought careers in the military service and distinguished themselves for their bravery and leadership.

Captain Pierre Martin (1777–1865) and his wife Fanie Bureau Martin (1800–1883) were the paternal grandparents of the greatest saint of modern times. His father, Jean Martin (1752–1806), was Thérèse's great grandfather. Jean's sister, Marie-Henriette Martin (1779–?) was the greatgrandmother of the last surviving member of the Martin family who was living when Thérèse was alive—Dr. Poirier (1885–1974). A journalist interviewed the doctor at one time and four years after the doctor died his interview appeared in the September/October 1978 edition of *Les Annales de Sainte Thérèse de Lisieux*. Much of the information herein recorded was derived from this interview. Born in the small market town of Athis, the doctor, a brilliant student, studied medicine in Lille and Paris and began his medical practice in his hometown. In 1912 his first wife died leaving one son. Seven years later he married again. An engagingly unique person, the doctor was noted as a fervent Christian, strict, and pious. During the German occupation in World War I, he helped French resistance groups. He also entered the ambulance corps and received the Legion of Honor medal for heroic service. Later he served in Lourdes at the medical bureau. At the request of Mother Agnès and her sisters at the Carmelite monastery in Lisieux, he, his wife, and son represented the Martin family in Rome at the canonization of St. Thérèse in 1925. Dr. Poirier died in 1973 at the age of eighty-nine.

Zélie (Guérin) Martin too came from a rich heritage of religion, military service, and patriotism. She was born in Gandelain, a tiny village close to Alençon in the Department of the Orne. Her father (1789–1868) became a captain in the military service under Napoleon I who ruled as emperor from 1804–1815. At the canonization ceremonies in 1925, Madame Sadi-Carnot and M. Houdayer represented the Guérin side of St. Thérèse's family.

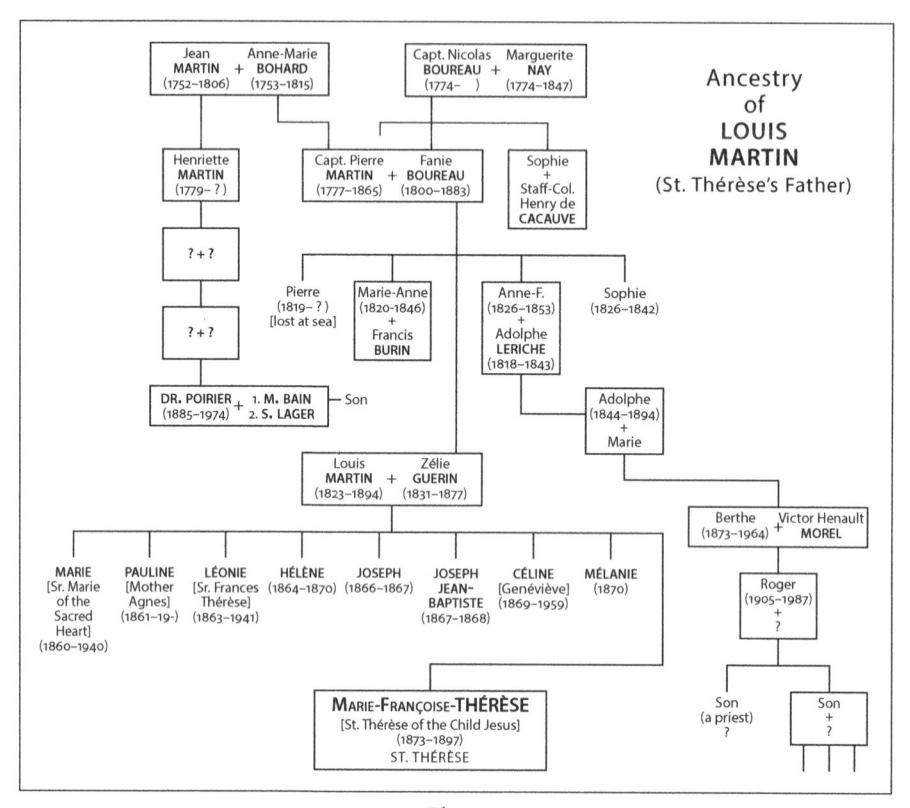

Ancestry of LOUIS MARTIN (St. Thérèse's Father)

- Jean MARTIN (1752–1806) + Anne-Marie BOHARD (1753–1815)
- Capt. Nicolas BOUREAU (1774–) + Marguerite NAY (1774–1847)
- Henriette MARTIN (1779–?)
- Capt. Pierre MARTIN (1777–1865) + Fanie BOUREAU (1800–1883)
- Sophie + Staff-Col. Henry de CACAUVE
- ? + ?
- Pierre (1819–?) [lost at sea]
- Marie-Anne (1820–1846) + Francis BURIN
- Anne-F. (1826–1853) + Adolphe LERICHE (1818–1843)
- Sophie (1826–1842)
- ? + ?
- DR. POIRIER (1885–1974) + 1. M. BAIN 2. S. LAGER — Son
- Adolphe (1844–1894) + Marie
- Louis MARTIN (1823–1894) + Zélie GUERIN (1831–1877)
- Berthe (1873–1964) + Victor Henault MOREL
- MARIE [Sr. Marie of the Sacred Heart] (1860–1940)
- PAULINE [Mother Agnes] (1861–19–)
- LÉONIE [Sr. Frances Thérèse] (1863–1941)
- HÉLÈNE (1864–1870)
- JOSEPH (1866–1867)
- JOSEPH JEAN-BAPTISTE (1867–1868)
- CÉLINE [Geneviève] (1869–1959)
- MÉLANIE (1870)
- Roger (1905–1987) + ?
- MARIE-FRANÇOISE-**THÉRÈSE** [St. Thérèse of the Child Jesus] (1873–1897) ST. THÉRÈSE
- Son (a priest) ?
- Son + ?

Plate 3

B. Parents

1. **Louis Martin**: *Father of St. Thérèse*
2. **Zélie Martin**: *Mother of St. Thérèse*

1. Louis Martin (1823–1894)
Father of St. Thérèse

When I think of you, dear little Father, I naturally think of God, for it seems to me that it is impossible to see anyone more holy than you on the earth.[1]

— Thérèse

Louis Martin's mother, Anne Fannie Martin (née Boureau) was the only grandparent Thérèse knew since the others died before she was born. She married Louis's father Pierre François Martin on April 7, 1818. They had five children, Louis being the third, was born of this union on August 22, 1823, in Bordeaux where Captain Martin (Thérèse's grandfather) was garrisoned. Though he was privately baptized right after birth, the full official church baptism took place in October when Captain Martin returned from a campaign in Spain. The Baptismal Certificate reads:

> In the year one thousand eight hundred and twenty-three on the twenty-eighth of October, has been baptized by me, priest, undersigned, Louis-Joseph-Aloys-Stanislas Martin, born the twenty-third [*sic*] of the month of August last, legitimate son of Monsieur Pierre-François Martin, Captain in the Nineteenth Light Infantry, and dame Marie-Anne-Fanny Boureau his wife, living at No. 3, rue Servandoni. He had for godfather Léonce de Lamothe, and for godmother Ernestine Beyssac who have signed with me.
>
>
>
> *Jn-Ant. Martegoute*, priest, *de licentia parochi*
> *Léonce de Lamothe*
> *Ernestine Beyssac, Jules Guibre*
> *Fanie Martin, née Boureau*
> Copy conformable to the original:
> *Jaure*, Curé de Sainte-Eulalie
> Followed by the attestation of Mgr. d'Aviau.[2]
>
>

The church was that of St. Eulalie where by chance the Archbishop of Bordeaux, Monseignor d'Aviau de Bois de Sanzay, was present. He prophetically announced to the parents, "Rejoice, this child is a child of destiny." In the Church there is a monument commemorating this event.

Very little is known about Louis's infancy and childhood except that he was reared in a deeply religious family rooted firmly in their faith. Some of his

---
[1] LT 58, Thérèse to her father, M. Martin, on July 31, 1888.
[2] Laveille, *op. cit.*, p. 2.

106　　　　　　　　　　CHAPTER 1: *St. Thérèse of Lisieux*

Plate 4

St. Thérèse's Parents, Grandparents, and Paternal Cousins

PARENTS

A. Louis Martin

B. Zélie Guérin Martin

GRANDPARENTS

C. Capt. Pierre-François Martin

D. Fanie Bureau Martin

E. Isidore Guérin

PATERNAL COUSINS

F. Adolphe Leriche

G. Marie Leriche

father's men in military service with him were amazed at his piety during Mass especially after the consecration. He told his chaplain the reason why: "Tell them that it is because I believe!"[1] His mother too referred all things to God. In one of her letters to Louis she wrote:

> Yet we must bear the crosses which God sends us, and thank him every day for the favors he has bestowed.... With what joy I pressed you to my heart, for you, dear son, are the dream of my nights and the constant subject of my thoughts.
>
> How many times do I not think of you when my soul, in prayer, follows the leading of my heart and darts up even to the foot of the divine throne. There I pray with all the fervor of my soul that God may bestow on my children the interior happiness and calm which are so necessary in this turbulent world.[2]

The Martins moved to various towns where Captain Martin was stationed, as in Strasbourg where Louis attended school. When little Louis was seven his father retired and settled permanently in Alençon after which his parents most likely enrolled him, at least for a while, in the school there conducted by the Christian Brothers. Not much factual information is available about his early formal education, but he did learn sufficiently on his own. It is known, though, that he did not have the privilege of obtaining a secondary school education. He loved to read and would read to his daughters in the evening. The list of books he possessed indicates his interest in religion, French history, Church history, lives of the saints, and other pious literature.

Upon reaching young manhood, Louis established himself in the business of clock and watch making. In the meantime, he enjoyed several activities and hobbies. His favorite sport was fishing which he pursued even during his later years. He was a good swimmer and once saved the son of a friend from drowning. Louis had a good voice, liked to sing, playfully imitated the voice and actions of people, enjoyed playing billiards, was fond of walking in the woods, and delighted in visiting various chapels in and out of town. Another one of his pleasures was traveling, perhaps attributable to his early life when his father's military duties necessitated moving to different localities with his family.

When in Alençon he joined the Vital-Romet Club, a social, recreational, and religious association of middle class men who met in the home of one of its presidents, Vital Romet, on the Rue de Mans across the street from the Church of Saint Léonard. The chaplain was Abbé Hurel, dean of Saint Léonard, the priest who married Louis and Zélie.

He began his training in the craft of making clocks and watches when he was nineteen, studying in Rennes, Strasbourg, and Paris. At thirty-three he set up his own business in Alençon. In the meantime he immersed himself in reading not only religious books but also history accounts mostly concerning his beloved France—particularly Brittany and Normandy. Besides reading at home, he would often withdraw to his retreat house not far away he called the

---
1 Piat, *op. cit.*, p. 10.
2 Laveille, *op. cit.*, pp. 3–4.

Pavilion located on Rue des Camions (now Rue du Pavillon) in the southern part of Alençon. This narrow hexagonal tower-like structure of three stories with one small room on each floor still exists. It is situated at the end of a garden belonging to a private family whose house is at the other end of the grounds. A high wall to which the Pavilion is attached completely surrounds the property. In the building he had his crucifix and pious sayings on the wall such as "God sees me," "Blessed are they who keep the commandments of the Lord!" and "Eternity is drawing near." Here he stored all his fishing equipment. Outside in the garden he placed the statue of the Blessed Mother given to him by Mlle. Baudouin who had helped him set up his business. This statue later became known as "Our Lady of the Smile" after Thérèse was cured of a strange sickness when she saw the Virgin smile at her.

When he was approaching his mid-thirties, Louis's mother began to be concerned about the future of her son. She realized that he gave up his longing to become a priest nearly ten years before so she thought of finding a suitable young lady to become his wife. Fortuitously, she came to know Zélie Guérin who was studying lacemaking with her and she seemed the ideal one for her son. Fortunately, while the two young people passed each other one day on the bridge of St. Leonard in Alençon, Zélie heard an interior voice tell her that he was the man who was to be her husband. It proved true for around three months later they were married. This ceremony took place at Zélie's parish church of Notre-Dame in Alençon on July 13, 1858. An extract from the church register reads:

> On Tuesday, the thirteenth of July, eighteen hundred and fifty-eight, after publication in the churches of Notre-Dame and Montsort of the banns of the future marriage between Louis Martin, watchmaker, living in Alençon, parish of Montsort, eldest son of Pierre-François Martin, retired captain, knight of St. Louis, and Marie-Anne-Fanny Boureau.
>
> And Zélie-Marie Guérin, manufacturer of *Point d'Alençon*, living in this parish of Notre-Dame, eldest daughter of Isidore Guérin and Louise-Jeanne Macé.
>
> No impediment or opposition having been found—dispensation from the other two publications of banns having been obtained—and the civil formalities gone through, after the ceremony of betrothal, we, dean of Saint-Leonard, with delegation from M. l'abbé Jamot, *Curé-Archiprêtre* of Notre-Dame, having received their mutual consent to matrimony, and having given them nuptial blessing, in the presence of their relations and friends who have signed their names with ours.
>
> *Louis Martin, Azélie Guérin, F. Martin, Guérin, F.P. Martin, Louise Guérin, A. Leriche, Lefort, Tessier, I. Guérin.*
>
> *F. Hurel*, Curé-Doyen de St-Léon[3]

The newly-wedded couple began their married life together on the rue du Pont Neuf where Louis had his watch and clock establishment. Both Louis

---

3 Laveille, *op. cit.*, p. 374.

and Zélie vowed, nevertheless, that they would remain in the celibate state and each would live very much as monk and nun. Both attended the daily five-thirty Mass, went to Communion frequently, and strictly observed the Church laws concerning fast and abstinence. They prayed in common, studied Scripture, and read about the saints and other pious subjects. He regularly attended "Nocturnal Adoration" in Alençon. Eventually ten months later, upon the wise counsel of a priest, their thoughts changed. He made them understand that they should consider marriage as their vocation and as such God desires them to bear children so that they may someday be consecrated to Him in the religious life. Within a year, the first of nine children was born to them: Marie (1860–1940), followed by Pauline (1861–1951), Léonie (1863–1941), Hélène (1864–1870), Joseph-Louis (1866–1867), Joseph-Jean-Baptiste (1867–1868), Céline (1869–1959), and Thérèse (1873–1897).

Family love abounded in the Martin household. Father and mother held a deep and abiding affection for each other. They in turn dearly loved all their children who reciprocated with their own exceptionally tender devotion. Thérèse wrote in later years: "God was pleased all through my life to surround me with *love*, and the first memories I have are stamped with smiles and the most tender caresses." [4] Again in her autobiography Thérèse describes the strong feelings she had for her father:

> I cannot say how much I loved Papa; everything in him caused me to admire him. When he explained his ideas to me (as though I were a big girl), I told him very simply that surely if he said this to the great men of the government, they would take him to make him *King*, and then France would be happy as it had never been before. But in the bottom of my heart I was happy that it was only myself who *knew* Papa *well*, for if he became *King of France and Navarre*, I knew he wouldn't be happy because this is the lot of monarchs; but above all he would no longer be my King alone! [5]

An indication of pure spousal love is reflected in the correspondence between Zélie and Louis. He, though, wrote few letters all of which were composed when he was away from home on business or vacation. One deep felt closing of a letter to Zélie tells all: "Your husband and true friend who loves you forever." [6] Zélie on the other hand was an inveterate letter writer, having written some 218 known letters, all to family members except one to the director of the Visitation school her daughters attended in Le Mans. Below are two typical samples of the touchingly warm feelings she had for her husband:

- I am always very happy with Louis. He makes my life very sweet. My husband is a saintly man. I admire him as well as love him dearly. I wish every woman had such a husband; that is my New Year's wish for them! [7]

---
4 *Story of a Soul*, chapter I, p. 17.
5 Ibid., p. 48.
6 CF 2, written on October 8, 1863, to Zélie from Paris.
7 CF 1, dated January 1, 1863, sent by Zélie to her sister-in-law, Mme. Guérin.

- I long to be home with you, Louis. I love you with all my heart, and I feel my affection redoubled from being deprived of your daily companionship. *It would be impossible for me to live separated from you....*[8]

Louis Martin's strong commitment to prayer in his private life spilled over into his social involvements. He displayed an unusually great degree of charity towards his neighbor in helping indigent families, homeless men, and the poor in general. Céline tells us of several charitable groups with which he was associated:

> [The] Catholic Circle of Alençon, and the Conference of St. Vincent de Paul, of which he was an active member. Later on he was inscribed on the list of the founders of the Parish Association of St. James at Lisieux, for us the best known work of apostolic zeal to which each year our parents gave a very substantial sum.[9]

Another lay organization he belonged to was the Society of the Blessed Sacrament which basically atoned for the sacrilegious actions against the Blessed Sacrament and for the widespread and even hostile irreligious fervor then so prevalent in France. Furthermore, he became a shareholder of the Social Action in Alençon which he had organized in the parish of Notre Dame in 1875.[10]

Louis was a wonderful father to his children. He played games with them, told them stories, read to them, and took them on walks and picnics in the countryside. After the death of Zélie, Thérèse says; "And still I continued to be surrounded with the most delicate *tenderness*. Our Father's *very affectionate heart* seemed to be enriched now with a truly maternal love!"[11]

When Thérèse was fourteen she had made the decision to become a Carmelite like her two elder sisters. But she knew it would be difficult to tell her dear father, her "King" of this intense desire. She says in her autobiography: "Ah! what interior struggles I went through before feeling courageous enough to speak."[12] She chose the feast of Pentecost, May 29, 1887, to tell her father and get his permission. The narration that follows is truly poignant:

> I found the opportunity to speak to my dear little Father only in the afternoon after Vespers. He was seated by the well contemplating the marvels of nature with his hands joined.... Papa's handsome face had a heavenly expression about it, giving me the feeling that peace flooded his heart. Without saying a word, I sat down by his side, my eyes already wet with tears. He gazed at me tenderly, and taking my head he placed it on his heart, saying: "What's the matter, my little Queen? Tell me." Then rising as though to hide his own emotion, he walked while still holding my head on his heart.
>
> Through my tears, I confided my desire to enter Carmel and soon his tears mingled with mine. He didn't say one word to turn me from my vocation,

---

8 CF 108, dated August 31, 1873, from Zélie to Louis.
9 Sister Geneviève, *The Father of the Little Flower*, p. 16.
10 Emert, *Louis Martin: Father of a Saint*, p. 38.
11 *Story of a Soul*, chapter II, p. 35.
12 Ibid., chapter V, p. 107.

simply contenting himself with the statement that I was still very young to make such a serious decision. I defended myself so well that, with Papa's simple and direct character, he was soon convinced my desire was God's will, and in his deep faith he cried out that God was giving him a great honor in asking his children from him....

Papa ... spoke just like a saint, and I'd love to recall his words and write them down, but all I preserved of them is a memory too sacred to be expressed. What I do recall, however, is a *symbolic* action my dear King performed, not realizing its full meaning. Going up to a low wall, he pointed to some *little white flowers*, like lilies in miniature, and plucking one of them, he gave it to me explaining the care with which God brought it into being and preserved it to that very day. While I listened I believed I was hearing my own story, so great was the resemblance between what Jesus had done for the *little flower* and *little Thérèse*. I accepted it as a relic and noticed that, in gathering it, Papa had pulled all its *roots* out without breaking them. It seemed destined to live on in another soil more fertile than the tender moss where it had spent its first days....

I placed the little white flower in my copy of the *Imitation* [*of Christ*] at the chapter entitled: "One must love Jesus above all things," and there it is still, only its stem has broken close to the roots, and God seems to be saying by this that He'll soon break the bonds of His little flower, not allowing her to fade away on this earth![13]

After some unwillingness on his part, Uncle Guérin eventually gave Thérèse his consent for her to become a Carmelite. Next course was to seek approval of the ecclesiastical superior of the Carmel, Father Delatroëtte, who immediately opposed her entrance on the basis of her young age. Because of this, she went to Bayeux to seek the approval of the ultimate authority, Bishop Hugonin. "The Bishop, believing he'd please Papa, tried to have me stay with him a few more years, and he was very much *surprised* and *edified* at seeing him take my part, interceding for me to obtain permission to fly away at fifteen.... The Bishop said an interview with the *Superior of Carmel* was indispensable before making his decision."[14] This was a stunning blow to Thérèse. A few days later, however, she, her father, and sister Céline embarked on a pre-scheduled pilgrimage to Rome where she personally asked Pope Leo XIII at a papal audience for permission to enter. His response was just as disappointing: " 'Well, my child, do what the Superiors tell you!' Resting my hands on his knees, I made a final effort, saying in a suppliant voice: 'Oh! Holy Father, if you say yes, everybody will agree!' He gazed at me steadily, speaking these words and stressing each syllable: 'Go ... go ... *you will enter if God wills it!*' "[15]

Thérèse eventually was accepted and entered on Monday, April 9, 1888, at the age of fifteen. Almost every day in the beginning, Louis Martin sent gifts to the monastery of various kinds including fish that he caught. His health,

---

13 Ibid., pp. 107–108.
14 Ibid., pp. 116–117.
15 Ibid., pp. 134–135.

though, deteriorated rapidly and after several strokes he was sent to the hospital of Bon Sauveur in Caen. Three years later on May 10, 1892, he was released and returned home where he was cared for by Céline and Léonie. During the time their father was experiencing mental problems stemming from various physical attacks, the Martin sisters suffered greatly knowing he was in pain which, however, he accepted stoically. The subservience and embarrassment he underwent, coupled with the vicious rumors of various people in Lisieux, added to the misery of it all. Two days after his release he went to see his three daughters in Carmel which proved to be the last time he saw them:

> Ah! what a visit that was! You recall it, Mother [Agnès, her sister Pauline]!
> When he was leaving and we were saying good-by, he lifted his eyes to heaven and remained that way a long time and had only one word with which to express his thoughts: "In heaven!" [16]

Shortly after her father's death on July 29, 1894, at the Chateau de la Musse where he had been vacationing, Thérèse wrote one of her most important poems: "Prayer of a Child of a Saint" (PN 8) in which she reminisces about her dear father. Here are the first and last stanzas which she signed with a pet name her father gave her: "The Orphan of Bérèsina."

> Remember that formerly on earth
> Your only happiness used to be to love us dearly.
> Grant your children's prayer.
> Protect us, deign to bless us still.
> Up there you have again found our dear Mother,
> Who had gone before you to our Holy Homeland.
> Now in Heaven
> You both reign.
> Watch over us!...
>
> ...
>
> Remember that at the Vatican
> The Holy Father's hand rested on your brow,
> But you could not understand the mystery
> Of the Divine seal imprinted on you....
> Now your children pray to you.
> They bless your Cross and your bitter suffering!...
> On your glorious brow
> Nine Lilies in bloom
> Shine in Heaven!!!...

It might be of interest to know that after Louis's death, the gross capital bequeathed to his family totaled 280,000 franks. In the lifetime of Louis and Zélie, they accumulated together the large sum of 360,000 franks—before the expenditure of dowries, gifts, etc.[17]

---

16 *Story of a Soul*, chapter VIII, footnote 214, p. 177.
17 Piat, *op. cit.*, footnote 4 on p. 378.

SOME IMPORTANT DATES IN THE LIFE OF LOUIS MARTIN	
1823–1830	Louis was born on August 22 in Bordeaux. His father, a captain in the French army, was at the time in Spain involved with the Spanish campaign. When Louis was seven the family had lived, necessitated by his father's military assignments, in Avignon and in Strasbourg where Louis went to school.
1830	In December, Louis' father retired from the army and the Martin family moved from Strasbourg to Alençon in 1831.
1842–1843	At 19, Louis went to Rennes to learn the clock and watch-making craft with his father's cousin, Louis Bohard.
1843	Louis went to Strasbourg for two or three years to continue studying his craft with Aimé Mathey, his father's friend. As a pilgrim he visited the Monastery of St. Bernard in the Alps.
1845	Louis again visited the Monastery in Switzerland, this time to join the Order of Canons Regular of Saint Augustine but was told he had to study Latin before he could be admitted as a candidate for the priesthood.
1846–1847	He studied Latin without success with Father Jamot of St. Léonard's in Alençon and with M. Wacquerie (about 120 lessons). He finally gave up Latin and concentrated on watchmaking. In order to complete his apprenticeship, he went to Paris for two or three years where he lived with his grandmother, Mme. Boureau-Nay, and a cousin.
1850	On November 9, Louis (27), with the financial help of Mlle. Felicité Baudouin, bought a store and established his own business as a clock maker at 15 Rue du Pont Neuf in Alençon. His parents moved into an apartment in the same building.
1857	On April 26, Louis bought the "Pavilion." Mlle. Baudouin gave him a statue of the Blessed Mother which he set up in the garden. Later it became known as the statue of Our Lady of the Smile.
1858	Louis (35) married Zélie Guérin (27) on July 13 in Zélie's parish church of Notre-Dame in Alençon.
1860–1873	During these years, nine children were born to Louis and Zélie.
1870	Adolphe Leriche took over his uncle Louis Martin's jewelry business in Alençon. Louis, thereupon, worked exclusively for Zélie's business.
1877	Zélie died at 45 on August 28 upon which the family (Louis and his five daughters) moved to Lisieux. They settled in at Les Buissonnets on November 16.
1878	June 17 to July 8—Louis visited the "Exposition" in Paris with Marie and Pauline.
1882	Pauline entered Carmel on October 2 and received the name of Sister Agnès of Jesus.
1885	From August 22 to October 10–17, Louis went on an extended tour to Rome and Constantinople with Father Marie, curate of St. Jacques in Lisieux.
1886	Marie entered Carmel on October 15 and received the name of Sister Marie of the Sacred Heart.
1887	On May 1, Louis (64) had his first paralytic stroke which left him partially paralyzed on one side. Tolerably improved, he went on a pilgrimage to Rome with Thérèse and Céline from November 4 to December 2.

SOME IMPORTANT DATES IN THE LIFE OF LOUIS MARTIN	
1888	Thérèse entered Carmel on April 9 and assumed the name of Sister Thérèse of the Child Jesus. Louis had two relapses: August 12 and October 31. He paid for a new main altar at the cathedral of St. Pierre in Lisieux and lost 50,000 fr on his Panama Canal investment plus some on real estate sales.
1889	Louis attended Thérèse's Clothing on January 10. He was hospitalized on February 12 at Bon Sauveur in Caen.
1892	Louis returned to his family in Lisieux on May 10. Two days later he went to the Carmel and saw Pauline, Marie, and Thérèse for the last time.
1894	On June 5, Louis had a serious heart attack. On July 29 he died at La Musse and was buried on August 2 in the Lisieux cemetery.
1994	On March 26, Pope John Paul II proclaimed Louis and Zélie Martin "Venerable."
2008	On October 19 he and Zélie were beatified at the ceremony held in Lisieux.

The preeminent roles Louis and Zélie played as Catholic parents resulted in their causes for beatification being presented and opened between 1957 and 1960 in Lisieux and then forwarded to Rome. On October 13, 1957, Louis and Zélie's coffins were exhumed and transferred to an honored spot behind the Basilica of St. Thérèse in Lisieux. On March 26, 1994, Pope John Paul II declared them "Venerable" by which is meant that these "Servants of God" had reached the state where their heroic virtues have been affirmed and dogmatically attested to by a decree signed by the pope.

In the meantime, the official prayer for the beatification of Louis Martin and for graces through his intercession had been widely circulated. The complete text follows:

> Lord Jesus, Who made Your servant Louis Martin an exemplary husband and father, we ask You to glorify him who gave to the Church St. Thérèse of the Child Jesus, because of his fidelity to Your service and admirable resignation in time of trial. From Your Goodness, be pleased to make known Your designs concerning him by granting us, through his intercession, the graces and favors we ask. Amen.

2. Zélie Martin (1831–1877)
Mother of Saint Thérèse

God gave me a father and a mother more worthy of heaven than earth.[18]

— Thérèse

Zélie Guérin was born on December 23, 1831 in Gandelain, a little village just outside of Alençon. She was baptized the next day, Christmas Eve, in the church of St. Denis-sur-Sarthon with the name Marie Azélie, but she was always called Zélie. Today on the baptismal font of the church is a plaque commemorating this event. This and a statue of her daughter Saint Thérèse, were placed there one hundred years later in 1931. Below is a short extract from

---
18 LT 261, Thérèse to Bellière, July 26, 1897.

the Baptismal Register of the Parish of Saint-Denis-sur-Sarthon of the baptism of Zélie-Marie Guérin, St. Thérèse's mother:

> Today, the twenty-fourth of December, eighteen hundred and thirty-one, has been baptized by us, the undersigned *vicaire*, Azélie-Marie, born yesterday of the legitimate marriage of Isidore Guérin, gendarme, and Louise Massey. The godfather, François-Michel Septier, Brigadier gendarme, and the godmother, Marie Berrier, cousin of the child, have together with the father signed their names with ours.
>
> *Signed*: F. Hubert, *vicaire*
> Marie Berrier, Septier, Guérin[19]

Zélie's father was Captain Isidore Guérin, a veteran of the Imperial Army and a member of the constabulary; her mother was Louise-Jeanne Macé. They were joined in holy matrimony in 1828 in Pre-en-Pail, Mayenne. They had three children: Marie Louise (1829–1877) who became a Visitation nun; Zélie, the mother of St. Thérèse; and Isidore (1841–1909), a pharmacist and eventually Thérèse's "second father."

Captain Guérin, upon his retirement in 1844, moved with his family to 36 rue Saint-Blaise, in Alençon—the same house where Saint Thérèse was born twenty-nine years later.

Zélie's mother, though deeply religious, was too strict, showed little maternal love, and did not understand Zélie's delicate and sensitive nature. Her father too had faults chiefly a result perhaps of his military training which manifested itself in his rather domineering and dictatorial manner. This description of the Guérin parents is quite incisive:

> They were strongly marked types, both in their own way. They were rough, authoritative, hard to please. Contrary to what one would imagine, there was more kindness in the husband than in the wife, and the children born of their union were the first to feel the effects of this contrast. Moreover, the demanding will of the Guérin couple asserted itself in a fortunate way in their concern for moral integrity and religious fidelity. Great would be the influence of this in the education of their children.[20]

An inveterate letter writer, Zélie[21] once confessed to her brother: "I have never had pleasure in my life, no, nothing that can be called pleasure. My childhood and youth were as sad as a winding sheet [shroud], because if our mother spoiled you [Isidore], she was much too severe with me as you know. Good, as she was, she did not know how to treat me, and I suffered much in my heart."[22] Céline later in life recalled memories of her mother and grandmother:

---

19 Laveille, *op. cit.*, p. 373.
20 Quoted from the *Summarium* (II, 91) which is from the cause for Zélie's beatification as recorded in DeMeester (Editor), *Saint Thérèse of Lisieux: Her Life, Times, and Teaching*, p. 12. See *Zélie et Louis Martin: Correspondance Familiale* (1863–1885), p. 394.
21 She has written some 218 letters, most of them to her sister-in-law (93) and to her brother (56).
22 CF 15, Letter from Zélie to her brother Isidore dated November 7, 1865.

Her mother [Zélie's], a woman of strong faith, but rather too austere, did not understand her [Zélie] and treated her highly-sensitive nature too harshly, which caused her to write, later on, that her youth was "as sad as a winding-sheet." A single detail shows us the picture: though she would have given anything for it when she was a child, Zélie never had a doll, even the smallest one. She suffered from frequent headaches, and this added to the painful atmosphere.[23]

The Guérin parents nonetheless reared their children in an atmosphere of piety and faith. They sent their two daughters as day pupils to the boarding school of the Perpetual Adoration (*Dames de l'Adoration*) in Alençon run by the Sisters of the Sacred Hearts of Picpus.[24] Their brother Isidore, ten years younger than Zélie, spent his early school years at the Lycée. Zélie proved to be an excellent student in school. Years later, in one of her letters to her brother who had just received his bachelor of science degree in Paris, mildly chiding him on the possibility that he would tease her on her writing style, reminded him of her academic accomplishments: "Still I won the first prize for style [in French composition]. Out of eleven compositions I won ten times the first prize and besides I was placed in the first division and in the upper class...."[25]

In this profoundly religious environment, the girls developed further and more deeply their religious inclinations. Both girls eventually expressed their desire to become nuns. Only Marie-Louise succeeded in becoming one. She was admitted into the Visitation Order assuming the name Sister Mary Dosithée (Dorothy) and lived her religious life as a teacher in Le Mans for almost twenty years until her death in 1877 of the same disease, tuberculosis, that took her saintly niece's life.

Zélie too sought admission to a convent—the Daughters of Charity of St. Vincent de Paul—at the General Hospital in Alençon but was not accepted. The very kind and motherly superior believed she had a calling to be a mother rather than a nun. Her evaluation greatly disappointed Zélie, but she made this little prayer when she was convinced the superior was correct: "My God, since I am not worthy to be Your Spouse like my sister, I shall enter the married state to accomplish Your holy will. I beg You then, let me have many children, and may they all be consecrated to You, my God."[26] Her wish came true for all five of her daughters became nuns and one even a saint.

Zélie decided to acquire an occupation while waiting for marriage. One day an interior voice suddenly and unexpectedly spoke to her on December 8, 1851, telling her to "undertake the making of Point d'Alençon lace."[27] She took this as a sign from God, thereupon she entered a professional school of lacemaking in Alençon. By 1853 she had mastered this delicate and intricate art so well that she established in her own home the center of a lace business. She employed

---

23 Sister Geneviève, *The Mother of the Little Flower*, p. 1.
24 Named after Rue Picpus in Paris where the first houses of the order were purchased in 1805 by the founder, Father Coudrin.
25 Translation by the author of a portion of a letter (CF3) Zélie wrote to her brother on Nov. 12, 1863.
26 Sister Geneviève, *op. cit.*, p. 2.
27 Ibid.

a number of ladies who did the lace work basically in their own homes and brought their creations to Zélie who put the pieces together. Her sister, not yet a nun, under the advice of their mother, managed the whole operation. For a while she ran her center as an independent enterprise. But then she sought connections in Paris where she was successful in becoming an important client of the prestigious Maison Pigache.[28] At the industrial Exposition in Alençon,[29] her products were highly acclaimed for their beauty and "richness of designs."

Meanwhile, back at the lacemaking school, Louis Martin's mother, also a student there, noticed and admired Zélie's extraordinary personal characteristics and imagined that she would make an ideal wife for her thirty-five-year-old son, Louis. Purely by chance, Zélie, then twenty-seven, while crossing the bridge of St. Leonard in Alençon, passed a handsome young man who happened to be Louis Martin. They did not speak to each other but Zélie heard that familiar interior voice speak to her again, this time saying, "That is he whom I have prepared for you."[30] Indeed he was, for shortly after they were formally introduced and amazingly after only three months they were married on July 13, 1858, at midnight (a custom then) in the church of Notre Dame in Alençon.

Louis and Zélie were kindred spirits. First of all he too was the son of a retired army captain. He was, however, born eight years before her in Bordeaux on August 22, 1823. Like her, he longed for the religious life and applied for admission to the Order of the Great St. Bernard in Switzerland. The only requirement he lacked was knowledge of Latin; therefore, he returned home and obtained a tutor to instruct him in the language. The task of learning Latin proved difficult and he did not progress satisfactorily. He, therefore, returned to his watch-making studies in Paris and eventually opened a jewelry shop at his home at 15 (later 23) rue de Pont Neuf in Alençon. He believed this decision was a sign from God that he should not pursue a religious vocation.

The married couple decided they would live together in the virginal state; but in the meantime they took a little boy into their home to take care of for a while. After serious counseling from their confessor, they decided to serve God in the family life and have many children of their own whom they could offer to God, especially with a boy child who would become a priest.[31]

Zélie was born to be a mother. One time she stated, "I am madly fond of children. It is such sweet work to take care of babies."[32] Another time she wrote:

> "We lived only for them; they were all our happiness and outside of them we desired no other. For their sakes, nothing gave us trouble; the world meant nothing without them. For myself they compensated for everything. And so I desired to have many of them in order to present them to Heaven.[33]

---

28 Redmond, *Louis and Zélie Martin*, p. 23.
29 De Meester, *Saint Thérèse of Lisieux: Her Life, Times, and Teaching*, p. 14.
30 Ibid., p. 3.
31 Ibid., p. 5.
32 Ibid., p. 6.
33 Sister Geneviève, *op. cit.*, p. 9.

Mme. Martin was not only an ideal wife, a superb mother, an excellent housekeeper, but an astute business woman. The task of managing a house with many children and a maid was enormous, yet she attended the daily 5:30 Mass, prepared all the meals, managed her lace business, and was the last to retire for the night. Louis, to be sure, did lend his assistance as much as he could. Pauline, when she was Mother Agnès, testified at the Diocesan Process of her sister Thérèse about the remarkable qualities of her mother and her father:

> It always seemed to me that my parents were saints. We were filled with respect and admiration for them. At times I would ask myself if it were possible to find their equals on earth. I could not see their likeness anywhere around me.
>
> Our mother was the personification of abnegation, being gifted with great courage, and a character of extraordinary energy. She had a heart which was very sensitive and very generous, always turned toward God, in Whom she had a truly heroic trust.[34]

Louis and Zélie were blessed with nine children: four died young, five lived to maturity, all of whom became nuns—and one a saint:

1. **Marie** (1860–1940) became a Carmelite—Sister Marie of the Sacred Heart—and died at 80.
2. **Pauline** (1861–1951) became a Carmelite—Mother Agnès of Jesus—and died at 90.
3. **Léonie** (1863–1941) became a Visantine—Sister Françoise-Thérèse—and died at 78.
4. **Hélène** (1864–1870) lived five years and four months.
5. **Joseph-Louis** (1866–1867) lived six months.
6. **Joseph-Jean Baptiste** (1867–1868) lived eight months.
7. **Céline** (1869–1959) became a Carmelite—Sister Geneviève of the Holy Face—and died at 90.
8. **Thérèse** (1873–1897) became a Carmelite—Sister Thérèse of the Child Jesus and the Holy Face—and died at 24.

Joy was unbounded at the birth of each child. On the other hand, their sorrow was intense with the death of four of their young children. Notwithstanding this, their courage and abandonment to the will of God were exceptional. Zélie's philosophical attitude toward all these trials was succinctly expressed in a letter she wrote to her sister-in-law: "Everyone in the world has troubles; the happiest are only the least unfortunate. The simplest and the wisest thing in all cases is to submit to God's will, and to prepare in advance to bear one's cross as bravely as possible."[35]

Of all the Martin children, only Léonie, their third child, gave the Martins trouble. She did not possess the same extraordinary intellectual and personality traits as her other daughters, which she explained in one of her letters to

---
34 Foley, *Zelie Martin: Mother of St. Thérèse*, p. 35.
35 Letter to Mme. Guérin on February 12, 1870.

Pauline: "She is less privileged than you in natural gifts, but in spite of that, she possesses a heart desirous of loving and being loved. It is only a mother who can continually show her the love that she needs, and can follow her closely enough to do her constant good."[36] Two years before this, Zélie wrote: "I am not dissatisfied with Léonie. If we could overcome her stubbornness, and make her will more flexible, she would become a good, devout girl who would be afraid of nothing."[37]

One admonition Zélie stressed with her girls was for them to become saints. This frequent exhortation was accomplished, indeed, by Thérèse, and in fact by Zélie and Louis themselves who have been beatified and are on the way to canonization: "You must serve the good God faithfully my dear girls, and beg to be, one day, in the number of those saints whose feast we celebrate today."[38]

Sixty-nine days after Thérèse was born she was sent to the countryside hamlet of Semallé to be nursed by Rose Taillé for a year since Zélie was not able to do so ever since the birth of her fourth child. She returned home a healthy baby a little over a year later. A few years after, Thérèse made a startling and unexpected comment. Zélie said that one day Thérèse flung her arms around her and said, "Oh, how I wish you would die, my poor little mother." Shocked, she reproached Thérèse for this remark to which Thérèse responded: "But it is that you may go to heaven, since you say we must die to go there." Zélie added this note to her letter, "She expresses the same wish to her father in the fervor of her love for him."[39]

Zélie reported to Pauline another quite amusing conversation between mother and daughter:

> Little Thérèse asked me the other day if she would go to heaven. I told her "Yes if she were good." She answered: "Yes, but if I'm not good, I'll go to hell. But I know what I will do. I will fly to you in heaven, and what will God be able to do to take me away? You will be holding me so tightly in your arms!" I could see in her eyes that she was really convinced that God could do nothing to her if she were in her mother's arms.[40]

The year before, in November 1875, when Thérèse was two, Zélie told Pauline about a childish habit Thérèse had: "She will not climb the stairs alone, but cries at each step: 'Mama, Mama!' If I forget to say: 'Yes, my child,' she stops and won't go any further."[41]

Both parents as well as the older sisters were completely enchanted with the baby of the family, Thérèse, though the family did not believe they spoiled her. Zélie said once, "How glad I am to have her. I believe I love her more than all the others, doubtless because she is the youngest.... Oh, how I should grieve

---

36 June 25, 1877.
37 Letter from Zélie to Mme. Guérin in 1875.
38 Letter dated Nov. 1, 1873 (All Saints Day), from Zélie to Marie and Pauline away at school in Le Mans.
39 Zélie to Pauline, December 5, 1875.
40 Letter of Mme. Martin to Pauline, October 29, 1876, CF 170.
41 From footnote 6 on p. 18 in *Story of a Soul*, chapter I.

were I to lose this child! And my husband adores her.... It is unbelievable all the sacrifices he makes for her by day and by night."[42]

Sadly, by 1876 Zélie developed cancer of the breast which she believed was the result of a childhood injury. She delayed seeing a doctor for some time and when she did he diagnosed it as incurable. The news struck a terrible blow to Louis and the children. Eventually, eleven weeks before she died, she went with her three oldest daughters on a pilgrimage to Lourdes to pray for a cure. Before she went she wrote a letter to her sister-in-law, Mme. Guérin: "If the good God wills to cure me, I shall be very happy, for in the depths of my heart I desire to live; it is a sacrifice to leave my husband and my children. But, on the other hand, I repeat: 'If I am not cured, it will be because it is better for them that I die.'"[43]

After a long period of suffering, she died in her forty-fifth year at 1:00 A.M. on August 28, 1877, in a state of calm resignation. Thérèse recorded in her autobiography the memory of this tragic loss and tells how it affected her life:

> The details of my Mother's illness are still present to me and I recall especially the last weeks she spent on earth.... The touching ceremony of the last anointing is also deeply impressed on my mind. I can still see the spot where I was by Céline's side. All five of us were lined up according to age, and Papa was there too, sobbing.
>
> The day of Mamma's departure or the day after, Papa took me in his arms and said: "Come, kiss your little Mother for the last time." Without a word I placed my lips on her forehead. I don't recall having cried very much, neither did I speak to anyone about the feelings I experienced. I looked and listened in silence. No one had any time to pay any attention to me, and I saw many things they would have hidden from me. For instance, once I was standing before the lid of the coffin which had been placed upright in the hall. I stopped for a long time gazing at it. Though I'd never seen one before, I understood what it was. I was so little that in spite of Mamma's small stature, I had to *raise* my head to take in its full height. It appeared *large* and *dismal*.
>
> I must admit, Mother [Agnès, her sister], my happy disposition completely changed after Mamma's death. I, once so full of life, became timid and retiring, sensitive to an excessive degree. One look was enough to reduce me to tears, and the only way I was content was to be left alone completely. I could not bear the company of strangers and found my joy only within the intimacy of the family.[44]

Zélie and Louis wanted all their children to be consecrated to God and hopefully become saints. She, too, had the same desire for herself: "I often say during the day: 'My God, how I wish I were a saint!' But then I do not accomplish the works of a saint."[45] Months later she stated humbly in a letter: "I want to become a saint; it will not be easy at all. I have a lot of wood to chop [strenuous

---

42 Piat, *op. cit.*, p. 205.
43 In a letter from Zélie to her sister-in-law, February 20, 1877, CF 189.
44 *Story of a Soul*, chapter II, pp. 33–34.
45 Letter to Pauline on February 26, 1876, CF 154.

work] and it is as hard as stone. I should have started sooner, while it was not so difficult; but, in any case, 'better late than never.'"[46]

All the Martin offspring who lived to adulthood became nuns and lived holy and exemplary lives. Thérèse, however, won the crown of sainthood and was even declared a Doctor of the Church. Much of the credit goes to her parents who proved to be such superb models of Christian spouses and parents that their causes for sainthood were drafted between 1957 and 1960. At first there were two separate causes: one for Louis and the other for Zélie Martin, but soon, however, they were considered as one single cause. On May 2, 1991, two volumes on the "Position on the Heroic Virtues (the *positio*)" were given to the Congregation for the Causes of Saints (CCS), approved, and eventually presented to the pope who highly endorsed their cause. Louis and Zélie Martin were declared "Venerable" on March 26, 1994, by Pope John Paul II. The authentication of one miracle through the intercession of Louis and Zélie was obtained. Beatification took place on October 19, 2008, in Lisieux under the authoritative approval of Pope Benedict XVI. The last step is canonization which requires an additional miracle.[47]

The official prayer, listed below, for beatification of Zélie Martin and for graces through her intercession was circulated worldwide:

> God, our Father, in return for her simplicity and childlike confidence in You, You glorified Your servant Thérèse of the Child Jesus. Grant, in answer to our prayer that her mother, Zélie Martin, be proposed by Your Church as a model of those virtues which she practiced with such a spirit of faith in all the duties and difficulties of family life. We ask You to manifest her power with You by granting us heavenly favors. Amen.

---

46 Letter to Marie and Pauline dated November 1, 1873, CF 110.
47 Redmond, *op. cit.*, p. 275.

C. Children

1. **MARIE-LOUISE MARTIN: "MARIE" (SISTER MARIE OF THE SACRED HEART)** *Oldest sister and godmother of Thérèse*
2. **MARIE-PAULINE MARTIN: "PAULINE" (MOTHER AGNÈS OF JESUS)** *The "little Mother" of the Little Flower*
3. **MARIE-LÉONIE MARTIN: "LÉONIE" (SISTER FRANCES THÉRÈSE)** *The least gifted and emotionally troubled sister*
4. **MARIE-HÉLÈNE MARTIN: "HÉLÈNE"** *The first Martin child to die, at six*
5. **MARIE-JOSEPH-LOUIS MARTIN: "JOSEPH"** *The first son who died in infancy*
6. **MARIE-JOSEPH-JEAN-BAPTISTE MARTIN: "JOSEPH"** *The second son who died in infancy*
7. **MARIE-CÉLINE MARTIN: "CÉLINE" (SISTER GENEVIÈVE OF THE HOLY FACE)** *Thérèse called her "The sweet echo of my soul"*
8. **MARIE-MÉLANIE-THÉRÈSE MARTIN: "MÉLANIE"** *The third Martin child who died in infancy*
9. **MARIE-FRANÇOISE-THÉRÈSE: "THÉRÈSE" (SISTER THÉRÈSE OF THE CHILD JESUS AND OF THE HOLY FACE)** *Canonized in 1925 (See Chapter 1. A for her biography)*

---

1. **MARIE-LOUISE MARTIN—"MARIE" (1860–1940)**
   (SISTER MARIE OF THE SACRED HEART—SŒUR MARIE DE SACRÉ-CŒUR)
   Oldest sister and godmother of Thérèse

MARIE-LOUISE MARIE, THIRTEEN YEARS OLDER THAN THÉRÈSE, PLAYED A most important part in Thérèse's spiritual and educational formation. She was the very first child born of Louis and Zélie Martin in Alençon on February 22, 1860. On the same day she was baptized in the church of St. Pierre-de-Montsort. Louis said to the curate that: "It is the first time that you have seen me here for a baptism but it will not be the last!"[1] Indeed it wasn't, for seven more children were baptized there. The ninth and last child, Thérèse, however, received this sacrament at the church of Notre-Dame not far away from the family home. Zélie informed her close and much loved sister-in-law, Céline Guérin, years later about this first birth: "I was very fortunate when I raised my firstborn. She had such good health. I was too proud. The good God did not want that this last. All the other children I had after were difficult to rear and gave me many worries."[2]

---

[1] Piat, *op. cit.*, p. 51.
[2] From CF 32, an excerpt from Zélie's letter to her sister-in-law dated May 1868 as freely translated by the author.

C. Children 123

Plate 5

The Sisters of St. Thérèse

BEFORE ENTERING CONVENT | AS A NUN

A. Marie Martin

B. Sr. Marie of the Sacred Heart

C. Pauline Martin

D. Mother Agnès of Jesus

E. Léonie Martin

F. Sr. Frances Thérèse

G. Céline Martin

H. Sr. Geneviève of the Holy Face

The Martin children were brought up in a deeply religious household. Their parents taught them to love God above all. Both parents were themselves instilled with a solid faith that came as a result of their own heritage and religious family traditions. In fact, they each attempted religious life well before they were married but providentially they were unsuccessful. Inbred in each of the Martin children was a firm belief in the value of suffering, sacrifice, and self-denial. They were assured that each act of self-denial merited for them a new "pearl in a crown" they would inherit in heaven.

Marie exhibited early on characteristics that seemed to continue throughout her life. One was a spirit of independence. As a child she displayed this trait with the maid Louise who was at times demanding and officious with the girls under her charge. Marie would have none of this and once told her boldly, "Leave me alone, Louise, I am quite free!" As a result, the maid gave her the nickname "I-Am-Quite-Free."[3]

Another interesting and unique trait the young Marie showed is clear in this quotation from a note she wrote to her sister Pauline:

> [I] never liked to bow to persons of our acquaintance. It humiliated me to bow.... Convinced that politeness and bowing were necessary before others would love me, I said to myself, "It is decidedly unpleasant to try to make others love me. No, I'll not so demean myself!" And I said to mother: "I don't care if other people do not love me; if you love me, that is enough."[4]

Marie Martin's Uncle Guérin wrote a rather candid word portrait of her in a letter dated June 21, 1900, when Marie had been a nun for fourteen years. In it he describes her personality which did not appear to be vastly different from the way it was when she was young. Because of her close and loving relationship with him and his wife, he often called her his daughter:

> You are my oldest daughter, my incorrigible child [*enfant terrible*], whose heart I've known for forty years.... It's very nice to return a little affection to such a heart that expands so easily, that explodes like a bomb to be divided into little particles so as to be lavished on everyone. You are truly the perfect model of devotion and affection.... You have your whims, your outbursts, but we don't love you any less for it because we know that you love.[5]

When Marie was eight and a half years old, she and her sister Pauline, then seven, were sent to Le Mans in October 1868 to attend the boarding school run by the Visitation nuns. Here their aunt, their mother's sister, Sister Mary Dosithée, was a teacher. This separation from the family and especially their parents was a traumatic experience for both. Apparently the reason for their education far from home under the care of their teaching aunt was motivated by the overpowering situation at home resulting from the deaths of two children and the exhaustive maternal concerns of a not-too-well Zélie. Maria is quoted as saying decades later:

---

3 Mother Agnès, *Marie, Sister of St. Thérèse*, p. 15.
4 Ibid., p. 16.
5 As quoted in Kenney (trans.), *The Poetry of Saint Thérèse of Lisieux*, p. 54.

> Indeed, it would be impossible for me to say how much I suffered in being separated from my parents.... Ah, had it not been for my aunt whom I did not wish to grieve, I would never have remained seven years behind a grill, for at that time I had no vocation to live behind grills.... Now that He [Jesus] has drawn me, I find myself behind the grill, the happiest of creatures. I find myself in possession of true liberty. Ah, it is now that I can really say, "I am quite free!"[6]

Though Marie and Pauline loved the Visitation school, they admitted that if they were not together they would not have endured. They went home only for Christmas, Easter, and other long holidays. Marie was an excellent student and received awards and honors for her scholarly accomplishments. She spent seven years at the school during which time she received her First Communion and Thérèse was born. She graduated in 1875 at the age of fifteen-and-a-half.

Interestingly, because of her association and friendship with girls of nobility who attended this prestigious school, she for a while acquired some of their foibles and supercilious attitudes. Her mother recounted to her daughter Pauline Marie's ambitions which fortunately did not last too long:

> There is Marie dreaming of going to live in a fine house, opposite the Poor Clares, in the Rue de la Demi-Lune. She talked about it all yesterday evening; one would have thought it was Heaven. Unfortunately, her desires cannot be realized. We must stay where we are; not for all her life, but for my part I shall leave this house only at my death. Although your sister has so little worldliness about her, she is never content where she is. She is ambitious for something better; she must have beautiful rooms, spacious and well furnished.... When she has something different, perhaps she will feel its insufficiency still more.[7]

Immediately upon returning home, Marie became immersed in the daily routine and obligations of family life, especially with the care of her younger siblings—Céline (six) and baby Thérèse (two). Soon she would be approaching marriageable age and when the subject was mentioned, she would have none of it. Nor did she contemplate a religious vocation; in fact, she opposed any thoughts of it.

The year 1877 turned out to be a difficult one for Marie and the entire family. Their beloved aunt, Sister Mary Dosithée, died on February 2, their mother passed away on August 28, and the remaining Martin family moved to Lisieux on November 15. At this time Marie was seventeen-and-a-half years old and Thérèse four. For the next nine years Marie, and for a while Pauline, took charge of the Martin household with their father's supervision and served admirably as mother-substitute and teacher. Thérèse tells us in her life's story about her sister Marie at this time:

> I was very fond of my *godmother*. Without appearing to do so, I paid close attention to what was said and done around me. It seems to me I was judging things then as I do now. I was listening carefully to what Marie was teaching Céline in order to do what Céline did. After Marie came out of the Visitation,

---

6 Ibid., pp. 19–20.
7 Letter of January 16, 1876 (CF 150) as given in Wust, *op. cit.*, p. 82.

to obtain permission to go into the room where she was giving Céline her lessons, I was very good and did everything she wanted. She gave me a lot of gifts, and in spite of their insignificant value these pleased me a lot.[8]

In 1881 Thérèse, then eight, became a day-boarder at the Benedictine Abbey school in Lisieux. The next year Pauline left to become a Carmelite (October 2, 1882) at the Lisieux Carmel leaving Marie at the age of twenty-two to conduct the household affairs by herself. Marie at this juncture in her life was still not certain about her future vocation. An acquaintance told her of a saintly Jesuit priest, Father Pichon, whom she eventually met in 1882 and who became her spiritual director. In the confessional one time, this rather amusing conversation ensued:

> After putting a few questions to me, he asked if I wanted to be a religious, to which I replied, "No, Father."
> "Do you wish to get married, then?" Again, I said, "Oh no, Father!"
> "But what do you want to do—be an old maid?" And even more emphatically I answered, "Oh, by no means!"[9]

For the next four years Marie remained a laywoman taking care of the Martin household.

In March of 1883, Thérèse became seriously ill with a strange uncertain malady at the home of the Guérins where she was staying while her father and older sisters were in Paris attending, at the invitation of Father Pichon, the Easter Triduum given at the Gesù, a Jesuit church. Thérèse recorded the story of her sickness in her autobiography:

> When Papa returned from Paris with my older sisters, Aimee [the Guérins' cook] met them at the door with such a sad face that Marie believed I had died.... Ah! How she [Marie] suffered because of me, and how grateful I am to her for the care she lavished upon me with such unselfishness. Her heart dictated what was necessary for me and really a *mother's* heart is more *discerning* than a doctor's, for it knows how to *guess at* what is suitable for its child's sickness.
> Poor Marie was obliged to come and live at Uncle's because it was impossible to bring me back at the time to Les Buissonnets.[10]

When Thérèse recovered slightly, she was brought home. For a total of seven weeks, attacks of this sickness plagued her. On Pentecost Sunday, May 13, 1883, she was suddenly cured which she attributed to Marie's fervent prayers to the Blessed Virgin:

> Marie was always by my bedside, taking care of me and consoling me with a mother's tenderness. Never did she show the slightest sign of annoyance, and still I gave her a lot of trouble, not even allowing her to be away from me....
> A miracle was necessary and it was Our Lady of Victories who worked it.... Marie finally returned [to the sick room from the garden]. I saw her

---
8 *Story of a Soul*, chapter I, p. 20.
9 Mother Agnès, *op. cit.*, p. 30.
10 *Story of a Soul*, chapter III, p. 61.

enter, but I cannot say I recognized her and continued to call her in a louder tone: "Mamma." I was suffering very much from this forced and inexplicable struggle and Marie was suffering perhaps even more than I. After some futile attempts to show me she was by my side, Marie knelt down near my bed with Léonie and Céline. Turning to [the statue of] the Blessed Virgin and praying with the fervor of a mother begging for the life of her child, *Marie obtained what she wanted....* The Blessed Virgin smiled at me.... Marie who was looking down at me lovingly ... seemed moved and appeared to surmise the favor the Blessed Virgin had given me. Ah! it was really to her, to her touching prayers that I owed the grace of the Queen of heaven's *smile.* Seeing my gaze fixed on the Blessed Virgin, she cried out: "Thérèse is cured!"[11]

Another milestone in Thérèse's life was her First Communion on May 8, 1884, for which Marie helped prepare her. Pauline, by now two years in the Carmelite monastery, also did her share by giving Thérèse a little notebook three months before the great event which Thérèse followed diligently:

> [I] sat on her [Marie's] lap and listened *eagerly* to everything she said to me. It seemed to me her *large* and *generous* heart passed into my own. Just as famous warriors taught their children the art of war, so Marie spoke to me about life's *struggles* and of the palm given to the victors. She spoke also about the eternal riches that one can so easily amass each day, and what a misfortune it was to pass by without so much as stretching forth one's hand to take them. She explained the way of becoming holy through fidelity in little things; furthermore, she gave me a little leaflet call "Renunciation" [by Father Pichon] and I meditated upon this with delight.
> Ah! how eloquent my dear godmother was!...
> At this time in my life nobody had ever taught me how to make mental prayer, and yet I had a great desire to make it. Marie, finding me pious enough, allowed me to make only my vocal prayers.[12]

Thérèse freely reveals a winsome little incident connected with her preparations for Communion while she was a boarder for four days at the Benedictine Abbey school:

> In the morning, I found it very nice to see all the students getting up so early and doing the same as they; but I was not yet accustomed to taking care of myself. Marie was not there to comb and curl my hair, and so I was obliged to go and timidly offer my comb to the mistress in charge of the dressing rooms. She laughed at seeing a big girl of eleven not knowing how to take care of herself, and still she combed my hair but not as gently as Marie. I didn't dare cry, which happened every day under the gentle hand of godmother.[13]

A profoundly moving and memorable event in Thérèse's life was indeed her First Communion and so was the following day. "The day after my First Communion was still beautiful, but it was tinged with a certain melancholy. The

---

11 Ibid., chapter IV, pp. 63–66.
12 Ibid., p. 74.
13 Ibid., p. 75.

beautiful dress Marie had bought me, all the gifts I had received did not satisfy my heart. Jesus only could do this, and I longed for the moment when I could receive Him a second time.[14]

For two years Father Pichon was Marie's spiritual advisor and close friend of the Martin family. Then a great disappointment hit them. Father Pichon's long desire to become a missionary came to fruition when on October 4, 1884, he left for Canada. Marie and her father saw him off at Le Havre. On his return two years later, they met him by chance in Paris after mixed-up directions misled them on a frantically circuitous search to Calais and Douvres.

During his sojourn in Canada, Father Pichon and Marie maintained a steady correspondence, especially on Marie's part, for she sent him scores of letters, none of which Father Pichon kept, just as he did not retain, unfortunately, any of Thérèse's priceless letters to him. In his letters to Marie there was an undercurrent of urgings for her to become a nun—a Carmelite in fact. He even chose a name for her—Sister Marie of the Sacred Heart (his nickname for her was "Lion of Jesus").

She finally made up her mind, told her saddened father, and her incredulous uncle and aunt: "They were absolutely astonished. I, the independent one! I who had always had an air of not being able to endure convents! I was going to become a nun! They could not recover from their astonishment."[15] The date chosen for her entrance into the Lisieux Carmel was October 15, 1886. Because he was ill with jaundice, Father Pichon was unable to escort her to the cloister door as he planned. Happily he did manage to be present when she received the habit on March 19, 1887, and to preach the sermon. Many years later she commented about this day to her sister Pauline:

> It was especially during the days that followed my reception of the habit that I best appreciated my good fortune. Every morning, it seemed, I put on a garment of liberty, and it was also a festive garment to me. Even as when I was a child, I could say, "I am quite free."... My happiness was unbelievable![16]

About her succeeding years in Carmel she said: "I have found Jesus within these four walls and, in finding Him, I have found heaven! Yes, it is here that I have passed the happiest days of my life."[17]

For the third time, Thérèse, now thirteen, was left without a mother figure. She began then to focus her future dreams toward Carmel. The seventeen-year-old Céline assumed charge of the Martin home. Léonie, though older, was experiencing her own struggles concerning her vocational ambitions and could not be relied upon to assume any serious responsibilities at home. Later that year on October 12, Céline chose Father Pichon to be her spiritual director and became eventually his favorite Martin sister.

---

14 Ibid., p. 79.
15 Mother Agnès, *op. cit.*, p. 32.
16 Ibid., p. 34.
17 Ibid., p. 33.

C. Children

On April 9, 1888, Thérèse followed her two sisters, Pauline and Marie, into the cloistered habitat of Carmel and for a very short time Thérèse and Marie were novices together. Sister Marie was her "angel" during her novitiate. Marie had this to say about Thérèse's entrance at the age of fifteen:

> I cannot say that I was happy when I saw her cross the threshold of the cloister. No, because I was thinking of our father who was going to be deprived of his treasure. But she! What a heavenly creature! And how my little Thérèse had grown! Such things are hard to judge through the parlor grill. Yes, how she had grown, and beautiful she was! The good God had endowed her with all graces.[18]

Marie spent the next nine years under the same monastic roof with Thérèse, participating in the same conventual life and for nearly seven of those years painfully enduring from afar the dreadful progression of their father's humiliating affliction. On the other hand, there was happiness, love, and communion with God that they experienced and shared. Here is a delightfully down-to-earth word sketch written by Sister Marie of the Angels (novice mistress) of Sister Marie of the Sacred Heart that one would not generally conjure up as being representative of a contemplative nun:

> She is a soul of faith, with the humility that knows no touchiness. As a flower gardener, her favorite get-up is a rustic canvas apron, large hobnailed shoes, a spade, a rake, a wheelbarrow, a watering can, and pruning shears. Her gardening, however, does not prevent her from being marvelously successful at very delicate pieces of needlework.[19]

Thérèse wrote at least eighteen letters to Marie and when she was in the convent composed six poems for her or at her request: numbers 5, 6, 9, 23, 33, and 54 (Thérèse's swan song). They are among the most beautiful and spiritual Thérèse wrote. In the important poem "Prayer of a Child of a Saint" (Pri 8), Thérèse gives a brief affectionate portrait of each daughter of their recently deceased father. Here is stanza 2 about Marie:

> Remember your beloved Marie,
> Your eldest daughter, the dearest to your heart.
> Remember that she filled your life
> With her love, charm, and happiness....
> For God you gave up her sweet presence,
> And you blessed the hand that offered suffering to you....
> O! your Diamond
> Always more sparkling
> Remember!...

A clear revelation of Marie's independent character displayed itself when Thérèse asked her if she would like to say the prayer she composed (Pri 6), "Act of Oblation to Merciful Love: Offering of myself as a Victim of Holocaust to

---

18 Ibid., p. 35.
19 De Meester, *Saint Thérèse of Lisieux*, p. 112.

God's Merciful Love." Marie's first response was: "Certainly not. I am not going to offer myself as a victim; God would take me at my word, and suffering frightens me too much. In the first place, this word 'victim' displeases me very much." [20] After Thérèse explained that she would not be offering herself to God's justice but to his love, Marie gave in and was the third, after Thérèse and Céline, to make this offering.

In reading many of the letters exchanged between the godmother (Marie) and her goddaughter (Thérèse), one finds an exquisite and profound exegesis of Thérèse's "little way of spiritual childhood" and other facets of her spirituality. One of Sister Marie's letters explains her feelings well:

> Dear little Sister, I have read your pages burning with love for Jesus. Your little godmother is very happy to possess this treasure and very grateful to her dear little girl who has revealed the secrets of her soul in this way. Oh! What should I say about these lines marked with the seal of love? [21]

Finally, at the end of December 1894, Marie suggested to her Carmelite blood sisters that Thérèse write down memories of her childhood which she did only because of obedience to her other sister Pauline, the prioress at the time, who then ordered her to do so. Thus Thérèse wrote her incomparable *Story of a Soul*. The second of the three manuscripts (Ms B)—a gem among all Thérèse's writings in which she proclaims, "MY VOCATION IS LOVE!" was written to and for Marie. It came about this way:

> I am writing to you, not because I have something to say to you but to get something from you, from you who are so close to God, from you who are His privileged little spouse, to whom He confides His secrets. The secrets of Jesus to Thérèse are sweet, and I want to hear them once again. Write me a short note. This is perhaps your last retreat....[22]

After reading it, Marie, very moved by it all, wrote back to Thérèse:

> Dear little Sister, I have read your pages burning with love for Jesus. Your little godmother is *very happy* to posses this treasure and very grateful to her dear little girl who has revealed the secrets of her soul in this way. Oh! What should I say about these lines marked with the seal of love?... Oh! I wanted to cry when I read these lines that are not from earth but an echo from the Heart of God.... Do you want me to tell you? Well, you are possessed by God... absolutely possessed, just as the wicked are possessed by the devil.
>
> I would like to be possessed, too, by the good Jesus. However, I love you so much that I rejoice when seeing you are more privileged than I am.[23]

Marie was present in the infirmary where Thérèse was suffering in the last drawn-out stages of the disease that took her life. Because of various reasons,

---

20 From the *Notebook of Sister Marie of the Incarnation*, June 6, 1934, p. 137, as quoted in footnote 6 of LC 170, the letter from Thérèse to Sister Marie of the Sacred Heart, September 17, 1896.
21 Letter from Sister Marie of the Sacred Heart to Thérèse, LC 170, September 17, 1896.
22 Letter from Sister Marie of the Sacred Heart to Thérèse, LC 169, September 13, 1896.
23 Letter from Sister Marie of the Sacred Heart to Thérèse, LC 170, September 17, 1896.

however, Marie was not there as often as her other sisters. Still, she jotted down, as the others did, some of Thérèse's last perceptive words. As early as July 13, 1897, she recorded this prophetic statement:

> "If you only knew the projects I'll carry out, the things I shall do when I'm in heaven.... I will begin my mission."
>
> "What are your projects?" I [Marie] asked.
>
> "Projects such as coming back with my sisters, and going over there to help the missionaries, and then preventing little pagans from dying before being baptized."

After Thérèse's death (a scene Marie witnessed), the knowledge of Thérèse's holiness began to be known especially after the publication of *Story of a Soul*. The meteoric rise in her popularity greatly affected the Carmel and all the Martin sisters. The Carmel was inundated with letters requesting prayers, mementos, and even relics. Many reported blessings received, conversions, and miracles attributed to Thérèse—a "shower of roses" as some called them. Marie read thousands of these messages. The other nuns were also involved with matters connected with Thérèse and eventually with the cause for her beatification and canonization.

When Marie was interrogated by the Canonical Process as to why she thought her sister should be beatified, she replied:

> I desire it because I think the good God desires it and will be glorified by it....
>
> Sister Thérèse of the Child Jesus teaches us to go to Him with confidence and love....
>
> Therefore I regard Sister Thérèse of the Child Jesus as the apostle, the chosen messenger of the Lord in these times, who is to announce to all the infinite Love He has for us.[24]

The one and only reunion of the four remaining Martin sisters when they were nuns took place in 1915 at the Lisieux monastery when they were all interviewed by the legates of the Holy See as witnesses to the virtues of Thérèse:

> We were seated together, all four of us, on the flight of steps near the infirmary. The sky was blue and cloudless. In a moment, time vanished before me: our childhood, the Buissonnets, all seemed to me a single instant. I saw Léonie a religious, beside us! Past and present were blended in a unique moment. The past was like a flash; I seemed already to live in an eternal present, and I understood eternity which contains all joys in the all-embracing now.[25]

As the years sped by, Marie suffered from rheumatism. By 1929 she had to leave her cell and was confined to the infirmary. This disease persisted causing great pain in her legs and knees. Her feet became swollen and inflamed with sores. During these trying years she always remained serene and stoically accepted this suffering with the same spirit that her saintly sister did. The evening before

---

24 Mother Agnès, *op. cit.*, p. 42.
25 Ibid., p. 36.

she died, her sister Pauline asked her if she feared death. She answered, "Not at all." Her last audible words were, "I love you" as she grasped and kissed her crucifix. She was gazing at the statue of Our Lady of the Smile as death came to her at two o'clock in the morning of January 19, 1940. She is buried in a vault along with her sisters Pauline and Céline in the monastery close to the shrine of her saintly goddaughter.

2. Marie-Pauline Martin—"Pauline" (1861–1951)
(Mother Agnès of Jesus—Mère Agnès de Jésus)
The "little Mother" of the Little Flower

PAULINE MARTIN WHOSE NAME IN RELIGION WAS MOTHER AGNÈS OF JESUS, played a very significant part in the formation and development of the sanctity of her youngest sister Thérèse, now known as St. Thérèse of Lisieux, or as the Americans like to call her, the Little Flower. Their parents were exceptionally holy people who brought up their children with an exquisite attention to love of God, family, and Church. In fact, each parent thought seriously of entering religious life but by Divine Providence their vocations led instead to the married state and to the birth of the "greatest saint of modern times," their youngest daughter Thérèse. In 1994 both parents were declared Venerable, in 2008 they were beatified; and now they are on the way to canonization. There has also been a great deal of interest in the holiness of another daughter, Léonie, who surprisingly caused the greatest amount of anxiety and disturbance in the family because of her emotionally disordered personality. In addition to Thérèse, the other three sisters—Marie, Pauline, and Céline—became Carmelites and lived very holy lives in the same monastery in Lisieux. The example and teaching of Pauline were crucial in the training of her younger sisters, particularly Thérèse. It may be claimed that Thérèse is the masterpiece created by Louis and Zélie, and formed by Pauline.

Marie-Pauline Martin was born in Alençon on September 7, 1861, and baptized in the ancient church of St. Pierre de Montsort. Pauline was the second child in the Martin family, the first being Marie who was born the year before. She was not named after St. Paul, the Apostle of the Gentiles, but after St. Paulinus of Nola (354–431). He, whose feast day is June 22, was born in Bordeaux, the birthplace also of Louis Martin. He often called Pauline "my little Paulinus."[26]

In anticipation of Pauline's birth, Mme. Martin wrote the following. Note the prophetic last statement concerning her own desire for sainthood:

> I begged our Mother in Heaven to give me a little Pauline. I cannot think of it now without laughing, for I was just like a child demanding a doll from its mother, and I went about it the same way. I wanted a Pauline just like the one I have, and I dotted all the i's and crossed all the t's, for fear that the Blessed Virgin might not understand exactly what I wanted. First of all, of course, she had to have a lovely little soul, good material for sanctity, but I also wanted

---
26 Redman, *Louis and Zélie Martin*, p. 38.

her to be very charming. As for that point, she is hardly pretty, but I find her beautiful—and very beautiful. She is just what I wanted.

This year I shall go very early to find the Blessed Virgin; I want to be the first arrival. I shall not ask for any more little daughters, I shall only ask that those she has given me may all be saints and that I may follow close behind them. But they must be very much better than me.[27]

Little Pauline proved to be just the kind of a child Zélie wished for. She loved her parents dearly and her sisters with as much depth. The other eight children included two boys and two girls who died young. Marie, Léonie, Céline, and Thérèse survived to adulthood. When Pauline was seven she and her sister Marie were sent as boarding students to a private school some distance away in Le Mans where their maternal aunt, Sister Marie Dosithée, was a teaching nun in the Visitandine Order. She said of her little niece Pauline that she "is a little jewel; gay as a lark, studious, and doing her little best at everything."[28] Zélie had glowing words to say about Pauline who later in life tells us that "One day Mother was lying down and I was watching her in silence. She took my hands and kissing them said: 'Oh, my Pauline, you are my treasure. I know well that you will be a nun, and that you will become a saint: I am not worthy to have a daughter like you, you are my glory and my happiness.'"[29]

At sixteen, a few weeks before Mme. Martin died in August of 1877, Pauline left school to be home with her dying mother. Thérèse, addressing Pauline, writes in quite a plaintive mode about their mother's death:

> The day the Church blessed the mortal remains of our dear Mother, now in heaven, God willed to give me another mother on earth. He willed that I also choose her freely. All five of us [Marie, Pauline, Léonie, Céline, and Thérèse] were gathered together, looking at each other sadly. Louise [the maid] was there too, and, seeing Céline and me, she said: "Poor little things, you have no mother any more!" Céline threw her arms around Marie saying: "Well, you will be my Mamma!" Accustomed to following Céline's example, I turned instead to you, Mother, and as though the future had torn aside its veil, I threw myself into your arms, crying: "Well, as for me, it's Pauline who will be my Mamma!"[30]

And that is exactly what Pauline became, her second mother—her "little Mother" as she was often called because she was not only a loving mother figure but also a superb model of littleness, humility, simplicity, and spiritual childhood. Incidentally, she was actually the shortest Martin sister (5'5") in stature with Thérèse (5'3") being the tallest.

Following the death of his wife, M. Martin placed the two older girls in charge of the general management of his household. Pauline, sixteen, assumed the task of educating her little sisters—Céline (eight) and Thérèse (four-and-a

---

27 As written in Pauline's obituary notice and printed in *Mother Agnès of Jesus O.C.D.*, p. 2.
28 Ibid, p. 7.
29 Ibid, p. 17.
30 *Story of a Soul*, chapter II, p. 34.

half). Marie, seventeen, handled the material operation of the house. Pauline tells us that "I took charge of her [Thérèse's] beautiful little soul, of her first studies, and of everything to do with her. She has said [in her autobiography] how I brought her up. But I reproach myself for certain severities quite unnecessary for this little creature of heaven...."[31]

Thérèse and the family lived a beautiful and tranquil life in their new home in Lisieux where they moved from Alençon to be near their aunt and cousins after Zélie's death. Five years later, though, Pauline, then twenty-one, sought permission to join the Carmelites in Lisieux and was readily accepted on October 2, 1882. This was the third time the young Thérèse (nine) suffered a separation from her "mother."

> I didn't know what Carmel was, but I understood that Pauline was going to leave me to enter a convent. I understood too, she would not wait for me [to become a nun with her] and I was about to lose my second Mother! Ah! How can I express the anguish of my heart. In one instant, I understood what life was; until then, I had never seen it so sad; but it appeared to me in all its reality, and I saw it was nothing but a continual suffering and separation. I shed bitter tears because I did not yet understand the joy of sacrifice. I was weak, so weak that I consider it a good grace to have been able to support a trial which seemed to be far above my strength! If I had learned of my dear Pauline's departure very gently, I would not have suffered as much perhaps, but having heard about it by surprise, it was as if a sword were buried in my heart.
>
> I shall always remember, dear Mother, with what tenderness you consoled me. Then you explained the life of Carmel to me and it seemed so beautiful! When thinking over all you had said, I felt that Carmel was the desert where God wanted me to go also to hide myself.... I wanted to go to Carmel not for Pauline's sake but for Jesus alone.[32]

Difficult as it was for her emotionally and physically because of the two separations and a subsequent serious illness, she managed to persevere. Pauline received the habit on April 6, 1883, and on May 8 the next year she was professed. That same day the eleven-year-old Thérèse made her First Holy Communion. In preparing for this great event, Pauline (now Sister Agnès of Jesus) put together a booklet for Thérèse in which she was to record all her acts of virtue and sacrifice:

> Do you remember, dear Mother [Agnès], the attractive little book you made for me three months before my First Communion? It aided me in preparing my heart through a sustained and thorough method. Although I had already prepared it for a long time, my heart needed a new thrust; it had to be filled with fresh flowers so that Jesus could rest there with pleasure. Every day I made a large number of fervent acts which made up so many flowers, and I offered up an even greater number of aspirations which you had written in my little book for every day, and these acts of love formed flower buds.[33]

---

31 Lisieux Carmelites, *op. cit.*, p. 8.
32 *Story of a Soul*, chapter III, p. 58.
33 Ibid., p. 73–74.

The great day finally arrived and Thérèse continues her story:

> In the evening of that beautiful day, I found myself once more with my family. Already in the morning at the Mass, I had embraced Papa and all my relatives. But now this was the real reunion and Papa took the hand of his little Queen and brought her to Carmel. There I saw my Pauline who had become the spouse of Jesus; I saw her with her white veil, one like mine, and her crown of roses. Ah! My joy was without any bitterness. I hoped to be with her soon and to await heaven with her![34]

Though Pauline was not with Thérèse in body for six years, she certainly was in spirit. There was a constant flow of letters from her to Thérèse exhorting, advising, and teaching her in matters primarily spiritual and specifically later on in encouraging her in her desire to become a Carmelite. Finally Thérèse joined her and their oldest sister Marie (who entered in 1886) on April 9, 1888, in the same convent to begin life as a cloistered and contemplative nun at the tender age of fifteen. Once she was in the convent, Thérèse progressed rapidly in holiness under the guidance and example of Pauline who encouraged Thérèse not only to love God but also to write plays, poetry, and paint as she did on special occasions in the convent.

The Lisieux Carmel Archives has in its possession six playlets with dialogue alone, sung verse, or both, written by Sister Agnès between the years 1884 and 1889. The first four were performed before Thérèse entered the monastery and the last two after:

1. *The Virtues at Jesus' Cradle* (Christmas 1884).
2. *The Magi at the Lisieux Carmel* (Epiphany 1884).
3. *The Feast of the Rosary* (October 1886).
4. *The Feast of the Kings at the Lisieux Carmel* (Epiphany 1887).
5. *St. Agnès* (Feast day of the prioress, Mother Gonzague, January 21, 1888). The postulant Thérèse played St. Agnès beautifully with unpretentious reverence.
6. *The First Dream of the Child Jesus* (Christmas 1889). The novice Thérèse deeply impressed the community by her portrayal of the Virgin Mary.

Pauline was elected prioress on February 20, 1893, and served in this capacity for three years. At the end of 1894 she ordered Thérèse (Sister Thérèse of the Child Jesus and of the Holy Face) to write down an account of her childhood memories which became the first of the three manuscripts that comprise her famous autobiography. It was given the title *Story of a Soul* which it really is, more so than strictly a story of her life. Concerning this, it was during Thérèse's last illness that Mother Agnès wrote a touching and revealing note expressing her sorrow, pride, and surprisingly accurate prediction of future circumstances:

> My dear little Angel, I feel very sorry for having made you undertake you know what [the part of the Autobiography addressed to Mother Gonzague], however, if you only knew how much this pleases me!... You know that the saints in

---
34 Ibid., p. 78.

heaven can still receive glory until the end of the world and that they favor those who honor them.... Well, I shall be your little herald, I shall proclaim your feats of arms. I shall take care to make God loved and served by means of all the lights which He has given you and which will never be extinguished. Then you will favor me with your caresses, will you not, little Angel? You will come to spread around me the little gilded dust from your golden wings; I shall have to feel your presence everywhere....

There is still one thing I wanted to tell you. You well know, my little girl, that it is not usual for my character to have accepted the trial of these recent days so well; this morning, I was astonished at this, and God said to me: "But your little girl has prayed for you, that is the secret of your strength." I come, then, to thank you and to press you to my little heart. If you are already so powerful on earth, what shall I see, what shall I feel when you will be up above? [35]

Sr. Thérèse wrote four poems for Pauline: PN 22, PN 26, PN 34, and PN 45.

It must be mentioned here that during Thérèse's last months, her sisters (Marie, Pauline, and Céline) and other nuns wrote down her conversations with them. Pauline in particular jotted them down in what is known as *The Yellow Notebook*. She combined all her notes and those of the others into a compilation called *Novissima Verba* (Latin for "Last Words"): *Derniers Entretiens de Ste. Thérèse de l'Enfant-Jésus — Mai–Septembre 1887*. Pauline's copied conversations comprise the majority of Thérèse's words.

Now as far as *Story of a Soul* is concerned, Thérèse exhorted her sister to edit her manuscript as she saw fit, after it was intimated that it might be published as Thérèse's death-circular (obituary notice) to be sent to all the French Carmels. Mother Agnès justifies her actions in a letter she wrote to the vice-postulator of Thérèse's cause of beatification:

> She told me, and I would swear to this on oath: "Little Mother, I entrust my manuscript to you. Our Lord will make use of it to do a great deal of good, but you must be very careful how you set about getting it ready for publication, omitting many things, and altering anything I have done badly. Whatever you do, it is I who do it." [36]

It was indeed published, with 2,000 printed copies in 1898, one year after Thérèse's death, not as the customary short death notice but in a bound volume of 475 pages. Interest in it spread rapidly and a second edition followed the next year. It soon became a best seller, with countless editions and translations in many languages. For the rest of Mother Agnès' life after Thérèse's death, she was involved at first with the publication of *Story of a Soul,* then the consequential spread of Thérèse's fame; huge correspondence and dissemination of material concerning Thérèse; and finally the long process dealing with the beatification and canonization. During this time also she was heavily occupied as prioress with the management of the monastery. She had been re-elected for six years as

---
35 LC 185, from Mother Agnès of Jesus to Thérèse, June 4, 1897.
36 As quoted in *Sicut Parvuli*, September 1984.

prioress on April 19, 1902. In 1923, at the time of Thérèse's beatification, Pope Pius XI gave a special indult bestowing the position of prioress of the Lisieux Carmel to Mother Agnès for life. With the exception of eighteen months (1908–1909), she held this office for a total of fifty-one years until her death.

Mother Agnès and all of her community suffered greatly, as did all the citizens of Lisieux, when in June of 1944 the Allied forces invaded Normandy and bombed the town as part of the strategy to rid the world of the Nazi menace that plagued Europe and the world during World War II. The nuns were forced to flee the monastery and seek refuge (for 80 days) in the huge basilica on the hill nearby. Miraculously the monastery buildings and the basilica were spared destruction despite the complete annihilation of nearly three-quarters of Lisieux. The magnificent basilica was built in honor of Pauline's baby sister, Thérèse, who by then had been declared not only a saint of the Catholic Church but also, among other honors, the Patron Saint of the Universal Missions, and Second Patron Saint of France with St. Joan of Arc.

Mother Agnès lived seven more years. She died peacefully on July 28, 1951, at almost the age of ninety, having endured a slow and progressive deterioration of her health that began with a simple fall. People came from all over the world to pay their last respects to this remarkable woman. Hundreds of telegrams and letters arrived to express their sorrow including one signed personally by Pope Pius XII. She is buried in a vault next to her sisters at the Carmel she loved so much.

3. Marie-Léonie Martin—"Léonie" (1863–1941)
(Sister Frances Thérèse—Sœur Françoise-Thérèse)
The least gifted and emotionally troubled sister

"I BELONG TO A FAMILY OF SAINTS, AND I MUST NOT STAIN THE RECORD." Thérèse's older sister Léonie said this when she was a nun. Although, when she was a girl of fourteen, her frustrated mother complained to her other daughter Pauline that Léonie was "a model of insubordination, having never obeyed me except when forced to do so."[37] Through the years a remarkable behavioral conversion slowly evolved and Léonie eventually became a truly saintly member of the holy Martin family.

Léonie, the third of nine children of Louis and Zélie Martin, entered the world on June 3, 1863, in Alençon, and was baptized Marie-Léonie. Her godmother was Mme. Tifenne. This tiny, blond, blue-eyed girl had a frail constitution that remained with her for the rest of her life. Right from the beginning she suffered from chronic whooping cough, intestinal inflammations, eczema, severe headaches, nausea, and a continuous lassitude. Added to these were other deficiencies such as her difficult personality traits and her slow learning ability. Unlike her sisters, she was a poor student, disruptive in class, and physically unattractive. Léonie's nature has been commonly classified as insubordinate, quarrelsome, capricious, excitable, stubborn, emotionally unstable, rebellious, incorrigible, headstrong, and

---
37 Letter (CF 194) dated March 12, 1877, as quoted in Dolan's *God Made the Violet Too*, p. 30.

prone to having temper tantrums. In contrast, though, she possessed "a heart of gold," was generous, and even called "good Léonie" by her father.

When Léonie, nicknamed "Lolo," was only sixteen months old she became seriously ill, so much so that Mme. Martin wrote to her sister, Sister Marie-Dosithée (a Visitation nun in Le Mans), urging her to make a novena to the then Blessed Margaret Mary (a Visitantine nun), to bring about a cure for the little girl. Their prayers were answered and Léonie recovered.

Various circumstances affected Léonie's personality and character. It naturally happened that the two older girls—Marie and Pauline—formed a close relationship because of the proximity of their ages. That was true also of Céline and Thérèse. The death in 1870, however, of Léonie's closest sister and playmate, Hélène, five and she six, surely influenced Léonie psychologically. Furthermore, the loss of the two boys born into the family prior to Hélène's death also must have influenced Léonie emotionally. All of this plus her mental inferiority perhaps prevented intimate ties with her sisters and led her to become a kind of outsider and a loner in the family. In fact, one time the bewildered girl once even asked her mother if she had been exchanged at birth for another infant because she was so different from all her sisters.

While Thérèse was still living in Alençon, a childish incident involving Léonie turned out to be a remarkably symbolic forecast of Thérèse's philosophy later in life:

> One day, Léonie, thinking she was too big to be playing any longer with dolls, came to us with a basket filled with dresses and pretty pieces for making others; her doll was resting on top. "Here, my little sisters, *choose*; I'm giving you all this." Céline stretched out her hand and took a little ball of wool which pleased her. After a moment's reflection, I [Thérèse] stretched out mine saying: "I choose all!" and I took the basket without further ceremony....
>
> This little incident of my childhood is a summary of my whole life.... Then, as in the days of my childhood, I cried out: "My God '*I choose all!*' I don't want to be a *saint* by *halves*, I'm not afraid to suffer for You, I fear only one thing: to keep my *own will*; so take it, for '*I choose all*' that You will!"[38]

Prior to her eighth birthday, Léonie pursued her studies with the Sisters of Providence in Alençon. Then in 1871 her aunt, Sister Marie-Dosithée (Zélie's sister), a teacher at the Visitation Convent school in Le Mans, volunteered to tutor her niece before the Christmas holidays with the hope that she would be able to stabilize and improve her complex and uncontrollable behavior, and thus have her accepted as a regular student in the next semester or school year. Her pedagogical, theraputic, and charitable techniques proved unsuccessful. Before long, Sister Marie-Dosithée wrote to her brother in Lisieux this disappointing assessment: "At the moment I am taking care of Léonie, that terrible little girl; she certainly keeps me on my toes. It's a continual little battle; she isn't afraid of anyone except me!"[39] Léonie obviously did not stay for the next year.

---

[38] *Story of a Soul*, chapter I, p. 27.
[39] Baudouin-Croix, *Léonie Martin*, p. 17.

Léonie's teaching nun aunt, despite her failure with controlling Léonie, was able to discern some underlying good features in the child:

> She is a difficult child to train, and her childhood will not show any attractiveness, but I believe that eventually she will be as good as her sisters. She has a heart of gold, her intelligence is not developed and she is backward for her age. Nevertheless, she does not lack capabilities, and I find that she has good judgment and also remarkable strength of character.... In short, by nature she is strong and generous, quite to my taste. But if the grace of God were not there, what would become of her?[40]

Nonetheless, the disturbed youngster returned home with this explanation from her aunt:

> But despite the best will in the world, it was necessary to separate her from the rest of the children. As soon as she is with companions, she seems to lose control of herself, and you never saw anything like her unruliness. Well, I have no longer any hope of changing her nature, save by a miracle.... At eighteen months, she was cured of a malady from which she should have died; why did God save her from death if He had not merciful designs for her?[41]

The Martin parents had to be content with sending Léonie back to the Sisters of Providence in Alençon and for a while also with a qualified young woman tutor.

Finally in January of 1874, Léonie returned to the school in Le Mans. Zélie's mother thought Léonie would behave by this time and follow all directions in preparation for her First Communion. She lasted only to April. From then on Zélie prepared Léonie for this sacrament herself and even took her on a pilgrimage to the Shrine of the Immaculate Conception in Sées as part of the rather long training. Léonie received her First Communion at the Church of Notre Dame in Alençon on May 23, 1875.

She continued to have her ups and downs in her personal behavior patterns. About a year later Sister Marie-Dosithée was diagnosed as having tuberculosis. Aware of this, Léonie wrote her this guileless note: "My dear aunt, when you are in Heaven, please ask God to give me the grace of conversion, and also to give me a vocation to be a true religious, because I think about it every day. Please, please, don't forget my little message, because I am sure God will listen to you."[42] Her aunt died at the age of forty-eight on February 24, 1877.

Around this time Léonie exhibited some really unusual and inexplicable behavior. Unknown to anyone, Louise Marais, the maid in the Martin household, had been terrorizing Léonie by forcing her to obey only her and no one else, not even her mother. Through close observation, Marie began to realize that Louise held Léonie completely under her power. She seemed actually proud that only she was able to control the unruly Léonie but in doing so she made her a slave by

---

40 Dolan, *op. cit.*, p. 16.
41 Ibid., p. 18.
42 Baudouin-Croix, *Léonie Martin: A Difficult Life*, p. 25.

frightening and even physically abusing her if she did not obey. Marie revealed this to her mother who was utterly shocked and ordered Louise to leave. Zélie, however, changed her mind because of Louise's pleadings, tears, and her promise never to do so again. She, however, forbade Louise to speak to Léonie and in fact to avoid her entirely. Zélie also stipulated that after her death, Louise must be dismissed from the household—which did come to pass. Fortunately Zélie was somewhat able successfully but slowly to form Léonie as she did the other girls.

Sadly, though, when Léonie was fourteen, Zélie was in the last stages of the deadly breast cancer that claimed her life on August 28, 1877. She expressed her intense anxiety about Léonie shortly before her death, wondering who would take care of poor Léonie after she died. No matter how good, well intentioned, and hard a father tries, he could never replace a mother. Who could therefore possibly love her like a mother? Her seventeen-year-old daughter Maria promised she would and did assume the role of mother for Léonie.

Mme. Martin was so concerned about Léonie that when she went on a pilgrimage to Lourdes in June 1877, accompanied by Pauline, Marie, and Léonie, she prayed more for Léonie than for herself: "I shall bring Léonie with me so that if Our Lady does not cure me, I will beg her to cure my child, to open her intelligence and to make her a saint." [43]

The year 1877 certainly was a sad one for Léonie as well as the entire family. It included the death of Sister Françoise-Dosithée, the disturbing affair with Louise Marais, Zélie's tragic death, and the family's move to Lisieux shortly thereafter. Upon Zélie's passing, Céline proclaimed Marie as her mother and Thérèse chose Pauline. Léonie was left out.

In January 1878, two months after the Martins settled in Lisieux, Léonie was sent as a boarder at the Benedictine Abbey school while Céline attended as a day student. Marie and Pauline stayed home to manage the household affairs and to care for the little ones. Then on October 3, 1881, Thérèse tells us that "I was eight and a half when Léonie [eighteen] left boarding school and I replaced her at the Abbey." [44]

On May 13, 1883, Thérèse was miraculously healed of a mystifying illness that beset her for months and ended when she saw the statue of the Blessed Virgin smile at her. Marie, Céline, and Léonie witnessed this amazing cure. Thérèse confessed in her autobiography that during her illness "Léonie was also very kind to me. She tried to amuse me as well as she could. I sometimes caused her some pain as she was easily able to see that Marie could be replaced by no one." [45]

Thérèse made her First Communion on May 8 in the Abbey chapel of Notre-Dame du Pré. Léonie was deeply impressed by the intense reverence Thérèse displayed during the liturgy. Shortly after, on June 14, Bishop Hugonin, confirmed Thérèse which she recalls in her autobiography: "It was my dear little Léonie

---

43 Letter (CF 200) of Mme. Martin to Mme. Guérin from Dolan's *op. cit.*, pp. 34-35, dated May 10, 1877.
44 *Story of a Soul*, chapter III, p. 53.
45 Ibid., p. 64.

who acted as my godmother, and she was so much moved that she was unable all through the ceremony to hold back her tears. She received Holy Communion with me, for I had the happiness on that beautiful day to unite myself with Jesus."[46]

Two years later when Léonie was twenty-three, she made her first unsuccessful try at religious life. Below is a detailed chart of her four attempts to become a nun.

LÉONIE'S ATTEMPTS AT RELIGIOUS LIFE			
DATE ENTERED	AGE	WHERE	DATE LEFT	WHY SHE LEFT
1. October 7, 1886	23	Poor Clares in Alençon.	Dec. 1, 1886 (Lasted 2 months)	Too austere a life.
2. July 16, 1887	24	Visitation Order in Caen.	Jan. 6, 1888 (Lasted 6 months)	Health failed.
3. June 24, 1893	30	Visitation in Caen. Received name Sr. Thérèse Dosithée.	July 20, 1895 (Lasted 2 years)	Poor health, eczema returned.
4. January 28, 1899	35	Visitation in Caen. Received name Sr. Françoise-Thérèse.	Remained 42 years until death on June 16, 1941	Death at 78.

From the time Léonie first tried religious life in 1886 (and even before to some extent) until Thérèse's death in 1897, Léonie eagerly sought, anticipated, and humbly accepted Thérèse's spiritual encouragement, advice, and comfort.

In October 1886, M. Martin with his daughters Léonie, Céline, and Thérèse went to Alençon for a few days. Thérèse was thirteen at the time and wrote about it in the story of her life:

> It was during this trip that Léonie made her attempt to enter the Poor Clares [Thursday, October 7]. I was saddened by her *extraordinary* entrance, for I loved her very much and I hadn't even the chance to kiss her before her departure. Never will I forget the kindness and embarrassment of this poor little Father of ours when he came to announce that Léonie had already received the habit of the Poor Clares. He found this very strange, just as we did, but he didn't want to say anything when he saw how unhappy Marie was about the matter. He took us to the convent and there I experienced a sort of *contraction of my heart* such as I never felt at the sight of a monastery. This monastery produced the opposite effect which Carmel produced in me, for there everything made my heart expand. The sight of the religious didn't attract me in the least, and I was not tempted to remain among them. However, poor Léonie was very attractive in her new costume, and she told us to get a good look at *her eyes* because we would no longer see them (the Poor Clares have a custom of going around with eyes downcast), but God was content with only two months of sacrifice, and Léonie returned to show us *her blue eyes* which were frequently moist with tears.
>
> When leaving Alençon I believed she would remain with the Poor Clares, and so it was with a heavy heart I left the sad street of *Demi-lune* (half moon).

---

46 Ibid., chapter IV, p. 80.

We were only three now and soon our dear Marie was also to leave. The 15th of October was the day of separation! From the happy and numerous family of Les Buissonnets, there remained only the two youngest children.[47]

Léonie found life with the Poor Clares so extremely trying that her weak constitution could not withstand the rigors and mortifications imposed by the austere Rule. She left and went home after only two months.

She clearly realized the great spiritual qualities of her ten years younger sister Thérèse and her need for assistance from her. Before Thérèse, Céline, and their father left for Rome in November 1887, Léonie wrote to Thérèse from her convent in Caen. This was during her second attempt at religious life:

> Dear little sister, it does me good to talk to you; I know that even though you are so young, you understand me. I want to share with you my soul's desire for intimate union with Jesus. We can find happiness only in Him.... until now, I didn't know how to control my poor heart. But your pure heart ... will come to Jesus in all its freshness. I am so happy for you! Tomorrow is the feast of Blessed Margaret Mary, who cured me miraculously. She is no stranger to the happiness I have found here in the Visitation Order. Pray that she will intercede for a second miracle to make me a holy Visitandine.[48]

Léonie, however, lasted only six months with the Visitandine nuns in Caen. Thérèse wrote: "When Léonie left the Visitation, he [Louis Martin] was not disturbed and made no reproaches to God for not having answered the prayers he offered up to obtain his daughter's vocation. It was even with joy that he left to go and bring her home." [49]

At the time of Léonie's third try at becoming a nun, life for the Martins underwent a drastic change: Les Buissonnets was no longer their home; M. Martin returned from three years at a mental institution in Caen; Céline was the sole caretaker of her father; the Guérins sold their pharmacy and upstairs flat and moved to another house in Lisieux, both Marie and Pauline were professed Carmelites, and Thérèse was a Carmelite for five years.

On July 20, 1895, after two years with the Visitation, Léonie left along with the entire novitiate, basically because of the extreme austerity imposed upon them by a severe mistress of novices. Another problem Léonie had there, perhaps due to her slowness, was difficulty in keeping her place in the Divine Office.[50] After this third try, Léonie again returned to lay life. Her uncle and aunt Guérin welcomed her like a daughter and had her live with them. Léonie thereby filled a void in their lives created by the departure of their own two daughters. By this time Jeanne Guerin had married Dr. La Néele (1890) and was living in Caen, Louis Martin had died (1894) after which Céline entered Carmel (1894), and Marie was about to enter in August 1895 the same monastery as her four Martin

---

47 Ibid., p. 92.
48 LC 56, from Léonie to Thérèse dated October 15, 1887.
49 *Story of a Soul*, chapter VII, p. 153.
50 Martens, "Thérèse as Léonie's Spiritual Guide," from *The Apostolate of the Little Flower*, July/August 2000.

cousins. Léonie remained with her aunt and uncle for four years during which she was in constant contact with Thérèse who died just two years later.

Léonie's third withdrawal from religious life troubled Thérèse who wrote to her the day she left the Caen convent:

> [We] were plunged into a very great sorrow because of our dear Léonie, it was like a real agony. God, who willed to try our faith, was sending us no consolation whatever, and, as for me, I was unable to offer any other prayer but that of Our Lord on the Cross: "My God, my God, why have You abandoned us!" Or like that in the garden of agony: "My God, may Your will be done and not ours...."
>
> I had left aside my letter yesterday without finishing it, for Marie [Guérin] arrived with Léonie; our emotion was very great when seeing her. We were unable to make her say a word, she was crying so much; finally, she ended up by looking at us, and everything went off well.[51]

During Thérèse's final painful months, the Guérins and others sent gifts to the Carmel for her. Among them was a music box from Léonie that Thérèse found joy in listening to, even though the music was not religious in nature. A few weeks before Thérèse passed away she said to Céline: "I'd love to have something, but only Aunt [Guérin] or Léonie could be able to get it for me. Since I'm eating now, I'd love to have a little chocolate cake, soft inside ... it's long, narrow, I believe it's called an éclair ... only one, however! Thank you. Thank you."[52] This request was quite unusual in view of the fact that Thérèse never really found any pleasure in eating.

Thérèse wrote seventeen extant letters to Léonie. In the last one she began with one of her characteristic exhortations: "The only happiness on earth is to apply oneself in always finding delightful the lot Jesus is giving us."[53] She then follows with a heavenly promise:

> You want me to pray in heaven to the Sacred Heart for you. Be sure that I shall not forget to deliver your messages to Him and to ask all that will be necessary for you to become a *great saint*.
>
> *Adieu*, dear sister; I would like the thought of my entrance into heaven to fill you with gladness since I shall be able to love you even more.[54]

Léonie went to the Carmel often to receive news of Thérèse's condition and especially when Thérèse was nearing the end. On the evening of September 30, 1897, she and the Guérins prayed as usual in the Carmelite chapel. While there they were handed a note from Pauline: "Our angel is in Heaven. She breathed her last at 7 o'clock [actually 7:20] while pressing her crucifix to her heart and saying 'Oh, I love you!' Her eyes were raised to Heaven. What did she see?"[55]

Unfortunately, M. Guérin was unable to attend the funeral services on October 4 because he was suffering from a painful attack of gout. Léonie, therefore,

---
51 From a letter (LT 178) of Thérèse to her aunt Guérin, dated July 20–21, 1895.
52 A letter from Céline [Sister Geneviève] to her aunt, Mme. Guérin in the beginning of September 1897.
53 LT 257, July 17, 1897.
54 Ibid.
55 Martens, "Thérèse as Léonie's Spiritual Guide," *The Apostolate of the Little Flower*, July/August 2000, p. 8.

was appointed to represent the family and lead the funeral procession to the town cemetery for the burial.

Despite her death, Thérèse continued to be Léonie's spiritual guide from heaven. Exactly one year later Thérèse's *Story of a Soul* was published and quickly required another edition until through the years millions of copies were sold. It was tremendously influential in Léonie's spiritual formation.

On January 28, 1899, twenty-one months after her saintly sister passed into eternity, Léonie tried for the fourth time to become a nun. Right after she entered the cloister door she told the Mother Superior: "I am here for always. This is my sole ambition: to hide myself like *a humble violet* under the leaves of perfect submission, so that my Superiors can do with me whatever they wish."[56] This time she was successful and remained there until she died forty-two years later.

Thérèse knew for certain that Léonie would in time become a nun. Her prediction came true as Léonie revealed in a statement she made at the Diocesan Process for Thérèse's beatification in 1910:

> In early 1888, Thérèse had said prophetically to a Benedictine sister in Lisieux: "We must not worry about the fact that Léonie's attempts at religious life have been unsuccessful. After my death, she will enter the Visitation Order, and this time she will succeed; she will take my name, and that of St. Frances de Sales."[57]

On April 23, 1899, A month after she entered the Visitation, Léonie wrote a letter to Mother Marie Gonzaga, the prioress of Lisieux at the time, expressing the sentiments she held for the rest of her life:

> I think of Thérèse constantly. Every moment I call her to my side. I do not want to be without her for an instant.... I humbly ask you to allow my sisters to take turns writing to me biweekly until my profession. Their letters do me much good. I am so sure you will grant me this wish that I thank you in advance.[58]

Mother Marie Gonzaga did allow the Martin sisters to correspond with Léonie which they gladly occupied their time in doing on a regular basis. Pauline, especially, was most comforting and consoling in her letters to Léonie who, so far from her sisters, became at times lonely, discouraged, and despondent.

Isidore and Céline, Léonie's aunt and uncle, missed Léonie now that they were left alone. Léonie's postulancy was short. After four months she received the habit and was given the name Sister Frances Thérèse, as Thérèse predicted. She completed her stay in the novitiate, was professed, and on July 2, 1900 (the Feast of the Visitation) she made her vows. Uncle Isidore, with both joy and sadness, wrote these lines to his beloved niece on this important day: "For many years, have you not been our daughter? We tried to do our part to bring you to this happy day. Today our mission is terminated. Help us, dear daughter, to

---

56 Dolan, *op. cit.*, p. 59.
57 Ibid.
58 As quoted in "Visitation: Home at Last," *op. cit.* by Sr. Martens, in *The Apostolate of the Little Flower*, September/October 2000.

thank God with and for you, and believe that your sweet presence is missed terribly by both aunt and me." [59]

Convent life still proved difficult but she persisted to the end. She was keenly aware of her deficiencies and humbly accepted corrections and reprimands. Her work assignments never ascended beyond "assistant" in all the tasks she was given such as in the bursar's office, in the infirmary, the sacristy, the dining room, or when making altar linens.

A decade after Léonie became a nun, the cause for Thérèse was introduced. While hanging up the community's laundry one day she learned of this and rather surprisingly remarked that "Thérèse was sweet but to canonize her? It is true that no one ever had anything to reproach her for." [60]

The time arrived when she was asked to give testimony before the tribunal for the Cause of the Beatification at the Informative Process held in Bayeux. She had not left her convent since she entered and experienced for the first time an automobile ride to Bayeux on November 27, 1910, escorted by her superior, Mother Jeanne-Marguerite. When the interrogation was completed, she returned on December 4. The next time she left her convent home was during the Apostolic Process held at the Carmelite convent in Lisieux which began in April 1915. It was a grand pleasure for her and indeed for her three sisters, Marie, Pauline, and Céline to be together for eight days since they had not seen each other for seventeen years. They all had their pictures taken together and separately.

Upon her return to Caen, she deeply felt the loss of her sisters. They also felt her loss. Léonie made these pathetic comments in a note to her Carmelite sisters in Lisieux: "... I believe I am loved, even though I am not at all lovable. Well, since you think I look well, I shall agree with you; this poor littlest one feels so inferior to you, in every respect." [61] And in regard to photos taken of her, she conceded to her sister Céline that "It is not your fault that I am so ugly and so untidy; it is mine." [62]

The sisters in Lisieux kept Léonie constantly and fully informed of all that was occurring in the "storm of glory" [63] that surrounded Thérèse's rise to fame and sainthood. Throughout all the dazzling celebrations and in view of the many incredible honors bestowed on Thérèse, Léonie preferred to be unrecognized and hidden. Once a priest came to the Visitation Convent and asked the nun at the door if he could see the sister of St. Thérèse. The nun replied, "We will ask our Mother, but I don't think that will be possible." The priest then said, "Oh, that would be a great disappointment!" Whereupon the nun answered: "However, Father, I can assure you that you won't be missing anything—it isn't worth the trouble!" The startled priest departed quite bewildered. When the

---

59 Dolan, *op. cit.*, p. 65.
60 Baudouin-Croix, *A Difficult Life*, p. 102.
61 Ibid., p. 106.
62 Ibid.
63 Pius XI mentioned the concept of Thérèse as "The storm, the deluge of glory which has descended upon Lisieux..." when addressing French pilgrims on May 18, 1925, the day following Thérèse's canonization.

convent chaplain happened to pass by, he told him about his amazing conversation. "My poor Father," he said with a chuckle, "you have been tricked—you were talking to Léonie herself!" [64]

Léonie's extreme humility and self demeaning attitude were characteristics that seemed to become more pronounced as she advanced in age. In a letter to her sister Pauline she wrote: "I correctly see myself as the least of all people. I have suffered much on account of my inferiority. I have experienced much loneliness of heart. But now I am above such rubbish and have only one dream: to efface myself more and more." [65] Four years before she died she penned this pitiful self-evaluation: "I am indeed becoming old, and I am glad of it.... Our dear Mother Superior redoubles her attention towards her aged child [she was 73] and I do not understand why she is so fearful of losing me, a good-for-nothing like me, a cracked window pane so easily replaced, a tottering, shaking, old building." [66]

Death struck many of Léonie's family members while she was in the convent. Her Aunt Guérin died in 1900; her cousin Marie (Sister Marie of the Eucharist) in 1905; Uncle Guérin, in 1909; Dr. Francis La Néele in 1916; Jeanne Guérin (Mme. La Néele) in 1938; and Marie Martin (Sister Marie of the Sacred Heart) in 1940.

In the winter of 1941, with Léonie's health failing, she was sent to the infirmary. The community celebrated her seventy-eighth birthday on June 3, 1941, at which time the pope honored her with a special blessing for the fortieth anniversary of her religious profession, presented a year late, though, because of the war. Nine days later she had a stroke and fell to the floor in her room. She passed peacefully into the afterlife four days later during the night of June 16/17, 1941. She is buried beneath a marble slab in front of the tomb of the foundress in the crypt of the Visitation Convent at 3 rue de l'Abbatiale in Caen.

By the 1960s an amazing and unexpected interest in the former nearly-forgotten Léonie emerged. Her story and example have encouraged people who have similar problems or who have family members or friends who do. Despite Léonie's early uncontrollable nature, her difficult childhood, slow learning capability, and her many failures, she was able to rise triumphantly above them all. Added to this was her underlining deep holiness which has drawn many to advocate submitting her cause for beatification.

4. Marie-Hélène Martin—"Hélène" (1864–1870)
The first Martin daughter to die, at six

Zélie and Louis Martin's fourth child, Marie-Hélène, was born on October 13, 1864, in their home at Louis's watch making and jewelry shop at 15 Rue du Pont Neuf in Alençon. By now Zélie could not nurse her own infants because of the onset of breast cancer and thus for the first time had to hire a wet nurse. They chose the dependable and robust Rose Taille who lived in Semallé,

---

64 Baudouin-Croix, *op. cit.*, p. 111.
65 Dolan, *op. cit.*, p. 89.
66 Ibid.

about six miles away in the farmlands. It was she who saved the very ill infant Thérèse from death nine years later. Zélie sent her brother notes giving her impression of her newest baby daughter:

> Last Tuesday, I went to see my little Hélène. I set off alone, at seven in the morning, in rain and wind which accompanied me there and back. Imagine how tired I was on the road, but I was upheld by the thought of soon holding my treasure in my arms. She is a daintly little jewel, enchantingly pretty....[67]
>
> I never remember experiencing such a thrill of happiness as when I took her in my arms, and she smiled so charmingly at me that I seemed to be looking at an angel. In short, I cannot describe it. I do not think I have ever yet seen or ever will see again such an enchanting little girl. Oh, when shall I have the pleasure of possessing her completely? I cannot realize that I have the honor to be the mother of such a delightful little creature. No indeed, I do not repent of having married.[68]

Hélène developed into an intelligent, charming, and affectionate child. Her health, however, was not always the best. When she was three she developed a serious inflammation of the inner ear (otitis) which the doctors were unable to remedy. Zélie began to appeal for the intercession of her baby boy Marie-Joseph-Louis who died in 1867:

> The inspiration came to me to turn to my little Joseph, who had died five weeks previously. So I took the child, and made her say a prayer to her little brother. The next morning, the ear was perfectly healed, the discharge had stopped all at once, and the little one has not felt any pain since. I have obtained several other graces also, but less obvious than this one.[69]

The little girl was five years old and already attending kindergarten when her sudden and unexpected demise occurred on February 22, 1870. In a letter to her brother and his wife, Zélie related Hélène's last tragic moments:

> I was looking at her sadly. Her eyes were dull, there was no more life in her, and I began to cry. Then she put her little arms round me and did her best to comfort me. All day she kept saying: "My poor little mother has been crying." I sat with her, and she had a very bad night. In the morning, I asked her if she would take her bouillon. She said yes, but could not swallow it. However, she made a last effort, saying to me, "If I eat it, will you love me better?"
>
> Then she took it all but suffered dreadfully afterwards, and I did not know what was happening. She looked at a bottle of medicine which the doctor had ordered, and wanted to drink it, saying that when it was all drunk, she would be better. Then about a quarter-to-ten, she said to me, "Yes, I shall soon be well again ... yes, very soon...." [And] at that very moment her little head fell on my shoulder, her eyes closed, and five minutes later she was dead....

---

67 An excerpt from CF 12, a letter by Zélie to her brother Isidore on March 5, 1865, in an English translation from Piat's *op. cit.*.

68 An excerpt from CF 13, a letter by Zélie to her brother Isidore on April 28, 1865.

69 An excerpt from CF 72, a letter of October 17, 1871, from Zélie to her sister-in-law, Mme. Guérin, translated into English from Piat's *op. cit.*, p. 77.

I shall never forget the impression it has made upon me. Neither I nor my husband expected this sudden end. When he came in and saw his poor little daughter dead, he burst out sobbing, and crying: "My little Hélène. My little Hélène." Then we offered her to God together. I spent the whole night beside the poor little darling. She was even lovelier in death than in life. I dressed her myself and laid her in her coffin. I thought I should die myself, but I did not want others to touch her. The church was full for the funeral. Her grave is by that of her grandfather.[70]

Zélie was scrupulous about maters religious in the training of her children. In a note Pauline wrote (as Mother Agnès of Jesus years later) we read: "After our little sister Hélène's death, Mamma was disturbed at the thought of a little lie the child had told. She was praying in front of the statue [the future "Miraculous statue of the Virgin of the Smile"], regretting she hadn't brought the child to confession and fearing she was in purgatory, when she heard these words: "She is here by my side."

For some time both parents were overwhelmed by this tragic death. A month later Zélie wrote these sad notes:

Sometimes I imagine myself slipping away very gently, like my little Hélène. I assure you, I scarcely cling to life since I lost this child. I am aware of an ardent longing to see her again. However, those who remain need me, and for their sakes I pray God to leave me a few years longer on earth.[71]

I feel deeply the loss of my two little boys, but I have suffered still more at losing this child. I was beginning to rejoice in her. She was so good, so loving and so advanced for her age. There is not a moment of the day when I do not think of her. The Sister who taught her in school told me ... and it is well said ... that children like her do not live. Well she is in Heaven, far happier than here below, but for me it seems as though all happiness has flown.[72]

Zélie's nun sister, Sister Dosithée, was always ready to console and uplift her sister's spirits:

Oh my dear little sister. How glad I am to see your deep faith and your resignation. You will soon find again those you now mourn. Yes, your crown will be beautiful ... very beautiful. Just now, your heart is broken, but by your acquiescence in all that God wills, there will come a fragrance which will delight the Heart of God.

One day, your faith and trust that never flinch will have a magnificent reward. Be sure God will bless you, and that the measure of your sorrows will be that of the consolations reserved for you. For, after all, if God is pleased with you and wills to give you the great saint you have so desired for His glory, will you not be well repaid?[73]

---

70 An excerpt from CF 52, a letter by Zélie to her brother and his wife, dated February 24, 1870, in an English translation also from Piat's *op. cit.*, p. 89.
71 Footnote 57, p. 64 in *Story of a Soul*.
72 An excerpt from CF 54, a letter Zélie wrote to her sister-in-law dated March 27, 1870, and translated in Piat's book mentioned above.
73 From Sister Dosithée to Zélie, as translated in Piat's *op. cit.*, p. 91.

5. Marie-Joseph-Louis Martin—"Joseph" (1866–1867)
The first son who died in infancy

THE MARTIN FAMILY—PARENTS AND FOUR DAUGHTERS—WERE ECSTATIC over the birth of their first boy on September 20, 1866, two years after the last child, Hélène, was born. Zélie reported to her nineteen-year-old sister-in-law, Mme. Guérin: "Oh, the beautiful little boy who is big and strong! It is impossible to wish for a better. I have never had an infant born so easily. Ah! If you knew how I love my little Joseph! I believe my fortune is made!"[74]

Zélie and Louis Martin chose their five-year-old daughter Pauline to be his godmother since at that time in France it was permissible to have a godparent that young. "Look how beautiful his hands are!" she indicated to her husband. "What a glorious day when he'll ascend the altar, or preach from a pulpit!"[75]

But soon the infant Joseph became ill. Because breast cancer was worsening, Zélie had arrived at a point where she absolutely could no longer nurse her own babies. She, therefore, entrusted him to Mme. Rose Taillé, the reliable wet nurse who lived on a farm in Semallé some six miles away. It was she who saved Thérèse's life six years later. Despite excellent care, little Joseph's condition worsened and a slow steady decline set in.

All were delighted, though, when on New Year's Day Joseph was brought home for just a few hours. The next day, however, the situation changed drastically and Zélie, quite distressed, informed Mme. Guérin:

> As a New Year's gift, I dressed him like a little prince. If you knew how nice he looked, and how he laughed! My husband said I treated him like a wooden statue of a saint!… Next day, at 3 A.M. we heard a loud knock at the door. We got up to open it, and someone said, "Come quickly! Your little boy is very ill. They are afraid he will die." You can imagine that I did not take long to dress, and there I was on the way to the country on an intensely cold night, in spite of snow and a slippery frost. I did not ask my husband to come with me, for I was not frightened and would have crossed a forest alone, but he would not let me go without him.[76]

The infant lingered on in pain for another two and a half months until the malady, then diagnosed as erysipelas or St. Anthony's Fire (caused by some variety of streptococcus) claimed his short life of eight months on February 14, 1867. When Zélie's sister, Sister Marie-Dosithee, a Visitation nun in Le Mans, heard of this tragic death she wrote to her grieving sister this prophetic statement:

> Dear little sister, I received your telegram yesterday evening, at half past five. Our little angel was then already in Heaven. How shall I comfort you, dear? I greatly need comforting myself. I am all shaking, but for all that, quite resigned to God's will. The Lord gave and the Lord hath taken away; blessed be the name of the Lord. Whilst I was praying to Our Lord this morning, at Holy

---
74 An excerpt from Zélie's letter (CF 19) to her brother Isidore dated November 18, 1866. English translation by the author.
75 Sister Geneviève, *op. cit.*, p. 58.
76 From Zélie's letter (CF 21) to Mme. Guérin dated January 13, 1867, as quoted in Piat's *op. cit.*, p. 75.

Communion, to leave us the poor little one, whom we wished to bring up only for His glory and the salvation of souls, I seemed to hear interiorly this answer: that He wished to have the first fruits, and would give you another child, later on, who would be such as we desire.[77]

The child's death was a tragedy deeply felt for years. Thérèse and her sisters often spoke of their deceased brothers and sisters and prayed for them. In one of her poems, Thérèse refers to the four deceased Martin children in a delightfully imaginative way:

> Together you play with the little angels
>   Near the altar,
> And your childish songs, gracious armies,
>   Charm Heaven.
> God is teaching you how He makes roses,
>   Birds, the winds.
> No genius here below knows as many things
>   As you, Children![78]

Again, in a lengthy letter she composed for her sister Céline's profession a quarter of a century later, Thérèse created fanciful situations and allusions which she beautifully weaves into the creative fabric of an allegorical tale worthy of any storyteller today. Part of it follows:

> Dear little Sister, you have asked me to tell you how things will go in heaven on your wedding day [Profession day]. I will try to do this....
> On February 24, at midnight, St. Peter will open the portals of heaven, and immediately the angels and saints will go forth with incomparable joy to form the court of the King and His fiancée.... Suddenly, a *Mother* [Zélie Martin] of incomparable beauty comes among them, she stops, and taking *four* charming cherubs [her dead children] by the hand she dresses them in clothes whiter than lilies and in diamonds glistening like dew in the sunlight.... A venerable Old Man [Louis Martin] with silvery hair is there, too, who bestows caresses on them, and all the other children are surprised at such preference. One of them timidly comes to little Thérèse [Mélanie-Thérèse, one of the deceased Martin girls], asking her why this beautiful Lady is dressing them so richly. Little Thérèse answers in her silver-toned voice: "It is because we are the sisters and brothers of the happy fiancée of Jesus, the King. Hélène and I will be bridesmaids, and our two little Josephs will hold us by the hand. Papa and Mamma, whom you see near us, will lead us, along with our little sisters still exiled on earth, and, the entire family reunited, we shall rejoice with unequalled joy....
> Little Hélène and the little Josephs will make some delightful remarks on their joy at belonging to the family of the Queen of so beautiful a celebration....
> I [Thérèse] have no wedding present to give my Céline, but tomorrow, I will take up into my arms the *charming cherubs* I have spoken about, and it is they themselves whom I will offer to her. Since we want to remain as children, we must

---

77 Letter dated February 15, 1867 as quoted in Redman, *Louis and Zélie Martin*, pp. 53–54.
78 PN 44, "To My Little Brothers in Heaven."

unite ourselves to them, and in this way I shall be *demoiselle's* bridesmaid, carrying a beautiful bouquet of lilies. All is *ours*, all is for *us*, for in Jesus we have all![79]

Six years before in 1890, Pauline, then Sister Agnès, also wrote a brief allegorical description of the celebration that would be held in heaven when Thérèse was professed:

> Our angel [Thérèse] is perfectly prepared; if only we could see the celebration that is in preparation in heaven!... Ah! How all the magnificent weddings of this earth would pale before this spectacle!
>
> [May] Jesus, then, have the two pretty boys of honor, namely, the two little Josephs, and she, the two darling little maids of honor, namely, little Hélène, holding hands, take up the collection before God's throne from the Trinity itself, saying: "Lord, for our little exiled sisters on earth, if you please.... For our dear Father that he may come soon to be with us always...."[80]

6. Marie-Joseph-Jean-Baptiste Martin—"Joseph" (1867–1868)
The second son who died in infancy

ALTHOUGH THE MARTIN FAMILY WAS DEVASTATED BY THEIR FIFTH CHILD'S premature death, joy soon returned at the next child's birth—their second and last son—on December 19, 1867. He was christened Joseph in memory of his brother. His full name was Marie-Joseph-Jean-Baptiste Martin. Pauline, now six years old, was chosen as his godmother. Custom then allowed a young a person as godparent.

Zélie, his mother, wrote to her brother and his wife two days later that "He is very strong and lively, but I had a terrible time and the infant was in the greatest danger. I suffered for four hours more severely than I have ever done, the poor little creature was nearly asphyxiated and the doctor administered clinical Baptism."[81] The infant recovered.

Baby Joseph seemed to be quite intelligent and had a beautiful disposition; but soon he began to follow the same sad decline in health that his late brother underwent. Following the advice of their doctor, the parents again sought the assistance of the faithful wet nurse Rose Taillé who lived in the nearby village of Semallé. The devoted mother trudged the twelve mile round trip twice a day at 7 A.M. and 8 P.M. to be with and comfort her ailing baby Joseph. She wrote to her brother that "He is as pretty as a little flower, and laughs like a cherub, till he chokes. I do so wish God would let me keep him. I pray and beseech Him daily to do so. If, however, He wills otherwise, we must resign ourselves."[82]

Despite the excellent nursing and comfort from both mother and "foster mother," little Joseph suffered greatly and ultimately died at eight months of age on August 24, 1868. In anguish Zélie notified her brother and his wife: "My dear little Joseph died at 7 o'clock this morning. I was alone with him. He had

---

79 LT 182, Thérèse to Sister Geneviève, February 23, 1896.
80 Letter of Sister Agnès of Jesus to Céline, September 7, 1890.
81 From Zélie's letter (CF 23) to her brother Isidore and his wife on December 21, 1867, as quoted in English in Wust, *op. cit.*
82 From Zélie's letter (CF 26) to Isidore, February 14, 1868, as quoted in Piat's *op. cit.*, pp. 77–78.

a night of cruel suffering, and I begged with tears for his deliverance. My heart felt lighter when I saw him give his last sigh.[83]

Rev. Piat, the noted biographer of the Martin family, adds some poignant details to this pathetic account:

> She [Zélie] put a wreath of white roses round his head, laid him in a tiny coffin and, valiant in her faith, kept him to the end beside her, in the room where she received her workers. "Oh God," she groaned at times, "must I put that in the ground! But, since You will it, may Your will be done!"[84]

Death struck again shortly after and left the family in more sorrow and pain. For some time Zélie's father was living in her home under her and her husband's loving care. He died a holy death on September 3, 1868, at the age of seventy-nine. Zélie wrote: "Yesterday I went to the cemetery [*Cimetière Notre-Dame* in Alençon].... I knelt by my father's grave but I could not pray. A few steps away I knelt by that of my two little angels.... I had trodden the road by which I had come five weeks previously with my little son and my father, and I could not tell you all I felt.... Never in my life did I feel such heart-rending grief."[85]

7. MARIE-CÉLINE MARTIN—"CÉLINE" (1869–1959)
(SISTER GENEVIÈVE OF THE HOLY FACE—SŒUR GENEVIÈVE DE LA SAINTE-FACE)
Thérèse called her "The sweet echo of my soul"

CÉLINE WAS BORN THE SEVENTH OF NINE CHILDREN AT THE HOME OF HER parents, Zélie and Isidore Martin, on the rue du Pont-Neuf in Alençon on April 28, 1869. She was baptized the same day and received the name Marie-Céline Martin. Her patron saint is the rather obscure St. Celina, the mother of St. Remigius, a 6th century bishop who baptized the adult, former pagan, Frankish King Clovis. Thérèse was always annoyed that Céline's feast day, October 21, that of St. Celina, was rarely if ever recorded on calendars.

As an infant Céline was frail and sickly, and again her mother was unable to care for her properly so she sent her to a wet nurse (Little Rose) in Semallé for several months. She recovered and soon became a normal active child. In fact, she was even called "mischievous as a little devil."[86] Nonetheless, her mother wrote:

> "What a sweet little thing she is! No one has ever been so attached to me.... My little Céline is altogether given to virtue; it is the innermost feeling of her being; she has a candid soul and has a horror of evil. I think this child is going to give me great consolation; she has a noble nature. She displays the best dispositions and is going to be a very pious child. It is truly rare to see such inclinations to piety in one so young.[87]

---
83 From Zélie's letter (CF 36) to her brother dated August 24, 1868. Translation by the author.
84 Piat, *op. cit.*, p. 79.
85 Ibid., p. 83.
86 Piat, *Céline*, p. 14.
87 Ibid., p. 15.

Besides these virtues, she proved to be intelligent, charming, witty, determined, and loving. Later in life her father and others gave her the nicknames "the intrepid," "the brave one," "Bobonne," "Demoiselle Lili" (or Lili), and "Monsieur Toto" (or just Toto).

Céline was four years old when Thérèse was born in 1873. She and Thérèse became inseparable and remained so until death separated them in 1897. Even after death, Thérèse had a tremendous influence on Céline. When they were children, Mme. Martin remarked that "I have never seen children love each other more." [88] Even Thérèse herself admitted this closeness which began very early. Their mother commented further in letters she wrote to her older daughter Pauline away at school in Le Mans:

> Céline and she [Thérèse] are very fond of each other, and are sufficient unto themselves for passing the time. Every day as soon as they've eaten dinner Céline takes her little rooster; she catches Thérèse's little hen with one swoop of her hand, something I can never do, but she's so lively she gets it in one bound. Then they come with their little pets and sit before the fireplace and amuse themselves for long hours at a time.[89]
>
> When Marie comes to get Céline for her classes, poor Thérèse begins to cry. Alas, what's going to become of her, her little friend is leaving! Marie pities her and takes her along too, and the poor little thing sits in a chair for two or three hours on end; she is given some beads to thread or a little piece of cloth to sew, and she doesn't dare budge but heaves deep sighs.[90]
>
> [The] other day ... Thérèse [upstairs] had heard Céline and had come down to be with her. Louise [the maid] said: "You don't want to get dressed?" Thérèse answered: "Oh!, no, Louise, we are like the two hens, we're inseparable!" Saying this they embraced each other and both held each other tightly." [91]

Thérèse tells us in her own words about her childhood days with Céline:

> I remember that I really wasn't able to be without Céline. I'd sooner leave the table without taking my dessert than not to follow her as soon as she got up.... Sometimes we went [across the street from their house] with the Mayor's little daughter, and I liked this because of the park and all the beautiful toys she showed us. But most of the time I went there only to please Céline, much preferring to stay in our own little garden....[92]

Upon graduation from the Abbey school, Marie was put in charge of instructing Céline though their mother guided Marie in important tasks. Mme. Martin was satisfied with the progress Marie obtained from her teaching: "I am very pleased with Céline; she is a very good child, says her prayers like an angel, learns her lessons well, and is very docile with Marie. With God's grace, we shall certainly make something good of her...." [93]

---

88 Ibid., p. 17.
89 Nov. 8, 1876.
90 March 4, 1877.
91 March 8, 1876. As quoted in *Story of a Soul*, chapter I, p. 25.
92 *Story of a Soul*, chapter I, p. 26.
93 Piat, *The Story of a Family*, pp. 202–203.

The death of Zélie Martin was a tremendous shock to her husband Louis and their five daughters. Thérèse provides details about her mother's death including this incident also involving the maid Louise:

> The day the Church blessed the mortal remains of our dear Mother, now in heaven, God willed to give me another mother on earth. He willed also that I choose her freely. All five of us were gathered together, looking at each other sadly. Louise was there too, and, seeing Céline and me, she said: "Poor little things, you have no mother any more!" Céline threw her arms around Marie saying: "Well, you will be my Mamma!" Accustomed to following Céline's example, I turned instead to you, Mother [Pauline], and as though the future had torn aside its veil, I threw myself into your arms, crying: "Well, as for me, it's Pauline who will be my Mamma!" [94]

Under the care of their older sisters and father, Céline and Thérèse lived a happy life at Les Buissonnets in Lisieux where they moved after their mother's death. Nonetheless, the personal behavior of both young girls changed perceptibly which Céline testifies to in the following note: "I, who had been so sweet became an imp full of mischief, while her [Thérèse's] high-spiritedness was instantly cloaked under the appearance of excessive timidity and sensitivity. Except for that, the roles were changed, for she was constantly the image of moral strength, and I was of the greatest weakness." [95]

In 1878, just a few months after the Martin family moved to Lisieux, the eight-and-a-half-year-old Céline entered as a part-time boarder and student at the Benedictine Abbey in Lisieux where she was an excellent student (except in mathematics) and won many awards for her academic achievements. Amazingly, by the time she left school in 1885 she had been absent only two days. A most important event during these years for Céline was her First Communion which took place on May 13, 1880, when she was eleven. Pauline devised a little devotional booklet to prepare Céline for this occasion (as she likewise did for Thérèse five years later). On each page was a picture of a different flower with a short prayer to be recited daily. Céline had to record each little act of mortification and virtue. Thérèse talks about this moving experience of Céline's First Communion in her autobiography:

> [Yes], our [Thérèse's and Céline's] joys were in common. I felt this especially on the beautiful day when Céline made her first Communion. I wasn't going to the Abbey as yet because I was only seven, but I have preserved a very sweet memory of the preparation you, my dear Mother [her sister Pauline], had Céline make. You took her, each evening, on your knees and spoke to her of the great action she was about to perform; I listened eagerly in order to prepare myself also, but very often you told me to go away as I was too little. Then my heart was very heavy and I thought four years was not too long to prepare to receive God.
>
> One evening, I heard you say that from the time one received one's First Communion, one had to commence living a new life, and I immediately made

---

94 *Story of a Soul*, chapter II, p. 34.
95 Piat, *Céline*, p. 18.

the resolution not to wait for that day but to commence the very same time as Céline. Never had I felt I loved her as much as I did during her three-day retreat; for the first time in my life, I was separated from her and I didn't sleep in her bed.... The day of Céline's First Communion left me with an impression similar to my own First Communion. When awakening in the morning all alone in the big bed, I felt *inundated with joy*. "It's today! The great day has arrived." I repeated this over and over again. It seemed it was I who was going to make my First Communion. I believe I received great graces that day and I consider it one of the most beautiful in my life.[96]

Thérèse became a student at the Abbey the next school year on October 3, 1881, when she was eight. She tells us of the new title she received about this time:

I had received the name: "Céline's little girl," and when she was irritated with me, her greatest sign of displeasure was to say: "You're no longer my little girl; that's over with, and I'll *always remember it!*" All I had to do was to start crying like a Magdalene, begging her to consider me still as her "little girl." Very soon she kissed me and promised me to *remember nothing*. To console me once she took one of her dolls and said: "My dear, embrace your Aunt!" The doll was in such a rush to embrace me tenderly that her two little arms went up *my nose*. Céline, who hadn't done it purposely, looked at me stupefied; the doll was dangling from my nose. *Aunt*, of course, was not long in warding off the excessively tender embraces of her *niece* and began laughing heartily at such a strange incident.[97]

The next quotation further typifies the relationship between the two sisters—both from Thérèse's autobiography:

I have said nothing of my close relationship with Céline and if I had to recount everything I would never come to an end. At Lisieux the roles had changed, for Céline had become a naughty little rascal and Thérèse was no longer anything but a sweet little girl, much given to crying. This did not prevent Céline and Thérèse from loving each other more and more, but at times there were little arguments. These were not of a serious nature and basically they were both of the same mind. I can truly say that *never* did my sister cause me any *trouble*, but was always a ray of sunshine for me, giving me much joy and consolation. Who can say with what intrepidity she defended me at the Abbey when I was accused of something? She took such good care of my health that I was wearied with her at times. What never wearied me, though, was *to see her at play*. She arranged our group of little dolls and conducted class like a truly clever teacher. She took care that her girls were always good, while mine were often put out of class because of bad behavior. She used to tell me all the new things she had just learned in class, which amused me very much; I looked upon her as a fountain of knowledge.[98]

During her school days, Céline's artistic talent and interest blossomed. Her father, impressed by her drawing and painting ability, provided professional art

---

96 *Story of a Soul*, chapter III, p. 57.
97 Ibid., p. 56.
98 Ibid., pp. 55–56.

lessons from a local teacher, Mlle. Godard, in 1882. Thérèse too wished for art lessons but was not allowed as Céline explains in her preparatory notes of 1908 for the Diocesan Process:

> I was thirteen when my father told me he was going to have me take drawing lessons. We were together, Thérèse and I, and I saw her eyes light up with envy, expecting to receive the same favor. In fact, my father said: "And you, my little Queen, would you like to learn how to draw?" She was about to answer when Marie spoke up, saying that the house was already cluttered with "smearings" that had to be framed, and she won the case. Thérèse didn't answer, and we did not think about what she was experiencing. Later on, some weeks before her death, she recalled this incident, and she told me that she experienced such a strong desire to complain that she wondered still, after so many years, how she had the strength to resist it.

Their uncle Isidore was acquainted with a well-known Norman artist, Édouard Krug (1829–1901), a student of one of the Flandrin brothers—three prominent Parisian artists. A painting by him of the Guardian Angel hangs in the Lisieux Cathedral today. At one point, Isidore introduced Céline to Krug who accepted her as his pupil. He was quite pleased with her work and recommended that she take some art courses in Paris and thereby be introduced to the famous Salon noted for its annual art exhibition. She was flattered, no doubt, but refused because her prime aim in life was to devote herself to God as a nun. When this goal was attained, M. Krug visited her a few times at the Carmel to check on how she was doing. In fact, he was so pleased with her progress that he gave her one of his palettes.

At the end of March 1883, Thérèse suddenly came down with a strange nervous sickness that doctors were not sure how to diagnose. This terrible condition affected the whole family. It lasted until May 13 when she was suddenly cured upon seeing the statue of the Blessed Virgin smile at her. Céline and her sister Léonie were present when it happened. This is what Thérèse wrote about the care and concern showered upon her by her sisters:

> And dear Céline, what did she not do for her Thérèse? On Sundays, instead of going out for a walk, she would close herself in for hours to be with a poor little girl who was like an idiot. Really, it took love for anyone not to fly far from me. Ah! my dear little sisters, how I made all of you suffer! No one ever caused you as much *trouble* as I, and no one ever received as much *love* as you bestowed on me.[99]

Three years later on Christmas Day of 1886 a drastic change in Thérèse's character occurred which she called her "conversion." She was to be fourteen in nine days. Again in Thérèse's words we learn the story:

> On that *night of light* began the third period of my life.... The work I had been unable to do in ten years was done by Jesus in one instant....

---
99 Ibid., p. 64.

C. Children

It was December 25, 1886, that I received the grace of leaving my childhood, in a word, the grace of my complete conversion.... We had come back from Midnight Mass.... Upon arriving at Les Buissonnets, I used to love to take my shoes from the chimney-corner and examine the presents in them; this old custom had given us so much joy in our youth that Céline wanted to continue treating me as a baby since I was the youngest in the family. Papa had always loved to see my happiness and listen to my cries of delight as I drew each surprise from the *magic shoes*.... He [Jesus] permitted Papa, tired out after the Midnight Mass, to experience annoyance when seeing my shoes at the fireplace, and that he speak those words which pierced my heart: "Well, fortunately, this will be the last year!" I was going upstairs, at the time, to remove my hat, and Céline, knowing how sensitive I was and seeing the tears already glistening in my eyes, wanted to cry too, for she loved me very much and understood my grief. She said, "Oh, Thérèse, don't go downstairs; it would cause you too much grief to look at your slippers right now!" But Thérèse was no longer the same; Jesus had changed her heart! Forcing back my tears, I descended the stairs rapidly; controlling the poundings of my heart, I took my slippers and placed them in front of Papa, and withdrew all the objects joyfully. I had the happy appearance of a Queen. Having regained his own cheerfulness, Papa was laughing; Céline believed it was all a *dream*! Fortunately, it was a sweet reality; Thérèse had discovered once again the strength of soul which she had lost at the age of four and a half, and she was to preserve it forever.[100]

For some time Thérèse felt "consumed with a *thirst for souls*. As yet, it was not the souls of priests that attracted me, but those of *great sinners*; I *burned* with the desire to snatch them from the eternal flames."[101] Eventually her chance came when she read of the criminal Henri Pranzini who was accused of brutally murdering two woman and a young girl in Paris in March 1887. His capture, trial, guilty verdict, and death sentence were headline news for months. Thérèse prayed fervently for his conversion without telling anyone, but finally revealed her wishes to Céline. She was happy to know and also wanted to help in his conversion. Thérèse sought a "sign" of repentance from Henri Pranzini which did come about just before he was guillotined on August 31, 1887. "He had mounted the scaffold," Thérèse writes, "and was preparing to place his head in the formidable opening, when suddenly, seized by an inspiration, he turned, took hold of the *crucifix* the priest was holding out to him and *kissed* the *sacred wounds three times*!... I had obtained the "sign" I requested...."[102]

Thérèse continues to write about her closeness to Céline:

> Céline had become the confidante of my thoughts. Ever since Christmas we could understand each other; the distance of age no longer existed because I had grown in both height and grace. Before this epoch I'd often complained at not knowing Céline's secrets, and she told me I was too little, that I'd have

---

100 Ibid., chapter V, p. 98.
101 Ibid., p. 99.
102 Ibid., p. 100.

to grow "as high as a stool" so that she could have confidence in me. I loved climbing up on that precious stool when I was standing by her side and tell her to speak intimately to me; but all to no avail, a distance separated us still!

Jesus, wanting to have us advance together, formed bonds in our hearts stronger than blood. He made us become *spiritual sisters*....[103]

Thérèse finally disclosed to Céline her burning desire to become a Carmelite, possibly even before her fifteenth birthday, at the monastery in Lisieux where her two older sisters Pauline and Marie were already nuns. This she hoped to be accomplished before her fifteenth birthday. Right from the start Céline and her father consented, sadly but with a sense of reverential pride. Thérèse compliments her sister in this quotation:

> [My] dear Céline did not rebel for one instant. And still it wasn't she whom Jesus was calling first, and she could have complained, for having the same vocation as I, it was her right to leave first!... thus Céline allowed her Thérèse to leave and she stayed for a the glorious and bloody struggle to which Jesus had destined her as the *privileged one of His love*![104]

However, there were objections from many quarters particularly from the superior of the Lisieux Carmel who adamantly refused to permit Thérèse to enter. She therefore sought higher ecclesiastical approval. Accompanied by her father, she went to Bayeux to obtain the bishop's permission. His answer was devastating since he told her to get permission from Canon Delatroëtte, the Carmel's superior!

Well before this interview with the bishop, Louis Martin paid for a pilgrimage to Rome for himself and his two daughters Thérèse and Céline which had been planned to start in four days on November 4, 1887. A papal audience with Pope Leo XIII was scheduled on November 20 at which no one was permitted to speak to the pope. Nonetheless, Thérèse's only resort and thus her explicit aim at this point was to ask the pope for his consent. Céline agreed with her bold plan and strongly insisted that she: "Speak! Speak!" She did. "Holy Father, in honor of your Jubilee permit me to enter Carmel at the age of fifteen!" His answer was for her to do as the superiors say. "Oh! Holy Father, if you say yes, everyone else will too." His non-committal, disappointing response was "Go... go.... You will enter if God wills it."[105]

Despite not receiving a favorable answer from the pope, Thérèse and Céline managed to enjoy the trip and all the wonderful sights they saw and shared together. Céline, "the intrepid one," encouraged Thérèse at a number of places to go beyond what was allowed of tourists. They hurried down to the floor of the Colosseum to pray where the martyrs died, picked some earth from the catacomb tomb where St. Cecilia's body had lain, and took a piece of red stone that had detached from a mosaic in the church of St. Agnès. Paris, Milan, Venice,

---
103 Ibid., p. 103.
104 Ibid., pp. 106–107.
105 Ibid., chapter VI, p. 135.

Padua, Loreto, Pompeii, Assisi, Florence, Pisa, Nice, Marseille, and Lyon all provided their secular and religious sites that charmed the girls. At Bologna the two sisters experienced this intriguing episode:

> Céline reported that when they were getting off the train, her Father was separated from them for a moment as he was looking for his baggage. Many students crowded into the station, and one of them took hold of Thérèse, trying to drag her off. Thérèse said: "But I gave him such a look he soon let go! Besides, Céline had seen what happened and was coming to my rescue."[106]

Twenty-six days after this trip, the bishop, Monsignor Hugonin, gave his permission for Thérèse to become a Carmelite. Actually, however, she had to wait until April 9, 1888, to enter the Carmel. Thus began a new epoch in the lives of both Céline and Thérèse. Céline remained at home with her father and Léonie. He suffered paralytic strokes which affected him not only physically but mentally. Within eleven months after Thérèse's entrance, Louis Martin was hospitalized on Feb. 12, 1889, at Bon Sauveur hospital in Caen where he remained for three years. In the beginning, the two sisters stayed at a convent near the hospital in order to see him as often as possible. This lasted for about thirteen weeks until they were allowed to visit only on weekends, so they went home and saw their father just at those times. He returned home finally on May 10, 1892, and was taken care of tenderly by Céline and Léonie. This extract from Céline's spiritual notebook clearly explains her extremely tender feelings about attending to her invalid father:

> My joy was great at being able to care for my beloved father myself.... I never grew tired of embracing him; I showed him my affection in a thousand different ways and did everything I could to please him.... And I was so happy that even to stay in a dungeon with him would have seemed sheer delight to me. Nothing, nothing would have made any difference to me in his company.... No, it was not ordinary filial love that I had for my father; I repeat, it was a kind of worship.[107]

But there were unexpected trials, humiliations, and sufferings also included in Céline's life as a caregiver. Pauline, in her *Souvenirs intimes, 1905*, p. 84, referred to these problems: "Outside the monastery, many persons made us responsible for this misfortune [their father's mental condition], caused, they said, by his extreme sorrow, especially when Thérèse entered the Carmel." Thérèse in her inimitable way encouraged Céline concerning these accusations which she refers here to as "pinpricks." Pauline gave, as indicated below, Céline the nickname "Lily Immortelle" a few years before:

> The more our heart is in heaven the less we feel these *pinpricks*.... But believe that this is a *grace* and a *great grace* to feel these pinpricks, for, then, our life is a martyrdom, and one day Jesus will give us the palm. To suffer and to be *despised*!... what *bitterness* but what glory. That is the Lily Immortelle's motto!... No other could suit her. My heart is following you in the *noble task*

---

106 Note of Mother Agnès as given in footnote 141, p. 128 in *Story of a Soul*.
107 Piat, *Céline*, pp. 48–49.

that Jesus has entrusted to you. You are not a soldier but a General.... Suffer both again and always.... But all passes.[108]

Thérèse extolled her two sisters who lovingly took care of their father:

> What marvels the trial worked in my dear Céline's soul! All the letters she wrote at this epoch are filled with resignation and love. And who could express the visits we had together? Ah! far from separating us, Carmel's grilles united our souls more strongly; we had the same thoughts, the same desires, the same *love for Jesus* and *for souls*. When Céline and Thérèse were speaking together, never did a word concerning the things of the earth mingle in their conversations which were already in the heavens. As formerly in the *belvédère*, they dreamed about things of *eternity*.[109]

From the years 1888 to 1894 when Thérèse and Céline were separated, a steady stream of letters flowed between them. Thérèse's thoughts, doctrine, and counsel therein are of incalculable spiritual richness. Unfortunately many of Céline's letters to her from this time are lost. Five major concerns occupied Céline during these years: charge of the Martin household; care for her sick father; the possibility of going to Canada to assist her spiritual director Father Pichon in his apostolate; marriage proposals; and the most compelling—becoming a Carmelite.

Céline was an attractive and charming young lady who declined marriage proposals from two ardent male admirers. In fact, on the very day that Thérèse entered Carmel, April 9, 1888, she received an offer of marriage from her aunt Guérin's nephew Henry Maudelonde (1864–1937). She recalled years later when she was a nun that:

> ... either at his house or ours, he always had to be near me. Since he demanded this boldly when he was not, we ended up by placing him definitively next to me at table in order to avoid scenes. Dinner over, he used to take me in his arms, whether I liked it or not, and made me dance.... My cousin Marie ... believed she was pleasing me by reporting.... "If you only knew how much Henry loves you." What struggles! ... I belonged to Jesus alone.[110]

Needless to say, she refused him. In 1892 he married another woman who died three years later. Four years after her death, he married for the second time.

Aware of Céline's marriage proposals and worldly associations, Thérèse had this to say:

> I had already suffered very much when knowing she was exposed to dangers in the world which were unknown to me. Since my entrance into Carmel, I can say that my affection for Céline was a mother's love rather than a sister's. When she was to attend a party [the wedding of Henri Maudelonde on April 20, 1892] one day, the very thought of it caused me so much pain that I begged God to *prevent her from dancing*, and (contrary to my custom) I even shed a torrent of tears. Jesus deigned to answer me. He permitted that His little fiancée *be*

---
108 LT 81, from Thérèse to Céline, January 23–25, 1889.
109 *Story of a Soul*, chapter VII, p. 157.
110 Note 2, p. 733 to LT 130, a letter from Thérèse to Céline dated July 23, 1891.

unable to dance that evening (even though she was not embarrassed to dance gracefully when it was necessary). She was invited to dance and was unable to refuse the invitation, but her partner found out he was totally powerless to make her dance; to his great confusion he was condemned simply *to walking* in order to conduct her to her place, and then he made his escape and did not reappear for the whole evening.[111]

Father Pichon thought that Céline should consider his missionary plans for her since he did not believe the Lisieux Carmel would ever allow four sisters to be together in the same convent. Despite some objections from various quarters including those who thought the convent would become a Martin monopoly, she was ultimately accepted. Father Pichon, though disappointed, acquiesced and extended his blessings to her.

Less than two months later (47 days), after her father died, Céline, now twenty-five, entered Carmel on September 14, 1894, where as a postulant she was called Marie of the Holy Face, the name Thérèse suggested she take. Thérèse wrote: "But the most intimate of my desires, the greatest of them all, which I thought would never be realized, was my dear Céline's entrance into the same Carmel as ours."[112]

When in the world, Céline and her cousin Marie Guérin developed an interest in what became a fashionable pastime for many in France at the time—photography. They had even participated in an amateur photo exhibition.[113] Fortuitously, Céline's sister Pauline (Mother Agnès, the prioress at the time) permitted her to bring her camera, a 13/18 Darlot, and all the photographic accessories with her when she entered the convent. She also allowed her to develop and print the pictures she took in one of the rooms in the convent cellar. Because of Céline, we now have some forty-two images of Thérèse out of a total of forty-three photographs that she herself took in the convent or that she set up for another nun (usually Sr. St. John of the Cross) to take when Céline was posing in the picture. Unfortunately, Céline received a considerable amount of criticism for retouching some of the photographs of Thérèse which she did with the strong belief that by so doing she was producing a true likeness of her sister which some of the photos failed to do.

On February 5, 1895, she received the habit and had to change her name from Sister Marie of the Holy Face to Sister Geneviève of St. Teresa. By this her superiors wanted to retain the memory of the foundress of the Lisieux Carmel, Mother Geneviève of Saint Teresa (1805–1891). Later, in 1916 she changed her name to Sister Geneviève of the Holy Face. At the time Céline entered, Thérèse, twenty-one, had been six years a Carmelite and the un-official novice-mistress. Céline was a conscientious novice, listened attentively, and followed her counsel; but, strangely, it wasn't until two months before Thérèse died that she became a true and permanent follower of the "little way of love and confidence." Céline tells quite candidly about her novice days with Thérèse:

---
111 *Story of a Soul*, chapter VIII, p. 176.
112 Ibid.
113 Piat, *op. cit.*, p. 64.

Because she had been given charge of the novices, my communications with my dear Thérèse were very frequent, but even in that I was to encounter the cross. Since I was not the only "kitten drinking out of the Infant Jesus' bowl," I was not supposed to take more than the others or to go back to it more often but, on the contrary, I was, through my discretion, to try to win forgiveness for the privilege of being her sister. This was the source of great sacrifices for me.[114]

Thérèse's written material to Céline during her days in the convent is rather large and includes letters, prayers, poems, and messages on holy cards. Out of a known fifty-seven letters to Céline, eighteen were addressed to her when they were together in the convent. The most imaginative and fanciful letter Thérèse wrote to her was on the occasion of her profession which was considered her marriage to Jesus. Thérèse composed it at Céline's request and relates in her own inimitable way her "wedding" as it would be celebrated in heaven. It is a long, imaginative, and feminine description in a style Céline admired. Part of it goes this way: "Thus all the pontiffs, the glorious martyrs, the warriors (at their head, St. Sebastian), in a word, the whole heavenly nobility will take glory in giving the spouse of Jesus the name of sister, and the wedding will be composed of one great and identical family."[115] The next day, Thérèse placed a large envelope in Céline's cell containing a beautifully painted illuminated parchment she made which was the "Contract of Marriage of Jesus and Céline." It begins: "I, JESUS, ETERNAL WORD, THE ONLY SON OF GOD AND OF THE VIRGIN MARY, espouse today CÉLINE, exiled princess, poor and without titles. I give Myself to her under the name of KNIGHT OF LOVE OF SUFFERING AND CONTEMPT." With it Thérèse included Céline's coat of arms that had the motto, "Who loses wins."[116] It too was meticulously and artistically executed.

Thérèse composed ten poems and four prayers especially for her, at her request, or suggested by her. The poems are listed below with brief explanations:

1. PN 3   "Saint Cecilia," written for Céline's 25th birthday.
2. PN 4   "Canticle to Obtain the Canonization of Joan of Arc," is dedicated to Céline, the "Galant Knight C. Martin."
3. PN 8   "Prayer of a Child of a Saint," contains word portraits of the daughters of the recently deceased Louis Martin.
4. PN 13 "The Queen of Heaven to Her Beloved Child Marie of the Holy Face," written as her 1894 Christmas gift to Céline.
5. PN 16 "Song of Gratitude of Jesus' Fiancée," written for Céline's clothing day, February 5, 1895.
6. PN 17 "Living on Love," stanza 4 was written at Céline's advice.
7. PN 18 "The Canticle of Céline," written for Céline's 26th birthday.
8. PN 24 "Jesus, My Beloved, Remember," depicts the life of Jesus that Céline requested.

---
114 Ibid., p. 71.
115 LT 182, Feb. 23, 1896, from Thérèse to Sr. Geneviève (Céline).
116 LT 183, February 24, 1896, Thérèse to Sr. Geneviève.

9. PN 27 "Remembrance of February 24, 1896," written in memory and honor of Céline's profession.
10. PN 48 "My Weapons," written for Marie Guérin, but alluding also to Céline to strengthen their religious profession.

All of Thérèse's poems were composed with a specific purpose in mind. For her third one (PN 3), for example, she clearly specifies her motive. Céline was alone at home taking care of her father. Thérèse addressed a deepfelt letter to her, part of which follows:

> Dear Little Lyre of Jesus ... Céline! I am sure you will understand all my canticle would like to tell you, alas, I would need a tongue other than that of this earth to express the beauty of a soul's abandonment into the hands of Jesus. My heart was able only to babble what it feels.... Céline, *the story of Cecilia* (the Saint of ABANDONMENT) is your story too![117]

The four prayers Thérèse composed concerning Céline are:

1. Pri 6 "Act of Oblation to Merciful Love," written for herself and for Céline.
2. Pri 9 "Prayer of Céline and Thérèse," composed for and given to Céline on Christmas, 1895.
3. Pri 12 "Consecration to the Holy Face," composed for herself and two of the novices, Céline and Sister Marie of the Trinity.
4. Pri 18 "O holy Innocents, O Saint Sebastian," composed for Céline at the time she was completing a year of profession.

The Carmelites from the time of St. Teresa of Avila were encouraged to have some time for recreation. Following this custom, the nuns at the Lisieux Carmel often would perform little skits written by the Carmelites themselves. Thérèse was asked to write them after she entered and as a result composed eight during her life there. The novices always performed in them. Thérèse played the lead in five and Céline also was involved. The most important one perhaps is *Joan of Arc Accomplishing Her Mission* (RP 3) from which we have five photos of Thérèse and Céline posing in costumes. It was performed on January 21, 1895, with Thérèse as Joan and Céline as Saint Margaret. No other plays or characters from them were ever photographed. Céline took four photos of Thérèse alone as Joan and one with the two of them together that was snapped by another nun, most likely Sister St. John of the Cross.

In the fall of the next year, 1896, Thérèse was greatly concerned that Pauline (Mother Agnès) would be sent to Saigon for a Carmelite foundation in Hanoi. This was cancelled. "However, a few months after this, they spoke of the departure of Sister Geneviève and Sister Marie of the Trinity. Then this was another kind of suffering, very intimate, very deep; I imagined all the trials, the disappointment they would suffer, and my heaven was covered with clouds;

---

[117] LT 151, dated April 26, 1894.

calm and peace remained only in the depth of my heart."[118] Fortunately, this departure never came to fruition and Céline remained at Lisieux.

Sadly, Thérèse became a victim of the dreaded and, unfortunately, the common disease of the time, tuberculosis. By July of 1897, her condition worsened and she was sent to the infirmary where Céline became her infirmarian. During the last months of her life her sisters recorded Thérèse's conversations. Céline jotted down on little slips of paper those words that were most pertinent to her. Then in 1898 she transferred some of them into a notebook, and in 1925 into a larger notebook with the title *Last Conversations of Thérèse to Céline*.[119] Throughout the days and months of her suffering, Thérèse often told Céline that after she died she would come down and get her since they could not be separated for long. One example of this is when Céline was with her in the infirmary, Thérèse looked at the picture of her beloved friend, the future Saint Theophane Venard (1829–1861), and said to him: "Bobonne [Thérèse's nickname for Céline] is taking good care of me, and as soon as I'm up there, we shall come looking for her together, right?"[120] Her wish, thankfully, did not come true, for Céline spent the rest of her long life in working for the cause, message, and glorification of her saintly sister.

On the last day of Thérèse's life, Céline was present at her bedside and made this telling observation:

> During her final agony, a few moments before she expired, I was passing a little piece of ice over her burning lips, and at this moment she lifted her eyes to me and looked at me with prophetic insistence. Her look was filled with tenderness, and there was in it a superhuman expression of encouragement and promise as though she were saying to me:
> "Go, go! Céline, I shall be with you!"
> Did God reveal to her the long and laborious career I was to carry out here on earth for her sake, and did He will through this look to console me in my exile? For the memory of that last look, so much desired by all and given to me, sustains me always and is an inexpressible strength for me.[121]

Céline as Sister Geneviève continued her artwork when she entered the convent and worked at it through the years prior to Thérèse's death. It wasn't until after her death that she produced the oil portraits of Thérèse such as the oval one, considered the authentic picture of Thérèse, that appeared in the second edition of the *Story of a Soul*. In addition, she is responsible for the sketches and paintings of Thérèse on her deathbed, Thérèse as a ten-year-old first communicant, her mother, her father, Thérèse with a harp, Christ at the Pillar, Christ Crucified, and many others. One of her paintings was done in grisaille and based on a photograph (1898) of Christ's face on the Shroud of Turin. It won the grand prize in an international religious art show in Bois-le-Duc (the Netherlands).[122]

---

118 *Story of a Soul*, chapter X, p. 217.
119 *Her Last Conversations*, p. 313.
120 Ibid., September 11, 1897, p. 226.
121 Ibid., September 30, 1897, p. 229.
122 Descouvemont, *op. cit.*, p. 312.

Interestingly, the inescapable portrayal of Thérèse holding a crucifix and roses did not originate with Céline or anyone else at the Carmel. Céline eventually did paint a picture of Thérèse that way in 1912 but it "was inspired by the wish of the Postulator of the Cause that the custom be followed of discerning in the Servants of God some symbolic attribute." [123]

In addition to her artwork, Céline wrote by herself much material in the course of the years about Thérèse and her family, in collaboration with Pauline, or with artists. Her published works include: [124]

1. 1914   *La petite Thérèse: Histoire de Soeur Thérèse de l'Enfant-Jésus.* The English edition is titled *Little Thérèse, The Life of Sister Thérèse of Lisieux for Children* written by Céline under the pseudonym of Père J. Carbonel, S.J., 1925. The artist Charles Jouvenot did the illustrations.

2. 1919   *La Petite Voie* (The Little Way). Another title inside the cover is *Ascension mystique de la Montagne de la Perfection par la Voie d'Amour et d'Enfance Spirituelle de la Servante de Dieu Thérèse de l'Enfant-Jésus.* Subsequent editions after Thérèse's canonization replaced the word "Servante" with "Sainte." English translations followed under the title *The Little Way,* with the subtitle, *Mystical Ascent to the Mountain of Perfection by the Way of Love and Spiritual Childhood of Saint Thérèse of the Child Jesus.* This book is an allegorical poem with 31 stanzas and 31 pictures in color for which Céline is reported to have supplied all the words and made corrections to some of the drawings by the artist Charles Jouvenot. The Abbé Ernest Langlois composed the music.

3. 1922   *L'Esprit de la bienheureuse Thérèse de l'Enfant Jésus d'après ses éscrits et les témoins oculaires de sa vie. The Spirit of Blessed Thérèse of the Child Jesus according to Her Writings and Witnesses to Her Life* is the name of the English edition of 1923.

4. 1932   *Petit catéchisme de l'Acte d'Offrande de Sainte Thérèse de L'Enfant-Jésus comme Victime d'Holocauste a L'amour Miséricordieux du bon Dieu.* The English edition is entitled *The Little Catechism of the Act of Offering of Saint Thérèse of the Infant Jesus as a Victim of Holocaust to the Merciful Love of the good God.*

5. 1951   *Vie en Images de Sainte Thérèse de L'Enfant-Jésus en 77 Tableaux avec Couplets et Musique pour Séances de Projections Epilogue illustré: Prières* (Life in Pictures of Saint Thérèse of the Infant Jesus with 77 pictures and the words and music for Projection). Pauline did all the writing. The artists Jouvenot, Blanchard, Dewinter, and Arnould did the art work with retouching by Céline.

6. 1952   *Conseils et Souvenir recueillis / Soeur Geneviève de la Sainte-Face, soeur et novice de Sainte Thérèse de l'Enfant-Jésus,* 1952. The English edition it is called *A Memoir of My Sister St. Thérèse,* 1959.

7. 1953   *Le Père de sainte Thérèse de l'Enfant-Jésus (1823–1894).* The 1955 English edition had the title *The Father of The Little Flower (Saint Thérèse*

---

123 Piat, *op. cit.*, p. 119.
124 Ibid., pp. 113–117.

of the Child Jesus) 1823–1894: The Sister of St. Thérèse tells us about her father. Translated by Rev. Michael Collins, S.M.A.

8. 1954   *La Mère de sainte Thérèse de l'Enfant-Jésus (1831–1877)*. The English edition appeared in 1957 with the title *The Mother of the Little Flower (Saint Thérèse of the Child Jesus) 1831–1877: The sister of St. Thérèse tells us about her mother*. Translated by Rev. Michael Collins, S.M.A.

Throughout the years, Sister Geneviève was an indefatigable promoter of her sister's mission and provided first-hand information to a number of authors writing about Thérèse. She had the privilege of testifying at the process of Thérèse's beatification and canonization and the joyful pleasure of being a witness at the early stages of process of beatification (the Informative Process) for both her parents in 1958.

At the death of her sister Pauline (Mother Agnès) in 1951, Céline was the last surviving member of the Martin family. For the next eight years she suffered intermittently from various ailments due to old age: influenza, arthritis, pneumonia, and heart failure. Her last day of life was on Wednesday, February 25, 1959, and her last spoken word was "Jesus." She expired quietly at 9:30 in the morning at the age of eighty-nine years and ten months. The funeral ceremony and burial attended by numerous bishops, clergy, and lay people took place on Saturday, February 28. Carmelite Fathers with their white mantles carried the coffin of their sister Carmelite who had spent sixty-four years in religion, to the vault at the Carmel chapel where they placed her next to her sisters Pauline and Marie. The memorial plaque reads: "You have hidden us, Lord, in the secret of your Face."[125]

8. Marie-Mélanie-Thérèse Martin—"Mélanie" (1870)
The third Martin child to die in infancy

During the Franco-Prussian war (1870–1871), Alençon experienced a number of military incidents and much deprivation. Many families, including the Martins, were required to billet the victorious enemy soldiers in their own homes. Amidst all the turmoil, Marie-Mélanie Thérèse, their eighth child, was born on August 16, 1870, at the Martin home on the Rue du Pont Neuf where M. Martin also had his watchmaking shop and jewelry store. Just six months before, the family witnessed the sudden death of their five-year-old daughter Hélène, and this new child came as a joy that helped lighten their personal sorrow and soften the turbulence of the war and its ramifications of it around them. Another happy occurrence six days later was the birth of Thérèse's cousin Marie, Uncle and Aunt Guérin's second daughter.

Because she was physically unable to nurse her last three babies, Zélie again sought the trustworthy wet nurse Rose Taillé who, unfortunately, was not available this time which forced the Martins to engage a comparative stranger. Medical agencies guaranteeing nurses' character and qualifications did not exist

---
125 Ibid., p. 195.

then. The woman chosen lived nearby on the Rue de la Barre and proved to be a fatal selection. As a result of her shameful negligence, malnutrition set in and Mélanie's health rapidly declined. When the parents discovered their child's terrible state, M. Martin rescued her in the middle of the night, but it was too late. Frantically, Zélie attempted to restore her infant's health. It was of no avail for the pitiable sixty-two day old infant died on October 8, 1870. In a note written to her devoted sister-in-law Céline Guérin the day Mélanie passed away in her mother's lap, Zélie expressed her overwhelming sorrow:

> My little Thérèse [Mélanie] is dead, today, Saturday at one o'clock in the afternoon.... Her agony began this morning at half past ten and you cannot imagine what she suffered. I am so broken-hearted, I so loved this child. At each new bereavement for me it seems that I love the one I have lost more than the others. She was so pretty ... like a bouquet of flowers. Besides which I took care of her myself. Oh, I wish I could die also. I am fatigued these past two days. I have eaten almost nothing and stayed up all night in mortal anguish.[126]

And later she wrote to her brother Isidore:

> It was such a pretty little girl. She had eyes such as one never sees in babies of that age, and such delicate features. And to think that she was allowed to die of hunger! Is it not terrible? You do not know what a delight it was going to be to bring up this little one all by myself. I was as glad to have her as though it was my first child. Ah well! It is all over and there is no remedy, and the best thing I can do is to resign myself. The child is happy and that consoles me.[127]

Incidentally, Zélie never went near the Rue de la Barre from then on for the tragic association with this street was too painful for her.

Despite the anguish of Mélanie's loss, Zélie was not in despair or abandoned all hope of having other children. She told her brother: "I wish however that the good God will give me another. I do not desire a little boy, but another little Thérèse who will not go out to a nurse (because this time I will bring a nurse into the house). No, if the good God grants me other children they will not go out of the house."[128] God did grant her "another little Thérèse" three years later, but the devoted and trustworthy wet nurse Rose Taillé was unable to stay at the Martin home, as they begged her to do, because she had her own large family to manage. The future saint of Lisieux, therefore, had to go to Rose's farmhouse in the country.

9. MARIE-FRANÇOISE-THÉRÈSE — "THÉRÈSE" (1873–1897)
(SISTER THÉRÈSE OF THE CHILD JESUS AND OF THE HOLY FACE)
Canonized in 1925 (See Chapter 1. A for her biography)

---

[126] From Zélie's letter (CF 60) to Mme. Guerin, dated October 8, 1870, as translated by the author.
[127] From Zélie's letter (CF 61) to Isidore, dated October 1870, as quoted in Piat's *The Story of a Family*, p. 96.
[128] From Zélie's letter to Isidore (CF 61) as quoted in Redman, *op. cit.*, pp. 64–65.

D. Grandparents

1. CAPTAIN PIERRE-FRANÇOIS MARTIN:
   Thérèse's paternal Grandfather
2. FANIE BOUREAU MARTIN: *Thérèse's paternal Grandmother*
3. ISIDORE GUÉRIN: *Thérèse's maternal Grandfather*
4. LOUISE-JEANNE MACÉ GUÉRIN: *Thérèse's maternal Grandmother*

1. CAPTAIN PIERRE-FRANÇOIS MARTIN (1777–1865)
Thérèse's paternal Grandfather

TWELVE YEARS BEFORE THE FRENCH REVOLUTION (1789–1799), PIERRE-Françoise Martin, St. Thérèse's paternal grandfather, was born on April 16, 1777, in Athis-de-l'Orne. He came from a family enriched with a history of fortitude, military distinction, and deep religious faith. At the end of the Revolution on August 36, 1799, when he was twenty-two, Pierre enlisted in the army. His father, Jean Martin (1752–1806)—Thérèse's great-grandfather—also served in the army when he was a young man and in the course of time became a captain. For the next thirty-one years Pierre likewise exercised his military duties honorably and rose through the ranks during the Napoleonic Wars (1799–1815) and the upheavals that followed. He progressed honorably in his military career from his entrance to his retirement. Following is a detailed record of his military service:[1]

> Enlisted in the 65th regiment of Infantry (made 61st in 1814) on the August 26, 1799; became corporal on December 22, 1800; sergeant on March 7, 1804; sub-lieutenant on April 14, 1813; lieutenant October 25, 1813; captain (provisional) June 27, 1815; commission ratified August 21, 1816, ranking from the January 1 preceding.
>
> Passed in 1816 into the departmental Legion of the Loire-Inférieure in 1821 to the 19th regiment of Light Infantry, and in 1828 was placed on the military staff at Strasbourg from which position he retired on the December 12, 1830.
>
> CAMPAIGNS:
> 1779–1801   Army of the Rhine
> 1803   Belle-Ile en Mer
> 1804–1805   Sous Brest
> 1806   Army of Nord
> 1807   Prussia and Poland
> 1814   Army of Nord and campaign in France
> 1815   Royal army in Morbihan
> 1823–1824   Spain

While in Spain he was honored with the royal and military Cross of a Knight of St. Louis. During the Restoration (1814–1848), he was stationed in a number

---
[1] Laveille, *op. cit.*, 375.

of French towns including Bordeaux, Avignon, Strasbourg, and Lyons. While doing garrison duty in Lyon he met Captain Nicolas-Jean Boureau.[2]

Captain Boureau had a young daughter, Marie-Anne-Fanie (1800–1883), with whom Captain Martin became romantically involved, soon engaged, and finally married on April 4, 1818.[3] He at the time was forty-one and she eighteen. In that era, a dowry was a fundamental requisite for an officer's wife-to-be. Fanie's family had experienced financial setbacks but through the magnanimity of Captain Martin's remarkable character, he supplied the required amount. Below is an extract from the Register of the Parish of Saint-Martin d'Ainay, Lyon, that recorded the marriage of Pierre and Fanie:

> On the seventh of April, eighteen hundred and eighteen, after one duly made publication of banns (dispensation from the other two having been obtained) without having found any impediment or opposition whatever to the consent of the respective parties, the civil formalities required by the mayoralty of Lyons having been complied with on the _____ [left blank] [4th of April, 1818], I, the undersigned, have solemnized the marriage of M. Pierre-François Martin, legitimate son of the late John Martin and Marie-Anne Bohard of Athis, captain on active service of the 42nd regiment of the line, residing at Lyons, bridegroom, on the one part.
>
> And Mlle. Marie-Anne-Françoise [Fanie], legitimate daughter of M. Nicolas Boureau and Marie Ney [Nay], with whom she lived at Lyons, rue Vaubecourt, bride, on the other part.—The witnesses were M. the Count de Labesse, colonel of the Legion of the Loire-Inférieure, M. Averin battalion commandant in the same Legion, M. Moyat, major of that Legion, M. Larue and M. Gourd, who with other relatives and friends have affixed their signatures with mine.
>
> Signed: BOURGANEL, Vicaire[4]

In the course of their married life they parented five children:

1. **Pierre** (1819–?), died in a shipwreck.
2. **Marie-Anne** (1820–1846), married Francis Burin.
3. **Louis-Joseph** (1823–1894), married Azélie Guérin, and was the father of St. Thérèse.
4. **Anne-Fanie** (1826–1853), married Adolphe Leriche.
5. **Sophie** (1833–1842), Louis's favorite sibling who died at 9.

On December 12, 1830, Captain Martin retired at the age of fifty-three. He moved with his family from Strasbourg to his beloved Normandy, the land of his ancestors, and settled down in Alençon where he knew his children would receive a good education. Their first home was on the Rue des Tisons (1830–1842) and later they moved to the Rue du Mans (1842–1850).[5] In 1850 the Martins relocated to 15 rue du Pont Neuf to be with their son and his wife. Louis's watchmaking and jewelry shop was on the ground floor and so was the

---

2 Piat, *op. cit.*, p. 7.
3 *Œuvres Thérèse de Lisieux Complètes*, p. 1477.
4 Laveille, *op. cit.*, pp. 371–372.
5 Piat, *op. cit.*, p. 9.

newly wedded couple's living quarters.⁶ (They also occupied the third floor.) His parents had their own rooms on the second floor.

Captain Martin, a dedicated and proud member of the Catholic Church, was a steadfast mainstay of his family. A lady active in the social life of Alençon described him to his Carmelite granddaughters: "He won our admiration by his immaculate appearance; he looked very fine in his greatcoat, decorated with the red ribbon which one did not meet in the streets in those days. What a lineage of saints you have in your family!"[7] Added to this accolade are two others. The first is the opinion the soldiers under him had of their leader. They observed with amazement his deep devotion and piety, particularly observable when he recited his prayers and his immersion in the mystery of the Mass especially during the consecration. His response to those who wondered why he evinced so much intensity was: "Tell them that it is because I believe!"[8] Another example is evident from one of his letters:

> "Praised be Jesus Christ!"
> Alençon, August 7th, 1828
>
> Monsieur,
>
> I have received your letter from which I learn that, by my communication, the consent to your marriage has safely reached you. At last, thank God!, my task is fulfilled to the best of my ability; now I desire, with all my heart, that our divine Master may deign to bless your union with my beloved niece, and that you may be as happy as one can be in this world, and that when you draw your last breath God may receive you into His mercy and place you among the number of the blessed, there to live forever. Kindly greet your estimable parents and ours. We all send you affectionate greetings.
>
> Yours sincerely in Jesus and Mary,
MARTIN [9]

In April 1865 the Captain, stricken with paralysis from a stroke, lingered on until June 26 when he died peacefully at home at the age of eighty-eight. Zélie, who dearly loved her father-in-law, described his death to her brother:

> My father-in-law died yesterday at 1 P.M. He had received the sacraments last Thursday. He had a holy death and died as he had lived. I should never have believed it could have affected me so much. I am overwhelmed....
>
> I own to you that I am terrified of death. I have just been to see my father-in-law. His arms are so stiff and his face so cold! And to think that I shall see my loved ones like that, or that they will see me!
>
> If you are used to looking upon death, I have never seen it at such close quarters.[10]

---

6 *Sicut Parvuli*, January 1974, p. 8.
7 Piat, *op. cit.*, p. 9.
8 Ibid., p. 10.
9 Ibid. This letter was written by Captain Martin to Nicholas Moulin who was to marry the Captain's niece.
10 Ibid., p. 74.

Thérèse was born eight years after her paternal grandfather died. She not only never knew him but neither did she see any of her father's four other siblings who all passed away twenty years before her birth.

2. Fanie Boureau Martin (1800–1883)
Thérèse's paternal Grandmother, the only grandparent Thérèse knew

THÉRÈSE'S PATERNAL GRANDMOTHER, MME. FANIE MARTIN, WAS THE ONLY grandparent living at Thérèse's birth. Marie-Anne-Fanie, the daughter of Maria Nay and Captain Jean Nicolas Boureau, was born in Blois (in the Loir Valley) on January 12, 1800, into a noted and distinguished military family. The parish priest of Ainay wrote a glowing account of the Captain's character:

> M. Nicholas-Jean Boureau, Captain, domiciled in this parish at no. 4, Rue Vaubecourt, with his wife and two daughters [Sophie and Fanie] had led a life grounded upon principles of honor, right conduct, and religion, and that on account of its virtues this honorable family is worthy of the esteem and admiration of the citizens of this town.[11]

The two captains—Pierre Martin (Thérèse's paternal grandfather) and Jean Boureau—served in the royal army in Lyon (1816–1817) where Pierre was introduced to and infatuated by Fanie. It came then as no real surprise that Fanie married Captain Pierre Martin on April 7, 1818, in the church of Saint-Martin d'Ainay in Lyons. They had five children, none of whom lived beyond their twenties except Louis:

1. **Pierre**, born in 1819, died young—lost in a shipwreck.
2. **Marie-Anne** (1820–1846) married François-Burin, and died childless at twenty-six.
3. **Louis** (1823–1894), the father of St. Thérèse, died at seventy-one.
4. **Anne-Fannie** (1826–1853) married François Leriche (1818–1843), had one son Adolphe (1844–1894), and died at twenty-seven.
5. **Sophie** (1833–1842), a favorite of Louis, died a child of nine.

After the death of Grandmother Martin, Adolphe Leriche was Thérèse's only close living relative on her father's side of the family.

Camp life in those days permitted the wife and family of officers to follow them on tours of duty which explains why the Martins lived in a number of cities including Avignon and Strasbourg in the early years of their marriage. When Louis was away on trips or when studying his watch making trade, his parents, particularly his mother, often wrote him letters which reveal their love and true Christian nature. A typical letter from Louis's mother (Thérèse's grandmother) attests to her noble character and tender concern for him. Her ideas sound remarkably Theresian:

> Yet we must bear the crosses which God sends us, and thank him every day for the favors he has bestowed.... With what joy I pressed you to my heart, for you, dear son, are the dream of my nights and the constant subject of my

---
11 Piat, *op. cit.*, p. 7.

thoughts.... How many times do I think of you when my soul, in prayer, follows the leading of my heart and darts up even to the divine throne. There, I pray with all the fervor of my soul that God may bestow on my children the interior happiness and calm which are so necessary in this turbulent world.... Remain always humble, dear son.[12]

Upon retirement in 1830, Captain Martin and his family moved to Alençon and within twenty years they lived in two different houses. They settled down for good at the residence quarters of their son's clock and watchmaker's business on the rue du Pont Neuf. There they lived a respectable family existence in the fervent practice of their religion and involvement with various charitable activities.

Fanie Martin was not content to see her thirty-five-year-old son Louis, pious and diligent as he was, end his days as a bachelor so she urged him to seek a compatible mate. Unsuccessful at this, she attempted to find one for him herself. A fortuitous incident occurred that solved the problem. By chance, Louis passed an attractive young lady one day at dusk while crossing the Bridge of Saint Leonard over the River Sarthe. The lady noticed him and was very impressed. They did not speak but she knew, with storybook foresight, that he was to be her husband. An inner voice told her, "This is he whom I have prepared for thee."[13] Fanie Martin was absolutely delighted when she heard about this from the lady who was Zélie Guérin, a fellow student in a class they both attended on *Point d'Alençon* lace. She had greatly admired her and secretly thought she would be an ideal woman for her son. She certainly proved to be the ideal woman. They were formally introduced and marriage ensued only three months later on July 13, 1858. The married couple made their home on the first floor at Louis's establishment. It provided privacy for both the newlyweds and the in-laws who resided in the rooms above.

Thirteen years later the Martins moved to rue Saint-Blaise not far away. Although Grandmother Martin remained at the rue du Pont Neuf house, she frequently visited her son and his family especially on Sundays. Thérèse mentions her grandmother concerning one of her visits after she and her father returned home from a walk:

> Very often Papa, finding the walk too long for his little Queen [Thérèse herself], brought her back to the house before the others (which pleased her very much). And to console her, Céline filled her pretty little basket with daisies and gave them to her when she got back; but alas! grandmother found her granddaughter had too many, so she took a large part of them for her statue of the Blessed Virgin. This didn't please little Thérèse, but she kept from saying anything, having got into the habit of not complaining ever, even when they took what belonged to her or when she was accused unjustly. She preferred to be silent and not excuse herself. There was no merit here but natural virtue. What a shame that this good inspiration has vanished![14]

---

12 Laveille, *op. cit.*, pp. 3–4. Letter from Mme. Martin to Louis, August 25, 1842.
13 Ibid., p. 9.
14 *Story of a Soul*, chapter I, p. 30.

D. Grandparents

Zélie's letter (CF 14, dated June 27, 1865) to her brother Isidore after Captain Martin's death reveals the great respect she held for her mother-in-law: "My poor father-in-law died yesterday at 1 P.M.... My poor mother-in-law spent her nights nursing him during two and a half months, refusing to have anyone to help her. It was she who prepared him for death and watched him day and night. Indeed, she possesses extraordinary courage and very fine qualities." [15]

An interesting extract from one of Mme. Martin's letters to her daughter Pauline away at the Le Mans boarding school displays the universal frustration a mother endures during an ordinary day at home, even though the home may be inhabited by a saint—possibly by more than one:

> At this moment I don't have any idea of what I am doing: Grandmother is talking to me while I am writing, the maid [Louise Marais] just came in with the little ones [Thérèse and Céline], and they are making lots of noise.... Good! here I am again pestered by the little ones; this time I am leaving my letter aside, for I have a headache. My God! how unfortunate I am that it is raining, otherwise all would be sent off on a walk! [16]

After Zélie's untimely death at forty-five, Louis was left with five motherless young daughters and a dearly loved seventy-seven-year-old widowed mother who had been living alone the past twelve years. It was a most difficult decision to make but Louis decided to move to Lisieux some sixty miles away to be near the devoted Guérins—Zélie's brother and his family—where they would receive maternal nurturing, attention, companionship, and love. Fanie Martin enjoyed her independence and did not wish to leave Alençon. Louis made arrangements to have her live in a country house in nearby Valframbert under the care of a nurse-companion, the reliable Mme. Rose Taillé (affectionately called "Little Rose") who moved from Semallé to Valframbert. Years before Rose had nursed several of Zélie's infants including Thérèse herself. Louis made many trips back to Alençon, usually every three months, to see his mother and visit the graves of his wife and family.

When Thérèse was ten years old, Fanie Martin died on April 8, 1883, at the age of eighty-three. Pauline, as Sister Agnès, recalled a visit Thérèse made to the Carmel shortly after the death of their grandmother: "... [It was] a very pleasant visit the one when Thérése came after her cure [from an undetermined sickness]; I remember she was still in mourning for Grandmamma and her black clothing made her look even prettier." [17]

It might be noted that Thérèse's great grandfather (her grandmother Fanie Martin's father, Captain Nicolas Boureau) had enlisted in the army at seventeen in 1791. He served during the last turbulent years of the French Revolution, fought in the Napoleonic Wars, and eventually suffered captivity by the Prussians together with his twelve-year-old son Jean-Prosper who died on September 21,

---
15 CF 14, dated June 27, 1865.
16 CF 198, dated April 29, 1877, from Mme. Martin to Pauline.
17 *Souvenirs intimes*, p. 16.

1813 while a prisoner in the course of the Silesian campaign. The captain was discharged in 1817.

Fanie's older sister Sophie married Staff-Colonel de Lacauve who had been highly decorated and became the governor of two towns in 1823–1824. Their son also garnered high military honors and gained the rank of major. He died in 1899.[18]

3. Isidore Guérin (1789–1868)
Thérèse's maternal Grandfather

ST. THÉRÈSE'S MOTHER'S SIDE OF THE FAMILY INCLUDED A RICH HERITAGE of religious dedication and military valor. Her grandfather Isidore Guérin was born at the start of the French Revolution in Saint-Martin-l'Aiguillon (Orne) on July 6, 1789. It was a time of great civil upheaval and persecution of the Church. As a young boy toward the end of the Revolution, he became involved in a fascinating and really edifying story of bravery and quick-wittedness involving him and his uncle, his father's brother, Rev. William Guérin. All religious services were forbidden especially the Mass which, when and where possible, had to be celebrated in secret. Sometimes little Isidore would go along with his uncle on his clandestine priestly business throughout the vicinity. On one occasion when his uncle was hiding in his brother Isidore's house, soldiers came to arrest him. When Uncle Guérin heard that they were coming, he quickly concealed himself in a kneading trough; whereupon clever little Isidore sat on the top of it and blithely played with his toys. The soldiers seeing the boy so pleasantly enjoying himself, passed by and thoroughly searched the rest of the house. Not finding their "criminal," they left.[19]

In 1809 when Isidore was twenty, he was conscripted into the Napoleonic army. He saw his first fighting at Wagram in Austria, then was transferred to the Oudinot division experiencing battle in Spain and elsewhere. Because of his fearless participation in these rough engagements, he received the St. Helena medal from Napoleon III. After the fall of the emperor, he returned home but did not retire from military life. Joining the foot and later the mounted gendarmerie (French horse and foot police) in 1823, he spent some time in the Vendée (*Compagnie de la Vendée*), followed by that of the 2nd Legion (*Compagnie de l'Orne*) at Saint-Denis-sur-Sarthon in which parish St. Thérèse's mother was born.

On September 16, 1828, he married Louise-Jeanne Macé in Pré-en-Pail. They had three children: Marie-Louise (1829–1877) who died a Visitation teaching nun (Sr. Marie Dosithée); Zélie (1831–1877) who was St. Thérèse's mother; and Isidore (1841–1909) who became a pharmacist and later was instrumental in the publication of St. Thérèse's autobiography. Finally, in 1844 after more than thirty years in the service, Isidore retired at the age of fifty-five to Alençon where he bought a house at 36 rue Saint Blasé where St. Thérèse was born twenty-nine years later.

---

18 Laveille, *op. cit.*, p. 376.
19 Redman, *Louis and Zelie Martin*, p. 6.

No doubt because of his rough military training and life, he developed a somewhat tough, domineering exterior but he did possess a righteous and loving spirit. He lived alone after his wife died in 1859 but in December 1866, not being able to find a suitable housekeeper, Louis and Zélie took him into their own home on the Rue du Pont Neuf where he lived happily with them and their children for almost two years. He died there at the age of seventy-nine on September 3, 1868, five years before his famous sainted granddaughter was born. Burial took place in Alençon, but in 1894 his and his wife's remains were transferred to the Martin plot in the Lisieux public cemetery near the Carmelite burial section where St. Thérèse was first interred.

After her father's death, Zélie wrote this sad note to her sister-law: "My heart is bruised with grief and at the same time filled with heavenly consolations. If you knew, dearest sister, in what holy dispositions our father prepared for death! At three A.M., he was still making the Sign of the Cross. I have the hope, and even the certitude that our poor, dear father has been welcomed by God...."[20]

4. LOUISE-JEANNE MACÉ GUÉRIN (1805–1859)
Thérèse's maternal Grandmother

LOUISE (NÉE MACÉ) GUÉRIN, ZÉLIE'S MOTHER AND THÉRÈSE'S MATERNAL grandmother, was born on July 11, 1805, in Pré-en-Pail. Her father, a wheelright, was Louis Macé (1778–1810), the son of a carpenter by the name of René (1732–1807) who lived some twenty or so miles west of Alençon in the little village of Le Horps. Louise's mother was Marie Lemarchand (1783–1829). Her parents were married in 1803.

At twenty-three, Louise married Isidore Guérin, a professional soldier, on September 16, 1828, in Pré-en-Pail. They settled down to bring up a family in the parish of Saint-Denis-sur-Sarthon where the mother of St. Thérèse was born. This marriage produced three children. The first was Marie-Louise who became a nun (Sister Marie Dosithée); the second, Azélie (Zélie), the mother of Saint Thérèse; and the last, Isidore, a pharmacist, who played a significant part in Thérèse's life and later after her death when she rose to fame.

Louise was a pious woman with great faith but with a strict disciplinary method of treating her daughters. In 1860, right after the birth of Zélie's first child, Marie, she wrote to her dearly loved nun sister these revealing lines about her upbringing:

> She [Marie] is a dainty little jewel, and sometimes I cannot believe that she is really mine! She is like a little doll! You know how our over-strict mother (God rest her soul) never allowed you and me to play with dolls in our childhood; well, this is my first doll. It will be so much fun to make pretty clothes for her.[21]

---

20 CF 38, dated September 3, 1868.
21 From Wust's *Zélie Martin*, p. 68. Only one letter (CF 138, dated August 31, 1875, and found in the Guérin family papers) exists that was written by Zélie to her sister. This quotation is not from it. The author's source is not given.

The complete opposite, however, was displayed by Louise's indulgent manner in rearing her only son Isidore. Years later as an adult of thirty-four, Zélie wrote to her ten years younger brother, whom she always loved, these pitiable remarks: "My childhood and youth were as sad as a winding sheet [shroud], because if our mother spoiled you, she was much too severe with me, as you know. Good as she was, she did not know how to treat me, so that I suffered much in my heart." [22]

After Louise's husband Isidore retired from the service in 1844, they moved to 36 Rue Saint-Blaise in Alençon. He enjoyed doing carpentry work during his retirement. In order to earn some extra needed money, Louise opened a small café on the ground floor and on the second they installed a billiard room. As a result of her propensity to moralize and preach to the patrons, her business failed to attract customers and consequently closed.

Thérèse's maternal grandmother never lived to see her world-known and loved granddaughter for she passed away fourteen years before Thérèse was born. She was fifty-four when she succumbed from congestion of the lungs on September 9, 1859, in Alençon, a year after Zélie and Louis were married.

---

22 CF 15. Letter from Zélie to her brother Isidore dated November 7, 1865.

E. Father's Other Relatives

THÉRÈSE ALLUDED IN HER WRITINGS ONLY TO THREE DIRECT RELATIONS on her father's side. The most important one was her grandmother, Mme. Fanie Martin (1880–1883), who was living alone at the time in Alençon on Rue Pont Neuf not far from where Thérèse and her family lived at 36 Rue Saint-Blaise. She is often mentioned in family letters and Thérèse herself relates an incident concerning her in her autobiography. Thérèse's Grandmother Martin died at 83 in Alençon when Thérèse was ten years old.

The second Martin relation who knew Thérèse was Adolphe Leriche (1844–1894), her first cousin—her father's sister's only child. Thérèse never names him but she does mention his wife who took care of her and her sister Céline during their mother's last illness.

A third relation, Berthe Madeline (1874–1921), rarely encountered in Theresian literature was a distant cousin of the Martins. She was born a year after Thérèse and died twenty-four years after her. For twenty-five years she was a member of the Religious of Providence of Portieux. Her great grandfather, François Bohard, was the brother of Anne-Marie Bohard (Mme. Jean Martin, 1753–1815), the great grandmother of Thérèse who was born in Athis de l'Orne in 1753. Athis is the ancestral town of this branch of Thérèse's family.

The last surviving descendents from this branch of the family were invited by Mother Agnès and her Carmelite sisters to represent the Martin family[1] at the canonization ceremonies of St. Thérèse at the Vatican in 1925 where they were particularly honored by the pope himself. Apparently the last surviving member of this family who lived during Thérèse's lifetime was Dr. Poirier (1885–1974). He, however, was only three years old when Thérèse entered Carmel and twelve when she died. He did recall that his mother and family sometimes would speak about his Carmelite cousins and even of Thérèse's parents. A magazine published by the Pèlerinage de Lisieux printed an account of it in 1978. The interviewer described him as an "original and engaging personality." He noted his distinguished career as municipal counselor of Athis, district counselor, and his courageous service during World War I in the front lines as doctor in the ambulance corps. He even won a Legion of Honor citation. Lourdes played a very important part in his life where he worked at its medical bureau, studied the miraculous cures, and examined the patients reporting there. Dr. Poirier went on to emphasize to his interviewer that many in the Martin family were truly saintly people. Here is a short excerpt from this article citing some pertinent data in his genealogical history:

> [My] father was a first cousin of the Martin sisters. My great grandmother—born in 1779, Marie-Henriette Martin—was the sister of Captain Pierre-François

---
[1] Two people who represented the Guérin side of the family were Mme. Sadi-Carnot and M. Houdayer.

Martin, grandfather of St. Thérèse. The Martin sisters and I are descendents of Jean Martin, born in Athis de l'Orne in 1752 and of Marie Anne Bohard, born in the same parish in 1753. The Martins are numbered and rooted for a long time in Athis ever since the XVIth century.[2]

Dr. Poirier lived a long life, dying at eighty-nine in 1974.

1. ADOLPHE LERICHE (1844–1894)
Thérèse's cousin who bought her father's jewelry store in Alençon

THÉRÈSE WROTE NOTHING IN *Story of a Soul* ABOUT ADOLPHE LERICHE, HER only cousin on her father's side. In stark contrast, she overflows in involvement with her three female maternal cousins, the Guérins. Yet the omission is quite understandable. When Thérèse was born, Adolphe was already twenty-nine years old, married, and immersed in his jewelry business in Alençon. Their age difference, especially in her early years, clearly militated against a close relationship. Obviously it was not as intimate as with her Guérin cousins who were all about her age. When Thérèse was four, the Martins moved from Alençon to Lisieux nearly sixty miles away, thus widening the tenuous relationship with the Leriches even further but strengthening those with the Guérins who lived within walking distance from them.

Thérèse does, however, mention in her autobiography Adolphe's wife, Marie, who helped the Martins in the very distressful last days of her mother's life when she was dying of breast cancer:

> All the details of my mother's illness are still present to me and I recall especially the last weeks she spent on earth [in August 1877]. Céline and I were like poor little exiles, for every morning Mme. Leriche came to get us and brought us to her home where we spent the day. One morning we didn't have time to say our prayers and during the trip Céline whispered: "Should we tell her we didn't say them," and placing us both in a large room, she left. Céline looked at me and we said: "Oh! this is not like Mamma! She always had us say our prayers with her."[3]

Thérèse's father, Louis Martin, was one of five children and the only one alive when Thérèse was born, the others having died years before. There were no nieces and only one nephew, Adolphe, in Louis's family. Louis's younger sister Ann-Fannie Martin (1826–1853) married Adolphe Leriche (1818–1843) in 1842 and from this union a boy, Adolphe, about whom this entry is concerned, was born on January 7, 1844. He married a lady named Marie and they had a daughter, Berthe (1873–1964), who married Victor Henault-Morel. Their son, Roger Henault-Morel (1905–1987), married and had two sons (both living in 1990); one became a priest and the other married and had three children.[4]

---

2 From an article by Paul Labutte published in the August-September, 1978, issue of *Les Annales de Sainte Thérèse de Lisieux*. Translation by the author.
3 *Story of a Soul*, chapter II, p. 33.
4 This information obtained from The Theresian Trust.

In 1870 Adolphe acquired a substantial inheritance and was able to buy his uncle Louis's watch making and jewelry shop as well as the dwellings in it on the rue du Pont Neuf. At any rate, by this time Louis was ready to relinquish his business in order to assist his wife Zélie in her lacemaking enterprise.

On December 7, 1894, Adolphe Leriche passed away at the age of fifty, three years before the death of his cousin Sister Thérèse of the Child Jesus.

F. Mother's Other Relatives

1. **Marie-Louise Guérin**: (Sister Marie-Dosithée) Thérèse's aunt who became a Visitation teaching nun
2. **Isidore Guérin**: Thérèse's uncle and "second father"
3. **Céline (Fournet) Guérin**: Thérèse's maternal aunt, wife of Isidore
4. **Jeanne (La Néele) Guérin**: (Mme. La Néele) Thérèse's cousin, wife of Dr. La Néele
5. **Marie Guérin**: (Sr. Marie de l'Eucharistie) Cousin and novice of St. Thérèse
6. **Dr. Francis La Néele**: Husband of Jeanne Guérin and Thérèse's cousin by marriage
7. **M. and Mme. Pierre Fournet**: Thérèse's Aunt Céline's parents
8. **The Maudelonde Family**: The family of Thérèse's Aunt Guérin's sister
    a. **César Maudelonde**: Father (Married Aunt Céline Guérin's sister)
    b. **Marie-Rosalie**: Mother (Sister of Thérèse's Aunt Céline Guérin)
    c. **Ernest**: Son (Eleven years older than Thérèse)
    d. **Henry**: Son (Wanted to marry Thérèse's sister Céline)
    e. **Marguerite-Marie**: Daughter (Married the athiest René Tostain)
    f. **Céline**: Daughter (Same age as Thérèse)
    g. **Hélène**: Daughter (Killed in the Allied bombings of World War II)

Plate 6

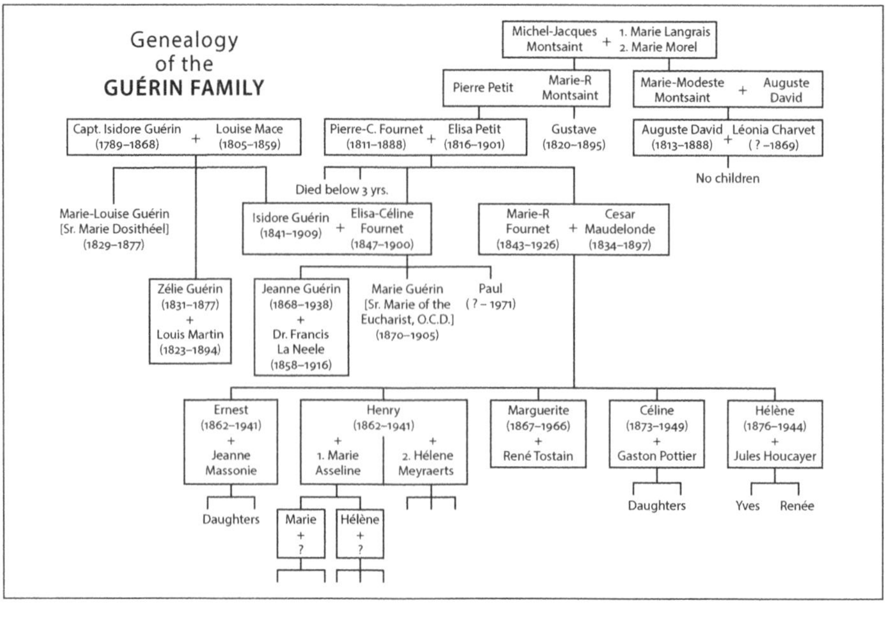

Genealogy of the GUÉRIN FAMILY

- Michel-Jacques Montsaint + 1. Marie Langrais / 2. Marie Morel
  - Pierre Petit + Marie-R Montsaint
  - Marie-Modeste Montsaint + Auguste David
    - Auguste David (1813–1888) + Léonia Charvet (?–1869) — No children

- Capt. Isidore Guérin (1789–1868) + Louise Mace (1805–1859)
  - Marie-Louise Guérin [Sr. Marie Dosithéel] (1829–1877)
  - Zélie Guérin (1831–1877) + Louis Martin (1823–1894)
  - Isidore Guérin (1841–1909) + Elisa-Céline Fournet (1847–1900)
    - Jeanne Guérin (1868–1938) + Dr. Francis La Neele (1858–1916)
    - Marie Guérin [Sr. Marie of the Eucharist, O.C.D.] (1870–1905)
    - Paul (?–1971)
    - Died below 3 yrs.

- Pierre-C. Fournet (1811–1888) + Elisa Petit (1816–1901)
- Gustave (1820–1895)

- Marie-R Fournet (1843–1926) + Cesar Maudelonde (1834–1897)
  - Ernest (1862–1941) + Jeanne Massonie — Daughters
  - Henry (1862–1941) + 1. Marie Asseline / 2. Hélene Meyraerts — Marie + ?, Hélène + ?
  - Marguerite (1867–1966) + René Tostain
  - Céline (1873–1949) + Gaston Pottier — Daughters
  - Hélène (1876–1944) + Jules Houcayer — Yves, Renée

F. Mother's Other Relatives

Plate 7

The Guérin Family

A. Isidore Guérin

B. Céline Guérin

C. Marie Guérin

D. Jeanne Guérin La Néele

E. Dr. Francis La Néele

F. César Maudelonde

G. Marie-Rosalie Maudelonde

H. Céline & Hélène Maudelonde

I. Marguerite Maudelonde Tostain

1. Marie-Louise-Pétronille Guérin (1829–1877)
(Sister Marie-Dosithée)
Thérèse's aunt who became a Visitation teaching nun

MARIE-LOUISE GUÉRIN WAS BORN ON MAY 31, 1829, IN THE HAMLET OF Gandelain in the parish of Saint-Denis-sur-Sarthon—the same place where her sister Zélie (the mother of St. Thérèse) and brother Isidore were born. Marie-Louise was a sickly child, particularly during the ages of seven to twelve. In 1844 the family moved to Alençon, just within two miles away. The two pious teenage girls were educated there by the sisters of the Congregation of Picpus[1] at whose school they were day students. Their house, founded in 1828 by a saintly nun, maintained a school with a reputation of high standards. When Isidore was of age he attended the Lycée for boys.

From their early years, the Guérin girls were rigidly reared by both parents especially the mother which surely helped unite the sisters in a strong bond of love and friendship that otherwise was so lacking in their lives. Sadly, their mother did not believe in bestowing much affection toward them. Céline tells us in the biography she wrote of her mother that "though she would have given anything for it when she was a child, Zélie never had a doll, even the smallest one. She suffered from frequent headaches, and this added to the painful atmosphere."[2] Their mother, however, treated her son Isidore just the opposite. Much to their credit, the two sisters always showed love and concern for their brother and never harbored any animosity, jealousy, or dislike for him. Zélie summed up not only her young life but also her sister's when she wrote, "My childhood and youth were as sad as a winding sheet [shroud], for if our mother spoiled you [Isidore], as you know, she was much too severe with me. She, nevertheless, was good, but she did not know how to treat me, so that I suffered much in my heart."[3]

In spite of their loveless upbringing, the two sisters both grew to be kind, loving, and deeply religious. Élise, as Marie-Louise was called, became especially scrupulous, as time passed. She was often warned against sinning which, though proper to a Christian upbringing, became perhaps extreme:

> the phrase "that's a sin" stopped the poor child [Élise] in her strongest inclinations.... Madame Guérin, who taught her daughters this excessive fear of offending God, used to harp on the phrase "that's a sin" to curb their least imperfections. Marie-Louise worked a lot and played too little.[4]

---

[1] The full correct title is the Congregation of the Sacred Hearts of Jesus and Mary and of the Perpetual Adoration of the Blessed Sacrament of the Altar. It was founded in 1768. Picpus is the name of the street in Paris where its Generalate was located. Saint Father Damian of Molokai was a member of this congregation.
[2] Sister Geneviève, *op. cit.*, p. 1.
[3] Letter (CF 15) from Zélie to her brother Isidore dated November 7, 1865. Author's translation. Most of the other English translations from *Correspondance Familiale* recorded here are from Wust's *Zélie Martin* unless otherwise indicated.
[4] As quoted from the obituary Circular of Sister Marie-Dosithée in De Meester's *Saint Thérèse of Lisieux; Her Life, Times, and Teaching*, p. 13.

Having been brought up in such a stern milieu, one can understand why, for example, when Élise danced or played with other children she "feared to commit the grave sin of finding herself near a little boy; she would slip away trembling, as skillfully as possible, sometimes bringing malicious teasing upon herself because of what others interpreted as her wild temperament." [5]

At any rate, from early childhood she wanted to enter a religious order and thought of the Poor Clares, but for various reasons she did not attain her vocational goal for quite some time. In the succeeding years, though, she assisted her sister as her manager in establishing a lace producing business in Alençon where the family had moved in 1844 after their father retired from the army. In 1853 she, accompanied by her father, successfully negotiated important business matters in Paris for her sister. At this point she became seriously ill with what appeared to be manifestations of consumption, but she lived for many years longer. *À propos* of this, during her final illness, Zélie, with hopeful thoughts, recalled this incident in a letter to her daughter Pauline:

> I trust that God will do for me what He did for your aunt, for it is twenty-four years now since she was condemned to death. The doctor had told my mother that she could hardly live more than three months. She prayed and made a novena to Our Lady of La Salette, to obtain the grace of dying a nun. The disease never disappeared but she lived twenty-two years longer.[6]

Her health, further shaken by various penances, led to a serious relapse in 1856. Nonetheless, on April 7, 1858, overcoming these impediments and the threat of tuberculosis, the twenty-nine-year-old Marie-Louise entered the Visitation Order and taught at its school in Le Mans. She received the religious habit on February 24, 1859, with the name Sœur Marie-Dosithée (Sister Mary Dorothy), and pronounced her vows of profession. For six years she served with fidelity and devotedness as assistant novice mistress. During her entire religious life of nearly twenty years, she maintained close ties with her sister and her family, though she was not allowed to leave her convent. Thérèse's older sisters Marie, Pauline, and later Léonie were boarders at her school. Sister Dosithée was highly respected for her devout life and work and was even admired by the illustrious Benedictine monk Dom Guéranger from Solesmes whose *L'Année Liturgique* was read every night by Louis Martin to Thérèse and her sisters.

Thérèse made brief references to her aunt in two of her letters (LT 148 and LT 163). She recorded a more lengthy account in her autobiography of a visit she made on March 29, 1875, when she was two to see her aunt and her sisters Marie and Pauline who were students at the school:

> I recall also the trip I made to Le Mans; it was my first train ride. What a joy to see myself on a trip alone with Mamma. I don't know why I began to cry, but my poor little Mother had nothing to introduce to Aunt at Le Mans but a plain little girl all

---

5 Ibid.
6 CF 195. Letter from Mme. Martin to her daughter Pauline dated March 22, 1877.

red with the tears she shed on the way. I remember nothing about the visit except the moment when Aunt handed me a little white mouse and a little cardboard basket filled with candies, on top of which *were enthroned* two pretty sugar rings, just the right size for my finger. Immediately I exclaimed: "How wonderful! There will be a ring for Céline also!" I took my basket by the handle. I gave the other hand to Mamma and we left. After a few steps, I looked at my basket and saw that my candies were almost all strewn out on the street like Tom Thumb's pebbles.[7]

This is Sister Marie-Dosithée's account of that visit:

On Easter Monday I had a delightful little visit I was not expecting. Zélie brought me her little Thérèse, thinking I would enjoy seeing her. She is a darling little girl, remarkably obedient; she did whatever she was told at once, and was so sensible that she would have sat still all day. I was very pleased to see her.[8]

Zélie in turn wrote to her sister-in-law, Louise Guérin, this amusing addition to the narrative of Thérèse's visit to see her aunt: "I took little Thérèse to my sister.... The Superior came to see her and gave her some small gifts. I said to her, 'Ask the good Mother to bless you.' She did not understand, and said 'Mother, will you come and visit us.' Everyone had to laugh."[9] Thérèse mistook the French word *"bénir"* (to bless) with *"venir"* (to come).

Thérèse's older sister Léonie had been a student at the Visitation school for a little while but she exhibited poor scholarship, behavior, and social skills. She was even dismissed a few times. Despite her incorrigible behavior and below standard academic achievement, her Aunt, Sister Marie-Dosithée, believed she would turn out well even to the point of becoming a religious. She told her sister Zélie in a letter that "As for little Léonie, I cannot refrain from believing that she will become a Visitandine."[10] Her prediction came true thirty years later when Léonie finally joined the Visitation Order in Caen on January 28, 1899. There she lived a humble and exemplary life as a nun for forty-two years up to her holy death in 1941.

Thérèse was four years old when her forty-eight-year-old aunt died on February 24, 1877, of tuberculosis—the same disease that ended her sainted niece's life at twenty-four, twenty years later. On Sister Marie-Dosithée's death, one of the Visitation nuns wrote this adulatory statement to Zélie:

The life of our dear Sr. Marie-Dosithée, that was so edifying, closed this morning by a death one might envy. She was quite conscious and preserved an admirable calmness to the end. One evening, almost the last before her death, she said to our mother: "O Mother, I have no other thoughts but of love, trust, and abandonment. Help me to thank God for it all. We can say that we have now another protectress in heaven, for it would be difficult to find a more saintly ending to a holier life.[11]

---

7 *Story of a Soul*, chapter I, p. 23.
8 As quoted on p. 3 in *Collected Letters of St. Thérèse*, edited by Abbé Combes in a letter by Sister Dosithée to Mme. Louise Guérin, her sister-in-law on April 4, 1875.
9 Letter (CF 131) dated April 29, 1875, written by Zélie to her brother Isidore and his wife Louise.
10 From a letter written by Sister Marie-Dosithée to her sister Zélie dated April 28, 1869.
11 As cited by Zélie in a letter (CF 190) to her brother dated February 26, 1877. This is a free translation by Laveille in his book *The Life of the Little Flower: St. Thérèse of Lisieux*, p. 54.

2. Isidore Guérin (1841–1909)
Thérèse's uncle and "second father"

THE ONLY MAN OTHER THAN HER FATHER WHO WAS INTIMATELY INVOLVED with and influential in the life of St. Thérèse was her Uncle Guérin. He was born on January 2, 1841, in Saint-Denis-sur-Sarthon (Orne) to Captain Isidore Guérin and Louise-Marie Macé, their third child and only son. Fifty-two years later when his niece Thérèse Martin was twenty, she wrote a New Year's greeting to him:

> I am not forgetting that January 2 is dear Uncle's birthday. I am proud to have been born on the same day as he, and I hope he will not forget to pray for his little Thérèse, who will soon be an old girl of twenty. How time flies!... It seems only yesterday that good Uncle used to bounce me on his knees, singing the romance of Blue Beard, with terrible eyes that almost made me die of fright.... The little *tune of Mirlitir* was more to my taste.... The remembrance of this song is enough to make me laugh still.[12]

Isidore's sisters were Marie-Louise who was twelve years old at her brother's birth and who later became a Visitation nun (Sr. Marie-Dosithée); and Zélie, ten, who was destined to be St. Thérèse's mother. The entire family loved, doted on, and spoiled their little boy right from the beginning. Their mother in particular openly favored Isidore over both girls which greatly affected Zélie as she revealed in a letter written years later when they were both adults: "My childhood and youth were as sad as a winding sheet [shroud]. For if our mother spoiled you, for me, you know it, she was too severe. She, therefore, as good as she was, did not know how to treat me, thus I suffered deeply in my heart."[13] Despite this disclosure, Zélie loved her brother tenderly her whole life and actually assumed a maternal role toward him after their mother died.

This pampered upbringing created in the otherwise intelligent Isidore a blunt, self-willed, tactless, fun-loving, and obstinate character. When in 1862 he left his home in Alençon to study medicine in Paris instead of the priesthood as his family wished, both sisters exhorted their debonair younger brother to beware the dangers of hedonistic Paris. Here is one of Zélie's letters firmly imploring him what to do:

> I beg of you, dear Isidore, to do as he [her husband Louis] did; pray, and you will not let yourself be carried along with the stream. If once you give in, you will be lost. It is only the first step that costs, on the way of evil as on that of good. After that, you will be borne along by the current.
>
> If you would only consent to do one thing I am going to ask of you, and which you may well give me for a New Year's gift, I should be happier than if you sent me all Paris. Here it is: You live close to *Our Lady of Victories.* Very well! Go in, just once a day, to say an *Ave Maria* to her. You will see that she will protect you in a quite particular way, that she will make you succeed in this world and give you an eternity of happiness hereafter.[14]

---

12 Letter (LT 139) from Thérèse to M. and Mme. Guérin dated December 30, 1892, translated by the author.
13 CF 15 from Zélie to Isidore, dated November 7, 1865.
14 CF 1, dated January 1, 1863, from Zélie to Isidore.

To the great disappointment of his family, Isidore failed to complete his medical studies, switched to pharmacy, and eventually received his diploma in this profession in 1866.

On April 22, 1866 he settled in Lisieux and on May 12 took over his future father-in law, M. Fournet's flourishing pharmacy business which was situated close to the Cathedral of St. Pierre on the corner of the market square at Place Saint-Pierre and the Grand Rue (later called Place Thiers and now Rue Henry Chéron). It was and still is (re-built, however) the location of pharmacies that date back centuries. This area, except for the cathedral, was completely destroyed in the World War II Allied bombardments of June 1944.

On September 11, 1866, five months after Isidore moved to Lisieux, he married the daughter of the former owner of the business, Elisa-Céline Fournet, a young lady of nineteen whose charm, attractiveness, piety, and amazing maturity belied her tender years. They settled in rooms on the second floor of the pharmacy they named "*Pharmacie Guérin.*" Thérèse and her family regularly visited their home for supper especially on Sundays after Vespers at the Cathedral.

Isidore and his wife had three children: Jeanne (1868–1938) who married Dr. Francis la Néele, Marie (1870–1905) who became a nun and one of Thérèse's novices in the Lisieux Carmel, and Paul (1871) who was delivered stillborn.

In February 1873 Isidore went into partnership with his brother-in-law, César Maudelonde, and they established a pharmaceutical factory next door which unfortunately burned down a month later but was shortly thereafter rebuilt.

Despite his somewhat frivolous youth and carelessness in religion, Isidore became, after he settled down to business and marriage, a pious, loyal, and active Catholic. His intelligence, forceful personality, and shrewd knowledge of the world and business gained for him success and wealth.

Before Zélie's premature death in 1877, she entrusted her daughters to the care of her young devoted sister-in-law Mme. Guérin. Isidore helped Louis Martin and his five daughters move from Alençon to Lisieux a few months after Zélie's funeral and chose their home, Les Buissonnets, not far from his own. Subsequent to Louis Martin's physical and mental debilitations caused by a series of strokes, Isidore willingly assumed legal guardianship of the Martin girls. He supported and sustained the Martins with love and care throughout all their lives.

Thérèse received permission from her ailing father to enter the Carmelite Convent in Lisieux (May 29, 1887) at the age of fifteen but she was also obliged to seek the consent of her Uncle Isidore who at first flatly refused:

> It was with trembling I confided my resolution to Uncle [October 8, 1887]. He showed me great tenderness but did not grant me his permission to leave. He forbade me to speak about my vocation to him until I was seventeen. It was contrary to human prudence, he said, to have a child of fifteen enter Carmel. This Carmelite life was, in the eyes of many, a life of mature reflection, and it would be doing a great wrong to the religious life to allow an *inexperienced*

> *child* to embrace it. Everybody would be talking about it, etc., etc. He even said that for him to decide to allow me to leave would require a *miracle*. I saw all reasoning with him was useless and so I left, my heart plunged into the most profound bitterness. My only consolation was prayer. I begged Jesus to perform the *miracle* demanded, since at this price only I'd be able to answer His call.... A long time passed by [only two weeks] before I dared speak to him again. It was very difficult for me to go to his home, and he himself seemed to be no longer considering my vocation. I learned later on that my great sadness influenced him very much.... [On October 22] I went to see Uncle. What was my surprise when I saw him looking at me, and, without expressing any desire to speak to him, he had me come into his study! He began by making some gentle reproaches because I appeared to be afraid of him, and then he said it wasn't necessary to beg for a miracle, that he had only asked God to give him "a simple change of heart" and that he had been answered. Ah! I was not tempted to beg for a miracle because *the miracle had been granted*; Uncle was no longer the same. Without making any allusion whatsoever to "human prudence'" he told me I was a *little flower God wanted to gather*, and he would no longer oppose it![15]

After surmounting several other trying oppositions, Thérèse entered Carmel on April 9, 1888, where she lived without ever leaving the premises until her death nine years later.

On August 22, 1888, the forty-seven-year-old Isidore inherited the sizeable fortune of his wife's cousin, Auguste David, which included the vacation home called the Château de la Musse near Evreux. Earlier in the month, Isidore went to see the very ill Auguste who at the time was staying at La Musse and under his strong influence managed to have him return to his faith and belief in God. In the first of two existing letters Thérèse wrote to her uncle, she consoles and praises him for what he did:

> Good Monsieur David's condition saddens us very much. I understand, dear Uncle, how much you must be suffering, for there is nothing so painful as seeing those whom we love suffering....
>
> It was impossible, Uncle, that God not grant you this consolation after all you've done for His glory.[16]

Then on December 8, 1888, he sold his business to Victor Lahaye (1855–1936), a close family friend, and retired. Isidore and his family left their pharmacy/home, stayed at Les Buissonnets for a short time, and moved again into a house at 16 rue Condorcet whose backyard was adjacent to *Le Jardin de l'Evêché* (today it is the Lisieux public gardens). After a short stay here they made their permanent residence a few blocks away into a new house M. Guérin purchased at 19 rue de la Chaussée (now 19 rue Paul Banaston).

The freedom he now had allowed him to devote more time to his many interests. He concentrated on politics, but he also focused on his independent studies, social

---

15 *Story of a Soul*, chapter V, pp. 109–110.
16 LT 59 from Thérèse to her Uncle Guérin dated August 22, 1888, the day M. David died.

duties, the many activities on behalf of parish concerns, Catholic education, and defense of the faith. He became more involved with the *Cercle catholique*, Saint Vincent de Paul conferences, and the work of Nocturnal Adoration which he founded in 1885. As a journalist he wrote countless religious and political articles from 1891 to 1896 for *Le Normand*, a conservative Lisieux newspaper published twice a week. He was a staunch monarchist, an anti-Dreyfusard,[17] and an expert in social and fiscal matters which he also wrote about in his articles. Father Piat has some intriguing facts to add concerning Isidore's entry into journalistic writing:

> [In] 1891, Céline intervened to persuade her uncle to set the journal *Le Normand* on its feet again and to assume its direction. He was hesitating, and his wife even more so, sensing strongly that this would threaten their peace. In a curious detail that reveals something about the period, he particularly dreaded, in his honor as a man as well as in his Christian conscience, possible challenges to a duel. His niece, with her usual spirit, swept away the objection. There were the interests of God and the Church, which *Le Progrès Lexovien* [a very liberal, Anti-Catholic paper] was holding up to ridicule throughout its columns. "Well! You have won, my big-hearted girl," concluded the former pharmacist who was becoming an impromptu journalist.[18]

Thérèse's father's physical condition and mental state were seriously affected by a series of paralyses. His doctor, accordingly, decided that confinement in the Hospital of the Good Savior (*Hôpital du Bon Sauveur*), the mental institution in Caen, was imperative. So on February 12, 1889, he was taken there by Isidore and his friend Vital Romet with the distraught Céline and Léonie accompanying them. He remained for a little over three years until he was permitted to return home on May 10, 1892, not because his condition improved but because he became completely incapable of moving about by himself which thus rendered him more controllable and easier to care for.

M. Martin was welcomed into the home of the Guérins where Céline and Léonie were living since the lease of their house, Les Buissonnets, had expired and was not renewed. About a month after their father's release, the Martin girls moved with him into a rented house across the street from the Guérin's back property where he lived until his death. During their father's hospital stay, the two sisters were well taken care of by the Guérins who also gladly welcomed them to their newly acquired country estate La Musse. Isidore even asked them to accompany him, which they did, and his family in May 1890 on a pilgrimage to Lourdes, Tours, and elsewhere in France and northern Spain. After his release from the hospital, M. Martin was invited with his daughters to La Musse, a secluded area he truly enjoyed. Sadly, though, it was the place of his death following a heart attack in 1894.

---

17 Captain Alfred Dreyfus (a Jew) was the center of a famous contentious political scandal called "The Dreyfus Affair." He was sent to the penal colony Devil's Island in French Guiana for being a German spy. Years later he was found not guilty, released, and reinstated in the French army in 1906. He served loyally during World War I and ended his military career with the rank of Lieutenant-Colonel.

18 Piat, *Céline*, p. 49.

F. Mother's Other Relatives

Isidore became involved in his way when the four Martin sisters joined the Carmelites and the fifth, Léonie, finally entered the Visitandine Order in 1899. With a broken heart in 1895, he allowed his own daughter Marie to join her four cousins in the Lisieux Carmel.

For a half year before Thérèse died, her uncle, aunt, and cousins were quite aware of her serious health condition. Her cousin Marie Guérin, then Marie of the Eucharist, kept her family informed of Thérèse's physical state, sometimes writing to them several times a week to keep them well abreast of the latest in her condition. They often sent food and other amenities to the Carmel in an effort to help the situation. Dr. La Néele, the husband of Thérèse's cousin Jeanne Guérin, also offered his assistance whenever he was allowed to.

Two months before Thérèse died, Isidore wrote her a poignant letter with the greeting "My dear little Angel" which so effusively discloses his great love for her:

> Your letter[19] was the cause of an inexpressible surprise and joy; it moistened my eyes with tears. What was the nature of these tears? I cannot analyze it. A crowd of different sentiments brought them about. The pride of having such an adopted daughter, admiration for so great a courage and so great a love of God, and I cannot hide it, my darling.... You were your good mother's [his sister's] little pearl; you were your aged father's little queen; and you are the most beautiful little flower of the lily-wreath crowning, scenting, and giving me a foretaste of the perfections of heaven.... Each time one of my five little Carmelite daughters crossed the threshold of the cloister, I experienced an inner rending similar in every way to what one feels at the loss of a beloved person.... When I think of you, a flower so pure and so chaste, I begin to despise humanity.... *Adieu*, my beloved child, precious pearl, whom your good mother entrusted to me; the remembrance of your virtues and your innocence will never leave me, and I hope that your prayers will make me worthy of being reunited with all my own in the eternal abode. The one who has perhaps the right to call himself your second father and who kisses you from the very bottom of his heart.[20]

Thérèse died on September 30, 1897, and was buried on October 4. Unfortunately, Isidore was confined to bed with a severe attack of gout on the very day his beloved niece became the first one interred, by an ironic twist of fate, in the plot he had recently purchased for the Lisieux Carmel.

Isidore played a major role in the posthumous life of Thérèse. From the very beginning he was enthusiastic about the publication of her autobiography, *Story of a Soul*. In fact he personally financed the first edition of 2,000 copies, was in charge of all the business arrangements, and even checked the editorial work that was done on it. One time he told Mother Agnès that he was "convinced by this publication. It will make a huge noise." "That is exactly word for word what he said. I am [still] struck by his words."[21] He was absolutely correct, yet

---

19 Probably LT 255, dated July 16, 1897, from Thérèse to M. and Mme. Guérin.
20 A letter (LC 192) by Isidore at La Musse to Thérèse dated July 24–25, 1897.
21 From the article "Vie posthume de Sainte Thérèse" (The Posthumous Life of Saint Thérèse) that appeared in the March 1981 issue of *Les Annales de Ste. Thérèse*. Translation by the author.

when Thérèse's fame and sanctity increased and steps were taken toward her glorification by the Church he strongly objected to it believing that her life which he had followed so intimately did not contain the true essence of which saints (as he thought of them) are made. It took a priest friend (Father Prévost, 1860–1946), heavily engaged in Thérèse's cause, who eventually broke down the reservations which Isidore so tenaciously held.

Isidore's latter years were saddened by the untimely deaths of his wife at fifty-three in 1900 and of his daughter Marie at thirty-five in 1905 of the same disease that took the life of her cousin Thérèse in 1897. On September 28, 1909, Isidore, sixty-nine, passed away at his residence on the rue Paul Banaston of hepatitis complicated by acute rheumatoid arthritis. His last words were "*Appelez-moi, Jésus!*" ("Call me, Jesus!")[22] The funeral Mass took place at the Cathedral of Saint Pierre in Lisieux amidst a large group of mourners. He was buried in the Guérin family plot in the Lisieux public cemetery right next to the space he purchased for the Carmel. Just a few feet away is the first grave of his beloved "adopted" daughter Thérèse.

This laudatory obituary notice appeared in the local newspaper *La Dépêche de Lisieux, héritière du Normand*:

> M. Guérin, great Christian, great Frenchman, writer of talent, and patron of many Catholic works of charity, ranks as one of the outstanding personalities of Lisieux. His death was, like his life, a good act of faith. He held the honorable title of Uncle of a Saint and of having intervened for good in her life on several decisive occasions.[23]

3. Élisa-Céline Fournet Guérin (1847–1900)
Thérèse's maternal aunt, wife of Isidore

> Dear little Aunt ... who is the dearest to me in this life, after my father....[24]
> — Thérèse

The story of the rapport between Thérèse and her aunt Guérin can be succinctly stated as a paean of mutual love and gratitude. Most of the incidents and remarks recorded by both are of humble, innocent, common things that are perfect examples of Thérèse's precept of the Little Way.

Élisa (Elizabeth)-Emilie-Céline Fournet was born on March 15, 1847, in Lisieux to Pierre-Célestin Fournet, a pharmacist, and Elisa-Ernestine (*née* Petit). At nineteen she married Thérèse's uncle Isidore Guérin on September 11, 1866. In May of the same year, Isidore acquired his future father-in-law's prosperous pharmaceutical business located at Place Saint Pierre in Lisieux. They had three children: Jeanne, who married Dr. Francis La Néele; Marie, who became a Carmelite nun and novice under her cousin Thérèse's direction; and Paul who died at birth.

---

22 Piat, *Marie Guérin*, p. 125.
23 From *The Saint of Lisieux*, April 1950, p. 31, vol. III, no. 2.
24 Letter (LT 133) from Thérèse to her Aunt Guérin dated November 16, 1891.

F. Mother's Other Relatives

A strong relationship between the Guérin family and that of the Martins developed while Zélie, Thérèse's mother, was alive. This bond increased over the years especially through the steady correspondence between Zélie Martin in Alençon and Céline Guérin in Lisieux. Zélie (sixteen years older than her sister-in-law Céline Guérin) wrote, from 1867 to1877, 94 letters to her that are preserved today. When Zélie realized that she had incurable cancer, she informed Céline and entrusted her daughters to her care:

> I am very anxious that this should not torment you too much and that you should be resigned to the will of God. If He thought I was necessary on this earth, He would certainly not allow me to have this disease. I have so often prayed that He might not take me from this earth so long as I was necessary to the children....
>
> They will be very happy in having you when I am no longer here. You will help them by your good counsel and should they have the misfortune to lose their father, you would take them to your home, wouldn't you?[25]

She gladly consented and received in turn the love of the Martin girls proving beyond measure that she was truly a worthy "second mother" to the girls. Years later Mme. Guérin wrote to her Carmelite niece Sister Thérèse of the Child Jesus recalling Zélie's wish:

> I am very much moved when seeing all the affection you are showing me and of which your sisters and yourself have already given me so many proofs.
>
> What have I done, then, that God has surrounded me with such loving hearts! I did nothing but answer the last look of a mother whom I loved *very much, very much*. I believed I understood that look, which nothing will be able to make me forget [on August 27, 1877, the night before Zélie died]. It is engraved within my heart. Since that day, I have tried to replace her whom God had taken away from you, but, alas! nothing can replace a Mother![26]

Thérèse was four when her family moved into their new home in Lisieux called Les Buissonnets, not very far from the Guérins, which her Uncle Isidore selected for them. From then on the friendship, intimacy, and love solidified. Thérèse visited them often and had dinner with them on Sundays, walked to school with the Guérin girls, and was always invited to go with them to the seaside resort towns of Trouville or Deauville. The Guérins never left the Martins out of any holidays or events. This excerpt is typical of the life, chores, and activities the two families shared together by the shore:

> We are doing some needlework, cooking, and today we are doing the wash. What work for ladies! Our little Thérèse [12] slept perfectly in the beautiful big bedroom, and this morning she looks very good. I told her she had to eat with all her might and that from today I'll not relent in this matter. She seems to be very happy here and she isn't lonesome. The weather is not very good

---
25 Letter (LT 177) from Zélie to her sister-in-law Céline Guérin dated December 17, 1876.
26 Letter (LC 148) from Mme. Guérin to Thérèse dated November 16, 1891.

this morning, but yesterday we were able to go to the beach. All our little girls were at the water's edge, waiting for the waves to come in. Thérèse was armed with a spade, and all of them were very happy.[27]

Another earlier example of Aunt Guérin's tender motherly concern is evident in this note she wrote to her niece Pauline while she was taking care of little six-year-old Thérèse:

> Well! Would you believe it? Thérèse isn't at all bored with me. She will, however, be delighted to see her Papa and her sisters again, but she's happy, very happy; she laughs so heartily that her good laugh wins me over. Just now I was saying to her, must I write Pauline that you're bored? Oh! No, Aunt, oh! No. We've hardly gone out these days because of the great heat. I put her into a light skirt, with a little blue blouse of Marie's [her daughter, two years older than Thérèse], and this way she'll not suffer so much from the heat as she would with her dress, and she's very delighted with this arrangement....
>
> Thérèse wanted very much to write you, so you will receive a beautiful letter *from her hand*.[28]

The major part of Thérèse's letter follows which she (5 yrs. old) wrote with her own hand but guided by her Aunt: "Marie Guérin is at the country [her grandmother's house] since Monday, but I'm enjoying myself all alone with Aunt. I bought some gray stockings with Aunt, and the lady gave me some pearls. I'm going to make a ring with them."[29]

When she was ten, Thérèse endured a mysterious sickness the doctors could not definitively diagnose that initially involved the Guérins. She tells us about it in her autobiography:

> Papa had gone to Paris with Marie and Léonie, and Aunt had taken me and Céline with her into her home. One evening Uncle took me for a walk and spoke about Mamma and about past memories with a kindness that touched me profoundly and made me cry. Then he told me I was too softhearted, that I needed a lot of distraction, and he was determined to give us a good time during our Easter vacation. He and Aunt would see to it. That night we were to go to the Catholic Circle meeting, but finding I was too fatigued, Aunt made me go to bed; when I was undressing, I was seized with a strange trembling. Believing I was cold, Aunt covered me with blankets and surrounded me with hot water bottles. But nothing was able to stop my shaking which lasted almost all night. Uncle, returning from the meeting with my cousins and Céline, was very much surprised to see me in this state which he judged to be very serious. He didn't want to say this in order not to frighten Aunt.
>
> He went to get Doctor Notta the next day, and he judged, as did Uncle, that I had a very serious illness and one which had never before attacked a child as young as I.[30]

---

27 Letter dated May 4, 1885, from Mme. Guérin to Marie Martin.
28 Letter dated June 26, 1878.
29 Letter (LT 5) dated June 26, 1878, from Thérèse to Pauline.
30 *Story of a Soul*, chapter III, pp. 60–61.

F. Mother's Other Relatives

The family felt it inadvisable to transfer Thérèse to her own home until the next month, July, at which time she received many sympathetic visitors:

> Uncle and Aunt were very good to me; dear little Aunt came every day to visit me and brought a thousand goodies. Other friends of the family came to visit me also, but I begged Marie to tell them I wanted no visits. It displeased me to *see people seated around my bed* LIKE A ROW OF ONIONS, *looking at me as though I were a strange beast*. The only visit I liked was that of Uncle and Aunt.[31]

Thérèse was suddenly cured after seeing the statue of the Blessed Mother smile at her.

Two years later when Thérèse was twelve and staying with her aunt at her aunt's mother's farm in Saint-Ouen-le-Pin, Aunt Guérin let her husband know how the two girls, Thérèse and her cousin Marie, were enjoying themselves:

> Mme. Papinau's[32] lessons are falling a little behind; however, we should take advantage of the country. They've neglected their homework and lessons for only a few days. Besides, Marie and Thérèse are enjoying themselves very much. Thérèse is delightfully happy. Mamma was telling me yesterday that she had never seen Thérèse so gay, with her face so frankly happy.[33]

Before and after Thérèse entered religious life, she sent letters of greetings to her family and to the Guérins particularly on feast days and New Year's Day. One typical greeting, overflowing with sincere love and appreciation, follows which Thérèse wrote to her aunt during her trip to Rome:

> If you only knew how happy your little daughter would be if she could be near you to wish you a happy feast [that of Saint Elizabeth of Hungary, November 19], but since this happiness is refused her, she wants at least that a short note from her heart depart from beyond these mountains to take her place. Poor little note, how insufficient it will be to tell dear Aunt all the love I have for you....
>
> Dear Aunt, I'd like to be able to have you read into my heart. You would see in it much better than a letter all I wish for your feast. I am far, very far, from you, dear little Aunt, but it is incredible how this evening I seem to be close to you. I'd like to tell you how much I love you and how much I think of you. However, there are things that cannot be said in words, they can only be divined....
>
> *Au revoir*, dear little Aunt. I beg you to kiss dear Uncle for me. I'm sending you dear Aunt, the best wishes I have ever addressed to you, for it's when we're separated from those we love that we feel all the affection we have for them.
>
> [Signed] *Your little daughter,*
Thérèse
e.m.[34]

---

31 Ibid., p. 63.
32 Thérèse's private tutor after she left the Abbey school and apparently Marie's also.
33 Letter dated July 29, 1885, from Mme Guérin to her husband Isidore.
34 Letter (LT 32) from Thérèse to Mme. Guérin, dated November 14, 1887. The "e.m." after the signature is an abbreviation for *"enfant de Marie"* (Child of Mary) since Thérèse was a member of the "Children of Mary."

On another one of Thérèse's Aunt Guérin's feast day years later, Thérèse wrote a note of gratefulness for all she had done for her as a child:

> How many memories for me there are in this date of November 19. For a long time in advance I used to take delight in it, first, because this date was dear Aunt's feast day, and also because of the nice treats I was given on this day. Now time has passed by, the little birds have grown, they have spread their wings and have flown from the very sweet nest of their childhood. But, dear little Aunt, while I was growing up, your little daughter's heart was growing also in tenderness for you, and now especially it understands all it owes you.... To pay my debt I have only one means. Being very poor and having as my spouse a powerful and very rich King, I entrust Him with pouring out in profusion on dear Aunt the treasures of His love and thus making return to her for all the motherly acts of kindness with which she surrounded my childhood.[35]

Continuing in the same vein of deep appreciation, Thérèse wrote five years later to her aunt these unintended prophetic words about herself as a saint and her relatives as the "blessed lot" living in her company:

> I love the reading of the lives of the saints very much, the account of their heroic deeds sets my courage on fire and attracts me to imitate them; but I admit that, at times, I happen to envy the blessed lot of their relatives who had the joy of living in their company and of enjoying their conversations.[36]

The Guérins' loving care and generosity followed the Martin "daughters," as they called them, into the convent. Aunt Guérin sent cakes, candies, fish, and even plants to the convent on a regular basis for the nuns and food particularly for Thérèse during the course of her final sickness. When Thérèse received the habit on January 10, 1889, she wore a crown of artificial lilies which kept the bridal veil in place. Her Aunt gave it to her as a gift which totally delighted Thérèse:

> Your little daughter is at the height of her joy!... How kind you are to her, it's really too much ... and how to thank you.... But isn't a Mother able to read into her little daughter's heart, so I am not going to worry, being sure that you are going to understand my gratitude.
>
> The lilies are RAVISHING; I would say they have just been picked! How good of my little *sisters* to offer them to me.
>
> [Thanks], dear Aunt. If you only knew how good I find you are.[37]

M. And Mme. Guérin took Céline and Léonie into their own home during their father's hospital confinement and also after he died. Céline entered Carmel in 1894 while Léonie stayed with the Guérins until she was accepted by the Visitation nuns in Caen five years later. The next year, 1900, Mme. Guérin died leaving her husband forlorn and disconsolate. His demise came in 1909.

---
35 Letter (LT 125) from Thérèse to Mme. Guérin dated November 17, 1890.
36 Letter (LT 178) from Thérèse to Mme. Guérin dated July 20–21, 1895.
37 Letter (LT 73) dated January 2, 1889, from Thérèse to Mme. Guérin.

During the long final months of Thérèse's fatal illness, Sister Marie of the Eucharist (Marie Guérin, Thérèse's cousin) supplied her parents with all the details, almost daily at times, of Thérèse's suffering. They are the most informative and valuable of all the facts of Thérèse's sickness.

Mme. Guérin lived all her life in Lisieux as a devoted wife, mother, and aunt. After Thérèse died and her fame spread, Lisieux was inundated with countless numbers of people anxious to see the places where their little saint lived and died. As a result, the Guérin's home and privacy were continually invaded almost forcing them to leave town.

In 1899 Aunt Guérin's health deteriorated despite medical treatment from her son-in-law, Dr. LaNéele. Neither did a trip for a cure to Royat, a small town in the Auvergne noted for its thermal spa and curative waters improve her condition. A severe attack of influenza struck her on January 29, 1900, and ultimately took her life at the age of fifty-three on February 13. Abbé Ducellier, who was closely associated with the many religious celebrations connected with Thérèse and her sisters in religion, assisted her in her final hours. He recalled that "feeling death approaching, this noble woman had held in one hand the crucifix used by her saintly niece and in the other her own daughter Marie's profession candle." He also noted that "I was called yesterday to give the Last Sacraments to your dear aunt. I will never forget the spectacle I saw with my eyes. After more than twenty-five years that I was a priest, I never saw the supreme acceptance of religion received with a piety so angelic."[38]

4. JEANNE-MARIE-ELISA GUÉRIN (1868–1938)
Thérèse's cousin, wife of Dr. La Néele

JEANNE GUÉRIN, COUSIN, PLAYMATE, AND SCHOOL COMPANION OF ST. THÉRÈSE, was born on February 24, 1868, in Lisieux—one of the three children from the marriage of Isidore Guérin (Thérèse's mother's brother) and Céline Fournet Guérin. The first two were Jeanne and Marie and the last a boy who was stillborn in 1871.

From the time that the Martin family moved from Alençon to Lisieux in 1877 to 1895, Thérèse was in continuous contact with Jeanne Guérin (five years older than she) and her family until Thérèse's death in 1897. Thérèse often accompanied the Guérins and their daughters Jeanne and Marie on vacations to Trouville or Deauville. When they were children, Thérèse and her sister Céline, accompanied by one of the servants or at times by their father, walked every day from their home, Les Buissonnets, to the Guérin home at the pharmacy in the main square of Lisieux. Here they joined their cousins Jeanne and Marie and all the girls proceeded to the Benedictine Abbey school a little distance away. One time this amusing incident occurred:

> Cousin Marie and I were always of the same opinion and our tastes were so much the same that once our *union of wills* passed all bounds. Returning one

---
[38] Piat, *op. cit.*, pp. 108–109.

evening [around 6 o'clock] from the Abbey, I said to Marie: "Lead me, I'm going to close my eyes." "I want to close mine too." She replied.[39] No sooner said than done; without *arguing,* each did *her will.* We were on a sidewalk and there was nothing to fear from vehicles; having savored the delights of walking without seeing, the two little scamps fell *together* on some cases placed at the door of a store, or rather they tipped them over. The merchant came out in a rage to lift up his merchandise, while the two blind ones lifted themselves up alone, and walked off at *great strides, eyes wide open*, listening to the just reproaches of Jeanne who was as angry as the merchant! To punish us she decided to separate us, and since that day Marie and Céline went together while I made the trip with Jeanne. This put an end to our great *union of wills.* And this wasn't a bad idea since the two older ones, Jeanne and Céline, were never of the same opinion and used to argue all the way home. Peace was then complete.[40]

Another time, also during her school years, Thérèse unsuccessfully attempted to obtain some sympathy from her Aunt and others the way her cousin Marie Guérin did:

> Marie [Guérin] ... was almost always ailing ... and then Aunt babied her, giving her all kinds of endearing names, but my dear cousin continued her crying and said she had a headache. I, who had a headache almost every day and didn't complain, wanted to imitate Marie. So one evening, sitting in an armchair in the corner of the parlor, I set about the business of crying. Soon Jeanne and Aunt hurried over to me, asking me what was the matter. I answered like Marie: "I have a headache." It seemed that complaining didn't suit me, for I was unable to convince them that a headache would make me cry; instead of babying me, they spoke to me as to an adult, and Jeanne scolded me for lacking confidence in Aunt, for she was convinced something was bothering my conscience. Getting nowhere for all my trouble, I made the resolution never to imitate others again.... I did get what I deserved and this cured me for life of any desire to attract attention.[41]

In the next account Jeanne had a headache. Thérèse this time is a bit whimsical as well as self-deprecating:[42]

> I am coming, dear Jeanne, to annoy you for a few moments. I hope your migraine headache has entirely passed away. Now that the tall English lady [Thérèse herself] has left, you will be less tormented and certainly everybody will be much better.
>
> I suppose you are very happy not to be listening any longer to my sermons on death....
>
> [Signed] *Au revoir,* dear Jeanne. I always love you with my whole heart.
> *Thérèse*
> e.m.[43]

---

39 By lowering or closing their eyes they believed they were imitating the modesty of hermits.
40 *Story of a Soul*, chapter III, p. 55.
41 Ibid., pp. 89–90.
42 Letter (LT 24) from Thérèse to Jeanne Guérin dated June 27, 1887.
43 See footnote 33.

F. Mother's Other Relatives

Jeanne gave testimony at the Diocesan Process in 1911 and was asked what Thérèse was like as a child. Here are two of her answers:

- When she was little, Thérèse was a very pious and an extraordinarily good child. I cannot remember ever seeing her disobey or tell the tiniest lie.... My parents loved her as if she were their own daughter, and she returned their affection, as her letters to them testify.... I cannot recall her ever offending my father or mother in the slightest; they were full of admiration for her virtues and angelic life.
- The Servant of God was not expansive; in fact, she spoke very little. I can remember only very few occasions when I saw her enjoy playing [regular] games.... I would never have suspected then that she was so holy.[44]

A few years after Thérèse's canonization, an American priest visited Mme. La Néele at her home in Lisieux and asked the same questions about Thérèse playing games as a child. He wondered if she played with Thérèse. "Oh, yes, hundreds of times":

> I was older than the Little Flower and it was my sister Marie who played with her more than I, but I would say that the Little Flower did not care a great deal to play as other girls would and neither did my sister Marie.... [They] played, but their games were religious in character. They played at hermit and at mass, benediction, vespers and so on.
>
> Oh, they were never long-faced even while they were playing those religious games. They were always very joyous. The Little Flower never seemed sad. My father used to call her his little ray of sunshine. And it was an experience to see her smile. I have never seen such a charming smile.[45]

Thérèse entered the Lisieux Carmel in April of 1888. Six months later when she was a postulant she wrote this atypical, prosaic, feminine letter:

> Thérèse is coming to ask for another favor. Sister Agnès [her blood sister] just told me that I need a pair of boots lined with fur [since the weather was frigid], just like the ones I saw you with many times in the winter; they are a kind of little ankle-boot that are bordered with Astrakhan fur. If Aunt wanted to buy them for me, I would be very happy. Jeanne could try them on, for she has exactly the same foot as I.[46]

After an engagement of four months, Jeanne married Dr. Francis La Néele on October 1, 1891, in Caen. In her autobiography, Thérèse composed in imitation of Jeanne's wedding invitation an extended form of an invitation to her own "spiritual wedding" to Christ in very florid language that some judge to be overly sentimental but nonetheless quite typical of the sentiments prevalent at the times, especially as composed by a teenage girl of seventeen. A portion of it follows:

> Jeanne's wedding took place eight days after I received the Veil. It would be impossible ... for me to tell ... how much I learned from her example concerning

---
44 O'Mahony, *op. cit.*, p. 267.
45 Dolan, *Collected Little Flower Works*, p. 112.
46 Letter (LT 69) from Thérèse to Marie Guérin dated November, 1888.

the delicate attentions a bride can bestow upon her bridegroom. I listened eagerly to what she was saying so that I would learn all I could since I didn't want to do less for my beloved Jesus than Jeanne did for her Francis; true, he was a perfect creature, but he was still only a creature.

I even went so far as to amuse myself by composing a letter of invitation which was comparable to Jeanne's own letter, and this is how it was written:

> Letter of Invitation to the Wedding of Sister Thérèse
> of the Child Jesus and the Holy Face.
>
> God Almighty, Creator of Heaven and Earth, Sovereign Ruler of the Universe, and the Most Glorious Virgin Mary, Queen of the Heavenly Court, announce to you the Spiritual Espousals of Their August Son, Jesus, King of kings, and Lord of lords, with little Thérèse Martin, now Princess and Lady of His Kingdoms of the Holy Childhood and the Passion, assigned to her in dowry by her Divine Spouse, from which Kingdoms she holds her titles of nobility—of the Child Jesus and the Holy Face.[47]

At her wedding, Jeanne wore a beautiful long white wedding gown made of satin that she later donated to the Carmel. The nuns made two long curtain panels out of it and arranged them on each side of the tall opening in the choir where they received communion. They also had enough for a valance above the curtains. on which Thérèse painted symbols of the Eucharist—lilies, angels, and a chalice.[48]

Two weeks after Jeanne's nuptials, Thérèse wrote her a letter in which she said: "I was very much touched when seeing that the name of Francis accompanied that of Jeanne in wishing me a happy feast [October 15], so it is to both of you that I am sending thanks.... I hope that soon God will send a little Isidore as perfect as his Papa or else a little Jeanne resembling exactly her Mamma."[49] For years Thérèse prayed, comforted her, and truly believed they would have a baby. She wrote three poems (PN 37-38-39) dedicated to Francis and Jeanne for Jeanne's feast day, August 21,[50] expressing her certitude in this regard:

> Jesus, hear my prayer.
> Grant my ardent desire.
> Exile an angel on earth.
> Give Jeanne a little baby!
> ...
> "With exquisite tenderness
> My [Christ's] hand is preparing her,
> Since she is to give to my Church:
> A Pontiff, a great Saint!"[51]

---

47 *Story of a Soul*, chapter VIII, p. 168.
48 Footnote 8 to LC 128, letter from Céline to Thérèse dated June 17, 1890.
49 LT 131. Letter from Thérèse to Mme. La Néele (Jeanne Guérin) dated October 17, 1891.
50 August 21 is the feast day of St. Jane Frances de Chantal (1572-1641), foundress with St. Francis de Sales, of the Order of the Visitation known also as the Visitandines and as the Nuns of the Visitation of Mary.
51 PN 38 entitled "Confidential Message from Jesus to Thérèse."

F. Mother's Other Relatives

Sadly, their marriage was childless. After her husband died in 1916, however, she adopted an orphan girl, one of her grand nieces, which afforded her much happiness and fulfillment.

Thérèse's sisters Céline and Léonie cared for their father in the last years of his life. After his death on July 29, 1894, Céline's dream of becoming a Carmelite came true when she entered the Lisieux Carmel forty-seven days later on September 14. Like her sister Thérèse, Céline encountered opposition to her entrance from, surprisingly, Jeanne and her husband. The many reasons they expressed with so much acrimony lacked understanding, empathy, and charity:

> Jeanne and Francis are really dead set against me, they are talking with great bitterness. They reproach me with many things.... First, they say that I do not have a vocation, that I was destined to be the mother of a family, that I should have spoken earlier about this attraction to the religious life, that I am foolish to decide so quickly, that if they were to offer me a good match, I would take it, that it is an impulse, out of desperation that I am entering the convent, etc.; afterward, it is about yourselves [the Carmelites], you are monopolizers, and you and I are low in their estimation, etc.; afterward, it is because I am ungrateful to be leaving so quickly after Papa's death! I should have finished my time of mourning in the world, strengthened my vocation, and given at least one year to Uncle and Aunt out of gratitude, etc., etc.... And they are pitiless when it comes to souls consecrated to God; it seems that religious deserve everything when it comes to contempt and trouble....[52]

Thérèse's response was short and sagacious:

> I am not surprised at the storm raging at Caen. Francis and Jeanne have chosen a road so different from ours that they cannot understand the sublimity of our vocation!... But they laugh best who laugh last.... After this life of one day, they will understand who will have been the most privileged, *we or they*....[53]

Jeanne and her husband lived some distance away in Caen where her husband had his medical practice. Visits to the Carmel, therefore, were infrequent. When Jeanne's sister Marie became a Carmelite in the same monastery as Thérèse and her three sisters, Marie kept not only Jeanne but their parents abreast of all the news at the Carmel. During Thérèse's last months of life suffering greatly from tuberculosis, Marie quite frequently notified Jeanne and her parents of Thérèse's condition.

A year after Thérèse died, her *Story of a Soul* was published and distributed to thousands. After Jeanne read it, she confided to her sister Marie (her name in religion was Sister Marie of the Eucharist) these thoughts:

> I am telling no one what Thérèse has said to me when reading her *Life*. I have said it only to my dear husband from whom I keep nothing hidden. I am telling you, my dear, but do not speak of it.... I have seen the truth of this saying

---

52 LC 160. Letter from Céline in Caen to Thérèse dated August 19, 1894.
53 Letter (LT 169) from Thérèse to Céline dated August 19, 1894.

of our little saint: "I shall spend my heaven in doing good...." The favors she is granting me are much more precious than if she were to send me the little fair-haired child she promised. She consoles me spiritually, she suggests that I offer up my little sufferings for a priest, and what good this thought has done me! I shall not be able to be the mother of a priest (what I was dreaming about all my life), but I shall be able to bring forth spiritually a servant of God by uniting my sorrows to the merits of Jesus Christ.[54]

Thérèse's fame as a sainted nun spread throughout France and beyond, motivating crowds of people to visit Lisieux to see the grave where Thérèse was buried, the monastery where she died, and Les Buissonnets, the home where she lived. Dr. La Néele bought this home in 1909 and in 1911 he rented it to Mme. Hazebrouck and her family who took charge of greeting the multitudes that were continually visiting it. In 1922, six years after the death of her husband Francis, Jean sold Les Buissonnets to the *Pèlerinage Sainte-Thérèse*. The Castel family served as guardians. In 1931 the Oblates of Saint Thérèse took over the care of Les Buissonnets and have been in charge ever since.

In the early years, Jeanne received many letters and visitors requesting souvenirs, pictures, and relics of Thérèse. This became quite a burden and invasion of her privacy which almost caused her and her husband to move out of town.

Around 1913, one contentious affair disturbed the normally tranquil relationship between Jeanne and Céline. It concerned certain paintings and photographs of Thérèse by Céline. Jeanne and her husband did not approve of Céline's work and preferred the photographs Abbé Gombault had taken of Thérèse. Their sharp criticism caused hurt feelings on both sides, mostly for Céline, though, but which in time were amicably healed.

Jeanne's later life was saddened by the early deaths of her sister at age thirty-five in 1905 and her husband at fifty-eight in 1916. She did, however, derive much pleasure in caring for her adopted daughter and in doing charitable work in the community. She died on April 25, 1938, at the age of seventy at Nogent-le-Rotrou, a town east of Alençon where she had retired. Fortunately she lived to see her cousin receive the highest honor from the Church when she was proclaimed the "greatest of the modern saints."[55]

5. MARIE GUÉRIN (1870–1905) (SISTER MARIE OF THE EUCHARIST)
Cousin and novice of St. Thérèse

THOUGH MARIE GUÉRIN WAS TWO YEARS AND FOUR MONTHS OLDER THAN Thérèse Martin, her cousin, they were close friends from childhood to Thérèse's death in 1897. She ranked next after Thérèse's own sisters in her close relationship with Thérèse. Born in Lisieux, the second of three children on August 22, 1870, she was christened Marie-Louise-Hélène the same day. Her father was Thérèse's uncle, Isidore Guérin—Thérèse's mother's brother—and Marie's mother was

---
54 Footnote 3, p. 1147, to a letter (LT 255) from Thérèse to M. and Mme. Guérin dated July 16, 1897.
55 Pope Pius X.

F. Mother's Other Relatives

Céline (*née* Fournet). They chose Louis Martin to be her godfather. M. and Mme. Guérin's two other children were a girl, Jeanne (1868–1938) and a little brother by the name of Paul who died at birth in 1871. Shortly after the death of Thérèse's mother in 1877 when Thérèse was four, M. Martin moved with his five daughters from Alençon to Lisieux to be near M. and Mme. Guérin and their two daughters—Marie, then seven-and-a-half and Jeanne, ten. The Martin and Guérin girls quickly became close friends and playmates.

Thérèse was eight in 1881 when she became a day student at the Benedictine Abbey school which her two cousins attended. All the girls—Thérèse, Céline, Marie, and Jeanne Guérin—walked to school together. In addition to this daily association, the Martin and Guérin children spent Thursdays and Sundays together and shared family gatherings and even lengthy vacations. The intimate friendship between Thérèse and Marie is amusingly illustrated in a passage from Thérèse's autobiography about their "hermit game":

> What pleased me was when by chance I was alone with little Marie and, not having Céline Maudelonde (Marie's cousin) dragging her into *ordinary games*, she left me free to choose, and I chose a game that was entirely new. Marie and Thérèse became two *hermits*, having nothing but a poor hut, a little garden where they grew corn and other vegetables. Their life was spent in continual contemplation; in other words, one *hermit* replaced the other at prayer while she was occupied in the active life. Everything was done with such mutual understanding, silence, and so religiously that it was just perfect. When Aunt came to fetch us to go for our walk, we continued the game even on the street. The two hermits recited the rosary together, using their fingers in order to screen their devotion from the inquisitive public; however, one day the younger hermit [Thérèse] forgot herself completely: having received a piece of cake for lunch, she made a big sign of the Cross over it before eating it, causing people to laugh.
>
> Cousin Marie and I were always of the same opinion and our tastes were so much the same that once our *union of wills* passed all bounds. Returning one evening from the Abbey, I said to Marie: "Lead me, I'm going to close my eyes." "I want to close mine too," she replied. No sooner said then done; without *arguing*, each did her *will*. We were on a sidewalk and there was nothing to fear from vehicles; having savored the delights of walking without seeing, the two little scamps fell *together* on some cases placed at the door of a store, or rather they tipped them over. The merchant came out in a rage to lift up his merchandise, while the two blind ones lifted themselves up alone and walked off at *great strides, eyes wide open*, listening to the just reproaches of Jeanne who was as angry as the merchant! To punish us she decided to separate us, and since that day Marie and Céline went together while I made the trip with Jeanne. This put an end to our great *union of wills*. And this wasn't a bad idea since the two older ones, Jeanne and Céline, were never of the same opinion and used to argue all the way home. Peace was then complete.[56]

---

56 *Story of a Soul*, chapter III, pp. 54–55.

Another humorous episode Thérèse experienced, but which resulted in a psychologically more valuable lesson learned, happened in May of 1885 when she was on vacation at Deauville with the Guérins:

> Marie, who was almost always ailing, often *whimpered*; and then Aunt babied her, giving her all kinds of endearing names, but my dear little cousin continued her crying and said she had a headache. I, who had a headache almost every day and didn't complain, wanted to imitate Marie. So one evening, sitting in an armchair in the corner of the parlor, I set about the business of crying. Soon Jeanne and Aunt hurried over to me, asking me what was the matter. I answered like Marie: "I have a headache." It seemed that complaining didn't suit me, for I was unable to convince them that a headache would make me cry; instead of babying me, they spoke to me as to an adult, and Jeanne scolded me for lacking confidence in Aunt, for she was convinced something was bothering my conscience. Getting nowhere for all my trouble, I made the resolution never to imitate others again, and I understood the fable about *"The donkey and the pet dog"* [by La Fontaine]. *I was the donkey* that saw the caresses the little dog was getting; he came and placed his clumsy hoof on the table to get his share of kisses. Although I didn't get the blows of the cudgel like the poor animal, I did get what I deserved and this cured me for life of any desire to attract attention. The one effort I had made was far too costly! [57]

Marie and Thérèse regularly corresponded throughout the years. (Thérèse wrote her about ten letters before she entered Carmel and five after. Marie sent Thérèse seven before Thérèse entered and three when Thérèse was a Carmelite.) Their early letters were generally prosaic, sentimental, and affectionate. Thérèse often used pet names (common at the time) in addressing her such as "Louploup," "little imp," "little rascal," "beautiful doll" (a reference to a recreation playlet acted by the novices). Her parents and others called her "Benoni" and "Benjamin" who, like the youngest son of the Biblical Jacob and Rachel, was the youngest of the family. Another nickname Maria had before and after she became a Carmelite was "Little Doctor." She nursed her often sick mother and sister and as a result earned that title. Her brother-in-law, Francis La Néele, was a real doctor whom they called the "Big Doctor."

Marie was endowed with a rather complex character. She was very intelligent and gifted with musical talent including a beautiful soprano voice and the ability to play the piano with great skill. At the time of her novitiate, Thérèse made the comment that "her beautiful voice is the joy and delight of our recreations." [58] As a matter of fact, when Marie entered Carmel she brought with her some of her own music, both sacred and profane, which Thérèse used as melodies to be sung to her lines of poetry. Other aspects of Marie's multifaceted personality, though less complimentary, were her extreme sensitivity, impulsivity, capriciousness, and scrupulosity. These traits she clearly revealed in a number

---

57 Ibid., chapter IV, pp. 89–90.
58 Letter (LT 180) dated October 14–17, 1895, from Thérèse to Mme. La Néele.

of her letters. For example, while in Paris with her family in May of 1889, she visited the Paris Exhibition and told Thérèse of her concerns:

> Paris was not made for healing the scrupulous. I no longer know where to turn my eyes. If I flee from one nudity, I meet another, and so it goes on all day long. It's enough to make you die of sorrow; it seems to me I do this out of curiosity.... How do you expect me to receive Holy Communion tomorrow and Friday? I am obliged to abstain from it; this is a great trial.... I don't know how one can live here. As far as I am concerned, this is a veritable hell.... I look upon Paris with horror.[59]

Thérèse's reply is both consoling and wise:

> You haven't committed the *shadow of any evil*; I know what these kinds of temptations are so well that I can assure you of this without any fear.... We must despise all these temptations and pay no attention whatsoever to them.
>
> Should I tell you something that has given me *much* sorrow? It is that my little Marie has given up her Communions.... When the devil has succeeded in drawing the soul away from Holy Communion, *he has won everything*.... And Jesus weeps!... so don't listen to the devil, mock him, and go without any fear to receive Jesus in peace and love!... [Receive] *Communion often*, very often.... That is the *only remedy* if you want to be healed.[60]

Throughout the succeeding years, spiritual advice continued to flow from Thérèse's pen in her correspondence with Marie. Then, some seven years after Thérèse entered Carmel, Marie joined her and her other cousins—Pauline, Marie, and Céline—on August 15, 1895, which happened to be her feast day. Thérèse became Marie's novice mistress. The prioress, Mother Marie de Gonzague, granted the rare privilege of allowing five women from the same family group to live together in one convent.

Her parents were quite distraught over her leaving them to join her cousins in religion. Eventually, however, they came to realize the beauty of her vocation, though it was difficult to lose their youngest and only daughter living with them at the time. Two years after Marie entered Carmel, her father wrote these beautiful words of praise and acceptance of his daughter's and four nieces' Carmelite vocation:

> Thank You, one thousand times thank You, Lord, for having given me such angels here below; thank You, Lord, for having made me experience, in preference to so many others, the beauties of Your love and the holiness of Your law.
>
> [I] thank Him and glorify Him for the glory with which He has made my house renowned.... It will be twenty-seven years ago on Sunday since He has entrusted me with the most precious pearl in my jewelry box [his daughter Marie]. It was necessary to fashion and polish her from her birth, and, if I have contributed little to this, her very gentle and good mother has cut off the rough edges, and you, my dear [Thérèse], have contributed by giving her all her splendor [through her role as mistress of novices].[61]

---

59 Letter (LC 113) dated May 29, 1889, from Marie to her cousin Thérèse.
60 Letter (LT 92) dated May 30, 1889, from Thérèse to Marie.
61 Letter (LC 195) from M. Guérin to Thérèse, dated August 18, 1897, four days before Marie Guérin's 27th birthday.

Msgr. Guy Gaucher, the ultimate authority on St. Thérèse, has these prudent insights concerning the relationship between Thérèse and Marie Guérin:

> Family ties did not facilitate Thérèse's task. We have seen this already in the case of Sister Geneviève. It is true, too, for her cousin Marie, who has now become Sister Marie of the Eucharist. Being introduced to the contemplative religious life by one's companions in games, when one is both compulsive and scrupulous, can give rise to many difficulties. It was not without some difficulty, then, that Thérèse won the confidence of her cousin. The health reports which Marie was very soon to be writing to her family give proof of the admiration and attachment she had for her Mistress.[62]

For the day of Marie's entrance, just a week before her twenty-fifth birthday, Thérèse composed the first of three poems dedicated to her, "Canticle of a Soul Having Found the Place of Its Rest" (PN 21). Though focused on Marie's vocation, this poem as well as the others, really expresses Thérèse's own spiritual journey. Most of her poems were written to be sung. Marie sang this poem before the community in the evening of her entrance, since it was expected that the young postulant herself "sing something."[63] The music Thérèse chose was the main melody from a well-known aria *"Connais-tu-le pays."*[64] In it she sang, "Lord, if I have left my dear family, / You will know how to heap heavenly favors on them." Also, "Jesus, soon I must follow you / To the eternal shore when my days will come to an end. / ... I shall live in Heaven / To love you and never to die again...."

On the very day Marie received the Carmelite habit, March 17, 1896, Céline donned the black veil. Marie's father Isidore Guérin wrote a justifiably prideful account of these ceremonies in the newspaper with which he was associated, *Le Normand*:

> This morning at eight-thirty, Mademoiselle Céline Martin, accompanied by her three sisters who preceded her into monastic life, pronounced her final vows and received the veil of the professed nun.
>
> His Excellency the Bishop of Bayeux and Lisieux presided over this impressive ceremony during which Father Ducellier, the Dean of Trevieres, developed its lofty and religious significance in a moving and eloquent allocution....
>
> His Excellency presided over this second ceremony at which a friend of Monsieur Guérin, Father Levasseur, pastor of Saint Germain-de-Navarre-les-Evreux, delivered a pious and insightful sermon.
>
> Morning and afternoon, the chapel was filled with people who came to show their affection for these young women and for this honored family on which God has poured such great and numerous blessings.[65]

Six months later, Thérèse wrote her second poem (PN 36), "Jesus Alone," for her cousin, now Sister Marie of the Eucharist, and presented it to her on August 15, 1896, which was again on her feast day. It is truly a love song for Jesus:

---
62 *Her Last Conversations*, pp. 248–249.
63 Kinney, *The Poetry of Saint Thérèse of Lisieux*, p. 111.
64 From Ambroise Thomas' opera *Mignon* (1866).
65 Descouvement, *Therese and Lisieux*, p. 255.

> Jesus, you alone can satisfy my soul.
> Nothing can charm me here below.
> True happiness cannot be found here....
> My only peace, my only happiness,
> My only love is you, Lord!...

Then later on she cries out, "Like a child full of little attentions,/Lord, I want to overwhelm you with caresses."

Because Thérèse was assistant novice mistress, she was asked to write something for Sister Marie of the Eucharist's profession which took place on March 25, 1897. The poem (PN 48) that resulted is entitled "My Weapons" and was sung before the community on the same night of the profession. Its basic premise was to fortify Marie's vocation but, again, it personifies Thérèse's own vocation, realities of life, and struggles as she was embarking on her own last days of suffering which culminated in her own death six months later. In it she says she put on the "weapons of the All-Powerful" which are her religious vows: poverty (lance and helmet), chastity (celestial sword), and obedience (breastplate and shield). The final lines are: "Smiling, I bravely face the fire./And in your arms, O my divine Spouse,/I shall die singing on the battlefield,/My weapons in hand!" Incidentally, the music Thérèse chose to write these words to is Charles Gounod's "Song at the Departure of the Missionaries" that was customarily sung at the seminary of the Paris Foreign Missions before the new missionaries left for their foreign assignments.

Sister Marie of the Eucharist was active as a novice in the production of recreations for the community. On Christmas Eve, 1895, Thérèse's playlet, *The Divine Little Beggar of Christmas* (RP 5), was put on in which each sister picked a folded note (Thérèse was #26) from a basket and gave it to Sister Marie of the Eucharist. She represented an angel and sang the verses written on the papers that exhorted each nun to offer her best quality to the Child Jesus.

For the feast day of Mother Marie de Gonzague, June 21, 1896, the novices performed another play for the community (RP 5) composed by Thérèse. Entitled *The Triumph of Humility*, it was based on the *Mémoires d'une Ex-Palladiste* by Diana Vaughan (then not known as being a deceitful, fictitious character). Sister Marie of the Sacred Heart (Marie Martin) informed Sister Marie of the Eucharist's parents of this performance:

> Yesterday and today, two little plays by the novices. Yesterday, the Benjamin [Marie Guérin], dressed up as a gardener with blouse and wig, enacted the part of the innocent one to perfection. Today, transformed into St. Michael, she combated Satan and his devils.... It was a current event. Asmodée [Marie Guérin] was there, speaking about Diana Vaughan, etc., etc.; it was composed by Sister Thérèse of the Child Jesus.... These are the amusements of the Carmelites.[66]

---

[66] This is from a letter dated June 21, 1896, from Sister Marie of the Sacred Heart to M. and Mme. Isidore Guérin. See *General Correspondence—Vol. 2*, p. 1265.

A little humorous incident occurred at the convent on November 30, 1896, involving the three cousins—Thérèse, her sister Marie, and Marie Guérin—which the latter informed her father of in a letter she wrote to him the next day (December 1):

> If I had had the space, I would have told you the story of a thief in Carmel. Yesterday evening, in the sacristy, Sister Thérèse of the Child Jesus heard movement in the room next to the one where she was. She came looking for us; five or six went armed; you will laugh at our arms of defense: a broom, some forks, heavy sticks. Not seeing them return, Sister Marie of the Sacred Heart left with me with tongs and shovels. There was one who had taken a fistful of ashes to throw on the head of the thief. All these arms were useless; we looked everywhere, and no thief.... As this was during recreation, the incident was not without some excitement.[67]

Thérèse served as Marie's novice mistress for nearly two years. Her spiritual tutelage had no peer. As such she was a loving, sympathetic, wise, but punctilious teacher. Though Thérèse considered Marie a kindred spirit, she did not hesitate to let her know where she needed improvement. For example, she corrected her occasional "foolish gaiety."[68] She reminded her that she "shouldn't sit sideways in the chair; it is forbidden!"[69] Marie recalled Thérèse's words to her about her scruples:

> "I beg you, be busied a little less with yourself, occupy yourself with loving God, and forget about yourself. All your scruples, these are just a lot of self-seeking. Your griefs, your sorrows, all that is centered on yourself, it is like spinning around on the same pivot. Ah! I beg you, forget yourself, think of saving souls." She used to be repeating this every time I [Marie] was with her for direction.[70]

Marie received the veil on June 2, 1897, about a month before Thérèse was brought to the infirmary on July 8. And in a letter dated four days after on the 12th, Marie disclosed to her father the spiritual advice Thérèse gave her and casual announcement of her forthcoming death:

> [There] is something, dear Father, which has afforded me much happiness; it's something Thérèse said to me a few days before I received the veil. I regard it as her "will and testament" to me.... There was, at this time, no question of her death, her condition was not yet known; she said to me all of a sudden, looking at me with such a profound gaze that I'll never forget it: "Oh, little Sister, promise me you'll become a saint, a great saint."
>
> When I looked at her in amazement, she continued: "Yes, and if I say this to you, it's because I find in you all that is necessary for this; and if you don't become one, believe me, you'll be unfaithful to grace. Oh! I beg you, become a

---

67 *General Correspondence*, Vol. 2, p. 1268. From Sister Marie of the Eucharist (Marie Guérin) to her father, Dec. 1, 1896.
68 See note 5 in LT 180, letter of Oct. 14–17, 1895, from Thérèse to Mme. La Néele.
69 *Last Conversations*, August 19, 1897.
70 As quoted in note 6 to LC 183, letter of Mother Agnès to Thérèse, June 2, 1897.

saint. God is begging this from you. When I'm no longer on earth, you'll have to be a saint for two, in order that God lose nothing; I feel that your soul is being called to the same type of perfection as my own, and you must replace me when I'm gone."[71]

There is an abundance of information available about Thérèse's last conversations with her sisters and cousin in the monastery. This includes additional conversations recorded by other nuns also. Sister Marie of the Eucharist kept her family regularly informed of Thérèse's physical condition and gradual deterioration. She was quite aware of medical practices and health symptoms since her father was a pharmacist, her brother-in-law was a doctor (Francis La Néele), and she took care of her often sick mother and sister. Her steady flow of letters were really detailed medical reports. Without them we would not have all the important medical facts about Thérèse's illness. The letters of course also included non-medical or non-health related comments. One observation Marie reported to her father in a letter three months before Thérèse died is absolutely amazing: "If you were to see our little patient [Thérèse], you wouldn't be able to stop laughing. She has to be always saying something funny. Ever since she has become convinced she is going to die, she has been as gay as a little finch. There are times when one would pay to be near her."[72]

The love and admiration Marie and others show in their writings pertaining to the ailing Thérèse at this point are revealing. Thérèse is referred to frequently as "our dear little angel" and often as "our little Queen." Marie summed up her opinion of Thérèse, as well as a résumé of Thérèse's spirituality, in a letter she wrote to her first cousin, Céline Maudelonde, during a period Thérèse was suffering severely:

> I thank God for permitting me to know this little saint, for here in the community she is loved and appreciated as such.... Hers is not an extraordinary sanctity; there is no love of extraordinary penances, no, only love for God. People in the world can imitate her sanctity, for she has tried only to do everything through love and to accept all little contradictions, all little sacrifices that come at each moment as coming from God's hands. She saw God in everything, and she carried out all her actions as perfectly as possible. Daily duty came before everything else; as for pleasure, she knew how to sanctify it even while enjoying it, offering it up to God.... I asked her the other day: "Did you sometimes refuse God anything?" She said: "No, I don't remember refusing Him anything. Even when I was very little, at the age of three, I began to refuse God nothing He was asking from me." This is saying everything, isn't it, to be able to make such an answer, and it's rare to hear it even in our Carmels. Never to have refused God anything!...[73]

---

71 Correspondance Générale, 1, p. 486, as quoted in *Last Conversations*, p. 250.
72 From a letter by Sister Marie of the Eucharist (Marie Guérin) addressed to her father on July 9, 1897, as quoted on p. 274 in *Her Last Conversations*.
73 From a letter dated July 20, 1897, by Sister Marie of the Eucharist to Mme. Gaston Pottier [Céline Maudelonde] as quoted on p. 250 in *Her Last Conversations*.

Sadly, Marie lived barely eight years after Thérèse, dying at the age of thirty-four years and seven months on April 14, 1905, of the same dreadful disease, tuberculosis, that claimed the life of Thérèse. She is buried along with a few other nuns in the same deep grave where Thérèse's coffin once rested in the public cemetery of Lisieux. Her family's plot is just a few feet away.

During those few years after Thérèse's death, Marie lived to see the knowledge and fame of her holy cousin's sanctity spread far and wide, leading possibly to her canonization. Thérèse's autobiography sold in the thousands, went through six French editions, and was translated into Polish and English.

A grievous blow struck the Guérin and Martin households with the death of Mme. Guérin, Marie's mother, who passed away in 1900. Just four months before Marie's own demise, Mother Marie de Gonzague, who played a crucial part in the life of Thérèse and, in fact, all the Carmelites of Lisieux, succumbed to cancer. The deaths of Mme. Guérin and her daughter Marie greatly affected Isidore Guérin who eventually died in 1909.

As a faithful and loving disciple of her cousin Thérèse, Marie's last words echoed exactly those Sister Thérèse of the Child Jesus uttered before she entered eternity: "*Mon Jésus, je vous aime!*"—"My Jesus, I love you!"

6. Dr. Francisque-Lucien-Sulpice La Néele (1858–1916)
Husband of Jeanne Guérin and Thérèse's cousin by marriage

Dr. Francis La Néele was Thérèse's cousin by his marriage to her first cousin Jeanne Guérin. He was born in Paris on October 18, 1858, and educated by the Jesuits. Upon finishing his higher education he was qualified with two degrees—as a pharmacist (1887) and a doctor (1888). At twenty-nine he began his career as a pharmacist at his own shop in Caen, where he was living at 123 rue Saint-Jean. After an engagement of four months, he married Jeanne on October 1, 1890, in Caen. A year later on November 26 he was compelled to sell his pharmacy; a new government law concerning the practice of medicine was passed forbidding one from holding two professions. He thereupon purchased an eighteenth-century hotel at 24 (26?) rue de l'Oratoire and established his medical practice there. This building and scores of others in that area were completely destroyed in the June 1944 bombings during the Allies' invasion of Normandy.

Dr. La Néele and his wife enjoyed many of their holidays at La Musse, the Guérins' vacation home near Evreux. The doctor was noted as an accomplished hunter, a sport he engaged in apparently when he was at La Musse. Through Marie Guérin he gave some of his catch to the chaplain of the Carmel and to those nuns there who were allowed to eat meat.[74] In the middle of July 1894, the La Néeles had a delightful time sharing pleasurable moments and activities with Céline Martin, Marie Guérin, and Abbé Joseph de Cornière, the twenty-year-old son of the Carmel's doctor. Céline conveyed her impressions and reactions

---

74 See note 7 to LT 192.

in detail of this vacation to her sister Thérèse in the convent.[75] (Marie Guérin, incidentally, was often referred to as the "Little Doctor" while Dr. Francis La Néele was called the "Big Doctor.")[76]

Marie Guérin joined her four Carmelite cousins Marie, Pauline, Céline, and Thérèse on April 15, 1895, at the Carmel in Lisieux. In fact, she became one of Thérèse's novices. Thérèse wrote a letter to her cousin Jeanne La Néele telling her of her sister Marie (Guérin) who "delights the whole community":

> If you had only seen her the other day with your photograph and that of Francis, it would have made you laugh!... Our Mother [Agnès, Pauline Martin] had brought them into our recreation and was having them passed around to each Sister; when Sister Marie of the Eucharist's turn came, she took the photographs one after the other, giving them her most *gracious smiles* and saying to each: "*Bonjour, Fifine* [Jeanne].... *Bonjour, Séraphin* [Francis]." These expressions of tenderness made all the Carmelites laugh, who are very happy to have so nice a postulant.[77]

In 1896, Thérèse wrote a poem (actually an acrostic), "A Holy and Famous Doctor" (PN 39) for Dr. La Néele which he found very engaging. It refers to the fact that Francis, with his father-in-law, Isidore Guérin, were actively involved with combating the anti-clerical elements in Lisieux:

<pre>
F   Francis took this motto:
R   Nothing for man, everything for my God.
A   And so to defend the Church
N   Has he not a heart all on fire?
C   Fighting godless science,
I   He confesses it out loud:
S   His glory is Mary's![78]
</pre>

The child of the seraphic Doctor:
Saint Teresa
August 21, '96

Since childhood Thérèse was not always in good health. Her sister Pauline testified that she caught colds every winter, had difficulty in breathing at times, and endured ever-occurring painful headaches. Her other sister Céline stated that "As a child, Thérèse could not run because she easily became short of breath."[79] The early signs of tuberculosis, the disease that took her life, appeared in June 1894 when she was a nun. Dr. La Néele was informed about her symptoms and accordingly visited the Carmel (July 1) to investigate her health problem. Marie Guérin (Sister Marie of the Eucharist) systematically informed her family of

---

75 See LC 159, the letter Céline wrote to Thérèse dated July 17, 1894.
76 Marie was called the "little Doctor" because she was the daughter of a pharmacist, from whom she must have learned a great deal, and the sister-in-law of a doctor. She also cared for her mother and sister during the many times they were sick. She wrote excellent medical accounts to her family of Thérèse's physical condition during the last months of her life.
77 LT 180, dated October 14–17, 1895, from Thérèse to Mme. La Néele (Jeanne Guérin).
78 The English translation does not lend itself to form a proper acrostic except for lines 1 and 3.
79 See Footnote c on p. 35 in Gaucher's *The Passion of Thérèse of Lisieux*.

Thérèse's health since it began to fail. One of the first times she reported this: "At Carmel, they expect Francis on Sunday, who will see Thérèse, who has a persistent sore throat, hoarse voice, and some pains in her *chest*. They would have liked Francis to examine her, but this is a very delicate matter with Dr. D. [de Cornière, the official Carmel physician]...."[80] Thérèse had her first coughing up of blood (hemoptysis) on April 2–3, 1896 (Holy Thursday and Good Friday). Dr. La Néele did manage to see Thérèse after this occurred though under most unsatisfactory and unusual conditions. He was not allowed to examine her the normal way but had to arrive at a medical assessment merely by checking her as she put her head through a small opening in the oratory grille.[81] He thus apparently did not attach much significance to Thérèse's spitting of blood. It is perplexing, though, why it took until the summer (July 15) for Dr. de Cornière to come for the first time to check Thérèse's condition.

After that initial visitation, Dr. Francis La Néele saw Thérèse only a few times in the last two months of her life.[82] Below are some extracts from written statements about each of his last visits that record quite touching and poignant moments:

1. AUGUST 17, 1897

I [Dr. La Néele] told her [Sister Marie of the Eucharist] to ask Mother Prioress if I could examine Thérèse.... I was brought in immediately, and what a favor this was! I kissed our little saint on the forehead for you, Mamma [Mme. Guérin, his mother-in-law and Thérèse's aunt], and the whole family. I asked permission, as a matter of form, from Mother Prioress, and without waiting for the answer that perhaps the Rule forbade it, I took what was your right. What a heavenly face! What a radiantly smiling Angel! I was moved to tears when I was speaking to her, holding her transparent hands burning with fever. After I examined her, I had her sit up on her pillows. She asked: "Am I going to heaven soon?" "Not yet, dear little sister. God wants you to wait for a few more weeks so that your crown will be more beautiful in heaven." "Oh! No, I'm not thinking of that! It's only to save souls that I want to suffer more." I answered: "That's very true, but when you save souls, you climb up higher in heaven, you are closer to God." She answered with a radiant smile which lighted up her face as though heaven had opened before her eyes, flooding her with its divine brightness. "You'll really remember us up there?" I asked: *"Oh! yes, and I'll ask God to send you a little cherub. Yes, that's quite settled! I'll ask for one that is like you."* I said: "No, not like me, but like his mother who is much better than I." *"May he be like both of you. How many days do I have before going to heaven?"* I said: "In your sickness, little sister, it's very hard to say. In a few weeks, a month, perhaps more, unless you have an accident or you're in a hurry to go to see God." She said: *"I'll wait as long as God wills. Besides, I don't want to cause you any inconvenience, you nor Uncle. I'll wait*

---

80 From a letter by Marie Guérin to Mme. La Néele dated June 28, 1897.
81 Gaucher, *op. cit.*, pp. 39–40.
82 Since Dr. de Cornier was the regular convent doctor, he saw her many more times—at least thirty-two—while Dr. La Néele was in effect, a substitute.

F. Mother's Other Relatives

till you return [from Lourdes]. *You will pray for me at Lourdes. Tell Uncle and Aunt how much I love them, kiss them for me, as well as Léonie and Jeanne. In heaven I'll be always with you.*" I remained a good half hour with her, along with Céline and Mother Prioress. I kissed her again before I left and she accompanied me to the door with her smile which I'll never forget.

The right lung is totally lost, filled with tubercles in the process of softening. The left lung is affected in its lower part. She is very emaciated, but her face still does her honor. She is suffering very much from intercostal neuralgia,[83] and it was because of this that I had the happiness of seeing her. I returned there the following Wednesday [August 18], hoping to enter once more, but Marie and the little prioress [Mother Agnès—Pauline] didn't dare ask Mother Marie de Gonzague's permission for me to do so. I gave her a prescription to calm her pains, for she was suffering very much that day, and I made Céline get permission to see me so as to give her some advice.[84]

2. AUGUST 17, 1897

[Dr. La Néele] found our little patient admirably cared for, and he said that with all the care Dr. de Cornière has given her, if she was not restored to health, it was because God willed to take her to Himself in spite of everything.[85]

3. AUGUST 30, 1897

As he [Dr. La Néele] was leaving, Francis remarked rather curtly to Mother Marie de Gonzague that his cousin's sufferings were such that she should have seen a doctor every day.[86]

Dr. La Néele came and he said to her [Thérèse]: "It will be soon, little Sister, I'm sure of it." She looked at him with a smile of happiness.[87]

4. AUGUST 31, 1897

Dr. La Néele said that Thérèse could die suddenly turning in her bed.[88]

5. SEPTEMBER 5, 1897

Dr. La Néele told her: "You're like a ship that neither advances nor goes back." Surprised, she said: "You heard, you see how it changes! But I don't want to change, I want to continue abandoning myself entirely to God."[89]

6. SEPTEMBER 14, 1897

Dr. La Néele had told her that she wouldn't have any agony, and when she still suffered more and more:

"And yet they told me that I wouldn't have any agony!... But, after all, I do want to have one."

I asked: "If you were made to choose one or the other, which would you choose?"

"I would choose nothing!"[90]

---

83 Acute pain along the nerves between the ribs.
84 From a letter by Dr. La Néele to M. Guérin dated August 26, 1897.
85 From a letter by Sr. Marie of the Eucharist to M. Guérin, her father, dated August 17, 1897.
86 Gaucher, *op. cit.*, p. 89.
87 *Her Last Conversations*, August 30, 1897.
88 Ibid., September 5, 1897, entry no. 4.
89 Ibid.
90 Ibid.

Thérèse died on Thursday, September 30, and for the next three days her body was on view in the Carmel chapel behind the grille where many mourners passed by including Léonie Martin, the Guérins, the Maudelondes, and Jeanne and Francis La Néele. The burial Mass was scheduled on Monday morning, October 4, at nine. The hearse containing the body of Sister Thérèse of the Child Jesus was drawn by two horses and slowly climbed the hill up to the city cemetery (roughly two miles from the Carmel behind the present day basilica built in her honor). The funeral procession was led by Léonie followed by a number of priests, the Guérins (Isidore had to remain at home because of a painful attack of the gout), and the La Néeles. Sister Mary Elizabeth, an extern sister at the Carmel, represented the Carmelite community of Lisieux.

Thirteen years after Thérèse's death, proceedings began for her beatification which included exhumation of the body. The question arose as how best to preserve Thérèse's remains. For this purpose, Dr. La Néele asked the local authorities for permission to do so. On September 6, 1910, at 3 o'clock in the afternoon Thérèse's simple pine coffin was unearthed in the presence of hundreds of people among whom were Doctors La Néele and de Cornière. They examined the body of which only the skeleton and the deteriorated remnants of her habit were left. Dr. La Néele wrote to Léonie Martin (Sr. Françoise Thérèse) an account of this exhumation. In it he said, "I held the head of the little Saint in my hands and I asked her to grant that my wife and I should love God as she had." [91] Her remains were kept in the original coffin (without the cover) but covered with a new habit, veil, and some flowers. This coffin was then put into a new lead-lined oaken coffin and transferred to another grave a few yards away.[92]

Among the many people summoned to testify at the Diocesan Process was Dr. La Néele who in August of 1911 gave his testimony concerning the miraculous cures of two people—Mme. Dorans and M. F. Aubrey. On September 6, 1911, he presented the findings of his examination of Thérèse's remains the year before.

In the same year, 1911, Dr. La Néele founded a Norman Soldiers' Circle, one among many that were forming into National Congresses honoring Sister Thérèse whom the soldiers came to love. Also, Dr. La Néele organized a "military festival day" which was held in Lisieux on May 21, 1911. Sixty-five soldiers from nine different garrisons attended. The agenda included a "military Mass," a study class, a visit to the Carmel, Les Buissonnets, and the cemetery.[93]

Thérèse's sister Céline (Sister Geneviève) received praise but also criticism for her paintings and her retouchings of some of the photos she took of Thérèse. Sadly, in 1913 a disquieting rapport between the La Néeles and Céline arose concerning these photographs and paintings by Céline and two taken by a priest, Abbé Gombault, of Thérèse as a novice which Céline retouched. The Guérins and the La Néeles preferred the photographs and greatly disliked the pictures

---

91 *Sicut Parvuli*, May 1983, p. 52.
92 Ibid.
93 Ibid., January 1983, p. 10.

by Céline who wrote to her sister Léonie explaining this problem: "Francis [La Néele] came to the parlor on business the other day and he scolded all of us, especially me, claiming that none of my portraits resembled Thérèse. He also said he had Abbé Gombault's photograph enlarged, and it was the only one he cared to see circulated."[94] Years later after the doctor's death, his wife Jeanne asked Céline to pardon her and her husband for all the distress and hurt feelings they gave her about this matter.

On January 1, 1916, the fifty-seven-year-old Dr. La Néele suffered an *attaque cérébrale* (a stroke or cerebral hemorrhage)[95] which left him partially paralyzed until he died on March 19, 1916, in the middle of the Apostolic Process (1915–1917) in which he had so faithfully participated. He was buried in the Lisieux cemetery in the Guérin family plot just a few feet from where Thérèse was first interred.

7. Mme. Elisa-Ernestine Petit Fournet (1816–1901) and M. Pierre-Célestin Fournet (1811–1888)
Thérése's Aunt Céline's Parents

Dear Aunt (Guérin), tomorrow I will offer my Holy Communion for you and also for Madame Fournet [her mother who was recovering from a heart attack]. I think very often of her and beg our Lord to preserve her a long time still for your sake.[96]
— Thérèse

THÉRÈSE'S LOVING CONCERN FOR MME. FOURNET, WHO WAS NOT A BLOOD relative, is apparent in her letters and manifestly in the fact that she often referred to her as *"bonne-maman"* ("grandmamma"). In the above quotation, Thérèse "begged our Lord to preserve her a long time" which He indeed did for she passed away four years after Thérèse at the age of eighty-five. She fortunately lived to witness Thérèse's rapid rise in esteem as an exceptionally holy person—possibly a "saint"; the widespread popularity of her autobiography; and the first amazing favors and cures attributed to her intercession.

Mme. Fournet was the mother of Thérèse's devoted Aunt Céline Guérin (Thérèse's mother's brother's wife) who assumed the role of mother for the Martin girls following the death of Zélie Martin when Thérèse was four.

Mme. Fournet lived on a farm near the little village of Saint-Ouen-le-Pin, just about six miles northwest of Lisieux. It remains today almost unchanged except for the address which is now No. 5 Dunroain. The landscape here is typical of the Auge country of Normandy with its meadows, woodland, and apple orchards. Thérèse spent three summer vacations here when she was ten (1883) eleven (1884), and twelve (1885). During this time Mme. Fournet was a mature woman in her mid-forties who later on in life suffered from heart troubles which her son-in-law, Dr. La Néele, treated. Céline describes in her writings what she and her sister Thérèse did on their day trips to the farm:

---

94 *The Photo Album of St. Thérèse of Lisieux*, p. 46.
95 Lisieux Carmel Archives.
96 LT 152, dated November 17, 1893, from Thérèse to Mme. Guérin.

> We used to go there and spend a whole day in September, gathering hazelnuts on the property of Mme. Fournet, Aunt Guérin's mother.... We went in a large wagon, and we left with the Guérin family.... It was a modest little house on a farm which was rented to some farmers, but we enjoyed ourselves there very much.... At Saint-Ouen everything was rustic, even to the dishes, and this pleased us.[97]
>
> Thérèse stayed there for several days with our aunt and our cousins Jeanne and Marie Guérin. She was there in order to get a change of air during a spell of whooping cough. Thérèse was very much interested in the ponds and the little brook on the farm, and, beyond the meadows, a tiny little woods, perhaps a section of a former park, called "le Theil." This woods was often the goal of our walks. We also went, but not very frequently, into the village by way of a pretty little road, which was well shaded.[98]

We also learn of Thérèse's stays at the farm from her Aunt Guérin who depicts her as an active, joyous youngster:

> We are very happy here. Thérèse's face is always radiant with joy. She is enjoying herself very much at sketching; she and Marie have undertaken to do the house on the farm.... Céline and Jeanne are doing another landscape. They are sketching the buildings on the farm taken from different angles. We're very fortunate for having discovered this delightful distraction, for the heat is such that we can't dream of going very far. Yesterday morning, we went to Mass at seven. It was charming. We were witnesses, it seemed, of nature's awakening. In the afternoon, we went with Ernest [Maudelonde, the twenty-two-year old nephew of Aunt Guérin] to Mourerie, and we were present, in the evening, at the milking of the cows. We go there every evening and each has a glass of very warm milk. I think this is a good remedy for the whooping cough, although I still can't see any great change in our patients. However, I think Thérèse is coughing less frequently. She is throwing up *very, very little* and last night she did so only twice, one spell being very, very bad; she slept very well. Her appetite is always good.[99]

The next year Mme. Guérin reported to her husband that "Marie [their daughter, Thérèse's cousin] and Thérèse are enjoying themselves very much. Thérèse is delightfully happy. Mamma was telling me yesterday that she had never seen Thérèse so gay, with her face so frankly happy."[100]

In a number of Thérèse's letters she inquires about Mme. Fournet or prays for the improvement of her health as in these examples: "We are praying *very much* for Mme. Fournet,"[101] "I will offer my Communion for you [Aunt Guérin] and for our dear Grandmamma,"[102] "Neither will I forget to fête dear Grandmamma

---

97 From G/NPHF, p. 553. This is a translation recorded on p. 207 in *General Correspondence*, vol. I.
98 Sister Geneviève, *Notes on Thérèse's Trips*, p. 1, as quoted on p. 207 in *General Correspondence*, vol. I.
99 Letter from Mme. Guérin to her husband Isidore dated August 7, 1884.
100 From a letter by Céline Guérin addressed to her husband Isidore dated July 29, 1884.
101 LT 153 from Thérèse to her Uncle Guérin dated December, 1893.
102 LT 181 from Thérèse to Aunt Guérin dated November 16, 1895.

with the riches of the saints; they will be so generous that my heart will have nothing more to desire."[103]

Mme. Fournet was born Elisa-Ernestine Petit on April 8, 1816, in Lisieux, the daughter of Pierre-Antoine Petit and Marie-Rosalie (*née* Monsaint). On November 11, 1839, when she was twenty-three, she married Pierre Fournet, a pharmacist. This union produced four children; the first two (a boy and a girl) died in infancy, but the next two children lived to maturity: Marie, who became Mme. Maudelonde and lived to eighty-three; and Céline, Thérèse's Aunt Guérin, who succumbed at fifty-three.

Pierre was a successful pharmacist in Lisieux for thirty years and eventually sold his business on May 12, 1866, to his future son-in-law, Isidore Guérin, his daughter Céline's husband. A native of La Roque-Baignard (Calvados), he was born on Christmas Day, 1811, and died in Lisieux at seventy-six on February 15, 1888, shortly before Thérèse's entrance into Carmel. His wife Elisa, despite her periods of serious illness, survived him by thirteen years, dying in the same town on December 10, 1901, age eighty-five.

8. The Maudelonde Family
The family of Thérèse's Aunt Guérin's sister

a. **César Maudelonde:** *Father (Married Aunt Céline Guérin's sister)*
b. **Marie-Rosalie:** *Mother (Sister of Thérèse's Aunt Céline Guérin)*
c. **Ernest:** *Son (Married Twice)*
d. **Henry:** *Son (Wanted to marry Thérèse's sister Céline)*
e. **Marguerite-Marie:** *Daughter (Married the atheist René Tostain)*
f. **Céline:** *Daughter (Same age as Thérèse)*
g. **Hélène:** *Daughter (Killed in the Allied bombings of World War II)*

Mme. Guérin, Thérèse's aunt by her marriage to her mother's brother Isidore, had a sister, Marie-Rosalie Fournet (1843–1926) who married César-Alexandre Maudelonde in 1861. They had two sons and three daughters. The boys were Ernest (1862–1941), and Henry (1864–1937), and the girls were Marguerite (1867–1966), Céline (1873–1949), and Hélène (1876–1944). Since the two boys were eleven and nine years older than Thérèse, they were not closely involved as children with their female cousins, the Guérins, and their cousins, the Martin girls. Marguerite was six years older than Thérèse; Céline, the same age; and Hélène, three years younger.

Calling intimate and dear friends "aunts," "uncles," and "cousins," though they were not related by blood, was not unusual in French society (as well as American) at that time and even today. This was true of the affiliation between the Maudelonde and Martin families. As early as 1873, Thérèse's mother wrote a letter to her sister-in-law Céline Guérin concerning this appellation matter:

---
103 LT 202 from Thérèse to her Aunt Guérin dated November 16, 1896.

"Pauline [Martin] wants Marguerite [Maudelonde] absolutely as her cousin; she says that since Jeanne [Guérin] is her first cousin and also Marguerite's cousin, it is impossible that the letter [sic] [latter?] be nothing to her. It is agreed then that Marguerite is a cousin to all!"[104] And so it was for the years to come that Thérèse and her sisters called the Maudelonde girls their cousins.

Thursday was a holiday from school in France. Thérèse and her sister Céline usually spent the afternoon of this day in at the home of the Maudelondes with the Guérin sisters Jeanne and Marie, and the Maudelonde girls. They often danced the quadrille and round dances. Unlike the other girls, this activity elicited little enthusiasm from Thérèse who made this comment in her autobiography:

> Each Thursday afternoon was a holiday, but this wasn't like Pauline's holidays; and I wasn't in the belvedere with Papa. I had to play, not with Céline, which pleased me very much when I was alone with her, but with my little cousins and the little Maudelondes. This was a real penance for me because I didn't know how to play like other children and as a consequence wasn't a very pleasant companion. I did my best, however, to imitate them but without much success. I was very much bored by it all, especially when we spent the whole afternoon *dancing quadrilles*. What I really liked, though, was going to the park,[105] for there I was first in everything, gathering flowers in great profusion and, knowing how to find the prettiest, I excited the envy of my companions.
>
> What pleased me was when by chance I was alone with little Marie [Guérin] and, not having Céline Maudelonde dragging her into *ordinary games*, she left me free to choose, and I chose a game that was entirely new. Marie and Thérèse became two *hermits*, having nothing but a poor hut, a little garden where they grew corn and other vegetables. Their life was spent in continual contemplation; in other words, one *hermit* replaced the other at prayer while she was occupied in the active life. Everything was done with such mutual understanding, silence, and so religiously that it was just perfect. When Aunt came to fetch us to go for our walk, we continued the game even on the street. The two hermits recited the rosary together, using their fingers in order to screen their devotion from the inquisitive public; however, one day the younger hermit forgot herself completely: having received a piece of cake for lunch, she made a big sign of the Cross over it before eating it, causing people to laugh.[106]

Some of the time with the Maudelonde girls, however, was pleasant as Thérèse noted in a letter she sent to her cousin Marie Guérin: "We went yesterday to spend the afternoon at Madame Maudelonde's home, and I had a lot of fun with Céline and Hélène."[107]

The Maudelondes inherited with the Guérins a rather large fortune from their lawyer cousin August David who died on August 22, 1888. It included a 100 acre estate known as the Château de la Musse situated on a picturesque hill

---

104 A letter (CF 107) from Mme. Martin to Mme. Guérin, dated August 20, 1873.
105 *Le jardin de l'étoile*, very close to Thérèse's home, Les Buissonnets.
106 *Story of a Soul*, chapter III, pp. 54–55.
107 LT 20 from Thérèse to Marie Guérin, dated July 15, 1886.

F. Mother's Other Relatives

some five miles or so from Evreux. Now instead of vacationing at the shores of Deauville and Trouville, the Martins went to the country estate of their cousins the Guérins. The Guérins stayed there from May to mid-August and the Maudelonde family from mid-August to October—the height of the hunting season. Céline and Léonie vacationed there regularly from 1889 through 1894 with their aunt, uncle, and cousins. The year after their father was released from the hospital in Caen the girls decided that their father was capable of spending time there also, so in 1893 and 1894 they took him with them convinced that the country atmosphere would be advantageous to his health. Thérèse never saw La Musse since she had entered the Carmel a few months before M. David died.

The first time we hear of one of the Maudelonde brothers—Ernest—is in connection with Louis Martin's surprising disappearance from his home in Lisieux on June 23, 1888. Penniless and bewildered, Louis wrote to his daughter Céline that he was stranded in Le Havre—where he had gone without notifying anyone—but not telling where in the city he was. M. Guérin and Céline went in search of him accompanied by the twenty-six-year-old Ernest Maudelonde. After a frantic pursuit, the distraught trio found him at the city post office, confused and disoriented.

Henry, the other Maudelonde brother—a lawyer in Caen—was much more closely involved with Céline, his junior by five years. He often met her and her sister Léonie at the home of their mutual "relations," the Guérins, or at their country estate La Musse where they held great parties. Soon he developed a serious interest in her. Years later, she put in writing her impressions about his method of approach and her reactions to it:

> [He was a] true military type of man, who had renounced this career only for the sake of his parents.... Either at his house or ours, he always had to be near me. Since he demanded this boldly when he was not, we ended up by placing him definitively next to me at the table in order to avoid scenes. Dinner over, he used to take me in his arms, whether I liked it or not, and made me dance.... My cousin Marie [Guérin], who loved me very much, believed she was pleasing me by reporting certain conversations that she had had with her cousins: "If you only knew how much Henry loves you; he is crazy about you." Ah! I had no need of anyone's telling me this, I was well enough aware of it!... What struggles!... I belonged to Jesus alone, I had given Him my pledge, but I found the marriage vocation beautiful also; I had, so to speak, two vocations, two attractions.... I would have to speak only one word, give only one look! When I think back on it, I am seized with fright, my vocation was so close to floundering! It seems it was holding on only by a thread.[108]

Henry proposed to Céline on April 9, 1888, on the day Thérèse entered Carmel, and of course she refused. He consequently sought romance elsewhere and eventually married Marie Asseline on April 20, 1892, and had two daughters. Several years after his wife's early demise, he married Hélène Maynaerts.

---

108 *Souvenirs autobiographiques*, pp. 95–99. See footnote 110.

Marguerite-Marie, the oldest daughter of M. and Mme. Maudelonde, and their third child, was born on February 24, 1867, in Lisieux. At twenty-two, on October 14, 1889, she married a deputy public prosecutor of the Republic in Lisieux, René Tostain, a thirty-one-year-old confirmed atheist but a morally upright man. Of this marriage of forty-seven years there were no children.

Marguerite Tostain visited Thérèse in the monastery on April 3, 1891, at which time she disclosed the doubts she had about her faith and the hereafter, probably much influenced by her husband's own non-belief in God. Thérèse promptly wrote to her sister Céline who was still at home but regularly visiting their father at the hospital in Caen:

> Marguerite confided to us intimate secrets that she tells no one. We really must pray for her, for she is exposed to danger.... She says that no book does her any good. I thought that the mysteries of the future life[109] would strengthen her faith which, alas, is really endangered!... She told us she could read books without her husband's knowing it.
>
> You should give her that book, telling her that we thought it would interest her, but to begin it only at the third chapter.... We would prefer that Mme. Maudelonde and Aunt do not know that we are lending this book to Marguerite.[110]

Just twenty-eight days before she died, the gravely ill Thérèse told her sisters that "I've offered up my trial against faith especially for a member united to our family [René Tostain] who has lost his faith." [111]

Seven years later which was a year after Thérèse died, Marguerite still harbored doubts and told Pauline (Mother Agnès) about them:

> You recall that a few days after Thérèse's death I wrote you that I reached a point of doubting the existence of a second life? Since then I doubted even more, I doubted *everything*. Well! The life of Sister Thérèse [*Story of a Soul*] has done me much good. She, too, suffered as I do, but she did not reason it out; she submitted to the trial God was sending her by means of this temptation. And I can do as she did; instead of thinking and losing myself in suppositions of all kinds, I can also think that if the faith God placed in us appears to be darkened at times, this is a trial to which I must submit while continuing to act as though I had before my eyes a dazzling light.[112]

Marguerite survived her husband by thirty years, dying at the advanced age of ninety-nine in 1966, forty-one years after her erstwhile friend Thérèse was canonized.

The next Maudelonde girl was Céline, born in 1873, the same year as Thérèse. Unlike Thérèse who died at twenty-four, she passed away at seventy-six in 1949, having lived over a half century longer than Thérèse. She was fortunate to have witnessed Thérèse's meteoric rise to fame and her glorious canonization.

---

109 *The End of the World and the Mysteries of the Future Life* by Abbé Arminjon.
110 LT 126, from Thérèse to Céline dated April 3, 1891.
111 *Her Last Conversations*, September 2, 1897.
112 Letter from Marguerite Tostain to Pauline (Mother Agnès) dated November 18, 1898.

F. Mother's Other Relatives

Céline Maudelonde and Thérèse were playmates as children and were often together with the Guérin girls Jeanne and Marie. Thérèse confesses in her autobiography this little bit of childhood memories: "What pleased me was when by chance I was alone with little Marie [Guérin] and, not having Céline Maudelonde dragging her into *ordinary games*, she left me free to choose, and I chose a game that was entirely new. Marie and Thérèse became two *hermits*...." [113]

Many years later when Thérèse was a Carmelite and Céline was three months away from her marriage to Gaston Pottier, a notary at Fervaques (a little town south of Lisieux), Thérèse wrote to Céline this affectionate and prayerful message:

> While you are following the path God has traced out for you [marriage], I will pray for my Céline, the companion of my childhood. I will beg that all her joys be so pure that she may always be able to enjoy them under the eyes of God. I ask, especially, that she may experience the incomparable joy of bringing back a soul to Our Lord, and that this soul be the one that must soon form only one with her.
>
> I do not doubt this grace will soon be granted to you, and I would be happy if my weak prayers had contributed a little bit to it.[114]

Céline and Gaston were married on June 19, 1894, and the next month Thérèse wrote the second of her letters to the now Mme. Pottier:

> I marvel at how the Blessed Virgin is pleased to answer all your desires. Even before your marriage, she willed that the soul to whom you were to be joined form only one with yours by means of an identity of feelings. What a grace for you to feel you are so well understood, and, above all, to know your union will be everlasting, that after this life, you will still be able to love the husband who is so dear to you!
>
> They have passed away, then, for us both the blessed days of our childhood! We are now at the serious stage of life [21 years old]; the road we are following is different, however, the goal is the same. Both of us must have only one same purpose: *to sanctify* ourselves in the way God has traced out for us.
>
> [You] ask, dear little cousin, that I pray for your dear husband; do you think, then I could fail in this?... No, I could not separate you in my weak prayers. I am asking Our Lord to be as generous in your regard as he was formerly to the spouses at the wedding of Cana.
>
> [I] dare, dear little *cousin*, to beg you to offer my respectful regards to *Monsieur* Pottier, whom I cannot refrain from considering also as my *cousin*.[115]

This long and happy marriage of Céline and Gaston produced two children.

The last and youngest Maudelonde child was Hélène, born in 1876, about whom there is very little mention in Theresian literature as compared to the quantity there is regarding her siblings. One note specifying her is from a letter by Thérèse to Marie Guérin where Thérèse makes this charming remark:

---

113 *Story of a Soul*, chapter III, p. 54.
114 LT 159 from Thérèse to Céline Maudelonde dated March 26, 1894.
115 LT 166 from Thérèse to Mme. Pottier (Céline Maudelonde), dated July 16, 1894.

I was very sorry that dear Aunt was sick; I think very much of her, and I am praying for her prompt cure. Hug her very TIGHTLY for her little daughter, however, not in a way to hurt her!...

Hug, too, for me DEAR little Jeanne and Céline and Hélène [Mondelonde]. For those who are not sick I have no pity, so I beg you to hug them as tightly as you can."[116]

Hélène married a man in the law profession, Jules Houdayer. She died tragically in 1944 during the bombings of Normandy by the Allies in World War II.

---

116 LT 62 from Thérèse to Marie Guérin, dated September 1888.

CHAPTER 3

NON-FAMILY RELATIONS

A. Family Friends
B. Domestic Help
C. Doctors, Tutors, and Others
D. Thérèse's School Companions

A. Family Friends

1. **Mlle. Félicité Baudouin**: *Helped Louis Martin set up his business in Alençon*
2. **M. and Mme. Victor Besnard**: *Became friends of the Martins on the Rome trip*
3. **Paul-Albert Boul**: *Thérèse's godfather*
4. **Auguste David**: *The Guérins inherited his country estate, La Musse*
5. **Victor Lahaye**: *Bought the pharmacy of Thérèse's Uncle Isidore*
6. **Louise Magdelaine**: *Thérèse wrote her first letter to her*
7. **François Nogrix**: *Long time friend of Thérèse's father*
8. **The Pallu du Bellay Sisters**: *Friends of Thérèse's sister Pauline*
9. **The Pigeon Sisters**: *Older friends of the Guérins and the Martins in Lisieux*
10. **The Primois Sisters**: *Friends of the Martins in Lisieux*
11. **The Rabinel Family**: *Wealthy friends of the Martins living near Alençon in Semallé*
12. **The Romet Family**: *The Martins' long time friends in Alençon*
13. **Mme. Léonie Tifenne**: *Close friend of the Martins in Alençon*

The people profiled in this section are classified as friends of the Martins, distant relatives of the Guérins, or just acquaintances. They exemplify the many normal and fond associations individuals and families acquire in life. Their presence in St. Thérèse's story weave in and out of her life, but in reality most of them did not exert any profound influence upon her or her mission notwithstanding their fidelity, love, benevolence, or amiability. One important group, however, that did make an impression on the young Thérèse were the affluent who made her realize the insignificance of wealth and fame in

Plate 8
Family Friends 1

A. Dr. Alexandre de Cornière

B. Marcelline Husé (as a nun)

C. Desiré Lejuif

D. Marie Lejuif

E. François Nogrix

F. Dr. Notta

G. The Pallu du Bellay sisters

H. Mme. Papinau

I. Victoire Pasquer

A. Family Friends 223

Plate 9

Family Friends 2

J. Clémence Pigeon

K. Josephine Pigeon

L. Louis Rabinel

M. August Romet

N. Pauline Romet

O. Vital Romet

P. Rose Taille

Q. Mme. Tifenne

R. Tom

relation to the soul's destiny. In order to obtain an in-depth portrait of a person, any contacts with people and places, though they may be peripheral, do add in their own way to the totality of the individual under consideration and help form a concept and dimension of that person which is more complete, distinct, and human.

Two families described here in some detail are the Romets and the Tifennes who lived in Alençon. M. Martin and his daughters stayed with these two families when they made return visits to their birthplace. These friends escorted Thérèse and her family to their prosperous friends, Mme. Monnier in Arçonnay, and the Rabinals in Semallé. Mme. Monnier was the sister of the Martin's dear friends, M. and Mme. Tifenne. On Thérèse's return trip to Alençon in 1883 she stayed at Mme. Monier's lovely country home called "Grogny" some six miles south of Alençon where Thérèse rode side-saddle. About the same distance east, the Rabinal family, old friends of Thérèse's father, lived in the magnificent Manoir de Lanchal with its huge estate where Louis enjoyed himself fishing in the stream that traversed the property. Thérèse was to comment later in life about this experience:

> My joy was great when seeing the places where I had spent my childhood days.... I can say it was during my stay at Alençon that I made my *first entrance* into the *world*. Everything was joy and happiness around me; I was entertained, coddled, and admired; in a word, my life during those two weeks was strewn only with flowers. I must admit this type of life had its charms for me. Wisdom [4:12] is right in saying: "*The bewitching of vanity overturns the innocent mind* [Wisdom 4:12]!" At the age of ten the heart allows itself to be easily dazzled, and I consider it a great grace not to have remained at Alençon. The friends we had there were too worldly; they knew too well how to ally the joys of this earth to the service of God. They didn't think about *death* enough, and yet *death* had paid its visit to a great number of those whom I knew, the young, the rich, the happy! I love to return in spirit to the *enchanting* places where they lived, wondering where these people are, what became of their houses and gardens where I saw them enjoy life's luxuries?[1]

A name that is encountered on occasion in the literature of St. Thérèse, but not by the saint herself, is Alexandre-Alphonse Colombe (1835–1889), a friend of the Guérins who was born and died in Lisieux. He lent his house, the Chalet des Roses, in Deauville to the Guérins during holiday seasons. Thérèse stayed with the Guérins there for a week in May 1885. The address was, and still is, 17 quai de la Touques. She enjoyed herself and even sketched a scene in the garden (*Jardin Colombe*) of the property. Colombe's five daughters were friends of the older Martin girls, especially Alice (Mme. Boyer). Her sisters were Marie (Mme. Manoury), Blanche, Aurélie, and Adrienne (Mme. Delandre).

---

1 *Story of a Soul*, chapter IV, pp. 72–73.

1. Mlle. Félicité Baudouin
Helped Louis Martin set up his business in Alençon

MLLE. BAUDOUIN, A VERY PIOUS WOMAN, RECOGNIZED AND ADMIRED THE skills and saintly qualities of the young bachelor Louis Martin. She was instrumental in helping the twenty-seven-year old Louis establish his business on November 9, 1850, in the building he owned at 35 rue du Pont Neuf in Alençon next to the bridge over the Sarthe River. The watchmaker and repair shop was set up on the ground floor with a jewelry store that he added later. He lived behind the shop and after marriage his eight children were born there, except Thérèse, who was born several blocks away in Louis and Zélie's second home on rue Saint-Blaise. Directly above on the second floor resided his parents. Sometime during the 20th century, these buildings were destroyed by war or otherwise and replaced by new ones. After all these years it is interesting to see a store on the same spot and others on both sides of the street flourishing as of old.

Seven years after Louis opened his shop, success and prosperity enabled him to purchase a retreat place not too far way in town that he called the Pavilion. It is a relatively narrow, hexagonal in shape, three-story tower-like structure with an adjoining garden in which he placed a statue of the Blessed Virgin—a gift from Mlle. Baudouin. Following Mme. Martin's untimely death, the family moved to Lisieux and took with them that statue which is a replica of the original in Saint-Sulpice church in Paris. On May 13, 1883, when Thérèse was ten years old, seriously ill, and bedridden, the statue appeared to come alive, smile, and cured her. This statue now stands over St. Thérèse's shrine in the Carmelite Chapel in Lisieux. Known as "Our Lady of the Smile," it has been reproduced countless times in statue and picture form.

2. M. and Mme. Victor Besnard
Became friends of the Martins on the Rome trip

THESE TWO FELLOW CITIZENS OF LISIEUX CAN CERTAINLY BE CALLED acquaintances rather than long-time friends for they are heard of only in connection with the 1887 pilgrimage to Rome that Thérèse made with her father and sister Céline. M. and Mme. Besnard shared the same train compartment during that long journey. In Rome they stayed at La Albergo del Sud where the Martins also lodged. It was Mme. Besnard who chaperoned Thérèse and Céline on their side trip to Naples and Pompei while their father remained in Rome to visit an old friend. A half century later we learn from the death notice of their daughter, who had become a nun, of an interesting detail about the Besnards' brief connection with Thérèse: "Mme. Besnard loved to tell how on the night of the first day [of the trip], little Thérèse, only fourteen, was so tired that she stretched out on the floor, leaned her head on her knees where she slept for a part of the night." [2]

---
2 Obituary notice of Sister Pauline de Sales Besnard, September 7, 1937.

3. Paul-Albert Boul (1860–1883)
Thérèse's godfather

PAUL-ALBERT BOUL IS A RATHER SHADOWY FIGURE IN THÉRÈSE'S LIFE despite the religious significance of his role. We know he was the son of an Alençon friend of Thérèse's father and was chosen as her godfather, yet he never again appears in Theresian literature.

Marie Martin, Thérèse's oldest sister, was selected as her godmother. She and Paul were both only twelve years old which at the time was not considered too young to be godparents. Traditionally, children were baptized the day after birth. For some uncertain reason Paul was not available for the christening that day which caused some concern for Thérèse's mother Zélie (nickname for Azélie). However, he did appear for the ceremony the second day on Saturday afternoon, January 4, 1873, at the Martins' parish church of Notre Dame.

The Notre Dame Registry lists all the people who were present including the clergy. The section naming the lay persons follows: "The godfather has been Paul-Albert Boul, and the godmother Marie-Louise Martin, sister of the child. These together with the child's father, have signed their names with us. Marie Martin, Paul-Albert Boul, Louis Martin, P. Boul, F. Boul, Pauline Martin, Léonie Martin, Léontine Boul, Louise Marais."[3]

Note that in attendance were four members of the Boul family and Louise Marais, the Martins' maid, who held the infant Thérèse during the ritual.

Paul Albert lived to the age of twenty-three, almost as long as his godchild. He died on February 18, 1883, when Thérèse was ten years old.

4. Auguste David (1812–1888)
The Guérins inherited his country estate, La Musse

BORN IN AUGUST 1812, AUGUSTE DAVID WAS THE FIRST COUSIN OF THÉRÈSE'S aunt Guérin's mother, Mme. Fournet. He was also a good friend of Thérèse's uncle, Isidore Guérin. Because they were such close friends, Isidore was summoned to Auguste's bedside at La Musse during his final sickness. Through Isidore's efforts he brought the dying man back to God. Thérèse, then a postulant in the Lisieux Carmel, penned a consoling letter to her Uncle Guérin:

> We just received a letter from Aunt [Guérin] in which she was telling us about all your sorrows. Although far away from you, your little niece is sharing in your pain. She would like to be near her good Uncle to console him, but, alas! what would she be able to do?... No it is better for her to be in Carmel; there, at least, she can pray as much as she wants to Him who alone can give consolation and pour it abundantly into her dear Uncle's heart.
>
> Good Monsieur David's condition saddens us [Thérèse and her sisters Pauline and Marie] very much. I understand, dear Uncle, how much you must be suffering, for there is nothing so painful as seeing those whom we love suffering. However, I thank God with my whole heart for the great grace He willed to grant

---
3 The Martins' maid, age 24. From Laveille's *op. cit.*, p. 371.

this beautiful soul. What a disposition he has for appearing before Him; it is really admirable. Everything dear Aunt told us about him has touched me very deeply.

It was impossible, Uncle, that God not grant you this consolation after all you've done for His glory....

[I] beg you to remember me to Madame Fournet; I share her pain. For you, Uncle, I'm sending all the love my heart contains, and I will continue to pray unceasingly for good Monsieur David.

Your little niece, who would like to be able to lessen your sorrow a little.[4]

Despite all the prayers, M. David succumbed after which Thérèse sent a letter of condolence, this time to Mme. Guérin:

Yesterday evening, we heard of the death of good Monsieur David. Although we were expecting to receive this sad news at any moment, when learning the reality I was very much touched. I am praying that God may take this very holy soul into His paradise; perhaps his soul is already there, for with dispositions as perfect as this one can go straight to heaven.

[Dear] Aunt, when we consider the death of the just man, we cannot refrain from envying his lot. The time of exile no longer exists for him; there is no longer anything but God, nothing but God.[5]

Upon M. David's death, the Guérins and their relations the Maudelondes inherited the country estate near Evreux called the Chateau de la Musse where Thérèse's father died six years later. The Guérins together with Thérèse and her family were accustomed to vacations at the seaside resorts of Deauville and Trouville. After M. David died, they transferred their vacations to La Musse with its beautiful house and vast woodland property located around fifty miles from Lisieux. Thérèse's father and sisters Céline and Léonie spent many enjoyable days at the estate but Thérèse never saw the place since she was by then a cloistered nun.

5. VICTOR LAHAYE (1855–1936)
Bought the pharmacy of Thérèse's Uncle Isidore

VICTOR LAHAYE WAS A FRIEND OF THÉRÈSE'S UNCLE ISIDORE AND BY EXTENsion of the Martin family also. On December 8, 1888, he bought Isidore's pharmacy at the busy corner of the Place Saint-Pierre and the Grande Rue in Lisieux. He was, in addition, the pharmacist for the Carmelite Monastery when Thérèse was dying of tuberculosis, the same disease his own wife succumbed to a year later.

A writer concerned with civic documentation, he became at one point president of the Historical Society of Lisieux. His memoir of Thérèse, published on March 19, 1923, is entitled *Portrait descriptif de la Bienheureuse, Thérèse de l'Enfant Jésus* (A Descriptive Portrait of the Blessed Thérèse of the Infant Jesus). In another account, "*Souvenirs d'un témoin aux cérémonies de Vêture et de Profession*" ("Reminiscences of a witness at the ceremonies of the reception of the veil and profession"), he offers his own graphic description of Thérèse:

---
4 LT 59 from Thérèse to M. Guérin dated August 22, 1888.
5 LT 60 from Thérèse to Mme. Guérin, August 23, 1888.

During her profession ceremony, I was standing in the sanctuary and could see her behind the grill. The black veil she was going to receive was covered with a crown of roses and lying on the altar. The white veil she was still wearing had been raised and I could see the fine symmetry of her features. Nevertheless, her forehead was slightly convex, the nose short, the mouth almost large, the chin quite large and rounded, and although her cheeks were not hollow, her cheek-bones were a little prominent. Her eyes possessed a brilliance that was tempered by candor and purity, but on that moving occasion their natural gentleness was supplanted by a certain gravity. Her color was like new ivory, transparent with a hint of amber and rose color. She seemed slender despite her heavy religious habit.[6]

"A certain gravity" indeed, further intensified by the absence of the three leading men in her life at this time: her hospitalized father, the sick bishop (Msgr. Hugonin), and her spiritual father in distant Canada, Father Pichon.

A native of Aignerville (Calvados), Victor Lahaye married a seamstress, had seven children, and died at the age of eighty-one in 1936.

6. LOUISE MAGDELAINE (1860–1939)
Thérèse wrote her first letter to her

Dear little Louise,

I don't know you, but I love you very much just the same. Pauline told me to write you; she is holding me on her knees because I don't know how to hold a pen. She wants me to tell you that I'm a lazy little girl, but this isn't true because I work all day long playing tricks on my poor little sisters. So I'm a little rascal who is always laughing. *Adieu*, little Louise. I'm sending you a big kiss. Kiss the Visitation for me, that is Sister Marie Aaolysia [sic][7] and Sister Louise de Bonzague [sic],[8] for I don't know anyone else.

— *Thérèse*[9]

THÉRÈSE WROTE HER FIRST LETTER (HERE COMPLETE) ON APRIL 4, 1877, when she was just four years and three months old; although her hand was guided by her older sister Pauline, then almost sixteen. Louise was a companion of Marie and Pauline Martin at the Visitation boarding school in Le Mans. Pauline and Louise continued their friendship and correspondence for the rest of their lives.

A native of Écommoy (Sarthe), Louise was born on April 10, 1860, married, and became Mme. Edouard Fournier. She bore two children: a girl, Madeleine who died in 1961, and a boy, Jacques who survived her by four years. Their mother lived to be seventy-nine and passed away in Le Mans on December 17, 1939, fourteen years after the little girl who wrote her first letter to her was canonized a saint of the Church.

---

6 From *The Photo Album of St. Thérèse of Lisieux*, p. 22.
7 Marie-Aloysia Valée, school mistress Pauline admired.
8 Gonzague, directress of the school.
9 LT 1 from Thérèse to Louise Magdelaine, dated April 4, 1877.

7. François Nogrix (1823–1898)
Long time friend of Thérèse's father

We read about Louis Martin's friend M. Nogrix, a fellow native of Brittany, only from the letters[10] Louis wrote to him relaying information about his family or reminiscing about the past and the mutual friends of their youth:

> I must tell you that Thérèse, my little Queen—that is what I call her, for she is a lovely slip of a girl, I assure you—is quite all right. The numerous prayers carried Heaven by storm, and God, who is so good, was willing to give in [and miraculously cured her of a serious illness through the smile of the Virgin Mary].[11]

The day after Thérèse's admittance into Carmel, Louis notified his friend of the momentous event: "Thérèse, my little Queen, entered Carmel yesterday! God alone can exact such a sacrifice; but He helps me so mightily, that in the midst of my tears my heart overflows with joy." [12]

At one time M. Nogrix had not been to the sacraments. Overjoyed at learning of his return to the faith, Louis responded:

> I really want to congratulate you, or rather with you to thank Our Lord with my whole heart, for the great favor which He granted you last December—a date never to be forgotten! It is only later on that that grace will be appreciated at its real worth.
>
> If "God hath blessed the house of Aaron [Psalm 113:13]," He has also blessed the house of Nogrix, for the family is "sailing at top speed." Let us trust that the wind will not change till all have safely reached the port.
>
> Your letter pleased me all the more that I now live mainly on memories. Those old-time reminiscences are so enjoyable that in spite of the trials I have undergone, there are moments when my heart abounds in joy....[13]

Then Louis added these words about his family: "Recently I spoke to you of my five girls, but I forgot to tell you that I have four other children, who are with their saintly mother, where we hope to rejoin them some day.... With Hélène are two Josephs and a pretty little Thérèse (full name is Marie-Mélanie-Thérèse)."

Louis reveals his affectionate regard for Nogrix at the end of the letter just quoted: "Good-bye, my dear old friend, whom I love as a brother. Give my best good wishes to Madame Nogrix and to your children."

8. The Pallu du Bellay Sisters
Friends of Thérèse's sister Pauline

The relationship between the two Pallu du Bellay sisters—Marie and Marguerite—and Thérèse was peripheral. Marie-Thérèse-Henriette, the older of the two, was a school companion and lifelong friend of Pauline Martin

---

10   We have only two letters in existence that M. Martin wrote to him (CF 220) and one to the Nogrix family (CF 230).
11   CF 220 written by M. Martin in Lisieux to M. Nogrix, dated just 1883.
12   CF 230 dated April 10, 1888, from M. Martin to the Nogrix family.
13   CF 220 from Louis Martin to M. Nogrix, dated simply 1883.

and, by asssociation, with her sister Thérèse. Born on November 2, 1862, in Château-Gontier (Mayenne), Marie-Thérèse married, became Countess de Feydeau de Saint-Christophe, and had six children.

Actually Thérèse Martin was eleven years younger than Marie Pallu du Bellay and thus nearer in age to her younger sister Marguerite. In one of her earliest letters, the eight-year-old Thérèse mentions the two sisters to Pauline who at the time was vacationing at Marie-Thérèse's home in Houlgate (Calvados): "*Au revoir*, dear little Pauline. I'm kissing you with all my heart. Kiss Marie-Thérèse and little Marguerite for me." [14] Pauline replied shortly after, "Marguerite would like to meet you both [Thérèse and, no doubt, Céline]; she's a nice little girl, well-mannered and very darling. She kisses you from her heart." [15]

Pauline and Marie-Thérèse maintained their friendship and correspondence throughout their lives. Both died close to ninety in 1951: Marie in Poitiers (Vienne) in January, and Pauline (Mother Agnès) in Lisieux in July.

9. The Pigeon Sisters
Older friends of the Guérins and Martins in Lisieux

THE TWO ELDERLY LADIES, VICTOIRE AND LOUISE PIGEON, WERE DEAR friends of Louis Martin and his four daughters, though more intimately of the Guérins. Their names frequently appear in the Guérin correspondence and sometimes in the Martin letters. On one occasion Pauline wrote to her Aunt Guérin relating an act of kindness on the part of the Pigeons toward the motherless Martin girls:

> Mademoiselle Pigeon left just this instant.... Would you believe, dear Aunt, that she came to look for us in order to take us to the *"jardin de l'Etoile"* [a private park near Les Buissonnets]? It was very good on her part; we [Pauline and her other sisters] weren't able to go with her ... [six year old] Thérèse went alone, very happy at the opportunity. This baby loves flowers so much ... to listen to her, she's very soon going to pick all there are of lilies of the valley in the *"jardin de l'Etoile."* [16]

At another time Thérèse briefly mentioned them in a letter she sent to her cousin Jeanne Guérin after a vacation with her and her family in Trouville: "I suppose you are very happy not to be listening any longer to my sermons on death, to no longer see my eyes which fascinate you so, and to be no longer pushed when going to see the Pigeon ladies." [17] The two sisters were in their fifties when Thérèse entered Carmel in 1888. Both were born in Lisieux a year apart and apparently never married. Marie-Victoire-Joséphine (March 8, 1833–November 3, 1905) was photographed several times in Guérin family groups. She survived her sibling by six years and died at seventy-two in Lisieux. Marie-Louise Clémence

---

14 LT 7 from Thérèse to Pauline, dated July 4, 1881.
15 LC 3 from Pauline to Thérèse, dated July 5–11, 1881.
16 Letter of Pauline to Mme. Guérin dated June 4, 1879.
17 LT 24 dated June 27, 1887, from Thérèse to Jeanne Guérin.

(February 24, 1834–May 13, 1899), whom Marie Guérin called "*Tante Clémence*" (Aunt Clemence), lived to her sixty-fifth year.

10. THE PRIMOIS SISTERS
Friends of the Martins in Lisieux

ALTHOUGH MARIE AND JEANNE-MARIE PRIMOIS (1864–1897) WERE FRIENDS of the Martins, albeit primarily of Thérèse's older sisters Pauline and Marie, they were rarely mentioned in Martin correspondence or other writings. They lived at 33 rue Paul Banaston not far from where the Guérins settled after selling their pharmacy and where Thérèse's sisters and father lived for a short time upon leaving Les Buissonnets. Jeanne, the younger sister died in Lisieux at thirty-three, just three months before Thérèse's death. Even less biographical data is available about her older sister Marie.

Thérèse referred to them in a letter she wrote as a novice asking her cousin Marie in an endearing and human way to fetch a book for her from Les Buissonnets (her former home):

> I'd be very happy if I could have it [a First Communion gift book Mme. Tifenne gave her] as soon as possible, as well as another *smaller* book that the *Mesdemoiselles* Primois had given me. It's a brown book surrounded with a gold border; I think these are meditations on the Eucharist. This book is on one of the shelves of the cupboard in Céline's bedroom (the cupboard next to the cupboard door). Dear little sister, pardon me for asking you this favor![18]

After Jeanne-Marie's death, the doctor at the Carmel made a rather morbid reference to her that Thérése in the midst of her own final sickness heard. This is what she said:

> One of our friends had died [Jeanne-Marie Primois], and Dr. de Cornière had spoken about her illness in the presence of Thérèse; she had a tumor that he was not able to define exactly. This case interested him very much from the medical viewpoint. "What a pity I was unable to make an autopsy," he said. She said later: "Ah! it's in this way that we are indifferent towards one another on earth! Would he say the same thing if it were a question of his own mother or sister? Oh! how I would love to leave this sad world!"[19]

11. THE RABINEL FAMILY
Wealthy friends of the Martins living near Alençon in Semallé

IN THE SMALL VILLAGE OF SEMALLÉ, BUT ON QUITE A DIFFERENT SOCIAL strata than the Taillés, resided the well-to-do Rabinel family, friends of Louis Martin. Louis Rabinel, his wife (*née* Henriette Enaux), and their daughter Louise lived in the Château de Lanchal which Louis Rabinel bought in 1866. Interestingly, the word "lanchal" in the local French dialect means "a little stream." M. Martin took pleasure visiting his friend Louis whose prosperous business in

---
18 LT 88 from Thérèse to Marie Guérin, dated April 24, 1889.
19 *Her Last Conversations*, July 3, 1897.

Alençon dealt with wines and spirits. Both men shared a passion for fishing especially in the stream (the Sarthe) that flows through this vast estate. Louis Martin usually visited his friend on Sundays where, besides fishing, he enjoyed a meal with him and his family.

Tragically, a sudden accident took the life of Louis Rabinel at the age of sixty-six when a bicyclist going at top speed ran into him and thrust him to the ground unconscious. Shortly after, he died from the terrible head injuries he received.

Thérèse's oldest sister Marie Martin became a friend of Louise and both attended the same classes when they were young. They maintained a correspondence well after she married Auguste Colombe. Louise and her husband had a daughter Suzanne who married a M. Onfray. This marriage produced ten children. Two of the boys, Jean François Onfray and his brother Pierre now own the property.

A nun relation of the Rabinel family years ago recalled this story of little Thérèse who was three or four years old, fell and scraped her knees: "Childish tears followed. Her mother, relieved, said to her not to cry but to offer her pain up to Jesus." When Thérèse was ten in 1883 and living in Lisieux, she stayed at this large manor on her first trip back to Alençon after her mother died.[20]

12. THE ROMET FAMILY
The Martins' long time friends living in Alençon

THE ROMET FAMILY, STEADFAST FRIENDS OF THE MARTINS, CONSISTED OF eight children,[21] the offspring of Pierre-Charles Romet (1775–1854) and Julienne Charlotte Gauthier (1797–1857):

1. **Pierre** (1819–1904)* lived to 85
2. **Vital** (died 1821)
3. **Pauline** (died 1822)
4. **Auguste** (1823–1880) lived to 57
5. **Hortense** (1825–1898)* lived to 73
6. **Pauline** (the 2nd, 1829–1889)* lived to 60
7. **Vital** (the 2nd, 1830–1916)* lived to 86
8. **Adrien** (1837–1922) lived to 85

Four of the above children (with the asterisk) played interesting though minor roles in the St. Thérèse story. The strong bonds of friendship between the Martins, especially Louis Martin, and the Romets began before Louis and Zélie were married. Vital, Auguste, Adrien, and Louis belonged to the Catholic Circle, familarily known as the Vital-Romet Club. This association of middle class men gathered each week at Vital's home at 72 rue du Mans opposite the Church of Saint Leonard in the main district of Alençon. Its purpose was social, recreational, as well as religious. The chaplain was Abbé Hurel, dean of Saint Leonard, the priest who married Thérèse's parents. On one occasion they dabbled in "table turning," a

---
20 The quote and the other information above are from an article about Louis Rabinel that appeared in the October 2006 issue of *Thérèse de Lisieux*. Translation by the author.
21 Names and dates courtesy of M. And Mme. Gerault of Alençon who live in the former home of Mme. Tifenne.

popular diversion of those days. Some members considered this ouija board type activity harmless but Louis thought it could have satanic associations. He therefore refused to participate, irritating some no doubt but decidedly convincing others.

Vital was a pharmacist by profession. In fact, it was in his pharmacy that Thérèse's uncle Guérin did part of his training as a pharmacist. A bachelor all his life, Vital lived with his maiden sister Pauline. Both devoted much of their efforts to charitable and social causes. At one time, we are told, she had a strong desire to marry the youthful Louis Martin. At any rate, after the Martins moved to Lisieux following Mme. Martin's premature death, their friendship continued. Whenever Louis returned to Alençon for visits by himself or with his children, he often stayed at Vital's home.

The relationship between the Martins and the Romets deepened when Vital and Pauline became godparents of Céline and Pauline Martin respectively. Close ties are quite evident in their correspondence. In the first known letter that Thérèse wrote herself when she was seven, she tells her sister Pauline to "Kiss *Mademoiselle* Pauline for me." [22] Though not related by blood, the Martin girls always referred to Pauline Romet as "Aunt Pauline." For instance, in a letter from Céline to Pauline Romet she wrote: "Dear Aunt Pauline.... The consolation of friends are very sweet too, especially when they are dictated by a heart like that of our good Aunt. My regards to M. Vital." [23] In another correspondence written to Pauline we read that "Sister Thérèse of the Child Jesus hugs you *very, very tightly* also." [24] The next year Pauline Romet died and a few months later Céline informs Vital Romet that "The Carmelites and ourselves think often of her, each day she is the subject of our prayers, for we love to recommend her to God and to recommend ourselves to her so that she may protect us.... The Carmelites and Léonie join me in offering you their regards and prayers." [25]

Vital and Pauline's sister Hortense-Scholastique married Charles-Jean-Joseph-Auguste Benoît (1826–1903) in 1857. They had three daughters: Marie, Amélie, and Pauline who became friends of Thérèse's older sisters Pauline and Marie. In February 1889, Auguste and Isidore Guérin disarmed Louis Martin who believed he was protecting his daughters from some imagined attackers. As a result, Isidore Guérin and Vital Romet, fearing Louis could accidentally do harm to the girls, had Louis admitted into Bon Sauveur hospital in Caen. The Benoits settled in Caen.

On one of her regular visits to see her father, Céline wrote:

> When going for the visit [in the "visiting" room, not the off limits hospital room], I met M. Vital [Romet] and Mme. [Hortense] Benoît, who were going there; they stopped their carriage and we climbed up with them. Poor little Father was really touched; it gives such evident joy when he sees his old friends.

---

22 From LT 6 dated Dec. 1, 1880, from Thérèse to Pauline.
23 From Céline to Pauline Romet, dated Feb. 18, 1889.
24 From Sister Agnès to Pauline-Rose-Marie Romet, November 29, 1888.
25 From Céline to Vital Romet, January 7, 1890.

He [Father] was charming. M. Vital, wishing to leave, said to him: "Now, I am going to leave you with your children." With a very kind look in his face, he replied: "Oh! stay a while, you are not in the way!" Finally, they left.[26]

Pierre, the oldest, was a successful business man who lived in an imposing chateau about five miles northwest of Alençon in Saint-Denis-sur-Sarthon, not far from where Thérèse's mother was born. In the summer of 1883 when Thérèse was ten years old she visited his large estate. She alludes to the luxurious living she was exposed to here in her autobiography: "Everything was joy and happiness around me; I was entertained, coddled, and admired; in a word, my life during those two weeks [in the Alençon area] was strewn only with flowers. I must admit this type of life had its charms for me.... At the age of ten the heart allows itself to be easily dazzled, and I considered it a great grace not to have remained at Alençon."[27]

Vital lived the longest of all. He was born in 1830 and died at eighty-six on July 21, 1916, having survived long enough to witness Thérèse's beatification proceeding. His sister Pauline passed away on September 15, 1889, also in Alençon, age sixty. Hortense went to her reward on July 6, 1898 in Caen at seventy-three while her husband Auguste outlived her by ten years, dying in Caen in 1903 at seventy-seven.

13. Mme. Léonie (Gilbert) Tifenne (1843–1930)
Close friend of the Martins in Alençon

MADAME LÉONIE TIFENNE WAS A LIFELONG FRIEND OF M. AND MME. MARTIN and family in Alençon and the godmother of their daughter Léonie. As a young girl she lived with her family, the Gilberts, opposite the Martin's home and watchmaker and jeweler's shop on the rue du Pont Neuf before St. Thérèse was born. Since Thérèse's grandparents lived for some time in the same house as her parents but on the second floor, Madame Tifenne's father, mother, and she knew them well.

Marie-Hyacinthe-Léonie Gilbert was born in Alençon on June 4, 1843, thirty years before Thérèse entered the world and died at eighty-seven in the same town on June 9, 1930, thirty-three years after Thérèse's death. She was buried in the family burial plot in Notre Dame Cemetery in Alençon where Thérèse's mother and her four young siblings were originally interred.

In 1866 she was twenty-three years old when she married a pharmacist, Jacques Tifenne, (1838–1905), who studied for a while with Thérèse's pharmacist uncle Isidore Guérin. He was born in the little hamlet of Roiville (Orne) near Camembert. No children resulted from this union but her maternal instincts emerged when she assumed custody of her orphaned niece and nephew—Thérèse (1872–1932)[28] and Pierre (1874–1955). They lost their father (Albert Gilbert) in 1885 when they were thirteen and eleven respectively, and their mother (Léontine Croisé) two years later. Madame Tifenne lived all her married and widowed life

---

26 Letter from Céline to her Carmelite sisters Pauline, Marie, and Thérèse dated May 20, 1890.
27 *Story of a Soul*, chapter IV, p. 73.
28 She married Charles Vetillard (1856–1919) in 1892 and had a son who died in World War I.

at 6 Place du Plénitre in a three-story dwelling in a row of houses located in a square just behind Notre Dame Church in Alençon. It is still there,[29] occupied by a gracious, hospitable private family who are true devotees of St. Thérèse.

After nearly two decades in Alençon, the Martin family left for Lisieux following Mme. Martin's death in 1877. Louis, and on occasion his daughters, frequently revisited Alençon. At these times they would stay with Madame Tifenne or at the home of the Romets who were also close friends of the Martins. Céline recorded in the biography she wrote of her mother that "Thérèse and I used to spend a part of our holidays with her [Mme. Tifenne], in a large room covered with red damask. St. Thérèse referred to it as the "Cardinal's room."[30] John Beevers in his enlightening book *Storm of Glory* mentions a white goatskin rug in a bedroom that fascinated Thérèse who liked to run her fingers through its thick hair. Madame Tifenne, whom Céline called "*Tante Bonbon*" (Sweet Aunt), taught the two girls how to make colored clay flowers with which they decorated earthenware objects that were then baked in an oven. During the August 1883 return visit to Alençon, Thérèse was invited to the country home of Madame Tifenne's sister, Madame Monnier, in Arçonnay ("Grogny") where she rode side-saddle on her wooded grounds.

In 1926, a year following Thérèse's canonization, Madame Tifenne told an American priest[31] visiting her about the last time Thérèse came to see her:

> Just before she entered the convent the Little Flower came to Alençon to bid goodbye to the Alençon friends and relatives of the family. I, as the godmother of Léonie and intimate friend of the family, had the honor of entertaining Thérèse and her father and this was the room which Thérèse occupied, and of course, I allow no one now to occupy this room.[32]

This same priest asked Mme. Tifenne many questions about Thérèse and her family. One of them was if she ever thought that Thérèse would some day become a saint:

> "Oh, no," she laughed, "I never dreamt that Thérèse would become a saint. I looked upon her merely as an unusually good little girl. I was not surprised at her goodness because both her mother and her father were saints—saints," she repeated. "*C'etait une famille vraiment patriarchale*," she declared, that is "It was a truly patriarchal family." She paused before the adjective "patriarchal," which was the best word that she could find in her vocabulary to characterize her admiration for the goodness of the Martin family.[33]

As the priest continued his interview with Madam Tifenne, she detailed some pleasurable moments of intimacy with Thérèse and her family:

---

29 It has no markings outside indicating Thérèse stayed there.
30 Sister Geneviève, *The Mother of the Little Flower*, p. 120.
31 Rev. Albert H. Dolan, O. Carm. who was the National Director of the Society of The Little Flower in Chicago, U.S.A.
32 Dolan, *Living Sisters of the Little Flower*, pp. 173–174.
33 Ibid., p. 177.

The greatest thrill of the interview came when she told me that she, the lady talking to me, had been present at the first Communion of the Little Flower and was present also at the first Communion feast at the Martin home in the evening. The Little Flower gives a whole chapter [actually only part of it] in the Autobiography to her First Communion and many pages to her First Holy Communion day. You can imagine therefore the thrill of sitting there listening to one who had been actually present at the scene which the Little Flower describes....

Madame Tifenne then went on and reconstructed for me all those scenes of that first Holy Communion day. She described for instance the tranquil joy of the little girl, evident to all and edifying all; she described the Little Flower's enthusiasm when her father presented the watch which was his first Communion gift to her.[34]

The priest described Mme. Tifenne as being "a little, short, agile, bright eyed, red cheeked Normandy lady ... [with] all courtesy and kindness." He asked her if all the pictures of Thérèse were faithful likenesses of Thérèse as she knew her. Her surprisingly candid response was:

"No," she declared, "they flatter her."

"Do you mean that the Little Flower was not beautiful?" I asked.

"No," she said, "I do not think that I would call her beautiful; not more beautiful than hundreds of other girls one sees, at least as regards her features. But there was a most unusual, arresting, and charming expression on her countenance, an expression of placidity which we always remarked from her earliest childhood, and her eyes—her eyes were very beautiful, large and mystic, as it were. By mystic I mean that her eyes always seemed to be looking into the next world. I remember that often while we had company Thérèse would be sitting in this very parlor as a little girl seemingly attentive, but if one looked into her eyes one would see that her thoughts were far away."

"I do not understand, Madam," I said, "how you can maintain that the pictures of the Little Flower flatter her, because her sister Céline is the artist who painted the pictures of the Little Flower that are in general circulation."

"Well, Céline," declared Madam Tifenne, "idealized her then; she idealized her."

"Well, did you ever see a picture of the Little Flower that you thought was a faithful likeness, Madam?" I asked.

"Yes." She said, "there is one. It is the face on the marble statue of the Little Flower that has been erected over her tomb in the cemetery at Lisieux...."[35]

Six months after Thérèse entered Carmel, M. and Mme. Tifenne and their niece and nephew visited the postulant Thérèse. Thérèse informs her cousin about it in a playful, adolescent way:

Yesterday, I received a visit, and I give you a hundred guesses.... A beautiful woman of the WORLD, her dear husband, a tall *Mademoiselle* of sixteen, a *Monsieur of fourteen*. Did you guess?... It is the godmother [of Lèonie], who used to plant verbena.... She was accompanied by her niece Th. Gilbert and

---

34 Ibid., pp. 178–181.
35 Ibid., pp. 175–176.

her nephew Pierre. High society! If you had only seen her in the speakroom. She was almost singing: "*Que mon coeur, que mon coeur a de peine*" [a song the Martins sang at Les Buissonnets], when seeing us behind the grille.[36]

In a letter written a half year later, again to her cousin Marie Guérin, Thérèse makes a very prosaic request:

> I'm coming to ask you for a favor, and it's to you I am addressing myself, for I know that Les Buissonnets, now, alas! deserted, was formerly your domain.
> Do you recall a book which Mme. Tifenne had given me at the time of my First Communion?... It was entitled: "The Young Girl's Bouquet." This book must be in one of the drawers of the bureau belonging to poor little Father [who was at the hospital in Caen]. I'd be very happy if I could have it as soon as possible.... If it were possible you could perhaps explain to the maid [Marcelline Husé] what you want without going to Les Buissonnets yourself![37]

When Therese was very ill in the monastery infirmary before she died, her sister Pauline (Mother Agnès) jotted these touching words in her notebook:

> She was trying to recall sins she could have committed through her senses in order to confess them before being anointed; we were considering the sense of smell, and she said:
> "I remember during my last trip from Alençon to Lisieux that I used a bottle of *eau de Cologne* which was given to me by Mme. Tifenne, and I did this with pleasure."[38]

The publication of *Story of a Soul* in 1898 appeared a year after Thérèse's death. When Madame Tifenne finished reading it, she sent a letter to the living sisters of Sister Thérèse in the Lisieux Carmel: "It was with heartfelt interest that I read all the details given about your family and ancestors. Those whom I knew, together with your father and your saintly mother, made me realize what a line of saints you possess in your family."[39]

The widowed Madame Tifenne recalled again about two years before she died how saintly the Martin family was:

> I pictured your mother to myself again, in the corner of her window with little Thérèse, and I repeated to myself: "Oh! if I had known the gift which God granted me, when I used to breathe the air of all that holy family, how much better would I have profited by it!"[40]

When she was nearing death in June 1930, five years after Thérèse's canonization, Mme. Tifenne uttered these tender words, "I am recommending myself to M. Martin. He was so good; I loved him dearly."[41]

---

36 LT 62 written by Thérèse and sent to Marie Guérin in September 1888.
37 LT 88 written on April 24, 1889, by Thérèse and addressed to Marie Guérin.
38 From *Her Last Conversations*, July 8, 1897.
39 From a letter by Mme. Tifenne written to the Lisieux Carmel as quoted in Sister Geneviève's *Mother*, p. 113.
40 Ibid.
41 Piat, *The Story of a Family*, p. 417.

B. Domestic Help

1. **Marie-Françoise-Félicité Hubert (Mme. Alfred Saffray):** Served the Martins in Lisieux for two years after Victoire Pasquer left
2. **Marcelline-Anna Husé:** Thérèse's aunt's maid who often cared for Thérèse
3. **Desiré and Marie Lejuif:** Louis Martin's manservant and maid in Lisieux after his release from the hospital
4. **Louise Marais:** The Martins' maid in Alençon who victimized Thérèse's sister Léonie
5. **Victoire Pasquer:** The Martins' servant at Les Buissonnets for seven years

---

Though both Louis and Zélie Martin were of distinctly Norman provincial origins that could be traced back to a sturdy ancient peasant stock, they both soon entered the rising bourgeois class in Alençon through their own tireless energies and talents as entrepreneurs. Even before marriage, Louis was a successful watchmaker and owner of a jewelry store, and Zélie headed her own lacemaking business. By their "hard work," as Céline states, "they were in financially easy circumstances"[1] which allowed them, as well as their similarly enterprising relatives the Guérins, to enjoy a lifestyle that provided them with lovely homes, long pleasure trips to the seaside, a family vacation chateau, boarding school, and sundry private lessons for their children. In addition they employed maids and servants to assume tasks for which they actually had not the time to execute themselves.

Besides the obvious household chores, the maids generally escorted the young girls to school, a custom Céline admitted years later she disliked:

> At that time school children were never allowed to go out alone, and young girls of our environment were always accompanied. Truly it was slavery. Every morning someone had to go with us, and call for us in the evening, for we were half-boarders. Sometimes it was the maid, but often Papa was asked to take his turn.[2]

Mme. Martin chose the help carefully and, once engaged, treated them as members of her own family as can be seen from a letter she wrote to her brother Isidore:

> It is not always high wages that assure the attachment of servants. They must feel that they are liked; we must show them marks of kindness and not be too stiff with them. When people are fundamentally good, we may be sure that they will serve us with attachment and thoroughness. You know I have a

---

[1] Sister Geneviève, *The Father of the Little Flower*, p. 36.
[2] Ibid., p. 54.

quick temper, yet all the maids I have had have liked me, and I keep them as long as I wish.... It is true that I never treat my servants less well than I do my children. If I tell you this, it is not to set myself up as a model; I assure you I do not think of that, for everyone tells me I do not know how to treat maids.[3]

Except for the last sentence, Céline corroborates what her mother said: "Our parents took affectionate care also of the servants employed at home, treating them with consideration. The same care was extended to the lace-makers who worked on the *Point d'Alençon* for my mother. She visited their homes, and saw to it that they needed nothing." [4]

This benevolent attitude toward the domestic help certainly was reciprocal even regarding Thérèse as substantiated by Léonie's testimony at the Diocesan Process in 1910:

At this time of her life [after she left school and was receiving private lessons], Thérèse was always at home, and was the family's pride and joy. Even the servant-maids loved her, because her whole person radiated peace and kindness. She was always forgetful of her own convenience, in order to please others; making everybody happy was her element.[5]

There were times, however, when Zélie became overwrought, specifically during her final months, and dreamed of not having servants:

The maid [Louise] must definitely leave soon; I still have no one in mind. Oh! if God were to do me the favor of curing me [of breast cancer], I would no longer want any servants. Marie is good regarding the management of the house, taking care of the bedrooms, attending to her little sisters, Pauline and Léonie would also help and we would be happy as I have never been before....[6]

In total we come across the names of twelve servants connected with the Martins and the Guérins who were associated with Thérèse in one way or another. The two domestics we hear of who worked in the Martin's Alençon home were Virginia Cousin and Louise Marais. Virginia was employed for about three years but nothing much else about her is known. On the other hand, Louise's service lasted twelve years and references to her abound in Martin family writings.

Zélie Martin's brother Isidore Guérin, his wife Céline, and their two daughters were always very close to the Martins even when they lived miles apart. After Zélie's death in 1877, Louis Martin and his five daughters moved from Alençon into their new home in Lisieux not far from the Guérins; whereupon, Mme. Guérin assumed a tender and enduring maternal role toward the motherless girls. Thus mutual affection led the two families to share much of their lives together. The Guérins' maids consequently were intimately involved with the Martins. Aimée Roger was their cook for a while and has the distinction of being mentioned in

---
3 CF 29 from Zélie to her brother Isidore, March 2, 1868, as quoted in English on p. 168 in Piat's *op. cit.*
4 Sister Geneviève, *op. cit.*, p. 25.
5 O'Mahony, *op. cit.*, p. 175.
6 Letter (CF 212) from Mme. Martin to Mme. Guérin, dated July 8, 1877.

Thérèse's autobiography, albeit only once. During Thérèse's serious and strange illness at ten, Thérèse observed that "everybody was puzzled [about her ailment]. Aunt [Guérin] was obliged to keep me at her home, and she took care of me with a truly *maternal* solicitude. When Papa returned from [Holy Week in] Paris with my older sisters [Marie and Léonie], Aimée met them at the door with such a sad face that Marie believed I had died. This sickness was not 'unto death.'"[7]

Three maids whose names occasionally turn up in Theresian literature—Alexandre Mariette, Maria Cosseron, and Maria Detettre—appear to be insignificant as far as their actual relevance to the story of St. Thérèse is concerned, primarily because they worked for the Martins after Thérése left home. One other domestic was dismissed because of a drinking problem.

Alexandre Mariette was hired by the Guérins on June 27, 1892, but played a minor role in the family affairs, especially Thérèse's since by then, she had already been living five years in the monastery.

Maria Cosseron worked for the Martins from Pentecost 1888 until the summer of 1889, dismissed no doubt because her services were no longer needed since only Céline and Léonie were left at home following the admission of their father into the hospital in Caen. In February of 1889 he suffered another attack of paralysis, which apparently affected his nervous system causing hallucinations. He imagined wild scenes of slaughter and violence. In order to protect his daughters he carried a revolver which alarmed all and at one point brandished it. Maria witnessed this as well as Louis's brother-in-law Isidore Guérin who feared for the safety of the girls. Consequently he was admitted into the mental hospital. Marie Cosseron was then engaged by the Guérin family and remained with them for some time. She was born in 1867 in Saint-Samson (Mayenne), the same town as another maid, Marcelline Husé, and died in Lisieux, fifty-eight years later (1945).

The third woman, Maria Detettre, worked for only about four or five months for the Martins at Les Buissonnets while Thérèse was still at home. When Thérèse was on her trip to Rome in November 1887 she sent her regards from Venice to this maid in a letter she wrote to her sister Marie in the Lisieux Carmel. Unfortunately she had to be dismissed on New Year's Day 1888 because of a serious drinking problem.[8]

One other servant named Auguste[9] was employed to help Céline and her father after he returned home from the hospital. He did not last long because of his frequent episodes of inebriation. For fear of causing harm to the Martins he was dismissed. In order to ensure better protection for Céline and her father, Isidore Guérin even considered rearranging "his laboratory quarters into a bedroom for M. Martin, with a bedroom above which he would make in the attic for the servant."[10]

The six people whose biographies follow were important enough in the life of Thérèse or her family to merit more lengthy profiles.

---
7 *Story of a Soul*, chapter III, p. 61.
8 In a footnote to LT 31A, dated Nov. 10, 1887, from Thérèse to Marie Guérin.
9 See p. 133 in Gaucher's *The Story of a Life*.
10 Letter from Mme. Guérin addressed to her daughter Mme. La Néele, dated May 22, 1894.

1. MARIE-FRANÇOISE-FÉLICITÉ HUBERT (1860–1930)
(MME. ALFRED SAFFRAY)
The Martins' servant in Lisieux for nearly three years

MARIE-FRANÇOISE-FÉLICITÉ HUBERT TOOK THE POSITION OF MAID AT LES Buissonnets that was left vacant with Victoire Pasquer's departure in 1884. She remained, though, only about three years—during the time Thérèse was twelve and thirteen—and then left in the winter of 1886–1887 to marry Paul-Adolphe Catherine shortly after on November 23, 1886. Sadly, in time Félicité, as she was called by the Martins, became a widow, then remarried—this time to Alfred Saffrey, a saddler (in the harness trade) in Lisieux. Her name is rarely mentioned in her employer's letters but when it is, it is with affection and thoughtfulness. One example is from a letter Thérèse wrote to her sister Marie away on a trip from Lisieux: "Don't forget especially our messages and the stool for Aunt [Guérin]. Félicité sends her regards; she's in a delightful mood ever since you left." [11]

Marie in Lisieux wrote to Thérèse on vacation in Deauville in 1885. In her closing remarks she says, "*Au revoir*, darling little big baby. I have to go and pour the soup on the bread. That is altogether different from going out on the beach. It is seven o'clock and Félicité hasn't yet brought back the Abbey's lover [Léonie]." [12] More meaningful, however, is Louis's admonition to Marie: "Take good care of Félicité, and do not forget to give her the wages for the three months." [13]

Here are two written statements Felicité made years after Thérèse and her father died. "I have heard that some evil-minded people found fault with the dear little saint; she who was so gentle and so lovable, always afraid of hurting you! I was three years in service with M. Martin, and I can say that she never gave me any trouble." [14] On May 25, 1926, Felicité, now a married woman (Mme. Saffray), wrote a letter from Paris to Thérèse's sisters in Carmel a year after Thérèse's canonization, commenting on their father's unique personality: "M. Martin above all was a saint, and so brave. He was afraid of nothing. Truly, there are few families such as you were." [15]

She was born in Villiers-le-Pré (Manche) on October 27, 1860, and died almost seventy years later in Lisieux on August 25, 1930, five years after Thérèse was proclaimed a saint.

2. MARCELLINE-ANNA HUSÉ (1866–1935)
(SISTER MARIE-JOSEPH OF THE CROSS, O.S.B)
Thérèse's aunt's maid who often cared for Thérèse

PERHAPS THE MOST SIGNIFICANT OF ALL THE DOMESTIC HELP ASSOCIATED with the adolescent Thérèse was Marcelline Husé. Though she was not a member

---
11 From a letter (LT 21) dated October 2, 1886, written by Thérèse to her sister Marie.
12 From a letter (LC 40) dated May 3, 1885, written by Marie to Thérèse.
13 From a letter (CF 223) dated August 30, 1885, written by M. Martin to his daughter Marie. See p. 138 in Sr. Geneviève's *The Father of the Little Flower*.
14 Piat, *The Story of a Family*, p. 324.
15 As quoted in Emert's *op. cit.*, p. 64.

of the Martin household *per se*, she got to know Thérèse very well during the eight years prior to Thérèse's entrance into Carmel. A bond of mutual love and concern existed between the two. Marcelline had this to say about Thérèse at the Diocesan Inquiry on December 12–15, 1910:

> Later, during her first year in Carmel, I confided to her that I intended becoming a nun. On this occasion, too, she gave me some excellent advice. Her last recommendation to me before I left the parlor was: "Dear Marcelline, we must always love God a great deal, and to prove that love we must make all the sacrifices he asks of us. Don't worry; I'll be praying for you. Love God so that you won't be afraid of him; he is so kind really! Remember too to pray for those who do not love him, so that we can convert many souls."[16]

Seven months after her admission into Carmel, Thérèse wrote a postscript in a letter to her cousin: "I often think of my dear Marcelline."[17]

In the course of the two processes leading to Thérèse's canonization, Marcelline provided much valuable information under oath. She confirmed and elucidated upon many aspects of Thérèse's life and personality recounted by the Martin family or revealed by Thérèse herself in her autobiography and letters. Following are some excerpts from the testimony she gave during the Diocesan Process from December 12 to 15, 1910:

- In 1880, when I was thirteen years old, I entered the service of M. Guerin, the Servant of God's uncle, as maid and governess. The Servant of God [Thérèse][18] was then seven, and had been in Lisieux two or three years. She came to her uncle's house every day, and I took care of her, as I did of her little cousins Jeanne and Marie, M. Guérin's daughters. I was always with them and took part in their games. I remained with the Guérin family until 1889—the year after the Servant of God entered Carmel....

- I do not know whether Thérèse in her simplicity was aware that she was loved more than the others, because all the members of this family were very fond of each other. In any case, she was not a spoiled child, and she never took advantage of her privileged position. As for her sisters, they loved her so much themselves that they were in no way jealous of her....

- Whenever she was alone with me on the way to school or at home, she was always very affectionate and trusting, and freely confided in me. These intimate conversations always seemed to veer spontaneously towards pious subjects. She was exceptionally intelligent and thoughtful for her age. I particularly remember how, even before her first communion, whenever she heard workmen using foul language, she would explain to me, in order to excuse them, that these people had received less grace than we had, and were more unfortunate than blameworthy....

- She always had the highest marks in her class, but found no pleasure in the noisy games of children her own age. Her idea of enjoyment was to pick flowers,

---

16 O'Mahony, *op. cit.*, p. 187.
17 Letter (LT 69) from Thérèse to Marie Guérin, November, 1888.
18 At this stage in the process toward canonization, the candidate for sainthood is called the Servant of God.

or to go away by herself in the garden or the country "to play the hermit." She loved nature and the singing of birds. I knew that the doctors found her illness strange [in 1883 when she was ten], and that their energetic treatment was of no avail. On the contrary, she seemed to grow worse. I prayed fervently for her with her sisters. Then suddenly on May 10 someone came to tell us that Therese was well again; the following day she came to see us herself. The only trace of her illness was a certain weakness, and that quickly disappeared.... But at the time, I knew nothing of an apparition of the Blessed Virgin....

- While I was still with her, I was already convinced that her virtue far surpassed that usually seen in children, even very pious ones. I do not know how to put it any better, but she was a soul apart, something special, and not at all like the rest....
- I also noticed her delicate love for her neighbor. The first time she was introduced to me at [the] Guerin's, she was only seven. Someone had told her that I was still lonely for my mother, and she took it upon herself to comfort me with a great demonstration of affection. When out walking, she was always delighted to be sent to give an alms to the poor. Later on, when she was about fourteen, she used to visit poor families herself, and teach their children the catechism....
- One characteristic of her charity towards her neighbor which I remember especially was that even before her first communion, she used to do little acts of charity for her cousin Marie Guérin who was always ill. What patience she had with her! Though three years younger, she lavished the most charming care upon her, giving in to all her whims, dissipating the boredom and sadness caused by her illness, teaching her how to live alone, and inviting her to practice virtue.
- One felt about her that she was a person who always lived in God's presence, because if one spoke to her of little matters of female vanity there was no holding her attention for very long, but when I talked with her on pious subjects, she immediately opened up and her heart overflowed with happiness.[19]

Marcelline was born the daughter of Norbert Husé and Françoise Baubier in the little town of Saint-Samson (Mayenne) in the diocese of Laval on July 19, 1866. The Guérins hired her as a maid and a governess for their two daughters on March 15, 1880. She also took care of Thérèse and Céline when their father and older sisters were away from Lisieux. After nine years with the Guérins she left to join the Benedictines of the Blessed Sacrament on the rue Saint-Loup in Bayeux on July 12, 1889, just one day before her twenty-third birthday. She took the name Sister Marie-Joseph of the Cross, received the habit on April 13, 1889, and made her profession on August 10, 1892.

She declared in her deposition at the Apostolic Process (1915–1916) that after she left the employ of the Guérins she no longer had any communication with Thérèse except through some letters. The following is an excerpt from a note to Sister Marie-Joseph of the Cross, [the only one in existence that is purportedly written by Thérèse to Sister Marie-Joseph when she was a Carmelite]:

---
19 O'Mahony, *op. cit.*, pp. 182–189.

Dear Sister,

I was very much touched by your letter, and I thank you for the prayers you offered for me. As for me, I have not forgotten you, and I have recommended all your intentions to God....

How good it is to be a religious in order to pray and to appease God's justice; yes, the mission which is entrusted to us is very beautiful, and eternity will not be long enough to thank Our Lord for the lot He has given us....

Your little Sister,
Thérèse of the Child Jesus
rel. carm. ind.[20]

Sister Marie-Joseph of the Cross was faithfully devoted to St. Thérèse during her forty-six years as a lay sister (*soeur converse*) at the Bayeux convent where she died the day after Christmas, 1935, at the age of sixty-nine following a long period of acute suffering.

3. Desiré Lejuif (1861–1916) and Marie Lejuif (1863–1916)
Louis Martin's manservant and maid in Lisieux after his release from the hospital

THE HUSBAND AND WIFE TEAM OF DESIRÉ (AGE 31) AND MARIE (AGE 29) was employed to assist Céline and Léonie at the time their dearly loved father was released from the hospital and returned home on May 10, 1892. A paralytic attack in 1887 marked the beginning of a five-year period of declining health for Louis Martin. Further emotional and mental problems arose forcing the family eventually to admit him in February 1889 into Bon Sauveur, a large hospital in Caen dealing with such cases.[21] Three years later he was permitted to return to Lisieux after a severe stroke which left his legs permanently paralyzed. Since there was no longer any fear of his wandering or disappearing as he did in the past at home, the family felt secure in caring for him. Isidore Guérin, Louis Martin's brother-in-law, brought him back to his own home in Lisieux at 19 rue Paul Banaston. Céline writes of the homecoming and of the new domestic help:

> Some time afterwards [July 1892], in order that we might be freer, our uncle rented a small house for us at 7 Rue Labbey. It faced our uncle's back garden, of which I had the key, by the tradesmen's entrance. We were very often, if not practically always, in the garden. We [Céline and Léonie] used to take Papa there [across the narrow road] in his wheel-chair. We had engaged a married couple to help us with the household work.... His manservant, Desiré, had a very cheerful disposition; he was tall, and Papa, whose arms were not paralysed, had only to put one arm around Desiré's neck to be lifted out of his carriage or to be placed in his armchair.[22]

Marie was hired to do all the housework and her husband was assigned to assist M. Martin in every regard including eating. The Martin girls must have

---
20 From a letter (LT 121) Thérèse addressed to Sister Marie-Joseph of the Cross dated September 28, 1890.
21 The hospital still exists for the same purposes. It was greatly demolished during WWII but it has since been rebuilt.
22 Sister Geneviève, *op. cit.*, pp. 113–114.

been pleased that he had two sisters who were nuns at the Providence Nuns' convent in Lisieux, but he himself had not been practicing his religion for some time. Under the Martin influence, though, he soon returned to the faith. Rev. Piat in his book on Céline has this to say about his conversion:

> She [Céline] told also of the emotion she felt at the end of a novena to Saint Joseph for the conversion of one of the servants when she saw this person fall at her feet and humbly confide: "I am a miserable wretch; for many years I have been separated from God, I have committed sacrileges, but I want to change. It is just now, while looking at the picture of the Blessed Virgin [painted by Céline] that my heart melted like wax." [23]

Céline, certainly delighted about the conversion, with all humility did not attribute it to the power of her painting but to the inspiration of love, as she explains: "That painting was just a lot of daubing, which proves that when God wants to touch a human heart he would rather use a work where love had directed the brush than a work of art." [24]

About a year later, Céline informed her Carmelite sister Marie about Désiré's gratifying relationship with her father:

> When entering Papa's room one night, I was surprised to hear him singing, for Désiré was not helping him. He had only intoned the *Kyrie*, and Papa was continuing it with his beautiful voice, very precise but a little muffled.
>
> Frequently Papa and Désiré sing psalms and all kinds of church hymns in this way. This pleases Papa very much. [25]

Désiré's wife Marie, on the other hand, had a serious problem with alcoholism that the Martins learned about after they employed her. Thérèse, by now nearly six years in the convent, learned of this and responded with consummate charity in a letter she wrote to Céline:

> All the problems you are having with your maid have upset us [Pauline, Marie, and Thérèse].... Your poor maid is very unfortunate in having such a bad habit, especially in being deceitful, but could you perhaps convert her as you did her husband? For every sin, mercy and God is powerful enough to give *stability* even to people who have none. I will really pray for her; perhaps were I in her place, I would be still less good than she is, and perhaps, too, she would have been already a great saint if she had received one half the graces God has granted to me. [26]

On June 5, 1894, Céline notified her three Carmelite sisters that their father had a severe heart attack: "This morning again, Papa had an extremely violent attack while I was at Mass; they came to get me. This attack was no longer a paralytic attack like the last one [on May 27, 1894], it was a heart attack." Desiré was present and, believing Louis was dying since he had turned "blue," called M. Guérin, Louis's brother-in-law. Two hours later M. Martin appeared to have completely recovered.

---

23 Piat, *Céline*, p. 49.
24 François de Sainte-Marie, *op. cit.*, chapter V, p. 42.
25 Dated around July 20, 1893, this letter was from Céline to Sister Marie of the Sacred Heart.
26 From a letter (LT 147) Thérèse wrote to Céline dated August 13, 1893.

On July 4, 1894, a month after this frightening incident, Louis's rather satisfactory physical condition prompted Céline to take her father, accompanied by Desiré, to join her Uncle and Aunt at their vacation home in the country, the Château de la Musse. While there a sudden heart attack took the life of Louis Martin on July 29, 1894. Désiré and Marie henceforth played no further part in the life of the Martin family members.

Records at the Archives in the Lisieux Carmel indicate that Louis Désiré Lejuif was born in 1861, a descendent of the Fosse family. He lived twenty-two years after he left the employ of the Martins and died at the age of fifty-five in 1916. His wife, *née* Marie-Augustine Amélie Rigot, died at fifty-three, the same year as her husband.

4. LOUISE MARAIS (1849–1923)
The Martins' maid in Alençon who victimized Thérèse's sister Léonie

LOUISE MARAIS ENTERED THE SERVICE OF THE MARTINS IN 1865 AT SIXTEEN and remained with them for almost twelve years—the longest of any other servants—until Mme. Martin's death. She was with the Martins during Thérèse's first five years of life. References to her are numerous in Martin family correspondence, Thérèse's autobiography, and elsewhere. One of the earliest notable allusions to Louise is in a letter from Mme. Martin to her brother Isidore where she explains her method of handling domestics: "[all] the maids I had liked me, and I keep them as long as I want. The one I have now [Louise Marais] would be sick if it was necessary that she leave. I am sure that if someone would offer her two hundred francs more she would not want to leave us. It is true that I do not treat them less than my own children." [27]

Zélie was naturally compassionate, wise, understanding, and did indeed know how to treat her maids. If they were sick she nursed them like a mother. When Louise suffered for several weeks with a serious attack of articular rheumatism, Mme. Martin cared for her continually until she got better and then allowed her to return to her own home for a complete recovery.[28] The saintly Zélie Martin attempted to instill in Louise, as well as all around her, solid Christian ethics usually by her constant good example or more directly by persuasion as in the following case which unfortunately was not a success:

> M. De C [Gaucherin], our neighbor, was buried yesterday, which event has affected Louise a lot. She cannot understand how anyone can die "when they are so happy on earth!" I believe she [Louise] would voluntarily sacrifice her part in Paradise in order to be eternally here below as happy as are the rich, who, she imagines, [live] in perfect happiness. It was useless to tell her that the rich are no more happy than others! She does not want to believe it! [29]

In the next episode Zélie was successful eventually in having her exhortations heeded:

---

[27] Letter (CF 29) from Mme. Martin to her brother Isidore, dated March 2, 1868, translated by the author.
[28] *The Story of a Soul*, chapter VII, p. 169.
[29] Letter (CF 164) from Mme. Martin to Pauline, July 16, 1876, translated by the author.

> The maid [Louise] has spent a week at home. Her father is dangerously ill, and he will not hear of confession. I had strongly urged her to notify the priest, in order that he might pay a visit and gradually prepare him; but she did not want to do so. She is like her mother, who repeats: "There is plenty of time: he is not so ill as that!" That infuriates me to the utmost, and makes me very annoyed with her.[30]

Louise, despite her loyalty, love for the children, and years of devoted work, presented at one time a very serious problem for the family. It dealt with the third Martin girl Léonie who had showed signs since babyhood of being a disturbed child with personality traits directly opposite of all the other sisters: disobedience, stubbornness, egocentricity, and poor scholarship. It gradually became apparent that the only one who could control Léonie was Louise. Her method, however, was unscrupulous. She terrified the child into submission and caused her to become rebellious. The oldest sister Marie discovered her machinations and reported to her mother who was appalled and declared, "Brutality never reformed anyone; it only makes slaves, and that is what has happened to this poor child."[31] She explains it all in a letter she wrote to her daughter Pauline away at school:

> You know what your sister [Léonie] was like: a model of insubordination, having never obeyed me saving when forced to do so. In a spirit of contradiction, she would do the precise contrary of what I wished, even when she would have wished to do the thing asked of her. In short, she obeyed only the maid.
>
> I had tried by every means in my power to win her. Everything had failed up to this day, and it was the greatest sorrow I have ever had in my life. Since your aunt [her sister, Sr. Marie-Dosithée] died, I have implored her to win the heart of this child for me, and on Sunday morning I was heard. I now have it as completely as I could have. She will no longer leave me for a moment, kisses me till she nearly stifles me, does anything I bid her without question, and works beside me all day long.
>
> The maid has entirely lost her authority and it is certain that she will never again have any ascendancy over Léonie after the manner in which things have turned out. She, the servant, wept and moaned when I told her to leave immediately, but I no longer wished to have her in my sight. She has so besought me to let her remain, that I am going to wait a little yet, but she is forbidden to address a word to Léonie. I am now treating the child so gently that, little by little, I hope to succeed in correcting her faults.[32]

Zélie did gain control over Léonie but maintained her strong convictions about Louise:

> I am very necessary to this child. After I am gone, she will be too unhappy and no one will be able to make her obey, saving the woman who has victimized her. But no! That shall not do, for as soon as I am dead, she must leave at once

---

30 Letter (CF 198) from Mme. Martin to Pauline, dated April 29, 1877, as quoted on pp. 65–66 in Sr. Geneviève's *Mother*.
31 Letter (CF 195) from Mme. Martin to Pauline, dated March 22, 1877, p. 238 in Piat's *Story of a Family*.
32 Letter (CF 194) from Mme. Martin to Pauline, dated March 12, 1877, p. 238 in Piat's *op. cit.*

[which she did]. I believe they will not refuse to carry out this my last wish.... I beseech Him to leave me long enough here that Léonie may no longer need me.[33]

Notwithstanding this shocking affair and Zélie's subsequent feelings, Louise was an excellent housemaid and clearly played an integral part in the Martin household right to the end. She had been working eight years for the family at the time of Thérèse's birth. It was she who carried the two-day-old Thérèse to Notre-Dame church for her baptism. Among the letters mentioning her is one written by Mme. Martin at the time that Thérèse was away from home being nursed by Mme. Taillé ("Little Rose") on her farm in Semallé several miles away:

> We did not expect Thérèse. The nurse arrived with her four children at half-past eleven, just as we were sitting down to table. She put the baby [Thérèse] in my arms and went off immediately to [Sunday] Mass.
>
> Yes, but the little one would not have this; she cried until we thought she would swoon away. Everyone in the house was upset. I had to send Louise to ask the nurse to come back immediately after Mass, as she had intended to make some delay in purchasing shoes for her children. She left before Mass was half finished and came running up to the house. I was vexed at that; the babe would not have died from crying. She became happy immediately.[34]

Louise was again involved with little Thérèse, then two years old:

> Some weeks ago she [Thérèse] was taken for a walk on Sunday. She had not been "at Mass" as she said herself. On returning from a walk she began to cry vigorously, saying that she wanted to go to Mass. She opened the hall door and ran away, in torrents of rain, towards the church [Notre-Dame]. When we [Louise and Zélie] had run after her and brought her back, her tears and lamentation lasted a good hour.[35]

Regrettably all the letters written by Mme. Martin to her oldest daughter Marie to prepare her for her First Communion were destroyed by Louise who thoughtlessly had them burned.

Twenty-two years later Thérèse herself mentions Louise by name at least a half dozen times in her autobiography. The first time is in Chapter 1 when she states candidly that "with a nature such as my own, had I been reared by parents without virtue or even if I had been spoiled by the maid, Louise, as Céline was, I would have become very bad and perhaps have even been lost."[36] Two paragraphs later Thérèse quotes from one of her mother's letters, again to Pauline:

> The other day Céline slept with me [Mme. Martin] and Thérèse had slept on the second floor in Céline's bed; she had begged Louise to take her downstairs to dress her. Louise went up to get her but found the bed empty. Thérèse had heard Céline and had come down to be with her. Louise said: "You don't want to get dressed?" Therese answered: "Oh! no, Louise, we are like the two hens, we're inseparable!" Saying this they embraced each other and both held each other

---

33 Letter (CF 195) from Mme. Martin to Pauline, dated March 22, 1877, p. 240 in Piat's *op. cit.*
34 Letter (CF 98) from Mme. Martin to Pauline, dated May 5, 1873, p. 26 in Laveille's *op. cit.*
35 Letter (CF 130) from Mme. Martin to Mme. Guérin, dated March 14, 1875, p. 31 in Piat's *op. cit.*
36 *Story of a Soul*, chapter I, pp. 24–25.

tightly. Then in the evening, Louise, Céline, and Léonie left for the meeting of the Catholic circle and left little Thérèse all alone. She understood she was too little to go to the meeting ... and fell into a sound sleep fifteen minutes later.[37]

The next excerpt contains an episode and a quotation often cited that reveals one aspect of Thérèse's unique spirituality—and Louise is mentioned:

> One day, Léonie, thinking she was too big to be playing any longer with dolls, came to us with a basket filled with dresses and pretty pieces for making others; her doll was resting on top. "Here, my little sisters, *choose*; I'm giving you all this." Céline stretched out her hand and took a little ball of wool which pleased her. After a moment's reflection, I stretched out mine saying: "I choose all!" and I took the basket without further ceremony. Those who witnessed the scene saw nothing wrong and even Céline herself didn't dream of complaining (besides, she had all sorts of toys, her godfather gave her lots of presents, and Louise found ways of getting her everything she desired).... This little incident of my childhood is a summary of my whole life.... Then, as in the days of my childhood, I cried out: "My God '*I choose all!*' I don't want to be a saint by halves, I'm not afraid to suffer for You, I fear only one thing: to keep my *own will*; so take it, for '*I choose all*' that You will!"[38]

Thérèse copied another passage from one of her mother's letters in relaying the anecdote of her childhood method of making little acts of sacrifice and counting them on beads which she called "practices":

> The other day she [the four-year-old Thérèse] was at the grocery store with Céline and Louise. She was talking about her practices. She was doing this rather loudly with Céline and the woman in the store said to Louise: "What does she mean by these little practices? When she's playing in the garden that's all she talks about. Mme. Gaucherin listens at the window trying to understand what this debate about practices means.[39]

When the slowly dying Zélie was finally incapable of attending to her lace workers, the oldest daughter Marie assumed the task with the valuable added assistance of Louise. We learn also of how attentive Louise was to her mistress from one of the last letters Zélie was able to write to her beloved brother and sister-in-law a month before she died: "Louis [Martin], Marie, and the maid [Louise] stayed beside me the whole time [during a night of painful suffering]. Poor Louis would take me, from time to time, into his arms, like a child."[40]

Thérèse tells us in *Story of a Soul* of a poignant moment for the grief stricken children after their mother's death on August 28, 1877:

> All five of us were gathered together, looking at each other sadly. Louise was there too, and, seeing Céline and me, she said: "Poor little things, you have no mother any more!" Céline threw her arms around Marie saying: "Well, you will be my Mamma!" Accustomed to following Céline's example, I turned instead

---

37 Letter (CF 172) from Mme. Martin to Pauline, dated Nov. 3, 1876, as quoted on p. 25 in *Story of a Soul*.
38 *Story of a Soul*, chapter I, p. 27.
39 Letter (CF 192) from Mme. Martin to Pauline, dated March 4, 1877, p. 40 in *Story of a Soul*.
40 Letter (CF 216) from Zélie to Isidore, dated July 27, 1877, as quoted on p. 100 in Sr. Geneviève's *Mother*.

to you, Mother [Pauline, Sister Agnès in religion], and as though the future had torn aside its veil, I threw myself into your arms, crying: "Well, as for me, it's Pauline who will be my Mamma!" [41]

On October 18, 1877, Louise Marais left the employ of the Martins. Eight-year-old Céline comments about her departure in a school-type exercise letter she wrote to her sister Marie: "DIARY. Friday. I was very sad yesterday. Louise left (that is, my maid). Thérèse cried a little; I did not cry, but I was very sad just the same, and when saying this, I am still sad." [42]

In time Louise married and became Mme. Edouard Legendre (or Le Gendre). After Thérèse's beatification forty-six years later, she contacted the Lisieux Carmel. Céline indicated in the biography she wrote of her mother that:

> Towards the end of her life, our former housemaid, Louise Marais, wrote July 22, 1923: "In my acute sufferings, I invoke the aid of little Thérèse, and at the same time, of her good and saintly Mamma. If little Thérèse is a saint, I believe that her mother is also a great saint. She had a great many trials during her life, and she accepted them all with resignation. And how eager she was to sacrifice herself constantly!" [43]

In the same book Céline states:

> When she could not go herself, Mamma frequently sent Louise, the maid, to render assistance to needy families. In after years, Louise testified to these acts of charity: "I alone know how many two franc pieces (of money) as well as the many dishes of stew she sent through me to poor persons around Alençon." [44]

Five months after she wrote this letter, Louise Marais, then Mme. Edouard Le Gendre, passed away in Gacé (Orne) on December 12, 1923. She was born seventy-four years before in Merlerault (Orne) on May 5, 1849.

5. VICTOIRE PASQUER (1857–1935)
The Martins' servant at Les Buissonnets for seven years

"VICTOIRE WAS VERY FOND OF ME AND I WAS ALSO FOND OF HER," DECLARES Thérèse in her autobiography.[45] Yet there were times during the seven years she worked for the Martins when they both got entangled in some rather amusing but at times petulant childhood incidents at Les Buissonnets, the Martin's home in Lisieux. Thérèse details four involving her May altar, an inkstand, a water bucket, and the fireplace:

> Since I was too little to attend May devotions, I remained at home with Victoire, carrying out my devotions before *my little May-altar*. This I had arranged according to my taste; everything was so small, the candlesticks, the flower pots, etc. *Two tapers* lit it up perfectly. Sometimes Victoire would surprise me with a gift of two candle stubs. But this was rare. All was in readiness one

---

41 *Story of a Soul*, chapter II, p. 34.
42 Céline wrote this after her signature.
43 Sister Geneviève, *The Mother of the Little Flower*, pp. 112–113.
44 Sister Geneviève, *op. cit.* The quote is from a letter by Mme. Le Gendre dated July 22, 1923.
45 *Story of a Soul*, chapter II, p. 39.

evening for us to commence our prayers, so I said to her: "Victoire, will you begin the Memorare? I'm going to light the tapers." She pretended to begin but said nothing and looked at me, laughing. I watched my *precious tapers* burning away rapidly and begged her to recite the prayer, but she still said nothing. Then rising from my knees, I shouted at her and told her she was very wicked. Laying aside my customary gentleness, I stamped my foot with all my might. Poor Victoire stopped laughing. She looked at me in amazement and then showed me the two candle stubs she'd brought along. After shedding tears of anger, I poured out tears of repentance, having a firm purpose of not doing it again!

Another time there was another incident with Victoire, but this time I had no repentance because I had kept calm. I wanted an inkstand which was on the shelf of the fireplace in the kitchen; being too little to take it down, I very nicely asked Victoire to give it to me, but she refused telling me to get up on a chair. I took a chair without saying a word but thinking she wasn't too nice; wanting to make her feel it, I searched out in my little head what offended me the most. She often called me "a little brat" when she was annoyed at me and this humbled me very much. So *before jumping off* my chair, I turned around with *dignity* and said: "Victoire, you are a brat!" Then I made my escape, leaving her to meditate on the profound statement I had just made. The result wasn't long in coming, for soon I heard her shouting: "M'amz'elle Marie Therese just called me a brat!" Marie came and made me ask pardon, and I did so without having contrition. I thought that if Victoire didn't want to stretch her *big arm* to do me a *little service*, she merited the title *brat*.

And still Victoire was very fond of me and I was also fond of her. One day, she drew me out of a *great peril* into which I had tumbled through my own fault. She was ironing the clothes and she had at her side a bucket filled with water. I was watching her and at the same time was swinging on a chair which was a habit of mine. All of a sudden, the chair slipped from under me and I fell, not on the floor, but into the bucket. My feet met my head and I filled the bucket like a little chick fills an eggshell! Poor Victoire gaped at me with great surprise, having never seen anything like it in her life.... With a little trouble she saved me from my *great peril* but not my dress and all the rest of my clothes which she had to change. I was soaked to the skin!

Another time I fell into the fireplace where fortunately there was no fire lighted at the time. Victoire had to draw me out and shake off the ashes which covered me completely. These incidents happened to me on a Wednesday when you [her sister Pauline for whom she is writing this account] were at singing practice with Marie.[46]

Directly after this, Thérèse mentions the parish priest who came calling at the front door which Victoire answered: "It was on Wednesday also that Father Ducellier came to pay a visit. Victoire told him nobody was home except Thérèse, and so he came out into the *kitchen* to see me and look over my homework; I was very proud to receive my *confessor*, for a short time before I made my first confession to him."[47]

One time when M. Martin was away from Alençon on business, Thérèse, while in her attic room, believed she saw him down in the garden and he appeared

---

[46] Ibid., pp. 38–40.
[47] Ibid.

to have a covering over his head. She called out to him, "Papa! Papa!" Her sister Marie ran to her and asked why she called out:

> [I] told her what I had just seen. To calm me down Marie said it was no doubt Victoire who hid her head in her apron to frighten me, but when asked about it, Victoire said she hadn't left her kitchen. Besides, I was very sure I'd seen a man and this man had Papa's appearance. Then all three of us [Thérèse, Pauline, and Marie] went behind the screen of trees, but when we found no mark indicating the passage of anyone, you [Pauline] told me to think no more about it.[48]

The last time Victoire is cited in the *Story of a Soul* occurs during Thérèse's strange sickness when she was ten. Thérèse was bedridden most of the time and very well taken care of by all especially Marie:

> [Never] did she [Marie] show the slightest sign of annoyance, and still I gave her a lot of trouble, not even allowing her to be away from me. She had to go and eat her meals with Papa, but I never stopped calling her all the time she was away. Victoire, who was taking care of me was at times obliged to go and get my dear "Mama" as I called her.[49]

It was the Guérins who engaged Victoire to work for the Martin family. She started in November 1877 right after the Martins moved to Lisieux from Alençon following the death of Mme. Martin. Thérèse was four years old at the time and when Victoire ended her employ with them in 1884, Thérèse was eleven.

In 1926, a year after the canonization of St. Thérèse, Victoire (then in Paris) defended the strict upbringing of the Martin girls:

> [Those] young ladies [the Martin sisters] never went out alone; and when their father did not accompany them, it was I who went with them. I always saw them very reserved, and models of good style. There were not many families like them. I have been in service in all classes of society, but I have met only one other family to compare with them.[50]

Victoire further stated that "little Thérèse was very well brought up, and I admired her for her sweetness and angelic ways. She was always obedient and a little angel of gentleness. She was very shy."[51]

After leaving the Martins in 1884, Victoire Pasquer established herself as a laundress in Lisieux for about three years. Then she moved and worked in Saint-Ouen (Seine) in 1887, in Louveciennes (Seine-et-Oise) in 1907, and Paris off and on from 1914 to 1932. When she was seventy-seven she visited the Lisieux Carmel (October 1934) and spoke to Sister Marie of the Sacred Heart (Marie Martin) who encouraged her to make the "Act of Offering to the Merciful Love" that St. Thérèse had composed. Almost a year later Victoire died in Villejuif (Seine) on August 10, 1935.

---

48 *Story of a Soul*, chapter II, p. 46. (The mystery was never solved.)
49 Ibid., p. 63.
50 Piat, *op. cit.*, p. 275.
51 Ibid., p. 324.

C. Doctors, Tutors, and Others

1. MLLE. GODARD AND EDOUARD KRUG: *Art teachers*
2. DR. NOTTA: *The Martins' family doctor in Lisieux*
3. MME. PAPINAU: *Thérèse's private tutor*
4. ROSE TAILLÉ: *Infant Thérèse's wet nurse*
5. TOM: *Thérèse's childhood pet dog*

1. MLLE. GODARD AND EDOUARD KRUG
Art teachers

YOUNG LADIES IN THE SAME SOCIAL CLASS AS THE MARTIN AND GUÉRIN girls often took art, sculpture, or music lessons especially if they had the interest or the aptitude. This was true of Céline Martin and Jeanne Guérin who loved to do art work. Jeanne's sister Marie Guérin was gifted with a lovely voice and in playing the piano.

Two art teachers played a significant part in the artistic development of the two girls mentioned above and, by association, with Thérèse herself though she never took lessons from a professional art instructor. They were Mlle. A. Godard and Edouard Krug. The elderly Mlle. Godard who lived in Lisieux was a somewhat eccentric teacher who had been a student in Paris of Léon Cogniet (1794–1880). He was an officer of the Legion of Honor, won the *prix de Rome in 1817*, decorated a ceiling at the Louvre, and taught at prestigious art academies in Paris. Mlle. Godard gave drawing, painting, and clay modeling instructions to Céline and Jeanne for a while. Thérèse also loved drawing and eagerly wished she could have received art lessons as well, but, unfortunately, was not given the opportunity.

Thérèse, her sisters, and her cousins often sketched the picturesque Norman countryside on short trips and holiday visits to their Aunt Guérin's mother, Mme. Fournet, who lived on a farm in Saint-Ouen-le-Pin, some six miles from Lisieux. Mme. Guérin recorded the experience the girls had on one such sketching excursion that provides insight into the pedagogical methods of Mlle. Godard:

> We are all very happy here. Thérèse's face is always radiant with joy. She is enjoying herself very much at sketching; she and Marie [her daughter] have undertaken to do the house on the farm. I am [assuming the role of] *Mademoiselle* Godard, and I supervise my pupils closely. Like her, I am very severe but also very much inclined to compliments, so I see two future *artists* in my pupils.[1]

---

[1] From a letter by Mme. Guérin to her husband Isidore dated August 7, 1884.

The second art teacher was Edouard Krug (1829–1901), also a pupil of Cogniet as well as of the more famous religious painter, Flandrin (one of three brothers who were all artists). He is classified as a painter of history and of portraits. At the *Exposition Universelle* of 1889 he won a bronze medal and received the honor of Chevalier de la Légion d'Honneur in 1897. His work was also on exhibition at the Exposition Universelle in 1900 and at the art museum in Caen. One of his large pictures entitled "The Guardian Angel," painted in 1875, hangs above the altar in a right side aisle chapel of the Lisieux Cathedral of St. Pierre. He executed frescoes in the Benedictine Abbey; particularly noteworthy was an apotheosis of the Blessed Virgin that adorned the dome on the wall high above the main altar of the Abbey chapel. The Abbey was completely destroyed during the Second World War, therefore all the work he did there does not exist. Father Piat describes Céline's contact with him:

> M. Guérin [Thérèse's uncle] had become a prominent figure in Lisieux. Thus it was that he became acquainted with M. Krug, a well-known artist, originally from Normandy and a student of Flandrin. He invited him to give lessons to Céline, who derived a great deal of profit from such training. Under the supervision of this master, she tackled some subjects that were difficult to execute. He praised her highly for her skill at composition and was committed to introducing her to the Salon [that held an annual art exhibition in Paris] if she would consent to take some courses of study in the capital. (The young girl did not hesitate to climb up the scaffolding in order to admire, at close range, the frescoes with which her patron was adorning the choir of the Abbey.) On several occasions, M. Krug went to see her at Carmel to inspect her progress, which gave her more confidence. He even offered her his large palette.[2]

Despite her inadequate artistic training, Céline received orders for religious paintings including a large picture of the Assumption above the main altar of the Hotel-Dieu in Bayeux that she painted in 1892, two years before she entered Carmel. She never pursued her art studies any further since her religious vocation became the all-important goal in her life. Yet after becoming a cloistered nun she did not abandon her artistic vocation. With the addition of her photographic accomplishments, her entire artistic output is rather substantial, having produced many drawings, paintings, decorations, miniatures, and some sculpture.

Thérèse learned from Céline's lessons (in the fall of 1887) for she tells us, "I studied, took lessons from Céline, and my clever teacher recognized in me an aptitude for her art."[3] As a result, she apparently felt confident in doing a great deal of art work in the monastery including little color decorations on holy cards, painting statues, pictures in oil or watercolor on canvas and cloth, etc. She even painted a fresco above the altar in the invalids' oratory.

Mlle. Godard died at the end of 1899 or the beginning of 1900. Edouard Krug passed away a year later in 1901.

---

2 Piat, *Céline*, p. 51.
3 *Story of a Soul*, chapter V, p. 112.

2. Dr. Alphonse-Henri Notta (1824–1914)
The Martins' family doctor in Lisieux

In December of 1876, before Dr. Notta was brought into the case, Dr. Prévost in Alençon was consulted by the Martins regarding Zélie's painful symptoms that eventually led to her death. His blunt manner in announcing his diagnosis that she had a terminal disease startled everyone. Nonetheless, he did prescribe a medication. Zélie asked him, "Of what use will it be?" In a somber tone he replied, "It is useless; I give it to please patients."[4] After a subsequent visit Marie wrote: "He ordered a sedative for the pains in her neck which, he explained, are the effect of her illness. I thought so myself, for a simple strain would not last so long. He was very polite and very kindly. I think he does not frighten her so much now."[5]

Zélie's brother Isidore, quite disturbed by Dr. Prévost's prognosis, urged his sister to see his friend Dr. Notta, a distinguished surgeon and long time general practitioner in Lisieux. Zélie agreed and reported the ominous results of this visit in a letter to her disconsolate husband back home: "The doctor considers it very regrettable that an operation was not performed at the very first, but it is now too late. However, he seemed to think I can go on for a very long time like this. So let us leave it all in God's hands."[6] Five months later on August 28, 1877, Zélie, age forty-six, died in Alençon.

Six years after this sad death, in March of 1883, the Martins, again at the insistence of Isidore, consulted Dr. Notta. However, this time the patient was Isidore's ten-year-old niece, Thérèse Martin. For a while she had been experiencing severe headaches and weakening health. The death of her mother and the recent loss of her "second mother" (her sister Pauline who had entered the cloistered Carmelite Monastery in Lisieux) affected her deeply. Suddenly, bizarre and unexplainable attacks of convulsive tremblings and even hallucinations struck Thérèse while she was at the home of her relatives, the Guérins. She recorded her memory of this in her autobiography: "He [Uncle Guérin] went to get Doctor Notta the next day, and he judged, as did Uncle, that I had a serious illness and one which had never before attacked a child as young as I. Everybody was puzzled."[7]

Dr. Notta was on the case from March to May and diagnosed her condition as extraordinary, but not hysteria, and thereupon prescribed hydrotherapy. He really treated it as a nervous disease. Thérèse's cousin Jeanne Guérin who later married a doctor (Francis La Néele) recalled: "The doctor treating the case called this disease St. Vitus' dance.[8] Nevertheless, it seems to me that he was somewhat hesitant about this disease and suggested that something else might

---

4 Laveille, *op. cit.*, p. 55.
5 From a letter of Marie Martin to her Aunt Guérin, July 28, 1877.
6 CF 179 from Mme. Martin to her husband, dated December 24, 1876.
7 *Story of a Soul*, chapter III, p. 61.
8 *Chorea minor*—a convulsive nervous disease that occurs generally in early life affecting girls more commonly than boys.

be present—but what?"⁹ These severe symptoms lasted off and on for seven weeks and disappeared almost instantly on Pentecost Sunday, May 13, 1883, when Thérèse said she saw the statue of the Blessed Virgin in her bedroom come alive and smile at her.

The next time we hear of Dr. Notta is during the period Louis Martin suffered paralytic strokes which affected not only his body but his mind. Dr. Notta treated him from 1887 to 1889 and finally found it necessary to have him admitted to Bon Sauveur hospital (*Hôpital du Bon Sauveur*) in Caen on February 12, 1889.

The following year we learn that Céline began to have heart problems that were believed derived from her concerns about her father's medical and mental condition. Her aunt wrote, "This poor Céline was very sick yesterday at your home.... We decided now not to allow her to go so frequently to see her father, and she was the first to agree to this. She is getting so emotional that her health is really being affected. I think it is time to remedy this."¹⁰ Almost fifty years later, Céline wrote: "The problems were such that Dr. La Néele did not want to take sole responsibility for his diagnosis, and he had Dr. Notta come, who prescribed a strong treatment and recommended especially the avoidance of emotional upsets."¹¹

Alphonse-Henri Notta was born in Fourqueux in the department of Seine-et-Oise on February 26, 1824, and died in Lisieux at the age of ninety on July 23, 1914.

3. Mme. Valentine Papinau (1835–1898)
Thérèse's private tutor

THÉRÈSE'S OLDER SISTERS MARIE AND PAULINE WERE HER FIRST TEACHERS from the age of five to eight-and-a-half. Then on October 3, 1881, she was enrolled as a day pupil in the Benedictine Abbey boarding school, *Notre Dame du Pré*, located at the other end of Lisieux. From the very beginning, she was an excellent student, but periodically suffered from severe headaches, emotional problems, and scruples of all kinds together with several physical ailments. She wrote years later that "the five years I spent in school were the saddest in my life, and if I hadn't had Céline with me, I wouldn't have remained there and would have become sick in a month."¹²

When Céline finished her studies at the Abbey in 1885, Thérèse had to go to school without her. As a result she became ill and was withdrawn by her father in March 1886, in the second trimester of the 1885–1886 academic year, when she was thirteen-and-a half. Thérèse as a matter of fact never completed her formal education in a school which normally should have lasted two more years. However, without any delay, her father provided private lessons for her

---

9 As cited in Goerres, *The Hidden Face*, p. 417.
10 Letter written by Mme. Guérin to her daughter Jeanne La Néele, dated March 18, 1891.
11 From a letter of Sister Geneviève dated September 19, 1940, as quoted in note 1, p. 714 to LT 124 (October 1890) in *General Correspondence*.
12 *Story of a Soul*, chapter III, p. 53.

C. Doctors, Tutors, and Others

with the fifty-year-old Mme. Papinau who lived with her mother and a cat at 57 Grand Rue, off of Place Saint-Pierre, not far from where her cousins the Guerins lived.

Thérèse went three or four times a week accompanied by her father for one-hour sessions. She received lessons from September 21, 1886, to April 1887. In all, she attended for ten months and received sixty-two lessons. Then after her trip to Rome (November 4 to December 2, 1887) she resumed lessons with Mme. Papinau. They amounted to about thirteen from December 1887 to March 1888.[13] She entered Carmel on April 9, 1888. Thérèse describes in her own delightful way and with quite a bit of insight what transpired at the Papinau residence when she was taking private lessons:

> I left the Abbey, then, at the age of thirteen, and continued my education by taking several lessons a week at the home of *Mme. Papineau* [sic]. She was a very good person, *very well educated* but a little old-maidish in her ways. She lived with her mother, and it was charming to see the little household they made up together, all three of them (for the cat [named "Monoti"] was one of the *family*, and I had to put up with its purring on my copybooks and even to admire its pretty form). I had the advantage of living within the intimacy of the family; as Les Buissonnets was too far for the somewhat old limbs of my teacher, she requested that I come and take the lessons in her home. When I arrived, I usually found only old lady Cochain [her mother] who looked at me *"with her big clear eyes"* and then called out in a calm, sententious voice: *"Mme. Papineau ... Ma ... d'moizelle Thê ... rèse est là!..."* Her daughter answered promptly in an *infantile* voice: "Here I am, Mamma." And soon the lesson began. Who could believe it! In this antiquely furnished room, surrounded as I was by text books and copybooks, I was often present at the visits of all types of persons: priests, ladies, young girls, etc. Mme. Cochain took on the burden of the conversation as well as she could in order to allow her daughter to conduct my lesson, but on those days I didn't learn very much. With my nose in the book, I heard everything that was said around me and even those things it would have been better for me not to hear because vanity slips so easily into the heart. One lady said I had pretty hair; another, when she was leaving, believing she was not overheard, asked who the very beautiful young girl was. These words, all the more flattering since they were not spoken in my presence, left in my soul a pleasurable impression which showed me clearly how much I was filled with self-love.[14]

The gifted American writer Frances Parkinson Keyes depicts the same academic scene at Mme. Papinau's but with some additional descriptive details:

> She went, several times a week, to the home of an accomplished woman, Mlle. Papineau [sic], who directed her studies expertly. Scholastically, she progressed even more rapidly than she had ever done before. But her lessons were by no means confined to textbooks; they included, both through precept and by

---

13 These facts are from p. 21 in *Les Cahiers d'école de Thérèse de Lisieux*.
14 *Story of a Soul*, chapter IV, pp. 85–86.

example, considerable instruction in the social graces. She was installed in the family parlor, charmingly furnished with valuable antiques, in which her teacher's mother, a lady of the old school, was accustomed to receive her visitors. A bright fire burned on a well-garnished hearth, suitable refreshments were served during the course of the afternoon, and Thérèse's recitations were made to the accompaniment of elegant conversation. Distracting as this occasionally proved, it was not without its beneficial side: the atmosphere, though formal, was distinctly friendly.... Cheered, instead of depressed, by the milieu in which she found herself, she began to expand like a flower.[15]

Thérèse was a fine student and received high honors. One persistent and noticeable weakness, however, was her spelling. There is on record one of Madam Papinau's pedagogical methods for correction of faults. During a dictation exercise on February 16, 1888, Thérèse made some errors; she confused "ou" and "où" as well as "a" and "à." Madane Papinau wrote: "The pupil, Thérèse Martin, will copy ten times: 'The verb *avoir* never takes the *grave* accent.'" This did not help for Thérèse still seemed to have made the same error. Some other repeated errors were with: "*déja*," "*celà*," "*bientot*," as well as "*Jesus*," "*repondre*," "*rejouir*," etc. Surprisingly she even wrote Papinot for Papinau.[16]

Marie Guérin, not quite three years older than her cousin Thérèse, attended the Abbey school with Thérèse, ending her schooling there at fifteen in August 1885 at the same time as Céline Martin. Apparently she was absent a lot from school. It seems that she continued her education with Madame Papinau for while on vacation with her family in Trouville in the summer of 1886, Marie wrote to Thérèse asking about Madame Papinau in a typical school girl manner: "How is Madame Papinau? Is she as monotonous as ever? And are your lessons always going well? Tell me all this in your next letter."[17] Thérèse replied from her home, Les Buissonnets, in Lisieux:

> You asked me in your letter to give you some news about Madame Papinot [*sic*]; she is very well and often inquires about your health. Regarding my lessons, all goes well; for some time now, their number has been increased, and this is why I wasn't able to write you on Sunday.[18]

Thérèse entered Carmel two years later in April of 1888, received the habit on January 10, 1889, was professed on September 8, 1890, and received the black veil on September 34, 1890.

The next time we come across the name of Thérèse's teacher is during Thérèse's retreat before her profession. She asked her sister Pauline (Sister Agnès of Jesus) if Madame should receive a special invitation to attend her Profession which was essentially a private ceremony: "Must I write to Mme. Papinot?... It seems to me that there is no point in doing so, she would not understand. It

---

15 Keyes, *Thérèse: Saint of a Little Way*, p. 91.
16 Note 27, p. 68, in *General Correspondence*, Vol. I.
17 Letter from Marie Guérin to Thérèse, dated June 23, 1886.
18 LT 19 from Thérèse to Marie Guérin, dated June 26, 1886.

would be better perhaps to wait until the receiving of the Veil?"[19] It was consequently deemed more prudent to invite her to the veiling since it was a public one.

Mme. Papinau was born Valentine Cochain in June 1835 in Saint-Pierre-la Rivière (Orne). Her marriage to Jules Papinau produced no children. She died in Lisieux at the age of sixty-three on January 22, 1898, having survived five months after her former student's death little realizing that her pretty, intelligent, and humble blond girl would someday become a glorious, world-famous, and well-loved saint and even doctor of the Roman Catholic Church.

4. Rose Taillé (1836–1908)
Infant Thérèse's wet nurse

Shortly after Thérèse's birth on January 2, 1873, she fell seriously ill with feeding and intestinal problems. The family physician, Dr. Belloc, diagnosed the ailment as enteritis and advised natural feeding to save the infant's life. In the past Zélie had entrusted her two baby boys to Rose Taillé, a wet nurse, who lived in Semallé, a hamlet in flat farm lands—quite a walking distance from Alençon. Her thatched roof peasant cottage consisted of two rooms with one stove. She lived with her rather strong-willed husband Louis-Moïse whom she called "Father Moses" and her four children, the youngest being thirteen-month-old Eugène. She, affectionately called "*La Petite Rose*" ("Little Rose"), was a healthy, good-natured, reliable thirty-seven-year-old woman with a happy disposition.

One day in March, little Thérèse became gravely ill causing her mother to fear for her life. She determined to get Rose immediately. Zélie reported what happened that night to her sister-in-law, Céline Guérin, in Lisieux:

> The night seemed long for Thérèse would take scarcely any food. All the gravest symptoms which had preceded the deaths of my other cherubs were showing themselves, and I was very sad for I was convinced that, in the state of exhaustion she was, I could do nothing more for the poor darling. So I set off at daybreak for the nurse, who lives at Semallé, about six miles from Alençon. My husband was away and I did not want to entrust the success of my enterprise to anyone else. On the lonely road I met two men who rather frightened me, but I said to myself, "I should not care if they killed me!" I felt death in my soul.[20]

Rose went back with Zélie notwithstanding objections from Rose's husband Moïse. When the two women arrived at the Martin home, Thérèse looked as if she was near the end. Zélie continues her story:

> As for me, I went up to my room at once, knelt down before the statue of St. Joseph, and asked him to obtain the grace that my little girl might recover; at the same time, resigning myself to God's will, should He see fit to take her. I do not often cry, but my tears fell whilst I was uttering that prayer.

---

19 LT 112 from Thérèse to Sister Agnès, dated September 1, 1890.
20 From a letter (CF 89) Zélie wrote to Mme. Guérin, March 1873, as quoted in Piat's *Story of a Family*, pp. 127–128.

I scarcely dared to go downstairs; at last I made up my mind. And what did I see but the child feeding greedily! She did not cease until one o'clock; then she rejected a few mouthfuls and lay like one dead on the nurse's lap.

There were five of us around her. All were shocked. One of my lace-workers was there crying, and I felt my blood freeze. The baby did not seem to be breathing. We bent over her, trying in vain to find a sign of life. We saw none, but she was so quiet and peaceful that I thanked God she had died so easily.

At last, after a quarter of an hour, my Thérèse opened her eyes and began to smile. From that moment she was completely cured. Her healthy look returned, as also her liveliness. Since then, all is as well as could be.

But my baby has gone away. It is very sad to have brought up a child for two months and then be compelled to entrust her to the care of strangers. It consoles me to know that God so wills it, since I have done my utmost to nurse her myself. So I have nothing with which to reproach myself on that score.

I should have preferred to keep the nurse in the house, and so would my husband;[21] he did not want the others, but he was very willing to accept this one, for he knows that she is an excellent woman.[22]

So Thérèse was put under the competent care of Little Rose on March 16, 1873. The fresh country air, sunshine, fields, flowers, and of course the excellent nursing care all helped to improve Thérèse's health and might conceivably have instilled in her at this early stage a fondness for nature. She grew to love her nurse as a mother. Little Rose often kept her next to her when selling her farm products at the market in Alençon and even sometimes tied her on top of their only cow, the reddish colored one named "*La Rousette*" ("The Little Russet Lady" or "Redskin"). On occasions when she was left without her, Thérèse was inconsolable. Once when Rose took Thérèse with her to Alençon, she let her off at her parents' home while she went to the market where she had a stall and sold her produce. Thérèse was so distraught over not being with Rose that she had to be taken to the market to calm her down: "As soon as she saw her nurse, she looked at her laughing, and then did not utter another sound. She remained like that all day, whilst the latter sold her butter with all the good country-women."[23] Another time Zélie wrote: "Thérèse is a big baby. She is sun burnt. Her nurse wheels her in the fields, perched on top of bundles of grass, in a wheel-barrow. 'Little Rose' says that one cannot see a more darling child."[24]

Finally, after over a year's separation from her anxious family, Thérèse was allowed by her doctor to return home on April 2, 1874, where her loving parents and sisters greeted her with joyous and thankful hearts.

Three years later, following the untimely death of his wife in 1877, Louis Martin with his five daughters moved to Lisieux leaving his aging but independent mother settled in a country house in Valframbert near Alençon under the

---

21 Rose could not leave her own children and husband the length of time necessary for Thérèse to regain her health.
22 CF 89 from Zelie to Mme. Guérin, March 1873, pp. 128–129. As quoted in Piat's *op. cit.*
23 CF 102. Letter of Zélie to Pauline, May 22, 1873. As quoted in Piat's *op. cit.*, p. 134.
24 CF 106, Zélie to Mme. Guérin, July 20, 1873, as quoted in Piat's *op. cit.* p. 134.

charge of Little Rose whose family and she were then living in this quiet hamlet. She acted as a nurse-companion to Mme. Fannie Martin who died there six years later at the age of eighty-three.

One little amusing incident reported in the correspondence between Marie and Pauline Martin in 1881 deals with Little Rose's ten-year-old son Eugené:

> Papa arrived Saturday morning [from Alençon to Lisieux]. Do you know what he brought Thérèse [eight years old] from her little foster brother [Eugené]? Guess if you can.... A magpie which is being cared for each moment as a child in a cradle. This is Thérèse's sole occupation; she remains whole hours contemplating it in a squirrel cage which Papa bought for her. I'd say it's a doll's house; never have I seen a cage like it.[25]

Sister Geneviève years later added more details to a humorous story that happened to end unhappily:

> We taught it to talk. Then Papa gave it its freedom. This is when our terrors began. If we were seated, the magpie used to come clandestinely, pulling at the buttons on our boots. If we were standing up, it bit at the calves of our legs.... At this time, Thérèse and Céline, having calculated that it took forty turns around the garden to make one league, set out courageously on the road like the wandering Jew. Like him, too, they provided themselves with sticks, a supply of which was placed at the entrance to the garden, to defend themselves from the magpie, which followed them tirelessly, calling out: "Thérèse! Thérèse!"... We closed the magpie within the greenhouse to withdraw ourselves from its persecution. One day, it found the door open and, out of despair, undoubtedly, took advantage of its freedom only by drowning itself in a bucket which was close by.

Years later Sister Geneviève described Little Rose's humble home:

> I thought back to my childhood, when I used to visit my little Thérèse at the home of her nurse, and we were ushered into the one and only room, which served as a kitchen, bedroom, and parlor all at the same time. The floor was hard-packed.... I reflected that truth and freedom, and therefore happiness, dwelled under the old dark beams rather than under artistic ceilings, and I looked forward to the happy moment when I would be transplanted to a poor cell.[26]

La Petite Rose was born Rosalie-Euphrasie Cosnard on January 15, 1836, in Goragains (Sarthe). She married Moïse-Louis Taillé and had four children by him: Rose, born in 1861; Auguste, born in 1863; Marie, born in 1866; and Eugéne, born in 1871. Rose lived to be seventy-three, dying on May 17, 1908, in Ste. Marguerite Carrouges (Orne) and was buried in the little cemetery next to the country church in the adjoining hamlet of Carrouges. A lacey-type metal cross at the head of the flat, earth-covered grave has a heart-shaped plaque in

---

25 This is a fragment of a letter Marie sent to Pauline dated July 11–12, 1881. The next quote is from Note 3 for this letter. This is all originally from CMG III, pp. 61–62.
26 Piat, *Céline*, p. 53.

the middle of which these words are engraved: "Here reposes Rosalie Gosnard, wife [of] Taille died the 17th of May 1908 in her 73rd year. Sincere regrets to her family. Pray to God for her."[27]

The Taille cottage still exists today and is privately owned by people who live across the street from it. A plaque with a small statue of St. Thérèse resting in a little niche above it has these words in French written on it: "The house of the 'Petite Rose' where St. Thérèse of the Child Jesus spent her infancy 1874." It is not open to the public but one is allowed to walk around the building and on the grounds adjoining it. Flat open farmland surrounds the area.

5. TOM
Thérèse's childhood pet dog

AS A CHILD AT *Les Buissonnets* (THE NAME OF THE MARTIN HOUSE IN LISIEUX), Thérèse Martin was accustomed to having animals around the home—rabbits, hens, birds, and goldfish. By the time she was eleven she longed for a more responsive pet, "an animal with hair" as she put it. Her father reminded her that she had "animals with hair; you have rabbits." "That's true," she said, "but I'd like an animal with hair that follows me everywhere and jumps around me!"[28] Whereupon her father gave her a dog on June 26, 1884, fourteen days after her Confirmation. They named the white and black Breton spaniel Tom. He provided an additional amount of joy to the family and indeed a degree of protection also. Thérèse immediately heaped her loving attention on him. When he was sick she prepared food for him, and when she studied he rested protectively under her chair.

One of Tom's favorite places outdoors was under a shady tree in front of the house. He waited patiently for anyone leaving who might walk or play with him. Generally on Mondays beggars and poor people sought help at the gate of Les Buissonnets. Tom, like any dutiful watchdog, barked his resentment at intrusions such as when M. Martin, with the eager assistance of the youthful Thérèse, distributed money that the family set aside during the week for this particular purpose. He followed the family everywhere including visits to church where he would wait forlornly outside until they came out. On one walk with Thérèse and her father, Tom jumped into a lily pond and, in typical canine fashion, rolled in the dirt. M. Martin promptly remarked to Thérèse, "See, that reminds us of a spotless, white soul which becomes soiled by sin."[29]

Thérèse's sister Marie wrote to her father away on a trip to Constantinople, informing him of the humdrum goings-on at home: "What will I say more, dear little Father? We are all well. Thérèse took a walk in the garden yesterday with Tom for more than half an hour because he had not gone out in the morning. She seemed happy to see herself followed so faithfully by her 'hairy beast.'"[30]

---

27 Freely translated by the author.
28 *Manuscript Notebook III* of Sister Geneviève.
29 Wust, *Louis Martin: An Ideal Father*, p. 171.
30 September 3, 1885.

Letters written by family members show that Tom really missed them when they were away and would not eat especially when M. Martin was on any of his long trips. He referred to Tom in one of his few letters as a "brave faithful dog." While a day student at the Benedictine Abbey School in Lisieux, the twelve-year-old Thérèse wrote to her father a letter she used as a composition homework assignment. She concludes with a reference to her dog: "All of us want you to return as soon as possible. [He was on the Constantinople trip] I'm sure that Tom has the same opinion as I, for he is lonesome because of your absence, and I am sure that, for your arrival, he is preparing to wag his tail in the same way that Tobias' dog did [Tobit 11:4] and to welcome you with his joyful bounds."[31]

Thérèse's Aunt Guérin mentions the dog in a letter she wrote to her nieces Céline and Thérèse in Rome during the pilgrimage there with their father: "We always feel very sorry for Tom. He is crying all the time over your departure; however, Maria [her daughter] takes him out every day, she tells me. But see how faithful this beast is and how he loves you. And so beasts and people long for you. You are missed everywhere and we can't get accustomed to your absence."[32] On the same day Marie also wrote a letter to her cousins illustrating again Tom's deep attachment to the family:

> In spite of the winter cold, we paid a visit to your cellar. There were a few pears lost, but what most attracted our attention and our compassion was your dog. Tom does nothing but whimper day and night; he arouses deep pity in us. If, at least, I had a place to put him at our house, I would take him and this would distract him.[33]

Thérèse entered the Carmelite Monastery of Lisieux in April 1888, four months after her fifteenth birthday. Her two older sisters Pauline and Marie were already nuns there. It was quite apparent how much Tom missed the members of the Martin family as each one left the home on vacations or permanently, particularly when Thérèse entered Carmel.

In February 1889 Céline and Léonie left Les Buissonnets for good. The girls stayed temporarily in convent boarding rooms in Caen in order to be near their father who was hospitalized nearby. He had leased Les Buissonnets since their arrival in Lisieux twelve years before. The girls' cousin Marie Guérin regularly went to the house to check on the work done by the gardener, M. Guéret, and laundry women, and to see how the rabbits, birds, and the dog were faring: "Poor Tom," she noted once, "was so happy to see me that he broke his collar."[34] The lease for Les Buissonnets was cancelled on December 25, 1889.

Sometime in October 1889 during the transfer of a few pieces of furniture from Les Buissonnets to the Carmel, the ever-devoted Tom followed the furniture

---
31 LTS 18a, from Thérèse to her father, October 15, 1885.
32 Letter (LD) from Mme. Guérin to Céline and Thérèse, dated November 17, 1887.
33 LC 63, letter from Marie Guérin to Thérèse, dated November 17, 1887.
34 Note 3 to letter (LT 84) from Marie Guérin to Léonie Martin, dated March 14, 1889.

laden wagons through the streets and into the monastery by way of the workmen's entrance. Even though a veil covered her face, he instantly recognized Thérèse who was then a novice and the portress for the convent. Céline describes the poignant encounter:

> Once inside the cloister, the faithful Tom raised his ears, then, looking in all directions as if to get his bearings, he sprang on his little mistress, leaping up at her face and making a thousand bounds in all directions. She was obliged to lift her large veil and hide Tom under it, for he could not control his joy. Then tears shone in Thérèse's eyes, a flood of memories pulled at her head, [and] she was forced to tear herself away from all this, so great was her emotion.[35]

The Martin household eventually dispersed with the death of Thérèse's father in 1894 and the subsequent joining of Céline with her three sisters at the Lisieux Carmel; thus leaving Léonie the only one left of the Martins "in the world." Whereupon poor old Tom was "adopted" by the Guérins who also took in Léonie. Two years after Thérèse died, Léonie too entered a convent and became a Visitation nun in Caen. What happened to Tom at this point is not certain for no further news or reference to Tom is available.

---

[35] *Manuscript Notebook III*, p. 103, by Sister Geneviève.

D. Thérèse's School Companions

1. **Hélène Doise:** *In same catechism class with Thérèse*
2. **Alexandrine and Marie Domin:** *The Chaplain's nieces, First Communicants with Thérèse*
3. **Jean-Louise Raoul:** *Thérèse tried in vain to gain her friendship*
4. **Marie-Blanche Dupont:** *Older student at the Abbey school*
5. **Marguerite-Leonie-Augustine Leroy:** *Older Abbey student*

Today millions of people love St. Thérèse. Yet when she was a young girl, Thérèse Martin was at times, bullied, intimidated, or ignored by many of her classmates. On the other hand, some did appreciate her as an excellent student and even perhaps envied her. The teachers of course were aware of her superior academic ability and her rare spirituality. They truly loved and admired her.

It is quite startling to know that Thérèse's uncle and aunt held the following unexpected opinion of her intelligence and academic competence as a young girl:

> I succeeded very well in my studies, was almost always first, and my greatest successes were history and composition. All my teachers looked upon me as a very intelligent student, but it wasn't like that at Uncle's house where I was taken for a little dunce, good and sweet, and with right judgment, yes, but incapable and clumsy.
>
> I am surprised at this opinion which Uncle and Aunt had of me, and no doubt still have, for I hardly ever spoke, being very timid. When I wrote anything, my *terrible scrawl* and my spelling, which was nothing less than original, did not make much of an impression on anyone. In the little tasks of sewing, embroideries, and others, I succeeded well, it is true, in the estimation of my teachers; but the stiff and *clumsy* way I *held my work* justified the poor opinion they had of me. I look upon this as a grace: God, wanting my heart for Himself alone, answered my prayer already "changing into bitterness all the consolations of earth." [*The Imitation of Christ*, III, 26:3] They often spoke highly of the intelligence of others in my presence, but of mine they never said a word, and so I concluded I didn't have any and was resigned to see myself deprived of it.[1]

Thérèse Martin's closest early childhood friends were really only her own sisters. This was exclusively so during her first four years of life when her mother was still alive and they were living in Alençon. Actually no need presented itself to find friends outside the home. Her sister Céline, almost four years her senior, was her inseparable playmate. Their mother wrote about this from time to time

---
[1] *Story of a Soul*, chapter IV, p. 82.

in her letters one of which Thérèse quotes in her autobiography: "Céline and she [Thérèse, age three] are very fond of each other, and are sufficient unto themselves, for passing the times." [2] Later on Thérèse confesses that "Céline had become the confidante of my thoughts. Ever since Christmas [1886] we could understand each other; the distance of age no longer existed because I had grown in both height and grace." [3] The ultimate harmony of friendship was expressed in Thérèse's calling Céline the "sweet echo of my soul." [4]

In 1877, after Mme. Martin died, M. Martin and his daughters moved to their new home in Lisieux within walking distance of their uncle and aunt, the Guérins. Consequently, Thérèse's contacts with her Guérin cousins, Jeanne and Marie, increased and friendships cemented. At this point Marie Guérin became Thérèse's next closest friend. "Cousin Marie and I were always of the same opinion and our tastes were so much the same that once our *union of wills* passed all bounds." [5]

Thérèse's association with others expanded to the Guérin's relatives, the Maudelonde sisters: Marguerite, Céline, and Hélene—all around her age. Though not blood related, Thérèse considered these girls as cousins.

Thérèse had been at home under the tutelage of her older sisters Marie and Pauline until eight-and-a-half years of age. Then beginning in October 1881 and for the next five years she was enrolled as a day student at the Benedictine Abbey of Notre-Dame-du-Pré in Lisieux. She, Céline, and the Guérin sisters walked to and from school together. The school enrollment then amounted to around sixty girls. The age at graduation was usually sixteen. In France at that time children were placed according to ability (assessed by an entrance exam) and not by age group.

The students soon learned that this young, shy, sensitive girl Thérèse surpassed them in intelligence, refinement, and spirituality, thus engendering envy and antagonism on the part of some older girls—one in particular:

> [When] I went to boarding school I was the most advanced of the children of my age. I was placed, as a result, in a class where the pupils were all older than I. One of them was about thirteen or fourteen and she wasn't too intelligent, but she was really adept at influencing the students and even the teachers. When she noticed I was so young, almost always first in the class, and loved by all the Sisters, she experienced a jealousy pardonable in a student. She made me pay in a thousand ways for my little successes. [6]

Thérèse's superior qualities coupled with extreme shyness, ineptitude in sports (she suffered from shortness of breath), inability to defend herself, and the ready flow of tears in face of adversities contributed to her isolation from

---

2 CF 172, from Mme. Martin to her daughter Pauline, dated November 3, 1876, in *Story of a Soul*, chapter I, p. 25.
3 *Story of a Soul*, chapter V, p. 103.
4 LT 89 from Thérèse to Céline, April 26, 1889.
5 *Story of a Soul*, chapter III, p. 55.
6 Ibid., p. 53.

the other children and her overall discomfort at school. Even at her young age, Thérèse understood her difficulty in forming friendships: "I didn't know how to play like other children and as a consequence wasn't a very pleasant companion. I did my best, however, to imitate them but without much success. I was very much bored by it all, especially when we spent the whole afternoon *dancing quadrilles* [with her cousins' cousins, the Maudelonde girls]."[7] She herself confessed that "the five years I spent at school were the saddest in my life, and if my dear Céline had not been with me I could not have stayed there for a single month without becoming ill."[8]

In a testimony she offered nearly thirty years later at the Diocesan Inquiry held in Lisieux in 1910 and 1911, a fellow student (Marguerite Leroy) gave her perceptive reasons why she thought Thérèse was unable to relate to her peers: "… it was the contrast between the exquisite delicacy of the mutual understanding and forms of piety that existed in the family milieu, and the composition of the boarding school students that, at the time, comprised a certain number of rather coarse students."[9] Thérèse with her exceptional gentility also realized the differences:

> [I] had to come in contact with students who were much different, distracted, and unwilling to observe regulations, and this made me very unhappy. I had a happy disposition, but I didn't know how to enter into games of my age-level; often during the recreations, I leaned against a tree and studied my companions at a distance, giving myself up to serious reflections![10]

Thérèse insightfully evaluated her own attempts at forming friendships:

> I tried to make friends with little girls my own age, and especially with two of them [Jeanne Raoul and Félicie Malling]. I loved them and they, in their turn, loved me insofar as they were *capable*. But alas!… I was unable to succeed.… How can a heart given over to the affection of creatures be intimately united with God? I feel this is not possible. I encountered only bitterness where stronger souls met with joy.… I have no merit at all, then, in not having given myself up to the love of creatures. I was preserved from it only through God's mercy![11]

Because of sickness and her inability to function in a regular classroom or school environment, Thérèse left school at thirteen in the winter of 1886 and received private tutoring lessons. A year later, however, she asked to become a member of the Association of the Children of Mary at the Abbey school:

> I left the Abbey without being received into the Association of Mary. Having left before completing my studies, I did not have permission to enter as a student; I admit this privilege didn't excite my envy, but, thinking that all my sisters had been "children of Mary," I feared I would be less a child of my

---

7 Ibid., p. 54.
8 Ibid.
9 *Vie Thérèsienne*, July 1980, page 194.
10 *Story of a Soul*, chapter IV, pp. 82–83.
11 Ibid.

heavenly Mother than they were. I went very humbly (in spite of what it cost me) to ask for permission to be received into the Association at the Abbey. The mistress didn't want to refuse me, but she placed as a condition that I come twice a week in the afternoon in order to prove my worthiness. Far from giving me any pleasure, this permission cost me very much.... I was content ... to greet the one in charge, and then go and work in silence until the end of the [sewing] lesson....[12]

She continues, revealing her thoughts about friendship:

No one paid any attention to me, and I would go up to the choir of the chapel and remain before the Blessed Sacrament until the moment when Papa came to get me. This was my only consolation, for was not Jesus my *only friend*? I knew how to speak only to Him; conversations with creatures, even pious conversations, fatigued my soul.... Ah! it was really for the Blessed Virgin alone that I was coming to the Abbey. Sometimes I felt *alone*, very much alone, and as in the days of my life as a day-boarder when I walked sick and sad in the big yard. I repeated these words which always gave rise to a new peace and strength in my heart: "Life is your barque not your home!" [Wisdom 5:10][13]

The girls most involved with Thérèse include these four among the six who received their First Communion with her in 1884:[14] Amélie-Alexandrine and Marie Domin, Félicie Malling, and Jeanne Raoul. (The other two were J. Lesforgettes and L. Delarue.)

Thérèse might have thought that "no one paid attention" to her but she was indeed noticed as we shall see in the profiles of Helene Doise,[15] Marguerete Leroy, and Marie Dupont.

1. Hélène Doise
(Mère Ste. Marie)
In same catechism class with Thérèse

HÉLÈNE DOISE WAS NOT ACTUALLY A FRIEND OF THÉRÈSE BUT ATTENDED the same catechism classes with her taught by Father Domin on Thursdays and Sundays[16] which were held in the convent chapel and on other days in the wainscoted *grand parloir* of the Abbey school. Frances Parkinson Keyes (1885–1970), the noted writer of novels, non-fiction, and winner of the Nobel Prize for Literature, wrote a unique biography of St. Thérèse of Lisieux. She interviewed a number of people who knew Thérèse personally. One of them was Mother Saint Marie who before she became a nun was Helen Doise, a school companion of Thérèse Martin. In her delightful book, Keyes describes, in her

---

12 Ibid., pp. 86–87.
13 Ibid., p. 87.
14 Descouvemont, *op. cit*, p. 58.
15 She apparently did not receive her First Communion with Thérèse but attended catechism classes with her. She later became a Benedictine nun named Mère Ste. Marie.
16 See p. 44 in Gaucher's *op. cit.*

own colorful and graphic style, Thérèse and others in the room where the girls learned their catechism:

> [Three] benches were arranged to form a double L opposite the seat occupied by Monsieur l'Abbé Domain, the grave-faced, round-cheeked, full-bodied chaplain of the Abbey.... Thérèse herself was always so early [to class] that she secured the seat nearest to him, where she fastened her eyes eagerly upon him and drank in every word that he said. The little girl who sat opposite her, Helen Doise, remembers to this day how she looked as she sat there, her gentle little face kindled with interest, the sun, streaming in through the mullioned windows behind her, falling full on her golden hair. After a lapse of over half a century, the expression on the fine old face of Mother Ste. Marie, the Benedictine nun who "in the world" was Helene Doise, lights to radiance as she talks about Thérèse's hair with the sun streaming across it. "It was the most beautiful hair I ever saw in my life, Madame," she says, her rich voice suddenly vibrant, as she sits talking about Thérèse with a privileged visitor who has been admitted to the same *parloir* where those famous catechism classes were held. "I shall never forget it, never, never ... never...."[17]

Incidentally, Mme. Keyes wrote that years later she heard from a man who observed Thérèse at church when he was a little boy and gave her a similar description of Thérèse's hair: "Illumined by the shafts of light which streamed from the stained glass window, these [Thérèse's bountiful golden curls] took on added radiance. 'I have never seen such hair before or since.... It was simply superb.'"[18]

2. AMÉLIE-ALEXANDRINE AND MARIE DOMIN
The Chaplain's nieces, First Communicants with Thérèse

THÉRÈSE MARTIN AND SIX OTHER GIRLS RECEIVED THEIR FIRST COMMUNION on May 8, 1884, at the Benedictine Abbey in Lisieux. A year later the same group attended a ceremony commemorating the one year anniversary of their First Communion which the French called the Second Communion. The then current episcopal dictum stated that a child must receive First Communion within the year of his or her eleventh birthday. Thérèse just turned eleven on January 2, 1884, and wanted to receive her First Communion with her classmates in May 1883. Despite her birthday falling only two days after the start of the new year, the authorities refused to wave the rule. Petitioning by family members, including her socially prominent Uncle Guérin who even went to the bishop in Bayeux seeking a dispensation, was of no avail.

The school chaplain and catechism instructor Abbé Domin happened to have two of his nieces—Amélie-Alexandrine and Marie Domin—preparing for First Communion at the same time with Thérèse. Traditionally the girl who received the best grades in catechism read on behalf of all the other

---
17 Keyes, *op. cit.*, pp. 84–85.
18 Ibid., Endnote 19-A, pp. 180–181.

communicants the Act of Consecration to the Blessed Virgin at Vespers on First Communion day. Since the Abbé's two nieces were among the group, the nuns thought they should chose one of them. When Thérèse heard of this she was quite disturbed because she had been the top student. In fact, during classes the Abbé even called her his "Little Doctor of Theology." She was eventually given the honor after much pleading by Thérèse's oldest sister Marie and her Aunt Guérin with the directress Mother Saint-Placid and the chaplain. Years later Thérèse wrote that "in the afternoon, it was I who made the Act of Consecration to the Blessed Virgin. It was only right that I *speak* in the name of my companions to my Mother in heaven. I who had been deprived at such an early age of my earthly Mother."[19]

Amélie-Alexandrine-Marie Domin (1873–1944) married Joseph Dupont and died at seventy-one in Caen during World War II.

3. JEANNE-LOUISE RAOUL (1873–1936)
Thérèse tried in vain to gain her friendship

THÉRÈSE REFERS IN HER AUTOBIOGRAPHY TO TWO GIRLS WHOSE FRIENDSHIP she sought but never obtained. Though she does not mention their names, Jeanne-Louise Raoul is most likely the one she especially liked. Biographical data on the other girl, Félicie Malling, is not available.

> My heart, sensitive and affectionate as it was, would have easily surrendered had it found a heart capable of understanding it. I tried to make friends with little girls my own age, and especially with two of them. I loved them and they, in their turn, loved me insofar as they were *capable*. But alas! how *narrow* and *flighty* is the heart of creatures! Soon I saw my love was misunderstood. One of my friends was obliged to go back to her family and she returned to school a few months later. During her absence, I *had thought about her*, treasuring a little ring she had given me. When I saw my companion back again my joy was great, but all I received from her was a cold glance. My love was not understood. I felt this and I did not beg for an affection that was refused, but God gave me a heart which is so faithful that once it has loved purely, it loves always. And I continued to pray for my companion and I still love her.[20]

Jeanne-Louise Raoul was born near the Abbey in the Saint-Desir district of Lisieux, on November 26, 1873. She and Thérèse received their First and Second Communion together. Jeanne was also Céline's confirmation godmother.

Jeanne's first husband, Monsieur Chaumont, died, after which she married a Monsieur Vandier. On August 30, 1936, she passed away in Lons-le-Saunier (Jura) at the age of sixty-three—eleven years after a friend she rejected was canonized as one of the greatest saints of modern times, proclaimed patroness of the universal missions, and at that point under consideration as a candidate for Doctor of the Church.

---

19 *Story of a Soul*, chapter IV, p. 78. Thérèse was the only First Communicant whose mother was not living.
20 Ibid., pp. 82–83.

4. **MARIE-BLANCHE DUPONT** (1867–1935)
   (SISTER SAINT JOHN THE EVANGELIST, O.S.B.)
   Older student at the Abbey school

MARIE-BLANCHE DUPONT (SIX YEARS THÉRÈSE'S SENIOR AND ONE OF FATHER Domin's nieces) always appreciated Thérèse's rare spiritual and mental qualities, though she was not in constant contact with her. She met Thérèse for the first time on the day of Thérèse's First Communion, May 8, 1884, which she attended because her two cousins, the Domin girls Marie and Alexandrine, were also first communicants.[21] At that time her mother noticed Thérèse's eyes were red as if she had been crying which was true, however, not because of sadness but because of joy.

The next time Marie Dupont met Thérèse occurred when she returned to the Benedictine Abbey boarding school in June 1885 at the age of eighteen to study and prepare for her exams as a teacher. She found Thérèse edifying, shy, serious, and somewhat withdrawn. Thérèse gave a most telling answer to Marie Dupont when she asked her if she was always silent in school when she was supposed to be. Thérèse, taken aback by this question, responded that she never talked when it was not allowed. Marie, in a kind of teasing way, pretended to doubt her sincerity. But Thérèse, now very hurt, retorted with a surprisingly curt but certainly true rebuttal: "Marie!... I never lie." ("*Marie!... je ne mens jamais.*")[22]

Before Thérèse became a member of the Children of Mary on May 31, 1887, she had to return to the Abbey two or three times a week to be properly certified for admission. Marie Dupont was then not only the president but the secretary of the association. She reported on August 11, 1911, at the Diocesan Inquiry a minor thing that seemed to bother her. When making out a list of all the members, she forgot Thérèse's name. It was not until after Thérèse's death that she noticed this error and corrected it.

Marie-Blanche Dupont was born on May 11, 1867, in Balleroy, in the diocese of Bayeux. Her father was Théodore Dupont, a merchant, and her mother Léontine Domin. She became a Benedictine nun with the name Sister Saint John the Evangelist and taught at the same school she and Thérèse had attended. Her profession took place on August 12, 1890. On March 19, 1935, she died at the age of sixty-eight, after having been a religious for forty-five years.

5. **MARGUERITE-LÉONIE-AUGUSTINE LEROY** (1867–?)
   (SISTER MARIE OF THE HOLY ROSARY)
   Older Abbey student

SEVERAL OF THÉRÈSE'S FELLOW STUDENTS AT THE ABBEY SCHOOL BECAME nuns and years later one of them, Marguerite Leroy, entered the Benedictine Order and assumed the name Sister Marie of the Holy Rosary. The thirty-second witness, part of the testimony follows that she gave at the Diocesan Inquiry held

---

21 When Marie was Sister St. John the Evangelist, she claimed at the Diocesan Inquiry on August 11, 1911, that there was some kind of a family connection with the Martins.
22 Marie was the 31st witness on August 11, 1911 and gave this testimony.

on August 12, 1911, in Lisieux, concerning the life and virtues of Sister Thérèse. These hearings in the early phases of the process led to Thérèse's beatification in 1923.

> During the two years that I knew Thérèse Martin at the Benedictine school (1882–1884) I found her shy and sensitive. Because of that, and also because I was six years older than her, I left her with the "little ones" and did not establish any close relationship. But I still saw in her, without being too clearly aware of it, an exceptional delicacy of conscience which inspired one with real respect for her....
>
> I remember her asking me one day [Thérèse was nine at the time] if she could talk to me during playtime. I was president of a kind of sodality in the house ["Child of the Holy Angels"], and, as such, the younger girls used to sometimes ask me for advice or encouragement concerning their conduct. I expected something similar on this occasion, but to my surprise and, indeed, embarrassment, she said, "Marguerite, I would like you to teach me how to meditate." I remember this incident clearly.[23]

Sister Marie was born Marguerite-Leonie-Augustine Leroy on June 27, 1867, in Lisieux and made her profession as a Benedictine nun in the same town on July 2, 1900, at the age of thirty-three.

---

23 O'Mahony, *op. cit.*, pp. 276–277.

CHAPTER 4

NUNS

A. At the Benedictine Abbey of Notre-Dame-du-Pré
B. At the Carmel in Lisieux
C. In Other Orders

A. At the Benedictine Abbey of Notre-Dame-du-Pré

1. Mère Saint-Francis de Sales: *Teacher at the abbey school*
2. Mère Saint Léon: *Teacher who wrote a book about Thérèse at the abbey school*
3. Mère Saint-Placide: *Director of the abbey school*

> *I have often heard it said that the time spent at school is the best and happiest of one's life. It wasn't this way for me. The five years I spent in school were the saddest in my life, and if I hadn't had Céline with me, I couldn't have remained there and would have become sick in a month.*[1]
> — St. Thérèse

This unhappy revelation opens chapter 3 of Thérèse's autobiography and continues with an explanation of why these five years at the Benedictine Abbey convent school in Lisieux were so distressing for her:

You [Pauline] had instructed me so well, dear Mother, that when I went to boarding school I was the most advanced of the children of my age. I was placed, as a result, in a class where the pupils were all older than I [Thérèse was eight years and ten months old]. One of them was about thirteen or fourteen and she wasn't too intelligent, but she was really adept at influencing the students and even the teachers. When she noticed I was so young, almost always first in the class, and loved by all the Sisters, she experienced a jealousy pardonable in a student. She made me pay in a thousand ways for my little successes.

As I was timid and sensitive by nature, I didn't know how to defend myself and was content to cry without saying a word and without complaining *even to you* about what I was suffering. I didn't have enough virtue, however, to rise above these miseries of life, so my poor little heart suffered very much. Each evening I was back at home, fortunately, and then my heart expanded.

---
[1] *Story of a Soul*, chapter III, p. 53.

274   CHAPTER 4: *Nuns*

Plate 10

Nuns 1

(CC) = Carmelite Choir Sister   (CL) = Carmelite Lay Sister   (CE) = Carmelite Extern Sister

A. Sr. Amy of Jesus

B. Sr. Anne of the Sacred Heart (CC)

C. Rev. Mother Geneviève (CC)

D. Mother Hermance of the Heart of Jesus (CC)

E. Sr. Margaret Mary of the Sacred Heart (CC)

F. Mother Marie de Gonzague (CC)

G. Sr. Marie of Jesus (CC)

H. Sr. Marie of the Trinity (CC)

I. Sr. Marie of St. Joseph (CC)

J. Sr. Marie of the Angels (CC)

K. Sr. Marie Emmanuel (CC)

L. Sr. Marie Philomena (CC)

A. At the Benedictine Abbey of Notre-Dame-du-Pré

Plate 11

Nuns 2

(CC) = Carmelite Choir Sister   (CL) = Carmelite Lay Sister   (CE) = Carmelite Extern Sister

M. Sr. St. John the Baptist (CC)

N. Sr. St. John of the Cross (CC)

O. Sr. St. Raphael of the Heart of Mary (CC)

P. Sr. St. Stanislas (CC)

Q. Sr. Teresa of Jesus (CC)

R. Sr. Teresa of Saint Augustine (CC)

S. Sr. Marie of the Incarnation (CL)

T. Sr. Mary Magdalene

U. Sr. Martha of Jesus (CL)

V. Sr. St. Vincent de Paul (CL)

W. Sr. Marie Elizabeth (CE)

X. Mother St. Léon, Benedictine nun

I would jump up on Papa's lap, telling him about the marks they were giving me, and his kiss made me forget my troubles. How happy I was to announce the results of my *first composition*, one in sacred history, where I missed getting the maximum grade by *one point* only, and this because I didn't know the name of Moses' father [Amram]. I was then the first and was wearing a beautiful silver badge.... The poor little thing needed these family joys very much [love, recognition, praise, and little prizes], for without them life at the boarding school would have been too hard.[2]

Thérèse's older sisters Léonie (a boarder from 1878 to 1881) and Céline (a day student from 1878 to 1885) were students at the Abbey before Thérèse was admitted. Prior to Thérèse's admission to the Benedictine Abbey school, she was home schooled for three years (1878–1881) beginning at age four-and-a-half. Her teachers were her two older sisters: Marie (17) and Pauline (16). The former taught her penmanship and the latter, reading, grammar, spelling, arithmetic, sacred history, and catechism. The last two were her favorite subjects.

Thérèse enrolled at the school right after Léonie finished her schooling there at eighteen. Céline went to school with Thérèse until she completed her studies at sixteen, leaving Thérèse all alone at school without her moral support. She lasted only five months, then left, continuing her studies with a private tutor.

The Benedictine Abbey of Notre-Dame-du-Pré was located in a section of Lisieux almost a mile (1.5 km) south-west of Thérèse's home, Les Buissonnets. In Thérèse's time it consisted of several ancient buildings built originally as a monastery for contemplative Benedictine nuns. Its foundress and first abbess was the widow Countess de Les Céline, first cousin of William the Conqueror. She established her first foundation, however, not in Lisieux, but at Saint-Pierre-sur-Dives, a little town south of Lisieux, in the year 1011. Thirty-five years later in 1046, she and her nuns moved to a small piece of land in Lisieux that William the Conqueror granted them called Saint-Désir. It wasn't until the seventeenth century that the nuns began to give instructions to young girls of the area. These nuns suffered much during the French Revolution as did all religious communities and were finally forced to leave their abbey. Shortly after they were arrested and imprisoned. Luckily they were spared the guillotine because of the fall of Robespierre (1758–1794). He was the last and perhaps the most dreaded leader of the Reign of Terror who himself was guillotined. With his demise, fortunately, no others were executed. When the horror of this period ended, Napoleon allowed the nuns to return to their abbey under the condition that they resume their educational work.[3]

The school prospered especially during the nineteenth century but eventually closed in 1904. Following this, the nuns gradually permitted a few pensioners and paying guests to stay at the monastery. But suddenly the very buildings themselves came to a tragic and instant end when everything was completely destroyed during the night bombings by the Allied forces of liberation on June 6 and 7, 1944. Nineteen of the nuns and the Mother Prioress were killed. The

---

2   Ibid., pp. 53–54.
3   Descouvemont, *op. cit.*, p. 43.

surviving forty nuns found refuge in a grand Norman chalet in Monteille just a few miles south-west of Lisieux. A new church and monastic cloister were built over the site of the old buildings and the nuns returned in 1954. This place served for a time, even while under construction, as a hostel (*hôtellerie*) for pilgrims who came to witness the consecration of the Basilica of Saint Thérèse. On June 4, 1963—just nineteen years almost to the day of the bombings—the monastery was consecrated marking the end of reconstruction and the return to full monastic life.[4] Unfortunately, the thirty-two nuns were not able to continue living there and were transferred in October of 1994 to a twelfth century abbey in Valmont, six miles (10km) from Fécamp,[5] a seaport north of Le Havre.

Today a school stands on the premises of the former site of the ancient Benedictine Abbey. A wax museum called The Diorama offering a thirty-minute spectacle showing the major stages in the life of St. Thérèse also occupied part of the grounds but closed in the early part of the twenty-first century. In the Saint's day the school's address was listed on the rue de Caen but it was changed after the Second World War to 36, avenue du 6 juin.

In Thérèse's time the nuns of the Abbey of Notre-Dame-du-Pré [Our Lady of the Meadow] were justifiably known as excellent teachers imbued with genuine maternal qualities. Their students received a sound academic education along with a thorough knowledge of their religion, proper deportment, and a spirit of piety. Included in the curriculum were: French, English, composition, mathematics, history, geography, penmanship, drawing, music (piano, violin, or mandolin if desired), religion, Church history, Scripture, catechism, needlework, and even dancing if requested by the parents.[6] There were five designated classes of about a dozen pupils in each class that was further divided into two divisions (or three, depending on the number of pupils). The school year followed a trimester system. Students spent two years in a class totaling ten years to complete the schooling at the abbey. Diplomas were awarded on the elementary and the upper-level. Generally there were about sixty young ladies attending the Abbey school every year but sometimes the enrollment might be over seventy. The faculty when Thérèse was there included the school chaplain and about forty nuns who were addressed as "Madame" by their pupils. The students in each of the five classes were identified by the color of the belts and suspender-like ribbons they wore over their black serge dresses:

    5th Class—Red—(the youngest children)
    4th Class—Green
    3rd Class—Violet
    2nd Class—Orange
    1st Class—Blue

There was an additional class known as the White Class that consisted of graduate students who wanted to receive advanced or supplementary courses.

---
[4] *Vie Thérèsienne*, 1980, p. 191.
[5] Descouvemont, *Sur les pas de Thérèse*, p. 142.
[6] Chalon, *op. cit.*, p. 45.

Special awards were given for scholastic excellence. A silver pin shaped like a palm or laurel wreath was awarded each week to pupils who achieved high academic marks. If a pupil obtained one for four consecutive weeks, she received a scarlet pin.

The children came primarily from the middle class with some from farming families if they could afford it. Those who lived at a distance were accepted as boarders while Lisieux residents were sent there as day pupils (sometimes referred to as "half-boarders" or "*demi-pensionnaires*"). Thérèse, her sisters, and cousins were in the latter category. Céline and Thérèse walked to their cousins' house in the center of town. Jeanne and Marie Guérin and a Guérin maid, normally Marcelline Husé,[7] joined them there and all the girls walked together to school. Sometimes Louis Martin would escort his daughters all the way to school. Felicité Saffray, another Guérin maid, occasionally accompanied the girls back home from school to the Guérin's house. They had to be in school at eight and left for home in the late afternoon around six. Sundays and Thursdays were days off. Students attended school on Saturday morning with the afternoon free. The summer vacation started the first week of August and ended the first week of October when the new school year began.

The huge monastic complex included the abbey chapel, classrooms, dormitories, and other components; outside was a courtyard, play area, and an orchard on a small hill in the rear called Mont Cassin. Here the pupils went for relaxation and even on days off. Directly next to the abbey was the parish church of Saint-Désir.

Each room had a statue of the Blessed Mother and a crucifix on the wall, otherwise the classrooms were plain and somber. Silence was required in the rather dark halls and stairways.

Religion naturally played a significant role in the life of the school. Pupils attended Mass regularly, recited the rosary daily, and participated at the short weekly service devoted to the Blessed Mother. In addition, they were allowed to visit the Blessed Sacrament during recreation period if they wished. Thérèse gladly availed herself of this great privilege and would often go to the choir beyond the grille of the chapel to meditate and pray. She did not enjoy the rough, noisy games during recreation but preferred to tell stories to the children in the primary classes; or if some students found a dead bird she would help them bury it "honorably."

Besides of course the classrooms and the imposing chapel, there was the students' dining hall (refectory), a large room twenty feet wide with a high ceiling. Two huge shuttered windows on opposite walls supplied light; a fireplace, a statue of the Blessed Mother, and pious paintings on the walls furnished decorative additions to the otherwise somber room. In the center were three long tables: the middle one was reserved for the day pupils and the other two were designated for the boarders. Each girl had to provide her own silver knife, fork, spoon, and napkin ring. The food was healthy but not always very appetizing: "a thin bread soup," boiled beef, stews, roasts, *pain brillé* (the regional bread), apple cake, and galettes (traditional French round flatcakes) at four o'clock tea. As in

---

[7] She gave testimony at the Diocesan Process in December of 1910.

every cloistered monastery, no talking was permitted while a nun read aloud something religious such as the story of a saint, martyr, or other pious literature.[8]

One of the students at the school who became a Benedictine nun after Thérèse's death (Mother Marie du Saint-Rosaire, née Marguérite Leroy) was about six years older than Thérèse. Her testimony at the Diocesan Process reveals her astute perception of Thérèse's character and that of the other students. There was, she says, a "contrast between the exquisite delicacy of the mutual understanding and the forms of piety in her home, and the composition of the boarding school, which at that period included a considerable number of extremely common pupils...."[9]

During the five years Thérèse spent at the convent school, she enrolled in a number of pious associations including: the Association of the Holy Angels (1882), the Works of the Holy Childhood (1882), the Holy Rosary Confraternity (1884), the Confraternity of the Holy Face (1885), the Apostolate of Prayer (1885), and as an aspirant into the Sodality of the Children of Mary (1886). After she left school she became a full-fledged member (May 1887) of the latter.

Also, in the course of those five academic years, four outstanding events for Thérèse occurred: a serious nervous and physical condition in 1883 that culminated with a sudden cure after she saw the statue of the Blessed Virgin smile at her, First Communion (May 8, 1884), Confirmation (June 1884), and second Solemn Communion (1885).

Louis Martin withdrew Thérèse from the abbey school at the beginning of March 1886 because of her poor health and sent her to the "highly respectable" Madame Papinau for private tutoring where she received around 75 lessons. Thérèse progressed quite well with her until February 1888, two months before she entered Carmel.

In Theresian literature the following list of Benedictine nuns from the abbey school are mentioned:

1. **Mother de l'Immaculée Conception**—Céline's favorite teacher
2. **Sister Marie Henriette**—teacher
3. **Sister Marie Marguerite**—converse sister
4. **Mother Saint André**—a young lay teacher who later became a nun, and finally prioress at the school
5. **Mother Saint Arsène**—in charge of the school before Sr. St. Placid
6. **Mother Saint Benoit**—teacher
7. **Mother Saint Chantal**—mother of Mother Saint-François de Sales
8. **Mother Saint Exupère**—prioress who died just before Thérèse's First Communion
9. **Mother Saint François de Sales**—teacher
10. **Mother Saint Léon**—teacher who later wrote a book about Thérèse at the abbey
11. **Mother Saint Placide**—director of the school and prioress
12. **Sister Sainte Scholastique**—portress

---

8 Keyes, *Written in Heaven*, pp. 55–56.
9 Görres, *The Hidden Face*, p. 64, footnote, as quoted from Summarium I, xv, 160.

Sister Henriette, a humble, young, and petite lay sister, was Thérèse's speech teacher who recalled an incident that occurred the day of Thérèse's First Communion. During the Mass some noticed that Thérèse was crying; however, it was not from sorrow but from joy at receiving Our Lord. She also realized that death would reunite her with her mother and deceased family members:

> At the two-hour party which followed, a child said to me [Sister Henriette]: "Do you know, Sister, what Thérèse asked God during her Thanksgiving—to die, Sister. How frightening!" But Thérèse looked at them with pity and said nothing. I then said to them: "You don't understand. Thérèse did indeed ask, like her holy patron, to die of love." Then she came up to me and looking me in the eye said: "Sister, you understand—but they—"[10]

Even at her tender school age, Thérèse was very concerned about how to meditate:

> One day, one of my teachers at the Abbey asked me what I did on my free afternoons when I was alone. I told her I went behind my bed in an empty space which was there, and that it was easy to close myself in with my bed-curtain and that "I *thought*." "But what do you think about?" she asked. "I think about God, about life, about ETERNITY ... I *think*!" The good religious laughed heartily at me, and later on she loved reminding me of the time when I *thought*, asking me if I *was still thinking*. I understand now that I was making mental prayer without knowing it and that God was already instructing me in secret.[11]

Thérèse would on occasion ask some friendly and trustworthy soul at school how to meditate and Sister Henriette was one of them. This piece of information Thérèse certainly took to heart:

> I do not know how the others do it, but as for me [Sr. Henriette], I imagine I do it a bit like you do, Thérèse, when you get home in the evening with your papa, whom you have not seen since the morning. You throw your arms around his neck, you show him your good marks, you tell him about all sorts of little things, everything is gone over—your joys and your sorrows. Well, I do the same with the good Lord; He is my Father. In my thoughts I put myself near Him, I adore Him, making myself very little, like you, I speak to Him; it is with my heart that I pray, and how the time goes by quickly![12]

Frances Parkinson Keyes in her delightful biography of the saint tells in her engaging style this brief encounter Thérèse had with one of the nuns:

> One day when she was playing with her doll, Soeur Marie-Marguerite, the *Converse* who had charge of the dishes for the pupils' dining hall, stopped to speak to her [Thérèse], looking her over reflectively. "Well, little Thérèse," she said shrewdly, "you think a great deal of that doll, don't you? You want to become a Carmelite yourself perhaps, like your sister?" The little girl gazed directly into the nun's eyes with that ethereal expression which was already so arresting to

---

10 Gaucher, *op. cit.* p. 52.
11 *Story of a Soul*, chapter IV, pp. 74–75.
12 Chalon, *op. cit.*, p. 49.

all those who saw it; then she turned back to her doll and continued to play without answering. "I could say nothing more to her." The Sister confessed, in relating the episode afterwards. "I instinctively knew that I had struck closer home than I had intended, that I had been indiscreet in my question."[13]

The school chaplain, Father Domin, gave instructions during the preparatory retreat to the youngsters who were about to receive their First Communion in 1884,[14] and Thérèse was one of them. She even copied down notes of Father's instructions in a small exercise book. To her, however, his talks about hell, punishment, death, and the Last Judgment were rather frightening. "Who knows whether any of you who are making this retreat will die before Thursday?" he forewarned them. Well, there was a death. The prioress of the abbey, Mère Saint-Exupère, died, which then prevented the chaplain from spending time with his retreatants. Obviously this had a chilling effect on the students including Thérèse.

A number of nuns were living while the cause for the beatification and that of the canonization of Sister Thérèse of the Child Jesus and of the Holy Face were underway and accomplished. The following gave testimony. Two did so at both processes.

Ordinary Process (*Procès de l'ordinaire*):
Mère Saint-André
Soeur Saint-Jean-l'Évangéliste
Soeur Marie du Saint-Rosaire

Apostolic Process (*Procès apostolique*):
Soeur Saint-André
Soeur Saint-François-de-Sales
Soeur Marie du Saint-Rosaire

Of all the twelve nuns listed who are mentioned in Theresian literature, eight in particular are discussed below. The first five are given brief notations while the last three merit lengthier accounts because they played more important roles with regards to Thérèse; and, thankfully, much more documentation is available concerning them.

1. **Mother Saint André** (1863–1942) became a member of the abbey faculty staff three months after Thérèse entered. In 1884 she was admitted to the Benedictine Order in 1884 and was professed in 1886. Ten years later she succeeded Mother Saint Placide as prioress in 1886. Throughout all the years Thérèse attended the abbey school, Mother Saint-André had innumerable occasions to see and observe Thérèse which she elaborated on in the testimony she offered at the Diocesan and Apostolic Processes.

Four other Benedictine nuns occasionally cited in Theresian literature are:

2. **Mère L'Immaculée** (1845–1924, a teacher and priores Céline was particularly fond of.)
3. **Soeur Saint Scholastique** (a portress.)

---
13 Keyes, *op. cit.*, p. 66.
14 In addition to Fr. Domin's instructions, there were three weekly lessons by the teacher in charge of the communion candidates. (Gaucher, *op. cit.*, p. 44.)

4. **Mère Saint Benoit** (1858–1929, teacher and niece of a Carmelite nun, Sister Madeleine, whom Thérèse found dead of influenza when she was an infirmarian in the Carmel.)
5. **Mère Saint Arsène** (head directress of the school before Mother Saint Placid who, according to Rev. Piat, was in someway connected to the Martin family.)

The following three biographies deal with **Mother Saint Francis de Sales**, **Mother Saint Léon**, and **Mother Saint Placide**.

1. Mère Saint François de Sales, O.S.B. (1848–1933)
(Mother Saint-Francis de Sales, de Sales, O.S.B.)
Teacher at the abbey school

MOTHER ST. FRANCIS DE SALES WAS BORN ON MARCH 15, 1848, IN THE PARISH of Saint-Désir, Lisieux. Her name was Marie-Joséphine-Aurélie Pierre, daughter of Jean-Edouard Pierre, an artisan, and Françoise-Alexandrine Etienne. She entered the Order of the Benedictines of Notre-Dame-du-Pré and was professed at twenty-three on May 17, 1871. During the years that Thérèse attended the abbey school, Mother St. Francis de Sales was Thérèse's regular class teacher (1881–1883) and also her religion instructor (1883–1886). She was a valuable witness at the Diocesan (1911) and Apostolic Process (1915). Father Piat cited one of the pertinent quotes from her testimony in his classic Theresian biography, *The Story of a Family*:

> I followed Thérèse practically all the time she spent at school. As her class mistress, I noticed that she was always at her work. I never had to reprove her. With her the thought of God was habitual and everything in her lessons recalled this to her. It was particularly striking in her little essays, where she always introduced a supernatural note despite the childish simplicity of the matter (p. 304).

A year after St. Thérèse's canonization, Mother St. Francis de Sales was interviewed at her monastery by an American priest, Father Albert Dolan, O. Carm. who asked her a number of questions which she graciously answered. Below is a portion of the interrogation:

- **Did you find the Little Flower, when she was in your class, an ordinary pupil?**
  In some ways, yes, she was ordinary, but in other ways she was most extraordinary. First, she was extraordinarily intelligent. She was very talented and precocious.... Then too she was extraordinarily obedient, scrupulously faithful to the minutest particulars of the rules of the school. And then again she was extraordinarily pious; her heart and mind were always on God, and she always wanted to talk of God and of the Saints.
- **Did you think that she would one day be a saint, Sister?**
  Oh, no, one doesn't guess that of a girl eight or nine years old. It was evident to all of us however, that she had never lost her baptismal innocence. I remember that one of the sisters said to me one day: "Did you notice the angelic expression on the countenance of Thérèse Martin? One sees other children with features as fine, but this child has Heaven in her eyes." We knew, Father, that we had a little treasure in Thérèse Martin, but we didn't estimate her at that time at her true worth.

- **Would you tell me something, Sister, about her life in school?**
  Well, she didn't care much to play with the others on the playground. She preferred the garden with its birds and flowers.... I remember once she astonished me during recreation by asking me, "Sister, how does one make a meditation?" A meditation is an advanced form of mental prayer practiced by nuns and priests and religious, and it is of course most extraordinary that a little girl of nine should ask how to make a meditation.... She was so perfect in catechism and showed such a sure knowledge of spiritual things and asked so many questions about subtle religious problems that the Chaplain of the school [Father Domin] used to call her "his little doctor of theology"—his little doctor of theology at nine or ten years of age. "She seemed endowed with a marvelous intuition." He said, "for things pertaining to the spiritual world."
- **Did the other pupils like her, Sister? Was she popular?**
  With the sisters, yes, she was a general favorite, but with the pupils, no. They were jealous of her intellectual superiority and outside the classroom they made her pay in a thousand little ways for her little classroom triumphs. Secondly, the fact that she was never punished because she was never disobedient prevented popularity. This immunity from punishment acted as kind of a barrier between her and the others who were punished frequently.... [Thérèse was always quiet during disorder in the classroom when the teacher was not present] was a rebuke to the disturbers and brought upon her head their displeasure. And even children do not tolerate rebukes, even though silent from one of their companions.
- **The Little Flower's obedience therefore, her desire to please God in all things was one of the causes of her unpopularity.**
  Again, Thérèse didn't like games... and the others took full opportunity on the playground to make fun of the awkwardness and lack of skill of her who put them all to shame in the classroom.... [The] Little Flower was always gentle, kind, and most patient with her companions, who, except those who were utterly blinded by jealousy, couldn't help but like her a little and in their hearts admire her and guess her worth.
- **Sister, do you remember anything that happened in the classroom while you were teaching the Little Flower that is worth recording?**
  [While explaining to the class the fate of those little children who die without baptism, Thérèse raised her hand and asked] "Sister, does God not love all souls?" Yes, my child. "Does He not love the souls of little children?" Yes. "Well then, how can He punish them; they never did any wrong; they never committed any sins themselves." [Sister Saint Francis explained that they were extremely happy; they were just deprived of seeing God.] "Well, if I were God, Sister, I would let the little children see me at least once."[15]

Father Rohrbach in his *The Search for St. Thérèse* quotes on page 87 what Mother Saint-Francis de Sales thought about Thérèse's kindness toward a poorly dressed, unattractive fellow student: "I am convinced that in her solicitude for that student there was no natural attraction of any kind; Thérèse was motivated by fraternal charity and the good of the child's soul."

---
15 Dolan, *op. cit.*, pp. 99–106.

Mother Saint Frances de Sales' death occurred at the abbey on February 25, 1933, when she was eighty-five—eight years after her former pupil was proclaimed a glorious saint of the Church.

2. Mère Saint Léon (1861–1938)
(Mother Saint-Léon)
Teacher who wrote a book about Thérèse at the abbey school

MOTHER SAINT LÉON WAS BORN MARIE LOUTREL IN LISIEUX ON JULY 24, 1861. She was professed as a Benedictine nun in 1884 at twenty-three when Thérèse, eleven, was in her third year at the school. She was noted to be lively, empathetic, and spontaneous—all qualities desirable in a teacher. On April 28, 1938, in the seventy-seventh year of her life, she went to her eternal reward thirteen years after Thérèse was declared a saint.

During the course of Mother Saint Léon's career she became Thérèse's sister Céline's friend and carried on a correspondence with her for many years. Five years after Thérèse's canonization, Mother Saint Léon wrote a small book entitled *La Petite Thérèse à l'Abbaye* (1930). Her younger sister, Valentine Loutrel (1874–1955), was one of Thérèse's classmates who later in life became an Augustinian nun by the name of Sister Saint-Stanislas. She provided useful firsthand information and anecdotes for her sister's book about St. Thérèse. In it Mother Saint Léon gave her impression of Thérèse:

> Outwardly there was nothing studied, nothing extraordinary about her. For the rest, she was obedient, showing a minute fidelity to the smallest detail of the rules, alarmed with even the semblance of a fault, sometimes to the extent of giving the appearance of being over scrupulous. Habitually gentle and reflective, she occasionally seemed inclined to dreaminess; a slight sadness sometimes pervaded her features.... Was she not already acquainted with inward suffering?[16]

Another selection from Mother Saint Léon's book records a perceptive description of the young student Thérèse by someone who certainly spent some time in observing her:

> Indeed Thérèse was a beautiful and gracious child with long golden curls framing her sweet face, delicate coloring, and a celestial expression about the eyes and the mouth.... I can still see her, holding her little prayer book in her hand; the union of childish grace with childish gravity was one of her great characteristics. I was so struck with her that even after fifty years, my first impression of her, confirmed afterwards by many like it, has never been effaced.
>
> Her usual expression was characterized by an exquisite smile as soon as her tears, which fell rather too facilely and frequently, it must be confessed, had been dried. Her manners were sweet and amiable, her spirit of devotion very deep, her sense of duty meticulous, her aversion to boisterous games and large crowds very marked.

Three years later she became involved in an unpleasant discussion concerning the photographs of Thérèse taken by Abbé Gombault and the portraits Céline

---
16 Keyes, *Thérèse: Saint of a Little Way*, pp. 76–77.

painted of her. She commented about the photographs in a letter to a priest, Abbé Robin: "The picture of Thérèse as a novice with that nice smile looks just like her. I have it also on postcards—one retouched and the other unretouched, so they can be compared. This way you are sure of knowing the truth."[17] Actually Mother Saint Léon was more in agreement with Thérèse's cousins—Dr. and Mme. La Néele—who favored the realism of a photograph.

Jean Chalon in his insightful biography of Thérèse relates a conversation she had with Mother Léon one day in school about her home schooling with Pauline. The curt response from Mother Léon produced tears in Thérèse's eyes: "Pauline is mistress at Les Buissonnets, whereas I am the mistress here."[18] This rather common tearful occurrence in school was observed by her teacher who noted that "the child's face expressed a melancholy which surprised me. Some callous students (mentioned on p. 25 in *Les Cahiers*) also noticed her tears and nicknamed her "*La Pleureuse*" ("The Weeper").

In retrospect, years later when she heard that Thérèse was up for canonization, Mother Saint Léon exclaimed that "when I think that I scolded a saint! But perhaps it is because I scolded her that she became a saint."[19]

3. Mère Saint-Placide (1845–1909)
(Mother Saint-Placide)
Director of the abbey school

THE WELL-LOVED HEAD MISTRESS OF THE BENEDICTINE ABBEY SCHOOL WAS Mother Saint Placide. Frances Parkinson Keyes discloses in detail her impressive ancestry:

> "The well-rounded education of this lady"—the annals of the Abbey tell us—"had dowered her with a variety of learning which rendered her instruction attractive. Extreme kindness of heart was an outstanding characteristic of her daily existence: she loved children profoundly, and took pains, in every way, to make their life at the school pleasant and as much as possible like family life." These annals also reveal that in the world Mère Ste. Placide had been Isabelle Fallery [born in Limoges in 1845], a lady of most noble lineage; her grandmother, Aglae Henriette de Boulert, had been lady-in-waiting to the Empress Josephine. Her grandfather, Nicholas François Martin Le Clerc, Esquier [sic], had been a Chevalier of St. Louis and an Officer of the Legion of Honor. Her father had been François Auguste Fallery, Chevalier of the Legion of Honor, and Departmental Treasurer, first at Limoges and later at Saint-Lô. Her mother, Henriette Charlotte Desire Le Clerc-Fallery, a chatelaine [the mistress of a chateau] worthy of all these great traditions, had desired to retire to a convent as soon as she became a widow, but she had waited to this until her daughter Isabelle could enter it with her. At a most impressive ceremony, they had taken the veil together, the elder as Mère Ste. Chantalle, the younger as Mère Ste. Placide; and in the cloister they were the admiration of all beholders, as they had been in the world.

---

17 François de Sainte-Marie, *op. cit.*, p. 47.
18 Chalon, *op. cit.*, p. 52.
19 Ibid., p. 50.

The mother was slender, erect, and highly strung; the daughter tall, fair, and tranquil: her name was happily chosen, for "Placide" described her well. "Their carriage was so arresting that merely to see them enter the choir was to be conscious of their distinction and their dignity."[20]

Like Thérèse, Mother Saint Placide entered religion at fifteen in 1860. She became director of the boarding school in 1882 and held this position until 1896. Her death occurred on December 10, 1909, when she was sixty-four years old.

Thérèse mentions Mother Saint Placide in her autobiography and the kindness she bestowed on her:

> The three months of preparation passed by quickly, and very soon I had to go on retreat and for this had to become a real boarder, sleeping at the Abbey. I cannot express the sweet memory this retreat left with me. And truly, if I suffered very much at the boarding school, I was largely repaid by the ineffable happiness of those few days spent in waiting for Jesus. I don't believe one can taste this joy anywhere else but in religious communities. The number of children was small, and it was easy to give each child particular attention, and certainly our teachers gave each of us their motherly care and attention. They spent more time with me than with the others, and each night the first mistress came [Mother Saint Placid], with her little lantern, and kissed me in my bed, showing me much affection. One night, touched by her kindness. I told her I was going to confide a *secret* to her; and drawing out my *precious little book* [containing a record of her many sacrifices in preparation for her First Communion] which was underneath my pillow, I showed it to her, my eyes bright with joy.[21]

Thérèse was in the Carmel eight months when she received a letter of invitation to attend the 25th anniversary of the installation of the Children of Mary Sodality which Thérèse had joined the year before. It was impossible for her to attend but she assured them she would be present in spirit. In her response letter to Mother Saint-Placide, Thérèse gave kind greetings to her "happy" classmates, but more significantly indicated her loving appreciation for her former teachers:

> I could not forget, dear Mistress [Mother Saint-Placide], how kind you were to me at the time of these great events in my life [First Communion and reception into the Children of Mary], and I cannot doubt that the remarkable grace of my religious vocation germinated on that blessed day when surrounded by my good teachers, I made the consecration of myself to Mary at the foot of the altar, taking her for my Mother in a special way.... I am thinking frequently of all my good teachers, and I love to name each in particular to Jesus during the blessed hours I spend at His feet. I dare to beg you, dear Mistress, to speak for me to them and to remember me to them, especially to *Madame la Prieure*, for whom I retain a most filial and grateful affection. Please, too, remember me to my happy companions, whose little sister in Mary I remain always.[22]

---

20 Keyes, *Written in Heaven*, pp. 64–65.
21 *Story of a Soul*, chapter IV, p. 75.
22 LT 70, presumably at the beginning of December 1888.

B. At the Carmel in Lisieux

Sœurs de Chœur (*Choir Sisters*)

Choir nuns (*moniales*) are members of contemplative orders, take solemn vows, and say the Divine Office every day in choir. Prayer, requiring many hours of concentration, takes priority over all other duties. Though they become involved with kitchen work and other manual tasks as the lay sisters, choir nuns more often would accomplish the genteel skills of needlework, calligraphy, creative or letter writing, and art. During the nine years of Thérèse's residence at the Lisieux Carmel there were at one time or another around twenty-four choir nuns.

Officially choir nuns should be called "nuns" not "sisters" because they take solemn vows. They, nonetheless, are addressed as "Sisters" and each has the word Sister affixed to her name. Lay sisters ("converse sisters"), on the other hand, should be called "sisters" exclusively; but in reality all women in religion are called interchangeably nuns or sisters.

In Thérèse's day the summer schedule began with rising at 4:45 in the morning followed during the day by six and a half hours of vocal prayer, two hours of silent prayer, and four and a half for Mass and the choral office. They spent the rest of the day with spiritual reading, involvement with personal projects such as artwork, writing, and free time in silence—about an hour at noon and the same around 8:00 in the evening. The nuns generally shared recreation periods together. They retired at night between 10:30 and 11:00 P.M. The winter schedule was about the same except they rose in the morning an hour later.

SŒURS DE CHŒUR (Choir Sisters)
1. **Révérende Mère Agnès de Jésus** (Reverend Mother Agnès of Jésus): *Pauline, Thérèse's sister (See Chapter 2, St. Thérèse's Family)*
2. **Sœur Aimée de Jésus et du Cœur de Marie** (Sister Amy of Jesus and of the Heart of Mary): *Opposed Céline's entrance into the Lisieux Carmel*
3. **Sœur Anne du Sacré-Cœur** (Sister Anne of the Sacred Heart): *Eurasian nun from the Saigon Carmel*
4. **Sœur Febronie de la Sainte-Enfance** (Sister Febronie of the Holy Infancy): *Thérèse was her nurse when she died during the flu epidemic*
5. **Sœur Geneviève de la Sante-Face** (Sister Geneviève of the Holy Face): *Thérèse's sister Céline (See Chapter 2, St. Thérèse's Family)*
6. **Révérende Mère Geneviève de Sainte-Thérèse** (Reverend Mother Geneviève of St. Teresa): *Saintly foundress of the Lisieux Carmel whose death Thérèse witnessed*

7. **Mère Hermance du Coeur de Jésus** (Mother Hermance of the Heart of Jésus): *A nun with a difficult personality*
8. **Sœur Marguerite-Marie du Sacré-Cœur** (Sister Margaret Mary of the Sacred Heart): *Likable nun who developed a mental disorder*
9. **Mère Marie de Gonzague** (Mother Marie de Gonzague): *An enigmatic prioress*
10. **Sœur Marie de Jésus** (Sister Marie of Jésus): *She unconsciously irritated Thérèse*
11. **Sœur Marie de la Trinité et de la Sainte-Face** (Sister Marie of the Trinity and of the Holy Face): *Thérèse's favorite novice*
12. **Sœur Marie de L'Eucharistie** (Sister Marie of the Eucharist): *Thérèse's cousin Marie Guérin (See Chapter 2, St. Thérèse's Family)*
13. **Sœur Marie de Saint-Joseph** (Sister Marie of Saint Joseph): *A nun with a violent temper who left the convent*
14. **Sœur Marie des Anges et du Sacré-Cœur** (Sister Marie of the Angels and of the Sacred Heart): *Thérèse's saintly novice mistress*
15. **Sœur Marie-Emmanuel** (Sister Marie Emmanuel): *A kind nun and widow with three deceased children*
16. **Sœur Marie-Philomène de Jésus** (Sister Marie Philomena of Jésus): *Older novice in the novitiate with Thérèse*
17. **Sœur Marie du Sacré-Cœur** (Sister Marie of the Sacred Heart): *Thérèse's oldest sister Marie (See Chapter 2, St. Thérèse's Family)*
18. **Sœur Saint-Jean Baptiste du Cœur de Jésus** (Sister Saint John the Baptist of the Heart of Jesus): *Her spirituality was too severe for Thérèse*
19. **Sœur Saint-Jean de la Croix** (Sister Saint John of the Cross): *An older nun who sought Thérèse's advice*
20. **Sœur Saint-Raphael du Cœur de Marie** (Sister Saint Raphael of the Heart of Mary): *Diabetic nun whose character flaws tried the nuns' patience*
21. **Sœur Saint-Stanislas des Saints-Cœurs** (Sister Saint Stanislas of the Sacred Hearts): *Oldest community member and Thérèse's infirmarian*
22. **Sœur Thérèse de Jésus du Cœur de Jésus** (Sister Thérèse of Jesus of the Heart of Mary): *Eccentric nun who left the monastery in 1909*
23. **Sœur Thérèse de Saint-Augustin** (Sister Teresa of Saint Augustine): *Thérèse had a natural but hidden dislike for her*

1. **RÉVÉRENDE MÈRE AGNÈS DE JÉSUS** (1861–1951)
   (REVEREND MOTHER AGNÈS OF JESUS)
   Thérèse's sister Pauline (See Chapter 2, St. Thérèse's Family)

2. **SŒUR AIMÉE DE JÉSUS ET DU CŒUR DE MARIE** (1851–1930)
   (SISTER AMY OF JESUS AND OF THE HEART OF MARY)
   Opposed Céline's entrance into the Lisieux Carmel

SISTER AMY OF JESUS OPPOSED HAVING THREE MEMBERS OF ONE FAMILY (Marie, Pauline, Thérèse Martin) in the same convent; therefore, she was firmly against the admission of one more sister, Céline, to join the "Martin clan," as she called it. Perhaps because of her rural upbringing, she also disliked the bourgeois style of the Martin sisters. She even announced that "Carmel does not need artists. It has far greater need of good infirmarians and laundresses!"[1] Nonetheless, Thérèse's wished-for change of heart on the part of Sister Amy came about at a most provocative moment which Thérèse reveals in her autobiography:

> When the difficulties seemed insurmountable one day, I said to Jesus during my act of thanksgiving: "You know, my God, how much I want to know whether Papa went straight to heaven; I am not asking You to speak to me, but give me a sign. If Sister A. of J. [Sister Amy of Jesus] consents to Céline's entrance or places no obstacle to it, this will be an answer that Papa went straight to You." This Sister, as you are aware, dear Mother [Sister Agnès, her blood sister Pauline], found we were already too many with three, and she didn't want another of our family to be admitted. But God who holds the hearts of His creatures in His hand, inclining them to do His will, changed this Sister's dispositions. The first one to meet me after my thanksgiving was Sister Aimée, and she called me over to her with a friendly smile and told me to come up with her to your [Pauline's] cell. She spoke to me about Céline and there were tears in her eyes. Ah! How many things I have to thank Jesus for; He answers all my requests![2]

Though she lived in the same convent with Thérèse, Sister Amy of Jesus was never closely involved with her in any assigned duties except at the end of Thérèse's life. As a religious she had working experience with the sick. One of Sister Amy's first tasks after profession was, in fact, as aide to the infirmarian. Sister Amy's obituary notice of January 30, 1930, mentions a poignant incident relating to Amy's skill working with the sick, this time to Thérèse:

> In the last days of September, 1897, when the weakness of our dear Saint prevented her from being moved, it became necessary to place her for a few moments on a temporary bed in order to make up her own bed. Seeing the embarrassment of the infirmarians who were afraid to hurt her, she said: "I believe that Sister Aimée of Jesus would easily take me into her arms; she's big and strong and very gentle around the sick."
>
> They called, then, our good Sister, who lifted the holy little patient as though she were a light burden, without giving her the least jolt. At this moment, with

---
[1] Descouvemont, *op. cit.*, p. 208.
[2] *Story of a Soul*, chapter VIII, pp. 177–178.

her arms around Sister's neck, this Angel thanked her with such a smile of affectionate gratitude that she will never forget that beautiful smile. It even became for her a compensation for her regrets at having been the only one not to hear the infirmary bell which convoked the Sisters at the last moment of the most beautiful death which was ever seen at the Carmel of Lisieux.[3]

Mother Agnès recorded in *The Yellow Notebook* another doleful service Sister Amy rendered for Thérèse:

> After her death [September 30, 1897], she had a heavenly smile. She was ravishingly beautiful. She was holding her Crucifix so tightly that we had to force it from her hands to prepare her for burial. Sister Marie of the Sacred Heart [Thérèse's sister Marie] and I performed this office, along with Sister Aimée of Jesus, and we noticed she didn't seem any more than twelve or thirteen years old.[4]

Sister Amy of Jesus was remarkably forthright in her replies on March 17, 1911, to the interrogation of the Promoter of the Faith (the Devil's Advocate) at the Diocesan Process. She was called to answer questions most likely because she at first could not understand why someone like Sister Thérèse who had done nothing extraordinary would be even considered for canonization.

- I esteem and love the Servant of God as a very holy person, but not with any enthusiasm or natural liking.
- I was one of the instruments God made use of to sanctify her. The charitable way she bore with my defects brought her to an outstanding degree of holiness. Her fraternal charity was unselfish and supernatural.
- From the very beginning of her stay in Carmel her religious comportment was remarkable. In spite of her youth, there was nothing childish or frivolous in her behavior. She gave no opening for becoming the plaything of the community; her seriousness insured that she would not be treated as a child.
- I am sure she would have made an excellent prioress.
- I noticed the delicacy of the Servant of God's humility in the way she never said a word to make us feel grateful for the many gifts bestowed on us by her family.... To my own shame, I admit that I did not come to appreciate soon enough the rare qualities God had endowed her with.[5]

Born on January 24, 1851, Léopoldine-Marie-Céline Féron, the future Sister Amy, was the second of seven children in a farming family living in Anneville-en-Saire, a little town east of Cherbourg near the English Channel. Her parents were Ambroise-Auguste Feron and Cécile Énault. She attended the private school Notre-Dame de Saint-Pierre as a boarding student and proved to be gifted in her studies, robust, and truly pious. However, she remained all her life a woman of the soil and not as well-bred or cultured as some of the other nuns, especially the Martin sisters.

---

3 From "Additional Conversations" in *Her Last Conversations*, p. 269.
4 September 30, 1897.
5 O'Mahony, *op. cit.*, p. 278–280.

On October 11 (or 13), 1871, when Léopoldine was twenty, Mother Geneviève of St. Thérèse (prioress and foundress of the Lisieux Carmel) accepted her as a postulant. On the feast of St. Joseph, March 19, 1872, she took as her religious name Sister Amy of Jesus and the Heart of Mary (Sœur Aimèe de Jésus et du Cœur de Marie). Another nun, Sister St. John the Baptist, shared the identical profession dates and consequently they often were referred to as "twins" by the community.

The strong and hard working Sister Amy of Jesus had several duties including woodworking, linen room tasks, and as infirmarian. She saw no need for a Carmelite to be involved with the fineries of upper class people with their artistic, musical, and literary pursuits. She preferred having potatoes around the Calvary in the cloister instead of roses.[6] Interestingly, Thérèse and roses are forever linked in pictures and writings of her. The story of how she and her novices would cast rose petals at the figure of the crucified Christ in the cloister courtyard is well-known.

Sister Amy expressed her dismay when the cause for Thérèse was introduced. She believed it was due solely to the instigation of Thérèse's doting sisters. "We shall see," she once remarked. She finally did "see" and was convinced. In fact she gladly participated in the various festivities relative to Sister Thérèse's glorification. Furthermore, she attributed a favor her niece received in 1902 to the intercession of St. Thérèse.

A few years before her death from pneumonia at the age of seventy-nine on January 7, 1930, ill health had set in: deafness, diminished vision, and finally an anthrax malady requiring much surgery. On her deathbed she prayed for "the grace of a holy death ... through the intercession of our little Saint," who was canonized five years before.[7]

3. Sœur Anne du Sacré-Cœur (1850–1920)
(Sister Anne of the Sacred Heart)
Eurasian nun from the Saigon Carmel

In faraway Macao (a Portuguese colony of China just south of Hong Kong), Maria de Souza was born in 1850 of a Portuguese father and a Chinese mother. At twenty-four she entered the Carmelite Order in Saigon (capital of South Vietnam) in 1874 and assumed the religious name of Sister Anne of the Sacred Heart. This Carmel was founded thirteen years earlier by a group of French Carmelites from Lisieux. Sister Anne received the habit on May 1, 1875, and was professed on September 8, 1876. For various reasons she developed a great desire to be transferred to the Lisieux monastery which became a reality in June 1883 when all the Lisieux nuns welcomed her with open arms: "This dear sister was received into our monastery with happiness as a double bond that unite us with our dear foundation in Saigon."[8]

---

6 Descouvemont, *op. cit.*, 208.
7 *Les Annales de Sainte Thérèse de Lisieux*, No. 603, June 1982, p. 14.
8 From the Chronicle of the Monastery as quoted in *Les Annales de Sainte Thérèse de Lisieux*, No 622., March 1984.

Thérèse's novice mistress, Sister Marie of the Angels, after living with Sister Anne for ten years wrote as subprioress these favorable comments about her in May 1894: "A true Chinese type.... Full of spirit, knowledge, talents, a marvelous worker, but her lack of strength did not permit her to have many jobs. Fervent as a seraphim and a source of edification by her courage and piety." [9]

A week after Thérèse entered Carmel, Sister Anne gave Thérèse (on April 17, 1888) a holy card showing the Christ Child in a crib staring ahead at a vision of the cross He was to die on. This picture inspired Thérèse six years later to paint a similar one which she named "The Dream of the Child Jesus." The Visitation Monastery in Chartres now has it.

Thérèse too had a strong desire to be a missionary in foreign lands as a girl and when she became a nun she wanted to live in a Carmel mission in the East. Her Order was already firmly established in Saigon and were seeking nuns for a new foundation in Hanoi, the capital of Tong-king (or Tonkin) which is now called North Vietnam where St. Théophane Vénard was martyred. She wished to go there but obedience and poor health prevented such a move.

Sister Anne managed to stay twelve years in France. Eventually, though, she found it difficult adapting to the climate. The switch from the torrid weather of Saigon to the damp, foggy, and often freezing conditions of Normandy proved a hard adjustment to make. She eventually left Lisieux on July 29, 1895, and took the long journey back to the Saigon Carmel. Incidentally, the very evening Sister Anne left, Thérèse and her novices presented before the community her fourth play entitled *Jesus at Bethany* in honor of all the lay sisters.

Thérèse certainly never forgot Sister Anne, the foreign nun who represented the mission ideal for her. Two years after her departure, Thérèse wrote her only letter to her:

> Very dear Sister,
>
> You will undoubtedly be very much surprised to receive a letter from me. So that you may pardon me for coming to disturb the silence of your solitude, I shall tell you how it happens I have the pleasure of writing you. The last time I went for spiritual direction from our good Mother [Gonzague], we spoke about you and the dear Saigon Carmel. Our Mother told me she was allowing me to write you if this pleased me. I accepted this suggestion with joy, and am taking advantage of the free day [a rare privilege for the community] for the feast of the Good Shepherd to come and speak for a few moments with you.
>
> I hope, dear Sister, you have not forgotten me; as for myself, I think often of you. I recall with joy the years I spent in your company, and you know, for a Carmelite to think of a person whom she loves is to pray for her. I ask God to bestow His graces upon you and to increase each day His holy love in your heart.... Oh, Sister! I beg you, ask Jesus that I increase each day His holy love in your heart.... Oh, Sister! I beg you, ask Jesus that I myself also may love Him (as you do) and that I may make Him loved. I would like to love Him

---

[9] Ibid.

> not with an ordinary love but like the Saints who did foolish things for Him. Alas! How far I am from being like them!
>
> Ask Jesus, too, that I may always do His will; for this I am ready to traverse the world.... I am ready also to die!
>
> [If] it does not bore you, I shall come back to speak with you at greater length on another occasion.[10]

Though she lived seven years under the same monastic roof with Thérèse, Sister Anne did not really get to know Sister Thérèse well. Years later during the process for Thérèse's canonization she was asked to answer some questions about Sister Thérèse. The most telling comment was that "There is nothing to say about her; she was very good and very self-effacing, one would not notice her, never would I have suspected her sanctity."[11] What a magnificent testimony to the simple "little way" Thérèse lived and professed so frequently in her writings and indeed in her life. In her autobiography we read: "true wisdom consists in desiring to be unknown and counted as nothing, in placing one's joy in the contempt of self. Ah! I desire that, like the Face of Jesus, my face be truly hidden, that no one on earth would know me."[12]

After leaving Lisieux, Sister Anne of the Sacred Heart spent the next twenty-five years in the Saigon Carmel where she died at the age of seventy on July 24, 1920.

4. Sœur Febronie de la Sainte-Enfance (1819–1892)
(Sister Febronie of the Holy Infancy)
Thérèse was her nurse when she died during the flu epidemic

WHEN THE FIFTEEN-YEAR-OLD THÉRÈSE ENTERED THE CARMELITE MONastery in Lisieux, Mother Febronie, then subprioress, was sixty-eight. Four years later during the terrible influenza epidemic of 1891–1892, Mother Febronie, who had been taken care of by the slightly stricken Thérèse herself, died of the disease. Thérèse recorded in her autobiography a sorrowful yet uplifting account of Mother Febronie's last night on earth:

> The night Mother subprioress died I was all alone with the infirmarian. It's impossible to imagine the sad state of the community at this time; the ones who were up and about can give some idea of the conditions, but in the midst of this abandonment I felt that God was watching over us. It was without effort that the dying passed on to a better life, and immediately after their death an expression of joy and peace covered their faces and gave the impression almost that they were only asleep. Surely this was true because, after the image of this world has passed away, they will awaken to enjoy eternally the delights reserved for the Elect.[13]

---

10 LT 225, May 2, 1897.
11 In a note from the Saigon Carmel to the Lisieux Carmel, dated December 21, 1947 [*sic*].
12 *Story of a Soul*, chapter seven, p. 152. Thérèse would have found a kindred spirit in the modest, unassuming American poetess Emily Dickinson (1803–1886) who wrote: "I'm nobody! Who are you? / Are you nobody, too? / Then there's a pair of us.... How dreary to be somebody! / How public, like a frog / To tell your name the livelong day / To an admiring bog!"
13 *Story of a Soul*, chapter VIII, p. 172.

Another time Thérèse tells how well this good nun understood her innermost feelings:

> It was only with great effort that I was able to take directions, for I had never become accustomed to speaking about my soul and I didn't know how to express what was going on within it. One good old Mother [Febronie] understood one day what I was experiencing, and she said laughingly during recreation: "My child, it seems to me you don't have very much to tell your Superiors." "Why do you say that, Mother?" "Because your soul is extremely simple; but when you will be perfect, you will be even more simple; the closer one approaches to God, the simpler one becomes." [14]

One duty she had as subprioress required her to make sure that the community closely followed the Rules of the Order, a task she was well qualified for since she herself was a model of obedience, piety, and silence. She occasionally conversed with Thérèse about theological matters and God's justice which she held was not, as Thérèse believed, tempered with mercy and love. Thérèse said one day to Sister Febronie, "You want God's justice? You will get God's justice. The soul receives exactly what it expects of God.... This justice, which has terrified so many souls, is the reason for my joy and my confidence." [15]

Several months after Febronie died, Thérèse had a startling dream in which she saw a procession of Carmelites among whom was the rueful figure of Sister Febronie. The next morning Thérèse related this vivid dream to Mother Gonzague:

> O my Mother, my Sister Febronie came this night to ask that we pray for her. She is in purgatory without doubt, for she did not count enough on the mercy of the good God. By her suppliant and profound look, she seemed to tell me: "You had reason, all justice is accomplished in me, but it was my fault; if I had believed you, I would have gone straight to Heaven...." [16]

Thérèse did not mention the above dream in her writings; but she did state in her autobiography "that the Fire of Love is more sanctifying than is the fire of purgatory. I know that Jesus cannot desire useless sufferings for us...." [17]

Sister Febronie was born Marie-Julie Malville in Paris on October 31, 1819. Her father, a tailor, moved to Rennes with his two daughters Marie and Pauline after his twenty-four-year-old wife died. The girls attended school there; then the family moved to Lisieux after M. Malville's second marriage to a deeply religious woman. Marie-Julie joined the Lisieux Carmelites in January 1842 and received the habit and veil in 1843. The community elected her sub-prioress from 1860 to 1866 and again from 1877 to 1883. Lastly, she held the same position from 1886 until her death six years later at eighty-three on January 4, 1892, just eleven days away from celebrating her golden anniversary as a Carmelite.

---

14 Ibid., chapter VII, p. 151.
15 Gaucher, *op. cit.*, p. 141.
16 Author's translation of a quote by Sister Marie of the Angels written in *Les Annales de Sainte Thérèse de Lisieux*, February 1983.
17 *Story of a Soul*, chapter VIII, p. 181.

5. Sœur Geneviève de la Sante-Face (1869–1959)
(Sister Geneviève of the Holy Face)
Thérèse's sister Céline (See Chapter 2, St. Thérèse's Family)

6. Révérende Mère Geneviève de Sainte-Thérèse (1805–1891)
(Reverend Mother Geneviève of St. Teresa)
Saintly foundress of the Lisieux Carmel whose death Thérèse witnessed

MOTHER GENEVIÈVE WAS ONE OF THE FOUNDRESSES AND SECOND PRIORESS of the Lisieux Carmel. She was born Claire-Marie-Radegonde Bertrand on July 19, 1805, in Poitiers. At the age of thirty she entered the Carmelite Order in the city of her birth on March 26, 1830. She served five terms as prioress that amounted to a total of twenty-seven years. For fifty years this saintly nun endured austerity, privation, poverty, and physical suffering from the very first days of the Lisieux monastery in March 1838 through 1888 when Thérèse Martin entered the Carmelite Monastery. Mother Geneviève was then eighty-five and Thérèse fifteen. She was always a caring and accessible person even in her old age. All considered her a saint.

On the very first day Thérèse entered the monastery she tells us:

> I was led, as are all postulants, to the choir immediately after my entrance into the cloister. The choir was in darkness because the Blessed Sacrament was exposed and what struck me first were the eyes of our holy Mother Geneviève which were fixed on me. I remained kneeling for a moment at her feet, thanking God for the grace He gave me of knowing a saint, and then I followed Mother Marie de Gonzague into the different places of the community. Everything thrilled me....[18]

Thérèse's great esteem for Mother Geneviève couldn't be any more heartfelt and praiseworthy than this excerpt from her autobiography:

> I haven't said anything to you [Mother Agnès, her sister Pauline] as yet concerning my good fortune at knowing our holy Mother Geneviève. This certainly was a priceless gift; God, who had given me so many graces, willed that I should live with a saint. Not one that was inimitable, but one who was made holy by the practice of the hidden virtues, the ordinary virtues. On more than one occasion I received great consolations from her...."[19]

Thérèse continues and gives an example of one of her consolations when Mother Geneviève spoke softly to her:

> [My] little child, I am going to say just a little word to you; every time you come you ask for a spiritual bouquet. Well, today, I will give you this one: Serve God with *peace* and *joy*; remember, my child, *Our God is a God of peace*" [1 Corinthians 14:33]. After thanking her very simply, I left but was moved to the point of tears and was convinced that God had revealed the state of my soul to her. That day I had been severely tried even to the verge of sadness; I

---
18 Ibid., chapter VII, p. 148.
19 Ibid., chapter VIII, p. 169.

was in such a night [period of worry, pain, sorrow, etc.] that I no longer knew whether God loved me. You can readily understand, dear Mother, the joy and consolation I then experienced![20]

Just before Thérèse's profession she had doubts about her vocation as a Carmelite nun and Mother Geneviève dispelled all her uncertainty. Thérèse did not forget when she wrote that "On the day of my Profession I was also very much consoled to learn from Mother Geneviève's own mouth that she had passed through the same trial as I did before pronouncing her Vows."[21] In the same paragraph she gives details of her death which she witnessed. Profoundly moved, she called it *"ravissant"*—enrapturing:

> [The] memory which Mother Geneviève left in my heart is a sacred memory. The day of her departure for heaven [December 5, 1891], I was particularly touched; it was the first time I had assisted at a death and really the spectacle was ravishing. I was placed at the foot of the dying saint's bed, and witnessed her slightest movements. During the two hours I spent there, it seemed to me that my soul should have been filled with fervor; however, a sort of insensibility took control of me. But at the *moment itself* of our saintly Mother Geneviève's birth in heaven, my interior disposition changed and in the twinkling of an eye I experienced an inexpressible joy and fervor; it was as though Mother Geneviève had imparted to me a little of the happiness she was enjoying, for I was convinced she went straight to heaven. While she was still living, I said to her one day: "Mother, you will not go to purgatory!" She answered gently: "I hope not." Ah! Surely, God does not disappoint a trust so filled with humility; the many favors we have received since are a proof of this.
>
> After Mother's death, each of the Sisters hastened to claim some relic, and you know the one I have the happiness of possessing. During her last agony, I had noticed a single *tear* glistening like a diamond on her eyelash, *and this tear, the last she was to shed on earth*, never fell; I saw it still glistening there when she was laid out in the choir. So when evening came, unseen by anyone, I made bold to approach her and with a little piece of linen I took *the saint's tear as a relic*. Since then I have carried it in a little container which holds my Vows.[22]

Following Mother Geneviève's death, Thérèse reminisced: "Fifteen years later [after her own mother's death], I was to stand before another coffin, Mother Geneviève's. It was similar in size.... I had no need to *raise* my head to see and, in fact, no longer *raised* it but to contemplate *heaven* which to me was *filled with joy*."[23]

Not long after Mother Geneviève's death, Thérèse had a dream about her:

> I dreamed she was making her last will and testament, giving each of the Sisters something which she possessed. When my turn finally came, I thought I would get nothing as there was really nothing left to give; however, she said: "To you I leave my *heart*." She repeated this three times with great emphasis.[24]

---

20 Ibid.
21 Ibid., p. 170.
22 Ibid.
23 Ibid., chapter II, p. 34.
24 Ibid., chapter VIII, p. 171.

The heart Mother Geneviève mentioned in her dream was in fact put into a reliquary as the nuns had requested the monastery physician, Dr. de Cornière, to do after the death of their holy foundress so that they would have a first-class relic they could venerate of the nun they all considered a saint. The nuns also wanted their foundress buried in their chapel next to Father Sauvage who was responsible for the construction of the chapel and was so instrumental in having the Carmel located there in Lisieux. The actual burial did not take place until three weeks after her death. The answer to their wish took such a long time because under the Third Republic municipal governments would permit burial in a cloister only under extraordinary situations.[25]

The eighty-seven-year-old Mother Geneviève was the first of four nuns to die during the bitter winter of 1891–1892 on December 5, 1891. She had suffered for seven years both physically and spiritually and after a long painful final illness she finally succumbed. The other three nuns died within eight days after Christmas when a widespread influenza epidemic struck the Carmel. Thérèse was assigned to arrange the flowers around Mother Geneviève's coffin when one of the lay sisters (Sister St. Vincent de Paul) made this cutting remark to her: "Ah, you know well how to put in the foremost place the wreath sent by your own family, while you leave in the background the bouquets of the poor." Thérèse sweetly replied, "I am thankful to you, Sister. You are right. Give me the moss-covered cross sent by the workmen [one was from Sr. St. Vincent's brother Louis], I am going to place it in front. That's where it belongs. I hadn't thought of it."[26]

Mother Geneviève's name and memory are encountered in much of the written material by Thérèse and others. During the months preceding Thérèse's death she was mentioned a number of times but mostly, one might say, in a rather morbid context. Nevertheless, sickness, suffering, and death are the shocking realities of life. For example, on July 8, 1897, Thérèse was taken down to the infirmary and placed in the same bed in which Mother Geneviève received Extreme Unction three times and died. Thérèse knew this of course and remarked that "They have placed me in an 'unlucky bed,' in a bed that makes me [also] miss the train [to the afterlife]."[27]

Mother Agnès was terribly worried that Thérèse would suffer greatly from the tuberculosis that ravaged her body. Thérèse consoled her with these words: "If by the agonies of death you mean the awful sufferings which manifest themselves at the last moment through sighs which are frightful to others. I've never seen them here in those who have died under my eyes. Mother Geneviève experienced them in her soul but not in her body."[28] Even before this date, Thérèse said,

> After my death, do not place wreaths on my coffin as was done for Mother Geneviève but ask that the money which would have been spent on them be

---

25 Descouvemont, *op. cit.*, p. 184.
26 From Mother Agnès' testimony at the Diocesan Process.
27 From *Her Last Conversations*, July 8, 1897 in a dialogue from Thérèse to her sister Marie.
28 Ibid., July 20, 1897.

used, rather, to ransom some poor little Negroes from slavery. Say that this it is which will give me pleasure. I should like a little Théophane [Vénard] and a little Marie-Thérèse.[29]

Thérèse rarely expressed verbally any serious doubt about her mission after death except this time a month before she passed away: "I want to do good after my death, but I will not be able to do so! It will be as it was for Mother Geneviève: We expect to see her work miracles, and complete silence fell over her tomb...."[30]

And finally, Mother Agnès told Thérèse that she would like to have her (Thérèse's) heart preserved the way they had Mother Geneviève's. Thérèse replied, "Do whatever you wish!" Then Mother Agnès wrote: "I changed my mind because even the thought repelled me, and I told her this. She appeared to be sad about it. I guessed at what she was thinking: We would be depriving ourselves of a consolation which she wouldn't grant us through a miracle, for we knew she would not be preserved after death."[31]

The aged saintly Mother Geneviève died in 1891 and the pious young Sister Thérèse six years later in 1897. Little did either, or for that fact, anyone, imagine twenty-eight years after the young one's death that she would be canonized a saint and before the end of the next century she would be proclaimed the third woman Doctor of the Church.

7. Mère Hermance du Cœur de Jésus (1834–1898)
(Mother Hermance of the Heart of Jesus)
A nun with a difficult personality

SISTER GENEVIÈVE (THÉRÈSE'S SISTER CÉLINE) IN HER TESTIMONY AT THE Apostolic Process revealed the opinion Thérèse had concerning Mother Hermance:

> Her [Thérèse's] preferences were for the less sympathetic sisters; "I [Thérèse] always placed myself close to her in recreation.... One day ... she confided in me the efforts she had to overcome her natural antipathy for a certain sister [Mother Hermance]. [She had] a nervous malady, [but] besides that, educated and intelligent.... [with] a thousand bizarre quirks which frightened the infirmarians." It was about this matter that Thérèse told me: "The work of the infirmarian pleases me the most."[32]

At another time Thérèse reiterated to her sister Marie her thoughts about Mother Hermance who was so demanding of the infirmarians that they had to give in to her many whims:

> Oh! How I wish I had been infirmarian, not by natural inclination but "through the attraction of grace." And it seems to me that I would have made Mother Heart of Jesus happy! Yes, I would have had an inclination for all that. And I'd have put so much love into the work, thinking of God's words: "I was

---
29 *Novissima Verba*, May 21–26, 1897, p. 7.
30 Ibid., August 1897.
31 Ibid., August 2, 1897, from "Additional Conversations" with Mother Agnès.
32 Testimony Sister Geneviève gave at session 32, August 24, 1915. English translation by the author.

sick and you visited me." [Matthew 25:36] It's very rare to find this beautiful opportunity in Carmel.[33]

Two days later Pauline jotted this down in her own *Yellow Notebook*: "Poor Mother C. of J. [Mother Hermance was called Mère Cœur de Jésus—Mother Heart of Jesus] was becoming more and more demanding, and the infirmarians were complaining because they had to give in to her whims: "Ah! What an attraction I would have for all that!" [34]

Céline claimed that Mother Hermance often openly showed great respect for Thérèse. For example, few in the community were as deeply absorbed with the writings of the Carmelite mystic and Doctor of the Church, St. John of the Cross, as was Sister Thérèse. Mother Hermance, quite aware of this, showed her amazement after hearing Thérèse speak about him during recreation. She remarked to Pauline (Mother Agnès), "How is it possible that a child of seventeen years understands these things and discusses them in such a way! It's admirable, I can't get over it!" [35]

Actually Mother Hermance knew Thérèse when she was a very young girl, surely from the time Thérèse and her family visited the monastery to see Pauline during her early years in the monastery. The Carmel Archives have a note written on a sheet of paper that wrapped a holy card which Mother Hermance sent to the ten- or eleven-year-old Thérèse: "For our dear little sister Térérsita, sister of our little lamb, all white." [36] This is most likely a reference to Pauline who was at the time either a novice wearing a white veil or later on when she wore a wedding gown on her clothing day.

One method Thérèse used in dealing with Mother Hermance as well as with everyone else, was not to do anything that might annoy her. For example, Thérèse loved to place fresh flowers by one of her favorite statues, that of the Child Jesus in the cloister walkway. However, since Mother Hermance claimed the scent of flowers displeased her, Thérèse would often place artificial ones there instead.

Mother Hermance was born Madelaine Hermance Pichery on February 12, 1834, in Honfleur, Normandy. Her father, a merchant, was Pierre Pichery, husband of Rose Jacquette. Incidentally, they lived very near to the Church of St. Catherine which Thérèse, happened to visit with her father and sister when she was fourteen. Madeleine and her younger sister received an excellent education and on completion of her training taught school for a while before entering the Lisieux Carmel. Against her mother's wishes, Mlle. Pichery entered the Carmel on May 14, 1858, received the habit on November 24, of the same year, and professed on December 2, 1859. After serving as mistress of novices for several months in 1866, she was asked to take part in the founding of a convent in Coutances

---

33 *Her Last Conversations*, August 20, 1897.
34 Ibid., September 3, 1897.
35 Mother Hermance's comment to Mother Agnès of Jésus as recorded in the Preparatory Notes of the Carmelites for the Apostolic Process (NPPA) which Guy Gaucher quotes on p. 9 in his book *John and Thérèse: Flames of Love*.
36 LC 17 written by Mother Hermance sometime in 1883–1884.

(Manche), became sub-prioress, and later its prioress. In 1882 she returned to the Lisieux Carmel where she began showing signs of neurasthenia, a nervous disorder, that plagued her the rest of her life and at times, irritatingly affected the community. As Thérèse remarkably predicted, she died after considerable suffering on October 30, 1898, at the age of sixty-three.

8. Sœur Marguerite-Marie du Sacré-Cœur (1850–1926)
(Sister Margaret Mary of the Sacred Heart)
Likable nun who developed a mental disorder

The Carmelite nuns in the Lisieux monastery were truly fond of Sister Margaret Mary throughout her twenty-three year stay with them, even during her most distressing last years. St. Thérèse's sister Pauline (Mother Agnès) in evaluating her stated that she was a "dear sister, most edifying" and "one of the pearls of our Carmel."[37] In 1893 Sister Marie of the Angels, novice mistress at the time, remarked that Sister Margaret Mary was the "daisy [marguerite] of the Good God, having the simplicity of that flower."[38] Decades later in 1948 another sister of the saint, Céline (Sister Geneviève), recalled that Sister Margaret was "sweet and good" and "one of those who rendered the communal life sweet and agreeable."[39]

The obscure village of Colombiers-sur-Seulles in Calvados, Normandy, was the birthplace on May 11, 1850, of Léa-Adolphine Nicolle, the future Sister Margaret Mary of the Sacred Heart. Her father, Alexandre, was a stone cutter in a region of many quarries and her mother, Affable, was a lace maker, one of thousands in the Bayeux area. After the birth of their fifth child, the family was left fatherless by the death of the forty-three-year-old Alexandre.

Abbé Hodierne of St. Pierre's Church in Lisieux recognized the contemplative vocation of Léa, the youngest living child in this family, and was influential in the decision to admit her into the Lisieux Carmel on July 15, 1873—the year of St. Thérèse's birth. Léa received the habit on December 8, 1873, and was professed on March 18, 1875. She, together with Sister Marie Philomene and Sister Amy of Jesus, formed a trio of nuns noted for their physical strength and willingness to volunteer for all the heavy tasks around the monastery.

Sadly, this pleasant and kind nun began exhibiting signs of a mental disease that plagued her the rest of her life. Around 1886 the community became aware of it and had to have her hospitalized at Bon Sauveur sanatorium in Caen in 1890. All the nuns were sympathetic to their dear confrère, especially the three Martin sisters (Marie, Pauline, and Thérèse) whose father was coincidentally a patient at that time in the same hospital (1889–1892).

The hospital released Sister Margaret Mary after a brief stay. She returned to the Lisieux Carmel where she lasted six more years until a recurrence of the disturbing symptoms. The nuns ardently prayed for her recovery but Sister Thérèse did not

---
37 *Les Annales de Sainte Thérèse de Lisieux*, No. 619, Dec. 1983.
38 Descouvemont, *op. cit.*, p. 149.
39 DeMeester, *op. cit.*, p. 110.

think she would be cured. She had a dream in which she saw Sister Margaret Mary enter the community room, amazing everyone with a brilliantly luminous cross on her shoulders.[40] She interpreted the cross as an affliction that would never leave her. Surprisingly, another nun, Sister Marie of the Angels, experienced the very same dream. She and Sister Thérèse believed that Sister Margaret's "heavy cross will surely follow her permitting her great glory in heaven."[41]

Eventually, on March 14, 1896, she was again admitted to Bon Sauveur, escorted there by Thérèse's Uncle Guérin and the nun's sister Armadine. The hospital discharged her after a few months but she never returned to the Carmelites. Her brother welcomed her back to Colombiers where she stayed for a quarter of a century until in 1922 she eventually entered another religious order, the Little Sisters of the Poor, in Caen. She died a pious death there on June 12, 1926, at the age of seventy-five.

9. Mère Marie de Gonzague (1834–1904)
(Mother Marie de Gonzague)
An enigmatic prioress

MOTHER MARIE DE GONZAGUE PLAYED A DOMINANT ROLE IN THÉRÈSE'S convent life and in that of all those under her. Her commanding personality was no doubt created and nurtured by her birth and upbringing in an aristocratic family whose lineage can be traced as far back as the fifteenth century to the Davy des Harpes family. The future prioress of the Lisieux Carmel was born on February 20, 1834, in Caen and named Marie-Adèle-Rosalie Davy de Virville. She was the daughter of a magistrate, Pierre-Louis Amédée Davy, who later became the Marquis of Virville. Her mother was Adelaïde, the daughter of a lawyer. They had seven children, the fourth one being Marie. Death claimed the life of Marie's mother in 1872 and of her father in 1876.

In her childhood, Marie studied at the Visitation in Caen near her home and developed there a life-long devotion to the Sacred Heart. At twenty-six she entered the Carmelite Order in Lisieux on November 29, 1860, took the habit on May 30, 1861, was professed on June 27, 1862, and the next month on July 16, she was given the black veil. Just four years later, she began her long career as superior of the monastery. The community elected her subprioress in 1866 and again in 1869.

The rapid advance of the Prussians during the final stages of the Franco-Prussian War (1870–1871) forced her and the other nuns to seek refuge in their family homes or elsewhere. Upon her eventual return to the Carmel, she held the office of prioress for a total of twenty-two years until 1893 when Thérèse's sister Pauline (Mother Agnès) was elected by a close call for one term of three years. The community then appointed Mother Gonzague prioress from 1896 to 1902. During this time, Marie de Gonzague functioned as Mistress of Novices with Thérèse acting as her aide.

---

40 From Sister Geneviève's preparatory notes for the Bishop's Process, 1908.
41 *Les Annales de Sainte Thérèse de Lisieux, op. cit.*

Mother Gonzague met Thérèse after Pauline entered the Carmel in 1882. Thérèse was nine at the time. She recalls in her autobiography that when she saw Mother Gonzague she told her she also wanted to become a Carmelite:

> Having listened to my *great confidences*, Mother Marie de Gonzague believed I had a vocation, but she told me they didn't receive postulants at the age of *nine* and that I must wait till I was sixteen. I resigned myself in spite of my intense desire of entering as soon as possible and of making my First Communion the day Pauline received the habit.[42]

In 1887 Mother Gonzague wrote a letter to "My dear Thérèsita" giving her some advice especially about eating her meals: "Doesn't my angel want to come and be with her older sisters, who are so happy in God's service? If you do not take the necessary nourishment, you won't be able to succeed. Courage, child of my heart, patience and hope."[43] Mother Gonzague often referred to Thérèse as "Thérèsita," the name of St. Teresa of Avila's niece (Teresita de Jesus) who entered the convent at the age of nine.

The time finally arrived when Thérèse made determined efforts to enter the Lisieux Carmel at fourteen which included seeking permission from her father, family, the Carmel superiors, the bishop, and even the pope. When she at last received permission, the date was delayed for several months causing her added disappointment. At any rate, when she did appear at the Carmel on the Rue de Livarot on April 9, 1888, at the age of fifteen, Mother Marie de Gonzague greeted her with open arms. She wrote a laudatory evaluation of Thérèse the day after her Profession (September 9, 1890): "This angelic child is only seventeen and a half; yet she has the judgment of a woman of thirty, the religious perfection of an old and accomplished novice, and very good self mastery; she is a perfect religious."[44] Here follows a more expanded characterization by Mother Gonzague three years later sent to the Visitation Convent in Le Mans:

> The jewel of Carmel, its dear Benjamin. She has the office of painter, in which she excels without having had any lessons other than observing our Reverend Mother, her sister [Pauline], at work. Mature and strong, with the air of a child, and with a sound of voice and manner of expression which veils the wisdom and perfection of a woman fifty years old. A soul which is always calm and in complete possession of herself at all times. A completely innocent saint, who needs no repentance to appear before God, but whose head is always full of mischief. Mystic, comic, she can make you weep with devotion, and just as easily die with laughter at recreation.[45]

Mother Marie de Gonzague was reelected in February 13, 1886, as prioress for seven more years. The next elections scheduled for February 1892 were

---

42 *Story of a Soul*, chapter III, p. 59.
43 LC 53, dated September, 1887.
44 From a letter to the Tours Carmel dated September 9, 1890.
45 François de Sainte-Marie, *op. cit.*, p. 18. This was written on the back of a photograph (lost) sent to the Carmel of Tours in 1893.

postponed for a year because of the severe influenza epidemic. Mother Agnès, elected this time as prioress on February 20, 1893, selected Mother Gonzague as Mistress of Novices. Mother Agnès chose Sister Thérèse to assist Mother Gonzague who was very willing to have her correct and sometimes instruct them, as she put it. Incidentally, Thérèse, then a senior novice, should have by then finished her novitiate on September 8, 1893. Thérèse wrote an analogy concerning her task as instructor and counselor to the novices: "Mother, you are the precious brush which the hand of Jesus lovingly holds when He wishes to do a *great work* in the souls of your children, and I am the *very small brush* He deigns to use afterwards for the smallest details."[46]

Thérèse dedicated her second poem "To Mother Marie de Gonzague for Her Sixtieth Birthday" (PN 2) on February 20, 1894. The fifth and last stanza is:

> Jesus, your Rose is the Mother
> Who directs our childlike hearts.
> Deign to listen to their prayer:
> May they celebrate her eightieth birthday!
>
> The three little novices
> Sr. Thérèse of the Child Jesus
> Sr. Martha of Jesus
> Sr. Marie-Madeleine

A large amount of severe criticism has been written about Mother Marie de Gonzague's personality defects most of which were based on her amazingly contradictory personality. Yet she has been lauded for her kindness, understanding, her very pleasant voice, and her possession of a reasonable amount of culture. But her negative traits included being too stern, unpredictable, jealous, changeable, moody, and domineering. She was also accused of violating Carmelite rules, or at best, relaxing some of them. For example, she openly campaigned for her own re-election which was forbidden. Another was her extremely close ties with her family. Her sister, a countess, often came to the monastery with her grandchildren and would stay for days, lodged, appropriately in the gatehouse, not the monastery itself, but with the sisters at her beck and call. Mother Gonzague's pet cat, Mira, at times received excessive attention, causing comment from some quarters.

Upon entering Carmel, Thérèse surprisingly experienced at times severe treatment from the prioress. Father Godefroy Madelaine, one-time prior of the Premonstratensian abbey of Mondaye and close friend of Mother Marie de Gonzague declared at the Apostolic Process that:

> Mother Marie de Gonzague confided to me that, in order to exercise Sister Thérèse's virtue [humility in particular], she had studiously sought to try her by affecting towards her a certain indifference and severity. She has, moreover, testified to me that this apparently harsh treatment had certainly been very painful to the Servant of God, but that no pain had ever caused her to deviate in the least from perfect obedience.

---

46 *Story of a Soul*, chapter XI, p. 235.

Even one of Thérèse's novices, Sister Marie of the Trinity, disclosed in the course of her testimony at the Diocesan Process in 1911 that she observed Mother Gonzague's startling harshness towards Thérèse. For example, whenever Thérèse had a stomach-ache her novice mistress ordered her to report it to her immediately which she would do out of obedience even though she did not want to complain openly to anyone. Then when Sister Marie of the Trinity asked Mother Gonzague to give Thérèse something to relieve her problem, her response was amazingly caustic one time: "For goodness sake, that child is always complaining. We come to Carmel to suffer, and if she cannot bear her little indispositions let her go home." [47]

Notwithstanding these personal reproofs, she did extend many favors to the Martin sisters who were granted services and exemptions, which under any other superior would most likely never have been tolerated. The fact that four blood sisters and a very close cousin were allowed in the same monastery was most uncommon. Furthermore, that Céline was permitted to bring her camera into the monastery with apparently no objections from anyone was a favor bestowed on few if any in other Carmelite convents at that time.

Thérèse explains in a manner only a saint could her reaction to the treatment she endured at the hands of Mother Gonzague:

> [Our] Mother Prioress, frequently ill, had little time to spend with me. I know that she loved me very much and said everything good about me that was possible, nevertheless, God permitted that she was VERY SEVERE *without her even being aware of it*. I was unable to meet her without having to kiss the floor, and it was the same thing on those rare occasions when she gave me spiritual direction. What an inestimable grace! How *visibly* God was acting within her who took His place! What would have become of me if I had been the "pet" of the community as some of the Sisters believed? Perhaps, instead of seeing Our Lord in my Superiors, I would have looked upon them as ordinary persons only and my heart, *so well guarded* while I was in the world, would have become humanly attached in the cloister. Happily I was preserved from this misfortune. I *loved* Mother Prioress *very much*, but it was a pure affection which raised me to the Bridegroom of my soul.[48]

Later on in her autobiography, Thérèse continues with the same thoughts:

> Dear Mother [Gonzague], you are the compass Jesus has given me as a sure guide to the eternal shore. How sweet it is to fix my eyes upon you and thus accomplish the will of the Lord! Since the time He permitted me to suffer temptations against the faith, He has greatly increased the spirit of faith in my heart, which helps me to see in you not only a loving Mother but also Jesus living in your soul and communicating His will to me through you. I know very well, dear Mother, you are treating me as a feeble soul, a spoiled child, and as a consequence I have no trouble in carrying the burden of obedience. But because of what I feel in my heart, I would not change my attitude towards you, nor would my love decrease

---

47 O'Mahony, *St. Thérèse of Lisieux*, p. 247.
48 *Story of a Soul*, chapter VII, pp. 150–151.

if it pleased you to treat me severely. I would see once more that it was the will of Jesus that you were acting in this way for the greater good of my soul.[49]

Despite all, the affection Thérèse had for Mother Gonzague was truly sincere and deep. In Manuscript C of the story of Thérèse's soul, she wrote "Dearest Mother" 21 times and "Beloved Mother" 39 times.[50] Some in the convent had an unduly strong attachment to the prioress which Thérèse, as an assistant to the novice mistress, observed in one of her charges, Sister Martha of Jesus, eight years Thérèse's senior:

> I was able to console her whom you [Mother Marie de Gonzague] had given me as a sister among the rest and to explain of what love really consisted. I pointed out to her that it was *herself* she was loving, not you. I told her, too, how I loved you and the sacrifices I was obliged to make at the commencement of my religious life in order not to become attached to you in a physical way as a dog is attached to its master....
>
> I remember when I was still a postulant that I had such violent temptations to satisfy myself and to find a few crumbs of pleasure that I was obliged to walk rapidly by your door [the prioress' office] and to cling firmly to the banister of the staircase in order not to turn back.... How happy I am now for having deprived myself from the very beginning of my religious life![51]

One of Mother Agnès' priorates ended on March 21, 1896, at which time the sixteen nuns who had the power to vote re-elected Mother Gonzague as prioress, though after a stressful runoff election of voting seven times. Despite the fact that her sister Pauline was not chosen, Thérèse accepted this choice as being the will of God. Not quite so for Mother Agnès whose time as prioress she recounted in these few words: "Mother Marie de Gonzague could not bear for me to take on too much authority. She would have wanted me always under her domination. How I suffered and cried during those three years! But I realize that this yoke was necessary for me. It matured me and detached my soul from honors."[52]

Thérèse was aware of the distressing feelings Mother Gonzague had concerning her relations with Mother Agnès and the community during and after the voting in which she won by a narrow margin. She wrote her a letter offering her conciliatory and soothing advice in the form of an allegorical story, "Legend of a very little Lamb." In it Thérèse concludes with Our Lord stating, "I want only that she [Mother Gonzague, the "shepherdess" in the story] may understand the truth and recognize that her cross is coming from heaven and not from earth."[53] The next day, June 21, 1896, was the feast day of St. Aloysius Gonzaga, and Thérèse's recreational play *The Triumph of Humility* (RP 7), written for Mother Gonzague, was performed in her honor at the monastery.

---

49 Ibid., chapter X, p. 219.
50 Gaucher, *The Passion of Thérèse of Lisieux*, footnote b, p. 24.
51 *Story of a Soul*, chapter XI, p. 237.
52 Chalon, *op. cit.* p. 202.
53 LT 190 from Thérèse to Mother Gonzague, dated June 20, 1896.

After Thérèse died, Mother Gonzague wrote in the margin of Thérèse's Act of Profession this evaluation of Thérèse's work as her assistant: "An accomplished model of humility, obedience, charity, prudence, detachment, and regular observance, Sister Thérèse carried out the difficult charge of mistress of novices with a wisdom and perfection that was equaled only by her love for God." [54]

In fact, Mother Gonzague praised Thérèse frequently and even called her "Carmel's treasure," especially in her correspondence with Thérèse's two "spiritual brothers." Sister Marie of the Trinity, testified at the Apostolic Process what Mother Marie de Gonzague told her a number of times about Thérèse: "If a prioress were to be chosen out of the whole community, I would not hesitate to choose Sister Thérèse of the Child Jesus in spite of her youth. She is perfect in everything. Her only drawback is having her three sisters with her [Pauline, Marie, and Céline]." [55]

One cold winter night in January 1895, Mother Agnès (then prioress) told Thérèse to write down all her childhood memories. She dutifully obeyed; the result was the masterpiece of spiritual writing, *Story of a Soul*. The first part, Manuscript A, is dedicated to Mother Agnès; the second to her other sister, Sister Marie of the Sacred Heart; and the third section—chapters X and XI—to Mother de Gonzague. It contains many passages of lavish praise of Mother Gonzague.

In October of 1895, a twenty-one-year-old seminarian, Maurice Bellière, wrote to Mother Agnès asking for a nun to pray for his vocation as a missionary. She chose the very pleased and willing Sister Thérèse. When Mother Marie de Gonzague became prioress the next year, another seminarian (Adolphe Roulland) asked for the same privilege of having a nun pray for his missionary apostolate. She assigned Thérèse this task. Thérèse's account of how it came about and her reaction to having a second "spiritual brother" follows:

> After having told me to be seated, you [Mother Gonzague] asked me: "Will you take charge of the spiritual interests of a missionary who is to be ordained and leave very soon [for China]?"... I believed I could not do it for the intentions of another, and that, besides, there were many Sisters better than I who would be able to answer his request. All my objections were useless. You told me that one could have several brothers.[56]

A delightfully witty little episode occurred when Father Roulland came to the Carmel on July 3, 1896 to say one of his first masses. When in the parlor, Mother Gonzague consented to have him catch a glimpse of Thérèse in the chapel. She told him, "The last one [since she was sacristan], who remains kneeling for a moment at the communion window after all the nuns have received communion, she is the one!" Without hesitating, Thérèse said: "And the first to receive communion, Father, is the prioress!" [57]

---

54 See p. 943 in *General Correspondence*, vol. II.
55 Gaucher, *op. cit.*, p. 23.
56 *Story of a Soul*, chapter XI, p. 253.
57 Descouvemont, *op. cit.*, p. 266.

The year 1894 signaled the first ill-omened signs of tuberculosis, the disease that would claim Thérèse's life. Her condition slowly worsened until July 8, 1897, when she was brought down to the infirmary. A month before, on June 7, the exhausted Thérèse posed for three photos that Céline, painfully convinced of her sister's approaching death, wished to have as a final remembrance of her appearance. She gave them to Mother Marie de Gonzague for her feast day on July 21. Thérèse gave her "the photograph album and some toques she had made with Sr. Marie of St. Joseph."[58] Along with this was Thérèse's poem "To Mother Marie de Gonzague" (PS 6):

> And yet, my darling mother,
> With great happiness I offer you
> A photograph album,
> My toques, and my little heart.
>
> *Thérèse of the Child Jesus*
> Unwor. carm. rel. [unworthy Carmelite religious]

Thérèse remained in the infirmary for two and a half months before she died. On April 6, her sisters and others jotted down Thérèse's "Last Conversations" which they considered as coming from the mouth of a saint. Mother Marie de Gonzague showed extreme kindness in allowing the Martin sisters and cousin free access to Thérèse. She permitted Mother Agnès to stay often at Thérèse's bedside and write the conversations she had with Thérèse. Furthermore, Céline became her primary infirmarian (nurse). The official infirmarian kindly yielded her rights to her. Moreover, Thérèse's cousin, Sister Marie of the Eucharist, received permission to write almost daily at times to her family informing them of Thérèse's condition. They in turn were granted the exceptional freedom of making visits to the parlor and sending Thérèse food. In addition, the prioress even allowed all three Martin sisters to be together with Thérèse at her bedside—another rare privilege indeed.

A few selections from *Her Last Conversations* pertaining to Mother Marie de Gonzague are printed below. All were spoken to Mother Agnès unless otherwise indicated:

- She [Thérèse] told me [Pauline] that formerly she had to undergo a rough battle with regard to a lamp to be prepared for Mother Marie de Gonzague's family that arrived unexpectedly to spend the night in the extern Sisters' quarters. The struggle was so violent, there came such thoughts against authority into her mind, that not to give in to them, she had to implore God's help with insistence.... "To conquer myself I imagined I was preparing the lamp for the Blessed Virgin and the Child Jesus; and then I did it with an incredible care.... From that day, I made the resolution never to consider whether the things commanded me appeared useful or not." (July 12, 1897)
- During Matins, with a reference to her autobiographical manuscripts: "After my death, you mustn't speak to anyone about my manuscript before it is

---
58 Note by Mother Agnès as quoted in *The Poetry of Saint Thérèse of Lisieux*, p. 231.

published ... you must speak about it only to Mother Prioress [Mother Gonzague]!" (August 1, 1897)
- We changed her tunic in the afternoon and were struck by her extreme thinness because her face hadn't changed. I went to ask Mother Prioress to come and see her back. Mother was long in coming, and I had to admire the gentle and patient way in which Thérèse awaited her arrival. Mother was painfully surprised and said kindly: "What is this little girl who is so thin?" [Thérèse responded] "A skeleton!" (September 20, 1897)
- One day, in her presence, Mother Prioress was speaking to the doctor about the purchase just made of a lot in the city cemetery because there was no longer any room in the old one. She added that they would henceforth dig the graves deep enough so that it would be possible to superimpose three coffins. Sister Thérèse of the Child Jesus said, laughing: "Then it's I who will do first honors to this new cemetery?" (September 1897)
- At Carmel, her great suffering had been not being able to receive Communion each day. She said, a short time before her death to Mother Marie de Gonzague, who was afraid of daily Communion: "Mother, when I'm in heaven, I'll make you change your opinion."
- That is what happened. After the death of the Servant of God, the chaplain gave us Communion every day, and Mother Marie de Gonzague, instead of being repelled by it, was very happy about it." (Words copied down by Sister Marie of the Sacred Heart [Marie Martin] in July 1897.)
- We had asked her: "Who will receive your last look?" She had answered a few days before her death: "If God leaves me free, it will be for Mother Prioress."

Critics have speculated about Mother Gonzague's care for Thérèse in her last suffering days. It is known that she refused to have Thérèse take any pain killers except for a few drops of morphine syrup. She decidedly prohibited morphine injections with the belief that it is shameful for Carmelites to have relief from pain since the purpose in their life is to suffer. Some critics even claim that Mother Gozague deprived Thérèse of a doctor in the crucial stages of her sickness. On the contrary, Dr. de Cornière, the official convent doctor, often visited his patient, but not as regularly, some contend, as he should have. Even Dr. La Néele, Thérèse's cousin by marriage, entered the enclosure to see her only four times despite the fact that he and Mother Gonzague did not get along well. Nonetheless, Sister Geneviève (Céline) wrote later on: "Mother Marie de Gonzague gave in to her jealousy, but it was not spitefulness. It was not because of any malice that St. Thérèse remained a long time without treatment. It was through negligence, not through malice." [59] But Thérèse's reason is truly worthy of a saint: "My dear sisters, one must not murmur against the will of God. It is He who does not allow Mother to give me any relief." [60]

In a letter from Thérèse's cousin, Marie Guérin (Sister Marie of the Eucharist) to her father, she states: "Mother Prioress takes good care of her, none could

---
59 Gaucher, *op. cit.* p. 244.
60 *Sicut Parvuli*, "Mother Marie de Gonzague," Sept. 1984, p. 88.

do better.... We are making a novena to Our Lady of Victories, and Mother Prioress is having Masses offered up there. Besides, during this novena, Mother is putting Lourdes water in everything Sister Thérèse takes" (June 5, 1897). In another letter to her father she added: "To mention the state the community is in, there are tears, sobs, and grief on all sides. Mother Agnès of Jesus is to be admired for her courage and resignation; our Mother Prioress has a real motherly tenderness towards all of us in the midst of the greatest of pains, for Sister Thérèse of the Child Jesus who was her greatest treasure" (July 8, 1897). A poignant note Sister Marie of the Eucharist wrote, this time to her mother, reads: "You cannot imagine how kind Mother Prioress is to us, especially to our little Thérèse. This dear little one said to her this morning, in her delightful, smiling way, "Mother, I want to die in your arms—not on the pillow but on your heart" (July 14, 1897).

Mother Gonzague lived only eight years longer than Thérèse. In 1896 she was elected prioress and held this position until 1902 when Mother Agnès replaced her and remained in this office for life (except for one year) by a special decree from the pope. Mother Gonzague underwent a gradual character transformation and realization of Thérèse's inestimable worth. When Sister Geneviève testified at the beatification process, she related this story about Mother Gonzague:

> Mother Marie de Gonzague told me of a favor she had received before a portrait of Thérèse as a child. It must have been a very vivid experience because our poor Mother could not look at this picture without crying. I often saw her moved in this way and she said to me, "Oh, the things she said to me! How much she reproached me with—but how gently." The good Mother often took up this picture and, in her later years there was much improvement in her, under the gentle influence of Sister Thérèse.[61]

Mother Marie de Gonzague spent her last years suffering from cancer of the tongue. Death came on December 17, 1904.

Interestingly, she herself refused any pain killers to alleviate her suffering but upon the persistence of the community, she consented at the end to take some narcotic relief.

For a total of twenty-two years, Marie de Gonzague served as prioress and six as sub-prioress. She died at the age of seventy, having survived all her siblings.

10. Sœur Marie de Jésus (1862–1938)
(Sister Marie of Jésus)
She unconsciously irritated Thérèse

SISTER MARIE OF JESUS STRAINED THÉRÈSE'S PATIENCE BY HER UNCONSCIOUS habit of clicking her teeth together during the long hours of prayer in the chapel. Thérèse tells us in her own words how she dealt with this irritation, a typical example of Thérèse applying her own philosophy of the Little Way:

---
61 Ibid., p. 89.

The practice of charity, as I have said, dear Mother [the prioress Mother Marie de Gonzague], was not always so sweet for me, and to prove it to you I am going to recount certain little struggles which will certainly make you smile. For a long time at evening meditation, I was placed in front of a Sister who had a strange habit and I think many lights [*sic*] because she rarely used a book during meditation. This is what I noticed: as soon as this Sister arrived, she began making a strange little noise which resembled the noise one would make when running two shells, one against the other. I was the only one to notice it because I had extremely sensitive hearing (too much so at times). Mother, it would be impossible for me to tell you how much this little noise wearied me. I had a great desire to turn my head and stare at the culprit who was very certainly unaware of her "click." This would be the only way of enlightening her. However, in the bottom of my heart I felt it was much better to suffer this out of love for God and not to cause the Sister any pain. I remained calm, therefore, and tried to unite myself to God and to forget the little noise. Everything was useless. I felt the perspiration inundate me, and I was obliged simply to make a prayer of suffering; however, while suffering, I searched for a way of doing it without annoyance and with peace and joy, at least in the interior of my soul. I tried to love the little noise which was so displeasing; instead of trying not to hear it (impossible), I paid close attention so as to hear it well, as though it were a delightful concert, and my prayer (which was not the Prayer of Quiet) was spent in offering this concert to Jesus.[62]

Thérèse recorded this anecdote in the last year of her life. Obviously that annoyance had no effect on Thérèse's relation with her. She considered her, in fact, one of the saintly nuns in the convent.[63] Just a few months before she died, Thérèse wrote her a letter evidently in response to a note (now lost) Sister Marie of Jesus wrote to her. It doesn't seem likely that Thérèse wrote letters or notes to every nun in the community. Therefore, it was a rare privilege that Sister Marie received one. In the letter below cited in its entirety she gives some of her characteristic spiritual advice. Apparently the thirty-five-year-old Sister had no qualms about seeking spiritual or other counsel from the twenty-four-year-old Thérèse.

The little spouse of Jesus must not be sad, for Jesus would be sad too. She must always sing in her heart the canticle of love, she must forget her little sorrows to give solace to the great sorrows of her Spouse.

Dear little Sister, do not be *a sad little girl* when seeing you are not understood, that you are judged badly, that you are forgotten, but lay a trap for everybody by taking care to do like others, or rather by doing for yourself what others are doing for you, that is, *forget all* that is not Jesus, *forget* YOURSELF for His love!... Dear little Sister, do not say that this is difficult; if I speak in this way, it is your fault, for you told me that you loved Jesus very much, and nothing seems impossible to the soul that loves....

Be assured that your note *pleased* me very much![64]

---

62 *Story of a Soul*, chapter XI, pp. 249–250.
63 *Histoire d'Une Âme*, edited by Conrad De Meester, footnote 1, p. 248.
64 From Thérèse to Sister Marie of Jesus, June–July, 1897.

Again, it was around the same time this was written that Sister Marie of Jesus assisted the infirmarians attending to the very ill Thérèse who was suffering from the long final stages of her illness. As such, Sister Marie witnessed the procedures Thérèse had to undergo involving very painful cauterizations. She not only lived with Thérèse during Thérèse's short nine years as a nun and witnessed her last sickness, but also experienced the joy of seeing her one-time colleague and advisor raised to sainthood, the greatest honor the church bestows on one of its spiritual luminaries.

Sister Marie of Jesus was born Eugéne-Henriette-Amélie Courceau in 1862 in Rouen, the town where St. Joan of Arc was burned at the stake. At twenty-one on April 26, 1883, she became a postulant at the Carmel in Lisieux and chose the name Sister Marie of Jesus. Her reception of the habit took place on October 15, 1883; profession followed the next year on December 5, 1884. Frequently she was known to say, "I can never do too much; I will never do enough." [65] She worked mainly as a seamstress at the convent. She passed to her eternal reward in 1938 after fifty-four years as a true daughter of St. Teresa of Avila.

11. Sœur de la Trinité et de la Sainte-Face (1874–1944)
(Sister Marie of the Trinity and of the Holy Face)
Thérèse's favorite novice—"The rogue of Carmel"

The story of sister marie of the trinity—the nun of many names— provides invaluable information on St. Thérèse's method of training her novices, her spirituality, her extraordinary personality, and her doctrine known as the "little way of spiritual childhood." This nun, only one year younger than Thérèse, lived throughout the entire ecclesial process leading to Thérèse's canonization and was directly involved with the myriad daily activities therein associated with it behind the cloistered Carmelite walls. After Thérèse's death and growing fame, Sister Marie's mother, father, and some siblings spent much of their lives partaking in Theresian matters that will be detailed at the end of this biography.

Sister Marie of the Trinity was born Marie-Louise-Joséphine Castel, the thirteenth of nineteen children, on August 12, 1874, in Saint-Pierre-sur-Dives, a little town located several miles south of Lisieux. Her father was an elementary school teacher in the same town. When the family moved to Paris, however, he became a merchant but also labored diligently with a priest who founded the institute "Work for First Communion" which prepared abandoned children for their first communion. He even traveled throughout France explaining and promoting this pious undertaking.

Having been reared in a very religious family especially devoted to the Holy Face, Marie-Louise soon expressed a desire to dedicate her life to Our Lord as a nun. On April 30, 1891, at the age of seventeen she entered the Paris Carmel on the Avenue de Messine and was given the name Sister Agnès of Jesus. A year later on March 12, she received the habit. On July 8, 1893, poor health forced

---

65 Conrad De Meester, *St. Thérèse of Lisieux: Her Life, Times, and Teaching*.

her to leave the convent. Hoping her condition would improve by being near the fresh air, beach, and water, her father took her to Trouville which indeed proved very beneficial.

Thérèse heard about this young novice who had left the Paris Carmel. Knowing that there was a legal plan proposed to forbid anyone to enter religious life in France before the age of twenty-one, Thérèse offered this winsome solution: "If they were to send me away, I know very well what I would do: I would go find little Sr. Agnès of Jesus and we would live together until we had reached the age to re-enter Carmel!" [66]

After Marie-Louise's health was restored, she wanted to return to a Carmelite monastery. By this time the family had settled in Lisieux. Since the Carmel on the Rue de Livarot was nearby, she visited the monastery a number of times, met Mother Agnès (Pauline) and Mother Gonzague, and made her wishes known. They eventually accepted her on June 16, 1894. She did not take the same name she had at the Paris Carmel; this time she chose Sr. Marie-Agnès of the Holy Face. Two years later, however, her name was changed to Sr. Marie of the Trinity and of the Holy Face because there was at times confusion with her name and that of Mother Agnès (Mère Agnès): Mère and Marie sounded almost the same especially when spoken with a local Norman accent.

The testimony Sister Marie of the Trinity gave at the process for the beatification of her beloved novice mistress is quite telling:

> It is really thanks to her [St. Thérèse] that I managed to be a Carmelite. My lack of virtue and health and the lack of sympathy I found in the [Lisieux] community because I came from another Carmel caused me a thousand almost insurmountable difficulties. In those painful times, only the Servant of God consoled me. She would cleverly make the most of every opportunity to plead my cause with the Sisters who were against me. "How I would willingly give my life for you to be a Carmelite!" she would tell me. On the day of my Profession, April 30, 1896, she confided that it was one of the most beautiful days of her life. Her joy seemed to equal mine." [67]

Sr. Thérèse became her "angel"—the name assigned to the nun who instructed the newly-entered on the customs, rules, and spirit of Carmel. Years later Sister Marie of the Trinity offered the following interesting information:

> Sister Thérèse had been about four years professed when I entered in 1894. But at her own request she had been left in the novitiate part of the convent [remaining officially still as a novice], where the observance is stricter. Mother Agnès, who was prioress at the time, knew that the other novices and I would benefit from her counsels, so she charged her with guiding us, and especially with correcting our faults. Mother Gonzague, the ex-prioress, was titular

---

[66] Descouvemont, *Thérèse of Lisieux and Marie of the Trinity*, p. 7.
[67] This quotation in the introduction to PN 29 on p. 144 in *Poetry of Thérèse of Lisieux* comes originally from Sister Marie of the Trinity's *Red Notebook*, a compilation of her notes on Sister Thérèse of the Child Jesus which she used at her interrogation during the Diocesan and Apostolic Processes.

B. At the Carmel in Lisieux

novice-mistress. When she became prioress again in 1896, she retained the title of novice-mistress and left Sister Thérèse as assistant with complete charge of the novices' training.[68]

Thérèse was happy now that she was not the youngest (the "Benjamin" as the nuns called them) in the convent. In fact, the new novice looked so young that Thérèse even playfully called her "my little doll." Her pleasant voice delighted Thérèse. She said to her once, "You have just the voice that I would wish to have. Now, I am no longer pained at not having one, since God has given me a daughter who has enough voice for both of us!"[69]

For various reasons the exuberant "little Parisian" found it difficult to adjust to the very strict rules of the Order which regulated the "exterior comportment" of every nun: i.e., her posture, glances, movement of feet, manner of sitting, standing, eating, etc. She often became discouraged during her formative period and would go to Thérèse in tears, especially when having doubts about her vocation. She of course received great counsel, tempered with kind criticism and wise advice. Thérèse's protégé was indeed blessed by this relationship and in due time not only did her spiritual life improve but a warm and fruitful friendship developed. Thérèse's own novice mistress (Sr. Marie of the Angels) wrote a brief sketch of Sr. Marie of the Trinity in 1901 describing her this way:

> Sr. Marie of the Trinity (age 27), the rogue of Carmel! Never feels embarrassed by anything and knows perfectly how to pull herself out of any affair, feeling herself accompanied on her joyous path by her angel-guide, Sr. Thérèse of the Child Jesus, to whose special guidance she owes the good fortune of being a Carmelite. Still now, at any moment, she feels the assurance of Thérèse's sensitive and constant protection and remembers with joy that from heaven above Thérèse does not abandon her little game of ninepins. She claims to be so happy that she feels she will one day die of joy.[70]

During Sr. Marie's novitiate Thérèse called her the "happy little Carmelite ninepin" and the "novice of the 'shell.' "[71] She chose these names from the way Sister Marie tried to practice virtues. Sister would imagine herself playing the game of bowling called "ninepins" with the Child Jesus. "I pictured these ninepins in all sizes and colors in order to personify the souls I wanted to reach out to in my prayers."[72] When Thérèse learned of this kind of childish spiritual game she expounded upon it in her 1896 Christmas Eve letter (LT 212) to her as if it were from Jesus. She addressed the envelope "Personal. To my dear little Spouse" and signed the note "Your little Brother Jesus":

> Oh! How pleased I am with you.... All year you have amused me very much by playing ninepins. I was so pleased that the angelic court was surprised

---

68 O'Mahony, *St. Thérèse of Lisieux by Those Who Knew Her*, p. 230.
69 Descouvemont, *op. cit.*, p. 10.
70 Ibid., p. 41.
71 Mother Agnès, *A Novice of Saint Thérèse*, p. 21.
72 From footnote 2 to Thérèse's note (LT 212) to Sr. Marie of the Trinity dated December 24, 1896.

and charmed: more than one little cherub asked me why I had not made him a child ... more than one asked me if the melody of his harp was not more pleasing to me than your joyful laugh when you knocked down a pin with the bowl of your love.... I told them, certainly, your smile was more sweet to me than their melodies because you could not play and smile except by suffering, by forgetting yourself....

The second name Thérèse gave to Sr. Marie of the Trinity, "the novice of the 'shell,' " was an appellation Thérèse used which Sister Marie of the Trinity herself explains:

> I often cried, and for nothing, and this caused my dear Mistress a lot of sorrow. One day she had a brilliant idea; taking from her painting table a moulding shell and holding my hands so I could not wipe my eyes, she started to gather my tears in the shell. Instead of continuing my crying, I could no longer keep from laughing.
> "All right," she said, "from now on you can cry as much as you want, providing you cry into this shell."[73]

In the same letter of December 24, 1896, Thérèse commented about another quaint spiritual game for Sister Marie of the Trinity. One Christmas all the nuns obtained little knickknacks for the Christmas tree. Sr. Marie of the Trinity received a spinning top which fascinated her but the other nuns thought unattractive and useless. Thérèse placed this charming little note in Sr. Marie's cell on Christmas Eve and signed it "Jesus":

> Beloved little spouse, I have something to ask you, will you refuse me?... Oh, no! you love me too much for that. Well, I shall admit I would like to change the game; the ninepins amuse me, but I would now like to spin the top, and if you wish you will be my top. I am giving you one as a model. You see it is not beautiful, whoever does not know how to use it will kick it away with his foot. But a child will leap with joy when seeing it and will say: "Ah! How amusing, this can spin all day long without stopping.... When I have been well entertained by you, I will take you up above and we shall play without any suffering." (LT 212)

Eight days before Thérèse died she noticed Sister Marie of the Trinity had been crying, and said, "You have been crying; did you cry into the shell?"[74] The repentant Sister promised she would follow her directions. Thérèse did, however, allow her to weep for the first few days after her death without the shell. Then she would have to return to using the shell. Forty-seven years later on the day after her death, the Mother Prioress discovered in the deceased sister's desk drawer the little tear shell and the top.[75]

Sister Marie of the Trinity was indeed blessed by her relationship with Thérèse not only because of the invaluable lessons she learned from her verbally and by

---

73 Mother Agnès, *op. cit.*, p. 23–24.
74 *Her Last Conversations*, p. 267.
75 Mother Agnès, *op. cit.*, p. 25.

example, but also from the nine letters she wrote to her. These nine letters (or notes) and eight poems Thérèse composed for her provide a wonderful insight into Thérèse's philosophy as well as the affection she had for Sr. Marie of the Trinity. The first two poems are in honor of her reception of the habit on December 18, 1894. The first one (PN 11) is entitled "The Time of Tears Has Passed at Last" and was actually sung by Marie of the Trinity at evening recreation on that day. After this the Carmelite choir welcomed her into the new community by singing the second one, (PN 12) "It's Close to You, Virgin Mary." These two poems are especially personalized reflections on the novice.

Thérèse composed PN 20 for her little novice's twenty-first birthday on August 12, 1895, entitled "My Heaven on Earth" which is a canticle to the Holy Face—a devotion they both shared. On April 30, 1896, Sister Marie of the Trinity's Profession of vows took place for which Thérèse wrote two more poems: PN 29, "How Sweet It Is for Us," and PN 30, "A Gloss on the Divine." On May 7 of the same year Sister Marie of the Trinity received her veil. Then at the end of the month on Trinity Sunday, May 31, Thérèse wrote PN 31 celebrating her feast day—"The Canticle of Sister Marie of the Trinity" ("I Thirst for Love").

Before Sister Marie of the Trinity entered the Lisieux Carmel she encountered some difficulties resulting in delaying her admittance. She attributed the overcoming of these delays to Our Lady of Perpetual Help for whom she had a special interest since childhood. Knowing this, in March 1897 Thérèse composed the seventh poem for her novice entitled "To Our Lady of Perpetual Help" (PN 49). The final one written during her last sufferings is PN 53, "For Sister Marie of the Trinity" ("A Lily Among Thorns") dated May 1897. This poem expresses Thérèse's deep conviction about God's love and mercy. "[The] one who has charmed me is you, my Sweet Jesus!... /And you alone, O Jesus! Could satisfy a soul / That needed to love even to the infinite."

For a while one of the duties Sr. Marie of the Trinity had was assistant infirmarian but when Thérèse was admitted into the infirmary she was dismissed because of fear she might contract the same disease Thérèse had. This greatly distressed Sr. Marie since she then was unable to see her as often as before. Nonetheless she was present, as well as all the community, at Thérèse's last agonizing moments. Shortly before the end, Thérèse was asked if it was God's will to continue this suffering, "Would you accept it?"

> With a tone of extraordinary heroism, she replied: "I will it!" And her head fell back on the pillow with an expression so calm, so surrendered, that we could no longer keep back our tears.... I left the infirmary, not having the courage to assist any longer at such a painful spectacle. I returned there only later with the community for the last moments and I witnessed her beautiful and long ecstatic look at the moment when she died, around 7 o'clock in the evening on Thursday, September 30, 1897.[76]

---

[76] Descouvemont, *op. cit.*, p. 40.

For nearly half a century until her own death, Sr. Marie of the Trinity assimilated and practiced Thérèse's teachings. For years she was intimately involved with Thérèse cause. Of tremendous importance were her depositions at the Process leading to Thérèse's canonization. She responded in writing to the tremendous quantity of mail the Carmel received. Because of this she was called "the Mother-archivist" by one of the prelates (Msgr. de Teil) connected with the cause who thought that she must be an elderly nun. In addition, she prepared and sent out photos and relics of our saint, contacted publishers, worked at bookbinding, copied out Thérèse's texts, and wrote her own memories of her former novice mistress known as the *Red Notebook*.

Despite a lifetime of bouts with frail health, she lived to be almost seventy. In February of 1923 the horrible disease that caused Sr. Marie's death manifested its first signs. It was a form of lupus that produced ulcerated patches on her face making her look like a "leper," a name she in fact called herself. She suffered heroically with St. Thérèse as her model for over twenty-one years until her death two decades after St. Thérèse's canonization and in the midst of World War II. Mother Agnès graphically describes the ravages of this horrible disease:

> After having completely eaten away the left ear, and having consumed the side of the face right up to the eye, which was threatening to pop out, it had covered the whole top of the head, and reached the other ear. The mouth was becoming swollen, and the process of eating was becoming very difficult.[77]

Death claimed the sixty-nine year old exemplary disciple of Thérèse on January 16, 1944, during a bout with the flu that had spread through the community. The last words spoken to her nurse were a touching culmination of her steadfast devotion to her erstwhile novice mistress: "In heaven I will follow little Thérèse everywhere."[78] Her mortal remains lie in the Lisieux town cemetery close to the first grave her dearly loved teacher was first interred.

About a third of her family of nineteen children and both parents became closely involved with the Theresian phenomenon that developed after Thérèse's passing. Following Victor Castel's demise (Sister Marie's father) in 1912, her mother and a sister took up residence as guardians at Les Buissonnets (the Martin family home in Lisieux). When her mother died, other sisters (including Violette) devoted themselves to the place as guides and caretakers. A priest brother likewise offered his service for years as a chaplain at the Carmel to the multitudes of pilgrims who flocked there. Another brother, Joachim Léon Castel, and their father in his time, worked assiduously with unfortunate orphans (*Orphelins-Apprentis* d'Auteuil—Orphans/apprentices of Auteuil) which is even now so closely related to the continuing story of St. Thérèse.

---

77 Mother Agnès, *op. cit.*, p. 57.
78 Descouvement, *op. cit.*, p. 64.

12. **Sœur Marie de l'Eucharistie**
 (Sister Marie of the Eucharist)
 Thérèse's cousin Marie Guérin (See Chapter 2, St. Thérèse's Family)

13. **Soeur Marie de Saint-Joseph** (1858–1936)
 (Sister Marie of Saint Joseph)
 A nun with a violent temper who left the convent

The nuns in the Lisieux Carmel generally avoided close contacts with Sister Marie of St. Joseph because of her impulsiveness, mood swings, and especially her displays of violent temper all of which were a genuine trial to the community. Sister Thérèse, however, was opposed to this ostracism and seriously undertook the task of helping her. Her sister, Sister Marie of the Sacred Heart (Marie Martin), gave pertinent testimony about this troubled nun in her deposition at the Diocesan Inquiry into the life and virtues of our Saint:

> This sister was subject to the blackest moods, and did scarcely any work. I saw her, when Sister Thérèse was already an invalid, come to her to call for the week's linen, which she had given her to repair, and because Sister Thérèse had not been able to complete her task, this sister reproached her severely instead of thanking her for what she had done in spite of being so ill. Sister Thérèse took the reproaches as if they were so much praise.
>
> This poor, unfortunate sister became the object of Sister Thérèse's tenderest compassion. One day, when I had confided to her how much trouble that sister gave me, the Servant of God said: "Ah! If you only knew how necessary it is to forgive her, how much she is to be pitied! It is not her fault if she is so poorly gifted; she is like an old clock that has to be re-wound every quarter of an hour. Yes, it is as bad as that. Well, wouldn't you have pity on it? Oh, how necessary it is to practice charity towards one's neighbor!"[79]

Thérèse recognized and appreciated Sister Marie of St. Joseph' positive qualities—tenderness, good memory, fine singing voice—and endeavored in her inimitable way to counteract the community's exclusionary treatment of her which induced feelings of rejection and isolation. Thérèse's remarkable tact, kindly manner, sweet smile, and intelligence, underscored by her own inborn psychological adeptness, proved successful in calming the disturbed spirit of Sister Marie. Furthermore, Thérèse's solid concentration on her own littleness, her weakness, her concept of being a child of Jesus and Mary, her abandonment, all had their part to play in her methodology. One feature of Thérèse's strategy involved writing letters (more appropriately "notes") to and even composing a poem for her. Though Sister Marie was fifteen years older than Thérèse, it is intriguing to read these sparkling notes in which she addresses her in very childlike terms. She calls her "little child," "bird," "naughty," and even "little brother." Most importantly, she associates Sister Marie with her own vocational

---

[79] O'Mahony, *St. Thérèse of Lisieux By those Who Knew Her*, p. 94.

and spiritual goals. In her first letter to Sister Marie, Thérèse actually expounds upon her own unique spirituality and vocation:

> I am delighted with the little child [Sister Marie of St. Joseph], and the one who carries her in His arms is still more delighted than I.... Ah! How beautiful is the little child's vocation! It is not one mission that she must evangelize but all missions. How will she do this?... By loving, by sleeping, by throwing flowers [sacrifices] to Jesus when He is asleep.... (A child, a missionary, and even a warrior, what a marvel.) [80]

And then in her second note she exclaims that:

> The most painful, the most loving martyrdom is ours since Jesus alone sees it.
> It will never be revealed to creatures on earth, but when the Lamb will open the book of life, what a surprise for the heavenly court to hear proclaimed with the names of missionaries and martyrs those of poor little children who will have never performed dazzling actions....[81]

Incidentally, the very first time Sister Marie of St. Joseph is mentioned in the story of St. Thérèse is around Christmas 1882 when she sent the nine-year-old Thérèse a holy card showing the little Child Jesus riding a sheep, with this note written on the reverse side: "To my gentle little Thérèse! May she think near Jesus of the little sister, her dear little Pauline. I promise her especially a little prayer so that she will always be nice and very quiet and good and so then she deserves always to carry the sweet name of Thérèse of the Infant Jesus." [82]

In a letter written possibly in January 1897, Thérèse refers to Sister Marie of St. Joseph's singing voice: "Sing your delightful refrains like a finch, and I, like a poor little sparrow, sigh in my corner, singing like the Wandering Jew, 'Death can do nothing to me, I can well see.' " [83]

In subsequent letters Thérèse encourages, advises, and instructs Sister Marie about some of the difficulties she apparently was experiencing with her fears and anxieties, and even with her sleeping. Added to this were some problems involving her duties in the convent particularly in the linen room. Later on Sister Marie of St. Joseph expressed her concern and worry over Thérèse's failing health. In fact she very much desired to see the dying Thérèse in the infirmary but was not allowed to enter. Visitors were restricted only to her blood sisters, the nursing nuns (generally Sister Geneviève—Céline), and a few others. In response to one of her attempted visits and refusals, Thérèse wrote to Sister Marie of St. Joseph: "I hope Sister Geneviève has consoled you; it is the thought that you are no longer grieved which makes mine disappear!... Ah! how happy we shall be in heaven; then we shall share in the divine perfections, and we shall be able to give to all without being obliged to deprive our dearest friends!" [84]

---

80 Thérèse's first letter (LT 194) to her written around Sept. 8–17, 1896.
81 LT 195, approximate date Sept. 8–17, 1896.
82 The author translated this from an article about Sister Marie of Saint Joseph in the November 1982 issue of *Les Annales de Sainte Thérèse de Lisieux*.
83 LT 217.
84 From Thérèse's last feebly written note (LT 250) to her, undated, but probably in July 1897.

A month later Mother Agnès copied these provocative words the dying Thérèse told her regarding Sister Marie of St. Joseph who wanted to confide in Mother Agnès even though she was no longer the prioress: "Don't ever listen to her, even though she be an angel; you would be unfortunate to do so because you wouldn't be doing your duty; it would be a weakness which would surely displease God." [85]

In the last month of Thérèse's life, on September 13, 1897, Sister Marie of St. Joseph picked a violet in the monastery garden and offered it to Thérèse through the window of the sick room that overlooked the garden area called the meadow. Thérèse commented about this scene to her sister Céline who jotted down this notation in her *Yellow Notebook*: [86]

> A sister had picked a violet for her in the garden; she offered it to her and then left. Our little Thérèse said to me, looking at the flower:
> "Ah! the scent of violets!"
> Then she made a sign to me to know if she would smell it without failing in mortification.

When Sister Marie of St. Joseph entered her cell the day after Thérèse died (October 1, 1897), she detected the scent of violets and searched around the room to find out where the flowers were. She found nothing. Then as she thought of the time she gave violets to Thérèse in the infirmary, the scent disappeared. Sister Marie of the Sacred Heart added this bit of information in her diocesan testimony: "In fact, nearly all the nuns in this community have smelt this mysterious perfume; I experienced it four or five times myself. We all experienced it when we least expected it. Anyway, I paid no heed to these phenomena; I consider them less important than an interior grace." [87]

Psychological problems plagued Sister Marie of St. Joseph through succeeding years. They persisted undiagnosed until Dr. La Néele (Thérèse's cousin through marriage) identified her affliction as neurasthenia, a condition characterized by over-all debility, depression, and bodily disorders. As a result, the fifty-one-year-old Sister Marie of St. Joseph was dismissed by the Carmel on June 29, 1909. She returned to "the world" she left twenty-eight years before.

In the lay world she was known as Marie Campain, born on January 29, 1858, into a well-to-do family in Valognes in the Cotentin Peninsula of Manche. Her father, a lawyer and businessman, was twenty-eight, and her mother, Marie Bois Campain, was twenty-one. Sadly, she died barely ten years later leaving her three daughters and a son motherless. Fortunately her two younger spinster sisters assumed some of the care of the four children. These aunts were gifted musically and imparted some of their ability in this field to Marie who made use of it when she was in the convent.

---

85 *Her Last Conversations*, August 7, 1897.
86 Ibid., September 13, 1897, p. 189.
87 O'Mahony, *op. cit.*, p. 107.

Despite the fact that Sister Marie was discharged from the convent, she continued to correspond with Mother Agnès and showered praise and respect for Sister Thérèse whom she considered such a help to her when in the convent as well as after she left:

> I am working hard to remain a little child and I want to remain docile and confident in her holy arms in order to be what she wanted me to be. I am nothing, my sweet Jesus, but this poor little nothing that I am, from now on is going to get lost in you.... I can tell you honestly now that my sojourn has become peaceful and I can leave now in total abandonment. Provided that I love my Jesus and I can satisfy Him and also little Thérèse. I don't care about what is left.[88]

Various serious physical infirmities attacked Sister Marie during her latter years, forcing her eventually to spend the last month of her life confined to her bed. She died in complete lucidity of mind at the age of seventy-eight on November 26, 1936, in Gavray (Manche).

14. Sœur Marie des Anges et du Sacré-Cœur (1845–1924)
(Sister Marie of the Angels and the Sacred Heart)
Thérèse's saintly novice mistress

THE NOVICE MISTRESS PREPARES THE YOUNG ASPIRANTS FOR THEIR RELIgious profession by guiding them in their spiritual life, teaching the rule of the order, explaining the customs of communal living, which includes training them how to move, dress, and eat. In her autobiography Thérèse calls her novice mistress, Sister Marie of the Angels, a saint and expresses her admiration for her, but also admits that some impediments existed in their relationship:

> Our novice mistress was really a saint, the finished product of the first Carmelites [of the Lisieux foundation in 1838]. I was with her all day long since she taught me how to work. Her kindness towards me was limitless and still my soul did not expand under her direction. It was only with great effort that I was able to take direction, for I had never become accustomed to speaking about my soul and I didn't know how to express what was going on with it.[89]

A few weeks before she died, Thérèse disclosed to her sister Pauline (Mother Agnès) the gratifying resolution to her relationship with Sister Marie of the Angels: "It was perhaps two years after I was here that God brought an end to my trial with regard to Sister Marie of the Angels, and I was able to open my soul to her; in the end, she consoled me very much."[90]

One consolation, for instance, happened on the night before Thérèse made her profession when she was suddenly struck with the idea that she really had no religious vocation. In *Story of a Soul* she relates how Sister Marie of the Angels helped her overcome this frightening doubt:

---

88 Letter of October 30, 1929.
89 *Story of a Soul*, chapter VII, p. 151.
90 *The Yellow Notebook*, notation of September 2, 1897.

It appeared to me ... that if I were to tell my Novice Mistress about these fears, she would prevent me from pronouncing my Vows. And still I wanted to do God's will and return to the world rather than remain in Carmel and do my own will. I made the Mistress come out of the choir and, filled with confusion, I told her the state of my soul. Fortunately, she saw things much clearer than I did, and she completely reassured me.[91]

If Thérèse believed Sister Marie of the Angels was a saint, then the feeling was mutual for Sister Marie gave under oath at the Diocesan Process (1910) these glowing assessments of Sister Thérèse:

- I cannot remember her ever saying a word against anybody. Whenever I was near her the effect it had on me was similar to what one feels before the tabernacle. A feature of her piety that struck me particularly, because I had never heard it spoken of in Carmel or in the lives of the saints, was the role she attributed to flowers. For her, every flower spoke a language of its own, in which it revealed God's infinite love and perfections to her ... plucking of petals from flowers was only a symbol of what she was doing for our Lord by means of the thousand and one sacrifices she made for him in every area of her life.

- She was an angel of peace for everybody. If someone needed advice, it was to her, the youngest, that her sisters turned, and her word was gospel.

- She found the cold very hard, but she never said a word to me about it; indeed, it was only lately that I discovered this. It would seem she suffered so much from it that it is a wonder she did not die of it. If I had only known! I would have done anything to remedy the matter. Today I say to myself: how heroic that dear child's virtue really was! Her mortification can be summed up in a few words: to suffer everything without complaint, whether it concerned clothing or food. How often I have been moved as I saw that frail young girl deprived of the consideration and dietary concessions which she should have been generously granted! But God permitted that all too often she was given only left-overs or food that even a healthy stomach would have had difficulty in putting up with. It was the same with sleep, but the dear child never said a word, so happy was she to have these opportunities of suffering.

- I have been told that even before she became a nun people were struck by her angelic expression. When Sister Stanislas's nephew saw her out walking with her father, the venerable M. Martin, he said to his sister: "Look at Mlle. Martin! She's like an angel. You know something? I think you'll see her canonized some day."

- It is marvelous to see how the Servant of God's "furor in the world" has gone on increasing since her death. The phrase I quote is the expression a religious used recently in the parlor. She seems to be everywhere — in communities, in seminaries, and in families.

- We turn out these pictures [asked for by people from around the world] by the thousand here, and still cannot meet the demand. Sometimes we receive as many as 100 letters in one day acknowledging favors and telling of the devotion they all have to the Servant of God.[92]

---

91 *Story of a Soul*, chapter VIII, p. 166.
92 All the above are from O'Mahony's translation in his book *St. Thérèse of Lisieux*.

In 1888, when Sister Marie of the Angels was still Thérèse's novice mistress, she wrote Thérèse a consoling letter after learning that her ailing father had another serious relapse:

> Yesterday, at the entrance to the choir, judging by what our beloved Mother [Gonzague] told us, I felt immediately that a sword of sorrow had transpierced your poor heart! Its sharp point entered even into my own heart, for I cannot sense a pain in my dear child but that pain becomes deeply my own!... How I would like to remain and talk with my little daughter, whom I love a thousand times over; oh! How I am going to pray to Jesus for her so that He may take my place by her side! He will be able to console her much better than I, and He will speak to her words that dry all tears and heal all wounds.[93]

Aristocratic blood flowed through Sister Marie of the Angels, the daughter of Count Amédée Chaumontel, a lieutenant of the first Regiment of the Royal Guard, Chevalier de St. Louis (1830), and Knight of the Legion of Honor (1858); and Elizabeth Gaultier de Saint-Basile. Born on February 24, 1845, at the Château de Meauty in Montpinçon, in the Bayeux Diocese. The future Carmelite was baptized Jeanne-Julia, the fourth of six children. As a very young child she was called "Lady Tempest"[94] by her two brothers and sisters because of her stormy disposition, but by the age of twelve she developed into a more placid person.

It was a difficult move for her to join the convent since family ties were very strong and remained so all her life. It fact it had to be by subterfuge that she managed to leave home on October 29, 1866, for the Lisieux Carmel. She went accompanied by her older sister Marie with the family believing she was going there for a retreat. The resentment of the parents was such that they did not even attend the ceremony for her reception of the habit a year later on March 19, 1867. Jeanne-Julia, now Sister Marie of the Angels and the Sacred Heart, was professed on March 25, 1868, at the age of twenty-three.

In the monastery she displayed great heroism during a fire incident even after receiving serious burns. Another time she came to the rescue when water inundated the property. Among other significant duties, that of subprioress headed the list. In this capacity she served a total of nine years from 1883 to 1886 and from 1893 to 1899. As mistress of novices she devoted the years 1886–1893 and 1897–1909 to the religious formation of the young ladies under her charge. Later on she became, lamentably, very absent-minded. For example, once during a procession she carried her cane with great solemnity thinking she was holding a candle.

In a little treasury of reminiscences entitled *Memories of My Little Thérèse*, Sister Marie of the Angels jotted down events, opinions, recollections, and favors concerning the saintly Thérèse that would otherwise be unknown.

She died at the age of seventy-nine on November 24, 1924, just six months before her erstwhile novice was canonized.

---

93 This letter (LC 92) from Sister Marie of the Angels to Thérèse was written Nov. 2–4, 1888.
94 Descouvemont, *Thérèse and Lisieux*, p. 115.

15. Sœur Marie-Emmanuel (1828–1904)
(Sister Marie Emmanuel)
A kind nun and widow with three deceased children

SISTER MARIE EMMANUEL FIRST MET THÉRÈSE IN 1882 WHEN THE FUTURE saint was only nine years old and she fifty-four, a nun for only three years. The occasion may have been during one of the Thursday visits to the Lisieux Carmel the Martin family made to see Pauline, Thérèse's older sister and "second mother," who had entered the Order in October 1882; or possibly when Thérèse came to tell the prioress Mother Gonzague that she too wanted to become a Carmelite.

Sister Emmanuel was jolly, zestful, industrious, and a truly humble woman with a great sense of sacrifice. She brought with her to the cloister particular attributes that those in a monastery normally do not possess or experiences they never went through: marriage, maternity, widowhood. Her three children were deceased. The first two died on the day of birth and the third, a girl named Elizabeth, fell victim of an epidemic at age six—not much younger than the little Thérèse she met in the convent parlor in 1882.

Though Sister Thérèse's and Sister Emmanuel's ages differed greatly, their cordiality, respect, and love for each other clearly did not. One of Sister Emmanuel's comments to Sister Geneviève (Thérése's sister Céline) clearly reveals her discerning perception of the saint: "This child is so mature and filled with so much virtue that I would like her to be prioress if she was not twenty-two." [95] At one time Sister Thérèse, with prophetic certainty of dying before the elder sister and with characteristic charm, promised, "At the moment of your death, I will come accompanied by your three little angels, and we will carry your soul off to eternity." [96]

The future Sister Marie Emmanuel entered the world as Bathilde-Virginie Bertin on September 10, 1828, in the Atlantic port city of Sables-d'Olonne (Vendée), the thirteenth of fourteen children. Her maternal grandfather was a sea captain and her father a captain of a sailing ship engaged in the coastal trade. From the age of seven until twenty she attended a school run by Ursuline nuns. Two years after the completion of her studies, she married a pastry cook, Germain-Louis Bérès, in Bordeaux. Her thirteen-year marriage ended with her husband's death in 1863. After the death of her third child during an epidemic, her youthful desire to be a nun became a reality on January 4, 1879, when she entered the Lisieux Carmel with apparently no serious objections from anyone. One can imagine the difficulties a fifty-one- year old woman had to face adjusting to convent life—especially a strictly cloistered and contemplative one—after having lived a full life of independence, worldly preoccupations, and family responsibilities.

She received the habit in 1879. The following year she made her profession and took the veil. Throughout nearly a quarter of a century in the Carmel, Sister Marie Emmanuel advanced spiritually and honorably until her death at seventy-six. Following a period of suffering from a stomach ailment, she died on June 21, 1904.

---

95 *Les Annales de Sante Thérèse de Lisieux*, December 1982.
96 Ibid.

16. Sœur Marie-Philomène de Jésus (1839–1924)
(Sister Marie Philomena)
Older novice in the novitiate with Thérèse

When the fifteen-year-old Thérèse Martin entered the novitiate in 1888, she joined a group of three other women—one of them, Sister Philomena, thirty-four years older than Thérèse. Reflecting on the age difference, she once said to Thérèse, "What do you think of our two vocations being so different? You giving so generously to God at the age of fifteen and I only at forty-five?" Thérèse replied, "I think that the Good God chooses fruits from all seasons. Isn't the charm of a garden but in the diversity of its flowers and fruits?" [97]

Sister Philomena had entered the Lisieux Carmel for a brief period in 1876 but returned home to care for her ailing mother for the next eight years. This devotion to her parent also extended to other relations including her nieces and nephews who called her "*tante maman*." It was not until November 17, 1884, after her mother died and all her familial duties were completed that she re-entered the Lisieux Monastery. Sister Philomena always had great admiration for Thérèse. She often told the postulants that having a cell next to Thérèse was a great pleasure for her. Every evening after Matins and Lauds she waited by her door to receive the beautiful smile that Thérèse always gave her before she entered her cell. "Oh! the sweet smile! It compensated for all the weariness of the day!" [98]

One of the assignments they both shared while they were novices entailed the making of communion hosts. Sister Philomena asked Thérèse a number of years later to write a poem about that artless task in order to help imbue it with a spiritual quality. What resulted was the ten-stanza poem of November 1896, "The Sacristans of Carmel" (PN 40):

> Here below our sweet office
> Is to prepare for the altar
> The bread and wine of the Sacrifice
> Which brings "Heaven" to earth!
> ...
> There are no queens on earth
> Who are happier than we.
> Our office is a prayer
> Which unites us to our Spouse
> This world's greatest honors
> Cannot compare
> To the deep, celestial peace
> Which Jesus lets us savor.
> ...
> Our happiness and our glory
> Is to work for Jesus.
> His beautiful Heaven is the ciborium
> We want to fill with souls!

---
97 Descouvemont, *op. cit.*, p. 116.
98 *Les Annales de Sainte Thérèse de Lisieux,* January 1982, p. 8. Translation by the author.

The actual purpose for writing another poem, "To My Guardian Angel" (PN 46), dated February 1897, is not certain. It might have been written at Sister Philomena's request or perhaps Thérèse made a copy of a poem she wrote on her own and gave it to her. At any rate, the last six lines especially deal with the subject of the sacred host which Thérèse tells Sister Philomena she made "with your celestial aid."

We learn from her death notice that a description of Sister Philomena indicated she was "a true lamb of God, and good batter for making hosts. She was all God's from head to toe." [99] Her death notice also recorded this observation: "How many recreations she spent turning the iron over and over on the stove, far from the company of her Sisters whom she loved so much! ... [Her] tall figure was prematurely bent from excessive work."

Thérèse and Sister Philomena would often talk together at recreation about God and even of Thérèse's premonition of dying young. Their spirituality, however, was not entirely the same. Sister Philomena had an inordinate fear of purgatory which Thérèse did not hesitate to assuage: "You do not have enough confidence, you are too fearful of the Good God.... If you choose to please God in everything ... you can be assured that you will not go to Purgatory." [100]

Regarding an early death, Sister Philomena believed that we should not rest in this life until all our work here for God is finished. Thérèse reminded her of St. Aloysius Gonzaga (1568–1591) who did not accomplish great things until after his death at the age of twenty-three. If he had lived a longer life he would still be considered a saint but Thérèse maintained that the marvels attributed to his intercession after death could not have been achieved during his lifetime.

Throughout her life Sister Philomena's esteem and appreciation for Thérèse never waivered. Her fear of purgatory vanished as she lived and practiced Thérèse's teachings on spiritual childhood, abandonment, and confidence in the goodness of God.

Born on October 28, 1839, in Langrune-sur-Mer (where the 1944 D-Day Normandy Invasion took place), Sister Marie Philomena was baptized Noéme-Colombe-Alexandrine Jacquemin, daughter of a carpenter. The third of six children, Noémi was nurtured in a religious atmosphere but her formal education was limited. A younger brother was ordained a priest and when he was curé of St. Michael de Vaucelles in Caen, he preached at her taking of the veil on March 19, 1885. The next year she made her profession at forty-six as a Carmelite on March 25. Thérèse was her companion in the novitiate from 1888 to 1889. Two nieces also became nuns in a religious order named "Virgine Fidele" which was later changed to Notre-Dame de Fidélité in La Délivrande, Normandy. A nephew of hers, Abbé Troude, was also a priest. He celebrated his first Mass in the Lisieux Carmel and gave communion to the dying Thérèse in the infirmary on July 16, 1897.

---

99 A quote from notes the Carmelite nuns of Lisieux wrote in 1893 concerning Sister Marie Philomena which Kenney translated into English in his *The Poetry of Saint Thérèse of Lisieux*, p. 169.
100 *Les Annales de Sainte Thérèse*, No. 597, December 1981.

What Sister Philomena might have lacked in physical beauty she compensated for by her goodness, humility, dignity, and common sense. This once tall, strong, and stout religious began to experience health problems in 1914 with the loss of sight in one eye followed a few years later with a developing heart disease. A cerebral hemorrhage paralyzed her in December 1923, causing her death shortly after on January 5, 1924, at the age of eighty-four.

17. **Sœur Marie du Sacré-Cœur** (1860–1940)
    (Sister Marie of the Sacred Heart)
    Thérèse's oldest sister Marie (See Chapter 2, St. Thérèse's Family)

18. **Sœur Saint-Jean Baptiste du Cœur de Jésus** (1847–1917)
    (Sister Saint-John the Baptist of the Heart of Jesus)
    Her spirituality was too severe for Thérèse

Sister St. John the Baptist believed in a very somber and severe spirituality, quite opposed to the joyous and confident philosophy Thérèse espoused. Sister St. John held that it is through great penances and prayers that true sanctity is acquired. God's justice is more imperative than His mercy. Thérèse's conviction was that God's justice is certainly paramount but it is tempered with mercy and love as from a father. Thérèse at one point, describing exactly what Sister St. John ascribed to, said she was the "image of God's severity."[101] Sister St. John told Thérèse that "If I were novice mistress I would not put up with a single black hair [infraction] on the fleece of my lambs [the novices]."[102]

Thérèse undertook the position of assistant novice mistress from 1893 to 1897. The linen room which Sister St. John the Baptist supervised was close to where Thérèse met the novices for consultation. She therefore could and did observe the novices going and leaving. As a novice, Sister Geneviève (Céline) observed that occasionally Sister St. John the Baptist would unexpectedly interrupt Thérèse's conferences on the pretext of some pressing concern. Céline wrote years later in 1948 that "our hearts used to beat fast as we passed by the linen room. The novices, witnesses to these matters, were indignant, but they were edified at the same time by the conduct and counsels of their prudent mistress, who remained calm."[103]

Thérèse was strict with her novices but softened all admonitions with mercy and love. These attributes Sister St. John the Baptist did not favor. In addition to this criticism, she even believed Thérèse was too young for holding such an important position as assistant novice mistress for she once told Thérèse: "You need to direct yourself more than to direct others!" Thérèse's reply was truly evidence of her saintly soul: "Ah! Sister, how right you are! I am even more imperfect than you think."[104]

---

101 Descouvemont, *op. cit.*, p. 236.
102 Ibid.
103 From Mother Agnès' preparatory notes for the Apostolic Process quoted here from Note 2 to LT 230 on p. 1102 in *General Correspondence*, dated May 28, 1897.
104 Descouvremont, *Thérèse and Lisieux*, p. 236.

One day four months before she died, Thérèse was feverish and exhausted but not yet bedridden. Sister St. John the Baptist rushed to her and asked for help at once about some art work she was doing for the feast day of Mother Gonzague. Pauline (Mother Agnès) who was present had some difficulty in convincing the insensitive nun that Thérèse, because of her weakened condition, should not possibly help her at that moment. Aware that her own expression showed some signs of disturbance or irritation, Thérèse later that evening wrote these lines to her sister:

> Ah! this evening I showed my *virtue*, my TREASURES of *patience*!... I who preach so well to others!!!!!!!!!!!!!!!!!!!!! I am happy you saw my imperfection. Ah, the good it does me for having been bad!... You did not scold your little girl, nevertheless, she deserved it; but your little girl is accustomed to this, your gentleness speaks more to her than severe words; you are the image of God's *mercy* for her. Yes, but ... Sister St. John the Baptist, on the contrary is *usually* the image of God's *severity*. Well, I just met her, and instead of passing coldly by my side, she embraced me, saying: (absolutely as though I had been the best girl in the world) "Poor little Sister, I felt sorry for you, I do not want to tire you out, I was wrong, etc., etc...." I, who felt contrition in my heart, was astonished at her not reproaching me in any way. I know that basically she must find me imperfect; it is because she believes I am going to die that she has spoken this way to me, but it does not matter. I heard only gentle and tender words coming from her mouth, and I found her very good and myself very bad.... When reentering our cell, I was wondering what Jesus was thinking of me, and immediately I recalled these words He addressed one day to the adulterous woman: "Has no one condemned you?" And I, tears in my eyes, answered Him: "No one, Lord.... Neither my little Mother, image of Your tenderness, nor Sister St. John the Baptist, image of your justice, and I really feel I can go in peace, for You will not condemn me either!..."[105]

Sister St. John the Baptist, an excellent embroiderer, had an attractive and noble appearance punctuated by a dignified stature. Little biographical data about her exists, not even the customary necrological circular. We do know, however, that she was born on October 10, 1847, in Coulcommers (Seine-et-Marne) and baptized Marie-Estelle Dupont, the first of three daughters of François-Denis Dupont, a basket maker, and Louise-Antoinette Dardenne. Before becoming a Carmelite she earned a living as a domestic. Fleeing from the dangers of the Franco-Prussian War, she, her family, and that of M. Hamel de la Barquerie, for whom she had worked, sought refuge in Lisieux.

Shortly after, the Carmelites accepted her on October 7, 1872. Room was available for her at the Lisieux monastery since some nuns had been disbursed to various new houses of the Order in Caen, Coutances, and even far-off Saigon. Sister St. John the Baptist—named in honor of the superior of the convent, Canon Jean-Baptiste Delatroëtte—received the habit on March 19, 1872, with Sister Amy of Jesus and professed with her on May 8, 1873. Because of identical

---
[105] LT 230 dated Nov. 28, 1897, from Thérèse to her sister Mother Agnès of Jesus.

religious profession dates, these two nuns were often referred to as the "twins" (*"jumelles"*). Up to her seventieth year she had been in good health and followed completely all the functions of community life. For some undisclosed reason she would not testify at the process for the canonization of Sister Thérèse of the Child Jesus. Sometime in October 1917 she became ill and lingered on until her death in the morning of October 27, 1917.

19. SOEUR SAINT-JEAN DE LA CROIX (1851–1906)
(SISTER SAINT JOHN OF THE CROSS)
An older nun who sought Thérèse's advice

ALICE-ÉMELIE, THE SECOND DAUGHTER OF LOUIS AND EUGENIE PANNIER-DES-rivières entered the world on July 25, 1851, in Torigny-sur-Vire (Manche). Her father managed to provide a comfortable living for his wife and four children as a seller of novelties which allowed him to provide a good education for Alice-Émelie, the future Sister St. John of the Cross, at the Pensionnat du Bon Sauveur in nearby St-Lô. Her exceptional sense of obedience, piety, and exactitude in observance of school regulations continued throughout her life. When she was twenty-five her parents, especially her father, reluctantly and with saddened and heavy hearts, gave their consent for her to become a nun. The Lisieux Carmel accepted her as a postulant at age twenty-five on April 21, 1876. She received the habit on December 8 of the same year, and was professed as a Carmelite nun on January 17, 1878.

Four years later in 1882 she met the nine-year-old Thérèse Martin for the first time when Thérèse visited the convent to see her sister Pauline who had just recently entered. Also present was Mother Gonzague who told Thérèse that when she becomes a nun she should have the four words "of the Infant Jesus" as part of her religious name. Some time after this, Sister St. John sent Thérèse a holy card commemorating the three hundredth anniversary of St. Teresa of Avila. Remembering what Mother Gonzague had proposed for Thérèse's future religious name, she wrote on the back of it: "My little Thérèse of the Infant Jesus. Say three times, 'O Mary, conceived without sin (etc.)' each day before this picture. With the intentions of Sister St. John of the Cross, rel.C.ind." [106]

Clearly Sister St. John held a very favorable feeling for little Thérèse but six years later when she learned Thérèse was allowed to enter Carmel at fifteen her attitude changed. Pauline (Mother Agnès) commented on this at the Apostolic Process:

> At her entrance, the Sisters, aware of her youthfulness, expected to see a child. Her presence, however, inspired them with respect; they admired her dignified yet modest bearing and her air of deep resolve. One of them, Soeur Saint-Jean de la Croix, who had been opposed to the entrance of so young a postulant, said to me some time afterwards: "I thought that you would soon be sorry for all you had done to give us your little sister. I said to myself, 'They will both be disappointed.' How deceived I was. Soeur Thérèse de l'Enfant Jésus is extraordinary; she is an example to us in everything." [107]

---
106 *Les Annales de Sainte Thérèse de Lisieux*, No. 604, July–August 1982, p. 7. Translation by the author.
107 Laveille, *op. cit.*, p. 149, as translated and quoted from *Summarium* of 1914, p. 679.

Despite the twenty-two year difference in age, she never seemed to hesitate in seeking spiritual advice from Thérèse. Thérèse in turn referred to her as a "faithful spouse" of Jesus in the poem she wrote at Sr. St. John's own request called "How I Want to Love" (PN 41). It is a paean of love for Jesus in which she wants to please, delight, console, and love Him on earth until He calls her to heaven.

Throughout her thirty years as a cloistered Carmelite, Sr. St. John's reserve, fastidious adherence to the Rule, punctuality, and patience were personal qualities particularly characteristic of this rather introverted nun. She found great comfort in reading, prayer, and devotion to Our Lord in the Blessed Sacrament.

Sr. St. John would often go to the infirmary to see the very ill Thérèse during the last months of her life. Not realizing, perhaps, the gravity of Thérèse's condition or maybe lack of experience with sick people may account for her rather provocative bedside behavior. The entry of August 25, 1897, in Mother Agnès's notebook of Thérèse's last conversations mentions one of these visits:

> One of the sisters [Sr. St. John of the Cross] had the habit of entering the infirmary every evening [during the silence between 8:00 and 9:00 P.M.] and placing herself at the foot of the bed, she continued to smile at Thérèse for a considerable time. Our little Saint smiled back in return. I surmised, however, that this indiscreet visit was fatiguing our invalid very much. When I asked her about this, she answered: "Yes, it is very painful to be the object of smiles when we are suffering, but I try to remember that Jesus on the Cross underwent the same experience in the midst of His sufferings. Is it not said in the Gospel: 'They blasphemed him, wagging their heads.' That thought helps me to offer up the sacrifice cheerfully." [108]

According to Mother Agnès, Sr. St. John's intentions were good when she smiled so much, apparently to cheer up Thérèse.

Sister St. John composed the following prayer after Thérèse passed away which she kept in her breviary and recited daily. It clearly shows the appreciation and esteem she had for Thérèse: "My dear Sister Thérèse of the Child Jesus, I thank the Sacred Heart for all the graces he showered on you. I ask you to let me share on earth the love that you have for him in heaven. Ask the angel [seraphim] who pierced your heart with the dart of divine love to please do for me what he did for *you*." [109]

About six months before Sr. St. John died, she experienced painful stomach problems. This persisted, worsened, and eventually caused her death. During those distressful periods her resignation, patience, and abandonment were noticed and admired by the other sisters. When her condition became critical she received the sacrament of Extreme Unction after which she uttered, "O my Mother, tell me always your will. When it appears difficult to accomplish, your grace strengthens me. I know that your will is that of the Lord, and I want to

---

108 Mother Agnès, *Novissima Verba*, p. 113.
109 Christopher O'Mahony, *op. cit.*, p. 163.

die according to the will of the Lord."[110] This heroic abandonment to the divine will decidedly resulted from what she learned as a disciple of Sister Thérèse of the Child Jesus. She was fifty-five when death claimed her on September 3, 1906.

20. Sœur Saint-Raphael du Cœur de Marie (1840–1918)
(Sister Saint Raphael of the Heart of Mary)
Diabetic nun whose character flaws tried the nuns' patience

SISTER ST. RAPHAEL HAD BEEN VERY KIND, INTELLIGENT, AND DEPENDABLE all of her fifty years as a Carmelite but she was slow in movement, a diabetic, and suffered disturbing attacks that affected her physically and possibly even mentally. In the latter case, it took the form of odd mannerisms and ways that, as one nun put it, "would try the patience of an angel."[111]

Thérèse's edifying contacts with Sister St. Raphael truly amazed the novices under her charge who could not understand how she so consistently displayed such great patience toward this idiosyncratic nun. She advised them:

> [Be] very gentle with her; she's not well. Besides, it's only charity to let her think she is rendering us a service, and it gives us an opportunity to practice patience. You are complaining after only a few words with her; what would you do if you had to listen to her all day, as I have to? Now you can do what I do. It's really very easy. All you have to do is to mellow your soul with charitable thoughts; you then feel such peace that you no longer get irritated.[112]

From the summer of 1893 to 1896 Thérèse held the post of "second portress," Sister St. Raphael's assistant who was in charge of the gatehouse. Thérèse itemizes the precision Sister St. Raphael expected of her: "Everything had to be done in a certain way, without hurrying; the broom had to be placed like this, a piece of paper like that, one box on its side, another always flat."[113]

Sister St. Raphael really cared for Thérèse and displayed her concern in many charitable but sometimes unexpected ways. One time Thérèse suffered with chilblains which Sister St. Raphael noticed and proceeded to treat her by wrapping up all her fingers in cotton batting. Only the tip of the little finger on each hand was visible which Thérèse said looked like they were protruding from "cocoons."[114] Another time, also worried about Thérèse's health, Sister St. Raphael called attention to the fact that "the little one was losing her health because she was not served a sufficient amount in the refectory."[115] Yet once at table she took for herself a bottle of cider that was intended for use by both Thérèse and herself but Thérèse ignored it in order not to disquiet her.

Pauline mentions Sister St. Raphael twice in her *The Yellow Notebook* and each time only in reference to work duties in which Thérèse and she were

---

110 See footnote 106.
111 *Procès de l'Ordinaire, 1910–1911*.
112 O'Mahony, *op. cit.*, p. 238.
113 Descouvement, *op. cit.*, 203.
114 Ibid.
115 Ibid.

involved. In the first entry she recorded an interesting episode that reveals Thérèse's method of self-control:

> She [Thérèse] told me that formerly she had to undergo a rough battle with regard to a lamp to be prepared for Mother Marie de Gonzague's family that arrived unexpectedly to spend the night in the extern Sisters' quarters. The struggle was so violent, there came such thoughts against authority into her mind, that, not to give in to them, she had to implore God's help with insistence. At the same time, she applied herself as well as she could to what had been demanded of her. It was during the night silence. She was portress, and Sister St. Raphael was first in charge:
>
> "To conquer myself I imagined I was preparing the lamp for the Blessed Virgin and Child Jesus; and then I did it with an incredible care, not leaving on it the least speck of dust, and, little by little, I felt a great appeasement and a great sweetness. Matins sounded and I was able to go to it immediately, but I experienced such a disposition of mind, I had received such a grace, that if Sister St. Raphael had come and had said, for example, that I was mistaken about the lamp, that I had to prepare another, I would have obeyed her happily. From that day, I made the resolution never to consider whether the things commanded me appeared useful or not."[116]

In the next day's conversation with Pauline, Thérèse enumerated the various assignments she held throughout her religious life: "During this time [June 1893] I was painting the angels in the oratory and was companion to the procuratrix (one in charge of purchasing food, supplies, and certain financial matters). After these two months I was assigned to the turn with Sister Raphael, while still being in charge of painting."[117]

Very little is known of Sister St. Raphael's life before her entrance into the Carmelite Order at twenty-eight. Her name, Laure-Stephanie Gayat is certain as well as her birth on February 18, 1840, in a poor section of Le Havre. She was the daughter of François Gayat, a wood turner and cooper, and Marie-Lucille Lavalee, an upholsterer in a residential area of Le Havre. On February 24, 1868, she entered the Lisieux monastery and received the holy habit on June 26 of the same year with Msgr. Hugonin presiding. She added the name "of the Heart of Mary" to "Sister St. Raphael" because the money from her dowry was used to pay in part for the construction cost of a wall recession with a statue of the Blessed Mother that was being built at the time she entered. The nuns including Thérèse and Sister St. Raphael had their picture taken in front of this statue. It is photo 36 in *The Photo Album of St. Thérèse of Lisieux*. Her profession occurred on July 6, 1869.

In time her physical and mental health deteriorated. Slowly she regressed into mental childishness. Paralysis of the legs set in, confining her to a wheelchair and finally to bed on August 16, 1918. She lived with great courage in the last stages of her sickness and offered up her extreme thirst "for the glory of God

---

116 July 12, 1897, in *Her Last Conversations*.
117 July 13, 1897, ibid.

and the salvation of souls."[118] Before she lapsed into a coma, her fellow nuns were amazed by the sudden recovery of her mental lucidity. Loyal to the saintly memory of her "little Thérèse" right to the end, she passed away on August 27, 1918, at the age of seventy. Thérèse's sister Marie (Sister Marie of the Sacred Heart) wrote after she died that Sister St. Raphael "is very happy today to run in the gardens of heaven."[119]

21. Sœur Saint-Stanislas des Sacrés-Cœurs (1824–1914)
(Sister Saint Stanislas of the Sacred Hearts)
Oldest community member and Thérèse's infirmarian

Mutual affection and esteem always existed between sister Thérèse, the youngest nun in the Lisieux Carmel at one time and Sister St. Stanislas, the oldest. One of the many assignments Sister St. Stanislas had during her sixty-nine convent years included that of infirmarian for Sister Thérèse during the early stages of Thérèse's last illness in the late spring of 1897 which she fulfilled with compassionate care. Sister St. Stanislas (then seventy-three) willingly relinquished her nursing duties in July 1897 to her assistant Sister Geneviève (Thérèse's blood sister Céline). Sister St. Stanislas observed that "during the sickness that led to her [Thérèse's] death, in spite of her great suffering, I never perceived on her face any sign that she was suffering so much; never a complaint...."[120]

Thérèse herself observed that Sister St. Stanislas "dressed the wounds [from cauterizing, vesicatories, etc.] with such tenderness! I saw her choose the most delicate linens, and she applied them with a velvet hand."[121] The ever solicitous sister concocted a cough medication for Thérèse of "snail syrup" (*sirop de limaçon*) which she consumed good-naturedly and jokingly quipped, "What does it matter if I take snail-syrup as long as I can't see their horns! Now I am eating snails just like the little ducks! Yesterday, I was acting like the ostriches, I was eating eggs raw!"[122]

On one occasion Sister St. Stanislas left Thérèse all alone in the infirmary to attend vespers, but did not close the door or window, thus exposing her to a strong draft. She had misunderstood Thérèse's motions to close the window and instead brought blankets and pillows to comfort her that caused added physical distress. Out of obedience Thérèse had to tell Mother Gonzague the circumstances:

> I told Mother Prioress the truth, but while I was speaking, there came to my mind a more charitable way of expressing it than the one I was going to use, and still it wasn't wrong, certainly. I followed my inspiration, and God rewarded me for it with a great interior peace.[123]

Céline recorded in her last conversations with Thérèse this tender incident:

---
118 *Les Annales*, June 1983.
119 Ibid.
120 *Les Annales de Sainte Thérèse*, No. 612, April 1983.
121 Death Circular of Sister St. Stanislas.
122 *Her Last Conversations*, June 6, 1897.
123 Ibid., August 6, 1897.

We were talking a sort of childish prattle which the others were unable to grasp. Sister St. Stanislas, the first infirmarian, said admiringly: "How charming these two little girls are with their unintelligible jargon!"

Later I said to Thérèse: "Yes, how charming we both are, but you're the only one that is charming; I am only charming when I'm in your company!"

She answered immediately: "That's exactly why I'll come and get you!" [124]

Sister St. Stanislas was a little deaf so Sister Thérèse would often thank her for any kindness by pressing her hand and giving her an appreciative smile which, some thought, prompted Sister Stanislas to call her an angel. Thérèse responded by saying, "It's in this way that I've taken God in, and it's because of this that I'll be so well received by Him at the hour of my death." [125]

Thérèse composed a poem commemorating one of Sister Stanislas' anniversaries that reflects the great fondness the entire community had for her:

> For fifty years on earth
> You have perfumed with your virtues
> Our humble little monastery,
> The palace of the King of the Elect.
>
> REFRAIN
>
> Let us celebrate, let us celebrate the happy entrance
> Of our senior sister in Carmel.
> All our hearts love her
> As a truly sweet gift from Heaven.
> You have received us all
> At our entrance into this place.
> Your kindness is well-known to us,
> Along with your tender love.
>
> Soon an even more beautiful feast
> Will come to gladden our hearts.
> We shall place new flowers
> On your head as we sing.[126]

Some time later, Thérèse composed her last recreational play *St. Stanislas Kostka* (RP 8) for Sister St. Stanislas' golden jubilee of her profession. Because of her own physical weakness, Thérèse was not able to participate in the acting as she had done in most of the previous plays. The Lisieux Carmel chronicles registered this entry for the play: "1897: February 8. The community celebrated with joy the golden wedding of our dear Sr. St. Stanislas.... In the evening the novices played an episode in the life of St. Stanislas which their young mistress, Sr. Thérèse of the Child Jesus authored."

Testifying at the Diocesan Process, Sister Marie of the Angels, Thérèse's novice mistress, related an incident she learned about Thérèse from a niece of

---

124 Ibid., August 24, 1897.
125 Ibid., September 4, 1897.
126 Supplementary Poem 3, "For Fifty Years."

Sister St. Stanislas: "When Sister Stanislas's nephew saw her [Thérèse] out walking with her father, the venerable M. Martin, he said to his sister: 'Look at Mlle. Martin! She's an angel. You know something? I think you'll see her canonized some day.' "[127] It was his sister who told Sister Stanislas this.

Sister St. Stanislas was born Marie-Rosalie Guéret in Lisieux on May 4, 1824, the fifth of six children of Nicholas-Joseph Guéret and Rosalie Valle, both involved with the linen industry in Lisieux. The eldest sister Caroline became a Carmelite and eventually was sent to a Carmel in Caen. However, Marie-Rosalie participated in the foundation of the Lisieux Carmel and as such was involved with the two Gosselin sisters who were its originators. Caroline assumed the name of Sister St. John of the Cross. Her twenty-one-year-old younger sister Rosalie, entered the Lisieux Carmel (then seven years old) on April 6, 1845, joining Caroline there. Taking the name Sister St. Stanislas of the Sacred Hearts, she was clothed in the Carmelite habit on January 15, 1847, and was professed on February 8, 1847.

When Thérèse Martin entered Carmel at fifteen in 1888, Sister St. Stanislas, then sixty-three, held the position of sacristan. Two years later Thérèse became her assistant in the sacristy and worked there from February 1891 to February 1893. While on this assignment the kind Sister St. Stanislas nicknamed Thérèse "little Sister amen" ("little Sister *ainsi soit-il*").[128] After Thérèse died, Sister St. Stanislas was chosen for the third time in her career as economic advisor to the prioress, but soon the painful infirmities of old age set in. She lived seventeen years after Thérèse's death with the memory of her dear "*petite fille*" never fading. Barely three weeks after her ninetieth birthday, she went to her eternal reward on May 23, 1914, from the grippe, a contagion that struck the Carmel community.

22. Sœur Thérèse de Jésus du Cœur de Marie (1839–1918)
(Sister Thérèse of Jesus of the Heart of Mary)
Eccentric nun who left the monastery in 1909

IN CHAPTER IV OF *Story of a Soul* THÉRÈSE RECOUNTS HOW, WHEN SHE WAS ten years old, she selected her name in religion:

> I wondered what name I would be given in Carmel. I knew there was a Sister Thérèse of Jesus; however, my beautiful name of Thérèse could not be taken away from me. All of a sudden, I thought of Little Jesus whom I loved so much, and I said: "Oh! how happy I would be if they called me Thérèse of the Child Jesus!"... But to good Mother Marie de Gonzague, who was asking the Sisters what name I should be given, came the idea of calling me by the name I had dreamed about.[129]

When finally in Carmel, Thérèse invariably seized the opportunity to practice charity toward her fellow nuns. Sister Thérèse of Jesus, for instance, would often ask her to do some unusual artwork that was either at an inconvenient

---
127 O'Mahony, *op. cit.*, p. 213.
128 As given in footnote 3 on p. 738 in *General Correspondence*, vol. II.
129 *Story of a Soul*, chapter IV, p. 71.

time or was of a disconcerting subject. In a message to Sister Agnès (Pauline, her sister), Thérèse sought advice on one such request: "I'm giving you a note from Sister Thérèse of Jesus. She gave it to me this morning. Must I do all this for her?... I don't have any models, and, then, it seems to me, that the linen [to be mended] and the Blessed Virgin [statue to be decorated] are more important, but I'll do what you tell me."[130] Years later Mother Agnès had to give examples of Thérèse's love of neighbor at the Apostolic Process for which she made reference to Sister Thérèse of Jesus:

> Because this poor Sister was rather eccentric, she used to ask for subjects that were very grotesque ... really bizarre and in poor taste, such as painting a lion surrounded by flowers and birds. In 1897, the last year of her life, in the month of June, Sister Thérèse of the Child Jesus painted two little works for this Sister. This was the last time that she used her brushes.[131]

Nonetheless, many nuns considered Sister Thérèse of Jesus "gay and amiable" and without the least bit of jealousy or pride in her character make up.

Sister Thérèse of Jesus was born Léonie-Anastasie in Rennes, Brittany, on August 6, 1839, of a Polish father, Erasme Jezewski, and a French mother, Julienne-Marie Chevrier. When her father (reportedly a descendent of a prince or nobleman) was fifteen, he and his family left Volhynia, a Polish region that had been annexed by Russia, and sought refuge in France. They apparently joined a group of Polish merchants who had settled there. Léonie's mother died when she was seven years old and was thereafter taken care of by her maternal grandmother, Mme. Chevrier, to whom she became closely attached. Absolutely nothing is known of her youthful years until 1870 when she joined the Carmelites in Rennes. In May 6, 1873, she transferred to the Lisieux Carmel at the age of thirty-three. Father Delatroëtte and Mother Marie de Gonzague gladly accepted her with apparently no reservations.

One source describes Sister Thérèse of Jesus as "being well-built, [but] in the absence of physical beauty (the photos reveal mannish traits and without doubt a divergent strabismus—an eye problem)."[132] After admittance into the Carmel, she soon received the habit on October 15, 1873, and made her profession in March 1875. A month later at a night ceremony presided over by Father Delatroëtte, she and another nun, Sister Marguerite Marie, took the black veil. Concerning Sister Thérèse of Jesus, Sister Geneviève rather honestly wrote in a "note of 1947–1948" that Sister Thérèse of Jesus had an "unpleasant disposition" (*"un mauvais esprit"*).[133]

She remained in the convent for thirty-six years, but due to serious health problems she left in 1909 at the age of seventy. Facts about her existence in the world during the nine remaining years of her life are completely unknown except for the date of her death on October 31, 1918.

---

130 LT 114, dated September 3, 1890. We do not know what Mother Agnès told her.
131 NPPA, p. 6.
132 *Les Annales*, November 1983. Translation by the author.
133 Ibid.

23. Sœur Thérèse de Saint-Augustin (1856–1929)
(Sister Teresa of Saint Augustine)
Thérèse had a natural but hidden dislike for her

THE RELATIONSHIP BETWEEN SISTER THÉRÈSE AND SISTER TERESA OF ST. Augustine is unique if not amazingly dichotomous. In a final frank revelation, Thérèse reports in her autobiography that there was one nun she found disagreeable in every regard. In fact she devotes almost two full manuscript pages to discussing her without, however, disclosing her name:

> There is in the community a Sister who has the faculty of displeasing me in everything, in her ways, her words, her character, everything seems *very disagreeable* to me. And still, she is a holy religious who must be very pleasing to God. Not wishing to give in to the natural anti-pathy I was experiencing, I told myself that charity must not consist in feelings but in works; then I set myself to doing for this Sister what I would do for the person I loved the most. Each time I met her I prayed to God for her, offering Him all her virtues and merits. I felt this was pleasing to Jesus.... I wasn't content simply with praying very much for this Sister who gave me so many struggles, but I took care to render her all the services possible, and when I was tempted to answer her back in a disagreeable manner, I was content with giving her my most friendly smile, and with changing the subject of the conversation, for the Imitation says: "It is better to leave each one in his own opinion than to enter into arguments" [*The Imitation of Christ*, III, 44: 1].
>
> Frequently, when I was not at recreation (I mean during the work periods) and had occasion to work with this Sister, I used to run away like a deserter whenever my struggles became too violent. As she was absolutely unaware of my feelings for her, never did she suspect the motives for my conduct and she remained convinced that her character was very pleasing to me. One day at recreation she asked in almost these words: "Would you tell me, Sister Thérèse of the Child Jesus, what attracts you so much towards me; every time you look at me, I see you smile?" Ah! what attracted me was Jesus hidden in the depths of her soul; Jesus who makes sweet what is most bitter [*The Imitation of Christ*, III, 5:3].[134]

Thérèse was so successful at disguising her true feelings that her oldest sibling, Sister Marie, became quite disturbed about her preference for Sister Teresa and remarked to their sister Pauline (Mother Agnès), "After all, I brought her up and now she likes this sister of all persons whom I find so repugnant, better than me."[135] Thérèse eventually confided to her sister Céline (Sister Geneviève) the truth: "It was absolutely a revelation to me, for she had such control of herself that not a jot of her effort was betrayed; and when on top of it all she named the object of her daily struggles, I was stunned—I had always thought this sister was her best friend."[136]

---

134 *Story of a Soul*, chapter X, pp. 222–223.
135 *I Summarium*, 18.
136 Goerres, *op. cit.*, p. 244.

B. At the Carmel in Lisieux

Shortly after Sister Thérèse died, Sister Teresa of St. Augustine, having been inspired by her conviction that the Saint loved her, wrote a short account called *Memoirs of a Holy Friendship* in which she explains their friendship as she saw it. In it she writes, "As soon as we met we experienced an irresistible attraction for another." Years later in February of 1911, Sister Teresa of St. Augustine testified in glowing terms and with invaluable information at the Diocesan Process leading to the beatification of her friend Sister Thérèse of the Child Jesus.

Just about a month before Sister Teresa of St. Augustine died—thirty-two years after St. Thérèse—she came to the staggering realization that she was the one disliked by Thérèse as well as by many others in the community who also found her burdensome. Initial unbelief soon turned into extreme embarrassment.

Thérèse's contacts with Sister Teresa of St. Augustine go back to when Thérèse was very young. On one visit to the Carmel to see her sister Pauline she recalls a pleasant encounter with her:

> It was on this day I received compliments for the second time. Sister Teresa of St. Augustine came to see me and did not hesitate to say that I was pretty. I had not counted on coming to Carmel to receive praises like this, and after the visit I did not cease repeating to God that it was for Him alone I wished to be a Carmelite.[137]

Thérèse also remembered that when she was eleven and getting ready for her First Communion—a joyous and important step in her early spiritual development—Pauline, then Sister Agnès, sent her youngest sister a little book of preparations for this holy event. Sister Teresa of St. Augustine's mother made the blue velvet cover and embroidered the white initials T M on it. Thrilled by the gift, the young Thérèse wrote to her sister Pauline:

> I had never seen anything so beautiful and I was unable to grow tired of looking at it.... What nice prayers there were at the beginning. I recited them to little Jesus with all my heart.... Thank Sister Thérèse of St. Augustine for me for her pretty little chaplet of practices [small acts of virtue and sacrifice which she counted on it] and for having embroidered the beautiful cover of my book.[138]

Sister Teresa of St. Augustine's mother and father donated the now famous granite cross (or Calvary) in the monastery which still stands on the grounds today. Without realizing it then, her parents' gift was to have a profound affect on Thérèse. After May when the twenty or so rose bushes nearby blossomed, Sister Thérèse of the Child Jesus would take her novices there after Compline around eight o'clock to strew rose petals at the cross. Sister Teresa made reference to this act in her 1911 deposition: "And then there were all those rose-petals which she used to spread at the foot of the Calvary in our cloister garth and on the feet of her crucified Lord when sickness nailed her to a bed of pain."[139]

---

[137] *Story of a Soul*, chapter III, p. 59.
[138] LT 11 from Thérèse to Sister Agnès of Jesus, March 1–6, 1884.
[139] O'Mahony, *op. cit.*, p. 195.

Thérèse mentions this activity in her autobiography and even wrote two poems concerning it: "An Unpetalled Rose" (PN 51), and "Strewing Flowers" (PN 34):

> Jesus, my only Love, how I love to strew Flowers
> Each evening at the foot of your Crucifix!
> ...
> This is my only delight in this valley of tears
> Soon I shall go to Heaven with the little angels
>   To strew Flowers!
>   ("Strewing Flowers," Poem 34)

It is therefore no coincidence that today the image of St. Thérèse, the Little Flower, in paintings and sculpture is that of a nun with cascading roses and a crucifix in her arms. Of all forty-seven photos we have of the Saint, ten were taken under this cross—more here than in any other place. Ever since her sanctity became known and her canonization proclaimed, clergymen and others from humble priests to popes have also had their pictures taken below this cross.

Thérèse worked closely with Sister Teresa many times; one of them making banners in celebration of the one-hundreth anniversery celebration of the martyrdom of the Carmelites of Compiègne. Sister Teresa mentioned this at the Diocesan Process in 1911 when she quoted Thérèse who exclaimed, "What joy if we were to have the same lot, the same grace!" Sister Teresa continued in her testimony:

> You could say that Sister Thérèse lived mostly in heaven; her spirit dwelt on it continually, and her heart longed unceasingly for the sovereign good. She spoke to me so many times about her desire to die.... "I cannot understand," she used to say, "why people get so upset when they see their sisters die; we are all going to heaven and we will meet one another then again." If she desired heaven it was only because of the love she could thus give to God; her own interest was entirely set aside.[140]

Sister Teresa provided further testimony in regard to Thérèse's desire for martyrdom at the same time as the above deposition:

> She had also an intense desire for martyrdom. I noticed this all the time. When she was ill, she wistfully remarked: "you are more fortunate than I am. I am going to heaven, but you might yet obtain the privilege of martyrdom." It showed how disappointed she was at not being able to reach that coveted crown.[141]

Close association also brought forth a somewhat demanding request by Sister Teresa that fortuitously resulted in the creation of over sixty Theresian poems. Thérèse had never written poetry before but though apprehensive at first, she embarked upon this new venture that began with "The Divine Dew" (PN 1), a poem about the Blessed Virgin that Sister Teresa asked her to write:

> One day I asked her to write a canticle on our favorite subject, the Holy Infancy of Jesus. "That's impossible," she replied, "I don't know anything about poetry."

---
140 Ibid., p. 192.
141 Ibid., pp. 93–94.

I answered, "What does that matter? We're not going to send it to the Académie française. This is just to make me happy and to satisfy a desire of my soul." ... She followed my advice and that is how she wrote her first poem.[142]

Thérèse also wrote for her a second poem, an allegory entitled "Abandonment Is the Sweet Fruit of Love" (PN 52).

Though praised for her gift of recollection, Sister Teresa of St. Augustine was otherwise a rather rigid and stern nun. An interesting episode occurred between her and the austere convent chaplain Father Youf. One day she rushed from the confessional to the prioress, Mother Marie de Gonzague, and in tears exclaimed that Father Youf "has just told me that I already have one foot in hell, and if I go on like this I will soon put the second one there!" Knowing the scrupulous Father very well, Mother Gonzague replied, "Don't worry, I already have both feet there!"

Sister Teresa of St. Augustine was born Julia Leroyer less than twenty miles southwest of Lisieux near Orbec in the Chateau de la Cressonnière where her parents worked—the father as a servant and the mother a chambermaid. When she was nineteen her father died of smallpox whereupon she entered the Lisieux Carmel on May 1, 1875, received the habit in six months on October 15, and made her profession vows two years later to the day. When the fifteen-year-old Thérèse Martin entered the Carmel, Sister Teresa was thirty-two. A nun for fifty years, she died at the age of seventy-three on June 9, 1929, four years after the canonization of the young nun she was associated with in "holy friendship."

Sœurs Converses (*Converse Sisters—Lay Sisters*)
IN THÉRÈSE'S DAY, A CARMELITE LAY SISTER WAS A RELIGIOUS WHOSE DUTIES involved primarily domestic chores such as cooking, housekeeping, gardening, and other manual work. Many came from farming and servant class families and were less educated than the choir nuns. Both the lay sisters and the choir sisters lived in the enclosed area of the monastery and attended daily mass. Their prayer periods were much shorter and simpler than the choir nuns. They did not attend choral office, were dispensed from the recitation of the breviary, and said instead a certain number of common prayers such as the Our Father and Hail Mary, most likely in the vernacular and not in Latin. They took simple vows, whereas the choir nuns took solemn vows. Their habits were exactly the same as the choir nuns except that the white veil of the novice became a permanent part of their habits. Because of that they were called the "white-veiled" sisters.

Lay sisters were also referred to as "converse sisters" (*Sœurs Converses*) a name derived from the Latin word "*convertere*" meaning "to turn around." Hence it followed that in becoming a religious they had renounced the world and in so doing they had "turned around" their lives, i.e., they were "converted."

While Thérèse was a nun in the Lisieux Carmel there were five lay sisters. The strict distinction between choir and lay sisters was abolished by the Holy See around 1967.

---
142 Page 36 and note 4 on page 37 of Kinnery's book *The Poetry of St. Thérèse of Lisieux.*

SŒURS CONVERSES (Converse Sisters—Lay Sisters)
1. **Sœur Marie de l'Incarnation** (Sister Marie of the Incarnation): *A kind lay sister*
2. **Sœur Marie-Madeleine du Saint-Sacrement** (Sister Mary Magdalene of the Blessed Sacrament): *A novice who avoided Thérèse*
3. **Sœur Marthe de Jésus du Bienheureux Perboyre** (Sister Martha of Jesus of Blessed Perboyre): *A novice with a temper*
4. **Sœur Saint-Joseph de Jésus** (Sister Saint Joseph of Jesus): *Died of influenza on Thérèse's 19th birthday*
5. **Sœur Saint-Pierre de Sainte-Thérèse** (Sister Saint Peter of Saint Teresa): *A crotchety old crippled sister Thérèse assisted*
6. **Sœur Saint-Vincent de Paul** (Sister Saint Vincent de Paul): *Often made cutting remarks to Thérèse*

1. **Sœur Marie de l'Incarnation** (1828–1911)
(Sister Marie of the Incarnation)
A kind lay sister

ONE WARM SUNNY DAY IN JUNE 1897, SISTER THÉRÈSE SAT WRITING HER autobiography in the shade of the chestnut walk in the Carmel garden. Resting in the same wheelchair her father used before his death, the ailing Thérèse concentrated on the virtue of charity when she was interrupted by a very caring nun, one of the many concerned about her condition. This little incident was duly recorded by Thérèse though she did not name the nun—Sister Marie of the Incarnation:

> When I begin to take up my pen, behold a Sister who passes by, a pitchfork on her shoulder. She believes she will distract me with a little idle chatter: hay, ducks, hens, visits of the doctor, everything is discussed; to tell the truth, this doesn't last a long time, but there is *more than one good charitable Sister*, and all of a sudden another hay worker throws flowers on my lap, perhaps believing these will inspire me with poetic thoughts. I am not looking for them at the moment and would prefer to see the flowers remain swaying on their stems....
>
> [I] would amuse you [Mother Marie de Gonzague], I believe, when telling you about all my adventures in the groves of Carmel; I don't know if I have been able to write ten lines without being disturbed; this should not make me laugh nor amuse me; however, for the love of God and my Sisters (so charitable towards me) I take care to appear happy and especially *to be so*. For example, here is a hay worker she is just leaving me after having said very compassionately: "Poor little Sister, it must tire you out writing like that all day long." "Don't worry," I answer, "I appear to be writing very much, but really I am writing almost nothing." "Very good!" she says, "but just the same, I am very happy we are doing the haying since this always distracts you a little." In fact, it is such a great distraction for

me (without taking into account the infirmarians's visits) that I am not telling any lies when I say that I am writing practically nothing.[143]

By the next month Thérèse's health deteriorated even more. Her sister Pauline (Mother Agnès) jotted down Thérèse's conversations into a pad called *The Yellow Notebook* because, realizing her young sister was approaching her end, she wanted to record her spiritually valuable words. One of the entries mentions Sister Marie of the Incarnation:

> When God wills that we be deprived of something there is nothing we can do about it; we must be content to go this way. Sometimes Sister Marie of the Sacred Heart [Thérèse's blood sister Marie] placed my bowl of salad so close to Sister Marie of the Incarnation, that I couldn't consider it my own, and I didn't touch it.
>
> Ah, little Mother, what poor omelet they served me during my life! They were convinced I liked it when it was all dried up. You must pay particular attention after my death not to give bad fare to the poor Sisters.[144]

In 1894, three years before this episode, Thérèse wrote a poem (PN 14) in 1894, at the request of Sister Marie of the Incarnation. Entitled "To Our Father Saint Joseph," it contemplates the poverty, humbleness, and privacy of the Holy Family "Like you [St. Joseph] we serve Mary and Jesus / In solitude"—an act which unites the Carmelite vocation with St. Joseph's.

After Thérèse died, the sisters collected all the photographs taken of the Saint and devised ways of utilizing some of them for publication and distribution. Sister Marie of the Incarnation suggested using one showing Thérèse sitting on a bench with her sisters (Photo 9), but cutting it out of context and pasting it on a photo of the convent cemetery. A few years later when she was in Caen, Léonie (Thérèse's sister, a Visitation nun in Caen), had it put on a souvenir card of her religious profession (July 2, 1900). Two years after this, it was included in an edition of *Story of a Soul* and titled "Thérèse in meditation in the monastery garden." It subsequently became a popular and well-known representation of St. Thérèse.

Of humble origin, Sister Marie of the Incarnation was born Zephirine (Josephine) Lecouturier on July 12, 1828, in Firfol, a small village near Lisieux. Her father worked at carpentry and masonry, and her mother, Marie-Rosalie *née* Homare, at spinning. As a youngster, Josephine exhibited intelligence, vitality, and piety. On August 10, 1852, she entered the Lisieux Carmel with the aim of becoming a converse sister. She received the habit on August 3, 1853, and made her profession the next year on November 14. During the fifty-nine years of her Carmelite life she worked at various tasks, most of the time as the sister in charge of the poultry yard. Her orderliness, charm, and giving of self gained her the admiration of the community. With a force similar to the one of 1891, an influenza epidemic struck in 1911 and claimed the life of eighty-one-year-old Sister Marie of the Incarnation on February 23.

---
143 *Story of a Soul*, chapter X, pp. 227–228.
144 *Her Last Conversations*, July 24, 1897.

2. Sœur Marie-Madeleine du Saint-Sacrement (1869–1916)
(Sister Mary Magdalene of the Blessed Sacrament)
A novice who avoided Thérèse

Sister Thérèse did not commit the least imperfection. Not only did she not follow the example of the imperfect nuns, she even seemed different from the several very edifying nuns as well. Her virtue was unfailing and always fervent. I even decided to see if I was possible to find some fault in her, because I had heard several criticisms of her that were inspired by party feelings. So I watched her everywhere—at the laundry, washing the dishes, at work in common and at recreation; I sometimes even tried to test her regularity. But I never succeeded in finding a single fault....

Sister Thérèse preferred to do good to those from whom she expected neither joy, nor comfort, nor tenderness. From the time I entered till she died I never felt any natural affection for her. I even avoided her. This was not because of any lack of esteem; quite the contrary. I found her too perfect; if she had been less so it would have encouraged me. I don't think I was ever a source of comfort to her. Still she never deserted me, but showed me a lot of kindness. Whenever I was depressed she went out of her way to distract me and cheer me up. She never stopped trying to help me, but she was very discreet about it.

[I've] never seen her in bad humor, nor have I ever found her the slightest bit angry with me, even though her charitable advances were not always returned in kind.... I never heard her complain.

[There] was one sister in the kitchen who did not like her and spoke of her with contempt (she is now dead). Once, when she saw Sister Thérèse coming, she said: "Look at the walk of her! She's not in any hurry [the Rule forbade hurrying]. When is she going to start working? She's good for nothing." Sister Thérèse heard her, but when she came in she gave this sister a big smile and did not show the slightest trace of hurt or bitterness.

[A] thing that increased my timidity with Sister Thérèse and made me speechless in her presence was that I found her too clear-sighted; I was afraid of being seen through. Especially if I had been guilty of some imperfection. I was afraid she would read it in my soul.[145]

Sister Mary Magdalene presented to the Diocesan Process, nearly twenty years after the Saint's death, the above quite penetrating analysis of Thérèse's character and her unreservedly frank personal feelings concerning her. She imposed her glum and uncongenial temperament not only on Thérèse but also on the whole community, so much so that at one point she was even considered for dismissal; yet she remained and even showed progress in her personal development, particularly in her later life.

At the same Diocesan Inquiry of March 16, 1911, Sister Mary Magdalene responded to a question concerning Sister Thérèse's love of God:

> One day when I was in her room she said to me in a tone of voice that I cannot reproduce : "God is not loved enough! And yet he is so good and kind.... Oh,

---

145 From the 1911 Diocesan Process as quoted from O'Mahony, *op. cit.*, pp. 260–264.

I wish I could die!" And she began to sob. Not understanding what it was to love God so vehemently, I looked on in amazement, and wondered what kind of an extraordinary creature I was standing in front of.

Thérèse's unending kindness and concern for this novice under her care expressed itself tangibly in the various compositions she wrote for her. To prepare her for her profession on November 20, 1894, Thérèse composed a set of prayers entitled "Mystical Flowers for making up my Wedding Gift" (Pri 5) which is a collection of "Aspirations" of love in the form of sixteen short pious ejaculations each headed by the name of a particular flower: roses, daisies, lilies, honeysuckles, etc. These flowers represented the sacrifices and virtues practiced each day, a concept reminiscent of the method Thérèse's sisters Marie and Pauline used to prepare her for her First Communion. From Thérèse's earliest years the symbolism of flowers played an important part in her spiritual vocabulary.

The second composition Thérèse penned for Sister Mary Magdalene's profession day is the engaging poem "Story of a Shepherdess become a Queen" (PN 10) which proved quite *à propos* for she actually worked as a shepherdess in her early childhood. The refrain encapsulates the essence of the poem: "Let us [the nuns] sing of the Shepherdess [Sister Mary Magdalene] / Poor on this earth. / Whom the King of Heaven / Weds this day in Carmel."

Two years later Thérèse composed her seventh play, *The Triumph of Humility* (June 21, 1896) in which she wrote a part not only for Sister Mary Magdalene but also for Sister Marie of the Trinity, and for herself. All the nuns kept their own religious names as characters in the play.

Sister Mary Magdalene was born Mélanie-Marie-Françoise Lebon, on the ninth of September 1869 in Plouguenast, a small town in Brittany. Her father, Eugène Lebon, married Mélanie's mother, Marie-Louise Bidan, and raised eleven children in their poverty stricken home. Mélanie, the eighth child, was forced to work at the tender age of five and became at fourteen a household servant which clearly precluded any opportunity for an education. She entered the Lisieux Carmel on July 22, 1892, (the feast of St. Mary Magdalene) at the age of twenty-three and received the habit on September 7, 1893. Interestingly, Thérèse's Uncle Guérin served as Sister Mary Magdalene's "godfather" at her clothing ceremony.

A dramatic character change transpired in 1908 when, after praying to Thérèse to cure her of a serious leg ailment, Sister Mary Magdalene completely recovered and attributed it entirely to the Saint's intercession. She honestly admitted that previously "I was not then in a state to profit from her advice, but since her entry into heaven, I've surrendered the care of my soul to her, and how she has changed me! It's incredible! I'm so peaceful and trusting. I don't recognize myself any more."[146]

She served as a lay sister, mostly in the kitchen, until her death at forty-seven on January 11, 1916.

---

146 From her Death Notice as quoted in *The Poetry of St. Thérèse of Lisieux*, p. 67.

3. Sœur Marthe de Jésus de Bienheureux Perboyre (1865–1916)
(Sister Martha of Jesus of Blessed Perboyre)
A novice with a temper

At the age of fifteen, when I [Thérèse] had the happiness of entering Carmel, I found a companion in the novitiate who had preceded me by several months; she was my senior in age by eight years, but her childlike character made one forget the differences in years, and very soon, Mother [Gonzague], you had the joy of seeing your two little postulants understanding each other marvelously and becoming inseparable companions.... My dear little companion charmed me by her innocence and her frank disposition, but she surprised me when I saw how much her affection for you differed from my own. Besides, there were many things in her conduct towards the Sisters which I would have liked to see her change....

I, placing her head upon my heart, told her with tears in my voice *everything I was thinking about her*, but I did this with such tender expressions and showed her such a great affection that very soon her tears were mingled with mine. She acknowledged with great humility that what I was saying was true, and she promised to commence a new life, asking me as a favor always to let her know her faults.... I pointed out to her that it was *herself* she was loving, not you. I told her, too, how I loved you and the sacrifices I was obliged to make at the commencement of my religious life in order not to become attached to you in a physical way as a dog is attached to its master.[147]

IN 1896 WHEN MOTHER GONZAGUE BECAME PRIORESS SHE ENTRUSTED Thérèse, a novice herself, with the training of the novices even though she was not officially given the title of "novice mistress." This explains why Thérèse corrected Sister Martha's faults as the above selection indicates. Though Thérèse added: "I would prefer a thousand times to receive reproofs than to give them to others; however, I feel it is necessary that this be a suffering for me."[148] Fourteen years later in Lisieux at the Diocesan Inquiry of February 1911, Sister Martha disclosed what some of her own behavioral problems were:

I inflicted a great deal of suffering on her [Thérèse] through my difficult temperament.... I was sometimes a bit jealous, and would get angry when she called attention to my shortcomings. On such occasions I used to go away and refuse to speak to her. But such was her charity that she always sought me out to try and help me, and her gentleness never failed to win me over. One day I was upset and said some very hurtful things to her. She just went on talking calmly and quietly.... Then I thought I would see how far her patience would be stretched so, to try her virtue, I decided not to answer when she spoke to me. But I failed to upset her, and ended up asking her to forgive me for being so rude.[149]

Sister Martha's esteem for Thérèse expanded under the Saint's tutelage and continued even after the Saint's death, lasting until her own demise at the age of

---
147 *Story of a Soul*, chapter XI, pp. 235–237.
148 Ibid., p. 239.
149 O'Mahony, *op. cit.*, p. 220.

fifty-one. In the same testimony given above, she acknowledged these amazing attributes of Thérèse:

- She was kindness and charity itself to me; only in heaven will it be realised how much she did for me, and the lengths to which she carried her self-sacrifice on my behalf.
- I found it very hard to understand how so young a nun could be as perfect as she was. What struck me most about her was her humility, piety, and mortification.
- No one who came in contact with Sister Thérèse of the Child Jesus could fail to be overwhelmed by a sense of the presence of God.
- Sister Thérèse was always my support, my comforting angel, and my guide through all the temptations and difficulties I had to endure.... Nothing earthly permitted itself to intrude itself on our conversations; they were entirely of spiritual matters.[150]

Thérèse wrote letters or notes, poems, and prayers specifically for her or at her request:

LETTERS (OR NOTES)

1. LT 80 This is the first known note to Sister Martha from Thérèse when they were both novices. It was written in pencil on the back side of a lace-edged holy card with the image of the Infant Jesus in His crib on the front: "Souvenir of my reception of the habit [on January 10, 1889], offered to my dear little Sister. Soon the divine Fiancé of Thérèse of the Child Jesus will also be the Fiancé of Sister Martha of Jesus! Ask Jesus that I become a great saint; I will ask the same grace for my dear little companion!"

2. LT 119 Thérèse gave this note to Sister Martha on her Profession day, September 23, 1890. Written in pencil along the edges of the reverse side of a lace-edged holy card are the words, "To my dear Companion. Souvenir of the most beautiful day of your life, unique day on which you were consecrated to Jesus."

3. LT 241 Thérèse offered encouragement to Sister Martha who was apparently going through moments of darkness and worry in June 1897.

4. LT 251 In this letter written sometime in June or July 1897, Thérèse again gave wise counsel to Sister Martha who was experiencing some troubling sorrows: "Dear little Sister, do not be *a sad little girl* when seeing you are not understood, that you are judged badly, that you are forgotten ... forget all that is not Jesus, *forget* YOURSELF for His love!"

5. LT 256 In this note written most likely on July 16, 1897, Thérèse says: "Dear little Sister, I remember just now that I did not celebrated your [32nd] birthday.... I wanted to offer you the prayer on humility [Pri 20]; I am not entirely finished copying it, but soon you will have it. Your little twin, who would be unable to sleep if she were not to send you this note." (She and Sister Martha were professed 16 days apart so Thérèse considered her a "twin.")

---

150 Ibid., pp. 217–221.

PRAYERS

1. Pri 3 "A Look of Love at Jesus," Thérèse composed in 1893 not only for Sister Martha but also for herself. It deals with the Carmelite custom of lowering the eyes in the refectory in imitation of Jesus before Herod.

2. Pri 4 "Homage to the Most Blessed Trinity," written in February 1894 for Sister Martha and Thérèse herself. It is a prayer praising God and promising Him that they will offer sacrifices to console and make amends to Him for all the blasphemies, insults, ingratitude, and unbelief shown by many including some religious.

3. Pri 7 "Prayer to Jesus in the Tabernacle" was composed in response to the request of Sister Martha who wanted it as an aid to help her make her evening examination of conscience. Thérèse gave it to her on her 30th birthday, July 16, 1895.

4. Pri 20 "Prayer for Acquiring Humility," composed for Sister Martha's 32nd birthday on July 16, 1897. It ends with the ejaculation, "Oh, Jesus, gentle and humble of heart, make my heart like yours!" Thérèse was at this time in the infirmary and not in contact with her or others except through written material.

POEMS

1. PN 7 "Song of Gratitude to Our Lady of Mount Carmel," written for Sister Martha's 29th birthday, July 16, 1894, which was also the feast of Our Lady of Mount Carmel.

2. PS 5 "For a Feast of Saint Martha," June 29, 1896, the day the community honored the lay sisters with a song, gifts, etc. The third stanza refers to Sister Martha as "Marthon," the masculine form of Martha:

> We offer our dear Marthon
> This delightful pig [toy animal].
> He will be her mount
> When he's chasing after rats.

PLAYS

1. RP 7 *The Triumph of Humility* was presented at the Carmel's recreation period on June 21, 1896. It deals with various aspects of Carmelite life which the devil tries to destroy. It ends with "Humility" overcoming him. Sister Martha played the role of Asmodeus, one of the evil spirits.

Sister Martha of Jesus was born Désirée-Florence-Marthe Cauvin on July 16, 1865, in Giverville, a hamlet just east of Lisieux. A deciding factor affecting her personality was the premature death of both parents when she was young. Her mother (Augustine Pitray Cauvin) died when she was six, and two years later her father (Alphonse Cauvin), a shepherd, followed her in death. Thereafter she grew up under the care of nuns in orphanages, pricipally by the Sisters of St. Vincent de Paul in Paris and in Bernay. At twenty-four the Lisieux Carmel accepted her on December 23, 1887. She received the habit on May 2, 1889, and made her profession as a lay sister on September 23, 1890, with the name Sister Martha of Jesus and of the Blessed Perboyre.[151]

Realizing the great spiritual benefits derived under Sister Thérèse's direction as acting novice mistress, Sister Martha asked to remain with her well beyond the required number of years. Fortunately we have a picture of her as a novice with Sister Thérèse beneath the cross in the cloister courtyard.[152]

The lengthy association with Thérèse benefited Sister Martha immeasurably. Thérèse voluntarily shared three of her annual private retreats with her in 1891, 1892, and 1893. Sister Martha and Sister Thérèse were two of the three untouched by the 1892 flu epidemic.

Sister Martha was present at Thérèse's death and quickly thereafter disposed of the Saint's sandals (alpargates) and other items by burning them all which she deeply regretted since, as later on when Thérèse's fame spread fast, anything connected with her was considered a relic. She had the task of supplying eager devotees of Sister Thérèse with "little pictures, to which we then attached little souvenirs of the Servant of God. I prepared 23,000 of them in one year, and they were not enough to satisfy the demand."[153]

For the rest of her nearly twenty years in Carmel after Thérèse died, Sister Martha was forevermore dedicated to the memory of her saintly mentor. She grew steadily in her spiritual and emotional life which ended after some months of suffering on September 4, 1916.

4. Sœur Saint-Joseph de Jésus (1809–1892)
(Sister Saint Joseph of Jesus)
Died of influenza on Thérèse's 19th birthday

SISTER ST. JOSEPH OF JESUS IS KNOWN IN THERESIAN LITERATURE PRIMARILY as the nun who died of the flu on St. Thérèse's nineteenth birthday. The influenza epidemic raging in France during the winter of 1891–1892 claimed an appalling 70,000 victims. It eventually struck the entire Lisieux Carmel except two: Sister Marie of the Sacred Heart (Thérèse's blood sister) and Sister Martha of Jesus, a novice under Thérèse's guidance. Thérèse, fortunately, had just mild symptoms so she was able to administer to the others. She tells us in her own words about this harrowing period:

> Influenza broke out in the monastery one month after Mother Geneviève's death. Two Sisters and myself were the only ones left on our feet. Never could I describe all the things I witnessed, what life appeared to be like, and everything that happened.
>
> My nineteenth birthday was celebrated with a death [Sister St. Joseph who died on January 2, 1892—at age eighty-two, the oldest nun in the community],

---

151 Rev. John Gabriel Perboyre (1802–1840), a Vincentian priest and martyr in China was canonized by Pope John Paul II on June 2, 1996.
152 Photo 28 in *The Photo Album of St. Thérèse of Lisieux*, taken by Sister Geneviève (Thérèse's sister Céline) on March 17, 1896.
153 O'Mahony, *op. cit.*, p. 228.

and this was soon followed by two other deaths. At this time I was all alone in the sacristy because the first in charge was seriously ill [Sister St. Stanislaus], I was the one who had to prepare for the burials, open the choir grilles for Mass, etc. God gave me very many graces making me strong at this time, and now I ask myself how I could have done all I did without experiencing fear. Death reigned supreme. The ones who were most ill were taken care of by those who could scarcely drag themselves around. As soon as a Sister breathed her last, we were obliged to leave her alone.[154]

Thérèse's maturity, patience, kindness, and competence—quite apparent during this dire crisis—stunningly impressed the superior of the monastery, Msgr. Delatroëtte. Three years before, he had obstinately opposed Thérèse's entrance into the Lisieux Carmel at fifteen and warned the nuns about the consequences of such an unwise decision, as he thought, in accepting her. However, after observing her at work not only with the sick and dying but in managing the various functions of the community, his opinion drastically changed.

The nineteenth century was just nine years old when Eugénie-Marie Lerebourg, the future Sister St. Joseph of Jesus, was born on February 16, 1809, in Saint-Méen-le-Grande, a village not far from Rennes. Her thirty-seven-year-old father Charles who sometimes used the surname Lerebourg, Larbourg, or d'Airbourg was a member of the Imperial Army and served with distinction and honor; but three years before his death in 1816 he was discharged with fifteen others for being "*mauvais sujets*" (bad subjects) of the king.[155] Her mother, Julienne, *née* Giclais, aged thirty-two, came from a farming community. Just a few hours before Eugénie was born, the second of her three little brothers died. Death took Julienne in 1813 leaving the four-and-a-half year-old Eugénie and her older brother motherless. A number of years later when she was still young her father died. The two orphans, nonetheless, were cared for and educated. Some reports indicate that Eugenie may have had an abusive or harsh teacher in those early years. At about twenty, she entered the *Communauté du Bon-Sauveur* in Caen as a boarder. She soon showed interest in religious life, a result no doubt of living in an exemplary religious atmosphere and witnessing the deep piety of the nuns. Application for admission into the order followed which the nuns gladly accepted. However, she lasted only up to the time she became a novice for poor health intervened, forcing her to leave. She took a position as a teacher's aide in a local school but eventually moved to Lisieux where she did the same kind of work.

The determined efforts of two Gosselin sisters from Pont-Audemer, who wanted to become Carmelites, brought about the foundation in 1838 of the Carmel in Lisieux. Most everyone considered the saintly Mother Geneviève its foundress, and Eugénie—Sister St. Joseph of Jesus—its first postulant. The first superior of the convent was the Sulpician curate of Saint Jacques in Lisieux, Msgr.

---
154 *Story of a Soul*, chapter VIII, p. 171.
155 *Les Annales de Sainte Thérèse de Lisieux*, January 1983.

Pierre-Nicolas Sauvage. He rekindled in Eugénie the desire to become a religious and at twenty-nine she entered the Carmelite Order where she remained for nearly fifty-four years. Her simplicity, humility, scrupulosity, obedience, and charity, particularly toward the young novices, gained for her a considerable amount of praise. In addition, her good memory and excellence at taking notes at sermons and especially retreats proved to be valuable personal assets.

5. Sœur Saint-Pierre de Sainte Thérèse (1830–1895)
(Sister Saint Peter of Saint Teresa)
A crotchety old crippled sister Thérèse assisted in walking

Sister St. Peter of St. Teresa was born Adélaide Lejemble on January 20, 1830 in the little village of Bruyère near Saint-Laurent-de-Cuves in the department of Manche. Her father, Louis, was thirty-three and her mother, Anne, *née* Pichon, thirty-six at the time of her birth. They were poor hard working farmers who had Adélaide start working early in life as a servant which she continued to do until her mid-thirties. Her desire to become a nun became a reality on October 22, 1866, when the doors of the Lisieux Carmel opened to welcome her as a lay sister. At thirty-seven, Adélaide with her religious name of Sister St. Peter of St. Teresa received the habit on July 16, 1867, and pronounced her vows of profession a year later on November 1, 1868—five years before Thérèse was born.[156]

With her strong constitution and good health she served the community tirelessly in the tasks allotted to her including assignments in the linen room and the making of altar hosts. Gout and arthritis, however, set in early and their painful and crippling symptoms persisted until she was unable to walk without crutches. Beginning somewhere in 1889 or 1890 Thérèse volunteered to help her get around. Before she would take her place in the refectory, Thérèse would cut the poor sister's bread and place the pieces neatly on her bowl. She writes in lengthy detail about her experience with this sister.

> I remember an act of charity God inspired me to perform while I was still a novice. It was only a small thing, but our Father who sees in secret and who looks more upon the intention than upon the greatness of the act has already rewarded me without my having to wait for the next life. It was at the time Sister St. Pierre was still going to the choir and the refectory. She was placed in front of me during evening prayer. At ten minutes to six a Sister had to get up and lead her to the refectory, for the infirmarians had too many patients and were unable to attend to her. It cost me very much to offer myself for this little service because I knew it was not easy to please Sister St. Pierre. She was suffering very much and she did not like it when her helpers were changed. However, I did not want to lose such a beautiful opportunity for exercising charity, remembering the words of Jesus: "whatever you do to the least of my brothers, you do to me." I offered myself very humbly to lead her, and it was with a great deal of trouble that I succeeded in having my services accepted! I finally set to work and had so much good will that I succeeded perfectly.

---

156 Facts in this paragraph are from *Les Annales de Sainte Thérèse de Lisieux*, April 1982, pp. 6–7.

Each evening when I saw Sister St. Pierre shake her hour-glass I knew this meant: Let's go! It is incredible how difficult it was for me to get up, especially at the beginning; however, I did it immediately, and then a ritual was set in motion. I had to remove and carry her little bench in a certain way, above all I was not to hurry, and then the walk took place. It was a question of following the poor invalid by holding her cincture; I did this with as much gentleness as possible. But if by mistake she took a false step, immediately it appeared to her that I was holding her incorrectly and that she was about to fall. "Ah! My God! You are going too fast; I'm going to break something." If I tried to go more slowly: "well, come on! I don't feel your hand; you've let me go and I'm going to fall! Ah! I was right when I said you were too young to help me."

Finally we reached the refectory without mishap; and here other difficulties arose. I had to seat Sister St. Pierre and I had to act skillfully in order not to hurt her; then I had to turn back her sleeves (again in a certain way), and afterwards I was free to leave. With her poor crippled hands she was trying to manage with her bread as well as she could. I soon noticed this, and, each evening, I did not leave her until after I had rendered her this little service. As she had not asked for this, she was very much touched by my attention, and it was by this means that I gained her entire good graces, and this especially (I learned this later) because, after cutting her bread for her, I gave her my most beautiful smile before leaving her alone.[157]

During the process of beatification Thérèse's sister (Sister Geneviève) answered questions regarding specific virtues of Thérèse. She mentioned her working with Sr. St. Peter in the light of Thérèse's heroic love of God. This is what she said of Sr. St. Peter:

Sister St. Peter gave me a detailed account of the charitable care which Sister Thérèse took of her. Then she added solemnly: "Such acts of virtue must not remain hidden under a bushel." The Servant of God's [Thérèse] virtue must have been of a very special gentleness to impress a rough temperament such as hers like that. What she had found particularly striking was the angelic smile with which her kindly helper left her on each occasion.[158]

Thérèse included another telling incident in her relation with Sister Peter:

One winter night I was carrying out my little duty as usual; it was cold, it was night. Suddenly, I heard off in the distance the harmonious sound of a musical instrument. I then pictured a well-lighted drawing room, brilliantly gilded, filled with elegantly dressed young ladies conversing together and conferring upon each other all sorts of compliments and other worldly remarks. Then my glance fell upon the poor invalid whom I was supporting. Instead of the beautiful strains of music I heard only her occasional complaints, and instead of the rich gildings I saw only the bricks of our austere cloister, hardly visible in the faintly glimmering light. I cannot express in words what happened in my soul; what I know is that the Lord illumined it with rays of truth which so

---

157 *Story of a Soul*, chapter XII, pp. 247–248.
158 O'Mahony, *op. cit.*, 129.

surpassed the dark brilliance of earthly feasts that I could not believe my happiness. Ah! I would not have exchanged the ten minutes employed in carrying out my humble office of charity to enjoy a thousand years of worldly feasts.[159]

In various ways the prioress provided for the increasingly debilitated Sister St. Peter who did express her appreciation for all that was being done for her. Despite her sufferings, she prayed continually and did not hesitate on special feasts to expound on her favorite subject, the Apocalypse.

Thérèse was not the only Martin sister who wrote poems. Her sister Pauline also composed them for special occasions; some were dedicated to particular nuns on their feast days or birthdays. She provided a few for Sister St. Peter, one of which follows in a rough translation:

> If you want a sermon
> Address yourself to [Sister] Saint Peter.
> She preaches without a fuss
> On the four last things.[160]

By 1892 Sister St. Peter became seriously incapacitated and in a great deal of pain. This sad condition persisted unabated for three years. Eventually the Carmel chaplain found it imperative to administer the sacrament of Extreme Unction on Saturday evening; on Sunday morning, November 10, 1895, she passed away peacefully. She was sixty-five. On seeing the serene features of the deceased Sister St. Peter, Thérèse remarked that "those who have a tender devotion to the Holy Face during their lifetime reflect after their death something of the divine Beauty."[161]

6. Sœur Saint-Vincent de Paul (1841–1905)
(Sister Saint Vincent de Paul)
Often made cutting remarks to Thérèse

OF ALL THE NUNS IN THE LISIEUX CARMEL, SISTER ST. VINCENT DE PAUL rarely missed an opportunity to make a cutting remark to or about Sister Thérèse, thirty-two years her junior. Even as she lay dying Thérèse heard someone repeat what Sister St. Vincent had just said about her at recreation: "I don't know why they are speaking so much about Sister Thérèse of the Child Jesus; she is not doing anything exceptional. One does not see her practicing virtue, you cannot even say she is a good nun." Thérèse's reply was extraordinary: "To hear on my deathbed that I am not a good nun, what joy! Nothing could give me greater pleasure."[162]

Thérèse experienced similar biting comments years before when she first entered Carmel. Sister St. Vincent would call her "the grand lady" and even a "big nanny-goat" (*grande biquette*) and complained that Thérèse was poor at manual work—an absolute requisite, she thought, for a true Carmelite. One day while

---
159 *Story of a Soul*, pp. 248–249.
160 *Les Annales de Sainte Thérèse*, April 1982, p. 14, translated by the author.
161 Ibid., p. 7.
162 Gaucher, *The Story of a Life*, chapter 11, p. 194.

fitting Thérèse for a pair of sandals (alpargates) that she made, Sister St. Vincent uttered some caustic words to her. This time, though, they hurt the young sensitive Thérèse. In a letter (LT 76) to her sister Pauline (Sister Agnès of Jesus) she wrote, "This morning [January 7, 1889], I had trouble with Sister St. Vincent de Paul. I went away with a heavy heart...." But a few lines later she added her philosophical resolution, "He [Jesus] knows well that if He were to give me a shadow of HAPPINESS, I would attach myself to it with all my energy. Since I can't find any creature that contents me, I want to give all to Jesus.... My Jesus always makes me understand that He alone is perfect joy, [even] when He appears to be absent."

Many other times Thérèse encountered these annoyances, or "pin-pricks" as she called them, from the same sister through the years. On July 25, 1897, for instance, the much loved and venerable foundress of the Lisieux Carmel, Mother Geneviève, died. Thérèse was assigned the task of arranging around the coffin the many flowers sent by the people of Lisieux—family, friends, and others. Sister St. Vincent carefully observed her at this task and brusquely interrupted her, commenting that "Ah, you certainly know how to place the wreaths sent by your family in the front row and the bouquets from the poor in the back." Thérèse sweetly replied, "Thank you, Sister, you are right. I'll put the moss cross sent by the workers in the front. That's where it belongs. I hadn't thought it!"[163] Years later Sister St. Vincent did confess that this response indicated to her Thérèse's unique piety. One of these workmen, incidentally, was Sister St. Vincent's brother whom Thérèse alluded to in a pun she made on his last name—Alaterre—just ten days before she died. He was at the time working on the construction of the extern sisters' building. She was speaking to Sister Geneviève (Céline) and Pauline who jotted these words down in her *Yellow Notebook*:

> When drying her [Thérèse's] eyes, a few eyelashes were detached from her eyelids:
> "Take these lashes, Sister Geneviève, for we must give as little as possible to the earth [*à la terre*].
> "Poor man, if this gives him any pleasure!"[164]

Ten weeks prior to her death, Thérèse responded quite philosophically to the opposite reactions two nuns made to and about her after she received the habit. She told the story to her sister, Mother Agnès, which she promptly recorded in her notebook:

> Listen to this little, very funny story: One day, after I received the Habit [January 10, 1889], Sister St. Vincent de Paul saw me with Mother Prioress [Mother Gonzague], and she exclaimed: "Oh! How well she looks! [literally, 'Oh! What a figure of prosperity!'] Is this big girl strong! Is she plump!" I left, quite humbled by the compliment, when Sister Magdalene stopped me in front of the kitchen and said: "But what is becoming of you, poor little Sister Thérèse of the Child Jesus! You are fading away before our eyes! If you continue at this pace, with an appearance that makes one tremble, you won't observe the Rule very long!" I couldn't

---
163 Descouvemont, *op. cit.*, p. 185.
164 *Her Last Conversations*, September 21, 1897.

get over hearing, one after the other, two such contrary appraisals. Ever since that moment, I have never attached any importance to the opinion of creatures, and this impression has so developed in me that, at this present time, reproaches and compliments glide over me without leaving the slightest imprint.[165]

How far from the truth Sister St. Vincent was when she remarked that "I wonder what our Mother Prioress will write about Sister Thérèse of the Infant Jesus [after she dies] and what can you say about a person who was all the time spoiled and who did not acquire virtue like us at the price of struggles and suffering? She is sweet and good but it is natural for her."[166]

Sister Geneviève noted a similar comment Sister St. Vincent made: "She's a sweet little Sister, but what will we be able to say about her after her death? She didn't do anything...."[167]

Apparently she did not consider the first four poems (PN 15, 19, 25, and 32) Thérèse wrote at her request as anything worthwhile. They all deal specifically with Sister St. Vincent's particular devotion to the Eucharist. In addition, four lines in a fifth poem (PS 5), "For a Feast of Saint Martha," concern among others, Sister St. Vincent and mention a little toy "pug dog" that was given to her as a "guardian" for her garden:

> We offer Sister Saint Vincent
> This smart little pug dog.
> Barking near her garden,
> He will be a good guardian.[168]

Years of misconception and ill will suddenly ended with an ironic twist at Sr. Thérèse's death. Edified by witnessing Thérèse's courageous and holy death and no doubt ashamed of her own ill-mannered behavior toward her, Sister St. Vincent bent down and kissed the dead saint's feet as she lay in her coffin. Instantly the cerebral anemia (lack of oxygen to the brain) she suffered with for years vanished. Thérèse bestowed her first miracle on the one who was perhaps the most unkind to her. She remained devoted to Thérèse for the rest of her life. In fact, a year after the Saint's death, Sister St. Vincent de Paul told Sister Geneviève: "You certainly can flatter yourself and consider it blessed to have been the sister of a saint."[169]

It should be born in mind that Sister St. Vincent de Paul had endured a difficult and sad childhood after the age of eight. She actually witnessed the tragic deaths of both parents and an aunt in the cholera epidemic of 1849 and from then on suffered the privations common to poor orphans lacking the basic family structure. Perhaps this experience, in addition to the cerebral anemia problem, contributed to her abrasive attitude toward the bourgeois Thérèse

---

165 Ibid., July 25, 1897.
166 Recorded by Mother Agnès and quoted in the article "Soeur Saint-Vincent de Paul," from the September 1982 issue of *Les Annales de Sainte Thérèse de Lisieux*.
167 Kinney, *op. cit.*, p. 152.
168 PS 5, a Supplementary Poem.
169 *Les Annales*, September 1982, p. 14.

whose family life was incredibly solid and loving. She had always considered Thérèse a pampered and spoiled young woman—even in the convent where she was still surrounded by her four doting family members.

Sister St. Vincent de Paul was born Zoé-Adéle Alaterre, on August 13, 1841, in Cherbourg, the second of six children, the offspring of a poor stone-cutter whose wife was the former Désirée Maurouard. Three children died before they reached the age of two. After the untimely demise of both parents within forty-eight hours of each other from cholera in 1849, she and her younger sister Ernestine were cared for and educated by the Sisters of St. Vincent de Paul in Caen. Ernestine died at sixteen, leaving only Zoé and her older brother Louis alive from a once large young family. Less than a year later, Zoé entered Carmel at the age of twenty-two on February 2, 1864, received the habit on December 8, 1864, and was professed the next year on December 14. During her forty-one years as a Carmelite, the energetic but fragile and tiny Sister St. Vincent de Paul served as cook, embroiderer, maker of alpargates, house-worker, and gardener. She had a booming off-key singing voice in choir which at times amused the others. Interestingly, of all the nuns in the convent, including Thérèse, she spent the longest hours in prayer and meditation before the Blessed Sacrament. She died of an internal tumor at the age of sixty-four on April 13, 1905.

Sœurs Tourières (*Extern Sisters*)

THE THIRD GROUP OF RELIGIOUS WOMEN IN THE LISIEUX CARMEL WERE the extern sisters (Latin, *externus*, outside) also called "Turn sisters"(*soeurs tourièrs*). Extern sisters were and are exclusively members of specific orders of cloistered nuns who communicate with the outside world. They live in the monastery but not in the enclosed area. For centuries the Carmelite extern sisters had their own special habits quite distinguishable from those of the cloistered nuns. On December 7, 1933, however, they were allowed to wear the same habits as the cloistered nuns. Their main function is to deal with business affairs and people from the outside world, do the shopping, and answer the door.

The extern sisters control the "turn" (sometimes called the "turning box") from which their name is derived. The turn is a relatively small cylindrically shaped cupboard or barrel-like structure built into the wall with shelves on which objects are placed then revolved so that the person on either side of the enclosure can receive or exchange items. In this way the cloistered nun could remain unseen by the person on the other side.

Turns in the Lisieux Carmel were located in the main entrance, the speakrooms, and in the sacristy. Thérèse served as sacristan in 1891 and 1892 but since she was a cloistered nun she was not allowed to have direct contact with the priest celebrating mass or any other liturgical ceremony. Therefore, after preparing the vessels and other material required for the liturgy, she handed them to him through the turn.

Four extern sisters lived at the Lisieux Carmel during the nine years Thérèse was there. There were only two externs at a time living in the Carmel:

1. Sœur Constance-Marie Jarry
2. Sœur Désirée Lebailly
3. Sœur Marie-Antoinette
4. Sœur Marie-Élizabeth de Sainte Thérèse

Sister Constance-Marie and Sister Désirée both left the Order in May 1889, about a year after Thérèse entered. They were replaced by Sister Marie-Antoinette and Sister Marie-Élizabeth de Sainte Thérèse, who both received the habit as extern sisters on August 15, 1890. These last two sisters were the only ones who really knew St. Thérèse.

EXTERN SISTERS (Soeurs Touriéres)
1. **Sœur Marie-Antoinette** (Sister Marie- Antoinette): *"The little lark of the turn"*
2. **Sœur Marie-Élizabeth de Sainte Thérèse** (Sister Marie Elizabeth of Saint Thérèse): *She represented the community at Thérèse's burial*

1. Sœur Marie-Antoinette (1863–1896)
(Sister Marie-Antoinette)
"The little lark of the turn"

Sister Marie-Antoinette was born on February 12, 1863, in Granville (Manche), a seaport town north of Mont Saint-Michel. On July 9, 1890, the Lisieux Carmel accepted her as a prospective member of the community and a month later clothed her with the habit of an extern. Because of her happy disposition, coupled with a pious and loving nature, she was called "the little lark of the turn."[170] Tuberculosis, that dreaded disease common at the time, attacked her and eventually caused her death on November 4, 1896, at the age of thirty-three.

2. Sœur Marie Élizabeth de Sainte Thérèse (1860–1935)
(Sister Mary-Elizabeth of Saint Thérèse)
She represented the community at Thérèse's burial

Sister Mary Elizabeth was an extern nun (*Sœur Tourièr*, "turn sister") who dealt essentially with the outside world. She did, however, get to know Thérèse when she worked in the sacristy and at the turn. On a number of occasions Sister Elizabeth, though, took care of the ailing Thérèse in the infirmary while the other nuns attended Sunday Mass. Three months before she died, Thérèse mentioned Sister Elizabeth to her blood sister Pauline (Mother Agnès):

> When I'm in heaven, I'll advance towards God like Sister Elizabeth's little niece, standing in front of the parlor grilles. You know how, when she recited her piece, and finished with a curtsy, she raised her arms, and said: "Happiness to all those whom I love."

---
170 De Meester, *Saint Therese of Lisieux: Her Life, Times, and Teaching*, p. 117.

God will say to me: "What do you want, my little child?" And I'll answer: "Happiness for all those whom I love." Then I'll do the same thing before all the saints.[171]

Sister Mary Elizabeth's niece, born in 1891, was Madeleine Prevost. On Thursdays Madeleine was accustomed to visiting her aunt whom she called "*tante Babeth.*" Sometimes she would see Sister Thérèse among the other nuns and recalled that Thérèse was always very kind to her. Madeleine married, became Mme. Martigny, and lived all her life in Lisieux. Before she died she often expressed the wish that "little Thérèse" (then St. Thérèse) would come and get her at the end of her life. Her death at ninety-one occurred on April 18, 1982. She is reported to have been the last living person who knew St. Thérèse.[172]

On October 4, 1897, Sister Mary Elizabeth, as the extern sister representing the Lisieux Carmel at Thérèse's burial, accompanied the group of mourners including a fair number of the clergy. The horse-drawn hearse wended its way up the hill from the Carmel to the city cemetery for the burial of the relatively unknown twenty-four-year-old Sister Thérèse of the Child Jesus. Thirteen years later she was present at the first exhumation of Thérèse's coffin on September 6, 1910. She often went on pilgrimage to the cemetery to pray.

As Thérèse's extraordinary life story spread far and wide, it did not take long for flocks of people to visit her grave and pray or request a cure. Many also went to the Carmel seeking information, prayers, souvenirs, and even relics. Sister Mary Elizabeth was ever present to welcome all graciously. She herself became a devoted disciple of the Saint of Lisieux. In fact, she gave her own personal testimony at the Apostolic Process on August 9, 1917.

Sister Mary Elizabeth was born Marie Hamard in Couterne (Orne) in the diocese of Sées on October 13, 1860. Her entire family was devoted to its religion, especially the father, a weaver. The Carmelites accepted her as an extern sister at the age of thirty on July 7, 1890 and on October 15, 1891, she made her profession.

When the new rules for the extern sisters (*Statuts des Sœurs Tourières*) were issued on December 7, 1933, allowing them to wear the same habit as the cloistered nuns, Sister Mary Elizabeth donned it with great joy and the next day renewed her religious vows.

Two years later following a short illness, she passed away on February 13, 1935, at the age of seventy-five. Just before she died, facing a picture of St. Thérèse which had been placed at the foot of her bed, she uttered softly, "Oh! How I wish to have her perfect abandonment." Then, after kissing her crucifix, she breathed her last while echoing the exact final words of Thérèse, "My God, I love you." [173]

---

171 *Her Last Conversations*, July 6, 1897, p. 75.
172 *Les Annales de Ste. Thérèse de Lisieux*, June 1982.
173 Ibid., Dec. 1984.

C. In Other Orders

1. **Mère Marie-Adélaid Costard** (1846–1897) (Mother Marie Adelaid Costard): *Louis Martin's nurse at Bon Sauveur Hospital in Caen*
2. **Sœur Marie-Aloysia** (1841–1903) (Sister Marie Aloysia): *Teacher in the Visitation Convent School in Le Mans to whom Thérèse wrote*

1. **Mère Marie-Adélaid Costard** (1846–1897)
(Mother Marie Adelaid Costard)
Louis Martin's nurse at Bon Sauveur Hospital in Caen

The story of Mother Costard is also that of St. Thérèse's saintly father in his later years at Bon Sauveur Hospital in Caen. This kind humble nun took great care of him during the years he was under her charge from 1889 to 1892. She regularly reported Louis Martin's condition directly to his daughters Céline and Léonie when they visited the hospital and contacted their other sisters in Lisieux by mail when the two girls were not at the hospital.

Mother Costard was forty-three and in charge of the psychiatric unit of the Bon Sauveur facility in Caen when Louis Martin was admitted on February 12, 1889. This huge, up-to-date establishment, founded in the eighteenth century, consisted of 1,700 inhabitants. It comprised not only buildings set apart for mental cases where Louis became one of 500 male patients, but also included a boarding school, a day school, a school for the deaf and dumb, a medical dispensary, and a large religious community (Order of Bon Sauveur).

Though much of Bon Sauveur was destroyed on July 9 during the Allied bombings of the 1944 Normandy campaign, it has been rebuilt and is flourishing again today as an important hospital for patients from many parts of Normandy. It is no longer owned by the sisters but is now the property of the state which purchased it in 1975.[1]

Louis was admitted there because it became difficult for Céline, Léonie, and others to care for him at home after several strokes which severely impaired his mental abilities. Once, after having disappeared for several days, his family found him in a confused state many miles away in Le Havre. But the final proof necessary for Louis's brother-in-law, Isidore Guérin, to convince everyone that for Louis's own welfare, he should be treated in a place specializing in cases similar to his own, was a terrifying incident involving a revolver. Louis, believing his daughters were in danger from burglars, brandished a revolver to protect them. Isidore and others believed he could potentially have unintentionally and

---
1 Emerts, *op. cit.*, note 11, p. 183.

unknowingly caused injury to someone. Shortly after this incident, Isidore and his friend Vital Romet took Louis to the hospital.

The assistant general of the Institution, Mother Lecoquil, informed Céline that "You can be assured that your dear patient, who inspires everyone with a deep veneration, is the object of our most considerate attention."[2] The daughters were indeed thoroughly pleased with the care he was receiving.

On February 19, a week after Louis's admission, Céline and Léonie obtained lodgings at a convent nearby where the Sisters of St. Vincent de Paul conducted an orphanage. They were able then to see their father every day to check the state of his health. In her letter of March 1, 1889, Céline informed Pauline, Marie, and Thérèse at the Lisieux Carmel about their father:

> When Papa sees me, he asks for news about all of you; he is thinking about all of you.... Since Sister Costard, after having talked about other patients, told me, when speaking about Papa: "This is not M. Martin's case, *he is paralyzed*." She claims he is rapidly approaching a general paralysis, she finds his tongue a little impaired, his movements slow, and he walks with difficulty.[3]

Following this letter, Céline wrote again on March 4, 1889, from Caen to the same cloistered Carmelite sisters:

> Sister Costard takes care of Papa simply as though he were her father; yesterday she was crying when she was giving me information about him: "You see, it's heartbreaking to see this handsome patriarch in such a condition; we are sad, deeply pained, and our staff is dismayed. In the short time that he has been here, he has made himself loved, and, then, there is something so venerable about him! He bears no ordinary stamp.... We can see that it is a trial; it doesn't suit him to have this illness, and this makes it all the more distressing!"
>
> This good religious kept repeating: "There is something so venerable about him!" Oh! How true this is. He seems to be incredibly good. The doctor wouldn't be surprised if paralysis were to follow this attack.[4]

At one point Céline wrote:

> Mother Costard has told me that she does all things for Papa, just as she would for her own father, who is in the same condition, but is cared for at home by his son. She says also it is a grace of God for her, and that she feels as deeply for our beloved father as for her own.[5]

Eventually, however, a change occurred that Celine explains in the biography she wrote of her father:

> On our visit of May 8 [1889], Mother Costard explained that since, according to the regulations, we could see Papa only once a week, it would be wiser for us not to stay on at Caen. Besides she promised that she would inform us of

---

2 Sister Genèvieve, *The Father of the Little Flower*, p. 97.
3 Ibid., pp. 99–100.
4 LD, March 4, 1899, in *General Correspondence*, p. 540.
5 Sister Geneviève, *op. cit.*, p. 99.

the least change. It was hard for Léonie and me, but it was beginning to affect our health, and our uncle [Guérin], as well as our sisters [including Thérèse], prevailed upon us to return to Lisieux, which we did on May 14. Every week we returned to Caen to visit our beloved father.[6]

At the hospital Louis chose from the very beginning to live in a ward instead of a private room where he remained for three-and-a-half years. The family decided to take Louis home after both his legs became paralyzed thus making it impossible for him to wander away as he did in the past. It was a happy day indeed when on May 10, 1892, Isidore brought the now sixty-eight-year-old Louis to his own home in Lisieux. Two months later Céline and Léonie, together with a married couple[7] employed as servants (the husband especially to help Louis), moved into a house close to the Guérin residence where they lovingly cared for their dear father. He had only two more years to live, dying on July 29, 1894.

After Louis's release from the hospital, Mother Costard was not involved any more in the life of the Martins. She died five years later in Caen on June 23, 1897, just four months before Thérèse's own death. She was born fifty-one years before in Coudeville (Manche) on August 15, 1846, entered religion in her teens, and was professed at twenty on October 9, 1866.

2. Sœur Marie-Aloysia (1841–1903)
(Sister Marie Aloysia)
Teacher in the Visitation Convent School in Le Mans to whom Thérèse wrote

THÉRÈSE APPARENTLY WROTE JUST TWO LETTERS, ONE OF WHICH IS LOST, to the much loved Sister Marie Aloysia, teacher at the exclusive girls' school in Le Mans conducted by the Sisters of the Visitation where Thérèse's older sisters, Pauline (1868 to 1877), Marie (1868 to 1875), and for a short time Léonie were boarding students. Their aunt, Sister Marie Dosithée (their mother's sister) was a teaching nun at that school. Pauline's favorite instructor was Sister Marie Aloysia. with whom she kept up a correspondence even after she became a Carmelite. Though Thérèse went to visit her sisters at their school in Le Mans in 1875, she never met Sister Marie Aloysia then or ever.

In memory of and love for her own aunt who died at the Visitation Convent in the last and ninth year of Pauline's education there (1877), Pauline, who was always fond of her, called Sister Marie Aloysia "Aunt" and urged Thérèse to refer to her also as Aunt.

On April 4, 1877, Pauline, then sixteen, wrote this charming letter to her school companion Louise Magdelaine during school vacation in which she tells her about her four-year-old baby sister Thérèse:

[How] are you spending your days? I hope you're seeing Sister Marie de Sales [Guyas][8] often. I want you to tell her that in a few years she will have a new novice,

---
6 Ibid., pp. 102–103.
7 Desiré and Marie Lejuive.
8 This sister lived from 1843 to 1909. She served as directress of the school from 1875 to 1876 after which she became mistress of novices. See note 4 on p. 109 in *General Correspondence I*.

guess whom? Like Madame de Sévigné, I'm going to give you ten, thirty, and even one hundred guesses.... Marie? No.... Léonie? No.... Me, you, then who?... Any more.... Well, this new postulant is, is, is ... Mademoiselle ... Thérèse Martin.... These are the motives that will guide her. Yesterday evening, she made her confession to me, and it was enough to make me die laughing. "I will be a religious in a cloister because Céline wants to go there, and, then, also Pauline ... it's not worth tormenting myself already, I'm too little, don't you see, and when I'll be big like you and Marie, I will be told what to do before entering the cloister...." "That's it, dear baby," I answered, covering her with kisses. "Now it's late; let's go to bed; I'll undress you.... Spend a few good nights before calling yourself Sister Marie Aolysia [sic] (this is the name she has chosen), you still have time to think it over." At that, both of us went upstairs. I put her to bed.

[Thérèse] is sending you a little letter; she is delighted with it and thinks herself *quite learned*.

The letter Pauline said Thérèse was sending was the very first letter Thérèse ever wrote (LT 1, April 4, 1877) but Pauline guided her little sister's hand. It was addressed to Louise Magdelaine and in it she mentions Sister Marie Aloysia. The last two sentences are: "Adieu, little Louise. I am sending you a big kiss. Kiss the Visitation for me, that is, Sister Marie Aolysia [sic] and Sister Louise de Bonzague[9] for I don't know anyone else."

Six months later, Céline, then eight, wrote about an amusingly childish moment in her life: "Thérèse is here at my back, talking to me about Sister Aolysia [Céline's spelling of Marie-Aloysia Vallée], but I told her to be silent.... Now that I lent my top to Thérèse she's no longer bothering me."[10]

Sister Marie Aloysia wrote a total of three letters to Thérèse. The first one was a reply to a letter, now lost, that Thérèse wrote to her when she was seven. These letters clearly reveal how kind and sweet a woman she was with qualities that easily won the love and affection Pauline and Marie had for her:

> Your letter gave us real pleasure, good little Thérèse, and all the more because we didn't need glasses to read it! [Thérèse wrote in large characters at the time] How proud your teacher [Pauline] must be of her pupil. Although your little fingers move so skillfully, and *all alone*, your heart is also able to find many pretty things!
>
> This should really merit a beautiful reward, and this poor aunt, presenting herself with empty hands, will surely not be well received. We would be very happy, however, Thérèse, to bring you some nice gifts, but I am so poor I can't even find a pretty picture to offer you. While you are waiting for us to make one, dear little one, we're going to send you a very little seal of the Sacred Heart, provided our letter doesn't weigh too much. We're sure it will please you, for you love the Heart of Jesus very much, don't you? And He loves "His child" even more because she is so good and obedient.
>
> Thank you for your good prayers. Please continue them for an aunt who loves her little Thérèse very much.[11]

---

9 Sister Marie-Louise de Gonzague Vétillart (1849–1884) was the directress of the boarding school at the time.
10 Letter from Celine to Marie dated October 13, 1877.
11 January 8, 1880.

A year almost to the day, Sister Marie-Aloysia wrote her second letter to Thérèse from her monastery in Le Mans:

> If little Thérèse is happy to write to her aunt at Le Mans, the latter is no less happy to answer her.... It is, then, from Jesus I will ask, not so much for pretty toys and candy,... but for very special graces which will make you grow "in age and wisdom" like the divine Child.
>
> I know, besides, from Pauline, that Thérèse is very good and very obedient, and that she loves God and the Blessed Virgin with all her heart. I can only want her, then, to continue and to remain, even while growing up, a good little girl for the consolation of her worthy father and her dear big sisters.
>
> Continue also, dear child, to speak a little word to God for this aunt, whom you don't know and for her other little nephews. She'll be very grateful to you.[12]

Fourteen years later when Thérèse was twenty-one and a Carmelite for six years, she painted a picture for Mother Agnès (Pauline) in the early part of January 1894 that she called "The Dream of the Infant Jesus" which illustrated some ideas Mother Agnès expressed in a few poems she had written. A letter accompanied the picture to her sister which gave an explanation of the allegorical painting. The painting shows the Christ Child holding flowers given to Him by Mother Agnès whose love for Him they represent. In the distance is depicted the dream the Child is having of His future passion:

> Dear Mother,
>
> You have just read the *dream* that your child wanted to reproduce for your feast day. But, alas! Only your artistic brush could paint such a sweet mystery!... I trust you will look only upon the good will of her who would be happy to please you....[13]

Mother Agnès in turn sent the picture to Sister Marie-Aloysia, her former teacher at the Visitation in Le Mans, together with her own startlingly candid opinion of it:

> This humble sketch was painted by Thérèse of the Child Jesus and given to me *for you* on the 21st by this dear little Angel. I assure you, she was very secretive about it, for I suspected nothing.... But, alas! When taking up the brush, she believed she was doing something marvelous, wanting to copy the divine Child, whom she saw in her heart, so easy to render, she thought, *for she saw* Him so *clearly*! The brush misguided her! And the result cost her much in tears; this was not what she wanted to give her dear Aunt Marie-Aloysia.... Really, this painting is a real daubing, but when we think it was made according to an inspiration, we are more indulgent, especially towards a child who has never learned sketching or painting. Well, I am sending it to you, in spite of the contrary opinion of Mother Marie de Gonzague, who does not like it.... She has painted such pretty things in flowers and landscapes, and the little Jesus could have been so attractive according to a model! But such as He is, it is always *a little Jesus*, and you will give Him a nice welcome, I am sure....[14]

---

12 LC 2 dated January 10, 1881.
13 LT 156 dated January 21, 1894.
14 January 29–30, 1894.

In response to this letter, Sister Marie Aloysia wrote her third letter (which is now lost) to Thérèse thanking her for the picture and praising it as a painting. Thérèse then wrote her own second letter to Sister Marie Aloysia in answer to her "Aunt's" letter. Below are a few excerpts from it which Thérèse signed, "Your unworthy little niece":

J. M. J. T.

April 3, 1894

Dearest Sister,

> I am unable to tell you how much your kind letter touched me. It was a great joy for me to know the painting of the little Jesus pleased you, and I was rewarded beyond all my hopes.... Dear *Aunt*, allow me to give you this name, I was thinking of you when I was meditating on the gift I wanted to offer our Reverend Mother [Agnès] for her first feast day as prioress.
>
> I knew she would be happy to send you a little souvenir, so I put all my heart into composing *The dream of the little Jesus*. But, alas! My unskilled brush was not able to reproduce what my soul dreamed about.... [And] to my great joy my little Jesus has gone *for me* to meet *good Aunt* at Le Mans. I painted this divine Child in order to show what He is in my eyes....
>
> I remember perfectly my trip to the Visitation at Le Mans at the age of three [actually two years and three months]; I have repeated it many times in my heart, and Carmel's grille is not an obstacle preventing me from visiting dear Aunt and all the revered Mothers who love little Thérèse of the Child Jesus without knowing her.
>
> I beg you, *good Aunt*, to pay your little niece's debt of gratitude by thanking your Reverend Mother and all your dear Sisters, especially Sister Joseph de Sales, whose affectionate regards really touched me.[15]

This is the last time we hear about any further communication, in writing at any rate, between Thérèse and Sister Marie Aloysia. Mother Agnès, however, continued to correspond with her until Sister Marie Aloysia's death.

By way of interest, the painting referred to above was returned to the Lisieux Carmel in 1927, two years after Thérèse's canonization. Sister Geneviève repainted the face, changing it considerably from its original baby look to one that was more to her liking. The painting now hangs in the Visitation in Chartres.

Sister Aloysia was born Marie-Hilaire-Aloysia Vallée in Argentin-Château (Deux Sèvres) on December 21, 1841. She entered the Visitation Order and was professed at the age of twenty-seven on July 1, 1868. After she entered into her eternal reward at sixty-two in 1903, the death circular recorded that she adapted the general concept of Thérèse's "spiritual childhood" to her own way of life, well before this doctrine of Thérèse became well known.

---

15 LT 160 dated April 3, 1894.

CHAPTER 5

CHURCHMEN

A. In Thérèse's Childhood
B. On the Pilgrimage to Rome
C. On the Carmel Staff
D. Carmel Retreat Masters
E. Others

A. In Thérèse's Childhood

1. **Abbé Crêté**: *Thérèse's mother's confessor*
2. **Abbé Domin**: *Stern school chaplain: Thérèse's catechist and confessor*
3. **Abbé Ducellier**: *Thérèse's first confessor*
4. **Abbé Dumaine**: *Erudite priest who baptized Thérèse*
5. **Abbé Hurel**: *Married Thérèse's parents*
6. **Abbé Jamot**: *Louis Martin's Latin teacher*
7. **Abbé Lepelletier**: *Thérèse's second childhood confessor*
8. **Abbé Marie**: *Louis Martin's travel companion and advocate in Thérèse's beatification process*
9. **Père Pichon**: *Martin family spiritual director, friend, and Carmel retreat master*

In an age when strong anticlericalism ran rampant in so-called Catholic France, respect for the clergy was obviously not universally held. Thérèse's family, however, took the same pride in their reverence for the clergy and religious that their forebears did. In fact, not only did Thérèse's parents, Louis and Zelie, concur with this deference but each seriously considered entering a religious order before they met and married. During their nineteen years of married life they never faltered in demonstrating their extraordinary regard for those in religion.

It became a custom in the Martin household to entertain at table once a year their parish priest and the family confessors. The Martins' awe of the priesthood actually limited their invitations to priests since they considered themselves unworthy to have clerics under their roof. When, however, a child received First Communion or other sacraments, the officiating priest was always invited.

364　CHAPTER 5: *Churchmen*

Plate 12

Clergymen 1

A. Abbé Charles Anne

B. Abbé Maurice Bellière

C. Abbé Joseph de Cornière

D. Abbé Jean-Baptiste Crêté

E. Canon Jean-Baptiste Delatroëtte

F. Abbé Louis-Victor Domin

G. Msgr. Pierre-Théophile Dubosq

H. Abbé Alcide Ducellier

I. Abbé Louis Gombault

J. Abbé Zacharie Hodierne

K. Bishop Flavien Hugonin

L. Abbé Alcide-Victor Leconte

A. In Thérèse's Childhood 365

Plate 13

Clergymen 2

M. Bishop Thomas Lemonnier

N. Père Godefroid Madelaine

O. Canon Alexandre Maupas

P. Père Alphonse Pichon

Q. Pope Leo XIII

R. Père Alexis Prou

S. Abbé Maurice Révérony

T. Père Adolphe Roulland

U. Frère Siméon

V. Msgr. Francis-Roger de Teil

W. Antonio Cardinal Vico

X. Abbé Louis Youf

Among the privileged guests were the Fathers Domin, Ducellier, Delatroëtte, Lepelletier, and especially Father Pichon who was the spiritual director for Marie, Pauline, Céline, and later Thérèse. They carried on a correspondence with him for some time even after he was sent to Canada to do missionary work.

Realizing the deep reverential sentiments the Martins held about the clergy, Abbé Ducellier, for instance, as he was approaching Les Buissonnets (the Martin home in Lisieux) to thank Thérèse's sister Pauline for a beautiful alb she embroidered for him, hesitated, felt uneasy, and left without knocking for entrance.

Céline wrote about her father's great admiration for the clergy:

> His respect for priests was so great that I never saw anything like it. I remember when I was a little child I imagined from what I had heard that priests were like gods; I was so accustomed to have them placed above the common level.... I never heard him express a criticism of the clergy, nor find fault with a sermon. He listened with a devout respect to the word of God, without considering the quality of the instrument which transmitted it.[1]

The following nine clerics—all but two parish priests—were eminently involved with the spiritual guidance and reception of various sacraments by Martin family members in the years preceding, and some during, Thérèse's convent years.

1. Abbé Jean-Baptiste Crêté (1809–1885)
Thérèse's mother's confessor

ABBÉ CRÊTÉ WAS THE PARISH PRIEST OF SAINT-PIERRE-DE-MONTSORT IN Alençon where all the children of M. and Mme. Martin, except Thérèse, were baptized. As Zélie Martin's confessor, she calmly revealed to him once in 1877 her imminent death from cancer. Nearly fifty years later, one of Zélie's former maids, Louise Marais, then Mme. Le Gendre, wrote to the Carmel in Lisieux telling them exactly what took place at this meeting with Abbé Crêté:

> During her illness, one day she received at her office a call from the parish priest of Montsort, who was her confessor, while I was present. She spoke to him of her death with so much resignation that the priest said: "Madame, I have met many valiant women, but never one like you." The good pastor was less calm than Madame.[2]

Abbé Crete was born on September 30, 1809, in Vimoutiers (south of Lisieux, near Camembert). He was ordained a diocesan priest on June 29, 1883. In Alençon on April 8, 1885, at the age of seventy-five, he passed on to his eternal reward.

---

[1] Sister Geneviève, *The Father of the Little Flower*, p. 14.
[2] Sister Geneviève, *The Mother of the Little Flower*, p. 90.

2. Abbé Victor-Louis Domin (1843–1918)
Stern school chaplain—Thérèse's catechist and confessor

ABBÉ VICTOR-LOUIS DOMIN WAS BORN ON OCTOBER 1, 1843, IN THE PARISH of Saint-Sauveur in Caen. His parents were Louis Domin, a printer, and Euphémie Delos Domin. He was ordained on December 19, 1868, at the age of twenty-five. For forty-four years he served as chaplain and religious instructor at the Benedictine Abbey School in Lisieux which the younger Martin sisters attended, Thérèse among them. She was a day student at this school from October 1881 to March 1886. During this time Abbé Domin taught catechism, gave the annual retreats, heard confessions, and presided over the First Communion ceremonies.

Thérèse wrote the following in her autobiography concerning the four-day retreat instructions prior to her First Communion which took place on May 8, 1884:

> The three months of preparation passed by quickly, and very soon I had to go on retreat and for this had to become a real boarder, sleeping at the Abbey. I cannot express the sweet memory this retreat left with me....
>
> In the morning, I found it very nice to see all the students getting up so early and doing the same as they; but I was not yet accustomed to taking care of myself. *Marie* was not there to comb and *curl* my hair, and so I was obliged to go and timidly offer my comb to the mistress in charge of the dressing rooms. She laughed at seeing a big girl of eleven not knowing how to take care of herself, and still she combed my hair but not as *gently* as Marie....
>
> I listened with great attention to the instructions Abbé Domin was giving us, even writing up a summary of them. As far as my own thoughts were concerned, I didn't want to write any of these down as I felt I would remember them. I was right. I was very happy to be able to go with the religious to recite the Divine Office. I made a spectacle of myself among my companions by wearing a *big crucifix* Léonie had given me and which I held in my cincture like the missionaries....[3]
>
> I grasped easily the meaning of the things I was learning, but I had trouble learning things word for word. As far as catechism was concerned, I received permission to learn it during my recreation periods almost every day of the year before my First Communion. My efforts were crowned with success and I was always first. If I lost my place accidentally by forgetting one single word, my sadness was shown by the bitter tears I shed, which Abbé Domin didn't know how to stop. He was very much pleased with me (not when I was crying), and used to call me his *little doctor* because of my name Thérèse. Once, a student who followed me did not know the catechism question to ask of her companion. Abbé Domin, having made the rounds of all the students in vain, came back to me and said he was going to see if I deserved my place as first. In my *profound humility* this was what I was waiting for; and rising with great assurance I said everything that was asked of me, to the great astonishment of everybody.... All my teachers looked upon me as a very intelligent student....[4]

---

3 *Story of a Soul*, chapter IV, p. 75.
4 Ibid., pp. 81–82.

Thérèse wrote notes on his talks into a small exercise book. They dealt with hell, punishment, death, and the Last Judgment, all of which seemed rather frightening topics for the young girls. Abbé Domin at one point cautioned the children by saying, "Who knows whether any of you who are making this retreat will die before Thursday?"[5] Coincidentally, there was a death. The prioress of the abbey, Mother Saint-Exupère, passed away, and this obviously was frightening for all the students including Thérèse.

Frances Parkinson Keyes, the eminent American writer, in her charming way meticulously describes the scene at the Abbey when Thérèse was receiving instructions for her First Communion. She derived her facts from the many conversations she had with the actual teachers of Thérèse at the Abbey in the 1930s prior to World War II. Tragically, during the war the Abbey complex was completely destroyed under the allied air bombings with the resulting deaths of some twenty nuns.

> Every day she [Thérèse] went bounding joyfully off to the catechism classes which took place in the convent chapel on Thursdays and Sundays and in the *grand parloir*, a noble apartment wainscoted in mellow paneling, on other days. In either case, three benches were arranged to form a double L opposite the seat occupied by Monsieur l'Abbé Domin, the grave-faced, round-cheeked, full-bodied chaplain of the Abbey, who was closely related to the two little girls [Alexandrine and Marie Domin] of the same name in Thérèse's own class. Thérèse herself was always so early that she secured the seat nearest to him, where she fastened her eyes eagerly upon him and drank in every word that he said....
>
> [The] little girls in their black dresses and white bonnets, the chaplain in his long cassock with a rug spread over his knees for warmth, the hard benches, the carved paneling, the shafts of sunshine.... Questions and answers were not merely a matter of dull routine for her, they were subjects for inquiry, for discussion, for consideration. She was not content that her teacher should glide swiftly as possible over the topic of Infant Damnation; she wished to have this dangerous doctrine explained. She also sought searchingly for the answer to another troubling question: "Since God is the ruler of all hearts and since He desires the salvation of all men, how does it happen that everyone is not converted? He *could* convert everyone!" Her eagerness aroused the torpid class.... The chaplain called her his "Little Doctor of Theology." After the first examination, he said to one of the nuns with a chuckle of pride, "I tried to trip Thérèse up, but I didn't succeed. All her answers were admirable."[6]

Abbé Domin called Thérèse "his little doctor" not only because of her name, referring to St. Teresa of Avila, a Doctor of the Church, but because he obviously discerned that she, only eleven years old, had the knowledge, intelligence, and intuition, to answer accurately difficult theological questions. How unknowingly prophetic he proved to be in view of the fact that 113 years later the Church declared her the thirty-third Doctor of the Church—the third woman so honored out of the Church's 2,000 years of history.

---

5 Gaucher, *op. cit.*, p. 51.
6 Keyes, *op. cit.* pp. 76–78.

Alexandrine and Maria Domin, Abbé Domin's nieces referred to earlier, were preparing for First Communion at the same time with Thérèse. Traditionally the girl who received the best grades in catechism read the Act of Consecration to the Blessed Virgin on behalf of all the other communicants at Vespers on First Communion day. Since the two girls were so closely related to the chaplain, the nuns thought they should chose one of them. When Thérèse heard of this she was quite disturbed since she had been the top student. Thérèse's Aunt Guérin and her sister Marie strenuously pleaded Thérèse's case with the directress of the boarding school, Mother Saint-Placid, and the chaplain himself. Eventually they conceded and she was given the honor. Years later Thérèse wrote that "in the afternoon, it was I who made the Act of Consecration to the Blessed Virgin. It was only right that I *speak* in the name of my companions to my Mother in heaven. I who had been deprived at such an early age of my earthly Mother." [7]

A year later, Thérèse spent five days as an over-night student at the Benedictine Abbey School preparing for her "second Communion" (the anniversary of the first as it is called in France). No longer a registered pupil there, she received private instructions at the home of her tutor, Mme. Papineau. The retreat master again was Abbé Domin whose discourses dealt with the foreboding subjects of death, the Last Judgment, and hell. In her retreat notes, Thérèse had this to record: "What the abbé told us was frightening. He spoke about mortal sin, and he described a soul in the state of sin and how much God hated it. He compared it to a little dove soaked in mud, and who is no longer able to fly." [8]

Despite his high praise for the young communicant Thérèse, Abbé Domin had a number of reservations later on when she entered Carmel. Thérèse, on the other hand, showed concern and respect for him as evident from a note she added to a letter she wrote to her sister Pauline (Sister Agnès): "M. l'abbé Domin doesn't know I'm making Profession; must I tell him? It seems to me that if Our Mother [Marie de Gonzague] hasn't yet written to the Abbey, she could tell these Sisters [there] to inform him about it?" [9]

Abbé Domin gave vital testimony at the Informative Process of 1911 as well as the Apostolic Process in 1915 where he made these rather candid and unrestrained remarks:

> It was my opinion (and that of many others, I believe) that she received far too much flattery and adulation from her relatives, especially from her father, who could not bear to be apart from her and continually called her "my little queen." It seemed to me that they were risking making her vain and preoccupied with herself, like so many other girls. I recall that this impression of mine persisted even after her entry into Carmel. During her novitiate I visited her once, and was considerably surprised when the Mother Prioress (!) [Marie de Gonzague] who was present at the interview began to praise the magnanimity of the little novice. I thought to myself that it was after all not wise to praise

---
7 *Story of a Soul*, chapter IV, p. 78.
8 See notes on p. 226 in *General Correspondence*, vol. I.
9 LT 114, September 3, 1890.

a young person to her face in that way. I have since concluded that she must have been firmly anchored in humility not to be shaken by all these praises.... The pastor of the house, the Reverend Monsieur Youf, also sometimes spoke to her in the highest terms.... This talk seemed to be simply claptrap and the consequence was that I no longer went to visit her. I always observed the greatest restraint because I found the general opinion of this child simply exaggerated and did not want to join the chorus of praises.[10]

On another occasion Abbé Domin commented about Thérèse's method of prayer during Mass; this time with a keener sense of understanding:

> She was supposed not to follow the Mass on Sundays very well; this statement requires some explanation. Children are generally expected to follow the different points of the Mass by reading their prayer-book. Thérèse was expected to do this, but the dear child did not do it.... When she was shown what she was to read, she thanked one with a charming smile, lowered her eyes to the book for a few moments, and soon raised her head again as if her attention were wandering. But of course her attention had not wandered. She was praying much better than her companions by giving herself to contemplative prayer.[11]

Actually, not until the beatification process began did Abbé Domin come to realize the truly exceptional spiritual qualities of his erstwhile pupil:

> I remember that the idea that people were flattering and adulating the Servant of God pursued me even after her entrance into Carmel. The chaplain of the Carmel at that date, the Abbé Youf, used also to talk to me sometimes about Sister Thérèse's extraordinary qualities. He told me in so many words: "Although she is so young, if the community wanted a prioress, she could be nominated without the slightest fear." These words of my confrere seemed to me to be bluff, as they say in English, and consequently I never went to see her in Carmel. Alas, it was I who was in the wrong, by not believing in her extraordinary virtue, as I now admit.[12]

In the final analysis, he confessed that he had a special devotion to her, wished for the success of her cause of beatification, and hoped that his former student would be ranked among the saints of the Church. Unfortunately he did not live to see Thérèse beatified and certainly not canonized for he died at the age of nearly seventy-five on June 13, 1918, in Lisieux—five years before her beatification.

3. ABBÉ ALCIDE-LEOIDA DUCELLIER (1849–1916)
Thérèse's first confessor

ALCIDE-LEOIDA DUCELLIER WAS BORN ON NOVEMBER 14, 1849, IN CHICHE-boville (diocese of Bayeux), France, the son of a masonry contractor, Louis-Adolphe Ducellier, and Céleste Philippe. He received his theological training at the

---
10 Goerres, *op. cit.*, p. 213.
11 Petitot, *op. cit.*, p. 53.
12 Ibid., pp. 170–171.

Seminary of Saint-Sulpice and was ordained at the age of twenty-five in 1874, a year after Thérèse's birth. Bishop Hugonin appointed him vicar at Saint-Gervais de Falaise (1874–1877) where he served for three years after which he was transferred to the Cathedral of Saint-Pierre in Lisieux. He served as assistant priest there for a period of seven years (1877–1884). For fifteen years (1884–1894) he was stationed as a parish priest in Mathieu, a town near Caen, followed by seven years at Trévières, a little northwest of Bayeux. Returning to Lisieux in 1899, he was elevated to archpriest of Saint-Pierre's where he worked diligently for seventeen years until his death there at sixty-seven of pulmonary congestion on December 20, 1916. He is buried not far from the original grave of St. Thérèse. Abbé Ducellier heard Thérèse's first confession at the end of 1879 or the beginning of 1880. She clearly remembered this event and recorded her memories of it:

> It was on Wednesday also that Father Ducellier came to pay a visit. Victoire [the maid] told him nobody was home except Thérèse, and so he came out into the *kitchen* to see me and look over my homework; I was very proud to receive my *confessor*, for a short time before I had made my first confession to him. What a memory for me!
>
> Oh! dear Mother [Mother Agnès, her sister Pauline]. With what care you prepared me for my first confession, telling me it was not to a man but to God I was about to tell my sins; I was very much convinced of this truth. I made my confession in a great spirit of faith, even asking you if I had to tell Father Ducellier I loved him with all my heart as it was to God in person I was speaking.
>
> Well instructed in all I had to say and do, I entered the confessional[13] and knelt down. On opening the grating Father Ducellier saw no one. I was so little my head was below the arm-rest. He told me to stand up. Obeying instantly, I stood and faced him directly in order to see him perfectly, and I made my confession like a *big girl* and received his blessing with *great devotion*.[14]

Abbé Ducellier remained her confessor until she entered the Benedictine Abbey school in 1881 at which time Abbé Domin assumed this office.

M. Martin greatly appreciated the cultivation of the minor arts with his daughters by providing art lessons, particularly for Céline, and encouraged embroidering, sewing, and crafts with shells, ivory, and the like. Pauline spent two industrious years embroidering an alb, a masterpiece of needlework, and gave it to her confessor, Father Ducellier, which after his death was returned to her when she was in the monastery. She had the great pleasure of seeing it worn by the Papal Legate, Cardinal Pacelli, the future Pope Pius XII, at a Mass he said in the infirmary where Thérèse died and the next day at the Mass celebrating the benediction of the Basilica in Lisieux on July 12, 1937.

When Pauline received the habit and the veil, Father Ducellier preached the sermon. He continued to be Pauline's spiritual director even while she was a nun. He also preached the sermon at the clothing of Sister Geneviève of the

---

13 The confessional is still at the same spot in the Cathedral of St. Pierre in Lisieux.
14 *Story of a Soul*, chapter II, p. 40.

Holy Face (Céline) on February 5, 1895. Some laudatory remarks and most discerning observations he made in this sermon reveal his thorough knowledge of and the great respect he had for members of the Martin family:

> My dear Sister, it seems fitting that at this time, when you are on the threshold of the Cloister, I speak for a moment about your vocation.... Seven years ago you spoke of it for the first time to him [her father] who rightfully merited all your filial devotion. There was some question, at that time, of whether or not to send you to Paris for further training at painting. More desirous of perfecting the art of painting, in your soul, the image and model of all perfection, our Savior Jesus Christ, you seized the favorable moment for making known your wishes for the future.... My dear Sister, your saintly father offered himself as a sacrifice—God judged the victim worthy of himself.... How well you understood then where your duty lay—by his side. You remained long years—night and day, until the last sigh, until the tomb ... this father, whom you surrounded with every care and the most tender pity—brought about your preparation for the life of devotion and sacrifice that is the lot of the daughters of Saint Teresa.[15]

Thérèse's concern for Father Ducellier shows in the remark she made to her sister Pauline two months before she died: "Don't tell Father Ducellier that I've only a few more days to live; I'm still not weak enough to die, and after these visits [from nuns and doctors] when I continue living, others are 'kaput.'"[16]

Being so closely associated with the Martin family as he was, he assisted Mme. Guérin, Thérèse's aunt, in the final hours of her holy death in 1900.

His testimony at the two processes for Thérèse's cause—the Diocesan and the Apostolic—was extremely valuable. This telling response to the ninth question he was asked during Session 76 on May 3, 1911, of the Diocesan Process reveal a great deal about his opinion of Thérèse: "I have a true devotion to the Servant of God, I invoke her every day; I desire and hope for her beatification because I am convinced of her sanctity and the power of her intercession."

Less than a year before he died he gave this laudatory testimony at the Apostolic Process:

> As a priest of the parish of Saint-Pierre in Lisieux, I can declare and affirm that all the Christian people of my parish who knew the Servant of God during her stay in Lisieux kept the memory of an exceptionally pious and edifying young girl whose virtues attracted attention; moreover, I do not believe there is today in my parish a Christian family who does not continually invoke the Servant of God.... With regard to the origin of this reputation of sanctity, I believe that the good God is served by the book *Story of a Soul* by making known the Servant of God.... The graces obtained have been the principal reason for this movement of piety.[17]

---

15 Piat, *The Story of a Family*, pp. 457–459.
16 This German word may mean "exhausted," "confused," "finished," or even "dead."
17 Given on February 7, 1916, Session 54 of the Apostolic Process and printed in the April 1974 edition of *Vie Theresienne*.

4. Abbé Lucien-Victor Dumaine (1842–1926)
Erudite priest who baptized Thérèse

FATHER DUMAINE LIVED THROUGH THÉRÈSE'S ENTIRE LIFE FROM HER inauspicious baptism in 1873 in the church of Notre-Dame in Alençon to her glorious canonization in Rome in 1925. Actually he knew Thérèse only when she was a young child living in Alençon between the years 1873 and 1877. However, from the time he was sent to Alençon in 1868 he knew her parents and recognized in both of them a rare degree of holiness.

Father Dumaine gave testimony at both processes during the progress of the cause of Thérèse. At the first one—the Diocesan or Informative Process—he gave this sincere comment: "I am moved to produce this testimony from a desire for the glory of God and through a very special affection that I have for the Servant of God, that I myself baptized." [18]

During the Apostolic Process he was questioned about the spread of the cult of Sister Thérèse of the Child Jesus:

> Perhaps somewhat too much zeal was applied to the distribution of books, pictures and other objects pertaining to Sister Thérèse. But I do not think these efforts were intended to manufacture a reputation of sanctity out of nothing. Her reputation was spread very normally among the people; I am convinced, for the strongest reasons, that nothing was done to hide anything which could harm the cause. Her sisters in the Carmel were certainly not indifferent to the success of their efforts—but I am certain that they acted with the greatest of intention.[19]

Lucien was born in Tinchebray (southwest of Caen) in the Orne region of Normandy on September 8, 1842. Though his mother died when he was only three years old, he owed his priestly vocation to her. In fact, on his own tombstone he had this tributary credit engraved: "I am, O my God, your servant and the son of your servant who was a saint." [20] He received his priestly training at the major seminary in Sées where he distinguished himself as a diligent and intelligent student not only in his theological studies but also in his special interests in ancient history and archeology.

Ordained a secular priest in Sées on June 15, 1867, he was sent for a short time to a small church in La Lande-Patry (close to his birthplace) then in 1868 to the church of Notre-Dame in Alençon. During the 1870–1871 war he worked with the soldiers as their chaplain. After the war he performed his priestly duties in Tourouvre and elsewhere, followed by becoming archpriest in the cathedral in Sées. In 1885 he was stationed as a parish priest at the church of Saint-Pierre de Montsort in Alençon. From 1899 to 1910 he functioned in the distinguished position of vicar-general in Sées. In 1918 he was appointed canon of the cathedral and also honorary vicar general. During this time he directed les Dames de Marie de Longny and the religious of *la Vierge fidèle de Saint-Hilaire-lès-Mortagne*.

---

18 From the testimony he gave during Session 40 on November 25, 1910.
19 This was given on April 20, 1915, at the Apostolic Process during Session 5.
20 *Vie Theresienne*, Tome 4, October 1961.

Many people regarded Father Domaine as a holy priest, ready to help anyone, a tireless worker, and an eloquent speaker. In the secular sphere, he gained prominence as a noted scholar in archeology and history. He died at the age of eighty-four on September 25, 1926, and is entombed in the old church of Notre-Dame des Montiers in Tinchebray.

5. Abbé Frédéric-Auguste Hurel (1795–1872)
Married Thérèse's parents

FATHER HUREL WAS THE DEAN (CURÉ-DOYEN) OF THE CHURCH OF ST. Léonard, one of three in Alençon. He married Louis Martin and Azélie Guérin, the future parents of St. Thérèse. The ceremony took place in the church of Notre-Dame—the parish church of the bride in Alençon—on July 13, 1858, at the unusual hour of midnight, a custom at the time. This sixty-year-old priest during the time of the marriage served as their confessor and formed a bond of friendship with them.

The Vital-Romet Club was a fraternal association of Alençon middle class men organized basically for recreational purposes. It did not lack, however, religious aspects. Both M. Martin and Father Hurel (the chaplain) were among the valued and active members which included three Romet brothers, M. P. Boul (the father of Thérèse's godfather), and Jacques Tifenne, the husband of Léonie Tifenne, a dear friend of the Martins. They regularly met at the home of M. Vital Romet who lived diagonally opposite the old church of Saint-Pierre de Montsort.

Frédéric-Auguste Hurel entered the world on December 18, 1795, in Laigné (Mayenne). He was ordained a priest on April 1, 1820. Among the parishes he was assigned to during his long career as priest was the church of Saint-Pierre de Montsort where he began on June 1, 1827, and served for seven years. Later in his career from 1849 on, he became the *curé-doyen* (senior parish priest) at the church of St. Léonard. Death came to him at the age of seventy-seven on October 31, 1872, just two months before Thérèse was born.

6. Abbé Jamot
Louis Martin's Latin teacher

IN THE FALL OF 1843 LOUIS MARTIN TRAVELED TO THE SWISS ALPS WHERE he visited the monastery of the Canons Regular of St. Augustine (Augustinian Fathers) some eight thousand feet above sea level. Located at the pass separating the Swiss Valais from the Val d'Aosta (Italy), this hermitage was known as the hospice of Mount-Joux. Those fearless men of prayer and action rescued, with the help of the famous St. Bernard dogs, people who lost their way in the snow or were caught in avalanches. Louis was quite impressed by their apostolate and the order itself.

For some time Louis ardently wished to devote his life to God as a religious. Finally in 1845, at the age of twenty-two, during the period he was living and studying in Strasburg, he once again visited the Augustinian Fathers and applied for admission into their order. He was deeply saddened when they did not accepted him purely on the grounds that he lacked knowledge of Latin—an absolute requisite of the order. He went home rather dejected but began the study of this language with Father Jamot, dean of St. Léonard's church in Alençon. He also pursued his study of Latin with a M. Wacquerie all of which lasted beyond a year with well over one hundred lessons. His valiant attempt ended, however, for unapparent reasons.[21]

Louis finally gave up his desire for the religious life and eventually completed his studies in the watchmaking craft. In 1858 he married and fifteen years later became the father of the future St. Thérèse of Lisieux.

7. Abbé Lepelletier (1853–1918)
Thérèse's second childhood confessor

WHILE VICAR AT THE CHURCH OF SAINT-PIERRE IN LISIEUX, ABBÉ LEPELletier was the usual confessor of Louis Martin and later of Thérèse. He served in this capacity from the time she left the Abbey school in 1886 until her entrance into Carmel in 1888, the year he left Lisieux. This priest had the honor of being one of the few clerics with whom Louis Martin socialized. At times Louis invited him for special meals at Les Buissonnets, and once (June 16, 1887) he accompanied Louis and his daughters Léonie, Céline, and Thérèse on one of their summer excursions into the country around Pont-l'Évêque. Louis, an avid fisherman, was anxious to give the thirty-four-year-old priest a lesson in fishing in the Touques River that flows through the area. The abbé, however, ended up giving Céline instructions in sketching and drew one of his own in one of the girls' sketchbook a sketch showing Thérèse in a field picking flowers with her busy sisters nearby. This drawing is quite unique since it is the only sketch from life, as far as can be ascertained, that was ever done of Thérèse, albeit not a closeup.

Knowing about the young Thérèse's strong belief in the miracle of the Eucharist and her fervent desire to receive Communion as often as possible, Abbé Lepelletier kindly allowed her the unusual privilege of receiving Communion several times a week. In her autobiography she comments about her thoughts on the reception of this sacrament:

> Jesus, aware of the desire and uprightness of my heart, allowed my confessor [Abbé Lepelletier] to tell me to receive Communion during the month of May four times a week; the month having passed, he added a fifth whenever a feast occurred. Sweet were the tears that flowed from my eyes when leaving the confessional. It appeared to be Jesus Himself who desired to give Himself to me, for I went to confession only a few times, and never spoke about my interior sentiments. The way I was walking was so straight, so clear, I needed no other guide but Jesus. I compared directors to faithful mirrors, reflecting Jesus in souls, and I said that for me God was using no intermediary, He was acting directly![22]

---

21 Piat in his *The Story of a Family* (pp. 23–25) thinks that illness caused Louis to quit Latin studies.
22 *Story of a Soul*, chapter IV, pp. 104–105.

Apparently Father Lepelletier was not aware of the various plans and actions Thérèse undertook regarding her vocation. While away on her Rome trip, he read in the November 24, 1887, issue of the newspaper *Univers* that a young girl of fifteen (actually fourteen) from Lisieux asked Pope Leo XIII during a papal audience for permission to become a Carmelite. Surmising it was Thérèse, he went to the Lisieux convent to seek an explanation from Thérèse's sister Pauline (Sister Agnès of Jesus). The kind and understanding priest must have been pleased with the answers she gave, for in a letter Pauline wrote to her Uncle Guérin she mentions that "M. l'Abbé Lepelletier knows everything. He came to see us on Saturday. He is full of admiration and says the child is a privileged soul and is destined for great things." [23]

She was indeed destined for great things but he did not play any further part in her life once he left Lisieux which happened to be the year she entered Carmel. He certainly did not forget her or her family for in 1910 he wrote to Thérèse's sisters at the monastery in Lisieux that "I love to recall the happy moments that I spent at Les Buissonnets with your father who was so holy, and his very dear children." [24]

Louis-Albert Lepelletier was born in Condé-sur-Noireau (Calvados) on December 16, 1853. At the age of twenty-four, on December 12, 1877, he was ordained a secular priest. Shortly thereafter, in the next year, he was stationed as a curate at the Cathedral of Saint-Pierre in Lisieux and remained there for ten years. Upon leaving Lisieux in 1888, he served one year as a curé at Lion-sur-Mer and three years at Saint-Etienne in Caen, the city where he died on November 27, 1918, in his sixty-fifth year.

8. Abbé Charles-Louis-Auguste Marie (1849–1912)
Louis Martin's travel companion and notary in Thérèse's beatification process

LITTLE DID THE THIRTY-EIGHT-YEAR-OLD PARISH PRIEST OF SAINT-JACQUES (from 1875 to 1885) in Lisieux know that twenty-five years after traveling with M. Martin to Central Europe and Constantinople[25] he would be involved with the procedures leading to the canonization of his travel partner's youngest daughter. He no doubt realized that his companion was an exceptionally holy person, but again, never that he would be beatified along with his wife 123 years later in 2008. In 1910 he was appointed deputy notary at the Diocesan Process, one of the lawyers of the Tribunal which was commissioned to advance the Cause of the Servant of God, Thérèse Martin (Sister Thérèse of the Child Jesus).

Back in the late summer of 1885, Father Marie urged and finally obtained the consent from Louis Martin to accompany him from August 22 to the middle of October on a tour of Central Europe as far as the Bosporus. It included these major cities: Paris, Munich, Vienna, Budapest, Bucharest, Varna (Bulgaria),

---

23 A letter dated November 28–29, 1887.
24 Sister Geneviève, *The Father of the Little Flower*, p. 60.
25 The largest city in Turkey, a port on the Bosporus founded by Constantine I. Formerly called Byzantium then Constantinople until 1923. Now it is called Istanbul (also Stambul).

A. In Thérèse's Childhood

Constantinople, Athens, Naples, Pompeii, Rome, and Milan. In the letters Louis Martin wrote to his five daughters back home who were being taken care of by their aunt, he reveals the high opinion he had for his clerical companion. Following are a few excerpts mentioning his priest companion who, it seems, was always in a youthful rush:

- Do not worry in the least about me, and do not be lonesome for me, children! If however you feel too sad, write to me frankly about it, my Marie ... and I'll abandon this good Abbé Marie.[26]
- I believe that this good Abbé Marie is happy to have me with him. We get along very well together; he is most genial and I like him very much.[27]
- Now, what shall I say next to you? That everything is getting on.... Abbé Marie is always radiant—he is almost tireless. I find it hard sometimes to keep up with him.[28]
- I have just a moment and am using it to send you a few lines—while Abbé Marie is taking a walk to Scutari.[29] We are feeling very well; and we are marvelously situated in this private house [of Mme. Matich], recommended by the Vincentian Fathers.[30]
- Excuse me, I am obliged to follow Monsieur l'Abbé and I write these lines very hastily.... Monsieur l'Abbé is on my back, and I am forced to finish [writing].[31]
- Abbé Marie was quite touched by the little note from Carmel, mentioned by my "fine Pearl" [Pauline] in her letter to me.[32]

Well after Thérèse died, Father Marie accepted the position of chaplain at the Carmel which he held for many years. The officials at the Diocesan Inquiry in 1910 appointed him deputy notary for the Tribunal commissioned to advance the cause of the Servant of God, Sr. Thérèse of the Child Jesus. In April of that year the Bishop ordered the enquiry into the writings of Sister Thérèse, a huge undertaking indeed. The Carmel had to submit every bit of written material by Thérèse. Her sister, Sister Marie of the Sacred Heart, wrote on April 14, 1910:

Not only had the manuscript [of her autobiography] to be copied, but all the letters as well, even those addressed to my uncle and aunt, together with all the poems, from the first to the last. M. l'abbe Marie (who has been chosen by Monsignor [the bishop] to help [as an assistant] the Canon [Deslandes]) read the copies, while Canon Deslandes read the originals. They were both utterly enchanted. They had not expected to find so many documents, particularly such splendid ones, and they declared to each other: "We have had a week in Heaven, we have just made a true Retreat."[33]

Father Marie died at the age of sixty-three in 1912 and is buried in Lisieux.

---

26 CF 221 to his "Very dear Children," dated Paris, August 2, 1885.
27 CF 222 to "Marie, my 'big girl,' " dated Munich, August 27, 1885.
28 CF 223 from Louis to Marie, dated Vienna, August 30, 1885.
29 A district of Istanbul on the Asian side of the Bosphorus.
30 CF 226 from Louis to Marie, dated Constantinople, September 16, 1885.
31 CF 227 from Louis to "My dear 'big girl' " (Marie), from Naples, dated September 25, 1885.
32 CF 228 from Louis to Marie, dated Rome, September 27, 1885.
33 *Sicut Parvuli*, September 1983.

9. Père Almire-Théophile-Augustin Pichon, S.J. (1843–1919)
Martin family spiritual director, friend, and Carmel retreat master

THE FIRST ENCOUNTER FATHER (PÈRE) PICHON HAD WITH ANY MEMBER OF the Martin family took place in 1882 when Marie Martin, then twenty-two, went to confession to him at the time he was giving a retreat for the women workers at one of the textile factories in Lisieux. From then on he gradually met other members of her family. Marie carried on a lengthy correspondence with him throughout the years, even after she entered Carmel. He became a close, respected, and admired friend, a rare privilege indeed since the only other male persons within the circle of family friends were Louis Martin, his brother-in-law, Isidore Guérin, and later on their cousin Jeanne's husband, Dr. La Néele. He delighted them all with his exuberant personality, great story telling, kindness, knowledge, oratorical ability, and above all his sound spiritual advice. Soon it became clear that he and the Martin family were kindred spirits. Their piety, manner of living, love of family, beliefs, and even style of writing were similar. Though the girls tended in their writing toward a feminine kind of sentimentality, he at times leaned toward extravagant or metaphorical language in order to stress certain points. Nonetheless, his emphasis on abandonment, suffering, self-abasement, and humility struck a resonant chord of harmony with all, especially Thérèse.

Here follows a terse, rather amusing second conversation Marie had in the confessional with Father Pichon in which he first asked her if she wanted to become a religious:

> No, Father.
> Do you want to get married?
> Oh no, Father.
> Then what do you want to do? Become an old maid?
> Oh of course not!
> I'm in a hurry. I have to catch the train in a few minutes, but I'm coming back to Lisieux in 15 days to preach a retreat at the Refuge. I'll meet you there. Write all your impressions about religious life, why you don't want it, and all the thoughts that come to you about your vocation. For my part, I hope to give you to Jesus.[34]

On April 27, 1882, Marie accepted Father Pichon, then thirty-nine, as her spiritual director. It took him four years to influence her decision to become a nun. She appeared the least religious of all the Martin sisters, the one people thought would not become a religious, let alone a strict contemplative Carmelite nun. In the meantime, Father Pichon received an assignment to do missionary work in Montreal, Canada. This news indeed saddened the Martin family. With a heavy heart, Marie went with her father to Le Havre on October 4, 1884, to see him off. His stay in Canada lasted two years. His return to France was announced on a certain date and place where he would arrive. Marie anxiously wanted to see him for the last time since she planned to enter Carmel in less than two weeks. However, misunderstanding or misinformation confused everything. M. Martin and

---
34 Coady, *The Hidden Way: The Life and Influence of Almire Pichon*, p. 33.

Marie went to Calais and Dover but did not see him. At any rate, the three luckily met by sheer coincidence in Paris at the Jesuit church of the Gesú. Here Father Pichon promised he would escort her to the door of the Carmel on her entrance day and preach in the chapel for the event. As fate would have it, he was unable to be there because of a severe attack of jaundice. His superior even proposed that she postpone her entrance until Father's health improved. It did not happen, and Marie entered on schedule on October 15, 1886, without him present.

Happily, Father Pichon was chosen to preach the 1887 annual retreat at the Lisieux monastery from October 6th to the 15th which consisted of the usual Spiritual Exercise of St. Ignatius,[35] and again the next year from May 24 to May 28. On May 23, 1888, Father attended Marie's reception of the black veil and preached the sermon. Her religious name became Sister Marie of the Sacred Heart.

Thérèse's involvement with Father Almire Pichon really began when she was ten. To a certain degree he served as her "second father." At this time she suffered a mysterious nervous sickness that forced her to remain in bed in a most distressful state. Marie kept Father Pichon informed of Thérèse's condition that began on March 25, 1883, and ended suddenly on May 13, 1883. In one of his letters he told Marie he was praying for her as if he were her grandfather.[36] Then after the cure, he wrote again:

> Do you know I have a lively affection for your dear little Thérèse? A grandfather is subject to having a weakness for his grandchildren. I love everything about this candid soul, even her demand to have you with her. Since she loves you so much, she has a foremost place in my heart. I am overjoyed to think that God is reserving for her a very privileged future and that the Blessed Virgin is watching over her with a maternal tenderness.[37]

To celebrate Thérèse's recovery, a holiday trip to Alençon three months later was arranged for the ten-year-old Thérèse. She met Father Pichon for the first time on August 22, 1883, while on this trip to her birthplace. In arranging for the meeting with Marie on that day, Father Pichon asked her in a brief note: "Above all, bring my little Thérèse and your charming imp [Céline] to me."[38]

Like the rest of her family, the young Thérèse too considered him a friend. Once when her father asked her to kiss Father Pichon, most likely in thanksgiving for his prayers during her recent illness, Thérèse felt quite willing to do so without any shy hesitation. She walked over to him and had to go on her tiptoes to kiss him. He later confessed that "It was the only kiss I ever received."[39]

For some time after Thérèse's miraculous recovery that transpired in her sick room as she saw the statue of the Blessed Virgin smile at her, she somehow had feelings of guilt about the cause of this sickness. She thought perhaps she became ill on purpose which created in her much psychological distress:

---

35 Ibid., pp. 56–57.
36 Letter of April 17, 1883, from Father Pichon in Nantes to Marie.
37 Letter dated May 21, 1883.
38 Card from Vitré (near Rennes), dated August 20–21, 1883.
39 Boncompain, *Un Directeur d'Ames*, p. 41.

I told Marie this and with her usual *kindness* she assured me. I told it too in confession and my confessor tried to calm me, saying it was not possible to pretend illness to the extent that I had been ill. God, willing no doubt to purify and especially to *humble me*, left me with this *interior martyrdom* until my entrance into Carmel, where the Father of our souls [Pichon], as with the wave of his hand, removed all my doubts. Since then I am perfectly calm.[40]

Just two days before Thérèse, now eleven, received her First Communion on May 8, 1884, Father Pichon sent her a letter from Paris with this greeting:

My good and blessed Child,

I am placing my good angel in charge of accompanying you to the Holy Table on Thursday and presenting you to Jesus, adorning you to please Him, and, above all, giving you to Him forever.... Your dear little letter pleased me very much. I was very happy to find in it the promise of a very childlike remembrance on this beautiful day when He, who will be the God of your heart, will be unable to refuse you anything. Ask for yourself, along with me, the grace of loving Him as much as He wills to be loved by your heart, and for myself a great number of souls to save.

I will offer the Adorable Victim at the altar for you and your Pauline.

I bless you just as a father blesses his youngest child on the day of her First Communion.

A.P. [Almire Pichon][41]

When Father Pichon preached his first retreat at the Lisieux Carmel in October 1887, he also visited Les Buissonnets and agreed to be Céline's spiritual director. Thérèse wrote to him in the same month about her vocation and the need for a spiritual director while in the convent. It's not certain, though, if this letter was actually ever mailed to him. Only a first draft exists from which this passage is quoted:

Reverend Father,

I thought that since you were attending to my sisters [Marie, Pauline, and Céline], you would be willing to take the last one also. I would like to be able to make myself known to you, but I am not like my sisters. I don't know how to express in a letter all I am feeling. I believe, Father, that, in spite of everything, you will understand me. When you come to Lisieux, I hope I will be able to see you at Carmel in order to open my heart to you.

Father, God has just granted me a great grace. For a long time I have wanted to enter Carmel, and I believe the moment has arrived. Papa is willing that I enter at Christmas.

[My] sisters told me that I could write you to tell you simply what was taking place in my heart. You see, Father, that I did this, hoping you would not refuse to accept me as your little daughter.[42]

---

40 Ibid., chapter III, p. 62.
41 LC 32 from Father Pichon to Thérèse, dated Paris, May 6, 1884.
42 LT 28 from Thérèse to P. Pichon, dated October 23, 1887.

Thérèse's hesitancy and humility are evident here. Father Pichon mentioned in his testimony that she was "timid and reserved," [43] "recollected and rather silent," [44] and "she did not express herself in a flow of words. She asked her questions very clearly but with great sobriety." [45] An interesting remark Father Pichon made to a friend clearly portrays Thérèse's relationship with Father Pichon at the time: "He told me that Thérèse was extremely uncommunicative; I can still picture the gesture he made which meant that he had to make the first moves in order to *delve* into her mind." [46]

The letters Thérèse wrote to Father Pichon do not exist because, unfortunately, he kept none of her correspondence which amounted to about fifty letters. In her autobiography, however, she refers to one of her letters to him:

> I had written to good Père Pichon recommending myself to his prayers, telling him that soon I would become a Carmelite and then he would be my director. (This is what happened four years later, since it was to him I opened my soul.) Marie gave me a *letter from him*, and my happiness was complete! All these good things came to me together. What pleased me very much in his letter was this sentence: "Tomorrow, I will ascend the altar to say Mass for you and your Pauline!" [47]

Once in the Carmel (April 9, 1888), Thérèse had this to say about Father Pichon's consoling remarks:

> [A] few months after I entered, Father Pichon, having come for the Profession of Sister Marie of the Sacred Heart [May 22, 1888] was surprised to see what God was doing in my soul. He told me that he was watching me at prayer in the choir one evening, and that he believed my fervor was childish and my way was very sweet. My interview with the good Father was a great consolation to me, but it was veiled in tears because I experienced much difficulty in confiding to him. I made a general confession, something I had never made before, and at its termination he spoke the most consoling words I ever heard in my life: "*In the presence of God, the Blessed Virgin, and all the saints, I DECLARE THAT YOU HAVE NEVER COMMITTED A MORTAL SIN.*" Then he added: "Thank God for what He has done for you; had He abandoned you, instead of being a little angel, you would have become a little demon." I had no difficulty in believing it.... The good priest also spoke these words which are engraved in my heart: "My child, may Our Lord always be your Superior and your Novice Master." [48]

This was the last time Father Pichon ever saw or spoke to her in person.

When commenting on her first years as a nun, Thérèse makes reference to some sage remark Father Pichon made:

---

43 PO 318.
44 PA 134.
45 PA 136.
46 DCL (Lisieux Carmel's Documentation).
47 *Story of a Soul*, chapter IV, pp. 76–77.
48 Ibid., pp. 149–150.

[I] had learned very much when I was teaching others [as assistant novice mistress]. I saw first of all that all souls have very much the same struggles to fight, but they differ so much from each other in other aspects that I have no trouble in understanding what Father Pichon was saying: "*There are really more differences among souls than there are among faces.*" It is impossible to act with all in the same manner.[49]

Sister Marie of the Sacred Heart asked Thérèse, since she was writing poetry for special occasions and people, if she would write something for the feast day of Father Almire Pichon away in Canada at the time. Of course Thérèse consented and composed "Prayer of an Exiled Child" (PN 9), dated September 11, 1894. It is in the form of an acrostic; obviously not translatable as such into English. The "exiled child" is Sister Marie, not Thérèse:

PRAYER OF AN EXILED CHILD

A   Near you, my God, I remember a Father
L   The beloved apostle of your Sacred Heart.
M   But he is exiled on a foreign shore....
I   It's time; bring back my Pastor at last!
R   Give your children back their guide and their light.
E   Call your apostle home to France, Lord.

This prayer certainly pleased Father who wrote these few words of appreciation: "Thank you for your feast day wishes, your delightful poetry. Everything coming from the little lamb does my heart good."[50]

His reassuring, supportive, affectionate, and positive counsel had a significant influence on Thérèse. She particularly found his general approval of her own spirituality, mainly her "little way," most gratifying. A few pertinent extracts from his letters illustrate the issues he stressed:

- Love all that comes to you from Jesus, everything, even the most bitter gall, the sharpest thorns, your most filial agonies, the divine absences. Be obstinate in smiling at Our Lord just the same.
- Yes, you are right, it is better to love Jesus on His terms; there is more love on Calvary than on Thabor.
- Yes, yes, take joy in being nothing since Jesus is all. Bless God that you feel nothing, possess nothing, find nothing in yourself.[51]
- Jesus has a weakness for nothingness, for our poor little nothings; let us rejoice, then, to be of such little consequence.[52]
- When advancing toward heaven, you will see better and better that to suffer is to love and to love is to suffer! Listen to Jesus when He reveals this admirable secret to you.
- Keep calm and serene in your whole exterior even when your interior is tossed by the tempest. This is holy hypocrisy.[53]

---

49   *Story of a Soul*, chapter XI, pp. 239–240.
50   CGII, p. 900 (from the French edition of the *General Correspondace, vol. II*).
51   LC 111 dated April 27, 1889.
52   LC 1287 dated March 27, 1890.
53   LC 146 dated February 16, 1891.

Céline always kept October 12 as a special day because on that day in 1887, when she was eighteen, she took Father Almire Pichon as her spiritual director, thus adding another Martin sister to his list of people under his spiritual care. This took place during Father's first time as retreat master at the annual fall retreat in the Carmel. She unknowingly became Father Pichon's favorite among her sisters. Eventually, after Father returned from Canada, he expressed his grand ambition of forming a religious community of nuns whose apostolate would be to serve the poor. This project he called "Bethany" and he decidedly wanted Céline to be part of it. This, plus several proposals of marriage after her father died, disturbed and confused her since she really felt destined to be a contemplative nun. In the end, she chose the Lisieux Carmel which she entered on September 14, 1894, thereby joining her three sisters there (Pauline, Marie, and Thérèse).

During the time Father Pichon labored in Canada (a total of almost twenty years), his influence and inspiration greatly affected particularly the well-known Vanier family. As ardent and faithful disciples of Father Pichon, they staunchly defended him whenever a problem arose. The Vanier family included the governor-general of Canada, a Trappist monk (still living in the Order near Montreal), and the founder of the world famous L'Arche ("The Ark"), a community devoted to working with people who have developmental and other disabilities.

Almire Théophile Augustin Pichon was born in Carrouges (Orne) on February 3, 1843. At twenty he entered the Jesuit Order and was ordained ten years later on September 8, 1873—the year Thérèse was born. He preached retreats at the Carmel and countless other places. Four years before his death, he was known to have given over a thousand retreats. He testified at both processes for the beatification and canonization of Thérèse, one of his directees who became not only a saint but also later on a Doctor of the Church. On April 23, 1915, during the proceedings and questioning at the Apostolic Process, he had this to say: "Yes, I have a great devotion to the Servant of God because I have always considered her an extraordinary soul, very privileged by God. I desire her beatification with all my heart and I pray for this intention. I am convinced I have obtained two times a cure through her intercession." [54]

One strong desire Father Pichon had all his life was to be able to celebrate Mass to his dying day. This came true while he was preparing to say Mass at the Jesuit seminary at rue Dantzig in Paris. He always spent an hour in meditation in preparation for the sacred liturgy. When younger, he would go down on his knees in the sacristy for part of the time, but when he became old and feeble, he sat down during the entire meditation. On November 15, 1919, he did exactly this. The brother sacristan came in an hour later at six o'clock and thought he was sleeping in the chair with his head bowed and hands folded. When he gently tried to awaken him, he found the seventy-six-year-old priest dead. Burial took place in the imposing Pichon family plot in Carrouges, the little village of his birth.

---

54 Translation by the author.

B. On the Pilgrimage to Rome

1. Msgr. Germain: *Bishop who led the pilgrimage*
2. Abbé Leconte: *Young priest friendly with the Martin sisters*
3. Msgr. Legoux: *Vicar general who organized the pilgrimage*
4. Pope Leo XIII: *Thérèse asked him for permission to enter Carmel*
5. Abbé Révérony: *Vicar general involved with Thérèse's vocation plans*
6. Père Vauquelin: *Complained of Thérèse and Céline's chatter in their Rome hotel*

LIKE HER FATHER, THÉRÈSE VIEWED PRIESTS AS GOD'S FLAWLESS REPresentatives on earth. After painfully experiencing Canon Delatroëtte's resolute opposition to her entrance into Carmel, her opinion began to change and was intensified during her pilgrimage to Rome where she observed at firsthand clerics as "mere humans" involved at times in somewhat mundane situations. Thérèse analyzes her significant change of mind in her autobiography:

> Having never lived close to them [priests], I was not able to understand the principal aim of the Reform of Carmel. To pray for sinners attracted me, but to pray for the souls of priests whom I believed to be as pure as crystal seemed puzzling to me!
>
> I understood *my vocation* in *Italy* and that's not going too far in search of such useful knowledge. I lived in the company of many *saintly priests* for a month and I learned that, though their dignity raises them above the angels, they are nevertheless weak and fragile men. If *holy priests*, whom Jesus in His Gospel calls the "salt of the earth," show in their conduct their extreme need for prayers, what is to be said of those who are tepid?[1]

Thérèse explains another bit of knowledge she gained on this trip:

> Ah! What a trip that was! It taught me more than long years of studies; it showed me the vanity of everything that happens and that *everything is affliction of spirit under the sun*. However, I saw some very beautiful things; I contemplated all the marvels of art and religion; above all, I trod the same soil as did the holy apostles, the soil bedewed with the blood of martyrs. And my soul grew through contact with holy things.
>
> [Having] never lived among the great of this world, Céline and I found ourselves in the midst of the nobility who almost exclusively made up the pilgrimage.[2] Ah! Far from dazzling us, all these titles and these "de" [before the surname] appeared to us as nothing but smoke.[3]

---

[1] *Story of a Soul*, chapter VI, p. 122.
[2] The majority of those French pilgrims were opponents of the Republic, staunch Royalists, and positively against Freemasonry.
[3] Ibid., p. 121.

The ecclesiastics Thérèse came into contact with on this trip were not only diocesan priests but also monsignori, monks, papal officials, a bishop and the pope himself. The travel group consisted of seventy-five priests out of a total of 197 pilgrims, the majority of which were of noble birth with impressive titles: dukes, viscounts, viscountesses, counts, countesses, and a few other aristocratic young ladies.

Two priests, besides the six portrayed more fully following this, are worthy of mentioning here. One was Msgr. August Pierre Laveille (diocese of Coutances and Avranches) a noted hagiographer who stayed at the same hotel in Venice that the Martins did, but was regrettably unaware of Thérèse, the teenager, whose authoritative biography of her he wrote after her canonization. The other cleric was Father Moulin, a curate of St. Denis, the church next to the Benedictine school in Lisieux that Thérèse attended.

The pilgrimage left Paris in the rain on Monday, November 7, 1887, and returned twenty-six days later on Friday, December 2.

1. Msgr. Abel-Anastase Germain (1833–1897)
Bishop who led the pilgrimage

Msgr. Germain, the bishop of Coutances (a city on the Cotentin Peninsula of Normandy), organized and led the grand pilgrimage to Rome basically to celebrate the golden jubilee of Pope Leo XIII's priestly ordination and to show support for him. He at the time was held a virtual prisoner in the Vatican amidst the virulent anti-clerical atmosphere at the time.

The tour group left Paris early on Monday morning, November 6, 1887, after the formal opening by Bishop Germain of the pilgrimage that began with a Mass he celebrated for the pilgrims. At that time the basilica was under construction (1875–1914), therefore, it was not possible to have religious services celebrated in the main part of the church. Céline wrote to her two sisters in Carmel, Pauline and Marie, telling them about Thérèse's and her doings at the basilica: "It was the steps at Sacred Heart that caused us so much fatigue. We made the tour of the underground church with Monseigneur de Coutances in a procession; it was very pretty. The Chancel is almost finished being covered. We received Holy Communion."[4]

Thérèse does not mention the bishop by his full name but does refer to him in her narrative of the trip:

> After our solemn consecration to the Sacred Heart in the Basilica [crypt] at Montmartre, we departed from Paris on Monday, at seven in the morning. We very quickly became acquainted with the different people on the pilgrimage. So timid that I usually dared not speak, I was surprised to find myself completely freed from this crippling fault. I was talking freely with the great ladies, the priests, and even the Bishop of Coutances.[5]

---

[4] An excerpt from the letter Céline wrote to her Carmelite sisters on November 5–6, 1887.
[5] *Story of a Soul*, chapter VI, p. 124.

The next time Thérèse mentions the bishop is when they were in Milan:

> The first Italian city we visited was Milan. We examined minutely its white marble cathedral in which its statues were so many they could have formed a small population. Céline and I were very brave; we were always the first and were following the Bishop closely in order to see everything pertaining to the relics of the saints and hear the explanations given by the guides. So while the Bishop was offering Mass on the tomb of St. Charles, we were behind the altar with Papa, resting our heads on the tomb enshrining his body which was clothed in its pontifical robes. And it was like this everywhere, except in those places reserved to dignitaries and then we did not follow his Excellency.[6]

It should be noted that Bishop Abel Germain is not Msgr. Octave Germain (1885–1957), founder of the Basilica of Lisiuex dedicated to St. Thérèse of the Child Jesus. Bishop Abel Germain died at the age of sixty-four in the same year as Thérèse—1897.

2. Abbé Alcide-Victor Leconte (1858–1907)
Young priest friendly with the Martin sisters

The Martin family knew the handsome, twenty-nine-year-old priest, Father Leconte, when he was curate at the church of Saint Pierre in Lisieux that they attended. As one of the members of the pilgrimage group to Rome, he was often seen with Céline and Thérèse, and of course M. Martin. His kind and obliging relationship with them was apparently noticed, causing some wags to gossip. At any rate, Thérèse refers to him only once and that is in her section on the visit to the Holy House of Loreto:

> Céline and I went in search of a priest who had accompanied us everywhere and who was just then preparing to say Mass in the Santa-Casa by special privilege. He asked for two small hosts which he laid alongside the large one on the paten and you can well understand, dear Mother [Pauline, her sister Mother Agnès], the joy we both experienced at receiving Communion in that blessed house! It was a totally heavenly happiness which words cannot express.[7]

Father Leconte served at one time as chaplain of a college in Lisieux and later on became Céline's confessor. He died in 1907 when he was only forty-nine.

3. Msgr. Arsène-Louis-Jean-Marie Legoux (1845–1921)
Vicar general who organized the pilgrimage

Msgr. Legoux, an advocate of ultramontanism, was the highly capable vicar-general to Bishop Germain of Coutances (Manche). He held the distinguished title of Pope's Chamberlain because of his many services to the Holy See. His task in 1887, together with the bishop, involved the organization of the 1887 pilgrimage to Rome for the dual purpose of displaying loyalty to the beleaguered Pope Leo XIII and to celebrate his golden jubilee of priesthood.

---
6 Ibid., p. 126.
7 Ibid., chapter VI, p. 129.

Each compartment in the train heading for Rome that left the Gare de l'Est in Paris on November 7 was placed under the patronage of a different saint. It came as a pleasant surprise when Msgr. Legoux announced to the group that the Martins' patron was St. Martin. Frequently thereafter, Thérèse's father was referred to as "Monsieur Saint Martin."

Thérèse made her daring request to enter the Lisieux Carmel at the age of fourteen at the papal audience. The Pope's vague, non-committal response was most disappointing. Thérèse recorded in vivid detail the incident and her feelings about this matter in her autobiography:

> My soul was plunged into sadness and still exteriorly I was the same, for I believed the request I made of the Holy Father was hidden; soon I was to be convinced of the opposite. Having remained alone in the car with Céline (the other pilgrims got off to eat during a short stop), I saw Monsignor Legoux, Vicar General of Coutances, open the door and looking at me with a smile, he said: "Well, how is our little Carmelite?" I understood then that the whole pilgrimage knew my secret; happily no one spoke to me about it, but I saw by their sympathetic way of looking at me that my request had produced no ill effect, on the contrary....[8]

Msgr. Legoux was born on August 8, 1845, and died on June 10, 1921, age seventy-six.

4. POPE LEO XIII (1810–1903, PONTIFICATE: 1887–1903)
Thérèse asked him for permission to enter Carmel

POPE LEO XIII REIGNED DURING ALL BUT THE FIRST FIVE YEARS OF THÉRÈSE'S life. When she was fourteen, she attended a papal audience on November 20, 1887, in the company of her father, her sister Céline, and 194 other French pilgrims who journeyed to Rome to honor the pope's golden jubilee as a priest. Thérèse tells us in her own words what occurred at this papal audience:

> Before entering the pontifical apartment [the Sala dei Palafreneri/Sala dei Chiaroscuri], I was really determined *to speak*, but I felt my courage weaken when I saw *Father Révérony* standing by the Holy Father's right side. Almost at the same instant, they told us on the Pope's *behalf* that *it was forbidden to speak*, as this would prolong the audience too much. I turned towards my dear Céline for advice: "Speak!," she said. A moment later I was at the Holy Father's feet. I kissed his slipper and he presented his hand, but instead of kissing it I joined my own and lifting tear-filled eyes to his face, I cried out: "Most Holy Father, I have a great favor to ask you!"
>
> The Sovereign Pontiff lowered his head towards me in such a way that my face almost touched his, and I saw *his eyes, black and deep,* fixed on me and they seemed to penetrate to the depths of my soul. "Holy Father, in honor of your Jubilee, permit me to enter Carmel at the age of fifteen!"

---

[8] Ibid., pp. 137–138.

Emotion undoubtedly made my voice tremble. He turned to Father Révérony who was staring at me with surprise and displeasure and said: "I don't understand very well." Now if God had permitted it, it would have been easy for Father Révérony to obtain what I desired, but it was the cross and not consolation God willed to give me.

"Most Holy Father," answered the Vicar General, "this is a child who wants to enter Carmel at the age of fifteen, but the Superiors are considering the matter at the moment." "Well, my child," the Holy Father replied, looking at me kindly, "do what the superiors tell you!" Resting my hands on his knees, I made a final effort, saying in a suppliant voice: "Oh! Holy Father, if you say yes, everybody will agree!" He gazed at me steadily, speaking these words and stressing each syllable: "Go ... go.... *You will enter if God wills it!*" (His accent had something about it so penetrating and so convincing, it seems to me I still hear it.)

I was encouraged by the Holy Father's kindness and wanted to speak again, but the two guards *touched* me *politely* to make me rise. As this was not enough they took me by the arms and Father Révérony helped them lift me, for I stayed there with joined hands resting on the knees of Leo XIII. It was with *force* they dragged me from his feet. At the moment I was *thus lifted*, the Holy Father placed his hand on my lips, then raised it to bless me. Then my eyes filled with tears and Father Révérony was able to contemplate at least as many *diamonds* [tears] as he had seen at Bayeux. The two guards literally carried me to the door and there a third one gave me a medal of Leo XIII.[9]

Nonetheless, she did enter at fifteen though not at the direct bidding of the pope. Three years later, Brother Siméon, a friend of the family and the Carmel stationed in Rome, obtained an Apostolic Blessing for her:

> I had the happiness of receiving the Holy Father's blessing for the day of my Profession [September 8, 1890]. The religious [Brother Siméon] who got it for me wrote how numerous are the enemies of the Church in Rome, the warfare against our Holy Father the Pope never ceases for an instant. It is heartbreaking....[10]

Thérèse was very grateful to Brother Siméon and in one of her letters to him wrote, "[You] have already obtained our Holy Father Leo XIII's blessing for us so many times."[11] Probably the pope did not realize these blessings were imparted to the little girl who begged him at one of his innumerable audiences for permission to enter Carmel before the usual age.

In 1898 the Carmel sent one of the first copies of *Story of a Soul* to Brother Siméon for the pope to bless which he did and then sent back to Lisieux. A year later on December 30, 1899, Cardinal Gotti, a Carmelite, presented to the pontiff another copy of the autobiography as a gift from the Lisieux Carmel. This time, beautifully printed and illustrated, it contained a drawing of Thérèse at the pope's feet that he must have seen. Whether or not he recalled the incident is not

---

9 Ibid., chapter VI, pp. 134–135.
10 From a letter, LT 121, written by Thérèse to Sr. Marie Joseph of the Cross (Marcelline Huse, a former housemaid of Thérèse's Aunt Guérin), dated September 28, 1890.
11 LT 218 dated January 27, 1897, from Thérèse to Brother Siméon.

known, but the Cardinal wrote to Mother Agnès (Pauline) that "His Holiness wished to acquaint himself with it straight away and carried on reading for a long time with marked satisfaction."[12]

This pope was born Gioacchino Pecci in Carpineto, central Italy, on March 2, 1810, the sixth of seven sons of the noble, but not wealthy, Colonel Ludovic Pecci and Anna Prosperi Buzi. His education consisted of studies at the Jesuit college in Viterbo, the Roman College, the College of Bobles, and finally at the University of Sapienza, at which point he was ordained in 1837. Soon after ordination he was sent as apostolic delegate to Benevento and proved particularly successful at controlling the banditry which ravaged that area. In 1843 he went to Belgium as papal nuncio where he gained valuable experience dealing with industrial and labor problems. Three years later he was made archbishop of Perugia and in 1853 created Cardinal by Pius IX. Cardinal Pecci insisted on religious instruction, the study of Aquinas, and spoke against social evils and the vehement anti-clericalism so rampant at the time. After the death of Pius IX in 1878, Cardinal Pecci succeeded him as Pope Leo XIII in a conclave that lasted only thirty-six hours.

As pope he condemned socialism and economic liberalism which became the subject of his most renowned encyclical *Rerum Novarum* (1891). During his long reign he produced eighty-six papal encyclicals, all models of "style and logic." He participated actively in the field of national and international politics, always striving to soothe strained relations among nations and with the Holy See. Above all, he encouraged biblical studies, opened the Vatican Archives (1881) to historians, urged sound doctrinal teachings in seminaries, and strove for understanding and conciliation with the Oriental, Slavic, and Anglican Churches.

Having completed twenty-five years as pontiff, Pope Leo XIII died a few months before his ninety-third birthday on July 20, 1903, not quite seven years after Thérèse.

5. Abbé Maurice-Joseph Révérony (1836–1891)
Vicar general involved with Thérèse's vocation plans

A CLERIC ACTIVELY INVOLVED WITH THÉRÈSE'S DETERMINED EFFORTS TO enter Carmel was the devout and capable assistant and advisor to the Bishop of Bayeux, the vicar general Father Révérony. He planned Thérèse's appointment with the bishop, accompanied her and the other pilgrims to Rome, introduced her to the pope, and became an arbiter in the final stages prior to her acceptance into the Carmel.

Thérèse's autobiography and the many letters she and her sisters wrote inform us in considerable detail of all the times Father Révérony was involved in her life. Thérèse introduces the vicar general in the fifth chapter of her book that deals with her visit to Bayeux to see the bishop on the rainy day of October 31, 1887:

---

12 *Sicut Parvuli*, "Posthumous Life of St. Thérèse," May 1982. This is an English translation from an article that appeared in the January and May 1981 edition of *Les Annales de Ste. Thérèse*.

> We went directly to Father Révérony's who was aware of our arrival as he himself had set the date of the trip.... Father Révérony was very friendly, but I believe the reason for our trip took him by surprise. After looking at me with a smile and asking me a few simple questions, he said: "I am going to introduce you to the Bishop; will you kindly follow me?" Seeing the tears in my eyes, he added: "Ah! I see diamonds; you mustn't show them to the Bishop!" He had us traverse several huge rooms in which portraits of bishops were hanging on the walls [as they still do today]. When I saw myself in these large rooms, I felt like a poor little ant, and I asked myself what I would dare say to the Bishop.
>
> The Bishop was walking on the balcony with two priests. I saw Father Révérony say a few words to him and return with him to where we were waiting in his study. There, three enormous armchairs were set before the fireplace in which a bright fire was crackling away. When he saw his Excellency enter, Papa knelt down by my side to receive his blessing; the Bishop had Papa take one of the armchairs, and then he sat down facing him. Father Révérony wanted me to take the one in the middle; I excused myself politely, but he insisted, telling me to show if I knew how to obey. And so I took it without further reflection and was mortified to see him take a chair while I was buried in a huge armchair which could hold four like me comfortably (more comfortably, in fact, for I was far from being so!...)
>
> The Bishop asked me if it had been a long time since I desired to enter Carmel. "Oh! yes, Bishop, a very long time." "Come, now," said Father Révérony with a smile, "you can't say it is fifteen *years* since you've had the desire." Smiling, I said; "That's true, but there aren't too many years to subtract because I wanted to be a religious since the dawn of my reason, and I wanted Carmel as soon as I knew about it. I find all the aspirations of my soul are fulfilled in this Order."... The Bishop said an interview with the *Superior of Carmel* was indispensable before making his decision. I couldn't possibly have heard anything that would cause me more pain than this because I was aware of his formal opposition. Without taking into account Father Révérony's advice, I did more than *show my diamonds* to the Bishop. I *gave* him some!
>
> He was very much touched by this and putting his arm around my neck, he placed my head on his shoulder and caressed me as no one, it appears, was ever caressed by him before....
>
> The Bishop brought us out as far as the garden.... Father Révérony wanted to accompany us to the end of the garden, and he told Papa that never had the like been seen before: "A father as eager to give his child to God as this child was to offer herself to Him!" [13]

Four days after this disappointing interview, Thérèse, with her sister Céline and their father, set out on their pre-scheduled pilgrimage to Rome where she was determined to ask the pope's authorization for her to enter the Carmelite Order.

On the way to Rome, whether on the train or sightseeing, Thérèse discreetly observed Father Révérony:

---

13 *Story of a Soul*, chapter V, pp. 115–117.

B. On the Pilgrimage to Rome

Father Révérony carefully studied all our actions, and I was able to see him do this at a distance. While eating, if I was not opposite him, he would lean over in such a way as to see me and listen to my conversation. He wanted to know me, undoubtedly, to see if I was really capable of becoming a Carmelite. I think he was favorably impressed by his study, for at *journey's end* he seemed well disposed towards me. At Rome he was far from being favorable to me as I will explain later on.[14]

Thérèse follows with a detailed account of what transpired at the audience with Pope Leo XIII on November 20, 1887:

Before entering the pontifical apartment, I was really determined to speak, but I felt my courage weaken when I saw *Father Révérony* standing by the Holy Father's right side. Almost at the same instant, they told us on the Pope's *behalf* that *it was forbidden to speak*, as this would prolong the audience too much. I turned towards my dear Céline for advice: "Speak!" she said. A moment later I was at the Holy Father's feet. I kissed his slipper and he presented his hand, but instead of kissing it I joined my own and lifting tear-filled eyes to his face, I cried out: "Most Holy Father, I have a great favor to ask you!"

The Sovereign Pontiff lowered his head towards me in such a way that my face almost touched his, and I saw *his eyes, black and deep*, fixed on me and they seemed to penetrate to the depths of my soul. "Holy Father, in honor of your Jubilee, permit me to enter Carmel at the age of fifteen!"[15]

Thérèse's story continues in this excerpt from a letter she wrote to her sister Pauline the very day she spoke to the pope:

I said what you were telling me in your letter but not all, for M. Révérony did not give me time. He said immediately: "Most Holy Father, this is a child who wants to enter Carmel at fifteen, but the superiors are considering the matter at this moment." (The good pope is so old that one would say he is dead; I would never have pictured him like this. He can hardly say anything. It is M. Révérony who talks.)[16]

Here is "the intrepid" Céline's version of the rest of this episode:

[M. Révérony] answered immediately with a sarcastic tone: "She is a child who is asking to enter Carmel at fifteen, but the matter is being examined by the superiors." Then, after Thérèse's *repeated entreaties*, the Holy Father answered: "My dear child, if God wills it, you will enter; leave it up to your superiors." This lasted hardly two minutes, and I came afterward. I had tears in my eyes, but would you believe that I had the audacity to say: "Most Holy Father, a blessing for the Carmel."[17] He blessed me, saying: "Oh, it is already blessed!"

After this request made by me, M. Révérony was careful not to say that I was Thérèse's sister, but he replied, laughing a little: "It is already blessed." The

---

14 Ibid., p. 124.
15 Ibid., p. 134.
16 LT 36 from Thérèse to Sister Agnès, dated November 20, 1897.
17 Céline said that her emotions at that moment made her forget to add the "Lisieux Carmel."

Holy Pontiff, who is so kind, seemed to understand it in another way, and it was then he said to me: "Oh, yes, it is already blessed!..." Then he extended his hand for me to kiss. Papa came afterward with the gentlemen. M. Révérony introduced him to the Holy Father, saying, "This is the father of two Carmelites and a Visitandine." But he did not say that he was Thérèse's father....[18]

Father Révérony apparently did not reprimand Thérèse or Céline for disobeying his orders not to speak to the pope. In fact, upon meeting them several times subsequently he appeared most gracious. While the two sisters were on a side trip to Naples and Pompeii, their father stayed in Rome and visited an old friend, Brother Siméon. He proudly spoke about his youngest daughter's desire to become a Carmelite and her meeting with the pope:

The Brother was charmed. Papa spoke to him frankly; he recounted the audience we had on Sunday, Thérèse's desires, her request, all the ups and downs, the sadness she experienced.... He was noting down what Papa was saying about Thérèse, and he offered to speak about her to M. Révérony. But listen to the very end: Papa stood up to leave and whom did he see enter but M. Révérony!... You may judge his surprise and that of the brother. M. Révérony was very much charmed by Papa; he seemed to be repentant. He reminded Papa that the Soverign Pontiff had spoken to him particularly because he [M. Révérony] had introduced him by telling the pope that two of his daughters were Carmelites. Papa asked him if he had heard anything regarding the bishop's decision, and he added: "You know very well that you had promised to help me." What a good Father! Then he recounted Thérèse's grief at the audience and especially when he had replied that the matter was being examined by the superiors, etc. M. Révérony was touched, I believe, and he is beginning to believe that Thérèse's vocation is extraordinary. He even said: "Well! I will assist at the ceremony; I'm inviting myself." Papa told him he would be happy to have him and all sorts of amiable things were exchanged between them. That is what Papa told us this morning....
[I] believe we have won M. Révérony's sympathy....[19]

On the way home, Thérèse had two unexpected encounters with Father Révérony involving a common type of tourist problem but with a humorous touch:

I had the opportunity at the little town of Assisi of climbing into Father Révérony's carriage, a favor granted to *no woman* during the whole trip. Here is how I obtained this privilege. After having visited the places made sacred by the virtues of St. Francis and St. Clare, I had studied the Saint's head [in a reliquary] at my leisure and was one of the last to leave when I noticed my belt was lost. I *looked* for it in the crowd; a priest had pity on me and helped in the search. After he found it, I saw him depart and I remained alone to *search*, for I had the belt but it was impossible to wear it as the buckle was missing. At last I saw it shining in a corner. Taking it and adjusting it to the belt was the work of an instant, but the work preceding this had taken up much time, and I was greatly surprised to find myself alone in front of the church. The numerous carriages

---
18 Letter from Céline to Sister Marie of the Sacred Heart (her sister Marie), dated November 20, 1887.
19 Letter dated November 23, 1887, from Céline to her two sisters in Carmel—Pauline and Marie.

had all disappeared, with the sole exception of Father Révérony's. What was I to do? Should I run after the carriages no longer in sight and expose myself to the danger of missing the train and thus upsetting my dear Papa, or else ask for a place in Father Révérony's coach? I decided on the latter. With my most gracious manner, trying to appear as little embarrassed as I could though I was greatly *embarrassed*, I explained my critical situation to him. I put him also in an *embarrassing situation*, for his carriage was filled with the most important *men* of the pilgrimage. There wasn't a single place left, but one good gentleman hastened to descend, made me climb into his place, and humbly took a seat beside the driver. I was like a squirrel caught in a trap and was far from being at ease, surrounded as I was by all these great personages and especially the most *formidable* of all; I was placed directly opposite to him. He was very friendly towards me, however, and even interrupted his conversation with the others from time to time to speak to me about *Carmel*. Before we reached the station, all the *great personages* took their *huge* purses out to give some money [25 cents] to the driver (already paid). I did the same thing, taking out my *very little* purse. Father Révérony did not agree with what I drew out from it, some pretty *little* coin, and instead he offered a *large* coin [50 cents][20] for both of us.

I was by his side, on another occasion, on a bus, and he was even more friendly, promising *to do all he could to have me enter Carmel*.[21]

The fourth time we read of Father Révérony on this trip involves a little incident when the pilgrims stopped at Nice. Céline wrote this account of it:

> This morning, when being taken to the station, we were in the *omnibus*[22] with M. Révérony. Papa was next to him, and he said in a whisper: "Would you say something to Thérèse." M. Révérony answered with a smile, and Papa said: "You know that she is always thinking of her little Christmas Jesus...." The same smile, the same response. Then without being aware of anything, we got up into the omnibus, Thérèse and I, and we were behind Papa. By God's permission, Thérèse was next to M. Révérony. She was very close to him, for we were sixteen in the carriage, eight on each side, crushed in like sardines. M. Révérony leaned over to Thérèse and said to her: "Well! Where will we go when we are at Lisieux?" Thérèse, searching for an answer, responded with a smile. M. Révérony repeated his question. Thérèse then said: "I will go to see my sisters at Carmel." He answered: "I *promise* to do all I *can*." Thérèse then answered with this word which came from her heart: "Oh! Thank you!..."[23]

Two weeks after returning home, Thérèse in her great determination to enter Carmel by Christmas, wrote to Father Révérony:

> All the distractions of the trip to Rome were not able to chase from my mind for one instant the ardent desire of uniting myself to Jesus. Ah! Why call me so strongly if it is only to make me languish far from Him.

---

20 Céline recorded the tip amounts in a letter to her Carmelite sisters, dated November 28, 1887.
21 *Story of a Soul*, chapter V, pp. 138–139.
22 A horse-drawn carriage.
23 Letter dated November 29, 1887, from Céline to her two sisters in Carmel—Pauline and Marie.

Monsieur l'Abbé, I hope you have pleaded my cause with Monseigneur [the bishop] as you promised me. If Jesus has consoled me in my trials it is through your intervention, and if I enter Carmel at Christmas, I know that I shall owe it to you. But I am not ungrateful, and all my life I shall remember this.[24]

Thérèse did not enter before Christmas. Mother de Gonzague, the prioress, received a letter from the bishop on December 28 authorizing Thérèse's admittance as an aspirant. She notified Thérèse of this on New Year's Day, 1888. Thérèse sent messages of gratitude to the bishop and Father Révérony. This is Father's reply: "I gladly share in your joy and with you I thank with my whole heart God, who is treating you as a very tenderly loved child.... Be His with all your heart and with all your strength."[25] Thérèse entered the Lisieux Carmel four months later at the age of fifteen on April 9, 1888.

Father Révérony did not attend Thérèse's Profession on September 8, 1890, but he did write a short letter to her about it: "When you receive these lines, all your desires, no doubt, will have been accomplished! You will belong to Jesus!... totally!... forever!... What a joy!... I am praying for you with all my heart and for your dear father whom Our Lord loves and blesses."[26]

A descendent of an old Italian family in France, Maurice-Joseph Révérony was born on September 9, 1836, in Caen. He was ordained a diocesan priest on January 17, 1864, was sent as a parish priest to Vaucelles (outside of Bayeux) the same year, remaining there until 1870. After this he served a short time as an army chaplain. Following his military duty from 1871 to 1878, he officiated as curate of Saint-Pierre, a church in Caen. He advanced to vicar general in the episcopacy of Bayeux on October 16, 1878. During his lifetime he acted as superior of various religious communities in the Caen area. He lived to be fifty, dying on October 10, 1891, six years before Thérèse died.

6. Père Vauquelin
Complained of Thérèse and Céline's chatter in their Rome hotel

BECAUSE OF OVERCROWDING AT THE SCHEDULED *Hôtel de Milan* IN ROME, twenty-three of the Normandy pilgrims were directed to the hotel *La Albergo del Sud* at 56 Via Capo le Case where they stayed from November 13 to 21, 1887. They included the three Martins (Louis, Céline, and Thérèse), three laymen, three elderly ladies, and fifteen priests among whom was Father (Père) Vauquelin, a religious of the Missionaries of La Délivrande. The two sisters shared the same room, No. 1, and Père Vauquelin occupied room No. 2. After each day's ventures in the exciting city, they would return to their long, dark hotel room and recount their wonderful experiences in exuberant conversation, unaware that their loud talking was preventing the priest next door from falling asleep. He soon registered a complaint to the hotel management. It is not known how

---
24 LT 39 from Thérèse to Father Révérony, dated December 16, 1887.
25 LC 72 from Father Révérony to Thérèse on January 12, 1888.
26 LC 139 from Father Révérony to Thérèse on September 7, 1890.

often it happened or what they did once they learned about the complaint. Many years later, after reading Céline's detailed memories, a Jesuit priest described this incident in one of his books:

> At night, overcome by fatigue from the comings and goings of the day and also somewhat intoxicated by the novelty of their encounters, the two sisters did not decide to go to bed immediately; they stretched out on the carpet in their bedroom, trying to relax, and they exchanged their impressions with each other so animatedly and joyfully that the sounds at times passed through the wall, preventing the good priest from falling asleep.[27]

Guy Gaucher asserts in his book *L' "Histoire d'Une Âme" de Thérèse de Lisieux* that Vauquelin "*tapant sur la cloison, l'abbé leur criait de se taire*" ("banging on the wall, the abbé screamed for them to be quiet").[28] Gaucher continues and states that years later, after reading the *Histoire d'Une Âme*, Father Vauquelin wrote to the Carmel on December 26, 1898, in which he praised Thérèse and hoped she would pray for him in heaven. He believed that for ten years that the angelic "perfume of the 'little spouse of the Infant Jesus'" (*parfums de la petite épouse de l'Enfant-Jésus*) filled the cloister and revived the spiritual ardor of the Lisieux Carmel. In his version of what happened in the hotel he omits his knocking on the wall. He did mention, though, that he heard the "prayers and bursts of joy of the two girls" ("*les priers et les éclats de joie des deux sœurs*"). Her room was adjacent to mine, from which I heard the prayers and the bursts of spiritual joy of the two sisters.... I am counting on the fact that she will pray for her old companion on the pilgrimage."

This simple story of Céline and Thérèse's adolescent behavior amazingly found its way to Lisieux. A friend of Carmel, Dom Madelaine, testified a quarter of a century later at the 1911 Diocesan Process that someone claimed Thérèse was *trop joviale* ("overly jovial") "but I thought he was too severe in his evaluation of a fifteen-year-old [actually fourteen] girl who was of a happy and gay character."

Shortly after her canonization in 1925, the room where Thérèse made so much "noise" was converted into an oratory in honor and remembrance of Thérèse's stay there. Today the building is no longer a hotel but houses various commercial and business establishments including a Chinese restaurant on the ground floor and apartments on the floors above. It is not possible now to see room No. 1, but a plaque on the outside under a second floor window states that "*Santa Teresa del Bambino Gesù*" (Saint Thérèse of the Child Jesus) stayed there.

---

27 Noché, *La Petite Sainte Thérèse de Maxence Van der Meerch devant la critique et devant les texts*, p. 296. This selection is a quote from footnote 6 to LC 68, dated November 23, 1887, written by Thérèse's aunt, Mme. Guérin, and sent to Thérèse.

28 This quote from p. 100 and the following two are from Gaucher's book *"L' Histoire d'une âme" de Thérèse de Lisieux*. Translation by the author.

C. On the Carmel Staff

1. ABBÉ BAILLON: *Extraordinary confessor who gave Thérèse good advice*
2. CANON DELATROËTTE: *Superior who opposed Thérèse's entrance into the monastery*
3. ABBÉ FAUCON: *Extraordinary confessor who heard Thérèse's last confession*
4. ABBÉ HODIERNE: *Friendly chaplain who fulfilled Thérèse's prediction about daily Communion*
5. CANON MAUPAS: *Superior who said Thérèse's funeral Mass*
6. ABBÉ YOUF: *Chaplain sympathetic to Thérèse*

1. ABBÉ EUGENE-AUGUSTE BAILLON (1836–1909)
Extraordinary confessor who gave Thérèse good advice

FATHER BAILLON SERVED FOR SIXTEEN YEARS AS EXTRAORDINARY CONFESsor to the nuns at the Carmelite Monastery in Lisieux from 1892 to 1908, the year before he died. Both he and Father Faucon heard Sister Thérèse's confession just a few times a year; therefore, they never really considered themselves particularly involved with her spiritual development. Thérèse said he gave her sound advice whenever she consulted him. About the year Father Baillon became confessor at the Carmel, Thérèse wrote a note preserved in the Carmel archives that quotes what he said to her: "If you do not act against your conscience, even though there would be a sin, you would not be sinning."[1]

Thérèse was a great storyteller and, like her father, could mimic certain people's manner of speaking. Father Baillon had a way of accenting specific words which Thérèse picked up and imitated. He would ask his penitents in the confessional: "Sister, are you truly 'soory' for your sins?" In kindhearted jest, Thérèse often stressed this word during conversations or at recreation by saying at the appropriate moments, "I am 'soo soory.'"[2]

Eugène-August Baillon was born on February 2, 1836, in Familly, a village south of Lisieux. He was ordained a secular priest on June 29, 1865, and in the same year at the age of twenty-nine was appointed the director of the Junior Seminary in Lisieux. From 1878 until 1906 he served as chaplain for the Sisters of Providence of Lisieux. On January 6, 1909, he died in Lisieux in his seventy-third year.

---

1 From Note 5 on p. 768 to a letter (LC 151) Father Pichon wrote to Thérèse on January 20, 1893.
2 Descouvemont, *Thérèse and Lisieux*, p. 106.

2. Canon Jean-Baptiste Delatroëte (1818–1895)
Superior who opposed Thérèse's entrance into the monastery

Though he served essentially as a priest at the nearby church of Saint Jacques in Lisieux, Canon Delatroëtte functioned as the ecclesiastical superior of the Lisieux Carmel for twenty-four years from 1871 to 1895 (seven of the nine years Thérèse was a nun there); though he was stationed essentially as a priest at the nearby church of Saint Jacques. Described by some as imperious and rigid, he was also known for his great faith, modesty, and devotion to works of charity. At the Carmel he, as all Superiors, was called "Our Father."

He had known Thérèse and her family since they arrived from Alençon in 1877 when he refused M. Martin's petition to reserve for his whole family seats in his church (a common practice at the time) for the times they would attend services. Whereupon, M. Martin went to the nearby church of Saint Pierre where he did obtain reserved seats.

When informed of Thérèse's desire to become a Carmelite at the age of fifteen, he made it known that he would not allow anyone to enter Carmel before the age of twenty-one. The Carmelite Constitution, however, specified eighteen or older as the age requirement for profession, but no age for aspirants or postulants. Perhaps Canon Delatroëtte's obstinacy resulted from the embarrassment he experienced in the recent past for permitting another young girl to enter which proved disastrous. Mother Agnès, Thérèse's blood sister, gave the following account at the Apostolic Process of Canon Delatroëtte's opinion of Thérèse's aspirations:

> One big feast day, Father Superior entered the cloister to visit Mother Geneviève, our Foundress, who was [sick] in the infirmary. Invited beforehand by Mother Marie de Gonzague, Mother Geneviève asked before the whole community for the favor of Thérèse's entrance at Christmas. Then the superior answered with emotion: "Again you speak to me about this entrance. You don't believe for an instant that the salvation of the community depends on this child?... Let her stay at the home of her father until her majority [twenty-one]. Besides, do you think I oppose this without consulting God? I insist that you do not speak to me again about this matter."[3]

Finally, after Bishop Hugonin gave permission for Thérèse to enter, Canon Delatroëtte acquiesced.

In one of the letters Thérèse wrote to Canon Delatroëtte, she asked him to bless her date of entrance into the Carmel:

> Please, Monsieur le Curé, bless the littlest of your children from a distance; at this moment, she is working to prepare her soul for the life of Carmel. I realize it is a great grace to be called so young, but I shall not be ungrateful, and God will give me, I trust, the means of being faithful to Him just as I desire with all my heart. I humbly beg you, Monsieur le Curé, not to forget me in your prayers.[4]

---
3 Testimony given on July 5, 1915 at the Apostolic Process as translated by the author.
4 LT 41 from Thérèse to Canon Delatroëtte, dated January 13–30, 1888.

Canon Delatroëtte promptly replied, concluding with a final cutting remark: "I am happy that you are asking God for the grace of being a holy Carmelite. With you, I will pray to Him with my whole heart to make you worthy of being numbered among the daughters of St. Teresa, but I cannot refrain from regretting that you pressed for your entrance with so much insistence. I fear that later on you and your own sisters will have to regret it." [5]

To appease him, the prioress delayed Thérèse's entrance three months and, in fact, later on for the same reason lengthened her postulancy to which normally would have lasted six months to well over a year. Finally, on April 9, 1888, Thérèse was admitted to the Carmel, and in the presence of the ailing M. Martin, guests, and the community, Canon Delatroëtte, just before Thérèse passed through the open enclosure door, announced in a clear voice these acrimonious words which certainly surprised and shocked those present: "Well, Reverend Mothers, you can sing a *Te Deum*. As the delegate of Monseigneur, the Bishop, I present this child of fifteen whose entrance you so desired. I trust she will not disappoint your hopes, but I remind you that if she does, you alone will have to bear the responsibility." [6]

Canon Delatroëtte came to visit the Carmel during the dreadful influenza epidemic of the 1891–1892 winter which claimed the lives of three nuns. Sister Thérèse (then nineteen), one of the three least affected by this malady, worked heroically and with great devotion for those more seriously stricken than she. He could not help but recognize in her that quality of holiness and dedication he least expected to see, and admitted, perhaps begrudgingly, his approval of her: "She shows great promise for this community." [7] Many years later, however, he did disclose to Mother Agnès and with deep sincerity: "Mother, that child is a real angel!" [8]

Not surprisingly, in 1894, two years later, he objected to Thérèse's sister Céline's wish to become a Carmelite also; this time claiming it would create a scandal by allowing four sisters to be united in the same convent. Nonetheless, he was again won over and permitted her to enter on September 14, 1894, with the religious name she had chosen—Sister Marie of the Holy Face. A year later she took the habit but, disappointingly, had to change her name to Sister Geneviève of St. Teresa. That was the name of the recently deceased foundress of their Carmel which Canon Delatroëtte suggested Céline assume as a way of honoring the memory of that saintly nun.

Despite his unyielding opposition to Thérèse's and Céline's entrance to the Carmel, Thérèse revealed her magnanimous sentiments about him to her missionary "brother," Father Roulland, in an 1896 letter in which she wrote, "his conduct was prudent, and I do not doubt that, in trying me, he accomplished the will of God, who willed to have me conquer the fortress of Carmel at the point of the sword." [9]

---

5 LC 74 from Canon Delatroëtte to Thérèse, dated January 30, 1888.
6 Reported by Mother Agnès of Jesus, AP, 370–371, as written in Note 1, of LC 78, March 27, 1888, from Sister Agnès to Thérèse.
7 Gaucher, *The Story of a Life*, p. 120.
8 Testimony given by Mother Agnès on July 6, 1915, at the Apostolic Process.
9 LT 201 from Thérèse to Father Roulland, dated November 1, 1896.

Jean-Baptiste Delatroëtte was born on July 23, 1818, in Saint-Martin-des-Besaces in the Normandy Bocage region. After his ordination on June 1, 1844, he was appointed vicar at the church of Saint-Jean in Caen, remaining there for twenty-three years. The bishop transferred him to the church of Saint-Jacques in Lisieux in 1867 where he stayed until his death on October 8, 1895, at the age of seventy-seven. His own nephew, Father (Canon) Maupas, replaced him as curé of Saint-Jacques where he stayed for twenty-five years (1895–1920) and as superior, like his uncle, of the Lisieux Carmel.

3. Abbé Pierre-Alexandre Faucon (1842–1918)
Extraordinary confessor who heard Thérèse's last confession

DURING HER LAST ILLNESS THÉRÈSE WAS DEPRIVED OF VISITS FROM THE convent chaplain Father Youf because of his own grave physical condition which ended with his death a few days after Thérèse's. In the evening of Wednesday, September 29, 1897, the day before Thérèse died, Father Faucon was summoned to substitute for Father Youf and heard her last confession. Deeply touched by this last meeting, he described it to his interrogators at the Apostolic Process:

> I entered the infirmary as if into a sanctuary. At the sight of her I was filled with profound respect.[10] Amidst her sufferings she was beautiful, so calm she appeared as if in heaven. The venerable Father Granger, diocesan missionary [of La Délivrande], knowing that I was to see the Servant of God, who without doubt considered her a saint, urged me to ask her to obtain for him two particular favors. She promised with simplicity and humility. I found out since then that Father Granger obtained these graces which pertained to the construction of the church of the Sacred Heart in Langannerie.[11]

When he left Thérèse's sick room, Father Faucon said to Mother Agnès: "What a beautiful soul! She seems to be confirmed in grace."[12]

The next day, Thérèse's Aunt Guérin in a letter to her married daughter told what occurred that day—September 30:

> Last night, she [Thérèse] wasn't too good, which is to be understood, but her condition is the same. She is truly a little victim chosen by God. In the midst of her sufferings, she always has the same appearance, the same angelic air about her. Father Faucon, who saw her yesterday, told me through Mme. Lahaye, the seamstress, that he admires her. He had to hear her confession, and she asked him for his blessing, always with her smiling and angelic manner which never abandons her. She has always remained lucid.[13]

---

10 He was able to see her face clearly because the veil Carmelites had to wear to cover their face when "outside" visitors were present was removed because Thérèse had great difficulty breathing, was in pain, and exceedingly weak.

11 Free translation by the author of Father Faucon's testimony at Session 57 of the Apostolic Process on February 9, 1916.

12 From Footnote X on p. 92 in Gaucher's *The Passion of Thérèse of Lisieux*.

13 An excerpt from a letter dated September 30, 1897, that Mme. Guérin wrote to Mme. La Néele.

Father Faucon reported when questioned at the Apostolic Process that the novices under Thérèse said she "enlightened them, dispelled their doubts, counseled them marvelously, encouraged them admirably, and appeared to read their souls."[14]

Pierre Faucon was born on February 15, 1842, in Ondefontaine (southwest of Caen), the son of a private guard (*garde particulier*) and of Aimée, *née* Besognet. He was ordained a diocesan priest at the age of twenty-six on June 29, 1868. His superior appointed him vicar at the eleventh century church of Our Lady in Guibray ("the village of mud"), a famous market town in a section of Falaise, south of Caen. Two years later he was transferred to the church of Saint-Jacques in Lisieux. In 1876 he held the position of chaplain of the Benedictine monastery in Caen. After seven years of ministry there, the bishop named him *curé-doyen* (senior curate) in Reyes (by the coast north of Caen). Returning to Lisieux in 1886 as chaplain of the Congregation of Orphans, he at the same time was appointed one of the extraordinary confessors at the Carmel where he heard Thérèse's confession about four times. At the Apostolic Process in 1916 he said he was currently an honorary canon of Bayeux and chaplain of the religious of Notre-Dame de Charité of Lisieux. He died two years later at the age of seventy-six.

4. Abbé Zacharie-Jules-Eugène Hodierne (1836–1900)
Friendly chaplain who fulfilled Thérèse's prediction about daily communion

A LINGERING FEATURE OF JANSENISM PERSISTING THROUGHOUT 19TH CENtury France insisted on the infrequent reception of the Eucharist. Mother Marie de Gonzague of the Lisieux Carmel firmly adhered to this custom. Religious even had to ask their superiors if they wanted to receive Communion more than the four times a week that was permitted. Many laymen and religious wished to receive Communion more frequently than allowed, Thérèse among them. Her belief was to "receive Communion often, very often.... When the devil has succeeded in drawing the soul away from Holy Communion, he has won everything.... And Jesus weeps!"[15] The empathetic convent chaplain Father Youf, however, would have given Thérèse daily Communion but was afraid to disgruntle Mother Marie de Gonzague so he abstained from doing so. Once he admitted to one of the Carmel retreat priests: "When I think that I do not have the freedom to permit daily communion to so perfect a religious!"[16]

Pope Leo XIII, quite aware that this Eucharistic deprivation caused unhappiness for many, granted chaplains of religious communities permission to allow those they considered qualified to received Communion often. One time during her last illness, this conversation took place between Thérèse and her sister Marie (Sister Marie of the Sacred Heart) regarding the curtailment of daily Communion:

---

14 The author's translation of Father Faucon's testimony on Feb. 9, 1916.
15 LT 92 dated May 30, 1889, from Thérèse to her cousin Marie Guérin.
16 Descouvemont, *op. cit.*, p. 192.

"It will not be always so. A time will come when we shall have perhaps as chaplain M. l'Abbé Hodierne, and he will allow us Holy Communion every day." ... "Why do you think of the Abbé Hodierne as our future chaplain?" "I hope," answered Thérèse, "that he will come and we shall be very fortunate to have him."[17]

A week after Thérèse died, her own ordinary confessor and the convent's chaplain, Abbé Youf, also passed away. Eight days later, Father Hodierne was appointed his successor, literally fulfilling that remarkable prediction Thérèse made a few months before her death. The newly selected chaplain took as the text for his first lesson the five words from Proverbs (9:5) "Come, and eat my Bread."[18]

Two months before she died, Thérèse had a short conversation with Sister Marie on the same topic. This is what Sister Marie wrote in her notebook:

> At Carmel, her great suffering had been not being able to receive Communion each day. She said, a short time before her death, to Mother Marie de Gonzague, who was afraid of daily Communion:
> "Mother, when I'm in heaven, I'll make you change your opinion."
> This is what happened. After the death of the Servant of God, the chaplain [Father Hodierne] gave us Communion every day, and Mother Marie de Gonzague, instead of being repelled by it, was very happy about it.[19]

5. Canon Alexandre-Charles Maupas (1850–1920)
Superior who said Thérèse's funeral Mass

THE FIRST TIME WE HEAR ABOUT CANON MAUPAS IS IN JANUARY 1896. HE had assumed the position of ecclesiastical superior of the Carmelites in Lisieux following the death of his uncle Canon Delatroëtte who passed away on October 8, 1895. In January, Mother Agnès (Pauline) still held the position of prioress. Two of Thérèse's novices were eligible for profession—Sister Geneviève (Céline) and Sister Marie of the Trinity. Mother Agnès's term of office was scheduled to end in March and a new prioress had to be elected. Mother Gonzague believed she would be chosen, even though Mother Agnès was up also for re-election. If she won, Mother Gonzague wanted to postpone the professions in order to officiate at the ceremony for both novices. She won the election by a small margin and then strongly expressed her desire about the professions. Céline, however, wanted her sister to do the honors. Much discussion followed with no solution until Canon Maupas was called in to settle the matter. He decided that both nuns should be professed in February. More discontent followed. Thérèse overheard one of the nuns say: "The novice mistress [officially Mother Gonzague] is entirely justified in trying these novices." Having been silent all along, Thérèse couldn't help making this pointed comment: "There are some forms of trial—postponing a religious profession out of jealousy, and endangering the loss of a vocation—which no

---

17 Laveille, *op. cit.*, p. 208.
18 Ibid.
19 Written down by Thérèse's sister, Marie of the Sacred Heart as quoted in *Her Last Conversations*, July 1897.

one has a right to impose."[20] This seemed rather harsh and uncharitable but it was justified, according to one of the ecclesiastical judges at the Process,[21] for Mother Gonzague herself was not obeying her superior Canon Maupas in forcing her will above his. At any rate, a compromise was reached: Céline was professed in February by her sister who was then the prioress whereas Sister Marie of the Trinity was professed in April under Mother Gonzague's priorate.

Throughout the course of Thérèse's final sickness, despite the pleas of several nuns, Canon Maupas did not think her condition warranted the administration of the Last Sacraments; ultimately he consented to do so on July 30, 1897. In the face of all her physical torments, Thérèse maintained a keen sense of humor even regarding this serious matter which her sister Pauline tells us about:

> Our Father [Canon Maupas] came to see her this morning and he exclaimed: "Oh! you're only trying to mislead us; you're not about to die, and very soon you'll be running in the garden. You don't look like one who is dying. Give you Extreme Unction? But the sacrament wouldn't be valid; you're not sick enough!" Father was a little rough, but, I believe, he did this purposely, for when he came out of the room, he was very much edified to see a child so young with such a desire to die and to see, with so much joy, death coming.
>
> When he left, our little patient was aggravated at him for not being willing to give her the last sacraments, and she said: "The next time I'll not go to so much trouble. I sat up in bed out of politeness, I was very pleasant with him, I paid him special respect, and he refused what I was asking of him! Another time, I'll sue a little pretence; I'll take a cup of milk before his arrival because then I always have a very bad face; I'll hardly answer him, telling him I'm in real agony." (Then she put on a real comedy for us.) "Yes, I really see I don't know my business; I don't know how to go about things!"[22]
>
> She's a charming little patient; extremely amusing; she knows only how to make us laugh; however, she's forbidden to talk lest she tire herself too much.[23]

And again four days later, Mother Agnès wrote these words on the day Thérèse received the Last Sacraments: "She [Thérèse] told me what Father Superior had said to her before the ceremony [at 6 o'clock in the evening]: 'You're going to be like a little child who has just received baptism.' Then he spoke to me only about love. Oh! how touched I was."[24]

Mother Agnès who had been transcribing Thérèse's last words and conversations added this little occurrence connected with Canon Maupas: "She was telling us with a smile that she had a dream in which she was being carried to the heated room [recreation room], between two torches in order to celebrate the feast of our Father Superior [Alexandre Maupas]."[25]

---

20 Rohrbach, *The Search for St. Thérèse*, p. 159.
21 Msgr. Toeschi.
22 Mother Agnès used the words "the trade of trickery" in place of Thérèse's words "I don't know how to go about things."
23 From a letter written by Sister Marie of the Trinity to her father, M. Guérin, on July 9, 1897.
24 *Her Last Conversations*, July 30, 1897.
25 Ibid., July 27, 1897.

Alexandre-Charles Maupas was born on August 27, 1850, in Mesnil-Auzouf (Calvados—southwest of Caen), the son of Alexandre Maupas, a farmer, and of Jeanne Marie. He did his priestly studies at the seminaries in Vivre, Sommervieu, and Bayeux culminating in his ordination as a secular priest on June 29, 1874. In 1876 he became a vicar at Bretteville-sur-Odon, a suburb of Caen, in 1889. Six years later he succeeded his uncle Canon Delatroëtte as curate (curé) of the church of Saint-Jacques in Lisieux and then as Superior of the Carmel located just a few blocks away. He functioned as Superior for the last two years of Thérèse's life and administered the Last Rites to her. As main celebrant at the funeral Mass for Sister Thérèse on October 4, 1897, he was assisted by Father Ronée, a parish priest and dean of the cathedral of St. Peter in Lisieux. Fourteen years later he gave testimony at the Diocesan Process as well as at the Apostolic Process. On August 7, 1911, he offered this loving testimony: "I have trusting devotion for the Servant of God and hope that the Church places her one day on the altars; my hope is founded on the esteem I have of her holiness and on the power of her constant intercession, not solely for others but also for me personally."

Canon Maupas was present at the exhumation of Thérèse's coffin on September 6, 1910. He was also involved with the second exhumation and recognition of the remains of St. Thérèse on August 9–10, 1917. He died at the age of seventy in Lisieux on February 19, 1920.

6. Abbé Louis-Auguste Youf (1842–1897)
Chaplain sympathetic to Thérèse

ABBÉ YOUF WAS THÉRÈSE'S ORDINARY CONFESSOR DURING THE NINE YEARS of her life as a contemplative nun. A pious but an austere priest, he served the convent dutifully for twenty-four years. From the outset he favored having Thérèse enter the order despite her very young age. Thérèse's sister Pauline, at that time five years a member of the community, informed her father about Abbé Youf's favorable opinion:

> I saw M. Youf just this moment, and told him our angel's whole affair [obstacles to her admission]. He could not get over Our Father's [the Carmel superior, Canon Delatroëtte] refusal. "She is such a charming child," he said. "Ah! I want her to enter!"... I admit that the interest which he seems to be taking in this matter really touched me. I saw a priest who understands perfectly that God is free to call souls at any age He pleases.[26]

Once Thérèse was admitted he clearly recognized besides her charm, her rare spirituality, but unfortunately did not seem to give her any substantive spiritual assistance. Because of her heroic efforts with the sick nuns during the terrible influenza epidemic, he allowed her to receive daily communion for a few months, something Thérèse had desired for a long time. At one of his visits to the infirmary to see the sick and dying, he noticed Thérèse's exemplary

---

[26] Letter dated October 25, 1887, from Pauline to her father.

demeanor. He remarked to her novice mistress that "Not one of you can match young Sister Thérèse in that perfectly calm and religious bearing of hers." [27]

Three years after Thérèse entered Carmel, she assumed the task of assisting the sacristan, Sister Saint Stanislas. As such she had to go along with Father Youf when he brought Communion to Mother Geneviève, the sick foundress. He revealed to Mother Agnès (Pauline) the impression that Thérèse made on him as he was on his way to Mother Geneviève: "When I see your sister so close to me under the cloister, when I am carrying the Holy Sacrament, she always makes me think of the votive candles that burn in the churches; just the sight of them inclines one to prayer and contemplation." [28]

Sister Aimée of Jesus offered this testimony of Father Youf's opinion of Thérèse: "In Sister Thérèse's time we had a chaplain called Fr. Youf. I would like to remember him here, and pay a tribute to his esteem for this little sister. One day I felt I had reason to complain about her elder sisters, but he said: 'Don't complain! Even if you do have something to suffer from one side, surely you must also be very happy to have a treasure like the younger sister. She is first class, and is making enormous strides in virtue. If only she were known, she would be the glory of this Carmel.'" [29]

Father Youf's acknowledged scrupulosity, however, is evident particularly in one of his grim reproaches to a choir nun (Sister Teresa of Saint Augustine) who informed Mother Gonzague, "Mother, the chaplain has just told me [in confession] that I already have one foot in hell, and if I go on like this I will soon put the second one there!" Mother Gonzague responded with this delightfully consoling rejoinder, "Don't worry, I already have both feet there!" [30]

Apropos of this, Mother Agnès of Jesus revealed that "one day Thérèse admitted to the confessor [Abbé Youf] her distress at suffering from exhaustion during the Mass even to the point of not being able to shake off sleep, and he gave her a severe reprimand and told her that she was offending God." [31]

During Thérèse's trial of faith at the time she was approaching her painful death, she commented to Mother Agnès about his advice to her:

> Father Youf told me with reference to my temptations against the faith: "Don't dwell on these, it's very dangerous." This is hardly consoling to hear, but happily I'm going to break my "little" head by torturing myself. Father Youf also said, "Are you resigned to die?" I answered: "Ah! Father, I find I need resignation only to live. For dying, it's only joy I experience." [32]

In an attempt to help Thérèse in her sufferings, Father Youf told her on July 9, 1897, "What is all this about your entering Heaven soon! Why, your crown is

---

27 From the testimony Sister Marie of the Angels offered at the Diocesan Process on February 16, 1911.
28 Chalon, *op. cit.*, p. 147. The author Jean Chalon does not cite his source.
29 Testimony given by Sister Aimée on March 17, 1911, as recorded by O'Mahony in *St. Thérèse of Lisieux*, p. 281.
30 Gaucher, *The Story of a Life*, p. 117.
31 Mother Agnès' preparatory notes for the Apostolic Process.
32 *Her Last Conversations*, June 6, 1897.

far from finished. You have only just begun to fashion it!" "Certainly, Father, that is true.... No, I have not yet woven my wreath, but God has finished it for me."[33]

Pauline recorded this simple example of Thérèse's profound spirituality and self-control in a conversation Thérèse had with her three months before her death:

> Just now I wanted to ask Sister Marie of the Sacred Heart [her own sister Marie], who had come back from a visit with Father Youf, what he had said about my condition after his visit to me. I was thinking to myself: This would perhaps do me some good; it would console me to know. When I thought the matter over further, I said: No, it's only curiosity; I don't want to do anything in order to learn what he said, and since God hasn't permitted her to tell me herself, this is a sign He doesn't want me to know. And I avoided bringing the conversation back to this subject lest Sister Marie be forced to tell me. I wouldn't have been happy.[34]

Father Youf, a constant visitor at the Carmel, saw and worked at times directly with Thérèse. He also went a number of times to see her in the infirmary during her last days. Following are five entries from the *Yellow Notebook* in which Mother Agnès recorded some of Thérèse's last conversations where Father Youf is mentioned:

- JULY 6   She had just coughed up some blood; I said: "You're going to leave us then?"
  "I am not." Father [Youf] said to me: "You're going to have to perform a great sacrifice in leaving your sisters." I answered: "But, Father, I find I'm not leaving them; on the contrary, I'll be closer to them after my death."
- JULY 8   She was so sick there was talk of giving her Extreme Unction. That day, she was taken down from her cell to the infirmary; she was no longer able to stand up, and she had to be carried down. While still in her cell, and knowing they were thinking of anointing her, she said in a tone of joy:
  "It seems to me that I'm dreaming! However, they aren't fools." She meant Father Youf, the chaplain, and Doctor de Cornière. "I fear only one thing: that all this will change."
- JULY 22   She repeated with a smile this remark of Father Youf after she had made her confession: "If the angels were to sweep heaven, the dust would be made of diamonds."
- AUGUST 26   She went to confession:
  "Little Mother, I would really like to talk to you, if I may. I don't know if I should tell Father Youf that I had thoughts of gluttony, because I thought of things I like, but I offer them to God."
- SEPTEMBER 25   I told her what was said in recreation regarding Father Youf, who had a great fear of death. The Sisters were speaking about the responsibility of those who were in charge of souls and those who lived a long life.
  As far as little ones are concerned, they will be judged with great gentleness [Wisdom 6:7]. And one can remain little, even in the most formidable offices,

---
33 Goerres, *op. cit.* p. 373.
34 *Her Last Conversations*, July 19, 1897.

even when living for a long time. If I were to die at the age of eighty, if I were in China, anywhere, I would still die, I feel, as little as I am today. And it is written: "At the end, the Lord will rise up to save the gentle and the humble of the earth." It doesn't say "to judge." But "to save."

Abbé Louis-Auguste Youf was born in Caen, Normandy, in 1842. As a young man, he attended both the minor and major seminary in Villiers-le-Sec and Bayeux. After ordination in 1869 at age twenty-seven, he accepted a clerical position at the church of Saint-Jacques in Lisieux. In 1873, the year of Thérèse's birth, he became chaplain of the Lisieux Carmel and remained in that post until his death in 1897—the period of time that encompassed Thérèse's entire life.

He suffered with poor health later on in life. Feeling sorry for him, Thérèse's cousin Sister Marie of the Eucharist (Marie Guérin) suggested to her father that he invite Father Youf to his beautiful country vacation home near Evreux called La Musse. She thought that this might help to improve his health, but certainly would dispel some of the tedium he must have been experiencing as a result of the rather solitary and sheltered life he led. He agreed and Father Youf, accompanied by the Carmel sacristan, Auguste Acard, spent the last days of July 1897 at La Musse, enjoying the hospitality and healthy rustic setting. It was during his absence that Canon Maupas had to give Thérèse the Last Sacraments which Father Youf most likely would have.

Father Youf fell seriously ill during Thérèse's last days on earth. With amazing accuracy he foretold their demise when he remarked to her a month before they both passed away: "we are finishing our ministry together, you as a Carmelite nun, I as a priest."[35] He resided a few blocks away from the Carmelite Monastery and when he, on his own deathbed, heard the convent bell tolling the death knell, he knew it was Thérèse who had died. He murmured: "She is dead ... she will not delay coming to look for me; she promised it to me. What a loss for Carmel! She is a saint."[36] On October 7, 1897, just a week later, he too went to his own reward, having lived only to his fifty-fifth year.

---

35 Ibid. August 30, 1897.
36 *Vie Thérésienne*, April 1966, No. 22. Translation by the author.

D. Carmel Retreat Masters

1. **Père Blino:** *Scolded Thérèse at one of his retreats*
2. **Père Déodat de Basly:** *Erudite preacher*
3. **Abbé Lechesne:** *His retreats pleased Thérèse*
4. **Père Lemonnier:** *Called Thérèse "the little flower"*
5. **Père Madelaine:** *Edited Thérèse's autobiography and testified at both processes*
6. **Père Prou:** *Approved of Thérèse's spirituality*
7. **Père Pichon:** *(See his biography in Chapter 5A—Churchmen, in Thérèse's Childhood)*

1. Père Laurent Blino, S. J. (1839–1908)
Scolded Thérèse at one of his retreats

SISTER THÉRÈSE IN HER SEARCH FOR PERFECTION EXPECTED TO OBTAIN wise and masterly counsel and reassurance from spiritual directors once she entered Carmel. Surprisingly, she did not receive what she eagerly desired but received instead unexpected criticism at times. Her sister Pauline (Mother Agnès of Jesus) maintained that some confessors and preachers of retreats disturbed her.[1] One such priest was the respected and experienced Jesuit preacher, Father (Père) Blino who had preached well over a thousand retreats before he died. Thérèse apparently felt quite open and free to reveal her innermost spiritual aspirations to him during the May 1890 retreat. A rather stunning response followed, however, which Mother Agnès recorded in her preparatory notes for the Apostolic Process:

> "Father, I want to become a saint; I want to love God as much as St. Teresa," she said to a retreat master [Father Blino]. "What pride and what presumption!" he replied. "Confine yourself to correcting your faults, to offending God no longer, to making a little progress in virtue each day, and temper your rash desires." She answered, "But, Father, I don't think that these are rash desires; I can aspire to sanctity, even to a more elevated sanctity, if I wish, than that of St. Teresa, since Our Lord said; 'Be as perfect as your heavenly Father is perfect.' See, Father, how vast the field is, and it seems to me I have the right to run in it!" The religious was not convinced, and the *Servant of God* was seeking, without being able to find it, the answer to her thoughts, her inner longings, someone in authority who would tell her: "Launch out into the sea and cast your nets, you are in the truth."[2]

Undaunted, Thérèse wrote to her sister Céline the same month as the retreat with Father Blino:

---
[1] See p. 43 in *Mother Agnes of Jesus*, the English translation of the obituary circular written in French of Mother Agnès.
[2] See Note 8 to LT 107 of Thérèse's letter to her sister Céline.

Céline, what a privilege to be unknown ["misjudged" in Sheed's translation] on this earth!... Ah, God's thoughts are not our thoughts. If they were, our life would be only a hymn of thanksgiving!...

Céline, do you think St. Teresa received more graces than you?... As for myself, I shall tell you not to aim for her *seraphic* sanctity, but rather to be perfect as your heavenly Father is perfect!... Ah! Céline, our *infinite desires* are not, then, either dreams or fancies, since Jesus Himself has given us this commandment![3]

Despite his harsh comments, Father Blino really held a high opinion of her. Sister Marie of the Trinity, one of St. Thérèse's novices, attended a retreat given by Father Blino at the Paris Carmel when she was sixteen and still a lay person. Part of her testimony includes this laudatory statement he made:

During this retreat, I saw Père Blino, S. J., extraordinary confessor at the Paris Carmel. He spoke to me with praise of Sister Thérèse of the Child Jesus at the Lisieux Carmel where he had just preached the "Ignatian Exercises," and he told me how she had even gone to the Holy Father to obtain entrance to the Carmel at fifteen....[4]

Father Laurent Blino was born on August 2, 1839, in Saint-Vincent-sur-Oust (Morbihan), south west of Rennes. He joined the Jesuits on October 12, 1861, and was ordained nine years later on August 15, 1870. He preached the retreats at the Lisieux monastery in 1883, 1888, and 1890. When he was sixty-eight years old, death came to him on February 25, 1908, in the town of Versailles.

2. Père Déodat De Basly (1862–1937)
Erudite preacher

In 1886 father (père) déodat preached a retreat in lisieux. He conducted the St. John of the Cross Centenary triduum at the Carmel in November of 1891. One year later he preached the community retreat. Though not referring to him or anyone specifically, Thérèse made the following comment in her autobiography: "Ordinarily, the retreats which are preached are more painful to me than the ones I make alone...."[5]

Joseph-Léon-Victor-Marie Déodat de Basly was born in the town that bears his name—Basly (Calvados, just north of Caen)—on October 11, 1862. When just seventeen in 1869, he entered the religious order of Franciscans known as Franciscan Recollects (now called Order of Friars Minor).

From the time of his ordination in 1885 until his death at seventy-five in 1937 in Le Havre, he led a distinguished life as a conscientious religious. He held the position of superior at a monastery in Rennes from 1890 to 1897, founded a convent in Le Havre in 1897, earned acclaim as a noted Duns Scotus theologian and scholar, and authored numerous literary works.

---
3 LT 107, dated May 19–20, 1890, by Thérèse to Céline.
4 Ibid., as quoted in note 8 from the *Circulaire de soeur Marie de la Trinité*, pp. 4–5.
5 *Story of a Soul*, chapter VII, p. 173.

3. Abbé Victor-Oscar Lechesne (1863–1931)
His retreats pleased Thérèse

THÉRÈSE REFERRED TO HIM ONLY ONCE IN HER WRITINGS IN A LETTER TO her Aunt Guérin in which she misspelled his last name. He preached on the same day as she wrote the note:

> I will soon be allowed to go to heaven with the little angels, not because of my health but because of another *declaration* made today in the Carmel's chapel by M. l'abbé Lechêne.... After having shown us the illustrious origins of our Holy Order, after having compared us to the Prophet Elias fighting against the priests of Baal, he *declared*: "Times similar to those of Ahab's persecution were about to begin again." We seemed to be flying already to martyrdom....
>
> What joy, dear little Aunt, if our whole family were to enter heaven on the same day. It seems to me that I see you smile ... perhaps you think this honor is not reserved for us.... What is certain about this is that, all together or one after another, we shall one day leave the exile for the homeland and then we shall take delight in all the things for which heaven will be the *prize*....[6]

Victor Lechesne was born in 1863 in Saint-Contest, a suburb north of Caen, and lived to be sixty-seven. While stationed as vicar at the church of St. Pierre in Lisieux, he preached at the Carmel. His superiors assigned him to churches in Rots, Trévières, and Orbec where he died in 1931, six years after Thérèse was canonized.

4. Père Armand-Constant Lemonnier (1841–1917)
Called Thérèse "the little flower"

OUTSIDE HER FAMILY AND THÉRÈSE HERSELF, FATHER (PÈRE) LEMONNIER is possibly the first to call Thérèse "the little flower" during her lifetime.

He officiated as retreat master for the customary fall community retreats in 1893, 1894, and 1895. Thérèse gained greatly from his preaching. She wrote these comments about his first retreat at the Carmel:

> We listened to a beautiful retreat to prepare us for the feast of our Holy Mother [St. Teresa of Avila, October 15]. The good Father [Lemonnier] spoke especially about union with Jesus and the beauty of our vocation. He pointed out to us all the advantages of the religious life, especially the contemplative life. He gave us a comparison that charmed me. He said: "Look at the oaks in our countryside, how deformed they all are; they spread out their branches to the right and left, nothing hinders them, so they never reach a great height. On the contrary, look at the oaks of the forest, hemmed in on all sides; they do not see the light except from *on high* so their trunks are without all these deformed branches that draw away the sap necessary to go upward. The oaks see nothing but the sky above, and all their strength is turned in that direction, so soon they attain a prodigious height. In the religious life, the soul like the young oak is hemmed in on all sides by the Rule, all its movements are hampered and thwarted by the trees of the forest.... But the soul has *light* when it looks

---
6 LT 192 dated July 16, 1896, from Thérèse to her Aunt Guérin.

upon HEAVEN, there alone it can rest its gaze, never must it fear climbing too much in this direction.⁷

At the next year's retreat in 1894, he again compared the Carmelites to objects in nature, this time more germanely "to the little fragrant flowers, whose sweet scent Jesus loves to breathe, the little flower He will come one day to gather to transport it to the delightful thickets where virgins follow the Lamb everywhere."⁸ Interestingly, two months later in the Christmas recreational play *The Angels at the Crib of Jesus* (RP 2) Thérèse wrote, she likewise compared human souls to flowers: "A soul is a perfumed flower."

In June of 1895, Thérèse experienced a powerful desire to offer herself as a victim to the merciful love of God. She thereupon composed her now well-known prayer "Act of Oblation to Merciful Love" (Pri 6) on June 9 which symbolically expressed her deep inner emotions and convictions. On June 11 she and her sister Céline (Sister Geneviève) knelt before the statue of the Virgin of the Smile and solemnly pronounced the words of this prayer, thus offering themselves together as "victims of holocaust to God's merciful love." Mother Agnès explained at the Ordinary Process years later details of this event:

> [She] composed the formula of her gift and submitted it to me. She also expressed the idea of submitting it to a theologian for examination. It was Père Lemonnier, superior of the Missionaries of *La Délivrande*, who examined it. He answered simply that there was nothing in it contrary to faith, however, she should not say "I feel within me infinite desires" but "I feel within me immense desires." This was a sacrifice for the Servant of God; however, she did it without any complaint. Besides, the substance was approved [also by Father Lemonnier's superior] and she showed much joy at this.⁹

Thérèse consequently requested Mother Agnès permission for some of the novices under her charge also to say the prayer.

At the Apostolic Process (1915–1917) Father Lemonnier testified that the novices under Thérèse's care regarded her highly and praised her as an exceptionally holy person who gave very sound and wise direction. He also reported that he heard similar laudable comments from one of the younger children at the Benedictine school, Alice Dumoulin, who became a religious of the Holy Family of Deliverance, whose company Thérèse preferred, as well as from other young girls during recreation when she told them stories and even showed them how to bury dead birds. At the time Thérèse was around ten or eleven and Alice was around seven. Alice said that "She [Thérèse] was very intelligent, above all very charitable in the care which she showered upon the young girls."¹⁰

Father Lemonnier, an ardent devotee of Thérèse's cause, stated at the Diocesan Process that: "I have trust in the Servant of God, but I have not adopted

---

7 LT 151, dated November 5, 1893, from Thérèse to her sister Léonie.
8 Quoted from note 2, page 905, to Father Lemonnier's letter to Sister Geneviève dated June, 1895.
9 As quoted from p. 62 in *The Prayers of Saint Thérèse of Lisieux*.
10 Testimony given by Father Lemonnier on April 9, 1915.

her personal devotional practices. I hope and ardently wish for the success of her beatification, which will be, I believe for the glory of God and the good of souls, because she already did a lot of good for those who invoke her."[11]

Besides affection for Thérèse, Father Lemonnier also showed interest in Céline ever since she entered Carmel. For some time after, he kept up a correspondence with her, always admonishing both sisters to do their best in the service of God. For a while he was also Céline's spiritual director. In one of his letters to Céline he wrote: "Dear child, I bless you with all my heart, you and your Angel of the Child Jesus.[12] I bless you, and I ask you to stir up one another in good, and that you not only be good and holy religious but that you do good, that your zeal may be a fire spreading itself and causing a real conflagration in your dear Carmel."[13]

Father Armand-Constant Lemonnier, born on November 1, 1841, in Vassy (diocese of Bayeux), was the son of a farmer, Auguste LeMonnier, and of a mother whose maiden name was Victoire Groult. His ordination as a priest of the Congregation of Our Lady of Deliverance took place on June 15, 1867, in Bayeux when he was twenty-six. The separation of church and state in 1904 caused the dissolution of his Congregation forcing all of them to leave the sanctuary of the Blessed Mother. He worked fourteen years in the colleges of his institute and about twenty years doing diocesan missionary work. Another assignment installed him as chaplain of the Religious of the Holy Family of Deliverance (Sainte Famille de la Délivrande). Besides officiating as retreat master for three consecutive years at the Carmel, he heard Thérèse's confession, and maintained a long correspondence with Martin family members. At the two processes for the cause of Sister Thérèse of the Child Jesus, he provided valuable testimony. He passed away at the age of seventy-six on February 20, 1917.

(Father Armand-Constant Lemonnier always spelled his name this way, but some sources give it as Le Monnier. He should not be confused with the bishop, Msgr. Thomas Lemonnier.)

5. Pere Godefroid Madelaine, O. Praem. (1842–1932)
Edited Thérèse's autobiography and testified at both processes

ONE YEAR AFTER THÉRÈSE'S DEATH, THE FIRST EDITION OF HER AUTOBIography appeared in print. The tentative name she gave to this work was *Printainère d'une Petite Fleur Blanche* ("Springtime of a Little White Flower"). The nuns at the Caramel involved with her book, however, offered a different title: *A Canticle of Love, or the Passing of an Angel*. Father (Père) Madelaine, who served as its editor and was instrumental in obtaining the *imprimatur*, advised the less sentimental and more appropriate *l'Histoire d'une Âme* (*Story of a Soul*) which the world now recognizes as the title of St. Thérèse of Lisieux's great religious classic.

---

[11] Testimony given by Father Lemonnier on April 7, 1911, at the Diocesan Process interrogations. (Translation by the author)
[12] Thérèse was Sister Geneviève's "angel" when she entered the Carmel.
[13] Letter from Lemonnier to Sister Geneviève in June 1895.

The Lisieux Monastery knew the well-known preacher Father Madelaine, prior of the Abbey of Mondaye, for he had visited them a number of times as preacher at the annual retreats of 1882, 1887, 1890, and 1896, and also at the triduum of 1896. Father Madelaine seemed to be one of the few who understood and appreciated the abstruse Mother Marie de Gonzague.

Furthermore, he was well acquainted with Thérèse's father whom he encountered many times at the rectory of the church of St. James (Église Saint-Jacques) in Lisieux. He recognized in him a man of profound sanctity who had a great love for his daughters all of whom he wished would someday consecrate themselves to God as nuns. When Thérèse's father was on vacation in Vienna, he mentioned Father Madelaine in one of his rare letters:

> Yesterday we visited the monastery of St. Norbert, where we could not have been better received. Abbé presented a letter from R. P. Godefroy, whom we had seen at St. James (Lisieux).... There are also Carmelites [in Vienna], but they have not such a good menu as we received at the Premonstratensians, for, imagine, we were served a whole pigeon or partridge a-piece, and enormous pieces of hare. Those good Religious have the reputation of being most charitable, and we have truly experienced it.[14]

Father Madelaine was very impressed with the young Sister Thérèse about whom he at one time wrote, "*Cette petite soeur est une âme chantante*" ("This little sister is a singing soul").[15] And again, "I don't believe that I ever encountered in my ministry a soul at once more humble and magnanimous."[16] As a friend of Canon Delatroëtte (Superior of the Carmel), he assisted at Thérèse's sister Marie's Clothing Day on March 19, 1887. He recalled that even as a postulant she begged the prioress to allow her to practice the Rule to the letter despite its rigors and persisted in this desire throughout her religious life even up to her painful last days.

For nearly the whole last year and a half of her life Thérèse battled but conquered her astonishing "dark night of the soul." She suffered bitter trials and temptations against faith and hope, and even questioned the existence of an afterlife, though she always believed in God and Christ's love. In her anguish she turned to Father Madelaine during his 1896 retreat in October. He considered her dilemma very serious and attributed it to diabolic intervention: "Her soul was passing through a spiritual crisis; she believed that she was damned and it was at that time that she increased her acts of confidence and abandonment to God."[17] Nonetheless, she never showed outwardly the trials of faith she was enduring. He recommended that she copy the Creed on paper which she did—in her own blood!—and place it in the pocket edition of Scripture she always carried on her person. When temptations assailed her she clung to it with a fervent prayer on her lips.

---

14 CF 223, from Louis Martin to his daughter Marie, dated August 30, 1885.
15 *Sainte Thérèse de Lisieux et l'abbaye de Mondaye*, Numéro spécial 178, p. 20.
16 Statement made by Father Madelaine at the Diocesan Process concerning Thérèse's humility on May 23, 1911. (The author's translation)
17 Gaucher, *The Passion of Thérèse of Lisieux*, p. 116.

Shortly after Thérèse's death, Mother Agnès sent him the manuscript of Thérèse's autobiography (about a third of which was written for her), to read, approve, and edit. He wrote to her in January 1898: "I am continuing my reading of this wonderful manuscript, it is all so fresh, so innocent, so uplifting! I hope to send it back to you by the end of February, together with the comments which I hope I may be *permitted* to make. I use this expression because I regard this autobiography as a holy relic."[18] And again he wrote:

> Dear Reverend Mother, I have read the whole manuscript and the poems. I am holding on to it because I must read it again. I shall then mark with blue pencil what I think should be omitted from the published edition. All of it, absolutely all of it, is precious for *you*. But there are some details that are so intimate and out of the ordinary, that it would be better, I think, not to print them for the public. There are slight mistakes in grammar and style; these are only slight blemishes and can easily be made to disappear. Finally, we have also noticed a certain repetitiousness; for the public it would be better to suppress some of these repetitions. I shall mark them. That's the critical part of the work. But, Mother, I can scarcely tell you the pleasure and spiritual delight with which I read those pages, so totally permeated by the love of God.[19]

In a letter to Mother Marie de Gonzague on March 8, 1898, he describes how he obtained the required *imprimatur*:

> Dear Mother, you can put your mind at rest about the *imprimatur*: we've got it. Yesterday I saw the bishop and after listening to my report, he granted it.
> What had happened was this. When the bishop [Msgr. Hugonin] heard of a manuscript by Sister Thérèse, his first reaction was one of distrust of the female imagination. But I was able to assure him in all conscience that I had studied the matter carefully and that I had been forced, in the present instance, to recognise that this whole manuscript bore evident marks of the Spirit of God, and that I had been unable to find any doctrinal error in it. On the strength of this testimony, the bishop granted his *imprimatur*.[20]

Godefroid Madelaine was born on November 14, 1842, in Le Tourneur in the diocese of Bayeux and baptized with the name Victor. His father, Jean-Baptiste Madelaine, farmed the land, and his mother, Marie Hamel Madelaine, tenderly brought up her family in a very religious household. He entered the Order of the Canons Regular of Premontre, the Premonstratensian Fathers, known in the U.S.A. as Norbertine Fathers, receiving his religious name of Godefroid (Godefroy) on November 3, 1861. Profession took place at the magnificent Abbey of Mondaye, just south of Bayeux on February 7, 1864, and ordination on December 23, 1865. During his lifetime he was prior of the Abbey of Mondaye (1879–1899),

---

18 Written on January 30, 1898, by Father Madeleine to Mother Agnès, as quoted in the January 1982 edition of *Sicut Parvuli*.
19 Letter written by Father Madelaine to Mother Marie de Gonzague on March 1, 1898, as quoted on p. 273 in O'Mahony's *St. Thérèse of Lisieux By Those Who Knew Her*. Father Madelaine read it at the Diocesan Process on May 23, 1911.
20 Ibid.

vice-provincial of the Order in France, and abbot of Saint-Michel in Frigolet (diocese of Aix) in 1899. Political-religious problems in France at the time were responsible for his and his entire community's expulsion by the French government from Frigolet in 1903 to one of their houses in Leffe, Belgium. In the first year of World War I the Germans overran Leffe and killed many civilians. On several terrifying occasions the Germans sentenced him and his monks to death but each time they claimed they were miraculously saved through the intercession of the saintly Sister Thérèse.

Father Madelaine's large volume on the life of St. Norbert, his order's 12th century founder, won him added recognition as a man of letters. He finally returned to the Abbey of Mondaye in 1920 and twelve years later on September 22, 1932, he died in Saint-Martin-des Besaces (south west of Caen), aged ninety.

6. Père Alexis Prou (1844–1914)
Approved of Thérèse's spirituality

THE PRIEST SCHEDULED BY MOTHER MARIE DE GONZAGUE TO CONDUCT the retreat for the week of October 8, 1891, was replaced at the last moment by forty-seven-year-old Reverend Alexis Prou whom the prioress and others in the Carmel thought not quite appropriate for a group of cloistered nuns since he was used to dealing with hardened criminals and tough factory workers. Thérèse, however, immediately found him a most understanding and ardent supporter of her ideas on abandonment and divine mercy. His spiritual direction was profound and appreciated, for up to then she had not been satisfied with the quality and amount of spiritual guidance and stimulation she was receiving. Thérèse poured out her feelings at some length about this wonderful, fully rewarding, but all too brief encounter:

> Ordinarily, the retreats which are preached are more painful to me than the ones I make alone, but this year it was otherwise. I had made a preparatory novena with great fervor, in spite of the inner sentiment I had, for it seemed to me that the preacher would not be able to understand me since he was supposed to do good to great sinners but not to religious souls. God wanted to show me that He was the Director of my soul, and so He made use of this Father specifically, who was appreciated only by me in the community. At the time I was having great interior trials of all kinds, even to the point of asking myself whether heaven really existed. I felt disposed to say nothing of my interior dispositions since I didn't know how to express them, but I had hardly entered the confessional when I felt my soul expand. After speaking only a few words, I *was understood* in a marvelous way and my soul was like a book in which this priest read better than I did myself. He launched me full sail upon the waves of *confidence and love* which so strongly attracted me, but upon which I dared not advance. He told me that *my faults caused God no pain, and that holding as he did God's place*, he was telling me *in His name* that God was very much pleased with me.
>
> Oh! how happy I was to hear those consoling words! Never had I heard that our faults *could not cause God any pain*, and this assurance filled me with joy,

helping me to bear patiently with life's exile. I felt at the bottom of my heart that this was really so, for God is more tender than a mother....[21]

This Franciscan priest's advice may have been a spark that eventually brought to light her doctrine of "spiritual childhood" or at least encouraged what she already conceptualized. For some unknown reason, the prioress strictly confined Father's solace to this one session only and, unfortunately, forbade Thérèse to speak to him any more about her spiritual concerns. It must have been a real torture to be so near to him as an assistant sacristan and not be permitted to converse with him about spiritual matters. Nonetheless, this brief experience with Father Prou proved a real joy for Thérèse as her sister Pauline stated when she was questioned at the Diocesan Process:

> She [Thérèse] was all the time scared of offending God in some way or other. Twice in her life she confided to me that she was extremely happy. The first time was when she was about fifteen and a half, and Fr. Pichon, S.J., assured her that she had never committed a mortal sin. The second was when, at the 1891 retreat, Fr. Alexis, a Recollect, taught her that her imperfections, which were all due to frailty, gave no offence to God. This latter statement was a source of great joy to her, because the fear of offending God was poisoning her life. She composed a little prayer for her profession, and always carried it next to her heart. One phrase in that prayer was: "Take me, Jesus, before I commit the least willful fault."[22]

Thérèse never, of course, forgot Father Prou's assurance, acquiescence, and comfort. Two months before she died, she remarked to her sister Pauline: "I'm very grateful to Father Alexis, he did me much good. Father Pichon treated me too much like a child; however, he did me much good also by telling me I'd not committed a mortal sin."[23] Three weeks later Thérèse again mentioned Father Alexis in her conversation with Pauline:

> After she had confided several little faults for which she reproached herself, she asked me if she had offended God. I answered simply that these little sins were nothing and that she had done me a lot of good in telling me about them; she appeared very much touched and she said later:
> "When I was listening to you, I was reminded of Father Alexis; your own words penetrated my heart as much as his."
> Then she began to cry; I gathered up these tears, drying them with a little piece of linen, which Sister Geneviève keeps as a relic.[24]

Jean-Marie Prou was born in Sainte-Pazanne, a town near Nantes in the Loire-Atlantique Department on November 13, 1844. During his student days in the seminaries his competence as a brilliant student manifested itself right

---

21 *Story of a Soul*, chapter VIII, pp. 173–174.
22 Testimony given by Mother Agnès at the Diocesan Process on August 19, 1910, as quoted in O'Mahony's *St. Thérèse of Lisieux By Those Who Knew Her*, pp. 44–45. August 19, 1910.
23 *Last Conversations*, July 4, 1897.
24 Ibid., July 25, 1897.

from the start. At twenty-five in 1869, he became a Franciscan Recollect (now called the Franciscan Order of Friars Minor) and was given his new religious name of Alexis. Ordination took place on June 29, 1871, in the Cathedral of Bayeux, and profession two years later. Father Prou became the superior of the Franciscan Convent of Saint-Nazaire in 1882, serving in this capacity for six years. He was noted for his writings, for always being well prepared for his work, and for delivering his sermons with great zeal and energy in the true spirit of St. Francis. His ministry included parish missionary work, directing retreats at various religious communities, and ministry to large groups of factory workers throughout Normandy and Brittany. Father Prou died in Caen on October 15, 1914, a month before his seventieth birthday.

7. **PÈRE ALMIRE PICHON, S.J. (1843–1919)**
Martin family spiritual director and friend
(*See his biography in Chapter 5. A—Churchmen, In Thérèse's Childhood*)

E. Others

1. ABBÉ BELLIÈRE: *Thérèse's first spiritual brother, missionary to Africa*
2. ABBÉ CHILLART: *Gave Louis Martin the Last Rites*
3. ABBÉ DE CORNIÈRE: *Convent doctor's son*
4. ABBÉ DE MAROY: *Said his first Mass at the Lisieux Carmel in 1897*
5. ABBÉ GOMBAULT: *Took two controversial photos of the novice Thérèse*
6. MSGR. HUGONIN: *Bishop who permitted Thérèse to enter the Lisieux Carmel*
7. PÈRE ROULLAND: *Thérèse's second spiritual brother, missionary to China*
8. FRÈRE SALUTAIRE: *Thérèse never answered his request*
9. FRÈRE SIMÉON: *Friend of the Martins in Rome*
10. ABBÉ TROUDE: *Gave Communion to the dying Thérèse*

1. ABBÉ MAURICE BELLIÈRE (1874–1907)
Thérèse's first spiritual brother, missionary to Africa

> *There is no doubt that Jesus is the Treasure, but I found Him in you.*[1]
> — Maurice

MAURICE MARIE LOUIS (BARTHÉLEMY) BELLIÈRE WAS BORN IN CAEN ON June 10, 1874 — a year and a half after Thérèse. His parents were Alphonse (1848–1897), a dyer, and Adèle Marie Louvel Bellière (1841–1874) who sadly died a week after the his birth, their only child. Fortunately his mother's sister Antoinette (1841–1907) and her sailor-husband Louis Barthélemy (1829–1877) gladly took him into their childless home and reared him as their own.[2] After dropping the infant Maurice at their home in the small fishing town of Langrune-sur Mer along the English Channel, the twenty-six year old father promptly disappeared from the scene, soon remarried, and was not heard from for years. Mme. Barthélemy's husband died three years later at sea during a long fishing stint leaving her alone to care for Maurice. It was not until he was eleven that he learned Mme. Barthélemy was his aunt and not his real mother; a fact that seemed to affect him more when he became an adult than when he was growing up. Out of love and gratitude to her, Maurice used the name Barthélemy as part of his full name.[3]

His father, Alphonse, appears again in Maurice's life when we learn that Maurice lived with him for a while in Paris around 1896, apparently after Maurice's military service.[4] For some reason, Maurice never told Thérèse that his real

---
[1] LC 193, from Maurice to Thérèse, dated August 5, 1897.
[2] *Vie Térésienne*, no. 69, January 1978.
[3] Descouvemont, *op. cit.*, p. 251.
[4] Vrai, *Thérèse de Lisieux et Ses Frères Missionnaires*, p. 14.

father was alive. Some writers have suggested that this omission of any reference to his father may be attributable to Maurice's embarrassment over the fact that he abandoned him as a child, remarried, or lived a rather dubious life style.

In 1894 Maurice was accepted as a student at the diocesan's major seminary in Sommervieu, not far from his home town. The next year, however, he applied for admission to the prestigious seminary of the Foreign Missionary Society of Paris (*Les Missionaires Étrangères de Paris*—sometimes called the MEP) but was not accepted, so he continued his studies at Sommervieu until 1897 where he did not do well in theology or philosophy. He, however, displayed ability in French literature and in English. His special talent clearly lay in the field of dramatics: staging, acting, and singing. Some fellow students later in life characterized him as "an agreeable and cheerful character." They remembered him as a:

> ... "class comedian" capable of amusing by his talents for hours the young men of the house [seminary], of good intelligence "although more brilliant than profound." He showed, in the face of the demands of discipline, a will rather inconstant; however, in spite of his whims, he had a very keen sensibility and an insufficiently strong family upbringing. He had an ardent soul capable of noble sentiments and enthusiasm.[5]

During these student years Maurice began his correspondence with Sr. Thérèse of the Child Jesus. When in his second year of study, he wrote to the Carmel of Lisieux asking that one of the nuns be allowed to pray for his vocation. The prioress at the time was Thérèse's sister, Mother Agnès, who assigned Thérèse as his spiritual sister. His letter of request includes this long excerpt that furnishes some insight into his personality:

> [I] am a seminarian of the Diocese of Bayeux, in second year at the Seminary of Sommervieu, guided into this house by the grace of God who wants me to become a priest. Moreover, while waiting for a definitive decision I am an aspiring missionary listed on the roster of the Seminary of Rue du Bac in Paris.... All of a sudden [during a retreat] it occurred to me that if someone prayed for me, I too would be fully and generously converted, and I said to myself: I'm going to write to a Carmelite community and I'll ask that a nun devote herself particularly to the salvation of my soul, and obtain for me the grace to be faithful to the vocation God has given me, that of a priest and a missionary.
>
> So I'm asking you, Mother, to propose that task to one of your Sisters. I am rash and for that I humbly ask pardon, but I'm so much in need of help!
>
> [In] the name of St. Teresa ... are you going to turn down my request?
>
> Perhaps, Reverend Mother, I shall obtain this favor from you, this grace, if you will take into account that within a month I'm going into the army, and I shall be subjected once again to the assaults of a world which is not entirely dead for me.[6]

---

5   *Vie Thérésienne*, no. 12, October, 1963, p. 175.
6   On November 12, 1895, he joined the military camp, 5th line, 4th company, in Caen. From Footnote 1 on p. 920 in *General Correspondence*.

> In return, I promise that once I am a priest I will always have a remembrance in the memento of the Mass both for the Religious who will have devoted herself to my salvation, as well as for you, Mother, and your community.[7]

When Mother Agnès sent a letter back to him a few days later stating that she chose someone to pray for him, he responded gratefully:

> How I thank you, Mother, for having exercised so much charity toward me ... you were so kind as to comply with my desperate request.... Whom have you given me as a Sister? A saint, an angel, as you express it yourself! I knew there were only saints among you, but I did not dare imagine that a saint among saints would become my sister. Oh, Mother, you are treating me like a son, permit me to consider myself as such, and to come into your family to pour out my sorrows and joys.
> [Signed] Your respectful and grateful son and brother forever, M. Barthélemy-Bellière, *Enf. de Marie et Joseph garde d'honneur de S.C. Asp. Mlle.* [Child of Mary and Joseph, Guard of Honor of the Sacred Heart, Missionary Aspirant][8]

Thérèse too was overjoyed to take on this assignment as she tells her sister Agnès in her autobiography:

> For a very long time, I had a desire which appeared totally unrealizable to me, that of having *a brother as a priest*. I often thought that had my little brothers not flown away to heaven, I would have had the happiness of seeing them mount the altar; but since God chose to make little angels of them, I could not hope to see my dream realized. And yet, not only did Jesus grant me the favor I desired, but He united me in the bonds of the spirit to two of His apostles, who became my brothers. [The other priest is Father Roulland.]
>
> [Mother], it would be impossible for me to express my happiness. My desire, answered in this unexpected way, gave birth in my heart to a joy which I can describe only as that of a child. I would really have to go back to my childhood days to recapture once more the memory of joys so great that the soul is too little to contain them, and not for years had I experienced this kind of happiness. I felt my soul was renewed; it was as if someone had struck for the first time musical strings left forgotten until then.[9]

Sometime during his early seminary days Maurice entered the army. For nine months he had been in the service, stationed in Caen, and not heard from. In desperation, though, he wrote to Mother Agnès disclosing his grave mental and spiritual dilemma: "I am a soldier, Mother. I have had many a fall. I am plunged into a deplorable situation, and my dear sister, Thérèse of the Child Jesus, must tear me away from it ... or I am lost.... Pardon me, have pity on me; and help me. I beg you."[10]

---

7 Letter from Maurice to Mother Agnès, dated October 15, 1895.
8 Letter dated October 23, 1895, from l'abbé Maurice Bellière to Mother Agnès of Jesus.
9 *Story of a Soul*, chapter XI, pp. 250–251.
10 July 21, 1896.

Three months later, he wrote again stating that his troubles were over and "the poor soldier has become again the seminarian of former days."[11] This twenty-one-year-old seminarian/soldier, one year younger than Thérèse, now was a second year student at the major seminary of Sommervieu, northwest of Caen. From this point on an intense and deeply spiritual correspondence flowed from the pens of Thérèse and Maurice.

Actually the very first written material Thérèse wrote for Maurice was a prayer (Pri 8) composed after she accepted the request to pray for him and his vocation. Mother Agnès enclosed it in her response letter to Maurice on October 22, 1895. In the prayer Thérèse thanks Jesus for "having fulfilled one of my greatest desires, that of having a brother, a priest, and apostle...." She continues by asking Him and Mary, the Queen of Carmel, to "keep him safe amid the dangers of the world." Then she states his and her mission:

> You know, Lord, that my only ambition is to make you known and loved. Now my desire will be realized. I can only pray and suffer, but the soul to whom you unite me by the sweet bonds of charity will go and fight in the plain to win hearts for you, while on the mountain of Carmel I will pray that you give him victory.... Keep him safe amid the dangers of the world. Make him feel increasingly the nothingness and vanity of passing things and the happiness of being able to despise them for your love....[12]

Thérèse understood from the start that she was not to write directly to Maurice (especially since he was a male) but through the prioress who at the time was her sister. In the meantime, Mother Marie de Gonzague was elected the new prioress, succeeding Mother Agnès. She wisely allowed Thérèse to write directly to him. She read each letter, however, and much to her credit she never corrected or criticized anything Thérèse wrote. At the end of her fourth letter to him Thérèse wrote this postscript: "It is clearly understood, is it not, that our relationship shall remain secret? No one except your Director must know of the union which has formed between our souls."[13]

There followed a correspondence between the two consisting of eleven letters from Maurice and ten from Thérèse. Her prayer for him, though, might be considered the eleventh message. It contained a holy card with the words "Last souvenir of a soul, sister of your own soul." A deep holy relationship between the two rather quickly developed. After he opened his soul to her, she wrote in her third letter to him, even though she still addressed him as Monsieur l'Abbé: "Truly, only in heaven will you know how dear you are to me. I feel our souls are made to understand each other."[14] She enclosed in this letter copies of nearly twenty of her poems (all complete except one) and excerpts from her playlet *The Triumph of Humility* (RP 7). Thérèse also included a prayer she wished him

---

11 October 14, 1896.
12 Prayer 8.
13 LT 224 from Thérèse to Maurice, dated April 25, 1897.
14 LT 220 Thérèse to Maurice, dated February 24, 1897.

to say daily for her: "Merciful Father, in the name of our lovable Jesus, of the Virgin Mary and of the Saints, I ask You to set my sister on fire with Your Spirit of Love, and to grant her the grace of making You deeply loved." Though it took him nearly two months to respond, he did so with sincere appreciation for her sending them and for the spiritual delight he experienced in reading them.[15]

Furthermore, she asked him to send her the memorable dates in his life which he did but listed only the day and month, leaving out the year. Below is the list he sent her with the year added by the present author:

> I celebrate my birth and baptism on the 10th of June [1874]. (The date of the latter is listed as June 25th, but the nun who took care of me at birth felt I should be baptized.) My first Communion day is June 7th [1885]. My admission to the Confraternity of St. Joseph took place on September 21st [1889], to that of the Blessed Virgin and St. Louis Gonzague on the 8th of December [1893], and on that same day, December 8th [1894], my reception of the cassock took place and my acceptance as an Aspiring Missionary. October 15th [1895], was the day of your kindness to me and of the promise I made to remember you in the memento of Mass....[16]

In her fourth letter she told him that "My pen, or rather my heart, refuses to call you "Monsieur l'Abbé," and our good Mother has told me that from now on, in writing you I may use the name I always use when I speak of you to Jesus."[17] He in turn was deeply appreciative of her council and theology. He addressed her in his last letter with "My dear and more than dear little Sister."[18] She never read this eleventh letter from him for she died five days before he wrote it.

Thérèse slowly unraveled to Maurice her "Little Way" as, for example, when she conceded to him that "the way of simple love and confidence is just made to order for you."[19] And again:

> I understand better than ever how much your soul is the sister of my own, since it is called to lift itself up to God by the ELEVATOR of love and not to climb the hard stairway of fear.... I am sure that I shall greatly help you to walk more surely by this delightful way once I have been delivered from my mortal envelope; and soon you will say like St. Augustine: "Love is the weight that pulls me forward."[20]

They exchanged not only photos of each other, the list of important dates in their lives, but also holy objects. Maurice sent Thérèse through her sister Mother Agnès a "Sacred Heart badge as a sign of our association in God, which lacks only her signature because you, Mother, and God have already given approval of it."[21] After he learned directly from her that she was dying, he wrote his sixth

---

15 His third letter was dated April 17, 1897.
16 LC 177 from Maurice to Thérèse, dated April 17–18, 1897.
17 LT 224 from Thérèse to Maurice, dated April 25, 1897.
18 LC 201 from Maurice to Thérèse, dated October 2, 1897.
19 LT 261 July 26, 1897.
20 LT 258 July 18, 1897.
21 October 23, 1895.

letter to her on July 17, 1897, in which he rather boldly made this request: "And you who will become my favorite Saint, you my very own sister, bless me and save me. And please leave me something of yourself, your crucifix if you will." The next month Thérèse answered his request in the last letter she wrote to him:

> Now dear little brother, I must speak to you about the *inheritance* you will receive after my death. Here is the share our Mother will give you: (i) the relic I received on the day of my reception of the habit, and it has never left me since then; (ii) a little crucifix which is incomparably more dear to me than the large one, for the one I have now is no longer the first one I had been given. In Carmel we exchange objects of piety at times; this is a good way to prevent us from becoming attached to them. I return to the little crucifix. It is not beautiful; the face of Christ has almost disappeared. You will not be surprised at this when you realize that since the age of thirteen this souvenir from one of my sisters [Léonie] has followed me everywhere. It was especially during my trip to Italy that this Crucifix became precious to me. Furthermore, it was blessed by the Holy Father [Pope Leo XIII]. Ever since my illness, I hold our dear little Crucifix almost always in my hands; when looking at it, I think with joy that, after having received my kisses, it will go to claim those of my little Brother. Here, then, is what your *inheritance* consists of, and in addition our Mother will give you the *last* picture that I have painted.[22]

Two days after she wrote this stunning bequest, she looked at a picture of Father Bellière in a soldier's uniform pinned to her bed curtains in the infirmary and said: "To this soldier, cutting such a dashing figure, I'm giving advice as to a little girl! I'm pointing out to him the way of confidence and love."[23] Two weeks before this Thérèse was again scrutinizing pictures of Maurice and Father Roulland (her other spiritual brother) and remarked quite wittily that "I'm much prettier than they are!"[24] Thérèse died on September 30, 1897. Maurice told Mother Gonzague in his letter of October 14, 1897, these quite prophetic words:

> [At] the very moment of 7:30 on Thursday night I was well out to sea, a hundred miles from France. That night—I don't recall the hour—I thought of her and was repeating the prayer she asked me to say for her every day until I died. Perhaps she was listening in heaven.... Well, I must face it, the last of life's treasures is gone and there is nothing left for me now.... [N]ow we have a saint in heaven who loved us while she was on earth. Now she becomes a powerful helper up there beyond. Never again shall I doubt my salvation.

He continued his contact with the Lisieux Carmel through his correspondence with Mother Gonzague, Mother Agnès, and sometimes with Céline who in turn kept him informed about the fame of Thérèse's autobiography, *Story of a Soul*, and no doubt even the desire of many to have Thérèse canonized.

---

22 LT 263, August 10, 1897.
23 *Her Last Conversations*, August 12, 1897.
24 Ibid. July 30, 1897.

Maurice left Marseille by boat with some sixty men and on September 30, the day Thérèse died, he was well out at sea heading for North Africa. Upon arrival, he set out for the novitiate of the White Fathers of Africa at Maison-Carrée in Algiers. Four years of intensive study faced him. On October 10 he received the habit of his order and ten months later his superiors sent him to the seminary in Carthage where he stayed from August 1898 to his ordination on June 29, 1901. His first assignment entailed secretarial work in the office of Bishop Livinhac in Algiers where his skill in English proved invaluable. After this he went back to his home in Normandy for a brief vacation which when ended, he left France from the port of Marseille on July 29, 1902 for Africa with ten companions, including his friend Brother Sébastien. Their assigned field of work was in Nyassaland (Malawi), a region that would try any man with its extremes of heat, humidity, disease, mosquitoes, and fear of harm from hostile Muslims and natives. Natives and foreigners alike dreaded the poisonous bite from the tse-tse fly that causes the deadly sleeping sickness (*maladie du commeil*). To reach their destination took sixty-seven days on water and two weeks on land.

In 1903 he contracted a dreaded tropical disease known as "Black Water" fever from which he luckily managed to survive. His nearly eight years doing missionary work in Malawi appeared rather successful but for unclear reasons, though obviously failing in health, he left without permission in 1905 for Maison-Carrée. He never arrived there but went back to France. It was determined later that he was displaying the early signs of the sleeping sickness which eventually did end his life. Some claim that he might have even had a brain tumor. At any rate, the community council in Algiers summoned him back to answer questions about his desertion which he did, however, without any realization of the seriousness of his actions. They ordered him back to his mission but allowed him to return home for a short rest with the promise of returning to Africa. He never returned. He arrived home in a confused state, was sent to the order's hospital in Autreppe, Belgium, where he stayed two weeks and then was released in the fall to go home. His pathetic state distressed all especially his foster mother who herself was ill and eventually died on January 15, 1907, at sixty-three.[25] His mental and physical condition deteriorated so much that after being found lost and meandering, an old priestly friend had him admitted on June 8, 1907, to Bon Sauveur mental hospital in Caen where Thérèse's father had been a patient. He died there a month after his thirty-third birthday on July 14, 1907. He is buried near his "foster" mother in the little cemetery on the property of the church he attended as a youth in Langrune-sur-Mer. For decades it was neglected but now a clearly marked sign on the grave as well as a plaque in the church rightfully acknowledge his association with St. Thérèse of Lisieux.

The list below indicates the dates and corresponding numbers assigned to the letters in *General Correspondence* that were exchanged between Sister Thérèse and Father Bellière:

---

25 Ahern, *Maurice and Thérèse*, p. 273.

LETTERS

THÉRÈSE'S	MAURICE BELLIÈRE'S
1. October 21, 1896 (LT 198)	1. November 28, 1896 (LC 172)
2. December 26, 1896 (LT 213)	2. January 21, 1897 (LC 174)
3. February 24, 1897 (LT 220)	3. April 17–18, 1897 (LC 177)
4. April 25, 1897 (LT 224)	4. June 7, 1897 (LC 186)
5. June 9, 1897 (LT 244) (not sent)	5. July 15, 1897 (LC 188)
6. June 21, 1897 (LT 247)	6. July 17, 1897 (LC 189)
7. July 13, 1897 (LT 253)	7. July 21, 1897 (LC 191)
8. July 18, 1897 (LT 258)	8. August 5, 1897 (LC 193)
9. July 26, 1897 (LT 261)	9. August 17, 1897 (LC 194)
10. August 10, 1897 (LT 263)	10. August 28, 1897 (LC 196)
11. August 25, 1897 (LT 266)[26]	11. October 2, 1897 (LC 201)

Maurice in the estimation of many was just an ordinary man, which of course he was, with all his faults, failures, weaknesses, sensitivity, and perhaps indiscretions. Yet he had soaring ambitions, noble ideals, and a deep love of God which Thérèse immediately recognized. Though the two never met in person, she was attracted to him because he honestly believed he was not an exceptional person, showed signs of true humility, desired martyrdom, and confessed that he had committed "blunders." She encouraged him by saying that "the good God has given you as a sister not a great soul, but one who is very little and very imperfect."[27] She knew the Merciful God of Love could never ignore a person like him; therefore, how could she do so, especially since he was her "brother." He perfectly exemplified the humble, little soul that she targeted in her "Little Way." Let us not forget that as a Carmelite, she dedicated her life to love of God, Mary, the Church, and especially to pray for priests, which she summarizes in one of the poems she sent to Maurice:[28]

> Living on Love, O my Divine Master,
> Is begging you to spread your Fire
> In the holy, sacred soul of your Priest.
> May he be purer than a seraphim in Heaven!...
> [PN 17, "Living on Love!" ("*Vivre d'Amour!*")]

2. ABBÉ CHILLART
Gave Louis Martin the Last Rites

ABBÉ CHILLART SERVED AS PASTOR OF THE LITTLE CHURCH OF ST. SÉBASTIEN in the village of Saint Sébastien de Morsent, a few miles west of Evreux. He often visited Thérèse's relatives, the Guérins, at their summer home called the Château de La Musse located about a mile or so from his church. They were happy to

---

26 This was actually not a letter. The envelope contained only a holy card on the front of which is a miniature of the last painting by Thérèse. It shows the two hands of a priest holding up a large host. The saying on the other side is: "Last souvenir of a soul, sister of your own soul."
27 LT 224, April 25, 1897.
28 LT 220, February 24, 1897.

have him join them because he usually would entertain them by relating his various gripping experiences as a military chaplain.

The ailing Louis Martin and his two daughters Céline and Léonie spent the month of July 1894 at La Musse with the Guérins when he became seriously ill. Céline tells us about the mournful situation leading up to her father's death on July 29, 1894:

> On July 28, our venerable father had another heart-attack, less violent than the last one, but more prolonged. During the evening, Abbé Chillart, the pastor of St. Sébastien, gave him Extreme Unction again. My uncle [Isidore Guérin] was absent, having left for Lisieux, to speak at the distribution of prizes at the Brothers' School. He was to return that night. On the 29th, at five o'clock in the morning, Desiré [the man servant], came to call me. Our poor father had his eyes closed, his breathing was strong and regular. Soon after, Desiré, Doctor and Madame La Néele [the Martin girls' cousin], with some servants, left by carriage for Evreux, in order to assist at an early Mass, and return in time to allow another group to go to St. Sébastien for the eight o'clock Sunday Mass.... I was watching by Papa almost alone.... [M]y aunt returned, followed by my uncle. The breathing became suddenly very weak, and quietly like a child going to sleep his happy soul took flight to Heaven. It was a quarter past eight. Papa was seventy-one years old lacking a month.[29]

Incidentally, Louis Martin did not die in the château itself but in an apartment on the ground floor of a building several yards opposite the main entrance to the château. Here it was easy to wheel him in and out whereas in order to enter the château one had to climb a number of steps (six or seven) before entering, which was a difficult, cumbersome, and dangerous maneuver to execute. Céline continues with her account of the funeral details:

> Our father was laid out in an oak coffin lined with lead. The pastor of St. Sébastien announced his death with much emotion at the Gospel of the Mass, and gave a eulogy of the venerable patriarch. On Thursday, August 2, the funeral service was held at the Cathedral of St. Pierre in Lisieux [some 50 miles away]. A large and sympathetic crowd followed the hearse to the cemetery hill. After so many humiliating trials his burial was in a sense a triumph.[30]

3. Abbé Joseph de Cornière (1874–1939)
Convent doctor's son

THE YOUNG SEMINARIAN ABBÉ JOSEPH DE CORNIÈRE WAS THE OLDEST SON of the Lisieux Carmel physician, Doctor Alexandre de Cornière. The first recorded time he was invited by the Guérins to spend vacation periods with them took place in 1893 and then again in 1894 at their summer place, the Château de La Musse, an impressive Louis XIII style house built on a large country estate near Evreux. As a novice in the Redemptorist Order he had been to Holland

---
29 Sister Geneviève, *op. cit.*, pp. 113–114.
30 Ibid., p. 116.

in 1892 and then from 1892 to 1893 in Chili, South America. In the summer of 1894 he spent a particularly joyous vacation with the Guérins and their cousin Céline which she cites in a letter she sent to her sister Thérèse, then six years in the monastery:

> I am going to write to you in haste, for these days I do not have time to turn around. Joseph de Cornière is here, and we are busy doing photography. We dress up and are making a whole story of travelers in living pictures; it will be very amusing. In the meanwhile, however, I am beginning to get enough of it. My days seem insipid to me, no more reading, no time to write, hardly any time to make meditation; we are always on the go....
>
> Lately, I have been going out of myself, and I am suffering much from this, a continual malaise. Furthermore, we spend our days in uncontrollable laughter, enough to split our sides, and I am thirsting for solitude. I can no longer breathe. Then I am unhappy ... not being accustomed to living with boys [Joseph, 20, and her cousin by marriage, Dr. Francis La Néele, 26], it seems strange to me to be spending my days in their company. As holy and pure and candid as they are, I cannot get used to it.[31]

Thérèse's response to Céline's letter referring to the "boys" is pragmatic but still quite Theresian: "I beg you to give my kindest regards to all the dear travelers who are enjoying themselves so much there. I understand what you feel regarding the boys.... But this is only for a passing moment, one day you will not see too much of them. Console yourself!..."[32]

The "living pictures" Céline mentions are the twenty-seven photographs Joseph took at La Musse to illustrate the entertainment he composed inspired by his experiences in Chili entitled *"Voyage excentrique aux Cordillères des Andes"* (Eccentric Voyage to the Cordilleras[33] of the Andes). The actors in this recreation were the Martin girls' cousins Marie Guérin and Jeanne La Néele, Jeanne's husband Francis, Céline Martin, and Joseph de Cornière. He wrote twenty-eight amusing quatrains for his actors to recite. The scenes in the photographs were of sites at La Musse: the river Iton down below the château proper, the woodland, the beautiful surrounding countryside, an abandoned quarry, and other sights.[34]

Joseph encountered some serious temptations before he was finally ordained. When Thérèse heard of them she offered up her sufferings for him. In August of 1897, Pauline (Mother Agnès) recorded Thérèse's comments regarding the self-effacing and sensitive letter he wrote to her:

> Oh, what consolation this letter brought to me! I saw that my sufferings were bearing fruit. Did you notice the sentiments of humility the letter expresses? It's exactly what I wanted.

---

31 LC 159, dated July 17, 1894.
32 LT 167, dated July 18, 1894.
33 One source freely interpreted it as—"A Faraway Voyage to the Franciscan Nuns of the Andes." The Cordilleras is an extensive system of ranges stretching from the Andes in South America north as far as Alaska.
34 From the Notes to LT 159.

And what good it did me to see how in such a short time we can have so much love and gratitude for a soul who has done us some good and whom we didn't know until then. What will it be then in heaven when souls will know those who saved them.[35]

After serious reflection, Joseph left the Redemptorists and continued his seminary studies in Bayeux as a diocesan priest. He was ordained a secular priest and worked in the Bayeux diocese the rest of his life. Death came to him at the age of sixty-five in Caen on October 8, 1938.

4. Abbé Joseph Denis de Maroy (1871–1962)
Said his first Mass at the Lisieux Carmel

ON SEPTEMBER 18, 1897, THIRTEEN DAYS BEFORE THÉRÈSE DIED, SHE LAY racked with pain on her bed in the convent infirmary. She lovingly watched her sister Céline (Sister Geneviève) sitting next to her with the embroidered altar cloth and vestments she had been working on for Abbé Denis de Maroy who was ordained that very day in Bayeux. The next day he celebrated his first Mass in the Carmel chapel. After it was over, Thérèse asked to see his chalice. When it was brought to her she stared at it for some time. After one of the nuns asked her why she was doing this so intently, Thérèse replied: "Because my reflection is there; when I was Sacristan, I used to love doing this. I was happy to say to myself: My features are reflected in the place where the Blood of Jesus rested and where it will descend again."[36]

Remembering the time she spoke to Pope Leo XIII ten years before at an audience in Rome on November 20, she continued with similar sentiments: "How many times, too, have I thought that in Rome, my face was reproduced in the eyes of the Holy Father."[37]

Joseph Denis de Maroy was born in Paris on March 3, 1871. Twenty-six years later on September 18, 1897, he was ordained a diocesan priest. In the years following his ordination he served as parish priest in Villerville-sur-Mer (1897) and Pont-l'Evêque (1900). During that time he became one of the initiators of the Catholic press and in 1907 its Diocesan Director. In 1919, just after World War I, he was chosen senior rector in Fontenay-le-Marmion, a suburb of Caen. Then in World War II he luckily survived the devastating bombardments that area underwent. Instead of retirement, he willingly accepted the position of curate of Saint-Michel-de-Hennequeville in Trouville by the sea. Later on, despite his eighty-eight years, the spry Abbé Denis was appointed chaplain of the Carmel Saint-Joseph (non-existent today) that was located near the Basilica of St. Thérèse in Lisieux. Abbé Denis died at the age of ninety-one on December 29, 1962, and was buried in Lisieux.

---

35 *Her Last Conversations*, August 23, 1897.
36 Ibid., September 19, 1897.
37 Ibid.

5. ABBÉ LOUIS GOMBAULT (1850–1920)
Took two controversial photos of the novice Thérèse

ABBÉ LOUIS GOMBAULT, PROFESSOR AT ST. MARY'S MINOR SEMINARY IN Lisieux, took two photographs of the sixteen-year-old novice Sister Thérèse in January 1889, sometime after her clothing day. These were the first photos ever taken in the Lisieux Carmel; in fact, it was a rare occurrence in any convent at that time. His position, however, at the time was bursar at the seminary and, having had a background in architectural work, was also diocesan inspector of religious buildings. Thus, with permission from the Bishop of Bayeux, he entered the enclosure of the Carmel monastery to give the nuns instructions concerning the installation and use of gaslight and to check the condition of the extern sisters' annex which was in dire need of repair. Sister Agnès of Jesus (Pauline, Thérèse's blood sister) found this the opportune time to ask him to take pictures of Thérèse for her father and sisters (Céline and Leonie) still at home at Les Buissonnets. The camera he used (a 13/18 Darlot) actually belonged to Céline. Photography as well as painting had been Céline's hobby for some time and when she eventually entered the monastery five years after Thérèse she brought her photographic equipment and art supplies with her—another rare privilege and a providential one indeed. All the camera work—posing of subjects, etc.—was done by Céline or under her direction. She even developed the pictures herself in her own darkroom in the monastery cellar.

Shortly after Abbé Gombault took the two pictures of Thérèse, Sister Agnès wrote an admonition to her sisters "in the world":

> Above all, tell dear little Father to show the photographs only to Uncle [Guérin] and not to tell anyone that M. Gombault photographed the angel [Thérèse]. People would believe that he entered the cloister precisely for this, which is not true, since Monseigneur [Bishop Hugonin] had given him the permission to come with the contractor to see the old house [of the extern sisters]. You say, in case you are asked, that someone had lent me the apparatus [Céline's own camera] for two or three days. This secret is very IMPORTANT.[38]

Years later in 1926 when Mother Agnès was prioress of the Carmel, she explained in writing what had occurred when they received the two negatives of the two pictures that Abbé Gombault took of Thérèse:

> This priest took two photographs: one long since made public, with the mantle (Photo #5), the other on the other side of the Cross without the mantle (Photo #6).[39] The light too harsh on that side, made the novice uncomfortable and in consequence of it altered her features. The community therefore accepted the first negative and refused the other, as it was defective.
>
> We believed it had been destroyed when, after the death of Blessed Thérèse, the unfaithful photograph was distributed to all sides. The original negative, having been restored to Carmel, Sister Geneviève [Céline], by touching up an

---
38 Letter from Sister Agnès to Leonie and Céline written at the end of January 1889.
39 The photo numbers are those used in *The Photo Album of St. Thérèse of Lisieux*.

enlargement, re-established the truth, so that one seems to see in it the servant of God at the age of sixteen.[40]

Céline, actually an artist with considerable skill, had painted several portraits of her sister after her death. Adhering to the religious mode of the day, Céline retouched at one time or another the Abbé's as well as her own photos of Thérèse with the purpose of idealizing reality. For all this she received considerable criticism for decades thereafter, even from her own Uncle Guérin as we learn from a letter by her sister Marie (Sister Marie of the Angels):

> [We] all feel rather badly that, despite his great love for Thérèse, he [Uncle Guérin] has all sorts of prejudices against her autobiography, and he communicates these prejudices to his daughter [Jeanne] and to his son-in-law, Doctor La Neele, who live with him. He is continually objecting to the illustrations in the book [*L'Histoire d'une âime—Story of a Soul*], and yet we published them only after we had asked advice from competent people.[41]

Almost a quarter of a century later in 1913, Céline still remembered Dr. Francis La Néele's criticism of her portraits and in contrast his approval of Gombault's photos:

> Francis came to the parlor on business the other day and he scolded all of us, especially me, claiming that none of my portraits resembled Thérèse. He also said he had Abbé Gombault's photograph enlarged, and it was the only one he cared to see circulated.[42]

After the doctor's death in 1916, his wife Jeanne apologized for his behavior and begged Céline's forgiveness for the pain he inflicted on her regarding this picture affair.

Despite the controversy surrounding Céline's paintings, they have enjoyed unbelievable success, having been reproduced in the millions. The Gombault photographs too have been circulated in untold numbers and likewise appreciated, especially since the publication in 1961 of *The Photo Album of St. Thérèse of Lisieux*, a scholarly and artistic volume edited by Françoise de Saint-Marie, O.C.D., that contains all forty-seven[43] photographs of St. Thérèse ever taken, and in their original, unretouched state.

Abbé Gombault's two photos, Céline's paintings, and the many other photographs of Thérèse, her family, friends, and co-religious, are a rare photographed record of any nineteenth century nun—and especially a saint.

Abbé Louis Gombault died at the age of seventy in 1920.

---

40 Robo, *Two Portraits of St. Thérèse of Lisieux*, pp. 38–39.
41 *The Photo Album*, chapter VI, p. 46.
42 Ibid.
43 Actually 46 because in Photo 8 Thérèse's back is barely discernable as she enters the doorway on the infirmary porch.

6. Msgr. Flavien-Abel-Antoine Hugonin (1823-1898)
Bishop who permitted Thérèse to enter the Lisieux Carmel

MSGR. HUGONIN, BISHOP OF BAYEUX AND LISIEUX, PARTICIPATED IN SOME of the most important religious events in the life of Thérèse before and during her convent years. An early experience with him occurred when she was eleven. Because of the strict diocesan laws, Thérèse was prevented from receiving First Holy Communion with her classmates in 1883. Her eleventh birthday was just two days short of the required time so she had to wait an entire year. This great disappointment was almost overcome when Thérèse happened by chance to see Bishop Hugonin going toward the Lisieux railroad station one day. She excitedly said to her sister: "Oh, Marie, shall I run and ask his permission to make my First Communion this year?"[44] It was with some effort that Marie prevented the eager Thérèse from approaching the Bishop. Sadly for Thérèse, she had to wait a year, thus she received the Sacrament of the Eucharist on May 8, 1884. Three years later she did go to him and asked permission—this time to enter the Carmelite Order at fifteen. In the meantime, in fact a month after receiving her First Communion, she was confirmed by Bishop Hugonin on June 14, 1884, at the Benedictine Abbey School in Lisieux.

Three years later, Thérèse had her next momentous meeting with the Bishop. The superior of the Carmelite Monastery in Lisieux, Canon Delatroëtte, would not consent to having the fourteen-year-old Thérèse become a nun there at fifteen but suggested she see the bishop. Here is her account in part about this meeting with Bishop Hugonin in Bayeux on October 31, 1887. After Thérèse and her father were escorted into the room at the Bishop's palace and seated comfortably in the presence of the Bishop, Thérèse has this to say:

> I had hoped that Papa would speak; however, he told me to explain the object of our visit to the Bishop. I did so as *eloquently* as possible and his Excellancy, accustomed to *eloquence*, did not appear touched by my reasons.... The Bishop asked me if it had been a long time since I desired to enter Carmel. "Oh! yes, Bishop, a very long time." ...
>
> The Bishop, believing he'd please Papa, tried to have me stay with him a few more years, and he was very much *surprised* at seeing him take my part, interceding for me to obtain permission to fly away at fifteen. And still everything was futile. The Bishop said an interview with the *Superior of Carmel* was indispensable before making his decision. I couldn't possibly have heard anything that would cause me more pain than this because I was aware of his formal opposition. Without taking into account Father Reverony's advice, I did more than *show my diamonds* [tears] to the Bishop. I *gave* him some!
>
> He was very much touched by this and putting his arm around my neck, he placed my head on his shoulder and caressed me as no one, it appears, was ever caressed by him before....
>
> The Bishop brought us out as far as the garden. Papa *amused him very much* by telling him that in order to appear older I had put up my hair. (This

---
44 Laveille, *op. cit.*, p. 95.

wasn't lost on the Bishop, for he never spoke about "his little daughter" without telling the story of the hair.)[45]

Disappointed after receiving no solid assurances from the Bishop, Thérèse went a few days later with her father and sister Céline on a pilgrimage to Rome which had been planned well in advance. Against all protocol, she desperately pleaded her cause with the pope himself, Leo XIII, before a large general audience. This too proved futile. Thérèse, with continued persistence, wrote these lines excerpted from a letter (one of three) to the Bishop, explaining the importance of his future decision in her regard. This one plea is typical: "Oh, Monseigneur! Christmas is approaching and I am awaiting your answer with a great confidence.... I will never forget that it is to Your Excellency that I will owe the accomplishment of God's will."[46] Bishop Hugonin finally gave the Mother Prioress authorization on December 28, 1887, to accept Thérèse. She thanked him with heartfelt emotion for the "beautiful New Year's gift,"[47] as she called it.

Bishop Hugonin was under the impression that since all had agreed to have Thérèse enter the convent by February, she would have been there already. The following episode was transcribed into the chronicles of the monastery:

On February 21 [1888], Bishop Hugonin entered the cloister with P. Basile, a Carmelite and the Lenten preacher in the diocese that year. Before the assembled community, the bishop asked: "Where is my little novice?" Mother Marie de Gonzague, then prioress, told him that because of the winter and Lent she had postponed her entrance until after Easter. Monseigneur approved the delay.[48]

A week before Thérèse's entrance on April 19, 1888, she received this warm and thoughtful letter from Bishop Hugonin:

Dear Child,

I bless you with all my heart. Your wishes have been answered. Our Lord is receiving you among His faithful spouses, whom He has chosen one by one through a privileged grace. Unite yourself more and more to Our Lord in order to be more and more detached from yourself. Such will be your program.

I recommend myself and the whole diocese to the prayers of your community.
All yours in Our Lord,

† *Flavien*[49]

The following passages recount some of the other times Bishop Hugonin became involved with situations connected with Thérèse:

1. The time for my reception of the habit had arrived.... Nothing was missing, not even the *snow*! At the termination of the ceremony [January 10, 1889] the Bishop intoned the *Te Deum*. One of the priests remarked to him that

---

45 *Story of a Soul*, chapter VI, pp. 116–117.
46 LT 38 A, dated December 3–8, 1887, from Thérèse to Bishop Hugonin.
47 LT 40 from Thérèse to Bishop Hugonin, dated the beginning of January 1888.
48 *Foundation du Carmel de Lisieux*, III, p. 154, as indicated in Note I of a letter from Thérèse to Bishop Hugonin dated March 27, 1888.
49 LC 79 from Bishop Hugonin dated March 31, 1888.

this hymn of *thanksgiving* was usually sung only at Professions, but, once begun, it was continued to the end. And indeed it was fitting that the feast be thus completed since in it were united all the others....⁵⁰

2. The Bishop came into the cloister after the ceremony and was very kind to me. I believe he was very proud I had succeeded and told everyone I was "*his* little girl."⁵¹

He was always kind to me on his return trips to the Carmel. I remember especially his visit on the occasion of our Father St. John of the Cross' Centenary. He took my head in his hands and gave me a thousand caresses, never was I so honored.⁵²

3. The ceremony of my reception of the Veil took place on the 24th of September [1890] and the day was veiled in tears. Papa [hospitalized in Caen] was not there to bless his Queen; Father Pichon was in Canada; the Bishop, who was supposed to come and dine with Uncle, did not come at all since he was sick. [His brother, Canon Jean-Baptiste Hugonin, came in his place.]⁵³

After their father's death, Céline undertook the necessary steps to accomplish her long time desire to become a Carmelite. Since her three sisters were nuns at the Carmel, Bishop Hugonin had some misgivings about allowing her, a fourth Martin sister, to join them. After considerable pondering on the matter, he gave his permission and Céline entered the Lisieux Carmel on September 14, 1894. Two years later, Bishop Hugonin gave her the black veil and the new name Sister Geneviève of the Holy Face.

When Thérèse's autobiography was seriously considered for publication, Bishop Hugonin was asked to approve the manuscript by supplying the *Imprimatur* which he did rather unenthusiastically by just verbally authorizing it.⁵⁴ He relied upon the wisdom and knowledge of Father Madelaine who edited it. Furthermore, he unexplainably declined to write a letter of Introduction to the book.

Flavien-Abel-Antoine Hugonin was born on July 3, 1823, in Thodure (a little distance from Grenoble) and ordained a priest at twenty-seven on May 25, 1850. His remarkable career commenced early with his achieving high honors as a student, earning doctorates in theology and literature. He was appointed professor of philosophy and literature at the school of the Carmelites in 1850, followed in 1859 as lecturer at the Sorbonne. In 1861 he became superior of the Carmelite Seminary. His consecration as bishop of Bayeux took place on July 13, 1866. A learned and scholarly man, he wrote many works on philosophy and law, and took part in the foundation of the Catholic University of Paris (1875). He, furthermore, staunchly maintained an affirmative stand on papal infallibility at Vatican Council I (1869–1870).

Bishop Hugonin died in Caen on May 2, 1898, (seven months after Thérèse) at the age of seventy-four.

---

50 *Story of a Soul*, chapter VII, p. 154.
51 Ibid., p. 156.
52 Ibid.
53 Ibid., p. 167.
54 Gaucher, "*L' Histoire d'Une Âm*" *de Thérèse de Lisieux*, p. 77.

7. Père Adolphe Roulland (1870–1934)
Thérèse's second spiritual brother, missionary to China

TWO YEARS BEFORE SHE DIED, THÉRÈSE GLADLY ACCEPTED THE YOUNG seminarian Maurice Bellière as her "spiritual brother" to encourage and sustain him in his struggles to become a missionary priest. Then when asked eight months later to take on another seminarian—Adolph Roulland—she hesitated at first, but agreed to accept him. He, three years older than Thérèse, recorded how this correspondence with her came about:

> I was about to leave for the missions. R. P. Norbert, a Premonstratensian of Mondaye, diocese of Bayeux, my compatriot, intervened at my request with the Lisieux Carmel to obtain permission from the prioress that a religious of the monastery be chosen to pray specially for me and my mission. Sister Thérèse, whom I did not know until then, was chosen.[55]

Thérèse likewise relates the genesis of this relationship but in more detail:

> Last year at the end of May [May 30, 1896], I remember how you [Mother Marie de Gonzague] called me one day before we went to the refectory. My heart was beating very fast when I entered your cell, dear Mother; I was wondering what you could have to tell me since this was the very first time you called me in this way. After having told me to be seated, you asked me: "Will you take charge of the spiritual interests of a missionary who is to be ordained and leave very soon [for China]?" And then, Mother, you read this young priest's letter in order that I might know exactly what he was asking. My first sentiment was one of joy which was immediately replaced by fear. I explained, dear Mother, that having already offered my poor merits for one future apostle, I believed I could not do it for the intentions of another, and that, besides, there were many Sisters better than I who would be able to answer his request. All my objections were useless. You told me that one could have several brothers. Then I asked you whether obedience could double my merits. You answered that it could, and you told me several things which made me see that I had to accept a new brother without any scruples. In the bottom of my heart, Mother, I was thinking the same way as you.... I hope with the grace of God to be useful to more than two missionaries and I could not forget to pray for all without casting aside simple priests whose mission at times is as difficult to carry out as that of apostles preaching to the infidels.[56]

Mother de Gonzague wrote to Adolphe Roulland that "of my good ones she is the best ... you have a very fervent auxiliary who will neglect nothing for the salvation of souls."[57] Once Thérèse accepted him as her second spiritual brother she eagerly settled down to work painting pictures on three items used by priests at Mass: a corporal, a purificator, and a pall. When finished, she gave them to Mother de Gonzague on her feast day, June 21, which she in turn made sure Adolphe received before his ordination on June 28, 1896. Five days, though,

---

55 From the introduction to Roulland's letter to Mother Marie de Gonzague of June 20, 1896, in *General Correspondence*, p. 954, as copied from the *Apostolic Process*, 55.
56 *Story of a Soul*, chapter XI, p. 253.
57 As recorded in the account of Adolph Roulland, the ninth witness giving testimony at the Apostolic Process.

before his reception of Holy Orders, Thérèse wrote her first letter to him in which she expressed her innermost feelings about the matter:

> I feel very unworthy to be associated in a special way with one of the missionaries of our adorable Jesus, but since obedience entrusts me with this sweet task, I am assured my heavenly spouse will make up for my feeble merits (upon which I in no way rely), and that He will listen to the desires of my soul by rendering fruitful your apostolate. I shall be truly happy to work with you for the salvation of souls. It is for this purpose I became a Carmelite nun; being unable to be an active missionary....
>
> For a long time I wanted to know an Apostle who would pronounce my name at the holy altar on the day of his first Mass....
>
> If I did not fear to be indiscreet, I would ask you, Reverend Father, to make each day at the holy altar a memento for me.... When the ocean will separate you from France, you will recall, when looking at the pall which I painted with so much joy, that on the mountain of Carmel a soul is praying unceasingly to the divine Prisoner of Love for the success of your glorious conquest.[58]

He commentated on the prayer Thérèse asked the "Reverend Father" (as she at first addressed him) to say at the "memento" of each Mass: "Each day, at the Holy Sacrifice, I will pronounce the name of Sister Thérèse of the Child Jesus. If as you hope you go to heaven before me, I will continue to pray for you. I will say: 'I offer this Sacrifice for the repose of the soul of my sister in Jesus.'"[59] Father (Père) Roulland testified years later that:

> ... the purpose of our apostolic union was to save souls: union of prayers, sacrifices, works, for this purpose. We had agreed between us that each morning at the memento of the living I would say: "Permit, my God, Sister Thérèse to make You loved by the souls who are dear to us." Our union was not broken at her death. On her recommendation, I retained for the memento of the dead the sentence she dictated to me for the memento of the living. I add that I never failed to carry out this request.[60]

Five days after his ordination in Paris, Father Roulland visited the Lisieux monastery (July 3, 1896) and said Mass. He spoke to both Mother de Gonzague and Thérèse at the covered grille before and after the service. Prior to the celebration of the Eucharist, an intriguing plan was arranged between the prioress and the young priest which would allow him to catch a glimpse of Sister Thérèse: "The last one who remains kneeling" (the sacristan—Thérèse), the prioress said, "for a moment at the communion window after all the nuns have received communion she is the one!" Thérèse immediately retorted with: "And the first one to receive communion, Father, is the prioress!"[61]

They also spoke about his forthcoming mission in south west China (Szechwan—*Su-Tchuen* in French). He gave Thérèse the book *The Su-Tchuen Mission*

---

58   LT 189, June 23, 1896.
59   LC 165 dated July 23, 1896.
60   Letter to Sister Geneviève, May 22, 1910.
61   Note 6 to LC 165 from Roulland to Thérèse on July 23, 1896.

in the 18th Century: The Life and Apostolate of Bishop Pottier by L. Guiot (Paris, 1892).[62] Thérèse's last words to the young priest which he never forgot were, *"Adieu, mon frère"* ("Good bye, my brother").

In her second letter to him dated seventeen days after this encounter,[63] she was happy to tell him that Mother de Gonzague:

> ... is allowing me to keep my brother's photograph [which he sent to the prioress on July 29, 1896]; this is a *very special* privilege.[64] A Carmelite does not even have the portraits of her closest relatives, but our Mother knows that your picture, far from reminding me of the world and earthly affections, will raise my soul to higher realms, and will make it forget itself for the glory of God and the salvation of souls. Thus, Brother, while I shall cross the ocean in your company, you will remain close to me, well hidden in our poor cell....
>
> All that is around me reminds me of you. I have attached the map of Su-Tchuen on the wall where I work, and the picture you gave me is resting always on my heart in the book of the Gospels which never leaves me.[65]

In this same letter Thérèse asked him to send her the principal dates of his life which he did under the title "Days of Graces granted by the Lord to His unworthy Missionary":

October 13, 1870	Birth at Cahagnolles
October 15, 1870	Baptism
July 3, 1881	First Communion
June 8, 1883	Confirmation
September 8, 1890	Vocation saved by Our Lady of Deliverance
October 1, 1890	Entrance into the Grand Seminary of Sommervieu
June 12, 1892	Entrance into the Seminary on the rue du Bac in Paris
June 29, 1892	Tonsure
September 24, 1894	Minor Orders
September 27, 1894	Subdiaconate
February 29, 1896	Diaconate
June 28, 1896	Ordination and apostolic union with Thérèse
[July 3, 1896	Mass at the Carmel of Lisieux (and interview with Thérèse and Mother Marie de Gonzague)]
July 9, 1896	Conversion of his father
August 2, 1896	Departure for China
August 2, 1896	First baptism of a pagan child and of a pagan adult

Before Father Roulland's departure for the Orient on August 2, 1896, Thérèse copied, at the end of a bound issue of Mother Geneviève's obituary circular, twelve of the poems she considered her best. These poems as they are numbered in *Œuvres Complètes* are: 3, 5, 15, 17, 20, 21, 22, 26, 30, 35, 44, and RP 39

---

62 She was photographed holding this book (VTL, #36) sometime in early July 1896.
63 LT 193, July 30, 1896.
64 She sent him a photo on July 27, 1897, showing her holding a rosary (VTL, #37).
65 It is a picture-souvenir of his ordination on which was written "Here below, let us work together—In heaven, we shall share the reward."

(a fragment). The poem "To Théophane Vénard" (PN 47) was sent in LT 221 at a later date—March 19, 1897. "To Our Lady of Victories: Queen of Virgins, Apostles, and Martyrs" (PN 35) dated July 16, 1896, was written especially for Father Roulland. Four of the twelve stanzas follow:

> ...
> You [Mary] have united me forever
> With the works of a Missionary,
> By the bonds of prayer,
> Suffering and love.
> ...
> He will cross the earth
> To preach the name of Jesus.
> I will practice humble virtues
> In the background and in mystery.
> ...
> Through Him, what a ravishing mystery,
> Even as far as East Szechuan
> I shall be able to make loved
> The virginal name of my tender Mother!
> ...
> Through Him, I'll be able to gather
> The palm for which my soul yearns.
> Oh what hope! Dear Mother,
> I shall be the sister of a Martyr!!!

During their correspondence which covered nearly fifteen months, they exchanged various mementos including books. Thérèse sent him a life of St. Teresa of Avila which he requested and he sent her *The Soul of a Missionary, Life of P. Nempon, Apostolic Missionary to Western Tonkin* by G. Monteuuis (3rd ed., Victor Retaux et Fils, Paris, 1895).[66] Thérèse explains one item she wanted from him in her third letter:

> You will perhaps find me really childish, but it does not matter. I confess that I committed a sin of envy when reading that your hair was going to be cut and replaced by a Chinese braid. It is not the latter I desire but very simply a little tress of the hair now become useless. You will no doubt ask me, laughing, what I will do with it? Well, it is very simple, this hair will be a *relic* for me when you will be in heaven, the palm of martyrdom in your hand. You find, no doubt, that I am going about this far in advance, but I know it is the only means of reaching my goal, for your little sister (who is known only as such by Jesus) will certainly be forgotten in the distribution of *your relics*. I am sure you are laughing at me, but this does not matter. If you consent to *pay* for the little amusement I am giving you with "the hair of a future Martyr," I shall be well recompensed.[67]

---

66 From Note 4, to LC 167, August 1, 1896.
67 LT 201, November 1, 1896.

In his letter of February 24, 1897, (LC 175) he did send her a clip of his hair which is preserved at the Carmel Archives along with the letter.

Despite her physical and mental anguish, Thérèse maintained her sense of humor and humanity. She had displayed the photos of her two spiritual brothers in the infirmary during her last days. Once when looking at their pictures she told her sister, "I'm much prettier than they are!" [68]

In one of her letters (LT 201), Thérèse tells Father Roulland about a special date of importance to her. He testified years later how that date was significant to him also:

> I am pleased to admit that I am somewhat indebted to her for my missionary vocation (PO, 1923). On September 8, 1890, I was having some hesitancy concerning my vocation and entrance into the Major Seminary. While I was praying in the chapel of Our Lady of Ransom, I suddenly and definitively came to a decision. I learned later that on the same September 8, 1890, the day of the Servant of God's Profession, she had asked Our Lord to give her the soul of a priest, and she pointed out the link between these two events (PA 2903).[69]

In the last letters to Thérèse, Father Roulland tells in great detail the story of his life in China: his sickness, difficulty with learning Chinese, travel hardships, conversions, persecution of Christians, famine, banditry, murder, etc. Despite all the trials, Thérèse managed to give him some comfort with her letters and prayers which he gratefully acknowledged. She reminded him of some of the sayings of Théophane Vénard: "The whole of a missionary's life is fruitful in the Cross," and then she quoted a line from one of his poems, "To be truly happy we must suffer, and to live we must die." [70]

Thérèse's last letter to him is quite prophetic:

> Ah! Brother, I feel it, I shall be more useful to you in heaven than on earth, and it is with joy that I come to announce to you my coming entrance into that blessed city.... I really count on not remaining inactive in heaven. My desire is to work still for the Church and for souls.... *Au revoir*, Brother; pray very much for your sister, pray for *our* Mother [Gonzague] whose sensitive and maternal heart has much difficulty in consenting to my departure. I count on you to console her.
>
> [Signed] *I am your little sister for eternity,*
> *Thérèse of the Child Jesus and of the Holy Face,*
> rel. carm. ind. (LT 254, July 14, 1897)

Father Roulland wrote not only to Thérèse but occasionally at the same time to the prioress relating to them the dangerous ventures he was experiencing in his ministry. Mother de Gonzague had extracts from these letters read to the community but edited them so as not to inform the nuns that they were sent to anyone other than to her, the prioress. He kept up a correspondence with

---

68 *Last Conversations*, July 30, 1897.
69 As quoted from note 3 to LT 201, from Thérèse to Roulland, dated November 1, 1896.
70 LT 226 from Thérèse to Roulland, dated May 9, 1897.

the Carmel well after Thérèse died, and was an important witness at the diocesan and apostolic inquiries that led to her beatification and canonization. He willingly presented all the evidence he knew of her sanctity and acknowledged that he continuously maintained a profound devotion to her.

Father Roulland was born on October 13, 1870, in Cahagnolles, a little village south of Bayeux. The full name given to him at baptism was Adolphe-Jean-Louis-Eugène Roulland, a son of Eugène Roulland and Marie Ledresseur. At twenty-two on October 1, 1892, he entered the Grand Seminary of the Foreign Mission Society in Paris located at 128 rue du Bac. He was ordained on June 28, 1896 and five weeks later on August 2, he left on his missionary assignment to China which at that time had a Catholic population of only 31,000 out of a total population of millions. It certainly was a dangerous place for foreigners. In fact, one of the seminarians ordained with Father Roulland, Father Mazel, who also accompanied him on his voyage to China, was murdered on April 1, 1897 at Lo-Ly in China. Persecution of Christians, famine, pillaging, and murder were common.[71]

It took Father Roulland a year of formation in the Yeou-Yang district to orientate himself to the new culture, mores, language, and missionary methods. The next year, 1898, he was in charge of the Leang-chan district. Following this, he was appointed professor at the seminary of Cha-pin-po where he distinguished himself as a splendid teacher and a person of dignity. Then in 1902 he headed the missionary district of Mao-pao-tchang.[72]

After thirteen years of missionary work in China and not having been martyred for his faith as he and Thérèse dreamed, he was recalled to Paris and given the post of director, and then procurator (bursar) at the Foreign Mission Society. In 1917 he refused out of humility an episcopal post for which his confreres at the seminary had voted him. He served as director of the novitiate of the Brothers of Dormans (northeast of Paris) and at the same time chaplain at the Convent of La Reconnaissance in Dormans where on June 12, 1934, at the age of sixty-four he died and was buried.

Below is a list of the dates and corresponding numbers assigned to the letters in *General Correspondence* exchanged between Sister Thérèse and Father Roulland:

LETTERS

THÉRÈSE'S
1. June 23, 1896 (LT 189)
2. July 30, 1896 (LT 193)
3. Nov. 1, 1896 (LT 201)
4. March 19, 1897 (LT 221)
5. May 9, 1897 (LT 226)
6. July 14, 1897 (LT 254)

ADOLPHE ROULLAND'S
1. July 23, 1896 (LC 165)
2. July 29, 1896 (LC 166)
3. August 1, 1896 (LC 167)
4. Sept. 25–26, 1896 (LC 171)
5. Jan. 20, 1897 (LC 173)
6. Feb. 24, 1897 (LC 175)
7. April 29, 1897 (LC 178)
8. Sept. 13, 1897 (LC 200)

---

71 Facts in this paragraph are from *Thérèse de Lisieux et Ses Frères Missionnaires*, pp. 30–34.
72 Ibid.

8. Frère Salutaire, F.S.C. (1821–1907)
Thérèse never answered his request

BROTHER (FRÈRE) SALUTAIRE WAS A MEMBER OF THE BROTHERS OF THE Christian Schools (*Frères des Ecoles Chrétiennes, F.S.C.*), a religious community commonly called Christian Brothers. He, a colleague of Brother Siméon—a longtime friend of the Carmel and of Louis Martin—was stationed at the College of St. Joseph, the school Brother Siméon helped found in Rome. Céline sent some of Thérèse's poems to Brother Siméon on February 1, 1897. The seventy-six-year old Brother Salutaire, a poet himself, also read them and decided to write to Thérèse asking a favor of her. He had written a book entitled *Mes Dévotions* (My Devotions), a collection of his own poems published in Rome in 1896. In his only letter to her dated "Rome, March 16, 1897," he asked Thérèse if she would write some laudatory comments about his work in a circular to be used advertising his book. A few excerpts from his unique letter clearly indicate his *modus operandi*. He begins with: "I come to give you a surprise [his book of poems], will you be pleased? I want you to be pleased. Your goodness makes me hope so." He proceeds by proposing that she use specific words, phrases, and sentences in her commendatory article:

> [You] are called by the beautiful name of Thérèse of the Child Jesus. It is important that people perceive this in your letter.... Jesus of Thérèse will be pleased with you.... Jesus, that is your theme.... Jesus, how much this name appears in the greatest part of my book. You will have noticed this easily. Now you are doing the talking: I have read with real interest the delightful book *Mes Dévotions* with which you have recently enriched the collection of pious manuals.... I must congratulate you on a work so suitable for preserving the precious seeds that a Christian education has sown in the impressionable heart of the child. It is not possible to single out or to analyze in so many beautiful pages the aspirations of love, the delightful tenderness of a soul for its God. What a holy inspiration are your pious affections on the Life of Jesus!... To know Jesus, to love Him, this is Religion.... This Life of Jesus! So compact, so well divided, with its little stanzas that are so easy to learn and to retain, is not all this simply an affectionate prayer in which the soul wills to remind the Divine Master of all He designed to do and suffer for it?[73]

He apologizes for being rather prescriptive yet continues in his fawning manner:

> I am not, however, imposing myself on you.... I have perhaps acted too quickly; you will please excuse me. You are so good, so indulgent! I dared too much! I imposed too much on your kindness....
>
> And if you judge it fitting, you begin immediately after the letter at the bottom of page three what I am suggesting to you, which you will send me as soon as possible. When sending your letter, you will thank me for the good and excellent news I gave you on Brother Siméon's health, etc.... I have entered

---
[73] LC 176, March 16, 1897.

into these details of arrangement to lighten the burden I am giving you and to lessen my mistakes.... If I am rushing you a little it is because I am in a hurry to print the circular in question.... I am dealing with a generous heart, devoted to Jesus ... a heart whose throbs charm her readers.

Perhaps because of his sycophantic approach, Thérèse never responded; or it may be that it was Lent and no correspondence was permitted. At any rate, there is no evidence Thérèse answered his letter. Céline, however, did respond in a letter dated April 25 to the one Brother Siméon sent her dated March 5 that may serve as an oblique way of answering Brother Salutaire's requests. "Thank you, very dear Brother Siméon for all you sent us, including *Mes Dévotions*; we cannot grow tired of reading and meditating on *all* that comes from Rome. Please accept ... the most affectionate regards from your two little Carmelites."[74]

It should be noted here that seven years before this incident, Thérèse wrote a letter (now lost) to Brother Siméon asking him to obtain an Apostolic Blessing for her religious profession (September 8, 1890) and for her father's health. Brother Siméon replied on August 31, 1890, with a letter and the text of the Apostolic Blessing. The actual wording of the blessing is believed to have been composed by Brother Salutaire:

Most Holy Father,

Sister Thérèse of the Child Jesus, Carmelite religious of Lisieux, prostrate at the feet of Your Holiness, humbly begs Your Apostolic Blessing for her religious Profession; she begs it, too, for her venerable Father, the saintly old man, tired by suffering.

And may Your Holiness, etc.
Romae e Secretaria Status, Die 29, Augusti 1890
SSmus D.N. Leo P.P. XIII benigne annuity pro gratia
† *Marius Mocenni Archiep. Aeliopolis*
Substitut. Secr. Stat.[75]

Brother Salutaire was born Barthélemi Avinens on January 30, 1821, in Viols-le-Fort, a town northwest of Montpellier (southern France) in the Department of Hérault. He entered the order of the Brothers of the Christian Schools in 1834 and was eventually assigned to teach in France and later at St. Joseph College in Rome where he taught for twenty-two years. He also conducted some evening classes in French to the members of the high society of Turin during the years 1845 to 1853. His character was described in a biographical notice in 1897 when he was seventy-six as a "lovable and jovial old man. Rarely a harsh or critical word, no sign of impatience, but a man with a happy propensity for the compliment, the expression of which was almost too familiar."[76]

He succumbed at the age of eighty-six in Rome on June 23, 1907.

---

74 Note 8, Brother Salutaire's letter to Thérèse (LC 176) in *General Correspondence*, vol. II, p. 1068.
75 LC 134 bis, from the letter by Brother Siméon to Thérèse, dated August 31, 1890.
76 Note 1, p. 1067, Brother Salutaire's letter to Thérèse (LC 176) dated March 16, 1897.

9. Frère Siméon, F.S.C. (1814–1899)
Friend of the Martins in Rome

The congregation of the brothers of the christian schools was founded in 1680 by St. John Baptist de la Salle, a priest in Rheims, France. Thérèse's father Louis Martin and his brother-in-law Isidore Guérin were benefactors of a school the Christian Brothers established in Lisieux in 1876. They also had schools in Alençon which Louis might have attended. It was through them that Louis knew Brother (Frère) Siméon. Louis sometimes spoke to his daughters about these teachers and certainly the girls at the Benedictine Abbey School which Thérèse attended must have had friends or relations as students of the Brothers. Isidore on occasions would speak there at the distribution of prizes which he did on July 28, 1894, the day Louis had a fatal heart attack.

Louis Martin visited Rome twice and each time paid a visit to Brother Siméon, one of the founders of the College of St. Joseph (a high school) in 1851, and who two years later became its director. Through his connections with the Vatican, he aided many of his fellow Frenchmen with their spiritual and other problems.

M. Martin's travel companion on his first trip to Rome and visit with Brother Siméon in the late summer of 1885 was Abbé Charles Marie, curate of his parish church of Saint Jacques in Lisieux. After considerable urgings, the abbé finally persuaded Louis to accompany him on this extensive European tour away from his beloved daughters who were then left in the care of their aunt and uncle.

Louis's second trip to Rome, this time on an actual pilgrimage, took place two years later in November 1887 and lasted twenty-nine days. On this occasion his companions included his two daughters Céline and Thérèse whose basic purpose was to plead Thérèse's case before the pope for his permission to allow her to enter Carmel at the uncustomary age of fifteen. They joined a large group of pilgrims going to Rome to celebrate Pope Leo XIII's fiftieth anniversary of ordination to the priesthood. Thérèse noted in her autobiography that while she and her sister Céline went on a side trip to Naples and Pompeii with a tour group, her father visited the seventy-three-year-old Brother Siméon:

> A few days after the audience with the Holy Father, Papa, having gone to see good Brother Siméon, found Father Révérony there, who was very friendly. Papa chided him gaily for not having aided me in my *difficult undertaking*, then he told his Queen's [Thérèse's] story to Brother Siméon. The venerable old man listened to his recital with much interest even took down notes, and said with emotion: "One doesn't see this in Italy!" I believe this interview made a good impression on Father Révérony; afterwards he never ceased proving to me that he was *finally* convinced of my vocation.[77]

Later in her autobiography Thérèse recorded: "A few days before my profession [September 8, 1890], I had the happiness of receiving the sovereign Pontiff's blessing. I had requested it through good Brother Siméon for both Papa and

---
77 *Story of a Soul*, chapter VI, p. 136.

myself, and it was a great consolation to be able to return to my dear little Father the grace he obtained for me when taking me with him to Rome."[78] Thérèse's letter of request does not exist but Brother Siméon's reply does:

> My very dear Sister,
>
> I just received the Apostolic Blessing which, upon your request, I asked for both you and Monsieur, your holy and Venerable Father....
>
> Beg Monsieur, your Venerable Father, to accept my respectful wishes, and tell him how much I share in his sufferings. Heaven will be the reward for these.[79]

Included was the text of the Apostolic Blessing which, it is believed, was most likely composed by Brother Salutaire, a colleague of Brother Siméon:

> Most Holy Father,
>
> Sister Thérèse of the Child Jesus, Carmelite religious of Lisieux, prostrate at the feet of Your Holiness, humbly begs Your Apostolic Blessing for her religious Profession; she begs it, too for her venerable father, the saintly old man, tried by suffering.
>
> And may Your Holiness, etc.
> *Romae e Secretaria Status, Die 29 Augusti 1890*
> *SSmus D.N. Leo P.P. XIII benigne annuity pro gratia*
> *† Marius Mocenni Archiep. Aeopolis*
> *Substitut. Secr. Stat.*[80]

Thérèse's sister Céline, and even Mother Gonzague carried on a friendly correspondence with Brother Siméon. They would seek favors of him and he in turn wanted some in return. In January of 1897, Celine asked Brother Siméon if he could acquire from Rome a special photograph for her:

> We [Céline and Thérèse] brought back from Rome a great devotion to St. Cecilia, and we remember a painting placed, I believe, near the room of the baths where she offered martyrdom. This painting represents an angel crowning Cecilia and Valerian with lilies and roses. It struck us very deeply, and it would be a sweet consolation for us to have a photograph of this painting; it exists, for we remember having seen it. Since then we have tried to get it; we have even written to the religious of the Convent, guardians of the tomb, but they did not answer. Then we thought that it would be only through a friend that this consolation could be given to us.... I am sending in this letter a set of verses composed by her [Thérèse]; this is only one flower detached from the beautiful bouquet that she is leaving to her religious family.[81]

Céline sent him a month later a photo of one of her paintings of the Baby Jesus as well as poems by Thérèse.[82] For her profession on February 24, 1896,

---

78 Ibid., chapter VIII, pp. 165–166.
79 LC 134, from Brother Siméon to Thérèse, dated August 31, 1890.
80 LC 134 bis.
81 From a letter dated January 10, 1897, written by Sister Geneviève to Brother Siméon.
82 See letter of Sister Geneviève to Brother Siméon, dated February 11, 1897, part of which is quoted on p. 1271 in *General Correspondence, Vol. 2*.

Céline also desired a papal blessing like the one Thérèse received, so she requested Brother Siméon to procure one for her. A year later, she asked the same for Sister Stanislas's golden jubilee:

> You may rest assured that your little Carmel of Lisieux thinks of you most dearly ... we remember good Brother Siméon, our father's friend, and both of us my sister Theresa [sic] of the Child Jesus and myself are quite proud to know you. We both try to become saints and we should like very much to be soon in heaven. She is well on the way thither, she is an angel. Love consumes her life. I send you a short poem which she wrote herself. It is her favorite and her most beautiful poem: "Living for love." [83]

Brother Siméon's answer included this comment:

> I have just read again the wonderful poem of your admirable sister. It is a sublime canticle which could have been found on the lips of the great Saint Teresa. My brothers vie with one another to have it and write it out for themselves. Our Holy Father Pope Leo XIII is enjoying perfect health; his secretary, a very close friend of mine, admires him.... Tell your holy sister I wish her the best of health.[84]

On January 27, 1897, just eight months before she died, Thérèse thanked Brother Siméon in a letter addressed to him at the College of Saint Joseph on the Piazza di Spagna, Rome:

> I am happy to join with my Sister Geneviève in thanking you for the precious favor you obtained for our Carmel.
> Not knowing how to express my gratitude, I want to show you how much I was touched by your kindness to us by means of my prayers at Our Lord's feet. A feeling of sadness is mingled with my joy when learning your health was impaired, so I am asking Jesus with my whole heart to prolong which is so precious for the Church the longest time possible. I know the divine Master must be eager to crown you in heaven, but I trust He will leave you still in exile so that, working for His glory as you have done since your youth, the immense weight of your merits may supply for other souls who will present themselves before God with empty hands.
> I dare to hope, very dear Brother, I shall be of the number of these blessed souls who will share in your merits. I believe my course here below will not be long ... when I shall appear before my Beloved spouse, I shall have only my desires to offer Him, but if you have preceded me into the homeland, I trust you will come to meet me and offer for me the merits of your very fruitful works.... You see, your little Carmelites cannot write you without asking some favor and without making an appeal to your generosity!!! ...
> *Monsieur le Directeur*, you are so *powerful* for *us* on earth, you have already obtained our Holy Father Leo XIII's blessing for us so many times that I cannot refrain from thinking that in heaven God will give you a very great power over

---

83 *Bulletin des F.E.C*, no. 211–212, December 1973.
84 Ibid.

His Heart. I beg you not to forget me in His presence if you have the joy of seeing Him before I do.... The only thing I beg you to ask for my soul is the grace of *loving* Jesus and of *making Him loved* as much as this is possible for me.

If it be myself whom the Lord comes to look for first, I promise to pray for your intentions and for all the persons who are dear to you.[85]

Céline with a heavy heart, petitioned a somber favor of Brother Siméon: to obtain an Apostolic Benediction and the indulgence "*in articulo mortis*" ["on the brink of death"]: "Our dear little sister Thérèse is going to breathe her last ... she is going away slowly.... Her illness is love.... She is actually dying of love, which she had yearned for so much."[86] He in turn wrote five days later:

> The sad news your letter brings me on the sad condition of your admirable sister is sorrowful and consoling. To die from love of Jesus, who died out of love for us, what is more sublime, more heroic, more worthy of envy!! I am praying and having others pray, however, that God preserve her and cure her for your consolation and the glory of your Lisieux Carmel.
>
> The Holy Father is not receiving at the moment; we are having suffocating heat and can hardly breathe. I asked for the Apostolic Blessing and the Indulgence *in articulo mortis* for your holy sister. The Holy Father granted all. It was through the intervention of the Prelate, his secretary, that the favor arrived just now.[87]

The report of Thérèse's passing arrived in a letter dated October 10, 1897—eleven days after she died.

A year after Thérèse's demise, 2,000 copies of her autobiography *Story of a Soul* were published. On October 4, 1898, Céline sent Brother Siméon three copies of it. One was for him who after reading it, notified her he was sure it would help many spiritually. He added that many of his fellow brothers were anxious to read it also. The second copy was for Brother Siméon's friend, the private secretary of the Holy Father. Brother Siméon asked him, as Céline wished, to give his opinion of the book in writing. The third copy was for Pope Leo XIII to bless and return to the Carmel which he did on November 6, 1898. One month later Brother Siméon died at eighty-five in Rome on January 4, 1899, two years after Thérèse's death.

Throughout the years there has been a depth of spiritual kinship expressed through correspondence between the Carmelites of Lisieux and the Brothers of the Christian Schools about which the Brothers are duly proud.

Charles-Joseph Perrier, Brother Siméon's name before he entered religion, was born in 1814 at Bourg-Saint-Andéol, in the Department of Ardèch, north of Avignon. He became a religious at age fifteen, the age Thérèse wished to enter Carmel but at first was not allowed; this was substantially because her order, unlike his, was extremely austere and deeply contemplative. On February 25,

---
85 LT 218, the only letter she wrote to him.
86 July 7, 1897.
87 Letter of July 12, 1897, from Brother Siméon to Sister Geneviève.

1830, he became a novice of the Brothers of the Christian Schools in the Christian Brothers house in Avignon, less than forty miles from his birthplace, and professed his final vows nine years later. He taught school in Béziers (near the western end of the French Riviera) with great success and later went to Rome where he helped found the French School for sons of French officers, diplomats, and upper class children. Later Italian children were admitted.

10. Abbé Paul Troude (1873–1900)
Gave Communion to the dying Thérèse

THÉRÈSE'S "SPIRITUAL BROTHER," MAURICE BELLIÈRE, INFORMED HER BY letter that "tomorrow, Sister, I shall closely be united with you and your community, especially in the Holy Communion that I shall receive with this intention. One of my friends, a newly ordained priest, my companion for several years [Abbé Troude], will sing your solemn Mass. He will be very blessed."[88] On July 16, 1897, Abbé Paul Troude gave Communion to Thérèse in the infirmary which happened to be the feast of Our Lady of Mount Carmel—a preeminent day for the Carmelites. Sister Marie-Philomène, a nun with Sister Thérèse at the Lisieux Carmel, was Abbé Troude's aunt.

Mother Agnès of Jesus, Thérèse's oldest sister Pauline, recorded the day before the Mass the following entry in the *Yellow Notebook*:

> We had made preparations for her to receive Holy Communion the next day from Sister M. Philomena's nephew who was coming to celebrate his first Mass at the Carmel and to bring her Communion afterwards. Seeing that she was sicker than usual, we feared she would cough up blood after midnight, and so we asked her to pray that no such unfortunate incident take place to interfere with our plans. She answered:
>
> "You know well that I cannot ask this myself, but you ask it for me.... This evening, in spite of my feelings, I was asking God for this favor in order to please my little sisters and so that the community might not be disappointed; but in my heart I told Him just the contrary; I told Him to do just what He wanted."[89]

The next day Thérèse described in her poignant last letter to her beloved Aunt and Uncle Guérin what had transpired:

> I would like, dear Relatives, to speak to you in detail of my Holy Communion this morning which you made so touching or rather so triumphant by your bundles of flowers. I am allowing dear little Marie of the Eucharist [their daughter Marie, Thérèse's cousin] to tell you all the details, and I want only to tell you that she sang, before Communion, a little couplet that I had composed for this morning. When Jesus was in my heart, she sang this couplet from *"Vivre d'Amour"*: "To die by love is a very sweet martyrdom." I cannot express to you how high and beautiful her voice was; she had promised me not to cry in order to please me, and my hopes were surpassed. Good Jesus must have

---

[88] LC 188, July 15, 1897.
[89] *Her Last Conversations*, July 15, 1897.

heard and understood perfectly what I expect from Him, and it was exactly what I wanted![90]

After the Mass in the Carmel chapel, Abbé Troude went in a solemn procession with the community through the flower bedecked corridors strewn especially with rose petals to bring Holy Communion to Thérèse in the infirmary.

A month later, Abbé Bellière wrote to Mother Gonzague:

> The sacrifice of a dear victim is then close to completion. What sorrow for a human creature whose angel guardian this dear soul was, and nevertheless what a consolation to know such a friend in heaven.
>
> In two days, I am going to Lourdes. I don't know what I must ask from the Queen of Miracles—the cure of this dear saint or her prompt union with Jesus.... Do you know, Mother, that my good confrere, l'Abbé Troude, was blest, I envied him in a singular way.... I trust that his joy of July 16 will one day be granted to me. Alas! the dear Sister whom Jesus has given to me will no longer be there. Mother! Oh, you will be there still and in spite of the absent one I shall still be blest.[91]

Thérèse went to her glorious reward on September 30, 1897, forty-five days after the above letter was written.

Paul-François Troude was born on January 30, 1873 (twenty-eight days after Thérèse) in Langrune, the same town where Maurice Bellière lived. He was ordained on June 29, 1897. Sadly, he lived less than three years longer than she did, dying at twenty-seven in March 1900.

---

90 LT 255, July 15, 1897.
91 Letter from Father Bellière to Mother Marie de Gonzague dated August 17, 1897.

CHAPTER 6

SAINTS AND "SINNERS"

INTRODUCTION
A. SAINTS
1. ANGELS: *Heavenly spirits, messengers of God*
2. THE BLESSED VIRGIN MARY: *Mother of Jesus Christ*
3. CARMELITE MARTYRS OF COMPIÈGNE: *16 nuns guillotined during the French Revolution*
4. LÉON DUPONT: *Layman who promoted devotion to the Holy Face of Christ*
5. PÈRE MAZEL: *Young missionary murdered in China*
6. SAINT AGNES: *A martyred Roman teenager, patroness of chastity*
7. SAINT ALOYSIUS GONZAGA: *Jesuit seminarian who died at 23, patron of youth*
8. SAINT CECILIA: *Virgin martyr of Rome: patroness of music*
9. SAINT JOAN OF ARC: *French heroine burned as a heretic*
10. SAINT JOHN OF THE CROSS: *Spanish Carmelite, writer, mystic, reformer, and Doctor of the Church*
11. SAINT MARY MAGDALENE: *Former sinner who followed Jesus*
12. SAINT SEBASTIAN: *Christian Roman soldier martyred for his faith*
13. SAINT STANISLAS KOSTKA: *Jesuit seminarian who died at 18*
14. SAINT TERESA OF AVILA: *Spanish Carmelite, mystic, writer, reformer of her Order, and Doctor of the Church*
15. SAINT THÉOPHANE VÉNARD: *Thérèse's favorite male saint martyred in Vietnam*
B. SINNERS
1. HENRI CHÉRON: *Once a family friend who became an anti-Catholic government official*
2. PÈRE LOYSON: *Contemporary apostate Carmelite priest*
3. HENRI PRANZINI: *Thérèse prayed for this murderer's repentance*
4. LÉO TAXIL: *Created the fictitious Diana Vaughan, an anti-Catholic hoax*
5. RENÉ TOSTAIN: *An atheist relative of Thérèse*

Introduction

All the saints are our relatives.[1] — St. Thérèse
During my short life I want / To save my fellow sinners.[2] — St. Thérèse

THÉRÈSE ADMIRED THE SAINTS AND CONSIDERED THEM HER HEAVENLY relations. The Blessed Virgin Mary headed the long list of favorites. Almost on a par with her was St. Joseph. Though she loved him tenderly, Thérèse does not mention him nearly as many times in her writings as she does his spouse Mary. A month before she met the two of them in heaven she uttered these tender words: "Good St. Joseph! Oh! How I love him."[3] She was secure with the feeling that he was always her protector particularly on her pilgrimage to Rome. Céline says that Thérèse did not fear anything regarding purity that she might see on this journey because she recited daily this short invocation, "St. Joseph, father and protector of virgins."[4] She even prayed to him for the privilege of receiving communion more often which did come about through the encyclical *Mirae Caritatis* of Pope Leo XIII on May 28, 1902, the vigil of the Solemnity of Corpus Christi. In this the pope stated that "the chief aim of our efforts must be that the frequent reception of the Eucharist may be everywhere revived among Catholic peoples.... For the soul, like the body, needs frequent nourishment, and the holy Eucharist provides that food...." She was convinced this would be accomplished through the intercession of St. Joseph.[5] Thérèse's poem "To Our Father Saint Joseph" (PN 14) was written in his honor. In it she asks that "Joseph, O tender Father, / Protect Carmel." He also appears as a leading character in her recreational play *The Flight into Egypt* (RP 6). Finally, this winsome little anecdote which Pauline recorded in her *Yellow Notebook* discloses Thérèse's fondness for Saint Joseph:

> She [Thérèse] had cast some flowers at a statue of St. Joseph which was in the garden at the end of the chestnut walk, saying in a childish tone of voice: "Take them!"
> I asked: "Why are you throwing flowers at St. Joseph? To obtain a special favor?"
> "Ah, no! It's just to please him; I don't want to give in order to receive."[6]

Besides the intimate circle of her special heavenly friends, those simple, humble, young saints Thérèse especially loved—Saints Cecilia, Agnes, Vénard, Joan of Arc—there were the Holy Innocents, St. Martin, St. Francis de Sales, St. Francis, and others. All in all, the Communion of Saints was a church dogma

---

1 *Her Last Conversations*, July 13, 1897.
2 "To My Guardian Angel," PN 46.
3 *Her Last Conversations*, August 20, 1897.
4 *Story of a Soul*, chapter VII, p. 124.
5 Sister Geneviève's testimony at the Diocesan Process of 1910.
6 On June 11, 1897, which is now part of *Her Last Conversations*.

Plate 14
One Saint and Five "Sinners"

A. Saint Théophane Vénard

B. Henri Chéron

C. Hyacinthe Loyson

D. Henri Pranzini

E. Léo Taxil

F. René Tostain

Thérèse firmly believed in throughout her life. These six quintessential Theresian quotations, both serious and whimsical, from her fertile mind pertain to saints:

- I love the reading of the lives of the saints very much, the account of their heroic deeds sets my courage on fire and attracts me to imitate them; but I admit that, at times, I happen to envy the blessed lot of their relatives who had the joy of living in their company and of enjoying their conversations.[7]

---

7 LT 178 written by Thérèse to her aunt Mme. Guérin and dated July 20–21, 1895.

- If the saints show me less affection than my sisters have shown me, this will appear very hard for me ... and I'll go and cry in a little corner.[8]
- Someone had given her [Thérèse] a fan from the Carmel of Saigon; she used it to shoo away the flies. When it became very hot, she began fanning her holy pictures pinned to her bed curtains, and she fanned us [the nuns at her bedside], too: "I'm fanning the saints instead of myself; I'm fanning you to do you some good because you, too, are saints!"[9]
- I pray often to the saints without receiving any answers; but the more deaf they are to my prayers, the more I love them.[10]
- The saints encourage me, too, in my prison [the convent]. They tell me: As long as you are in irons, you cannot carry out your mission; but later on, after your death, this will be the time for your works and your conquests.[11]
- Were some of the saints to return to earth, I wonder how many would recognize themselves when reading what has been written about them.[12]

One other serious concern in Thérèse's life was for sinners. Before she even entered Carmel, she had a strong desire to save sinners. On Christmas Day in 1886 when she was thirteen years old she underwent a "conversion" which meant the grace of leaving childhood. She says in her autobiography that Jesus:

> ... made me a fisher of *souls*. I experienced a great desire to work for the conversion of sinners, a desire I hadn't felt so intensely before.... The cry of Jesus on the Cross sounded continually in my heart: "I *thirst!*" These words ignited within me an unknown and very living fire. I wanted to give my Beloved to drink and I felt myself consumed with a *thirst for souls*. As yet, it was not the souls of priests that attracted me, but those of *great sinners*; I burned with the desire to snatch them from the eternal flames.[13]

The first sinner she prayed for and believed was saved through her petitions was Henri Pranzini, the criminal who had murdered two women and a girl in Paris on March 19, 1887, and was executed for this crime within six months.

On her deathbed Thérèse prayed for the five "sinners," all contemporaries, she was most concerned with: the murderer Pranzini, the apostate priest Father Loyson, the grand hoaxer Leo Taxil, the atheist family member Tostain, and the anti-Catholic Chéron. She sums up her simple prayer for sinners in perhaps her best poem "Living on Love!" (PN 17):

> Living on Love is wiping your Face,
> It's obtaining the pardon of sinners.
> O God of Love! May they return to your grace,
> And may they forever bless your Name....

---

8 *Her Last Conversations*, May 1897.
9 Ibid., July 30, 1897.
10 Ibid., August 11, 1897.
11 Ibid., August 10, 1897.
12 Sister Geneviève, *A Memoir of My Sister St. Thérèse*, p. 208.
13 *Story of a Soul*, chapter V, p. 99.

A. Saints

1. Angels
Heavenly spirits, messengers of God

> *I presented myself before the angels and saints and said to them: I am the smallest of creatures; I know my misery and my feebleness, but I know also how much noble and generous hearts love to do good. I beg you then, O Blessed Inhabitants of heaven, I beg you to* ADOPT ME AS YOUR CHILD. *To you alone will be the glory which you will make me merit.*[1]
>
> — St. Thérèse

THÉRÈSE CERTAINLY MERITED GLORY, THE GLORY OF SAINTHOOD. THE POWER of angels—those supernatural beings that she strongly believed in from her earliest days until her very last moments on earth—must have had a great deal to do with it. She tells us about her interest in them even when she was a school girl:

> Almost immediately after my entrance at the abbey, I was received into the Association of the Holy Angels. I loved the pious practices it imposed, as I had a very special attraction to pray to the blessed spirits of heaven, particularly to the one whom God gave as the companion of my exile. A short time after my First Communion, the ribbon of the aspirant to the Children of Mary replaced that of the Holy Angels.[2]

She was not unique in her belief in angels. The existence of angels was a tenet of the faith accepted and unquestioned by the faithful in Thérèse's day and for centuries before. Scripture alone mentions "angels" almost 300 times but specifies only three by name—Michael, Raphael, and Gabriel—all of them archangels. Thérèse herself refers to them countless times in her writings and conversations. She was intrigued by their being, knowledge, nearness to God, protection, and intercession.

The Church and Scripture describe them as spiritual, genderless, non-corporeal beings who praise, serve, and act as God's messengers. The Bible mentions nine choirs of angels, each group having specific duties: seraphim, cherubim, thrones, dominions, virtues, powers, principalities, archangels, and angels. They possess intelligence and will and constantly behold the face of God in Heaven. From creation onward throughout Biblical times and beyond they have been mentioned and reported to have appeared to and/or assisted Old and New Testament figures. They accompanied Christ in His earthly life, assisted many saintly individuals throughout Church history, and are invoked daily in the liturgy and life of the Church.

Thérèse was aware of the characteristics of angels, their duties, qualities, etc. All of this she acknowledged and from which she found solace and inspiration.

---
[1] *Story of a Soul*, chapter X, p. 195–196.
[2] Ibid., chapter IV, p. 86.

She, however, seemed to concentrate on the purely personal aspects of angels. In this passage she reveals her profound understanding of the angels: "Our Beloved [Jesus] has no need of our beautiful thoughts and our dazzling works. If He wants sublime thoughts, does He not have His angels, His legions of heavenly spirits whose knowledge infinitely surpasses that of the greatest geniuses of our sad earth?"[3]

While she was in the infirmary dying from tuberculosis she would often comment in her own whimsical way about angels to her sisters which are recorded in *Her Last Conversations*:

- This is what happened: when I was about to die, the little angels made all sorts of beautiful preparations to receive me; but they got tired and fell asleep.[4]
- The little angels amused themselves very much by playing little tricks on me. They all tried to hide from me the light which was showing me my approaching end.[5]
- Yes, I want to spend my heaven in doing good on earth. This isn't impossible, since from the bosom of the beatific vision, the angels watch over us.[6]
- [Someone suggested a rather noisy distraction to which Thérèse answered with a smile:] No little boys' games! No little girls' games either! Just the games of little angels.[7]
- All these images [of angels] do me no good; I can nourish myself on nothing but the truth. This is why I've never wanted any visions. We can't see, here on earth, heaven, the angels, etc., just as they are. I prefer to wait until after my death.[8]
- The angels can't suffer; therefore, they are not as fortunate as I am. How astonished they would be if they suffered and felt what I feel! Yes, they'd be very surprised because so am I myself.[9]
- [When she was told that after she died she would go to heaven among the Seraphim, Thérèse replied] Ah! But if I go among the Seraphim, I shall not do as they do! All of them cover themselves with their wings before God; I will be very careful not to cover myself with my wings.[10]
- Soon I shall speak only the language of the angels.[11] (She died six days later.)

Besides "angels" in general, Thérèse mentions cherubs, seraphim, archangels, and guardian angels. She sometimes coupled angels with saints in her allusions to them:

- God reminded me of the caresses He will bestow upon me in the presence of the angels and saints.[12]

---

3 LT 141, April 1893.
4 June 29, 1897.
5 July 8, 1897.
6 July 17, 1897.
7 July 25, 1897.
8 August 5, 1897.
9 August 16, 1897.
10 September 14, 1897.
11 September 24, 1897.
12 *Story of a Soul*, chapter VII, p. 156.

- I shall carry your messages faithfully to the Lord, to our Immaculate Mother, to the angels, and to the saints whom you love. I will ask the palm of martyrdom for you, and I shall be near you holding your hand.[13]

Many times Thérèse referred to her family members as angels though she usually classified her parents as "saints." Thérèse of course knew the distinction between angels and humans who died as infants or saints in heaven but she used the generic, affectionate, and symbolic meaning of "angel" when referring to living beings. She often called her deceased siblings "cherubs" or "little angels"; and her cousins or aunt "angels." Interestingly, when Thérèse was twelve[14] she wrote a letter to her father away on a tourist trip to the Balkans and included a poem written by her sister Pauline in which she fancied what she would do if she were an angel:

> If I were a beautiful Archangel
> With wings all garnished in gold
> Papa, if I were a little angel
> Towards you I'd take my flight.
> ...
> If you wanted white wings
> I'd bring you some from heaven
> And toward the eternal shores
> Both of us would fly.
> But I haven't any wings that shine
> I am not a Seraph
> I am only a little girl
> Whom you still hold by the hand.[15]

Her sister Pauline (Mother Agnès) was certainly an angel in Thérèse's eyes. In fact she wrote a poem (PN 22) for Pauline's thirty-fourth birthday entitled "To My Dear Mother, The Fair Angel of My Childhood." In it she gives an account of Pauline's life and the relationship she had with her:

> This fair Angel guides my steps.
> ...
> This fair Angel, O dear Mother!
> Sang by my cradle.
> ...
> O deep mystery! This fair Angel
> Called me her baby sister....
> ...
> One day the fair Angel,
> Seeking the Virgins' procession,
> Took her flight toward Carmel!

---

13 From the last letter, LT 253, that Thérèse wrote on July 14, 1897, to her spiritual brother, Father Roulland, in anticipation of her own death.
14 LT 18, August 25, 1885.
15 These are 3 of the 14 stanzas from the poem Pauline composed that Thérèse copied and would have read to her father if he were home on his feast day.

...
Jesus granted my desires.
Near my fair Angel in Carmel
I look forward to nothing but Heaven!...

Thérèse's sister Céline did not escape being called an angel. Below is an excerpt from a letter Thérèse wrote to Céline on her birthday when she was at home caring for their father:

> Dear Céline, you who used to ask me so many questions when we were little, I wonder how it happened that you had never asked me this question: "Why did God not create me an angel?" Ah, Céline, I shall tell you what I think. If Jesus did not create you an angel in heaven, it is because He wants you to be an angel on earth; yes, Jesus wants to have His heavenly court here below just as up above! He wants angel-martyrs, He wants angel-apostles, and He has created a little unknown flower, who is named Céline, with this intention in mind. He wills that His little flower save souls for Him; for this, He wills only one thing: that His flower look at Him while suffering her martyrdom....[16]

Just about a month after she entered Carmel, Thérèse jotted down these tender words to her oldest sister Marie (Sister Marie of the Sacred Heart) who was in the same monastery with her: "If you only knew how much I love you. When I meet you, it seems to me you are an angel."[17]

Thérèse's guardian angel was very real and important to her. In "To My Guardian Angel" (PN 46) she informs us that he/she leads her by the hand, is the "Glorious Guardian" of her soul, invites her "to look only at Heaven," and gives her "holy fervor." In Prayer 5 she wrote a number of pious aspirations one of which is: "O my Holy Guardian Angel! Cover me always with your wings so that I may never have the misfortune to offend Jesus."

Of the eight plays Thérèse composed for presentation during recreation periods on holidays or anniversaries at the Carmel, all but one (RP 4—*Jesus at Bethany*) have angels in speaking or singing parts; however, angels are mentioned here two times. Two plays deal with one of Thérèse's favorite saints, Joan of Arc. In the first one entitled *The Mission of Joan of Arc* (RP 1) St. Michael the Archangel is one of the leading characters. In the sequel to this play, *Joan of Arc Accomplishing Her Mission* (RP 3), both the Archangels, St. Michael and St. Gabriel, appear.

The two Christmas plays feature angels prominently, notably *The Angels at the Crib of Jesus* (RP 2) where practically all the characters are angels: The Angel of the Infant Jesus, The Angel of the Holy Face, The Angel of the Resurrection, The Angel of the Eucharist, and The Angel of the Last Judgment. The other work, *The Divine Little Beggar at Christmas* (RP 5) is not quite a play but a recitation (or more precisely, a singing) of twenty-six short poems. Each nun chose one from a basket and handed it to the Angel, a novice, who sang it. The

---
16 LT 127, April 26, 1891.
17 LT 49, May 12–20, 1888.

overall theme, typical of Thérèse, is an exhortation to the nuns and others to offer their lives to Jesus for the salvation of other people.

In *The Flight into Egypt* (RP 6) an Angel urges the Holy Family to flee into Egypt and at the end of the play she sings a rather long hymn extolling the value of poverty, the hidden life, and the mercy of God.

St. Michael the Archangel and Lucifer engage in verbal exchanges in *The Triumph of Humility* (RP 7) and angel voices sing the victorious final lines in which Thérèse hails Carmelite nuns with these words: "You are, you are the sisters of angels / O Virgins of Carmel." [18]

The last play is *Saint Stanislas Kostka* (RP 8) in which there is a short scene where the celestial voice of an angel is heard singing.

Thérèse showed a great interest in art and displayed a certain degree of talent in that field. Angels are featured in a few of her works one of which is of angels on a cloth hanging that went around the communion rail. She also re-painted several statues of angels. In 1893 she completed a beautiful large fresco on the wall of the invalid's oratory. It is still there and consists of fifteen angels surrounding the tabernacle where the chaplain would place the monstrance for adoration on certain occasions. One of the little angels represents Thérèse who is fast asleep holding some lilies in her hand.

One should not omit what others thought of the "angelic" Sister Thérèse of the Child Jesus or how they addressed her by using these affectionate words: "angel," "little angel," "dear angel," and "poor dear little angel." Doctor de Cornière, the monastery physician, profoundly touched by Thérèse's calm demeanor amidst intense suffering, her indomitable courage, and her serene acceptance of her fate, uttered this deep-felt assessment to Mother Agnès (Pauline): "She's an angel! She has the face of an angel; her face hasn't changed, in spite of her great sufferings. I've never seen that in others before. With her general state of getting thinner, it's supernatural." [19]

Finally, in depicting Saint Thérèse of Lisieux during and after her beatification and canonization at St. Peter's in Rome, the inclusion of angels and cherubim was not only unavoidable but inevitable. The huge painting that hung over the balcony from the façade of St. Peter's Basilica showed Thérèse surrounded by these heavenly creatures. At the Carmel chapel in Lisieux and elsewhere, sculptured figures and other representations of angels usually accompany the Saint.

Toward the end of the twentieth century, however, representations of St. Thérèse have tended to eliminate the inclusion of angels, though in the secular world, in the United States at any rate, much popular attention has been placed on angels in books, posters, paintings (especially by Bouguereau), sculpture, and various novelties. Perhaps, however, this interest and concentration is more engendered by their charm, prettiness, and supernatural attributes, rather than by their religiosity.

---

18 Translation by the author.
19 *Her Last Conversations*, September 24, 1897.

Thérèse's wish throughout her life was to be eventually with her heavenly Spouse, Jesus, in Paradise. In her poem "Jesus, My Beloved, Remember!" (PN 24) she concludes with this petition:

> Remember how I often long
> For the day of your great coming.
> Send the angel to tell us soon:
> "Wake up, time is no more!..."
> Then I'll swiftly pass through space.
> Lord, right near you I'll take my place.
> In the Eternal Home
> You're to be my Heaven,
> Remember!...

2. The Blessed Virgin Mary
Mother of Jesus Christ

Oh Mary, if I were Queen of Heaven and you were Thérèse, I would want to be Thérèse so that you might be Queen of Heaven!!! [20]

— St. Thérèse

ST. THÉRÈSE'S DEEP LOVE AND DEVOTION TO MARY BEGAN IN EARLY CHILDhood and continued to the moment of her death. She was reared in an exceptionally pious household intensely devoted to the Blessed Mother. Daily demonstrations of love for the Mother of God formed in Thérèse a striking degree of tenderness, confidence, and love for her. After Jesus, Thérèse speaks and writes about Mary the most.

The foundation of Thérèse's "Little Way of Spiritual Childhood" is based on the tenet that since God is our Father and Mary is our Mother we, therefore, are their children. Mary is the Mother of Jesus—the Word made flesh in her own body—hence she became Thérèse's spiritual Mother. She adamantly believed in the Fatherhood of God and the Motherhood of Mary. This spiritual doctrine permeates all her thoughts, writings, and conversations.

Thérèse's most important document is *Story of a Soul*, where, in the very beginning, she makes a supplication to Mary: "Before taking up my pen, I knelt before the statue of Mary (the one which has given so many proofs of the maternal preferences of heaven's Queen for our family), and I begged her to guide my hand that it trace no line displeasing to her." [21]

The miraculous cure by Mary on May 13, 1883, when Thérèse was ten, became a milestone in Thérèse's life. She had been suffering for seven weeks from a serious nervous disease that threatened her life. At the request of her family, a novena of Masses for her recovery was said at the church of Our Lady of Victories in Paris. At home in Lisieux, her three sisters prayed at her bedside. Thérèse also pleaded for help while looking at the statue of the Blessed Virgin (later to be called "Our Lady of the Smile" or *"La Vierge du Sourire"*—"The Virgin of the Smile"):

---
20 PN 21.
21 *Story of a Soul*, chapter I, p. 13.

[All] of a sudden the Blessed Virgin appeared *beautiful to me,* so *beautiful* that never had I seen anything so attractive; her face was suffused with an ineffable benevolence and tenderness, but what penetrated to the very depths of my soul was the *"ravishing smile of the Blessed Virgin."* At that instant, all my pain disappeared, and two large tears glistened on my eyelashes, and flowed down my cheeks silently, but they were tears of unmixed joy. Ah! I thought, the Blessed Virgin smiled at me, how happy I am, but never will I tell anyone for my *happiness would then disappear....* The memory of the ineffable grace I had received was a real spiritual trial for me for the next four years, and I was not to find my happiness again until I was kneeling at the feet of Our Lady of Victories [in Paris, November 4, 1887]. At that time, my happiness was restored to me in *all its fullness.*[22]

The "spiritual trial" Thérèse mentions above were her "scruples" or doubts about the reality of Mary's smile and the genuineness of the cure she obtained. She composed her first prayer (Pri. 1) to help her overcome this problem: "O my good Blessed Virgin, grant that your little Thérèse may stop tormenting herself."

Thérèse began her autobiography with an invocation to Mary and ended it with a symbolic representation of her. She designed and painted in watercolor her own original coat of arms consisting of two armorial shields: one with the letters JHS[23] over it and the other with FMT. Thérèse describes the one on the right: "The coat of arms FMT is that of Marie-Françoise-Thérèse, the little flower of the Blessed Virgin Mary; the flower is represented as receiving the lightsome rays of the sweet Morning-Star [Mary]."[24]

Thérèse mentions or alludes to Our Lady in most of her poems. Eight of them, though, are written entirely for and addressed to her:

1. PN 1 "The Divine Dew"
2. PN 7 "Song of Gratitude to Our Lady of Mount Carmel"
3. PN 11 Originally had no title. First line is: "Virgin Mary, in spite of my weakness"
4. PN 12 Originally had no title. First line is: It's close to you, Virgin Mary"
5. PN 13 "The Queen of Heaven to Her Beloved Child"
6. PN 35 "To Our Lady of Victories"
7. PN 49 "To Our Lady of Perpetual Help"
8. PN 54 "Why I Love You, O Mary"

Thérèse expands upon her love of Mary in her own distinctive way in letters also:

I surprise myself at times by saying to her, "But good Blessed Virgin, I find I am more blessed than you, for I have you for my Mother, and you do not have a *Blessed Virgin to love....* It is true you are the Mother of Jesus, but this Jesus you have given entirely to us ... and He, on the Cross, He gave you to us as Mother. Since we possess Jesus and since you are ours also. Formerly, in

---

22 Ibid., chapter III, pp. 65–66.
23 From the Latin: *"Iesus Hominum Salvato"* — "Jesus Savior of Men."
24 Piat, *Our Lady of the Smile*, p. 49.

your humility, you wanted one day to be the little servant of the happy Virgin who would have the honor of being the Mother of God, and here I am, a poor little creature, and I am not your servant but your child! You are the Mother of Jesus, and you are my Mother." [25]

Thérèse acknowledges that Mary is the Queen of Heaven (PN 13) but expands upon this in one of her last conversations:

> We know very well that the Blessed Virgin is Queen of heaven and earth, but she is more Mother than Queen; and we should not say, on account of her prerogatives, that she surpasses all the saints in glory just as the sun at its rising makes the stars disappear from sight. My God! How strange that would be! A mother who makes her children's glory vanish! I myself think just the contrary. I believe she'll increase the splendor of the elect very much.
>
> What the Blessed Virgin has more than we have is the privilege of not being able to sin, she was exempt from the stain of original sin; but on the other hand, she wasn't as fortunate as we are, since she didn't have a Blessed Virgin to love. And this is one more sweetness for us and one less sweetness for her! [26]

During her last illness, Thérèse told her sister Céline with deep conviction, "I have still something to do before dying. I always dreamed of expressing in a song to the Blessed Virgin all that I think about her." [27] She did so in her last poem, "Why I Love You, O Mary" (PN 54). In each of the twenty-five stanzas, she expounds upon her Marian love and spirituality. She refers to Mary as "beloved Mother," "Sweet Queen of the Angels," "Mother full of grace," "Queen of the elect," "Queen of martyrs," "Immaculate Virgin," "Refuge of sinners," and "afflicted Mother." Some consider this poem Thérèse's best and most beautiful. The last stanza tells all:

> Soon I'll hear that sweet harmony.
> Soon I'll go to beautiful Heaven to see you.
> You who came to smile at me in the morning of my life,
> Come smile at me again ... Mother....
>   It's evening now! ...
> I no longer fear the splendor of your supreme glory.
> With you I've suffered, and now I want
> To sing on your lap, Mary, why I love you,
> And to go on saying that I am your child! ...

References, invocations, and praises regarding the Blessed Virgin are countless in Thérèse's other writings: the 266 letters, 21 prayers, 8 plays, and 54+ poems. The Blessed Virgin is mentioned many times in the eight plays but she appears as a member of the cast in only one, *The Flight into Egypt* (RP 6). Discussions about Mary, of course, abounded in conversations with her sisters especially during her final illness which fortunately have been recorded in *Her Last Conversations*. In

---

25 LT 137, from Thérèse to Céline on October 19, 1892.
26 *Her Last Conversations*, August 21, 1897, pp. 161–162.
27 From the testimony Céline gave at the Apostolic Process on July 29, 1915.

all her writings Thérèse expounds upon an array of qualities and virtues that are completely in harmony with the life of the Blessed Virgin: poverty, obedience, humility, littleness, purity, silence, faith, peaceful suffering, and love.

On July 8, 1897, three months before Thérèse died, she was transferred from her cell on the second floor of the monastery to the infirmary on the ground floor. Tuberculosis had ravaged her body to such an extent that the move was absolutely necessary. In this room her sisters placed the statue of Our Lady of the Smile—the same one that was in their home, Les Buissonnets. They had it face her iron bed and on the brown bed curtains they pinned pictures of her favorite people: the Blessed Virgin, Théophane Venard, and her deceased little brothers and sisters.[28] During her stay here of almost three months, and even three months before in her cell upstairs, Thérèse's blood sisters, knowing she was dying, recorded significant moments of conversation with her. In a dialogue between Céline and Thérèse, a typically Theresian reasoning unfolded. Céline said to her, "The angels will come looking for you.... Oh! Perhaps we shall really see them!" Thérèse responded:

> I don't believe you'll see them, but that doesn't prevent their being there....
> I would, however, like to have a beautiful death to please you. I asked this from the Blessed Virgin. I didn't ask God for this because I want Him to do as He pleases. Asking the Blessed Virgin for something is not the same thing as asking God. She really knows what is to be done about my little desires, whether or not she must speak about them to God. So it's up to her to see that God is not forced to answer me, to allow Him to do everything He pleases.[29]

On her deathbed Thérèse confessed to her sister Pauline something Pauline was not aware of which occurred during Thérèse's novitiate eight years before. It was about an inexplicable grace she received in July of 1889 in the grotto of St. Mary Magdalene located behind the cemetery on the monastery property. While gazing at a statue of the Immaculate Conception above the grotto, she felt that the veil of Mary covered and protected her as a mother protects her child—a wish she always had of hiding under the mantel of Mary:

> [It] was as though a veil had been cast over all the things of this earth for me.... I was entirely hidden under the Blessed Virgin's veil. At this time, I was placed in charge of the refectory, and I recall doing things as though not doing them; it was as if someone had lent me a body. I remained that way for one whole week.[30]

Thérèse explains this concept in her Poem 13, "The Queen of Heaven to Her Beloved Child Marie of the Holy Face [her blood sister Marie]" where the Blessed Mother is speaking. It is basically an explanation of Thérèse's doctrine of Spiritual Childhood:

---

28 Gaucher, *The Story of a Life*, pp. 192–193.
29 *Her Last Conversations*, July 4, 1897, p. 55.
30 Ibid., p. 88.

> I will hide you under the veil
> Where the King of Heaven takes refuge.
> From now on my Son will be the only star
> That shines for you.
>
> But to shelter you always
> Under my veil beside Jesus,
> You must stay little,
> Adorned with childlike virtues. (Stanzas 4 and 5)

But perhaps the best explanation of Thérèse's conception of Mary's guardianship is from her autobiography in the chapter on her pilgrimage to Rome:

> We reached Paris ... and very soon we saw all the marvels of the Capital. I myself found *only one* which filled me with delight, *Our Lady of Victories*!
>
> Ah! What I felt kneeling at her feet cannot be expressed. The graces she granted me so moved me that my happiness found expression only in tears, just as on the day of my First Communion. The Blessed Virgin made me feel *it was really herself who smiled on me and brought about my cure*. I understood she was watching over me, that I was her child. I could no longer give her any other name but "*Mamma*," as this appeared ever so much more tender than Mother. How fervently I begged her to protect me always, to bring to fruition as quickly as possible my dream of hiding *beneath the shadow of her virginal mantle*! This was one of my first desires as a child. When growing up, I understood it was at Carmel I would truly find the Blessed virgin's mantle, and towards this fertile Mount I directed all my desires.[31]

Thérèse's last sufferings increased and by August of 1897 she at times experienced unbearable pain with no relief. Mother de Gonzague, the prioress, did not permit Thérèse to have morphine or any other pain killers: "I was asking the Blessed Virgin yesterday evening to stop me from coughing in order that Sister Geneviève [who was in the adjoining room] would be able to sleep, but I added: If you don't do it, I'll love you even more."[32] A little later that day Thérèse groaned: "I'm perhaps losing my wits. Oh! If they only knew the weakness I'm experiencing. Last night, I couldn't take anymore; I begged the Blessed Virgin to hold my head in her hands so that I could take my sufferings."

And again, on August 23, Thérèse asked Sister Geneviève: "Pray very much to the Blessed Virgin for me, you who are my little infirmarian, for if you were sick, I'd pray so much for you! But when it comes to praying for oneself, one doesn't dare." But five days later she did cry out, "O my good Blessed Virgin, take pity on me ... 'this time!' "

On Thursday, September 30, 1897, the day she died, Thérèse suffered intensely. The following words she addressed to Our Lady and Mother de Gonzague:

> O good Blessed Virgin, come to my aid!
> If this is the agony, what is death?!

---

[31] *Story of a Soul*, chapter VI, p. 123.
[32] Ibid., August 15, 1897.

Ah! My God!... Yes, He is very good, I find Him very good....
[Looking at the statue of Our Lady of the Smile]:
Oh! You know I'm suffocating!

...

O Mother [Gonzague], present me quickly to the Blessed Virgin; I'm a baby who can't stand anymore!... Prepare me for death. Never would I have believed it was possible to suffer so much! Never! Never![33]

Thérèse died around 7:20 that evening. While looking at her crucifix she whispered, "Oh! I love him.... My God ... I love you!" Shortly after her head fell back with her now bright eyes staring as if in ecstasy at a spot a little above the statue of Our Lady of the Smile. She remained in that position for a short time then slowly she became limp and closed her eyes in death.

Below in chronological order is a list of some of the memorable Marian related associations and events in St. Thérèse's life:

1. Thérèse's parents wanted all their children consecrated to the Blessed Mother by giving them the first name of Mary (*Marie* in French), even the boys. Thérèse, therefore, was baptized Marie-Françoise-Thérèse.
2. The Martin family always said their morning and night prayers before the statue of the Blessed Virgin (Our Lady of the Smile).
3. As a young child Thérèse made and decorated May altars to honor Mary.
4. Our Lady smiled at and cured the ailing Thérèse on May 13, 1883.
5. Thérèse read the Act of Consecration to Our Lady at her First Communion, May 8, 1884. "I cannot doubt that the remarkable grace of my religious vocation germinated on that blessed day when, surrounded by my good teachers, I made the consecration of myself at the foot of the altar, taking her for my Mother in a special way, when in the morning I had received Jesus for the first time."[34]
6. Thérèse joined the Confraternity of the Holy Rosary on September 25, 1884. "The Sweet Queen of Heaven cannot forget her children who ceaselessly repeat her praises. For the Rosary rises like incense to the very throne of God; and Mary sends down in return a beneficent dew that refreshes and vivifies the hearts of men. There is no prayer more agreeable to God than the rosary."[35]
7. Thérèse became an aspirant "member" of the Children of Mary sodality on February 2, 1886—the feast of the Purification of the Blessed Virgin.
8. On May 31, 1887, (feast of the Visitation) Thérèse became a full member of the Children of Mary. "O Mary, conceived without sin, wishing to place myself under your special protection I choose you this day for my patroness, my advocate, my mistress, and my mother."[36]
9. On November 4, 1887, Thérèse received a special grace of peace at Notre-Dame-des-Victories in Paris regarding the authenticity of the Blessed Mother curing her four years before. "The Blessed Virgin made me feel it was really herself who smiled on me and brought about my cure."[37]

---

33 *Her Last Conversations*, September 30, 1897.
34 LT 70, from Thérèse to Mother Saint Placid at the beginning of December 1888.
35 From a student composition Thérèse wrote about the rosary as quoted in Piat's *op. cit.*, p. 31.
36 Ibid., p. 32.
37 *Story of a Soul*, chapter VI, p. 123.

10. Thérèse visited the Holy House of Loreto in Italy on November 9, 1887. She wrote that it was here "where Mary had carried Jesus in her arms, having carried Him in her virginal womb. I beheld the little room in which the angel had appeared to the Blessed Virgin." [38]
11. On April 9, 1888, Thérèse entered the Carmelite Order dedicated to Our Lady of Mount Carmel which she called "the enclosed garden of the Virgin Mary." [39]
12. On Thérèse's profession day, September 8, 1890 — the feast of the Nativity of the Blessed Mother — she became the spiritual "Bride of Christ." "Our Lady helped me with my wedding-dress, and no sooner was it completed then all obstacles vanished, and my profession was set for September 8, 1890. Was not the Nativity of Mary a beautiful feast to become the spouse of Christ?" [40]
13. Thérèse offered herself as a "Victim of Holocaust to God's Merciful Love" in reciting her "Act of Oblation to Merciful Love" on June 11, 1895, before the statue of the Virgin of the Smile. Thérèse, with her sister Céline (Sister Geneviève), pledged: "I offer you, O Blessed Trinity! the love and merits of the Blessed Virgin, my dear Mother. It is to her I abandon my offering, begging her to present it to you."
14. Thérèse made many deathbed invocations to Mary between April and September 1897.

3. CARMELITE MARTYRS OF COMPIÈGNE (JULY 17, 1794)
16 nuns guillotined during the French Revolution

AT THE HEIGHT OF THE REIGN OF TERROR (1793-1794) DURING THE FRENCH Revolution (1789-1799), sixteen Carmelite nuns lost their lives. They hoped that by this martyrdom peace would be restored in France and that the violent persecution of the Catholic Church would end. These nuns from the Carmel of Compiègne were arrested, imprisoned, and tried before the tribunal of the Revolution. The Republic's Public Prosecutor condemned the nuns because of their "criminal hope of seeing the French people put back into the irons of its [former] tyrants and enslaved to priests whose thirst for blood equals their imposture, and also of seeing freedom swallowed up in torrents of blood shed through their infamous intrigues organized in the name of heaven." [41] A further preposterous reason was their "fanaticism and their foolish religious practices." [42] On July 17, 1794, just ten days before the end of the Reign of Terror they were guillotined in Paris. [43]

Two years before their execution, the nuns under the suggestion of their prioress, Mother Teresa of Saint Augustine, recited each day until their death an act of consecration wherein each sister offered herself in union with the community as a holocaust victim, even to the point of martyrdom, to God for

---

38 Ibid., chapter VI, p. 128.
39 Piat, *op. cit.*, p. 40.
40 Ibid., p. 45 as quoted from Thérèse's autobiography.
41 Newkirk, *The Martyrs of Compiègne*, pp. 41–42.
42 Ibid., p. 11.
43 The place is uncertain; sources vary: *Place du Trône Renversé* (modern *Place de la Nation*) or the *Barrière de Vincennes*.

the return of peace. When in prison each also renewed aloud her baptismal and religious vows and sang among others the *Veni Creator*. They were also a great comfort to the other prisoners by their serene presence and Christian behavior. As the tumbrels took them to the place of execution they sang the *Miserere*, *Salve Regina*, and the *Te Deum*. When each nun calmly ascended the scaffold, the other nuns chanted the *Laudate Dominum*.[44] The last to be killed was the youngest, Sister Constance (twenty-nine), the one St. Thérèse particularly favored. The fanatic, jeering crowds that witnessed executions were always boisterous and screamed curses at the condemned but this time they were surprisingly quiet and respectful. The sixteen martyrs included three lay sisters and two servants (*tourières*). Their remains were thrown into a sand-pit at Picpus where the bodies of over 1,298 victims of the Revolution are also buried.[45]

Pope Leo XIII, the same pope Thérèse asked in 1887 for permission to become a Carmelite, declared the martyred nuns Venerable in 1902. They were beatified by Pius X on May 27, 1906. Their canonization is still pending.

The story of the Carmelite martyrs of Compiègne has fascinated generations of people for the past two hundred years since they were killed. They include historians, authors, playwrights, film writers, composers, hagiographers, artists, and religious. Gertrud von le Fort (a convert to Catholicism) wrote a novella about the French martyrs that was published in 1931 in Germany when the Nazi party was in the process of gaining control. She chose as her title *Die Letzte am Schafott* ("The Last Woman on the Scaffold," sometimes translated into "Song at the Scaffold") which is based on the account of the executions written by Sister Marie of the Incarnation, one of the community who was absent at the time of the arrests and thus not killed. Ironically, she was of royal blood, a condition absolutely requiring death according to the revolutionary, murderous terrorists.

The well-known opera by the French composer Francis Poulenc (1899–1963), *Dialogues des Carmélites* ("Dialogue of the Carmelites"), is based on Gertrud von Le Fort's work. Georges Bernanos (1888–1948) wrote the opera's libretto. He first composed it as a film scenario but it was never filmed with his script. It was, however, staged as a play in Paris where Poulenc saw it twice. Then Poulenc used Bernanos's script for his libretto. In its own way it is an operatic masterpiece that cannot avoid touching deeply everyone who sees it. Though the leading character, Sister Blanche, is a fictional creation, the story rather accurately portrays the essence of the purpose and martyrdom of those sixteen courageous women. Especially riveting is the final scene, perhaps the most emotional in all French opera, where the soprano voices are eliminated one by one, punctuated by the swift descent and ghastly slashing sound and thud of the blade for each nun, until after the last nun meets her end, there is complete silence followed by the slow descent of the curtain.

---

44 Ibid., p. 45.
45 Ibid., p. 19.

Thérèse of course knew about the martyrdom of her predecessors, the nuns of Compiègne, and held them in high regard; but it was not until the centenary celebration of their martyrdom on July 17, 1894, that we find references to them regarding Thérèse. She helped one of the nuns in her convent, Sister Teresa of Saint Augustine, to make banners that were used to decorate the chapel of the Compiègne Carmel. In her testimony at the diocesan inquiry leading to Thérèse's beatification, Sister Teresa of Saint Augustine commented on Thérèse's opinion of martyrdom:

> She became even more fervent than usual when those who had shed their blood for our Lord were being honored. On 17 July, 1894, the centenary of the martyrs of Compiègne, the Carmel of Compiègne wanted to celebrate the event, and they asked the Lisieux Carmel to help them. The two of us were given the task of making little banners to decorate the chapel with. I was thus able to see the eagerness with which she set to work; she was almost beside herself with happiness as she explained: "If only we could be fortunate enough to share their lot! What a privilege!"[46]

Two years later in September of 1896, Msgr. Francis de Teil, canon of Notre Dame in Paris, went to the Lisieux monastery to speak about his work as vice-postulator for the beatification of the sixteen Carmelite martyrs. He asked if any of the nuns had heard of any miracles obtained through the intercession of those martyred nuns. After the lecture, Sister Thérèse of the Child Jesus remarked to one of the nuns: "How touching is the zeal of this postulator! How glad one would be to have miracles to make known to him!"[47] According to John Beevers in his book *Storm of Glory*, Msgr. de Teil ended his talk with the statement that "If any of you who are listening to me have the intention of being canonized, please have pity on the poor Vice-Postulator and work plenty of miracles!" Thérèse was among his audience. Monsignor de Teil's comment, years later, was: "And Sister Thérèse, obedient child, did precisely as she was told."[48] Little did anyone imagine then that just thirteen years later this same monsignor would be chosen postulator for the cause to canonize Thérèse herself. And many miracles did occur attributable to Thérèse after she died.

Thérèse took Sister Constance, the last and youngest of the nuns to be guillotined, as one of her special spiritual friends along with Father Mazel, and Saints Cecilia, Joan, and Théophane Vénard. They were all young, similar in temperament, and died martyrs. She offered some insightful opinions to her sister Pauline on July 12, 1897, when on her bed in the infirmary less than three months before she died: "With the virgins we shall be virgins; with the doctors, doctors; with the martyrs, martyrs, because all the saints are our relatives; but those who've followed the way of spiritual childhood will always retain the charms of childhood."[49]

---

46 O'Mahony, *St. Thérèse of Lisieux by Those Who Knew Her*, p. 195.
47 Laveille, *op. cit.*, footnote 1, p. 331.
48 Beevers, *Storm of Glory*, p. 136.
49 *Her Last Conversations*, July 13, 1897, pp. 93–94.

And just before this date, on May 26, she disclosed to her sister another one of her notions about saints which is a unique explanation of the Communion of Saints. "The saints know me, love me, smile upon me, and invite me to join them."[50] Besides the actual act of martyrdom which attracted Thérèse to the martyred Carmelite nuns of the French Revolution, there was their prayer of self-offering as victims to divine justice. It is similar in concept to Thérèse's own "Act of Oblation to Merciful Love" (Pri 6) composed on June 9, 1895. Note, however, Thérèse concentrates on God's love rather than justice as she says at the end:

> [I] offer myself as a victim of holocaust to your merciful love, asking you to consume me incessantly ... and that thus I may become a Martyr of your Love, O my God!... I want, O my Beloved, at each beat of my heart to renew this offering to you an infinite number of times, until the shadows having disappeared I may be able to tell you of my Love in an Eternal Face to Face!

Incidentally, Compiègne, located north of Paris in southern Picardy, played a meaningful part in French history. It was here where Joan of Arc was captured by the Burgundians in 1490, where in 1918 the Armistice of World War I was signed in a railway car, and where in the same car the French signed their surrender to Hitler in 1940.

4. LÉON-PAPIN DUPONT (1797–1876)
Layman who promoted devotion to the Holy Face of Christ

MONSIEUR LÉON-PAPIN DUPONT, A LAYMAN ALL HIS LIFE, NAMED BY HIS contemporaries "the Holy Man of Tours," promoted devotion to the Holy Face of Christ Crucified. St. Thérèse and her family were particularly attracted to this pious movement. In fact, she took the words Holy Face as part of her religious name.

M. Dupont was born into a well-to-do Creole family on January 24, 1797, in Martinique, an island in the West Indies, named after St. Martin of Tours. At one period of his life he served as a magistrate at the royal court in Martinique. He pursued his education in law at Paris, a city he thoroughly enjoyed at the time. For a while Parisian society life with all its glitter strongly held his interest including the theater, balls, and racing. In fact at one time he even owned several racehorses. Along with these mundane pleasures he did engage in helping the poor and in other charitable work. At this period he began a devotion to the Blessed Mother especially related to her appearance and message at La Salette (south of Grenoble in the French Alps). Léon then began to wonder about his vocation so he consulted many wise priests about it; he eventually decided to marry which he did at the age of thirty. His wife was twenty-four. They had one daughter, Henriette. Sadly, his wife died shortly after, but before that she urged her husband to have the Ursuline nuns in Tours educate their child. Léon, therefore, accompanied by his mother decided to settle in that town. After the

---
50 Ibid., May 26, 1897, p. 50.

death of his mother, he spent most of his time helping the indigent. His daughter had the misfortune of contracting typhoid fever and died at the age of fifteen. Notwithstanding the crushing blows from the deaths of his wife and child, his faith and courage sustained him.

He became actively involved with a number of religious and charitable causes. Among them was the organization of pilgrimages to places connected with St. Martin and his work for the construction of a new basilica in St. Martin's honor. The Little Sisters of the Poor were established in Tours due to his efforts. He founded an organization that provided clothing for the poor unemployed called appropriately St. Martin's Cloakroom (*Vestiaire Saint-Martin*). (Notice the number of times the name Martin is involved.) He also propagated the Work of Nocturnal Adoration in many parishes.

Years before in the same town where he lived, a saintly Carmelite nun, Sister Marie of Saint Peter (1816–1848), had revelations concerning Jesus and the blasphemies committed against Him which offend and disfigure His Holy Face. She wanted to create an association that would make reparations for these outrages, but as a cloistered nun she was not sure how this could come about. She died three years before Léon was aware of her ambitions; nonetheless, within a short time he became the means by which the devotion to the Holy Face was realized and spread. He converted one of the rooms in his home into a chapel that became the center of devotion to the Holy Face. Enshrined there was a replica of Veronica's veil with the tortured face of Jesus imprinted upon it. The original is preserved at St. Peter's Basilica in Rome. Many pilgrims and devotees of the Holy Face came to pray at the shrine and a number of cures and conversions took place there. Sister Marie of St. Peter's desire fully materialized when the Holy Man of Tours created the Archconfraternity of the Holy Face which the pope in time legalized. Thérèse Martin, her family, and thousands since then have joined it.

Monsieur Dupont spent the last twenty-five years of his life successfully spreading devotion to the Holy Face. He suffered from several diseases toward the end and died at the age of seventy-nine on March 18, 1876. After his death the shrine in his home was converted into an official oratory and is still visited by hundreds of people.

From early childhood, Thérèse and her family concentrated on the veneration of the Sacred Heart of Jesus with its stress on reparations due to Jesus because of the disrespect shown to Him, in the lack of piously observing Sunday, and in using His name so much in profanity. They likewise honored the Holy Face of Jesus as it is shown on Veronica's veil.[51] When Thérèse reached the age of twelve, she along with her father, Céline, Léonie, and Marie enrolled in the Confraternity of the Holy Face on April 26, 1885. Not until Thérèse entered Carmel, however, did she become completely immersed in the deep meaning of this devotion, primarily with the contemplation of God's love rather than with

---

51 Christ on the Shroud of Turin was not revealed until 1898, a year after Thérèse died.

reparation. The saintly foundress of the Lisieux Carmel, Mother Geneviève of Saint Teresa, encouraged the young novices under her charge to acquire devotion to the Holy Face. Sister Agnès, Thérèse's sister, also influenced Thérèse in realizing the depth of meaning in contemplating the agonized face of Jesus. In her autobiography Thérèse explains this:

> Until my coming to Carmel, I had never fathomed the depths of the treasures hidden in the Holy Face. It was through you, dear Mother, that I learned to know these treasures. Just as formerly you had preceded us into Carmel, so also you were first to enter deeply into the mysteries of love hidden in the Face of our Spouse. You called me and I understood.... Ah! I desired that, like the Face of Jesus, "my face be truly hidden, that no one on earth would know me." I thirsted after suffering and I longed to be forgotten.[52]

When Thérèse Martin entered Carmel she assumed the name Sister Thérèse of the Child Jesus. As the youngest in her family, she always considered herself a child of God the Father, and especially so when she was a religious. Consequently, the dominant characteristic of her philosophy evolved into what is called "Spiritual Childhood," or "The Little Way." The exact opposite of the Child Jesus' visage is His suffering Face. And because she wanted to imitate and resemble Him in both forms she added the phrase "of the Holy Face" to her name on January 10, 1889, the day she received the habit.

One of the duties Thérèse had at the monastery was painting pictures, statues, etc. Among the many pieces of art work she produced was the image of the Holy Face on holy cards, vestments, and on her coat of arms which she did in watercolor on the last page of Manuscript A of her autobiography.

In all of her writings—letters, autobiography, poems, prayers, plays—and in her conversations, Thérèse routinely mentioned the Holy Face. The shortest prayer she wrote is "Make Me Resemble You, Jesus" (Pri 11); that is, hidden in imitation of Christ whose Holy Face was concealed under the blood, scars, and marks received during His passion. She wrote this on a holy card with a picture of the Christ on Veronica's veil and wore it over her heart.

When Thérèse was six or seven, she believed she saw her father in the back garden of their home even though at the time he was far from there in another town. This is the story of her interpretation of that vision *vis-à-vis* Christ's hidden Face:

> It was indeed *Papa* whom I had seen advancing, bent over with age. It was indeed Papa, who was bearing on his venerable countenance and white hair the symbol of his *glorious* trial [strokes causing paralysis and mental problems]. Just as the adorable Face of Jesus was veiled during His Passion, so the face of His faithful servant had to be veiled in the days of his sufferings in order that it might shine in the heavenly Fatherland near its Lord, the Eternal Word![53]

---

[52] *Story of a Soul*, chapter VII, p. 152.
[53] Ibid., chapter II, p. 47.

Sister Thérèse as novice mistress wrote "Consecration to the Holy Face," a prayer (Pri 12) that she and two of her novices, Sister Geneviève, and Sister Marie of the Trinity of the Holy Face, recited most likely on the Feast of the Transfiguration, August 6, 1896, as a means of consecrating themselves to the "Adorable Face of Jesus."[54] The final paragraph summarizes its content: "*O beloved Face of Jesus!* As we await the everlasting day when we will contemplate your infinite Glory, our one desire is to charm your *Divine Eyes* by hiding our faces too so that here on earth no one can recognize us.... O *Jesus!* Your *Veiled Gaze* is our *Heaven!*..." All three nuns had "of the Holy Face" added to their names:

Sr. Thérèse of the Child Jesus and of the Holy Face
Sr. Marie of the Trinity of the Holy Face
Sr. Geneviève of the Holy Face[55]

Two more prayers come from the pen of Thérèse dealing with the Holy Face: "Eternal Father, Since You Have Given Me" (Pri 15) and "[To the Holy Face] I am the Jesus of Thérèse" (Pri 16). In the first of two paragraphs of Prayer 16 Thérèse identifies herself with Jesus: "O Adorable Face of Jesus, the only Beauty that captivates my heart, deign to imprint in me your divine Likeness so that you may not behold the soul of your little bride without seeing Yourself in her."

One of the two Christmas plays she wrote, *The Angels at the Crib of Jesus* (RP 2, performed in 1894) lists five angels among the characters who speak and sing. One of them is the Angel of the Holy Face who engages in a dialogue with the Infant Jesus in the course of which she reveals Jesus' awareness of His future Passion.

Thérèse composed one poem (PN 20) specifically concerning the Holy Face which she titled "My Heaven on Earth (Canticle to the Holy Face)." The fifth stanza expresses beautifully her convictions about the Holy Face. The last two lines have prophetic significance:

> Your Face is my only wealth.
> I ask for nothing more.
> Hiding myself in it unceasingly,
> I will resemble you, Jesus....
> Leave in me the divine impress
> Of your Features filled with sweetness,
> And soon I'll become holy.
> I shall draw hearts to you.

During Thérèse's last conversations with her sisters and others in the monastery infirmary before she died, she often commented on the Holy Face of Jesus. Below is one of the references that Mother Agnès transcribed:

[To] celebrate the feast of the following day, August 6, feast of the Transfiguration, we took from the choir the picture of the Holy Face [from the one on Veronica's

---

54 This feast is one of the principle feast days of the Confraternity of the Holy Face.
55 See p. 92 in *The Prayers of Saint Thérèse of Lisieux*.

veil preserved at St. Peter's in Rome] she so much loved and hung it on the wall to the right, decorating it with flowers and lights. She said, looking at the picture:

"How well Our Lord did to lower His eyes when he gave us His portrait! Since the eyes are the mirror of the soul, if we had seen His soul, we would have died from joy.

"Oh! How much good that Holy Face has done me in my life! When I was composing my canticle: '*Vivre d'Amour*,' it helped me to do it with great ease. I wrote from memory, during my night silence, the fifteen couplets that I had composed during the day without a rough draft. That same day, when going to the refectory after the examination of conscience, I had just composed the stanza:

> To live from love is to dry your Face,
> It's to obtain pardon for sinners.

"I repeated this to Him while passing by, doing so with great love. When looking at the picture, I cried out of love."[56]

5. Père Frédérique Mazel, M.E.P. (1871–1897)
Young missionary murdered in China

THE TWENTY-SIX-YEAR-OLD FELLOW STUDENT OF FATHER ROULLAND, Thérèse's "spiritual brother," was brutally murdered on April 1, 1897, in his chapel in Lo-Li, China, just because he was a European and a Frenchman.

The Lisieux Carmel learned about Father (Père) Mazel's death on May 1, 1897. Among Thérèse's "Diverse Writings" (*Écrits Diverse*)[57] is a brief biography of Father Mazel at the end of which she wrote in pencil, "Blessed Martyr, pray for me!"

Mother Agnès, Thérèse's older sister Pauline, providentially jotted down her dying sister's last words and actions during the final agonizing months of her life. The day after they learned about the murder, May 2, 1897, she recorded what Thérèse said about this missionary:

> You [Pauline] weren't at recreation this evening. Reverend Mother [Mother Marie de Gonzague] told us that one of the missionaries [Père Mazel] who embarked with Father Roulland was dead before he reached his mission. This young missionary received Communion on the ship with hosts from our Carmel that were given Father Roulland.... And now he is dead!... He didn't have to carry out any apostolate whatsoever, nor go to any trouble, for example, learning Chinese. God gave him the palm [symbol of martyrdom] of desire; see how He needs no one.[58]

And again in Thérèse's fifth letter to Rev. Roulland she expressed her ideas about missionaries and martyrdom:

> Brother, the beginnings of your apostolate are marked with the seal of the Cross; the Lord is treating you as a privileged one. It is more by persecution and suffering than by brilliant preaching that He wills to make His kingdom

---

56 *Her Last Conversations*, August 5, 1897.
57 From "3. *TEXTES DIVERS*," p. 1239, in *Œuvres Complètes*.
58 *Her Last Conversations*, May 1, 1897.

firm in souls. You say: "I am still a child who cannot speak." Father Mazel, who was ordained the same day as you, did not know how to speak either; however, he has already taken up the palm.... Oh! How the divine thoughts are above ours! When learning about the death of this young missionary whom I heard named for the first time, I felt drawn to invoke him; I seemed to see him in heaven in the glorious choir of Martyrs. I know that in the eyes of men his martyrdom does not bear this name, but in the eyes of God this sacrifice without any glory is not less fruitful than the sacrifices of the first Christians, who confessed their faith before tribunals.... I wanted simply to say that it seems to me all missionaries are *martyrs* by desire and will and that, as a consequence, not one should have to go to purgatory.[59]

September 22, 1871, marks the date of Father Mazel's birth which took place in Rodelle (Aveyron), a town in the Massif Central section of south western France. At twenty he entered the seminary of the Foreign Mission Society of Paris (*Les Missionaires Étrangères de Paris*—MEP) on October 21, 1891, and was ordained a priest on June 28, 1896. The next month on the 29th he left for China where a mere eight months later he was murdered.

6. Saint Agnes (died 303–304 A.D.?)
A martyred Roman virgin, patroness of chastity

MUCH OF ST. AGNES'S RECORDED LIFE IS BASED UPON LEGENDS AND, THEREfore, not completely reliable. We do know for a fact, however, that she was born of a noble Roman family and suffered martyrdom at the early age of twelve or thirteen under the Roman Emperor Diocletian in 303 or 304. Some accounts, though, place her death years later under Emperor Valerian.

Her path to martyrdom began when she refused to marry Sempronius, the son of a Roman prefect who was struck by her beauty. She said she was betrothed to another—Jesus Christ—and preferred death rather than renounce Him and her vow of virginity. Thereupon, as was customary in that era, they sent her to a brothel to defile her. As she entered the place, her hair grew miraculously long covering her body like a coat while a celestial light illuminated the room helping to protect her virginity. The love-smitten lad touched her body, though, and instantly dropped dead. He, nevertheless, was restored to life after Agnes prayed to God for this miracle. Another judge then ordered her to be burned and, again miraculously, the fire did not touch her but consumed her torturers instead. In frustration they beheaded her. The famous medieval work *The Golden Legend* says, however, that she died from a sword thrust into her throat. Legends also tell us that not long after her death, her parents saw a vision at her grave of a procession of virgins with their daughter Agnes holding a snow-white lamb among them.

Above the site of her grave which was in what has been called for centuries the Catacombs of St. Agnes, is the impressive basilica of *Sant' Agnese Fuori le Mura* (St. Agnes Outside the Walls) by the Via Nomentana that contains the remains

---

[59] LT 226 Thérèse to Père Roulland dated May 9, 1897.

of Agnes. Above the place where Agnes was killed is the baroque church of *Sant' Agnese in Agone* (St. Agnes in Agony) where her head is enshrined in a reliquary. The daughter of the Emperor Constantine, Princess Costanza (Constantia or Constantina) was cured of a skin disfiguration (perhaps leprosy) and in gratitude founded in 342 the basilica of St. Agnes Outside the Walls. Adjacent to it is the circular mausoleum, now the church of St. Constanza erected between 337 and 354, the year Constanza died. For centuries it held her remains and those of her sister Helen. Now they are in the Vatican Museum.

The feast day of St. Agnes is celebrated on January 21 (a day after that of St. Sebastian)—the date attributed to the day of her burial. St. Agnes had another blood sister or foster-sister named Emerenziana (Emerentina), a virgin who was stoned to death while praying at the grave of Agnes. Around 1600 St. Emerenzians's remains were found next to those of St. Agnes. Since then she was canonized and we celebrate her feast day on January 23, two days after her sister's. In some places it is a custom to bless lambs on this day.

Even when St. Thérèse was very young she loved everything about St. Agnes, particularly her martyrdom. She wrote in her autobiography that "martyrdom was the dream of my youth and this dream has grown with me within Carmel's cloisters." [60] She wanted to die for Christ by any method—scourging, crucifixion, boiling water, or "with St. Agnes and St. Cecilia I would present my neck to the sword and like Joan of Arc, my dear sister, I would whisper at the stake Your Name, O JESUS." [61]

Early in her autobiography, Thérèse tells the story of her pilgrimage to Rome including this incident at the basilica of St. Agnes Outside the Walls:

> The visit to the church of St. Agnes was also very sweet to me; she was a childhood friend whom I was visiting in her own home. I spoke a long time to her about the one [Mother Agnès, her sister Pauline] who carries her name so well, and I exerted all my efforts to get one of the relics of my Mother's angelic patroness and bring it back to her. But it was impossible to get any except a small piece of red stone which was detached from a rich mosaic, the origin of which goes back to St. Agnes' time. She must often have gazed upon it. Wasn't it charming that the lovable saint herself should give us what we were looking for and which we were forbidden to take? I've always considered it a delicate attention on her part, a proof, too, of the love with which the sweet St. Agnes looks upon and protects my Mother! [62]

Thérèse later gave her sister Pauline the loose fragment she found which is now preserved in a golden reliquary.

The person, name, and feast day of St. Agnes were always very dear to St. Thérèse right from her childhood days when the family would celebrate the virgin saint's day. It became more significant when Pauline became a Carmelite

---
60 *Story of a Soul*, chapter IX, p. 193.
61 Ibid.
62 Ibid., p. 132.

and assumed the name of Sister Agnes. Two months after entering Carmel, the postulant Thérèse, dressed in a white tunic with her long luxuriant golden hair flowing down to her shoulders, took the part of St. Agnes in a play (*St. Agnès*) Sister Agnès wrote for the feast of their prioress, Mother Marie de Gonzague, June 21, 1888. For added touches to her costume, Thérèse had her sister Céline bring to her from Les Buissonnets a few clothing accessories including some from her First Communion dress.[63]

The feast day of a prioress is the feast day of the saint whose name the prioress has, so it is a special community holiday. When Mother Agnès became prioress, January 21 was therefore celebrated by the community. Thérèse presented her first play about Joan of Arc on this day in 1894 and on the same day the next year she performed her second play also about Joan of Arc. It is interesting to note that on January 20, 1896, though a day before St. Agnes's feast day, Thérèse gave the first manuscript of her famous autobiography to her sister Mother Agnès.

An important original work given to Mother Agnès on January 21, 1896 is the so-called betrothal poem, "The Responses of Saint Agnes" (PN 26). Thérèse's purpose was to form her own poetic interpretation of the "Responses" from the Divine Office as said by the martyr St. Agnes. Composed as if written by St. Agnes, it is actually a personal engagement poem of Thérèse—a nun bride of Christ—who identifies herself with St. Agnes:

> Christ is my Love, He is my whole life.
> He is the Fiancé who alone delights my eyes.
> ...
> So I fear nothing, neither sword nor flame.
> No, nothing can trouble my ineffable peace,
> And the fire of love which consumes my soul
> Shall never go out!

Throughout Church and art history St. Agnes has been pictured with a lamb, the symbol of purity, and a palm, a symbol of martyrdom. In fact, the word Agnes is derived from the Latin *agnus* meaning "lamb." Rather appropriately, one of the nicknames the family gave Thérèse was "the little lamb," while her sister Pauline was named simply "the lamb." Quoting a few lines from one of Thérèse's letters to Pauline, she refers to these symbolic names: "The palm of Agnes is needed for the lamb and the little lamb and if this is not through blood, then it has to be through love...."[64]

The Church proclaimed St. Agnes the patroness of young girls, virgins, children, and engaged couples. She is also numbered as one of the few female saints in the canon of the Mass as well as in the Litany of the Saints.

It is interesting to notice that Thérèse's favorite saints had a great deal in common with Thérèse herself. They were virgins, loved their family, and died young—most of them of martyrdom, a death Thérèse longed for all her life.

---

63 LT 53 from Thérèse to Céline dated June 17, 1888.
64 LT 54, July, 1888.

7. Saint Aloysius Gonzaga (1568–1591)
Jesuit seminarian who died at 23, patron of youth

Though St. Thérèse admired St. Aloysius, she did not have any special devotion to him. Three similarities between them are: both died in their early twenties (he at 23, she at 24); family life was important to both, and both believed penance and suffering were necessary ingredients in their spiritual life. St. Aloysius said in this regard that "he who wishes to love God does not truly love Him if he has not an ardent and constant desire to suffer for His sake." [65] These words are completely Theresian. They both were excited about seeing God as their deaths became imminent. In her last days Thérèse referred to St. Aloysius several times, though not all favorably:

- Théophane Vénard [not canonized until 1988] pleases me much more than St. Louis [Aloysius] de Gonzague, because the life of the latter is extraordinary, and that of Théophane is very ordinary. Besides, he is the one who is talking, whereas for the Saint [Aloysius] someone is telling the story and making him speak; so we know practically nothing about his "little" soul! [66]
- Did you notice during the reading in the refectory, the letter addressed to the mother of St. Louis de Gonzague, in which it was said of the saint that had he lived to the age of Noah he would not have learned more or become more holy? [67]
- Saint Louis de Gonzague was serious, even during recreation, but Théophane Vénard was always cheerful. [68]

Every prioress's feast day was especially celebrated by the Lisieux Carmel and since the prioress, Mother Marie de Gonzague, was named after St. Aloysius Gonzaga, her feast day was honored during most of Thérèse's life there. There is an intriguing aspect of St. Aloysius' life with respect to St. Thérèse. During the reading of his life in the monastery refectory from May to June 1897, the following anecdote was related. A German priest asked for St. Aloysius's intercession to cure his sickness. The saint appeared to him and caused a shower of roses to fall on his sickbed as a sign of the healing grace he would receive. After Thérèse heard the reading of his story, she shortly after told her sister, Sister Marie of the Sacred Heart, that "I too will send a shower of roses after my death." [69] How prophetic, for since her death an untold number of miracles, favors, and even roses appearing have been attributed to St. Thérèse of the Child Jesus.

Aloysius (Luigi, Aluigi, Louis) Gonzaga lived his short life during the High Renaissance, a period of extremes — violence, sexual excesses, intrigue, wars, corruption, religious fervor, but above all glorious artistic accomplishments. St. Aloysius's heritage included noble blood, wealth, prominent ecclesiastical ancestors and relations, and royal connections. Born on March 9, 1568, in the

---

65 *New Catholic Dictionary*, (Patron Saints Index).
66 *Her Last Converzations*, May 21, 1897.
67 Ibid., May 27, 1897.
68 Ibid.
69 Descouvemont, *op. cit.*, p. 290.

castle of Castiglione delle Stivieri near Mantua, Lombardy, Italy, he was the eldest son of Marquis Ferdinand (Don Ferrante) Gonzaga and his wife, the noble born Marta de Tana Santena. His parents met at the court of King Philip II and Queen Isabella of Spain where his mother, a very religious woman, was then a lady-in-waiting to the Queen. The Marquis was a military commander and strongly desired that Aloysius become a great military leader also. In fact he started him early by sending him at the tender age of four or five to a military camp for five months which he apparently enjoyed. Nonetheless, all his life he deeply regretted the fact that there he learned some of the foul language the soldiers used. When he learned the meaning of these words he was appalled and considered he committed serious sins, even though he was unaware of what he was saying.

Aloysius began to display a propensity toward holiness, purity, prayer, and even penance at a very early age. When only nine, he made a vow of perpetual virginity which he maintained all his life. He also expressed his wish to become a religious, much to his mother's satisfaction. About this time he was initiated into the life of a courtier at the court of Francesco de'Medici in Florence where he and his brother Rudolfo were placed under the care of tutors who taught them Latin and the pure Italian of Tuscany.

Two years later in 1579 the two brothers were sent to the court of the Duke of Mantua for the continuation of their schooling. Aloysius, now eleven, developed a kidney disorder which restricted his activities, but he did manage to visit churches, pray more, and teach little boys the catechism. In 1581 Louis' father Ferdinand Gonzaga was appointed grand chamberlain to the king of Spain, Philip II. The brothers went to Spain with their parents where they were made pages to the king's son, Prince James (the *Infante* at the royal court in Madrid).

During his stay in Spain, Aloysius revealed to his mother that he wanted to become a Jesuit which pleased her very much. When his father, however, learned of this he was furious since he expected his eldest son to continue in his footsteps, inherit his title and fortune, and become both a soldier and a ruler. He spent three years attempting to dissuade Aloysius with the help of others including clergymen, but he finally relented and gave his consent. It appears that after Aloysius entered the Jesuits his father became less worldly, controlled his fits of anger, decreased his gambling, and even devoted more time to pious practices. Sadly, though, he died less than a year later. Other family tragedies followed. His brother Rudolfo was murdered and his mother nearly died from stab wounds inflicted by an enemy.

At seventeen Aloysius entered the Jesuit novitiate in Rome on November 25, 1587. There he met Pope Sixtus V who, aware of his social standing and wealth, wondered whether he would last as a Jesuit. The Pope, needless to say, was quickly convinced of his vocation and remarkable character. As a novice he was most privileged to have Father Robert Bellarmine, a future saint of the Church, as his confessor and spiritual director.

As a seminarian he astonished the community with his mature spirituality, leadership, strict adherence to the Rule, intelligence, penances, prayer life, and his intense holiness. Even the saintly Father Bellarmine was impressed by Aloysius's profound sanctity and his extraordinary insights into the contemplative sphere. His youthful vow of chastity manifested itself in what is called the "custody of the eyes" which he practiced before women, even his mother. His lifelong struggle against pride is quite understandable considering his breeding, training, and wealth. Some have called him "the impossible prig." Nevertheless, all acknowledged that his kindness and holiness were quite remarkable.

A terrible plague and famine struck Rome in 1587. The Jesuits opened a hospital to serve the suffering and dying where many young Jesuits including Aloysius and his superiors worked. They helped the victims by begging alms for them, and washing and feeding them. No wonder he contracted a disease, some say, after carrying a terminally ill man from the streets to the hospital. The holy young Jesuit became bedridden on March 3, 1891, and was on death's doorstep when St. Robert Bellarmine gave him the last rites. His condition, however, improved and he was on the way to recovery when fever and cough set in. For three months he lingered on but finally succumbed on June 21, 1591. He was buried in the Church of St. Ignatius in Rome where thirty years later his spiritual guide and admirer St. Robert Bellarmine was himself buried at his own request near the tomb of Aloysius. Incidentally, St. Bellarmine (declared a Doctor of the Church in 1931) died the same year that Aloysius was beatified.

Knowledge of Aloysius's sanctity spread far and wide after his death and hundreds of miracles and cures were attributed to his intercession. Pope Benedict XIII canonized him on December 31, 1726, the same year as another young (18 years old) Jesuit seminarian, St. Stanislas Kostka, was canonized. St. Aloysius Gonzaga was declared Patron of students, young men, and seminarians. His feast day is celebrated on June 21.

8. SAINT CECILIA (D. APPROX. 280)
Virgin martyr of Rome, patroness of music

THE VIRTUES AND CHARACTERISTICS THÉRÈSE ESTEEMED THE MOST WERE all embodied in her cherished role model, St. Cecilia: virginity, youth, apostolic zeal, abandonment, fortitude, martyrdom, and music. The one virtue Thérèse perfectly imitated to the very last tortured days of her life was fortitude. St. Cecilia was left for three days to suffer and die with her neck severely slashed by the executioner who failed in his attempt to behead her. Thérèse too lay suffering but for many months, enduring it all like Cecilia with heroic courage and perseverance.

Thérèse explains very clearly how, when, and where her interest in St. Cecilia (*Cécile* in French) began:

> Before my trip to Rome I didn't have any special devotion to this saint, but when I visited her house transformed into a church, the site of her martyrdom, when learning that she was proclaimed patroness of music not because of her beautiful

voice or her talent for music, but in memory of the *virginal song* she sang to her heavenly Spouse hidden in the depths of her heart, I felt more than devotion for her; it was the *real tenderness of a friend*. She became my saint of predilection, my intimate confidant. Everything in her thrilled me, especially her *abandonment*, her limitless confidence which made her capable of virginizing souls who had never desired any other joys but those of the present life. St. Cecilia is like the bride in the Canticle; in her I see "a choir in an armed camp" [*Canticle of Canticles* 7:1]. Her life was nothing else but a melodious song in the midst of the greatest trials, and this does not surprise me because "the Gospel *rested on her heart*" [from the Office of the saint], and in her heart reposed the *Spouse* of Virgins![70]

Thérèse, furthermore, felt that the story of Cecilia was also the story of her sister Cèline. In fact, she compared her relationship to her sister like that of Cecilia to Valerian (Cecilia's husband), calling her "My little Valerian."[71] In a letter addressed to Céline on her twenty-fifth birthday, Thérèse tells her that "*the story of Cecilia* (the *Saint* of ABANDONMENT) is your story too! Jesus has placed near you an angel from heaven who is always looking after you...."[72]

Two days later Thérèse gave Céline her first long poem, "Saint Cecilia" (PN 3), in which she sums up her beliefs with these last lines:

> Your chaste union will give birth to souls
> Who will seek no other spouse than Jesus,
> ...
> You can be pure, and you can suffer!...
> Cecilia, lend me your sweet melody.
> I would like to convert so many hearts to Jesus!
> Like you, I would like to sacrifice my life.
> I would like to give him both my blood and my tears....
> Obtain for me to taste perfect abandonment,
> That sweet fruit of love, on this foreign shore.
> O my dear saint! Soon, far from earth,
> Obtain for me to fly beside you forever.

Concerning abandonment, Thérèse wrote:

> I cannot think without delight of the dear little St. Cecilia.... In the midst of the world, plunged into the center of all dangers, at the moment of being united with a young pagan who longs only for profane love, it seems to me that Cecilia would have had to tremble and to weep ... but, no, while hearing the sounds of the instruments that were celebrating her nuptials, Cecilia was singing in her heart [from the Office of St. Cecilia, November 22]. What abandonment!... she was hearing no doubt other melodies besides those of earth, her divine Spouse was singing too, the angels were making resound in Cecilia's heart the sound of their celestial concerts.... Yes, the chaste generation of virgin souls is beautiful. The Church sings of it often, and these words are still true today as in the time of the virgin Cecilia....[73]

---

70 *Story of a Soul*, chapter VI, p. 131–132.
71 *Her Last Conversations*, July 12, 1897.
72 LT 161 dated April 26, 1894.
73 LT 149 from Thérèse to Céline dated October 20, 1893.

Another quote from *Story of a Soul* specifically mentions martyrdom in all its forms:

> Martyrdom was the dream of my youth and this dream has grown with me within Carmel's cloisters. But here again, I feel that my dream is a folly, for I cannot confine myself to desiring one kind of martyrdom. To satisfy me I need all. Like You, my Adorable Spouse, I would be scourged and crucified. I would die flayed like St. Bartholomew. I would be plunged into boiling oil like St. John; I would undergo all the tortures inflicted upon the martyrs. With St. Agnes and St. Cecilia, I would present my neck to the sword, and like Joan of Arc, my dear sister, I would whisper at the stake Your Name, O JESUS.[74]

As Thérèse lay in the monastery infirmary three months before she died, her sister Pauline (Mother Agnès) talked to her about some saints whose lives were quite remarkable, to which Thérèse commented, "I myself prefer the saints who feared nothing, for example, St. Cecilia, who allowed herself to be married and didn't fear."[75]

Saint Cecilia is among the most popular saints in the Church. She is listed in the Canon of the Mass and is invoked in the Litany of the Saints. Though she probably did not play a musical instrument—at least there is no firm evidence that she did—she is honored as the patron saint of music in general, musicians, church music, singers, instrument makers, organists, and also of poetry. Her patronage of music is derived mainly from a passage in an account of her life, sufferings, and death as a martyr written centuries after her death which states that at Cecilia's nuptials "while the musical instruments resounded, the virgin Cecilia sang in her heart only to the Lord."[76] From this passage it was deduced that she sang songs and some also surmised that it infers she also played a musical instrument—perhaps a kind of organ.

A truly reliable and accurate biography of St. Cecilia is impossible to obtain; therefore, we have to rely upon several questionable sources including her *passio* (the story of a martyr's life and sufferings), *The Roman Martyrology*, the *Acta* of Cecilia, *The Golden Legend*, and a number of other early resources.

The Golden Legend contends that the name Cecilia may possibly be derived from *coeli lilia*, Latin for "lily of heaven." At any rate, she was born into an ancient and noble Roman family and was devoted to prayer from an early age. She made a vow to remain a virgin and to serve Christ only. However, her parents had her betrothed to a pagan by the name of Valerian. At the time they were imperial Rome's most prominent young couple, both from patrician families, rich, intelligent, and attractive. After their marriage, though, she informed him that her true spouse was another—Christ. She said an angel protected her virginity whereupon Valerian demanded to see this angel. It is not possible, she informed him, unless you are converted to Christianity and are baptized, to which he willingly agreed. She then sent him to a saintly old man, probably a bishop whose name some sources

---

74 *Story of a Soul*, chapter IX, p. 193.
75 *Her Last Conversations*, June 30, 1897.
76 Original Latin is "… *cantantibus organis Cecilia virgo in corde suo soli Domino decantabat*," from *Encyclopedia of Saints* by Clemens Jöckle, p. 92.

say was Urban, but apparently not Pope Urban since he reigned from 222 to 230, long before Cecilia was born. The pope at the time was living undercover for fear of persecution. Valerian, deeply impressed by Urban's eloquence and persuasive discourse, was converted and baptized. When he returned to his wife he did see an angel standing next to her who thereupon put a heavenly crown on their heads—roses on Cecilia and lilies on Valerian. His brother Tiburtius was soon also converted through Cecilia's convincing conversations with him about Jesus.

The two brothers, because of their unusual zeal, alms giving to the poor, and overall Christian kindness, especially in burying the bodies of the martyrs, became suspect, were arrested, and condemned to death by beheading. Maximus, a Roman officer under whom they were placed, was so touched by their courage and conviction that he declared he also wanted to be a Christian which he did become. As a result, he too suffered martyrdom by being clubbed to death.

After burying the three bodies, Cecilia was called in for interrogation by the Roman authorities. She was given two choices: repudiate her faith and sacrifice to the pagan gods or refuse and die. She chose the latter. The form of death was unique—suffocation by steam in her own bathroom. Though the furnace was heated to an extreme degree she remained unharmed after a day and a night. (Some accounts report that she was placed in boiling water in the caldarium [hot bath] of her own house.) A soldier was subsequently ordered to behead her. He struck her three times and was not successful in severing her head so he left her to die in that state. A fourth blow was apparently forbidden by law. It took three days for her to die during which time many Christians flocked to see her. She commended her household to Urban and willed her house to the Church. Christians buried her in the St. Calixtus Catacombs on the Appian Way. In the ninth century her remains as well as those of Valerian, Tiburtius, Maximus, and Pope Urban were transferred to the church of St. Cecilia in Trastevere, which was built over the foundations of Valerian's villa.

Devotion to St. Cecilia spread extensively from the earliest times and continued throughout all the ages right down to the present.

9. SAINT JOAN OF ARC (C. 1412–1431)
French heroine burned as a heretic

> Sweet martyr, our monasteries are yours.
> You know well that virgins are your sisters,
> And like you the object of their prayers
> Is to see God reign in every heart.[77]
> — St. Thérèse

THÉRÈSE, DEEPLY INSPIRED BY THE STORY OF JOAN OF ARC (*Jeanne d'Arc* IN French), felt a close attachment to her as a holy teenager, a virgin with child-like characteristics, one who wished all souls loved God and one who would undergo martyrdom.

---

77 From Thérèse's "Canticle to Obtain the Canonization of Joan of Arc," PN 4.

After the humiliating defeat of the French in the Franco-Prussian War (1870–1871), a new interest in Joan of Arc arose in France. Republicans, royalists, non-religious, Freemasons, free-thinkers, and even anti-clericals became infatuated with her. Perhaps it was a means of soothing the French pride. Despite that, the valiant, patriotic, triumphant young French lady Joan of Arc (also called Joan of Lorraine, the Maid of Orleans, the Liberator of France) was in the minds and hearts of many a loyal French man, woman, and child. Of great influence, no doubt, was the publication of books, poems, plays, operas (e.g. Verdi's *Giovanna d'Arco* and Tchaikovsky's *The Maid of Orleans*), paintings (by Ingres, etc.), her life, and her infamous trial. Notable was her biography by the well-known historian and politician Henry Wallon (1812–1904) that appeared in 1877. Thérèse's Uncle Guérin gave her a copy of this book which she read and used as the source material for her two Joan of Arc plays.

Clergymen like Msgr. Dupanloup (Bishop of Orleans) were successful in initially championing the introduction of her cause for beatification. The preliminary investigations necessary (the Diocesan Process) was formally begun by Pope Pius IX in 1869. Eventually on January 27, 1894, the promulgation by Pope Léo XIII of the heroic virtues of this martyr and Servant of God officially allowed the faithful to honor and pray to her publicly as the "Venerable" Joan of Arc.

As a result of Henry Wallon's efforts, May 8, the date of the liberation of Orleans by Joan of Arc in 1429 was proclaimed an annual national holiday honoring her. All France participated. Lisieux too was caught up in this patriotic and religious fervor. Thérèse's sister Céline and her cousin Marie Guérin, as members of their parish ladies' committee for the holiday, made a dozen banners for the decoration of their church, the Cathedral of Saint Pierre.

Thérèse, despite the fact that she was then a cloistered Carmelite, did not exclude herself from all the excitement and activity. For this grand holiday she composed her fourth poem, "Canticle to Obtain the Canonization of the Venerable Joan of Arc" and dedicated it to her intrepid sister, the "Gallant Knight C. Martin." The first eight lines sum up the message of the poem:

> God of hosts, the whole Church
> Soon wishes to honor at the Altar
> A Martyr, a warrior Virgin
> Whose sweet name resounds in Heaven.
>
> REFRAIN
>
> By your Power,
> O King of Heaven,
> Give to Joan of France
> The Halo and the Altar. (PN 4)

Interestingly, the two towns where Thérèse lived have a direct connection with Joan of Arc: Alençon where she was born and Lisieux where she died. Jean le Beau, the first Duke of Alençon, became a friend and a companion in arms with Joan of

Arc. Ironically, a year after Joan was burned at the stake in Rouen, the prelate Pierre Cauchon, who betrayed her to the English, thus influential in causing her death, was "rewarded" the position of Bishop of Bayeux-Lisieux (1432–1442) because of the aid he accorded to the English. He is buried in the Our Lady chapel in St. Pierre Cathedral in Lisieux where Thérèse and her family routinely attended Mass and where on May 8, 1894, a flag paying homage to Joan was placed.

Unlike the *petite bourgeoise* Thérèse, Joan was born into a simple peasant family on January 6, 1412, in Domrémy, a tiny village in Champagne (on the border of Lorraine), a region east of Paris. Her father, Jacques d'Arc, was a farmer and his wife, Isabelle *née* Romée, a kind and affectionate mother to their five children. Joan was a simple shepherdess, uneducated but a deeply religious young girl who spent many hours in prayer.

At the time of her birth all of northern France was under the power of the English who were supported by the leaders of Burgundy, the large region south of Champagne. This period in history is called the Hundred Years' War (1337–1453), a title used because of the long series of battles between France and England. At the end, England lost all its territory in France except Calais, the port city on the English Channel. Joan had a great deal to do to with solidifying French rule under Charles VII (1403–1461) and the expulsion of the foreigners from her soil, though it took an additional two decades to accomplish the complete removal of the English.

Joan first began to hear supernatural voices when she was in her early teens. Soon she was able to actually see these heavenly manifestations and identify them as St. Michael and two early Christian virgin martyrs—St. Catherine of Alexandria, and St. Margaret. By the time she was sixteen they slowly disclosed to her the mission she had to accomplish—to drive the English out of France.

Joan's two saints told her in May 1428 to become active in pursuing the course they wanted her to follow: to appear before the Dauphin,[78] obtain soldiers for her to lead in the rescue of the city of Orléans, and then to have him finally and decisively crowned King of France in Reims.

The holding of Orléans at this point was extremely crucial since it was the most significant remaining stronghold of the French. If it fell, it would mean the end of French rule. Joan was successful in eventually convincing the indecisive and weak Dauphin that he should muster French troops under her leadership, and rally to deliver Orléans from the English who had been besieging the city for some time. This resulted in a brilliant victory on May 8, 1429. The fearless shepherdess led the King's soldiers in other significant military conflicts and victories. She was also successful in having the Dauphin crowned King in Reims Cathedral. By this time she had become a living heroine to the general populace.

A year later, unfortunately, the Burgundians captured Joan and handed her over to the English for 10,000 gold francs. The ungrateful and cowardly King during this time and afterwards did not make the slightest effort to help her. She

---

78 The prince, son of the deranged Charles VI, who died in 1422.

appeared before an ecclesiastical court presided over by Msgr. Pierre Cauchon who after heavy cross-examination declared her a heretic and sorceress and then handed her over to the secular arm for sentencing. The nineteen-year-old Joan was condemned to death and burned at the stake in the market place of Rouen on May 30, 1431. Her ashes were ignominiously cast into the River Seine.

Twenty-five years later, through the efforts of her mother and two brothers, Joan's case was opened and reviewed under a commission appointed by Pope Callistus III which declared her innocent of all the evil accusations that brought about her death. It took another 453 years before she was beatified on April 11, 1909, by Pope Pius X and an additional eleven for her canonization on May 16, 1920, by Benedict XV.

While still very young, Thérèse was inspired by reading about France's heroines. She tells her spiritual brother Abbé Bellière about it:

> When I was beginning to learn the history of France, the account of Joan of Arc's exploits delighted me; I felt in my heart the desire and the courage to imitate her. It seemed the Lord destined me, too, for great things. I was not mistaken, but instead of voices from heaven inviting me to combat, I heard in the depths of my soul a gentler and stronger voice, that of the Spouse of Virgins, who was calling me to other exploits, to more glorious conquests, and into Carmel's solitude. I understood my mission was not to have a mortal king crowned but to make the King of heaven loved, to submit to Him the kingdom of hearts.[79]

In her third play, Thérèse has Joan sing her own thoughts:

> I want to fight for Jesus...
> To win Him countless souls.
> I want to love Him more and more!...
> My life will pass like a single day
> And soon without veil or cloud
> I will see Jesus, my love.
> There.... On that Heavenly shore,
> He will embrace me forever!!!...[80]

Thérèse clearly crystallizes her entire philosophy of life in her references to Joan of Arc. The affinity to her is striking and flows constantly through the years in her writings and conversations even to her dying days. A few examples follow as recorded in *Her Last Conversations* (*Derniers Entretiens*) where Thérèse is talking to her sister Pauline in the infirmary during her last months of life:

- I have read over again the play on Joan of Arc that I composed [RP 3]. You will see there my sentiments on death; they are all expressed; this will please you. But don't believe I'm like Joan of Arc when she was afraid for a moment.... She was tearing her hair out!... I myself am not tearing out my "little" hair (July 5, 1897).

---

79 LT 224 from Thérèse to l'abbé Bellière, dated April 25, 1897. Incidentally, Mark Twain too was fascinated by Joan of Arc. In 1904 he stated that "She is easily and by far the most extraordinary person the human race has ever produced." He said his best book is on Joan of Arc.
80 From Thérèse's play, *Joan of Arc Accomplishing Her Mission*, RP 3, Part I, Scene 5.

- They [nuns questioning her when she was ill] plague me with questions; it reminds me of Joan of Arc before her judges. It seems to me I answer with the same sincerity (July 20, 1897).
- [Pauline envisioned difficulties with the publication of Thérèse's autobiography:] Well, I say with Joan of Arc: "And the will of God will be carried out in spite of the envy of men!" (July 27, 1897)

Thérèse wrote more about Joan of Arc than she did of any other saint. This includes the passages she refers to her in *Story of a Soul*, the poems, prayers, letters, and most especially the three plays she composed: *The Mission of Joan of Arc or the Shepherdess of Domrémy Listening to Voices* (RP 1) presented on January 21, 1894; *Joan of Arc Accomplishing her Mission* (RP 3) given exactly a year later; and *The Triumph of Humility* (RP 7), given on June 21, 1896. The last one does not deal with Joan of Arc in depth, but Thérèse refers to Diana Vaughan as "the new Joan of Arc." It deals with the power of humility needed to combat the evil Satan employs to destroy the Carmelite vocation. (Thérèse did not realize at the time that this Diana Vaughan was completely fictional, and as such, a notoriously anti-Catholic character who never experienced the conversion that her creator claimed.)

These three plays widen our understanding of Thérèse's spirituality and unfold the similarities between Joan's character and Thérèse's. They mirror perfectly Thérèse's own aspirations, thoughts on death, love, humility, courage, and to some degree the Carmelite ethos.

The second play, *Joan of Arc Accomplishing Her Mission*, is the longest play Thérèse wrote, the most elaborate to present, and the one for which Thérèse received the most acclaim by her fellow nuns, not only for its compositional merits, but for her excellence in acting the part of Joan. (She portrayed Joan in the first play also.) This is the only play (RP 3) of the eight that had photographs (five) taken connected with it. The first two pictures show Thérèse wearing a wig over her toque, and standing in her blue gown decorated with silvery *fleurs-de-lis* sewn on it. She is holding a sword in one hand and a large flag in the other. The third, fourth, and fifth photos depict Thérèse as Joan in prison, during a vision of St. Margaret (played by Céline), and in heaven wearing a crown of flowers and holding a palm branch in her hands. Incidentally, during one of the scenes, flames from an alcohol lamp representing fire at the stake hit a piece of scenery that started to burn. Thérèse stood behind but luckily was not harmed.

Thérèse sent one of the photos of herself and Céline, signed with the inscription to "a new Joan of Arc," to the current celebrity, Diana Vaughan—unknown at this point as the imaginary creation of the infamous hoaxer Léo Taxil. "She" at first became notorious throughout Europe as a malicious anti-Catholic as well as the author of a book exposing a secret Masonic cult that reveled in satanic practices, which was equally fictitious. In time she related her sudden, extraordinary conversion to Catholicism. After this sensational revelation, she devoted her efforts to combating the evil in which she had been involved.

Diana attributed this spiritual transformation to the impact that Joan of Arc's story had on her. Furthermore, Diana's writings, particularly *The Eucharistic Novena of Reparation* (1895), and her wish to become a nun especially impressed Thérèse. It was after Thérèse heard about her remarkable conversion and that of Léo Taxil's, that she sent her the photo (Number 14 that Céline retouched) of herself as Joan of Arc in prison with her sister Céline as St. Margaret. This picture, vastly enlarged, was the only image on display in the auditorium of the Paris Geographical Society (*Société de Géographie*, founded in 1821) on the Boulevard St. Germain before a huge assembly of journalists, clergy, Masons, and others on April 19, 1897. Léo Taxil finally appeared before the anxiously waiting crowd and with a contemptuous air brazenly divulged his egregious hoax, the main purpose of which he admitted was to embarrass the Catholic Church, the Pope, and ridicule devotion to Joan of Arc. Fortunately Thérèse and Céline were not identified by name or location during the talk. Needless to say, Thérèse was appalled by Taxil's treachery, fraud, hatred, and ability to deceive and not be detected.

Clearly Thérèse strove for sainthood as intensely, rigorously, and persistently as an athlete does to win an Olympic medal. Yet one wonders if she really believed she would ever be called a "new Joan of Arc," especially by a reigning pontiff (Pope Pius XI); let alone be proclaimed by another pontiff, Pope Pius XII the "secondary patroness of France" on a par with St. Joan of Arc. And to crown even these supreme accolades, Pope John Paul II in 1997 declared her a "Doctor of the Universal Church," one of only three women in two thousand years of history so honored.

10. Saint John of the Cross (1542–1591)
Spanish Carmelite, writer, mystic, reformer, and Doctor of the Church

> *Lord, what I should like you to give me is trials to suffer for you, to be despised and esteemed as of little worth.*
>
> — St. John of the Cross

THE ABOVE QUOTATION COULD EASILY BE CONSIDERED FROM THE PEN OF St. Thérèse of Lisieux, but it is by St. John of the Cross.[81] He was her inspiration, guide, and master in the spiritual realm. Yet the two were worlds apart in origin, culture, time, and gender.

He was born Juan de Yepes y Alvarez, son of a poor silk-weaver, Gonzalo de Yepes, and Catalina, *née* Alvarez, in Fontiveros, near Avila, Old Castile, Spain, in 1542, some 331 years before St. Thérèse of Lisieux. Gonzalo died when John was an infant, leaving the family truly impoverished. John did not do well as an apprentice weaver or at any other trade. At seventeen the director of the hospital in Medina del Campo accepted him as a humble worker. While working there he pursued his education with the Jesuits (1559–1563) through the financial help of a kind benefactor, Alvarez of Toledo. He entered the Carmelite Order at Santa

---
81 Crisógono de Jesús, O.C.D., *The Life of St. John of the Cross*, p. 268.

Ana in Medina in 1563 and received the religious name John of St. Mathias. The next year he was professed. From 1564 to 1568 he attended the University of Salamanca. After profession they permitted him to follow the strict rules of the old order in preference to the more liberal ones then prevalent. At first he wanted to be a lay brother, but because of his intellect and learning capacity, they urged him to study for the priesthood, which he did, and was ordained in 1567 at the age of twenty-five. In a short time, though, he wanted to become a Carthusian.

Fortuitously, John met St. Teresa of Avila who was in the midst of reforming her order of Carmelite nuns. He became most interested in her cause, dropped his idea of becoming a Carthusian, and joined her in the furtherance of her endeavors. John then, with a few others, in 1568 founded the first house of the reform for Discalced (barefooted) Carmelite men in a run-down house in Duruelo. In the same year John took the new name of John of the Cross (Juan de la Cruz). Soon he established several more houses. He was also made the rector of a college of the university in Alcalá. In 1571 St. Teresa became the prioress of an unreformed monastery in Alcalá called the Incarnation, and through her wishes John was chosen its spiritual director and confessor for five years.

St. Teresa's undertakings to reform the Order met with violent opposition. Eventually John too was severely censured, abducted in Avila in 1577, and finally committed to a monastery prison in Toledo by friars of the old relaxed Order—the Calced (wearing shoes) Carmelites, sometimes called the "mitigated" Carmelites. In prison he suffered from beatings, insults, and slanders but he would not abandon his aim of reform. Managing to escape after nine months of confinement in a tiny filthy cell with very little light, John found refuge at several reformed friaries in Spain.

Eventually, in 1580, Pope Gregory XIII recognized the Discalced Carmelites and gave them a special honor by establishing a province just for them. John became in succession the head of a college, provincial, prior, and founder of numerous Carmelite houses not only in Spain but also in Portugal. In 1582 his companion in reform St. Teresa of Avila died.

Ultimately, controversy and heated disputes within the Discalced Carmelites arose resulting in the demotion of John who was sent to an out-of-the-way monastery in Ubeda where he contracted a fever. Even here friars of his own order tormented him with harsh treatment for three months. In addition, he suffered from gangrene in his foot and eventually died there at the age of forty-nine on December 14, 1591. His body was transferred to Segovia where it remains today in an incorrupt state.

St. John of the Cross has been designated as one of the greatest mystics and spiritual writers of the Christian world. His most acclaimed works of mystic theology are: *The Dark Night of the Soul, The Spiritual Canticle, The Ascent of Mount Carmel,* and *The Living Flame of Love.*

In 1675, eighty-four years after his death, John was beatified. Fifty-one years later Pope Benedict III canonized him on December 27, 1726. It took two hundred more years for him to be proclaimed a Doctor of the Church by Pope Pius XI in 1926—a year after Thérèse Martin was canonized. Thérèse always believed that he merited this honor and several times expressed this wish to her novice, Sr. Marie of the Trinity.

A distinct and profound kinship exists between St. Thérèse and St. John of the Cross, similarities obvious in their manner of expression, their spiritual concepts, and the development of their spiritual life. The strong influence he exerted on Thérèse's thoughts and doctrines is quite obvious and considerable. Not only did she specifically make references to St. John of the Cross and his works in her writings but also in conversations and oral teachings. She quotes him twenty-one times in her letters, eight times in *Her Last Conversations*, and in her autobiography fourteen times.[82] In one excerpt from *Story of a Soul*, she tells us how she is indebted to him: "Ah! How many lights have I not drawn from the works of our holy Father, St. John of the Cross! At the ages of seventeen and eighteen (1890–1891) I had no other spiritual nourishment."[83]

Thérèse absorbed his *The Living Flame of Love* and *The Spiritual Canticle*, the latter being the work she preferred. In fact, among the few books she had in her convent cell and later on at her night stand in the infirmary were these two books bound in one volume, with certain passages, particularly on dying of love, underlined.

There clearly are differences in gender, nationality, temperament, family background, upbringing, education, age at writing, length of life, and era; yet in the spiritual domain the similarities are striking. Notice their theories on faith, hope, love, humility, littleness, suffering, death, Mary, and the Church. The manner of conveying these subjects is not necessarily identical, but the essence is the same despite Thérèse's simplification, modification, amplification, and synthesis. And herein lies her genius, her uniqueness, her creativity. St. John's approach is mystic, philosophical, and theological whereas Thérèse's is simple, concise, generally more poetic, down-to-earth, clearer to understand, more precise in verbiage, and if you will, more feminine.

It was from him that Thérèse derived much insight for her "Act of Oblation to Merciful Love" and even her "little Way." Thérèse said to one of her novices, Sr. Marie of the Trinity, a statement that alludes to this "little Way": "The only means of making rapid progress on the way of love is to remain very little. Also, I now sing with our Father St. John of the Cross: The lower and more subdued / and abased I became. / I … sank, ah, so low, / that I was so high, so high, / that I took the prey."[84]

Another time Thérèse wrote a poem for Sr. Marie of the Trinity named "A Gloss on the Divine" (PN 30) and gave it to her on the day she was professed, April 30, 1896. It is an interpretation of a poem St. John wrote which in Spanish

---

82 Miller, *The Trial of Faith of St. Thérèse of Lisieux*, p. 116.
83 Chapter viii, p. 179.
84 Poem VI, "More Stanzas Applied to Spiritual Things" from *The Collected Works of St. John of the Cross*, p. 722.

is "Glosa a lo Divino." She wrote it on a card in black and red lettering on the top of which she drew a picture of the Holy Face. When this sister received the veil seven days later, Thérèse gave her another holy card on the front of which was a photograph of a painting Mother Agnès did of St. John of the Cross and on the back Thérèse wrote three sayings by the Spanish Mystic.

Surprisingly, in Thérèse's time St. John of the Cross was considered a rather obscure author and thus not generally read or referred to even in Carmelite houses. The third centenary celebration of the death of St. John of the Cross (December 14, 1891), however, generated an interest in him and the Lisieux Carmel made necessary preparations for it. Though Thérèse most likely did not read the complete works of the Doctor of Carmel, she did have access to at least major portions of his principle works, read and assimilated them, and soon became his disciple, sister, and daughter; and he in return, her master, father, and brother.

When Thérèse was still a lay person at Les Buissonnets, she had heard of St. John of the Cross primarily from her older sisters Marie and Pauline who were then in the Lisieux Carmel. Surprisingly, her father forbade her to read his writings for fear they might hinder in some ways her spiritual growth. Upon entering the Carmel her favorite readings besides Scripture were the lives of the saints, *The Song of Songs*, and the works of St. John of the Cross. Thérèse's mistress of novices reported this of Thérèse:

> One day, I do not know if she was seventeen years old, she spoke to me of certain passages from mysticism [by St. John of the Cross] with an intelligence so much above her age that I was astonished. A little time after she left the novitiate she told me [during recreation] of the magnificent things that she expressed later on in her splendid canticle "*Vivre d'amour*." ["Living on Love," PN 17][85]

In her autobiography and letters Thérèse quotes St. John of the Cross a number of times from his *The Spiritual Canticle* and other works especially on suffering, love, the state of being despised, and abandonment. For example, on love she writes: "O my Jesus! I love You! I love the Church, my Mother! I recall that 'the smallest act of pure love is of more value to her than all other works together.'"[86] She writes these same words to Father Roulland in Letter 221 of March 19, 1897.

Another passage from *The Spiritual Canticle* that had its imprint on St. Thérèse is from stanza 9, no. 7: "Love is paid only with love itself." She repeats this in her autobiography: "Oh Jesus, I know it, love is repaid by love alone."[87] Furthermore, when she devised her coat of arms and painted it at the end of Ms. A of her autobiography, she incorporated that phrase on it: "Love is repaid by love alone" which in the original French is "*L'Amour ne se paie que par l'Amour*."

---
85 From the testimony given by Sister Marie of the Angels at the Apostolic Process on September 7, 1915. The translation is by the author.
86 *Story of a Soul*, chapter IX, p. 197. This is a quote from *The Spiritual Canticle*, stanza 29, no. 2.
87 Ibid., p. 195.

Two months before she died, Thérèse reminded her sister Mother Agnès of these words from *The Living Flame of Love*: "Tear through the veil of this sweet encounter!"[88] Then Thérèse added:

> I've always applied these words to the death of love that I desire. Love will not wear out the veil of my life; it will tear it suddenly.
>
> With what longing and what consolation I repeated from the beginning of my religious life these other words of St. John of the Cross: "It is of the highest importance that the soul practice love very much in order that, being consumed rapidly, she may be scarcely retained here on earth but promptly reach the vision of God face to face" [*The Living Flame of Love*, stanza 1].

St. John of the Cross wrote a significant amount on "the death of love" that played a crucial part in molding and strengthening Thérèse's final spiritual convictions.

> Ah! It is incredible how all my hopes have been fulfilled. When I used to read St. John of the Cross [*The Living Flame of Love*, stanza 1], I begged God to work out in me what he wrote, that is, the same thing as though I were to live to be very old; to consume me rapidly in Love, and I have been answered![89]

This death of love Thérèse so ardently wished for she indeed attained. Her very last words were: "Oh!... I love Him!... My God! I love You!"[90]

For the third centenary of St. John of the Cross's death, Sister Thérèse of the Child Jesus and Mother Agnès were given the task of illuminating holy cards [preserved in the Carmel Archives] of the great mystic father. Other reminders of St. John of the Cross exist in the monastery today. In the rear of the Carmel Chapel which is open to the public stands a statue of St. John of the Cross embracing a huge cross. When Thérèse was alive it stood in the heated parlor in the cloistered area of the monastery.

A maxim St. Thérèse often meditated upon as a young girl and in conversations with her sister Céline is a reply St. John of the Cross gave to Christ: "To suffer and be despised" to which Thérèse added "for love." The origin of this quotation follows. The confessor of St. John was Padre Carro, a Jesuit of Medina, to whom St. John related this incident:

> After I had put it [a crucifix or picture] in the church as reverently as I could, when I was praying before it one day, a voice said to me, "Fray [Brother] John, ask me what you like, for I will grant it you for this service you have done me." I said to him: "Lord, what I should like you to give me is trials to suffer for you, and to be despised and esteemed as of little worth."[91]

This affirms the essence of Thérèse's religious life and longing as it did of her spiritual mentor St. John of the Cross centuries before.

---

88 *Her Last Conversations*, July 27, 1897.
89 Ibid., August 31, 1897.
90 Ibid., September 30, 1897.
91 Crisógono de Jesús, O.C.D., *op. cit.*, p. 268.

11. SAINT MARY MAGDALENE (FIRST CENTURY)
Former sinner who followed Jesus

Most of all I imitate the conduct of Magdalene; her astonishing or rather her loving audacity which charms the Heart of Jesus also attracts my own. Yes, I feel it; even though I had on my conscience all the sins that can be committed, I would go, my heart broken with sorrow, and throw myself into Jesus' arms, for I know how much He loves the prodigal child who returns to Him.[92]

—St. Thérèse

IT SEEMS MOST TELLING THAT THÉRÈSE WROTE THIS STRONG STATEMENT of just two sentences before the very end of her autobiography. Saint Mary Magdalene, nonetheless, was not included in that inner circle of youthful and martyred saints Thérèse loved so dearly such as Saints Théophane Vénard, Agnès, Cecilia, and Joan of Arc. Yet she admired her and tried to imitate her "loving audacity" as she called it. An example would be her boldness at the Colosseum in Rome where, despite the barrier and the rules of the tour guide, she went down to the floor of the arena and picked up a few stones as souvenirs:

In the Gospel, we read that Mary Magdalene stayed close to the tomb, and *every once in a while* she stooped down to peer inside. She initially saw two angels. Like her, while recognizing the impossibility of seeing my desires fulfilled, I continued to look towards the ruins into which I wanted to descend; I didn't see any angels, but I did see *what I was looking for* and I cried to Céline: "Come quick! We can get through!"[93]

Also, at the ancient tomb of St. Cecilia, the two sisters, determined to take some souvenir from the catacombs, stealthily slipped away from the rest of the tourists and removed a small piece of earth from the spot where the martyr's body had lain. But the most audacious action Thérèse took on this pilgrimage was to speak to the pope despite the regulations forbidding anyone to talk to him at this papal audience.

Thérèse expounded upon St. Luke's scriptural account (Chapter 7: 37–50) where the well-known sinner named Mary Magdalene displayed her loving audacity at the house of Simon the Pharisee when she approached Jesus at dinner, washed his feet, and anointed them and His head with precious oil:

I know that without Him, I could have fallen as low as St. Mary Magdalene, and the profound words of Our Lord to Simon resound with a great sweetness in my soul. I know that *"he to whom less is forgiven,* LOVES *less,"* (Luke 7:47) but I also know that Jesus has *forgiven me more* than St. Mary Magdalene since He forgave me *in advance* by preventing me from falling.... He wants me to *love* Him because He *has forgiven* me not much but ALL. He has not expected me to *love Him much* like Mary Magdalene, but He has willed that I KNOW how He has loved me with a love of *unspeakable foresight* in order that now I may love Him unto *folly!*[94]

---

92 *Story of a Soul*, chapter XI, pp. 258–259.
93 Ibid., chapter IV, p. 130.
94 Ibid., chapter IV, pp. 83–84.

The qualities Thérèse loved about Mary Magdalene were not only her "loving audacity" but her enduring love and her sincere repentance:

> You [Abbé Bellière] love St. Augustine, Saint Magdalene, these souls to whom "many sins were forgiven because they loved much" [Luke 7:47]. I love them too, I love their repentance, and especially ... their loving audacity! When I see Magdalene walking up before the many guests, washing with her tears the feet of her adored Master, whom she is touching for the first time, I feel that *her heart* has understood the abysses of love and mercy *of the Heart of Jesus*, and, sinner though she is, this Heart of love was not only disposed to pardon her but to lavish on her the blessings of His divine intimacy, to lift her to the highest summits of contemplation.[95]

St. Thérèse was much impressed by the episode from the gospel account of St. Luke when Jesus is invited to the house of Mary and her sister Martha who lived with their brother Lazarus. Martha is annoyed that Mary is listening to Jesus speak and not helping her in preparing to serve Him. Jesus responds: "Martha, Martha, thou art anxious and troubled about many things; and yet only one thing is needful. Mary has chosen the best part, and it will not be taken away from her."[96] This incident had such an impact on Thérèse that she composed a play about it, *Jesus at Bethany* (RP 4). She presented it before the entire Carmelite community on the feast of St. Martha, July 29, 1895, to honor the lay sisters, the "Marthas" of the community, who did most of the manual work. Thérèse, however, mistakenly assumed, as was widely believed at the time, that this Mary of Bethany was the repentant sinner Mary Magdalene.

Thérèse has her own distinctive interpretation of Our Lord's response to Martha when in her play she has Jesus say to her: "Work is indeed necessary and I came to make it holy. But it is always essential to accompany work with fervent prayer."[97] In all probability she omitted "Mary has chosen the best part" from Luke's account in order not to imply in any way that choir nuns were better than or superior to lay sisters.

Two years after she composed this play, Thérèse commented about the same story in her autobiography, again believing that this Mary Magdalene was the sister of Martha:

> [A] soul that is burning with love cannot remain inactive. No doubt, she will remain at Jesus' feet as did Mary Magdalene, and she will listen to His sweet and burning words. Appearing to do nothing, she will give much more than Martha who torments herself with many things and wants her sister to imitate her. It is not Martha's works that Jesus finds fault with; His divine Mother submitted humbly to these works all through her life since she had to prepare the meals of the Holy Family. It is only the *restlessness* of His ardent hostess that He willed to correct.[98]

---

95 Thérèse's letter to the Abbé Bellière, LT 247, June 21, 1897.
96 Luke 10:41.
97 RP 4, p. 868 in *Œuvres Complètes*.
98 *Story of a Soul*, chapter XI, pp. 257–258.

In one of her letters to Céline, Thérèse defends Mary Magdalene's loving actions and relates them to the contemplative life:

> Jesus has defended us in the person of the Magdalene. He was at table, Martha was serving, Lazarus was eating with Him and His disciples. As for Mary, she was not thinking of taking any food but of *pleasing* Him whom she loved, so she took a jar filled with an ointment of great price and poured it on the head of Jesus, after *breaking the jar*, and the whole house was scented with the ointment, but the APOSTLES *complained* against Magdalene.... It is really the same for us, the most fervent *Christians*, *priests*, find that we are *exaggerated*, that we should serve with Martha instead of consecrating to Jesus the *vessels* of our *lives*, with the ointments enclosed within them....[99]

Six months after she wrote this letter, Thérèse continues the same thought lyrically in stanza 12 of one of her best poems, "Living on Love!" (PN 17):

> Living on Love is imitating Mary,
> Bathing your divine feet that she kisses, transported.
> With tears, with precious perfume,
> She dries them with her long hair....
> Then standing up, she shatters the vase,
> And in turn she anoints your Sweet Face.
> As for me, the perfume with which I anoint your Face
>   Is my Love!...

In July of 1889, when Thérèse was in her novitiate year, an unusual thing happened to her in the Carmel garden area. While she was praying at the grotto of St. Mary Magdalene that had a statue of the Blessed Mother above it, she experienced the extraordinary sensation of being covered with the protective veil of the Virgin Mary. She described this strange phenomenon to her sister Pauline (Mother Agnès) nine years later when she was in the infirmary: "I recall I was doing things as though not doing them; it was as if someone had lent me a body. I remained this way for one whole week."[100]

Mary Magdalene was born in Magdala (now called Migdal), a small town in Galilee near Tiberius on the western shore of the Sea of Galilee. In the Bible she is also called "the Magdalene," "the sinner," and the woman "from whom seven devils had gone out." This exorcism by Jesus is the first time we hear of her in Scripture The next occasion is at the home of Simon the Pharisee where she lavishly anoints Jesus who says to Simon:

> "Wherefore I say to thee, her sins, many as they are, shall be forgiven her, because she has loved much. But he to whom little is forgiven, loves little." And He said to her: "Thy sins are forgiven." ... And they who were at table with him began to say within themselves, "Who is this man, who even forgives sins?" But he said to the woman, "Thy faith has saved thee; go in peace."[101]

---

99 LT 169, dated August 19, 1894.
100 *Her Last Conversations*, July 11, 1897.
101 Luke 7:47–50.

Another Gospel account states that six days before Jesus was arrested, Mary anointed Jesus at the home of Lazarus which annoyed the sanctimonious Judas Iscariot because, as he said, that money could have been given to the poor. Jesus replied, "Let her be—that she may keep it for the day of my burial. For the poor you have always with you, but you do not always have me."[102]

Most likely Mary Magdalene saw the scourged Jesus on Pilate's balcony, heard the crowd roar, "Crucify Him!" and, with the other women, followed Him carrying His cross to Calvary. She witnessed His crucifixion and with the Blessed Mother and the young John she stood nearby as He uttered His seven last words, gazed at Him when He died, and helped His mother bury Him.

Furthermore, Mary Magdalene had the unique honor of being the first person Jesus appeared to after His resurrection. It was through her that He relayed His instructions to the Apostles. Thérèse was clearly impressed by the passage in Scripture when Mary did not at first recognize Jesus at the tomb until he spoke her name. She composed one of her most deeply felt poems, "To the Sacred Heart of Jesus" (PN 23), in which she reflects upon this episode in her own inimitable way, associating herself with Mary while expressing her profound love for Jesus:

> At the holy sepulcher, Mary Magdalene,
> Searching for her Jesus, stooped down in tears.
> ...
> Close by the tomb, the last one to stay,
> She had come well before dawn.
> Her God also came, veiling his light.
> Mary could not vanquish him in love!
> Showing her at first his Blessed Face,
> Soon just one word sprang from his Heart.
> Whispering the sweet name of: Mary,
> Jesus gave back her peace, her happiness.
> ...
> O my God, one day, like Mary Magdalene,
> I wanted to see you and come close to you.

After His ascension, Mary's life is shrouded in mystery since the sources are not entirely reliable. Some historians tell us that Mary Magdalene spent a number of years with the Mother of Jesus. She helped spread the message of Jesus Christ first to the people of Ephesus where the Blessed Virgin and John are purported to have lived after they left the Holy Land. And from there she went as far as Marseille with her brother and sister where tradition says she died.

Devotion to St. Mary Magdalene seems to have spread throughout Europe beginning in the eleventh century. Many chapels and shrines have been built in her honor in Paris and elsewhere. Today, however, there is an unusual shrine twenty-five miles northeast of Marseille at Le Plan d'Aups-Sainte Baume where her relics are preserved high up in a grotto. From here an expansive view of the

---

102 John 12:7–8.

distant Mediterranean Sea, forty miles away, can be seen. Thousands of pilgrims each year visit this site believed to be the place where Mary Magdalene died and was buried.

Throughout the ages, Mary Magdalene has fascinated famous artists and sculptors who have depicted her generally as a tearful woman repenting her sins. Even as a young child, Thérèse was aware of this customary portrayal of her:

> I had received the name: "Céline's little girl," and when she was irritated with me, her greatest sign of displeasure was to say: "You're no longer my little girl; that's over with, and I'll *always remember it!*" All I had to do was to start crying like a Magdalene, begging her to consider me still as her "little girl." Very soon she kissed me and promised me to *remember nothing*.[103]

Another amusing example of Thérèse as the weeping Magdalene, is also from the autobiography: "I was really unbearable because of my extreme touchiness; if I happened to cause anyone I loved some little trouble, even unwittingly, instead of forgetting about it and not *crying*, which made matters worse, I *cried like a Magdalene* and then when I began to cheer up, I'd begin to *cry again for having cried*."[104]

Saint Mary Magdalene has been proclaimed the patroness of towns and locations such as Naples, Provence, and Sicily. She is also the patroness of an amazing variety of occupations and conditions including prisoners, penitent women, the seduced, hairdressers, comb-makers, perfume manufactures, winegrowers, children with difficulty in walking, and many others.[105]

12. Saint Sebastian (d. 288)
Christian Roman soldier martyred for his faith

ONE OF THE BOOKS THÉRÈSE AVIDLY READ AS A YOUNG GIRL WAS CARDINAL Wiseman's *Fabiola* or *the Church of the Catacombs*, a popular novel of early Christianity about a young pagan Roman lady who became a Christian and died as a martyr for her faith. Saint Sebastian plays a very significant part in this book. Thérèse and her sister Céline were fascinated by this saint and felt an affinity toward him as a courageous soldier who willingly endured martyrdom, a fate Thérèse especially longed for: "Martyrdom was the dream of my youth and this dream has grown with me within Carmel's cloisters.... I would undergo all the tortures inflicted upon the martyrs."[106] This, though, is only one of several roles she longed for: "I feel the vocation of the warrior, the priest, the apostle, the doctor, the martyr."[107]

Ever since childhood, Céline was called "the intrepid" and "the brave one," nicknames her father gave her because she proved to be more courageous and

---
103 *Story of a Soul*, chapter III, p. 56.
104 Ibid., chapter V, p. 97.
105 Jöckle, *Encylopedia of Saints*, p. 311.
106 *Story of a Soul*, p. 193.
107 Ibid., p. 192.

dauntless than any of his other daughters. During their student days together, Céline was unafraid to defend Thérèse boldly when the occasion arose. Her childhood interest in knights of old and chivalry did not diminish when she became a nun. As a matter of fact, her sister Pauline (Mother Agnès) used to compare her to Saint Sebastian.

At Céline's request, Thérèse (a nun at the time) wrote in a long letter to her a fanciful account of how the heavenly beings would celebrate Céline's "wedding day"—February 24, 1896, the day of her profession as a Carmelite nun: "Thus all the pontiffs, the glorious martyrs, the warriors (at their head, St. Sebastian), in a word, the whole heavenly nobility will take glory in giving the spouse of Jesus the name of sister, and the wedding will be composed of one great and identical family."[108]

Thérèse composed a prayer about St. Sebastian for her sister Céline, writing it in beautiful calligraphy on a holy card. At the time Céline was struggling with some difficulties in her novitiate and this was intended to give her encouragement:

> O Saint Sebastian! Obtain for me your love and your courage so that like you, I may be able to fight for the glory of God!
>
> O Glorious Soldier of Christ! You fought victoriously for the honor of the God of hosts and received the palm and crown of Martyrdom. Listen to my secret: "Like the angelic Tarcisius I carry the Lord." I am only a child and yet I must fight each day to preserve the priceless Treasure that is hidden in my soul.... Often I must redden the arena of combat with my heart's blood.
>
> O Mighty Warrior! Be my protector, sustain me by your victorious arm and I will not fear my powerful enemies. With your help I will fight until the evening of my life, then you will present me to Jesus and from his hand I will receive the palm that you will have helped me to win![109]

During her final illness as the feast of St. Sebastian approached, Thérèse recited the words of an old refrain: "O great Sebastian / To whom God refuses nothing...." She was asking him to hasten her entrance into heaven, but it did not occur until almost a month later. Disappointed, during the interim she remarked that "I am going to do as Saint Sebastian; I am going to be healed of my first wounds. I will die not believing in my death."[110]

The story of Saint Sebastian is derived from legends all of which are clouded with uncertainty and conjecture. Perhaps of noble parentage, Sebastian may have been born in Milan, Narbonne (in southern France), or in Rome. As a young man he enlisted in the imperial Roman army of the infamous Emperor Diocletian (245–313). Because of his noble bearing and exceptional bravery, he rose to the enviable position of captain of the Praetorian Guard, thus becoming the emperor's personal protector.

---

108   LT 182, February 23, 1896.
109   Pri 18, "O Holy Innocents, O Saint Sebastian."
110   Piat, *Céline*, p. 184.

In the meantime, he secretly comforted and aided the Christians who were arrested and sentenced to death. Whether he was already a Christian himself or if the Christian prisoners converted him is not certain. Inevitably the Emperor learned that Sebastian was a Christian and deeply involved with helping the imprisoned Christians. He had him arrested for ingratitude and criminal conspiracy and sentenced him to death. The soldiers tied him to a stake and shot him with arrows—a form of "firing squad" common in those Roman times. As he was left for dead, Irene, the widow of another martyr, Castulus, sought the body with the purpose of burying it. She was surprised to discover him alive and thereupon nursed him back to health. But Sebastian, zealous as ever, appeared before the astounded emperor and reproached him for his ordering the senseless shedding of innocent blood. Completely enraged, Diocletian ordered Sebastian to be clubbed to death. This time he did die and his body was thrown into the main Roman sewer.

Another Roman lady, the young Luciana, learned through a dream the exact location of Sebastian's corpse, removed it, and buried it in a catacomb on the Old Appian Way. This, now called the Catacomb of Saint Sebastian, is considered the first and earliest catacomb. In the fourth century a church named the Basilica of Saint Sebastian was built over it, possibly by Constantine. There is no evidence available, however, that Thérèse visited this shrine when she was on her pilgrimage to Rome.

Saint Sebastian is honored as the patron saint of soldiers, archers, athletes, crusaders, plague victims, and others. His feast day is celebrated on January 20.

An interesting side note is that Thérèse's father, Louis Martin, died at La Musse, the vacation home of her cousins which is situated in the village of Saint Sébastien-de-Morsent. The vicar of the church of St. Sébastien administered the last rites.

Thérèse is always pictured as an angelic, meek young nun holding beautiful roses. Her expression is always serene and trouble free. She certainly possessed these personality traits; nonetheless, she was a tenacious and courageous fighter beneath her sweet and peaceful facade. As certain proof of this, in the final months of her life she stoically suffered from her trial of faith, from the terrible pains incurred during the administration of the current rather primitive medical treatments, and most noticeably from the intense agony she endured from the tuberculosis that caused her death—and all of this without any relief from pain killers that were denied her.

Thérèse's poem "My Weapons" (PN 48), though written for her cousin, is really about herself as the spouse of Christ. Composed in the midst of her sufferings, it includes as a kind of preface this potent excerpt from *The Song of Songs*: "The Spouse of the King is terrible as an army ranged in battle; she is like a choir of music in an armed camp." The stirring final lines, blended with her characteristic musical allusions, are worthy of any martyr, saint, or soldier like St. Sebastian:

> If I have the powerful armor of the Warrior,
> It I imitate him and fight bravely,
> ...
> Then I can sing of the strength and sweetness
> Of your Mercies.
> Smiling, I bravely face the fire.
> And in your arms, O my Divine Spouse,
> I shall die singing on the battlefield,
> My Weapons in hand!

13. Saint Stanislas Kostka (1550–1568)
Jesuit seminarian who died at 18

ALL THE SAINTS THÉRÈSE FAVORED DIED YOUNG; AND ST. STANISLAS INDEED was one of them. In addition to that, and quite striking, is the fact that both she and he had the desire to do good on earth after their death.

Sister Thérèse composed a play for the golden jubilee of the kindly nun, Sister St. Stanislas, entitled simply "Saint Stanislas Kostka" (RP 8) and presented it at the Carmel on February 8, 1897. Sister St. Stanislas was the oldest member of the community and later Thérèse's infirmarian when she was dying of tuberculosis. Thérèse wrote it in prose except for nine quatrains of music sung to two different melodies at the end by celestial voices: an Angel, St. Barbara, and the Blessed Virgin. The play takes place entirely in the chamber of St. Francis Borgia in Rome. The major events in Stanislas's life are featured: his family opposition, travel to Germany, entrance into the Jesuit community, and the vision he experienced of St. Barbara, accompanied by angels, giving him Communion.

Thérèse harbored two strong desires in her life which she presents in this play: the wish to exercise priestly duties (like St. Barbara) and the hope (like St. Stanislas) of doing good on earth after death. In the vision Stanislas has at the very end, the Blessed Virgin assures him that his wish will be granted:

> Dear child, you will protect
> The souls struggling in this world.
> The more their harvest will be fertile,
> And the more in heaven you will shine!...[111]

That is exactly what happened concerning Thérèse after she died.

Stanislas was born on October 28, 1550, in Rostkovo, Poland, of a noble Polish family; the son of John Kostka, a senator of the Kingdom of Poland and Lord of Zakroczmy, and Margaret de Drobniy Kryska, the sister and niece of the Dukes Palatine of Masovia and the aunt of the noted Chancellor of Poland, Felix Kryski. The second of seven children, Stanislas was closest to his older brother Paul who eventually, because of envy and irritation with his brother's piety, treated him violently—verbally and physically.

---
111 RP 8. Author's translation into English.

At first the two sons were taught at home with particular emphasis on holiness, obedience, and firm discipline. When Stanislas reached the age of fourteen he and Paul were sent to the Jesuit school in Vienna with their tutor Belinksi where they remained for three years. Here Stanislas distinguished himself as a friendly, cheerful, and an exceptionally "angelic" student. During this time he sought admittance into the Jesuit order, but was not accepted by the superior because he feared he would encounter serious difficulties with Stanislas's noble father who was opposed to his son entering religion. His brother Paul, who lived until the time of Stanislas's beatification in 1605, gave testimony during the process of the cause declaring that his brother "devoted himself so completely to spiritual things that he frequently became unconscious, especially in the church of the Jesuit Fathers at Vienna."[112] This type of mystical behavior not only occurred there but apparently also back home, at least once during an Easter meal.

Stanislas joined the popular congregation of St. Barbara at the college in Vienna. He revealed to his tutor and others that during a serious illness he prayed to St. Barbara (d. about 235) for help and she, attended by two angels, appeared before him and gave him Holy Communion. The Blessed Virgin to whom he was especially devoted all his life cured him of this sickness.

Eventually Stanislas summoned up enough courage to leave on foot for Rome where he wanted to enter the Jesuit novitiate of Saint Andrew. His angry brother and tutor attempted to catch up with him and take him back, but they failed. Before reaching Rome, Stanislas stopped in Dillingen, Germany, where he met St. Peter Canisius (1521–1597), the provincial of that community and future Doctor of the Church, who straightaway discerned in him a remarkable degree of sanctity. Fearing, however, the potentially violent reaction from Stanislas's father, he sent the young man after a month's stay on his way to Rome where he met another future Jesuit saint, Francis Borgia (1510–1572), the Superior General of the order. Finally on October 25, 1867, he reached Rome, just two days before his seventeenth birthday. His holiness soon was recognized and he was admired as a model of religious perfection.

Ten months later, exhausted from his hasty flight and arduous traveling, his physical condition slowly weakened. Eventually he developed a fever, possibly malaria. Realizing his own critical state, he wrote a letter on the feast of St. Lawrence (August 10), addressed it to the Blessed Mother, and placed it before an image of St. Lawrence. In it he asked St. Lawrence to present the note to Mary whom he was imploring to grant his wish to die on the feast day of her Assumption. He received the last sacraments and died in the early morning of August 15, 1568—the Feast of the Assumption. His fame as a holy person spread wide and fast. Beatification was proclaimed thirty-seven years later in 1605 followed by canonization in 1726.

St. Stanislas, whose feast day is November 13, was declared patron saint of Poland, of Warsaw, students, and Jesuit novices. He is invoked against fever and palpitations of the heart.

---

112 *The Catholic Encyclopedia*, "St. Stanislas Kostka."

14. Saint Teresa of Avila (1515–1582)
Spanish Carmelite, mystic, writer, reformer of her Order, and Doctor of the Church

ON MARCH 28, 1515, A BABY GIRL BY THE IMPRESSIVE NAME OF TERESA SANchez Cepeda Davila y Ahumada, was born of a noble family in Avila, Spain. Her father was Alonso de Cepeda, a saintly man, and her mother Doña Beatriz Davila y Ahumada, a loving and pious woman. She had two sisters and nine brothers. All the boys eventually found their way to the West Indies. One brother by the name of Rodrigo was near her age and shared many of her ambitions. For example, when children they both at one time wanted to become martyrs and at another time to be hermits. Not unremarkably, neither of these ambitions came to fruition.

When Teresa was around thirteen her mother died. In 1530 her father sent her to the Augustinian nuns of Avila for her schooling, but two years later she returned home because of poor health. At twenty she left her father to become a Carmelite nun in the convent of the Incarnation outside Avila. While there she contracted a serious disease and was on the point of death. Despite this problem, she somehow recovered sufficiently and was able to be professed. Her religious name was Teresa of Jesus. Regardless of the fact that she became a professed nun, her father who was always very concerned about her health, had her leave the convent. After three years of suffering from this same malady, she was restored to good health and returned to the convent. However she suffered almost all her life with various ailments: backaches, fevers, headaches, kidney and liver problems. The Rule at the time was greatly relaxed in most Carmelite convents including the Incarnation which consisted of 140 nuns, an amazingly large number. The nuns were allowed to spend too much time outside the monastery on business and lived a life less than ascetic.

After twenty years of difficulties with her prayer life and the pleasures of secular conversations, she finally, with the advice of some wise laymen and clerics, changed her ways and understood that she owed God her entire being. From then on she devoted all her energies to prayer, meditation, and the beginning of her attempts to reform the order. She soon began to experience apparitions of Christ, ecstasies, spiritual espousal ("mystical marriage"), piercing of her heart (*transverberatio*), and even levitation.

She specifically aimed at restoring the Order to its primitive observance and to found new monasteries under her reformed rules. The first convent she established was in Avila and authorized by Rome in 1562 with the full name Discalced Carmelite Nuns of the Primitive Rule of Our Lady of Mount Carmel. The monastery was dedicated to St. Joseph. Teresa's niece and three other novices were the first occupants. The town, however, believing, among other reasons, that there were enough convents already in town, vehemently objected to this new monastery but after four months things calmed down and Teresa with four other nuns went there to live. Here Teresa stayed for the next five years with a final total of thirteen nuns.

The rule was harsh, entailing perpetual silence, abstinence, and extreme poverty. Their habits were of coarse serge and they wore sandals not shoes. It was because of the latter that they were called Discalced (without shoes) Carmelites.

New reformed houses were founded in Medina del Campo, Malagon, Valladolid, Toledo, Salamanca, Alba, and elsewhere. It was in Medina del Campo that she met a soul mate—Fray (Brother) John of the Cross (1542–1591)—who became her confessor and friend. He incidentally was twenty-five when they met and she twenty-seven years his senior.

In 1568 St. Teresa of Jesus founded a Carmelite monastery for men in an old farmhouse in the small village of Duruelo and a year later one in Pastrana where the friars also lived in abject poverty and austerity. St. John of the Cross directed the Duruelo reformed community. In him St. Teresa found the one who would help her fulfill all her desires for reform.

Theresa's superior sent her to her old convent of the Incarnation in Avila for the purpose of reforming it where she, not surprisingly, met opposition, jealousy, and intrigue.

In time, the prior general, Father John-Baptist Rubeo, began to believe that Teresa of Jesus was going too far in her reform measures. Eventually she was told to cease making any more foundations and ordered her to retire to one of the convents. St. John of the Cross too was reprimanded and was finally imprisoned by his own superiors. He managed to escape after nine tormented months. King Philip II of Spain favored Teresa's efforts and through his interest and others the newly formed Discalced Carmelites separated from the rest of the order (the Calced Carmelites) in 1580 by a mandate from Rome and were given their own autonomy and province.

At this time St. Teresa was sixty-five, worn out, and ill. In her life she had accomplished a great deal, the reform of her order being the prime achievement. She established a total of seventeen foundations, the last being in Burgos in 1852. Besides, she continued experiencing apparitions, visions of hell, and other supernatural phenomena. As an author she wrote several books including an autobiography and three masterpieces of religious literature: *The Interior Castle*, *The Way of Perfection*, and *Foundations*.

St. Teresa's last days were ones of suffering and privation. After having traveled for two months visiting several of her convents, she arrived on the verge of death at a monastery in Alba de Tormes where she met Maria Henriquez, the Duchess of Alba. Three days later on October 4, 1582, the sixty-seven-year-old St. Teresa died with her holy assistant Sister Anne-of-St.-Bartholomew (later beatified) by her side.

Her incorrupt remains are preserved in Alba de Tormes. Thirty-two years after her death she was beatified (1614) and eight years later canonized by Gregory XV (1622). In 1970 Pope Paul VI declared her a Doctor of the Church together with St. Catherine of Sienna—the first two women to be so honored. (St. Thérèse of Lisieux was the third woman Doctor of the Church, proclaimed by Pope John Paul II in 1997). St. Teresa of Avila is also the patron saint of Spain.

Her feast day is not on the day of her death. The day after she died the Gregorian reform of the calendar came into effect thus changing dates which thereby put St. Teresa's feast day on October 15, eleven days after her death.

St. Teresa's wit, affectionate nature, intelligence, courage, and psychological acumen charmed many. Her spiritual daughter of three hundred years later, St. Thérèse of Lisieux, said, "what I liked best about St. Teresa of Avila were her cheerfulness and simplicity: Long live her drum and its beating."[113] When Thérèse Martin entered the Lisieux Carmel she was well acquainted with St. Teresa (called also by the nuns "the Seraphic Saint" and "our holy Mother, St. Teresa"). She was her patron saint since she bore her name in baptism. Her father brought this to her attention once at services in the Cathedral of Saint Pierre in Lisieux when Thérèse was a little girl:

> I listened attentively to the sermons which I understood very poorly. The first I did understand and which touched me deeply was a sermon on the Passion preached by Father Ducellier and since then I've understood all the others. When the preacher spoke about St. Teresa, Papa leaned over and whispered: "Listen carefully, little Queen, he's talking about your Patroness."[114]

On one occasion when Thérèse was nine she visited the Lisieux Carmel to see her sister Pauline (then Sister Agnès). She managed to be alone for a short time with the prioress, Mother Marie de Gonzague and told her that she too wanted to become a Carmelite. Soon after, Mother Gonzague suggested that if Thérèse became a Carmelite she should take the name of Sister Thérèse of the Child Jesus. Thérèse was delighted since that was the exact name she had hoped she could have. She knew the story of her namesake and that Teresa's niece Teresita entered Carmel as a boarder when she was only nine years old. Thérèse thereafter happily signed some letters and notes not only to the prioress but to others as well, "Térèsita."

Of interest is the dubious but popular legend that St. Teresa of Avila had a vision once of the Child Jesus who embraced her and uttered the words "I am Jesus of Teresa." In the two prayers Thérèse wrote, Pri 14 ("To the Child Jesus") and Pri 16 ("To the Holy Face"), the subtitles are "I am the Jesus of Thérèse" in imitation of what the Child Jesus said to St. Teresa of Avila.

The Lisieux Monastery contained a variety of representations of the great Spanish reformer. Even on Thérèse's cell wall hung a picture of St. Teresa and two of her sayings: "To suffer or to die" and "Forever I will sing the mercies of the Lord." Note that Thérèse echoes the latter one in the first paragraph of her autobiography: "I am going to be doing only one thing: I shall begin to sing what I must sing eternally: 'the Mercies of the Lord'" (which is actually a quote from Psalm 88:2).

As a novice Thérèse had to study the Rule and Constitutions of Carmel formulated by St. Teresa of Avila; and as assistant mistress of novices she was

---

113 Descouvemont, *op. cit.*, p. 240.
114 *Story of a Soul*, chapter II, p. 42.

required to impart this knowledge to her charges. One significant requisite was to pray for priests—the basis of the Carmelite vocation which St. Thérèse also stipulates in her autobiography:

> How beautiful is the vocation that has as its goal the preservation of the salt intended for souls. This is the vocation of Carmel, since the sole end of our sacrifices is to be the apostle of the apostles [priests], praying for them as they evangelize souls.[115]

In many portions in her writings and certainly in her conversations, Thérèse cites, alludes to, or agrees with her holy Mother, St. Teresa of Avila. A few examples follow:

- *Sainthood*: Father [Blino, a retreat priest], I want to become a saint. I want to love God as much as Saint Teresa did.[116]
- *Answering prayers*: I am praying to St. Teresa to obtain through her intercession the favor of being an aunt myself. I do not doubt that she will answer me by sending to my dear little Jeanne [Guérin La Néele, her cousin] a blessed family that will give to the Church some great saints.[117]
- *Love of God*: How well I understand Our Lord's words to St. Teresa, our holy Mother: "Do you know, my daughter, who are the ones who really love me? It's those who recognize that everything that can't be referred to me is a lie."

  Oh, little Mother, I really feel that this is true! Yes, everything outside of God is vanity.[118]
- *Sending her a spiritual brother, Abbé Belliere*: It was our holy Mother St. Teresa who sent me my first little brother as a feast-day gift in 1895. I was in the laundry, very much occupied by my work, when Mother Agnès of Jesus took me aside and read a letter she had just received. It was from a young seminarian, inspired, he said, by St. Teresa of Avila. He was asking for a Sister who would devote herself especially to the salvation of his soul.... Mother Agnès of Jesus told me she wanted me to become the sister of this future missionary.[119]
- *The will of God*: O little Mother [her sister Pauline], I don't love one thing more than another; I could not say like our holy Mother St. Teresa: "I die because I cannot die." What God prefers and chooses for me, that is what pleases me more.[120]
- *Sacrifices*: But alas! God, who knows the rewards He is reserving for His friends, often loves to have them win His treasures by means of sacrifices. Our Holy Mother Teresa said smilingly to Our Lord these very true words: "My God, I am not surprised You have so few friends, You treat them so badly."[121]
- *Purgatory*: I don't know whether I'll go to purgatory or not, but I'm not in the least bit disturbed about it; however, if I do go there, I'll not regret having done nothing to avoid it. I shall not be sorry for having worked solely for the

---

115 *Story of a Soul*, chapter III, p. 122.
116 Mother Agnès, NPPA, Hope, p. 2.
117 LT 150, October 22, 1893, from Thérèse to Mme. La Néele.
118 *Her Last Conversations*, June 22, 1897, spoken to Mother Agnès, her blood sister.
119 *Story of a Soul*, chapter XI, p. 251.
120 *Her Last Conversations*, September 4, 1897, p. 183.
121 LT 155, December 29, 1893, from Thérèse to her Uncle and Aunt Guérin.

- *Strength*: He [Jesus] transformed me in such a way that I no longer recognized myself. Without this change I would have had to remain for years in the world. Saint Teresa, who said to her daughters: "I want you to be women in nothing, but that in everything you may equal strong men" [from *The Way of Perfection*] ... would not [*sic*] have wanted to acknowledge me as her child if the Lord had not clothed me in His divine strength, if He had not Himself armed me for war.[123]
- *Daughter of the Church*: Finally, I want to be a daughter of the Church as our holy Mother St. Teresa was [and said on her death bed] and to pray for the Holy Father's intentions which I know embrace the whole universe.[124]

Saint Thérèse of the Child Jesus certainly proved to be "a daughter of the Church" as her holy Mother St. Teresa even to the point of equaling her as a sublime Doctor of the Church.

15. SAINT THÉOPHANE VÉNARD (1829–1861)
Thérèse's favorite male saint martyred in Vietnam

THÉRÈSE REALLY BECAME ACQUAINTED WITH THE LIFE OF THE YOUNG French missionary martyr Théophane Vénard just over a year before she died and instantly developed a deep and pure love for him whose life, spirit, and ideas were so similar to hers. Though not yet canonized, he promptly joined the close association of saints Thérèse loved and with whom she clearly identified. She found in him a kindred spirit; one with a cheerful, humble soul who deeply loved his family, and who also lost his mother when he was a child. He possessed a strong contemplative mentality, loved the Blessed Mother, showed a feeling of littleness like hers, and longed as she did for martyrdom in a far-off pagan land.

Jean-Théophane Vénard was born on November 21, 1829, in St. Loup-sur-Thouet, a little French town in the department of Deux-Sèvres in the diocese of Poitiers. His father, Jean Vénard, was a village schoolmaster and later a justice of the peace. His mother, the former Marie Guéret, was a devout and loving woman but with a fragile constitution. His parents had six children: two died in infancy and the others lived much longer—Mélanie, Théophane, Henry, and Eusebius. When Théophane was only nine years old while in the fields on the hillside of Bel-Air caring for the family goats, he and his sister or friends would sing or read pious material. Once after reading about the martyrdom in 1837 of a priest from his own diocese, the Venerable Charles Cornay, he said, "And I too will go to Tong-king, and I too will be a martyr."[125]

While attending a school in Doué-la-Fontaine where he remained for six years, his beloved mother died. In 1847 Théophane entered a preparatory school

---

122 *Her Last Conversations*, June 4, 1897.
123 LT 201 from Thérèse to Father Roulland dated Nov. 1, 1896. See note 12 to this letter in *General Correspondence*, vol. II.
124 *Story of a Soul*, chapter XI, p. 253.
125 Walsh, *A Modern Martyr*, p. 3.

called *"Le Petit Séminaire"* in Montmorillon near Limoges founded for the training of boys who showed interest in the priesthood. He left after a year of philosophy and entered the major seminary (*"Grand Séminaire"*) in Poitiers and received minor orders in 1850. On March 3, 1851, he entered the Paris Seminary for Foreign Missions (*Séminaire des Missions Étrangères* [MEP]) at 128, Rue du Bac where, after recovering from a serious illness, he was ordained on June 5, 1852, at the young age of twenty-three. He left with four other priests for the Far East four months later on September 19.

After over four months on the sea, the ship carrying the French missionaries finally arrived at Singapore on New Year's day, 1853. Three weeks later, they sailed for Hong Kong where he stayed at the motherhouse, regaining his health and studying Chinese. Then after fifteen months, he was sent to a mission in Tonkin (Vietnam) where Christians were terribly persecuted. He, called Father Ven by the natives, labored for seven difficult years in Vietnam under terrible conditions and in constant danger of being caught and punished for teaching the banned religion—Christianity. He was betrayed and captured on November 30, 1860, tried before a mandarin, tortured, refused to apostatize, and imprisoned in a small bamboo cage.[126] During this time he was permitted to write letters home. In a letter dated January 20, 1861 that he sent to his father, Théophane mentioned his approaching death in words and thoughts that could have been penned by Thérèse herself:

> A slight cut of the saber will separate my head, as a spring flower that the Master of the garden picks for his pleasure. We are all flowers planted on this earth which God picks in his time; a few early, a few later, one a crimson rose, another a virginal lily, another a humble violet. We all endeavor to please, according to the fragrance or brightness [like flowers] we are given by our sovereign Lord and Master. I wish you, dear Father, a long, peaceful, and virtuous old age. Carry gently the cross of this life behind Jesus as far as Calvary, to a happy death. Father and son shall meet in Paradise. I, a little may-fly, shall leave the first. Adieu.[127]

His father never read the letter for he died on August 26, 1859, a year and a half before Théophane wrote it. Three months after Théophane sent the letter, he was cruelly beheaded by a half-drunk, deformed executioner, on February 2, 1861, near Hanoi, witnessed by hundreds of people. He was thirty-one.

Théophane's siblings led somewhat interesting lives, though not nearly as dramatic as his. His brother Eusèbe (Eusebius) (1825–1913) finished seminary training for the diocesan priesthood and became vicar of the Cathedral at Poitiers. For many years he served as the Curé of Assai, a small town less than four miles from the family home in St. Loup. Confident that his brother was a saint, he saved

---

126 Apparently he spent time in that bamboo cage in the mandarin's palace where he could be heard singing hymns. Some sources, though, say he was held at the citadel.
127 Translated into English by the author from the November 1984 issue of *Les Annales de Sainte Thérèse de Lisieux*.

all his letters, wrote a martyr-play about him (*Captivity and Martyrdom*), and his biography.[128] Mélanie (1827-1887) was not only Théophane's much loved sister but also his dearest friend and confidante. At the age of thirty-five, following her father's death, she accomplished her life-long dream and became a teaching nun of the Sisters of the Immaculate Conception[129] with the name Sister Marie Théophane. Théophane never knew she became a nun. After an unsuccessful marriage and the death of his wife and only son, Henry, the less gifted of all and an alcoholic, died in 1909 under the care of his devoted brother Eusebius.

Thérèse's "spiritual brother" Père Roulland, shortly after his ordination, introduced her to the life of Théophane Vénard when he visited the Carmel on July 3, 1896. They conversed at the monastery grille and he gave her two books for the monastery library, one of which was *Life and Letters of J. Théophane Vénard* written by the saint's brother, Abbé Eusèbe Vénard (7th edition, 1888). In 1897 Thérèse wrote to Father Roulland: "Since your departure, I have read the *Life* of several missionaries.... I have read, among others, the *Life of Théophane Vénard*, and it interested me and touched me more than I could express. Under its influence, I composed some couplets that are totally personal, however, I am sending them to you."[130] In this poem (PN 47) entitled "To Théophane Vénard," composed on February 2, 1897, the thirty-sixth anniversary of his beheading, she plainly expresses her own feelings, particularly in her last sufferings, which are fully in harmony with Théophane's:

> Blessed Martyr, at the moment of your death
> You savored the happiness of suffering.
> To you suffering for God seemed a delight.
> Smiling, you knew how to live and to die....
> You hastened to say to your executioner
> When he offered to shorten your torment:
> "The longer my painful martyrdom lasts,
> The better it will be and the happier I'll be!!!"
> ...
> Ah! If I were a springtime flower
> That the Lord soon wanted to pluck,
> O Blessed Martyr! I implore you,
> Descend from Heaven at my last hour.
> Come embrace me in this mortal dwelling,
> And I'll be able to fly with the souls
> That will make up your eternal procession!...

Thérèse had been considered for transfer to the Hanoi Carmel in Tonkin founded on October 15, 1895, by the Carmel in Saigon which in turn had been founded by nuns from the Lisieux Carmel. In May of 1887 she reminded Mother Agnès of it:

---

128 Walsh, *op. cit.*, p. 221.
129 In Father Walsh's book, he says she became a member of *Les Religieuses d'Espérance*, p. 219.
130 LT 221 dated March 19, 1897.

CHAPTER 6: *Saints and "Sinners"*

> At the time when my departure for Tonkin was planned, around November [1896], you recall how we began a novena to Théophane Vénard in order to have a sign of God's will? At this time, I returned to all the community exercises, even Matins. Well! During the novena precisely, I began to cough again, and since then I've gone from bad to worse. He's the one who's calling me! Oh, I would love to have his portrait [which she received on August 10]; he's a soul that pleases me. St. Louis de Gonzague was serious, even during recreation, but Théophane Vénard was always cheerful. At this time we were reading the life of St. Louis de Gonzague in the refectory.[131]

Just a few days prior to making the above comments and comparing Théophane with St. Louis de Gonzague, Thérèse also mentioned why she liked Théophane better:

> Théophane Venard pleases me much more than St. Louis de Gonzague [same person as St. Aloysius Gonzaga], because the life of the latter is extraordinary, and that of Théophane is very ordinary. Besides, he is the one who is talking, whereas for the Saint someone is telling the story and making him speak; so we know practically nothing about his "little" soul!
>
> Théophane Venard loved his family very much, and I, too, love my "little" family very much. I don't understand the saints who don't love their family.... My little family of today, oh! I love it very much! I love my little Mother very, very much.[132]

During her final illness Thérèse displayed many signs of devotion to Théophane. She was so impressed with the thoughts conveyed in his letters home during his imprisonment before execution that she copied four pages from them into her own scripture notebook. And from this source she copied on one side of a memento card the following sentences and placed the card in a letter to her three sisters in her convent, Pauline, Marie, and Céline, as a final testimony to them. One can clearly see that her thoughts and even words and phrases were very similar to his. Here is one paragraph from this poignant message:

> I do not long for the life of this world, my heart is thirsting for the waters of eternal life.... I do not depend on my own strength but on the strength of Him, who on the Cross has overcome the powers of hell. I am a springtime flower that the Master of the garden is plucking for His pleasure.... We are all flowers planted on this earth that God gathers in His own time, a little earlier, a little later.... I, a little short-lived creature, am going there the first! One day we shall find one another again in Paradise, and we shall enjoy true happiness.
> (SIGNED)
> Thérèse of the Child Jesus borrowing the thoughts
> of the angelic Martyr, Théophane Vénard.[133]

Because of her worsening condition, Thérèse was brought down from her cell to the infirmary on July 8, 1897. On August 10 she pinned to the curtain over

---
131 *Her Last Conversations*, May 27, 1897.
132 Said sometime between May 21 and May 26 and recorded in *Her Last Conversations*.
133 LT 245 dated June 1897.

her bed a portrait of Théophane Vénard that Mother Agnès had given her. This was placed above five other little pictures: a *Mater Dolorosa*, a photograph of her three dead siblings, Saint Joseph holding the Baby Jesus, Saint Cecilia, and Guido Reni's famous oval portrait of Jesus titled *Ecce Homo*. These five images actually were glued above a touching inscription: "Farewell! Farewell! We will see each other again in heaven!"[134] Concerning Théophane's picture, it might be interesting to know that his head on it is an actual photograph that was cut out and pasted over a drawn figure or etching which would explain why the head and the body don't seem to match correctly. Théophane is holding a hat in his left hand and his right arm is raised with a finger pointing to heaven. Regarding this gesture, Thérèse remarked to her sister, "Do you believe he knows me? Look at what he's pointing to."[135] Thérèse was very happy whenever she looked at this portrait of Théophane and was moved to tears when on September 6 she was given a relic of Théophane.[136]

Following are six of the comments Sister Thérèse of the Child Jesus made that her sister Pauline jotted down in her notebook entitled the *Yellow Notebook* which, when it was eventually published, was called *Derniers Entretiens* (*Last Conversations*):

- With a happy and very beautiful look when gazing at the picture of Théophane Vénard [she said]:
  "Ah! But!..."
   Sister Geneviève asked: "Why do you say: 'Ah! But!'"
  "It's because each time I look at him, he looks at me, too, and then he seems to look at me out of the corner of his eye with a kind of mischievous look." [August 10, 1897]
- She stroked Théophane Vénard on the cheeks. [His picture, though, was pinned to the curtain of her bed, at a little distance from her.]
  I asked: "Why are you stroking him like that?"
  "Because I can't reach him to kiss him." [August 19, 1897]
- It's you who have given me the consolation of having Théophane Vénard's portrait; It's an extremely great consolation.... [August 20, 1897]
- I [Pauline] was saying when looking at the picture of Théophane Vénard: "There he is hat in hand, and to top it all, he doesn't come to get you!"
   With a smile she said:
   "I myself don't make fun of the saints.... I love them so much!... They want to see...."
   "What?" I asked, "If you're going to lose patience?" With a mischievous but grave look, she said:
   "Yes.... But especially if I'm going to lose confidence.... [A]nd how far I'm going to push my confidence...." [September 22, 1897]

---

134 Descouvemont, *op. cit.*, p. 297.
135 *Her Last Conversations*, August 10, 1897.
136 Father Walsh of the Maryknoll Fathers (The Catholic Foreign Mission Society of America) claims on p. 206 in *A Modern Martyr* that Father Eusebius sent a relic of his brother to the "Little Flower of Jesus" at the Lisieux Carmel.

- As she was caressing her "Théophane," I said: "He is very much honored."
  "These are not honors...."
  "What are they?"
  "Caresses, that's all!" (She hugged the picture of Théophane Vénard.) [September 24, 1897]

The cause of his beatification was submitted to Rome in 1879 when Thérèse was six years old. Thirty years later he was beatified on May 2, 1909, fourteen years before her beatification. The only member of Théophane's family who lived to see his brother beatified was Father Eusebius. Thérèse was canonized in 1925, twenty-eight years after her death, whereas Théophane was canonized (along with nineteen other martyrs of Vietnam) on June 19, 1988, by Pope John Paul II, 187 years after he died.

The two saints were linked together even by the Church when in 1937 an approved prayer for the canonization of Théophane Vénard was issued, part of which reads as follows:

> O little St. Thérèse of the Child Jesus, we seek your powerful intercession to obtain from God the necessary miracles for the canonization of your "favorite saint," Blessed Théophane Vénard. We ask you to allow a share in your glory to him whom you called "a little saint," an "angelic martyr." Remember that you said: "my soul is as his is," that you relied upon him "to come and find you," that, as you breathed your last, you clutched his relic in your hand.[137]

---

137 From p. 10 in an article entitled "Thérèse and Théophane" in the January 1986 issue of Sicut Parvuli. This is an English translation of the article that originally appeared in the November 1984 issue of *Les Annales de Sainte Thérèse de Lisieux*.

B. "Sinners"

1. Henry Chéron (1867–1936)
Once a family friend who became an anti-Catholic government official

WHEN ONLY SEVENTEEN YEARS OLD, HENRY CHÉRON INTERNED OR SIMPLY worked for a while at the Pharmacie Guérin. He often frequented the Guérin home above the drugstore, and even gave music lessons to Marie Guérin, Thérèse's cousin.[1] During one of these visits he first met Thérèse Martin, then eleven years old, whom he would often recall in later years when Thérèse's sainthood and popularity were spreading throughout the world. His reminiscence included the time he played the accordion in the back room of the pharmacy which Thérèse heard and enjoyed. This intelligent and ardent Catholic at the time eventually received a degree in law and later became intensely involved with politics, especially the radical left. Soon he strayed from his faith and became quite hostile toward the Church, the pope, and the clergy. He started writing inflammatory articles which Isidore Guérin adroitly counterattacked in the conservative and monarchial newspaper *Le Normand* which he wrote for and helped subsidize. Isidore answered the intense twenty-four-year-old Henry with fervid rebuttals one of which was entitled "Two questions to be resolved."[2]

In August 1893 Sister Thérèse of the Child Jesus wrote to her Aunt Guérin: "Is it not for His glory that Uncle's hand never grows tired of writing these admirable pages which must save souls and make demons tremble?"[3] "These admirable pages" referred to those written by her Uncle Isidore Guérin in *Le Normand* refuting Chéron's violent anti-Catholic articles, especially those in the radical liberal journal *Le Progrès Lexovien* blatantly founded by his one-time friend Henry Chéron.

In the sixty-nine years of his life which began on May 13, 1867, Henry Chéron enjoyed a brilliant career in politics and government. It all started when he was elected district counselor at the age of twenty-five in 1892. By twenty-seven he was mayor of Lisieux serving for eleven years from 1894 to 1908 and later at sixty-five he held the same office from 1932 to 1936. His career skyrocketed rapidly during the two periods he functioned as the Lisieux mayor. He was also a member of the anti-clerical ministry of Émile Combes (1902–1905) in Paris. From 1906 to 1909 he was Under-Secretary of State for War after which he became Under-Secretary of the Navy (1909–1910). At forty-six he was elected Senator from Calvados (1913). Nine years later he acquired the prestigious position of Minister of Agriculture (1922) for France. At sixty-one, Henry was chosen Minister of Finance

---

1 *The Saint of Lisieux*, April 1950.
2 *Le Normand*, November 3, 1891 as referenced in footnote 2 of LT 146, dated August 10, 1893, from Thérèse to Mme. Guérin.
3 Ibid.

(1928–1930), followed by Minister of Justice from 1930 to 1931 and again in 1934.[4] Because of his successful political career, a street—the Rue Henry Chéron—in the main business section of Lisieux bears his name. Ironically the corner of the site where the Guérin pharmacy existed is on the Rue Henry Chéron.

As he grew older, however, his stance against the Church seems to have changed, at least outwardly. During his tenure as mayor in later years, he was instrumental in the preparation and operation of the many functions—processions, pilgrimages, etc.—honoring the town's illustrious daughter Saint Thérèse whom he knew years before as a little, quiet, pious girl. He was obviously aware of the commercial, tourist, and other benefits that Lisieux derived from her cult which he clearly encouraged. Perhaps his spiritual life went full circle for after he died a cross and a medal of St. Thérèse were discovered on his body.

2. Père Hyacinthe Loyson (1827–1912)
Contemporary apostate Carmelite priest

IN THE FINAL WEEKS OF HER LIFE, THÉRÈSE WAS UNABLE TO SWALLOW EVEN Communion without intense suffering since it produced breathing difficulties, vomiting, and extreme weakness. Her last agonizing reception of the Eucharist on August 18, 1897, the feast of St. Hyacinthe, was offered up for the conversion of Hyacinthe Loyson, an ex-Carmelite priest who had left the Church three years before Thérèse was born and for whom she prayed much of her life.

Hyacinthe Loyson was born in Paris in 1827. He began his vacillating religious career as an ordained priest in the Society of Saint Sulpice in 1851. Eight years later he became a Dominican novice, but after five months he left. He then joined the Order of Discalced Carmelites, making his religious profession two years later in 1860. In this role he distinguished himself as a brilliant preacher in various parts of France, especially at Notre Dame Cathedral in Paris, and in Rome. He managed to rise to the position of provincial of his order. His extreme liberalism finally surfaced when he openly opposed papal authority, advocated a married priesthood, pressured for the liturgy in French, and wanted bishops to be elected by the people and the clergy not the pope. This led to his official excommunication on October 10, 1869. A coincidental fact that must have irked him took place shortly after when Vatican Council I proclaimed the dogma of papal infallibility (July 1870).

In the meantime, an American Protestant widow by the name of Emily Meriman, became so impressed by Loyson's preaching in Rome that she sought instructions in Catholicism from him. She was converted and four years later on September 3, 1872, she and Loyson were married in a civil ceremony in England. A liberal Protestant, Paul Sabatier, said of Mme. Loyson that her husband "converted her to Catholicism, she converted him to marriage."[5] This union in time produced one son in 1873, the same year Thérèse was born.

---

4 Descouvemont, *op. cit.*, p. 180.
5 Ibid., p. 178.

In Paris he founded his own French national church in 1879 calling it *L'Église Catholique Gallican* (Gallican Catholic Church) and traveled throughout France preaching, holding conferences, and disseminating his ideas to gain membership.

No doubt Thérèse knew about Loyson for quite some time before she became a religious. Her purpose as a Carmelite was "to save souls and especially to pray for priests."[6] She, therefore, devoted much of her daily life of prayer and penance for his conversion. Believing that since she was successful praying for the murderer Pranzini, she would be so also with Loyson.

Through reading articles from *Le Croix du Calvados* (the locally available supplement to the Parisian paper *La Croix de Paris*) that perhaps Céline sent, Thérèse learned of Loyson's exploits to gain converts in Normandy during the summer of 1891. She wrote to her sister Céline on vacation at the Château de La Musse detailing her knowledge and opinions concerning this "renegade monk," as he was called by some members of the religious press. She, however, referred to him more benignly as "this poor sheep" and "the unfortunate prodigal":

> Yes, dear Céline, suffering alone can give birth to souls for Jesus.... Is it surprising that we are so favored, we whose only desire is to save a soul [i.e. Hyacinthe Loyson] that seems to be lost forever?... The details interested me very much, while making my heart beat very fast.... But I shall give you some other details that are not any more consoling. The unfortunate prodigal went to Coutances where he started over again the conferences given at Caen. It appears he intends to travel throughout France in this way.... Céline.... And with all this, they add that it is easy to see that *remorse* is gnawing at him. He goes into churches with a huge Crucifix, and he seems to be making great acts of adoration.... His wife follows him everywhere. Dear Céline, he is really culpable, more culpable than any other sinner ever was who was converted. But cannot Jesus do once what He has not yet ever done? And if He were not to desire it, would He have placed in the heart of His poor little spouses a desire that He could not realize?... No, it is certain that He desires more than we do to bring back this poor stray sheep to the fold. A day will come when He will open his eyes, and then who knows whether France will not be traversed by him with a totally different goal from the one he has in mind now? Let us not grow tired of prayer; confidence works miracles. And Jesus said to Blessed Margaret Mary: "*One just soul* has so much power over my Heart that it can obtain pardon for a thousand *criminals*." No one knows if one is just or sinful, but, Céline, Jesus gives us the grace of feeling at the bottom of our heart that we would prefer to die rather than to offend Him; and then it is not our merits but those of our Spouse, which are *ours*, that we offer to Our Father who is in heaven, in order that our brother, a son of the Blessed Virgin, return vanquished to throw himself beneath the mantle of the most merciful of Mothers....[7]

Thérèse cut four articles from *La Croix* concerning Father Loyson and kept them among her papers which were found after her death. She may have

---

6 *Story of a Soul*, chapter VII, p. 149.
7 LT 129, July 8, 1891.

obtained one bit of hope for Loyson's conversion from a statement he made in one of those pieces which Thérèse underlined: "If the Church were to prove me wrong, I will gladly acknowledge my error and take my place once again humbly in Christian unity." [8] She resolutely continued to pray for him even to the end of her life and often said that we should never tire of praying because through it, and trust in God, miracles can happen. One of St. Thérèse's novices, a lay sister named Sister Mary Magdalene of the Blessed Sacrament, testifying at the Informative Process of 1914 stated that Thérèse told the novices:

> We ought to like suffering for priests. The more the trials, annoyances, and all sorts of sufferings you have, the happier you should be. God will call us to account for the priests whom we could have saved by prayer and sacrifices, and didn't, because of our unfaithfulness and laxity. Let us not miss even one of these little sacrifices for them.[9]

In January 1911, fourteen years after Thérèse's death, during the period when the cause for her beatification was well underway, the Lisieux Carmel sent Hyacinthe Loyson Thérèse's autobiography, the *Story of a Soul*. The next month after reading it, he sent a reply to Mother Agnès from Geneva thanking her for the book and added:

> Some notes written in pen indicated that this beautiful soul had offered to God her prayers and sufferings for what she called "my conversion," that is, my submission to the teachings imposed by the Pope on consciences that surrender themselves into his hands.... I insist on telling you that I was touched, very much touched, by many of the things I read in this book. I must add that I am far from being convinced, and I cannot refrain from applying to Sister Thérèse what Saint Paul said of the good Jews, his contemporaries and adversaries: "They are zealous for God but not according to knowledge." I can be mistaken, Reverend Mother, I have been mistaken more than once in my life, but I am convinced that what God condemns in man is not error when this is sincere, but selfishness, pride, and hatred. I believe I can say, in the very face of death and before God, that such were never the motives of my mind and my life. Very respectfully, Hyacinthe Loyson, former superior of the Paris Carmel.[10]

Sister Geneviève (Céline) corresponded with him from then on and at one point sent him a copy of Msgr. de Teil's *Articles*, a book recounting Thérèse's life and miracles attributed to Thérèse after her death. In his reply he stated that he "was touched, not shaken" and promised "to read the book of the *Articles* which you sent me. Because of all I know about her, your good and heroic sister is far from being a stranger to me, and, without giving approval to everything concerning her, I admire her and am grateful to her."[11]

---

8 See footnote 6 on p. 730 in *General Correspondence*. In it is this quote from *La Croix du Calvados*, (nos. 23–30, July 1891).
9 O'Mahony, *St. Thérèse of Lisieux By Those Who Knew Her*, p. 261.
10 See footnote 6 on p. 730 to LT 129 of July 8, 1891, in General Correspondence.
11 Ibid.

No reconciliation with the Church ever occurred even on his deathbed. He died on February 9, 1912, in Paris in his eighty-fifth year. At his side were a cleric from the Armenian Church, a schismatic Greek Church priest, and three Protestant ministers. Loyson repeatedly exclaimed before the end, "O my sweet Jesus."[12] Years later the Jesuit priest Père Flamérion, grand exorcist of France, was asked his opinion of Loyson's spiritual state: "You have asked us in the Virgin's name if Hyacinthe is damned, we are forced to answer you that he is saved, through the intercession of Thérèse and the prayers of Holy Souls in the cloister, saved by a glance cast upon him by Our Lord before he was judged, an instant before."[13]

3. HENRI-JACQUES PRANZINI (1853–1887)
Thérèse prayed for this murderer's repentance

THOUGH THÉRÈSE NEVER SAW OR KNEW HIM PERSONALLY, HENRI PRANZINI was one of the most important persons in her life. After she learned about him and the murders he committed, she prayed intensely for his repentance and conversion. Before him, she prayed in general for sinners; but he then became the first one she specifically prayed for. She called him her "first child." As a result of this affair, she was even more so determined to become a Carmelite and thereby offer her life and prayers for sinners.

Henri Pranzini's story is most engrossing. Henri, a tall handsome Italian born in Alexandria, Egypt, in 1853, with the name Enrico, was brought up a good Catholic by his pious mother, Antonietta, a florist. His father, Gandolfo, was an archivist at the Alexandria post office. Because of his education (Brothers of the Christian Schools) and ability to speak eight languages (French, Italian, English, Greek, Turkish, Arabic, Russian, and one or more of the Hindu languages) he easily obtained a position as interpreter in his native land. Unfortunately he drifted toward criminal activities involving acceptance of stolen goods, swindling, and robbery for which he spent nine months in jail in 1877.[14] Gradually he lost all his money and wended his way to Persia, Afghanistan, and Burma, and then to Italy. He eventually returned to North Africa where he accompanied the English Army as an interpreter in the Sudanese War of 1885.

A year later Enrico Pranzini landed in Paris completely destitute. Now calling himself Henri Pranzini, he did anything to obtain money. Openly he assumed a number of legitimate jobs including interpreter, tour guide, and even a Pullman car employee; undercover, he again resorted to criminal pursuits even those that entailed sexual affairs whether normal or deviant as long as they were financially profitable.

A most intriguing bit of parenthetical information on Pranzini surfaced in studies concerning the artists Paul Gauguin (1848–1903) and Vincent van Gogh (1853–1890). The eminent art historian Douglas W. Druick of the Art Institute of Chicago reveals the following about these two artists:

---
12 Laveille, *op. cit.*, p. 176.
13 From footnote 11, p. 162 in *Collected Letters of Saint Thérèse of Lisieux*, edited by the Abbé Combes.
14 Irving, *Studies of French Criminals of the Nineteenth Century*, p. 161.

The press drew parallels between Prado's[15] handiwork with the razor and that of his acquaintance the notorious Henri Pranzini, an erstwhile runner in the Paris art trade who had been convicted of murder and executed in 1887. A ladies' man like Prado, Pranzini had been a boyfriend of Agostina Segatori[16]—or so Vincent informed Gauguin, citing confidences received from the owner of the café Le Tambourin in Paris, where he claimed that both Pranzini and Prado had hatched their plots.[17]

With his exotic demeanor, amazing intelligence, and seductive charm, Henri Pranzini managed to inveigle his way into the company of elegant society women, actresses, titled ladies, and even wealthy industrialists' wives—all apparently attracted by his alluringly intriguing persona and his enigmatic exploits. H. B. Irving[18] gives a perceptive explanation of Pranzini's methodology in his book on criminals in nineteenth century France published only fourteen years after "The Pranzini Affair."

> For the seduction of women he was well equipped by art and nature.... Pranzini was a man of singular muscular development, for which his feminine adorers could find no milder adjective than "magnificent." With this hopeful physique he combined an easy and insinuating address that seems to have been absolutely immediate in its effect. His favorite method of courtship was to invite a lady's attention by his seductive glance, after which he slipped his visiting-card into her hand, and a meeting was speedily arranged.[19]

The newspaper *Le Journal illustré* published this typical description of Pranzini:

> A peculiar fellow, this Levanter [a person from the eastern Mediterranean or northern Egypt]; one must have traveled to have come across anything like him. He is not at all the lackey of good families who has been described. With his little raised mustache, his frizzy, carefully combed beard, his lithe, insinuating appearance, his self-complacent air, his elegant clothing—white piqué waistcoat, impeccable linen, handkerchief corner showing in the side pocket—Pranzini completely carries off the hotel interpreter in Austria or Italy, half cicerone [a tourist guide], half procurer, who by day shows the city's curiosities and who, when evening comes, guides the romantic wanderings of generous travelers.[20]

Pranzini's nefarious career peaked with the brutal murder and robbery of three people at 17 Rue Montaigne in Paris on the night of March 19, 1887. The unfortunate victims were all females: a woman, her maid, and a young girl. This sensational murder created immediate interest throughout France and beyond. The thirty-four-year-old Pranzini was arrested two days later in Marseille in the

---

15 Louis Prado was a contemporary murderer referred to by a balladeer as a "pale follower of Pranzini."
16 Owner of Le Tambourin where the Impressionists often exhibited their works. She was a model for van Gogh, Manet, Corot, and Degas.
17 Druick, *van Gogh and Gauguin: The Studio of the South*, pp. 257–258.
18 Son of the famous British actor Sir Henry Irving (1838–1905).
19 Irving, *op. cit.*, p. 161.
20 Chalon, *op. cit.*, p. 81.

Grand Theatre during a performance of Rossini's opera, *The Barber of Seville*. That night he tried to commit suicide though he consistently proclaimed his innocence, even on his way to the scaffold. He was easily traced to Marseille since prostitutes told the police that Pranzini tried to sell them jewelry identical with those belonging to the murdered woman, Mme. De Montille. In addition, police found three visiting-cards with the name "Pranzini" at the murder scene.

The preeminent authority on St. Thérèse, Msgr. Guy Gaucher, vividly recounts the story of the horrendous murder in his excellent study of the case:

> On March 20, 1887, the lifeless bodies of Régine de Montille, Annette Grémeret, her chambermaid, and that of a little girl of twelve years, Marie (in reality, the daughter of Régine, who made her pass for the daughter of her servant) were found in Paris at 17, rue Montaigne (now called avenue Matignon). The throats of all three had been savagely cut; the jewels of the mistress had disappeared. The real name of Mme. Régine de Montille was Marie Regnaud. Beautiful, she had been seduced at a very young age and abandoned in the capital city. The comte de Montille noticed her there. She was seen in every social gathering of fashionable Paris, which was trying to forget 1870 and the Commune. And a good girl besides, playful, watching over her child.... This triple crime caused enormous reverberations as much because of the personality of the victim as of the conditions in which it was committed. All the newspapers the next day related the triple murder on the rue Montaigne with a wealth of horrible details that were to make this crime a subject of unprecedented sales. It must be admitted that there was much here to entice the public: a sinner of great beauty, a servant devoted to the point of death, and the lamb of sacrifice: the little Marie Grémeret, to say nothing yet of the guilty party, who could only be a splendid beast.[21]

Msgr. Guy Gaucher continues his fascinating narration of what transpired after Pranzini was caught in Marseille and returned to Paris:

> When the police brought Pranzini back to Paris from Marseille, it was decided not to let him get out at the Gare de Lyon since there was a crowd waiting for him—though not to lynch him. It was largely made up of women—a first sign of an exclusively feminine infatuation which was later to make this executioner of women into a legend. Getting out at Charenton, Pranzini entered Paris in a convoy of five cabs. His trial opened in a court-room packed so full that even people with special tickets of admission signed by the presiding judge, M. Onfroy de Bréville, could not get in. The latter had been besieged by hordes of society ladies, and the appearance of the court-room was most unseemly. You might have thought you were at the theatre or, to be more precise, in the Presidential Enclosure at the races, since the summer's day (Saturday, 9 July) was radiantly sunny, calling for little white veils, parasols and fans. There were even feminine hands to focus lorgnettes in the prisoner's direction. The presiding

---

21 From *Vie Thérèsienne*, No. 48, October 1972, in the entry "*Thérèse Martin et l'affaire Pranzini*," pp. 275–286. This (on p. 128) and the other quotations from this article are translations by Alan Neame found in *Saint Thérèse of Lisieux: Her Family, Her God, Her Message* by Bernard Bro.

judge got angry and had to order the society women to stop their chattering. Maitre Demamge—Pranzini's defence counsel—spoke to such effect that he drew applause from the people present in the court-room.[22]

The list of evidence against Pranzini increased each day. It soon became evident that a young American girl, Cassidi Weil, from New York visiting Paris with her wealthy parents had joined the number of women infatuated by Pranzini. Even after she returned home, she carried on a fervid correspondence with him with the hope that he would marry her. The police conjectured that perhaps in order to cover the cost of a passage to the United States he committed the robbery.[23]

A much more compelling source of information came from Pranzini's mistress at the time, Madame Sabatier, a woman over fifty who worked in a fashionable store in Paris. She at first claimed he spent that fateful night[24] at her apartment. A few days later she recanted and admitted that he did not stay with her then. In court she confronted the prisoner and implored him to tell the whole truth. She also introduced other details that proved quite incriminating, but all he would say is, "*Je ne suis pour rien dans cette affaire.*" ("I know nothing of this affair.")[25] Every bit of evidence presented by others also turned out to be futile for Pranzini's cause.

On the last day of the trial which went on for only five days, the defense lawyer Demange gave his final desperate, surprising plea and revelation to the jury. He said a cabman somehow knew and swore that a "brown man" ("*l'homme brun*") was the real murderer who gave Pranzini the stolen property.[26] Notwithstanding all the evidence, fictitious or true, and Pranzini's persistent pleas of innocence, he was pronounced guilty and sentenced to death by guillotine:

> Noisy demonstrations and shouts of "Quash the case! Quash the case!" ["*Cassation! Cassation!*"] marked Pranzini's transfer to Grande-Roquette prison. His photograph was on sale on the boulevards, so were broadsheets telling his story. Of all the many letters addressed to him, often accompanied by chocolates or cigarettes, the only ones he was allowed to receive were those from his mother. And once the President of the Republic refused him a pardon, a veritable riot broke out round the walls of Grande-Roquette. At nightfall, on a word given by no one knows whom, the fashionable world united *en Masse* to advance on the prison. A long queue of carriages along the Boulevard Voltaire disgorged women dressed to the nines and men in top-hats, and these marched forward alongside men in cloth caps and bareheaded girls. Such singleness of purpose had never been seen; it suggested the very passing of a social order. And this composite crowd, squeezing into the square where the execution was scheduled to take place, shout for Pranzini's pardon.[27]

---

22 Bro, *The Little Way*, p. 71.
23 Irving, *op. cit.*, pp. 162–164.
24 Irving cites the night of March 16 and 17 as the date of the murders, whereas all other sources report it as March 19 and 20.
25 Irving, *op. cit.*, pp. 166–167.
26 Ibid., p. 178.
27 Bro, *op. cit.*, pp. 71–72.

B. "Sinners"

The Martin girls were not allowed to read any of the newspapers, not even the Catholic *La Croix* which their father regularly received. Yet Thérèse learned about "the Pranzini affair" (as it was and is still called) from discussions at home with her father and other family members and relatives. Thérèse, then fourteen, was determined that this man should be saved from eternal damnation, whereupon she embarked upon a regimen of private prayer and sacrifices. She kept her pledge a secret but finally had to confide in her sister Céline who then also felt a need to convert the sinner. Thérèse tells us in her own words about the Pranzini affair:

> I heard talk about a great criminal just condemned to death for some horrible crimes; everything pointed to the fact that he would die impenitent. I wanted at all costs to prevent him from falling into hell, and to attain my purpose I employed every means imaginable. Feeling that of myself I could do nothing, I offered to God all the infinite merits of Our Lord, the treasures of the Church, and finally I begged Céline to have a Mass offered for my intentions. I didn't dare ask this myself for fear of being obliged to say it was for Pranzini, the great criminal. I didn't even want to tell Céline, but she asked me such tender and pressing questions, I confided my secret to her. Far from laughing at me, she asked if she could help convert *my sinner*. I accepted gratefully, for I would have wished all creatures would unite with me to beg grace for the guilty man.
>
> I felt in the depths of my heart *certain* that our desires would be granted, but to obtain courage to pray for sinners I told God I was sure He would pardon the poor, unfortunate Pranzini; that I'd believe this even if he went to his death without *any signs* of *repentance* or without *having gone to confession*. I was absolutely confident in the mercy of Jesus. But I was begging Him for a "sign" of repentance only for my own simple consolation.[28]

Fifty days after Pranzini was condemned to death, Thérèse read the following account with every morbid detail of his execution in the August 31, 1887, issue of the journal *Le Croix*:

> The sinister blackguard who murdered the three victims of the rue Montaigne was executed this morning, and with him ends the vile scandal of recent days. At a very early hour crowds overran the Roquette Plaza and neighboring streets. At 11:30 detachments of the republican guard, on horseback and foot, and the Seine police came to take their place on the plaza. At precisely 3:00 the venerable Abbé Faure arrived, in carriage no. 3751, drawn by a white horse. He was followed closely by M. Athalin, the examining magistrate, Taylor, head of the Sureté [criminal investigation department], Garon, second in command, and Martigny, secretary. At 4:45, M. Bauquesne, director of the Roquette, M. Baron, police commissioner, his secretary, and M. Faure went for the first time to cell no. 2, occupied by the condemned. M. Caubet accompanied these gentlemen.
>
> Pranzini slept soundly. M. Bauquesne shook him twice to wake him up. The assassin of Marie Regnaud sat up on his bed, cast haggard eyes all around him and uttered a hoarse cry. What an awakening! In reality, the miserable one had

---
28 *Story of a Soul*, chapter V, p. 99–100.

not ceased to rely on his pardon. He made violent efforts to speak a little. "You are going to commit a crime. I am innocent!" And he added, making a violent effort to appear calm: "The only thing I regret is not having been able to kiss my mother." In a few seconds, his face became livid. "Courage, Pranzini," M. Bauquesne said to him. "Your crime was too great; M. the President of the Republic was not able to grant you a pardon. Die a good death, and redeem your fault that way." "I am innocent! I am innocent!" he screamed. The two Sureté agents passed him his boots. He put them on slowly, while the clerk read the sentence. He dressed while trembling, mumbling incoherent phrases. Then he asked for some cold water in order to wash his face and hands. The chaplain, M. Faure, then remained next to him for a few moments. He said to him: "I will be as calm as you, for I die innocent." Finally, he was led to the clerk's office, where Deibler and his assistants had been waiting for several minutes for him to be delivered to them. There, they cut his hair, cut out the neck of his shirt, bound him hand and foot, and, at two minutes to five, while the birds were singing in the trees of the plaza, while a confused murmur arose from the crowd, the command "saber in hand" rang out, a clinking of iron resounded, swords shone, and on the threshold of the prison, whose door opened, the murderer appeared, livid. The chaplain placed himself in front of him to hide the sinister machine from him. The assistants supported him. He pushed away both the priest and the executioners. There he was before the bascule [*sic*]. Deibler pushed him and threw him onto it. One assistant, placed on the other side, grabbed his head, brought it under the blade, holding it by the hair.

But before this movement could be produced, perhaps a flash of repentance crossed his conscience. He asked the chaplain for his crucifix. He kissed it twice. And when the blade fell, when one of the assistants seized the detached head by an ear, let us say to ourselves that if human justice is satisfied, perhaps this final kiss will also have satisfied divine justice, which asks above all for repentance.[29]

Reading this powerful account deeply affected Thérèse:

> My prayer was answered to the letter! In spite of Papa's prohibition that we read no papers, I didn't think I was disobeying when reading the passages pertaining to Pranzini. The day after his execution I found the newspaper "*La Croix*." I opened it quickly and what did I see? Ah! My tears betrayed my emotion and I was obliged to hide. Pranzini had not gone to confession. He had mounted the scaffold and was preparing to place his head in the formidable opening, when suddenly, seized by an inspiration, he turned, took hold of the *crucifix* the priest was holding out to him and *kissed the sacred wounds three times*![30] Then his soul went to receive the merciful sentence of Him who declares that in heaven there will be more joy over one sinner who does penance than over ninety-nine just who have no need of repentance! [Luke 15:7]
>
> I had obtained the "sign" I requested, and this sign was a perfect replica of the grace Jesus had given me when He attracted me to pray for sinners. Wasn't

---

29 English translation on pp. 125–126 in Bernard Bro's *Saint Thérèse of Lisieux*.
30 Writing years later, Thérèse's memory seems to have failed her since newspaper reports had stated Pranzini kissed the crucifix "two times."

B. "Sinners"

it before the *wounds of Jesus*, when seeing His divine *blood* flowing, that thirst for souls had entered my heart? I wished to give them this *immaculate blood* to drink, this blood which was to purify them from their stains, and the lips of my "first child" were pressed to the sacred wounds!

What an unspeakably sweet response! After this unique grace my desire to save souls grew each day, and I seemed to hear Jesus say to me what he said to the Samaritan woman: "*Give me to drink!*" [John 45:7] It was a true interchange of love: to souls I was giving the *blood of Jesus*, to Jesus I was offering these same souls refreshed by the *divine dew*.[31]

The chaplain of the prison, Father Faure, served for six years in this capacity and had attended twenty prisoners before their death. In his book *Souvenirs de la Roquette* (Memories of La Roquette) he wrote that he talked to Pranzini the day before his execution: "Our interview was more cordial and more intimate than ever. We conversed for more than two hours and, when I left him, he told me he was sorry to see our conversation end so soon."[32] During this and other conversations with Father Faure, Pranzini touchingly mentioned his pious mother who lived in Alexandria and how sorry he was not able to give her his last kiss. He also attended Mass at the prison. At the Diocesan Inquiry many years later Céline made the following explanation of what happened at Pranzini's last moments:

> Recently, I had a visit from Fr. [Jean-Auguste] Valadier, who used to be chaplain to Roquette prison (a prison for those condemned to death), and was the successor of Fr. Faure, who assisted Pranzini at his death. He confirmed the fact of Pranzini's unexpected conversion; Fr. Faure himself had told him all about it. Pranzini had ascended the scaffold still refusing any help from religion; it was only after they had bound his hands that he cried out in an anguished voice that was full of repentance and faith: "Chaplain, give me the crucifix!" He kissed it effusively and exchanged a few words with the chaplain just before the executioner took him away.[33]

This episode of the Pranzini affair[34] definitively convinced Thérèse that she had to become a Carmelite and spend her life in prayer for the salvation of sinners. The prioress permitted Thérèse to have a Mass said each year for Pranzini because she said that after the many crimes of his life he certainly needed prayers and Masses.

Ten years later in the year of her death she confirmed this purpose when she wrote "During my short life I want to save my fellow sinners."[35]

---

31 *Story of a Soul*, chapter V, p. 100.
32 Descouvemont, *op. cit.*, p. 79.
33 At Session 30, September 20, 1910.
34 This case has held such interest through the years that even a novel based on Pranzini's story was written in French by Viviane Janouin-Benanti called *Le Chéri magnifique: Histoire d'un Crime* (*The Splendid Darling: Story of a Crime*), published in 2001 by Cheminements, Canada.
35 PN 46, "To My Guardian Angel."

4. LÉO TAXIL (1854–1907)
Created the fictitious Diana Vaughan, an anti-Catholic hoax

WHILE THÉRÈSE WAS GRAVELY ILL WITH TUBERCULOSIS THAT TOOK HER life six months later, she underwent an emotional ordeal caused by Léo Taxil and Diana Vaughan who she believed were then helping the cause of Catholicism in a France rampant with anti-clericalism and hostile freemasonry.

This woman by the name of Diana Vaughan was supposedly a Protestant, born in 1864 in Lexington, Kentucky, of an American father and a French mother who came from a wild remote region in southern France. While still in the United States she was initiated by her father into a Masonic Luciferian sect called Palladism allegedly connected somehow with the American Albert Pike, one of the luminaries of international freemasonry. Her strange story progressed following her arrival in France in 1884 at the age of twenty. She asserted that as a daughter of Lucifer she had become "engaged" to the demon Asmodeus in 1889.[36] Apparently she traveled back and forth from America and Europe getting more enmeshed in the rituals of this cult and more notorious as a result. In 1893 she met a Dr. Bataille and Léo Taxil, the latter a well-known and virulent opponent of Catholicism.

Léo was born into a bourgeois family in Marseille on March 21, 1854, and baptized with the full name of Marie-Joseph Gabriel Antoine Jogand Pagès. His father was Charles Jogand and his mother Josephine, *née* Pagés. He attended a Jesuit elementary school in Ville-franche-sur-Saôn, just south of Lyon from 1863 to 1865 and was confirmed by the Archbishop of Lyon. At fourteen he went to the high school of St. Louis in his hometown but did not last long there. Because of the problems caused by his severe disruptive behavior at school and his troubles at home, he ran away and headed for Italy. It took no time for the police to apprehend and usher him back home. His father, whereupon, sent him to a boys' correction facility in the small village of Mettray, just north of Tours, known as the Mettray Penal Colony (1839–1937).[37] He hated this place, the teachers, the discipline, and especially his father for sending him there. After only two months, he couldn't stand the place and decided to go home again—for a while. By 1870 at the age of sixteen, however, he was on his own.

For the next few years he managed to write articles for not only anti-clerical but revolutionary periodicals under the pen-name of Léo Taxil. From here on his infamous career as a master hoaxer and fraud began with a made-up story about a school of sharks in Marseille harbor. He was nineteen at the time and three years later he initiated another fantastic deception about a sunken city in Lake Geneva which at first even convinced many including a Polish archeologist. Léo happened to be in the Swiss capital because he fled there to escape a juridical case involving some illegal activity.

---

36 Chalon, *op. cit.*, p. 214.
37 Jean Genet (1910–1986), the famous French dramatist, novelist, poet, and political activist was an inmate here at 15.

At twenty-three in 1877 he was in Paris and deeply involved with his career as an anti-Catholic writer. In the meantime, his private life moved along quite dramatically. At this point he was living in a small flat at 1499 rue de Rennes and frequented his favorite tavern. He had a liaison with a married woman, a dressmaker from Marseille by the name of Marie who had two children. She had been convicted of stabbing a man who had told her husband about her deceptive and immoral ways. Somehow acquitted, she later married Léo.[38] By now Léo had long left the Church, became a Freemason, and had delved into pornography.

To further promote his anti-Catholic hatred, he established a newspaper with the title *L'Anticlérical* (The Anticlerical) and wrote around 130 pamphlets in what was known as the "Anticlerical Library." Especially notorious were his "*A bas la calotte*" ("Down with the Priesthood"), "*Les soutanes grotesques*" ("Ludicrous Cassocks"), and the salacious "*Les Maîtreses du Pape* [Pius IX]" ("The Mistresses of the Pope"). In 1881 he founded The Anti-clerical League. Meanwhile, not having abandoned his skill as a creator of hoaxes, he perpetrated other creative frauds that proved quite successful and generally undetected.

Finally, he experienced financial difficulties followed by expulsion from the Freemasons because of his false assertions that they were involved with demonic practices. With a totally unexpected and surprising move, he reverted to Catholicism in 1885 which he claimed came about while studying the trial of Joan of Arc. As a result of this marvelous transformation, he wrote *Confessions d'un libre penseur* ("Confessions of a Free Thinker") which became so popular that it managed to go through forty-five editions.

In the meantime, Diana's own bizarre story emerged and was widely covered by the press which seemed quite intrigued by her and a reading public equally so. The Catholic newspaper *La Croix* in a May 1895 issue particularly commented on Diana and urged its readers to pray to Joan of Arc for her conversion. A month later it happened. She claimed that she was showered with divine grace specifically inspired by Joan of Arc and, like her associate Léo Taxil, was converted. Shortly after she was apparently baptized, composed a eucharistic novena (*La Neuvaine eucharistique*), and announced that she had a strong desire to become a nun. In 1885 her extraordinary story was published with the long title of *Memoirs of an Independent, Fully Initiated, ex-Palatine: unveiling the mysteries and satanic practices of Luciferian triangles* (meeting places). In it she confessed she had been a priestess of Lucifer and that her sudden conversion was due to the influence of Joan of Arc who, incidentally, had been proclaimed Venerable by the Pope just a year before. Diana's fame spread throughout Europe with many in the Catholic world truly believing in her existence including priests, bishops, and even Pope Léo XIII. Léo Taxil got into the act and claimed at the sensational press conference in 1897 that he had an audience with the Pope who

---

38 Alex Mellor, "*A Hoaxer of Genius—Leo Taxil*," Last Modified Saturday November 03, 2001, http://www.cix.co.uk/~craftings/leo.htm.

asked him, "My son, what do you wish?" He answered, "Holy Father, to die at your feet, right now!... This would be my greatest happiness."[39]

Thérèse learned of this amazing young lady primarily from her Uncle Guérin's writings in the newspaper *Le Normand*. Diana's eucharistic novena and the offering of herself on June 13, 1895, as a victim of divine justice deeply stirred Thérèse. Mother Agnès urged her to compose a poem for Mlle. Vaughan and send it to her. Somehow lacking poetic inspiration, Thérèse sent instead a short letter with a photo of herself as Joan of Arc and her sister Céline as St. Margaret, two characters in the play, *The Mission of Joan of Arc* (RP 1), that Thérèse wrote for a convent recreation in 1894. Diana replied with a gracious note of thanks.

Actually Thérèse composed her seventh convent play directly under the spell of Diana's story, named it *The Triumph of Humility*, and had it performed at the monastery on June 21, 1896, the feast day of the prioress, Mother Marie de Gonzague. In it Thérèse calls Diana a "new Joan of Arc." Of all her eight plays this is the only one with a contemporary topic and setting. Just one year before, Diana had declared that Lucifer revealed to her his war of destruction on all convents, especially those of the Carmelites. Thérèse's play took this theme and, as the title indicates, humility vanquishes evil. The novice mistress in the play, portrayed by Thérèse, concludes with a final exhortation:

> [We] know now the means to overcome the demon and that from now on we have only one desire, that of practicing humility.... [B]ehold our weapons, our shield; with this omnipotent force, we will know, the new Joan of Arc, will chase the stranger from the kingdom, that is, to prevent proud Satan to enter into our monasteries.[40]

Thérèse, Céline, and her other novices apparently enjoyed this diversion acting their parts as saints, devils, and other characters, some of which were derived from Diana Vaughan's writings. Sister Marie of the Sacred Heart, Thérèse's blood sister, wrote to her Uncle Guérin telling him about this production:

> Yesterday and today, two little plays by the novices. Yesterday, the Benjamin [nickname for Thérèse's cousin Marie Guérin—Sister Marie of the Eucharist] dressed up as a gardener with blouse and wig enacted the part of the innocent one to perfection. Today, transformed into St. Michael, she combated Satan and his devils.... It was a current event. Asmodée [an evil destructive spirit in Jewish demonology] was there [played also by Marie Guérin], speaking about Diana Vaughan, etc., etc. It was composed by Sister Thérèse of the Child Jesus.... These are the amusements of the Carmelites.[41]

As time went by some perceptive journalists and others began to have suspicions about the sincerity, fantastic claims, amazing conversion, and eventually

---

39 Taxil, "The Confessions of Léo Taxil."
40 *Œuvres Complètes*, p. 926, translated by the author.
41 June 21, 1896, on p. 1265 in *General Correspondence*.

even the reality of this mysterious, shadowy, and elusive Diana Vaughan. A number of German Jesuits also joined this skeptical group. Eventually the Vatican started an inquiry under the supervision of Msgr. Lazzareschi, a distinguished prelate of the Church. Upon hearing that Mlle. Vaughan lashed out aggressively against him, Thérèse began to have doubts about Diana Vaughan since "it is not possible that that would come from the good Lord." [42]

Finally, in order to dispel all suspicions, Léo Taxil, her exclusive spokesman, announced that he and Diana would hold a press conference which would include a speech by him and the projection of many images. He said this was not previously proposed since Diana feared some form of retaliation, possibly physical harm from members of the Freemasons she had so flagrantly maligned. In fact, he asked the police to be present in order to ensure her safety which they willingly consented to by providing sixty policemen.[43] They in turn insisted that all the men who carried canes or umbrellas leave them at the door.[44] The newspaper announcement regarding this meeting that appeared in *Le Normand*, Saturday, April 17, 1897, follows in a rough translation:

> We announce a meeting promised by Diana Vaughan at the Geographic Society of Paris for Easter Monday.
> Here is the program published by several newspapers:
> This meeting will be preceded by a talk by Léo Taxil entitled *Twelve years under the banner of the Church* in which he declared he separated from the anti-Masonic strife.
> The conference of Diana Vaughan will have the title: *Palladism Vanquished*. The light projections will show the legal family documents of Diana Vaughan and other Masonic papers and portraits.
> We announce a series of other similar meetings in a great number of cities in Europe and America.[45]

The long awaited day arrived, Easter Monday morning, April 19, 1897, when over 350 French and foreign journalists, Freemasons, clerics, freethinkers, and others assembled in the large hall of the Geographic Society on Boulevard Saint-Germain in Paris. This was one of the largest rooms in Paris for meetings at the time which the Society rented out to various organizations. When Taxil appeared at the entrance to the building, a raucous crowd brazenly surrounded the unnerved Taxil forcing the police to dispurse them. In the hall itself, the only picture projected on a large screen was the photo Thérèse sent to Diana a year before! And the only one to appear was Léo Taxil, a stocky forty-three-year-old bald headed man with a bushy beard. During a lengthy speech of some two dozen single-spaced typed pages that he read with his Marseille accent, Taxil arrogantly declared that he still maintained his old beliefs against Catholics, never

---

42 Chalon, *op. cit.*, p. 241.
43 *La Croix*, Wednesday, April 21, 1897.
44 Descouvemont, "*Thérèse a l'écran ... de son vivant!*," *Les Annales*, July–August, 1990.
45 Descouvemont, *Thérèse and Lisieux*, p. 283. Translated by the author.

converted, and most significantly, was delighted that he so shrewdly deceived society, the press, the Masons, and especially the gullible Catholic Church for the past twelve years. The audience was not only shocked but infuriated. The astounding climax came when he announced with smug arrogance that Palladism was a fiction he invented, that he created the characters Dr. Bataille as well as the provocative Diana Vaughan, and that all the writings attributed to her were by himself including the famous eucharistic novena. Boos, shouts, screams, laughter, hissing, as well as applause from the delighted anti-clerics erupted after each stinging salvo by Taxil.[46]

He tried in vain to convince the audience that the photo of the Carmelites was authentic, but the now untrusting and angry crowd did not believe him. At one point he even referred to the nun who sent the photo as a *"pauvre imbécile"* ("poor imbecile")![47] Whether Thérèse ever heard about this scurrilous epithet is uncertain. At any rate, amidst all the excitement and furor, the triumphant Taxil departed safely from the hall under the obliging protection of the police, after which he found refuge and solace in his favorite brasserie Lipp (now called Chez Lipp) on the Boulevard Saint-Germain not far from the Geographic Society building.

After the conference, a lengthy front page article labeled "The Confessions of Léo Taxil" appeared in *Le Normand* relating the details of this tumultuous news session. Toward the end it stated:

> What remains to be said about that meeting? Of the pictures he was to have had there by the hundreds—there was only one, a photo representing Joan of Arc's vision of St. Catherine,[48] from a play which had been put on in honor of Diana Vaughan in a Carmelite Convent. What convent? Probably Taxil's house! The farce is ended … until the actor begins again his practice.[49]

Of course it was not Taxil's house; it was Thérèse's convent and its sole purpose certainly was not to honor Diana Vaughan. But the Joan of Arc was Thérèse and the St. Margaret was Céline. It must be realized, however, though Taxil was truly vicious, it is to his credit that he did not reveal Thérèse's name nor the monastery where she lived.

This diabolic and embarrassing deception mortified Thérèse and the other nuns who were appalled at being duped by that hoaxer. Thérèse promptly threw the letter "Diana" sent into the garden dung heap. Never again did she mention the incident but she surely must have considered him another soul like the murderer Pranzini to be prayed for and saved. Thérèse wrote the following pertinent lines a few months later with him no doubt in mind:

---

46 According to some sources the name Diana Vaughan was the name of an actual person, but not with such a bizarre background. One author says she was Taxil's secretary who typed all his writings (Patrick Ahern, *op. cit.*, p. 100).
47 Schmidt, *Everything is Grace: The Last Eighteen Months in the Life of Thérèse of Lisieux*, p. 282.
48 Céline in the picture represented St. Margaret not St. Catherine.
49 Descouvemont, *op. cit.*, p. 283.

Your child, however, O Lord, has understood Your divine light, and she begs pardon for her brothers.... May all those who were not enlightened by the bright flame of faith one day see it shine. O Jesus! If it is needful that the table soiled by them be purified by a soul who loves You, then I desire to eat this bread of trial at this table until it pleases You to bring me into Your bright Kingdom.[50]

Léo Taxil eventually moved to a stately home at 11 rue de Fontenay in Sceaux, a suburb just south of Paris, where he enjoyed a comfortable life with his wife. Writing continued to occupy his time. In fact, in 1904 he had the sanctimonious audacity to write a book—*The Art of Buying*—which gives advice to people about how not to be fooled by false advertising.[51] And to top it off, he used his old trick—the pseudonym, and a female one too: Jeanne Savarin![52]

His fame as a hoaxer *par excellence* has persisted internationally even to the present. He has also been called a "mythomaniac charlatan."[53] The noted American magazine *U.S. News & World Report* in its August 26/September 2, 2002 issue featured Léo Taxil in an article by Dan Gilgoff entitled "Devil in a red fez: The lie about the Freemasons lives on." It summarizes the case of Léo Taxil, that ribald French prolific journalist:

> Taxil himself had no intention of aiding any Christian cause: He wanted to embarrass Rome. After promising to present Diana Vaughan to the public in April 1897, he instead used the occasion to reveal himself as a fake and to thank the church for its gullibility. "Palladism, my most beautiful creation, never existed except on paper and in thousands of minds," he told a crowd of 300. They were incensed, but Taxil had once more outwitted his audience: He had requested that all umbrellas and canes be checked at the door.
>
> [Taxil] had a personal ax to grind with Rome: He'd been successfully prosecuted by the church for libel, though he managed to avert a prison sentence. "Taxil had so many enemies," says William Harman, a religion professor at the University of Tennessee-Chattanooga, "that I'm amazed he was able to walk around freely."

Leo Taxil did exactly that, walk around freely until his death on September 3, 1907, at the age of fifty-three.

5. RENÉ TOSTAIN (1858 – 1936)
An atheist relative of Thérèse

"I'VE OFFERED UP MY TRIAL AGAINST FAITH ESPECIALLY FOR A MEMBER united to our family who has lost his faith." The gravely ill Sister Thérèse made this magnanimous pledge on September 2, 1897, just twenty-eight days before she died. Her sister Pauline (Mother Agnès of Jesus) copied these words down in her *Yellow Notebook*—the record of Thérèse's last conversations with her blood sisters and other nuns in the Lisieux Carmel. The "member united" to her family was René Tostain, a morally decent and upstanding man but a professed

---
50 *Story of a Soul*, chapter X, p. 212.
51 Ahern, *op. cit.*, p. 101.
52 Éditions du Cerf, *Le Triomphe de L'Humilité*, p. 97.
53 Jean-François Six in his *Light of the Night* quotes these words from Rioux's *Chronique* (n. 71), p. 212.

atheist. He was married to Marguerite Maudelonde (1867–1966), the daughter of Thérèse's Aunt Guérin's sister. Marguerite and her sisters Céline and Hélène with their cousins Marie and Jeanne Guérin were close friends and schoolmates of Thérèse and her sister Céline.

René held the position of deputy public Prosecutor of the Republic in Lisieux and at one time served as president of the Civil Tribunal of Mortagne-au-Perche, a town a little distance from Alençon. He married Marguerite on October 14, 1889, with no children produced by this union.

Marguerite Tostain visited Thérèse in the monastery on April 3, 1891, at which time she disclosed the doubts she had been having about her own faith and the hereafter, no doubt much influenced by her husband's philosophy of life. Thérèse promptly wrote to her sister Cèline who was still at home during the time their father was a patient at the hospital in Caen:

> Marguerite confided to us intimate secrets that she tells no one. We really must pray for her, for she is exposed to danger.... She says that no book does her any good. I thought that the mysteries of the future life[54] would do her some good and would strengthen her faith which, alas, is really endangered!... She told us she could read books without her husband's knowing it.
>
> You should give her that book, telling her that we thought it would interest her, but to begin it only at the third chapter where there is a little holy picture, because the first three chapters would have little interest for her.... As for myself, I have the greatest desire that she read a book in which she will really find the answer to many doubts![55]

Seven years later Marguerite still had doubts and told Pauline about them:

> You recall that a few days after Thérèse's death I wrote you that I reached a point of doubting the existence of a second life? Since then I doubted even more, I doubted *everything*. Well! The life of Sister Thérèse [*Story of a Soul*] has done me much good. She, too, suffered as I do, but she did not reason it out; she submitted to the trial God was sending her by means of this temptation. And I can do as she did; instead of thinking and losing myself in suppositions of all kinds, I can also think that if the faith God placed in us appears to be darkened at times, this is a trial to which I must submit while continuing to act as though I had before my eyes a dazzling light.[56]

After a long period of suffering, René died at seventy-eight on June 11, 1936, eleven years after Thérèse was canonized. Even to the end he remained a radical atheist. On his deathbed, however, he whispered three times "*Ainsi soit-il*" (French for "Amen").[57]

Marguerite survived him by thirty years, dying at the age of ninety-nine in 1966.

---

54 Abbé Arminjon, *The End of the Present World and the Mysteries of the Future Life*.
55 LT 126 from Thérèse to Céline dated April 3, 1891.
56 Letter from Marguerite Tostain to Pauline dated November 18, 1898.
57 See "*Notes sur le Carnet Jaune*" in *Derniers Entretiens*, p. 551 (2.9.7).

CHAPTER 7

PLACES ASSOCIATED WITH ST. THÉRÈSE

A. In Normandy
B. The Rome Trip
C. Other Places Visited by St. Thérèse's family

A. In Normandy

1. ALENÇON
   a. **St. Thérèse's Birthplace:** *House at 50 rue Saint-Blaise*
   b. **The Prefecture:** *Opposite the Birthplace House where Thérèse and Céline's little girlfriend lived*
   c. **Louis Martin's Watchmaking and Jewelry Shop:** *Louis Martin's business establishment and first home after his marriage*
   d. **Notre-Dame Church:** *Where Thérèse's parents were married and she was baptized*
   e. **The Church of Saint Leonard:** *Thérèse's parents attended services here*
   f. **The Church of Saint-Pierre de Montsort:** *Thérèse's parents' church during their early marriage years where all their children except Thérèse were baptized*
   g. **The Pavilion:** *Louis Martin's retreat place*
   h. **The Bridge of Saint Leonard:** *Where Thérèse's parents first met*
   i. **The Monastery of the Poor Clares:** *Where Thérèse's mother often visited and Léonie first tried religious life*
   j. **The Railroad Station:** *Regularly frequented by the Martins who lived nearby*
   k. **The Promenades:** *A public park the Martins often visited*
   l. **Our Lady's Cemetery:** *Where Thérèse's mother and four siblings were first buried*
   m. **Mme. Tifenne's House:** *Home of the Martins' friends where Thérèse stayed at times*
   n. **Vital Romet's House:** *Home of Louis Martin's good friend and his family*

526 CHAPTER 7: *Places Associated with St. Thérèse*

Plate 15

Alençon

A. St. Thérèse's Birthplace

B. Vital Romet's House

C. Convent of the Poor Clare Nuns

D. The Pavilion

E. Saint Leonard's Bridge

F. The Prefecture

G. "The Cardinal's Room"

H. Notre-Dame Church

I. Notre Dame Cemetery

J. Mme. Tifenne's House

1. ALENÇON

ALENÇON, THE CAPITAL OF THE ORNE, IS LOCATED ON THE BORDER BETWEEN two departments—the Orne and the Sarthe—in the southern frontier of Normandy about 105 miles west of Paris. It is one of the 83 original departments created during the French Revolution (1790). Called the City of the Dukes, it has a long history dating back to before the time of the famous William Duke of Normandy, better known as William the Conqueror, who laid siege to the town. During the Anglo-Norman Wars of 1113 to 1203 the British occupied Alençon. Then from 1415 the city became the seat of a dukedom under the command of the sons of the Kings of France until the Revolution (1789–1799). Napoleon visited the town in 1811 and ordered the building of the law courts which opened in 1827. During the Franco-Prussian War (1870–1871) Alençon was occupied by the Prussians and experienced many hardships. In World War II it became a key town in the Mortain-Falaise pocket battle during the Battle of Normandy in the summer of 1944. The German army occupied it from June 17, 1940, until August 12, 1944, when it became the first town in France that was liberated by the French army under General Leclerc.

Alençon has been recognized since the seventeenth century as the center for the extremely intricate and painstaking technique of needle lacemaking called *Point d'Alençon*. For example, it requires 25 hours of work to create a lace pattern the size of a postage stamp. For religious-minded people, though, Alençon is primarily known as the birthplace of St. Thérèse of the Child Jesus.

The famous novelist Honoré de Balzac (1799–1850) placed two of his novels in Alençon: *La Vielle Fille* (1837) and *Le Cabinet des Antiques* (1838). The French poet Charles Baudelaire (1821–1867) had one of his works printed here.

In the Saint's day, this bustling little town had a population of over 16,000 inhabitants (more than double that size by 2000) and was distinguished not only for its lace, but also for its fabric industry, horse dealing, and printing business.

St. Thérèse's much visited birthplace is located on the main road (Rt. N 138) from Lisieux to Alençon at 50 (formerly 36 and 42) rue Saint-Blaise. It is now a museum and shrine honoring the saint's birth there on January 2, 1873. Thérèse's mother Zélie Guérin lived at this address for fifteen years with her parents (1843–1858) before she married. She possessed a truly entrepreneurial spirit and in 1853 when she was twenty-two, established in her home her own lacemaking business. At times she employed up to twenty workers who brought their hand-sewn lace to her every Thursday. From this supply she put together the finished product ready for sale. After her wedding to Louis Martin in 1858, she moved to his home at 15 rue du Pont Neuf not far away and managed her thriving industry from there for thirteen years. Upon the death of her parents, she inherited their property on rue Saint-Blaise and moved back to it in 1871 with her husband and four daughters. She continued her business at their new home with the assistance this time of her husband who after twenty years in his own successful profession (1850–1870) sold his watch and jewelry store to his nephew and became her manager and salesman "to be able to give up more of his time to her lacemaking enterprise and to lighten her work of correspondence."[1]

For almost five years until her mother's death in 1877, Thérèse lived here after which the disconsolate family moved to Lisieux almost sixty miles away. Louis thought it would be best for his girls to be near his wife's brother, his sympathetic and loving wife, and their daughters who had been living there for some time. Céline gives us additional insight into the reason for the move: "In after years I wanted to know why he decided to leave Alençon in spite of the contrary views that were presented to him. He wished 'to take us away from influences that he considered too worldly among some of his friends, and from the liberal ideas of others.'"[2]

When she was ten, Thérèse went on her first visit back to Alençon for a much needed vacation that lasted from August 20 to September 3, 1883:

> Three months after my cure [from a serious illness] Papa took us [Marie, Léonie, Céline, and Thérèse] to Alençon. This was the first time I had gone back. My joy was very great when seeing the places where I had spent my childhood days and especially when I was able to pray at Mamma's grave and ask her to protect me always.
>
> God gave me the grace of knowing the world just enough to despise it and separate myself from it. I can say it was during my stay at Alençon that I made my *first entrance* into the *world*. Everything was joy and happiness around me; I was entertained, coddled, and admired; in a word, my life during those two weeks was strewn only with flowers. I must admit this type of life had its charms for me. Wisdom [4:12] is right in saying: "*The bewitching of vanity overturns the innocent mind!*" At the age of ten the heart allows itself to be easily dazzled, and I consider it a great grace not to have remained in Alençon. The friends we had there were too worldly; they knew too well how to ally the joys of this earth to the service of God. They didn't think about *death* enough, and yet *death* had paid its visit to a great number of those whom I knew, the young, the rich, the happy! I love to return in spirit to the *enchanting* places where they lived, wondering where these people are, what became of their houses and gardens where I saw them enjoy life's luxuries?[3]

Three years later on October 5, 1886, Thérèse took her second trip back to Alençon with her father, accompanied again by her sisters Marie, Léonie, and Céline. Their father wanted Marie to pay a final visit to her mother's grave before entering the convent:

> A month [actually a few days] before her [Marie's] entrance into Carmel [October 15, 1886], Papa brought us to Alençon, but this trip was far from resembling the first; everything about it was sadness and bitterness for me. I cannot express the tears I shed on Mamma's grave because I had forgotten to bring the bouquet of corn-flowers I had gathered especially for her. I really

---

1 Sister Geneviève, *The Father of the Little Flower*, p. 33.
2 Ibid., p. 47.
3 *Story of a Soul*, chapter IV, pp. 72–73.

made a big fuss over *everything!* I was just the opposite of what I am now, for God has given me the grace not to be downcast at any passing thing.... I was still only a child who appeared to have no will but that of others, and this caused certain people in Alençon to say I had a weak character.[4]

She stayed overnight at the home of Mme. Tifenne at 6 Place du Plénitre, located a short distance behind the church of Notre-Dame. Her husband was a pharmacist friend of Isidore Guérin (Thérèse's uncle) and a close family friend of the Martins. Mme. Tifenne recalled this memorable visit to an American priest in 1926:

> Just before she entered the convent the Little Flower came to Alençon to bid goodbye to the Alençon friends and relatives of the family. I, as the godmother of Léonie and intimate friend of the family, had the honor of entertaining Thérèse and her father and this was the room which Thérèse occupied, and of course, I allow no one now to occupy this room.[5]

Céline has additional words to say about Mme. Tifenne's room: "Thérèse and I used to spend a part of our holidays with her, in a large room covered with red damask. St. Thérèse used to refer to it as the 'Cardinal's room.'"[6]

a. St. Thérèse's Birthplace
House at 50 rue Saint-Blaise

THE THREE STORY RED BRICK AND WHITE STONE HOUSE AT 50 (FORMERLY 34 and 42) rue Saint-Blaise, where St. Thérèse was born on January 2, 1873, rises directly beside the sidewalk on the street named after the fourth century Saint Blaise. From earliest days Alençon held a special devotion to this martyred Armenian bishop who is noted for having saved a boy's life by removing a fishbone from his throat. The Church blesses throats every year on his feast day, February 3 in remembrance of this incident.

Just two steps lead up from the pavement to the front door on the right. Shortly after the Martins moved here in 1871, Thérèse's father joined his wife in her lacemaking business and installed a marble tablet above the door with the words "Louis Martin, Maker of Point d'Alençon." Today, however, a sign indicating the birthplace of St. Thérèse—"*La Maison Natale de Saint Thérèse*"—is attached to the middle of the balcony railing on the second floor. Two large windows spread out to the left of the main door. On the second floor three French doors span the width of the house and in front of them a balcony with an iron railing runs along the entire length of the building. The third floor has a solitary gabled window jutting out in the center of the slanted roof.

Thérèse's oldest sister Marie points out the exterior balcony in a letter she wrote to their sister Pauline who was attending a boarding school in Le Mans at the time:

---
4 Ibid., p. 91.
5 Dolan, *op. cit.*, pp. 173–174.
6 Sister Geneviève, *The Mother of the Little Flower*, pp. 119–120.

Just now she [Thérèse] was on the balcony and was looking very pensively [to the right] at the street leading to the train station. I asked her what she was thinking about: "Ah! I'm thinking it is this way the *petit Paulin* (family nickname for Pauline] returns from Le Mans." So you see the little baby isn't forgetting you either.[7]

The actual front of the house remains today as it was in Thérèse's time, but some changes have been made in the interior, on the property adjacent to it, and in the rear. The buildings on both sides were torn down and replaced on the left by a chapel (1925) and on the right by an alleyway that leads to an open garden beyond, dominated by a statue of the saint, and an annex to the left. The façade of the chapel is recessed a short distance in from the front sidewalk and is enclosed by a wall with an opening in the middle. Two curved stairways, one on each side, ascend to a landing with a two-door entrance into the sanctuary that contains six wall paintings depicting scenes in Thérèse's early life. The main feature, inside on the right, cannot fail to impress the visitor: a glassed-in room with the original furniture where Thérèse was born and where her mother died. A large dome above the chapel outside is a distinctive and dominant feature of the chapel edifice.

Directly inside the house on the ground floor a hallway meets a winding staircase on the left in the rear. Thérèse's mother wrote about these steps: "She [Thérèse] will not climb the stairs all alone, but cries at each step: 'Mamma, Mamma!' If I forget to say: 'Yes, my child,' she stops and won't go any further."[8]

Céline presents a clear and authoritative description of the rest of the house in the biography she wrote of her mother:

> The ground floor of the home, facing the street, comprised three rooms. The front room [on the left], lighted by two windows, was both sitting room and office. It was here that mother worked her "Point d' Alençon," and received her workers. [Zélie's work-table and Louis's desk and other original memorabilia are now displayed in this room].
>
> Behind a glass partition [on the right] was the dining room. But when guests came, or there was a large dinner, the front room was used, the central table being moved against the wall.
>
> Opening into the regular dining room was the kitchen, which faced a small yard at the back. This serves, at present, as a sacristy and parlor for the Sisters [of the Congregation of Oblates of St. Thérèse] who act as custodians of the place.
>
> On the first floor [second to non-Europeans] there are two rooms, facing the (street) balcony. The one on the left—a guest room—has two windows. If necessary, it became a reception room, for the bed was completely hidden in an alcove, closed by a double folding door....
>
> The other room, facing the balcony, was the bedroom of the older girls, Marie and Pauline. It was there that Marie gave lessons to her young sisters.

---

7 Letter from Marie to Pauline dated May 9, 1877.
8 Letter (CF 146) from Zélie to Pauline dated November 1875, as quoted in footnote 6 of *Story of a Soul*, chapter I, p. 18. In the original French letter, the word is not "climb" (*"monterait"*) but *"descendent"* ("descend"). The footnote explains it.

Behind the "big room" was that of our parents; an opening has been made from it into the present-day chapel. This room was directly over the kitchen, and was lighted by a window looking out over the small year....

On the second floor [third] were the rooms of the children and the maid.

To go from the house to the garden [then about 36 ft. by 24 ft.], one has to pass by a narrow alley, between the high walls of the adjacent houses; the passage is about forty feet long. At the alley, on the left, is the sheltered recess where Thérèse and Céline used to count their "sacrifices." That used to mystify their neighbor [Mme. Gaucherin] who from her overlooking window could hear their "debates" about the "sacrifices." Her house was afterwards purchased and is now occupied by the Sisters, who are custodians of the house.

On the right of the passage, at its extremity, is the "annex"—the addition, which grandfather built for the house. It comprised on the lower floor, a large room, which was used as a laundry and linen room. In the mysterious dream which Thérèse had in her childhood, it was here she saw two little devils, terrified by the gaze of the child....

After the beatification of St. Thérèse, in order to arrange the property as a place of pilgrimage, the neighboring property was purchased. This allowed for the construction of the chapel, and the placing of a statue of St. Thérèse, which occupies the exact spot of the annex-building, which was torn down.[9]

Two extracts from Thérèse's autobiography mention the garden swing:

> Your father just installed a swing, and Céline's joy knows no bounds. But you should see the little one [Thérèse, a year and a half old] using it; it's funny to see her trying to conduct herself as a big girl. There's no danger of her letting the rope go. When the swing doesn't go fast enough, she cries. We attached her to it with a rope, but in spite of this I'm still uneasy to see her perched so high.[10]

> One day when I was swinging contentedly, he [her father] passed by and called out to me: "Come and kiss me, my little Queen!" Contrary to my usual custom, I didn't want to budge, and I answered boldly: "Come and get it, Papa!" He paid no attention to me and was right to do so. Marie was there. She said: "You naughty little girl! How bad it is to answer one's father in this way! Immediately I jumped off my swing for the correction was not lost on me! The whole house resounded with my cries of sorrow. I climbed the stairs quickly, and this time I didn't call "Mamma" each step, for I thought of nothing but finding Papa and being reconciled to him. This was done very quickly.[11]

Today, at the end of the alley that leads from the street to the back of the house, there is a garden with a life-size statue of St. Thérèse atop an elegant pedestal. In the rear can be seen the place where Céline and Thérèse used to count their "sacrifices." A plaque attached to the ivy-covered wall reads in French: "*ICI SE TROUVAIT LA TONNELLE OU THÉRÈSE ENFANT COMPTAIT SES PRACTIQUES DE VERTU AVEC SA SOEUR CÉLINE.*" ("Here was located the arbor

---

9 Sister Geneviève, *op. cit.*, pp. 116–119.
10 Thérèse quotes this excerpt in chapter I of *Story of a Soul*, p. 17, from her mother's letter of June 25, 1874 (CF119) written to her daughters Marie and Pauline.
11 *Story of a Soul*, chapter I, footnote 8, p. 19.

where the child Thérèse counted her practices of virtue with her sister Céline.") Against the rear wall is the tombstone that was originally in the Martin plot at the Cemetery of Our Lady (*Cimetière Notre-Dame*) not very far away on the rue de la Fuie des Vignes. Next to it is a plaque, here translated into English, informs the reader that:

> ST. THÉRÈSE OF THE CHILD JESUS
> USED TO KNEEL AT
> THIS BURIAL STONE
> WHICH COVERED
> THE MORTAL REMAINS
> OF HER PIOUS MOTHER
> AND THAT OF
> SEVERAL MEMBERS OF HER FAMILY
> FROM 1877 TO 1894
> THE DATE WHEN THEY WERE TRANSFERRED
> FROM THE CEMETERY OF NOTRE DAME IN ALENÇON
> TO THAT OF LISIEUX

b. The Prefecture

Opposite the birthplace house where Thérèse and Céline's little girlfriend lived
DIRECTLY OPPOSITE THE HOUSE WHERE THÉRÈSE WAS BORN (*La Maison Natale de Sainte-Thérèse*) is the huge red brick and stone 17th century *Hôtel de la Préfecture* (the Prefecture of the Orne) constructed in the grand Louis XII style with a large courtyard in front. A huge long wing on the right of the recessed rear main building extends to the fence at the street. On the left another building reaches as far as the one on the right but is not attached to the mansion. Two stone entrance pillars in the center of a long and high wrought-iron fence separate the estate from the street. Originally a town house for the pious Duchess of Guise, it later served as a residence for royal commissioners, a military headquarters, and finally after 1809 as a home for the administrators of the department. Today it still functions as a civic building.

Occasionally Céline's friend, Jeanne Béchard, the prefect's daughter, whom Thérèse called "the little prefect," would invite them to play with her. In her diary of October 19, 1877, Céline recorded the family's move away from Alençon, and in it she writes about their friend: "We leave for Lisieux after 'All Saints.' Papa already brought some things by train yesterday. I forgot to say that the day before yesterday I played with the little prefect; she has a beautiful swing. We used to swing, and I was also in the bedroom of the lady."

Thérèse was awed by the luxurious surroundings and the spacious grounds behind the mansion and, to be sure, she enjoyed all of Jeanne's toys and her see-saw. She admitted, nonetheless, that she went there primarily to please Céline for she really preferred the quiet and solitude of her own backyard garden.

Even though they lived across the street from the Béchards, Thérèse's parents apparently never really socialized with them. The Martins did not find time to visit any of their neighbors or attend their parties. Their main interests, besides their lace business, concerned the upbringing of their children, attending daily religious services, and visiting primarily their relations and a few very close friends.

The Prefecture fence was the scene of a very humane action on the part of Louis Martin. Céline cites this incident as well as other charitable ones in her book about her father:

> Many persons in need were thus helped, in particular an aristocratic family reduced to poverty. My father had noticed the husband leaning sorrowfully against the grating of the Prefecture buildings, and seemingly in the greatest distress. After having relieved his immediate needs, Father found an honorable position for the head of the family. It was the son of that gentleman who at the birth of Thérèse brought to our home a welcome for the baby. Written in verse, it was from the pen of the grateful father.[12]

The following incident took place in front of the Prefecture, but it most certainly was not humane. It exemplifies the class envy so prevalent at the time:

> A curious adventure took place recently in connection with a lady whose barouche[13] was standing opposite to our house, outside the Prefecture. The coachman wore gorgeous livery lavishly trimmed with fur. A discontented individual carrying a canvas sack in his hand was just passing by. He stopped for a moment to survey the coachman and then the lady inside the carriage. Then he turned to the open door, undid his bag and threw the contents into her lap.
>
> At once, she cried out in terror. The coachman came to her assistance, the passers-by ran up. There they saw her convulsed in a nervous attack, and swarming over her were about twenty frogs. They were even on her head; in fact she was covered with them.
>
> The wretched assailant watched her struggling when the policeman arrived on the scene and asked him why he had done such a thing. He quietly replied, "I had just caught these frogs to sell, but when I saw this aristocrat, with her coachman all decked out in furs, I preferred to give her a good fright, rather than sell my frogs. They took him to the gaol [jail]; he did not try to escape.[14]

c. Louis Martin's Watchmaking and Jewelry Shop
Louis Martin's business establishment and first home after his marriage

NEAR THE PONT NEUF BRIDGE OVER THE RIVER SARTHE IN ALENÇON STANDS a store at 35 rue du Pont Neuf built on the exact spot where the business establishment and home of Thérèse's parents and paternal grandparents existed. All the original buildings in the area have disappeared including M. Martin's. In his day, to the left of his shop were one or two other stores that ended at the edge of the bridge. A parking lot has replaced them. Now, as formerly, the entire

---

12 Sister Geneviève, *The Father of the Little Flower*, p. 23.
13 A carriage with four wheels that had a folding top. There were four seats inside and a special seat outside for the driver.
14 An English translation from Piat's *The Story of a Family* of part of a letter (CF 112) dated November 30, 1873, written by Mme. Martin to her daughters Marie and Pauline.

street on both sides contain a row of upscale stores. A sign facing the parking lot on the side of the new building where Louis Martins' shop stood, indicates the importance of this edifice: "MAISON MARTIN *Ancienne demeure et magasin d'horlogerie de Monsieur* MARTIN *père de Sainte Thérèse de l'Enfant Jésus.*" [15]

Many significant events in the life of Thérèse's close relatives occurred there. Of the nine Martin children, all but Thérèse were born in that house and four of them died there as did both her grandfathers. Although Thérèse never resided at this address, she as a very young girl visited this house where the only grandparent she knew, Fanie Martin, was living at the time.

In 1850, after studying his craft in Strasbourg and Paris, Louis Martin settled down with his parents in Alençon. On November 9 of the same year he purchased and moved into his new watch and clock making shop where he later sold jewelry on the ground floor of the building on the Rue du Pont Neuf.[16] His parents went to live in the second floor apartment above the store. After his marriage, he and his wife lived in separate quarters on the first floor behind the store.

Louis Martin and Zélie Guérin were married in 1858 at the bride's parish church of Notre-Dame, not far away, and for the next thirteen years lived at this place, then numbered 15 rue du Pont Neuf. Their parish during this period was Saint-Pierre de Montsort.

Thérèse's grandfather, Captain Martin, died in the house in 1865, ending his thirty-five year retirement residence in Alençon. His widow Fanie continued living there for twelve more years, the last six by herself after her son and his family moved to their own home. In the meantime, Zélie's father, Captain Guérin, had been living alone for seven years after the death of his wife. The time finally came when Zélie realized he could not manage on his own much more, so she and Louis willingly accepted him into their home where he was tenderly cared for until he died almost two years later in 1868.

The house on the rue du Pont Neuf played a role, almost insignificant though it was, in the Franco-Prussian War (1870–1871). When the Prussians invaded France, Alençon experienced a brief bombardment then occupation and billeting of thousands of enemy soldiers who had marched triumphantly along the rue du Pont Neuf. Despite the war's terrible disruptions, Zélie's letters to her devoted sister-in-law Céline recounting in detail those woeful days reached their destination miles away in Lisieux:

> [About] three o'clock on Monday, every door was marked with a certain number of enemy soldiers to be billeted there. A tall sergeant came and demanded to look over our house. I took him up to the first floor [second floor in America] and told him we had four children. Happily for us, he made no attempt to go up to the second floor. Finally he assigned us nine, and we cannot complain.

---

15 "MARTIN HOUSE The former residence and watch and clock-making store of M. Martin, the father of Saint Thérèse of the Child Jesus."
16 Two words in large bold print indicated the type of store it was: "HORLOGERIE and BIJOUTERIE."

In our neighborhood small shopkeepers, who have only two-storied houses, are being sent fifteen, twenty and even twenty-five....

[We] have been obliged to give up the entire first floor to them, and to come down to the ground floor. If I told you everything, I should have to write a book. The town refused to pay the sum demanded and we were threatened with reprisals....

[The] town is desolated and everyone, except ourselves is in tears. I was not much afraid. I no longer fear anything.[17]

One soldier attempted to steal some jewelry from Louis's establishment but Louis caught him in the act and threw him out. He reported the incident to the proper officials. The penalty for such misconduct, he soon discovered, was death but he managed to have the authorities spare the man's life.

Realizing that his wife's prosperous lace business required augmented managerial assistance, Louis sold his own shop and the building to his nephew, Adolphe Leriche, in 1870. The next year Louis and Zélie moved a short distance away to their new home at 36 rue Saint-Blaise, the property she inherited from her father. Here the last child of this marriage was born—the future Saint Thérèse of the Child Jesus.

Zélie's untimely death in 1877 changed the lives of all dramatically. Barely three months later, Louis left Alençon with his five motherless daughters for Lisieux in order to be near his wife's brother and family and benefit from their benevolent influence. He did, though, provide a new dwelling in the quiet little hamlet of Valframbert (just north of Alençon) for his rather independent mother who had been living at the rue du Pont Neuf address. Here her nurse-companion for the final six years of her life was none other than Thérèse's erstwhile wet nurse Rose Taillé.

d. Notre-Dame Church
Where Thérèse's parents were married and she was baptized

IN THE CROWDED CENTER OF ALENÇON ON THE BUSY RUE SAINT-BLAISE stands the beautiful Gothic church of Notre-Dame built between 1444 and 1506 during the war between England and France known as the Hundred Years' War (1338–1453). In the French Revolution it was sacked and greatly damaged. About 150 years later, at the time of the 1944 bombings of World War II, Alençon experienced some amount of damage, but this church luckily escaped destruction. Eleven sixteenth century stained glass windows were removed and safely stored before the bombings. The stained glass windows in the side chapels, though, were destroyed but replaced between 1986 and 1996. Then in 1999, due to a huge storm, some of the architectural features, especially the magnificent three-sided front porch, built in 1517, required restoration, a process lasting three years.

The distinctive features of this church are the aforementioned luminous stained glass windows and the grand front porch constructed in the flamboyant

---
17 Letter (CF 64) dated January 17, 1870, written by Zélie to her sister-in-law Mme. Guérin.

style that reaches out to the street. Inside the church on the left is the baptistery closed off by an ornate wrought-iron grille where Thérèse was christened on January 4, 1873, two days after her birth. It is now a chapel with the original font and an altar on the right surmounted by a statue of the saint. Encased in the left wall are some of Thérèse's baptismal clothes; the rest is displayed in the museum of St. Thérèse memorabilia connected with the Lisieux Carmel. Overlooking all in this chapel is a large new stained glass window depicting Thérèse's baptism.

Only two and a half blocks away on the same side of the road is the house where St. Thérèse was born and lived for nearly five years. In 1871, the Martins moved from rue du Pont Neuf in the Saint-Pierre de Montsort parish to the house Zélie inherited from her father in the Notre-Dame parish. The first family ritual celebrated at Notre-Dame in fact had been performed thirteen years before on July 13, 1858, with the wedding of Louis and Zélie at midnight—a custom for marriages at that time. Only family friends in Alençon and the witnesses were present. The civil ceremony took place the evening before at the town hall (*Hôtel de Ville*). Notre-Dame was the bride's parish church before her union with Louis in Holy Matrimony. From their wedding day until their move, the Martins were, however, members of Saint-Pierre de Montsort. Then from 1871 to 1877, they were enrolled in the parish of Notre-Dame. Zélie's early death in 1877 marked the end of their affiliation with this church. She was buried from there on August 29 and interred in the Notre-Dame Cemetery, a number of blocks away on rue de la Fuie des Vignes.[18]

The Register of Notre-Dame d' Alençon contains the record of Thérèse's parents' marriage:

> On Tuesday, the thirteenth of July, eighteen hundred and fifty-eight, after publication in the churches of Notre-Dame and Montsort of the banns of the future marriage between Louis Martin, watchmaker, living in Alençon, parish of Montsort, eldest son of Pierre-François, retired captain, knight of St. Louis, and Marie-Anne-Fanny Boureau.
>
> And Zélie-Marie Guérin, manufacturer of *Point d'Alençon*, living in this parish of Notre-Dame, eldest daughter of Isidore Guérin and Louise-Jeanne Macé.
>
> No impediment or opposition having been found—dispensation from the other two publications of banns having been obtained—and the civil formalities gone through [on the evening of July 12], after the ceremony of bethrothal, we dean of Saint-Leonard, with delegation from M. l'abbé Jamot, *Curé-Archiprêtre* of Notre-Dame, having received their mutual consent to matrimony, and having given them nuptial blessing, in presence of their relations and friends who have signed their names with ours.
>
> *Louis Martin, Azélie [Zélie], F. Martin, Guérin, F. P. Martin, Louise Guérin, A. Leriche, Lefort, Tessier, I. Guérin.*
> *F. Hurel, Curé-Doyen de St. Léon*[19]

---

18 After Louis Martin's death on July 29, 1894, Zélie's coffin and those of her four deceased young children, her father, and her mother-in-law were transferred to the public cemetery in Lisieux on October 11, 1894.
19 Lavielle, *Life of the Little Flower*, p. 374.

A. In Normandy

Thérèse Martin's baptism was also recorded in the Register at Notre-Dame and signed by Abbé Dumaine who lived to give testimony at Thérèse's process of beatification and then to see the tiny infant he christened fifty-two years before, canonized a saint of the Church:

> On Saturday, the fourth of January, eighteen hundred and seventy-three, has been baptized by us the undersigned, Marie-Françoise Thérèse, born on the second of January of the legitimate marriage of Louis-Joseph-Aloys-Stanislas Martin and Zélie-Marie Guérin, both of this parish (rue St-Blaise, 36). The godfather has been Paul-Albert Boul [13 years old], and the godmother Marie-Louise Martin [13 years old], sister of the child. These, together with the child's father, have signed their names with us. Marie Martin, Paul-Albert Boul, Louis Martin, P. Boul, Pauline Martin, Léonie Martin, Léontine Boul, Louise Marais [maid who carried the baby].
>
> *Dumaine*, Vicaire de N.-D.[20]

Thérèse's parents attended the 5:30 A.M. Mass daily at Notre-Dame and on Sundays they attended the Solemn High Mass and afternoon Vespers. Zélie never failed to go to Holy Communion on the first Friday of each month, a long held Church custom practiced by many even today. In addition, she was a faithful member of all the church societies. M. Martin was one of the founders of the Catholic Club established at Notre-Dame. Céline informs us of her parents' attendance at church services:

> Our father went daily to Mass, and also to Holy Communion as often as the custom of the time allowed. Accompanied by our mother he left the house early, so much so that the neighbors used to say at the sound of the closing door: "That is the holy Martin couple going to Mass, let us sleep some more!" While they lived at St. Blaise Street, where Thérèse was born, it was to Notre Dame (Our Lady's, Alençon) that they went. The church has a marvelous outside porch, a fact which lent itself to a popular but rather irreverent local saying:
>
>> In such a way the Church was made,
>> That to prepare the choicest spot
>> Wherein to place Our Lord, they said,
>> Outside the door would be His lot!
>
> [Every] afternoon he used to pay a visit to the Blessed Sacrament, and whenever there was a "Corpus Christi" Procession he never missed being directly behind the canopy. On no account would he have stayed away, even when the sun was very hot—something he minded very much as obviously he always had his head uncovered. This devotion to Our Lord in the Tabernacle manifested itself also by his exemplary fidelity to Nocturnal Adoration. He was one of the first to arrive at the appointed hour; and when free to choose he selected the most inconvenient hours, and gladly changed with someone else if a more favorable hour fell to his lot.[21]

---

20 Ibid., p. 371.
21 Sister Geneviève, *op. cit.*, pp. 5–7.

The next excerpt provides another interesting perspective into M. Martin's character related to going to Notre-Dame Church:

> Our venerable father was careful to avert from us anything that might disturb our souls. Every morning when we were going to early Mass, he used to tell us not to look up at the windows which, in summer, would be open, lest we see persons dressing, or half-dressed. For the same reason, we should be modest on our walks in the country if, perchance, we passed a bathing place.[22]

It is not surprising that Thérèse too possessed a great love for the church and its sacred rituals even from her earliest years. Zélie described to her sister-in-law this unique fascination that the two-year-old Thérèse displayed:

> She already knows how to pray to the good God, and goes every Sunday to a part of Vespers; if, unfortunately, she is left at home she cries and will not be comforted.
>
> Some weeks ago she was taken for a walk on Sunday. She had not been "at Mass" ["*a la mette*"] as she said of herself. On returning from a walk she began to cry vigorously, saying that she wanted to go to Mass. She opened the hall door and ran away, in torrents of rain, towards the church [Notre-Dame]. When we had run after her and brought her back, her tears and lamentation lasted a good hour.
>
> Once she said out loud to me in church: "I have been at Mass here, and I have prayed well to the good God too." When, on her father's return home this evening, she did not see him say his prayers, she said: "Why do you not say your prayers, papa? Have you already been to church?"[23]

Further exemplifying Thérèse's delight in matters religious, Céline recorded this incident: "During May we used to assist at the May devotions in the church. Besides that, mother wanted to keep a special month of Mary at home. The shrine had to be so beautiful that my sister used to joke about it, good-naturedly, and say 'that it rivaled the decorations of the parish church,' Notre-Dame, Alençon."[24]

Even in her last days of suffering, Zélie would not abandon going to church regardless of the pain it caused her. The second to last time she attended Mass, Marie reveals some agonizing struggles that ensued:

> She needed unheard-of courage and effort to reach the church. Every step she took caused pain in her neck; sometimes she was forced to stop in order to regain a little strength. When I saw how weak she was, I implored her to return home, but she would go on to the end, thinking that this pain would pass. Nothing of the kind happened. On the contrary, she had great difficulty in returning from church.... I never thought I should bring her home alive. Oh, in what anguish I heard that Mass! Several people looked at us astonished, doubtless wondering how anyone could have made a sick person come out in such a pitiable state. But, cost what it might, she would go, thinking she was not ill enough to miss Sunday Mass.[25]

---

22 Ibid., p. 52.
23 Letter (CF 130) dated March 14, 1875, by Zélie to Mme. Guérin.
24 Sister Geneviève, *The Mother of the Little Flower*, pp. 50–51.
25 Piat, *op. cit.*, pp. 251–252.

Years later in May 1888, Louis Martin offered himself to God in a special way at this church. Thérèse reminisces about this poignant moment:

> O Mother [Agnès, her sister Pauline], do you remember the day and the visit when he [their father] said to us [Marie, Pauline, and Thérèse in the convent parlor]: "Children, I returned from Alençon where I received in Notre-Dame church such great graces, such consolations that I made this prayer: 'My God, it is too much! Yes, I am too happy, it isn't possible to go to heaven this way. I want to suffer something for you! I offer myself....'" the word victim died on his lips; he didn't dare pronounce it before us, but we had understood.[26]

Two days before Zélie died, Louis in much torment sought a priest to administer the Last Rites to her:

> On the evening of the 26th, he went to *Notre-Dame* to fetch the priest and insisted upon himself accompanying the holy Viaticum. The whole family gathered round the dying bed; their hearts made one in the same prayer. Thérèse has recorded this memory: "The ceremony of Extreme Unction has remained imprinted upon my memory. I still see the spot where they made me kneel. I still hear our poor father's sobs."[27]

Notre-Dame Church, from its inception over half a millennium ago to the present, has witnessed untold numbers of events, felicitous as well as tragic. The Martin family perhaps ranks at the very apex of its dramatic history, having intensely provided the myriad elements of idealistic parochial life that culminated in the glorification of one of its members as "the greatest saint of modern times" and the third woman "Doctor of the Universal Church." Behind this grand apotheosis stand her holy parents who themselves are progressing on the glorious path to sainthood.

e. The Church of Saint Leonard
Thérèse's parents attended services here

THE THIRD CATHOLIC CHURCH IN ALENÇON IS THE 15TH CENTURY GOTHIC church of Saint Leonard, a fine example of the Flamboyant style of architecture, on Grand-Rue, several blocks south on the same road where Thérèse was born; there, however, the road is called the rue Saint-Blaise. This splendid edifice, built between 1489 and 1505, has a tall impressive nave with, however, no triforium[28] which apparently was usual at the time. Through the actions of Blessed Margaret of Lorraine, niece of Margaret of Anjou, queen of Henry VI of England, the reconstruction of the building was accomplished.

The Martins were not members of this parish, though Louis and Zélie often attended missions, retreats, and other services there. Apropos of this is a letter Zélie wrote that reveals her intense devotion to church rituals: "In spite of a fever, which has been weakening me for six weeks, I have even arisen every morning

---
26 *Story of a Soul*, chapter VII, footnote 182, p. 154.
27 Piat, *op. cit.*, p. 257.
28 On both sides of the nave in a Gothic church there are generally 3 divisions in its height: arcade, triforium, and clerestory (or "clear-story"). The center one, the triforium, has no windows to the outside, and thus often called a "blind-storey."

at 5:30 for the past two weeks to go to St. Leonard's to assist at the mission, given by the Capuchin Fathers."[29]

Louis was well acquainted with the priests stationed there, particularly the dean, Abbé Hurel, who served as chaplain of a men's association called the "Vital-Romet Club." The curate, Father Jamot, taught the young bachelor Louis Latin for a while. Both priests participated in the Martin wedding ceremony. On return visits to Alençon, Louis would regularly stay at Vital Romet's home at 72 rue du Mans opposite the church of Saint-Pierre de Montsort. Vital, a pharmacist, was Thérèse's sister Céline's godfather. Incidentally, Louis belonged to the Nocturnal Adoration Society (a monthly obligation in honor of the Blessed Sacrament) and the Conference of St. Vincent de Paul which helped people in distress.[30]

f. The Church of Saint-Pierre de Montsort
Thérèse's parents' church during their early married years where all their children except Thérèse were baptized

On November 9, 1850, the twenty-year-old bachelor Louis Martin settled down at 23 (some sources say 15) rue du Pont Neuf after five years studying his watch-making and jewelry craft in Strasbourg and Paris. His parents, who had been living not far away, went to live with him. Their parish church was Saint-Pierre de Montsort, a number of blocks away in the south end of town at the fork between the rue du Bas-de-Montsort and the Avenue du General-Leclerc (Route N 138). It is located in the general vicinity of Louis's retreat place called the Pavilion.

When Louis married Zélie Guerin in 1858, the wedding, following a custom of the time, took place at midnight, at her parish church of Notre-Dame. The newly married couple went to live at his parents' residence in the quarters behind the store while his parents lived above on the second floor. They faithfully attended the daily 5:30 A.M. Mass and all the religious functions at their church during the next thirteen years. Concerning her parents' church attendance there, Céline comments briefly in her biography of her father:

> Our father went daily to Mass, and also to Holy Communion as often as the custom of the time allowed. Accompanied by our mother he left the house early, so much so that the neighbors used to say at the sound of the closing of the door: "That is the holy Martin couple going to Mass, let us sleep some more!"[31]

Louis happily presented their first child, Marie, born on February 22, 1860, at the baptistery of Saint-Pierre. He joyously greeted the curate with the prediction: "This is the first time that I have come here for a Baptismal Ceremony, but it will not be the last!"[32] Seven more children were baptized there and, sadly, four of them died young and were buried from the same church. Thérèse was the only child of the nine who was baptized elsewhere.

---

29 Letter (CF 51) by Zélie to her sister-in-law Mme. Guérin dated February 12, 1870.
30 Sr. Geneviève, *The Father of the Little Flower*, p. 16.
31 Ibid., p. 5.
32 Ibid., p. 39.

After the death of her father, Zélie inherited his house on Rue Saint-Blaise and in 1871 moved back to the home she had lived in before her marriage. Two years later Thérèse was born on January 2, 1873 and baptized in the church of their new parish—Notre-Dame. Céline gives an example not only of her mother's exceptional fortitude but also of her continued ties with Saint-Pierre's even after their move. She quotes from a letter by their former family maid, Louise Marais (later Madame Le Gendre) that she received forty-six years later when she was a nun in the Lisieux Carmel:

> During her illness [terminal breast cancer], one day she [Zélie] received at her office [in her home] a call from the parish priest of Montsort [Abbé Crêté], who was her confessor, while I was present. She spoke to him of her death with so much resignation that the priest said: "Madame, I have met many valiant women, but never one like you." The good pastor was less calm than Madame.[33]

g. The Pavilion
Louis Martin's retreat place

I recall the days Papa used to bring us to the pavilion; the smallest details are impressed in my heart.... Oh! everything truly smiled upon me on this earth.[34]
—Thérèse

THESE HAPPY THOUGHTS APPEAR TOWARD THE END OF THE FIRST CHAPTER of Thérèse's renowned autobiography. "The Pavilion," located not a great distance from where Louis Martin was living, was the name given to the property which included a little building. He bought it on April 24, 1857, fifteen months before his marriage when he was thirty-four years old. It served as a retreat from the cares of his business and the distractions of his home. In those days, the street had the name Rue des Lavoirs, but, recognizing its significance, the town changed its name many years later to 26 Rue du Pavilion Sainte-Thérèse. The small plot of land, surrounded by a high wall, was and still is hidden from the road beside it. Louis converted the grounds into a delightful garden area with a walnut tree, plentiful daisies, poppies, strawberries, currants, and roses which the young Thérèse delighted in and often joyfully picked and carried home after pleasant visits with her father.

This narrow three-story hexagonal structure in the shape of a tower adjoins the wall at the far end of the property with one room on every floor. The ground floor has an entrance at the right and an outside stairway on the left leading to the second floor room that contains a wooden spiral staircase leading to the third level (or attic space). Louis Martin furnished his unique little hideaway with only the barest necessities: fishing gear, chairs, a desk, pious pictures, a crucifix, and select religious books. On the walls he hand-painted some thoughtful sayings: "God sees me," "Eternity is drawing near," and "Blessed are they who keep the Commandments of the Lord."[35]

---

[33] Sister Geneviève, *op. cit.*, p. 90.
[34] *Story of a Soul*, chapter I, p. 29.
[35] Sister Geneviève, *The Father of the Little Flower*, p. 4.

The great Franciscan writer on St. Thérèse, Father Stéphane-Joseph Piat, a friend of Mother Agnès, provides intimate knowledge of things Theresian. He gives a detailed description of a day at the Pavilion enjoyed by the entire Martin family:

> During the holidays the outings most appreciated by the small ones had as their goal the Pavilion, that chalet which M. Martin had furnished in the *Rue des Lavoirs*. No party gave them so much pleasure as those afternoons when they romped freely round the old fir and the walnut tree amid the flowers and fruit. If the father did not produce his fishing tackle, he retired with his books to the ground floor room with the rustic furniture: the farmhouse clock, the armchair, the folding table and perhaps best of all the two framed water colors over the fireplace, which testified to Pauline's budding artistic talent. The mother would bring her needlework and talk to her daughters while they picked strawberries, made posies, or worked at the small garden patches which had been assigned to each of the three elder girls. When tired with their games the sisters came, one after another, to settle themselves closely on the straw-seated bench; the picnic basket was opened, and there was a fresh outburst of laughter and joyous exclamations. Was there not a whole education in this simplicity that led them to delight in little things, in the family circle, without having useless recourse to the fallacious attractions wherewith those who cater for the leisure hours of the public think proper to cheer the incurable boredom of worldly folk?[36]

Louis was not the only one besides his family who came to this solitary little haven. On occasion, fellow members of the St. Vincent de Paul Society, a men's group from his parish of St. Pierre, met there to discuss their charitable and missionary work. For a while he had as company a greyhound who one day when Louis arrived became so excited that he fell from the second floor landing to the ground below and broke his legs.

Later, after marriage and children, Louis frequented the place much less, but one day his daughter Marie invited a friend there. The lady was taken aback by the austerity of it all and remarked, "Oh, Marie! Take me out of this place! It sends a chill down my spine! It's too much like a monastery for me! Let's go into the garden again."[37] Interestingly, decades later in 1929, after learning that the Pavilion was to be repainted, the same lady wrote to Marie, "It would be unfortunate to have all these aspirations of a saint, which your father was, painted over."[38]

Msgr. Laveille recounts in his book about Thérèse a little humorous reference to the Pavilion:

> One morning Céline was tormenting her father to bring her and Thérèse to the "Pavillon," as he had done the evening before. In a half-jesting, half-serious tone, M. Martin said: "Are you joking? Do you imagine that I can bring you there every day?" Thérèse was over in a corner amusing herself with a little wand and seemingly quite occupied with her toy. Suddenly she turned with a nonchalant air: "Oh, we need not flatter ourselves with the notion that

---

36 Piat, *op. cit.*, p. 174.
37 Ibid., p. 31.
38 Sister Geneviève, *op. cit.*, p. 4.

papa will bring us there every day!" Céline hung down her head, and "papa" laughed heartily.³⁹

At one place on the grounds, Louis placed a thirty-five inch high statue of the Blessed Mother that Mlle. Félicité Baudouin, a pious lady of the town, had given him. Some years before, she assisted him financially to set up his watchmaking business. The statue was a plaster copy reduction of an original silver-gilt figure by Bouchardon, the "Sculptor of the King," made for the Church of Saint-Sulpice in Paris in 1734. Unfortunately it disappeared during the French Revolution. All succeeding reproductions were taken from an engraving of a painting of the original made a few years after the statue was modeled. Subsequent to his marriage, Louis brought this statue to his home where it was always the center for prayers and especially the May devotions:

> [The] statue of Our Lady, which was to smile on Thérèse as a child, was always venerated by her with honor. One day Marie, our eldest sister, thinking this statue too big for the room in which it was placed, said: "It looks like a school statue," and wanted to have it changed. Mamma protested at once:
> "When I am gone, child, you can do what you like, but as long as I live, this Blessed Virgin will not leave this place."⁴⁰

After Zelie's death in 1877, Louis and his five motherless daughters moved to a new home in Lisieux the girls named Les Buissonnets (sold to them with the name *Maison Le Valois aux Bissonnets*).⁴¹ Louis maintained the ownership of the Pavilion with the knowledge that he would be staying there on return trips to Alençon. The statue went with them and was put in the older girls' bedroom where it continued to be the center of the family's great Marian devotions. They said their daily prayers there, decorated it lavishly for their May ceremonies, and arranged the Christmas crib before it each year as they had done in Alençon when their mother was alive.

Thérèse suffered for three months from a grave and unexplainable physical and mental illness when she was ten-and-a-half. She was cured instantly on May 13, 1883, as she gazed imploringly at the statue near her bed of the Blessed Mother who smiled at her.

When the lease of Les Buissonnets terminated on December 25, 1888, Léonie, and Céline—the only girls still at home—went to live with the Guérins. Upon their father's release from the hospital three years later, the two girls moved to their own dwelling, just behind the Guérin's house at 7 Rue Labbey where they cared for him until he died two years later.

Within two months after her father's death, Céline joined her three sisters in the Lisieux Carmel. The statue preceded her there by one day. They placed it on top of a set of drawers donated by the Martins in the art workroom next

---

39 Quoted from Leveille's *Life of the Little Flower*, p. 49. The actual quote is from Zelie's letter to Pauline, CF 169, dated October 22, 1876.
40 Sister Geneviève, *The Mother of the Little Flower*, p. 50.
41 See note 9 on p. 129 to a letter dated September 10, 1877 from M. Guérin to M. Martin.

to Sister Thérèse's cell. When in 1897 Thérèse was taken down to the infirmary several months before she died, the statue followed her. Just a short time before she died, Thérèse stared at the statue and gasped, "Oh, good Blessed Virgin, come to my aid!"[42]

Today, this statue that began its life with the Martins is enshrined in a niche above the Theresian shrine in the Carmelite Chapel in Lisieux. Many copies exist in various places where Thérèse lived or visited including the one today in the garden of the Pavilion in Alençon. Incidentally, Céline stated in her book about her father that the original granite tombstone of the Martin family in the cemetery in Alençon was placed in the garden of the Pavilion. It was transferred on Good Friday, April 1, 1983 to the garden behind the house where Thérèse was born. It is kept very clean by being regularly washed with a high-pressure pump called a "karcher."[43]

The Pavilion is at present privately owned and cannot be visited. The upper part of the tower, however, is clearly visible from the street—the Rue du Pavilion Ste. Thérèse. A high wall surrounds the property from public view. Several yards along the rear wall where the tower is attached is an elaborate entrance door surmounted by a statue of St. Thérèse.

h. The Bridge of Saint Leonard
Where Thérèse's parents first met

THE BRIDGE OF SAINT LEONARD PLAYED A SIGNIFICANT PART IN THE LIFE of St. Thérèse's parents. When traveling on the Rue de Fresnay past the church of St. Leonard and a hospital, one passes over this bridge, the fourth in Alençon crossing the Sarthe River that flows its long gentle winding way through the town. Zélie Guérin (twenty-seven) and Louis Martin (thirty-five) happened to pass each other here with virtually a "love at first sight" reaction, at least on Zélie's part. Céline, their future daughter, mentions this fleeting encounter in the biography she wrote years later of her mother: "One day, as she [Zélie] was crossing St. Leonard's bridge at Alençon, the same inspiration which had directed her in regard to her professional work [lacemaking], now made her feel within herself, on meeting a man who had passed her on the way: *That is he whom I have prepared for you.*"[44] They were married just three months later at Zélie's church, Notre-Dame.

i. The Monastery of the Poor Clares
Where Thérèse's mother often visited and Léonie first tried religious life

THE MONASTERY OF THE POOR CLARES, AN AUSTERE CLOISTERED FRANCIScan community, is located at 3 Rue de la Demi-Lune. This street runs directly behind the large rear area of the Prefecture that contains a well-cultivated garden and spacious lawns. Zélie Martin often visited the nuns at the convent to unfold her problems to the them and ask for their prayers. Her husband Louis also visited

---
42 *Her Last Conversations*, September 30, 1897.
43 Carmel Archives.
44 Sister Geneviève, *op. cit.*, p. 3.

the place and often gave the sisters the results of his many fishing jaunts. Zélie was admitted into their lay branch, the Franciscan Tertiaries, in a ceremony held in the chapel, and regularly attended all the meetings of the chapter. Her daughter Léonie frequently accompanied her and gradually developed a desire to become a Poor Clare nun herself. Zélie disclosed to her daughter Pauline what Léonie had in mind: "Yesterday she [Léonie] came for a walk with me and we went to the Poor Clares. She whispered to me, 'Mother, ask the enclosed nuns to pray for me that I may be a nun.' In short, all is going well; let us hope that it will last."[45]

Zélie has these comments on her eldest daughter Marie's high ambitions:

> There is Marie dreaming of going to live in a fine house, opposite the Poor Clares, in the *Rue de la Demi-Lune*. She talked about it all yesterday evening; one would have thought it was Heaven. Unfortunately, her desires cannot be realized. We must stay where we are; not for all her life, but for my part I shall leave this house only at my death.[46]

This selection from Thérèse's autobiography gives her impression of the monastery as well as her family's opinion of Léonie's vocation:

> It was during this trip [to Alençon in 1886] that Léonie made her attempt to enter the Poor Clares. I was saddened by her *extraordinary* entrance, for I loved her very much and I hadn't even the chance to kiss her before her departure. Never will I forget the kindness and embarrassment of the poor little Father of ours when he came to announce that Léonie had already received the habit of the Poor Clares. He found this very strange, just as we did, but he didn't want to say anything when he saw how unhappy Marie was about the matter. He took us to the convent and there I experienced a sort of *contraction of my heart* such as I never felt at the sight of a monastery. This monastery produced the opposite effect which Carmel produced in me, for there everything made my heart expand. The sight of the religious didn't attract me in the least, and I was not tempted to remain among them. However, poor Léonie was very attractive in her new costume, and she told us to get a good look at *her eyes* because we would no longer see them (the Poor Clares have a custom of going around with eyes downcast), but God was content with only two months of sacrifice, and Léonie returned to show us *her blue eyes* which were frequently moist with tears.
>
> When leaving Alençon I believed she would remain with the Poor Clares, and so it was with a heavy heart I left the sad street of *Demi-Lune* (half moon).[47]

The monastery still exists today. The outside apparently has not changed much from the time of Thérèse. A sign on the wall along the street reads "MONASTÈRE DES CLARISSES." A very plain, hardly noticeable light blue door indicates the entrance at 7 Rue de la Demi-Lune. The chapel inside, because of its very simple, rather modern appearance and lack of ornamentation, does not seem

---

45 Piat, *op. cit.*, p. 239. This itself is a quote from CF 194, dated March 12, 1877, written by Zélie to her daughter Pauline.
46 Ibid., p. 193. This is a translation of an excerpt from a letter (CF 150) written by Zelie to Pauline, dated January 16, 1876.
47 *Story of a Soul*, chapter IV, pp. 91–92.

to be the original one. No altar railing separates the sanctuary which rises four steps from the congregation area. A huge San Damiano Crucifix hangs on the rear wall. On the left the tall white figure of the Madonna and Child adds a feeling of tenderness to the surroundings. The small inside cloistered quadrangle contains a lovely, rather well-kept garden. The nuns now wear a modified habit with no veil. An elderly priest who has his own street entrance and private quarters inside serves as the resident chaplain.

j. The Railroad Station
Regularly frequented by the Martins who lived nearby

A PLACE IN ALENÇON THAT PLAYED AN IMPORTANT PART IN THE TRAVEL life of the Martins, as indeed of all the citizenry, was the railroad station located a short distance from the home of the Martin family on the Rue Saint-Blaise. They routinely went by train to visit family and friends, for business, to go to boarding school in Le Mans, to vacations spots, and to religious shrines. Thérèse mentions this station in her autobiography when quoting a letter her mother wrote to Pauline away at school:

> Thursday evening we took a walk in the direction of the train station, and she [Thérèse] wanted absolutely to go into the waiting room to go and see Pauline; she was running on ahead with a joy that was pleasant to see, but when she saw we had to return without getting on the train to go to visit Pauline, she cried all the way home.[48]

Two paragraphs later, Thérèse reminisces further: "I recall also the trip I made to Le Mans [some fifty miles away]; it was my first train ride. What a joy to see myself on a trip alone with Mamma." She had gone on March 29, 1875, when she was two, to see her aunt, her mother's older sister (Sister Marie-Dosithée), a religious at the Visitation Convent and teacher at the school that the three older Martin girls attended.

Five months later, Mme. Martin in one of her many letters to her sister-in-law, Mme. Guérin, wrote these lines about a time when the whole Martin family congregated at the railroad station:

> Yesterday, my husband ran to the station to see my brother [Isidore] on the train; I would have liked to go there too....
>
> I was very sorry that the little girls did not go with him to greet their uncle. It was their fault. I had repeated in vain: "Get dressed early." But they knew better, so they were not ready in time. They wanted to dress when it was time to leave for the station. Louis chatted with my brother for nearly ten minutes. I so deplored this disappointment that I was really saddened by it and so was Marie. However, I hope to make up for it on Friday, at five-thirty, upon the return of my brother [from a pilgrimage to Lourdes]. We shall all be at the station: father, mother, and the five daughters.[49]

---
48 Letter (CF 159) dated May 14, 1876, from Mme. Martin to Pauline as quoted in Thérèse's *Story of a Soul*, chapter I, p. 22.
49 CF 137, dated August 31, 1875.

In one of her letters to Pauline, Marie informs her that "just now she [Thérèse] was on the balcony and was looking pensively at the street leading to the train station. I asked her what she was thinking about: 'Ah! I'm thinking it is this way that *petit Pauline* [nickname for Pauline] returns from Le Mans.'" [50]

Thérèse's parents continually displayed exceptional acts of charity and compassion that clearly influenced her; interestingly, the railroad station was the scene for several of them. Once when her father and mother were returning home on the train they observed a poor woman with two children whose presence seemed to annoy another woman on the train. After reprimanding the irritated woman, though in a most kindly manner, they helped the mother off with her children and luggage, and even accompanied the poor woman to her home. Their act of mercy consumed a considerable amount of time, making them arrive at their own home well after midnight. On another occasion Céline had this to say about her father's benevolence:

> [Having] seen in the railway station a poor epileptic who had not enough money for his fare, Father took off his hat, placed an offering in it, and went round to all the passengers begging for him. Then after collecting the price for the journey, he settled the man in the railway carriage himself.[51]

Thérèse alluded to trains and railroad stations occasionally in conversations even when in the convent where she could hear the distant sound of the trains going to and from the railroad station not very far away. She remarked during her last illness: "Ah!... this evening, I was listening to some beautiful music in the distance, near the train station, and I was thinking that very soon I was going to hear much more beautiful harmonies." [52] And again she made this related comment: "I cough and cough! I'm just like a locomotive when it arrives at the station; I'm arriving also at a station: heaven, and I'm announcing it!" [53]

The old railroad station was replaced by a more modern structure in the twentieth century.

k. The Promenades
A public park the Martins often visited

ZÉLIE MARTIN WAS FOND OF STROLLING ALONE OR WITH HER FAMILY IN *Les Promenades*, a public park situated within a short distance from her home. This spacious area faces the Hôtel de Ville, the Château des Ducs, and the Palais de Justice. It is now a very busy section with a large crowded parking area in the center that takes up much of the area that once was a lovely park.

Thérèse's parents, Louis and Zélie, went through a civil marriage—a mandatory formality—at the Hôtel de Ville in the evening of July 12, 1858. The next

---

50 May 9, 1877.
51 Sister Geneviève, *The Father of the Little Flower*, pp. 25–26.
52 From a letter Mother Agnès wrote to her Aunt Guérin, dated July 16, 1897.
53 *Her Last Conversations*, May 7, 1897.

day, July 13, at midnight (a French custom at the time) the two were solemnly wedded at the church of Notre-Dame a number of blocks away.

On the street directly leading into it, the Rue Porte-de-la-Barre, lived the wet nurse who cared for the Martins' eighth child Mélanie. Mme. Martin's encroaching breast cancer prevented her from performing this necessary function herself; therefore she sought outside help. The poor infant died in 1870 as a result of the nurse's extreme negligence and from then on, because of the horrid memories it evoked, Mme. Martin found it impossible to walk down that street.

l. Our Lady's Cemetery
Where Thérèse's mother and four siblings were first buried

THIS OLD CEMETERY IS LOCATED IN ALENÇON ON THE RUE DE LA FUIE DES Vignes. Thérèse's four young brothers and sisters were buried here before Thérèse was born: Joseph Louis who died at five months in 1867, Joseph John at eight months in 1868, Hélène at six years in 1870, and Mélanie at seven weeks in 1870. In 1877 when Thérèse was four, her mother died and was likewise buried here next to her children. When her husband Louis passed away in 1894, his brother-in-law, Isidore Guérin, had Louis buried in the Lisieux cemetery. Eleven weeks later he had the remains of Mme. Martin, her four children, father and mother-in-law removed from Alençon to the public cemetery in Lisieux situated less than a mile behind the present basilica dedicated to St. Thérèse. Céline wrote about this transferal:

> When he [Isidore Guérin] told us about the exhumation of mother, my uncle said that the coffin was quite intact after 17 years, although another, more recently interred, had entirely disintegrated. He noticed, with emotion, that in the interior nothing had collapsed, and that the folds of the coffin drapery had remained in place, just as when she had been placed in the coffin. But he did not dare to raise them....
>
> As the earth in which the coffin had been placed was damp, some small openings were bored at the base of the coffin, and a little water seeped through. That may explain how in the interior nothing had changed in volume.
>
> The granite tombstone was later placed in the garden of the Pavilion at Alençon where it can still be seen.[54]

The tombstone is now in the rear garden of the house where Thérèse was born.

In 1883, the ten-year-old Thérèse accompanied her father and sisters on a vacation to Alençon and the vicinity. She naturally visited Our Lady's Cemetery and wrote of this visit: "Three months after my cure [of a strange but serious illness] Papa took us to Alençon. This was the first time I had gone back. My joy was very great when seeing the places where I had spent my childhood days and especially when I was able to pray at Mamma's grave and ask her to protect me always."[55] A little later on in this excerpt from her autobiography, Thérèse tells us of her second visit to Alençon in 1886 when she was thirteen:

---
54 Sister Geneviève, *The Mother of the Little Flower*, pp. 120–121.
55 *Story of a Soul*, chapter IV, pp. 72–73.

A month before her [Marie, her sister's] entrance into Carmel, Papa brought us to Alençon, but this trip was far from resembling the first; everything about it was sadness and bitterness for me. I cannot express the tears I shed on Mamma's grave because I had forgotten to bring the bouquet of corn-flowers I had gathered especially for her. I really made a big fuss over *everything*! I was just the opposite of what I am now, for God has given me the grace not to be downcast at any passing thing.[56]

In view of the fact that the cause for the canonization of both of Thérèse's parents was underway, on October 13, 1958, the coffins of each were exhumed and placed in a new plot of ground directly behind the basilica in honor of St. Thérèse. A beautiful statue of St. Thérèse stands between the two slabs of granite that cover the graves of her parents. On her father's are these words:

HERE REPOSES
THE SERVANT OF GOD
LOUIS MARTIN
FATHER OF ST. THÉRÈSE OF THE INFANT JESUS
1823-1894

On her mother's grave these words are engraved:

HERE REPOSES
THE SERVANT OF GOD
ZÉLIE MARTIN
MOTHER OF ST. THÉRÈSE OF THE INFANT JESUS
1831-1877

In the same cemetery in Alençon the remains of Mr. and Mme. Tifenne and other members of their family rest in coffins under one large horizontally placed flat light gray granite slab with the names of the deceased on it. Not too far away is the grave of Mr. and Mrs. Grant, two English converts to Catholicism, who for many years were custodians and guides at the house where Thérèse was born. The Romets, friends of the Martins, also have a large family plot there containing all the family members.

m. Mme. Tifenne's House
Home of the Martins' friends where Thérèse stayed at times
(For the biographies of the Tifennes and description of their house, see Chapter 3—Non-Family Relations, A. 12)

n. Vital Romet's House
Home of Louis Martin's good friend and his family
(For a description of the house and biographies of the Romet family, see Chapter 3—Non-Family Relations, A. 11)

---

56 Ibid., p. 91.

2. Vicinity of Alençon

a. **Athis de l'Orne:** *Birthplace of Thérèse's paternal grandfather*
b. **Arçonnay** *(at an estate called Grogny or Groigny): Where Thérèse rode side-saddle*
c. **Roulée:** *Louis Martin bought some land here*
d. **Saint-Denis-sur-Sarthon:** *Thérèse stayed at a chateau here*
   Gandelain: *Birthplace of Thérèse's mother*
   Pré-en-Pail: *Where Thérèse's maternal grandparents were married*
e. **Sées:** *The child Thérèse went to the cathedral here on a pilgrimage*
f. **Semallé:** *The infant Thérèse was nursed here for over a year*
g. **Valframbert:** *Where Thérèse's paternal grandmother died*

a. Athis de l'Orne
Birthplace of Thérèse's paternal grandfather

A LITTLE TOWN THÉRÈSE MOST LIKELY NEVER VISITED BUT IS WORTH MENtioning is Athis de l'Orne located some distance northwest of Alençon toward Caen. Here Thérèse's paternal grandfather, Captain Pierre-François Martin (1777–1865) was born. Because of his granddaughter's universal fame, a street was named after him—*Rue du Captaine Martin*—and a plaque commemorating his baptism was installed in the local church. Louis Martin very often went to Athis to pray at the graves of his family members buried in the local cemetery.

b. Arçonnay (at an estate called Grogny or Groigny)
Where Thérèse rode side-saddle

ON HER FIRST JOURNEY BACK TO ALENÇON IN AUGUST 1883, THÉRÈSE AND her family stayed at the home of a dear family friend, Madame Tifenne, Thérèse's sister Léonie's godmother. On return trips, if they did not stay with her, they lodged at the home of Vital Romet, a pharmacist friend, and his sister Pauline, both of whom were godparents of two other Martin girls. On this trip of 1883, Madame Tifenne took them to see her sister, Madame Monnier, who lived in an attractive home in Arçonnay around five or so miles south of Alençon. Before arriving there and on the right side of the rather sequestered roadway is the grand *"Château des Chevaliers"* with its impressive large entrance gateway framed by two columns leading to the courtly mansion in the distance.

It was at Mme. Monnier's home where Thérèse rode side-saddle, perhaps the only time in her life she ever attempted to ride a horse. When she was a baby, though, her wet nurse "Little Rose" would sometimes tie Thérèse on the back of her cow named *La Rousette* and go about her farm duties. On vacation in Trouville in September of 1885, Thérèse enjoyed a donkey ride.

When Thérèse was living in Alençon, she visited with her mother this attractive country estate with colorful fields beyond the front property. She mentions one such trip in her autobiography with her childish vanity specifically targeted:

A. In Normandy 551

Plate 16

Vicinity of Alençon

A. Cathedral in Sées

B. The Basilica of the Immaculate Conception in Sées

C. Rose Taille's Grave in Carrouges

D. "Grogny" in Arçonnay where Thérèse rode side-saddle

E. Rose Taillé's Cottage in Semallé

F. Home of Pierre Romet in Saint-Denis-sur-Sarthon

G. Lanchal Manor, home of the Rabinels in Semallé. A relative stands at left.

Another time we had to go to Grogny to Mme. Monnier's home. Mamma told Marie to dress me in my sky-blue frock with the lace trimmings but not to leave my arms bare lest the sun burn them. I allowed myself to be dressed with the indifference a child of my age [around three] should really have, but I thought within myself that I would look much more pretty with my arms bare.[57]

Commenting philosophically, however, about the trip of 1883, Thérèse wrote:

God gave me the grace of knowing the *world* just enough to despise it and separate myself from it. I can say that it was during my stay at Alençon that I made my *first entrance into the world*. Everything was joy and happiness around me. I was entertained, coddled, and admired; in a word, my life during those two weeks was strewn only with flowers. I must admit this type of life had its charms for me. [Wisdom 4:12] is right in saying: "*The bewitching of vanity overturns the innocent mind!*" At the age of ten the heart allows itself to be easily dazzled, and I consider it a great grace not to have remained in Alençon. The friends we had there were too worldly; they knew too well how to ally the joys of this earth to the service of God. They didn't think about *death* enough, and yet *death* had paid its visit to a great number of those whom I knew, the young, the rich, the happy! I love to return in spirit to the *enchanting* places where they lived, wondering where these people are, what became of their houses and gardens where I saw them enjoy life's luxuries? And I see that all is vanity and vexation of spirit under the sun, that the *only good* is to love God with all one's heart and to be *poor in spirit* here on earth.[58]

Today the privately owned gray plastered, medium-sized château with white shutters has a somewhat large lawn in front with a driveway on the right leading to the main door at the center of the building. Along the public road, an ivy-covered stonewall extends the length and side of the front property providing privacy. At the driveway entrance on the right side wall is a sign, partially covered with ivy, on which is inscribed "Groigny."

c. Roullée
Louis Martin bought some land here

LOUIS MARTIN BOUGHT SOME PROPERTY IN THIS TINY VILLAGE ABOUT SIX miles west of Alençon after he sold his jewelry and watch making shop in 1870. Céline explains why in the book she wrote about her father: "[To] be able to give up more of his time to her [Zélie's] lacemaking enterprise and to lighten her work of correspondence, etc., he sold out his own jewelry shop." [59]

This little incident involving this property deals with boasting:

At the end of one of the summer vacations Marie [Thérèse's oldest sister] was walking with our good father in our modest family estate, Roulee. She began plucking flowers, saying: "I am going to take these flowers to the Visitation [School] as a souvenir of Roulee." Papa answered archly, "Ah, yes! Then you will

---

57 *Story of a Soul*, chapter I, p. 24.
58 Ibid., chapter IV, p. 73.
59 Sister Geneviève, *The Father of the Little Flower*, p. 33.

put on airs with your friends, and show them flowers from your estate." Provoked at herself for allowing her motives to be so evident, she quickly cast her bouquet to the ground to show that she was quite indifferent.[60]

d. Saint-Denis-sur-Sarthon
Thérèse stayed at a chateau here
Gandelain
Birthplace of Thérèse's mother
Pré-en-Pail
Where Thérèse's maternal grandparents were married

LOUIS MARTIN'S AFFLUENT FRIENDS PIERRE ROMET (BROTHER OF VITAL Romet who lived in Alençon) and his family were among those who "entertained, coddled, and admired" Thérèse, as she admits in her autobiography, on her first trip back to Alençon during the family summer holiday of 1883. One of the places she visited was in Saint-Denis-sur-Sarthon, a few miles northwest of Alençon. Here was and is, privately owned, the Romets' stately country residence with its spacious grounds, its immaculately manicured front lawn, and long driveway leading to the grand mansion. An impressive, rather intimidating entrance gate protects the property from the busy highway (N 12) in front of it. Thérèse says that "it was during my stay at Alençon [and here] that I made my *first entrance* into the *world* ... in a word, my life during those two weeks was strewn only with flowers. I must admit this type of life had its charms for me."[61]

Nearby is the hamlet of Gandelain which is within the Saint-Denis-sur-Sarthon parish district. It was here that Thérèse's maternal grandfather Captain Guérin made his home after his marriage in 1828. He and his wife, Louise-Jeanne Macé, were married, however, in Pré-en-Pail a short distance away. After a vibrantly active military career, he continued with civic affairs, mainly as a member of the constabulary. Zélie, the second of their three children, was born in Gandelain and baptized in the church of Saint-Denis on Christmas Eve 1831, the day after her birth. The font she was baptized in still remains there. Thérèse's sister Céline states that "on the occasion of the centenary of the birth of my mother in 1931, the Reverend Pastor of St. Denis-sur-Sarthon erected in the baptistery of his church, a statue of St. Thérèse, and a commemorative tablet of the baptism of my mother."[62]

e. Sées
The child Thérèse went to the cathedral here on a pilgrimage

THE MARTINS TRAVELED TO VARIOUS PLACES IN THE ALENÇON AREA. AMONG them was Sées, a quiet old town on the main road (N 138) less than twenty miles north of Alençon. In the center of the town stands the splendid thirteenth century Norman Gothic Cathedral with its two tall spires, the destination of

---
60 Mother Agnès, *Marie, Sister of St. Thérèse*, p. 23.
61 *Story of a Soul*, chapter IV, p. 73.
62 Sister Geneviève, *The Mother of the Little Flower*, p. 114.

countless pilgrims throughout the centuries. It had been the seat of the bishop's see since the fifth century when St. Latuin settled there, converted the natives to Christianity, and became its first bishop.

Thérèse accompanied her mother and sisters on one such pilgrimage to pray for her older sister Léonie, a child with disruptive personality traits. In the chapel of St. Godegrand behind the main altar is a wooden statue of Thérèse installed there to commemorate Thérèse's visit. Mme. Martin came here with Léonie in May 1875 to consecrate her to the Virgin Mary before she received her First Communion.

The other church the Martins visited, especially the father, is a smaller edifice, the Basilica of the Immaculate Conception, not far from the Cathedral off Rue Conté (N 138). It was elevated to the status of a basilica in 1902 because of the vast number of pilgrims who came here to worship. Actually it is the first church dedicated to the Blessed Mother under this title after her appearance to Bernadette Soubirous at Lourdes in 1858 which occurred four years after the Pope's proclamation of the doctrine of the Immaculate Conception. Around it is a large compound of several buildings basically schools for primary and secondary school children. Incidentally, Sées is the birthplace of the eminent chemist and inventor Nicolas-Jacques Conté (1755–1805) who developed the principle of the modern pencil and created those widely used by artists today known as Conté pencils.

f. Semallé
   The infant Thérèse was nursed here for over a year
   BECAUSE OF HER ENCROACHING BREAST CANCER WITH ITS MANY SERIOUS complications, Mme. Martin was unable to nurse her infant daughter Thérèse. She entrusted this essential function to the wet nurse Rose Taillé who lived around six miles from Alençon in the flat farmland near Semallé with her husband Moses and their four children. It was here in her small, humble thatched farmhouse that Rose, or "Little Rose" as they affectionately called her, nursed the sickly three-month-old Thérèse from March 1873 to April 1874. Rose owned a cow named "Roussette" ("The Little Russet Lady" or "Redskin") on which Thérèse was often tied in order to accompany Rose while she did her farm work. Thérèse truly thrived under her care and seemed to become part of the family.

Thérèse's mother confesses in her letters to her sister-in-law the concerns and worries she had during this time:

> At daybreak I set out for Semallé to get Little Rose, the special nurse....
>
> [Ah], how well I know that road to Semallé! My husband was away on business and I did not want to entrust the success of my enterprise to anyone else, so I walked all the way, alone.
>
> [But] today my baby has gone away. Our doctor [Belloc] advised me to let Little Rose take the baby back with her to the country for a while.... Of course, Little Rose is not a "stranger" to us; but still I would like to have our baby at home.

> [And] the doctor assures us that Thérèse will thrive in her temporary farmhouse-home in the country.[63]

Four months later Zélie joyfully reports the improvement Thérèse had made:

> Thérèse is a big baby; she is sunburned. Her nurse wheels her in the fields, perched on top of bundles of grass in a wheelbarrow; she hardly ever cries. "Little Rose" says that one could not find a sweeter child. Thus, as you see, my dear sister, all goes well. I had a sad beginning this year, according to all appearances, the end will be better.[64]

Less than nine months later, a healthy and happy Thérèse returned home to the welcoming arms of her loving family.

Many years later, Céline wrote a description of Little Rose's humble home:

> I thought back to my childhood, when I used to visit my little Thérèse at the home of her nurse, and we were ushered into the one and only room, which served as a kitchen, bedroom, and parlor all at the same time. The floor was hard-packed.... I reflected that truth and freedom, and therefore happiness, dwelled under the old dark beams rather than under artistic ceilings, and I looked forward to the happy moment when I would be transplanted to a poor cell [in the Carmelite monastery in Lisieux].[65]

This cottage still exists today and is privately owned by people who live across the street from it. On the street a plaque with a small statue of St. Thérèse in a little niche above it has these words in French written on it: "The house of the 'Petite Rose' where St. Thérèse of the Child Jesus spent her infancy 1874." It is not open to the public but one can walk around the building and on the grounds adjoining it. Extensive flat farmland surrounds the area.

In the same village of Semallé, but on quite a different social strata than the Taillés, resided the well-to-do Rabinal family, friends of Louis Martin. (See Chapter 3, A. Family Friends)

g. Valframbert
Where Thérèse's paternal grandmother died

THE INFANT THÉRÈSE'S WET NURSE ROSE TAILLÉ LIVED IN SEMALLÉ FOR years; but some time after the Martins moved from Alençon to Lisieux in 1877, she and her family made their home in the sparsely-populated hamlet of Valframbert not far from Alençon. Rose was employed by Louis Martin to care for his mother who had been living in Valframbert after her son and his family moved away. Louis visited her every three months during which time he stayed with her for a few days.

Thérèse probably paid Rose a call on her first trip back to her birthplace in 1883. Most likely she also went to the local cemetery to pray at her grandmother's grave since it was just six months before that she had died.

---

63 CF 89 written by Mme. Martin to Mme. Guérin in March 1873.
64 CF 106 written by Mme. Martin to her sister-in-law Mme. Guérin on July 20, 1873, translated by the author.
65 Piat, *Céline*, p. 53.

3. Lisieux

a. **Les Buissonnets:** *Thérèse's home before she became a nun*
b. **Jardin de l'Etoile:** *Thérèse often visited this private park near her home*
c. **The Cathedral of St. Peter:** *Where Thérèse attended Mass and made her first confession*
d. **Saint Jacques Church:** *The Martins' parish church*
e. **The Place Thiers Area** *(now called Place Mitterand)*
   i. The Guérin Pharmacy and first home
   ii. The Post Office
   iii. The Episcopal Palace
   iv. The Public Gardens
f. **The Benedictine Abbey School:** *Thérèse attended school here from 1881 to 1886*
g. **The Carmel Chapel:** *At the monastery where Thérèse lived*
h. **The Second Guérin Home:** *Their home after selling the pharmacy*
i. **The Second Martin Home:** *After the Martins left Les Buissonnets*
j. **The Hermitage:** *Theresian spiritual center for retreats, conferences, etc.*
k. **The Basilica:** *Large church honoring St. Thérèse*
l. **The Cemetery:** *Thérèse's original burial place and location of the Martin family plot*

AFTER THE DEATH OF ZÉLIE MARTIN IN 1877, THE MARTIN FAMILY CONSISTing now of M. Martin, Thérèse, and her four sisters moved to Lisieux to be near their closest relatives, the Guérins. This town with a population of over 18,000 inhabitants earned the reputation of being the foremost prosperous industrial and commercial city in Calvados, a department (1 of 101 in France today), located in the Basse-Normandie region (1 of 22 in France today). Specifically, Lisieux was noted for its cider factories, tanneries, distilleries, and textile factories which employed several thousand workers. In 1873, the year of Thérèse's birth, this quotation from *Le Grand Larousse*[66] stated:

> Lisieux is above all a manufacturing town; the district possesses close to 300 industrial establishments. The manufacture of fabrics [printed in colored patterns] and of sheets constitutes a very important industry in the town. M. Fournet's factory is one of the more important ones in all Normandy. The cotton mills and the tanneries acquire day by day more importance and occupy a considerable number of workers.[67]

---

66 An encyclopedic dictionary in French consisting of ten volumes.
67 Translated by the author from an excerpt that appears in *Lisieux au Temps de Thérèse*, p. 15. A wealthy factory owner in Lisieux by the name of Jean Fournet was a relative of Thérèse's Aunt Guérin who inherited through his son the Chateau La Musse.

A. *In Normandy*

Plate 17

Lisieux

A. Cathedral of Saint-Pierre

B. Les Buissonnets

C. Saint Jacques, Church

D. Site of the Guérin Pharmacy

E. Exterior of the Carmel Chapel

F. The Guérins' 2nd Home

G. The Martin's 2nd Home

H. Rear grounds of former Benedictine Abbey

I. Where Thérèse was first buried

The Place Thiers was always filled every Saturday with people buying Norman country products in the open market. Children enjoyed the circus when it would come to town and have fun on the carousel. They and others participated in the frequent religious processions that passed through. Bastille Day (July 14) was a special holiday celebrated by all. The military battalions stationed nearby impressed everyone with their display of arms and music as they performed at the Place Thiers and paraded through the quaint medieval streets.

The history of Lisieux began centuries ago in the land known as ancient Gaul where the natives in this area were called Lexovians. Around 56 B.C., when Julius Caesar's army invaded and occupied the town, it became known as *Noviomagus*[68] *lexoviarum*. It was destroyed by the Saxons at the end of the fourth century and replaced by a new town called Lexove. The Franco-English wars of the 14th and 15th centuries (the Hundred Years' War), and the religious conflicts of the 16th, added to the continuing assaults on this land and its people. In 1562 Protestants conquered Lisieux, pillaged, and burned the interior of the cathedral. During the French Revolution, the Cathedral was turned into a Temple of Reason honoring the god of nature. This lasted until 1802 when the Cathedral was returned to the Catholic Church. The worst affliction the town experienced occured during World War II (1939–1945) when much of it was destroyed and more than 1,200 inhabitants were killed or went missing in 1944. Fortunately, most of the Theresian landmarks escaped annihilation.

The Roman Catholic Church apparently has flourished in Lisieux since the sixth century when the first known Bishop of Lisieux, Theodibandes, was mentioned in ancient documents regarding a council held there in 538. Down through the ensuing centuries Lisieux maintained its own bishop until the Concordat of 1801 when the bishopric of the Lisieux diocese was united with the one of Bayeux. Then in 1854 from a papal mandate, the Bishop of Bayeux was called the Bishop of Bayeux and Lisieux, a title which exists to the present day. The church connected with a bishop is always called a cathedral; however, in this case, the term is still used for the Cathedral of St. Pierre in Lisieux despite the fact that no bishop occupies an office there.

All the major places in Lisieux connected with the story of St. Thérèse are dealt with in detail in the succeeding pages; nonetheless, two buildings not covered are the Refuge and the Delaunay barracks. The Refuge consisted of a large four-story building with an attic area built the year Thérèse was born—1873. It was founded by Father Rolau to house former prostitutes and was directed by the Sisters of Our Lady of Mercy. It housed as many as two hundred residents. Thérèse often accompanied her father on his visits there to offer them some of the fish he caught on his frequent fishing jaunts in the area. Thérèse tells us about this experience in a conversation she had with one of her novices, Sister Marie of the Trinity:

> If I had not been accepted in Carmel, I would have entered a shelter [like the Refuge] in order to live there unknown and despised in the midst of the poor

---
68 "*Neuf-marché,*" Ibid., p. 14.

unfortunates. My happiness would have been to pass for one of them. I would have made myself the apostle of my companions, telling them what I think about the merciful love of God.

"But how would you have managed to hide your innocence from your confessor?"

I would have told him that I had made a general confession before entering and that this protected me from mentioning it again.[69]

The other place, very close to Les Buissonnets on the Boulevard Nicolas Oresme, was the Delaunay barracks (*La Casernie Delaunay*) built in 1874–1875 to serve the 119th Infantry Regiment. Named after a general of the Empire (Jean-Charles René Delaunay, 1738–1825), it took only three years to build and lasted less than fifty years. Thérèse often heard military band music emanating from it. Even as a child it impressed her deeply:

> Without knowing what it was to meditate, my soul was absorbed in real prayer. I listened to distant sounds, the murmuring of the wind, etc. At times, the indistinct notes of some military music reached me where I was, filling my heart with a sweet melancholy. Earth then seemed to be a place of exile and I could dream only of heaven.[70]

It took a humble, unpretentious young lady of twenty-four to raise the town of Lisieux to a prominence it never had. Thérèse Martin, a holy cloistered nun with the name Sister Thérèse of the Child Jesus became not only a saint but a Doctor of the Universal Church—the third woman to be so honored in 2,000 years of the Roman Catholic Church's history. Visited by millions every year, Lisieux ranks second only to Lourdes as the most popular pilgrimage site in France.

a. Les Buissonnets
Thérèse's home before she became a nun

> *It is a charming house, cheerful and gay, with a large garden in which Céline and Thérèse will be able to play.*[71]
>
> —Marie

Les Buissonnets ("LITTLE BUSHES") IS THE NAME OF THE HOUSE LOUIS MARTIN, Thérèse's father, rented in Lisieux in 1877 almost twelve weeks after his wife Zélie died in Alençon, roughly fifty miles south of Lisieux, on August 28, 1877. Thérèse lived here for almost eleven years from the age of four to fifteen when she entered the Carmelite Monastery in the same town.

M. Martin, fifty-four, decided to move to Lisieux so that his five daughters would be near their mother's brother, Isidore Guérin; his wife, Céline; and their two daughters: Jeanne, 9, and Marie, 7. The Martin girls' ages at the time of their move to Lisieux were: Marie, 17; Pauline, 16; Léonie, 14; Céline, 8; and Thérèse, 4.

---

69 CRN 80–82. This is a quote from p. 78 in Descouvemont's *Thérèse of Lisieux and Marie of the Trinity.*
70 *Story of a Soul,* chapter II, p. 37.
71 A letter dated November 16, 1877, from Marie to her father.

Thérèse's mother Zélie had held in her heart for some time a strong longing that after her death her family should move to Lisieux where her relations lived. Isidore Guérin, aware of his sister's wishes, went searching for a house for the Martins to rent. A month after Zélie's death he found the perfect place and described it in a detailed, lengthy, and persuasive letter to Louis:

> Taking my stand on your word, I set out in search of a house capable of lodging seven [the 6 Martins and their maid, Victoire]. We searched as much as possible in our own vicinity [the center of Lisieux] and in a healthful section for a house with a garden or, at least, a little flower bed for the children. This was a recommendation made to me by my poor sister [Zélie].
>
> Of the twenty-five houses for rent, having as much space as yours, we weren't able to find one which didn't have a redhibitory defect [legal term regarding defects in a thing sold].
>
> Finally, we discovered one such as I'd desire to have if I were retired from business [he owned a pharmacy in the center of town]:
>
> A beautiful gate facing the public thoroughfare.
>
> You then enter a little landscape garden. Shrubs on each side. A delightful house topped by a belvedere.
>
> On the ground floor, four rooms, one of which is a beautiful dining room paneled in oak. Behind this room, a cellar divided into a wine cellar and a storeroom for fruit.
>
> Above the ground floor, a first floor level with a large garden situated behind the house; three magnificent bedrooms and a smaller one; two dressing rooms.
>
> Above: a belvedere with a fireplace and three attics well-lighted and papered. The whole in perfect condition, newly painted and papered.
>
> At the side of the house, a beautiful well, a water pump. At the rear of the house, a spacious garden, at least as large as M. Vital's [Vital Romet, Céline's godfather and Martin family friend who lived in Alençon]; a beautiful cistern; a carriage gateway for bringing in provisions (wood, cider) opening onto another road; a shed; a laundry; a greenhouse; a very comfortable shelter for poultry and rabbits; an enclosure with a shelter and bath for ducks, etc., etc. All is surrounded by walls and overlooks part of the town; it is set behind the *"jardin de l'Etoile"* [a park open to keyholders only. It does not exist today].
>
> Distance from the church [Saint-Jacques], seven hundred paces, and from my house, seven hundred and sixty-four, which is almost equivalent to the distance of your house to that of M. Tifenne [Alençon friend of Messrs. Martin and Guérin].
>
> But there is a difficulty and a big one, it's the access: from the entrance of the *"jardin de l'Etoile,"* which is on the boulevard, there are one hundred paces to reach the house, on a narrow and steep road [which Louis Martin later called "The Way to Paradise"] but clean, well-lighted, for a lamppost is right in front of the door.
>
> From the house, you are not seen from any direction, and you see no road but simply a delightful panorama of the town.
>
> I prayed to my poor sister to guide me, and I was so happy with my find that I wasn't able to sleep all night. In such a pretty property, you will forget the Pavilion [an hexagonal tower in Alençon, two stories high, surrounded by a large

garden where M. Martin went for relaxation and meditation] and all Alençon's attractions; however, I'm told that the trout and the eels have begun to take flight at the news of your arrival. [Louis Martin was an accomplished fisherman.][72]

On September 19, 1877, M. Louis signed the lease for this property owned by M. and Mme. Levallois (or *Le Valois*) which was officially located in the quarter of the town known as the "*village du Nouveau-Monde*" ("village of the New World" because it was on the edge of the town).[73] The property was rather old for records show that as far back as 1784 it was owned by a M. Bourcheville.[74] The Martin girls changed the incorrect spelling of the name (Les Bissonnets) to its proper form, Les Buissonnets.

The Martin sisters arrived in Lisieux on Thursday evening, November 15, 1877, and stayed at the home of their uncle and aunt that night. The next day they settled down at Les Buissonnets. Their father was away in Alençon settling the estate and the lace business his wife had established. He did not join his daughters at Les Buissonnets until Friday, November 30—fifteen days later.

Today the house and grounds are almost the same as in Thérèse's day except for the area in front of the Martin house beyond the road which has been changed drastically but necessarily for parking and to accommodate the large number of visitors that arrive every day from all over the world.

One can visit the house at its present address of 22 chamin des Buissonnets by taking the main road north from the center of Lisieux on the way to Deauville and Trouville which is called in town the Boulevard Jeanne d'Arc; but the name soon changes to the Boulevard Duchesne-Fournet and Herbet-Fournet. A little distance up this road on the right is a clearly marked sign with the words "Les Buissonnets." As you turn here, the chamin des Buissonnets, a very narrow inclined road, leads up to Les Buissonnets, the first house on the left. Just before this, however, you pass on the same side a small gift shop and opposite it on the right a large parking area for busses and private cars. Formerly along this little alleyway (or road) a wall on both sides provided privacy for the dwellings on both sides even beyond the Martin home. A number of private homes still exist there. This road today is composed of cobblestones with a narrow depressed gutter down the center through which rainwater flows. A low wall on the right overlooking the large parking lot has replaced the former high wall.

When one opens the heavy door to the front yard of Les Buissonnets and walks up about six steps, the same sight that Thérèse and her family saw on their first day there presents itself before you. It was at this very door that the young Thérèse, under her father's influence, would offer food or money to poor people who came for help, usually on Monday afternoons. From the very beginning, the house charmed Thérèse. *Story of a Soul* gives her initial impression of her new home:

---

72 Letter to M. Martin from Isidore Guérin dated September 10, 1877.
73 ChrIG, p. 31.
74 Descouvemont, *Sur les pas de Thérèse*, note 2, p. 268.

> The next day, November 16, we were brought to our new home, Les Buissonnets, which was situated in a quiet section next to a park named: "Jardin de l'Étoile," The house appeared very charming to me: a belvedere from which a view extended far into the distance, an English garden in front, and a large vegetable garden in the rear of the house, all this was a new joy to my young imagination. In fact, this smiling habitation became the theater of many sweet joys and unforgettable family scenes. Elsewhere, as I said above, I was an exile, I wept, I felt I no longer had a mother! There, my heart expanded and I smiled once more at life.[75]

The rather imposing red brick building with white trim around all the doors and windows, some of which is of white cut stone, comes as a pleasant surprise when entering the grounds. It consists of three stories in the front and two in the back because the ground elevation there is higher than in the front. Two wooden doors in the front of the building provide entrance to the house; the one on the left is the entrance for visitors. On the facade of the second floor, a rather large white bas-relief by the Trappist monk, Father Marie-Bernard, placed in the middle of the six windows, informs the visitor of the importance of the building. It depicts the moment Thérèse was suddenly cured of a serious illness by the smile of the Blessed Mother. On the first floor on the left is the room (living or sitting room) where the older girls worked during the day. In the evening the family gathered there after meals, played games, and their father read to them Guéranger's *The Liturgical Year* and other religious books. On the right is the kitchen where the Martins had their breakfast. Here at the fireplace Thérèse left her shoes every Christmas Eve. At this place, a momentous turning point in Thérèse's life occurred:

> It was December 25, 1886, that I received the grace of leaving my childhood, in a word, the grace of my complete conversion. We had come back from Midnight Mass where I had the happiness of receiving the *strong and powerful* God. Upon arriving at Les Buissonnets, I used to love to take my shoes from the chimney-corner and examine the presents in them; this old custom had given us so much joy in our youth that Céline wanted to continue treating me as a baby since I was the youngest in the family. Papa had always loved to see my happiness and listen to my cries of delight as I drew each surprise from the *magic shoes*, and my dear King's gaiety increased my own happiness very much. However, Jesus desired to show me that I was to give up the defects of my childhood and so He withdrew its innocent pleasures. He permitted Papa, tired out after the Midnight Mass, to experience annoyance when seeing my shoes at the fireplace, and that he speak those words which pierced my heart: "Well, fortunately, this will be the last year!" I was going upstairs, at the time, to remove my hat, and Céline, knowing how sensitive I was and seeing the tears already glistening in my eyes, wanted to cry too, for she loved me very much and understood my grief. She said, "Oh, Thérèse, don't go downstairs; it would cause you too much grief to look at your slippers right now!" But Thérèse

---

75 *Story of a Soul*, chapter II, footnote 34, p. 35.

was no longer the same; Jesus had changed her heart! Forcing back my tears, I descended the stairs rapidly; controlling the poundings of my heart, I took my slippers and placed them in front of Papa, and withdrew all the objects joyfully. I had the happy appearance of a Queen. Having regained his own cheerfulness, Papa was laughing; Céline believed it was all a *dream*! Fortunately, it was a sweet reality; Thérèse had discovered once again the strength of soul which she had lost at the age of four and a half [when her mother died], and she was to preserve it forever.

On that *night of light* began the third period of my life, the most beautiful and the most filled with graces from heaven. The work I had been unable to do in ten years was done by Jesus in one instant....[76]

Two very amusing incidents happened at the kitchen fireplace when the very little Thérèse was home alone with the maid, Victoire. Since Thérèse was too small to reach the mantel to get an inkstand she wanted, she asked the maid to give it to her. Victoire refused and told Thérèse to get up on a chair and get it herself which Thérèse thought was not very nice of her. Just before she jumped off the chair with the inkstand, Thérèse "turned around with *dignity* and said: 'Victoire, you are a brat!'"[77] She then quickly made her "escape." (Victoire often called Thérèse a "brat"—"*mioche*" from whence Thérèse got the idea to call her the same.) When Marie heard of this she made Thérèse apologize to Victoire. "I did so without having contrition. I thought that if Victoire didn't want to stretch her *big arm* to do me a *little service*, she merited the title *brat*."[78] Another time Thérèse fell into the fireplace, though luckily there was no fire in it. She was completely covered with ashes which Victoire nicely cleaned off of her.

To the right of the kitchen fireplace is the dining room which has two windows, but it is not accessible to the public today. It is a charming and cozy room with wood paneled walls, parquet floors, oak furniture, a round table, and a fireplace over which is a painting of the Holy Family painted by Céline. The main meal was taken here as was Thérèse's last meal before she left to enter the monastery:

> The day chosen for my entrance into Carmel was April 9, 1888, the same day the community was celebrating the feast of the Annunciation, transferred because of Lent. The evening before, the whole family gathered round the table where I was to sit for the last time. Ah! How heartrending these family reunions can really be! When you would like to see yourself forgotten, the most tender caresses and words are showered upon you making the sacrifice of separation felt all the more.
>
> Papa was not saying very much, but his gaze was fixed upon me lovingly. Aunt cried from time to time and Uncle paid me many affectionate compliments. Jeanne and Marie gave me all sorts of little attentions, especially Marie, who, taking me aside, asked pardon for the troubles she thought she caused me. My dear little Léonie, who had returned from the Visitation a few months

---

76 Ibid., chapter V, p. 98.
77 Ibid., chapter II, p. 39.
78 Ibid.

previously, kissed and embraced me often. There is only Céline, about whom I have not spoken, but you can well imagine, dear Mother [Agnès, her blood sister Pauline], how we spent that last night together.[79]

On the second floor are the four bedrooms and two bathrooms. The older girls, Marie and Pauline, slept in the room on the left. When the ten-year-old Thérèse became seriously ill in 1888, the family sent Thérèse there to be closely cared for by Marie. (Pauline at this time was a nun at the Carmel.) Here Thérèse was miraculously cured on May 13 when she saw the face on Our Lady's statue by her bedside smile at her.

> Marie knelt down near my bed with Léonie and Céline. Turning to the Blessed Virgin and praying with the fervor of a mother begging for the life of her child, *Marie* obtained what she wanted.
>
> Finding no help on earth, poor little Thérèse had also turned toward the Mother of heaven, and prayed with all her heart that she take pity on her. All of a sudden the Blessed Virgin appeared *beautiful* to me, so *beautiful* that never had I seen anything so attractive, her face was suffused with an ineffable benevolence and tenderness, but what penetrated to the very depths of my soul was the *"ravishing smile of the Blessed Virgin."* At that instant, all my pain disappeared.... Seeing my gaze fixed on the Blessed virgin, she [Marie] cried out: "Thérèse is cured!"[80]

After Marie entered the Carmelite Monastery in Lisieux in 1886, Thérèse and Céline used her room as their sleeping quarters. Thérèse tells us she would often go behind her bed and meditate, "think", as she called it. Their father occupied the bedroom next to theirs with three windows facing the street. You can view it only through a glass partition. In this same area behind a large glass window is another room that once served as Léonie's bedroom. Many objects connected with Thérèse's childhood are on display here including some of her school books, tiny religious objects, skipping rope (Thérèse holds it in Photo 2 when she was eight), her First Communion dress, and the little wooden boat Céline gave her on Christmas night of 1887, fifteen weeks before Thérèse entered religious life at the Carmel:

> When I returned from Midnight Mass I found in my room, in the center of a charming basin, a *little* boat carrying the *Little* Jesus asleep with a *little* ball at His side, and Céline had written these words on the white sail: "I sleep but my heart watches" [Canticle of Canticles 5:2], and on the boat itself this one word, "Abandonment!"[81]

The intriguing third floor, or attic area is, unfortunately, not open to the public. From the front lawn view, the architecture of the upper part of Les Buissonnets attracts the observer. The mansard roof slopes down with four large closely fit dormer windows forming one large gable in the center. In addition, on the right

---
79 Ibid., chapter VII, p. 147.
80 Ibid., chapter III, pp. 65–66.
81 Ibid., chapter VI, pp. 142–143.

and on the left, small dormer windows or gables extend out from the building. White carved wooden ornaments top all the windows. The center windows give light to the Belvedere, the main room there that served as Louis's study. From these windows a splendid view spreads out revealing the Lisieux skyline with its church spires clearly visible. Pauline had her painting room in one of the two adjoining attic rooms which Thérèse took over after Pauline entered the convent:

> Since my leaving the boarding school, I set myself up in *Pauline's* old painting-room and arranged it to suit my taste. It was a real bazaar, an assemblage of pious objects and curiosities, a garden, and an aviary. Thus, at the far end on the wall was a *big cross* in black wood, without a corpus, and several drawings I liked. On another wall, a basket, decorated with muslin and pink ribbons, contained some delicate herbs and flowers. Finally, on the last wall, was enthroned all by itself the portrait of *Pauline* at the age of ten. Beneath the portrait was a table and upon it was a *large cage* which enclosed a *great* number of birds; their melodious song got on the nerves of visitors but not on those of their little mistress who cherished them very much. There was also the *"little white piece of furniture"* filled with my schoolbooks, and on it was set a statue of the Blessed Virgin, along with vases always filled with natural flowers and candles. Around the statue was a number of small statues of the saints, little baskets made out of shells, cardboard boxes, etc.! My garden was *suspended* in front of the window, and there I cultivated pots of flowers (the rarest I could find). I also had on the inside of "my museum" a flower-stand on which I placed my privileged plant. In front of the window was a table covered with a green cloth, and in the center were an *hour-glass*, a small statue of St. Joseph, a watch-case, baskets of flowers, an ink-well, etc. A few *rickety* chairs and a beautiful *doll's* cot belonging to *Pauline* completed my furnishings.
>
> Truly, this poor attic was a world for me and like M. de Maistre I could compose a book entitled: "A Walk around my Room." It was in this room I loved to stay alone for hours on end to study and meditate before the beautiful view which stretched out before my eyes.[82]

Thérèse loved the little animals and birds she had but Tom, a spaniel, gave her special delight when her father gave him to her in 1884 when she was eleven. She had told her father she wanted "an animal with hair that follows me everywhere and jumps around me!"[83] So he gave her this dog that proved to be not only a faithful friend and plaything but also a good watchdog. He remained with the family for many years.

Marie and Pauline home schooled Thérèse until she was eight:

> My dear godmother [Marie] took charge of the writing lessons and you, Mother [Pauline], all the rest. I enjoyed no great facility in learning, but I did have a very good memory. Catechism and sacred history were my favorite subjects and these I studied with joy. Grammar frequently caused me to shed many tears. You no doubt recall the trouble I had with the masculine and feminine genders!

---

82 Ibid., pp. 90–91.
83 Sister Geneviève, CMG III, p. 102.

As soon as my classes were over, I climbed up to the belvedere and showed my badge and my marks to Papa. How happy I was when I could say: "I got *full marks*, and it's *Pauline* who said so *first!*"[84]

When Thérèse was a little older, she and Céline found spiritual comfort in the Belvedere upstairs where they would look out the windows and admire God's beautiful creations in nature. Their conversations about pious and religious matters provided a great source of joy for both of them. Much of this they derived from the inspirational readings their father read to them each day. Thérèse reminisces about this room and her father in one of her most important poems, "Prayer of a Child of a Saint" (PN 8):

> Remember that in the belvedere
> You [her father] always sat her [Thérèse] on your lap,
> And then whispering a prayer,
> You rocked her with your sweet refrain....
>   Remember!

In the rear of the second floor a door opens to the backyard containing a garden, wash house, shed, greenhouse, swing, and other memorable features in Thérèse's childhood. A life-sized sculpture of Thérèse asking her father's permission to become a Carmelite highlights the area. Thérèse's anecdotes in the garden area are most endearing and show how typically human a child she was:

> After a walk [with her father] ... we returned to the house; then I did my homework and the rest of the time I stayed in the garden with Papa, jumping around, etc., for I *didn't know* how to play with dolls. It was a great joy for me to prepare mixtures with little seeds and pieces of bark I found on the ground, and I'd bring them to Papa in a pretty little cup. Poor Papa stopped all his work and with a smile he pretended to drink. Before giving me back the cup he'd ask me (on the sly) if he should throw the contents out. Sometimes I would say "Yes," but more frequently I carried away my precious mixture, wanting to use it several times.
>
> I loved cultivating my little flowers in the garden Papa gave me. I amused myself, too, by setting up little altars in a niche in the middle of the wall [of the wash house in the left rear]. When I completed my work, I ran to Papa and dragged him over, telling him to close his eyes and not open them till I told him. He did all I asked him to do and allowed himself to be led in front of my little garden, then I'd cry out: "Papa, open your eyes!" He would open them and then go into an ecstasy to please me, admiring what I believed was really a masterpiece![85]

Thérèse loved using the swing attached to a beam in the back shed. When either her father or sisters would push her, she wanted them to push her really high so she could see the neighbor lady's bonnet. This lady, known as Mother Gadet, worked in her garden and wore a cotton bonnet.[86]

---

84 *Story of a Soul*, chapter II, p. 36.
85 Ibid., chapter II, p. 37.
86 Descouvemont, *Thérèse and Lisieux*, p. 38.

Céline tells us about the kind of work their father did around the house:

> For his manual work besides gardening at Les Buissonnets my father took over the care of the poultry yard and the rabbits, providing their food and not allowing anyone to help him in the cleaning of the yard. We had an aviary for pet birds, which he took care of as well. As an amusement for us, he succeeded in teaching a tame magpie to speak. He also took charge of the cellar, and bought apples for cider, which he brewed at home himself. Along with all that he sawed and chopped and stacked in the laundry house all the firewood that was required for the household.[87]

Thérèse observed a rather frightening thing one bright summer afternoon when she was six or seven. Louis Martin was away in Alençon on business. While looking out a window in the attic that faces the garden she observed this strange vision:

> [I] saw a man dressed exactly like Papa standing in front of the laundry which was just opposite. The man had the same height and walk as Papa, only he was *much more stooped*. His *head* was covered with a sort of apron of indistinct color and it hid his face. He wore a hat similar to Papa's.... I called out very loudly: "Papa! Papa!," my voice trembling with emotion. But the mysterious personage, appearing not to hear, continued his steady pace without even turning around.... [T]he prophetic vision had vanished [behind the trees]![88]

No one else saw the vision nor did anyone find any trace of the mysterious person. It took fourteen years later for the Martin sisters, then nuns, to realize that this scene prophetically foretold the mental condition that attacked their father years later.

The potential annihilation of Les Buissonnets was averted one time as an article in the Lisieux journal *Le Normand* of Tuesday, June 26, 1888 reported:

> This morning, shortly before five o'clock, a fire broke out in Lisieux, *chemin des Bissonnets* [sic], in a little house rented by a M. Prévost.... Under the direction of Captain Lepage, two pumps were put in action and extinguished the fire; the first from the hydrant at the City Hall, brought in by Corporal Leminoux, was able to preserve the house occupied by M. Martin and his family; a piece of wood in the roof was beginning to burn.[89]

For the purposes of enlarging the land on the right side of his house, Louis bought the burnt property next door the following month. Today on this site, stairs lead up to this flat area converted now into a beautiful garden.

On December 25, 1889, the lease of Les Buissonnets ended. The Martins had lived there for twelve years. The furniture was dispersed to different places. Some items, including a clock, went to the Carmel. Sister Agnès wrote to Céline on December 31, 1889 about this clock: "Ah, who could have told us on

---

87 Sister Geneviève, *The Father of the Little Flower*, pp. 34–35.
88 *Story of a Soul*, chapter II, pp. 45–46.
89 As quoted from note 3 to a letter from Mme. Guérin to Pauline and Thérèse in Carmel, dated June 26, 1888.

December 31, '88, that Papa's clock would ring 'midnight' in the Carmel's choir on December 31, '89.... What upheavals there are in life!"[90] The day before the lease was up, Céline wrote to Thérèse: "Tomorrow, Les Buissonnets will no longer be ours. I was there, yesterday, to visit it for the last time. I took some moss and some branches for my crib.... As a souvenir, not finding the smallest flower, I took several ivy leaves. This is *the* souvenir of so many souvenirs!!!..."[91]

Subsequently, Céline and Léonie lived with their Aunt and Uncle, after which they rented a house behind them at what is now 7 rue Labbey in Lisieux.

The story of Les Buissonnets after the Martins left is quite interesting. From 1900 Thérèse's fame and influence spread far beyond Lisieux and France. Even the possibility of her future canonization was circulating. A lawyer (notary) in Lisieux purchased the house in 1904 for 1,500 francs but he eventually sold it for 10,000 francs to Thérèse's cousin by marriage, Dr. Francis La Néele. A year later the first visitors began to arrive and have not ceased coming even to the present day.

Dr. La Néele rented Les Buissonnets in 1911 to a Mme. Hassebroucq who came with her three daughters, great devotees of the future Saint. She was responsible for returning the original Martin furniture given to the Carmel in 1889. Finally Mme. Hassebroucq went back to her native Belgium and new guardians took over, Mme. Castel (a recent widow) and her sister, Mikaëlle. Mme. Castel happened to be the mother of Sister Marie de la Trinity, Thérèse's favorite novice. She died at Les Buissonnets in 1915, and her sister continued to serve at Thérèse's home for about ten years when her sister, Violette, took over. Dr. La Néele died in 1916 and in 1922 his widow Jeanne La Néele sold the property to the *Société immobilière de pèlegrinages* with the assurance that the Castel family could continue their valuable guardianship there. Finally, in 1932 the Congregation of the Oblates of Saint Thérèse, founded in 1928 by Father Gabriel Martin, assumed the task of welcoming pilgrims to Les Buissonnets. They also maintain guardianship of Thérèse's birthplace in Alençon even to the present.[92]

Improvements and necessary maintenance work continually have to be made.

b. Jardin De l'etoile

Thérèse often visited this private park near her home

THIS PRIVATE PARK, THE *Jardin de L'Etoile (Garden of the Star),* WAS LOCATED on the outer limits of Lisieux with the main entrance on the left along the main road going north to Pont l'Evecque, Trouville, and Deauville. Across from the entrance a road led directly to Les Buissonnets. This park was created a century before the Martins moved to Lisieux. Doctor Caumont at one time attended to Louis XV, retired to Lisieux, and developed this area in 1778. Forty stockholders purchased the property in 1824 with the stipulation that the park be used only

---
90 As quoted in note 2 to LC 121, from Céline to Thérèse, dated December 24, 1889.
91 LC 121.
92 Descouvemont, *Sur les pas de Thérèse,* pp. 77–80.

by a certain number of people with bought passes. By the time of the Martins, the Guérins, and the Maudelondes, the annual pass cost thirty francs which included a key for each holder to use when entering. For a while Célestin Fournet (Thérèse's Aunt Guérin's father) served as president of the *Société du Jardin de l'Etoile*. He sold his pharmacy to Isidore Guérin in 1866.[93] The meticulously cared for grounds of the *Jardin de l'Etoile* contained many large and rare trees and flowers. Nearby stood the Delaunay barracks, built in 1875 to house about six hundred soldiers. Military music could sometimes be heard here as well as at Les Buissonnets about which Thérèse commented, "the indistinct notes of some military music reached me where I was, filling my heart with a sweet melancholy."[94] Neither the barracks nor the park exist today. An apartment building and a parking lot occupy the former site of the park.

Thérèse loved going to the Jardin and especially to pick flowers, an activity allowed by the authorities:

> Each Thursday afternoon was a holiday.... I had to play ... with my little cousins and the Maudelondes. This was a real penance for me because I didn't know how to play like other children and as a consequence wasn't a very pleasant companion. I did my best, however, to imitate them but without much success. I was very much bored by it all, especially when we spent the whole afternoon dancing quadrilles. What I really liked, though, was going to the park, for there I was first in everything, gathering flowers in great profusion and, knowing how to find the prettiest, I excited the envy of my companions.[95]

One time Mademoiselle Pigeon, a friend of the family, took Thérèse, then six, to the park. Pauline wrote to her Aunt Guérin about this little venture:

> Mademoiselle Pigeon left just this instant.... Would you believe, dear Aunt, that she came to look for us in order to take us to the "jardin de l'Etoile"? It was very good on her part; we weren't able to go with her as you well know because of the above-mentioned workers. Thérèse went alone, very happy at the opportunity. This baby loves flowers so much ... to listen to her, she's very soon going to pick all there are of lilies of the valley in the "jardin de l'Etoile."[96]

It is interesting to note that over one hundred years later this little six-year-old who loved flowers so much is known the world over as "The Little Flower."

c. The Cathedral of Saint Peter
Where Thérèse attended Mass and made her first confession

THE GREAT NORMAN GOTHIC CATHEDRAL OF SAINT PIERRE REMAINS TO this day the central focus of the Place Mitterand (*La Place François Mitterrand*) which in Thérèse's day was called Place Thiers and even at one time Place St. Pierre—the main market square in Lisieux. Bishop Arnould, after returning

---

93 Six, *Lisieux au temps de Thérèse*, footnote 1, p. 11.
94 *Story of a Soul*, chapter II, p. 37.
95 Ibid., chapter III, p. 54.
96 LD June 4, 1879.

from the Second Crusade, had construction of the church begin in 1149.[97] Some Medieval scholars, however, believe it was in 1160.[98] The cathedral was completed in 1250. Bishop Arnould was an advisor to the Duke of Normandy and a friend of two French kings, Louis VI and Louis VII. He also assisted at the coronation of Henry II in Westminster Abbey in London and knew Thomas à Becket. Actually, the cathedral was built over the site of a former Romanesque church in the sixth century and dedicated to St. Peter. Throughout the centuries many changes had been made and reconstructions carried out, all necessary because of the damages caused by fires and the natural ravages of time. Luckily the bombardments of Lisieux in 1944 did not touch the cathedral itself but many of the nearby buildings were completely destroyed.

Since the Napoleonic Concordat of 1802, bishops of the diocese of Lisieux have not resided at the cathedral but in Bayeux. Despite this fact, the church of Saint Pierre retains the title of cathedral. The present bishop has jurisdiction not only over Bayeux but also Lisieux.

Les Buissonnets lies within the parish of Saint-Jacques; therefore, when Louis Martin arrived in Lisieux, he went to see Father Delatroëtte, the pastor, to rent seats in the church for his family and the maid, making a total of seven. It was the custom to do so for families each year. There were no seats available so he went to the other church, Saint-Pierre. This church was actually closer to Les Buissonnets and the church the Guérins attended since they lived just a few houses away from it. He did obtain seats here though not in the nave but in the ambulatory on the right side (the south aisle) at the little chapel of Saint Joseph of Cupertino directly opposite the high (main) altar. From here they were able to follow carefully the Sunday Mass and Vespers despite the slight obstruction from the choir grille. It was not possible, however, to hear clearly or see the priest delivering the sermon, so directly after the gospel was read, the family left their places *en masse* and went to the nave of the church to hear the sermon:

> [When] we had to go down into the body of the church to listen to the sermon, two chairs had to be found side by side [for Thérèse and her father]. This wasn't too difficult, for everyone seemed to think it so wonderful to see such a *handsome old man* with such a *little daughter* that they went out of their way to give them their places. Uncle [Guérin], sitting in the warden's pews, was always happy to see us come. He used to call me his little ray of sunshine."
>
> I wasn't too disturbed at being looked at by people. I listened attentively to the sermons which I understood very poorly. The first *I did understand* and which *touched me deeply* was a sermon on the Passion preached by Father Ducellier [when she was five-and-a-half] and since then I've understood all the others. When the preacher spoke about St. Teresa, Papa leaned over and whispered: "Listen carefully, little Queen, he's talking about your Patroness." [99]

---

97 Descouvemont, *op. cit.*, p. 102.
98 Clark, "The Nave of Saint Pierre at Lisieux," p. 29.
99 *Story of a Soul*, chapter II, pp. 41–42.

When the sermons were over, the Martins returned to their assigned places on the right side near the main altar.

Céline in the biography of her father wrote: "Every afternoon he [her father] used to pay a visit to the Blessed Sacrament, and whenever there was a 'Corpus Christi' procession he never missed being directly behind the canopy. On no account would he have stayed away...."[100] From the same source we read what Thérèse observed while her father was listening to a sermon at the Sunday High Mass: "I must own that I often looked at papa more than at the preacher, I read so many things in his noble face. Sometimes his eyes would fill with tears, which he strove in vain to keep back. And as he listened to the eternal truths, he seemed no longer of this world...."

Thérèse tells of the joy she experienced at church during feast days:

> The *feasts*! what memories this word brings back to me. How I loved the *feasts*!... I loved above all the processions in honor of the Blessed Sacrament. What a joy it was for me to throw flowers beneath the feet of God. Before allowing them to fall to the ground, I threw them as high as I could and I was never so happy as when I saw my roses *touch* the sacred monstrance.[101]

This imposing cathedral dominates the eastern end of the spacious and busy square before it. Two features make it rather distinctive. The first are the two tall towers of different architectural design. The left (north) one being half the size of the right one that is topped by a lofty stone spire. The other feature is the closeness of the buildings to the church on both sides. In fact, the left one (on the north side) is actually connected with a long building spreading along the north side of the Place Thiers which used to be part of the Episcopal palace. On the south side of the cathedral a narrow way along the side of the building separates the church from a long row of houses and shops that form the eastern end of the market square. A grand flight of steps the length of the façade leads to a wide landing followed by more stairs facing the three entrance doors.

Upon entering the cathedral, one passes through the unlighted narthex and into the great nave that stretches some distance ahead. Flanked on each side, seven large Norman pillars support graceful Gothic arches. Six side chapels form a line along the left, the first of which, the Chapel of the Annunciation, contains the 18th century wooden confessional where the tiny six-year-old Thérèse made her first confession:

> Oh! Dear Mother [Agnès—her sister Pauline], with what care you prepared me for my first confession, telling me it was not to a man but to God I was about to tell my sins; I was very much convinced of this truth. I made my confession in a great spirit of faith, even asking you if I had to tell Father Ducellier I loved him with all my heart as it was to God in person I was speaking.
>
> Well instructed in all I had to say and do, I entered the confessional and knelt down. On opening the grating Father Ducellier saw no one. I was so

---
100 Sister Geneviève, *op. cit.*, p. 7.
101 *Story of a Soul*, chapter II, p. 41.

little my head was below the arm-rest. He told me to stand up. Obeying him instantly, I stood and faced him directly in order to see him perfectly, and I made my confession like a *big girl* and received the blessing with *great devotion* for you had told me that at the moment he gave me absolution the *tears of Jesus* were going to purify my soul. I remember the first exhortation directed to me. Father encouraged me to be devout to the Blessed Virgin and I promised myself to redouble my tenderness for her. Coming out of the confessional I was so happy and light-hearted that I had never felt so much joy in my soul. Since then I've gone to confession on all the great feasts, and it was truly a *feast* for me each time.[102]

From *Story of a Soul* (*Histoire d'une Ame*) we read a little more about what Thérèse did just after she finished confessing her "sins": "I then passed my rosary through to have him bless it. It was evening and on the way home when we passed under a streetlight I looked at it from all sides. 'What are you looking at, Thérèse?' you asked. 'I want to see what a blessed rosary looks like.' This amused you. I remained a long time affected by the grace I received."[103]

In front of the high altar two long rows of choir stalls face each other. The high altar was in need of replacement in 1888 and M. Martin, in December, during the time of his mental problems, paid completely for the installation of a new one at a cost of 10,000 francs which his brother-in-law, Isidore Guérin, a member of the Board of Consultors of the Cathedral, considered rather excessive on his part. (Incidentally, he was married in this church in 1866.) Thérèse, however, approved of this generosity. (It happened to be the exact amount given for her dowry upon entrance into Carmel.)[104] A plaque behind the altar states, "This altar was donated by M. Martin Father of Saint Thérèse of the Infant Jesus."

Directly behind the high altar is the Lady Chapel (the absidal chapel) where Thérèse and her family attended weekday 6:00 A.M. Mass. Here the Blessed Sacrament is reserved. Construction of this late Gothic Marian chapel began in 1432 and completed in 1442 with the financial backing of Msgr. Cauchon (1371–1442), who was chosen Bishop of Lisieux (1432 to 1442). He is noted as the principal judge in the trial and conviction of Joan of Arc. Later on he was severely censured for having favored English involvement in France and imposing his secular interests on an ecclesiastical trial. Joan's verdict of being a relapsed heretic was overturned in 1456, a quarter of a century after her brutal death. Some sources contend that he had this chapel built "in expiation for the iniquitous judgment rendered against Joan of Arc."[105] Bishop Cauchon died in Rouen but his body was brought back to his see and buried in a vault under the floor of the Lady Chapel in the Cathedral of St. Pierre. In 1931 excavations took place here and the bishop's ivory crosier was discovered on his leaden casket. It is now in the Vieux Lisieux Museum.

---

102 Ibid.
103 See footnote 38 on p. 41 in *Story of a Soul*, chapter II.
104 Gaucher, *The Story of a Life*, p. 97.
105 Descouvemont, *Therese and Lisieux*, p. 40.

On the left wall of the Lady Chapel are two rather large bas-reliefs, one of which shows Christ crucified between the two thieves with a group of mourners below. In the summer of 1887 the horrendous murder of two women and a girl in Paris by Henri Pranzini was the great topic of discussion in all the newspapers of the time. He was condemned to death by the guillotine. When Thérèse heard of this she believed that if Christ forgave the "good thief" before he died (as she observed in the bas-relief), he would also do so for Pranzini if he repented. She fervently prayed for an indication of this and was completely convinced when she learned that Pranzini asked the priest present for a crucifix which he kissed just before his execution. Thérèse wrote:

> I had obtained the "sign" I requested, and this sign was a perfect replica of the grace Jesus had given me when He attracted me to pray for sinners. Wasn't it before the *wounds of Jesus*, when seeing His divine *blood* flowing [as in the bas-relief], that thirst for souls had entered my heart? I wished to give them this *immaculate blood* to drink, this blood which was to purify them from their stains, and the lips of my *"first child"* were pressed to the sacred wounds! What an unspeakably sweet response![106]

When one proceeds to the right of the Lady Chapel along the ambulatory to the south aisle of the choir, one encounters the small side (apsidal) chapel where the Martin family observed Sunday Mass. Plaques on the walls indicate that this was the chapel where Thérèse attended Sunday Mass. A small altar, votive lights, and a modern statue of Thérèse fill the area. This statue was made by the Polish sculptor J. Lambert Rucki (1888–1967), a friend of the famous artists Modigliani and Soutine. Here Thérèse received the first of two special graces at Midnight Mass which she realized after she returned home:

> It was December 25, 1886, that I received the grace of leaving my childhood, in a word, the grace of my complete conversion. We had come back from Midnight Mass where I had the happiness of receiving the *strong* and *powerful* God. Upon arriving at Les Buissonnets, I used to love to take my shoes from the chimney-corner and examine the presents in them....[107]

She continues to tell the rest of the story of how she instantly overcame her childish habits, self-centeredness, and incessant tears.

> On that *night of light* began the third period of my life, the most beautiful and the most filled with graces from heaven. The work I had been unable to do in ten years was done by Jesus in one instant.... He made me a fisher of *souls*. I experienced a great desire to work for the conversion of sinners....[108]

A year later, just before she became immersed in the salvation of Pranzini, Thérèse received her second eucharistic grace in this chapel. When Sunday Mass ended, a picture of the crucifixion with the sole figure of a kneeling woman

---

[106] *Story of a Soul*, chapter V, p. 100.
[107] Ibid., p. 98.
[108] Ibid., pp. 98–99.

embracing Christ's feet slid out of her missal. This picture suddenly produced a deep and lasting impact on her:

> One Sunday, looking at a picture of Our Lord on the Cross, I was struck by the blood flowing from one of the divine hands. I felt a great pang of sorrow when thinking this blood was falling to the ground without anyone's hastening to gather it up. I was resolved to remain in spirit at the foot of the Cross and to receive the divine dew. I understood I was then to pour it out upon souls.... As yet, it was not the souls of priests that attracted me, but those of *great sinners*; I *burned* with the desire to snatch them from the eternal flames.[109]

Leaving this chapel and proceeding down the south choir aisle, one reaches the south transept (the right arm of this cruciform church). Here is the side door of the Cathedral Thérèse and her family generally used called The Gate of Paradise (*le Portail du paradis*) because long ago after a funeral Mass the coffin was carried through this door while the choir chanted "*In paradisum ...* May the Angels lead you into Paradise." In this transept a statue of Joan of Arc stands on a pedestal at the right side wall.

After this rather large entrance area, continuing along the right side aisle, there are seven recessed chapels. The first one contains a statue of Our Lady of Mount Carmel which was originally in the church of St. Jacques. Somehow it managed to survive the bombings of 1944 that nearly destroyed all of St. Jacques, leaving basically only the side walls intact. It was recovered from the rubble and placed here. Thérèse's sister Pauline prayed before this statue on February 16, 1882, which she explains herself:

> I was at the 6 o'clock Mass at St. Jacques, in the Chapel of Notre Dame du Mont Carmel with father and Marie. Suddenly a light flashed through my soul, and God showed me clearly that He did not wish me to go to the Visitation [Order] but to Carmel.... I had *never* thought of the Carmel, and in one moment I found myself being impelled there with an irresistible attraction.[110]

The next chapel contains on the left wall above a small altar a large painting of "The Guardian Angel" by Edouard Krug (1829–1901) painted in 1875. He was Céline's art teacher for a while and encouraged her to study art in Paris. However, her strong desire to enter Carmel overcame her wish to become an artist. Even after she entered the convent, Krug visited her and urged her to continue her artwork. In fact, on one occasion he offered her one of his own palettes.

The succeeding two chapels contain representations of images particularly significant to St. Thérèse: an image of Our Lady of Perpetual Help and an image of the Holy Face.

The last recessed area next to the narthex is the baptistery with an ornate wrought iron fence (or low grille) enclosing the area with a baptismal font in the middle. Here Thérèse's cousins Jeanne and Marie Guérin were baptized.

---

109 Ibid., p. 99.
110 Obituary Notice of Mother Agnès of Jesus, p. 9.

d. The Church of Saint Jacques
The Martins' Parish Church

LOUIS MARTIN MOVED WITH HIS FIVE DAUGHTERS TO LISIEUX IN NOVEMBER 1877, two-and-a-half months after his wife died, in order to be near his wife's brother and family. The house they settled in, called Les Buissonnets, fell within the parish of Saint Jacques. Louis immediately went to see the pastor of the church, Father Delatroëtte (1818–1895), to make arrangements for his family to have assigned seats in the church (a custom at the time). Unfortunately there was not a block of seats available so Louis went to the nearby Cathedral of Saint Pierre where he did obtain them. They were located in the south ambulatory section at the little side chapel of St. Joseph of Cupertino that afforded a perfect side view of the nearby high altar. To hear the sermons, however, the Martins had to leave their rented places and find seats in the nave of the cathedral. They returned to their side chapel when the sermons were over. The Martins did not completely abandon Saint Jacques, however, but would sometimes attend Mass there. Generally, the Martins went to the daily 6 A.M. Mass at St. Pierre's.

A memorable occurrence for Pauline concerning her vocation took place at the Church of Saint Jacques on February 16, 1882, while she was praying before the statue of Our Lady of Mount Carmel:

> I was at the 6 o'clock Mass at St. Jacques, in the Chapel of Notre Dame du Mont Carmel with father and Marie. Suddenly a light flashed through my soul, and God showed me clearly that He did not wish me to go to the Visitation [Convent where her maternal aunt had been a nun] but to the Carmel.... I had *never* thought of the Carmel, and in one moment I found myself being impelled there with an irresistible attraction.[111]

The priests of Saint Jacques play an important part in the history of the Carmel in Lisieux. The first superior of the Carmelites was the curate of Saint Jacques, the Sulpician priest Rev. Pierre-Nicolas Sauvage (1794–1853). He closely and vigorously assisted the nun founders of the Carmel, became their first superior, and was responsible for the construction of their main chapel that was completed in 1852. Sadly, he died a few months later and was buried near the choir grille of the chapel since he was a founder. Interred next to him is Mother Geneviève who is considered the principal foundress. Rev. Xavier Cagniard, also curate of the Cathedral of Saint Pierre,[112] succeeded him as superior. He in turn was followed by Canon Delatroëtte who served from 1867 to 1895 and vigorously objected to Thérèse's entrance into Carmel at the age of fourteen or even fifteen. However, he finally reluctantly gave permission for her to enter at fifteen, but warned the whole community that if she did not succeed it would be their responsibility. His convictions changed when he came to realize the great holiness and dedication Thérèse displayed. He died two years before Thérèse, whereupon his nephew, Canon Maupas (1850–1920) assumed his position as

---
111 Ibid.
112 *Les Annales*, Nov. 1988, pp. 2–3.

superior of the Carmel. At the death of Sister Thérèse of the Child Jesus, he performed the funeral ceremonies.

Thérèse's father became a friend of Father Charles-Louis Marie (1849–1912), a young priest at Saint-Jacques, who accompanied Louis Martin on a tour of Central Europe, Constantinople, and Rome in 1885. Louis highly respected Abbé Marie and the two got along very well despite the differences in their ages. In a letter home to his daughters he wrote, "Abbé Marie is always radiant—he is almost tireless. I find it hard to keep up with him."[113] He served as chaplain of the Carmel for a number of years.[114]

Years later, Bishop Lemmonnier chose him as one of the notaries in the Diocesan Process charged with pursuing the cause of the Servant of God, Louis Martin's daughter, Sister Thérèse of the Child Jesus. Part of his task included the reading of Thérèse's complete written works in copied form.

The very first stone of the church of Saint-Jacques was laid in 1496 during the reign of Louis XII (1462–1515). Wealthy nobles by the name of Le Vallois, from the nearby town of Mesnil-Guillaume just south of Lisieux,[115] lent their financial assistance for its construction. It took, however, a half-century to build this magnificent church which was completed in 1546, almost at the end of the reign of Francis I (1515–1547). It had a single belfry tower and a double flight of steps leading to the large entrance door. The Allied bombardments of June 1944 completely gutted the edifice leaving only the outer walls standing. The Department of Historical Buildings restored the church including stained glass windows. It is now used not as a church but as an exhibition hall run by the municipality. At the time of the beatification of Thérèse's parents in October 2008, a wonderful exhibit relating to them and St. Thérèse was held, which included many rare pieces of furniture, photographs, and other objects from the Martin home and elsewhere.

e. The Place Thiers Area (Now called Place Mitterand)
   i. The Guérin Pharmacy
   ii. The Post Office
   iii. The Episcopal Palace
   iv. The Public Gardens

THE PLACE FRANÇOIS MITTERAND, FORMERLY PLACE ST. PIERRE AND PLACE Thiers in Thérèse's time, was and is a large and busy square in the center of Lisieux. It serves as a market place, amusement center for children, parade ground, and processional area on various religious feast days. The imposing Cathedral of St. Pierre dominates the entire plaza.

Thérèse crossed this area nearly every day, not only to attend daily Mass at the cathedral, but on her way to the Abbey School. She and Céline would meet their cousins, Marie and Jeanne, at the Guérin pharmacy located just a few

---

113 CF 223, dated August 30, 1885, Vienna. Translated by the author.
114 *Sicut Parvuli*, "The Posthumous Life of St. Thérèse," Sept. 1983.
115 Descouvemont, *op. cit.*, p. 48.

houses down from the cathedral on the corner of Place Thiers and rue Henry Cheron (then called Grand Rue). The Guérins lived in the apartment above the pharmacy from 1866 to 1889. Though this building was completely destroyed in the June 1944 air raids, it has been rebuilt to resemble the original. For many generations a pharmacy existed on this exact corner.

> Papa, to please Uncle, used to permit Marie or Pauline to spend Sunday evenings at his home; I was happy when I was there with one of them. I preferred this to being invited all alone because then they paid less attention to me. I listened with great pleasure to all Uncle had to say, but I didn't like it when he asked me questions. I was very much frightened when he placed me on his knee and sang Blue Beard in a formidable tone of voice. I was happy to see Papa coming to fetch us.[116]

Another building in the Place Thiers located on the north side (left of the cathedral) is the post office that Thérèse went to daily as she anxiously expected a letter from the bishop permitting her to enter Carmel at the age of fifteen: "ten days before Christmas [1887] my letter was on its way! Convinced the answer would not be long in coming, I went every morning after Mass with Papa to the Post Office, believing I would find the permission to take my flight. But each morning brought with it a new disappointment which, nevertheless, didn't shake my faith."[117]

The former Episcopal Palace, a rather grandiose structure next to the cathedral, extends above the level of the market square. Now called the Palace of Justice, it functions primarily as a courthouse, but parts of it include a museum, library, and at one time even a prison. In the past it contained the king's apartment (later, the Bishop's Reception Room)—the glistening "Golden Room" (*Salle Dorée*). On her way to and from the square below, Thérèse would climb the stairway up past the courtyard in front of the Episcopal Palace and go down a few steps to the grand Public Gardens (*Le Jardin de l'Evêche*). This sprawling and meticulously maintained park was designed in the style of the great French landscape architect André Le Nôtre (1613–1700) who planned the royal gardens of Versailles and other sumptuous parks and gardens. On the left side of the park, Isidore Guérin, after he sold his pharmacy, rented for a short time a house at 16 rue Concorcet whose back property can be seen from the park. Thérèse writes what happened once when she strolled through the park with her father:

> When we were on our way home, I would gaze upon the *stars* which were twinkling ever so peacefully in the skies and the sight carried me away. There was especially one cluster of *golden pearls* which attracted my attention and gave me great joy because they were in the form of a T. I pointed them out to Papa and told him my name was written in heaven. Then desiring to look no longer upon this dull earth, I asked him to guide my steps; and not looking where I placed my feet I threw back my head, giving myself over completely to the contemplation of the star-studded firmament![118]

---

116 *Story of a Soul*, chapter II, p. 42.
117 Ibid., chapter VI, p. 141.
118 Ibid., chapter II, pp. 42–43.

f. The Benedictine Abbey School of Notre Dame du Pré
36, avenue du 6 juin
Thérèse attended school here from 1881 to 1886

THIS LARGE, GRAND HISTORIC PLACE EXISTED FOR OVER 900 YEARS UNTIL the night air raid bombings in Normandy of June 7–8, 1944, completely annihilated it. A new unimpressive convent replaced the old one not long after the war. Today the area is occupied not by nuns but by an institution that provides care and education for orphaned and abandoned children, the *Apprentis-Orphelins d'Auteuil* (The Orphan-Apprentices of Auteuil [Paris]). Father Daniel Brottier (1876–1936), a director of this institution and tireless promoter of its cause, was beatified by Pope John Paul II in 1984. Also in recent years a wax museum on the grounds called The Diorama offered a thirty-minute presentation showing the major stages in the life of St. Thérèse.

The Benedictine Abbey of Notre-Dame-du-Pré was located on the rue de Caen, now 36 avenue du 6 June, in a section of Lisieux almost a mile (1.5 km) south-west of Thérèse's home, Les Buissonnets. In Thérèse's time it consisted of several ancient buildings built originally as a monastery for contemplative Benedictine nuns. Its foundress and first abbess, the widow Countess Lesceline, first cousin of William the Conqueror, established her monastery in 1011 at Saint Pierre sur Dives (southwest of Lisieux). In 1046 she and her community settled in Lisieux on land called Saint-Désir given to them by her famous cousin. About seven hundred years later the Benedictine nuns opened a school for girls. The French Revolution caused great havoc with all religious including these nuns. Nonetheless, later on Napoleon permitted the nuns to return to the abbey with the stipulation that they resume their educational work. The school prospered during the nineteenth century and garnered for itself honors in the field of education. Eventually it closed in 1904. Then tragically the 1944 bombings killed twenty of the nuns who were living there. Those who survived sought refuge in a nearby town and returned after a new convent was constructed in 1954. They opened rooms as a hostel for the many pilgrims who came on pilgrimage to the Basilica, the Carmel, and other Theresian places. In order to live a more secluded and quiet life, the nuns moved to an old abbey in Valmont (north of Le Havre) in 1994. Thus ended the 948 years' presence of the Benedictines of Notre-Dame du Pré in Lisieux.

Thérèse's five years at the Abbey School from 1881 to 1886 turned out to be joyless and unpleasant:

> I was eight and a half when Léonie left boarding school and I replaced her at the Abbey. I have often heard it said that the time spent at school is the best and happiest of one's life. It wasn't this way for me. The five years I spent in school were the saddest in my life, and if I hadn't had Céline with me, I couldn't have remained there and would have become sick in a month.[119]

---

119 Ibid., chapter III, p. 53.

A. In Normandy

Thérèse, nonetheless, experienced some happy days at the school especially at the time of her First Communion (May 8, 1884) about which she wrote: "The time of my First Communion remains engraved in my heart as a memory without any clouds."[120] Her narrative continues:

> The three months of preparation passed by quickly, and very soon I had to go on retreat and for this had to become a real boarder, sleeping at the Abbey. I cannot express the sweet memory this retreat left with me. And truly, if I suffered very much at the boarding school, I was largely repaid by the ineffable happiness of those few days spent in waiting for Jesus. I don't believe one can taste this joy anywhere else but in religious communities. The number of children was small, and it was easy to give each child particular attention, and certainly our teachers gave each of us their motherly care and attention.... In the morning, I found it very nice to see all the students getting up so early and doing the same as they.... Ah! how sweet was that first kiss of Jesus! It was a kiss of love; I *felt* that I *was loved*, and I said: "I love You, and I give myself to You forever!"...
>
> In the afternoon, it was I who made the Act of Consecration to the Blessed Virgin. It was only right that I *speak* in the name of my companions to my Mother in heaven, I who had been deprived at such an early age of my earthly Mother.[121]

A month later on June 14, 1884, another unforgettable ceremony took place here—her Confirmation:

> A short time after my First Communion, I entered upon another retreat for my Confirmation. I was prepared with great care to receive the visit of the Holy Spirit, and I did not understand why greater attention was not paid to the reception of this sacrament of *Love*.... Like the Apostles, I awaited the Holy Spirit's visit with great happiness in my soul.... Finally the happy moment arrived.... On that day I received the strength to *suffer*.[122]

In early 1886 M. Martin removed Thérèse from the school because of her poor health and had her receive special lessons from Mme. Papinau, a private tutor in Lisieux. A year later, Thérèse returned for the last time to the Abbey school two afternoons a week in preparation for becoming a member of the Association of the Children of Mary to which she was admitted on May 31, 1887.

The last time we hear of the Abbey school is in an 1888 letter Thérèse wrote to her former teacher at the Benedictine Abbey school, Mother Saint-Placide. Thérèse had been in the Carmel almost nine months when she received an invitation to attend at the Abbey the twenty-fifth anniversary celebration of the creation of the Children of Mary Sodality:

> I received the dear circular letter of the Children of Mary with pleasure. Certainly, I won't fail to be present in spirit at this beautiful celebration, for was it not in this beautiful chapel that the Blessed Virgin adopted me on the beautiful day of my First Communion and on the day of my reception into the Children of

---

120 Ibid., chapter IV, p. 73.
121 Ibid., pp. 75–77.
122 Ibid., p. 80.

Mary. I could not forget, dear Mistress, how kind you were to me at the time of these great events in my life, and I cannot doubt that the remarkable grace of my religious vocation germinated on that blessed day when, surrounded by my good teachers, I made the consecration of myself to Mary at the foot of the altar, taking her for my Mother in a special way, when in the morning I had received Jesus for the first time....

[So] I am thinking frequently of all my good teachers.... I dare to beg you, dear Mistress, to speak for me to them and to remember me to them.... Please, too, remember me to my happy companions, whose little sister in Mary I remain always.[123]

g. The Carmel Chapel
37 Rue du Carmel
At the Monastery where St. Thérèse lived

FROM HER EARLY CHILDHOOD THÉRÈSE'S WANTED TO BE A CARMELITE NUN in the fifty-year-old Carmel in Lisieux. She did become a nun and lived there for almost ten years from the age of fifteen in 1888 to twenty-four in 1897. The monastery is still an active community of cloistered nuns; therefore, the public is not allowed to visit any parts of it except the chapel and museum. Many changes have been made to the exterior of the complex and inside the chapel notably in 1919, 1923, and later on in the century. Drastic but necessary changes in the interior and exterior portions of the chapel were undertaken and completed in 2008 in order to accommodate the great number of people who came to celebrate the beatification of Thérèse's parents. On the other hand, the chapel's façade, despite modifications, looks generally how it did when Thérèse resided there.

In the space in front of the Carmelite Monastery before the wrought-iron fence and gate that encloses the chapel, extends a large paved promenade with beautifully landscaped areas on both sides and a few benches placed here and there where visitors can rest. A statue of St. Thérèse made by the Trappist sculptor Father Marie-Bernard highlights the area. This rather impressive foreground to the chapel did not exist in St. Thérèse's day. A street then called the rue de Livarot ran directly in front of the fence and gate. (It was named after a nearby town, Livarot, that produced the first Norman cheese.)

Opposite this broad area, across the street now called the rue du Carmel, is the Librairie du Carmel—Office Central—the large store selling books, photographs, and other materials relative to St. Thérèse.

A small gift shop within the gated area on the right of the chapel building sells photos, postcards, religious objects, etc. Inside the church, to the left next to the sacristy is the entrance to a little museum. Here objects related to Thérèse are displayed in large lighted cases including her long-flowing blonde hair cut off over two years after she entered Carmel. The interior of the chapel is noticeably different from the way it was in the 19th century. It was widened by the inclusion of an aisle on the left side. The original florid bits of architecture, the high altar,

---
123 LT 70, dated sometime in the beginning of December 1888.

the sculptured group above it, and other aspects in the chapel have been removed and replaced by much simpler features. About halfway down the aisle on the right is the shrine where the recumbent figure by Father Marie-Bernard of St. Thérèse dressed in her habit lies in a large glassed-in golden case. She holds in her right hand a golden rose given by Pope Pius XI. A copy of the coat of arms Thérèse designed for herself is attached to the center top of the golden case. For years in the past, this shrine was very ornately decorated and had grandiose life-sized statues of angels on each side of the case; however, much of the excessive ornamentation was removed apparently for the sake of simplicity. Above the shrine and placed in front of the blue stained-glass window in the center stands the actual statue of Our Lady of the Smile that Thérèse saw smile and cure her on May 13, 1883. Behind and to the left of this shrine is a recessed area on the wall with a plaque indicating that the bodies of St. Thérèse's Carmelite blood sisters, Mother Agnès, Sister Marie, and Sister Geneviève are entombed there.

The single unpretentious main altar, installed above two steps, now consists of only a flat piece of material held up by a plain wide pedestal. A large figure of Christ crucified hangs on the wall behind the altar. Many tall long but narrow panels of wood now flank the sidewalls partially covering up the columns behind them. The color scheme is generally off-white, ivory, and beige. The nuns' choir grille remains in the same place on the right of the altar. On the floor at the foot of the grille a tablet indicates the tomb containing the bodies of the founder, Father Sauvage who built the chapel, and the foundress, Mother Geneviève. The whole sanctuary is framed by two beige pillars that support the archway. No altar rail separates the sanctuary from the congregation now but there are two steps leading up to the sanctuary floor.

A statue of St. Teresa of Avila and one of St. John of the Cross have been placed in front of the rear wall at the entrance to the chapel. At the time of Thérèse these two statues were positioned one on each side of the main altar: St. John on the left and St. Teresa on the right.

Close to the chapel's entrance door in the back left side is the sacristy which is ordinarily not accessible to the public. Inside, besides cabinets containing the usual liturgical clothing and vessels, are the turn through which Thérèse passed things from the cloister area to the sacristy, and the priests' side of the confessional that Thérèse used once a week. One can also see the grille a few feet away through which some of the nuns gave their testimony during the steps dealing with the cause of Thérèse's canonization. Also the door there to the cloister remains the same as when Thérèse passed through it on April 9, 1889, when she entered the cloister to become a nun and through which the coffin containing her body left on its way to the cemetery on October 4, 1897.

Thérèse became acquainted with the Carmel chapel at a very young age. When she accompanied her father on some of his walks through Lisieux visiting churches, he sometimes would take his "little Queen" to this chapel to pray or meditate.

> Each afternoon I took a walk with Papa. We made our visit to the Blessed Sacrament together, going to a different church each day, and it was in this way we entered the Carmelite chapel for the first time. Papa showed me the choir grille and told me there were nuns behind it. I was far from thinking at the time that nine years later I would be in their midst.[124]

The very day Thérèse entered the monastery she was delighted by what she saw and experienced. Below, she verbalizes this and then submits her reasons for entering Carmel:

> I was led, as are all postulants, to the choir immediately after my entrance into the cloister. The choir was in [semi-] darkness [to prevent the people seeing the Carmelite nuns] because the Blessed Sacrament was exposed and what struck me first were the eyes of our holy Mother Geneviève [now buried near the grille] which were fixed on me. I remained kneeling for a moment at her feet, thanking God for the grace He gave me of knowing a saint, and then I followed Mother Marie de Gonzague [the prioress] into the different places of the community. Everything thrilled me; I felt as though I was transported into a desert; our [her] little cell, above all, filled me with joy.... With what deep joy I repeated those words: "I am here forever and ever!"
>
> This happiness was not passing. It didn't take its flight with "the illusions of the first days." *Illusions*, God gave me the grace *not to have* A SINGLE ONE, when entering Carmel. I found the religious life to be *exactly* as I had imagined it, no sacrifice astonished me and yet,... my first steps met with more thorns than roses!... I had declared at the feet of Jesus-Victim, in the examination preceding my Profession, what I had come to Carmel for: "I came to save souls and especially to pray for priests." When one wishes to attain a goal, one must use the means; Jesus made me understand that it was through suffering that He wanted to give me souls, and my attraction for suffering grew in proportion to its increase.[125]

The public may participate in the daily and the Sunday Masses celebrated in the morning at 8:00, 9:00 (the community Mass), and 11:30. The nuns sing the Divine Office during the week at 7:15 A.M. and 1:45 P.M. (Vespers). In the afternoon, the last service is at 6:00 P.M. during the week and at 5:00 P.M. (Vespers) on Sunday.

h. The Second Guérin Home
19 rue Paul Banaston
Their home after selling the pharmacy

THÉRÈSE'S UNCLE ISIDORE GUÉRIN LIVED FROM 1866, THE DATE OF HIS marriage, to his death in 1909 entirely in Lisieux. His wife and children were born and lived their whole lives there except for the oldest daughter who at her marriage lived elsewhere. For over twenty-two years, from the time of Isidore's marriage to Céline Fournet in 1866, the family lived above their pharmacy on the corner of Place Saint Pierre and Grande Rue. The name above the store was

---
124 *Story of a Soul*, chapter II, p. 36.
125 Ibid., chapter VII, pp. 148–149.

"GUÉRIN – FOURNET." (Sometime since then the street Grande Rue changed to rue Henry Chéron.) On December 8, 1888, Isidore retired and sold his business to a friend, Victor Lahaye. Thérèse spent many hours visiting her relations there, especially on Sunday:

> Papa, to please Uncle, used to permit Marie or Pauline to spend Sunday evenings at this home; I was happy when I was there with one of them. I preferred this to being invited all alone because then they paid less attention to me. I listened with great pleasure to all Uncle had to say, but I didn't like it when he asked me questions. I was very much frightened when he placed me on his knee and sang Blue-Beard in a formidable tone of voice. I was happy to see Papa coming to fetch us.[126]

Another reference to the Guérin home by Thérèse in her autobiography is quite revealing: "All my teachers looked upon me as a very intelligent student, but it wasn't like that at Uncle's house where I was taken for a little dunce, good and sweet, and with right judgment, yes, but incapable and clumsy. I am not surprised at this opinion which Uncle and Aunt had of me, and no doubt still have, for I hardly ever spoke, being very timid."[127] On October 8, 1887, the fourteen-year-old Thérèse went to see her Uncle Isidore, to tell him of her desire to become a Carmelite:

> It was with trembling I confided my resolution to Uncle. He showed me great tenderness but did not grant me his permission to leave.... A long time passed by [just two weeks] before I dared speak to him again. It was very difficult for me to go to his home.... I learned later on that my great sadness influenced him very much.[128]

On April 20, 1889, Isidore bought a three-story house (with a large attic) at 19 rue Paul Banaston, a number of blocks away from his pharmacy home. Before he and his family eventually settled there, however, they lived at La Maison Sauvage, 16 rue Condorcet, from March 25 to June 7, 1889. Then from this last date they moved into Thérèse's former home, Les Buissonnets, to live temporarily with Céline and Leonie while waiting to move into their new home. Céline and Leonie had just returned from living in Caen to be near their father who was hospitalized there. Finally in July, the Guérins moved into their new house on the rue Paul Banaston (formerly the rue de la Chaussée) opposite the wall of the former Lisieux College where Banaston was a student.

Céline and Leonie went to live with the Guérins on July 20, 1889, where they remained until 1892 when their father returned from the hospital in Caen on May 10. In July 1892, the two sisters rented a house at 7 Rue Labbey just opposite the rear entrance (the carriage gate) to the Guérin property. It was easy, therefore, to push their wheelchair-bound father across the narrow rue Labbey into the Guérin garden and then into their house. They, their father, and two servants resided there until after Louis Martin died on July 29, 1894. Upon

---

126 Ibid., chapter II, p. 42.
127 Ibid., chapter IV, p. 82.
128 Ibid., chapter V, p. 109.

Céline's departure in September to become a Carmelite, the Guérins welcomed Léonie with open arms to live with them.

The new house provided more room for the Guérin family than the one they occupied in the Place Thiers. Now it is the second building from the corner of rue Labbey and rue Paul Banaston. On the Rue Labbey side of the Guérin's house a long high brick wall with a wrought iron gate at the entrance to the back yard and garage provides privacy. In this rear area of the property Céline took pictures of her family which are extant today.

This house, presently privately owned, is not open to visitations by the public.

i. The Second Martin Home
7 rue Labbey
After the Martins left Les Buissonnets

THE MARTINS NAMED THE FIRST HOME THEY HAD IN LISIEUX LES BUISSONnets. They lived there for seventeen years from 1877 to 1889. After Thérèse's mother died in Alençon in 1877, her father moved with his five daughters to Lisieux to be near their family relations, the Guérins. In February of 1889 Louis Martin was hospitalized for almost four years at Bon Sauveur Hospital in Caen. By the end of 1889 the lease of Les Buissonnets expired, whereupon Céline and Léonie took up residence with the Guérins. Louis was released from the hospital on May 10, 1892. Isidore Guérin brought him to his own home to stay temporarily:

> Some time afterwards [July 1892], in order that we might be freer, our uncle rented a small house for us at 7, Rue Labbey. It faced our uncle's back garden, of which I had the key, by the tradesmen's entrance. We were very often, if not practically always, in the garden. We used to take Papa there in his little wheel-chair. We had engaged a married couple [Desiré and Marie] to help us with the household work.
>
> Father occupied a room on the ground floor, for one could not dream of taking him upstairs. He was as happy as he could be. His manservant, Desiré, had a very cheerful disposition; he was tall, and Papa, whose arms were not paralysed [*sic*], had only to put one arm around Desiré's neck to be lifted out of his carriage or to be placed in his armchair.[129]

The second Martin home is a two-story house, one among others in a long row of attached houses—a typical urban housing structural plan in French towns. An attractive backyard with a garden still exists where the Martins on one occasion had their now well-publicized picture taken with the Guérins. The long garden area leads to a stone stairway down to the rushing waters of a narrow stream where Céline and Léonie used to wash their clothes.

On June 24, 1893, Léonie entered the Visitation convent in Caen leaving Céline to care for her father with the help of the two servants. She did not return home until the death of her father on July 29, 1894. About seven weeks later, Céline entered the Carmelite convent (September 14).

---

129 Céline, *op. cit.*, pp. 113–114.

This house still exists today, unaffected by the 1944 bombings, but it is privately owned and not open to the public. Some changes have been made since the nineteenth century, one of which is the narrowing of the back yard to make way for the expansion of the property on the right side of the Martin house.

The beatification of St. Thérèse's parents took place in Lisieux on October 19, 2008. In July 2009 a plaque commemorating the fact that Louis Martin lived at 7 rue Labbey for a while was posted on the front of the building. Translated into English it says: "Louis Martin Father of Saint Thérèse of the Child Jesus lived in this house from 1892 to 1894."

j. The Hermitage
The Theresian spiritual center for retreats, conferences, etc.

THE HERMITAGE AT 25 RUE DU CARMEL, SERVES AS A SPIRITUAL CENTER that promotes, encourages, and advances Thérèse's message to the world by means of seminars, conferences, and retreats for priests, religious, and lay people. The building, located near the Carmel, accommodates large groups of people. It contains a chapel, conference rooms, a library, dining area, and sleeping quarters.

In 1670, a hotel known as the Hôtel du Maure stood on the present site. Over two centuries later, Msgr. Octave Germain (1885–1957) purchased it and named it the Hermitage. As the cult of Thérèse greatly enlarged after her canonization, a demand for such a venue became quite necessary. For over thirty years Msgr. Germain worked tirelessly for the honor and glory of Thérèse. He founded, built, promoted, directed pilgrimages, and functioned as rector of the Basilica. In addition, he opened a music school for young boys (*"jeunes clercs"*) he called *"Petits Clercs"* who were specially trained for the altar and sanctuary; many of them eventually entered the seminary. Furthermore, he founded a monthly magazine in 1925 devoted to the Saint initially named *Les Annales de Ste. Thérèse de Lisieux*, but in March 1992, sixty-seven years later, the title was changed to *Thérèse de Lisieux*. A trimestral supplement called *Vie Thérèsienne: Etudes et Documents* was initiated in 1961 which presents articles that deal in more depth with Theresian doctrine. Both periodicals flourish today with subscribers from all over the world.

A chronological listing of significant events in the history of the Hermitage follows:

1928   Msgr. Germain bought the Hotel du Maure at 31 Rue du Carmel, and named it the Hermitage.

1929   The first retreatants arrived in August. Bishop Suhard blessed it on May 17, 1930.

1939   At the beginning of World War II (1939–1945) the place was converted into an ambulance headquarters, then a military hospital under the direction of the Oblates of Saint Thérèse founded by Blessed Father Gabriel Martin. In June it closed.

1940   The Nazis occupation forces turned it into a barracks for the German army. On June 21, France surrendered to Germany.

1942   The Seminary of the Mission of France opened here with 30 seminarians under the direction of the Sulpician priest Father Louis Augros.
1944   On June 7, the Allied Forces bombed Lisieux. The Hermitage was spared. The Canadian army took over the building.
1945   With war's end in May, the seminarians, who had taken refuge in the Basilica during the bombings, returned to the Hermitage.
1952   The Seminary of the Mission of France moved to Limoges.
1953   The Oblates de Saint Thérèse took charge of the house.
2000   The Oblates left. Now the Travailleuses Missionnaires de l'Immaculée manage it.
2003   The foundation-stone of the newly restored Hermitage (Spiritual Center) was laid on September 27, 2003.
2004   It opened on March 13 and was blessed on September 25.

In 1928 when the retreats began at the Hermitage, Msgr. Germain remarked that "In building it, I gave Lisieux its spiritual basilica." It remains as such even to this day.

k. The Basilica
Large church honoring St. Thérèse

THE BASILICA OF ST. THÉRÈSE IN LISIEUX IS THE LARGEST RELIGIOUS EDIFICE constructed in Europe during the twentieth century.

Throughout the course of the beatification of Thérèse in 1923 and her canonization in 1925, thousands of pilgrims from all over France, and indeed the whole world, flocked to Lisieux to pray and honor the Little Flower whom they loved dearly. They visited the cemetery where she was first buried and the Chapel of the Carmelite Monastery where she lived and died. The Chapel, however, soon proved much too small to accommodate the huge numbers that arrived. At first the solution seemed to be to construct nearby a chapel in her honor or possibly to utilize one of the two churches—the Cathedral of St. Pierre or the Church of St. Jacques—for this purpose. Some, including a few of the local clergy were opposed to any plan, deeming it unnecessary. Eventually the construction of a basilica on the top of the hill behind the town cemetery was proposed and accepted. On January 26, 1926, the bishop of Bayeux and Lisieux, Msgr. Thomas Lemonnier (1853–1927), published a text in favor of the church and its location. A widespread campaign for funds began headed by Father Dellattre which proved very successful.

The Basilica's actual founder, promoter, director of construction, and rector was Msgr. Octave Germain (1886–1957). This indefatigable and foremost leader succeeded in bringing about a smooth and rapid construction of the Basilica. Monsignor Durand succeeded him after his death. The inevitable, sagacious, and ever-present advisors were Thérèse's two blood sisters, Pauline (Mother Agnès) and Céline (Sister Geneviève).

Louis-Marie Cordonnier-Lussigny (1854–1940), one of the foremost internationally renowned architects, was chosen to design the basilica. He had a remarkable career, winning first place in many contests in his field including the design for the Stock Exchange in Amsterdam in 1885, the Grand Prix at the World Exposition of Paris in 1900, and the Peace Palace at The Hague in 1906. Other accomplishments involved the planning of a number of chateaux, hotels, and churches.

Louis Cordonnier chose to apply the Roman-Byzantine style similar to the Basilica of the Sacred Heart in Montmartre, Notre-Dame de la Garde in Marseille, and Notre-Dame de Fouvière in Lyon (incidentally, Thérèse visited all three churches on her pilgrimage to Rome). The total area comprised about 48,500 square feet; the length and the height to the top of the dome both come to about 312 feet.

The family Cordonnier consists of a long line of great architects beginning with the father of Louis:

- Jean-Baptiste Cordonnier Cambron (1820–1902)
- Louis-Marie Cordonnier-Lussigny (1854–1940), 75, when asked to design the plans for the Basilica in 1929
- Louis-Stanislas Cordonnier-Tacquet (1884–1960), succeeded his father Louis-Marie in this work
- Louis-Marie Cordonnier-Delemer (1913–2007) finished in 1955 the work begun by his grandfather[130]

Construction began in 1929 with the complete approval of Pope Pius XI who called St. Thérèse "the star of his pontificate." After the death of Bishop Lemonnier, the pope informed the new bishop of Bayeux, Msgr. Suhard, that he wanted this building to be "very big, very beautiful, and completed as quickly as possible."[131] The immense Basilica was indeed finished in record time. The future Pope Pius XII, Cardinal Pacelli, solemnly blessed it in 1937.

The Reynès and Caralp company did the formidable excavation work with hundreds of workers. They encountered some unexpected difficulties at the outset. In order to reach a base strong enough to withstand the tremendous weight of the massive Basilica, they had to dig down to almost 100 feet (30 meters) below surface level.[132] Between the surface and the hard limestone base, they dredged through layers of soft silt, black clay, sand, and a number of streams and springs. Despite this enormous task, the building was successfully completed within the scheduled time.[133] In addition to the architect, many artists and craftsmen were required: sculptors, workers in mosaics, painters, stain-glass experts, etc. The vast amount of mosaics and stained glass was accomplished by a father and son who came from a long line of brilliant artists. Jean Gaudin (1879–1954), the father, did all the mosaics in the crypt during a period of thirty years. His son, Pierre Gaudin (1908–1973), finished what his father began and ended with the work

---

130 Main facts obtained from Maze's *La Basilique Sainte Thérèse de Lisieux*, pp. 8–9.
131 Descouvemont, *op. cit.*, p. 324.
132 Maze, *op. cit.*, pp. 10–11.
133 Ibid.

in the main part of the Basilica. Following the Liberation of France in 1944, he spent ten years in repairing or replacing the stained-glass and mosaics damaged or destroyed during the war. Estimates indicate that around 8,000 square meters of mosaics cover just the upper, main part of the Basilica.

The sculptors chosen to do the decorations on the façade, inside, and on the grounds of the Basilica were also masters in their field. The sculptor who did most of the work was Robert Coin whom Louis-Marie Cordonnier had recommended. Son of a sculptor, Mr. Coin had also won prizes for his accomplishments. He devoted fifty years of his life to this Herculean undertaking from 1932 to 1982. His task entailed the carving of all the sculptured figures and the bas-reliefs on the inside and outside of the Basilica. The results turned out to be magnificent; notably the Way (Stations) of the Cross in the rear of the Basilica, the huge crucified Christ over the main altar, and the tympanum over the large entrance door.[134]

Another sculptor whose works are known by all devotees of St. Thérèse is Father Marie-Bernard (1883–1975), a Trappist from the motherhouse of the Order near the town of Soligny-la-Trappe (Orne), northeast of Alençon. His outstanding creations include among others, the recumbent figure of St. Thérèse in the Carmel Chapel, the statue in the Basilica of Thérèse with outstretched arms, the one of her holding a crucifix and roses before the entrance to the Carmel Chapel, the seated Thérèse in the courtyard of the Hermitage, and the bas-relief on the façade of Les Buissonnets depicting the young Thérèse gazing at the statue of Our Lady smiling at her.[135]

In 1996 a welcome center called Le CAPI (*Le Centre d'accueil pastoral international*) opened at the far end of the large area (*parvis*) directly opposite the main entrance to the Basilica. Steps lead down to the large facility under the esplanade that provides information, souvenirs, books, gifts, pastoral assistance, conference space, and other services. A door downstairs in the rear leads to the parking area in the back.

Some significant dates in the history of the Basilica:

- 1927 Louis Cordonnier's architectural plan was accepted.
- 1929 On September 30, excavation started and then the first stone was laid.
- 1931 The inauguration of the esplanade (*parvis* or plaza) in front of the Basilica took place on May 17. The first bell of the Basilica was consecrated at the same time.
- 1932 The crypt was opened on July 3.
- 1934 The Way of the Cross was blessed on April 2.
- 1935 The construction of the avenue to the Basilica began.
- 1937 Cardinal Pacelli (the future Pope Pius XII) blessed the Basilica on July 11 during the Eleventh Eucharistic Congress held this year in Lisieux.
- 1939 The dome was completed and on July 22 Cardinal Piazza, a Carmelite and Patriarch of Venice, blessed it.

---

134 Ibid., pp. 26–27.
135 Descouvemont, *op. cit.*, October and November 1992.

1944   R.A.F. aircraft bombarded Lisieux on June 6–7. In all some 150 bombs and shells fell on the hill. Stray bombs exploded on the esplanade, and two actually hit the Basilica but did not blow up. On the evening of June 7 Mother Agnès, Sister Geneviève, and all the nuns left the Carmel and sought refuge in the crypt of the Basilica, making their living quarters in the Chapel of Our Lady of the Smile at the right of the main altar. They remained there for 80 days until August 27 when it became safe for them to return to the monastery.[136]

1954   Once all the restoration work was completed, Msgr. Martin, Archbishop of Rouen, consecrated the Basilica on July 11.

1957   Msgr. Germain died on November 6.

1958   On October 13, the coffins of Louis and Zélie Martin, Thérèse's parents, were transferred from the public cemetery nearby to an honored place just behind the Basilica.

1975   The blessing of the bell tower (campanile) took place on May 18.

1980   On June 2, Pope John Paul II, the first pope to visit Lisieux, celebrated Mass on the esplanade in front of the Basilica.

2000   The carillon was completed. It consists of 51 bells, each "christened" with a name engraved on it relating to St. Thérèse, such as: "Saint Thérèse of the Child Jesus and of the Holy face—Doctor of the Church" and on the great bell, "Thérèse, the patroness of all peoples. I ring to call all peoples to be united in love."

2008   Louis and Zélie Martin were beatified at the Basilica on October 19, Mission Sunday. The ceremony was presided over by José Cardinal Saraiva Martins, prefect emeritus of the Congregation for the Causes of Saints who represented Pope Benedict XVI.

l. The Cemetery
Thérèse's original burial place and the location of the Martin family plot

THROUGHOUT THE YEARS AT THE CARMEL FROM 1838 UNTIL 1877, THE deceased nuns were buried in the small cemetery in the rear garden area of the Carmel cloister. After that date, the authorities under the Third Republic (1870–1940) forbade burials on monastery premises. Only extraordinary people, however, were allowed to be interred there such as the founders of the Carmel, Father Sauvage (who built the chapel) in 1853, and a foundress of the community, Mother Geneviève in 1891. Otherwise, all the nuns who died were buried in the town cemetery. The nuns, therefore, had to buy a plot in the town cemetery which at the time was called Champs-Rémouleux.

Before Thérèse died, her Uncle Guérin bought for the Carmel additional burial space right next to his own family plot that is practically within the shadow of St. Thérèse's life-size white statue that now stands over her last grave before her remains were transferred to the Carmel. Thérèse's cousin Marie Guérin (Sister Marie of the Eucharist) and all the other nuns Thérèse lived with including Mother Gonzague lie within this space. The Guérin granite funeral monument

---

136 Ibid., June 1994.

surmounted by a cross has the inscription: "FAMILLE GUÉRIN FOURNET ET DR. LA NÉELE † O CRUX AVE!" Below are buried: Isidore Guérin (1841–1909), Céline Fournet Guérin (1847–1900), Jeanne Guérin La Néele ((1868–1938), and Dr. Francis La Néele (1858–1916).

Also located in this cemetery not too far from the Carmelite plot is the Martin family tomb. After Louis Martin died in 1894, his brother-in-law Isidore Guérin had the coffins of Zélie Martin and her four deceased young children removed from the cemetery in Alençon and placed in this burial site. Also interred are Grandmother Martin and Grandfather Guérin. The tomb, topped by a granite cross, has this inscription on it: *"FAMILLE MARTIN O CRUX AVE, SPES UNICA! La Race Des Justes Sera Bénie"* ("Martin Family. Hail Holy Cross, Our only hope! The race of the just will be blessed"). On October 13, 1958, the remains of Louis and Zélie were exhumed and buried in two separate graves next to each other in a prominent spot behind the Basilica with a beautiful statue of their saintly daughter a little behind and between the two graves. In March 1994, Pope John Paul II proclaimed the Martin spouses "Venerable."

Other contemporary people connected with St. Thérèse are buried in this cemetery including Canon Delatröette (1818–1895), the Ecclesiastical Superior of the Lisieux Carmel who opposed Thérèse's entrance; and Abbé Ducellier (1849–1916), Thérèse's first confessor who also testified at the Apostolic Process (1915–1917).

When Thérèse died, she became the very first nun to be interred in the new cemetery plot that her uncle purchased for the Carmel. Though he knew his niece was ill, he most likely did not think that perhaps she would be the first one who would be laid to rest there. It is ironic also that an attack of gout prevented him from attending Thérèse's funeral. Her burial took place on Monday, October 4, 1897—five days after her death. Thérèse's sister Léonie led the funeral procession followed by the Guérins, Dr. and Mrs La Néele, a few friends, and a group of priests, totaling perhaps nearly thirty. After the liturgical prayers, the coffin was lowered slowly into a grave over eleven feet deep (3.50 meters) in order to accommodate three coffins.[137] Mother Agnès had a large wooden cross placed at the head of the grave a few days later with Thérèse's birth and death years (1873–1897) imprinted at the top of the vertical piece of the cross. On the crossbar her name was listed (Soeur Thérèse de l'Enfant Jésus), and below on the upright piece her prophetic announcement was written: "I will spend my heaven in doing good upon earth."

Within thirteen years an amazing "storm of glory" arose as a result of the rapidly growing popularity and love for the saintly young nun. It has been estimated that some 80,000 people visited the grave every year and miracles occurred even before her beatification. This large amount of pilgrims would have been impossible if Thérèse had been buried in the small cloister cemetery.

---

137 *Sicut Parvuli*, September 1981, p. 69. This and the following three excerpts are English translations from *Les Annales de Sainte Thérèse de Lisieux*.

Msgr. Roger de Teil, the Vice-Postulator for the cause wrote an account in the newspaper *L'Univers* explaining the reason for this exhumation:

> The rapid spread of the name of Sr. Thérèse of the Child Jesus and the Holy Face, who died in the Carmel at Lisieux scarcely thirteen years ago, the good produced by the reading of her works, the confidence of the ever growing number of pilgrims at her tomb, all explain the desire to learn any new facts about her glorification being prepared by the Church.[138]

Exhumation of the coffin is the first step that has to be taken prior to beatification. The second is inspection followed by reburial. The examiners opened the coffin and found only the skeleton with no trace of flesh remaining. On September 6, 1910, at 3:00 in the afternoon, her coffin was exhumed in the presence of Bishop Lemonnier, other clergymen, two medical examiners (Doctors de Cornier and La Néele), and several hundred bystanders. The Carmelite habit had deteriorated to some degree and was covered over (or replaced) with a new robe and a scapular. A black veil was placed over the skull. All of this was done by Dr. La Néele, Thérèse's cousin by marriage, who gave an account of the proceedings to Léonie Martin:

> The crucifix of her rosary was in her fingers, I offered it to Monseigneur [the Bishop] who was very pleased with this memento....
>
> Everybody, 700–800 people who had been waiting for two hours, praying, filed past and held out a multitude of objects. I lifted up the three planks from the lid of the coffin and the six sacks of earth which had been in contact with it. Everything was carried to Carmel. The Bishop instructed that nothing of the robes or the planks should be given away without his permission, except to the family. I held the head of the little saint in my hands and I asked her to grant that my wife and I should love God as she had.... This exhumation caused an enormous stir in the town.[139]

Though she was not there, Mother Agnès had a few words to say about this first exhumation: "There was no miracle except that of lifting the coffin from a depth of 3.50 metres. There was nothing holding it together and it took a great deal of effort to lift it.... Nothing out of the ordinary happened at the cemetery, which is just what we really expected."[140]

When all was finished, the coffin without the cover was put into a new oak coffin lined with lead then placed into a cement vault. It was transferred to a new grave several feet away on top of which a life-sized statue of St. Thérèse now stands.

The cause continued even during the course of World War I (1914–1918). On August 9 and 10, 1917, the second exhumation took place—another requirement in order to identify officially Thérèse's remains—after which the coffin was returned to the same burial spot.

---

138 Ibid., May 1983, p. 51.
139 Ibid.
140 Ibid.

A third and final exhumation was required before beatification. Under the direction of Bishop Lemmonier and the civil authorities, Thérèse's coffin was dug up on March 26, 1923. The remains then had to be transferred with great solemnity to the Carmel, the new and permanent location suitable to the exalted position of the "beatus." An estimated fifty thousand pilgrims went to Lisieux to witness all the ceremonies. A woman from Angers arrived at the grave and was allowed to lay her half-paralyzed god-daughter on soil that was originally very close to the coffin. The girl suddenly began walking on her own from the gravesite. Furthermore, workmen and spectators reported that they smelled the scent of roses emanating from the tomb. A grand and extremely long cortège (more than two kilometers) followed the coffin covered with a cloth of gold atop a splendidly decorated carriage drawn by four horses. Over 200 priests accompanied it, as well as a multitude of officers, delegates, guards representing various organizations, and a detachment of American military men with drawn swords.[141] Several other miracles were reported during the triumphant procession that wended its way through the streets and around the Place Thiers to the Carmel. At this time no hymns were sung or bells rung in honor of Thérèse because at this stage in the cause such homage was not permitted by Rome.

Sixty-two years after Thérèse's mother died and only fourteen years after Thérèse's own death, Thérèse's oldest sister, Marie of the Sacred Heart, reminisced about their mother while gazing from the Carmel grounds at the huge basilica in the distance built in honor of the baby of their family:

> A short while ago as I was looking at the basilica I was thinking of Mamma. When she used to come to Lisieux my aunt [Mme. Guérin, Mme. Martin's sister-in-law] would always take her to the cemetery. It was a beautiful spot; and then when members of the family were buried there Mamma loved to go there. If someone had said to her at that time: "Do you see this beautiful little hill where we are now? Well, in fifty years a magnificent basilica will be built here in honor of your little Thérèse." Poor little Mother! She would have said: "You are off your head!" She who had had so many sorrows would not have believed it. That's for sure![142]

---

141 Verde, *The Story of the Canonization of S. Thérèse of Lisieux*, p. 92.
142 Gaucher, *The Spiritual Journey of St. Thérèse of Lisieux*, pp. 213–214.

4. Vicinity of Lisieux

a. **Pont-l'Évêque:** *Where Louis Martin fished and Thérèse picked flowers*
b. **Ouilly-le-Comte:** *Within walking distance where Thérèse sketched and picked flowers*
c. **Rocques and Hermival-les-Vaux:** *The Martins enjoyed walking through Rocques on the way to Hermival*
d. **Saint-Ouen-le-Pin:** *Thérèse enjoyed day trips here*
e. **Beuvilliers and Saint-Martin-de-la-Lieu:** *Where Thérèse picked flowers while her father fished*
f. **Saint-Hippolyte-des-Pres:** *Louis Martin had a permit to fish on private property here while Thérèse picked flowers*

a. Pont-l'Evêque
Where Louis Martin fished and Thérèse picked flowers

AMONG THE MANY TRIPS THÉRÈSE MADE—ALWAYS ACCOMPANIED BY FAMILY members—was one to the active city of Pont-l'Évêque situated a little more than half way on the main road from Lisieux to Deauville on the Normandy coast. It has always been at the crossroads of the main highways of communication in that section of Normandy. Now it is known as it was 700 years ago for its local cheese which bears its name. Because of its strategic location, it underwent a great deal of destruction during World War II from the Allied bombings of 1944.

On June 6, 1887, however, Pont l'Évêque possessed the picturesque qualities of an old peaceful Norman town. That day Louis Martin invited the curate of the cathedral of St. Pierre in Lisieux, his friend and confessor, the thirty-four-year old Abbé Lapelletier, to accompany him on a fishing trip. M. Martin's three daughters, Léonie (24), Céline (18), and Thérèse (14) also came along. They all enjoyed the day and the beauties of nature. The young ladies sketched the scenery and picked flowers. The men did some fishing but apparently the abbé (who was also Thérèse's confessor up to the time she entered religious life) spent more time sketching with the sisters than learning how to fish from their father. In fact, he did a drawing in Céline's sketchbook of the three girls in a field of tall grass and flowers. This rendering of Thérèse wearing a large hat and picking flowers appears to be the only extant drawing of the saint.

b. Ouilly-le-Comte
Within walking distance where Thérèse sketched and picked flowers

AROUND TWO MILES NORTH OF LISIEUX IS THE LITTLE VILLAGE OF OUILLY-le-Comte where the Martin family loved to stroll. On the way there they would walk past the Woods of Rocques (*Bois de Rocques*) on the right hand side and a little farther inland the village of Rocques where they would also on occasion stop and M. Martin would fish. Upon reaching Ouilly-le-Comte they turned left

Plate 18
Vicinity of Lisieux

A. The church in Hermival-le-Vaux

B. The church in Rocques

C. The church in Saint-Ouen-le-Pin

D. The church in Ouilly-le-Vicomte

E. Mme. Fournet's house in Saint-Ouen-le-Pin

F. The church in Saint Martin-de-la-Lieue

G. The manor in Saint-Hippolyte-des-Pres

and visited the quaint country church where they all would inevitably stop to pray. To enter the church one must walk on the cemetery pathway from the right side of the building. An antique wooden porch with a tall-pointed arch graces the main door to the church. Just at the end of the property a bridge crosses over the narrow rushing stream, La Paquine, a tiny tributary of the Toques River, in whose waters Louis enjoyed fishing. On one such day excursion, April 12, 1887, fourteen-year-old Thérèse brought along her sketchbook and made a drawing of the rustic church showing its old cemetery and the trees and fields in the surrounding area. Concerning these idyllic days with her family Thérèse wrote:

> They were beautiful days for me, those days when my "dear King" took me fishing with him. I was very fond of the countryside, flowers, birds, etc. Sometimes I would try to fish with my little line, but I preferred to go alone and sit down on the grass bedecked with flowers, and then my thoughts became very profound indeed! Without knowing what it was to meditate, my soul was absorbed in real prayer. I listened to distant sounds, the murmuring of the wind, etc.... Earth then seemed to be a place of exile and I could dream only of heaven.[143]

c. **Rocques and Hermival-les-Vaux**
   The Martins enjoyed walking through Rocques on the way to Hermival

THÉRÈSE USED TO WALK WITH HER FATHER FROM THEIR HOME IN LISIEUX (named Les Buissonnets) northeast around two miles to the little hamlet of Rocques where they would stop to pray at the small church dedicated to St. Ouen, a seventh-century bishop of Rouen. The parish cemetery surrounds the building on three sides. The two wooden porches in the front were built in the sixteenth century and the pointed towers and the sanctuary date back to the thirteenth century. The stained glass windows, the porches, and part of the transept were damaged during the liberation of the French from Nazi control in August of 1944, but restored beautifully in 1948–1949. Because of its ancient origin, interesting history, architecture, belfry with its noteworthy bells, and religious *objets d'art*, it was designated as an historical monument (*Monument Historique*) in 1946.[144]

In the wake of the phenomenal popularity of St. Thérèse even before she was canonized, a diocesan priest, Father Gabriel Martin (known as "Père Martin") founded the first community of nuns to follow Thérèse's simple and humble way of life. They were canonically recognized by the Church in 1933 as the Congregation of the Oblate Sisters of St. Thérèse of the Child Jesus (or simply Oblates of St. Thérèse). Their motherhouse, an elegant building, is nestled in a beautifully sylvan setting at Rocques. These nuns were from the start and still are the guardians and guides at the various Theresian landmarks in Lisieux and in Alençon.

From Rocques, father and daughter would proceed a little farther down to the tiny village of Hermival-les-Vaux where they inevitably would stop at the elegant church of St. Germain situated on the main road to this community.

---
143 *Story of a Soul*, chapter II, p. 37.
144 These facts were obtained from a pamphlet at the church titled *Eglise de Rocques près Lisieux*.

Behind it stands a very impressive chateau with its large estate where local rumor has it that Louis Martin might have stayed at one time and fished in the narrow La Pâquine that flows alongside the mansion. The religious Community of the Beatitudes now occupies this building and take care of the property.

As they followed the meandering La Pâquine abounding with fish, M. Martin did not hesitate to cast his line in anticipation of a good catch. Whenever he did succeed, he often gave it to the Carmel or to the Refuge in Lisieux where the Sisters of Our Lady of Mercy conducted a home for former prostitutes. A few months after Thérèse entered the Carmel in Lisieux, she wrote a letter to her father thanking him for the fish he donated to the sisters:

> If you only knew the pleasure your carp, your monster, gave us. The dinner was held back for half an hour. Marie of the Sacred Heart [her sister Marie] made the sauce, and it was delicious. It tasted like *"la cuisine du monde."* It was even better than the sumptuous *"cuisine d'Italie,"* and that is not saying little, for what banquets ... and what company! Do you remember, little Father?... [Referring to the food they had in Rome when they were there on a pilgrimage.] But it isn't always that that gives appetite, at least to me, for I haven't eaten so much since I've been in Carmel.[145]

d. Saint-Ouen-le-Pin
Thérèse enjoyed day trips here

NEAR THE SMALL VILLAGE OF SAINT-OUEN-LE-PIN, LESS THAN SIX MILES west of Lisieux, Mme. Elise Fournet, the mother of Thérèse's Aunt Guérin maintained her charming country home. The address now is No. 5 Dunroan and is privately owned. This brick building with two floors and six windows with shutters in the front is an excellent example of the quintessential Norman country house. Behind this structure, vast grounds with several farm buildings extend well into the distance. Thérèse made a detailed drawing of one of them which looks exactly like it does today. The surrounding landscape typifies the Auge country of Normandy with its meadows, woodlands, and apple orchards. During the summers of 1883, 1884, and 1885 when Thérèse was ten, eleven, and twelve, she came here for day outings and sometimes for extended periods of time. She, her sisters, and cousins went on long walks in the nearby country to see castles, abbey ruins, and enjoyed picnics and sketching in the fields. Their father took great delight in fishing for trout and other fish in the ponds on the property.

A little distance from here the Guerins and Martins attended Mass at the village church where a statue of the saint now stands in the churchyard.

In preparing information to assist Father Piat in writing the story of her family, Céline recorded these notes:

> This [the Fournet farm] was over five miles from the town. We used to go there and spend a whole day in September, gathering hazelnuts on the property of Mme. Fournet, Aunt Guérin's mother.... We went in a large wagon, and we

---

145 LT 58 from Thérèse to her father, dated July 31, 1888.

left with the Guérin family.... It was a modest little house on a farm which was rented to some farmers, but we enjoyed ourselves there very much.... At Saint-Ouen everything was rustic, even to the dishes, and this pleased us.

The adjacent property spread out into the surrounding countryside studded with castles that we could see in the distance. In one of these castles [formerly a Cistercian abbey], no doubt the most ostentatious, less than half a mile from the Fournet home, François Guizot [French statesman and historian] had died about ten years previously. It was there that Louis-Phillipe's former minister had written several of his works on French history. He rests in the parish cemetery.[146]

When Céline was a Carmelite, she wrote notes on Thérèse's various trips. In the very beginning she commented on the vacation they spent at Saint-Ouen-le-Pin in July and August of 1884:

Thérèse stayed there for several days with our aunt and cousins Jeanne and Marie Guérin. She was there in order to get a change of air during a spell of whooping cough. Thérèse was very much interested in the ponds and the little brook on the farm, and, beyond the meadows, a tiny little woods, perhaps a section of a former park, called "*le Theil*." This wood was often the goal of our walks. We also went, but not very frequently, into the village by way of a pretty little road which was well shaded.[147]

Through frequent letters, Mme. Guérin informed her husband back home in Lisieux of the health and the various activities at her mother's home of the busy children under her watchful eye:

We are very happy here. Thérèse's face is always radiant with joy. She is enjoying herself very much at sketching [particularly Mme. Fournet's main farm building]; she and Marie have undertaken to do the house on the farm.... Céline and Jeanne are doing another landscape. They are sketching the buildings on the farm taken from different angles. We're very fortunate for having discovered this delightful distraction, for the heat is such that we can't dream of going very far. Yesterday morning, we went to Mass at seven. It was charming. We were witnesses, it seemed, of nature's awakening. In the afternoon, we went with Ernest [Maudelonde, the twenty-year-old nephew of Aunt Guérin] to Mourerie, and we were present, in the evening, at the milking of the cows. We go there every evening and each has a glass of very warm milk. I think this is a good remedy for the whooping cough, although I still can't see any great change in our patients. However, I think Thérèse is coughing less frequently. She is throwing up *very, very little*, and last night she did so only twice, one spell being very, very bad; she slept very well. Her appetite is always good.... This morning, Mme. Grip gave us a whole dissertation on her honeybees. She even gave our children some wax cells where the bees place the honey. This piece had fallen to the ground and she picked it up. The children were in admiration over the work of the bees.[148]

---

146 Introductory note on pp. 207–208 to the letters about Saint-Ouen-le-Pin in Vol I of *General Correspondence*.
147 Sister Geneviève, "Notes on Thérèse's Trips," p. 1, as cited on p. 207 in *General Correspondence*, Vol. I.
148 Extract from a letter Mme. Guérin wrote to her husband on August 7, 1884.

And again a year later, Aunt Guérin wrote about the fun the girls were having at her mother's farm:

> I have just allowed all four of them [her daughters Jeanne and Marie and her nieces Thérèse and Céline] to make a tour of the property by way of the field, the meadow, and the Theil woods; they left filled with delight. Mme. Papinau's[149] lessons are falling a little behind; however, we should take advantage of the country. They've neglected their homework and lessons for only a few days. Besides, Marie and Thérèse are enjoying themselves very much. Thérèse is delightfully happy. Mamma was telling me yesterday that she had never seen Thérèse so gay, with her face so frankly happy. Yesterday, she and Marie came home all decked out in little bouquets. Marie had cornflowers, Thérèse had forget-me-nots. All was perfectly arranged. They were wearing their Breton aprons, with well-made bouquets at each of the corners, on their heads, at the end of their pigtails, and even on their shoes. One was Rosette, the other Bluette....[150]

e. **Beauvilliers and Saint-Martin-de-la-Lieue**
Where Thérèse picked flowers while her father fished

ON THE MAIN ROAD LEADING SOUTH FROM LISIEUX TO ALENÇON ONE PASSES three picturesque villages the Martin family often visited: Beauvilliers (over a mile from Lisieux), followed by Saint-Hippolyte-des-Prés (around two miles), and finally Saint-Martin-de-la-Lieue, a bit farther south. The Orbiquet stream flows by Beauvilliers where Louis loved to fish. At one time the Guerins owned property in Beauvilliers.[151] Of course, they would never hesitate to stop and pray at the village church. Little would they have imagined that in just over half a century later a massive basilica would be visible in the distance from this spot that would be dedicated to the youngest one of this family.

Not far south of this place is Saint-Martin-de-la-Lieue. The Martins certainly must have visited the typical Norman church there, seemingly still in use, just off the main road. A low brick wall mostly stucco covered surrounds the church with a wrought iron gate on the right side. This entrance to the churchyard and cemetery leads immediately to some rather large family tombstones.

In one of the earliest and perhaps the best account of the family life of St. Thérèse, Stephanie-Joseph Piat, O.F.M., records that "At Saint-Martin-de-la-Lieue where the kindly owner of the country estate had given him [Louis Martin] a permit which protected him from the thunders of the keeper, he teased the pike."[152]

---

149 Apparently both girls, not only Thérèse, were tutored by Mme. Papinau.
150 Extract from a letter Mme. Guérin wrote to her husband on July 29, 1885.
151 See footnote 8 on p. 279 in *Her Last Conversations*.
152 Piat, *The Story of a Family*, p. 283.

f. Saint-Hippolyte-des-Pres
Louis Martin had a permit to fish on private property here while Thérèse picked flowers

GOING SOUTH AT SAINT-HIPPOLYTE-DES-PRÉS ONE CAN SEE AT THE RIGHT side of the main road in the near distance the attractive sixteenth-century manor of Saint Hippolytus with its unusually shaped dovecote near it. These buildings are separated from the road by a large field and the narrow River Touques that originates at Deauville on the coast and continues to flow for many more miles south beyond Saint-Hippolytus. Here Louis Martin often fished while Thérèse gathered wild flowers in the fields nearby and maybe even sketched.

Today this mansion and its vast property have been converted into a museum called *Domaine de Saint Hippolyte*. It is open to the public from May through September and provides guided tours, demonstrations, and exhibits showing the traditional methods of producing cider, cheese, milk, and meat. It appears that basically few drastic changes have been made to it since the time of Thérèse. At the northern end of the property one can see in the distance the Basilica of St. Thérèse.

5. Elsewhere

a. **Bayeux:** *Where Thérèse sought the bishop's permission to become a Carmelite*
b. **Caen:** *Where Thérese's father was hospitalized and Léonie died a nun*
c. **Deauville and Trouville:** *Thérèse enjoyed vacationing at these seaside resort towns with her relatives, the Guérins*
d. **La Musse:** *Vacation home of the Guérins near Evreux where Louis Martin died*
e. **Honfleur and Le Havre:** *Thérèse visited the churches in Honfleur and saw the 1887 International Maritime Exposition in Le Havre*
f. **Le Mans:** *Thérèse's older sisters attended the convent school here where their nun aunt taught*

a. Bayeux
Where Thérèse sought the bishop's permission to become a Carmelite

BAYEUX, ABOUT FORTY-FOUR MILES FROM LISIEUX, IS ONE OF THE MOST historically significant locations in Normandy. At one time or another it was occupied by Romans, Bretons, Saxons, Vikings, and Germans. It came to be the homeland of the Dukes of Normandy with William the Conqueror (1027/1028–1087) as its most prominent citizen. His conquest of England in 1066 is depicted on a huge piece of embroidery known as the Bayeux Tapestry (called in French *La Tapisserie de la Reine Mathilde*—The Tapestry of Queen Matilda)[153] that draws multitudes of tourists to its permanent display in the William the Conqueror Center (*Centre Guillaume-le-Conquerant*), a former 18th century seminary. Not far away stands the Cathedral of Notre Dame on the Rue du Bienvenu, a splendid example of Norman Gothic architecture, dedicated to Our Lady in 1077 in the presence of William the Conqueror. Throughout the ages, Bayeux weathered many disasters but, remarkably, survived undamaged during the mammoth D-Day invasion of June 6, 1944, that took place on the shoreline just a few miles away. The next day Bayeux became the first main French town liberated from the Nazis.

For many years Thérèse Martin dreamed of becoming a Carmelite in the Lisieux Monastery like her two older sisters. The superior of the monastery, Canon Delatroëtte, flatly refused to allow her, then a child of fourteen, to enter the Order; he also thought fifteen too young. Eventually[154] he conceded: "I am only the delegate of Monseigneur [Bishop Hugonin]. If he allows you to enter, I shall have no more to say."[155] Before that, M. Martin offered to take Thérèse to the Bishop in Bayeux to plead her case. Thérèse wrote with much detail and length the scenario of this disappointing one-day trip:

---

[153] According to a number of contemporary scholars, Queen Matilda, William the Conqueror's wife, did not design or sew the tapestry.
[154] Six months later she entered Carmel (April 9, 1888).
[155] Laveille, *op. cit.*, p. 121.

A. In Normandy 601

Plate 19

Elsewhere in France

A. Our Lady of Victories, Trouville

B. *La Pluie* de Rose, Trouville

C. *Notre Dame*, cathedral in Bayeux

D. *Chalet des Roses*, Deauville

E. *La Musse* (near Evreux)

F. Orphanage of St. Vincent de Paul, Caen

G. *Notre-Dame de Grace*, near Honfleur

H. Thérèse first saw the "sea" at Trouville

I. Villa *Marie-Rose* (center), Trouville

J. Visitation school in Le Mans

October 31 [1887] was the day set for the [train] trip to Bayeux. I left alone with Papa, my heart filled with hope, but also rather scared at the thought of meeting the Bishop. For the first time in my life, I was to make a visit unaccompanied by my sisters and this visit was to a *Bishop!*... It *was raining* in torrents when we arrived at Bayeux. Papa, unwilling to have his little Queen enter the Bishop's house with her *beautiful dress* soaking wet, made her get on a bus and brought her to the cathedral. There my miseries began. The Bishop and all the clergy were attending an important funeral. The cathedral was filled with ladies in mourning and, as a consequence, I was stared at by everybody, dressed as I was in a bright frock and white hat. I would have much preferred to go out of the church, but this was out of the question because of the rain. To humiliate me more, God permitted that Papa in his fatherly simplicity made me take a front seat in the cathedral. Not wishing to give him any trouble, I executed this with great grace and thus procured this distraction for the good inhabitants of Bayeux, whom I would have preferred never to have known.

Finally, I was able to breathe freely in a small chapel behind the main altar and stayed there a long time praying fervently and waiting for the rain to stop and allow us to leave. When we were leaving, Papa had me admire the beauty of the edifice which appeared much larger when empty.... We went directly to Father Révérony's [the Bishop's Vicar-General] who was aware of our arrival as he himself had set the date of the trip, but he was absent; we had to wander through the streets which appeared *very sad* to me. Finally we returned close to the Bishop's residence, and Papa brought me into a magnificent hotel where I did not do the honors to the excellent cooking....

Father Révérony was very friendly, but I believe the reason for our trip took him by surprise. After looking at me with a smile and asking me a few simple questions, he said: "I am going to introduce you to the Bishop; will you kindly follow me?" Seeing the tears in my eyes, he added: "Ah! I see diamonds; you mustn't show them to the Bishop!" He had us traverse several huge rooms in which portraits of bishops were hanging on the walls. When I saw myself in these large rooms, I felt like a poor little ant, and I asked myself what I would dare say to the Bishop.

The Bishop was walking on the balcony with two priests. I saw Father Révérony say a few words to him and return with him to where we were waiting in his study. There, three enormous armchairs were set before the fireplace in which a bright fire was crackling away.... [All but Father Révérony sat down] I had hoped that Papa would speak; however, he told me to explain the object of our visit to the Bishop. I did so as *eloquently* as possible and his Excellency, accustomed to *eloquence* did not appear touched by my reasons....

The Bishop asked me if it had been a long time since I desired to enter Carmel. "Oh! yes, Bishop, a very long time." "Come, now," said Father Révérony with a smile, "you can't say it is fifteen *years* since you've had the desire." Smiling, I said: "That's true, but there aren't too many years to subtract because I wanted to be a religious since the dawn of my reason, and I wanted Carmel as soon as I knew about it. I find all the aspirations of my soul are fulfilled in this Order...."

The Bishop, believing he'd please Papa; tried to have me stay with him a few more years, and he was very much *surprised* and *edified* at seeing him take my part, interceding for me to obtain permission to fly away at fifteen. And still everything was futile. The Bishop said an interview with the *Superior of Carmel* [Canon Delatroëtte] was indispensable before making his decision. I couldn't possibly have heard anything that would cause me more pain than this because I was aware of his formal opposition. Without taking into account Father Révérony's advice, I did more than *show my diamonds* to the Bishop. I *gave* him some!

He was very much touched by this and putting his arm around my neck, he placed my head on his shoulder and caressed me as no one, it appears, was ever caressed by him before. He told me all was not lost, that he was very happy I was making the trip to Rome to strengthen my vocation, that instead of crying I should rejoice. He added that the following week, before going to Lisieux, he'd speak about me to the pastor of St. James [Canon Delatroëtte] and I would receive an answer from him in Italy [which did not happen]. I understood it was useless to make further entreaties, and besides I had nothing to say having exhausted all the resources of my *eloquence*.

The Bishop brought us out as far as the garden. Papa *amused him very much* by telling him that in order to appear older I had put up my hair. (This wasn't lost on the Bishop, for he never spoke about "his little daughter" without telling the story of the hair.) ...

When in the street again my tears began to flow, not so much because of my sorrow but because of my little Father who had made a useless trip.... It seemed my future was ruined forever....

As soon as we arrived at Lisieux, I went looking for consolation at Carmel....[156]

b. Caen
Where Thérèse's father was hospitalized and Léonie died a nun

THÉRÈSE, WHILE TRAVELING BY TRAIN TO BAYEUX TO SEEK THE BISHOP'S permission to become a Carmelite, passed through Caen, the capital city of Lower Normandy (*Basse-Normandie*), over thirty miles from Lisieux. Her cousin Jeanne and her husband Dr. La Néele resided in Caen, though a few years later when Thérèse was already in the convent; therefore, communication with her Caen relations was carried on by mail only.

This large industrial port city at the confluence of two rivers—the Orne and the Orlon—is less than ten miles from the English Channel to which it is connected by a canal built in the middle of the 19th century. William the Conqueror declared Caen his favorite of all cities and with his wife Matilda of Flanders founded abbeys and hospitals there. Miraculously, the Abbey for Women (*Abbaye aux Dames*) and the Abbey for Men (*Abbaye aux Hommes*) where William and his wife are buried, were spared the destruction that three-quarters of the city suffered during the bombings of the 1944 Invasion and Battle of Normandy in World War II.

Thérèse's first association with Caen was through her sister Léonie, ten years her senior, who tried religious life but failed there on three different occasions (1886, 1887, 1893). Finally, on January 29, 1899, at the age of thirty-six (two years after her saintly sister's death), she was admitted and remained for forty-two

---

[156] *Story of a Soul*, chapter V, pp. 114–118.

years in the Order of the Visitation (also called Nuns of the Visitation of Mary, Visitandines, or simply, Visitation Nuns). The convent on the rue de l'Abbatiale is situated directly in the town's center close to the Church of Saint-Étienne—the church of the Abbaye aux Hommes. Léonie (Sister Françoise-Thérèse) died in 1941 and was buried in a special crypt with only one other nun, the foundress of the monastery.

In 1890, Thérèse's cousin Jeanne Guérin—school companion and playmate, five years older than Thérèse—married Dr. Francis La Néele in Caen where the couple spent most of their married lives. His office was at 26 Rue de l'Oratoire. He also owned a pharmacy that he eventually had to give up in 1891 because of recent legal restrictions on maintaining two professions. His office in downtown Caen was completely demolished in the World War II bombings of 1944. The folks in Lisieux and the married ones in Caen maintained a constant flow of correspondence throughout the years. The doctor was summoned a number of times to the Lisieux Carmel to examine Thérèse during her last illness and was later involved with the medical aspects of the beatification process.

Mme. Guérin, Jeanne's mother, who assumed the role of mother for the Martin sisters after their own mother died, often visited her daughter in Caen. At one time she recuperated from a temporary sickness at the home of her daughter. Thérèse wrote from Carmel to her and her other cousin Marie: "when I am in spirit near my dear little sister [cousin Marie] at Caen, immediately the good Saint Anne returns to my memory, and I entrust the one whom I love to her. I see with pleasure, dear little Marie, the air of the city of Caen is causing in you no melancholy...." [157]

The most important and poignant connection Thérèse had with Caen involved her father's three-year residence from February 12, 1889 to May 10, 1892, as a mental patient in Bon Sauveur, a hospital on Rue Caponiere not far from the Visitation Convent. It was and still is a large establishment with a medical dispensary, a school for the deaf and dumb, and a residence for mental patients. The Martin family was very pleased with the excellent care from the nuns, especially Mother (Mère) Costard, in charge of the section where Louis stayed. Great filial devotion and desire to be near their physically and mentally afflicted father, led Céline and Léonie to board for three months at the nearby Orphanage of Saint Vincent de Paul at 59–61 rue de Bayeux conducted by the Sisters of Charity who still occupy the building. When visitations were restricted to only one day a week, they returned to Lisieux and traveled faithfully by train to Caen for their weekly call. Less than a year after Thérèse's entrance into Carmel, her father was hospitalized causing great anxiety and mortification for her and indeed her entire family:

> O dear Mother [Thérèse's sister Pauline]! how sweet our great trial was since from our hearts came only sighs of love and gratitude! We were no longer walking in the way of perfection, we were flying, all five of us. The two poor

---

157 LT 136, dated October 16, 1892.

little exiles of Caen [Céline and Léonie], while still in the world, were no longer of it. Ah! what marvels the trial worked in my dear Céline's soul! All the letters she wrote at this epoch are filled with resignation and love. And who could express the visits we had together? Ah! far from separating us, Carmel's grilles united our souls more strongly; we had the same thoughts, the same desires, the same *love for Jesus* and *for souls*.[158]

Bon Sauveur, now known as the *Centre Hospitalier Spécialisé de Caen* (or just *Hôpital Psychiatrique*), was partially destroyed in the bombings of 1944 but shortly after the war it was restored and is still in use. The chapel and crypt were also rebuilt after the war and can be visited today.

c. **Deauville and Trouville**
Thérèse enjoyed vacationing at these seaside resort towns with her relatives, the Guérins

> *Never will I forget the impression the sea made upon me.*[159] — Thérèse

BEFORE THE 1800S GENTEEL SOCIETY IN FRANCE AND ELSEWHERE AVOIDED the seaside and its concomitant exposure to the sun. The therapeutic value of sea water began to be realized early in the nineteenth century and doctors soon recommended it as an aid to health. People, therefore, flocked to the seaside, mountains, and open spaces in an attempt to absorb the natural benefits of the environment. The Romantic movement in art, music, and literature, which seems to have run its course by the mid-nineteenth century, also discovered nature and found great inspiration in it. Significant too was the industrialization of large urban areas which with its accompanying problems compelled people from northern France particularly to seek temporary relief by the shore, notably the Channel Coast. Parisians could easily reach this area by means of a rapidly developing railway system.

The most famous seaside resorts along the Normandy coast in Thérèse's day as well as now are Deauville and Trouville, less than twenty miles from Lisieux. They stand like guards on opposite sides of the mouth of the river Touques that empties into the English Channel within sight of distant Le Havre. Deauville on the left (west) bank of the river is the more exclusive resort noted for its brilliant international clientele lured there by the annual horse race (Deauville Grand Prix), regattas, yachting, casino, galas, and luxury hotels. The popular boardwalk (*Promenade des Planches*) stretching along its nearly two-mile long beach also attracts socialites and tourists. On the other hand, Trouville on the right (east) bank, the older and quieter town, is more plebeian with its middle-class houses, markets, fishermen, and workers not concerned with tourism. Nonetheless, it does interest multitudes including artists fascinated by its own wonderful beach, very long boardwalk, picturesque quays and streets, casino, yacht basin, and aquarium. In Thérèse's time this area had been fashionable for only a few decades and was certainly not as prominent as it is today.

---

158 *Story of a Soul*, chapter VII, p. 157.
159 *Ibid.*, chapter II, p. 48.

The following chart provides data about the very first time Thérèse went to the seashore and the four times she stayed more than a day at villas rented by the Guérins on the coast of Normandy called the Côte Fleurie:

SIGNIFICANT TRIPS THÉRÈSE MADE TO THE CÔTE FLEURIE				
DATE	DAYS	VILLA	TOWN	HER AGE
1. Aug. 8, 1878	1	None	Trouville	5
2. May 3–10, 1885	8	Chalet des Roses at 17 quai de la Toques. Once called Chalet Colombe. Also called Chalet Bellevue.	Deauville	12
3. Sept. 21–30, 1885	10	Villa Maria-Rose (or Villa Rose) at rue Charlemagne. Now 25 rue Victor-Hugo.	Trouville	12
4. July 1–(?), 1886	3 or 4	Chalet des Lilas at 29 rue de la Cavée. Now called La Pluie de Roses.	Trouville	13
5. June 20–26, 1887	7	Chalet des Lilas	Trouville	14

Soon after the untimely death of Thérèse's mother in Alençon, the family moved to Lisieux in November 1878 to be near Isidore Guérin, Mme. Martin's brother, and his family. The Guérins began renting villas at the Normandy beaches in 1878 and continued doing so intermittently for years after. They shared the pleasures of seaside living with M. Martin and his five motherless daughters for the day, usually Sunday, and for longer periods of time. Thérèse was five in 1878 when she first went to Trouville with her father for a day on Thursday, August 8, in order to bring her sister Marie home. (Young ladies never traveled alone in those days.) Marie was staying with her cousins who had rented the Maison Leroux on the Grand-Rue (now named the Rue Georges Clemenceau). Thérèse enjoyed herself immensely as she accompanied the others fishing, boating, and walking on the beach. M. Guérin, back home at work in his pharmacy, received news of what the girls were doing during the week through letters his wife regularly wrote to him:

> [I] was very happy because of all this loving correspondence, and also to see good little Thérèse's beaming face at the sight of the great sea. M. Martin hardly enjoyed the spectacle of the sea, for he was busy the whole time fishing in the river [Toques]. He caught an eel for us as big as my little finger and two crabs (one of which escaped last night in the kitchen, and we haven't been able to find it this morning). Marie was very quick to tell him he used to do better than that at Lisieux.[160]

This first trip to Trouville proved a memorable one for little Thérèse who wrote of it in her autobiography years later:

> I was six or seven years old [actually five years and eight months old] when Papa brought us to Trouville. Never will I forget the impression the sea made upon me; I couldn't take my eyes off it since its majesty, the roaring of its waves,

---
160 August 9, 1878.

everything spoke to my soul of God's grandeur and power. I recall during the walk on the seashore a man and a woman were looking at me as I ran ahead of Papa. They came and asked him if I were his little daughter and said I was a very pretty little girl. Papa said "Yes," but I noticed the sign he made to them not to pay me any compliments. It was the first time I'd heard it said I was pretty and this pleased me as I didn't think I was.... I gave no great importance to the words or admiring glances of this woman....

In the evening at that moment when the sun seems to bathe itself in the immensity of the waves, leaving a *luminous trail* behind, I went and sat down on a huge rock with *Pauline*. [Not then but sometime between 1879 and 1881.] Then I recalled the touching story of the "Golden Trail" [from *La Tirelire aux histoires* by Madame Louise Belloc]. I contemplated this luminous trail for a long time. It was to me the image of God's grace shedding its light across the path the little white-sailed vessel had to travel. And near Pauline, I made the resolution never to wander far away from the glance of Jesus in order to travel peacefully towards the eternal shore.[161]

After this enjoyable experience at the seaside, Thérèse returned with her father and sisters for other one-day outings.[162] Deauville and Trouville constitute part of the shoreline known as the Côte Fleurie (Flower Coast) and were easily and quickly accessible by a short train trip of about eighteen miles from Lisieux.

Not until seven years later did the Guérins again rent a villa at the beach for a month from April 28 to June 5, 1885; and of course they invited the Martins. Thérèse stayed with them from the third of May to the tenth at the Chalet des Roses (formerly called the Maison [or Chalet] Colombe, owned by Isidore Guérin's friend Alphonse Colombe (1835–1889)[163] at 17 quai de la Touques in Deauville. Years later the name changed to the Chalet Bellevue (1972). Over the entrance on the left side of the building a plaque recalls Thérèse's stay there: "Saint Thérèse of the Child Jesus stayed at this villa during the month of May 1885."[164] She and the other girls sketched in the chalet's garden (*Jardin Colombe*) over which in time a small café-bar was built called "*au petit Navire*."[165]

As usual Mme. Guérin took charge of the girls, now much older: her daughters—Jeanne (seventeen) and Marie (fifteen), her niece Thérèse (twelve and a half), and maid Marcelline (almost nineteen). Céline did not spend this vacation with them. Mme. Guérin wrote to her husband welcoming Thérèse to stay with her on May 2, 1885:

> Little Thérèse will be welcome here if you judge it good and if her father allows it. So we expect you on Sunday, the children are counting on it. Now with regard to sleeping, I think I should keep her with me. I would not want to have her stay on the second floor. In any case, you know there is room enough and

---

161 *Story of a Soul*, chapter II, pp. 48–49.
162 Exact number of times is difficult to determine.
163 LC 39, note 1, p. 217 to the letter dated May 1, 1885, written by Marie Guérin to Thérèse.
164 Today a wooden sign a few feet from the commemorative plaque has these words engraved on it: "VILLA BELLEVUE • ANCIENT CHALET COLOMBE."
165 In 2003 the name of the place was "*Au bout d'un bar*."

that we'll be very happy to have one more little girl. However, follow whatever your heart tells you.... We are expecting you, then, tomorrow with Thérèse at 9:15 in the morning. You know, too if one of the older ones wants to come with her, being acquainted with our accommodations, you know this is possible. Whatever you do will be all right....

The children thoroughly enjoyed the days there at the seaside. They watched the fishing boats in the busy harbor, took the very short ferry boat ride across the narrow harbor to Trouville,[166] collected shells on the sandy beach, walked the boardwalk, fished, and sketched different scenes including the garden in their chalet which Thérèse herself did. Mme. Guérin, nonetheless, assured Thérèse's sister Marie back home that all was not just fun and play:

> [Don't] get the idea we are staying here without any work to do. We're doing some needlework, cooking, and today we are doing the wash. What work for ladies! Our little Thérèse slept perfectly in the beautiful big bedroom, and this morning she looks very good. I told her she had to eat with all her might and that from today I'll not relent in this matter. She seems to be very happy here and she isn't lonesome. The weather is not very good this morning, but yesterday we were able to go to the beach. All our little girls were at the water's edge, waiting for the waves to come in. Thérèse was armed with a spade, and all of them were very happy. We were at High Mass [most likely at Notre-Dame-des-Victoires] this morning at Trouville, and in the afternoon we attended Vespers at [the church of] Bon Secours.[167] [Abbé Fournier was the pastor there.]

The Martins and Guérins visited these two churches in Trouville almost every day. The main road in Trouville, now called the Boulevard Fernand Moureaux, follows the Toques. Perpendicular to this, the short uphill Rue Notre Dame runs directly into the church of Notre-Dame-des-Victories (Our Lady of Victories). Here Thérèse confessed her scruples about feeling pleasure in having pretty blue ribbons in her hair. Marie Guérin mentions this church in a letter she wrote to Thérèse stating that "we were at Notre-Dame-des-Victoires this morning for Mass; the flight of steps is very steep, so steep that I fell. Everybody is falling this week."[168] The other church is Notre-Dame-de-Bon-Secours (Our Lady of Good Help) farther north on the rue Victor Hugo. In this section of the town, many narrow streets with cafes, antique shops, and other stores have enticed tourists even to the present.

Marcelline Husé, the Guérins' maid, gave this testimony at the Diocesan Inquiry about Thérèse's love of the Blessed Mother and of the Mass:

> I have one very vivid memory of her devotion to the Blessed Virgin. She was ten, or maybe twelve, and we were spending May by the seaside, at Trouville. Where we were staying was rather far from the church of Our Lady of Victories, but we usually went there every evening for the May devotions. If any of us pleaded weariness after a long day, or the distance as an excuse for our reluctance, Thérèse would insist that this was just not good enough. Her greatest

---

166 Today a short bridge connects Trouville to Deauville.
167 May 4, 1885.
168 May 1, 1885.

joy was to go to Mass every morning at this church of our Lady, and neither cold nor bad weather could put her off.[169]

Thérèse comments about the May 1885 vacation in her autobiography: "Aunt invited us to come every year, each in our turn, to her place at Trouville, and I should have loved going there, but with Marie [Guérin]! When I didn't have her with me, I was very much bored...."[170] The following experience concerning Marie surprised Thérèse but she gained a lesson from it. Marie often complained of a headache and inevitably received great consolation from her mother. Thérèse also suffered from headaches almost daily and one time craved the same kind of attention that Marie always received, so she copied her style sighing that she had a headache and then she began to cry. No similar sympathy, however, was shown:

> Getting nowhere for all my trouble, I made the resolution never to imitate others again, and I understood the fable about *"The donkey and the pet dog"* [from La Fontaine's *Fables*]. *I was the donkey* that saw the caresses the *little dog* was getting; he came and placed his clumsy hoof on the table to get his share of kisses. Although I didn't get the blows of the cudgel like the poor animal, I did get what I deserved and this cured me for life of any desire to attract attention. The one effort I had made was far too costly![171]

Thérèse's cousin Jeanne mentions in a letter to her father a trivial but interesting little occurrence at the waterfront: "Yesterday, we followed your advice, and we were at the Deauville pier. We saw several ships leaving, but Mamma and Thérèse got a little dizzy from the noise and motion of the sea."[172]

That same year from September 21 to 30, 1885, the Guérins again stayed at the seaside, this time at the Villa Marie-Rose on rue Charlemagne (now 25 rue Victor Hugo) in Trouville. This building with four floors is not as attractive as the Maison Colombe. Today a structure protrudes out from it to the street, obscuring half of the original façade. Thérèse and Céline vacationed there from the 20th to about the 30th:

> [It] was the year of Papa's trip to Constantinople [August 22 through October 1885]. To give us a little distraction (we were sad when we knew Papa was so far away), Marie sent us, Celine and me, to the seashore for two weeks. I enjoyed myself very much because I was with my Celine. Aunt provided us with all the amusements possible: donkey-rides, fishing for eels, etc. I was still very much a child in spite of my twelve and a half years, and I remember the joy I had putting on some pretty sky-blue ribbons Aunt had given me for my hair; I also recall having confessed at Trouville [Notre-Dame-des-Victories] even this childish pleasure which seemed to be a sin to me.[173]

---

169 Deposition given on December 14, 1910, during Session 47. This translated excerpt is from O'Mahony's *Thérèse of Lisieux By Those Who Knew Her*.
170 *Story of a Soul*, chapter IV, pp. 88–89.
171 Ibid., pp. 89–90.
172 May 5, 1885.
173 *Story of a Soul*, chapter IV, p. 89.

Jeanne Guérin also informs us of what they did during this off-season time in the resort town: "At the moment, Trouville isn't cheerful; all the visitors have left and the beach is deserted. We spent two hours there yesterday in the shelter of a cabin, where we weren't too badly off. Céline, Marie, and Thérèse took their shoes off to play a little at the seashore. It wasn't cold, and today I think the weather will be good...."[174]

The following year, 1886, the Guérins once again vacationed at Trouville, this time during the height of the season from June 15 to July 31 at the Chalet des Lilas (now called "Pluie de Roses"), 29 rue de la Cavée, located several blocks from the church of Notre-Dame-des-Victoires. Today, a plaque high up above the front door and two windows has this inscription in French: "This villa was occupied by the Blessed THÉRÈSE OF THE INFANT JESUS as she tells us in her biography during the seasons of 1886–1887." One of Marie Guérin's letters describes the house and indicates an activity Thérèse enjoyed:

> If my Thérèse were here, she'd enjoy herself watching the children, for we are surrounded on the beach only by babies and they amuse us very much. We have cheerful lodgings, and our large room looks out upon a little garden where Jeanne and I have good games of shuttlecock. My bedroom is charming, and I like it very much. The view from it is delightful; I can see the ocean, especially from the Deauville side, shrimp boats with blue and red sails, boats fishing for eels, and a steamboat arriving.[175]

Thérèse admits what happened after her brief visit with them at the end of July 1886:

> The following year, that of my dear Marie's departure for Carmel, Aunt invited me again but this time all alone, and I was so much out of my element that after two or three days I got sick and they had to bring me back to Lisieux [the Martin sisters never traveled unescorted]. My sickness, which they feared was serious, was only an attack of nostalgia for Les Buissonnets, for hardly had I put my foot in the house when my health returned. And it was from a child such as this that God was taking away the only support which attached me to life![176]

In 1887, the Guérins rented the Chalet des Lilas in Trouville from June 20 to July 31, and invited Thérèse to spend the first week there with them from the 20th of June to the 26th. Céline remained at home but Jeanne Guérin let her know what they were doing there:

> The tall Thérèse[177] is very well and is enjoying herself, too, I believe. Yesterday, we gathered aspens in the park. Just picture to yourself a field with tall daisies and aspens; never had we seen anything like it, and we gathered two large bouquets of them. We went to the rocks to get some sea water, and

---

174 Letter from Marie Guérin to her father dated September 29, 1885.
175 Letter dated June 23, 1886, from Marie Guérin to Thérèse.
176 *Story of a Soul*, chapter IV, p. 90.
177 Sometimes they called her "the tall English lady" because her height was 5'3" (162 cm) which they thought was tall.

Thérèse removed her shoes for a moment. We go to the seashore every day, twice a day.[178]

The next day after returning home, Thérèse declined an invitation to stay again with the Guérins in Trouville because during that time her father would be away from Lisieux:

> It seems strange to me to be again at Les Buissonnets. This morning, I was surprised to see myself at Céline's side. We spoke to Papa about the cordial offer that good Aunt made to us, but it is absolutely impossible because Papa leaves on Wednesday and he will remain a very short time at Alençon on this occasion.[179]

This June vacation with her cousins in Trouville marked the final pleasure trip Thérèse took to the beaches in Normandy. She did travel, however, one day to Bayeux with her father on October 31, 1887, seeking the bishop's permission to become a Carmelite. Then five days later (November 4) she left on a twenty-nine day grand pilgrimage to Rome. Four months after her return she entered the Lisieux Carmel, which she never left during the nearly ten years she lived there until her death in 1897.

d. La Musse
Vacation home of the Guérins near Evreux

This magnificent château named La Musse played a significant part in the life of the Guérin family and their cherished relations the Martins. Thérèse, however, never visited this place that witnessed many happy vacations for her father, sisters, cousins, uncle and aunt. Sadly M. Martin succumbed there in 1894.

The history of the vast property on which the château de La Musse is located goes back to the 12th century and beyond. The word *Musse* is a hunting term meaning a narrow thicket or hedge where rabbits and other game such as geese and ducks find shelter. Nearby is the village of Saint-Sebastien de Morsent which is closely associated with the history of the area. Auguste David (1813–1888) a lawyer from Evreux had inherited the property and at his death bequeathed it to his second cousins Céline (Fournet) Guérin and her sister Marie (Fournet) Maudelonde. The château, constructed in the style of Louis XIII, is located on a plateau overlooking the vast grounds of the estate with a grand view of the Iton valley below. Céline in the biography she wrote of her father many years later described it briefly: "He [Uncle Guérin] had just inherited [through his wife] along with my aunt's sister, this beautiful property situated about five miles from Evreux, which included, besides the castle on the heights, some eighty [actually over 100] acres of woodlands and meadows, entirely enclosed by walls."[180] The Martins and the Guérins never again vacationed by the seashore at Deauville or Trouville.

---

178 Letter from Jeanne Guérin to Céline dated June 24–25, 1887.
179 LT 24 from Thérèse to Jeanne Guérin dated June 27, 1887.
180 Sister Geneviève, *The Father of the Little Flower*, p. 103.

Under a mutual agreement it was decided that the Guérins would have the use of the estate from May to mid-August each summer and the Maundelondes from August to the hunting season in October. Therefore, from 1889 through 1894 Céline and Léonie spent vacation periods at the château with their aunt, uncle, and cousins. Céline, a gifted amateur artist, described to her three sisters in Carmel a colorful picture of what she observed from her window at La Musse:

> From my window, my eyes sweep out on the flat open countryside, and there I see fields and meadows, but how limited all this is! These fields are only narrow strips of land, cut very sharply; some are yellow, this is ripe corn; others are light green, dark green. They blend together, forming a striped carpet. I can see men tossing hay, and how tiny they are! I look with surprise on the haystacks, and these, though very large, appear to me only like mudpies shaped by the hands of children. And yet both the happiness or the sadness of the workers consists in the odor and the color of this hay![181]

M. Martin had been a patient at a hospital in Caen from 1889 to 1892. A year after his return home, Céline and Léonie decided that he was capable of spending time at La Musse; so in the summer of 1893 they brought him there convinced that the wholesome environment would be advantageous to his health. Céline, however, explains the difficulties of taking an invalid to such a place:

> [When] Papa had returned home, it was not considered possible to take him to La Musse, on account of the problems of transportation. A thousand precautions were necessary for the dear invalid, besides transporting his invalid-bed, his wheel-chair, and other luggage. At that time there were no motor-cars, and one had to use either carriages more or less convenient, or the train, to get the invalid there. The property was quite far from the railway station. Even from the gateway lodge there remained almost two miles of winding road to reach the plateau. But for the summer of 1893 my uncle had resolved to try the experiment, which succeeded very well.[182]

M. Martin did not stay in the actual château of La Musse because it would have been extremely difficult to move him up the seven or so steps to the main door or any of the other entrances. They, therefore, lodged him in an apartment just several yards directly opposite the front of the château. Here he stayed on the ground floor with easy access by wheelchair. A stairway inside led to his manservant's quarters.

One of Thérèse's cousins describes the delight that her uncle, Thérèse's father, experienced at La Musse in June of 1893:

> My uncle is radiant since he arrived. He is much happier, he says, than at Lisieux. Céline and I wheel him for excursions through the woods, but what

---

181 Letter from Céline at La Musse, to Sister Agnès of Jesus, Sister Marie of the Sacred Heart, and Thérèse, dated July 22, 1890.
182 Sister Geneviésve, *op. cit.*, pp. 116–117.

entertains him best is to look at the beautiful panorama from the heights. A few days ago he just could not cease gazing at it with delight.[183]

Other guests were also invited to spend vacation time there with the Martins and the Guérins. Joseph de Cornière, the seminarian son of the Carmel doctor was one of them who came in 1893 and 1894. Céline, twenty-five at the time, informed her sister Thérèse of the many activities in which they were all involved:

> I am going to write to you in haste, for these days I do not have time to turn around. Joseph de Cornière is here, and we are busy doing photography. We dress up and are making a whole story of travelers in living pictures; it will be very amusing ... we are always on the go....
>
> We spend our days in uncontrollable laughter, enough to split our sides, and I am thirsting for solitude ... not being accustomed to living with boys [Joseph, twenty and Dr. La Néele, thirty-six], it seems strange to me to be spending my days in their company. As holy and pure and candid as they are, I cannot get used to it.[184]

Thérèse, well aware of Céline's desire to become a nun (which she did sixty days later), penned a quick response the next day from her cloistered cell in Lisieux: "I beg you to give my kindest regards to all the dear travelers who are enjoying themselves so much there. I understand what you feel regarding the boys.... But this is only for a passing moment, one day you will not see too much of them. Console yourself!"[185]

Mother Nature can be frightening at times, and this example describes how she performed one time at La Musse. Mme. Guérin informed Sister Thérèse at the Lisieux Carmel about it:

> If you knew, Thérèse, what a storm we had on Friday at six in the evening. We were at dinner. Lightning flashes followed each other without interruption, when one flash brighter than all the others lighted up the room, and the clap of thunder resounded almost at the same time. Jeanne was frightened and held on to her father and Marie. Struck by the commotion, I jumped up and cried out: "Ah! This time it is the end!" Then I sat down again and said very calmly: "But do not be frightened, we saw the flash, there is no longer any danger." The picture was so funny (if I add here that Léonie, who was not afraid and, dying with hunger, was not missing a bite) that your uncle began to laugh heartily. Then everything came out; my words, my tone of voice, my actions were all reproduced in all kinds of ways. I must add to this that Maria [their maid], who died from fright in her kitchen, threw herself in panic on the first person she met, and this was Alexandre [another maid]! You have now a painting of a storm scene at La Musse.... However, I must add that the lightning struck a tree at La Musse outside the wall of the park on the St.

---

183 Ibid., p. 117.
184 LC 159 from Céline to Thérèse, dated July 17, 1894.
185 LT 167 from Thérèse to Céline, dated July 18, 1894.

Sebastian side (Celine will understand) and Mother Simon, who was milking her cows at *La Vielle Musse*, felt the shock and was still upset by it yesterday. Her cows were dancing.[186]

The summer of 1894 found M. Martin again at La Musse. Two weeks after his arrival with his two daughters, a sudden heart attack struck him on July 28, 1894. In the evening, Abbé Chillart from the church of Saint Sébastien in the nearby village of Saint Sébastien de Morsent, administered the Last Rites. Louis passed away the next day at sunrise. The funeral service and burial were held, however, in Lisieux some fifty miles away.

The next year Marie Guérin, Thérèse's cousin, reminisced about her uncle in letters she wrote from La Musse to Céline:

> As soon as I got out of the carriage, I made my little pilgrimage to my uncle's room, which enshrines so many memories. I went over it all again.... I was lost in thought that there—in that room—he had his first vision of God, and had been well received by Him....
>
> I remember the least incidents of the last days during which we both used to remain beside him.
>
> Thus my stay here is mingled with joy and sorrow. I seem to hear again, every evening, on the door-steps the sound of the wheel-chair bringing back my good uncle, and I am quite surprised when I lean out of the window not to see anybody.[187]

Many years later Céline recorded the ensuing history of La Musse:

> In subsequent years the property of La Musse was sold and resold several times. The first purchaser was Count de la Bourdonnaye, and the Countess transformed the room in which our father expired into an oratory. Now this fine domain has become a sanatorium [on the grounds, not the chateau itself] for tubercular patients. One of the chief surgeons erected on the esplanade in front [actually on the left side] of the Chateau a bust of our venerated father with that of his saintly Benjamin [one of the pet names for Thérèse] leaning on his heart. This lovely monument is always kept decorated with flowers.[188] One of the doctors of the Institute wrote to us in 1937: "Thinking of M. Martin, I had the impression that I was entering a house which had been inhabited by a saint."[189]

No truer statement could have been made.

---

186 Mme. Guérin wrote this letter (LC 163) to her niece Thérèse, dated July 28, 1895.
187 Sister Geneviève, *op. cit.*, pp. 128–129.
188 The inscription on the pedestal reads in an English translation: "To the memory/of/Monsieur Louis Martin/Father of Saint Thérèse/of the Infant Jesus/Died the 29th of July 1894/at the Château de la Musse/ Then the property of M. Guérin/ his brother-in-law."
189 Sister Geneviève, *op. cit.*, pp. 130–131.

e. Honfleur and Le Havre
Thérèse visited the churches in Honfleur and saw the 1887 International Maritime Exposition in Le Havre

IN JUNE 1887, LOUIS MARTIN AND HIS THREE DAUGHTERS—THÉRÈSE, CÉLINE, and Léonie—traveled to Le Havre to see the International Maritime Exposition. They stopped first, however, at Honfleur across the estuary from Le Havre on the south bank of the Seine where it empties into the English Channel. It is about twenty-one miles from Lisieux and about nine from Trouville.

Honfleur gained its greatest glory in the 17th century with the remarkable French voyages of discovery that originated there, notably with Jacques Cartier who claimed the territory of Canada for France and Samuel Champlain. Centuries later this charming old town became a favorite of artists, musicians, and writers who created some of their best work there. Corot (1796–1875), Bonnington (1801–1828), Courbet (1819–1877), and Manet (1833–1883) are numbered among the earlier artists inspired by the atmosphere and character of Honfleur. Following them came the Impressionists among whom were Monet (1840–1926), Renoir (1840–1919), and Degas (1835–1917) who held some of their first meetings in 1874 in one of its little inns above the hill in the western end of Honfleur called the *Ferme Saint-Siméon* ("Farmhouse of Saint-Siméon"—recently rebuilt). Honfleur's most prominent citizens include the painter Eugène Boudin (1824–1898),[190] the composer Erik Satie (1866–1925), and the writer Lucie Delarue-Mardrus (1874–1945) who wrote two books about St. Thérèse. As can be seen, much of this artistic activity occurred during Thérèse's lifetime.

As usual on all their trips, the Martins visited chapels and shrines, one of which certainly stands out as the most important—the church of Sainte-Catherine located not far from the Old Dock, the Governor's House (La Lieutenance), and the narrow harbor. The church and bell-tower (set apart from the church) are quite unique since they are both constructed entirely of wood—a rarity in Western Europe. Built by shipwrights after The Hundred Years' War (1338–1453) in thanksgiving for the departure of the hated English, it was intended to be a temporary structure until the return of the stonemasons and architects who were called after the war for reconstruction work. It has survived in excellent condition to this day.

Thérèse's main interest unquestionably was the church of Notre-Dame de Grâce on higher ground a little distance west behind the town and overlooking Le Havre clearly visible in the distance. Here she prayed to Our Lady for help in obtaining permission to become a Carmelite. Countless seamen throughout the centuries also prayed here for safe voyages and for other favors; the most outstanding among them are Cartier (1491–1557), who discovered the Saint Lawrence River, and Champlain (1567–1635), who founded Quebec. In 1558 those early explorers were responsible for the creation of the Canadian shrine of St. Anne de Beaupré. The long list of other famous visitors to this shrine of Our Lady boasts such luminaries as King Louis XIII, Napoleon Bonaparte, and

---

190 The Eugène-Boudin Museum there features his and other artists' work.

numerous important Catholic prelates. Age-old elms surround this little chapel, built in 1653. Nearby a large Calvary and scenic overlook affords an expansive view of the Seine estuary and Le Havre.

This edifice dedicated to Our Lady of Grace had special significance for Thérèse because fifty years before, two girls came to this church and petitioned the Blessed Mother to have a Carmelite monastery established in Lisieux. Abbé Sauvage, the vicar of Saint Jacques church in Lisieux assisted these young natives of Le Havre, the Gosselin sisters. A year later on March 15, 1838, the Carmel of Poitiers founded the Carmel in Lisieux and accepted the two sisters as postulants.

Thérèse's cousin Marie Guérin describes the journey she and her family took to this shrine during their 1886 summer vacation in Trouville which doubtlessly was similar to the one Thérèse took in 1887:

> On Sunday, we went on an outing to La Grâce.... We had a carriage with two horses, a coachman in uniform, and off we went, then, for the whole afternoon. The route was charming. When going, we traveled along the edge of the Saint Gatien forest, where we stopped to go and see the home of our ancestors.... Afterward, we continued on our way to La Grâce. During the trip, we saw a balloon that came from the Honfleur carnival. When we reached La Grâce, we went into the chapel, and there I prayed for my Thérèse and her whole family. You cannot imagine the pretty panorama that unfolded before our very eyes. It was enchanting; the Seine flowing into the sea and, facing us, the coast of Le Havre, Barfleur, etc. On our return, we went along the side of the sea. We came back by way of Villerville.[191]

From Honfleur the Martins took the ferry boat ride across the estuary to Le Havre. This city provided regular steamship service to the United States since the 1860s. The artist Monet grew up in Le Havre and the village overlooking the beach of Le Havre called Ste-Adresse from which he derived much of his inspiration. The Martins visited Notre-Dame church situated in the old part of the town not far from the harbor and the docks. This impressive Gothic-Renaissance structure, built between 1539 and 1630, somehow survived the terrible annihilation of ninety percent of the city during the September 6, 1944 Allied Assault against the firmly entrenched Nazis who obstinately resisted even after the fall of Paris and the rest of Normandy. Le Havre (French for "harbor") is the second largest flourishing port in France after Marseille. Its strategic location at the northern end of the Seine estuary makes it the trading and transatlantic port of northern France.

The large Exposition consisting of nearly 3,000 exhibitors was held in buildings spread along the Bassin du Commerce and at the docks adjoining them where ships from many nations were on display. In addition, an international music competition was held with Belgium being the winner. The Martins enjoyed the exhibits, regattas, shopping, fireworks, and a meal on one of the ships, the novel "*Café-flottant*" (Floating Café)—a large three-masted barque utilized as a

---

[191] This letter (LC 45) from Marie Guérin to Thérèse is dated July 31, 1886.

restaurant for the occasion.[192] In addition, Thérèse bought two birds for Céline at one of the exhibitions but unfortunately they died shortly thereafter:

> [Céline] has a very sad one [mishap] to tell you: the death of her little bluebird which died last night. Papa told us this morning that the remaining one appears very joyful at being rid of his wife, he is making never-ending chirps. But I believe the poor little husband was crying; birds are not like people, they cannot show their sorrow in another way. Thérèse almost said a funeral prayer for the defunct. It seems she encouraged Céline to resignation; finally, to soften bitter regrets they have decided to have it stuffed.[193]

Thérèse concludes this little tale of woe: "Céline is mourning her two little finches; the male rejoined his companion the next morning, and now its mortal remains are at the taxidermist's."[194]

Louis Martin's physical and mental health slowly deteriorated after a paralytic stroke on May 1, 1887. He did improve enough, though, to go on the trip to the Le Havre Exposition and continue his normal routine for some time. The next year, however, on June 23, he acted out of character. Suddenly, and without telling anyone, he left his home in Lisieux and took a train to Le Havre. His absence and unknown whereabouts alarmed everyone until he finally notified his family that he was in Le Havre and without money. By this time Thérèse was in the convent and unable to help. Céline with her uncle Guérin and his nephew Ernest Maudelonde searched Le Havre, eventually found him at the General Post Office, and brought him back to Lisieux on June 27. He was much less confused by then, though he informed everyone that he was determined to become a hermit!

The final Martin association with both Le Havre and Honfleur, distressing as it was, happened during the journey Céline and Léonie made there with their father from October 31 to November 2, 1888 to see their family spiritual confessor and advisor Father Pichon off to Canada as a missionary. Just before reaching Le Havre, when they were in nearby Honfleur, Louis Martin had another sudden attack—essentially mental, it seems, rather than physical. They failed to meet the priest in Le Havre but did manage somehow to find him later in Paris after which they speedily returned to Lisieux. "Honfleur … Le Havre … most painful stages! Papa is very sick.…" wrote Céline in her *Manuscript Notebooks* years later in unhappy remembrance of this event.

f. Le Mans
Thérèse's older sisters attended the convent school here where their nun aunt taught

TODAY LE MANS IS BEST KNOWN INTERNATIONALLY FOR ITS FAMED TWENty-four hour car racing event held every June. In Thérèse's time no such affair lured people there. Then it was just another bustling city in the Sarthe Department,

---

192 Viquesnel, *Promenades en Normandie avec Sainte Thérèse de Lisieux*, p. 109.
193 From a letter dated June 28, 1887, from Marie, then Sister Marie of the Sacred Heart, to Marie Guérin.
194 Thérèse dated this letter (LT 25) July 14, 1887, and addressed it to her cousin Marie Guérin.

south of Normandy. Today in the center of town crowds of people (mostly young) mill around, motorcyclists abound, and noisy cars and busses add to the confusion.

The only significance Le Mans held for the Martin family was the Visitation Convent and its school located at the now very busy and congested Place Republique. The older Martin girls—Marie, Pauline, and for a short time Léonie—were boarding students where their mother's older sister, Sister Marie-Dosithée, taught school. Thérèse, however, visited Le Mans once on March 29, 1875, when she saw her aunt for the first and only time. With a remarkably good memory, she remembered the meeting clearly though she was but two years old:

> I recall also the trip I made to Le Mans [some thirty miles from her home in Alençon]; it was my first train ride. What a joy to see myself on a trip alone with Mamma. I don't know why I began to cry, but poor little Mother had nothing to introduce to Aunt at Le Mans but a plain little girl all red with the tears she shed on the way. I remember nothing about the visit except the moment when Aunt handed me a little white toy mouse and a little cardboard basket filled with candies, on top of which *were enthroned* two pretty sugar rings, just the right size for my finger. Immediately I exclaimed: "How wonderful! There will be a ring for Céline also!" I took my basket by the handle. I gave the other hand to Mamma and we left. After a few steps, I looked at my basket and saw that my candies were almost all strewn out on the street like Tom Thumb's pebbles. I looked again more closely and saw that one of the precious rings had undergone the awful fate of the candies. I had nothing now to give to Céline and so was filled with grief! I asked if I could retrace my steps, but Mamma seemed to pay no attention to me. This was too much and my *tears* were followed by loud *cries*. I was unable to understand why she didn't share my pain, and this only increased my grief.[195]

A month later, Mme. Martin wrote her version of this incident in an amusing letter to her sister-in-law explaining the childish but rather characteristic behavior of her little daughter:

> I brought her [Sister Marie-Dosithée] little Thérèse, who was very happy to get on the train. When we arrived at Le Mans, she was tired, she cried, but she remained in the visiting room all the time, good like a big girl. However, I do not know what was the matter with her; when we entered, she was heavy-hearted, and her tears came without any noise, she was choking. I do not know if it was the grilles that frightened her. Afterwards, all went well. She was answering all the questions as if she had passed an examination.
>
> The Superior came to see her and gave her some gifts. I said: "Ask the good Mother to bless you." But she did not grasp it [the confusion was between "*bénir*" ("to bless") and "*venir*" ("to come")] and answered: "Mother, will you come to our house?" This made everybody laugh.[196]

---

195 *Story of a Soul*, chapter I, p. 23.
196 Zelie wrote this letter (CF 131) to her brother and Mme. Guérin on April 29, 1875.

B. The Trip to Rome

1. **Paris**: *The starting point of the trip*
2. **Lucerne**: *The first overnight stop on the trip*
3. **Milan**: *The first Italian city visited*
4. **Venice**: *"I found this city sad."—Thérèse*
5. **Padua**: *Thérèse prayed at the shrine of St. Anthony*
6. **Bologna**: *A male student accosted Thérèse here*
7. **Loreto**: *"Loreto really charmed me."—Thérèse*
8. **Rome**: *"Rome! Rome! It was not a dream. I was in Rome!"—Thérèse*
9. **Naples and Pompeii**: *"In our honor Mount Vesuvius made a lot of noise."—Thérèse*
10. **Assisi**: *An embarrassing moment here for Thérèse*
11. **Florence**: *Thérèse visited the shrine of St. Mary Magdalen de Pazzi*
12. **Pisa and Genoa**: *Where Thérèse enjoyed pleasant diversions*
13. **Nice**: *Here Thérèse was given some hope of entering Carmel*
14. **Marseille**: *Thérèse visited its famous basilica*
15. **Lyon and Paris**: *Last phase of the trip*

WHEN THÉRÈSE ASKED THE POPE FOR PERMISSION TO BECOME A NUN AT FOURTEEN (NOVEMBER 4 TO DECEMBER 2, 1887)

THÉRÈSE DEVOTED THE ENTIRE CHAPTER VI IN HER AUTOBIOGRAPHY, *Story of a Soul*, to the twenty-nine day journey to Rome, the longest trip and the only excursion she took outside of France. M. Martin, a frequent traveler himself, decided to show his two teenage daughters, Thérèse and Céline, through this pilgrimage some of the wonders of Europe that he had seen in the past. It was not, as a few in Lisieux believed, to dissuade in some way his youngest from becoming a nun.

Four days before the much anticipated trip, he and Thérèse visited Bishop Hugonin in Bayeux to obtain his permission for her to enter the Lisieux Carmel before Christmas when she would still be fourteen. Disappointed with the indecisive reply she received, Thérèse eventually decided to make the same request of Pope Leo XIII at the audience the tourist group was scheduled to have with him in the Vatican. This encounter likewise proved disappointingly inconclusive.

The trip had been planned well in advance by Msgr. Germain, the "ultramontane" (favoring the pope) bishop of Coutances, to affirm loyalty to the beleaguered seventy-seven-year old pontiff and to celebrate his fifty-year jubilee as a priest. His capable vicar general, Abbé Legoux, assisted in making the arrangements and joined the travelers as well. The pilgrims, in large measure members of

Plate 20

The Itinerary of Thérèse's Trip to Rome

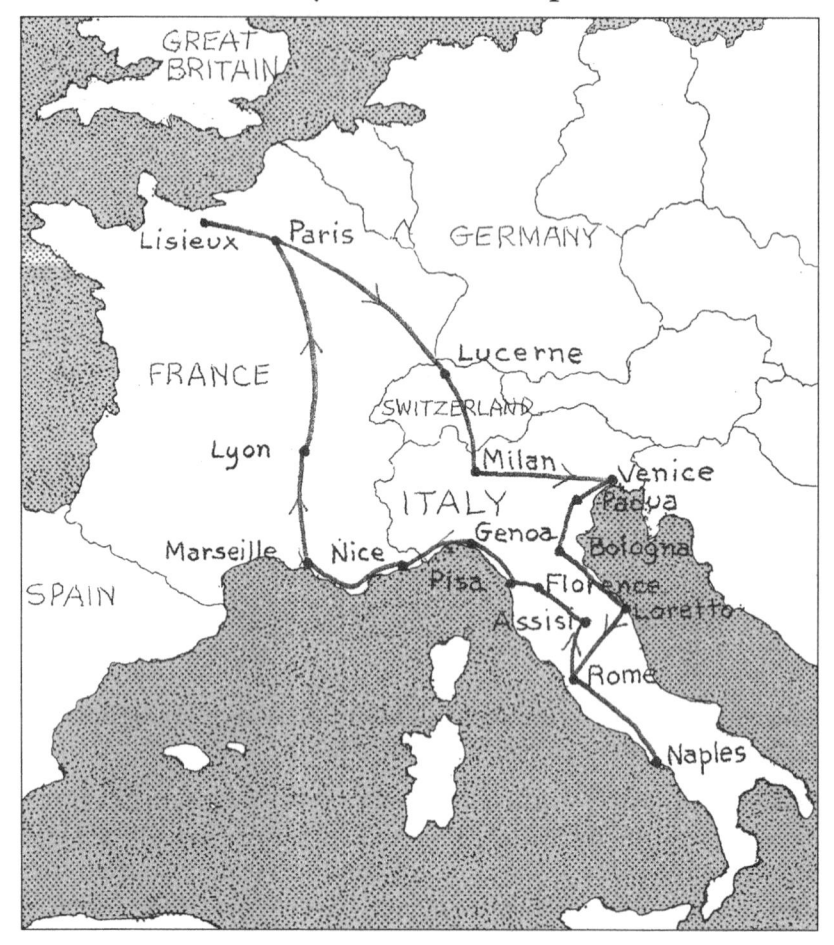

the aristocracy, comprised 197 people, seventy-five of whom were clergymen. The Bayeux group headed by Msgr. Révérony, Bishop Hugonin's vicar general, formed part of the contingency of various Normandy dioceses especially loyal to the papacy. Luxury and expense were not spared by the Agence Lubin (Lubin Agency) which provided the best hotels and travel amenities for them.[1] This second such pilgrimage from France was duly noted, as no routine religious trip had been before, by the press and the political factions active in the virulent anti-clerical and anti-royalist atmosphere of the time. Most French Catholics were royalists, disapproved of the Republic, and opposed Freemasonry whose anti-religious ideas permeated much of the contemporary society.

Thérèse plainly reveals in her writings the expanded knowledge she gained through this religious tour about the world, humanity, her vocation, and herself:

---
1 The cost of the trip: 1st class = 600 F, 2nd class = 565 F.

B. The Trip to Rome

> Ah! what a trip that was! It taught me more than long years of studies; it showed me the vanity of everything that happens.... I contemplated all the marvels of art and religion; above all, I trod the same soil as did the holy apostles, the soil bedewed with the blood of martyrs.... Having never lived among the great of this world, Céline and I found ourselves in the midst of the nobility who almost exclusively made up the pilgrimage. Ah! far from dazzling us, all these titles and these "de" appeared to us as nothing but smoke.
>
> [I] understood my vocation in Italy and that's not going too far in search of such useful knowledge. I lived in the company of many saintly priests for a month and I learned that, though their dignity raises them above the angels, they are nevertheless weak and fragile men.
>
> [We] very quickly became acquainted with the different people on the pilgrimage. So timid that I usually dared not speak, I was surprised to find myself completely freed from this crippling fault. I was talking freely with the great ladies, the priests, and even the Bishop of Coutances. It seemed to me I had always lived in this milieu. We were, I believe, very well loved by everybody....
>
> [When] I am a prisoner in Carmel and trials come my way and I have only a tiny bit of starry heavens to contemplate, I shall remember what my eyes have seen today. This thought shall encourage me and I shall easily forget my own little interests, recalling the grandeur and power of God, this God whom I want to love alone.[2]

During the many long hours of train travel, the passengers whiled away their time by playing cards and invited the Martins to participate. They declined politely, excusing themselves for lack of knowledge:

> Presently their [the passengers'] annoyance became evident, and then dear Papa began quietly to defend us, pointing out that as we were on a pilgrimage more of our time might be given to prayer. One of the players, forgetting the respect due to age, called out thoughtlessly: "Thank God, Pharisees are rare!" My father did not answer a word, he even seemed pleased; and later on he found an opportunity of shaking hands with this man, and of speaking so pleasantly that the latter must have thought his rude words had either not been heard, or at least were forgotten.[3]

Thérèse's reaction to another incident reveals her keen assessment of the typically unpleasant, querulous tourist common to any period or nationality:

> An old gentleman (French), who no doubt did not possess as poetic a soul, looked at us critically and said in bad humor, pretending he was sorry he could not share our admiration [of sights seen]: "Ah! what enthusiasts these French people really are!" I believe this poor man would have been better off to remain at home, for he did not appear to me to be happy with his trip. He was frequently close to us and complaints were coming from his mouth constantly: he was unhappy with the carriages, the hotels, the people, the cities, everything. Papa, with his habitual kindness, tried to console him by offering him his place, etc.;

---

2 *Story of a Soul*, chapter VI, pp. 121–125.
3 From *Histoire d'une âme*, as quoted on p. 355 in Piat's *op. cit.*

he himself felt at home everywhere, being of a temperament directly opposite that of his disobliging neighbor. Ah! what different personages we saw, and what an interesting study the world is when one is ready to leave it! [4]

During the entire excursion Thérèse and Céline fervidly wrote letters home which took up precious time from sightseeing and rest. In general, Thérèse described the beauties of God's creation, but in detail, only those things that really appealed to her. Her primary concerns of course were the shrines, churches, the audience with the pope, and the delicate but tense maneuvers (on both sides) with Father Révérony—the one man whom she and her sisters considered the key person at this stage in securing Thérèse's permission to enter the Lisieux Carmel. Later on the letters home and those the Martins received while on their journey dealt almost exclusively with the subject of her vocation.

Louis Martin gave as a departing gift to each of his daughters a golden chain bracelet. On the trip he bought them a watch in Rome, and a bejeweled pin shaped like a butterfly in Genoa. Every French pilgrim wore a badge artistically and symbolically designed identifying them as members of this particular pilgrimage: a white ribbon with blue pin stripes attached to a medal with a portrait of Pope Leo XIII.

To be sure, the Martin girls attracted attention among the travelers because of their beauty, youth, and personality. Abbé Leconte, the twenty-nine year-old curate of St. Peter's (their parish in Lisieux), was often seen with the Martin family causing some wags to gossip. Another person in the group, but unaware of Thérèse at the time, happened to be a noted hagiographer, Msgr. Laveille. He did hear by chance of a fourteen-year-old girl who had asked the pope for permission to become a nun; he even stayed in the same hotel with her in Venice. Many years later, the Carmelites of Lisieux chose him to write a biography of this girl and he ruefully conjectures in his 1925 biography, *Life of the Little Flower St. Thérèse of Lisieux*, that he perhaps passed her within the confines of the Hotel del la Luna in Venice without, unfortunately, ever noticing her.

The strict enclosure rules in Italian religious places and the consequential punishment if broken particularly distressed Thérèse:

> I still cannot understand why women are so easily excommunicated in Italy, for every minute someone was saying: "Don't enter here! Don't enter there, you will be excommunicated!" Ah! poor women, how they are misunderstood! and yet they love God in much larger numbers than men do and during the Passion of Our Lord, women had more courage than the apostles since they braved the insults of the soldiers and dared to dry the adorable Face of Jesus.... One day when we were visiting a Carmelite monastery [*Santa Maria della Vittoria* in Rome], not content with following the pilgrims in the *outer* galleries, I advanced into the *inner* cloisters, when all of a sudden I saw a good old Carmelite friar at a little distance making a sign for me to leave. But instead of going, I approached him and showing him the cloister paintings I made a

---
[4] *Story of a Soul*, chapter VI, p. 127.

sign that they were beautiful. He undoubtedly understood by the way I wore my hair and from my youthful appearance that I was only a child, so he smiled at me kindly and left. He saw he was not in the presence of an enemy. Had I been able to speak Italian I would have told him I was a future Carmelite, but because of the builders of the Tower of Babel it was impossible for me.[5]

The memory of this trip always remained with Thérèse who alluded to it on various occasions. She had a special talent, inherited from her father, of imitating people in their speech and mannerisms by which she amused her family and later the nuns—especially her impersonation of the tour guide they had in Rome. According to Léonie, "she mimicked him more than once during the recreations in Carmel." Thérèse, she says, "never ... [had] this little amusement ever degenerate into mockery.... Thérèse knew when to stop at a certain point, with perfect tact."[6] Relating to this, Marie, writing to Léonie, said Thérèse was "a mystic, a comedienne, she is everything! She can make you shed tears of devotion, and she can as easily make you split your sides with laughter during recreation."[7]

Thérèse and Céline naturally had many anxieties during this pilgrimage/vacation trip. The most important matter concerned the well-being of their beloved father. He had suffered a paralytic stroke six months before; though he recovered, it left him in a slightly weakened state. Céline recalled decades later that "one day in the train at Rome, our father, tired out from sight-seeing, closed his eyes; he was deathly pale and his lips were purple. I was frightened and, filled with anxiety, I said to him: "Papa, are you sick?"[8] These symptoms proved not to be serious and he soon returned to his normal state. Fortunately nothing undermined his health during the rest of the long, strenuous journey.

1. Paris
The starting point of the trip

WITH THE EMERGENCE OF THE ART NOUVEAU MOVEMENT DURING THE Belle Époque era, Paris in 1887 burst with vitality, excitement, invention, and creative energy in the arts. Elegantly clad women of fashion, eager flower sellers, and horse-drawn carriages crowded the tree-lined boulevards designed by Baron Georges Haussmann (1809-1891). The newly built bridges and railroad stations were likewise areas of great activity. In the political arena General Boulanger (1837-1891) elicited considerable attention. The reigning man of the theater, Victorien Sardou (1831-1908), presented his latest creation, the melodrama *La Tosca* (1887) with Sarah Bernhardt (1844-1923). Jules Massenet (1842-1912), Bizet (1838-1875), and Gounod (1818-1893) maintained their reputations as the foremost French operatic composers of the period. The music of Offenbach (1819-1880)

---
5 Ibid., p. 140.
6 From Léonie's deposition at the 1910 Diocesan Process.
7 From an 1893 letter.
8 From Sister Geneviève's *Preparatory Notes* for Piat's *Story of a Family* as mentioned in note 5, p. 320 for LD, Nov. 11, 1887, from Sr. Agnès to the three travelers in Rome.

624　CHAPTER 7: *Places Associated with St. Thérèse*

Plate 21

On the Trip to Rome

A. Our Lady of Victories Church, Paris

B. Grand Hotel de Mulhouse et de Champagne, Paris

C. Basilica of St. Anthony, Padua

D. Sacre-Coeur, Paris

E. Papal Audience Room

F. Hotel de la Luna, now Hotel Baglioni, Venice

G. Basilica of St. Peter, Rome

H. Saint-Pierre de Monmartre, Paris

I. La Albergo del Sud, Rome

J. Sant' Andrea della Fratti, Rome

continued to thrill the populace with his sparkling music, especially his *opérabouffe*. (He was called the "Mozart of the *Champs Elysées*.") The government supported the conservative Paris art Salon (*Académie des Beaux-Arts*) and lionized the academic painter Adolphe-William Bouguereau (1825–1905), among other realistic artists, while the younger avant-garde artists van Gogh (1853–1890), Toulouse-Lautrec (1864–1901), Monet (1840–1926), Renoir (1840–1919), Cezanne (1839–1906), and a host of other Impressionists were slowly gaining recognition.

The two pretty guileless teenagers from the tranquil Norman countryside, Thérèse and Céline, entered this cosmopolitan capital from the *Gare St. Lazare* at 8 o'clock, Friday morning, November 4, 1887, and their exciting venture began. This was the first railroad station built in France, in 1837. Particularly intrigued by this structure, Claude Monet obtained official permission to set up his art equipment there and painted many famous pictures of the interior and exterior of the building.

Thérèse tells her story:

> The pilgrimage left Paris on [Monday] November 7, but Papa had taken us there a few days before to visit the Capital. At three o'clock in the morning, I crossed the city of Lisieux which was still wrapped in sleep; many impressions passed through my soul at that moment. I had a feeling I was approaching the unknown, that great things awaited me out there. Papa was very happy; when the train began to move he sang the old refrain: "Roll, roll, my carriage, here we are on the open road." We reached Paris in the morning and commenced our visit without delay. Poor little Father tired himself out trying to please us and very soon we saw all the marvels of the Capital.[9]

M. Martin made certain their hotel was near the family's favorite church, *Notre-Dame-des-Victoires* (Our Lady of Victories); therefore, he obtained lodgings in the *Hôtel du Bouloi* at 5 rue du Bouloi.[10] On Sunday, though, they moved to the *Grande Hôtel de Mulhouse et de Champagne*[11] because it was situated (and still is) just across the plaza in front of the *Gare de l'Est* from where the tour left early the next morning, Monday, November 7, at 6:20. (Carriages were unavailable that early at the other hotel.) Msgr. Ahern in his book on Maurice Bellière reveals through his research a most intriguing bit of information. Thérèse, "the greatest saint of modern times," might have met by chance the greatest contemporary atheist, Friedrich Nietzsche (1844–1900),[12] who stayed at one of the same hotels at the exact time when Thérèse was there.

Louis Martin had spent about three years in Paris as a young man finishing his apprenticeship in the jewelry and watch making craft. Later on his function as a manager and salesman for his wife's lacemaking industry often took him on business to the City of Lights. Being familiar with the many tourist attractions

---
9 *Story of a Soul*, chapter VI, p. 123.
10 It does not exist today.
11 Now called Libertel Strasburg Mulhouse, located at 87 Blvd. Strasburg.
12 German philosopher noted also for his belief in the concept of nihilism, existentialism, and for coining the statement "the death of God."

Paris had to offer, he anxiously showed his youngest daughters all those city wonders which still fascinate wide-eyed tourists of the present. During their three busy days in Paris, Céline and Thérèse sent diary-like letters to their two Carmelite sisters back home informing them of the sights they saw. A few excerpts follow:

- I cannot go over all I am seeing. We have seen some beautiful things in Paris but all this is not happiness. Céline is going to tell you if she wants the marvels of Paris; as for myself, I'll tell you only that I am thinking very often of you. The beautiful things of Paris don't captivate my heart in the least.[13]
- Paris is very beautiful.... Today, we went to the *Champs Elysées*, the *Tuileries*; we saw the panorama and the diorama. This time, they were presenting the Bosphorus and Constantinople, and I believed I was actually there. We passed under the *arc de triomphe de l'Etoile*, climbed up to the tower of the *Bastille* (250 steps); we saw the statues of the Republique, Joan of Arc, and Louis XVIII. We saw the royal palace, the Bourse, the Louvre Museum.... We went to the Louvre [shopping area] to find some raincoats, and it was only last spring that I got my bargain. Papa was helping me buy them, asking everybody where the counters were for women's raincoats.... We were in the elevators [of the *Printemps* department store], and it was amusing. Although we went often either by [horse-drawn] carriage or tramway, we were tired.... We saw, too, the grand opera and several theaters and circuses, etc.[14]
- This afternoon, we saw *Guignol* [a marionette show] at *Champs Elysees*, the little wagons drawn by goats, the wooden horses, the *Invalides*, the *Vendôme* tower, a beautiful exhibition of machines for making beer, etc.[15]

In her autobiography written eight years later, Thérèse stresses the places that were significant to her. In Paris it was the church of Our Lady of Victories:

- We reached Paris in the morning and commenced our visit without delay.... and very soon we saw all the marvels of the Capital. I myself found only one which filled me with delight, Our Lady of Victories!
- Ah, what I felt kneeling at her feet [during the Mass on November 4] cannot be expressed.... The Blessed Virgin made me feel it was really herself who smiled on me and brought about my cure [of a strange malady over four years before].
- I prayed Our Lady of Victories to keep far from me everything that could tarnish my purity; I was fully aware that on a voyage such as this into Italy I could easily meet with things capable of troubling me.[16]

Thérèse acquired this love for Our Lady of Victories from both her parents. When her father lived in Paris as an apprentice watchmaker, he routinely stopped there for Mass or for prayer. In 1877 his wife Zélie was suffering from her final bout with cancer. She wrote to the priest there (Abbé Martignon) to pray for her recovery. Louis expressed his devotion to Our Lady in a letter he wrote to her when he went to Paris on her business: "I had the happiness of going to Holy

---
13 LT 30, letter from Thérèse to Pauline and Marie, dated November 6, 1887.
14 Letter from Céline to Pauline and Marie, dated, November 5–6, 1887.
15 Ibid.
16 *Story of a Soul*, chapter VI, p. 123.

Communion at Our Lady of Victories, which is like an earthly paradise. I also lighted a votive candle for the whole family." [17] Just a week before, the solicitous Zélie wrote to her brother Isidore then living in Paris:

> If you only agree to do something I am going to ask you, and if you want to offer me that for a New Year's gift, I should be happier than if you sent me all Paris. Here it is! You live close to Our Lady of Victories. Very well! Go in, just once a day to say an Ave Maria to her. You will see that she will protect you in a quite particular way.[18]

Father Roulland, one of Thérèse's two "spiritual brothers," following a custom of the Foreign Mission Society of Paris, said one of his first Masses there in 1896. During Thérèse's own debilitating illness when she was ten, novenas and Masses were also offered at this church for her recovery.

Our Lady of Victories church is really a basilica and the place of a popular Marian pilgrimage in Paris. Since 1836 suppliants have flocked there to pray and light votive candles which even today fill the walls inside, especially in the Virgin's chapel in the right arm of the transept. The basilica faces a little square, the Place des Petits-Pères, named after the Monastery of the *Petits-Pères* (Augustinian Fathers) that was originally connected to the church. A block or so away is the *Place des Victories* with its circle of elegant 17th century mansions containing the address of major names in the fashion industry. Within the same environs one can visit the *Palais-Royal*, the *Biblioteque Nationale*, and the Bourse district.

Paintings inside Our Lady of Victories church depict the dedication of the church to the Blessed Virgin in 1629 by Louis XIII who the year before gained victory over Protestant factions in a bitter battle at La Rochelle. Other huge pictures illustrate the story of St. Augustine of Hippo (354–430), the founder of the Order. Of interest to devotees of opera is the tomb on the left of the nave containing the remains of the celebrated opera composer Jean-Baptiste Lully (1632–1687) who lived in the vicinity.

Thérèse mentions another important church in Paris—*Sacré-Coeur* (the Basilica of the Sacred Heart), the starting point for the pilgrimage. Here all the pilgrims on her tour met for the first time. *Sacré-Coeur* rises on a hill 328 feet above the Seine on a terrace that provides a magnificent view of Paris. This hill and district on the top is called Montmartre (Mount of Martyrs) because of St. Denis—the patron saint of Paris—and two other priests were possibly beheaded there by the Romans for their faith around 250 A.D. For a long time it was considered a hallowed place, especially during the Middle Ages when multitudes of pilgrims went there to pray. St. Ignatius of Loyola (1491–1556) and the first Jesuits made their vows on this spot. In modern times this entire area, formerly known also for its picturesque windmills and streets, has become world famous not because of its religious associations but because of its spirited Bohemian

---

17 October 8, 1863.
18 October 1, 1863.

ambience, exuberant night life, and the Impressionists and others who have immortalized it in their paintings.

The basilica itself is of rather recent origin. It came about as a result of the French defeat in the Franco-Prussian War when the people petitioned its construction as an act of reparation to the Sacred Heart. The National Assembly under the presidency of MacMahon then voted to start a campaign to build the "Church of the National Vow" in 1873 (the year of Thérèse's birth). Construction began with the laying of the first stone in 1875 and finally completed in 1914. The towering white edifice with its gleaming domes, turrets, and rear campanile are patterned after Romano-Byzantine designs and in general well planned as a place for pilgrimages, capable of accommodating some nine thousand people. Through the years this familiar building has been fiercely criticized as an architectural monstrosity by some purists even more so than the other symbolic landmark of Paris, the Eiffel Tower.

A church Thérèse prayed at in *Montmartre* was *Saint-Pierre de Montmartre* in a square, the Place du Tertre, to the left of the basilica. A priest stationed there claims Thérèse attended Mass here just before her departure for Rome. A plaque on the left wall of the nave commemorates her brief visit:[19]

> A Remembrance of the visit of
> ST. THÉRÈSE OF THE CHILD JESUS
> to our ancient Church of ST. PIERRE
> at the time of her pilgrimage to
> Sacré-Cœur de Montmartre
> November 6, 1887
> before her departure for Rome
> *"I will spend my heaven doing good on earth"*
> *"I will let fall a shower of roses"*
> *"My God... I love you"*
> St. Thérèse[20]

Incidentally, located just behind the basilica of *Sacré-Coeur* at 34 rue de chevalier de la Barre is the Carmel de Montmartre founded in 1928, forty-one years after Thérèse came to Paris and three years after she was canonized.

Tourists assembled in the crypt of the Basilica because the upper area was under construction. Here the pilgrimage began formally with Msgr. Germain officiating at the opening ceremonies in one of the fourteen or so chapels (that of St. Peter) where Thérèse and the group pronounced their consecration to the Sacred Heart. A plaque at the entrance to the chapel contains these words in English translation:

---

19 The French artist Maurice Utrillo (1883–1955) painted a number of pictures of the exterior of this church. His funeral Mass was held here and interment was in the little cemetery called *Cimetière St. Vincent* a short distance away down the hill. Here also is buried the painter Eugène Boudin (1824–1898) who was born in Honfleur and painted many scenes of that area in Thérèse's day.

20 The author's free translation of the French on the plaque: *En Souvenir du passage de STE. THÉRÈSE DE L'ENFANT JÉSUS dans notre antique Eglise Ste. PIERRE lors de son pèlerinage au Sacré Cœur de Montmartre le 6 Novembere 1887 avant son depart pour Rome. "Je veux passer mon Ciel à faire du bien sur la Terre."/"Je ferai tomber une pluie de roses."/"Mon Dieu... je vous aime."* Ste. Thérèse.

ON SUNDAY NOV. 6, 1887
AT 9 O'CLOCK IN THE MORNING
THÉRÈSE MARTIN
14 YEARS OLD WHO WENT
TO ROME WITH HER FATHER AND
HER SISTER CÉLINE TO ASK
HIS HOLINESS POPE LEO XIII
PERMISSION TO ENTER
DESPITE HER YOUNG AGE
THE CARMEL OF LISIEUX
CAME IN PILGRIMAGE
TO THIS CRYPT
TO THE CHAPEL OF SAINT PETER
AND PRONOUNCED HER CONSECRATION
TO THE SACRED HEART.
AND AS SOON AS SHE RETURNED TO LISIEUX
SHE SENT TO THE SANCTUARY
HER GOLD BRACELET
TO BE USED IN THE COMPOSITION
OF A LARGE MONSTRANCE.
SAINT THÉRÈSE OF THE INFANT JESUS
PRAY FOR US.

The pilgrims sang the "Magnificat" as they processed up the stairs and outside. Thérèse succinctly ends the narrative of her Parisian interlude with these words: "After our solemn consecration to the Sacred Heart in the Basilica at Montmartre [on Sunday], we departed from Paris on [a rainy] Monday [November 7], at seven in the morning."[21]

Each car of the special train waiting for them at the Gare de l'Est was decorated with religious emblems and the individual compartments were given a saint's name. "When we heard ours was named after St. Martin," Thérèse exclaimed, "our father was so happy he went to thank the one in charge [Msgr. Legoux]. After that he was called M. St. Martin."[22]

2. LUCERNE
The first overnight stop

IT WAS RAINING ON MONDAY, NOVEMBER 7, WHEN THE EXCITED PILGRIMS destined for Rome left the Gare de l'Est Paris station at 6:35 in the morning. During the journey, the train stopped briefly at Vesoul, Belfort, and Basle (*Ligué Bâle* or Basel) where the tourists got off to dine at the railroad station restaurant. They reached Lucerne, the famed tourist resort in central Switzerland, at 12:30 that night where they stayed at the Hôtel du Lac. Not many hours later that same morning they left at eight o'clock which prevented any real sightseeing in this picturesque town on the lake. Passing through the impressive Lake Lucerne

---
21 *Story of a Soul*, chapter VI, p. 124. Gaucher says on p. 75 in his *Story of a Life* that it was at 6:35 A.M.
22 From *Histoire d' une Âme*, as quoted in note 138, p. 124 in *Story of a Soul*, chapter VI.

district and the spectacular St. Gothard Massif section of the country certainly had an impact on Thérèse:

> First, there was Switzerland with its mountains whose summits were lost in the clouds, its graceful waterfalls gushing forth in a thousand different ways, its deep valleys literally covered with gigantic ferns and scarlet heather. Ah! Mother [Agnes—her sister Pauline in religion], how much good these beauties of nature, poured out *in such profusion*, did my soul. They raised it to heaven which was pleased to scatter such masterpieces on a place of exile destined to last only a day. I hadn't eyes enough to take in everything. Standing by the window I almost lost my breath; I would have liked to be on both sides of the car. When turning to the other side, I beheld landscapes of enchanting beauty, totally different from those under my immediate gaze.
>
> At times, we were climbing a mountain peak, and at our feet were ravines the depths of which our glance could not possibly fathom. They seemed about to engulf us. A little later, we were passing through a ravishing little village with its graceful cottages and its belfry over which floated immaculately white clouds. There was, farther on, a huge lake gilded by the fires of the setting sun. All this presented to our enraptured gaze the most poetic and enchanting spectacle one could possibly imagine. And at the end of the vast horizon, we perceived mountains whose indistinct contours would have escaped us had not their snowy summits made visible by the sun not come to add one more charm to the beautiful lake which thrilled us so.
>
> When I saw all these beauties very profound thoughts came to life in my soul. I seemed to understand already the grandeur of God and the marvels of heaven.[23]

The pilgrim train passed through the St. Gothard Tunnel and into sunny Italy where it traveled by Lugano, Como, and finally that evening reached cosmopolitan Milan where the passengers alighted for a well-deserved rest.

3. MILAN
The first Italian city visited

MILAN WAS IN THÉRÈSE'S DAY, AND STILL IS, NOT ONLY THE MOST IMPORTant industrial, banking, and commercial center in Italy but also the second largest in population. Among the many famous people associated with this northern metropolis, the following men stand out as the most notable: Constantine (c. 288–337), Attila the Hun (c. 406–453), Leonardo da Vinci (1452–1519), and Giuseppi Verdi (1813–1901).

The geographical, political, and social center of the city is the area most frequented by tourists and citizens alike—the Piazza del Duomo and the surrounding buildings. At one end of the multi-colored tiled square is the grand Gothic cathedral (Duomo), the third largest church in the world. To the left of it, the famous Galleria—the glass-roofed gathering place with its many cafes and shops—leads to the Piazza della Scala dominated by the world-renowned opera house, the Teatro della Scala (La Scala).

---
23 *Story of a Soul*, chapter VI, pp. 124–125.

B. The Trip to Rome

The tourist group spent the second overnight stop at the Hotel Central, in the vicinity of the cathedral at the Via Pesce and Via Larga. They arrived around six o'clock Tuesday evening, November 8, and remained in this cosmopolitan city overlooking the Alps until the next afternoon after many hours of sightseeing and shopping. Just two places in Milan interested Thérèse enough to comment on: the cathedral and the cemetery. The first is a profusion of white lace-like marble bursting with pinnacles, gables, belfries, and statues (estimated at well over 3,000 in and outside the edifice); the second, besides being a huge resting place for the deceased, is an outdoor sculpture gallery—a marvel of artistic virtuosity and unabashed sentimentality called *Cimitero Monumentale* (Monumental Cemetery). Built in 1860-1897, it contains the graves of some of the most famous men in the world of opera and literature: Giuseppi Verdi (1813-1901), composer; Amilcare Ponchielli (1834-1886), composer; Alfredo Catalani (1854-1893), composer; Pietro Mascagni (1863-1945), composer; Arturo Toscanini (1867-1957), conductor; Alessandro Manzoni (1785-1873), poet and novelist; and Franco Corelli (1921-2003), operatic tenor. Thérèse had this to say about this place:

> The first Italian city we visited was Milan. We examined minutely its white marble cathedral in which its statues were so many they could have formed a small population. Céline and I were very brave; we were always the first and were following the Bishop [Msgr. Germain] closely in order to see everything pertaining to the relics of the saints and hear the explanations given by the guides. So while the Bishop was offering Mass on the tomb of St. Charles [Borromeo], we were behind the altar with Papa, resting our heads on the tomb enshrining his body which was clothed in its pontifical robes. And it was like this everywhere, except in those places reserved for dignitaries and then we did not follow his Excellency.
>
> We climbed up to the lower pinnacles adorning the roof of the cathedral, and leaving some timid ladies to hide their faces in their hands we followed the braver pilgrims and reached the *top* of the marble bell-tower. From this vantage point, we had the pleasure of seeing the city of Milan at our feet, its numerous inhabitants milling around like *so many tiny ants*. Descending from our high perch, we commenced a series of driven tours which lasted a whole month. I certainly satisfied my desire forever to ride around in comfort!
>
> *Compo Santo* [a "cemetery" by the name of *Cimetro Monumentale*] attracted us even more than the cathedral. All its marble statues, seemingly brought to life by the chisel of some great genius, are placed around the huge cemetery in a sort of haphazard manner which to me added greatly to their charm. One could almost be tempted to console these imaginary personages who were all around us. The expression on the faces is so real, the sorrow so calm and resigned, one can hardly fail to recognize the thoughts of immortality which must necessarily have filled the hearts of the artists creating these masterpieces. One saw a small child scattering flowers on the grave of its parents; the marble seemed to lose its heaviness as the delicate petals slipped through the child's fingers and the breeze scattered them. That same breeze appeared to move

the light veils of widows and ribbons adorning the hair of young girls. Papa was as thrilled as we were.[24]

The large tourist group left Milan on Wednesday, November 9, at three in the afternoon with the city of gondolas as the next stop on their itinerary.

4. Venice
"I found this city sad." — Thérèse

THEY REACHED VENICE FROM MILAN ON WEDNESDAY, NOVEMBER 9. Arriving at ten in the evening, the Martins and others went straight to their lodgings at the sumptuous *Hôtel de la Luna* (*Locanda della Luna*—Hotel of the Moon) which still exists today near Saint Mark's Square, but now under the name Luna Hotel Baglioni. Years later Céline wrote memories of this trip under separate covers known as "*Carnet de voyage*" and "*Souvenirs du voyage de Rome*" (unpublished). In one she copied an observation from a journalist, Abbé Hamel from Bayeux, made on the same trip that she too certainly must have noticed: "In this hotel, everything bears the moon coat of arms: the glasses, the dishes, even the pats of butter which they serve at our meals." Thérèse's recollections of Venice, however, reveal the melancholy that its history evoked in her:

> At Venice the scene changed completely; instead of the noise of the great cities one heard in the solitude nothing but the cries of the gondoliers and the murmur of the waves agitated by their oars. Venice was not without its charms, but I found this city sad. The palace of the doges is splendid, however it too is sad where gold, wood, the most precious statues and paintings of the masters are on display. For a long time now its arches have ceased to resound with the voices of Governors pronouncing the sentence of life or death in the rooms through which we passed. The unfortunate prisoners who were once locked up in these underground cells and dungeons have also ceased to suffer. When we were visiting these frightful prisons, I imagined myself living back in the days of the martyrs and would willingly have remained there in order to imitate them! However, we had to pass quickly from there and cross over the "Bridge of Sighs"; it was given this name because of the sighs of consolation heaved by the condemned when they saw themselves freed from the horrors of the underground caverns; they preferred death to these horrors![25]

A partial list of the places the pilgrims saw, besides the above-mentioned ones, includes what most tourists see today:

- Saint Mark's Square
- The Campanile (the two sisters climbed it)
- The Doges' Palace
- *Palais des Chambord*
- The lace factory
- *Santa Maria Gloriosa dei Frari* (or simply, The Frari), a Franciscan church

---

24 Ibid., pp. 126–127.
25 *Story of a Soul*, chapter VI, pp. 127–128.

where the painter Titian, the sculptor Canova, and the composer Monteverdi are buried. It is also called *Santa Maria Assunta* because of Titian's famous painting of the "Assumption" high above the main altar.
- *Santi Giovanni e Paolo (or San Zanipolo,* an abbreviated form of the two martyrs), a Gothic church founded by Dominicans which houses the tombs of many Doges.
- *Chiesa degli Scalzi (or Santa Maria di Nazareth),* a Carmelite church close to the railroad station.
- The glass factories[26]

Thérèse found time on Thursday—the one full day they had in Venice—to write to her cousin Marie Guérin:

> The country of Italy is beautiful. We are now enjoying its beautiful blue skies. This afternoon, we visited the monuments of Venice in a gondola: it is delightful.
>
> It appears strange to me to hear the language of Italy spoken around us. It is very beautiful, very musical. The people at the hotel call me *Signorella*, but I don't understand anything else but this word which means *"petite demoiselle."* [27]

One member of the French group registered at the same hotel included the noted hagiographer Msgr. Laveille who years later regretted not ever noticing the subject of his future popular biography—*Life of the Little Flower St. Thérèse of Lisieux.*

The one day and two nights' sojourn in Venice ended Friday morning, November 11, at nine when the pilgrimage train left for Padua, about twenty miles away.

5. Padua
Thérèse saw a relic of St. Anthony

THE PILGRIMS LEFT VENICE ON FRIDAY MORNING THE 11TH OF NOVEMBER and headed for Bologna. About twenty miles southwest of Venice they made a short stop at Padua, the cultural, commercial, and religious capital of Venetia, one of the many regions of Italy. It is best known for its associations with St. Anthony and for its ancient university founded in 1222. The only remark Thérèse makes about Padua in her autobiography is the short statement: "after Venice, we went on to Padua where we venerated the tongue of St. Anthony."[28]

Thérèse visited the Church of St. Justina, martyred in Padua as well as the impressive five-domed church of St. Justin that contains the tomb of St. Justin, a philosopher martyred in 166. For her, though, the chief point of interest was the large Romanesque-Gothic *Basilico del Santo* (Basilica of the Saint) that contains in the treasury chapel the relic of St. Anthony. Thirty-two years after St. Anthony's death in 1231, his body was exhumed and transferred to this basilica (built 1232–1307), but all that remained were the bones and the incorrupt tongue now preserved in a golden reliquary studded with precious gems. The Franciscan St.

---

26 From a list Céline wrote in her *"Carnet de voyage"* (her diary) as given in note 4, p. 319, to LT 31.
27 LT 31 A, from Thérèse to Marie Guérin, dated November 10, 1887.
28 *Story of a Soul,* chapter VI, p. 128.

Bonaventure, present at the removal, exclaimed in amazement: "O blessed tongue, you who have always praised the Lord and led others to praise him! Now we can clearly see how great indeed have been your merits before God!"[29] A stone sarcophagus containing the bones of the saint serves as the altar of the burial chapel.

1195 marks the year St. Anthony was born in Lisbon, Portugal, into an aristocratic family. At twenty-five he became a Franciscan and after a brief time in Morocco he spent most of his life in Italy where he soon became recognized as a miracle worker and an extraordinarily eloquent preacher—even to fishes! His short life of thirty-six years involved fifteen years of living at home, ten as a member of the Canons Regular of St. Augustine, and eleven years in the Order of Friars Minor. He died in a suburb of Padua and was canonized only a year after his death. For richly deserved reasons he ranks as the most popular wonder-working saint of the Church.

In art he is recognized by his brown Franciscan habit and is generally depicted holding the Child Jesus in one arm with a book and a lily in the other. The Church bestowed upon him the honor of patron saint of Portugal and Padua. Many devotees pray to him to find lost items.

During her last illness in the convent infirmary, Thérèse disclosed to her sister Mother Agnès that "I was begging St. Anthony during Matins to find our[30] handkerchief that I lost. Do you think he answered me? He did no such thing! But it doesn't make any difference; I told him I loved him just the same."[31]

6. Bologna
A male student accosted Thérèse here

THÉRÈSE INTRODUCES HER SHORT SECTION ON BOLOGNA WITH "AFTER Venice, we went on to Padua ... and then on to Bologna where we saw St. Catherine who retains the imprint of the kiss of the Infant Jesus."[32]

St. Catherine was born of noble parentage in Bologna on September 8, 1413. When a teenager, this beautiful and intelligent girl joined the Augustinians; eventually, though, she became a Poor Clare, and finally an abbess of that order. According to her own writings, the Blessed Virgin appeared to her one Christmas Eve and placed in her arms the Infant Jesus who kissed her tenderly. St. Catherine died at the age of fifty on March 9, 1463. Her body, darkened by time and exposure to lamp and candle smoke, has been in an upright sitting position since 1475 in the chapel specially designed to honor her. Clothed in the habit of a Poor Clare nun, her corpse was enshrined in the *Monastero del Corpus Domini* in this bizarre manner as a result of extraordinary circumstances. An exceptionally holy person, artist, writer, poet, mystic, and visionary, Catherine was canonized in 1712 and proclaimed the patron saint of artists.

---

29 From the *Catholic Encyclopedia*.
30 Thérèse used "our" instead of "my" handkerchief because for Carmelites all possessions belong to the community, not to individual nuns.
31 *Her Last Conversations*, July 2, 1897.
32 *Story of a Soul*, chapter VI, p. 128.

Actually Thérèse admitted to her sisters at the time she was facing her death that the sight of St. Catherine's body was a bit gruesome to behold: "I would rather be reduced to ashes than to be preserved like St. Catherine of Bologna."[33]

Bologna, the capital of Emilia-Romagna (a region south of Venice), boasts of its many titles that capture the essence of the city: "Bologna the learned" because of its fifth century university; "Bologna the red" because of the color of its rooftops; and "Bologna the fat" because of its excellent food. It also gained recognition as an important center of art, commerce, and industry. Some famous natives of Bologna include Pope Gregory XIII (1502-1585)—calendar reformer, the religious painter Guido Reni (1575-1642), the inventor Guglielmo Marconi (1874-1937), and the composer Ottorino Respighi (1879-1936).

The pilgrim group arrived in this large city about six on Friday evening, November 11. On November 12, 1887, a local newspaper reported the arrival of the pilgrim tour group. This might be the first account of several that appeared in print during Thérèse's lifetime which obviously referred to her but typically and fortunately did not mention her name:

> At 5:52 this afternoon a special train arrived containing two hundred French pilgrims. A large crowd gathered at the railroad station composed in major part of students. On the public concourse there was also a large audience; but all observed an irreproachable attitude worthy of a truly courteous city—and the preparations of the guards and police were perfectly useless. The first to get off the train was an old lady, disappointing the young men who were there. Each compartment had at least one priest. A short time after the men who formed a row at the exit turned [with all eyes] toward two beautiful young ladies [Thérèse and Céline?], then two others, then an endless line of priests all with the same look and color, big and red, austere and thin, young and old. A few looked about with an astonished eye, the others advanced with a dignity and lordly pride as if to say "We are the missionaries of the faith."[34]

The Martins stayed at the *Hotel dei Trei Re (Trois Rois)* which does not exist today, at least under that name, on the via Rizzoli until the next morning and boarded their train at eleven. Despite their short stay, the Martins managed to visit seven churches. Thérèse finishes her account of the city with an engaging disclosure:

> It was a great joy to leave Bologna since this city has become unbearable to me because of the students who filled it and formed long lines on the streets through which we had the misfortune to go on foot. I disliked it also because of the little incident which happened to me with one of the students. I was indeed happy to be on my way to Loreto.[35]

Céline explains "the little incident" involving one of the spirited students who had come out to observe the French pilgrims:

---

33 *Her Last Conversations*, July 8, 1897.
34 From a letter by M. Laisney that appeared in the newspaper *Il Resto del Carlino*.
35 *Story of a Soul*, chapter VI, p. 128.

We stood together on the station platform waiting for Papa to get our transport [luggage]. Thérèse looked very pretty and a number of times we heard admiring whispers [and whistles earlier when the ladies alighted from the train] from the passers-by. Suddenly a student rushed up to her and took her in his arms with some words of flattery. He was already carrying her off.[36]

Thérèse finishes the story with "But I gave him such a look that he took fright, let me go and fled shamefacedly.... Besides, Céline had seen what happened and was coming to my rescue."[37]

Years later Céline disclosed a similar incident that occurred on the trip:

On the way to Rome she [Thérèse] noticed that one young man was obviously attracted to her. When we were alone, she said; "How timely Jesus is withdrawing me from the poisoned breast of the world; I feel my heart could easily be captured by affection, and I, too, would perish where others do, for none of us is any stronger than the other."[38]

7. Loreto

"Loreto really charmed me." — Thérèse

LEAVING BOLOGNA AT 11 A.M. ON SATURDAY, NOVEMBER 12, THE TOURist-filled train wended its way down the east coast of Italy known as the Marches, hugging the blue Adriatic coastline. Its destination was Italy's second place of pilgrimage after Rome, the little town of Loreto, where they arrived at five in the afternoon. They stopped here to visit the *Santa Casa* (Holy House—also called the House of Mary), which has been the site of Marian pilgrimages for centuries. Church authorities believe that this building was carried by angels from Nazareth in the Holy Land to a hill in Slavonia (a region of Croatia in northern Yugoslavia) in 1291. Three years later angels again transported it, this time to its present location, setting it down in a woodland of laurel (*lauretum* in Latin, from whence the town received its name). Loreto, surrounded by spurs of the Apennines in the distance, lies on flat land that stretches out to the nearby shores of the blue Adriatic Sea.

The magnificent basilica that houses the Santa Casa was designed by Florentine architects with construction started in 1468. A large piazza extends far out in front of it. This is completely enclosed by an impressive complex of buildings all of which is encircled by a fortress-like wall. Inside the church, the oblong brick Holy House (about 31′ × 13′ × 14′) is situated at the transept crossing under the large dome above it. It, however, is entirely surrounded by a high, ornately carved, white marble edifice designed in the fifteenth century. The one-room structure inside contains an altar, a window on one side, and two doors—one for entering and the other for exiting. Pious legend has it that St. Peter celebrated Mass on this cube-shaped altar after the Ascension. Above it stands an image of the Virgin and Child thought to have been carved out of olive wood by St. Luke. The original was destroyed in 1921 but since then it was replaced by a copy.

---

36 As recorded in Gaucher's *The Story of a Life*, p. 75.
37 Comment of Mother Agnès. See p. 128 in *Story of a Soul*, note 141.
38 From Céline's deposition at the Process of Beatification.

B. The Trip to Rome

The Madonna of Loreto and her story have been the subject for illustrious artists and writers throughout the ages including Raphael (1483–1520), Tasso (1544–1596), Tiepolo (1693–1770), and Gabriele D'Annunzio (1863–1938). Among the many other renowned visitors to this shrine were Christopher Columbus (1446–1506), Galileo (1564–1642), Descartes (1596–1650), and Mozart (1756–1791). The following saints visited the Holy House: St. Charles Borromeo (1538–1584), St. Francis de Sales (1567–1632), St. John Bosco (1815–1884), St. Thérèse of Lisieux, and more than fifty popes. In 1920 the Church proclaimed the Madonna of Loreto the patroness of airmen.

Thérèse was happy indeed to be on her way to Loreto. She tells of the deeply religious feelings she experienced in Loreto:

> I am not at all surprised the Blessed Virgin chose this spot to transport her blessed house, for here peace, poverty, and joy reign supreme; everything is primitive and simple. The women have preserved their graceful Italian dress and have not, as in other cities, adopted the Paris fashions. Loreto really charmed me!
>
> And what shall I say about the Holy House? Ah! how deep was my emotion when I found myself under the same roof as the Holy Family; contemplating the walls upon which Jesus cast His sacred glance, treading the ground bedewed with the sweat of St. Joseph, under this roof where Mary had carried Jesus in her arms, having carried Him in her virginal womb. I beheld the little room in which the angel had appeared to the Blessed Virgin. I placed my rosary in the little bowl of the Child Jesus. What ravishing memories!
>
> *Our greatest consolation* was to receive *Jesus Himself* in His house and to be His living temple in the very place He had honored with His presence. As is the custom in Italy, the Blessed Sacrament is reserved on only one altar in the churches, and here alone can one receive Holy Communion. This altar was in the Basilica itself where the Holy House is to be found, enclosed like a precious diamond in a white marble casket. This didn't satisfy Céline and me! It was in the *diamond* not in the *casket* that we wanted to receive Holy Communion. Papa with his customary gentleness did like all the rest [attended Mass at another chapel in the basilica], but Céline and I went in search of a priest [Abbé Leconte] who had accompanied us everywhere and who was just then preparing to say Mass in the Santa-Casa by special privilege. He asked for *two small hosts* which he laid alongside the large one on the paten and you can well understand ... the joy we *both* experienced at receiving Communion in that blessed house! It was a totally heavenly happiness which words cannot express.[39]

Before leaving the Holy House and while their father was still attending Mass at another chapel in the huge Basilica, Thérèse and Céline searched discreetly and successfully for a particle from the brick walls to take home as a souvenir.

On Sunday afternoon, the thirteenth of the month, after packing their luggage in most likely the Hotel Marinelli, the Martins and the other tourists were driven to the railroad station, boarded their special train, and headed directly for the goal of their pilgrimage—Rome.

---

[39] *Story of a Soul*, chapter VI, pp. 128–129.

8. ROME

"Rome! Rome! It was not a dream, I was in Rome!" — Thérèse

It is about Rome I still have to speak, Rome the goal of our voyage, there where I believed I would encounter consolation [papal approval of her entrance into Carmel] but where I found the cross! It was night when we arrived and as we were all asleep we were awakened by the shouts of the porters crying: "Rome! Rome!" It was not a dream, I was in Rome![40]

THUS BEGINS THÉRÈSE'S FIVE-PAGE NARRATIVE OF HER STAY IN ROME. THE Martin trio (Louis, Céline, and Thérèse) left Loreto on Sunday afternoon, November 13, reached Rome around eight that evening, and checked in at *La Albergo del Sud* (Hôtel de Sud) on the Via Crispi (today it is at 56 Via di Capo le Case) where they stayed for seven rainy days. Actually they were scheduled for the Hotel de Milan but because of overcrowding they were transferred to La Albergo del Sud. This group included the two Martin sisters their and father, three other laymen, three old ladies, and fifteen priests. Among them were M. and Mme. Besnard of Lisieux, whom we shall meet later. The next morning everyone plunged headlong into sightseeing and gift buying for family and friends:

> The first day was spent outside the walls and was perhaps the most enjoyable, for the monuments have preserved their stamp of antiquity. In the center of Rome itself one could easily believe one was in Paris, judging by the magnificence of the hotels and stores. This trip through the Roman countryside left an indelible impression upon me. I will not speak of the places we visited, as there are enough guide books describing these fully, but I will speak only of the *principal* impressions I experienced.[41]

Céline informed those back home in more detail about what they were doing:

> Today, we visited ancient Rome, that is, outside the walls; we went through the Roman countryside, passed along the Appian Way, so famous because of historic and holy memories. St. Paul walked it to go to his martyrdom.... I drank some water from the fountain produced by the bounds made by the head of this great Saint. I saw the prison where he spent three days; it is walled in, but through a little window I was able to thrust in my hand quite far, perhaps farther than many people.... I could not begin to tell you all the things we see; each step uncovers something new.[42]

The guided tours and carriage drives were constant and furious as one of the tourists, Msgr. Leveille, indicates in his biography of St. Thérèse:

> Thus, to fulfill their programme, they [tourist/pilgrims] had usually to hasten along after a guide who too often allowed but little time for prayer even in the most venerated places.

---

40 Ibid., p. 129.
41 Ibid.
42 From Céline to Mme. Guérin dated November 14, 1887.

B. The Trip to Rome

To make matters worse, the rain never ceased to harass the pilgrims; every cupola and obelisk had for background a leaded sky.[43]

Besides the Vatican, the "principal" sights that impressed them were the Coliseum, the Catacombs, the church of St. Agnes, and the basilica of the Holy Cross in Jerusalem. The zealous sisters managed to obtain little mementos at these places such as dirt, a loose mosaic, or purchased items at gift shops.

Just beyond the perimeter of the ancient Roman Forum one sees perhaps the most recognizable structures in the world—the Colosseum (or *Colosseo*) so named because of the "colossal" statue of Nero that stood near it. Construction of this gigantic building 150 feet high, properly called the Flavian Amphitheater, was begun by Emperor Vespasian and completed ten years later by his son Titus in 80 A.D. It served as a sports entertainment center which could accommodate as many as 45,000 seated spectators and 5,000 standees who entered through eighty gateways. Gladiatorial contests, fights between men and animals, races, and even mock naval battles were held wherein millions of lives, both human and animal, were sacrificed for the amusement of the Roman citizenry. For example, on the day it opened 9,000 animals were slaughtered. It is inconceivable how and why the continuous spectacle of horror, cruelty, suffering, and death so pleased the insatiable pagan multitudes that this arena functioned for over 500 years. The last gladiatorial fight took place in 405 A.D. Thérèse, like most Christians today, viewed it primarily as the site of martyrdom for the countless early Christians massacred there. She spends a few pages on it in her autobiography:

> One of the sweetest memories was the one that filled me with delight when I saw the Colosseum. I was finally gazing upon that arena where so many martyrs had shed their blood for Jesus. I was already preparing to kneel down and kiss the soil they had made holy, but what a disappointment! The place was nothing but a heap of ruins, and the pilgrims were expected to be satisfied with simply looking at these. A barrier prevented them from entering the ruins.... But was it possible to come all the way to Rome and not go down into the Colosseum? For me it was impossible! One thought raced through my mind: get down into the arena!... I cried to Céline: "Come quick! We can get through!" We crossed the barrier where there was an opening, the fallen masonry hardly reaching up to the barrier, and we were climbing down over the ruins which rumbled under our feet.
>
> Papa stared at us, surprised at our boldness. He was calling us back, but the two fugitives no longer heard anything.... Céline had listened to the guide and remembering that he had pointed out a tiny bit of pavement marked with a cross as the place where the martyrs fought, we began looking for it. We soon found it and threw ourselves on our knees on this sacred soil, and our souls were united in the same prayer. My heart was beating hard when my lips touched the dust stained with the blood of the first Christians. I asked for the grace of being a martyr for Jesus and felt that my prayer was answered! All this was accomplished in a very short time; gathering up a few stones, we

---
43 Leveille, *Life of the Little Flower*, p. 135.

returned to the fallen walls and began the dangerous ascent. Papa, seeing us so happy, didn't have the heart to scold us and I could easily see he was proud of our courage. God visibly protected us, for the other pilgrims hadn't noticed our absence.

The ravaged corpses of untold numbers of courageous martyrs murdered in the Colosseum and elsewhere were laid to rest in the cold dark labyrinth of Catacombs, extensive burial areas for millions of non-pagan citizens, located some distance away from the Colosseum (Flavian Amphitheatre), on the Appian Way (*Via Appia Antica*), and elsewhere in Rome. They consist of endless areas of long underground passages, chambers, and galleries on several levels dug out of the sandstone-like bedrock. The precious remains were sealed up in recesses in the walls. Carvings and wall paintings honoring them reveal early Christian practices, beliefs, art style, and techniques. These subterranean tombs were in active use from the second until the ninth century when the relics of the martyrs were transferred to churches and shrines above ground.

The most frequented catacomb even today is that of St. Calixtus containing the empty tomb of St. Cecilia that Thérèse visited. The two sisters fortunately had as a guide a Trappist priest, Père Marie-Bernard (not the sculptor) from Normandy who led them through the maze of dimly lit passageways to the original tomb of St. Cecilia and allowed them to lie on the same spot where the saint's body rested for centuries. We learn from Céline's "Notebook of the Trip" that they saw "inscriptions, paintings, an altar where Mass was celebrated, tomb of St. Cornelius, the famous reclining sculpture of St. Cecilia, skeleton of a woman, skull of a child, an anchor, Jonas, the Chananean [*sic*] woman, a bird, a knife [the last five most likely all paintings], etc." Thérèse's venture into the catacombs gained for her some unexpected spiritual rewards:

> [The] Catacombs, too, left a deep impression upon me. They were exactly as I had imagined them when reading the lives of the martyrs. After having spent part of the afternoon in them, it seemed to me we were there for only a few moments so sacred did the atmosphere appear to me. We had to carry off some souvenir from the Catacombs: having allowed the procession to pass on a little, *Céline and Thérèse* slipped down together to the bottom of the ancient tomb of St. Cecilia and took some earth which was sanctified by her presence. Before my trip to Rome I didn't have any special devotion to this saint, but when I visited her house transformed into a church, the site of her martyrdom.... I felt more than devotion for her; it was the real tenderness of a friend. She became my saint of predilection, my intimate confidante. Everything in her thrilled me, especially her abandonment....[44]

The church of St. Agnes (*Sant'Agnese fuori le Mura*—St. Agnes Outside the Walls) was built by Constantine the Great near an ancient catacomb to house the relics of the saint. The thirteen-year-old Roman maiden, martyred around 304 in the Diocletian persecutions, is a special patroness of chastity who for

---
44 *Story of a Soul*, chapter VI, p. 131.

B. The Trip to Rome

centuries has been prayed to by devotees and even mentioned in the canon of the Mass. The original church was rebuilt and renovated in the 7th and 15th centuries, and more recently in 1856. Thérèse has this to say about her:

> [The] visit to the church of St. Agnes was also very sweet to me; she was a childhood friend whom I was visiting in her own home. I spoke a long time to her about the one [her sister Pauline, Mother Agnès who carries her name so well, and I exerted all my efforts to get one of the relics of my Mother's angelic patroness and bring it back to her. But it was impossible to get any [the monks there told her] except a small piece of red stone which was detached [stealthily by the girls] from a rich mosaic, the origin of which goes back to St. Agnes' time. She must often have gazed upon it. Wasn't it charming that the lovable saint herself should give us what we were looking for and which we were forbidden to take? [45]

Saints Cecilia and Agnes both remained "friends" of Thérèse throughout the rest of her short life. In fact she composed two poems especially about them that she dedicated to her sisters: "The Response of St. Agnes" (PN 26) written for Pauline's feast day in 1896, and "St. Cecilia" (PN 3) composed for Céline's twenty-fifth birthday in 1884.

Not far from the well-known Basilica of St. John Lateran is the less familiar church of the Holy Cross in Jerusalem (*Santa Croce in Gerusalemme*). Rebuilt in 1743, it is one of the Seven Roman Basilicas, popular stopping points for devout pilgrims. The eighty-year-old Empress Helena (St. Helen— c. 250–330), the mother of Constantine the Great (c. 288–337), is said to have found in 326 the cross on which Christ died and divided it into three sections: one she sent to her son in Constantinople, one she left in Jerusalem, and the third she brought back to Rome. The main relics of the passion include: three pieces of wood from the cross, one nail, two thorns from the crown placed on Jesus' head, part of the "titulus" (the top section with the sign inscribed in three languages), and even a finger of St. Thomas. All are now in six jeweled gold and silver reliquaries on display in the Chapel of the Relics. After Helena's death, her son or grandsons converted part of her palace into a church to house them. Thérèse has this to say about this place:

> I always had to find a way of touching everything. At the Holy Cross Church in Rome, we were able to venerate several pieces of the true Cross, two thorns, and one of the sacred nails. The nail was enclosed in a magnificent golden reliquary which did not have a glass covering. I found a way of placing my little finger in one of the openings of the reliquary and could touch a nail bathed in the blood of Jesus. Really, I was far too brazen! [46]

---

45 Ibid., chapter VI, p. 132.
46 Ibid, p. 139. The room where the relics of the true cross can be seen today was built in the 1930s. Thérèse did not see them there but in a small, dark, windowless chapel, not currently open to the public, located near the sacristy and refectory in the cloistered part of the monastery. The altar is now in the refectory and being restored. When finished, it will be placed where it was originally.

Italy has been known through the ages as one of the great centers of opera and song. Cognizant of this, Thérèse mentions Italy's artistic heritage in a letter to her close cousin Marie Guérin, an avocational pianist and future nun with her in Carmel:

> In Italy, we hear very much music. You realize it is the country of artists; you would be able to judge much better than I what is beautiful, for I'm not an artist. Jeanne [Marie's sister who was taking art lessons] would see some very beautiful paintings. You see, little sister, that there is nothing for me at Rome; it's all for the artists! If I could only have one word from the pope, I'd ask for nothing more.[47]

The anxiously awaited day finally arrived for the papal audience that was held on Sunday, November 20, in a room in the Vatican named "*Sala dei Palafrenieri*" (Hall of the Grooms). Thérèse best describes the scenario in her autobiography, though at the time she did relay the facts in letters to her concerned family members back home:

> Six days were spent visiting the principal attractions of Rome; it was on the *seventh* I saw the greatest of them all, namely, Leo XIII. I had both longed for and dreaded that day! On it depended my vocation....
>
> Sunday, November 20, after dressing up according to Vatican regulations, i.e., in black with a lace mantilla as head-piece, and decorated with a large medal of Leo XIII, tied with a blue and white ribbon, we entered the Vatican through the Sovereign Pontiff's chapel. At eight o'clock in the morning our emotion was profound when we saw him enter to celebrate Holy Mass....[48]

Céline informs us of the sequence of events at this point with most enlightening details:

> The pope's Mass was followed by a Mass "in thanksgiving," and this was attended by Leo XIII on his knees. The audience began immediately afterward by the presentation of some 125 [Gaucher says 197] pilgrims from Coutances. M. Révérony then offered the wishes of the Bayeux diocese and its jubilee gift, a lace rochet (surplice for prelates), which had required six thousand days of work. The Holy Father examined it closely. Then the pilgrims were presented to him in single file: ladies (about twenty-five; Thérèse and Céline were last); the clergy (some thirty priests); gentlemen (about twenty). At first, Leo XIII had a kind word for each one. But after the long preliminaries which had caused some fear of fatiguing the Holy Father, M. Révérony did not hesitate to forbid any speaking to him, and the audience was hurried up. The Nantes pilgrims came afterward.[49]

Thérèse next continues her narrative:

---

47 LT35, letter from Thérèse to her cousin Marie Guérin, dated November 19, 1887.
48 *Story of a Soul*, chapter VI, pp. 132–135.
49 From the account by Abbé Hamel, correspondent for the *Indicateur de Bayeux*, that sister Geneviève quoted on page 22 in her copybook *"Souvenirs du voyage de Rome 1887."*

B. The Trip to Rome

After the Mass of thanksgiving, following that of the Holy Father, the audience began. Leo XIII was seated on a large armchair; he was dressed simply in a white cassock, with a cape of the same color, and on his head was a little skullcap. Around him were cardinals, archbishops, and bishops. Before entering the pontifical apartment, I was really determined to speak, but I felt my courage weaken when I saw Father Révérony standing by the Holy Father's right side. Almost at the same instant, they told us on the Pope's behalf that it was forbidden to speak, as this would prolong the audience too much. I turned towards my dear Céline for advice: "Speak!," she said. A moment later I was at the Holy Father's feet. I kissed his slipper and he presented his hand, but instead of kissing it I joined my own and lifting tear-filled eyes to his face, I cried out: "Most Holy Father, I have a great favor to ask you!... in honor of your Jubilee, permit me to enter Carmel at the age of fifteen!"

[He] turned to Father Révérony who was staring at me with surprise and displeasure and said: "I don't understand very well."

"Most Holy Father," answered the Vicar General, "this is *a child* who wants to enter Carmel at the age of fifteen, but the Superiors are considering the matter at the moment." "Well, my child," the Holy Father replied, looking at me kindly, "do what the Superiors tell you!" Resting my hands on his knees, I made a final effort, saying in a suppliant voice: "Oh! Holy Father, if you say yes, everybody will agree!" He gazed at me steadily, speaking these words and stressing each syllable: "Go ... go.... You will enter if God wills it!"

I was encouraged by the Holy Father's kindness and wanted to speak again, but the two guards touched me politely to make me rise. As this was not enough they took me by the arms and Father Révérony helped them lift me.... The two guards literally carried me to the door and there a third one gave me a medal of Leo XIII.

One additional fact Thérèse mentions, not in her autobiography, but in a letter to her sister, Sister Agnès, describing the pope: "The good pope is so old that one would say he is dead; I would never have pictured him like this. He can hardly say anything. It is M. Révérony who talks."[50] Ironically, the pope lived for twenty-two more years until 1909, six years after Thérèse died.

Almost a half century later we learn of a remark made by one of those guards to his family the night of the audience. "Oh! it would be impossible ever to see a more charming girl ask for something so difficult."[51]

Céline reported to her Carmelite sister Marie that "I came afterward. I had tears in my eyes, but would you believe that I had the audacity to say: 'Most Holy Father, a blessing for the Carmel.' He blessed me, saying: 'Oh, it is already blessed!'" Their father was introduced with a group of men and when it was all over he tried to console the weeping Thérèse disappointed by the inconclusive papal response. "Ah! it was all over," Thérèse tells us in her autobiography, "my trip no longer held any attraction for me since its purpose had failed."[52]

---

50 LT36, letter from Thérèse to sister Agnès, dated November 20, 1887.
51 From an August 26, 1936, letter to the Carmel by the guard's daughter, then a nun in Egypt.
52 *Story of a Soul*, chapter VI, p. 136.

The people back home soon learned of the episode. Later when Thérèse and Céline discovered they knew, they were quite embarrassed but especially distressed by an article that appeared in the November 24, 1887 issue of the Parisian journal *L'Univers*. It reviewed the audience the pope had with a French group asserting that "among the pilgrims was a young girl of fifteen [unnamed], who begged the Holy Father for permission to enter a convent immediately to become a religious. His Holiness encouraged her to be patient, to pray very much, and to seek counsel from God and her conscience. This caused the young girl to break down into sobs."

The very same day Thérèse wrote a letter (LT 36) to her sister Pauline these emotionally charged feelings:

> Oh! Pauline, I cannot tell you what I felt. I was crushed. I felt I was abandoned, and, then, I am so far, so far.... I was crying a lot when writing this letter; my heart is heavy. However, God cannot give me trials that are above my strength. He has given me the courage to bear this trial. Oh! It is very great.... But Pauline, I am the Child Jesus' little ball; if He wishes to break His toy, He is free. Yes, I will all that He wills.

Years later Céline explained that because of the whole disheartening affair with the pope:

> We hardly ever spoke about it afterward. It was like a memory you wanted to cast far from you. I regarded it so much as a shameful humiliation that I used to think interiorly: If later on they write Thérèse's life, this fiasco will mar its beauty, and, when in Carmel Mother Agnes of Jesus gave her the command to write her memories, I said to myself: Poor little thing, she'll have to recount the audience with the pope which succeeded so poorly.[53] (*See also* Brother Siméon and Pope Leo XIII)

After the audience, Thérèse and Céline went on a side trip for two days to Naples and Pompeii. Their father stayed in Rome and visited his friend, Brother Siméon at the French College of St. Joseph on the Via Aurelia, to whom he told the story of Thérèse's religious calling and the papal audience. The Brother exclaimed in admiration, "One doesn't see this in Italy!" By sheer coincidence, Abbe Révérony also came to see Brother Siméon. Thérèse concludes that "I believe this interview made a good impression on Father Révérony; afterwards he never ceased proving to me that he was finally convinced of my vocation."[54]

Thérèse and her sister returned to Rome at midnight on Tuesday, the twenty-second, and still had the entire next day to continue their vacationing in the Eternal City. The girls were naturally ebullient about their daily experiences and excitedly recounted them at night in their hotel room number 1 at La Albergo del Sud on the Via di Capo le Case just a few feet from the corner of Via Gregoriana. In the room next door resided a crotchety priest, Père Vauquelin (See his biography in chapter 5, B) who was so annoyed by the chatter of these teenagers

---

53 From Céline's preparatory notes for the 1910 Diocesan Process.
54 *Story of a Soul*, chapter VI, p. 137.

that he yelled at them to be quiet and complained to the management! Again news traveled fast and the people of Lisieux learned about the "noisy" girls in their hotel room in Rome. Though the building still exists, it is no longer a hotel but an apartment building with business establishments on the ground floor. After Thérèse's canonization a memorial plaque was placed on the building inscribed thus: "In this house formerly Hotel of the South stayed in 1887 Saint Thérèse of the Infant Jesus."

The Martins visited two churches near their hotel. One is San Giuseppe a Capo le Case on the Via Francesco Crispi, a block away from the end of the street, that was built in the sixteenth century and originally occupied by Carmelite priests. Here Thérèse attended Mass with her father and Céline. The second is the more distinguished and beautiful *Sant' Andrea delle Fratte*, which Pope Benedict called "the Lourdes of Rome." It is located on the Piazza di S. Andrea just about two blocks down from Thérèse's hotel on the opposite side of the street. It is known in art circles for the two Bernini statues of angels. But more significant religiously is the fact that the Virgin of the Miraculous Medal appeared here in January 1842 at a side chapel on the left of the nave to the Alsatian Jew, Marie Alphonse Ratisbonne (1814–1884), who almost immediately converted to Catholicism and later became a priest. (His brother, whom he disdained before this conversion, was ordained a priest years before.) At this same altar St. Maximilian Kolbe (1894–1941) who was greatly influenced by Thérèse's spirituality said his first Mass on April 29, 1918, which happened to be exactly five years to the day she was beatified in Rome.

9. Naples and Pompeii
"In our honor Mount Vesuvius made a lot of noise." — Thérèse

MOST OF THE PILGRIMS, INCLUDING THÉRÈSE AND CÉLINE, LEFT ROME Monday morning at six, the day after the papal audience, for a two-day trip to sunny Naples. Their fatigued father for the first time remained alone to visit a friend but placed his two daughters under the trustworthy care of M. and Mme. Besnard, their travel companions on the train. We learn from the obituary notice of their daughter, a nun, that "Mme. Besnard loved to tell how on the night of the first day, little 'Thérèse, only fourteen, was so tired that she stretched out on the floor [of the train compartment], leaned her head on her knees where she slept for part of the night.'"[55] The tourists arrived early at Naples in the afternoon, left their luggage at the Hotel Metropole, very near the waterfront at 36 *Quai Chiatamone*, and rushed off for some sight-seeing.

The third largest city in Italy, the beautiful sunny Naples with its azure-hued bay and warm climate, was once the summer retreat for Virgil, Caesar Augustus, and Nero. Naples, justly noted for its melodious songs, proudly claims to be the birthplace of spaghetti and Neapolitan ice cream. Its profusion of

---

55 From the obituary notice of Sister Pauline de Sales Besnard, daughter of M. and Mme. Besnard, who died on September 7, 1937. This quote is from note 1 to a letter Céline wrote to her sister Marie in Carmel dated November 23, 1887.

crowded streets, churches, and art galleries did not seem to attract Thérèse, at least in her writing, except for the monastery of San Martino (Certosa di San Martino—Carthusian Monastery, or charterhouse, of St. Martin), an immense building on a hill that is now a museum and art gallery. Construction began in 1325 and completed in 1369 by Giovanna, of the French dynasty of Anjou (the family of St. Louis). It perfectly exemplifies the Neapolitan Baroque style and contains priceless works of art including the famous Neopolitan *presepio* (nativity Christmas scene with hundreds of figures).

From one of the rooms called a belvedere, which Thérèse no doubt entered, visitors behold a spectacular view of the city, the mountain, and the bay. She does comment on Mount Vesuvius, the volcanic mountain outside the confines of Naples. It rises abruptly from the Campania countryside some 3,900 feet above Pompeii which lies on a plain just below it. This ancient settlement was a sumptuous resort town of over 20,000 inhabitants when it was completely covered by 35 feet of hot ash and stone in the 79 A.D. eruption.

The following excerpt comprises all Thérèse wrote in her autobiography about Naples and Pompei:

> On the morrow of that memorable day, we had to leave early for Naples and Pompeii. In our honor, Mount Vesuvius made a lot of noise all day long; it allowed, along with its canon shots, a thick cloud of smoke to escape. The traces it has left upon the ruins of Pompeii are frightening and are a manisfestation of God's power: "*He looks at the earth and it trembles; he touches the mountains and they are reduced to smoke.*" [Psalm 103:32]
>
> I would have loved to take a walk all by myself in these ruins, meditating on the fragility of things human, but the number of travelers took away a great part of the charm of the destroyed city. At Naples it was just the opposite. The trip to the monastery of San Martino, placed on top a hill [Vomero] dominating the whole city, was made magnificent by the great number of carriages drawn by two horses. Unfortunately, the horses took the bit into their own mouths and more than once I was convinced I had seen my last hour. The driver vainly repeated the magic word of Italian drivers: "Appipau! Appipau!"; the horses wanted to turn the carriage upside down. Finally, thanks to our guardian angels we arrived at our magnificent hotel in one piece.[56]

The French travelers had almost the entire day on Tuesday, November 22, for tours and shopping. The train left in the evening, returning them to Rome at midnight.

10. Assisi

An embarrassing moment here for Thérèse

THE FRENCH PILGRIMS FINALLY BADE FAREWELL TO THE ETERNAL CITY ON Thursday November 24. At six o'clock in the morning they set out for Florence, the first night stop on their way home. The train halted briefly at one point for the passengers to get off about which Thérèse writes:

---
56 *Story of a Soul*, chapter VI, p. 137.

> Having remained alone in the car with Céline (the other pilgrims got off to eat during a short stop), I saw Monsignor Legoux, Vicar General of Coutances, open the door and looking at me with a smile, he said: "Well, how is our little Carmelite?" I understood then that the whole pilgrimage knew my secret; happily no one spoke to me about it but I saw by their sympathetic way of looking at me that my request had produced no ill effect, on the contrary....[57]

Half way to Florence they stopped again for just a few hours in the afternoon at Assisi, the town hallowed by the birth and presence of St. Francis and St. Clare. Assisi, built on the lower slopes of the Monte Subasio range, has maintained its Medieval charm even to this day with its heavy ramparts, narrow streets, and closely built ochre colored houses with light brick-colored tiled roofs. The chief point of interest is the Gothic Basilica of St. Francis (consecrated in 1253) consisting of two churches, a crypt, and an adjoining Franciscan monastery. Within the walls of this huge complex are many large frescoes and paintings by the 13th century masters Cimabue and Giotto, most of which pertain to St. Francis.

Thérèse makes no comment in her autobiography about any works of art in Assisi. We do know, however, that she went to the church of St. Clare and the Portincula and also visited the monastery of St. Agnes where she experienced a slight but disconcerting episode involving the priest she most wanted to help her get permission to become a Carmelite:

> I had the opportunity at the little town of Assisi of climbing into Father Révérony's carriage, a favor granted to *no woman* during the whole trip. Here is how I obtained the privilege. After having visited the places made sacred by the virtues of St. Francis and St. Clare, we were ending up in the monastery of St. Agnes, the sister of St. Clare. I had studied the Saint's head at my leisure and was one of the last to leave when I noticed my belt was lost. I *looked* for it in the crowd; a priest had pity on me and helped in the search. After he found it, I saw him depart and I remained alone to *search*, for I had the belt but it was impossible to wear it as the buckle was missing. At last I saw it shining in a corner. Taking it and adjusting it to the belt was the work of an instant, but the work preceding this had taken up much time, and I was greatly surprised to find myself alone in front of the church. The numerous carriages had all disappeared, with the sole exception of Father Révérony's. What was I to do? Should I run after the carriages no longer in sight and expose myself to the danger of missing the train and thus upsetting my dear Papa, or else ask for a place in Father Révérony's coach? I decided on the latter. With my most gracious manner, trying to appear as little embarrassed as I could though I was greatly embarrassed, I explained my critical situation to him. I put him also in an *embarrassing situation*, for his carriage was filled with the most important men of the pilgrimage. There wasn't a single place left, but one good gentleman hastened to descend, made me climb into his place, and humbly took a seat beside the driver. I was like a squirrel caught in a trap and was far from being at ease, surrounded as I was by all these great personages and especially the

---

[57] *Story of a Soul*, p. 138.

most *formidable* of all; I was placed directly opposite to him [Father Révèrony]. He was very friendly towards me, however, and even interrupted his conversation with the others from time to time to speak to me about *Carmel*. Before we reached the station, all the *great personages* took their *huge* purses out to give some money to the driver (already paid). I did the same thing, taking out my *very* little purse. Father Révérony did not agree with what I drew out from it, some pretty *little* coins, and instead he offered a *large* coin for both of us.[58]

Céline, in a letter to her two Carmelite sisters in Lisieux, fills in a few relevant details:

> The other day, Thérèse by accident found herself in the same carriage as himself [Father Révérony] with several handsome gentlemen who never leave him; at the end of the trip, they all gave twenty-five cents to the coachman. Thérèse took out her purse, but M. Révérony gave a fifty-cent piece, saying to Thérèse: "We have an account to settle together."[59]

Three months before her death, Thérèse made a comment about St. Francis that her sister Pauline, then Mother Agnes, jotted down in the notebook she kept of her sister's last utterances:

> In the afternoon, she [Thérèse] felt the need of going out of herself, and she said to us with a sad and gentle look:
> "I need some food for my soul; read a life of a saint to me."
> "Do you want the life of St. Francis of Assisi? This will distract you when he speaks of the little birds."
> "No, not to distract me, but to see some samples of humility."[60]

After a long train ride the weary tourists arrived at the railroad station in Florence at 9:45 in the evening and indulged in a well-deserved rest at the Hotel Porta Rossa where they stayed for two nights.

11. FLORENCE
Thérèse visited the shrine of St. Mary Magdalene dei Pazzi

THE PILGRIM TRAIN REACHED FLORENCE AT 9:45 P.M. ON A VERY RAINY Thursday evening, November 24. The passengers got off and headed for their hotels; the Martins easily finding theirs—the centrally located Hotel Porta Rosa where they were booked for two nights and a day.

Florence (*Firenze*) is an ancient city that traces its founding to around 200 B.C. Situated in the heart of Tuscany, it is divided by the Arno River and surrounded by the Tuscan Apennines in the distance. This world renowned center of art and culture, home of the Medicis, Dante, Machiavelli, Fra Angelico, Michelangelo, Raphael, and da Vinci, apparently held no artistic or historic interest for Thérèse since she makes no reference to anything else in her autobiography except the relatively obscure Carmelite Church of St. Mary Magdalene dei Pazzi:

---
58 Ibid., pp. 138–139.
59 Letter from Céline to Pauline and Marie, November 28, 187.
60 *Her Last Conversations*, July 4, 1897.

At Florence, I was happy to contemplate St. Magdalene dei Pazzi in the Carmelite choir. They opened the grille for us. As we did not know we would enjoy this privilege and many wanted to touch their rosaries to the Saint's tomb, I was the only one who could put my hand through the grating which separated us from the tomb. And so everybody was carrying rosaries to me and I was very proud of my office.[61]

Born into great wealth in Florence, St. Mary Magdalene dei Pazzi (1566–1607) encountered difficulties in becoming a nun. Like Thérèse, she overcame them and was admitted at sixteen into the Carmelite convent of *Santa Maria degli Angeli* in her native town. She died at forty-two after years of intense suffering in body and spirit. Nonetheless, she was privileged with many mystical experiences: visions of Jesus, Mary, and the saints, performance of miracles, and even levitation. Some of these supernatural doings we learn about from her writings.

Today St. Mary Magdalene dei Pazzi's body, remarkably incorrupt and supple for nearly four hundred years, rests in a crystal and bronze casket in the chapel of a Carmelite Monastery of cloistered nuns in the outer limits of Florence far from the bustling tourist center. The place is difficult to find but once there one must ring the bell at the entrance. The voice of a nun answers in Italian and permission to enter must be given in Italian. The chapel is on the second floor and a nun, unseen behind a turn there, will speak and unlock the door to the chapel by ringing a buzzer. Thérèse, though, must have seen the body of St. Mary Magdalene dei Pazzi when it was at the Monastery of the Carmelite nuns in the heart of the city.

Céline tells us they also saw the Cathedral, the Baptistry with its famous bronze doors, Holy Cross Church (*Santa Croce*) where Michelangelo is entombed, the Piti Palace, the Church of the Annunciation, and the Church of St. Lawrence.

Thérèse found time in Florence to write a letter to her cousin telling of her anxiety about returning home: "I assure you I will leave all Italy's marvels behind with pleasure. All this is very beautiful, but I can't forget those whom I have left at Lisieux. There is a kind of magnet which is attracting me to Lisieux, so I shall return there with very much pleasure."[62]

Departure time from Florence was set for two on Saturday afternoon, November 26, with Pisa as their next stopover.

12. Pisa and Genoa
Where Thérèse enjoyed pleasant diversions

Thérèse mentions only the following sentence in her autobiography about Pisa and Genoa: "After visiting Pisa and Genoa once more, we returned to France."[63] (Actually this was the only time they were there!) The tourist train from Florence arrived in Pisa on Saturday afternoon, November

---
61 *Story of a Soul*, chapter VI, p. 139.
62 LT 37, letter from Thérèse to Marie Guérin, November 25, 1887.
63 *Story of a Soul*, chapter VI, p. 140.

26, at four-thirty. The Martins stayed overnight at the *Hotel de la Minerve*. The following afternoon they left this city known as the birthplace of Galileo, but more popular because of its Leaning Tower which the sisters climbed. They arrived that evening at Genoa, nestled on a hilly slope overlooking the sparkling Ligurian Sea. This, the largest Italian seaport, is an important part of the luxuriant Italian Riviera. The Martins spent the night in the *Hotel Isotta* where a plaque there states that "In this building, now *Hotel Isotta*/Saint Thérèse of the Infant Jesus (Thérèse Martin) Discalced Carmelite/Doctor of the Church and Patroness of the Missions/Stayed November 27, 1887/on her return trip to Lisieux/during the pilgrimage to Rome/in celebration of the priestly jubilee of Pope Leo XIII."

After only a few hours of sightseeing, the homeward bound pilgrims left Genoa the next morning en route to France.

Half a year later when Thérèse was a postulant in Carmel, she wrote to her father reminding him of one of their whimsical diversions: "Do you recall, Papa, when at Genoa we were shadowing from a distance M. Benoit [one of the tourists, a magistrate from Caen] and the others? Ah! what fun we had." [64] Céline explains this "shadowing": "At times, when we had free time, we used to take walks without knowing too much where we were going. It was then that, seeing someone from the pilgrimage, Papa used to say to us playfully: 'Let's shadow him!' This amused us very much. But it was done out of curiosity, nor for a long time!" [65]

13. NICE
Here Thérèse was given some hope of entering Carmel

AFTER LEAVING GENOA AT NOON ON MONDAY THE 28TH, THE LARGE GROUP of French tourists enjoyed the stunning scenery along the French Riviera. They arrived at six in the early evening at the famous Mediterranean resort city of Nice where the Martins had accommodations at the *Hôtel Beau Rivage*. Thérèse glowingly describes in her autobiography the sights she beheld on the way there:

> [The] scenery was magnificent. We traveled at times along the side of the sea and the railroad was so close to it that it seemed the waves were going to come right up to us. This impression was created by a tempest which was in progress. It was evening and the scene became all the more imposing. We passed through fields full of orange trees laden with ripe fruit, green olive trees with their light foliage, and graceful palm trees. It was getting dark and we could see many small seaports lighted up by many lights, while in the skies the first *stars* were beginning to sparkle.
>
> Ah! what poetry flooded my soul at the sight of all these things I was seeing for the first time in my life! It was without regret I saw them disappear, for my heart longed for other marvels.[66]

---
64 LT 51, letter from Thérèse to her father, dated May 17, 1888.
65 From Céline's "Preparatory Notes" for Piat's *The Story of a Family*.
66 *Story of a Soul*, chapter VI, pp. 140–141.

A half dozen letters from home were waiting for the Martins at their hotel when they arrived. Most dealt with the sensitive incidents pertaining to Thérèse's vocation. Since the party left the next morning at seven o'clock for Marseille, they really had no time for answering them or even for much sightseeing in Nice with its famed seafront avenue and pebbly beach. Céline, nonetheless, informed her Carmelite siblings through her last letter home of a propitious meeting in Nice between Thérèse and the ubiquitous Abbé Révérony:

> This morning, when being taken to the station, we were in the omnibus [a horse-drawn vehicle] with M. Révérony. Papa was next to him, and he said in a whisper: "Would you say something to Thérèse." M. Révérony answered with a smile, and Papa said: "You know that she is always thinking of her little Christmas Jesus [her expression for entering Carmel by Christmas four weeks hence].... The same smile, the same response. Then without being aware of anything, we got up into the omnibus, Thérèse and I, and we were behind Papa. By God's permission, Thérèse was next to M. Révérony. She was very close to him, for we were sixteen in the carriage, eight on one side, crushed in like sardines. M. Révérony leaned over to Thérèse and said to her: "Well! where will we go when we are at Lisieux?" Thérèse, searching for an answer, responded with a smile. M. Révérony repeated his question. Thérèse then said: "I will go to see my sisters at Carmel." He answered: "I *promise* to do all I *can*." Thérèse then answered with this word [sic] which came from her heart: "Oh! Thank you!..."
>
> This was the whole little scene; I wrote it immediately [on the train] such as it took place.[67]

14. MARSEILLE
Thérèse visited its famous basilica

AFTER LEAVING NICE AT 7 A.M. ON TUESDAY, NOVEMBER 29, THE TRAINLOAD of homeward bound pilgrims traveled over seventy miles along the French Riviera coastline and arrived in the afternoon at Marseille, the largest port city in the Mediterranean. Founded about 600 B.C., it also ranks as the oldest French big city. The Martins slept that night at the *Hotel Belle-Vue* and left the next morning after some quick sightseeing of the city popularized by Alexandre Dumas' 1844 novel, *The Count of Monte Cristo*.

The Martins' chief interest here was the *Basilica of Notre-Dame-de-la-Garde* (Our Lady of the Guard), a celebrated pilgrimage center even to this day. Throughout the centuries, French seamen especially from Marseille were devoted to the Blessed Virgin under the title, *Notre-Dame-de-la-Garde*. Successive chapels stood on the site formally used as a lookout point. Eventually between 1853 and 1899 a magnificent church was built on the site of former chapels and consecrated under the present title. This grand Romano-Byzantine edifice, over five hundred feet above sea level, affords a wonderful panoramic view of the city and the sea, especially from the top of its grandiose 150 foot high tower

---
67 Letter by Céline to Pauline and Marie, dated November 29, 1886.

surmounted by a twenty-eight foot tall gilded statue of the Madonna. Inside the hollow metal figure, a staircase leads to the top with its spectacular sight of the whole area. Though neither sister mentions it in her writings, one wonders if they ventured to the pinnacle as they did to the *Arc de Triomphe*, the Milan cathedral, the dome of St. Peter's, the bell tower at St. Mark's Square, and the Leaning Tower of Pisa. While in the basilica, though, the grateful French pilgrims sang the "Magnificat" in thanksgiving for a safe and enjoyable journey. A marble plaque on the left side wall of the nave not far from the main altar commemorates Thérèse's visit there in 1887 and a chapel in the lower crypt is dedicated to her. The plaque states that on "November 29, 1887, Saint Thérèse of the Infant Jesus returning from Rome, came to pray [at] N.D. de la Garde. Blessed be the name of the Lord. Ave Maria!"

Four men who touched Sister Thérèse's life also spent a brief time in Marseille. The two "spiritual brothers" she corresponded with embarked from here for their assigned foreign missions: Père Roulland to China in 1896 and Abbé Bellière to Algeria on September 29, 1897—the day before Thérèse died. The third man, on the opposite end of social and moral conformity, was the criminal Pranzini for whose conversion Thérèse had prayed so fervently. He was arrested here on March 22, 1877, two days after he brutally murdered two women and a girl in Paris.

Ten years after her visit to Marseille, Thérèse underwent a mortifying experience through the diabolical deceit of one of Marseille's own citizens, Charles Jogand-Pagès, alias Léo Taxil. As a writer he created, among others, the fictitious person Diana Vaughan, an alleged atheist who spread her anti-Catholic, egregious ideas through his/her sensational writings. At one point Taxil penned a dramatic turn in her story and had her convert to Catholicism and even contemplate becoming a Carmelite. Sister Thérèse heard of this and, sufficiently intrigued, wrote to her (him), and enclosed a photo of herself as Joan of Arc—a character in a play she wrote for one of her convent recreations. Eventually, during a highly publicized press conference, Taxil revealed with arrogant pride his hoax and displayed only one photo—that of Thérèse as Joan of Arc! With further audacity, he referred to the "credulous" nun who wrote to him as a "*pauvre imbécile*" ("poor imbecile"),[68] thankfully he did not disclose her identity. Taxil, having hoodwinked a nation, let alone Thérèse and even the pope, craftily slipped away from the frenzied assemblage, never to surface prominently again. From then on, Thérèse, totally astounded by it all, never spoke of the incident.

Though posthumously done, Marseille made a kind of oblique restitution for this calumny perpetrated by one of its natives by building the first sanctuary to St. Thérèse—even before her canonization in 1925. The church, a small version of *Notre-Dame-de-la-Garde*, bears the name *Sainte Thérèse des Chutes-Lavie*.

---

[68] Schmidt, *Everything is Grace*, p. 282.

15. Lyon and Paris
The last phase of the trip

THE PILGRIM TRAIN LEFT MARSEILLE FROM THE ST. CHARLES RAILROAD Station at six o'clock on Wednesday morning, November 30, leaving behind the beautiful Mediterranean coastline. It headed inland, directly north for the evening's stop 122 miles away in Lyon, a hilly city divided by the confluence of two rivers—the Rhône and the Saône. Later in the day it arrived and the tourists dispersed to their hotels for the night—the *Hôtel Continental Collet* for the three weary Martins. It was at this hotel that Céline says they were pleased to go to their room by using an elevator again. Before departing the following morning on the last segment of the journey, Thérèse paid a visit with her father and sister to *Notre-Dame-de-Fourvière*, a basilica positioned atop the Fourvière hill in the old section of town reached by steep winding uphill streets or by funicular. Built in fulfillment of a vow after the disastrous Franco-Prussian War (1870–1871), it furnishes a grand view of the city, the Rhône River, and the countryside in the distance. At this point, though, the overriding concern for Thérèse did not involve the sights before her but the speedy attainment of her dream—entering Carmel by Christmas.

On Thursday morning at 10:30 the large contingency of tourists left Lyon on the 300 or so mile ride to Paris. Céline fills in the final plans of their itinerary in a letter she wrote to her Carmelite sisters:

> We arrive on Thursday at midnight at Paris. Being *very eager* to see all of you again, we shall probably not stay at Paris [during the day on Friday], and we are counting on taking the 11:45 [A.M.] train [from the Gare Saint-Lazare] which will bring us into Lisieux around 4:30 on Friday. If you don't receive any other letters or telegrams, it is because nothing has changed. It is understood that we shall stop at the Carmel immediately.[69]

And that is exactly what they did. Thérèse tells us: "we had hardly arrived at Lisieux when our first visit was to the Carmel. What an interview that was! We had so many things to talk over after the separation of a month which seemed very long to me and in which I learned more than in several years."[70]

One sentence in the autobiography perfectly sums up Thérèse's reaction to this marvelous trip: "[My] heart longed for other marvels. It had contemplated *earthly beauties* long enough; *those of heaven* were the object of its desires and to win them for souls I was willing to become a *prisoner!*"[71]

Six months later, after she attained her vocational objective and became a postulant in the Lisieux Carmel, Thérèse wrote to her father informing him that "the memory of this beautiful trip made with my dear little Father will always remain with me."[72] She did have her fill of traveling, however, for she

---

69 Letter from Céline to Pauline and Marie, dated November 28, 1887.
70 *Story of a Soul*, chapter VI, p. 141.
71 Ibid.
72 LT 51, May 17, 1888.

divulges in *Story of Soul* that "Papa suggested we take a trip to Jerusalem, but in spite of my attraction for visiting the places sanctified by Our Lord's passage there, I was tired of earthly pilgrimages." Céline succinctly finishes the story of Thérèse's struggles to become a Carmelite:

> On her return to Lisieux Thérèse anxiously awaited the authorization of the Bishop. At the advice of Pauline, she [Thérèse] wrote to him on 16 December a letter of reminder, and also to Father Révérony recalling his promise to help her.... It was on 1 January, 1888, that she learned through Mother Marie de Gonzague [the prioress] of the definite consent of Msgr. Hugonin. But at the suggestion of Sister Agnes of Jesus [Pauline] her entrance was postponed until after Easter [April 9, 1888] because of the Lenten season, and without doubt also to spare the feelings of Abbé Delatroëtte [who opposed her entrance from the start].[73]

---

73 Sister Geneviève, *The Father of the Little Flower*, pp. 76–77.

C. Other Places Visited by St. Thérèse's Family

1. THE BASILICA OF OUR LADY OF DELIVERANCE: *Popular Marian pilgrimage center*
2. LOURDES: *Thérèse's mother went here for a cancer cure*
3. THE TRAPPIST MONASTERY OF SOLIGNY: *Where Louis Martin made retreats*

1. THE BASILICA OF OUR LADY OF DELIVERANCE
Popular Marian pilgrimage center

THE OLDEST PILGRIMAGE SHRINE DEDICATED TO THE BLESSED MOTHER IN Normandy is the Basilica of Our Lady of Deliverance (*Notre-Dame de la Délivrande*) in Douvres-la-Délivrande, located some thirty-six miles northwest of Lisieux and about eight miles north of Caen on the Normandy coast. Tradition maintains that in the fifth century a Catholic chapel, replacing an old pagan temple, was erected there and dedicated to the Virgin Mary. By the twelfth century a church was constructed on the spot, likewise dedicated to the Virgin, which in turn was replaced, in the middle of the nineteenth century, by the present basilica. Throughout the centuries cures and exceptional conversions were reported to have occurred there through the intercession of "Our Lady who saves." Even today thousands of pilgrims go there not only from Normandy but beyond to pray and worship.

Our Lady of Deliverance is mentioned in Theresian literature but there is no definitive proof that she ever visited the place. Regarding this matter, Sister Geneviève (Céline) offered these two statements contradicting each other; the first in 1943 and the second in 1958:

> 1. In July 1887, our good father took us, Léonie, Thérèse, and myself, to the exhibition at Le Havre. We went there by way of Honfleur, stopping first at *Notre-Dame de Grâce*. It seems to me it was not the first time we went to Honfleur to pray to the Madonna. He brought us also to *Notre-Dame de la Délivrande*, about this same time.[1]
> 2. I cannot believe that Thérèse ever went without me, without all of us to *Notre-Dame de la Délivrande*, nor can I state that Papa ever set foot there. Yes, this is what I can unfortunately state, he never set foot there (Father S. J. Piat, February 21, 1958). [Since Sister Geneviève was eighty-nine at the time and evidencing many signs of lapse of memory, her testimony cannot be relied upon.][2]

---

[1] G/NPHF, p. 555. Actually the trip occurred in June 1887.
[2] This and the above information are taken from Note 5, to LC 186, the letter from Father Bellière to Thérèse written on June 7, 1897.

2. LOURDES
Thérèse's mother went here for a cancer cure

LOURDES IS PERHAPS THE WORLD'S MOST FAMOUS SHRINE DEVOTED TO THE Blessed Virgin where millions of pilgrims, both well and infirm, go to visit, meditate, and pray for physical and spiritual cures. Located at the foot of the Pyrenees Mountains in southwestern France, Lourdes is the birthplace of the peasant girl Bernadette Soubirous who at the age of fourteen experienced her first of eighteen visions of the Blessed Mother on February 11, 1858, in the Massabielle Grotto near the town. Up through the fifteenth apparition, Bernadette referred to the one she saw as "the Beautiful Lady." It wasn't until the sixteenth apparition that the Lady revealed her name when she said, "I am the Immaculate Conception." Since then the Church has officially recognized and authenticated well over sixty miracles attributable to the intercession of the Blessed Mother. Thousands of other physical healings have been reported and millions of spiritual and moral ones have taken place.

One of the earliest records of a Martin visiting Lourdes is that of Thérèse's father who went there some months before Thérèse's birth. He returned with two pieces of rock he had broken from the cave of Massabielle, just six feet from the spot where the Virgin appeared.[3] This brings to mind a similar thing Thérèse did on her pilgrimage to Rome in 1888 when she and her sister, contrary to the rules, climbed down onto the floor of the Colosseum and picked up a few stones as relics from the spot where martyrs died.

Because of the fame of this place of miracles, Thérèse's mother Zélie in June 1877 traveled the long and painful train trip of one hundred and seventy miles to pray for the cure of her cancer that finally took her life two months later. She was accompanied by her three oldest daughters, Marie (seventeen), Pauline (sixteen), and Léonie (fourteen). Since Thérèse was only four at the time and her sister Céline, eight, they had to remain at home under the care of their father. Zélie wrote this poignant letter to her brother and sister-in-law, M. and Mme. Guérin:

> Heaven has never seen, nor will it ever see, more fervent prayers, more lively faith, than those prayers which my little Pauline has offered for her mother. And then, I have my sister, the nun, now in Heaven praying for me.... And my four little angels in Heaven, my little ones who died so young. They are all praying for me. They will all be with us, in spirit, at Lourdes.[4]

In another letter Zélie, writing on the train home from Lourdes, gives details of her experience there:

> I have been immersed four times in the baths; the last time was two hours before we left Lourdes. I was in the icy water above my shoulders but it was less cold than in the morning. I stayed in, over a quarter of an hour, still hoping that

---
3 Emert, *Louis Martin: Father of a Saint*, p. 37.
4 CF 205, letter of June 7, 1877.

Our Lady might cure me.... *While I was immersed in the waters, I no longer felt any pain*; but as soon as I came out, the sharp twinges returned as usual....[5]

It is interesting to know that Zélie had previously corresponded with Bernadette's parish priest of Lourdes, Father Peyramale, who was most helpful in providing consolation and courage to her in her great physical affliction. Unfortunately, he was not in town during her visit but Zélie did see his housekeeper who also knew Bernadette and was present at some of her apparitions.

Zélie reminded her sorrow-stricken daughters, who were heartbroken that their mother was not cured, what Our Lady said to Bernadette: "I do not promise to make you happy in this world, but *in the next*." Confiding in her loving sister-in-law Mme. Guérin, she wrote: "I know very well that Our Lady *could* cure me; but I cannot help thinking that she does not will to do so, since the Will of God may be for me to die."[6] She was right. There was no miracle and the forty-six-year-old wife and mother of five daughters died on August 28, 1877.

Years after this tragic loss for the family, members of Zelie's immediate family or close relatives went to Lourdes several times seeking assistance from Our Lady. From May 6 to 17 or 18, 1890, Céline traveled with her sister Léonie and the Guérins, to various cities in France including Lourdes and Tours. In the former home of Léon Dupont ("The Holy Man of Tours") in Tours, the chapel now there became the center of devotion to the Holy Face; this became an important element in Thérèse's spiritual life and she chose "the Holy Face" as part of her religious name.

Both Céline and Léonie were experiencing at this time some health concerns: Céline, heart problems, and Léonie, skin eruptions. Apparently Céline received some solace at Lourdes for their cousin Marie Guérin wrote to Céline that: "Thérèse told me yesterday that certainly you [Céline] would receive consolations from the Sacred Heart just as the Blessed Virgin gave you at the grotto. You had not told me that you had received any consolations at Lourdes."[7]

Thérèse conveyed to her sister Céline this bit of wisdom, "[Do] you know it is a great grace to visit all these holy places?"[8] It was a different matter for herself, however, as she told her sister Pauline (Sister Agnès of Jesus): "How happy I am to be *always a prisoner* in Carmel; I have no desire to go to Lourdes to have ecstasies. I prefer 'the monotony of sacrifice'! What a joy to be so hidden that nobody thinks of you!... To be *unknown* even to persons with whom you live...."[9]

In August of 1897, Dr. Francis La Néele, and his wife, Thérèse's cousin, Jeanne, went on a national pilgrimage to Lourdes. (This, as it happened, left the dying Thérèse at the Carmel with no doctors at hand including the official convent physician.) In a letter dated August 26, 1897, Dr. La Néele informed his father-in-law, Isidore Guérin, that there were about fifty cures among the forty

---

5 CF 209, letter dated June 24, written by Zélie to her brother and sister-in-law.
6 CF 213, letter dated July 15, 1877.
7 LD, dated October 15, 1890.
8 LT 105, dated May 10, 1890.
9 LT 106, letter dated May 10, 1890, from Thérèse to Pauline.

thousand pilgrims who were there, "which, in the memory of man, had never been seen at Lourdes."[10] Thérèse's spiritual brother, the Abbé Bellière, was on the same pilgrimage. Aware of Thérèse's impending demise, he wrote to her:

> At Lourdes, I did not ask for your cure.... I prayed to the gentle Queen of Virgins and Martyrs to aid you in your final preparations and to open heaven to you. I do not know how to pray, so I asked to be a stretcher-bearer for the poor sick people, and I was doing this for your sake. Often when carrying them to the Grotto, to the baths, my thoughts went to you and ascending to Mary, saying: "Mother, this is for Sister Thérèse." ... [And] when the Blessed Sacrament passed close by me, blessing this crowd of unfortunate people gathered round it, I prayed fervently for you. That is what my prayer was. And when I saw these sick people, whom a few hours before I had carried in my arms, almost without any life, shocking at times in their illness, when I saw them made well, cured, and now forming the escort of honor for Jesus, I was thinking of you, suffering on your poor bed, and I asked from your Bridegroom for a consolation, a last preparation, and additional act of tenderness for you.[11]

Besides Lourdes and Nevers where the incorrupt body of St. Bernadette is venerated, Céline and Léonie and some relations made trips to Le Puy to honor the Blessed Virgin Mary at her shrine there; to Ars, where St. John Vianney (the "Curé of Ars") lived and his incorrupt body is enshrined; and to Paray-le-Monial on October 17, 1896, the feast of the bicentenary of the Blessed Margaret Mary's death. It was she who promoted devotion to the Sacred Heart of Jesus.

3. The Trappist Monastery of Soligny
Where Louis Martin made retreats

CÉLINE WROTE A PIOUS BIOGRAPHY OF HER FATHER, LOUIS MARTIN, IN which she disclosed that:

> Our father also used to make *Closed Retreats*. At the Trappist Monastery of Soligny they have on record the dates of one of his stays there. He also liked to make pilgrimages, to which he used to add some form of penance. Walking-stick in hand, he would start out fasting for Our Lady's of Seez [sic],[12] or some nearer shrine around Alençon. He visited Chartres also several times. His object was to implore some special grace, the cure of one of his sick children, or aid for France in some national crisis or calamity.[13]

Louis Martin, a loyal, conservative Frenchman, loved his country, her greatness, her mission. An example of one of Louis Martin's pilgrimages for blessings on his homeland is expressed in a letter he wrote to his daughter, Pauline, in May 1873—the year Thérèse was born: "Pray hard, my dear little one, for the success of the pilgrimage to Chartres [consisting of 20,000 other Catholics],

---

10 Footnote 2, LC 196, August 28, 1897.
11 LC 196, August 28, 1897.
12 Today the spelling is "Sées" which is in the Orne, not Séez, located in the French Alps (Savoie).
13 Sister Geneviève, *op. cit.*, p. 10.

in which I am to take part, and which will gather a great many pilgrims from our fair France at the feet of our Blessed Lady, in order to obtain the graces of which our fatherland [rampant with anticlericalism] stands in such great need, if it is to show itself worthy of its past."[14]

The Trappist Monastery, known as the Abbaye Notre-Dame de La Trappe, is about thirty miles south of Alençon, near the town of Soligny-la-Trappe. The land itself was originally known only to trappers, hence its name, La Trappe. On these grounds in the 12th century a count had a chapel built in memory of his departed wife. Eventually monks arrived and founded a monastery. It was not until the 17th century that some Cistercian monks, observers of the Rule of St. Benedict (c. 480–543), arrived there and under the direction of their abbot, Armand Jean de Rancé (1626–1700), born of a wealthy and noble French family, initiated serious reforms. He insisted on the penitential aspect of monasticism which bound the monks to eat small quantities of food and no meat. Hard manual labor and strict silence were mandatory. During the French Revolution (1789–1799), the monks were forced to leave, and under the leadership of their abbot, Dom Augustine de Lestrange (1754–1827), they survived and returned in 1815. The monastery was in ruins but a new one was built on the foundations of the old. Again in 1880 the Trappists were expelled for a short time and returned to construct a new church in 1895. As late as 1977 the interior was remodeled.

The large and impressive Trappist Monastery of Soligny is thriving today. The monks have a gift shop where they sell pottery and other goods they make themselves. An extremely gifted sculptor, Louis Richomme (1883–1975) became a Trappist in 1907 and was ordained a priest with the religious name Father Marie-Bernard. He had a very strong devotion to St. Thérèse and carved most of the familiar statues of her. He consulted Thérèse's sister Mother Agnès and received much inspiration, advice, and encouragement from her. His famous pieces include, among others, the recumbent figure of the deceased Thérèse in the Lisieux Carmel chapel and the one outside on the left of the entrance to the chapel. At the Basilica in Lisieux there are two by him—one outside and one inside above the main altar. On the façade of Les Buissonnets in Lisieux is a bas-relief of Thérèse gazing at a statue of the Blessed Virgin that smiled at her. Also in Lisieux at the Hermitage—a spiritual center for pilgrims and retreatants—is another beautiful sculpture depicting her sitting down with her hands folded on a book. At her birth town of Alençon, in the baptistery of the church of Our Lady, stands the conventional one depicting Thérèse strewing roses.

Trappist is the popular name for a member of this order of Cistercians of the Strict Observance. Today there are about seventy Trappist abbeys throughout the world consisting of monks and some for nuns who both wear long white habits with a black scapular extending far down the front.

---

14 CF 102 bis. Translated into English in Piat, *The Story of a Family*, p. 109.

CHAPTER 8

THE CARMELITES

A. History
B. The Lisieux Carmel

A. History

THE CARMELITE ORDER ORIGINATED FAR BACK IN THE 12TH CENTURY at Mount Carmel on a verdant mountain range in the northwest part of Israel. It began around 1154 in caves located there inhabited by ten Christian hermits from Europe headed by St. Berthold (d. 1185). They came to this area originally either as pilgrims or as crusaders. Then, in imitation of the ninth century B.C. saintly prophet Elias who lived in nearby caves, these hermits determined likewise to live secluded lives in the same spot, dwell also in little cells in the rocks, and emulate him in his desire to be always "in the presence of God." One of the most important aims of these first hermits was the construction of a small chapel in honor of Our Lady of Mount Carmel. By the end of the century, the community increased in number so much that in 1208 they requested the Italian Patriarch of Jerusalem, St. Albert (d. 1214), to draw up a written rule of life for them. Pope Honorius III (1216–1227) formally approved this rule in 1226, thereby allowing these hermits, now called Carmelites, to have the status given to the Dominicans who in 1216 and the Franciscans in 1223 had their rules legitimately approved. Nineteen years later in 1245, Pope Innocent IV elevated the Carmelites to the rank of a mendicant order rather than an eremitical one. The full title of the order became the "Order of Our Lady of Mt. Carmel."[1] The name "Carmel" means garden, orchard, or vineyard.

During the period of the Crusades (1096–1291), the cruel persecution of Christians in the Holy Land by the Muslims compelled many Christians to leave including some of the Carmelite brothers who were permitted by their superiors to do so on condition that they live the Rule of the Order wherever they settled. Thus around 1237 monasteries were founded in Cyprus, Sicily, Italy, and France. By 1240 the Carmelites settled in England and by the end of the century they had established other Carmelite monasteries in Spain, Germany, Ireland, and Scotland. These totaled 150, not only across Europe, but also back in the Holy Land.

---

[1] In Latin, *Ordo fratrum Beatæ Virginis Mariæ de monte Carmelo.*

Plate 22

The Lisieux Carmel

A. The courtyard and cloister of the Lisieux Carmel (north side) at the time of Saint Thérèse. (The cross below the window at the right indicates Saint Thérèse's cell.)

B. The courtyard and cloister of the Lisieux Carmel (south side) at the time of Saint Thérèse.

Plan of the Lisieux Monastery
(Drawing by Renzo Restani)

⊢——⊣ = 10 m

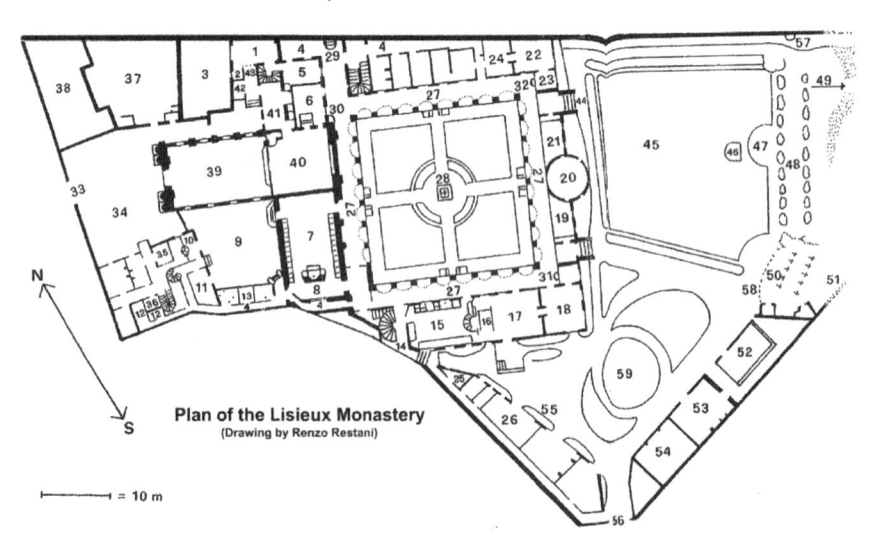

Inside the Cloister

1. Vestibules
2. Confessional (nun's side)
3. Sacristy courtyard
4. Hallways
5. Sacristy
6. Oratory
7. Choir
8. Entrance room to choir
9. Lourdes courtyard
10. Inner turn
11. Turn sisters' workroom
12. Sisters' side of parlors (speakrooms)
13. Storeroom
14. St. Alexis (refectorian's workroom)
15. Refectory
16. Procurature (pantry)
17. Kitchen
18. Recreation room
19. Hermitage of St. Joseph
20. Hermitage of the Sacred Heart
21. Room for making altar breads
22. Infirmary of the Holy Face
23. Infirmary's cell (Sr. Geneviève)
24. Infirmary of Our Lady of Lourdes
25. Lamp storeroom (?)
26. Cellar
27. Cloisters
28. Large cross in cloister courtyard
29. Statue of Immaculate Virgin
30. Thérèse's statue of the Infant Jesus
31. Statue of Our Lady of Mount Carmel
32. Statue of St. Teresa of Avila

Outside the Cloister

33. Entrance door
34. Chapel courtyard
35. Extern sisters' house
36. Visitors' side of parlors (speakrooms)
37. Chaplain's gardens
38. Chaplain's house
39. Chapel
40. Sanctuary
41. Sacristy
42. Confessional (priest's side)
43. Door into enclosure

Garden

44. Infirmary stairs
45. Meadow
46. Pond
47. Heritage of the Holy Face
48. Chestnut walk
49. Lower yard
50. Cemetery
51. Grotto of St. Mary Magdalen
52. Laundry
53. Washhouse
54. Shed
55. Satue of the Heart of Mary
56. Carriage gate
57. Statue of St. Joseph
58. Medlar tree
59. Flower garden

C. Plan of the Lisieux Monastery

In 1245 the first general chapter of the Order convened in Kent, England, at Aylesford and elected St. Simon Stock (1165–1265), then eighty years of age, as the sixth prior-general. As a youth, he lived for a while like a hermit in the hollow of a tree, hence his surname Stock, meaning "tree trunk." On July 16, 1251, near Winchester (some sources say Cambridge), England, St. Simon Stock experienced a vision of the Blessed Mother who gave him the brown scapular with the assurance that whoever died wearing it would be saved. Sadly, also in 1251, in the Holy Land of Palestine, a brutal persecution by the Muslims forced the Carmelites to abandon their hermitage on Mount Carmel and return to Europe.

Two centuries later another prior-general of the Carmelite Order, Blessed John Soreth (1395–1471), born in Caen, France, established the first French convent of Carmelite nuns in 1452 and at the same time attempted to restore the order to its original strict rule initiated by St. Albert. St. Teresa of Avila fully realized this dream a century later by founding the first house of Discalced Carmelite nuns at Avila, Spain, in 1562. She also brought about the re-formation of the order with the superb and energetic assistance of St. John of the Cross. As a result, the Carmelites separated into two branches: the Discalced Carmelites (O.C.D.) and the Calced Carmelites (O.Carm.).

By the middle of the 17th century, the Carmelites attained the height of their power and influence. The Jesuits, especially at this time as well as other orders, became involved with serious controversies with the Carmelites basically concerning the origin of their order and the source of the scapular. It wasn't until the end of the century that Pope Innocent XII (1615–1700) issued a brief (1698) which demanded and brought about an end to the controversy.

In the meantime, six Discalced Carmelite nuns arrived in Paris on October 15, 1604, among whom were four Spaniards and two Flemish. One of the Spaniards was the Venerable Anne of Jesus (1545–1621), born Anne de Lobera, counselor and companion of St. Teresa of Avila. Incidentally, in May of 1896, St. Thérèse of the Child Jesus had a dream wherein she saw a nun who told her of her imminent death. She, without any previous knowledge of her appearance, recognized the nun as Sister Anne of Jesus.[2]

All religious including the Carmelites suffered greatly during the French Revolution (1789–1799) by expulsion, imprisonment, or death; but in the end the Carmelites managed to return and resume their religious life on French soil.

After the Revolution, the Carmelite nuns in Pont-Audemer strove to re-establish their Carmelite monastery there, but in order to receive authorization to do so, the government compelled these nuns to open a school. Two blood sisters from Le Havre, Athalie and Désirée Gosselin, attended as boarding students. Deeply enamored of the Carmelite Order, they wanted to become Carmelite nuns. Poor health prevented them from enduring the strict life required by the then existing Carmelite rules. They prayed, nonetheless, for a Carmelite vocation at the chapel of Our Lady of Grace in Honfleur, the same place a half century later

---

2 See *Story of a Soul*, chapter IX, pp. 190–191.

where Thérèse also invoked Our Blessed Mother's help for her vocation. The bishop of Bayeux, Msgr. Dancel, directed them for guidance to the Sulpician priest Pierre Nicolas Sauvage (1794–1853), curate of the church of Saint-Jacques in Lisieux, who eventually became their future superior. In order to accomplish their objective, which he himself favored, he sought a Carmelite community that would be compatible to their abilities and willing to give them assistance. He found just the one in the Carmel of Poitiers. The nuns there agreed and accepted the two sisters and a friend, Caroline Gueret from Lisieux, to make their novitiate at their monastery. Another young lady joined them soon after. When the time came, the Poitier Carmelites offered two of their best professed nuns to direct and advise them once they moved to their new place in Lisieux. They appointed Sister Elizabeth of Saint Louis prioress (d. 1842) and Sister Geneviève de Saint-Thérèse (1805–1891) subprioress as well as mistress of novices.

They found their way to Lisieux on March 16, 1838, ready to commence their religious life. Since at this point the new Carmel was not ready for them, the gracious widow Madame Le Boucher welcomed the six women into her home on Chaussée de Beuvillers (Beuvillers Road)[3] in Lisieux, just a very short distance behind the present Carmel. Not long after, they moved into a slightly larger building nearby on the Rue de Livarot that would later become the present Carmel. The recently appointed Bishop, Msgr. Robin, blessed their new oratory on August 24, 1838, under the title of "Mary conceived without sin." A month later the two Gosselin sisters and Caroline Gueret made their profession there. The community received the first postulant on March 19, 1839.

Mother Elizabeth of Saint Louis died in 1842 after which Mother Geneviève became prioress, an office she held, except for intervals required by the Rule, until 1886. Though these two nuns were co-foundresses of the Lisieux Carmel, Mother Geneviève is regarded by many as the true foundress of the Lisieux Carmel. Mother Geneviève was still alive when Thérèse entered the monastery; Thérèse became very fond of her and considered her a saint. She was present at the eighty-six-year-old nun's deathbed.

Father Sauvage, keenly aware that a chapel for the monastery was of uppermost importance, consequently traveled throughout France to obtain the necessary funds for its construction. Finally, the new chapel was built and blessed by Bishop Robin on September 6, 1852. Only a half year later Father Sauvage died and was interred near the choir grille. Canon Delatroëtte (1818–1895), his successor as superior of the Carmel, served from 1867 to 1895. Upon his death, his own nephew, Canon Maupas (1850–1920) followed in his steps as the Carmel superior. He is remembered as the main celebrant at the funeral Mass of Sister Thérèse of the Child Jesus.

---

3 Descouvemont, *op. cit.*, p. 100. However, the present author when visiting this place in March 2006 noticed the sign indicating the name of the street: "*Rue du Père Zacharie auteur atirique du XVII ème siècle né a Lisieux*" (Street of Father Zachary satiric author of the 17th century born in Lisieux).

Despite years of poverty and struggle, spiritual strength prevailed and enabled four nuns from the Lisieux community, headed by Sister Philomène of the Immaculate Conception, to establish successfully in 1861 the first Carmelite monastery in the Far East in Saigon (now Ho Chi Min City), the then capital of the French colony of Cochinchina (South Vietnam).

It took about forty years to finish the construction of the Lisieux Carmel. The last major addition during that time was the second wing of the building that contained the library, chapter room, some cells, and the infirmary. Thérèse entered eleven years after the completion of all the structures. She died on September 30, 1897, in the infirmary that had been blessed exactly twenty years before on the same day and month.

During Thérèse's life at the Lisieux Carmel, the repair in 1889 of the house of the Extern Sisters took several months of work and inconvenience to the whole community. After Thérèse's death, major structural repairs, changes, and additions were made. Due to the the constant and huge volume of pilgrims visiting the Carmel chapel in the aftermath of Thérèse's canonization, the Rue de Livarot directly in front of the buildings was replaced by a large plaza. In 1933 the name of the road passing in front of the Carmel area was changed to the Rue du Carmel. Later in the twentieth century the interior of the original chapel was made less ornate to conform to contemporary standards of simplicity.

Further drastic changes were made in 2008 in time for the celebration of the beatification of St. Thérèse's parents, Louis and Zélie Martin, which entirely altered the manner of entering the grounds of the chapel, thus making it possible to handle the vast amount of pilgrims better. The museum too was renovated.

B. The Lisieux Carmel

1. Formation Stages
2. Daily Schedule and Regimen
3. Thérèse's Assignments
4. Lay Staff
   a. Dr. Alexandre-Demas de Cornière: *The Carmel doctor*
   b. Victor Bonaventure and August-Ferdinand Acard: *Sacristans and gardeners*

1. Formation Stages

THE LISIEUX MONASTERY OF DISCALCED[1] CARMELITES IN THÉRÈSE'S DAY consisted of three separate groups of religious: choir nuns with black veils, lay sisters (converse sisters) with white veils, and extern sisters (turn sisters) with their own distinctive habit. In order to become a full-fledged Carmelite (choir nun), the aspirant had to go through three stages—as postulant, novice, and professed. The constitution of the order did not specify an age for the admittance of postulants but it did stipulate that no one would be professed before the age of eighteen.[2] In Thérèse's case, the greatest objection to her entry at fourteen came from the ecclesiastical superior of the Lisieux Carmel, Canon Delatroëtte, who maintained that no one should be permitted before twenty-four. He finally gave in and Thérèse was allowed to enter at fifteen. She had already overcome some obstacles and resistance from other quarters.

The name postulant is derived from the Latin *postulare* meaning "to ask" which the aspirant does—ask to be admitted into a religious community. The length of time spent as a postulant varied but it was generally from six to twelve months.

The garb of the postulant consisted of a long dark blue dress, a black cape, and a small dark bonnet. Thérèse wore this dress from April 9, 1888 to January 10, 1889. The general norm required the candidate to submit a dowry. Thérèse's amounted to 10,000 francs.[3] The rule in Carmelite houses provided for each young postulant an "angel" who taught the aspirant the practices and customs of the Order. In Thérèse's case, her eldest sister Marie (Sister Marie of the Sacred Heart), a novice, twenty-eight years old and in the convent two years, was selected as her angel. Below are seven paragraphs of rules from the *Book of Decorum* regarding the formation of novices:

---

1 "Without shoes," i.e., these Carmelites wore sandals, not shoes.
2 Laveille, *op. cit.*, p. 120.
3 Ibid., p. 115.

- The Sisters must take great care to manage and compose their exterior appearance the best they can, in order to honor that of Our Lord Jesus Christ and of his most blessed Mother.
- They must always hold themselves erect and, whether speaking or walking, they must pay attention to make the least movement possible of the head, the hands, and the rest of the body.
- They must go about the house in a recollected and extremely modest manner, without turning the head, nor raising their gaze to look at anything out of curiosity or frivolity, and they must keep their hands under the scapular so that they will refrain from carrying anything that would hinder them.
- They must pay attention to train their feet to make so little noise while walking, that they will not be heard at all. Our Spanish Mothers were very exact in this practice, and they strongly urged it.
- When someone truly needs to speak, if two words will suffice, one must render this accuracy to God and not say three.
- During the Hours of the Office, one must be most modest and recollected, and pay great attention to not raise the eyes at all, and not turn the head at all, nor touch one's face or one's clothing.
- They ought always to have their eyes cast down and fixed before them, without turning the head, and without looking at others, even when serving them.... They ought always to hold themselves erect, leaning neither on the table nor against the wall.[4]

The day's schedule and regimen for everyone in the monastery below the age of twenty-one was practically the same for all the women except the postulants who were not allowed to fast. Abstinence from meat, however, was obligatory for everyone except in cases of illness or frailty.

Upon completion of postulancy, the young lady became a novice, a more stringent kind of probation period that lasted less than a year during which the candidate was tested more scrupulously for fitness to become a member of the community. The day Thérèse entered the novitiate—her clothing day, January 10, 1889—she discarded her simple postulant dress. In its place she put on a white veil, white velvet bridal gown embellished with flowers and lace, and a long train. Under her white veil crowned with lilies that her Aunt Guérin had given her,[5] her long luxuriant blond hair flowed gracefully down to her shoulders. She emerged from the enclosure and met her waiting father who escorted her down the aisle of the public chapel with members of her family following. Slowly they walked two-by-two as in a wedding procession to the sanctuary where she symbolically became the Bride of Christ. At the conclusion of all the pomp and ceremony, she proceeded to the sacristy where she kissed her family for the last time, knelt down on the tile floor to receive her father's blessing, and entered the door leading to the enclosure. All the nuns greeted her here. Each carried a lighted candle, headed by the prioress who took Thérèse's hand

---

4 Descouvemont, *Thérèse of Lisieux and Marie of the Trinity*, pp. 12–13.
5 Gaucher, *op. cit.*, p. 99.

and proceeded to the monastic choir where the actual clothing took place. In the meantime, the "wedding" party met the officiating priest in the sanctuary of the chapel and congregated at the grille that separated the faithful from the nuns inside. Here the officiating priest intoned the liturgical prayers while the prioress dressed the novice in her new religious habit that consisted of a long scapular over a rough homespun brown tunic with a leather belt from which dangled a rosary. On her head she wore a white wimple and white veil. Woolen stockings and sandals called alpargates completed her attire. This day was called the Clothing Day or "reception of the habit" day. At this time Thérèse Martin officially received the religious name of Sister Thérèse of the Child Jesus.

Normally at the end of one year the novice made her perpetual vows. (Temporary vows did not exist during that era.) The superiors decided in Thérèse's case that instead of the expected date of January 10, 1889, it should be postponed for eight months. Her official novitiate period thus lasted eighteen months until September 1890. In the eighth month she made her profession. On this day in the privacy of the chapter room she pronounced the three canonical vows—poverty, chastity, and obedience. The second part of this religious commitment took place seventeen days later on September 24 in the monastery chapel with the public present. This was called the "Veiling" when the black veil replaced the white one. Thérèse became the forty-eighth nun professed up to that time in the Carmel of Lisieux.[6] Usually three years after profession a Carmelite left the novitiate but in 1893, of her own accord, Thérèse requested an extension of her stay in the novitiate quarters. By remaining there she was considered a minor and not a full-fledged nun in the canonical sense of the word. Four years later she died.[7]

The final stage or period was that of the professed nun which lasted until the death of the Carmelite. When a nun passed away, the superior of the monastery sent an obituary notice (necrological circular) to other houses of the Order notifying them of the death of one of its members. It contained a brief account of the deceased person's life and requests for the repose of her soul. In Thérèse case, her autobiography *Story of a Soul* became her death circular. It was published on September 30, 1898, a year after her death, in one volume of 475 pages and 2,000 printed copies.

2. Daily Schedule and Regimen in St. Thérèse's Time

SUMMER SCHEDULE

A.M.

4:45 Rising
5:00 Mental Prayer (meditation in choir)
6:00 Prime, Terce, Sext, None (Little Hours of the Office)
7:00 Mass and Thanksgiving (8 o'clock on Sunday)

---

6 Ibid., p. 129.
7 Ibid.

8:00	Breakfast (nothing on fast days)
	Work
9:50	Examination of Conscience (in choir)
10:00	Lunch
11:00	Recreation (dishwashing for those assigned, lasting about ½ hr.)

P.M.

12:00	Siesta (nap and free time in silence)
1:00	Work
2:00	Vespers (in choir)
2:30	Spiritual reading (meeting of the novices in the novitiate)
3:00	Work (bell is rung to recall when Christ died. Each nun kisses the ground and her crucifix)
4:00	Work continues
5:00	Mental prayer (meditation in choir)
6:00	Supper
6:45	Recreation (dishwashing for those assigned to it)
7:40	Compline
8:00	Grand Silence (Free time—when Thérèse did her writing)
9:00	Matins and Lauds (the "morning office" lasting 1¼ hr. but 1 hr. and 40 min. on feast days)
	Examination of Conscience (10 minutes)
	Reading of the subject for meditation the next day
10:30–11:00	Bedtime

The year at Carmel was divided into two periods: the summer schedule (summer horarium) which started on Easter and ended on September 14, the feast of the Exaltation of the Holy Cross; and the winter schedule (winter horarium) that extended from September 14 to Easter. An extra hour of sleep was allowed in the winter; therefore, the day began at 5:45 instead of 4:45 A.M. There was no siesta in wintertime so the afternoon schedule was the same as in the summer.

REGIMEN

I. LITURGY AND PRAYER

4½ hours were devoted to the recitation of the Divine Office in choir and the celebration of Mass. Private meditation lasted two hours in choir. An additional half hour was dedicated to spiritual reading.

II. FOOD

There was perpetual abstinence from meat for everyone except for those who were sick or infirm. The basic element of the diet consisted of bread and a considerable amount of milk and starches. Nothing was allowed between meals. Drinking of water was permitted at 3:00 P.M. and after Matins in the evening.

Breakfast	8:00 A.M.
	Thick soup while standing at one's place on the outside of the tables. Nothing on fast days.
Lunch	10:00 A.M.

Fish or eggs, generous portion of vegetables, and dessert of cheese or fruit

Supper 6:00 P.M.
Soup, vegetables, dessert
At this time the readings varied according to the feast day and were selected from the following:
- "Lessons" of Matins read in French (not Latin)
- Martyrology
- Entire Office except Psalms
- Passages from *The Liturgical Year*
- Biography of a saint

III. FASTS

The Constitution prescribed numerous fasts during the liturgical year. No one was permitted to fast before the age of twenty-one. Some of the fast days included the vigil of the feast of the Sacred Heart, the Saints Peter and Paul, the Visitation, Assumption, etc. In these cases, the main meal was an hour later at 11:00 A.M., the nap (siesta) was cut to ½ hr., and the supper replaced by a light meal (Collation).

- Fast of the Order:
  Morning No food
  Midday The main meal at 11:00 A.M. with the regular food plus soup.
  Supper Collation at 6:00 P.M. with bread (7 ounces), butter or cheese, fruit, and sometimes jam. No soup or broth and nothing hot was served.
- Ecclesiastical Fast (during Lent, Forty-hours, and vigils):
  Morning No food
  Midday Main meal at 11:30 with the same menu as during the fast of the Order. Eggs and all milk products were excluded from the diet. The food was boiled prepared with oil.
  Supper Collation at 6:00 P.M. consisting of 6 ounces of bread, no jam, no fresh or dried fruit.

IV. WORK

Amounted to about five hours a day in solitude in one's cell or in rooms set aside for work in the laundry, art studio, sacristy, where altar breads were baked, or outside in the garden area.

V. RECREATION

This lasted around two hours and was generally held in the heated recreation room and sometimes outside. The plays Thérèse composed as recreational skits were almost all performed in the recreation room except for one or two when the chapter room might have been used.

VI. SLEEP

At night about six hours were allotted for sleep during the summer schedule and seven for the winter one. In addition, a nap during the one hour siesta was permitted or that time could be used as a free period.

3. Thérèse's Assignments

YEAR	AGE	STATUS	DUTIES
1888	15	Postulant	Mended in linen-room, worked in the refectory and laundry, swept a staircase and the dormitory corridor, and weeded the garden.
1989	16	Novice	Second in charge of the refectory. She rang bells, served at table, and took her turn reading during meals.
1890	17	Professed	Worked in refectory: set up water, bread, and cider on tables, and swept the floor.
1891	18	Assistant Sacristan	By the end of the year she was in full charge of the sacristy during and after the influenza epidemic.
1892	19	Sacristan until June then in August was portress	Worked as sacristan and was assigned as third portress.
1893	20	Assistant Novice Mistress	Did most of the work of novice mistress. She left the sacristy and painted pictures that were sold to the public. She also painted a fresco of angels in the infirmary oratory. For 2 months (June–July) she was the bursar's "tierce" and accompanied the bursar each time a workman entered the monastery. In September she was appointed second portress and also assisted the nun in charge of the gatehouse.
1894	21	Assistant Novice Mistress	She did the full work of novice mistress but without the title; produced some art work (painted holy pictures, and decorated church ornaments and objects); and wrote her first assigned play for the community.
1895	22	Assistant Novice Mistress	Same as previous year. Started to write her autobiography.
1896	23	Assistant Novice Mistress	Did work in linen room, art room, and again in the sacristy.
1897	24	Assistant Novice Mistress	Did some mending and art work early in the year until she became too ill to continue.

4. Lay Staff

a. **Dr. Alexandre-Demase de Cornière:** *Thérèse's doctor at the monastery*
b. **Victor Bonaventure and Auguste-Ferdinand Acard:** *Sacristans and gardeners during Thérèse's time in the Lisieux Carmel*

a. Dr. Alexandre-Demase de Cornière (1841–1922)
Thérèse's doctor at the monastery

ALEXANDRE-DEMASE DE CORNIÈRE WAS BORN ON OCTOBER 26, 1841, IN Bonnebosq, Calvados, Normandy. He studied medicine in Caen and Paris where he became the senior intern at St. Louis Hospital. In 1868 he settled in Lisieux, a year later began his general medical practice in Lisieux, and in 1891 was appointed chief surgeon at the Lisieux hospital. Between 1886 and 1920 he served as the doctor for the Carmelite monastery and never charged a fee for his services.

Dr. Cornière was an ardent Roman Catholic and a great benefactor of the poor in Lisieux, many of whom he treated also without exacting a fee. His son, Joseph (1874–1939), one of seven children, was ordained a priest in 1899.

He was friendly with the Guérin family who had him as a guest at their vacation home called the Chateau de la Musse. For many years Dr. Cornière maintained a long correspondence with Sr. Geneviève (Céline). He gave valuable testimony at the preliminary Informative Process that led to Thérèse's beatification. Together with Dr. La Néele (the husband of Thérèse's cousin, Jeanne Guérin), he had the task of examining the remains of St. Thérèse when they were exhumed—a necessary requirement for the process toward sainthood.

After Thérèse's apparently first meeting with Dr. Cornière, she commented about him in a letter she wrote to her Aunt Guérin:

> Dear Aunt, you ask me to give you some news about my health ... but if I tell you I am in excellent health, you will not believe me, so I shall allow the famous Doctor de Cornière to speak, to whom I had the distinguished honor of being presented yesterday in the speakroom. This illustrious personage, after having honored me with a look, declared that I looked well![8]

Thérèse and her family members were accustomed to using nicknames for themselves and others. She had one for her doctor: "*Clodion le chevelu*" (Clodion the Hairy—or the Long-haired) because the way he wore his hair reminded her of the barbarian Frankish chieftan Clodion who invaded Gaul in the 5th century. Sister Geneviève wrote in her *Manuscript Notebook IV* (CMG IV) that not only did Thérèse think his hairdo was like Clodion's, but he arranged it "*à la Jeanne d'Arc, en artiste*" (like an artist, in the style of Joan of Arc).

Except for the period from about August 10 to September 10, 1897, when he was on vacation at Plombiéres in the south of France, Dr. Cornière took charge

---
[8] LT 192 dated July 16, 1896.

of Thérèse during her final sickness, visiting her at least thirty-two times—about twenty-six before he left and six after he returned. Unfortunately, no replacement from the hospital for Dr. Cornière was called perhaps because of thoughtless procrastination or simply inaction on the part of Mother Gonzague, not maliciously as some contend. He did, however, send prescriptions for Thérèse whenever he was absent. The frank and outspoken young Dr. Francis La Néele, nonetheless, very concerned about his cousin's health, took it on his own to visit Thérèse a few times times, notwithstanding some opposition from Mother Gonzague. He strongly contended that she should be seen every day by a doctor.

Mother Agnès testified during the Apostolic Process that when "Doctor de Cornière returned in the early days of September [1897] he spoke of injecting morphine [because of Thérèse's severe pains] but the Mother Prioress would not allow it." She contended that it was "shameful" for a Carmelite to give in to taking sedatives.[9] At the very end, however, she rather reluctantly permitted her to have some small doses of morphine syrup.

Dr. Cornière is mentioned quite often by Thérèse and family members in letters and written conversations. In fact, detailed accounts of the medical condition, treatments, medications, progress, and mental state of Thérèse flowed steadily through the mail between the Carmel and the Martin and Guérin families. Besides this form of gaining information, family members on visits to the Carmel learned the latest health status. Mother Agnès copied this conversation in her "Yellow Notebook" about Dr. de Cornière months before her sister died:

> One of our friends had died [Jeanne-Marie Primois], and Dr. de Cornière had spoken about her illness in the presence of Thérèse; she had a tumor that he was not able to define exactly. This case interested him very much from the medical viewpoint. "What a pity I was unable to make an autopsy," he said. She [Thérèse] said later:
> "Ah! It's in this way that we are indifferent towards one another on earth! Would he say the same thing if it were a question of his own mother or sister? Oh! How I would love to leave this sad world!"[10]

In July, Mother Agnès wrote to her Aunt and Uncle Guérin telling them that Thérèse was not concerned about the seriousness of her illness or her appearance:

> [she] sees herself become emaciated and is happy about it: "How happy I am," she said, when looking at her hands. "How pleasant it is to see my destruction." And again: "This poor M. Clodion, you'll have to see him when he withdraws his head from my shoulder; he'll no longer know what to do, and he'll be so nettled, he'll jump around. And he will find nothing but rags, bones, and old habits!"[11]

Four days later, Pauline urged Thérèse to say some kind and uplifting words to the doctor which she did with this surprisingly candid and unreserved

---

9 Gaucher, *The Passion of Thérèse of Lisieux*, p. 244.
10 *Her Last Conversations*, July 3, 1897.
11 Letter of July 16, 1897.

reply: "Ah! Little Mother, this isn't my little style. Let Doctor de Cornière think what he wants. I love only simplicity; I have a horror for 'pretense.' I assure you that to do what you want would be bad on my part."[12]

Thérèse spoke more amiably ten days later: "If you want to give Doctor de Cornière some souvenir of me, give him a picture with the words: 'What you have done to the least of my brethren, that you have done to me'"[13] (Matthew 25:40).

Thérèse's sense of humor never left her even during her trying and painful last days. After a visit from the doctor, she stated that "I wanted to say to Dr. de Cornière: 'I'm laughing because you were not able to prevent me from going to heaven; but, for all your trouble, when I am there, I will prevent you from coming there soon.'"[14] Thérèse's plan worked, for Dr. de Cornière died twenty-five years later.

Thérèse concocted an amusing yarn involving Dr. Cornière a few months earlier which generated a bit of jollity for all: "We had caught a mouse in the infirmary, and she made up a whole story about it, begging us to bring her the wounded mouse so that she could put it in bed by her side and have the doctor examine it. We laughed very much over this, and she was happy for having distracted us."[15]

This example of her sense of humor is tinged with pathos as evidenced in a letter Thérèse's cousin Marie of the Eucharist sent to her father:

> If you were to see our little patient, you wouldn't be able to stop laughing. She has to be always saying something funny. Ever since she has become convinced she is going to die, she has been as gay as a little finch. There are times when one would pay to be near her. All of a sudden this morning she began to say: "But if I am going to be one of the two, alas!..." We looked at one another, wondering what she meant, and she went on: "Yes, one of the two percent; that would be unfortunate!" Very simply stated, because Mother Prioress told her that Dr. de Cornière said that only two percent of those in her present condition recover, she is afraid she might be one of those who will recover.[16]

This excerpt provides another example of her many poignant utterances:

> This evening, when you told me that Dr. de Cornière believed I still had a month or more to live, I couldn't get over it! It was so different from yesterday when he was saying that I had to be anointed that very day! However, it left me in deep peace. What does it matter if I remain a long time on earth? If I suffer very much and always more, I will not fear, for God will give me strength; He'll never abandon me."[17]

This quote from Pauline indicates how Thérèse thought she reacted to her pains:

---

12 *Her Last Conversations*, July 7, 1897.
13 Ibid., July 30, 1897.
14 Ibid., September 24, 1897.
15 Ibid., July 9, 1897.
16 July 9, 1987. See p. 274 in *Her Last Conversations*.
17 Ibid., July 31, 1897.

B. The Lisieux Carmel

Doctor de Cornière paid her a visit, and he told us that she still had to suffer a real martyrdom. When leaving, he remarked on her heroic patience, and I told her this:

> [Thérèse responded] "How can he say that I'm patient! It's not true! I never stop moaning and groaning; I'm crying all the time: Oh! Là là! And: My God, I can't stand it anymore! Have pity, have pity on me!"[18]

Thérèse's superior qualities of holiness, courage, and strength of will to withstand extreme pain were apparent to all. The following three selections disclose the opinion of Dr. Cornière who clearly realized the heroic features of the young dying nun, specifically the medical aspects:

> 1. She's an angel! She has the face of an angel; her face hasn't changed, in spite of her great sufferings. I've never seen that in others before. With her general state of getting thinner, it's supernatural.[19]
> 2. It appears Dr. de Cornière was admiring his patient's gentleness and patience. It seems she's suffering atrociously. He can't understand how she continues to live and attributes this prolongation to a supernatural cause; this was the case with Mother Geneviève formally.[20]
> 3. "My little patient isn't worse, but she isn't better. The sickness pursues its course," says Dr. de Cornière, and he adds that cavities are forming in the lung; this makes him fear the formation of sores, etc. He was telling us the other day: "She's going to win her canonization process!"[21]

Mother Agnès recorded this morbid but typical Theresian conversation that took place in September of 1987 (day unknown):

> One day, in her presence, Mother Prioress was speaking to the doctor [de Cornière] about the purchase just made [by Thérèse's uncle, Isidore Guérin] of a lot in the city cemetery because there was no longer any room in the old one. She added that they would henceforth dig the graves deep enough so that it would be possible to superimpose three coffins. Sister Thérèse of the Child Jesus said, laughing: "Then it's I who will do first honors to this new cemetery?"
>
> The doctor was surprised and told her not to be thinking of her burial. She replied:
>
> "However, it's a happy thought. But if the hole is so deep [hers was more than eleven feet], it will disturb me, because some accident could happen to those who were lowering me into it."
>
> And continuing in this same vein:
>
> "I already hear one undertaker crying out: 'Don't pull the cord there!' Another who answers: 'Pull it that way! Hey, be careful! So that's that!' They will throw some earth on my coffin and then everybody will leave."

---

18 Ibid., September 20, 1897.
19 Made by Dr. de Cornière to Pauline on September 24, 1897, and recorded by her in *Her Last Conversations*.
20 From M. Guèrin's letter to his daughter, Mme. La Néele on Sept. 25, 1897.
21 A truly prophetic remark made to Mother Agnès, though he probably never imagined it would actually happen. Céline wrote this in a letter to her Aunt Guèrin on July 22, 1897.

When Doctor de Cornière left, I asked her if she really felt nothing at the thought of being placed so deeply in the earth. She answered with surprise: "I don't understand you! What does it matter to me! I would not even experience the least repulsion at knowing that I will be thrown into a common grave."[22]

Some misgivings have circulated that Dr. de Cornière did not at first diagnose Thérèse's condition correctly, claiming that her problem was merely congestion in the right lung. This conjecture seems insubstantial in view of the fact that the records show all his prescriptions and treatments were indeed for tubercular patients. Others believe he knew her true condition and because it was incurable, he avoided upsetting the family and the Carmelite community by bluntly telling them the truth, especially in the early stages of the disease. On the other hand, Dr. La Néele seems to have been aware from the onset that she had tuberculosis and did not hide it, at least from her immediate family. At any rate, Dr La Néele was quite laudatory in his evaluation of the doctor as Thérèse's cousin Marie observed: "He found our little patient admirably cared for, and he said that with all the care Dr. de Cornière has given her, if she was not restored to health, it was because God willed to take her for Himself in spite of everything."[23]

Dr. Cornièr was present at the first exhumation of Thérèse's coffin in 1910 and examined her remains at the second one in 1917 for which he presented a detailed professional report of his findings to the tribunal at the Apostolic Process in August of 1917. He died at the age of eighty-one in Lisieux on June 25, 1922, after serving faithfully as the Carmel doctor gratis for thirty-four years.

b. Victor Bonaventure (d. 1889) and Auguste-Ferdinand Acard (1864–1931)
Sacristans and gardeners at Carmel during Thérèse's life there

OUT OF ABSOLUTE NECESSITY THE LISIEUX MONASTERY REQUIRED A LAYMAN to work as sacristan for tasks in the chapel open to the public, and as gardener and manual laborer. The Carmel employed two men during Thérèse's time at the convent—Victor Bonaventure and Auguste Acard. Victor was there when Thérèse entered in April 1888 but died about a year and a half later on August 27, 1889. During the month or so interval between Victor's death and the engagement of his successor Auguste, the novices, Sister Thérèse and Sister Martha, assumed the sacristan's duty of sweeping the chapel open to the public. The twenty-five-year-old Acard stayed on the job for twenty-three years until he left in 1912. A native of Calvados, he was born in Villers-Bocage on March 25, 1864, and died at sixty-seven in Lisieux on January 30, 1931, well after Thérèse was proclaimed a glorious saint of the Church.

Thérèse's sister Céline (Sister Geneviève), an avid amateur photographer, brought with her to the convent her camera and photographic equipment and even developed her own pictures there. She photographed most of the

---

22 See p. 258 in *Her Last Conversations*.
23 From a letter written by Sister Marie of the Eucharist (Marie Guérin) to her father on August 17, 1897.

forty-seven pictures taken in the convent—all but one in which Thérèse appears. (Those pictures in which Céline is seen were snapped by another nun.) Céline took three separate photos of Thérèse in the cloister courtyard which required some time to arrange a position for her and then for her to pose nine seconds for each shot. This proved quite grueling for Thérèse, just four months from death, weak, in pain, and suffering from a high fever. August Acard was at that moment working nearby and heard her say to Céline just before the final picture (No. 42), "Oh, quickly, I am exhausted!" [24]

Toward the end of the next month, Auguste and the Carmel chaplain, Abbé Youf, left for a few days vacation at Thérèse's Uncle Guérin's country estate, the Chateau de La Musse where Thérèse's father died three years before.

Léonie Martin had sent her sister Thérèse a music box with sweet melodies that all enjoyed in the convent, despite the fact that they were not religious in nature. In connection with this we hear for the last time of Auguste. Pauline recorded the incident:

> The little music box had been wound up too tightly and appeared to be broken. Auguste repaired it, but since then it missed (for one tune) the most beautiful note. I was rather disappointed, and I asked her [Thérèse] if she was too:
> "Oh! Not at all! But I am simply because you are." [25]

---

[24] *The Photo Album of St. Thérèse of Lisieux*, p. 201.
[25] September 9, 1897, in the *Yellow Notebook* (*Her Last Conversations*).

Selected Bibliography

Agnès of Jesus, Mother [Pauline Martin]. *At the School of St. Thérèse of the Child Jesus: Her True Doctrine Explained by Herself and Supported by the Writings of Doctors and Theologians of Holy Church*. Translated by Rev. Michael Collins in collaboration with the Carmel of Kilmacud. Dublin: M. H. Gill and Son, Ltd., 1952.

_____. *Marie: Sister of St. Therese: Her Life written by Pauline, Another Sister of the Little Flower*. Translated from the French by Rev. Roland Murphy and Rev. Albert H. Dolan. Chicago: The Carmelite Press, 1943.

_____. *A Novice of Saint Therese*. Translated by the Carmelite Nuns of the Ancient Observance at the Carmel of the Little Flower. Allentown, Penn: Carmelite Monastery of Saint Therese, 1946.

_____. *Novissima Verba: The Last Conversations of St. Thérèse of the Child Jesus. May–Sept. 1897.* Revised translation by the Carmelite Nuns of New York. New York: P. J. Kenedy & Sons, 1952.

Ahern, Patrick. *Maurice and Thérèse: The Story of a Love*. New York: Doubleday, 1998.

Les Annales de Sainte Thérèse. A monthly review founded in 1926. The name was changed in the March 1992 issue (#712) to *Thérèse de Lisieux*. Lisieux: Pèlerinage de Lisieux.

Apostolate of the Little Flower. A magazine published bi-monthly. San Antonio, Texas: Discalced Carmelite Fathers of San Antonio, Inc.

Ball, Ann. *Modern Saints: Their Lives and Faces*. Rockford, Illinois: Tan Books and Publishers, Inc., 1990.

Beevers, John. *Storm of Glory: St. Thérèse of Lisieux*. New York: Sheed & Ward, 1950.

Blanc, Mgr. Paul. *Notre-Dame-de-la Garde*. Lucon: Editions Quest-France, 2007.

Bro, Fr. Bernard. *Saint Thérèse of Lisieux: Her God, Her Family, Her Message*. San Francisco: Ignatius Press, 2003.

_____. *The Little Way: The Spirituality of Thérèse of Lisieux*. Westminster, Maryland: Christian Classics, 1980.

Carmel of Lisieux. *Les Musiques de Thérèse*. With an Introduction by Guy Gaucher. Paris: Les Éditions du Cerf, 1997.

Carmelites of Lisieux. *Vie en Images de Sainte Thérèse de L'Enfant-Jésus en 77 Tableaux avec Couplets et Musique pour Séances de Projections*. Paris: Office Central de Lisieux, 1944.

A Catholic Dictionary: The Catholic Encyclopaedic Dictionary. Third Edition. New York: The Macmillan Company, 1962.

Chalon, Jean. *Thérèse of Lisieux: A Life of Love*. Translated by Anne Collier Rehill. Liguori, Missouri: Liguori Publications, 1997.

Coady, Mary Frances. *The Hidden Way: The Life and Influence of Almire Pichon*. Toronto: Novalis, 1998.

Combes, Abbé André. *Saint Thérèse and Her Mission: The Basic Principles of Theresian Spirituality*. Translated by Alastair Guinan. New York: P. J. Kenedy & Sons, 1955.

Chrisógono de Jesús, O.C.D. *The Life of St. John of the Cross*. Translated by Kathleen Pond. New York: Harper & Brothers, 1958.

DeMeester, Conrad, ed. *Saint Thérèse of Lisieux: Her Life, Times, and Teachings*. Translated by Susan Conroy, et al. Washington, D.C.: ICS Publications, 1997.

Deshayes, Daniel. *Memoire en Images Lisieux*. Joué-lès-Toures: Alan Sutton, 1997.

———. *Memoire en Images Lisieux: Sainte Thérèse*. Saint-Cyr-sur-Loire: Alan Sutton, 2003.

Descouvemont, Pierre. *Sainte Thérèse de Lisieux: La Vie en Images*. Paris: Les Éditions du Cerf, 1995.

———. *Sur les pas de Thérèse: Guide Complete du Pèlerin*. Paris: Les Éditions du Cerf, 2001.

———. *Thérèse and Lisieux*. Translated by Salvatore Sciurba and Louise Pambrun. Toronto: Novalis, 1996.

———. *Thérèse of Lisieux and Marie of the Trinity: The Transformative Relationship of St. Thérèse of Lisieux and her novice, Sister Marie of the Trinity*. Translated by Plettenberg-Serban. New York: Alba House, 1997.

The Discalced Carmelites of Boston. *Carmel: Its History and Spirit Compiled from Approved Sources*. Boston: Flynn and Mahony, 1897

Dolan, Rev. Albert H. *God Made the Violet Too: Life of Leonie, Sister of St. Therese*. Chicago: Carmelite Press, 1948.

———. *The Living Sisters of the Little Flower*. Chicago: Carmelite Press, 1926.

———. *The Sisters of St. Therese Today*. Chicago: Carmelite Press, 1948.

Emert, Joyce R. *Louis Martin: Father of a Saint*. Staten Island, NY: Alba House, 1983.

Foley, Barbara. *Zelie Martin: Mother of Saint Therese of Lisieux*. Boston: Daughters of St. Paul, 1959.

François de Sainte-Marie. *The Photo Album of St. Thérèse of Lisieux*. Translated by Peter-Thomas Rohrbach. New York: P. J. Kenedy & Sons, 1962.

Freze, Michael. *The Making of Saints*. Huntington, Indiana.: Our Sunday Visitor Publishing Division of Our Sunday Visitor, Inc. 1991.

Frohlich, Mary. Frost, Christine. *A Guide to the Normandy of St. Thérèse: From the Cradle to the Grave*. Dublin: Co-Published by The Theresian Trust, Birmingham, 1994, and St. Thérèse Missionary League, 1994.

Gaucher, Guy. *John and Thérèse: Flames of Love: The Influence of St. John of the Cross in the Life and Writings of St. Thérèse of Lisieux*. Translated by Alexandra Plettenberg-Serban. Staten Island, N.Y.: Alba House, 1998.

———. *The Passion of Thérèse of Lisieux*. Translated by Sr. Anne Marie Brennan. New York: Crossroad Publishing Co., 1990.

———. *The Spiritual Journey of St. Thérèse of Lisieux*. Translated by Sr. Anne Marie Brennan. London: Darton, Longman and Todd, 1997.

———. *The Story of a Life*. Translated by Sr. Anne Marie Brennan. San Francisco: Harper & Row Publishers, Inc., 1987.

Geneviève de la Sainte-Face [Céline Martin]. *Conseils et Souvenirs*. Paris: Éditions du Cerf/Desclée de Brouwer, 1973.

———. *The Father of the Little Flower*. Translated by Michael Collins. Dublin: M. H. Gill & Sons, Ltd., 1959.

———. *A Memoir of My Sister St. Thérèse*. Translated by The Carmelite Sisters of New York of *Conseils et Souvenirs*. New York: P. J. Kenedy & Sons, 1959.

———. *The Mother of the Little Flower*. Translated by Michael Collins. Dublin: M. H. Gill & Sons, Ltd., 1957.

Goerres, Ida. *The Hidden Face: Life of Thérèse of Lisieux*. Translated by Richard and Clara Winston. New York: Pantheon Books, Inc., 1959.

Guéranger, Dom Prosper. *The Liturgical Year*. Translated by the Benedictines of Stanbrook Abbey. 15 vols. Fitz-William, N.H.: Loreto Publications, 2000.

Hardouin-Fugier, Élizabeth. *Fourvière: The story behind the basilica*. Châtillon-sur-Chalaronne: Éditions La Taillanderie, 2006.

Irving, H. B. *Studies of French Criminals of the Nineteenth Century*. London: William Heinemann, 1901.

Jamart, Rev. François. *Complete Spiritual Doctrine of St. Therese of Lisieux*. Translated by Rev. Walter Van De Putte. New York: St. Paul Publications, 1961.

Johnson, Vernon. *Spiritual Childhood*. London: Sheed and Ward, 1953.

Keyes, Frances Parkinson. *Therese: Saint of the Little Way*. New York: Julian Messner, Inc., 1950.

_____. *Written in Heaven: The Life on Earth of the Little Flower of Lisieux*. New York: Julian Messner, Inc. 1940.

Lang, Rev. Jovian. *Dictionary of the Liturgy*. New York: Catholic Book Publishing Co., 1989.

Laveille, Msgr. August Pierre. *Life of the Little Flower: St. Thérèse of Lisieux*. Translated by Rev. M. Fitzsimons. New York: McMullen Books, Inc., 1953.

Martin, Zélie. *Correspondance familiale: 1863–1877*. Lisieux: Carmel de Lisieux, 1958.

The Maryknoll Catholic Dictionary. Compiled and edited by Albert Nevins. New York: Dimensions Books (Grosset & Dunlap), 1965.

Maze, Fabrice. *La Basilique Sainte-Thérèse de Lisieux*. Grenoble: Editions Publialp, no date.

Morteveille, Blanche. *The Rose Unpetaled: Saint Thérèse of the Child Jesus*. Translated by Mother Paula, U.S.B. of St. Cecilia's Abbey, Ryde, Isle of Wight. Revised edition and eighth printing of the original 1942 printing. Milwaukee, The Bruce Publishing Co.

Newkirk, Terrys. *The Martyrs of Compiègne*. Washington, D.C.: ICA Publications, 1995.

O'Mahony, Christopher. *St. Thérèse of Lisieux by Those Who Knew Her: Testimonies from the Process of Beatification*. London: Veritas Publications, 1975.

Pascal, Abbé F. "*Sainte Thérèse de Lisieux et l'abbaye de Mondaye: Le Père Godefroid Madelaine prain de l'Histoire d'une Âme*" in Numéro speciale of *Courrier de Montaye*. (178–Mars, 1997) Juaye-Mondaye: Abbaye Saint-Martin de Mondaye, 1997.

Payne, Steven. *Saint Thérèse of Lisieux: Doctor of the Universal Church*. Staten Island, N.Y.: Alba House, 2002.

Petitot, O.P., Henri, *Saint Thérèse of Lisieux*. London, Burns Oates & Washbourne LTD., 1948.

Piat, R. P. Stéphane-Joseph. *Céline: Sister Geneviève of the Holy Face, Sister and Witness to St. Thérèse of the Child Jesus*. Translated by the Carmelite Sisters of the Eucharist of Colchester, Conn. San Francisco: Ignatius Press, 1997.

_____. *Marie Guérin: Cousine et novice de Sainte Thérèse de l'Enfant-Jésus, 1870–1905*. Lisieux: Office Central de Lisieux, 1953.

_____. *Our Lady of the Smile and Thérèse of the Child Jesus*. Translated by Michael Collins. Dublin: M. H. Gill & Sons, Ltd., 1958.

_____. *The Story of a Family: The Home of the Little Flower*. New York: P. J. Kenedy & Sons, Ltd., 1948.

Procés de Béatification et Canonization de Sainte Therese de l'Enfant-Jésus et de la Sainte-Face. 2 vols. Vol. 1: *Procès informative ordinaire*. Vol. 2: *Procès apostolique*. Rome: Teresianum, 1973, 1986.

Redmond, Paulinus. *Louis and Zélie Martin: The Seed and the Root of the Little Flower*. London: Quiller Press, 1995.
Robo, Etienne. *Two Portraits of St. Thérèse of Lisieux*. Chicago: Henry Regnery Company, 1955.
Rouée, Anne-Marie. *Thérèse Élève à l'Abbaye: La nuit de la conversion Noel 1886*. Paris: Éditions Médiaspaul, 1993.
Saint John of the Cross. The *Collected Works of St. John of the Cross*. Translated by Kavanaugh and Rodriguez. Washington, D.C.: ICS Publications, 1973.
The Saint of Lisieux. A quarterly review of the Lay Association of St. Thérèse of the Child Jesus published since 1948. In 1966 it united with the quarterly for priests only, *Sicut Parvuli* thus allowing both priests and laity to subscribe. London: The Saint of Lisieux publications.
Saint Thérèse of Lisieux. *Essential Writings: Selected with an Introduction by Mary Frohlich*. Maryknoll, New York: Orbis Books, 2003.
―――. *General Correspondence*. Translated by John Clarke. 2 vols. Washington, D.C.: ICS Publications, 1977.
―――. *Her Last Conversations*. Translated by John Clarke. Washington, D.C.: ICS Publications, 1977.
―――. *Les Cahiers d'école de Thérèse de Lisieux, 1877–1888*. Introduction and notes by Msgr. Guy Gaucher en collaboration avec le Carmel de Lisieux. Paris, France: Les Éditions du Cerf, 2008.
―――. *Œuvres complètes* [Complete Works in one volume]. Édition du centenaire. Paris: Éditions du Cerf/ Desclée de Brouwer, 1998.
―――. *The Plays of Saint Thérèse of Lisieux: "Pious Recreations."* Translated by Susan Conroy and David J. Dwyer. Washington, D.C.: ICS Publications, 2008.
―――. *Poems of Sr. Thérèse, Carmelite of Lisieux, known as The "Little Flower of Jesus."* Translated by S. L. Emery. Boston: Angel Guardian Press, 1907.
―――. *Poems of St. Thérèse of the Child Jesus Known as "The Little Flower of Jesus."* Translated by the Carmelites of Santa Clara, Cal., U.S.A. London: Burns Oates and Washbourne, Ltd., 1925.
―――. *The Poetry of Saint Thérèse of Lisieux*. Translated by Donald Kinney. Washington, D.C.: ICS Publications, 1996.
―――. *The Prayers of Saint Thérèse of Lisieux*. Translated by Aletheia Kane. Washington, D.C.: ICS Publications, 1997.
―――. *Story of a Soul: The Autobiography of St. Thérèse of Lisieux*. Translated by John Clarke. Third edition. Washington, D.C.: ICS Publications, 1996.
Sicut Parvuli. The quarterly review of the Association of Priests of St. Thérèse of the Child Jesus founded by Msgr. Vernon Johnson in 1939. In 1966 it incorporated the review *The Saint of Lisieux* which allowed the laity as well to subscribe to it. Hornchurch, Essex (formerly London), England.
Simonnet, Christian. *Théophane Vénard: a Martyr of Vietnam*. Translated by Cynthia Splatt. San Francisco: Ignatius Press, 1988.
Six, Jean-François. *Lisieux au temps de Thérèse*. Paris: Desclée de Brouwer, 1997.
―――. *Light of the Night: The Last Eighteen Months in the Life of St. Thérèse of Lisieux*. Translated by John Bowden. Notre Dame, Indiana.: University of Notre Dame, 1998.
Sullivan, John. "Experiencing St. Thérèse Today." In *Carmelite Studies*, no. 5. Washington, D.C.: ICS Publications, 1990.

Teil, Msgr. Roger de. *The Cause of Beatification of the Little Flower of Jesus*. Translated by Rev. L. Basevi. New York: P.J. Kenedy & Sons, 1913.

Thérèse de Lisieux. A monthly review, formerly called *Les Annales de Saint Thérèse*, that changed its name in March of 1992. Lisieux: Pèlerinage de Lisieux.

Vico, A. Cardinal. *The Story of the Canonization of St. Thérèse of Lisieux: With the Text of the Principal Documents in the Process*. London: Burns Oates & Washbourne Ltd., 1934.

———. *Proclamazione a Dottore Della Chiesa di Sasnta Teresa di Gesù Bambino e del Santo Volta*. Edited by the Office of the Celebration of the Liturgy of the Supreme Pontiff. Rome: Tipografia Vaticana, 1997.

Vie Thérèsienne. A trimestrial review founded in 1961 as a supplement to *Les Annales de Saint-Thérèse de Lisieux* (now called *Thérèse de Lisieux*). Lisieux: Pèlerinage de Lisieux.

Viquesnel, Jacques. *Promenades en Normandie avec Sainte Thérèse de Lisieux*. Cond-sur-Noireau: Éditions Charles Corlet, 1993.

Vrai, Suzanne. *Thérèse de Lisieux et Ses Frères Missionnaires*. Médiaspaul & Éditions Paulines.

Wust, Louis and Marjorie. *Louis Martin, an Ideal Father*. Derby, N.Y.: Daughters of St. Paul, 1953.

———. *Zélie Martin, Mother of St. Therese*. Boston: The Daughters of St. Paul, 1969.

Walsh, James A. *A Modern Martyr: Théophane Vénard*. Maryknoll, N.Y.: Catholic Foreign Mission Society of America, 1913.

Woodward, Kenneth L. *Making Saints: How the Catholic Church Determines Who Becomes a Saint, Who Doesn't, and Why*. New York: Simon & Schuster, 1990.

Picture Credits

Plate 1: *St. Thérèse of Lisieux*
All 10 images reproduced from *Visage de Thérèse de Lisieux*, Office Central de Lisieux.

Plate 2: *Miracles*
A: BT, p. 154
B: SA, p. 16
C: BT, p. 155
D: SA, p. 116

Plate 3: *Genealogy of the Martin Family*
Devised by the author

Plate 4: *Saint Thérèse's Parents, Grandparents, and Paternal Cousins*
A: LA,
B: TdeL, from the 2005 Calendar
C: TdeL, p. 16
D: AC
E: TetL, p. 14
F: AC
G: AC

Plate 5: *The Sisters of Saint Thérèse*
A: LA, Feb. 1958
B: LA, Sept. 1967
C: TdeL, from the 2005 Calendar
D: LA, Feb. 1992
E: LA, June 1973
F: TdeL, April 1993
G: LA, Jan. 1985
H: LA, June 1973

Plate 6: *Genealogy of the Guérin Family*
Devised by the author

Plate 7: *The Guérin Family*
A: LA, April 1950
B: TetL, p. 27
C: TdeL, Sept. 1994
D: TdeL, April 2002
E: TetL, p. 180
F: AC
G: AC
H: AC
I: AC

Plate 8: *Family Friends*
A: TetL. P. 295
B: LA, Dec. 1996
C: AC
D: AC

E: AC
F: AC
G: AC
H: LA, March 1993
I: TetL, p. 31

Plate 9: *Family Friends*
J: AC
K: AC
L: TdeL, Oct. 2006
M: AC
N: AC
O: AC
P: TetL, p. 22
Q: Through the courtesy of Louis and Christine Gérault
R: LA, May 1969

Plate 10: *Nuns*
A: V, Photo 21
B: V, Photo 18
C: TetL, p. 184
D: V, Photo 18
E: V, Photo 18
F: V, Photo 18
G: V, Photo 18
H: V, Photo 18
I: V, Photo 18
J: V, Photo 18
K: V, Photo 17
L: V, Photo 18

Plate 11: *Nuns*
M: V, Photo 18
N: AC
O: TetL, p. 203
P: V, Photo 18
Q: V, Photo 18
R: V, Photo 17
S: V, Photo 17
T: V, Photo 17
U: V, Photo 21
V: V, Photo 18
W: LA, Dec. 1984
X: LC, p. 40

Plate 12: *Clergymen*
A: LA, June 1969
B: LA, May–April 1977
C: AC
D: LA, Nov. 1957
E: LA, April 1963
F: TetL, p. 47

G: LA, April 1992
H: TdeL, April 2003
I: LA, Jan. 1964
J: LA, Dec. 1982
K: TetL, p. 81
L: AC

Plate 13: *Clergymen*
M: BT, p. 63
N: TdeL, Jan 1994
O: AC
P: AC
Q: STJ
R: TetL, p. 183
S: LA, April 1963
T: TetL, p. 265
U: FSC
V: BT, p. 63
W: BT, p. 77
X: TetL, p. 260

Plate 14: *One Saint and Five "Sinners"*
A: AC
B: TetL, p. 180
C: TdeL, Jan, 2005
D: TdeL, p. 79
E: TdeL, p. 282
F: LA, Feb. 1961

Plate 15: *Alençon*
All 10 photos taken by John Kochiss

Plate 16: *Vicinity of Alençon*
All 7 photos taken by John Kochiss

Plate 17: *Lisieux*
All 9 photos taken by John Kochiss

Plate 18: *Vicinity of Lisieux*
All 7 photos taken by John Kochiss

Plate 19: *Elsewhere in France*
All 10 photos taken by John Kochiss

Plate 20: *The Itinerary of Thérèse's Trip to Rome*
Map drawn by the author

Plate 21: *On the Trip to Rome*
All 10 photos taken by John Kochiss

Plate 22: *The Lisieux Carmel*
A: SA, p. 182
B: SA, p. 183
C: STL, p. 104–105

ABBREVIATIONS

AC: Reproduced by courtesy of the Archives du Carmel de Lisieux
BT: *La Bienheureuse Thérèse de l'Enfant-Jésus: Sa Béatification*
FSC: Reproduced by courtesy of *Fratelli delle Scuole Cristiane*, Rome
G: Through the kind permission of Louis and Christine Gérault of Alençon
LA: *Les Annales de Sainte Thérèse de Lisieux*, monthly French magazine
LC: *Les Cahiers d'école de Thérèse*
SA: *Sainte Thérèse de l'Enfant-Jésus: Sa Canonisation*
STJ: Reproduced by permission from the rector of St. Joseph's Seminary, Yonkers, New York
STL: *St. Thérèse of Lisieux* by Conrad de Meester, O.C.D.
TdeL: *Thérèse de Lisieux* (the magazine formerly called *Les Annales de Sainte Thérèse de Lisieux*)
TetL: *Thérèse et Lisieux* by Pierre Descouvemont
V: *Visage de Thérèse de Lisieux* (the Photo Album by the Office Central de Lisieux)

The 22 Plates
In *A Companion to Saint Thérèse of Lisieux*

PLATE NO.	PAGE NO.	NUMBER OF IMAGES	TITLE OF PLATE
1	xx	10	Saint Thérèse of Lisieux
2	79	4	Miracles
3	104	7	Genealogy of the Martin Family
4	106	7	Saint Thérèse's Parents, Grandparents, and Paternal Cousins
5	123	8	The Sisters of Saint Thérèse
6	180	1	Genealogy of the Guérin Family
7	181	9	The Guérin Family
8	222	9	Family Friends
9	223	9	Family Friends (Continued)
10	274	12	Nuns
11	275	12	Nuns (Continued)
12	364	12	Clergymen
13	365	12	Clergymen (Continued)
14	449	6	One Saint and Five "Sinners"
15	526	10	Alençon
16	551	7	Vicinity of Alençon
17	557	9	Lisieux
18	594	7	Vicinity of Lisieux
19	601	10	Elsewhere in France
20	620	1	The Itinerary of Saint Thérèse's Trip to Rome
21	624	10	On the Trip to Rome
22	662	3	The Lisieux Carmel
		169 (Total)	